Joint 5th Workshop on Statistical Machine Translation and MetricsMATR 2010

(WMT10)

Held at ACL 2010

Uppsala, Sweden
15-16 July 2010

ISBN: 978-1-61738-823-1

Printed from e-media with permission by:

Curran Associates, Inc.
57 Morehouse Lane
Red Hook, NY 12571

Some format issues inherent in the e-media version may also appear in this print version.

Printed by Curran Associates, Inc. (2010)

For permission requests, please contact the Association for Computational Linguistics
at the address below.

Association for Computational Linguistics
209 N. Eighth Street
Stroudsburg, Pennsylvania 18360

Phone: 1-570-476-8006
Fax: 1-570-476-0860

acl@aclweb.org

Additional copies of this publication are available from:

Curran Associates, Inc.
57 Morehouse Lane
Red Hook, NY 12571 USA
Phone: 845-758-0400
Fax: 845-758-2634
Email: curran@proceedings.com
Web: www.proceedings.com

Introduction

The Joint Fifth Workshop on Statistical Machine Translation and MetricsMATR (WMT10) took place on July 15 and 16 in Uppsala, Sweden, immediately following the 48th conference of the Association for Computational Linguistics (ACL).

This is the sixth time this workshop has been held. The first time was in 2005 as part of the ACL 2005 Workshop on Building and Using Parallel Texts. In the following years the Workshop on Statistical Machine Translation was held at HLT-NAACL 2006 in New York City, USA, at ACL 2007 in Prague, Czech Republic, at ACL 2008 in Columbus, Ohio, USA, and at EACL 2009 in Athens, Greece. MetricsMATR was previously held in conjunction with AMTA 2008 in Honolulu, Hawaii, USA.

The focus of our workshop was to evaluate the state of the art in machine translation for a variety of languages. Recent experimentation has shown that the performance of machine translation systems varies greatly with the source language. In this workshop we encouraged researchers to investigate ways to improve the performance of machine translation systems for diverse languages.

Prior to the workshop, in addition to soliciting relevant papers for review and possible presentation we conducted a shared task that brought together machine translation systems for an evaluation on previously unseen data. The shared task also included a track for evaluation metrics and system combination methods.

The results of the shared task were announced at the workshop, and these proceedings also include an overview paper that summarizes the results, as well as provides information about the data used and any procedures that were followed in conducting or scoring the task. In addition, there are short papers from each participating team that describe their underlying system in some detail.

Like in previous years, we have received a far larger number of submission than we could accept for presentation. This year we have received 24 full paper submissions. 15 full papers were selected for oral presentation and one for poster presentation.

We received 7 short paper submissions for the evaluation task, 9 short paper submissions for the system combination task, and 30 short paper submissions for the translation task. Due to the large number of high quality submission for the full paper track, shared task submissions were presented as posters. The poster session gave participants of the shared task the opportunity to present their approaches.

The invited talk was given by Hermann Ney (RWTH Aachen).

We would like to thank the members of the Program Committee for their timely reviews. We also would like to thank the participants of the shared task and all the other volunteers who helped with the manual evaluations.

Chris Callison-Burch, Philipp Koehn, Christof Monz, Kay Peterson, and Omar Zaidan

Co-Organizers

Organizers:

Chris Callison-Burch, Johns Hopkins University (United States of America)
Philipp Koehn, University of Edinburgh (United Kingdom)
Christof Monz, University of Amsterdam (The Netherlands)
Kay Peterson, NIST (United States of America)
Omar Zaidan, Johns Hopkins University (United States of America)

Program Committee:

Steve Abney, University of Michigan (United States of America)
Lars Ahrenberg, Linköping University (Sweden)
Yaser Al-Onaizan, IBM Research (United States of America)
Abhishek Arun, University if Edinburgh (United Kingdom)
Necip Fazil Ayan, SRI (United States of America)
Graeme Blackwood, University of Cambridge (United Kingdom)
Phil Blunsom, University of Oxford (United Kingdom)
Thorsten Brants, Google (United States of America)
Chris Brockett, Microsoft Research (United States of America)
Bill Byrne, Cambridge University (United Kingdom)
Michael Carl, University Saarbrücken (Germany)
Marine Carpuat, Columbia University (United States of America)
Simon Carter, University of Amsterdam (The Netherlands)
Francisco Casacuberta, University of Valencia (Spain)
David Chiang, ISI/University of Southern California (United States of America)
Adria deGispert, Cambridge University (United Kingdom)
Steve DeNeefe, ISI/University of Southern California (United States of America)
John DeNero, University of California at Berkeley (United States of America)
Kevin Duh, NTT (Japan)
Andreas Eisele, University Saarbrücken (Germany)
Marcello Federico, FBK-irst (Italy)
George Foster, Canada National Research Council (Canada)
Alex Fraser, University of Stuttgart (Germany)
Michel Galley, Stanford University (United States of America)
Daniel Gildea, University of Rochester (United States of America)
Jesus Gimenez, Technical University of Catalonia (Spain)
Kevin Gimpel, Carnegie Mellon University (United States of America)
Nizar Habash, Columbia University (United States of America)
Keith Hall, Google (Switzerland)
John Henderson, MITRE (United States of America)
Hieu Hoang, University of Edinburgh (United Kingdom)
Abe Ittycheriah, IBM (United States of America)
Howard Johnson, National Research Council (Canada)
Doug Jones, Lincoln Labs MIT (United States of America)
Damianos Karakos, Johns Hopkins University (United States of America)
Katrin Kirchhoff, University of Washington (United States of America)
Kevin Knight, ISI/University of Southern California (United States of America)
Greg Kondrak, University of Alberta (Canada)

Roland Kuhn, National Research Council (Canada)
Shankar Kumar, Google (United States of America)
Philippe Langlais, University of Montreal (Canada)
Alon Lavie, Carnegie Mellon University (United States of America)
Adam Lopez, Edinburgh University (United Kingdom)
Wolfgang Macherey, Google (United States of America)
Daniel Marcu, Language Weaver (United States of America)
Yuval Marton, Columbia University (United States of America)
Evgeny Matusov, Apptek (United States of America)
Arne Mauser, RWTH Aachen (Germany)
Arul Menezes, Microsoft Research (United States of America)
Bob Moore, Microsoft Research (United States of America)
Smaranda Muresan, Rutgers University (United States of America)
Patrick Nguyen, Microsoft Research (United States of America)
Miles Osborne, Edinburgh University (United Kingdom)
Chris Quirk, Microsoft Research (United States of America)
Stefan Riezler, University of Heidelberg (Germany)
Antti-Veikko Rosti, BBN Technologies (United States of America)
Jean Senellart, Systran (France)
Libin Shen, BBN Technologies (United States of America)
Wade Shen, Lincoln Labs MIT (United States of America)
Khalil Simaan, University of Amsterdam (The Netherlands)
Michel Simard, National Research Council Canada (Canada)
Jörg Tiedemann, University of Uppsala (Sweden)
Christoph Tillmann, IBM Research (United States of America)
Roy Tromble, Google (United States of America)
David Vilar, RWTH Aachen (Germany)
Clare Voss, Army Research Labs (United States of America)
Taro Watanabe, NTT (Japan)
Andy Way, Dublin City University (Ireland)
Jinxi Xu, BBN Technologies (United States of America)
Sirvan Yahyaei, University of Amsterdam (The Netherlands)
Omar Zaidan, Johns Hopkins University (United States of America)
Richard Zens, Google (United States of America)
Bing Zhao, IBM Research (United States of America)
Andreas Zollmann, Carnegie Mellon University (United States of America)

Invited Speaker:

Hermann Ney, RWTH Aachen

Table of Contents

Conference Program

Thursday, July 15, 2010

8:45–9:00 Opening Remarks

Full Paper Session 1

9:00–9:25 *A Semi-Supervised Word Alignment Algorithm with Partial Manual Alignments*
Qin Gao, Nguyen Bach and Stephan Vogel

9:25–9:50 *Fast Consensus Hypothesis Regeneration for Machine Translation*
Boxing Chen, George Foster and Roland Kuhn

Shared Translation Task

9:50–10:15 *Findings of the 2010 Joint Workshop on Statistical Machine Translation and Metrics for Machine Translation*
Chris Callison-Burch, Philipp Koehn, Christof Monz, Kay Peterson, Mark Przybocki and Omar Zaidan

10:15–10:45 Boaster Session 1: Translation Task

10:45–11:00 Morning Break

Poster Session: Translation Task

LIMSI's Statistical Translation Systems for WMT'10
Alexandre Allauzen, Josep M. Crego, İlknur Durgar El-Kahlout and Francois Yvon

2010 Failures in English-Czech Phrase-Based MT
Ondrej Bojar and Kamil Kos

An Empirical Study on Development Set Selection Strategy for Machine Translation Learning
Hui Cong, Zhao Hai, Lu Bao-Liang and Song Yan

The University of Maryland Statistical Machine Translation System for the Fifth Workshop on Machine Translation
Vladimir Eidelman, Chris Dyer and Philip Resnik

Further Experiments with Shallow Hybrid MT Systems
Christian Federmann, Andreas Eisele, Yu Chen, Sabine Hunsicker, Jia Xu and Hans Uszkoreit

Thursday, July 15, 2010 (continued)

The Cunei Machine Translation Platform for WMT '10
Aaron Phillips

The CUED HiFST System for the WMT10 Translation Shared Task
Juan Pino, Gonzalo Iglesias, Adrià de Gispert, Graeme Blackwood, Jamie Brunning and William Byrne

The LIG Machine Translation System for WMT 2010
Marion Potet, Laurent Besacier and Hervé Blanchon

Linear Inversion Transduction Grammar Alignments as a Second Translation Path
Markus Saers, Joakim Nivre and Dekai Wu

UPV-PRHLT English–Spanish System for WMT10
Germán Sanchis-Trilles, Jesús Andrés-Ferrer, Guillem Gascó, Jesús González-Rubio, Pascual Martínez-Gómez, Martha-Alicia Rocha, Joan-Andreu Sánchez and Francisco Casacuberta

Reproducible Results in Parsing-Based Machine Translation: The JHU Shared Task Submission
Lane Schwartz

Vs and OOVs: Two Problems for Translation between German and English
Sara Stymne, Maria Holmqvist and Lars Ahrenberg

To Cache or Not To Cache? Experiments with Adaptive Models in Statistical Machine Translation
Jörg Tiedemann

Applying Morphological Decompositions to Statistical Machine Translation
Sami Virpioja, Jaakko Väyrynen, Andre Mansikkaniemi and Mikko Kurimo

Maximum Entropy Translation Model in Dependency-Based MT Framework
Zdeněk Žabokrtský, Martin Popel and David Mareček

UCH-UPV English–Spanish System for WMT10
Francisco Zamora-Martinez and Germán Sanchis-Trilles

Hierarchical Phrase-Based MT at the Charles University for the WMT 2010 Shared Task
Daniel Zeman

Thursday, July 15, 2010 (continued)

12:30–14:00 Lunch

Invited Talk

14:00–15:00 Invited Talk by Hermann Ney

Full Paper Session 2

15:05–15:30 *Incremental Decoding for Phrase-Based Statistical Machine Translation*
Baskaran Sankaran, Ajeet Grewal and Anoop Sarkar

15:30–16:00 Afternoon Break

Full Paper Session 3

16:00–16:25 *How to Avoid Burning Ducks: Combining Linguistic Analysis and Corpus Statistics for German Compound Processing*
Fabienne Fritzinger and Alexander Fraser

16:25–16:50 *Chunk-Based Verb Reordering in VSO Sentences for Arabic-English Statistical Machine Translation*
Arianna Bisazza and Marcello Federico

16:50–17:15 *Head Finalization: A Simple Reordering Rule for SOV Languages*
Hideki Isozaki, Katsuhito Sudoh, Hajime Tsukada and Kevin Duh

17:15–17:40 *Aiding Pronoun Translation with Co-Reference Resolution*
Ronan Le Nagard and Philipp Koehn

Friday, July 16, 2010

Shared Task Presentations

9:00–10:00 Overview: MetricsMATR

10:00–10:30 Discussion

10:30–10:45 Boaster Session

10:45–11:00 Morning Break

Poster Session: Full Paper

Poster Session: System Combination Task

Friday, July 16, 2010 (continued)

CMU System Combination via Hypothesis Selection for WMT'10
Almut Silja Hildebrand and Stephan Vogel

JHU System Combination Scheme for WMT 2010
Sushant Narsale

The RWTH System Combination System for WMT 2010
Gregor Leusch and Hermann Ney

BBN System Description for WMT10 System Combination Task
Antti-Veikko Rosti, Bing Zhang, Spyros Matsoukas and Richard Schwartz

Poster Session: Metrics Task

LRscore for Evaluating Lexical and Reordering Quality in MT
Alexandra Birch and Miles Osborne

Document-Level Automatic MT Evaluation based on Discourse Representations
Elisabet Comelles, Jesus Gimenez, Lluis Marquez, Irene Castellon and Victoria Arranz

METEOR-NEXT and the METEOR Paraphrase Tables: Improved Evaluation Support for Five Target Languages
Michael Denkowski and Alon Lavie

Normalized Compression Distance Based Measures for MetricsMATR 2010
Marcus Dobrinkat, Tero Tapiovaara, Jaakko Väyrynen and Kimmo Kettunen

The DCU Dependency-Based Metric in WMT-MetricsMATR 2010
Yifan He, Jinhua Du, Andy Way and Josef van Genabith

TESLA: Translation Evaluation of Sentences with Linear-Programming-Based Analysis
Chang Liu, Daniel Dahlmeier and Hwee Tou Ng

The Parameter-Optimized ATEC Metric for MT Evaluation
Billy Wong and Chunyu Kit

12:30–14:00 Lunch

Friday, July 16, 2010 (continued)

Full Paper Session 4

14:00–14:25 *A Unified Approach to Minimum Risk Training and Decoding*
Abhishek Arun, Barry Haddow and Philipp Koehn

14:25–14:50 *N-Best Reranking by Multitask Learning*
Kevin Duh, Katsuhito Sudoh, Hajime Tsukada, Hideki Isozaki and Masaaki Nagata

14:50–15:15 *Taming Structured Perceptrons on Wild Feature Vectors*
Ralf Brown

15:15–15:40 *Translation Model Adaptation by Resampling*
Kashif Shah, Loïc Barrault and Holger Schwenk

15:40–16:00 Afternoon Break

Full Paper Session 5

16:00–16:25 *Integration of Multiple Bilingually-Learned Segmentation Schemes into Statistical Machine Translation*
Michael Paul, Andrew Finch and Eiichiro Sumita

16:25–16:50 *Improved Translation with Source Syntax Labels*
Hieu Hoang and Philipp Koehn

16:50–17:15 *Divide and Translate: Improving Long Distance Reordering in Statistical Machine Translation*
Katsuhito Sudoh, Kevin Duh, Hajime Tsukada, Tsutomu Hirao and Masaaki Nagata

17:15–17:40 *Decision Trees for Lexical Smoothing in Statistical Machine Translation*
Rabih Zbib, Spyros Matsoukas, Richard Schwartz and John Makhoul

A Semi-supervised Word Alignment Algorithm with Partial Manual Alignments

Qin Gao, Nguyen Bach and **Stephan Vogel**
Language Technologies Institute
Carnegie Mellon University
5000 Forbes Avenue, Pittsburgh PA, 15213
{qing, nbach, stephan.vogel}@cs.cmu.edu

Abstract

We present a word alignment framework that can incorporate partial manual alignments. The core of the approach is a novel semi-supervised algorithm extending the widely used IBM Models with a constrained EM algorithm. The partial manual alignments can be obtained by human labelling or automatically by high-precision-low-recall heuristics. We demonstrate the usages of both methods by selecting alignment links from manually aligned corpus and apply links generated from bilingual dictionary on unlabelled data. For the first method, we conduct controlled experiments on Chinese-English and Arabic-English translation tasks to compare the quality of word alignment, and to measure effects of two different methods in selecting alignment links from manually aligned corpus. For the second method, we experimented with moderate-scale Chinese-English translation task. The experiment results show an average improvement of 0.33 BLEU point across 8 test sets.

1 Introduction

Word alignment is used in various natural language processing applications, and most statistical machine translation systems rely on word alignment as a preprocessing step. Traditionally the word alignment model is trained in an unsupervised manner, e.g. the most widely used tool GIZA++ (Och and Ney, 2003), which implements the IBM Models (Brown et. al., 1993) and the HMM model (Vogel et al., 1996). However, for language pairs such as Chinese-English, the word alignment quality is often unsatisfactory (Guzman et al., 2009). There has been increasing interest on using manual alignments in word alignment tasks. Ittycheriah and Roukos (2005) proposed to use only manual alignment links in a maximum entropy model. A number of semi-supervised word aligners are proposed (Blunsom and Cohn, 2006; Niehues and Vogel, 2008; Taskar et al., 2005; Liu et al., 2005; Moore, 2005). These approaches use held-out manual alignments to tune the weights for discriminative models, with the model parameters, model scores or alignment links from unsupervised word aligners as features. Also, several models are proposed to address the problem of improving generative models with small amount of manual data, including Model 6 (Och and Ney, 2003) and the model proposed by Fraser and Marcu (2006) and its extension called LEAF aligner (Fraser and Marcu, 2007). The approaches use labelled data to tune parameters to combine different components of the IBM Models.

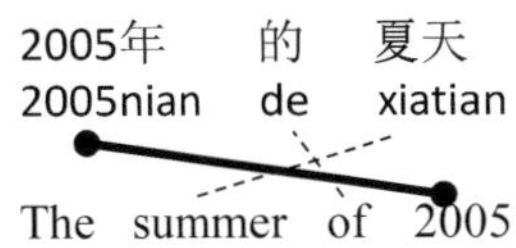

Figure 1: Partial and full alignments

An interesting question is, if we only have partial alignments of sentences, can we make use of them? Figure 1 shows the comparison of partial alignments (the bold link) and full alignments (both of the dashed and the bold links). A partial alignment of a sentence only provides a portion of links of the full alignment. Although it seems to be trivial, they actually convey different information. In the example, if the full alignment is given, we can assert *2005* is only aligned to *2005nian*, not to *de* or *xiatian*, but if only the partial alignment is given we cannot make such assertion.

Partial alignments can be obtained from various sources, for example, we can fetch them by manually correcting unsupervised alignments, by simple heuristics such as dictionaries of technical

Proceedings of the Joint 5th Workshop on Statistical Machine Translation and MetricsMATR, pages 1–10,
Uppsala, Sweden, 15-16 July 2010. ©2010 Association for Computational Linguistics

terms, by rule-based alignment systems that have high accuracy but low recall rate. The functionality is considered useful in many scenarios. For example, the researchers can analyse the alignments generated by GIZA++ and fix common error patterns, and perform training again. On another way, an application can combine active learning (Arora et al., 2009) and crowdsourcing, asking non-expertise such as workers of Amazon Mechanical Turk to label crucial alignment links that can improve the system with low cost, which is now a promising methodology in NLP areas (Callison-Burch, 2009).

In this paper, we propose a semi-supervised extension of the IBM Models that can utilize partial alignment links. More specifically, we are seeking answers for the following questions:

- Given the partial alignment of a sentence, how to find the most probable alignment that is consistent with the partial alignment.
- Given a set of partially aligned sentences, how to get the parameters that maximize the likelihood of the sentence pairs with alignments consistent with the partial alignments
- Given a set of partially aligned sentences, with conflicting partial alignments, how to answer the two questions above.

In the proposed approach, the manual partial alignment links are treated as ground truth, therefore, they will be fixed. However, for all other links we make no additional assumption. When using manual alignments, there can be links conflicting with each other. These conflicting evidences are treated as options and the generative model will choose the most probable alignment from them. An efficient training algorithm for fertility-based models is proposed. The algorithm manipulates the Moving and Swapping matrices used in the hill-climbing algorithm (Och and Ney, 2003) to rule out inconsistent alignments in both E-step and M-step of the training.

A similar attempt has been made by Callison-Burch et al. (2004), where the authors interpolate the parameters estimated by sentence-aligned and word-aligned corpus. Our approach is different from their method that we do not require fully aligned data and we do not need to interpolate two parameter sets. All the training is done within a unified framework. Our approach is also different from LEAF (Fraser and Marcu, 2007) and Model 6 (Och and Ney, 2003) that we do not use these additional links to tune additional parameters to combine model components, as a result, it is not limited to fully aligned corpus.

A question may raise why the proposed method is superior over using the partial alignment links as features in discriminative aligners? There are three possible explanations. First, the method preserves the power of the generative model in which the algorithm utilizes large amount of unlabeled data. More importantly, the additional information can propagate over the whole corpus through better estimation of model parameters. In contrast, if we use the alignment links in discriminative aligners as a feature, one link can only affect the particular word, or at most the sentence. Second, although the discriminative word alignment methods provide flexibility to utilize labeled data, most of them still rely on generative aligners. Some rely on the model parameters of the IBM Models (Liu et al., 2005; Blunsom and Cohn, 2006), others rely on the alignment links from GIZA++ as features or as training data (Taskar et al., 2005), or use both the model parameters and the alignment links (Niehues and Vogel, 2008). Therefore, improving the generative aligner is still important even when using discriminative aligners. Third, these methods require full alignment of sentences to provide positive (aligned) and negative (non-aligned) information, which limits the availability of data (Niehues and Vogel, 2008).

The proposed method has been successfully applied on various tasks, such as utilizing manual alignments harvested from Amazon Mechanical Turk (Gao and Vogel, 2010), and active learning methods for improving word alignment (Ambati et al., 2010). This paper provides the detailed algorithm of the method and controlled experiments to demonstrate its behavior.

The paper is organized as follows, in section 2 we describe the proposed model as well as the modified training algorithm. Section 3 presents two approaches of obtaining manual alignment links, The experimental results will be shown in section 4. We conclude the paper in section 5.

2 Semi-supervised word alignment

2.1 Problem Setup

The IBM Models (Brown et. al., 1993) are a series of generative models for word alignment. GIZA++ (Och and Ney, 2003) is the most widely used implementation of the IBM Models and the

HMM model (Vogel et al., 1996). Given two strings from target and source languages $f_1^J = f_1, \cdots, f_j, \cdots f_J$ and $e_1^I = e_1, \cdots, e_i, \cdots e_I$, an alignment of the sentence pair is defined as $a_1^J = [a_1, a_2, \cdots, a_J], a_j \in [0, I]$. The IBM Models assume all the target words must be covered exactly once (Brown et. al., 1993). We try to model $P(f_1^J|e_1^I)$, which is the probability of observing source sentence given target sentence e_1^I. In statistical models a hidden alignment variable is introduced, so that we can write the probability as $P(f_1^J|e_1^I) = \sum_{a_1^J} Pr(f_1^J, a_1^J|e_1^J, \theta)$, where $Pr(\cdot)$ is the estimated probability given the parameter set θ. The IBM Models define several different set of parameters, from Model 1 to Model 5. Starting from Model 3, the fertility model is introduced.

EM algorithm is employed to estimate the model parameters of the IBM Models. In E-step, it is possible to obtain sufficient statistics from all possible alignments with simplified formulas for simple models such as Model 1 and Model 2. Meanwhile for fertility-based models, enumerating all possibilities is NP-complete and hence it cannot be carried out for long sentences. A solution is to explore only the "neighbors" of Viterbi alignments. However, obtaining Viterbi alignments itself is NP-complete for these models. In practice, a greedy algorithm is employed to find a local optimal alignments based on Viterbi alignments generated by simpler models.

First, we define the neighbor alignments of a as the set of alignments that differ by one of the two operators from the original "**center alignment**".

- Move operator $m_{[i,j]}$, that changes $a_j := i$, i.e. arbitrarily set word f_j in source sentence to align to word f_i in target sentence.
- Swap operator $s_{[j_1,j_2]}$ that exchanges a_{j_1} and a_{j_2}.

We denote the **neighbor alignments** set of current center alignment a as $nb(a)$. In each step of hill-climbing algorithm, we find the alignment $b(a)$ in $nb(a)$, s.t. $b(a) = \arg\max_{a' \in nb(a)} p(a'|e, f)$, and update the current center alignment. The algorithm iterates until there is no update could be made. The statistics of the neighbor alignments of the final center alignment will be collected for normalization step (M-step). The algorithm is greedy, so a reasonable start point is important. In practice GIZA++ uses Model 2 or HMM to generate the **seed alignment**.

To improve the speed of hill climbing, GIZA++ caches the cost of all possible move and swap operations in two matrices. In the so called Moving Matrix M, the element M_{ij} stores the likelihood difference of a move operator $a_j = i$:

$$M_{ij} = \frac{Pr(m_{[i,j]}(a)|e, f)}{Pr(a|e, f)} \cdot (1 - \delta(a_j, i)) \quad (1)$$

and in the Swapping Matrix S, the element $S_{jj'}$ stores the likelihood difference of a swap operator between a_j and $a_{j'}$:

$$S_{jj'} = \begin{cases} \frac{Pr(S_{[j,j']}(a)|e,f)}{Pr(a|e,f)} \cdot (1 - \delta(a_j, a_{j'})) & \text{if } j < j' \\ 0 & \text{otherwise} \end{cases} \quad (2)$$

The matrices will be updated whenever an operator is made, but the update is limited to the rows and columns involved in the operator.

We define a **partial alignment** of a sentence pair (f_1^J, e_1^I) as $\alpha_I^J = \{(i, j), 0 \le i < I, 0 \le j < J\}$, note that the partial alignment does not assume 1-to-N restriction on either side, and the word from neither source nor target side need to be covered with links. If an index is missing, it does not mean the word is aligned to the empty word. Instead it just means no information is provided. We use a link $(0, j)$ or $(i, 0)$ to explicitly represent the information that word f_j or e_i is aligned to the empty word.

In order to find *the most probable alignment that is consistent the partial alignments*, we treat the partial alignment as constraints, i.e. for an alignment $a_1^J = [a_1, a_2, \cdots, a_j]$ on the sentence pair f_1^J, e_1^I, the translation probability $Pr(f_1^J, a_1^J|e_1^I, \alpha_I^J)$ will be zero if the alignment is inconsistent with the partial alignments.

$$Pr(f_1^J|e_1^I, a_1^J, \alpha_I^J) = \begin{cases} 0, a_1^J \text{is inconsistent with} \alpha_I^J \\ Pr(f_1^J|e_1^I, a_1^J, \theta), \text{otherwise} \end{cases} \quad (3)$$

Under the constraints of the IBM Models, there are two situations that a_1^J is inconsistent with α_I^J:

1. Target word misalignment: The IBM Models assume one target word can only be aligned to one source word. Therefore, if the target word f_j aligns to a source word e_i, while the constraint α_I^J suggests f_j should be aligned to $e_{i'}$, the alignment violates the constraint and thus is considered inconsistent.

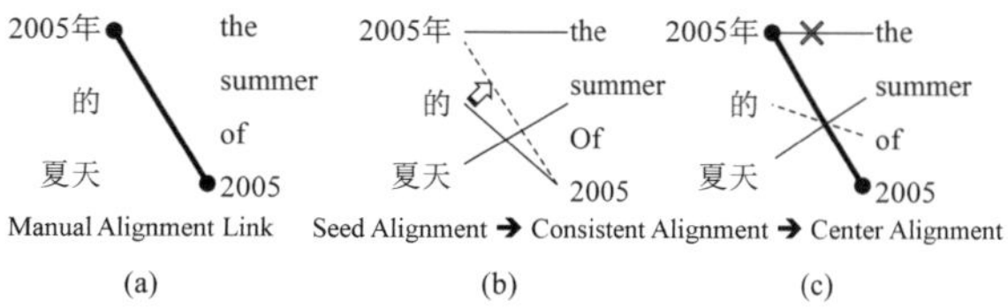

Figure 2: Illustration of Algorithm 1

2. Source word to empty word misalignment: Since one source word can be aligned to multiple target words, it is hard to constrain the alignments of source words. However, if a source word is aligned to the empty word, it cannot be aligned to any concrete target word.

However, we are facing the problem of conflicting evidences. The problem is not necessarily caused by errors in manual alignments, but the assumption of the IBM Models that one target word can only be aligned to one source word. This assumption causes multiple alignment links from one target word conflict with each other. In this case, we relax the constraints of situation 1 that if the alignment link a_{j^*} is consistent with any target-to-source links (i, j) that $j = j^*$, it will be considered consistent. Also, we arbitrarily assign the source word to empty word constraints higher priorities than other constraints.

In EM algorithm, to ensure the final model be *marginalized* on the fixed alignment links, and the final Viterbi alignment is *consistent* with the fixed alignment links, we need to guarantee that no statistics from inconsistent alignments be collected into the sufficient statistics. On fertility-based models, we have to make sure:

1. The hill-climbing algorithm outputs alignment links consistent with the fixed alignment links.
2. The count collection algorithm rules out all the inconsistent statistics.

With the constrained hill-climbing algorithm and count collection algorithm which will be described below, the above two criteria are satisfied.

2.2 Constrained hill-climbing algorithm

Algorithm 1 shows the algorithm outline of constrained hill-climbing. First, similar to the original hill-climbing algorithm described above, HMM (or Model 2) is used to obtain a seed alignment. To ensure the resulting center alignment be consistent with manual alignment, we need to split the hill-climbing algorithm into two stages, i.e. optimize towards the constraints and towards the optimal alignment under the constraints.

Algorithm 1 Constrained Hill-Climbing

1: Calculate the seed alignment a_0 using HMM model
2: **while** $ic(a_0) > 0$ **do**
3:   **if** $\{a : ic(a) < ic(a_0)\} = \emptyset$ **then**
4:     break
5:   **end if**
6:   $a_0 := \arg\max_{a \in nb(a_0), ic(a) < ic(a_0)} Pr(f|e, a)$
7: **end while**
8: $M_{ij} := -1$ if $(i, j) \notin \alpha_I^J$ or $(i, 0) \in \alpha_I^J$
9: **loop**
10:   $S_{jj'} := -1$ if $(j, a_{j'}) \notin \alpha_I^J$ or $(j', a_j) \notin \alpha_I^J$
11:   $M_{i_1 j_1} = \arg\max M_{ij}$; $S_{j_1 j_1'} = \arg\max S_{ij}$
12:   **if** $M_{i_1 j_1} \leq 1$ and $S_{j_1 j_1'} \leq 1$ **then**
13:     Break
14:   **end if**
15:   **if** $M_{i_1 j_1} > S_{j_1 j_1'}$ **then**
16:     Update $M_{i_1 *}, M_{j_1 *}, M_{* i_1}, M_{* j_1}$
      and $S_{i_1 *}, S_{j_1 *}, S_{* i_1}, S_{* j_1}$, set $a_0 := M_{i_1 j_1}(a_0)$
17:   **else**
18:     Update $M_{j_1 *}, M_{j_1' *}, M_{* j_1}, M_{* j_1'}$
      and $S_{j_1' *}, S_{j_1 *}, S_{* j_1'}, S_{* j_1}$, set $a_0 := S_{j_1 j_1'}(a_0)$
19:   **end if**
20: **end loop**
21: Return a_0

From a seed alignment, we first try to move the alignment towards the constraints by choosing a move or swap operator that:

1. has highest likelihood among alignments generated by other operators, excluding the original alignment,
2. eliminates at least one inconsistent link.

The first step reflects in line 2 through 7 in the algorithm, where we use $ic(\cdot)$ to denote the total number of inconsistent links in the alignment, and $nb(\cdot)$ to denote the neighbor alignments.

We iteratively update the alignment until no additional inconsistent link can be removed. The algorithm implies that we force the seed alignment to become closer to the constraints while trying to find the best consistent alignment. Figure 2 demonstrates the idea, given the manual alignment link shown in (a), and the seed alignment shown as solid links in (b), we move the inconsistent link to the dashed link by a move operation.

After we find the consistent alignment, we proceed to optimize towards the optimal alignment within the constraints. The algorithm sets the cells to negative if the corresponding operations are not allowed. The Moving matrix only need to be updated once, as in line 8 of the algorithm. Whereas the swapping matrix need to be updated every iteration, Since once the alignment is updated, the possible violations will also change. This is done in line 10.

If source words i_k are aligned to the empty word, we set $M_{i_k,j} = -1, \forall j$, as shown in line 8. The swapping matrix does not need to be modified in this case because the swapping operator will not introduce new links. Again, Figure 2 demonstrates the optimization step in (c), two move operators or one swap operator can move the link marked with cross to the dashed line, which can be a better alignment.

Because the cells that can lead to violations are set to negative, the operators will never be picked in line 11, therefore we effectively ensure the consistency of the final center alignment.

The algorithm will end when no better update can be made (line 12 through 14), otherwise, we pick the new update with highest likelihood as new center alignment and update the cells in the Moving and Swapping matrices that will be affected by the update. Line 15 through line 19 perform the operation.

2.3 Count Collection

After finding the center alignment, we collect counts from the neighbor alignments so that the M-step can normalize the counts to produce the model parameters for the next step. All statistics from inconsistent alignments are ruled out to ensure the final sufficient statistics marginalized on the fixed alignment links. Similar to the constrained hill climbing algorithm, we can manipulate the Moving/Swapping matrices to effectively exclude inconsistent alignments. We just need to bypass all the cells whose values are negative, i.e. represent inconsistent alignments.

By combining the constrained EM algorithm and the count collection, the Viterbi alignment is *guaranteed to be consistent* with the fixed alignment links, and the sufficient statistics is *guaranteed to contain no statistics from inconsistent alignments*.

2.4 Training scheme

We extend the multi-thread GIZA++ (Gao and Vogel, 2008) to load the alignments from a modified corpus file. The links are appended to the end of each sentence in the corpus file in the form of indices pairs, which will be read by the aligner during training. In practice, we first training unconstrained models up to Model 4, and then switch to constrained Model 4 and continue training for several iterations, the actual number of training order is: 5 iterations of Model 1, 5 iterations of HMM, 3 iterations of Model 3, 3 iterations of unconstrained Model 4 and 3 iterations of constrained Model 4. Because here we actually have more Model 4 iterations, to make the comparison fair, in all the experiments below we perform 6 iterations of Model 4 in the baseline systems.

3 Obtaining alignment links

Given the algorithm described in the Section 2, we still face the problem of obtaining alignment links to constrain the system. In this section, we describe two approaches to obtain the links, the first is to resort to human labels, while the second applies high-precision-low-recall heuristic-based aligner on large unsupervised corpus.

3.1 Using manual alignment links

Using manual alignment links is simple and straight-forward, however the problem is how to select links for human to label given that labelling the whole corpus is impossible. We propose two link selectors, the first is the random selector in which every links in the manual alignment has equal probability of being selected. Obviously, the random selecting method is far from optimal because it pays no attention on the quality of existing links. In order to demonstrate that by selecting links carefully we can achieve better alignment quality with less manual alignment links, we propose the second selector based on disagreements of alignments from two directions. We first classify the source and target words f_j and e_i into three categories. Use f_j as an example, the categories are:

- $C1$: f_j aligns to $e_i, i > 0$ in $e \rightarrow f$,[1] but in reversed direction e_i does not align to f_j but to another word.
- $C2$: f_j aligns to $e_i, i > 0$, in $f \rightarrow e$, but in reversed direction ($e \rightarrow f$), f_j aligns to the empty word.
- $C3$: no word aligns to f_j, in $f \rightarrow e$, but in reversed direction f_j aligns to $e_i, i > 0$.[2]

The criteria of e_i are the same as f_j after swapping the definitions of "source" and "target".

We prioritize the links $\alpha_I^J = (i, j)$ by looking at the classes of the source/target words. The order of

[1]Recall that f_j can align to only one word.

[2]This class is different from $C1$ that whether e_i aligns to concrete words or the empty word.

Order	Criterion	Order	Criterion
1	$f_j \in C1$	5	$e_i \in C2$
2	$f_j \in C2$	4	$e_i \in C1$
3	$f_j \in C3$	6	$e_i \in C3$

Table 1: The priorities of alignment links

priorities is shown in Table 1. All the links not in the six classes will have the lowest priorities. The links with higher priorities will be selected first, but the order of two links in a same priority class is not defined and they will be selected randomly.

3.2 Using heuristics on unlabelled data

Another possible way of getting alignment links is to make use of heuristics to generate high-precision-low-recall links and feed them into the aligner. The heuristics can be number mapping, person name translator or more sophisticated methods such as alignment confidence measure (Huang, 2009). In this paper we propose to use manual dictionaries to generate alignment links.

First we filter out from the dictionary the entries with high frequency in the source side, and then build an aligner based on it. The aligner output links between words if them match an entry in the dictionary. The method can be applied on large unlabelled corpus and generate large number of links, after that we use the links as manual alignment links in proposed method.

The readers may notice that GIZA++ supports utilizing manual dictionary as well, however it is different from our method. The dictionary is used in GIZA++ only in the initialization step of Model 1, where only the statistics of the word pairs appeared in the dictionary will be collected and normalized. Given the fact that Model 1 converges to global optimal, the effect will fade out after several iterations. In contrast, our method impose a hard constraint on the alignments. Also, our method can be used side-by-side with the method in GIZA++.

4 Experiments

4.1 Experiments on manual link selectors

We designed a set of controlled experiments to show that the algorithm acts as desired. Particularly, with a number of manual alignment links fed into the aligner, we should be able to correct more misaligned alignment links than the manual alignment links through better alignment models. Also, carefully selected alignment links should outperform randomly selected alignment links.

We used Chinese-English and Arabic-English manually aligned corpus in the experiments. Table 2 shows the statistics of the corpora:

	Number of Sentences	Num. of Words Source	Num. of Words Target	Alignment Links
Ch-En	21,863	424,683	524,882	687,247
Ar-En	29,876	630,101	821,938	830,349

Table 2: Corpus statistics of the corpora

First the corpora is trained as unlabelled data to serve as baselines, and then we feed a portion of alignment links into the proposed aligner. We experimented with different methods of choosing alignment links and adjust the number of links visible to the aligner. Because of the limitations of the IBM Models, such as no N-to-1 alignments, the manual alignment is not reachable from either direction. We then define the best alignment that the IBM Models can express *"oracle alignment"*, which can be obtained by dropping all N-to-1 links from manual alignment. Also, to show the upper-bound performance, we feed all the manual alignment links to our aligner, and call the alignment *"force alignment"*. Table 3 shows the alignment qualities of oracle alignments and force alignments of both systems. For force alignments, we show the scores with and without implicit empty links derived from the manual alignment.[3] The oracle alignments are the performance upper-bounds of all aligners under IBM Model's 1-to-N assumption. The result from Table 3 shows that, if we include the derived empty links, the force alignments are close to the oracle results. Then the question is how fast we can approach the upper-bound.

To answer the question, we gradually increase the number of links being fed into the aligner. In these experiments the seeds for random number generator are fixed so that the links selected in later experiments are always superset of that of earlier experiments. The comparison of the alignment quality is shown in Figure 3 and 4. To show the actual improvement brought in by the algorithm instead of the manual alignment links themselves, we compare the alignment results of the proposed method with directly fixing the alignments from original GIZA++ training. By fixing alignments we mean that first the conventional

[3]We can derive empty links if one word has no alignment link from the full alignment we have access to.

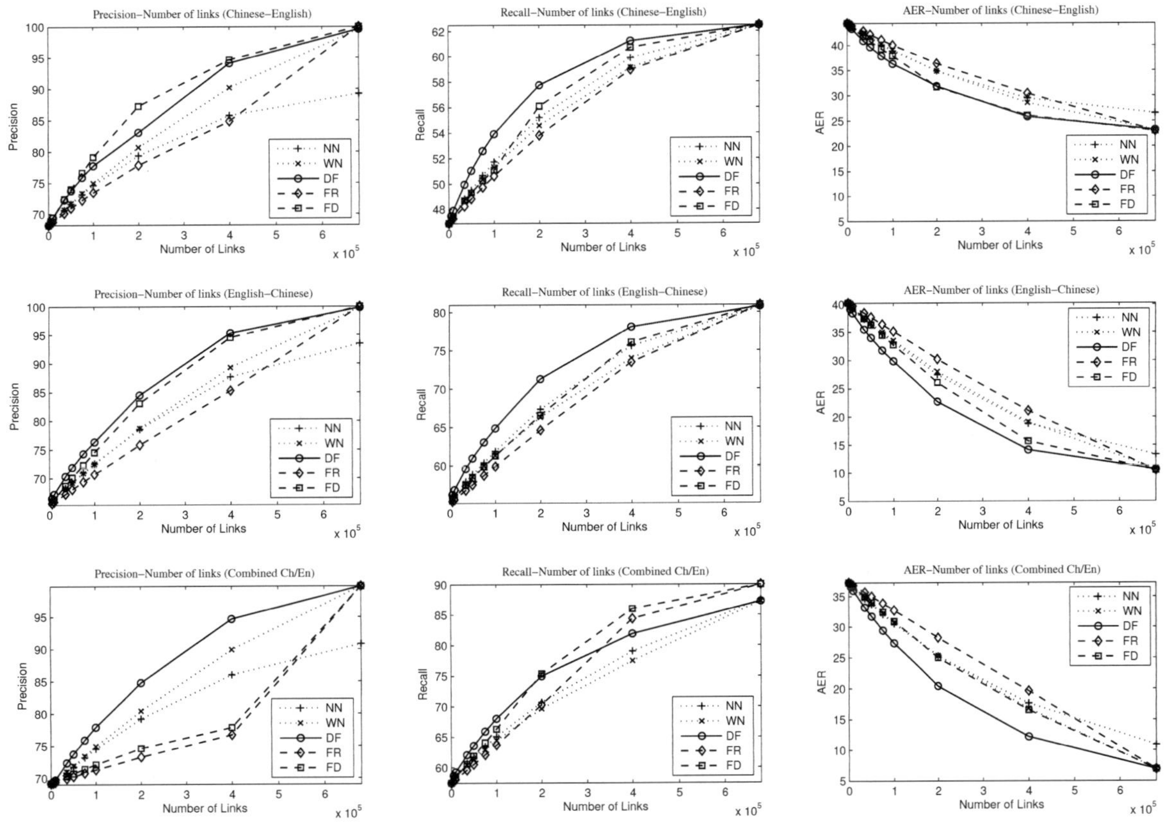

Figure 3: Alignment qualities of Chinese-English word alignment, NN: Random selector without empty links, WN: Random seletor with empty links, DF: Disagreement selector, FR: Directly fixing the alignments with random selector, FD: Directly fixing the alignments with disagreement selector. Each row shows the precision, recall and AER when applying different number of manual alignment links. The three rows are for Chinese-English, English-Chinese and heuristically symmetrized alignments (grow-diag-final-and) accordingly.

GIZA++ training is performed and then we add the manual alignment links to the resulting alignment. In case that the 1-to-N restriction of the IBM Models is violated, we keep the manual alignment links and remove the links from GIZA++.

We show the results as FR (dashed curves with diamond markers) and FD (dashed curves with square markers) in the plots, corresponding to alignments selected from the random link selector and the disagreement-based link selector. These two curves serve as baseline, and the gaps between the FR curves and the WN curves (dotted curves with cross markers) and the gaps between the FD curves and the DF curves (solid curves) show the amount of improvement we achieved using the method in addition to the manual alignment links. Therefore, they represent the effectiveness of the proposed alignment approach. Also the gaps between DF and WN curves indicate the differences in the performance of two link selectors.

The plots illustrate that when the number of links is small, the WN and DF curves are always higher than the FR/FD curves. It proves that our system does not just fix the links provided by manual alignments, instead the information propagates to other links. The largest gap between FD and DF is **8% absolute** in combined alignment of Chinese-English system with 200,000 manual alignment links. Also, we can see that the disagreement-based link selector (DF) always outperform the random selector (WN). It suggest that, if we want to harvest manual alignment links, it is possible to apply active learning method to minimize the user labelling effort while maximizing the improvement on word alignment qualities. Especially, notice that in the lower parts

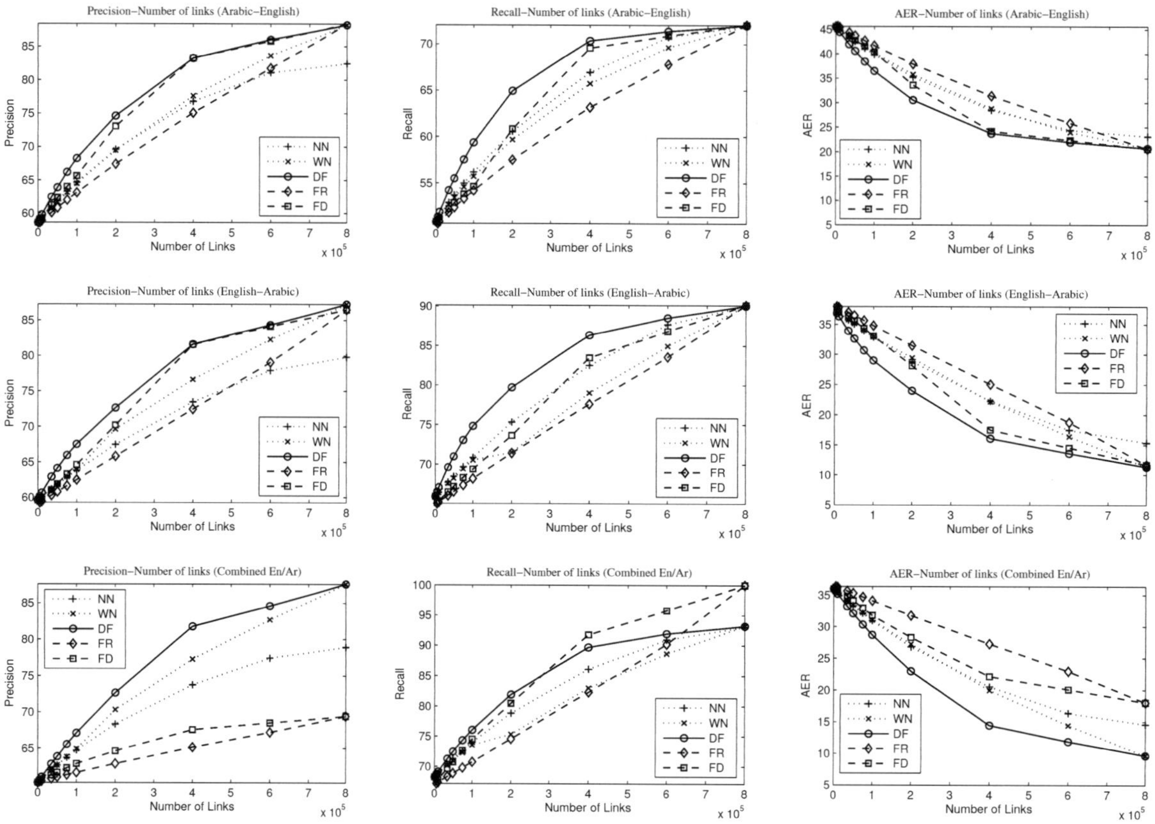

Figure 4: Alignment qualities of Arabic-English word alignment, NN: Random selector without empty links, WN: Random selector with empty links, DF: Disagreement selector, FR: Directly fixing the alignments with random selector, FD: Directly fixing the alignments with disagreement selector. Each row shows the precision, recall and AER when applying different number of manual alignment links. The three rows are for Arabic-English, English-Arabic and heuristically symmetrized alignments (grow-diag-final-and) accordingly.

of the curves, with a small number of manual alignment links, we can already improve the alignment quality by a large gap. This observation can benefit low-resource word alignment tasks.

4.2 Experiment on using heuristics

The previous experiment shows the potential of using the method on manual aligned corpus, here we demonstrate another possible usage of the proposed method that uses heuristics to generate high-precision-low-recall links. We use LDC Chinese-English dictionary as an example. The entries with single Chinese character and more than six English words are filtered out. The heuristic-based aligner yields alignment that has 79.48% precision and 17.36% recall rate on the test set we used in 4.1. By applying the links as manual links, we run proposed method on the same Chinese-English test data presented in 4.1, and the results of alignment qualities are shown in 5. As we can see, the AER reduced by 1.64 from 37.23 to 35.61 on symmetrized alignment.

We also experimented with translation tasks with moderate-size corpus. We used the corpus LDC2006G05 with 25 million words. The training scheme is the same as previous experiments, where the filtered LDC dictionary is used. After word alignment, standard Moses phrase extraction tool (Och and Ney, 2004) is used to build the translation models and finally Moses (Koehn et. al., 2007) is used to tune and decode.

We tune the system on the NIST MT06 test set (1664 sentences), and test on the MT08 (1357 sentences) and the DEV07[5] (1211 sentences) test sets, which are further divided into two sources (newswire and web data). A trigram language

[5]It is a test set used by GALE Rosseta Team

	MT02	MT03	MT04	MT05	MT08-NW	MT08-WB	Dev07NW	Dev07WB
Baseline	28.87	27.82	30.08	26.77	25.09	17.72	24.88	21.76
Dict-Link	**29.59**	*27.67*	**31.01**	27.13	25.14	17.96	**25.51**	21.88

Table 4: Comparison of the performance of baseline and the alignment generated by new aligner with dictionary links in BLEU scores

		Precision	Recall	AER
Ch-En	ORL	100.00	62.61	23.00
	F/NE	89.25	62.47	26.50
	F/WE	99.59	62.47	23.22
En-Ch	ORL	100.00	80.98	10.51
	F/NE	93.49	80.79	13.32
	F/WE	99.82	80.79	10.70
Comb	F/NE	90.79	87.49	10.89
	F/WE	99.78	87.23	6.92
Ar-En	ORL	100.00	72.07	16.23
	F/NE	82.46	72.00	23.13
	F/WE	94.25	72.00	18.36
En-Ar	ORL	100.00	90.14	5.18
	F/NE	79.81	90.06	15.37
	F/WE	93.27	90.10	8.34
Comb	F/NE	78.91	93.07	14.59
	F/WE	94.64	93.21	6.08

Table 3: Alignment quality of oracle alignment and force alignment, the rows with "ORL" in the second column are oracle alignments, "F/NE" and "F/WE" represent force alignments with empty links and without empty links correspondingly. For "F/NE" and "F/WE" we also listed the scores of heuristically symmetrized alignment[4]. ("Comb")

Chinese-English			
	Precision	Recall	AER
Baseline	68.22	46.88	44.43
Dict-Link	69.93	48.28	42.88
English-Chinese			
	Precision	Recall	AER
Baseline	65.35	55.05	40.24
Dict-Link	66.70	56.45	38.85
grow-diag-final-and			
	Precision	Recall	AER
Baseline	69.15	57.47	37.23
Dict-Link	70.11	59.54	35.61

Table 5: Comparison on alignment error rate by using alignment links generated by dictionaries

model trained from GigaWord V1 and V2 corpora is used. Table 4 shows the comparison of the performances on BLEU metric (Papineni et al., 2002). As we can observe from the results, the proposed method outperforms the baseline on all test sets except MT03, and has significant[6] improvement on MT02 (+0.72), MT04 (+0.93), and Dev07NW(+0.63). The average improvement across all test sets is 0.35 BLEU points.

As a summary, the purpose of the this experiment is to demonstrate an important characteristic of the proposed method. Even with imperfect manual alignment links, we can get better alignment by applying our method. This characteristic opens a possibility to integrate other more sophisticated aligners.

5 Conclusion

In this study, our major contribution is a novel generative model extended from IBM Model 4 to utilize partial manual alignments. The proposed method enables us to efficiently enforce subtle alignment constraints into the EM training. We performed experiments on manually aligned corpora to prove the validity. We also demonstrated using the method with simple heuristics to boost the translation quality on moderate size unlabelled corpus. The results show that our method is effective in promoting the word alignment qualities with small amounts of partial alignments and with high-precision-low-recall heuristics. Also the method of using dictionary to generate manual alignment links showed an average improvement of 0.35 BLEU points across 8 test sets.

The algorithm has small impact on the speed of GIZA++, and can easily be added to current multi-thread implementation of GIZA++. Therefore it is suitable for large scale training.

Future work includes applying the proposed approach on low resource language pairs and integrating the algorithm with other rule-based or discriminative aligners that can generate high-precision-low-recall partial alignments.

Acknowledgement

This work is supported by DARPA GALE project and NSF CluE project.

[6]We used the confidence measurement described in (Zhang and Vogel, 2004)

References

V. Ambati, S. Vogel, and J. Carbonell. 2010. Active semi-supervised learning for improving word alignment. In *Proceedings of the NAACL HLT 2010 Workshop on Active Learning for Natural Language Processing*.

S. Arora, E. Nyberg, and C. P. Rosé. 2009. Estimating annotation cost for active learning in a multi-annotator environment. In *HLT '09: Proceedings of the NAACL HLT 2009 Workshop on Active Learning for Natural Language Processing*, pages 18–26.

P. Blunsom and T. Cohn. 2006. Discriminative word alignment with conditional random fields. In *Proceedings of the 21st International Conference on Computational Linguistics and the 44th annual meeting of the Association for Computational Linguistics*, pages 65–72.

P. F. Brown et. al. 1993. The mathematics of statistical machine translation: Parameter estimation. In *Computational Linguistics*, volume 19(2), pages 263–331.

C. Callison-Burch, D. Talbot, and M. Osborne. 2004. Statistical machine translation with word-and sentence-aligned parallel corpora. In *Proceedings of the 42nd Annual Meeting on Association for Computational Linguistics*, pages 175–183.

C. Callison-Burch. 2009. Fast, cheap, and creative: Evaluating translation quality using amazons mechanical turk. In *Proceedings of the 2009 Conference on Empirical Methods in Natural Language Processing*, pages 286–295.

A. Fraser and D. Marcu. 2006. Semi-supervised training for statistical word alignment. In *ACL-44: Proceedings of the 21st International Conference on Computational Linguistics and the 44th annual meeting of the Association for Computational Linguistics*, pages 769–776.

A. Fraser and D. Marcu. 2007. Getting the structure right for word alignment: LEAF. In *Proceedings of the 2007 Joint Conference on Empirical Methods in Natural Language Processing and Computational Natural Language Learning (EMNLP-CoNLL)*, pages 51–60.

Q. Gao and S. Vogel. 2008. Parallel implementations of word alignment tool. In *Proceedings of the ACL 2008 Software Engineering, Testing, and Quality Assurance Workshop*, pages 49–57.

Q. Gao and S. Vogel. 2010. Consensus versus expertise : A case study of word alignment with mechanical turk. In *NAACL 2010 Workshop on Creating Speech and Language Data With Mechanical Turk*, pages 30–34.

F. Guzman, Q. Gao, and S. Vogel. 2009. Reassessment of the role of phrase extraction in pbsmt. In *The twelfth Machine Translation Summit*.

F. Huang. 2009. Confidence measure for word alignment. In *Proceedings of the Joint Conference of the 47th Annual Meeting of the ACL and the 4th International Joint Conference on Natural Language Processing of the AFNLP*, pages 932–940. Association for Computational Linguistics.

A. Ittycheriah and S. Roukos. 2005. A maximum entropy word aligner for arabic-english machine translation. In *Proceedings of Human Language Technology Conference and Conference on Empirical Methods in Natural Language Processing*, pages 89–96.

P. Koehn et. al. 2007. Moses: Open source toolkit for statistical machine translation. In *Proceedings of the 45th Annual Meeting of the Association for Computational Linguistics Companion Volume Proceedings of the Demo and Poster Sessions*, pages 177–180.

Y. Liu, Q. Liu, and S. Lin. 2005. Log-linear models for word alignment. In *ACL '05: Proceedings of the 43rd Annual Meeting on Association for Computational Linguistics*, pages 459–466.

R. C Moore. 2005. A discriminative framework for bilingual word alignment. In *Proceedings of the conference on Human Language Technology and Empirical Methods in Natural Language Processing*, pages 81–88.

J. Niehues and S. Vogel. 2008. Discriminative word alignment via alignment matrix modeling. In *Proceedings of the Third Workshop on Statistical Machine Translation*, pages 18–25.

F. J. Och and H. Ney. 2003. A systematic comparison of various statistical alignment models. In *Computational Linguistics*, volume 1:29, pages 19–51.

F. J. Och and H. Ney. 2004. The alignment template approach to statistical machine translation. In *Computational Linguistics*, volume 30, pages 417–449.

K. Papineni, S. Roukos, T. Ward, and W. Zhu. 2002. BLEU: A method for automatic evaluation of machine translation. In *Proceedings of ACL'02*, pages 311–318, Philadelphia, PA, July.

B. Taskar, S. Lacoste-Julien, and Klein D. 2005. A discriminative matching approach to word alignment. In *Proceedings of the conference on Human Language Technology and Empirical Methods in Natural Language Processing*, pages 73–80.

S. Vogel, H. Ney, and C. Tillmann. 1996. HMM based word alignment in statistical machine translation. In *Proceedings of 16th International Conference on Computational Linguistics)*, pages 836–841.

Y. Zhang and S. Vogel. 2004. Measuring confidence intervals for the machine translation evaluation metrics. In *Proceedings of The 10th International Conference on Theoretical and Methodological Issues in Machine Translation*, October.

Fast Consensus Hypothesis Regeneration for Machine Translation

Boxing Chen, George Foster and **Roland Kuhn**
National Research Council Canada
283 Alexandre-Taché Boulevard, Gatineau (Québec), Canada J8X 3X7
{Boxing.Chen, George.Foster, Roland.Kuhn}@nrc.ca

Abstract

This paper presents a fast consensus hypothesis regeneration approach for machine translation. It combines the advantages of feature-based fast consensus decoding and hypothesis regeneration. Our approach is more efficient than previous work on hypothesis regeneration, and it explores a wider search space than consensus decoding, resulting in improved performance. Experimental results show consistent improvements across language pairs, and an improvement of up to 0.72 BLEU is obtained over a competitive single-pass baseline on the Chinese-to-English NIST task.

1 Introduction

State-of-the-art statistical machine translation (SMT) systems are often described as a two-pass process. In the first pass, decoding algorithms are applied to generate either a translation *N*-best list or a translation forest. Then in the second pass, various re-ranking algorithms are adopted to compute the final translation. The re-ranking algorithms include rescoring (Och et al., 2004) and Minimum Bayes-Risk (MBR) decoding (Kumar and Byrne, 2004; Zhang and Gildea, 2008; Tromble et al., 2008). Rescoring uses more sophisticated additional feature functions to score the hypotheses. MBR decoding directly incorporates the evaluation metrics (i.e., loss function), into the decision criterion, so it is effective in tuning the MT performance for a specific loss function. In particular, sentence-level BLEU loss function gives gains on BLEU (Kumar and Byrne, 2004).

The naïve MBR algorithm computes the loss function between every pair of k hypotheses, needing $O(k^2)$ comparisons. Therefore, only small number k is applicable. Very recently, DeNero et al. (2009) proposed a fast consensus decoding (FCD) algorithm in which the similarity scores are computed based on the feature expectations over the translation *N*-best list or translation forest. It is equivalent to MBR decoding when using a linear similarity function, such as unigram precision.

Re-ranking approaches improve performance on an *N*-best list whose contents are fixed. A complementary strategy is to augment the contents of an *N*-best list in order to broaden the search space. Chen et al (2008) have proposed a three-pass SMT process, in which a hypothesis regeneration pass is added between the decoding and rescoring passes. New hypotheses are generated based on the original *N*-best hypotheses through *n*-gram expansion, confusion-network decoding or re-decoding. All three hypothesis regeneration methods obtained decent and comparable improvements in conjunction with the same rescoring model. However, since the final translation candidates in this approach are produced from different methods, local feature functions (such as translation models and reordering models) of each hypothesis are not directly comparable and rescoring must exploit rich global feature functions to compensate for the loss of local feature functions. Thus this approach is dependent on the use of computationally expensive features for rescoring, which makes it inefficient.

In this paper, we propose a fast consensus hypothesis regeneration method that combines the advantages of feature-based fast consensus decoding and hypothesis regeneration. That is, we integrate the feature-based similarity/loss function based on evaluation metrics such as BLEU score into the hypothesis regeneration procedure to score the partial hypotheses in the beam search and compute the final translations. Thus, our approach is more efficient than the original three-pass hypothesis regeneration. Moreover, our approach explores more search space than consen-

Proceedings of the Joint 5th Workshop on Statistical Machine Translation and MetricsMATR, pages 11–16,
Uppsala, Sweden, 15-16 July 2010.

sus decoding, giving it an advantage over the latter.

In particular, we extend linear corpus BLEU (Tromble et al., 2008) to n-gram expectation-based linear BLEU, then further extend the n-gram expectation computed on full-length hypotheses to n-gram expectation computed on fixed-length partial hypotheses. Finally, we extend the hypothesis regeneration with forward n-gram expansion to bidirectional n-gram expansion including both the forward and backward n-gram expansion. Experimental results show consistent improvements over the baseline across language pairs, and up to 0.72 BLEU points are obtained from a competitive baseline on the Chinese-to-English NIST task.

2 Fast Consensus Hypothesis Regeneration

Since the three hypothesis regeneration methods with n-gram expansion, confusion network decoding and re-decoding produce very similar performance (Chen et al., 2008), we consider only n-gram expansion method in this paper. N-gram expansion can (almost) fully exploit the search space of target strings which can be generated by an n-gram language model trained on the N-best hypotheses (Chen et al., 2007).

2.1 Hypothesis regeneration with bidirectional n-gram expansion

N-gram expansion (Chen et al., 2007) works as follows: firstly, train an n-gram language model based on the translation N-best list or translation forest; secondly, expand each partial hypothesis by appending a word via overlapped (n-1)-grams until the partial hypothesis reaches the sentence ending symbol. In each expanding step, the partial hypotheses are pruned through a beam-search algorithm with scoring functions.

Duchateau et al. (2001) shows that the backward language model contains information complementary to the information in the forward language model. Hence, on top of the forward n-gram expansion used in (Chen et al., 2008), we further introduce backward n-gram expansion to the hypothesis regeneration procedure. Backward n-gram expansion involves letting the partial hypotheses start from the last words that appeared in the translation N-best list and having the expansion go from right to left.

Figure 1 gives an example of backward n-gram expansion. The second row shows bi-grams which are extracted from the original hypotheses in the first row. The third row shows how a partial hypothesis is expanded via backward n-gram expansion method. The fourth row lists some new hypotheses generated by backward n-gram expansion which do not exist in the original hypothesis list.

original hypotheses	*about weeks' work .*			
	one week's work			
	about one week's			
	about a week work			
	about one week work			
bi-grams	*about weeks', weeks' work, ..., about one, ..., week work.*			
backward n-gram expansion	partial hyp.		***week's***	*work*
	n-gram	*one*	***week's***	
	new partial hyp.	*one*	***week's***	*work*
new hypotheses	***about one week's work***			
	about week's work			
	one weeks' work .			
	one week's work .			
	one week's work .			

Figure 1: Example of original hypotheses; bi-grams collected from them; backward expanding a partial hypothesis via an overlapped n-1-gram; and new hypotheses generated through backward n-gram expansion.

2.2 Feature-based scoring functions

To speed up the search, the partial hypotheses are pruned via beam-search in each expanding step. Therefore, the scoring functions applied with the beam-search algorithm are very important. In (Chen et al., 2008), more than 10 additional global features are computed to rank the partial hypothesis list, and this is not an efficient way. In this paper, we propose to directly incorporate the evaluation metrics such as BLEU score to rank the candidates. The scoring functions of this work are derived from the method of lattice Minimum Bayes-risk (MBR) decoding (Tromble et al., 2008) and fast consensus decoding (DeNero et al., 2009), which were originally inspired from N-best MBR decoding (Kumar and Byrne, 2004).

From a set of translation candidates E, MBR decoding chooses the translation that has the least expected loss with respect to other candidates. Given a hypothesis set E, under the probability model $P(e \mid f)$, MBR computes the translation $\tilde{e}$ as follows:

$$\tilde{e} = \arg\min_{e \in E} \sum_{e' \in E} L(e,e') \cdot P(e \mid f) \qquad (1)$$

where f is the source sentence, $L(e,e')$ is the loss function of two translations e and e'.

Suppose that we are interested in maximizing the BLEU score (Papineni et al., 2002) to optimize the translation performance. The loss function is defined as $L(e,e') = 1 - BLEU(e,e')$, then the MBR objective can be re-written as

$$\tilde{e} = \arg\max_{e \in E} \sum_{e' \in E} BLEU(e,e') \cdot P(e \mid f) \qquad (2)$$

E represents the space of the translations. For N-best MBR decoding, this space is the N-best list produced by a baseline decoder (Kumar and Byrne, 2004). For lattice MBR decoding, this space is the set of candidates encoded in the lattice (Tromble et al., 2008). Here, with hypothesis regeneration, this space includes: 1) the translations produced by the baseline decoder either in an N-best list or encoded in a translation lattice, and 2) the translations created by hypothesis regeneration.

However, BLEU score is not linear with the length of the hypothesis, which makes the scoring process for each expanding step of hypothesis regeneration very slow. To further speed up the beam search procedure, we use an extension of a linear function of a Taylor approximation to the logarithm of corpus BLEU which was developed by (Tromble et al., 2008). The original BLEU score of two hypotheses e and e' are computed as follows.

$$BLEU(e,e') = \gamma(e,e') \times \exp\left(\frac{1}{4}\sum_{n=1}^{4} \log(P_n(e,e'))\right) \qquad (3)$$

where $P_n(e,e')$ is the precision of n-grams in the hypothesis e given e' and $\gamma(e,e')$ is a brevity penalty. Let $|e|$ denote the length of e. The corpus log-BLEU gain is defined as follows:

$$\log(BLEU(e,e')) = \min\left(0, 1 - \frac{|e|}{|e'|}\right) + \frac{1}{4}\sum_{n=1}^{4} \log(P_n(e,e')) \qquad (4)$$

Therefore, the first-order Taylor approximation to the logarithm of corpus BLEU is shown in Equation (5).

$$G(e,e') = \theta_0 |e| + \frac{1}{4}\sum_{n=1}^{4} \theta_n \cdot c_n(e,e') \qquad (5)$$

where $c_n(e,e')$ are the counts of the matched n-grams and θ_n ($0 \le n \le 4$) are constant weights estimated with held-out data.

Suppose we have computed the expected n-gram counts from the N-best list or translation forest. Then we may extend linear corpus BLEU in (5) to n-gram expectation-based linear corpus BLEU to score the partial hypotheses h. That is

$$G(h,e') = \theta_0 |h| + \frac{1}{4}\sum_{n=1}^{4} \theta_n \cdot \sum_{t \in T_n} E[c_n(e',t)] \cdot \delta_n(h,t) \qquad (6)$$

where $\delta_n(h,t)$ are n-gram indicator functions that equal 1 if n-gram t appears in h and 0 otherwise; $E[c_n(e',t)]$ ($1 \le n \le 4$) are the real-valued n-gram expectations. Different from lattice MBR decoding, n-gram expectations in this work are computed over the original translation N-best list or translation forest; T_n ($1 \le n \le 4$) are the sets of n-grams collected from translation N-best list or translation forest. Then we make a further extension: the expectations of the n-gram counts for each expanding step are computed over the partial translations. The lengths of all partial hypotheses are the same in each n-gram expanding step. For instance, in the 5th n-gram expanding step, the lengths of all the partial hypotheses are 5 words. Therefore, we use n-gram count expectations computed over partial original translations that only contain the first 5 words. The reason is that this solution contains more information about word orderings, since some n-grams appear more than others at the beginning of the translations while they may appear with the same or even lower frequencies than others in the full translations.

Once the expanding process of hypothesis regeneration is finished, we use a more precise BLEU metric to score all the translation candidates. We extend BLEU score in (3) to n-gram expectation-based BLEU. That is:

$$Score(h) = BLEU(h,e') + \exp\left[\min\left(0, 1 - \frac{E[|e'|]}{|h|}\right) + \frac{1}{4}\sum_{n=1}^{4} \log \frac{\sum_{t \in T_n} \min(c_n(h,t), E[c_n(e',t)])}{\sum_{t \in T_n} c_n(h,t)}\right] \qquad (7)$$

where $c_n(h,t)$ is the count of n-gram t in the hypothesis h. The step of choosing the final translation is the same as fast consensus decoding (DeNero et al., 2009): first we compute n-

gram feature expectations, and then we choose the translation that is most similar to the others via expected similarity according to feature-based BLEU score as shown in (7). The difference is the space of translations: the space of fast consensus decoding is the same as MBR decoding, while the space of hypothesis regeneration is enlarged by the new translations produced via n-gram expansion.

2.3 Fast consensus hypothesis regeneration

We first generate two new hypothesis lists via forward and backward n-gram expansion using the scoring function in Equation (6). Then we choose a final translation using the scoring function in Equation (7) from the union of the original hypotheses and newly generated hypotheses. The original hypotheses are from the N-best list or extracted from the translation forest. The new hypotheses are generated by forward or backward n-gram expansion or are the union of both two new hypothesis lists (this is called "bi-directional n-gram expansion").

3 Experimental Results

We carried out experiments based on translation N-best lists generated by a state-of-the-art phrase-based statistical machine translation system, similar to (Koehn et al., 2007). In detail, the phrase table is derived from merged counts of symmetrized IBM2 and HMM alignments; the system has both lexicalized and distance-based distortion components (there is a 7-word distortion limit) and employs cube pruning (Huang and Chiang, 2007). The baseline is a log-linear feature combination that includes language models, the distortion components, translation model, phrase and word penalties. Weights on feature functions are found by lattice MERT (Macherey et al., 2008).

3.1 Data

We evaluated with different language pairs: Chinese-to-English, and German-to-English. Chinese-to-English tasks are based on training data for the NIST [1] 2009 evaluation Chinese-to-English track. All the allowed bilingual corpora have been used for estimating the translation model. We trained two language models: the first one is a 5-gram LM which is estimated on the target side of the parallel data. The second is a 5-gram LM trained on the so-called English *Gigaword corpus*.

			Chi	Eng
Parallel Train	Large Data	|S|	10.1M	
		|W|	270.0M	279.1M
Dev		|S|	1,506	1,506×4
Test	NIST06	|S|	1,664	1,664×4
	NIST08	|S|	1,357	1,357×4
Gigaword		|S|	-	11.7M

Table 1: Statistics of training, dev, and test sets for Chinese-to-English task.

We carried out experiments for translating Chinese to English. We first created a development set which used mainly data from the NIST 2005 test set, and also some balanced-genre web-text from the NIST training material. Evaluation was performed on the NIST 2006 and 2008 test sets. Table 1 gives figures for training, development and test corpora; |S| is the number of the sentences, and |W| is the size of running words. Four references are provided for all dev and test sets.

For German-to-English tasks, we used WMT 2006[2] data sets. The parallel training data contains about 1 million sentence pairs and includes 21 million target words; both the dev set and test set contain 2000 sentences; one reference is provided for each source input sentence. Only the target-language half of the parallel training data are used to train the language model in this task.

3.2 Results

Our evaluation metric is IBM BLEU (Papineni et al., 2002), which performs case-insensitive matching of n-grams up to $n = 4$.

Our first experiment was carried out over 1000-best lists on Chinese-to-English task. For comparison, we also conducted experiments with rescoring (two-pass) and three-pass hypothesis regeneration with only forward n-gram expansion as proposed in (Chen et al., 2008). In the "rescoring" and "three-pass" systems, we used the same rescoring model. There are 21 rescoring features in total, mainly translation lexicon scores from IBM and HMM models, posterior probabilities for words, n-grams, and sentence length, and language models, etc. For a complete description, please refer to (Ueffing et al., 2007). The results in BLEU-4 are reported in Table 2.

[1] http://www.nist.gov/speech/tests/mt

[2] http://www.statmt.org/wmt06/

testset	NIST'06	NIST'08
baseline	35.70	28.60
rescoring	36.01	28.97
three-pass	35.98	28.99
FCD	36.00	29.10
Fwd.	36.13	29.19
Bwd.	36.11	29.20
Bid.	36.20	29.28

Table 2: Translation performances in BLEU-4(%) over 1000-best lists for Chinese-to-English task: "rescoring" represents the results of rescoring; "three-pass", three-pass hypothesis regeneration with forward n-gram expansion; "FCD", fast consensus decoding; "Fwd", the results of hypothesis regeneration with forward n-gram expansion; "Bwd", backward n-gram expansion; and "Bid", bi-directional n-gram expansion.

Firstly, rescoring improved performance over the baseline by 0.3-0.4 BLEU point. Three-pass hypothesis regeneration with only forward n-gram expansion ("three-pass" in Table 2) obtained almost the same improvements as rescoring. Three-pass hypothesis regeneration exploits more hypotheses than rescoring, while rescoring involves more scoring feature functions than the former. They reached a balance in this experiment. Then, fast consensus decoding ("FCD" in Table 2) obtains 0.3-0.5 BLEU point improvements over the baseline. Both forward and backward n-gram expansion ("Fwd." and "Bwd." in Table 2) improved about 0.1 BLEU point over the results of consensus decoding. Fast consensus hypothesis regeneration (Fwd. and Bwd. in Table 2) got better improvements than three-pass hypothesis regeneration ("three-pass" in Table 2) by 0.1-0.2 BLEU point. Finally, combining hypothesis lists from forward and backward n-gram expansion ("Bid." in Table 2), further slight gains were obtained.

testset	Average time
three-pass	3h 54m
Fwd.	25m
Bwd.	28m
Bid.	40m

Table 3: Average processing time of NIST'06 and NIST'08 test sets used in different systems. Times include n-best list regeneration and re-ranking.

Moreover, fast consensus hypothesis regeneration is much faster than the three-pass one, because the former only needs to compute one feature, while the latter needs to compute more than 20 additional features. In this experiment, the former is about 10 times faster than the latter in terms of processing time, as shown in Table 3.

In our second experiment, we set the size of N-best list N equal to 10,000 for both Chinese-to-English and German-to-English tasks. The results are reported in Table 4. The same trend as in the first experiment can also be observed in this experiment. It is worth noticing that enlarging the size of the N-best list from 1000 to 10,000 did not change the performance significantly. Bi-directional n-gram expansion obtained improvements of 0.24 BLEU-score for WMT 2006 de-en test set; 0.55 for NIST 2006 test set; and 0.72 for NIST 2008 test set over the baseline.

Lang.	ch-en		de-en
testset	NIST'06	NIST'08	Test2006
baseline	35.70	28.60	26.92
FCD	36.03	29.08	27.03
Fwd.	36.16	29.25	27.11
Bwd.	36.17	29.22	27.12
Bid.	36.25	29.32	27.16

Table 4: Translation performances in BLEU-4 (%) over 10K-best lists.

We then tested the effect of the extension according to which the expectations over n-gram counts are computed on partial hypotheses rather than whole candidate translations as described in Section 2.2. As shown in Table 5, we got tiny improvements on both test sets by computing the expectations over n-gram counts on partial hypotheses.

testset	NIST'06	NIST'08
full	36.11	29.14
partial	36.13	29.19

Table 5: Translation performances in BLEU-4 (%) over 1000-best lists for Chinese-to-English task: "full" represents expectations over n-gram counts that are computed on whole hypotheses; "partial" represents expectations over n-gram counts that are computed on partial hypotheses.

3.3 Discussion

To speed up the search, the partial hypotheses in each expanding step are pruned. When pruning is applied, forward and backward n-gram expansion would generate different new hypothesis lists. Let us look back at the example in Figure 1.

Given 5 original hypotheses in Figure 1, if we set the beam size equal to 5 (the size of the original hypotheses), the forward and backward n-gram expansion generated different new hypothesis lists, as shown in Figure 2.

forward	backward
one week's work .	*one week's work .*
about week's work	*about one week's work*

Figure 2: Different new hypothesis lists generated by forward and backward n-gram expansion.

For bi-directional n-gram expansion, the chosen translation for a source sentence comes from the decoder 94% of the time for WMT 2006 test set, 90% for NIST test sets; it comes from forward n-gram expansion 2% of the time for WMT 2006 test set, 4% for NIST test sets; it comes from backward n-gram expansion 4% of the time for WMT 2006 test set, 6% for NIST test sets. This proves bidirectional n-gram expansion is a good way of enlarging the search space.

4 Conclusions and Future Work

We have proposed a fast consensus hypothesis regeneration approach for machine translation. It combines the advantages of feature-based consensus decoding and hypothesis regeneration. This approach is more efficient than previous work on hypothesis regeneration, and it explores a wider search space than consensus decoding, resulting in improved performance. Experiments showed consistent improvements across language pairs.

Instead of N-best lists, translation lattices or forests have been shown to be effective for MBR decoding (Zhang and Gildea, 2008; Tromble et al., 2008), and DeNero et al. (2009) showed how to compute expectations of n-grams from a translation forest. Therefore, our future work may involve hypothesis regeneration using an n-gram language model trained on the translation forest.

References

B. Chen, M. Federico and M. Cettolo. 2007. Better N-best Translations through Generative n-gram Language Models. In: *Proceedings of MT Summit XI.* Copenhagen, Denmark. September.

B. Chen, M. Zhang, A. Aw, and H. Li. 2008. Regenerating Hypotheses for Statistical Machine Translation. In: *Proceedings of COLING.* pp105-112. Manchester, UK, August.

J. DeNero, D. Chiang and K. Knight. 2009. Fast Consensus Decoding over Translation Forests. In: *Proceedings of ACL.* Singapore, August.

J. Duchateau, K. Demuynck, and P. Wambacq. 2001. Confidence scoring based on backward language models. In: *Proceedings of ICASSP 2001.* Salt Lake City, Utah, USA, May.

L. Huang and D. Chiang. 2007. Forest Rescoring: Faster Decoding with Integrated Language Models. In: *Proceedings of ACL.* pp. 144-151, Prague, Czech Republic, June.

P. Koehn, H. Hoang, A. Birch, C. Callison-Burch, M. Federico, N. Bertoldi, B. Cowan, W. Shen, C. Moran, R. Zens, C. Dyer, O. Bojar, A. Constantin and E. Herbst. 2007. Moses: Open Source Toolkit for Statistical Machine Translation. In: *Proceedings of ACL.* pp. 177-180, Prague, Czech Republic.

S. Kumar and W. Byrne. 2004. Minimum Bayes-risk decoding for statistical machine translation. In: *Proceedings of NAACL.* Boston, MA, May.

W. Macherey, F. Och, I. Thayer, and J. Uszkoreit. 2008. Lattice-based Minimum Error Rate Training for Statistical Machine Translation. In: *Proceedings of EMNLP.* pp. 725-734, Honolulu, USA, October.

F. Och. 2003. Minimum error rate training in statistical machine translation. In: *Proceedings of ACL.* Sapporo, Japan. July.

F. Och, D. Gildea, S. Khudanpur, A. Sarkar, K. Yamada, A. Fraser, S. Kumar, L. Shen, D. Smith, K. Eng, V. Jain, Z. Jin, and D. Radev. 2004. A Smorgasbord of Features for Statistical Machine Translation. In: *Proceedings of NAACL.* Boston.

K. Papineni, S. Roukos, T. Ward, and W. Zhu. 2002. BLEU: A method for automatic evaluation of machine translation. In: *Proceedings of the ACL 2002.*

R. Tromble, S. Kumar, F. J. Och, and W. Macherey. 2008. Lattice minimum Bayes-risk decoding for statistical machine translation. In: *Proceedings of EMNLP.* Hawaii, US. October.

N. Ueffing, M. Simard, S. Larkin, and J. H. Johnson. 2007. NRC's Portage system for WMT 2007. In: *Proceedings of ACL Workshop on SMT.* Prague, Czech Republic, June.

H. Zhang and D. Gildea. 2008. Efficient multipass decoding for synchronous context free grammars. In: *Proceedings of ACL.* Columbus, US. June.

Findings of the 2010 Joint Workshop on Statistical Machine Translation and Metrics for Machine Translation

Chris Callison-Burch
Johns Hopkins University
ccb@cs.jhu.edu

Philipp Koehn
University of Edinburgh
pkoehn@inf.ed.ac.uk

Christof Monz
University of Amsterdam
c.monz@uva.nl

Kay Peterson and **Mark Przybocki**
National Institute of Standards and Technology
kay.peterson,mark.przybocki@nist.gov

Omar F. Zaidan
Johns Hopkins University
ozaidan@cs.jhu.edu

Abstract

This paper presents the results of the WMT10 and MetricsMATR10 shared tasks,[1] which included a translation task, a system combination task, and an evaluation task. We conducted a large-scale manual evaluation of 104 machine translation systems and 41 system combination entries. We used the ranking of these systems to measure how strongly automatic metrics correlate with human judgments of translation quality for 26 metrics. This year we also investigated increasing the number of human judgments by hiring non-expert annotators through Amazon's Mechanical Turk.

1 Introduction

This paper presents the results of the shared tasks of the joint Workshop on statistical Machine Translation (WMT) and Metrics for MAchine TRanslation (MetricsMATR), which was held at ACL 2010. This builds on four previous WMT workshops (Koehn and Monz, 2006; Callison-Burch et al., 2007; Callison-Burch et al., 2008; Callison-Burch et al., 2009), and one previous MetricsMATR meeting (Przybocki et al., 2008). There were three shared tasks this year: a translation task between English and four other European languages, a task to combine the output of multiple machine translation systems, and a task to predict human judgments of translation quality using automatic evaluation metrics. The performance on each of these shared task was determined after a comprehensive human evaluation.

There were a number of differences between this year's workshop and last year's workshop:

- **Non-expert judgments** – In addition to having shared task participants judge translation quality, we also collected judgments from non-expert annotators hired through Amazon's Mechanical Turk. By collecting a large number of judgments we hope to reduce the burden on shared task participants, and to increase the statistical significance of our findings. We discuss the feasibility of using non-experts evaluators, by analyzing the cost, volume and quality of non-expert annotations.

- **Clearer results for system combination** – This year we excluded Google translations from the systems used in system combination. In last year's evaluation, the large margin between Google and many of the other systems meant that it was hard to improve on when combining systems. This year, the system combinations perform better than their component systems more often than last year.

- **Fewer rule-based systems** – This year there were fewer rule-based systems submitted. In past years, University of Saarland compiled a large set of outputs from rule-based machine translation (RBMT) systems. The RBMT systems were not submitted this year. This is unfortunate, because they tended to outperform the statistical systems for German, and they were often difficult to rank properly using automatic evaluation metrics.

The primary objectives of this workshop are to evaluate the state of the art in machine transla-

[1]The MetricsMATR analysis was not complete in time for the publication deadline. An updated version of paper will be made available on http://statmt.org/wmt10/ prior to July 15, 2010.

Proceedings of the Joint 5th Workshop on Statistical Machine Translation and MetricsMATR, pages 17–53,
Uppsala, Sweden, 15-16 July 2010.

tion, to disseminate common test sets and public training data with published performance numbers, and to refine evaluation methodologies for machine translation. As with past years, all of the data, translations, and human judgments produced for our workshop are publicly available.[2] We hope they form a valuable resource for research into statistical machine translation, system combination, and automatic evaluation of translation quality.

2 Overview of the shared translation and system combination tasks

The workshop examined translation between English and four other languages: German, Spanish, French, and Czech. We created a test set for each language pair by translating newspaper articles. We additionally provided training data and two baseline systems.

2.1 Test data

The test data for this year's task was created by hiring people to translate news articles that were drawn from a variety of sources from mid-December 2009. A total of 119 articles were selected, in roughly equal amounts from a variety of Czech, English, French, German and Spanish news sites:[3]

Czech: iDNES.cz (5), iHNed.cz (1), Lidovky (16)

French: Les Echos (25)

Spanish: El Mundo (20), ABC.es (4), Cinco Dias (11)

English: BBC (5), Economist (2), Washington Post (12), Times of London (3)

German: Frankfurter Rundschau (11), Spiegel (4)

The translations were created by the professional translation agency CEET[4]. All of the translations were done directly, and not via an intermediate language.

2.2 Training data

As in past years we provided parallel corpora to train translation models, monolingual corpora to train language models, and development sets to tune parameters. Some statistics about the training materials are given in Figure 1.

2.3 Baseline systems

To lower the barrier of entry for newcomers to the field, we provided two open source toolkits for phrase-based and parsing-based statistical machine translation (Koehn et al., 2007; Li et al., 2009).

2.4 Submitted systems

We received submissions from 33 groups from 29 institutions, as listed in Table 1, a 50% increase over last year's shared task.

We also evaluated 2 commercial off the shelf MT systems, and two online statistical machine translation systems. We note that these companies did not submit entries themselves. The entries for the online systems were done by translating the test data via their web interfaces. The data used to train the online systems is unconstrained. It is possible that part of the reference translations that were taken from online news sites could have been included in the online systems' language models.

2.5 System combination

In total, we received 153 primary system submissions along with 28 secondary submissions. These were made available to participants in the system combination shared task. Based on feedback that we received on last year's system combination task, we provided two additional resources to participants:

- Development set: We reserved 25 articles to use as a dev set for system combination. These were translated by all participating sites, and distributed to system combination participants along with reference translations.
- n-best translations: We requested n-best lists from sites whose systems could produce them. We received 20 n-best lists accompanying the system submissions.

Table 2 lists the 9 participants in the system combination task.

3 Human evaluation

As with past workshops, we placed greater emphasis on the human evaluation than on the automatic evaluation metric scores. It is our contention

[2] `http://statmt.org/wmt10/results.html`

[3] For more details see the XML test files. The `docid` tag gives the source and the date for each document in the test set, and the `origlang` tag indicates the original source language.

[4] `http://www.ceet.eu/`

Europarl Training Corpus

	Spanish ↔ English		French ↔ English		German ↔ English	
Sentences	1,650,152		1,683,156		1,540,549	
Words	47,694,560	46,078,122	50,964,362	47,145,288	40,756,801	43,037,967
Distinct words	173,033	95,305	123,639	95,846	316,365	92,464

News Commentary Training Corpus

	Spanish ↔ English		French ↔ English		German ↔ English		Czech ↔ English	
Sentences	98,598		84,624		100,269		94,742	
Words	2,724,141	2,432,064	2,405,082	2,101,921	2,505,583	2,443,183	2,050,545	2,290,066
Distinct words	69,410	46,918	53,763	43,906	101,529	47,034	125,678	45,306

United Nations Training Corpus

	Spanish ↔ English		French ↔ English	
Sentences	6,222,450		7,230,217	
Words	213,877,170	190,978,737	243,465,100	216,052,412
Distinct words	441,517	361,734	402,491	412,815

10^9 Word Parallel Corpus

	French ↔ English	
Sentences	22,520,400	
Words	811,203,407	668,412,817
Distinct words	2,738,882	2,861,836

CzEng Training Corpus

	Czech ↔ English	
Sentences	7,227,409	
Words	72,993,427	84,856,749
Distinct words	1,088,642	522,770

Europarl Language Model Data

	English	Spanish	French	German
Sentence	1,843,035	1,822,021	1,855,589	1,772,039
Words	50,132,615	51,223,902	54,273,514	43,781,217
Distinct words	99,206	178,934	127,689	328,628

News Language Model Data

	English	Spanish	French	German	Czech
Sentence	48,653,884	3,857,414	15,670,745	17,474,133	13,042,040
Words	1,148,480,525	106,716,219	382,563,246	321,165,206	205,614,201
Distinct words	1,451,719	548,169	998,595	1,855,993	1,715,376

News Test Set

	English	Spanish	French	German	Czech
Sentences	2489				
Words	62,988	65,654	68,107	62,390	53,171
Distinct words	9,457	11,409	10,775	12,718	15,825

Figure 1: Statistics for the training and test sets used in the translation task. The number of words and the number of distinct words is based on the provided tokenizer.

ID	Participant
AALTO	Aalto University, Finland (Virpioja et al., 2010)
CAMBRIDGE	Cambridge University (Pino et al., 2010)
CMU	Carnegie Mellon University's Cunei system (Phillips, 2010)
CMU-STATXFER	Carnegie Mellon University's statistical transfer system (Hanneman et al., 2010)
COLUMBIA	Columbia University
CU-BOJAR	Charles University Bojar (Bojar and Kos, 2010)
CU-TECTO	Charles University Tectogramatical MT (Žabokrtský et al., 2010)
CU-ZEMAN	Charles University Zeman (Zeman, 2010)
DCU	Dublin City University (Penkale et al., 2010)
DFKI	Deutsches Forschungszentrum für Künstliche Intelligenz (Federmann et al., 2010)
EU	European Parliament, Luxembourg (Jellinghaus et al., 2010)
EUROTRANS	commercial MT provider from the Czech Republic
FBK	Fondazione Bruno Kessler (Hardmeier et al., 2010)
GENEVA	University of Geneva
HUICONG	Shanghai Jiao Tong University (Cong et al., 2010)
JHU	Johns Hopkins University (Schwartz, 2010)
KIT	Karlsruhe Institute for Technology (Niehues et al., 2010)
KOC	Koc University, Turkey (Bicici and Kozat, 2010; Bicici and Yuret, 2010)
LIG	LIG Lab, University Joseph Fourier, Grenoble (Potet et al., 2010)
LIMSI	LIMSI (Allauzen et al., 2010)
LIU	Linköping University (Stymne et al., 2010)
LIUM	University of Le Mans (Lambert et al., 2010)
NRC	National Research Council Canada (Larkin et al., 2010)
ONLINEA	an online machine translation system
ONLINEB	an online machine translation system
PC-TRANS	commercial MT provider from the Czech Republic
POTSDAM	Potsdam University
RALI	RALI - Université de Montréal (Huet et al., 2010)
RWTH	RWTH Aachen (Heger et al., 2010)
SFU	Simon Fraser University (Sankaran et al., 2010)
UCH-UPV	Universidad CEU-Cardenal Herrera y UPV (Zamora-Martinez and Sanchis-Trilles, 2010)
UEDIN	University of Edinburgh (Koehn et al., 2010)
UMD	University of Maryland (Eidelman et al., 2010)
UPC	Universitat Politècnica de Catalunya (Henríquez Q. et al., 2010)
UPPSALA	Uppsala University (Tiedemann, 2010)
UPV	Universidad Politécnica de Valencia (Sanchis-Trilles et al., 2010)
UU-MS	Uppsala University - Saers (Saers et al., 2010)

Table 1: Participants in the shared translation task. Not all groups participated in all language pairs.

ID	Participant
BBN-COMBO	BBN system combination (Rosti et al., 2010)
CMU-COMBO-HEAFIELD	CMU system combination (Heafield and Lavie, 2010)
CMU-COMBO-HYPOSEL	CMU system combo with hyp. selection (Hildebrand and Vogel, 2010)
DCU-COMBO	Dublin City University system combination (Du et al., 2010)
JHU-COMBO	Johns Hopkins University system combination (Narsale, 2010)
KOC-COMBO	Koc University, Turkey (Bicici and Kozat, 2010; Bicici and Yuret, 2010)
LIUM-COMBO	University of Le Mans system combination (Barrault, 2010)
RWTH-COMBO	RWTH Aachen system combination (Leusch and Ney, 2010)
UPV-COMBO	Universidad Politécnica de Valencia (González-Rubio et al., 2010)

Table 2: Participants in the system combination task.

Language Pair	Sentence Ranking	Edited Translations	Yes/No Judgments
German-English	5,212	830	824
English-German	6,847	755	751
Spanish-English	5,653	845	845
English-Spanish	2,587	920	690
French-English	4,147	925	921
English-French	3,981	1,325	1,223
Czech-English	2,688	490	488
English-Czech	6,769	1,165	1,163
Totals	**37,884**	**7,255**	**6,905**

Table 3: The number of items that were collected for each task during the manual evaluation. An item is defined to be a rank label in the ranking task, an edited sentence in the editing task, and a yes/no judgment in the judgment task.

that automatic measures are an imperfect substitute for human assessment of translation quality. Therefore, we define the manual evaluation to be primary, and use the human judgments to validate automatic metrics.

Manual evaluation is time consuming, and it requires a large effort to conduct it on the scale of our workshop. We distributed the workload across a number of people, including shared-task participants, interested volunteers, and a small number of paid annotators. More than 120 people participated in the manual evaluation[5], with 89 people putting in more than an hour's worth of effort, and 29 putting in more than four hours. A collective total of 337 hours of labor was invested.[6]

We asked people to evaluate the systems' output in two different ways:

- Ranking translated sentences relative to each other. This was our official determinant of translation quality.
- Editing the output of systems without displaying the source or a reference translation, and then later judging whether edited translations were correct.

The total number of judgments collected for the different modes of annotation is given in Table 3.

In all cases, the output of the various translation systems were judged on equal footing; the output of system combinations was judged alongside that of the individual system, and the constrained and unconstrained systems were judged together.

3.1 Ranking translations of sentences

Ranking translations relative to each other is a reasonably intuitive task. We therefore kept the instructions simple:

> *Rank translations from Best to Worst relative to the other choices (ties are allowed).*

[5]We excluded data from three errant annotators, identified as follows. We considered annotators completing at least 3 screens, whose $P(A)$ with others (see 3.2) is less than 0.33. Out of seven such annotators, four were affiliated with shared task teams. The other three had no apparent affiliation, and so we discarded their data, less than 5% of the total data.

[6]Whenever an annotator appears to have spent more than ten minutes on a single screen, we assume they left their station and left the window open, rather than actually needing more than ten minutes. In those cases, we assume the time spent to be ten minutes.

Each screen for this task involved judging translations of three consecutive source segments. For each source segment, the annotator was shown the outputs of five submissions. For each of the language pairs, there were more than 5 submissions. We did not attempt to get a complete ordering over the systems, and instead relied on random selection and a reasonably large sample size to make the comparisons fair.

Relative ranking is our official evaluation metric. Individual systems and system combinations are ranked based on how frequently they were judged to be better than or equal to any other system. The results of this are reported in Section 4. Appendix A provides detailed tables that contain pairwise comparisons between systems.

3.2 Inter- and Intra-annotator agreement in the ranking task

We were interested in determining the inter- and intra-annotator agreement for the ranking task, since a reasonable degree of agreement must exist to support our process as a valid evaluation setup. To ensure we had enough data to measure agreement, we purposely designed the sampling of source segments shown to annotators so that items were likely to be repeated, both within an annotator's assigned tasks and across annotators. We did so by assigning an annotator a batch of 20 screens (each with three ranking sets; see 3.1) that were to be completed in full before generating new screens for that annotator.

Within each batch, the source segments for nine of the 20 screens (45%) were chosen from a small pool of 60 source segments, instead of being sampled from the larger pool of 1,000 source segments designated for the ranking task.[7] The larger pool was used to choose source segments for nine other screens (also 45%). As for the remaining two screens (10%), they were chosen randomly from the set of eighteen screens already chosen. Furthermore, in the two "local repeat" screens, the system choices were also preserved.

Heavily sampling from a small pool of source segments ensured we had enough data to measure inter-annotator agreement, while purposely making 10% of each annotator's screens repeats of previously seen sets in the same batch ensured we

[7]Each language pair had its own 60-sentence pool, disjoint from other language pairs' pools, but ach of the 60-sentence pools was a subset of the 1,000-sentence pool.

INTER-ANNOTATOR AGREEMENT		
	$P(A)$	K
With references	0.658	0.487
Without references	0.626	0.439
WMT '09	0.549	0.323

INTRA-ANNOTATOR AGREEMENT		
	$P(A)$	K
With references	0.755	0.633
Without references	0.734	0.601
WMT '09	0.707	0.561

Table 4: Inter- and intra-annotator agreement for the sentence ranking task. In this task, $P(E)$ is 0.333.

had enough data to measure intra-annotator agreement.

We measured pairwise agreement among annotators using the kappa coefficient (K), which is defined as

$$K = \frac{P(A) - P(E)}{1 - P(E)}$$

where $P(A)$ is the proportion of times that the annotators agree, and $P(E)$ is the proportion of time that they would agree by chance.

For inter-annotator agreement for the ranking tasks we calculated $P(A)$ by examining all pairs of systems which had been judged by two or more judges, and calculated the proportion of time that they agreed that $A > B$, $A = B$, or $A < B$. Intra-annotator agreement was computed similarly, but we gathered items that were annotated on multiple occasions by a single annotator.

Table 4 gives K values for inter-annotator and intra-annotator agreement. These give an indication of how often different judges agree, and how often single judges are consistent for repeated judgments, respectively. The exact interpretation of the kappa coefficient is difficult, but according to Landis and Koch (1977), $0 - .2$ is slight, $.2 - .4$ is fair, $.4 - .6$ is moderate, $.6 - .8$ is substantial and the rest is almost perfect.

Based on these interpretations the agreement for sentence-level ranking is *moderate* for inter-annotator agreement and *substantial* for intra-annotator agreement. These levels of agreement are higher than in previous years, partially due to the fact that that year we randomly included the references along the system outputs. In general, judges tend to rank the reference as the best translation, so people have stronger levels of agreement when it is included. That said, even when comparisons involving reference are excluded, we still see an improvement in agreement levels over last year.

3.3 Editing machine translation output

In addition to simply ranking the output of systems, we also had people edit the output of MT systems. We did not show them the reference translation, which makes our edit-based evaluation different from the Human-targeted Translation Edit Rate (HTER) measure used in the DARPA GALE program (NIST, 2008). Rather than asking people to make the minimum number of changes to the MT output in order capture the same meaning as the reference, we asked them to edit the translation to be as fluent as possible without seeing the reference. Our hope was that this would reflect people's understanding of the output.

The instructions given to our judges were as follows:

> *Correct the translation displayed, making it as fluent as possible. If no corrections are needed, select "No corrections needed." If you cannot understand the sentence well enough to correct it, select "Unable to correct."*

A screenshot is shown in Figure 2. This year, judges were shown the translations of 5 consecutive source sentences, all produced by the same machine translation system. In last year's WMT evaluation they were shown only one sentence at a time, which made the task more difficult because the surrounding context could not be used as an aid to understanding.

Since we wanted to prevent judges from seeing the reference before editing the translations, we split the test set between the sentences used in the ranking task and the editing task (because they were being conducted concurrently). Moreover, annotators edited only a single system's output for one source sentence to ensure that their understanding of it would not be influenced by another system's output.

3.4 Judging the acceptability of edited output

Halfway through the manual evaluation period, we stopped collecting edited translations, and instead asked annotators to do the following:

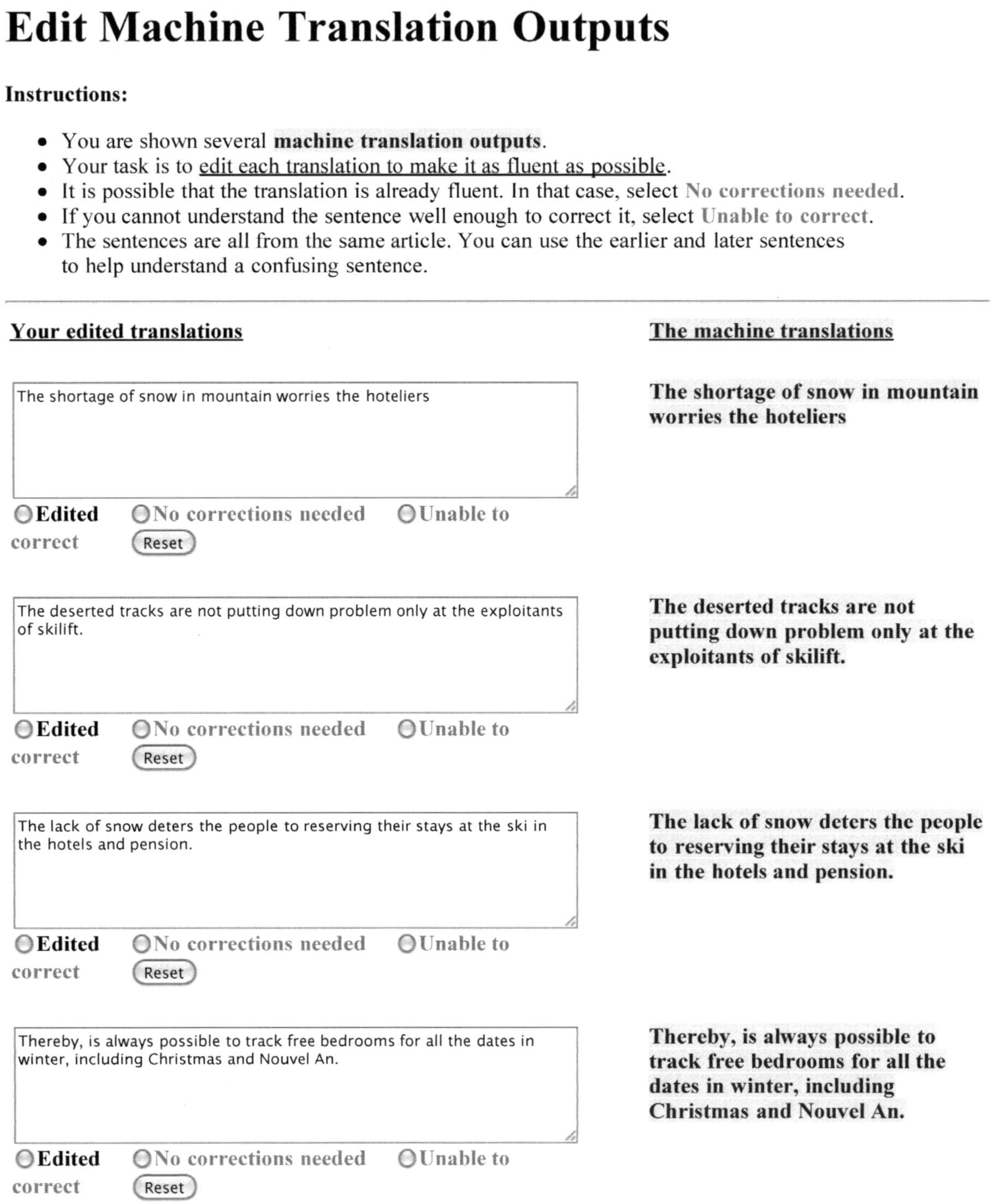

Figure 2: This screenshot shows what an annotator sees when beginning to edit the output of a machine translation system.

Indicate whether the edited translations represent fully fluent and meaning-equivalent alternatives to the reference sentence. The reference is shown with context, the actual sentence is **bold**.

In addition to edited translations, unedited items that were either marked as acceptable or as incomprehensible were also shown. Judges gave a simple yes/no indication to each item.

4 Translation task results

We used the results of the manual evaluation to analyze the translation quality of the different systems that were submitted to the workshop. In our analysis, we aimed to address the following questions:

- Which systems produced the best translation quality for each language pair?
- Did the system combinations produce better translations than individual systems?
- Which of the systems that used only the provided training materials produced the best translation quality?

Table 5 shows the best individual systems. We define the best systems as those which had no other system that was statistically significantly better than them under the Sign Test at $p \leq 0.1$. Multiple systems are listed as the winners for many language pairs because it was not possible to draw a statistically significant difference between the systems. There is no individual system clearly outperforming all other systems across the different language pairs. With the exception of French-English and English-French one can observe that top-performing constrained systems did as well as the unconstrained system ONLINEB.

Table 6 shows the best combination systems. For all language directions, except Spanish-English, one can see that the system combination runs outperform the individual systems and that in most cases the differences are statistically significant. While this is to be expected, system combination is not guaranteed to improve performance as some of the lower ranked combination runs show, which are outperformed by individual systems. Also note that except for Czech-English translation the online systems ONLINEA and ONLINEB where not included for the system combination runs

Understandability

Our hope is that judging the acceptability of edited output as discussed in Section 3 gives some indication of how often a system's output was understandable. Figure 3 gives the percentage of times that each system's edited output was judged to be acceptable (the percentage also factors in instances when judges were unable to improve the output because it was incomprehensible).

This style of manual evaluation is experimental and should not be taken to be authoritative. Some caveats about this measure:

- There are several sources of variance that are difficult to control for: some people are better at editing, and some sentences are more difficult to edit. Therefore, variance in the understandability of systems is difficult to pin down.
- The acceptability measure does not strongly correlate with the more established method of ranking translations relative to each other for all the language pairs.

5 Shared evaluation task overview

In addition to allowing the analysis of subjective translation quality measures for different systems, the judgments gathered during the manual evaluation may be used to evaluate how well the automatic evaluation metrics serve as a surrogate to the manual evaluation processes. NIST began running a "Metrics for MAchine TRanslation" challenge (MetricsMATR), and presented their findings at a workshop at AMTA (Przybocki et al., 2008). This year we conducted a joint MetricsMATR and WMT workshop, with NIST running the shared evaluation task and analyzing the results.

In this year's shared evaluation task 14 different research groups submitted a total of 26 different automatic metrics for evaluation:

Aalto University of Science and Technology (Dobrinkat et al., 2010)

- MT-NCD – A machine translation metric based on normalized compression distance (NCD), a general information-theoretic measure of string similarity. MT-NCD measures the surface level similarity between two strings with a general compression algorithm. More similar strings can be represented with

French-English
551–755 judgments per system

System	C?	≥others
LIUM •⋆	Y	0.71
ONLINEB •	N	0.71
NRC •⋆	Y	0.66
CAMBRIDGE •⋆	Y +GW	0.66
LIMSI ⋆	Y +GW	0.65
UEDIN	Y	0.65
RALI •⋆	Y +GW	0.65
JHU	Y	0.59
RWTH •⋆	Y +GW	0.55
LIG	Y	0.53
ONLINEA	N	0.52
CMU-STATXFER	Y	0.51
HUICONG	Y	0.51
DFKI	N	0.42
GENEVA	Y	0.27
CU-ZEMAN	Y	0.21

English-French
664–879 judgments per system

System	C?	≥others
UEDIN •⋆	Y	0.70
ONLINEB •	N	0.68
RALI •⋆	Y +GW	0.66
LIMSI •⋆	Y +GW	0.66
RWTH •⋆	Y +GW	0.63
CAMBRIDGE ⋆	Y +GW	0.63
LIUM	Y	0.63
NRC	Y	0.62
ONLINEA	N	0.55
JHU	Y	0.53
DFKI	N	0.40
GENEVA	Y	0.35
EU	N	0.32
CU-ZEMAN	Y	0.26
KOC	Y	0.26

Czech-English
788–868 judgments per system

System	C?	≥others
ONLINEB •	N	0.7
UEDIN ⋆	Y	0.61
CMU	Y	0.55
CU-BOJAR	N	0.55
AALTO	Y	0.43
ONLINEA	N	0.37
CU-ZEMAN	Y	0.22

German-English
723–879 judgments per system

System	C?	≥others
ONLINEB •	N	0.73
KIT •⋆	Y +GW	0.72
UMD •⋆	Y	0.68
UEDIN ⋆	Y	0.66
FBK ⋆	Y +GW	0.66
ONLINEA •	N	0.63
RWTH	Y +GW	0.62
LIU	Y	0.59
UU-MS	Y	0.55
JHU	Y	0.53
LIMSI	Y +GW	0.52
UPPSALA	Y	0.51
DFKI	N	0.50
HUICONG	Y	0.47
CMU	Y	0.46
AALTO	Y	0.42
CU-ZEMAN	Y	0.36
KOC	Y	0.23

English-German
1284–1542 judgments per system

System	C?	≥others
ONLINEB •	N	0.70
DFKI •	N	0.62
UEDIN •⋆	Y	0.62
KIT ⋆	Y	0.60
ONLINEA	N	0.59
FBK ⋆	Y	0.56
LIU	Y	0.55
RWTH	Y	0.51
LIMSI	Y	0.51
UPPSALA	Y	0.47
JHU	Y	0.46
SFU	Y	0.34
KOC	Y	0.30
CU-ZEMAN	Y	0.28

English-Czech
1375–1627 judgments per system

System	C?	≥others
ONLINEB •	N	0.70
CU-BOJAR •	N	0.66
PC-TRANS •	N	0.62
UEDIN •⋆	Y	0.62
CU-TECTO	Y	0.60
EUROTRANS	N	0.54
CU-ZEMAN	Y	0.50
SFU	Y	0.45
ONLINEA	N	0.44
POTSDAM	Y	0.44
DCU	N	0.38
KOC	Y	0.33

Spanish-English
1448–1577 judgments per system

System	C?	≥others
ONLINEB •	N	0.70
UEDIN •⋆	Y	0.69
CAMBRIDGE	Y +GW	0.61
JHU	Y	0.61
ONLINEA	N	0.54
UPC ⋆	Y	0.51
HUICONG	Y	0.50
DFKI	N	0.45
COLUMBIA	Y	0.45
CU-ZEMAN	Y	0.27

English-Spanish
540–722 judgments per system

System	C?	≥others
ONLINEB •	N	0.71
ONLINEA •	N	0.69
UEDIN ⋆	Y	0.61
DCU	N	0.61
DFKI ⋆	N	0.55
JHU ⋆	Y	0.55
UPV ⋆	Y	0.55
CAMBRIDGE ⋆	Y +GW	0.54
UHC-UPV ⋆	Y	0.54
SFU	Y	0.40
CU-ZEMAN	Y	0.23
KOC	Y	0.19

Systems are listed in the order of how often their translations were ranked higher than or equal to any other system. Ties are broken by direct comparison.

C? indicates constrained condition, meaning only using the supplied training data, standard monolingual linguistic tools, and optionally the LDC's GigaWord, which was allowed this year (entries that used the GigaWord are marked +GW).

• indicates a **win** in the category, meaning that no other system is statistically significantly better at p-level≤0.1 in pairwise comparison.

⋆ indicates a **constrained win**, no other constrained system is statistically better.

For all pairwise comparisons between systems, please check the appendix.

Table 5: Official results for the WMT10 translation task, based on the human evaluation (ranking translations relative to each other)

French-English
589–716 judgments per combo

System	≥others
RWTH-COMBO •	0.77
CMU-HYP-COMBO •	0.77
DCU-COMBO •	0.72
LIUM ⋆	0.71
CMU-HEA-COMBO •	0.70
UPV-COMBO •	0.68
NRC	0.66
CAMBRIDGE	0.66
UEDIN ⋆	0.65
LIMSI ⋆	0.65
JHU-COMBO	0.65
RALI	0.65
LIUM-COMBO	0.64
BBN-COMBO	0.64
RWTH	0.55

English-French
740–829 judgments per combo

System	≥others
RWTH-COMBO •	0.75
CMU-HEA-COMBO •	0.74
UEDIN	0.70
KOC-COMBO •	0.68
UPV-COMBO	0.66
RALI ⋆	0.66
LIMSI	0.66
RWTH	0.63
CAMBRIDGE	0.63

Czech-English
766–843 judgments per combo

System	≥others
CMU-HEA-COMBO •	0.71
ONLINEB ⋆	0.7
BBN-COMBO •	0.70
RWTH-COMBO •	0.65
UPV-COMBO •	0.63
JHU-COMBO	0.62
UEDIN	0.61

German-English
743–835 judgments per combo

System	≥others
BBN-COMBO •	0.77
RWTH-COMBO •	0.75
CMU-HEA-COMBO	0.73
KIT ⋆	0.72
UMD ⋆	0.68
JHU-COMBO	0.67
UEDIN ⋆	0.66
FBK	0.66
CMU-HYP-COMBO	0.65
UPV-COMBO	0.64
RWTH	0.62
KOC-COMBO	0.59

English-German
1340–1469 judgments per combo

System	≥others
RWTH-COMBO •	0.65
DFKI ⋆	0.62
UEDIN ⋆	0.62
KIT ⋆	0.60
CMU-HEA-COMBO •	0.59
KOC-COMBO	0.59
FBK ⋆	0.56
UPV-COMBO	0.55

English-Czech
1405–1496 judgments per combo

System	≥others
DCU-COMBO •	0.75
ONLINEB ⋆	0.70
RWTH-COMBO	0.70
CMU-HEA-COMBO	0.69
UPV-COMBO	0.68
CU-BOJAR	0.66
KOC-COMBO	0.66
PC-TRANS	0.62
UEDIN	0.62

Spanish-English
1385–1535 judgments per combo

System	≥others
UEDIN ⋆	0.69
CMU-HEA-COMBO •	0.66
UPV-COMBO •	0.66
BBN-COMBO	0.62
JHU-COMBO	0.55
UPC	0.51

English-Spanish
516–673 judgments per combo

System	≥others
CMU-HEA-COMBO •	0.68
KOC-COMBO	0.62
UEDIN ⋆	0.61
UPV-COMBO	0.60
RWTH-COMBO	0.59
DFKI ⋆	0.55
JHU	0.55
UPV	0.55
CAMBRIDGE ⋆	0.54
UPV-NNLM ⋆	0.54

System combinations are listed in the order of how often their translations were ranked higher than or equal to any other system. Ties are broken by direct comparison. We show the best individual systems alongside the system combinations, since the goal of combination is to produce better quality translation than the component systems.

- • indicates a **win** for the system combination meaning that no other system or system combination is statistically significantly better at p-level≤0.1 in pairwise comparison.
- ⋆ indicates an **individual system** that none of the system combinations beat by a statistically significant margin at p-level≤0.1.

For all pairwise comparisons between systems, please check the appendix.

Note: ONLINEA and ONLINEB were not included among the systems being combined in the system combination shared tasks, except in the Czech-English and English-Czech conditions, where ONLINEB was included.

Table 6: Official results for the WMT10 system combination task, based on the human evaluation (ranking translations relative to each other)

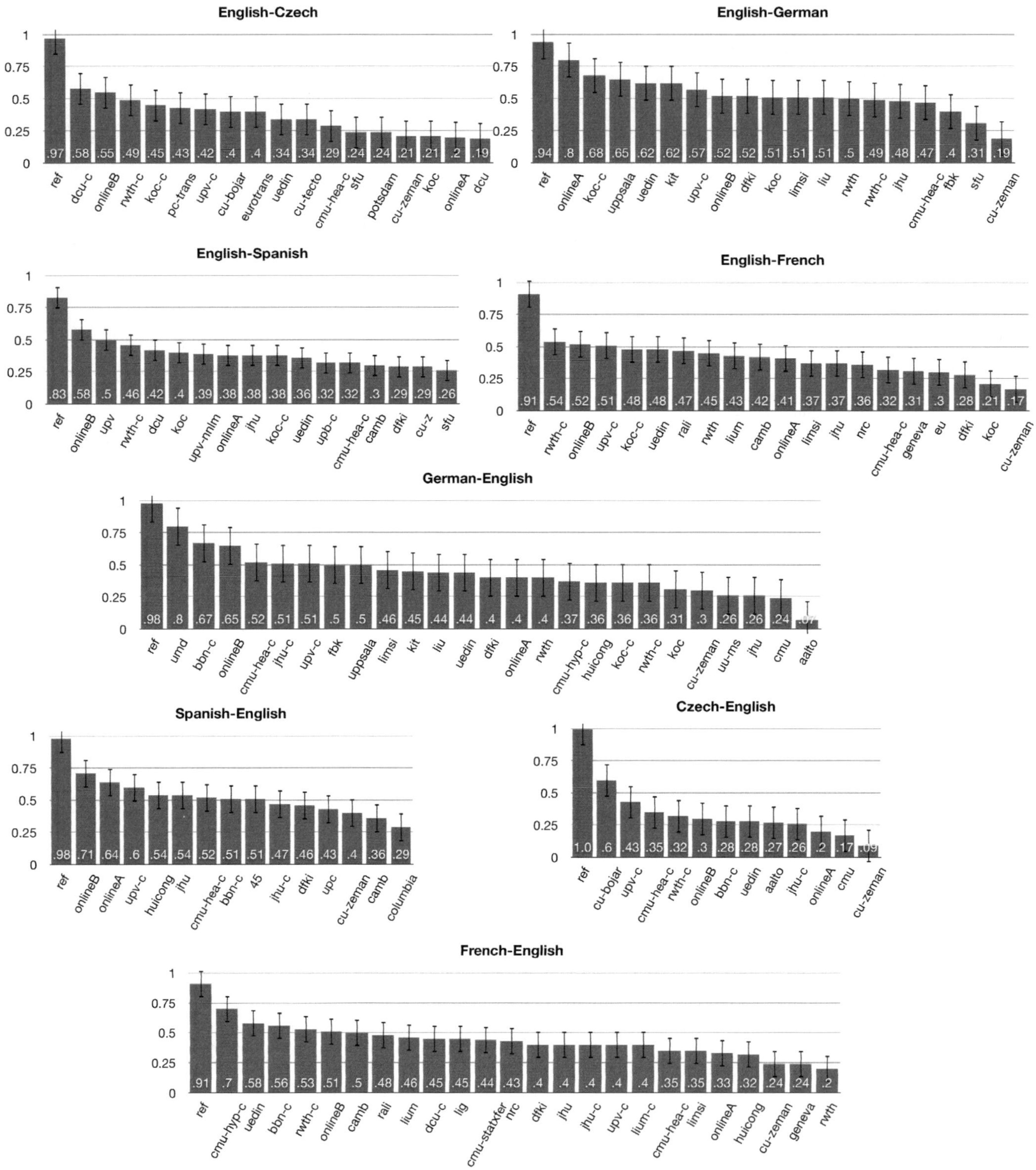

Figure 3: The percent of time that each system's edited output was judged to be an acceptable translation. These numbers also include judgments of the system's output when it was marked either *incomprehensible* or *acceptable* and left unedited. Note that the reference translation was edited alongside the system outputs. Error bars show one positive and one negative standard deviation for the systems in that language pair.

a shorter description when concatenated before compression than when concatenated after compression. MT-NCD does not require any language specific resources.

- MT-mNCD – Enhances MT-NCD with flexible word matching provided by stemming and synonyms. It works analogously to M-BLEU and M-TER and uses METEOR's aligner module to find relaxed word-to-word alignments. MT-mNCD exploits English WordNet data and increases correlation to human judgments for English over MT-NCD.

Due to a processing issue inherent to the metric, the scores reported were generated excluding the first segment of each document. Also, a separate issue was found for the MT-mNCD metric, and according to the developer the scores reported here would like change with a correction of the issue.

BabbleQuest International[8]

- Badger 2.0 full – Uses the Smith-Waterman alignment algorithm with Gotoh improvements to measure segment similarity. The full version uses a multilingual knowledge base to assign a substitution cost which supports normalization of word infection and similarity.

- Badger 2.0 lite – The lite version uses default gap, gap extension and substitution costs.

City University of Hong Kong (Wong and Kit, 2010)

- ATEC 2.1 – This version of ATEC extends the measurement of word choice and word order by various means. The former is assessed by matching word forms at linguistic levels, including surface form, stem, sense and semantic similarity, and further by weighting the informativeness of both matched and unmatched words. The latter is quantified in term of the discordance of word position and word sequence between an MT output and its reference.

Due to a version discrepancy of the metric, final scores for ATECD-2.1 differ from those reported here, but only minimally.

Carnegie Mellon University (Denkowski and Lavie, 2010)

- METEOR-NEXT-adq – Evaluates a machine translation hypothesis against one or more reference translations by calculating a similarity score based on an alignment between the hypothesis and reference strings. Alignments are based on exact, stem, synonym, and paraphrase matches between words and phrases in the strings. Metric parameters are tuned to maximize correlation with human judgments of translation quality (adequacy judgments).

- METEOR-NEXT-hter – METEOR-NEXT tuned to HTER.

- METEOR-NEXT-rank – METEOR-NEXT tuned to human judgments of rank.

Columbia University[9]

- SEPIA – A syntactically-aware machine translation evaluation metric designed with the goal of assigning bigger weight to grammatical structural bigrams with long surface spans that cannot be captured with surface n-gram metrics. SEPIA uses a dependency representation produced for both hypothesis and reference(s). SEPIA is configurable to allow using different combinations of structural n-grams, surface n-grams, POS tags, dependency relations and lemmatization. SEPIA is a precision-based metric and as such employs clipping and length penalty to minimize metric gaming.

Charles University Prague (Bojar and Kos, 2010)

- SemPOS – Computes overlapping of autosemantic (content-bearing) word lemmas in the candidate and reference translations given a fine-grained semantic part of speech (sempos) and outputs average overlapping score over all sempos types. The overlapping is defined as the number of matched lemmas divided by the total number of lemmas in the candidate and reference translations having the same sempos type.

[8] `http://www.babblequest.com/badger2`

[9] `http://www1.ccls.columbia.edu/~SEPIA/`

- SemPOS-BLEU – A linear combination of SemPOS and BLEU with equal weights. BLEU is computed on surface forms of autosemantic words that are used by SemPOS, i.e. auxiliary verbs or prepositions are not taken into account.

Dublin City University (He et al., 2010)

- DCU-LFG – A combination of syntactic and lexical information. It measures the similarity of the hypothesis and reference in terms of matches of Lexical Functional Grammar (LFG) dependency triples. The matching module can also access the WordNet synonym dictionary and Snover's paraphrase database[10].

University of Edinburgh (Birch and Osborne, 2010)

- LRKB4 – A novel metric which directly measures reordering success using Kendall's tau permutation distance metrics. The reordering component is combined with a lexical metric, capturing the two most important elements of translation quality. This simple combined metric only has one parameter, which makes its scores easy to interpret. It is also fast to run and language-independent. It uses Kendall's tau permutation.

- LRHB4 – LRKB4, replacing Kendall's tau permutation distance metric with the Hamming distance permutation distance metric.

Due to installation issues, the reported submitted scores for these two metrics have not been verified to produce identical scores at NIST.

Harbin Institute of Technology, China

- I-letter-BLEU – Normal BLEU based on letters. Moreover, the maximum length of N-gram is decided by the average length for each sentence, respectively.

- I-letter-recall – A geometric mean of N-gram recall based on letters. Moreover, the maximum length of N-gram is decided by the average length for each sentence, respectively.

- SVM-RANK – Uses support vector machines rank models to predict an ordering over a set of system translations with linear kernel. Features include Meteor-exact, BLEU-cum-1, BLEU-cum-2, BLEU-cum-5, BLEU-ind-1, BLEU-ind-2, ROUGE-L recall, letter-based TER, letter-based BLEU-cum-5, letter-based ROUGE-L recall, and letter-based ROUGE-S recall.

National University of Singapore (Liu et al., 2010)

- TESLA-M – Based on matching of bags of unigrams, bigrams, and trigrams, with consideration of WordNet synonyms. The match is done in the framework of real-valued linear programming to enable the discounting of function words.

- TESLA – Built on TESLA-M, this metric also considers bilingual phrase tables to discover phrase-level synonyms. The feature weights are tuned on the development data using SVMrank.

Stanford University

- Stanford – A discriminatively trained string-edit distance metric with various similarity-matching, synonym-matching, and dependency-parse-tree-matching features. The model resembles a Conditional Random Field, but performs regression instead of classification. It is trained on Arabic, Chinese, and Urdu data from the MT-Eval 2008 dataset.

Due to installation issues, the reported scores for this metric have not been verified to produce identical scores at NIST.

University of Maryland[11]

- TER-plus (TERp) – An extension of the Translation Edit Rate (TER) metric that measures the number of edits between a hypothesized translation and a reference translation. TERp extends TER by using stemming, synonymy, and paraphrases as well as tunable edit costs to better measure the distance between the two translations. This version of TERp improves upon prior versions by adding brevity and length penalties.

[10] Available at `http://www.umiacs.umd.edu/~snover/terp/`.

[11] `http://www.umiacs.umd.edu/~snover/terp`

Scores were not submitted along with this metric, and due to installation issues were not produced at NIST in time to be included in this report.

University Politècnica de Catalunya/University de Barcelona (Comelles et al., 2010)

- DR – An arithmetic mean over a set of three metrics based on discourse representations, respectively computing lexical overlap, morphosyntactic overlap, and semantic tree matching.
- DRdoc – Is analogous to DR but, instead of operating at the segment level, it analyzes similarities over whole document discourse representations.
- ULCh – An arithmetic mean over a heuristically-defined set of metrics operating at different linguistic levels (ROUGE, METEOR, and measures of overlap between constituent parses, dependency parses, semantic roles, and discourse representations).

University of Southern California, ISI

- BEwT-E – Basic Elements with Transformations for Evaluation, is a recall-oriented metric that compares basic elements, small portions of contents, between the two translations. The basic elements (BEs) consist of content words and various combinations of syntactically-related words. A variety of transformations are performed to allow flexible matching so that words and syntactic constructions conveying similar content in different manners may be matched. The transformations cover synonymy, preposition vs. noun compounding, differences in tenses, etc. BEwT-E was originally created for summarization evaluation and is English-specific.
- Bkars – Measures overlap between character trigrams in the system and reference translations. It is heavily weighted toward recall and contains a fragmentation penalty. Bkars produces a score both with and without stemming (using the Snowball package of stemmers) and averages the results together. It is not English-specific.

Scores were not submitted for BEwT-E; the runtime required for this metric to process the WMT-10 data set prohibited the production of scores in time for publication.

6 Evaluation task results

The results reported here are preliminary; a final release of results will be published on the WMT10 website before July 15, 2010. Metric developers submitted metrics for installation at NIST; they were also asked to submit metric scores on the WMT10 test set along with their metrics. Not all developers submitted scores, and not all metrics were verified to produce the same scores as submitted at NIST in time for publication. Any such caveats are reported with the description of the metrics above.

The results reported here are limited to a comparison of metric scores on the full WMT10 test set with human assessments on the human-assessed subset. An analysis comparing the human assessments with the automatic metrics run only on the human-assessed subset will follow at a later date.

The WMT10 system output used to generate the reported metric scores was found to have improperly escaped characters for a small number of segments. While we plan to regenerate the metric scores with this issue resolved, we do not expect this to significantly alter the results, given the small number of segments affected.

6.1 System Level Metric Scores

The tables in Appendix B list the metric scores for the language pairs processed by each metric. These first four tables present scores for translations out of English into Czech, French, German and Spanish. In addition to the metric scores of the submitted metrics identified above, we also present (1) the ranking of the system as determined by the human assessments; and (2) the metrics scores for two popular baseline metrics, BLEU as calculated by NIST's mteval software[12] and the NIST score. For each method of system measurement the absolute highest score is identified by being outlined in a box.

Similarly, the remaining tables in Appendix B list the metric scores for the submitted metrics and the two baseline metrics, and the ranking based on the human assessments for translations into English from Czech, French, German and Spanish.

As some metrics employ language-specific resources, not all metrics produced scores for all language pairs.

[12] ftp://jaguar.ncsl.nist.gov/mt/resources/mteval-v13a-20091001.tar.gz

	cz-en	fr-en	de-en	es-en	avg
SemPOS	.78	.77	.60	.95	**.77**
IQmt-DRdoc	.61	**.79**	**.65**	.98	.76
SemPOS-BLEU	.75	.70	.61	.96	.75
i-letter-BLEU	.71	.70	.60	.98	.75
NIST	**.85**	.72	.55	.86	.74
TESLA	.70	.70	.60	.97	.74
MT-NCD	.71	.72	.58	.95	.74
Bkars	.71	.67	.58	.98	.74
ATEC-2.1	.71	.67	.59	.96	.73
meteor-next-rank	.69	.68	.60	.96	.73
IQmt-ULCh	.70	.64	.60	**.99**	.73
IQmt-DR	.68	.67	.60	.97	.73
meteor-next-hter	.71	.66	.59	.95	.73
meteor-next-adq	.69	.67	.60	.96	.73
badger-2.0-lite	.70	.70	.56	.94	.73
DCU-LFG	.69	.69	.58	.96	.73
badger-2.0-full	.69	.70	.57	.94	.73
SEPIA	.71	.70	.57	.92	.73
SVM-rank	.66	.65	.61	.98	.73
i-letter-recall	.65	.64	.61	.98	.72
TESLA-M	.67	.67	.57	.95	.72
BLEU-4-v13a	.69	.68	.52	.90	.70
LRKB4	.63	.62	.53	.89	.67
LRHB4	.62	.65	.50	.87	.66
MT-mNCD	.69	.64	.52	.70	.64
Stanford	.58	.19	.60	.46	.46

Table 7: The system-level correlation of the automatic evaluation metrics with the human judgments for translation into English.

It is noticeable that system combinations are often among those achieving the highest scores.

6.2 System-Level Correlations

To assess the performance of the automatic metrics, we correlated the metrics' scores with the human rankings at the system level. We assigned a consolidated human-assessment rank to each system based on the number of times that the given system's translations were ranked higher than or equal to the translations of any other system in the manual evaluation of the given language pair. We then compared the ranking of systems by the human assessments to that provided by the automatic metric system level scores on the complete WMT10 test set for each language pair, using Spearman's ρ rank correlation coefficient. The correlations are shown in Table 7 for translations to English, and Table 8 out of English, with baseline metrics listed at the bottom. The highest correlation for each language pair and the highest overall average are bolded.

Overall, correlations are higher for translations to English than compared to translations from English. For all language pairs, there are a number of new metrics that yield noticeably higher correlations with human assessments than either of the two included baseline metrics. In particular, Bleu performed in the bottom half of the into-English and out-of-English directions.

	en-cz	en-fr	en-de	en-es	avg
SVM-rank	.29	.54	.68	.67	**.55**
TESLA-M	.27	.49	**.74**	.66	.54
LRKB4	.39	.58	.47	**.71**	.54
i-letter-recall	.28	.51	.61	.66	.52
LRHB4	**.39**	.59	.41	.63	.51
i-letter-BLEU	.26	.49	.56	.65	.49
ATEC-2.1	.38	.52	.44	.62	.49
badger-2.0-full	.37	.58	.41	.59	.49
Bkars	.22	.54	.52	.66	.48
BLEU-4-v13a	.35	.58	.39	.57	.47
badger-2.0-lite	.32	.57	.41	.59	.47
TESLA	.09	**.62**	.66	.50	.47
meteor-next-rank	.34	.59	.39	.51	.46
Stanford	.34	.48	.70	.32	.46
MT-NCD	.17	.54	.51	.61	.46
NIST	.30	.52	.41	.50	.43
MT-mNCD	.26	.49	.17	.43	.34
SemPOS	.31	n/a	n/a	n/a	.31
SemPOS-BLEU	.29	n/a	n/a	n/a	.29

Table 8: The system-level correlation of the automatic evaluation metrics with the human judgments for translation out of English.

6.3 Segment-Level Metric Analysis

The method employed to collect human judgments of rank preferences at the segment level produces a sparse matrix of decision points. It is unclear whether attempts to normalize the segment level rankings to 0.0–1.0 values, representing the relative rank of a system per segment given the number of comparisons it is involved with, is proper. An intuitive display of how well metrics mirror the human judgments may be shown via a confusion matrix. We compare the human ranks to the ranks as determined by a metric. Below, we show an example of the confusion matrix for the SVM-rank metric which had the highest summed diagonal (occurrences when a particular rank by the metric's score exactly matches the human judgments) for all segments translated into English. The numbers provided are percentages of the total count. The summed diagonal constitutes 39.01% of all counts in this example matrix. The largest cell is the 1/1 ranking cell (top left). We included the reference translation as a system in this analysis, which is likely to lead to a lot of agreement on the highest rank between humans and automatic metrics.

Metric	Human Rank				
Rank	1	2	3	4	5
1	12.79	4.48	2.75	1.82	0.92
2	2.77	7.94	5.55	3.79	2.2
3	1.57	4.29	6.74	5.4	4.46
4	0.97	2.42	3.76	4.99	6.5
5	0.59	1.54	1.84	3.38	6.55

No allowances for ties were made in this analysis. That is, if a human ranked two system translations the same, this analysis expects the metrics to provide the same score in order to get them both correct. Future analysis could relax this constraint. As not all human rankings start with the highest possible rank of "1" (due to ties and withholding judgment on a particular system output being allowed), we set the highest automatic metric rank to the highest human rank and shifted the lower metric ranks down accordingly.

Table 9 shows the summed diagonal percentages of the total count of all datapoints for all metrics that WMT10 scores were available for, both combined for all languages to English (X-English) and separately for each language into English.

The results are ordered by the highest percentage for the summed diagonal on all languages to English combined. There are quite noticeable changes in ranking of the metrics for the separate language pairs; further analysis into the reasons for this will be necessary.

We plan to also analyze metric performance for translation into English.

7 Feasibility of Using Non-Expert Annotators in Future WMTs

In this section we analyze the data that we collected data by posting the ranking task on Amazon's Mechanical Turk (MTurk). Although we did not use this data when creating the official results, our hope was that it may be useful in future workshops in two ways. First, if we find that it is possible to obtain a sufficient amount of data of good quality, then we might be able to reduce the time commitment expected from the system developers in future evaluations. Second, the additional collected labels might enable us to detect significant differences between systems that would otherwise be insignificantly different using only the data from the volunteers (which we will now refer to as the "expert" data).

7.1 Data collection

To that end, we prepared 600 ranking sets for each of the eight language pairs, with each set containing five MT outputs to be ranked, using the same interface used by the volunteers. We posted the data to MTurk and requested, for each one, five redundant assignments, from different workers. Had all the $5 \times 8 \times 600 = 24{,}000$ assignments been completed, we would have obtained 24,000 $\times$ 5 = 120,000 additional rank labels, compared to the 37,884 labels we collected from the volunteers (Table 3). In actuality, we collected closer to 55,000 rank labels, as we discuss shortly.

To minimize the amount of data that is of poor quality, we placed two requirements that must be satisfied by any worker before completing any of our tasks. First, we required that a worker have an existing approval rating of at least 85%. Second, we required a worker to reside in a country where the target language of the task can be assumed to be the spoken language. Finally, anticipating a large pool of workers located in the United States, we felt it possible for us to add a third restriction for the *-to-English language pairs, which is that a worker must have had at least five tasks previously approved on MTurk.[13] We organized the ranking sets in groups of 3 per screen, with a monetary reward of $0.05 per screen.

When we created our tasks, we had no expectation that all the assignments would be completed over the tasks' lifetime of 30 days. This was indeed the case (Table 10), especially for language pairs with a non-English target language, due to workers being in short supply outside the US. Overall, we see that the amount of data collected from non-US workers is relatively small (left half of Table 10), whereas the pool of US-based workers is much larger, leading to much higher completion rates for language pairs with English as the target language (right half of Table 10). This is in spite of the additional restriction we placed on US workers.

[13]We suspect that newly registered workers on MTurk already start with an "approval rating" of 100%, and so requiring a high approval rating alone might not guard against new workers. It is not entirely clear if our suspicion is true, but our past experiences with MTurk usually involved a noticeably faster completion rate than what we experienced this time around, indicating our suspicion might very well be correct.

Metric	*-English	Czech-English	French-English	German-English	Spanish-English
SVM-rank	39.01	41.21	36.07	38.81	40.3
i-letter-recall	38.85	41.71	36.19	38.8	39.5
MT-NCD	38.77	42.55	35.31	38.7	39.48
i-letter-BLEU	38.69	40.54	36.05	38.82	39.64
meteor-next-rank	38.5	40.1	34.41	39.25	40.05
meteor-next-adq	38.27	39.58	34.41	39.5	39.35
meteor-next-hter	38.21	38.61	34.1	39.13	40.18
Bkars	37.98	40.1	35.08	38.6	38.52
Stanford	37.97	39.87	36.19	38.27	38.09
ATEC-2.1	37.95	40.06	34.96	38.6	38.53
TESLA	37.57	38.68	34.38	38.67	38.36
NIST	37.47	39.54	35.54	37.13	38.2
SemPOS	37.21	38.8	37.39	35.73	37.69
SemPOS-BLEU	37.16	38.05	36.57	37.11	37.21
badger-2.0-full	37.12	37.5	36	36.21	38.62
badger-2.0-lite	37.08	37.2	35.88	36.23	38.69
SEPIA	37.06	38.98	34.6	36.46	38.52
BLEU-4-v13a	36.71	37.83	34.84	36.44	37.81
LRHB4	36.14	38.35	34.65	34.24	37.93
TESLA-M	36.13	37.01	34	35.79	37.6
LRKB4	36.12	38.72	33.47	35.25	37.63
IQmt-ULCh	35.86	37.64	33.95	35.81	36.45
IQmt-DR	35.77	36.27	34.43	34.43	37.74
DCU-LFG	34.72	36.38	32.29	33.87	36.49
MT-mNCD	34.51	34.93	31.78	35.73	35.13
IQmt-DRdoc	31.9	33.85	28.99	32.9	32.18

Table 9: The segment-level performance for metrics for the into-English direction.

	en-de	en-es	en-fr	en-cz	de-en	es-en	fr-en	cz-en
Location	DE	ES/MX	FR	CZ	US	US	US	US
Completed 1 time	37%	38%	29%	19%	3.5%	1.5%	14%	2.0%
Completed 2 times	18%	14%	12%	1.5%	6.0%	5.5%	19%	4.5%
Completed 3 times	2.5%	4.5%	0.5%	0.0%	8.5%	11%	20%	10%
Completed 4 times	1.5%	0.5%	0.5%	0.0%	22%	19%	23%	17%
Completed 5 times	0.0%	0.5%	0.0%	0.0%	60%	63%	22%	67%
Completed $\geq$ once	59%	57%	42%	21%	100%	99%	96%	100%
Label count	**2,583**	**2,488**	**1,578**	**627**	**12,570**	**12,870**	**9,197**	**13,169**
(% of expert data)	**(38%)**	**(96%)**	**(40%)**	**(9%)**	**(241%)**	**(228%)**	**(222%)**	**(490%)**

Table 10: Statistics for data collected on MTurk for the ranking task. In total, **55,082** rank labels were collected across the eight language pairs (**145%** of expert data). Each language pair had 600 sets, and we requested each set completed by 5 different workers. Since each set provides 5 labels, we could have potentially obtained $600 \times 5 \times 5 = 15{,}000$ labels for each language pair. The **Label count** row indicates to what extent that potential was met (over the 30-day lifetime of our tasks), and the "Completed..." rows give a breakdown of redundancy. For instance, the right-most column indicates that, in the cz-en group, 2.0% of the 600 sets were completed by only one worker, while 67% of the sets were completed by 5 workers, with 100% of the sets completed at least once. The total cost of this data collection effort was roughly $200.

INTER-ANNOTATOR AGREEMENT

	$P(A)$	K	K^*
With references	0.466	0.198	0.487
Without references	0.441	0.161	0.439

INTRA-ANNOTATOR AGREEMENT

	$P(A)$	K	K^*
With references	0.539	0.309	0.633
Without references	0.538	0.307	0.601

Table 11: Inter- and intra-annotator agreement for the MTurk workers on the sentence ranking task. (As before, $P(E)$ is 0.333.) For comparison, we repeat here the kappa coefficients of the experts (K^*), taken from Table 4.

7.2 Quality of MTurk data

It is encouraging to see that we can collect a large amount of rank labels from MTurk. That said, we still need to guard against data from bad workers, who are either not being faithful and clicking randomly, or who might simply not be competent enough. Case in point, if we examine inter- and intra-annotator agreement on the MTurk data (Table 11), we see that the agreement rates are markedly lower than their expert counterparts.

Another indication of the presence of bad workers is a low *reference preference rate* (RPR), which we define as the proportion of time a reference translation wins (or ties in) a comparison when it appears in one. Intuitively, the RPR should be quite high, since it is quite rare that an MT output ought to be judged better than the reference. This rate is 96.5% over the expert data, but only 83.7% over the MTurk data. Compare this to a randomly-clicking RPR of 66.67% (because the two acceptable answers are that the reference is either better than a system's output or tied with it).

Also telling would be the rate at which MTurk workers agree with experts. To ensure that we obtain enough overlapping data to calculate such a rate, we purposely select one-sixth[14] of our ranking sets so that the five-system group is exactly one that has been judged by an expert. This way, at least one-sixth of the comparisons obtained from an MTurk worker's labels are comparisons for which we already have an expert judgment. When we calculate the rate of agreement on this data, we find that MTurk workers agree with the expert workers 53.2% of the time, or $K = 0.297$, and when references are excluded, the agreement rate is 50.0%, or $K = 0.249$. Ideally, we would want those values to be in the 0.4–0.5 range, since that is where the inter-annotator kappa coefficient lies for the expert annotators.

7.3 Filtering MTurk data by agreement with experts

We can use the agreement rate with experts to identify MTurk workers who are not performing the task as required. For each worker w of the 669 workers for whom we have such data, we compute the worker's agreement rate with the experts, and from it a kappa coefficient $K_{exp}(w)$ for that worker. (Given that $P(E)$ is 0.333, $K_{exp}(w)$ ranges between -0.5 and $+1.0$.) We sort the workers based on $K_{exp}(w)$ in ascending order, and examine properties of the MTurk data as we remove the lowest-ranked workers one by one (Figure 4).

We first note that the amount of data we obtained from MTurk is so large, that we could afford to eliminate close to 30% of the labels, and we would still have twice as much data than using the expert data alone. We also note that two workers in particular (the 103rd and 130th to be removed) are likely responsible for the majority of the bad data, since removing their data leads to noticeable jumps in the reference preference rate and the inter-annotator agreement rate (right two curves of Figure 4). Indeed, examining the data for those two workers, we find that their RPR values are 55.7% and 51.9%, which is a clear indication of random clicking.[15]

Looking again at those two curves shows degrading values as we continue to remove workers in large droves, indicating a form of "overfitting" to agreement with experts (which, naturally, continues to increase until reaching 1.0; bottom left curve). It is therefore important, if one were to filter out the MTurk data by removing workers this way, to choose a cutoff carefully so that no criterion is degraded dramatically.

In Appendix A, after reporting head-to-head comparisons using only the expert data, we also report head-to-head comparisons using the expert

[14]This means that on average Turkers ranked a set of system outputs that had been ranked by experts on every other screen, since each screen's worth of work had three sets.

[15]In retrospect, we should have performed this type of analysis as the data was being collected, since such workers could have been identified early on and blocked.

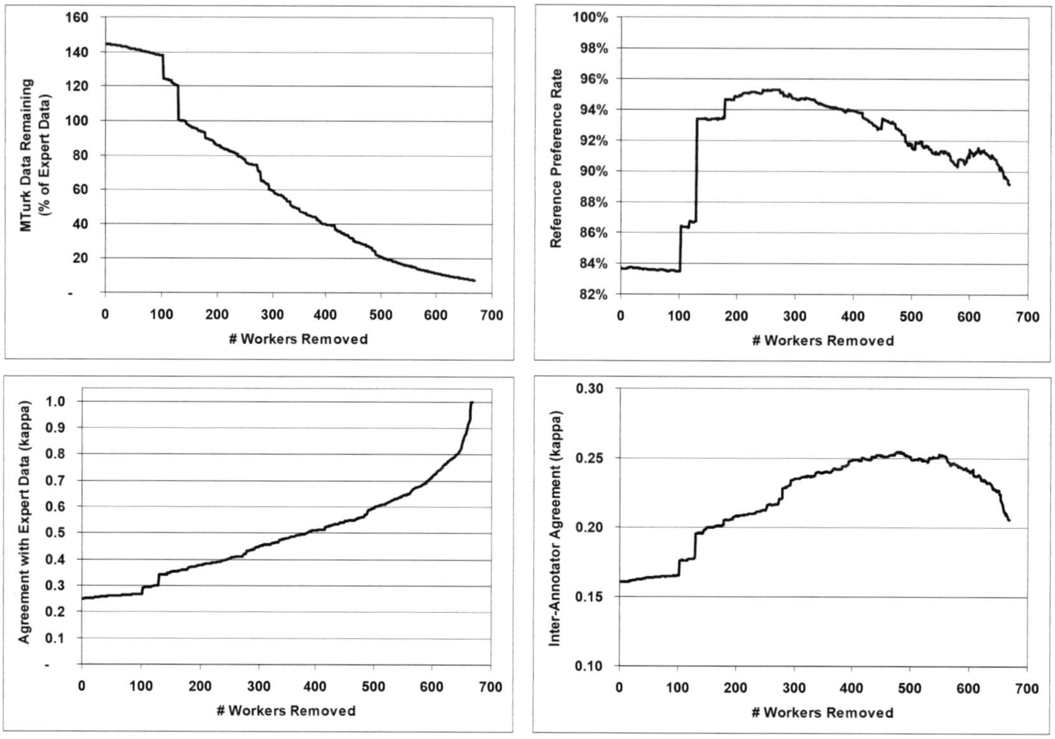

Figure 4: The effect of removing an increasing number of MTurk workers. The order in which workers are removed is by $K_{exp}(w)$, the kappa agreement coefficient with expert data (excluding references).

data *combined* with the MTurk data, in order to be able to detect more significant differences between the systems. We choose the 300-worker point as a reasonable cutoff point before combining the MTurk data with the expert data, based on the characteristics of the MTurk data at that point: a high reference preference rate, high inter-annotator agreement, and, critically, a kappa coefficient vs. expert data of 0.449, which is close to the expert inter-annotator kappa coefficient of 0.439.

7.4 Feasibility of using only MTurk data

In the previous subsection, we outlined an approach by which MTurk data can be filtered out using expert data. Since we were to combine the filtered MTurk data with the expert data to obtain more significant differences, it was reasonable to use agreement with experts to quantify the MTurk workers' competency. However, we also would like to know whether it is feasible to use the MTurk data alone. Our aim here is not to boost the differences we see by examining expert data, but to eliminate our reliance on obtaining expert data in the first place.

We briefly examined some simple ways of filtering/combining the MTurk data, and measured the Spearman rank correlations obtained from the MTurk data (alone), as compared to the rankings obtained using the expert data (alone), and report them in Table 12. (These correlations do not include the references.)

We first see that even when using the MTurk data untouched, we already obtain relatively high correlation with expert ranking ("Unfiltered"). This is especially true for the *-to-English language pairs, where we collected much more data than English-to-*. In fact, the relationship between the amount of data and the correlation values is very strong, and it is reasonable to expect the correlation numbers for English-to-* to catch up had more data been collected.

We also measure rank correlations when applying some simple methods of cleaning/weighting MTurk data. The first method ("Voting") is performing a simple vote whenever redundant comparisons (i.e. from different workers) are available. The second method ("K_{exp}-filtered") first removes labels from the 300 worst workers according to agreement with experts. The third method

("RPR-filtered") first removes labels from the 62 worst workers according to their RPR. The numbers 300 and 62 were chosen since those are the points at which the MTurk data reaches the level of expert data in the inter-annotator agreement and RPR of the experts.

The fourth and fifth methods ("Weighted by K_{exp}" and "Weighted by $K(RPR)$") do not remove any data, instead assigning weights to workers based on their agreement with experts and their RPR, respectively. Namely, for each worker, the weight assigned by the fourth method is K_{exp} for that worker, and the weight assigned by the fifth method is $K(RPR)$ for that worker.

Examining the correlation coefficients obtained from those methods (Table 12), we see mixed results, and there is no clear winner among those methods. It is also difficult to draw any conclusion as to which method performs best when. However, it is encouraging to see that the two RPR-based methods perform well. This is noteworthy, since there is no need to use expert data to weight workers, which means that it is possible to evaluate a worker using inherent, 'built-in' properties of that worker's own data, without resorting to making comparisons with other workers or with experts.

8 Summary

As in previous editions of this workshop we carried out an extensive manual and automatic evaluation of machine translation performance for translating from European languages into English, and vice versa.

The number of participants grew substantially compared to previous editions of the WMT workshop, with 33 groups from 29 institutions participating in WMT10. Most groups participated in the translation task only, while the system combination task attracted a somewhat smaller number of participants

Unfortunately, fewer rule-based systems participated in this year's edition of WMT, compared to previous editions. We hope to attract more rule-based systems in future editions as they increase the variation of translation output and for some language pairs, such as German-English, tend to outperform statistical machine translation systems.

This was the first time that the WMT workshop was held as a joint workshop with NIST's MetricsMATR evaluation initiative. This joint effort was very productive as it allowed us to focus more on the two evaluation dimensions: manual evaluation of MT performance and the correlation between manual metrics and automated metrics.

This year was also the first time we have introduced quality assessments by non-experts. In previous years all assessments were carried out through peer evaluation exclusively consisting of developers of machine translation systems, and thereby people who are used to machine translation output. This year we have facilitated Amazon's Mechanical Turk to investigate two aspects of manual evaluation: How stable are manual assessments across different assessor profiles (experts vs. non-experts) and how reliable are quality judgments of non-expert users? While the intra- and inter-annotator agreements between non-expert assessors are considerably lower than for their expert counterparts, the overall rankings of translation systems exhibit a high degree of correlation between experts and non-experts. This correlation can be further increased by applying various filtering strategies reducing the impact of unreliable non-expert annotators.

As in previous years, all data sets generated by this workshop, including the human judgments, system translations and automatic scores, are publicly available for other researchers to analyze.[16]

Acknowledgments

This work was supported in parts by the EuroMatrixPlus project funded by the European Commission (7th Framework Programme), the GALE program of the US Defense Advanced Research Projects Agency, Contract No. HR0011-06-C-0022, and the US National Science Foundation under grant IIS-0713448.

References

Alexandre Allauzen, Josep M. Crego, Ilknur Durgar El-Kahlout, and Francois Yvon. 2010. Limsi's statistical translation systems for wmt'10. In *Proceedings of the Joint Fifth Workshop on Statistical Machine Translation and MetricsMATR*, pages 29–34, Uppsala, Sweden, July. Association for Computational Linguistics.

Loïc Barrault. 2010. Many: Open source mt system combination at wmt'10. In *Proceedings of the Joint Fifth Workshop on Statistical Machine Translation*

[16] `http://www.statmt.org/wmt09/results.html`

	Label count	Unfiltered	Voting	K_{exp}-filtered	RPR-filtered	Weighted by K_{exp}	Weighted by $K(RPR)$
en-de	2,583	0.862	0.779	0.818	0.862	**0.868**	0.862
en-es	2,488	0.759	0.785	0.797	0.797	0.768	**0.806**
en-fr	1,578	0.826	**0.840**	0.791	0.814	0.802	0.814
en-cz	627	0.833	0.818	0.354	0.833	**0.851**	0.828
de-en	12,570	0.914	0.925	0.920	0.931	**0.933**	0.926
es-en	12,870	0.934	0.969	0.965	**0.987**	0.978	**0.987**
fr-en	9,197	0.880	0.865	**0.920**	0.919	0.907	0.917
cz-en	13,169	0.951	0.909	**0.965**	0.944	0.930	0.944

Table 12: Spearman rank coefficients for the MTurk data across the various language pairs, using different methods to clean the data or weight workers. (These correlations were computed after excluding the references.) K_{exp} is the kappa coefficient of the worker's agreement rate with experts, with $P(A) = 0.33$. $K(RPR)$ is the kappa coefficient of the worker's RPR (see 7.2), with $P(A) = 0.66$. In K_{exp}-filtering, 42% of labels remain, after removing 300 workers. In $K(RPR)$-filtering, 69% of labels remain, after removing 62 workers.

and MetricsMATR, pages 252–256, Uppsala, Sweden, July. Association for Computational Linguistics.

Ergun Bicici and S. Serdar Kozat. 2010. Adaptive model weighting and transductive regression for predicting best system combinations. In *Proceedings of the Joint Fifth Workshop on Statistical Machine Translation and MetricsMATR*, pages 257–262, Uppsala, Sweden, July. Association for Computational Linguistics.

Ergun Bicici and Deniz Yuret. 2010. L1 regularized regression for reranking and system combination in machine translation. In *Proceedings of the Joint Fifth Workshop on Statistical Machine Translation and MetricsMATR*, pages 263–270, Uppsala, Sweden, July. Association for Computational Linguistics.

Alexandra Birch and Miles Osborne. 2010. Lrscore for evaluating lexical and reordering quality in mt. In *Proceedings of the Joint Fifth Workshop on Statistical Machine Translation and MetricsMATR*, pages 302–307, Uppsala, Sweden, July. Association for Computational Linguistics.

Ondrej Bojar and Kamil Kos. 2010. 2010 failures in english-czech phrase-based mt. In *Proceedings of the Joint Fifth Workshop on Statistical Machine Translation and MetricsMATR*, pages 35–41, Uppsala, Sweden, July. Association for Computational Linguistics.

Chris Callison-Burch and Mark Dredze. 2010. Creating speech and language data with amazons mechanical turk. In *Proceedings NAACL-2010 Workshop on Creating Speech and Language Data With Amazons Mechanical Turk*, Los Angeles.

Chris Callison-Burch, Cameron Fordyce, Philipp Koehn, Christof Monz, and Josh Schroeder. 2007. (Meta-) evaluation of machine translation. In *Proceedings of the Second Workshop on Statistical Machine Translation (WMT07)*, Prague, Czech Republic.

Chris Callison-Burch, Cameron Fordyce, Philipp Koehn, Christof Monz, and Josh Schroeder. 2008. Further meta-evaluation of machine translation. In *Proceedings of the Third Workshop on Statistical Machine Translation (WMT08)*, Colmbus, Ohio.

Chris Callison-Burch, , Philipp Koehn, Christof Monz, and Josh Schroeder. 2009. Findings of the findings of the 2009 workshop on statistical machine translation. In *Proceedings of the Fourth Workshop on Statistical Machine Translation (WMT09)*, Athens, Greece.

Chris Callison-Burch. 2009. Fast, cheap, and creative: Evaluating translation quality using amazon's mechanical turk. In *Proceedings of the 2009 Conference on Empirical Methods in Natural Language Processing (EMNLP-2009)*, Singapore.

Elisabet Comelles, Jesus Gimenez, Lluis Marquez, Irene Castellon, and Victoria Arranz. 2010. Document-level automatic mt evaluation based on discourse representations. In *Proceedings of the Joint Fifth Workshop on Statistical Machine Translation and MetricsMATR*, pages 308–313, Uppsala, Sweden, July. Association for Computational Linguistics.

Hui Cong, Zhao Hai, Lu Bao-Liang, and Song Yan. 2010. An empirical study on development set selection strategy for machine translation learning. In *Proceedings of the Joint Fifth Workshop on Statistical Machine Translation and MetricsMATR*, pages 42–46, Uppsala, Sweden, July. Association for Computational Linguistics.

Michael Denkowski and Alon Lavie. 2010. Meteor-next and the meteor paraphrase tables: Improved evaluation support for five target languages. In *Proceedings of the Joint Fifth Workshop on Statistical Machine Translation and MetricsMATR*, pages 314–317, Uppsala, Sweden, July. Association for Computational Linguistics.

Marcus Dobrinkat, Tero Tapiovaara, Jaakko Väyrynen, and Kimmo Kettunen. 2010. Normalized compression distance based measures for metricsmatr 2010. In *Proceedings of the Joint Fifth Workshop on Statistical Machine Translation and MetricsMATR*, pages 318–323, Uppsala, Sweden, July. Association for Computational Linguistics.

Jinhua Du, Pavel Pecina, and Andy Way. 2010. An augmented three-pass system combination framework: Dcu combination system for wmt 2010. In *Proceedings of the Joint Fifth Workshop on Statistical Machine Translation and MetricsMATR*, pages 271–276, Uppsala, Sweden, July. Association for Computational Linguistics.

Vladimir Eidelman, Chris Dyer, and Philip Resnik. 2010. The university of maryland statistical machine translation system for the fifth workshop on machine translation. In *Proceedings of the Joint Fifth Workshop on Statistical Machine Translation and MetricsMATR*, pages 47–51, Uppsala, Sweden, July. Association for Computational Linguistics.

Christian Federmann, Andreas Eisele, Yu Chen, Sabine Hunsicker, Jia Xu, and Hans Uszkoreit. 2010. Further experiments with shallow hybrid mt systems. In *Proceedings of the Joint Fifth Workshop on Statistical Machine Translation and MetricsMATR*, pages 52–56, Uppsala, Sweden, July. Association for Computational Linguistics.

Jesús González-Rubio, Germán Sanchis-Trilles, Joan-Andreu Sánchez, Jesús Andrés-Ferrer, Guillem Gascó, Pascual Martínez-Gómez, Martha-Alicia Rocha, and Francisco Casacuberta. 2010. The upvprhlt combination system for wmt 2010. In *Proceedings of the Joint Fifth Workshop on Statistical Machine Translation and MetricsMATR*, pages 277–281, Uppsala, Sweden, July. Association for Computational Linguistics.

Greg Hanneman, Jonathan Clark, and Alon Lavie. 2010. Improved features and grammar selection for syntax-based mt. In *Proceedings of the Joint Fifth Workshop on Statistical Machine Translation and MetricsMATR*, pages 57–62, Uppsala, Sweden, July. Association for Computational Linguistics.

Christian Hardmeier, Arianna Bisazza, and Marcello Federico. 2010. Fbk at wmt 2010: Word lattices for morphological reduction and chunk-based reordering. In *Proceedings of the Joint Fifth Workshop on Statistical Machine Translation and MetricsMATR*, pages 63–67, Uppsala, Sweden, July. Association for Computational Linguistics.

Yifan He, Jinhua Du, Andy Way, and Josef van Genabith. 2010. The dcu dependency-based metric in wmt-metricsmatr 2010. In *Proceedings of the Joint Fifth Workshop on Statistical Machine Translation and MetricsMATR*, pages 324–328, Uppsala, Sweden, July. Association for Computational Linguistics.

Kenneth Heafield and Alon Lavie. 2010. Cmu multi-engine machine translation for wmt 2010. In *Proceedings of the Joint Fifth Workshop on Statistical Machine Translation and MetricsMATR*, pages 68–73, Uppsala, Sweden, July. Association for Computational Linguistics.

Carmen Heger, Joern Wuebker, Matthias Huck, Gregor Leusch, Saab Mansour, Daniel Stein, and Hermann Ney. 2010. The rwth aachen machine translation system for wmt 2010. In *Proceedings of the Joint Fifth Workshop on Statistical Machine Translation and MetricsMATR*, pages 74–78, Uppsala, Sweden, July. Association for Computational Linguistics.

Carlos A. Henríquez Q., Marta Ruiz Costa-jussà, Vidas Daudaravicius, Rafael E. Banchs, and José B. Mariño. 2010. Using collocation segmentation to augment the phrase table. In *Proceedings of the Joint Fifth Workshop on Statistical Machine Translation and MetricsMATR*, pages 79–83, Uppsala, Sweden, July. Association for Computational Linguistics.

Almut Silja Hildebrand and Stephan Vogel. 2010. Cmu system combination via hypothesis selection for wmt'10. In *Proceedings of the Joint Fifth Workshop on Statistical Machine Translation and MetricsMATR*, pages 282–285, Uppsala, Sweden, July. Association for Computational Linguistics.

Stéphane Huet, Julien Bourdaillet, Alexandre Patry, and Philippe Langlais. 2010. The rali machine translation system for wmt 2010. In *Proceedings of the Joint Fifth Workshop on Statistical Machine Translation and MetricsMATR*, pages 84–90, Uppsala, Sweden, July. Association for Computational Linguistics.

Michael Jellinghaus, Alexandros Poulis, and David Kolovratník. 2010. Exodus - exploring smt for eu institutions. In *Proceedings of the Joint Fifth Workshop on Statistical Machine Translation and MetricsMATR*, pages 91–95, Uppsala, Sweden, July. Association for Computational Linguistics.

Philipp Koehn and Christof Monz. 2006. Manual and automatic evaluation of machine translation between European languages. In *Proceedings of NAACL 2006 Workshop on Statistical Machine Translation*, New York, New York.

Philipp Koehn, Hieu Hoang, Alexandra Birch, Chris Callison-Burch, Marcello Federico, Nicola Bertoldi, Brooke Cowan, Wade Shen, Christine Moran, Richard Zens, Chris Dyer, Ondrej Bojar, Alexandra Constantin, and Evan Herbst. 2007. Moses: Open source toolkit for statistical machine translation. In *Proceedings of the ACL-2007 Demo and Poster Sessions*, Prague, Czech Republic.

Philipp Koehn, Barry Haddow, Philip Williams, and Hieu Hoang. 2010. More linguistic annotation for statistical machine translation. In *Proceedings of the Joint Fifth Workshop on Statistical Machine Translation and MetricsMATR*, pages 96–101, Uppsala, Sweden, July. Association for Computational Linguistics.

Patrik Lambert, Sadaf Abdul-Rauf, and Holger Schwenk. 2010. Lium smt machine translation system for wmt 2010. In *Proceedings of the Joint Fifth Workshop on Statistical Machine Translation and MetricsMATR*, pages 102–107, Uppsala, Sweden, July. Association for Computational Linguistics.

J. Richard Landis and Gary G. Koch. 1977. The measurement of observer agreement for categorical data. *Biometrics*, 33:159–174.

Samuel Larkin, Boxing Chen, George Foster, Ulrich Germann, Eric Joanis, Howard Johnson, and Roland Kuhn. 2010. Lessons from nrcs portage system at wmt 2010. In *Proceedings of the Joint Fifth Workshop on Statistical Machine Translation and MetricsMATR*, pages 108–113, Uppsala, Sweden, July. Association for Computational Linguistics.

Gregor Leusch and Hermann Ney. 2010. The rwth system combination system for wmt 2010. In *Proceedings of the Joint Fifth Workshop on Statistical Machine Translation and MetricsMATR*, pages 290–295, Uppsala, Sweden, July. Association for Computational Linguistics.

Zhifei Li, Chris Callison-Burch, Chris Dyer, Juri Ganitkevitch, Sanjeev Khudanpur, Lane Schwartz, Wren Thornton, Jonathan Weese, and Omar Zaidan. 2009. Joshua: An open source toolkit for parsing-based machine translation. In *Proceedings of the Fourth Workshop on Statistical Machine Translation*, Athens, Greece, March.

Zhifei Li, Chris Callison-Burch, Chris Dyer, Juri Ganitkevitch, Ann Irvine, Sanjeev Khudanpur, Lane Schwartz, Wren Thornton, Ziyuan Wang, Jonathan Weese, and Omar Zaidan. 2010. Joshua 2.0: A toolkit for parsing-based machine translation with syntax, semirings, discriminative training and other goodies. In *Proceedings of the Joint Fifth Workshop on Statistical Machine Translation and MetricsMATR*, pages 114–118, Uppsala, Sweden, July. Association for Computational Linguistics.

Chang Liu, Daniel Dahlmeier, and Hwee Tou Ng. 2010. Tesla: Translation evaluation of sentences with linear-programming-based analysis. In *Proceedings of the Joint Fifth Workshop on Statistical Machine Translation and MetricsMATR*, pages 329–334, Uppsala, Sweden, July. Association for Computational Linguistics.

Sushant Narsale. 2010. Jhu system combination scheme for wmt 2010. In *Proceedings of the Joint Fifth Workshop on Statistical Machine Translation and MetricsMATR*, pages 286–289, Uppsala, Sweden, July. Association for Computational Linguistics.

Jan Niehues, Teresa Herrmann, Mohammed Mediani, and Alex Waibel. 2010. The karlsruhe institute for technology translation system for the acl-wmt 2010. In *Proceedings of the Joint Fifth Workshop on Statistical Machine Translation and MetricsMATR*, pages 119–123, Uppsala, Sweden, July. Association for Computational Linguistics.

NIST. 2008. Evaluation plan for gale go/no-go phase 3 / phase 3.5 translation evaluations. June 18, 2008.

Sergio Penkale, Rejwanul Haque, Sandipan Dandapat, Pratyush Banerjee, Ankit K. Srivastava, Jinhua Du, Pavel Pecina, Sudip Kumar Naskar, Mikel L. Forcada, and Andy Way. 2010. Matrex: The dcu mt system for wmt 2010. In *Proceedings of the Joint Fifth Workshop on Statistical Machine Translation and MetricsMATR*, pages 124–129, Uppsala, Sweden, July. Association for Computational Linguistics.

Aaron Phillips. 2010. The cunei machine translation platform for wmt '10. In *Proceedings of the Joint Fifth Workshop on Statistical Machine Translation and MetricsMATR*, pages 130–135, Uppsala, Sweden, July. Association for Computational Linguistics.

Juan Pino, Gonzalo Iglesias, Adrià de Gispert, Graeme Blackwood, Jamie Brunning, and William Byrne. 2010. The cued hifst system for the wmt10 translation shared task. In *Proceedings of the Joint Fifth Workshop on Statistical Machine Translation and MetricsMATR*, pages 136–141, Uppsala, Sweden, July. Association for Computational Linguistics.

Marion Potet, Laurent Besacier, and Hervé Blanchon. 2010. The lig machine translation system for wmt 2010. In *Proceedings of the Joint Fifth Workshop on Statistical Machine Translation and MetricsMATR*, pages 142–147, Uppsala, Sweden, July. Association for Computational Linguistics.

Mark Przybocki, Kay Peterson, and Sebastian Bronsart. 2008. Official results of the NIST 2008 "Metrics for MAchine TRanslation" challenge (MetricsMATR08). In *AMTA-2008 workshop on Metrics for Machine Translation*, Honolulu, Hawaii.

Antti-Veikko Rosti, Bing Zhang, Spyros Matsoukas, and Richard Schwartz. 2010. Bbn system description for wmt10 system combination task. In *Proceedings of the Joint Fifth Workshop on Statistical Machine Translation and MetricsMATR*, pages 296–301, Uppsala, Sweden, July. Association for Computational Linguistics.

Markus Saers, Joakim Nivre, and Dekai Wu. 2010. Linear inversion transduction grammar alignments as a second translation path. In *Proceedings of the Joint Fifth Workshop on Statistical Machine Translation and MetricsMATR*, pages 148–152, Uppsala,

Sweden, July. Association for Computational Linguistics.

Germán Sanchis-Trilles, Jesús Andrés-Ferrer, Guillem Gascó, Jesús González-Rubio, Pascual Martínez-Gómez, Martha-Alicia Rocha, Joan-Andreu Sánchez, and Francisco Casacuberta. 2010. Upv-prhlt english–spanish system for wmt10. In *Proceedings of the Joint Fifth Workshop on Statistical Machine Translation and MetricsMATR*, pages 153–157, Uppsala, Sweden, July. Association for Computational Linguistics.

Baskaran Sankaran, Ajeet Grewal, and Anoop Sarkar. 2010. Incremental decoding for phrase-based statistical machine translation. In *Proceedings of the Joint Fifth Workshop on Statistical Machine Translation and MetricsMATR*, pages 197–204, Uppsala, Sweden, July. Association for Computational Linguistics.

Lane Schwartz. 2010. Reproducible results in parsing-based machine translation: The jhu shared task submission. In *Proceedings of the Joint Fifth Workshop on Statistical Machine Translation and MetricsMATR*, pages 158–163, Uppsala, Sweden, July. Association for Computational Linguistics.

Sara Stymne, Maria Holmqvist, and Lars Ahrenberg. 2010. Vs and oovs: Two problems for translation between german and english. In *Proceedings of the Joint Fifth Workshop on Statistical Machine Translation and MetricsMATR*, pages 164–169, Uppsala, Sweden, July. Association for Computational Linguistics.

Jörg Tiedemann. 2010. To cache or not to cache? experiments with adaptive models in statistical machine translation. In *Proceedings of the Joint Fifth Workshop on Statistical Machine Translation and MetricsMATR*, pages 170–175, Uppsala, Sweden, July. Association for Computational Linguistics.

Sami Virpioja, Jaakko Väyrynen, Andre Mansikkaniemi, and Mikko Kurimo. 2010. Applying morphological decompositions to statistical machine translation. In *Proceedings of the Joint Fifth Workshop on Statistical Machine Translation and MetricsMATR*, pages 176–181, Uppsala, Sweden, July. Association for Computational Linguistics.

Zdeněk Žabokrtský, Martin Popel, and David Mareček. 2010. Maximum entropy translation model in dependency-based mt framework. In *Proceedings of the Joint Fifth Workshop on Statistical Machine Translation and MetricsMATR*, pages 182–187, Uppsala, Sweden, July. Association for Computational Linguistics.

Billy Wong and Chunyu Kit. 2010. The parameter-optimized atec metric for mt evaluation. In *Proceedings of the Joint Fifth Workshop on Statistical Machine Translation and MetricsMATR*, pages 335–339, Uppsala, Sweden, July. Association for Computational Linguistics.

Francisco Zamora-Martinez and Germán Sanchis-Trilles. 2010. Uch-upv english–spanish system for wmt10. In *Proceedings of the Joint Fifth Workshop on Statistical Machine Translation and MetricsMATR*, pages 188–192, Uppsala, Sweden, July. Association for Computational Linguistics.

Daniel Zeman. 2010. Hierarchical phrase-based mt at the charles university for the wmt 2010 shared task. In *Proceedings of the Joint Fifth Workshop on Statistical Machine Translation and MetricsMATR*, pages 193–196, Uppsala, Sweden, July. Association for Computational Linguistics.

A Pairwise system comparisons by human judges

Tables 13–20 show pairwise comparisons between systems for each language pair. The numbers in each of the tables' cells indicate the percentage of times that the system in that column was judged to be better than the system in that row. Bolding indicates the winner of the two systems. The difference between 100 and the sum of the complimentary cells is the percent of time that the two systems were judged to be equal.

Because there were so many systems and data conditions the significance of each pairwise comparison needs to be quantified. We applied the Sign Test to measure which comparisons indicate genuine differences (rather than differences that are attributable to chance). In the following tables ⋆ indicates statistical significance at $p \leq 0.10$, † indicates statistical significance at $p \leq 0.05$, and ‡ indicates statistical significance at $p \leq 0.01$, according to the Sign Test.

B Automatic scores

The tables on pages 33–32 give the automatic scores for each of the systems.

C Pairwise system comparisons for combined expert and non-expert data

Tables 21–20 show pairwise comparisons between systems for the into English direction when non-expert judgments have been added.

The number of pairwise comparisons at the ⋆ level of significance increases from 48 to 50, and the number at the † level of significants increases from 79 to 80 (basically same number). However, the ‡ level of significance went up considerably, from 280 to 369. That's a 31% increase. 75 of ‡ are comparisons involving the reference, then the non-reference ‡ count went up from 205 to 294, a 43% increase.

	REF	CAMBRIDGE	CMU-STATXFER	CU-ZEMAN	DFKI	GENEVA	HUICONG	JHU	LIG	LIMSI	LIUM	NRC	ONLINEA	ONLINEB	RALI	RWTH	UEDIN	BBN-COMBO	CMU-HEAFIELD-COMBO	CMU-HYPOSEL-COMBO	DCU-COMBO	JHU-COMBO	LIUM-COMBO	RWTH-COMBO	UPV-COMBO
REF	–	.00‡	.00‡	.00‡	.00‡	.00‡	.04‡	.03‡	.00‡	.00‡	.00‡	.00‡	.04‡	.00‡	.04‡	.00‡	.00‡	.00‡	.00‡	.05‡	.06‡	.03‡	.09‡	.04‡	.04‡
CAMBRIDGE	**.79**‡	–	.36	.16‡	.12‡	.23†	.27	**.43**	.26†	.38	.24	.3	.28	**.51**	.34	.23	.37	.24	.32	**.46**	.24	.29	**.45**	**.59**⋆	**.44**
CMU-STATXFER	**.84**‡	**.58**	–	.16‡	**.48**	.14‡	.19	.39	.33	**.54**	**.54**⋆	**.50**†	.36	**.50**	**.70**‡	**.55**⋆	**.50**	.46	**.58**†	**.67**†	**.50**	**.56**†	**.48**	**.58**‡	**.52**†
CU-ZEMAN	**1.00**‡	**.77**‡	**.72**‡	–	**.76**‡	.37	**.73**‡	**.74**‡	**.79**‡	**.77**‡	**.77**‡	**.81**‡	**.75**‡	**.94**‡	**.86**‡	**.77**‡	**.89**‡	**.67**	**.77**‡	**.79**‡	**.81**‡	**.81**‡	**.77**‡	**.96**‡	**.86**‡
DFKI	**1.00**‡	**.72**‡	.45	.12‡	–	.32	**.48**	**.50**	**.52**	**.53**	**.56**	**.65**	**.53**	**.62**	**.55**	.43	**.61**⋆	**.50**	**.68**†	**.73**‡	**.70**†	**.60**	**.59**⋆	**.72**‡	**.71**‡
GENEVA	**1.00**‡	**.69**†	**.76**‡	**.48**	**.56**	–	**.47**	**.71**†	**.79**‡	**.72**†	**.79**‡	**.71**†	**.68**†	**.76**‡	**.83**‡	**.57**	**.86**‡	**.72**‡	**.71**†	**.69**†	**.76**†	**.65**‡	**.88**‡	**.96**‡	**.70**
HUICONG	**.86**‡	**.54**	**.29**	.12‡	.26	.37	–	**.48**	.31	**.43**	**.63**‡	**.62**†	**.53**	**.55**	**.53**‡	.44	**.50**	**.55**	**.52**	**.68**‡	**.52**⋆	**.51**	**.52**⋆	**.57**	**.53**
JHU	**.83**‡	.39	**.42**	.13‡	.33	.19†	.3	–	.3	.36	**.56**†	**.56**⋆	**.47**	**.52**	**.46**	.29	**.36**	**.42**	**.42**	**.59**†	**.50**	.31	.43	**.29**	**.37**
LIG	**.97**‡	**.63**†	**.36**	.15‡	.37	.18‡	**.40**	**.60**	–	**.62**⋆	**.57**‡	**.39**	.35	**.54**†	**.46**	.33	.34	.38	**.54**†	**.48**⋆	**.42**	**.44**	**.50**	**.61**⋆	**.56**
LIMSI	**.96**‡	**.41**	.23	.19‡	.31	.17†	.32	**.50**	.28⋆	–	**.35**	**.42**	.21	**.62**‡	.25	.21	.33	.22	**.42**	.35	**.43**	.32	.26	**.35**	**.41**
LIUM	**.83**‡	**.33**	.21⋆	.13‡	.41	.05‡	.13‡	.15†	.09‡	.3	–	.39	.19	.36	**.43**	.26	.23†	.28	.29	**.45**	.28	.26	.28	.33	.28
NRC	**.96**‡	.3	.10†	.10‡	.32	.24†	.15†	.22⋆	.22	.33	**.43**	–	.26	**.58**	.26	.24	.3	**.50**	**.36**	**.45**	**.47**†	.23	**.38**	**.36**†	**.35**
ONLINEA	**.96**‡	**.55**	**.57**	.14‡	.42	.16†	.42	.4	**.39**	**.53**	**.52**	**.47**	–	**.52**⋆	**.46**	.36	**.64**	**.57**	**.59**	**.50**	**.59**	**.42**	**.46**	.43	**.48**
ONLINEB	**.87**‡	.37	.33	.03‡	.29	.12‡	.31	.26	.16†	.12‡	**.39**	.35	.20⋆	–	.33	.38	.17†	.36	.29	.21	.33	.3	.3	.32	.21‡
RALI	**.89**‡	**.45**	.15‡	.06‡	.35	.04‡	.12‡	.42	.35	**.46**	.32	**.42**	.39	**.52**	–	.32	.31	.26	**.43**	**.41**	.27	**.43**	**.40**	**.63**⋆	.26
RWTH	**.91**‡	**.46**	.21⋆	.05‡	**.51**	.36	.44	**.46**	**.53**	**.39**	**.48**	**.48**	**.39**	**.48**	**.48**	–	**.39**	**.38**	**.39**	**.52**	**.46**	**.53**†	**.52**	**.50**‡	.25
UEDIN	**.96**‡	**.40**	.33	.03‡	.28⋆	.03‡	.28	.29	**.49**	**.38**	**.61**†	.3	.32	**.50**†	**.34**	.24	–	**.42**	**.33**	**.43**	**.48**	.18⋆	.13	**.27**	**.38**
BBN-C	**.90**‡	**.48**	.46	.29	.39	.22‡	.27	.27	**.46**	**.43**	.28	.35	.33	**.39**	**.29**	.34	.26	–	**.28**	**.44**†	**.33**	**.26**	**.62**⋆	**.36**	.28
CMU-HEA-C	**.89**‡	**.50**	.23†	.14‡	.30†	.21†	.26	.25	.17†	.33	**.43**	.16	.36	**.43**	.26	.29	.24	.24	–	**.48**	**.27**	.13	.25	**.30**	.15
CMU-HYP-C	**.81**‡	.17	.19†	.11‡	.19‡	.19†	.14‡	.14†	.19⋆	**.40**	.23	.18	.29	**.46**	.35	.29	.21	.15†	.17	–	.26	.18	.07‡	**.32**	.21
DCU-C	**.88**‡	**.27**	.25	.11‡	.22†	.24†	.20⋆	.28	.21	.35	**.50**	.10†	.31	**.44**	.27	.29	.22	.21	.2	**.30**	–	.12⋆	.26	**.26**	.08
JHU-C	**.86**‡	**.48**	.16†	.16‡	.33	.21‡	.35	**.41**	.32	**.44**	**.39**	**.35**	.39	**.37**	.26	.19†	**.50**⋆	.23	**.32**	**.43**	**.40**⋆	–	.36	**.27**	**.39**
LIUM-C	**.87**‡	.41	.36	.13‡	.31⋆	.08‡	.21⋆	**.48**	.31	**.47**	**.44**	.24	.39	**.52**	.28	.28	**.33**	.27⋆	.25	**.67**‡	.26	**.44**	–	**.54**‡	**.48**
RWTH-C	**.88**‡	.18⋆	.13‡	.04‡	.22‡	.04‡	.14	.24	.25⋆	.3	.33	.05†	.43	**.50**	.30⋆	.13‡	.23	.14	.18	.21	.19	.23	.11‡	–	.24
UPV-C	**.92**‡	.25	.12†	.10‡	.16‡	.3	.25	.34	.29	.31	**.34**	.29	.39	**.65**‡	**.39**	**.36**	.3	**.45**	**.27**	**.36**	**.23**	.16	.24	**.28**	–
> others	.90	.44	.31	.13	.33	.18	.29	.37	.34	.42	.44	.38	.37	**.51**	.41	.31	.38	.35	.38	**.48**	.39	.36	.40	.46	.37
>= others	.98	.66	.51	.21	.42	.27	.51	.59	.53	.65	**.71**	.66	.52	**.71**	.65	.55	.65	.64	.70	**.77**	.72	.65	.64	**.77**	.68

Table 13: Sentence-level ranking for the WMT10 French-English News Task

	REF	CAMBRIDGE	CU-ZEMAN	DFKI	EU	GENEVA	JHU	KOC	LIMSI	LIUM	NRC	ONLINEA	ONLINEB	RALI	RWTH	UEDIN	CMU-HEAFIELD-COMBO	KOC-COMBO	RWTH-COMBO	UPV-COMBO
REF	–	.08‡	.02‡	.00‡	.04‡	.08‡	.13‡	.06‡	.09‡	.09‡	.07‡	.16‡	.11‡	.12‡	.12‡	.12‡	.05‡	.07‡	.08‡	.09‡
CAMBRIDGE	**.82**‡	–	.16‡	.24†	.15‡	.07‡	.35	.10‡	**.42**	.36	.43	.27	**.67**‡	**.46**	**.39**	**.44**	**.40**	**.46**	**.48***	**.40**
CU-ZEMAN	**.98**‡	**.82**‡	–	**.47**	**.54***	**.62**‡	**.71**‡	**.41**	**.79**‡	**.82**‡	**.70**‡	**.67**‡	**.85**‡	**.90**‡	**.75**‡	**.72**‡	**.92**‡	**.82**‡	**.88**‡	**.82**‡
DFKI	**.95**‡	**.66**†	.31	–	**.46**	.25*	**.78**‡	.36	**.59**	**.62***	**.75**‡	**.65**†	**.45**	**.56***	**.75**‡	**.69**‡	**.71**‡	**.63***	**.57**	**.65**†
EU	**.96**‡	**.78**‡	.30*	.41	–	**.55**	**.68**‡	.16‡	**.76**‡	**.72**‡	**.82**‡	**.67**‡	**.63**‡	**.86**‡	**.78**‡	**.78**‡	**.76**‡	**.76**‡	**.75**‡	**.71**‡
GENEVA	**.86**‡	**.81**‡	.23‡	**.55***	.34	–	**.65**‡	.25‡	**.65**†	**.70**‡	**.69**‡	**.66**‡	**.77**‡	**.71**‡	**.70**‡	**.89**‡	**.75**‡	**.63**†	**.84**‡	**.75**‡
JHU	**.77**‡	**.42**	.15‡	.22‡	.22‡	.22‡	–	.06‡	**.58***	**.47**	**.52**†	**.49**	**.70**‡	**.61**†	**.53**	**.64**‡	**.53***	**.65**‡	**.68**‡	**.50**
KOC	**.85**‡	**.67**‡	.4	**.58**	**.55**‡	**.69**‡	**.82**‡	–	**.76**‡	**.85**‡	**.81**‡	**.72**‡	**.86**‡	**.82**‡	**.86**‡	**.85**‡	**.77**‡	**.77**‡	**.74**‡	**.79**‡
LIMSI	**.84**‡	.23	.08‡	.29	.09‡	.30†	.21*	.08‡	–	.33	**.37**	.17‡	**.51**	**.40**	.29	**.45**	**.49**	**.40**	**.61**‡	.28
LIUM	**.85**‡	**.39**	.07‡	.32*	.11‡	.21‡	.44	.07‡	**.46**	–	.44	.4	.32	.44	.37	**.64**†	.35	**.40**	**.35**	**.42**
NRC	**.91**‡	.43	.15‡	.20‡	.11‡	.25‡	.21†	.09‡	.31	**.45**	–	.32	**.48**	.44	**.49**	**.61**†	**.52**†	**.30**	**.58***	**.40**
ONLINEA	**.80**‡	**.51**	.21‡	.33†	.23‡	.15‡	.41	.14‡	**.60**‡	**.42**	**.54**	–	**.52***	**.56***	.36	**.67**‡	**.61**‡	**.45**	**.50**	**.44**
ONLINEB	**.87**‡	.23‡	.08‡	.43	.23‡	.11‡	.12‡	.08‡	.27	**.36**	.43	.25*	–	.38	.31	.33	**.52**	.33*	**.46**	.29
RALI	**.83**‡	.38	.05‡	.27*	.11‡	.15‡	.22†	.10‡	.36	.44	**.49**	.31*	**.50**	–	.38	**.44**	**.42**	.37	**.38**	**.34**
RWTH	**.76**‡	.33	.11‡	.12‡	.15‡	.17‡	.34	.05‡	**.34**	**.44**	.29	**.42**	**.49**	**.40**	–	**.56**	**.48**	**.44**	**.53**‡	**.50**
UEDIN	**.84**‡	.29	.20‡	.17‡	.12‡	.09‡	.19‡	.07‡	.33	.23†	.24†	.24‡	**.56**	.31	.3	–	**.36***	.27	**.51**	.18†
CMU-HEAFIELD-COMBO	**.90**‡	.23	.04‡	.23‡	.18‡	.12‡	.22*	.11‡	.32	**.41**	.20†	.23‡	.28	.31	.31	.11*	–	.29	.24	.3
KOC-COMBO	**.91**‡	.26	.08‡	.31*	.17‡	.28†	.20‡	.07‡	.23	.26	.19	.36	**.57***	.37	.32	**.32**	**.42**	–	**.38**	**.34**
RWTH-COMBO	**.85**‡	.21*	.02‡	.36	.16‡	.07‡	.12‡	.07‡	.16‡	.3	.30*	.4	.34	.32	.06‡	.26	**.35**	.16	–	.21*
UPV-COMBO	**.87**‡	.38	.08‡	.30†	.19‡	.19‡	.37	.11‡	**.39**	.24	.33	.37	**.44**	.27	.34	**.46**†	**.35**	.28	**.50***	–
> others	.87	.43	.15	.30	.22	.25	.38	.13	.44	.45	.46	.41	**.53**	.49	.44	.52	**.53**	.45	**.53**	.45
>= others	.92	.63	.26	.40	.32	.35	.53	.26	.66	.63	.62	.55	**.68**	.66	.63	.70	.74	.68	**.75**	.66

Table 14: Sentence-level ranking for the WMT10 English-French News Task

	REF	AALTO	CMU	CU-ZEMAN	DFKI	FBK	HUICONG	JHU	KIT	KOC	LIMSI	LIU	ONLINEA	ONLINEB	RWTH	UEDIN	UMD	UPPSALA	UU-MS	BBN-COMBO	CMU-HEAFIELD-COMBO	CMU-HYPOSEL-COMBO	JHU-COMBO	KOC-COMBO	RWTH-COMBO	UPV-COMBO
REF	–	.00‡	.03‡	.00‡	.06‡	.03‡	.00‡	.00‡	.05‡	.00‡	.00‡	.03‡	.06‡	.09‡	.06‡	.00‡	.09‡	.03‡	.03‡	.14‡	.03‡	.06‡	.03‡	.03‡	.06‡	.00‡
AALTO	**1.00‡**	–	**.50**	.31	**.60**	**.69‡**	**.39**	**.41**	**.71†**	.31	**.45**	**.60‡**	**.59†**	**.65‡**	**.66‡**	**.64‡**	**.81‡**	**.45**	**.41**	**.69†**	**.72‡**	**.75†**	**.55**	**.55‡**	**.76‡**	**.57†**
CMU	**.93‡**	.31	–	.29	**.49**	**.57‡**	**.38**	**.50**	**.74‡**	.13‡	**.44**	**.59‡**	**.57†**	**.59⋆**	**.60†**	**.67†**	**.59‡**	**.41**	**.50**	**.68‡**	**.67‡**	**.46**	**.64‡**	**.55⋆**	**.67‡**	**.54⋆**
CU-ZEMAN	**1.00‡**	**.44**	**.56**	–	**.58**	**.64‡**	.17	**.44**	**.75‡**	.38	**.50**	**.54†**	**.76†**	**.79‡**	**.73‡**	**.72‡**	**.72‡**	**.50⋆**	**.73‡**	**.78‡**	**.80‡**	**.68‡**	**.72†**	**.62†**	**.68⋆**	**.73‡**
DFKI	**.92‡**	.25	.32	.27	–	**.53**	.36	**.46**	**.65⋆**	.07‡	**.50**	**.47**	**.47**	**.69‡**	**.56**	.35	**.55**	**.58**	**.47**	**.67†**	**.61⋆**	**.52**	**.47**	.38	**.67†**	**.51**
FBK	**.97‡**	.20‡	.16‡	.14‡	.38	–	.11‡	.31	**.45**	.10‡	.22⋆	**.36**	**.50**	**.57†**	.37	**.43**	**.40**	.12‡	.17†	**.48⋆**	**.43**	**.35**	**.38**	.22	**.38**	**.39**
HUICONG	**.93‡**	.35	.28	**.46**	**.43**	**.75‡**	–	**.52**	**.69†**	.16†	**.39**	.42	**.64†**	**.79‡**	.31	**.51†**	**.78‡**	**.27**	**.41**	**.49**	**.74‡**	**.68‡**	**.60⋆**	**.37**	**.68‡**	**.56†**
JHU	**.86‡**	.34	.29	.16	.43	.31	.26	–	**.61‡**	.15‡	.35	.36	**.45**	**.69‡**	**.52⋆**	**.56⋆**	**.64†**	.27	**.36**	**.70‡**	**.53**	**.47**	**.66‡**	**.52**	**.68‡**	**.44**
KIT	**.89‡**	.21†	.10‡	.14‡	.29⋆	.33	.19†	.14‡	–	.03‡	.27	.21†	.36	**.46**	.17‡	.29	.24	.25‡	.25‡	**.48**	.23⋆	.31	.38	.2	**.36**	.12‡
KOC	**.96‡**	**.58**	**.77‡**	**.48**	**.70‡**	**.77‡**	**.58†**	**.71‡**	**.97‡**	–	**.77‡**	**.90‡**	**.72‡**	**.82‡**	**.76‡**	**.84‡**	**.81‡**	**.84‡**	**.66‡**	**.83‡**	**.87‡**	**.79‡**	**.77‡**	**.75‡**	**.93‡**	**.71‡**
LIMSI	**1.00‡**	.23	.28	.35	.35	**.53⋆**	.33	**.45**	**.41**	.19‡	–	**.49**	**.48**	**.63†**	**.49**	**.63‡**	**.52**	.36	.29	**.73‡**	**.53⋆**	.45	**.59‡**	.29	**.56†**	**.59†**
LIU	**.88‡**	.12‡	.15‡	.16†	.39	.21	**.46**	.36	**.61†**	.00‡	.27	–	**.44**	**.63†**	**.49**	**.45**	**.53**	.27⋆	.33	**.67‡**	**.55⋆**	**.46**	**.44**	.32	**.37**	**.55**
ONLINEA	**.92‡**	.15†	.23†	.24†	.42	.34	.21†	.35	**.50**	.10‡	.32	.36	–	**.41**	.4	.44	.37	.32	.34	**.36**	.4	**.47**	.3	.26	**.48**	.41
ONLINEB	**.68‡**	.18‡	.29⋆	.17‡	.26‡	.24†	.18‡	.23‡	.33	.18‡	.23†	.27†	.34	–	.3	.15‡	.29	.24†	.15‡	**.44**	.28	.33⋆	.20†	.21‡	.38	.3
RWTH	**.88‡**	.17‡	.20†	.20‡	.37	**.49**	**.41**	.23⋆	**.61‡**	.16‡	.4	.3	**.43**	**.56**	–	.39	**.50**	.26	**.49**	**.37**	.29	**.34**	**.41**	.26	**.44**	.2
UEDIN	**.89‡**	.14‡	.22†	.13‡	**.62**	.34	.18†	.22⋆	**.39**	.03‡	.17‡	.3	.44	**.67‡**	**.42**	–	.39	.15‡	.14‡	**.52⋆**	**.40**	.36	**.43**	.26	**.41**	.38
UMD	**.91‡**	.07‡	.14‡	.08‡	.36	.34	.11‡	.25†	**.48**	.16‡	.24	.34	**.52**	**.56**	.41	**.45**	–	.16‡	.21†	**.41**	.28	.29	**.43**	.29	.25	.23
UPPSALA	**.97‡**	.32	.34	.17⋆	.36	**.54‡**	.23	**.37**	**.70‡**	.00‡	**.41**	**.62⋆**	**.56**	**.68†**	**.57**	**.64‡**	**.59‡**	–	.2	**.63‡**	**.69‡**	**.51‡**	**.60⋆**	**.33**	**.69‡**	**.63‡**
UU-MS	**.82‡**	.22	.43	.14‡	.45	**.51†**	.19	.21	**.68‡**	.14‡	**.39**	**.52**	**.60**	**.64‡**	.44	**.53‡**	**.61†**	**.28**	–	**.36**	**.58‡**	**.52⋆**	**.53⋆**	**.30**	**.64‡**	**.44**
BBN-C	**.86‡**	.25†	.10‡	.07‡	.27†	.17⋆	.23	.18‡	.35	.07‡	.15‡	.12‡	.32	.41	.3	.19⋆	.22	.15‡	.27	–	**.39**	.06†	.23⋆	.11‡	.21	.18†
CMU-HEA-C	**.87‡**	.14‡	.15‡	.08‡	.29⋆	.33	.04‡	.26	**.53⋆**	.00‡	.20⋆	.24⋆	**.44**	**.31**	**.46**	.23	**.53**	.15‡	.13‡	.27	–	**.40**	.2	.14‡	.22	.28
CMU-HYP-C	**.94‡**	.25†	.24	.14‡	.44	.3	.15‡	.26	**.47**	.08‡	.45	.31	.42	**.67⋆**	.24	.36	**.46**	.14‡	.21⋆	**.50†**	.32	–	**.43**	.28	**.51⋆**	**.42**
JHU-C	**.97‡**	.34	.11‡	.20†	.29	.34	.29⋆	.03‡	.38	.12‡	.07‡	.29	**.55**	**.67†**	.34	.32	.23	.24⋆	.24⋆	**.48⋆**	**.40**	.32	–	.27	**.37**	**.31**
KOC-C	**.88‡**	.00‡	.23⋆	.21†	**.53**	**.44**	.29	.22	**.43**	.08‡	**.36**	**.50**	**.53**	**.63‡**	**.39**	**.37**	**.39**	.28	.19	**.64‡**	**.61‡**	**.38**	**.55**	–	**.48⋆**	**.46**
RWTH-C	**.82‡**	.09‡	.06‡	.29⋆	.25†	.25	.18‡	.18‡	.24	.03‡	.19†	.26	.36	**.54**	.25	.26	**.33**	.06‡	.14‡	**.29**	.22	.23⋆	.3	.17⋆	–	.13‡
UPV-C	**.97‡**	.17†	.21⋆	.17‡	.36	.36	.23†	.19	**.67‡**	.20‡	.18†	.29	.41	**.40**	**.40**	.38	**.48**	.17‡	.31	**.50†**	**.43**	.27	.27	.27	**.65‡**	–
> others	.91	.23	.25	.20	.39	.42	.24	.30	.53	.11	.31	.38	.47	**.59**	.42	.43	.48	.27	.30	**.53**	.49	.42	.44	.31	.51	.41
>= others	.96	.42	.46	.36	.50	.66	.47	.53	.72	.23	.52	.59	.63	**.73**	.62	.66	.68	.51	.55	**.77**	.73	.65	.67	.59	.75	.64

Table 15: Sentence-level ranking for the WMT10 German-English News Task

	REF	CU-ZEMAN	DFKI	FBK	JHU	KIT	KOC	LIMSI	LIU	ONLINEA	ONLINEB	RWTH	SFU	UEDIN	UPPSALA	CMU-HEAFIELD-COMBO	KOC-COMBO	RWTH-COMBO	UPV-COMBO
REF	–	.03‡	.06‡	.01‡	.02‡	.05‡	.00‡	.00‡	.01‡	.04‡	.03‡	.01‡	.01‡	.01‡	.02‡	.01‡	.01‡	.05‡	.06‡
CU-ZEMAN	**.97‡**	–	**.85‡**	**.67‡**	**.62‡**	**.78‡**	**.58⋆**	**.70‡**	**.64‡**	**.80‡**	**.85‡**	**.64‡**	**.52**	**.80‡**	**.61†**	**.79‡**	**.69‡**	**.76‡**	**.73‡**
DFKI	**.89‡**	.14‡	–	.36†	.24‡	.38	.30‡	.27‡	.36⋆	.36⋆	**.55**	.35†	.21‡	.41	.39	.46	.38⋆	.47	.37⋆
FBK	**.97‡**	.30‡	**.59†**	–	.35†	.42	.12‡	.36	**.48**	**.48**	**.64‡**	.39	.29‡	**.46**	.30†	**.44**	**.46**	**.48**	.38
JHU	**.98‡**	.27‡	**.72‡**	**.57†**	–	**.59‡**	.30‡	**.51**	**.53**	**.56⋆**	**.65‡**	.43	.39	**.66‡**	.45	**.56**	**.61‡**	**.52**	**.47**
KIT	**.92‡**	.18‡	**.55**	.42	.29‡	–	.23‡	.32	.32†	.43	**.53⋆**	.41	.27‡	.43	.23‡	**.41**	**.41**	**.42**	.37
KOC	**1.00‡**	.37⋆	**.64‡**	**.82‡**	**.62‡**	**.70‡**	–	**.74‡**	**.74‡**	**.74‡**	**.82‡**	**.63‡**	.48	**.62†**	**.65‡**	**.73‡**	**.67‡**	**.81‡**	**.71‡**
LIMSI	**.95‡**	.27‡	**.68‡**	**.39**	.45	**.49**	.17‡	–	**.49**	**.74‡**	**.70‡**	**.51**	.28‡	**.58‡**	.32	**.51**	**.53⋆**	**.52†**	.31
LIU	**.95‡**	.32‡	**.59⋆**	.4	.36	**.58†**	.21‡	.37	–	.39	**.74‡**	.33⋆	.23‡	**.55†**	.36⋆	.49	**.42**	**.46**	.38
ONLINEA	**.95‡**	.16‡	**.55⋆**	.4	.36⋆	**.45**	.21‡	.23‡	**.50**	–	**.56†**	.38	.23‡	.41	.23‡	**.48**	.4	**.50**	.33†
ONLINEB	**.92‡**	.12‡	.42	.26‡	.27‡	.33⋆	.14‡	.23‡	.21‡	.32†	–	.24‡	.14‡	.39	.19‡	.29‡	.27‡	.36	.32‡
RWTH	**.98‡**	.33‡	**.61†**	**.51**	**.47**	**.46**	.30‡	.33	**.52⋆**	**.55**	**.71‡**	–	.33†	**.57⋆**	**.45**	**.40**	**.51†**	**.47**	**.46**
SFU	**.98‡**	.42	**.77‡**	**.66‡**	**.51**	**.69‡**	.48	**.68‡**	**.69‡**	**.72‡**	**.77‡**	**.56†**	–	**.82‡**	**.53**	**.65‡**	**.69‡**	**.73‡**	**.62‡**
UEDIN	**.94‡**	.17‡	**.51**	.4	.31‡	**.49**	.34†	.25‡	.30†	**.52**	**.52**	.36⋆	.10‡	–	.33⋆	.31	**.42**	.38	.22‡
UPPSALA	**.97‡**	.36†	**.55**	**.51†**	**.47**	**.70‡**	.25‡	**.46**	**.57⋆**	**.67‡**	**.71‡**	.41	.38	**.54⋆**	–	**.53†**	**.42**	**.58‡**	**.40**
CMU-HEAFIELD-COMBO	**.96‡**	.17‡	**.49**	.36	.36	.37	.21‡	.35	.49	.42	**.64‡**	.38	.28‡	**.48**	.28†	–	.35	**.46**	.35
KOC-COMBO	**.99‡**	.27‡	**.56⋆**	.32	.27‡	.32	.23‡	.32⋆	.41	**.55**	**.64‡**	.30†	.21‡	.37	.36	**.41**	–	.34	.36
RWTH-COMBO	**.92‡**	.17‡	**.50**	.34	.35	.41	.09‡	.25†	.38	.4	**.54**	.38	.20‡	**.42**	.19‡	.28	**.35**	–	.16‡
UPV-COMBO	**.93‡**	.23‡	**.58⋆**	.38	.36	**.51**	.23‡	**.50**	**.49**	**.57†**	**.60‡**	.42	.28‡	**.51‡**	.3	**.38**	**.46**	**.48‡**	–
> others	.95	.24	.57	.44	.37	.48	.24	.39	.45	.51	**.63**	.40	.27	.51	.34	.45	.44	**.49**	.39
>= others	.98	.28	.62	.56	.46	.60	.30	.51	.55	.59	**.70**	.51	.34	.62	.47	.59	.59	**.65**	.55

Table 16: Sentence-level ranking for the WMT10 English-German News Task

	REF	CAMBRIDGE	COLUMBIA	CU-ZEMAN	DFKI	HUICONG	JHU	ONLINEA	ONLINEB	UEDIN	UPC	BBN-COMBO	CMU-HEAFIELD-COMBO	JHU-COMBO	UPV-COMBO
REF	–	.00‡	.01‡	.01‡	.01‡	.00‡	.00‡	.00‡	.00‡	.00‡	.01‡	.02‡	.05‡	.01‡	.04‡
CAMBRIDGE	**.95**‡	–	.23‡	.14‡	.34*	.31†	**.41**	.34	**.62**‡	**.45***	.35	**.40***	**.42**	.22†	**.44**
COLUMBIA	**.97**‡	**.58**‡	–	.25‡	**.52**	**.45**	**.59**‡	**.53***	**.65**‡	**.60**‡	**.47**	**.56**‡	**.55**‡	**.45**	**.58**‡
CU-ZEMAN	**.96**‡	**.71**‡	**.59**‡	–	**.60**‡	**.68**‡	**.79**‡	**.66**‡	**.75**‡	**.80**‡	**.66**‡	**.79**‡	**.78**‡	**.69**‡	**.75**‡
DFKI	**.97**‡	**.51***	.37	.23‡	–	**.43**	**.59**‡	**.52**†	**.66**‡	**.62**‡	**.48**	**.53**†	**.55**†	**.55**†	**.64**‡
HUICONG	**.95**‡	**.50**†	.34	.21‡	.41	–	**.45**	**.50**	**.66**‡	**.61**‡	**.39**	**.50***	**.59**‡	**.40**	**.52**‡
JHU	**.98**‡	.39	.22‡	.12‡	.30‡	.33	–	.37	**.56**‡	**.51**‡	.34	**.39**	**.34**†	.22‡	.34
ONLINEA	**.96**‡	**.46**	.37*	.23‡	.32†	.38	**.44**	–	**.59**‡	**.53**†	.4	**.50**	.36	.30†	**.54**‡
ONLINEB	**.88**‡	.25‡	.21‡	.16‡	.23‡	.21‡	.27‡	.23‡	–	.35	.24‡	.28‡	.34†	.22‡	.36
UEDIN	**.96**‡	.31*	.28‡	.10‡	.25‡	.19‡	.25‡	.31†	**.48**	–	.23‡	.27†	.31	.23‡	.2
UPC	**.94**‡	**.47**	.4	.20‡	.41	.33	**.43**	**.46**	**.66**‡	**.56**‡	–	**.50***	**.52**†	**.48***	**.49**†
BBN-COMBO	**.95**‡	.26*	.31‡	.09‡	.32†	.34*	.33	.37	**.54**‡	**.44**†	.33*	–	**.35**	.24‡	**.34**
CMU-HEAFIELD-COMBO	**.91**‡	.39	.21‡	.08‡	.34†	.22‡	.16†	**.42**	**.57**†	**.45**	.31†	.31	–	.14‡	.27
JHU-COMBO	**.95**‡	**.40**†	.32	.15‡	.36†	.31	**.44**‡	**.50**†	**.66**‡	**.50**‡	.32*	**.47**‡	**.43**‡	–	**.43**†
UPV-COMBO	**.92**‡	.35	.28‡	.16‡	.27‡	.23‡	**.38**	.28‡	**.47**	**.30**	.28†	.26	**.35**	.25†	–
> others	.95	.41	.30	.15	.33	.32	.39	.39	**.56**	.48	.34	.41	**.43**	.32	**.43**
>= others	.99	.61	.45	.27	.45	.50	.61	.54	**.70**	.69	.51	.62	**.66**	.55	**.66**

Table 17: Sentence-level ranking for the WMT10 Spanish-English News Task

	REF	CAMBRIDGE	CU-ZEMAN	DCU	DFKI	JHU	KOC	ONLINEA	ONLINEB	SFU	UEDIN	UPV	UCH-UPV	CMU-HEAFIELD-COMBO	KOC-COMBO	RWTH-COMBO	UPV-COMBO
REF	–	.00‡	.02‡	.07‡	.15‡	.07‡	.02‡	.11‡	.14‡	.07‡	.07‡	.03‡	.06‡	.09‡	.06‡	.03‡	.07‡
CAMBRIDGE	**.91**‡	–	.28†	**.45**	.38	**.45**	.11‡	**.52**	**.61**†	.21*	**.52**	**.47**	.35	**.54**	**.51**	**.39**	**.49**
CU-ZEMAN	**.95**‡	**.70**†	–	**.79**‡	**.75**‡	**.85**‡	**.49**	**.83**‡	**.82**‡	**.74**‡	**.87**‡	**.67**‡	**.85**‡	**.81**‡	**.80**‡	**.70**‡	**.74**‡
DCU	**.93**‡	.32	.21‡	–	.45	.32	.09‡	**.70**†	**.59**	.24‡	**.48**	.38	.29	.32	.36	.24	.14‡
DFKI	**.80**‡	**.41**	.15‡	.45	–	.38	.12‡	**.64**†	**.57**	.4	**.57**	.31	.41	**.59**	**.50**	**.48**	**.47**
JHU	**.90**‡	.37	.10‡	**.52**	**.56**	–	.17‡	**.67**†	**.67**‡	.26†	.34	.3	**.49**	**.54**	**.53**†	**.47**	**.35**
KOC	**.98**‡	**.87**‡	.47	**.88**‡	**.73**‡	**.76**‡	–	**.76**‡	**.87**‡	**.67**‡	**.83**‡	**.86**‡	**.90**‡	**.87**‡	**.90**‡	**.86**‡	**.86**‡
ONLINEA	**.82**‡	.42	.08‡	.30†	.18†	.24†	.20‡	–	**.49**	.36	.25†	.17‡	.25†	.45	.30*	.29	.18‡
ONLINEB	**.76**‡	.26†	.10‡	.32	.37	.22‡	.10‡	.34	–	.21‡	.28	.24†	.32	.33	.22‡	.19‡	.27*
SFU	**.91**‡	**.54***	.19‡	**.67**‡	**.51**	**.63**†	.27‡	**.64**	**.72**‡	–	**.74**‡	**.57***	**.68**‡	**.77**‡	**.71**‡	**.64**‡	**.46**
UEDIN	**.91**‡	.3	.08‡	.4	.38	.34	.14‡	**.71**†	**.49**	.09‡	–	.34	.4	**.58**	.33	.3	.31
UPV	**.94**‡	.34	.07‡	**.41**	**.53**	**.54**	.07‡	**.73**‡	**.61**†	.27*	**.45**	–	.37	**.51**	**.44**	**.38**	**.48**†
UCH-UPV	**.90**‡	**.55**	.07‡	**.58**	**.51**	.41	.08‡	**.69**†	**.52**	.24‡	**.51**	**.46**	–	**.47**	**.41**	**.49**	**.49**
CMU-HEAFIELD-COMBO	**.83**‡	.29	.13‡	**.37**	.38	.35	.07‡	**.48**	**.54**	.08‡	.29	.26	.28	–	.17†	.21*	.21
KOC-COMBO	**.88**‡	.27	.15‡	**.40**	.42	.24†	.03‡	**.62***	**.60**‡	.15‡	**.41**	.27	.34	**.53**†	–	.3	**.40**
RWTH-COMBO	**.92**‡	.36	.21‡	**.52**	.33	.31	.10‡	**.55**	**.65**‡	.14‡	**.37**	.22	.41	**.52***	**.48**	–	**.31**
UPV-COMBO	**.91**‡	.32	.13‡	**.69**‡	.4	.32	.09‡	**.76**‡	**.52***	.36	**.38**	.19†	.31	**.45**	.35	.28	–
> others	.89	.39	.15	.48	.44	.41	.14	**.61**	.58	.29	.46	.36	.42	**.51**	.44	.39	.40
>= others	.93	.54	.23	.61	.55	.55	.19	.69	**.71**	.40	.61	.55	.54	**.68**	.62	.59	.60

Table 18: Sentence-level ranking for the WMT10 English-Spanish News Task

	REF	AALTO	CMU	CU-BOJAR	CU-ZEMAN	ONLINEA	ONLINEB	UEDIN	BBN-COMBO	CMU-HEAFIELD-COMBO	JHU-COMBO	RWTH-COMBO	UPV-COMBO
REF	–	.04‡	.02‡	.03‡	.00‡	.02‡	.00‡	.03‡	.03‡	.04‡	.01‡	.04‡	.02‡
AALTO	**.88**‡	–	**.49**	**.51**	.22‡	.38	**.64**‡	**.55**†	**.57**⋆	**.71**‡	**.64**‡	**.65**‡	**.59**‡
CMU	**.97**‡	.35	–	.4	.14‡	.18‡	**.59**‡	**.49**†	**.45**†	**.57**‡	**.50**‡	.34	**.43**
CU-BOJAR	**.90**‡	.33	**.43**	–	.12‡	.20‡	**.64**‡	**.45**	**.45**	**.54**‡	**.42**	**.42**	.41
CU-ZEMAN	**.99**‡	**.60**‡	**.77**‡	**.75**‡	–	**.56**†	**.81**‡	**.78**‡	**.88**‡	**.79**‡	**.84**‡	**.84**‡	**.76**‡
ONLINEA	**.92**‡	**.46**	**.68**‡	**.59**‡	.28†	–	**.65**‡	**.54**‡	**.72**‡	**.75**‡	**.58**‡	**.57**‡	**.66**‡
ONLINEB	**.97**‡	.27‡	.28‡	.21‡	.10‡	.17‡	–	.25†	.32	.22	.21†	.32	.28
UEDIN	**.95**‡	.28†	.26†	.38	.07‡	.22‡	**.49**†	–	**.60**‡	**.52**‡	.33	**.31**	.32
BBN-COMBO	**.92**‡	.31⋆	.20†	.39	.08‡	.15‡	**.41**	.16‡	–	.27	.25	.3	.26
CMU-HEAFIELD-COMBO	**.90**‡	.13‡	.23‡	.25‡	.07‡	.15‡	**.31**	.23‡	**.34**	–	.18‡	.35	.28
JHU-COMBO	**.93**‡	.20‡	.19‡	.33	.08‡	.25‡	**.48**†	**.39**	**.38**	**.52**‡	–	**.37**	**.42**
RWTH-COMBO	**.92**‡	.18‡	**.37**	.38	.13‡	.25‡	**.34**	.28	**.43**	**.40**	.26	–	.25
UPV-COMBO	**.96**‡	.25‡	.36	.41	.11‡	.27‡	**.45**	**.35**	**.37**	**.44**	.31	**.34**	–
> others	.93	.28	.36	.38	.11	.23	**.49**	.38	.47	**.48**	.38	.40	.40
>= others	.98	.43	.55	.55	.22	.37	**.70**	.61	.70	**.71**	.62	.65	.63

Table 19: Sentence-level ranking for the WMT10 Czech-English News Task

	REF	CU-BOJAR	CU-TECTO	CU-ZEMAN	DCU	EUROTRANS	KOC	ONLINEA	ONLINEB	PC-TRANS	POTSDAM	SFU	UEDIN	CMU-HEAFIELD-COMBO	DCU-COMBO	KOC-COMBO	RWTH-COMBO	UPV-COMBO
REF	–	.04‡	.04‡	.03‡	.01‡	.05‡	.03‡	.08‡	.04‡	.04‡	.03‡	.02‡	.02‡	.04‡	.08‡	.04‡	.07‡	.04‡
CU-BOJAR	**.87**‡	–	**.46**	.27‡	.12‡	.28‡	.16‡	.17‡	**.44**	.4	.11‡	.27‡	**.41**	.28	**.52**‡	.28	**.42**	**.43**
CU-TECTO	**.88**‡	.36	–	.30†	.23‡	.38	.17‡	.28‡	**.56**†	**.44**	.29†	.27‡	.36	**.45**	**.51**†	.4	**.58**†	.35
CU-ZEMAN	**.91**‡	**.58**‡	**.51**†	–	.38	**.49**	.19‡	.39	**.62**‡	**.63**‡	.36	**.41**	**.48**	**.51**‡	**.58**‡	**.48**†	**.54**†	**.55**‡
DCU	**.98**‡	**.73**‡	**.52**‡	**.43**	–	**.59**‡	.22‡	**.47**	**.74**‡	**.63**‡	**.47**†	**.53**†	**.56**‡	**.77**‡	**.77**‡	**.62**‡	**.76**‡	**.71**‡
EUROTRANS	**.88**‡	**.61**‡	**.47**	.33	.30‡	–	.10‡	.33	**.51**	**.54**†	.25‡	.27‡	**.49**	**.57**‡	**.59**†	**.49**	**.57**‡	**.60**‡
KOC	**.93**‡	**.69**‡	**.67**‡	**.54**‡	**.49**‡	**.77**‡	–	**.54**‡	**.71**‡	**.70**‡	**.51**‡	**.55**‡	**.64**‡	**.72**‡	**.78**‡	**.65**‡	**.76**‡	**.78**‡
ONLINEA	**.91**‡	**.62**‡	**.57**‡	**.51**	.39	**.44**	.24‡	–	**.66**‡	**.62**‡	.39	**.43**	**.55**‡	**.60**‡	**.61**‡	**.59**‡	**.73**‡	**.61**‡
ONLINEB	**.91**‡	.31	.29†	.27‡	.13‡	.33	.14‡	.19‡	–	.44	.22‡	.09‡	**.39**	.19	.34	.24⋆	.22†	**.39**
PC-TRANS	**.88**‡	**.45**	.43	.24‡	.26‡	.29†	.21‡	.24‡	**.49**	–	.22‡	.27‡	.37	**.43**	**.55**†	.33†	**.49**	.41
POTSDAM	**.88**‡	**.60**‡	**.51**†	**.40**	.27†	**.59**‡	.25‡	**.47**	**.63**‡	**.64**‡	–	**.45**	**.52**‡	**.56**‡	**.69**‡	**.61**‡	**.70**‡	**.68**‡
SFU	**.95**‡	**.52**‡	**.56**‡	.4	.30†	**.61**‡	.27‡	.39	**.65**‡	**.64**‡	.29	–	**.55**‡	**.54**‡	**.76**‡	**.53**‡	**.70**‡	**.60**‡
UEDIN	**.94**‡	.39	**.44**	.33	.23‡	.32	.20‡	.26‡	.32	**.49**	.25‡	.26‡	–	**.43**	**.57**‡	.18	**.46**†	**.42**
CMU-HEAFIELD-COMBO	**.91**‡	**.42**	.39	.23‡	.10‡	.27‡	.14‡	.19‡	**.23**	.35	.24‡	.19‡	.28	–	**.48**‡	.28	**.34**	**.29**
DCU-COMBO	**.84**‡	.23‡	.27†	.23‡	.03‡	.31†	.10‡	.21‡	**.42**	.31†	.15‡	.10‡	.16‡	.20‡	–	.18‡	.27⋆	.22‡
KOC-COMBO	**.91**‡	**.37**	**.49**	.25†	.10‡	.39	.17‡	.32‡	**.42**⋆	**.55**†	.17‡	.27‡	**.26**	**.33**	**.41**‡	–	.32	.22
RWTH-COMBO	**.88**‡	.29	.34†	.28†	.05‡	.26‡	.10‡	.17‡	**.48**†	.43	.16‡	.15‡	.24†	.33	**.46**⋆	**.36**	–	.29
UPV-COMBO	**.92**‡	.37	**.52**	.22‡	.09‡	.25‡	.10‡	.19‡	.28	**.47**	.15‡	.25‡	.33	.24	**.49**‡	**.34**	**.39**	–
> others	.91	.45	.44	.32	.20	.39	.16	.29	**.49**	**.49**	.25	.28	.40	.43	**.54**	.39	.50	.45
>= others	.96	.66	.60	.50	.38	.54	.33	.44	**.70**	.62	.44	.45	.62	.69	**.75**	.66	.70	.68

Table 20: Sentence-level ranking for the WMT10 English-Czech News Task

Czech-English -- Metrics submited to NIST MetricsMATR 2010, plus two baseline metrics (BLEU and NIST). Scores for "all" (entire WMT10 testset) and "sub" (subset of the humanly assessed data) are shown.

	rank		MT-NCD		MT-mNCD		Badger full		Badger lite		ATEC 2.1		METEOR adq		METEOR hter		METEOR rank		SEPIA		SemPOS		SemPOS BLEU		DCU-LFG		LRKB4		LRHB4	
	(all)	(sub)	(all)	(sub)	(all)	(sub)	(all)	(sub)	(all)	(sub)	(all)	(sub)	(all)	(sub)	(all)	(sub)	(all)	(sub)	(all)	(sub)	(all)	(sub)	(all)	(sub)	(all)	(sub)	(all)	(sub)	(all)	(sub)
aalto	0.43		0.54		0.53		0.49	0.50	0.48	0.49	0.43		0.48		0.50		0.45		0.24		0.15		0.27		0.35		0.51		0.44	
bbn-combo	0.70		0.58		**0.56**		**0.54**	**0.54**	**0.54**	**0.54**	**0.50**		**0.55**		**0.57**		**0.51**		**0.29**		**0.17**		**0.37**		**0.44**		**0.56**		**0.49**	
cmu-HF-combo	**0.71**		0.58		0.55		0.54	0.54	0.53	0.53	0.50		0.54		**0.57**		0.50		**0.29**		**0.17**		0.36		**0.44**		**0.56**		0.48	
cmu	0.55		0.55		0.53		0.52	0.52	0.51	0.52	0.46		0.52		0.54		0.48		0.27		**0.17**		0.33		0.41		0.54		0.46	
cu-bojar	0.55		0.56		0.53		0.50	0.51	0.49	0.50	0.45		0.51		0.53		0.47		0.25		0.15		0.30		0.37		0.53		0.46	
cu-zeman	0.22		0.49		0.52		0.45	0.46	0.45	0.45	0.39		0.45		0.46		0.42		0.21		0.13		0.20		0.30		0.50		0.41	
jhu-combo	0.62		0.57		**0.56**		**0.54**	**0.54**	0.53	**0.54**	0.48		0.53		0.55		0.49		0.28		**0.17**		0.35		0.42		0.53		0.47	
onlineA	0.37		0.54		0.52		0.49	0.50	0.48	0.50	0.42		0.47		0.49		0.44		0.24		0.14		0.27		0.34		0.49		0.42	
onlineB	0.70		**0.59**		**0.56**		**0.54**	0.53	0.53	0.53	0.49		0.54		0.56		0.50		**0.29**		**0.17**		0.36		0.43		0.53		0.46	
rwth-combo	0.65		0.58		0.55		**0.54**	**0.54**	0.53	0.53	0.49		0.53		0.56		0.49		**0.29**		**0.17**		0.35		0.42		0.55		0.48	
uedin	0.61		0.57		0.54		0.52	0.53	0.51	0.52	0.48		0.53		0.55		0.49		0.28		0.16		0.34		0.42		0.55		0.48	
upv-combo	0.63		0.58		0.55		**0.54**	**0.54**	0.53	0.53	0.49		0.54		0.56		0.50		**0.29**		**0.17**		0.35		0.43		0.55		0.48	

	I letter BLEU		I letter recall		SVM Rank		TESLA M		TESLA		Stanford		TERp		DR		Drdoc		ULCh		BEwT-E		Bkars			BLEU v13a		NIST	
	(all)	(sub)	(all)	(sub)	(all)	(sub)	(all)	(sub)	(all)	(sub)	(all)	(sub)	(all)	(sub)	(all)	(sub)	(all)	(sub)	(all)	(sub)	(all)	(sub)	(all)	(sub)		(all)	(sub)	(all)	(sub)
aalto	0.49		0.52		4.97		**0.41**		0.02		0.07				0.27		0.42		0.25				0.52	0.52		0.18		6.20	
bbn-combo	0.54		**0.57**		5.46		**0.48**		**0.03**		0.11				**0.33**		**0.48**		**0.30**				**0.58**	**0.58**		**0.25**		**7.10**	
cmu-HF-combo	0.54		**0.57**		5.43		**0.48**		**0.03**		0.09				**0.33**		0.48		**0.30**				0.57	0.57		**0.25**		6.98	
cmu	0.50		0.53		5.10		0.45		0.02		0.09				0.31		0.46		0.28				0.54	0.54		0.22		6.66	
cu-bojar	0.52		0.55		5.23		0.45		0.02		0.05				0.30		0.45		0.27				0.55	0.55		0.19		6.24	
cu-zeman	0.47		0.49		4.77		0.36		0.02		0.03				0.23		0.37		0.22				0.49	0.49		0.14		5.45	
jhu-combo	0.53		0.55		5.25		0.46		0.02		0.03				0.32		0.46		0.29				0.56	0.56		0.23		7.00	
onlineA	0.49		0.51		4.87		0.42		0.02		0.07				0.27		0.43		0.25				0.52	0.52		0.18		6.13	
onlineB	**0.55**		**0.57**		5.41		**0.48**		**0.03**		**0.16**				0.32		0.47		**0.30**				**0.58**	**0.58**		0.24		6.13	
rwth-combo	0.54		0.56		5.40		**0.48**		**0.03**		0.07				0.32		0.47		0.29				0.57	0.57		0.24		7.06	
uedin	0.53		**0.57**		5.40		**0.48**		**0.03**		0.14				0.32		0.47		0.29				0.57	0.57		0.23		6.64	
upv-combo	0.54		**0.57**		**5.47**		**0.48**		**0.03**		0.07				**0.33**		0.47		0.29				**0.58**	**0.58**		0.24		6.99	

French-English -- Metrics submitted to NIST MetricsMATR 2010, plus two baseline metrics (BLEU and NIST). Scores for "all" (entire WMT10 testset) and "sub" (subset of the humanly assessed data) are shown.

	rank		MT-NCD		MT-mNCD		Badger full		Badger lite		ATEC 2.1		METEOR adq		METEOR hter		METEOR rank		SEPIA		SemPOS		SemPOS BLEU		DCU-LFG		LRKB4		LRHB4	
	(all)	(sub)	(all)	(sub)	(all)	(sub)	(all)	(sub)	(all)	(sub)	(all)	(sub)	(all)	(sub)	(all)	(sub)	(all)	(sub)	**(all)**	(sub)	(all)	(sub)	(all)	(sub)	(all)	(sub)	(all)	(sub)	(all)	(sub)
bbn-combo	0.64		0.60		**0.57**		**0.59**		**0.58**		0.53		**0.59**		**0.62**		**0.54**		**0.33**		**0.18**		0.41		**0.50**		**0.58**		0.50	
cambridge	0.66		0.60		**0.57**		0.58		**0.58**		0.53		**0.59**		**0.62**		**0.54**		**0.33**		**0.18**		0.40		0.49		**0.58**		0.50	
cmu-HF-combo	0.70		0.60		**0.57**		**0.59**		**0.58**		0.53		**0.59**		**0.62**		**0.54**		**0.33**		0.18		0.41		0.49		**0.58**		0.50	
cmu-hyp-combo	**0.77**		0.60		**0.57**		0.58		**0.58**		0.53		**0.59**		**0.62**		**0.54**		**0.33**		**0.18**		**0.41**		**0.49**		0.57		0.50	
cmu-statxfer	0.51		0.58		0.55		0.55		0.54		0.49		0.56		0.58		0.51		0.29		**0.17**		**0.37**		**0.43**		0.56		0.48	
cu-zeman	0.21		0.52		0.55		0.51		0.50		0.46		0.52		0.54		0.48		0.24		**0.15**		**0.23**		**0.37**		0.53		0.44	
dcu-combo	0.72		**0.61**		**0.57**		**0.59**		**0.58**		**0.54**		**0.59**		0.62		**0.54**		**0.33**		0.18		**0.43**		**0.50**		**0.58**		**0.51**	
dfki	0.42		0.56		0.53		0.52		0.51		0.46		0.53		0.54		0.49		0.25		0.17		0.32		0.40		0.55		0.46	
geneva	0.27		0.55		0.52		0.49		0.49		0.44		0.50		0.51		0.46		0.23		0.14		0.27		0.37		0.53		0.44	
huicong	0.51		0.56		0.55		0.55		0.54		0.50		0.56		0.58		0.51		0.28		0.17		0.32		0.44		0.55		0.47	
jhu-combo	0.65		0.60		**0.57**		0.58		**0.58**		0.53		0.58		0.61		0.53		0.32		**0.18**		0.40		0.48		**0.58**		0.50	
jhu	0.59		0.60		**0.57**		0.57		0.56		0.52		0.58		0.60		0.53		0.31		**0.18**		0.38		0.47		0.57		0.49	
lig	0.53		0.59		0.56		0.55		0.55		0.51		0.56		0.59		0.52		0.30		0.17		0.36		0.45		0.56		0.48	
limsi	0.65		0.59		0.56		0.57		0.56		0.52		0.57		0.60		0.53		0.31		0.17		0.38		0.47		0.57		0.48	
lium-combo	0.64		0.60		**0.57**		0.58		0.57		0.53		0.58		0.61		0.53		**0.33**		**0.18**		0.41		0.49		0.57		0.49	
lium	0.71		0.60		**0.57**		0.58		0.57		0.53		**0.59**		0.61		**0.54**		0.32		**0.18**		0.41		0.49		**0.58**		0.50	
nrc	0.66		0.60		**0.57**		0.57		0.56		0.52		0.58		0.61		0.53		0.32		**0.18**		0.39		0.48		0.57		0.49	
onlineA	0.52		0.59		0.56		0.55		0.55		0.50		0.56		0.58		0.51		0.30		0.17		0.36		0.44		0.54		0.46	
onlineB	0.71		0.60		**0.57**		0.58		**0.58**		0.53		0.58		0.61		**0.54**		0.32		**0.18**		0.42		0.49		0.57		0.49	
rali	0.65		0.60		0.56		0.57		0.56		0.52		0.58		0.61		**0.54**		0.32		**0.18**		0.40		0.48		0.57		0.49	
rwth-combo	**0.77**		0.60		**0.57**		0.59		**0.58**		**0.54**		**0.59**		**0.62**		**0.54**		**0.33**		0.18		0.42		**0.50**		**0.58**		0.50	
rwth	0.55		0.59		0.56		0.57		0.56		0.52		0.58		0.60		0.53		0.31		0.17		0.38		0.46		**0.57**		0.49	
uedin	0.65		0.60		0.56		0.57		0.57		0.53		0.58		0.61		**0.54**		0.32		**0.18**		0.40		0.49		**0.58**		0.49	
upv-combo	0.68		0.60		**0.57**		0.58		**0.58**		**0.54**		**0.59**		**0.62**		**0.54**		**0.33**		**0.18**		0.42		**0.50**		**0.58**		**0.51**	

	I letter BLEU		I letter recall		SVM Rank		TESLA M		TESLA		Stanford		TERp		DR		Drdoc		ULCh		BEwT-E		Bkars			BLEU 13a		NIST	
	(all)	(sub)	(all)	(sub)	(all)	(sub)	(all)	(sub)	(all)	(sub)	(all)	(sub)	(all)	(sub)	(all)	(sub)	(all)	(sub)	(all)	(sub)	(all)	(sub)	(all)	(sub)		(all)	(sub)	(all)	(sub)
bbn-combo	**0.58**		0.60		5.80		0.51		**0.03**		0.02				**0.37**		0.50		**0.34**				**0.61**			0.30		**7.81**	
cambridge	0.57		0.60		5.80		0.51		**0.03**		0.05				**0.37**		0.50		0.33				**0.61**			0.30		7.65	
cmu-HF-combo	**0.58**		0.60		5.81		**0.52**		**0.03**		0.03				**0.37**		**0.51**		0.34				**0.61**			0.30		7.69	
cmu-hyp-combo	**0.58**		0.60		5.84		**0.52**		**0.03**		0.03				**0.37**		**0.51**		**0.34**				**0.61**			0.30		7.69	
cmu-statxfer	0.55		0.57		5.56		0.48		**0.03**		0.03				0.34		0.49		0.31				0.58			0.25		7.16	
cu-zeman	0.51		0.54		5.30		0.40		0.02		0.02				0.27		0.40		0.27				0.55			0.19		6.12	
dcu-combo	**0.58**		**0.61**		5.87		0.52		**0.03**		0.03				**0.37**		**0.51**		**0.34**				**0.61**			**0.31**		7.78	
dfki	0.51		0.56		5.46		0.46		0.02		0.04				0.31		0.45		0.29				0.55			0.19		6.01	
geneva	0.49		0.55		5.29		0.45		0.02		0.05				0.29		0.43		0.27				0.54			0.17		5.67	
huicong	0.55		0.58		5.60		0.48		**0.03**		0.03				0.33		0.47		0.31				0.57			0.24		6.99	
jhu-combo	0.57		0.60		5.77		0.51		**0.03**		0.01				0.36		0.50		0.33				0.60			0.29		7.61	
jhu	0.57		0.59		5.74		0.50		**0.03**		0.08				0.35		0.50		0.32				0.60			0.28		7.44	
lig	0.55		0.58		5.62		0.48		**0.03**		0.05				0.34		0.49		0.31				0.58			0.26		7.13	
limsi	0.56		0.59		5.72		0.51		**0.03**		0.05				0.36		0.50		0.33				0.59			0.27		7.31	
lium-combo	0.57		0.60		5.77		0.51		**0.03**		0.03				**0.37**		**0.51**		0.33				0.60			0.29		7.70	
lium	**0.58**		**0.61**		**5.88**		**0.52**		**0.03**		0.06				**0.37**		**0.51**		**0.34**				**0.61**			0.29		7.59	
nrc	0.57		0.60		5.79		0.50		**0.03**		0.04				0.36		0.50		0.33				0.60			0.29		7.53	
onlineA	0.55		0.58		5.54		0.50		**0.03**		0.08				0.33		0.48		0.31				0.58			0.25		7.29	
onlineB	**0.58**		0.60		5.80		**0.52**		**0.03**		**0.11**				**0.37**		**0.51**		**0.34**				**0.61**			0.29		7.73	
rali	0.57		0.60		5.80		**0.52**		**0.03**		0.06				0.36		0.50		0.33				0.60			0.28		7.44	
rwth-combo	**0.58**		**0.61**		5.87		**0.52**		**0.03**		0.01				**0.37**		**0.51**		**0.34**				**0.61**			0.30		7.73	
rwth	0.56		0.59		5.73		0.50		**0.03**		0.04				0.36		0.50		0.33				0.60			0.28		7.39	
uedin	0.57		0.60		5.82		0.51		**0.03**		0.04				0.36		0.50		0.33				**0.61**			0.28		7.44	
upv-combo	**0.58**		**0.61**		**5.88**		**0.52**		**0.03**		0.03				**0.37**		0.50		**0.34**				**0.61**			0.30		7.64	

German-English -- Metrics submitted to NIST MetricsMATR 2010, plus two baseline metrics (BLEU and NIST). Scores for "all" (entire WMT10 testset) and "sub" (subset of the humanly assessed data) are shown.

	rank (all)	rank (sub)	MT-NCD (all)	MT-NCD (sub)	MT-mNCD (all)	MT-mNCD (sub)	Badger full (all)	Badger full (sub)	Badger lite (all)	Badger lite (sub)	ATEC 2.1 (all)	ATEC 2.1 (sub)	METEOR adq (all)	METEOR adq (sub)	METEOR hter (all)	METEOR hter (sub)	METEOR rank (all)	METEOR rank (sub)	SEPIA (all)	SEPIA (sub)	SemPOS (all)	SemPOS (sub)	SemPOS BLEU (all)	SemPOS BLEU (sub)	DCU-LFG (all)	DCU-LFG (sub)	LRKB4 (all)	LRKB4 (sub)	LRHB4 (all)	LRHB4 (sub)
aalto	0.42		0.54		0.53		0.50		0.49		0.43		0.50		0.52		0.46		0.25		0.15		0.25		0.35		0.48		0.36	
bbn-combo	0.77		0.59		0.55		0.55		0.54		0.50		0.56		0.59		0.52		0.31		0.17		0.36		0.46		0.54		0.42	
cmu-HF-combo	0.73		0.58		0.55		0.55		0.54		0.50		0.56		0.59		0.52		0.30		0.17		0.35		0.45		0.54		0.42	
cmu-hyp-combo	0.65		0.58		0.55		0.54		0.53		0.50		0.56		0.58		0.51		0.29		0.17		0.34		0.44		0.53		0.41	
cmu	0.46		0.54		0.51		0.50		0.50		0.44		0.51		0.53		0.47		0.26		0.16		0.30		0.38		0.51		0.38	
cu-zeman	0.36		0.51		0.53		0.47		0.47		0.42		0.48		0.50		0.45		0.23		0.14		0.20		0.32		0.50		0.36	
dfki	0.50		0.54		0.52		0.49		0.48		0.44		0.51		0.52		0.47		0.24		0.16		0.29		0.35		0.50		0.36	
fbk	0.66		0.58		0.54		0.51		0.51		0.49		0.55		0.57		0.50		0.27		0.16		0.31		0.42		0.52		0.39	
huicong	0.47		0.53		0.51		0.49		0.48		0.43		0.50		0.52		0.47		0.25		0.15		0.25		0.36		0.50		0.36	
jhu-combo	0.67		0.58		0.55		0.54		0.53		0.50		0.55		0.58		0.51		0.29		0.16		0.34		0.44		0.53		0.41	
jhu	0.53		0.55		0.52		0.52		0.51		0.45		0.51		0.54		0.47		0.27		0.16		0.29		0.37		0.49		0.37	
kit	0.72		0.58		0.54		0.53		0.52		0.49		0.55		0.57		0.51		0.29		0.16		0.34		0.44		0.53		0.40	
koc-combo	0.59		0.56		0.54		0.53		0.52		0.48		0.53		0.56		0.49		0.28		0.16		0.31		0.41		0.52		0.40	
koc	0.23		0.49		0.47		0.45		0.45		0.37		0.43		0.45		0.41		0.21		0.13		0.21		0.28		0.49		0.35	
limsi	0.52		0.57		0.54		0.52		0.51		0.48		0.54		0.56		0.50		0.28		0.16		0.32		0.41		0.52		0.39	
liu	0.59		0.57		0.54		0.51		0.50		0.47		0.53		0.55		0.49		0.27		0.16		0.32		0.41		0.52		0.39	
onlineA	0.63		0.57		0.54		0.52		0.51		0.48		0.53		0.55		0.49		0.27		0.16		0.31		0.40		0.49		0.36	
onlineB	0.73		0.59		0.56		0.55		0.54		0.52		0.57		0.60		0.53		0.31		0.18		0.37		0.47		0.54		0.41	
rwth-combo	0.75		0.58		0.55		0.54		0.54		0.50		0.56		0.59		0.52		0.30		0.17		0.35		0.45		0.54		0.41	
rwth	0.62		0.58		0.55		0.53		0.52		0.49		0.55		0.57		0.51		0.29		0.17		0.34		0.44		0.53		0.41	
uedin	0.66		0.58		0.54		0.53		0.52		0.50		0.55		0.57		0.51		0.29		0.16		0.33		0.43		0.53		0.39	
umd	0.68		0.58		0.55		0.53		0.52		0.50		0.56		0.58		0.51		0.29		0.17		0.33		0.44		0.53		0.40	
uppsala	0.51		0.55		0.53		0.50		0.50		0.45		0.51		0.54		0.48		0.26		0.15		0.28		0.38		0.51		0.38	
upv-combo	0.64		0.58		0.55		0.54		0.53		0.50		0.55		0.58		0.51		0.29		0.16		0.34		0.44		0.53		0.41	
uu-ms	0.55		0.55		0.52		0.50		0.49		0.45		0.51		0.53		0.47		0.26		0.15		0.29		0.37		0.51		0.38	

	I letter BLEU (all)	I letter BLEU (sub)	I letter recall (all)	I letter recall (sub)	SVM Rank (all)	SVM Rank (sub)	TESLA M (all)	TESLA M (sub)	TESLA (all)	TESLA (sub)	Stanford (all)	Stanford (sub)	TERp (all)	TERp (sub)	DR (all)	DR (sub)	Drdoc (all)	Drdoc (sub)	ULCh (all)	ULCh (sub)	BEwT-E (all)	BEwT-E (sub)	Bkars (all)	Bkars (sub)		BLEU 13a (all)	BLEU 13a (sub)	NIST (all)	NIST (sub)
aalto	0.50		0.52		5.01		0.41		0.02		0.01				0.29		0.42		0.25				0.53			0.19		6.38	
bbn-combo	0.55		0.57		5.46		0.48		0.03		0.04				0.35		0.47		0.30				0.58			0.26		7.28	
cmu-HF-combo	0.55		0.57		5.47		0.48		0.03		0.03				0.34		0.46		0.30				0.58			0.26		7.19	
cmu-hyp-combo	0.54		0.57		5.46		0.47		0.03		0.04				0.33		0.46		0.29				0.58			0.25		7.09	
cmu	0.50		0.53		5.08		0.42		0.02		0.03				0.30		0.44		0.26				0.52			0.21		6.47	
cu-zeman	0.48		0.51		4.98		0.37		0.02		0.02				0.26		0.39		0.23				0.51			0.16		5.71	
dfki	0.49		0.53		5.12		0.45		0.02		0.06				0.31		0.45		0.28				0.53			0.17		5.95	
fbk	0.54		0.57		5.43		0.47		0.03		0.02				0.33		0.46		0.28				0.58			0.22		6.67	
huicong	0.50		0.53		5.11		0.42		0.02		0.02				0.30		0.43		0.26				0.52			0.19		6.13	
jhu-combo	0.54		0.57		5.43		0.47		0.03		0.02				0.34		0.46		0.29				0.58			0.25		7.13	
jhu	0.51		0.53		5.12		0.42		0.02		0.05				0.31		0.44		0.27				0.54			0.21		6.73	
kit	0.54		0.58		5.51		0.48		0.03		0.05				0.34		0.47		0.30				0.58			0.24		6.91	
koc-combo	0.52		0.55		5.31		0.45		0.02		0.02				0.33		0.45		0.28				0.56			0.24		6.88	
koc	0.43		0.48		4.72		0.36		0.02		0.01				0.27		0.40		0.24				0.47			0.16		5.39	
limsi	0.53		0.56		5.35		0.47		0.02		0.04				0.32		0.46		0.28				0.57			0.23		6.73	
liu	0.53		0.56		5.34		0.46		0.02		0.03				0.32		0.46		0.28				0.56			0.22		6.60	
onlineA	0.53		0.55		5.24		0.46		0.02		0.10				0.33		0.46		0.29				0.56			0.21		6.88	
onlineB	0.56		0.60		5.71		0.52		0.03		0.17				0.36		0.49		0.32				0.61			0.26		7.18	
rwth-combo	0.55		0.58		5.50		0.48		0.03		0.02				0.35		0.47		0.30				0.59			0.26		7.20	
rwth	0.54		0.57		5.44		0.47		0.03		0.03				0.33		0.46		0.29				0.58			0.24		6.96	
uedin	0.54		0.58		5.53		0.49		0.03		0.06				0.34		0.48		0.30				0.58			0.23		6.80	
umd	0.55		0.58		5.50		0.48		0.03		0.07				0.33		0.47		0.29				0.58			0.23		6.77	
uppsala	0.51		0.54		5.21		0.43		0.02		0.02				0.31		0.44		0.27				0.54			0.21		6.51	
upv-combo	0.54		0.57		5.45		0.48		0.03		0.03				0.34		0.45		0.29				0.58			0.25		7.15	
uu-ms	0.50		0.54		5.18		0.44		0.02		0.02				0.31		0.45		0.27				0.54			0.20		6.32	

Spanish-English -- Metrics submitted to NIST MetricsMATR 2010, plus two baseline metrics (BLEU and NIST). Scores for "all" (entire WMT10 testset) and "sub" (subset of the humanly assessed data) are shown.

	rank (all)	rank (sub)	MT-NCD (all)	MT-NCD (sub)	MT-mNCD (all)	MT-mNCD (sub)	Badger full (all)	Badger full (sub)	Badger lite (all)	Badger lite (sub)	ATEC 2.1 (all)	ATEC 2.1 (sub)	METEOR adq (all)	METEOR adq (sub)	METEOR hter (all)	METEOR hter (sub)	METEOR rank (all)	METEOR rank (sub)	SEPIA (all)	SEPIA (sub)	SemPOS (all)	SemPOS (sub)	SemPOS BLEU (all)	SemPOS BLEU (sub)	DCU-LFG (all)	DCU-LFG (sub)	LRKB4 (all)	LRKB4 (sub)	LRHB4 (all)	LRHB4 (sub)
bbn-combo	0.62		0.61		0.58		0.59		0.59		0.54		0.60		0.63		0.55		0.34		0.18		0.43		0.53		0.59		0.51	
cambridge	0.61		0.60		0.58		0.58		0.57		0.53		0.59		0.62		0.55		0.34		0.18		0.41		0.52		0.59		0.51	
cmu-HF-combo	0.66		0.61		0.58		0.59		0.58		0.54		0.60		0.63		0.55		0.34		0.18		0.41		0.52		0.59		0.51	
columbia	0.45		0.58		0.56		0.55		0.54		0.50		0.56		0.59		0.52		0.30		0.17		0.35		0.47		0.57		0.48	
cu-zeman	0.27		0.55		0.58		0.52		0.52		0.48		0.54		0.56		0.50		0.27		0.15		0.25		0.41		0.55		0.45	
dfki	0.45		0.58		0.55		0.54		0.53		0.49		0.56		0.58		0.51		0.28		0.18		0.35		0.46		0.56		0.47	
huicong	0.50		0.57		0.56		0.56		0.55		0.51		0.58		0.61		0.53		0.31		0.17		0.35		0.47		0.57		0.48	
jhu-combo	0.55		0.60		0.58		0.58		0.58		0.53		0.59		0.62		0.54		0.33		0.18		0.40		0.51		0.58		0.50	
jhu	0.61		0.60		0.57		0.57		0.57		0.53		0.59		0.62		0.54		0.33		0.18		0.39		0.50		0.58		0.49	
onlinaA	0.54		0.60		0.57		0.57		0.57		0.53		0.58		0.61		0.54		0.32		0.17		0.39		0.48		0.55		0.46	
onlineB	0.70		0.63		0.59		0.62		0.61		0.56		0.62		0.65		0.57		0.36		0.20		0.47		0.55		0.59		0.50	
uedin	0.69		0.61		0.57		0.58		0.58		0.54		0.60		0.63		0.55		0.33		0.18		0.42		0.52		0.59		0.51	
upc	0.51		0.59		0.56		0.55		0.55		0.51		0.58		0.60		0.53		0.31		0.17		0.37		0.48		0.58		0.49	
upv-combo	0.66		0.61		0.58		0.59		0.58		0.54		0.60		0.63		0.55		0.34		0.18		0.42		0.53		0.60		0.51	

	I letter BLEU (all)	I letter BLEU (sub)	I letter recall (all)	I letter recall (sub)	SVM Rank (all)	SVM Rank (sub)	TESLA M (all)	TESLA M (sub)	TESLA (all)	TESLA (sub)	Stanford (all)	Stanford (sub)	TERp (all)	TERp (sub)	DR (all)	DR (sub)	Drdoc (all)	Drdoc (sub)	ULCh (all)	ULCh (sub)	BEwT-E (all)	BEwT-E (sub)	Bkars (all)	Bkars (sub)		BLEU 13a (all)	BLEU 13a (sub)	NIST (all)	NIST (sub)
bbn-combo	0.59		0.61		5.92		0.52		0.03		0.04				0.38		0.50		0.34				0.62			0.32		7.94	
cambridge	0.58		0.60		5.85		0.51		0.03		0.07				0.37		0.50		0.33				0.61			0.31		7.77	
cmu-HF-combo	0.59		0.61		5.90		0.52		0.03		0.04				0.37		0.50		0.34				0.62			0.31		7.87	
columbia	0.55		0.57		5.53		0.47		0.02		0.04				0.34		0.46		0.30				0.57			0.27		7.19	
cu-zeman	0.54		0.56		5.46		0.42		0.02		0.03				0.28		0.41		0.27				0.56			0.22		6.65	
dfki	0.54		0.58		5.63		0.50		0.02		0.08				0.34		0.47		0.31				0.58			0.23		6.60	
huicong	0.57		0.59		5.73		0.49		0.03		0.05				0.34		0.48		0.31				0.59			0.26		7.37	
jhu-combo	0.58		0.60		5.83		0.51		0.03		0.01				0.37		0.50		0.33				0.61			0.30		7.81	
jhu	0.58		0.60		5.83		0.51		0.03		0.08				0.36		0.49		0.33				0.61			0.29		7.72	
onlinaA	0.57		0.59		5.70		0.52		0.03		0.11				0.36		0.50		0.32				0.61			0.28		7.77	
onlineB	0.61		0.63		6.03		0.56		0.03		0.25				0.40		0.53		0.36				0.64			0.33		8.39	
uedin	0.59		0.62		5.97		0.54		0.03		0.12				0.38		0.51		0.34				0.62			0.30		7.68	
upc	0.56		0.60		5.75		0.50		0.03		0.03				0.35		0.48		0.32				0.60			0.26		7.25	
upv-combo	0.59		0.62		5.97		0.53		0.03		0.04				0.38		0.50		0.34				0.62			0.31		7.82	

English-Czech -- Metrics submited to NIST MetricsMATR 2010, plus two baseline metrics (BLEU and NIST). Scores for "all" (entire WMT10 testset) and "sub" (subset of the humanly assessed data) are shown.

	rank		MT-NCD		MT-mNCD		Badger full		Badger lite		ATEC 2.1		METEOR adq		METEOR hter		METEOR rank		SEPIA		SemPOS		SemPOS BLEU		DCU-LFG		LRKB4		LRHB4	
	(all)	(sub)	(all)	(sub)	(all)	(sub)	(all)	(sub)	(all)	(sub)	(all)	(sub)	(all)	(sub)	(all)	(sub)	(all)	(sub)	(all)	(sub)	(all)	(sub)	(all)	(sub)	(all)	(sub)	(all)	(sub)	(all)	(sub)
cmu-HF-combo	0.69		0.58		0.54		0.50		0.47		0.37						0.45				0.37		0.49				0.51		0.44	
cu-bojar	0.66		0.57		0.54		0.49		0.46		0.36						0.43				0.36		0.47				0.50		0.43	
cu-tecto	0.60		0.57		0.53		0.46		0.43		0.34						0.40				0.33		0.42				0.48		0.41	
cu-zeman	0.50		0.55		0.52		0.46		0.43		0.31						0.39				0.34		0.42				0.46		0.39	
dcu-combo	0.75		0.59		0.55		0.51		0.48		0.39						0.45				0.38		0.51				0.52		0.46	
dcu	0.38		0.54		0.51		0.46		0.43		0.32						0.39				0.33		0.41				0.49		0.43	
eurotrans	0.54		0.54		0.51		0.43		0.41		0.29						0.37				0.31		0.38				0.48		0.42	
koc-combo	0.66		0.57		0.54		0.49		0.46		0.37						0.43				0.37		0.47				0.51		0.45	
koc	0.33		0.52		0.49		0.44		0.41		0.29						0.36				0.33		0.39				0.49		0.42	
onlineA	0.44		0.55		0.51		0.45		0.41		0.31						0.38				0.33		0.41				0.48		0.42	
onlineB	0.70		0.58		0.54		0.49		0.46		0.37						0.44				0.37		0.48				0.51		0.45	
pc-trans	0.62		0.55		0.51		0.44		0.41		0.31						0.37				0.29		0.36				0.49		0.42	
potsdam	0.44		0.55		0.51		0.45		0.42		0.31						0.38				0.34		0.42				0.49		0.42	
rwth-combo	0.70		0.57		0.53		0.50		0.47		0.38						0.44				0.37		0.49				0.51		0.45	
sfu	0.45		0.55		0.52		0.44		0.41		0.31						0.38				0.33		0.41				0.49		0.43	
uedin	0.62		0.57		0.53		0.48		0.45		0.36						0.42				0.37		0.47				0.50		0.44	
upv-combo	0.68		0.58		0.55		0.50		0.47		0.38						0.45				0.37		0.49				0.51		0.45	

	I letter BLEU		I letter recall		SVM Rank		TESLA M		TESLA		Stanford		TERp		DR		Drdoc		ULCh		BEwT-E		Bkars		BLEU v13a		NIST	
	(all)	(sub)	(all)	(sub)	(all)	(sub)	(all)	(sub)	(all)	(sub)	(all)	(sub)	(all)	(sub)	(all)	(sub)	(all)	(sub)	(all)	(sub)	(all)	(sub)	(all)	(sub)	(all)	(sub)	(all)	(sub)
cmu-HF-combo	0.46		0.47		4.80		0.55		-0.02		0.05												0.53		0.17		5.62	
cu-bojar	0.45		0.46		4.70		0.53		-0.01		0.06												0.51		0.16		5.47	
cu-tecto	0.43		0.45		4.62		0.53		-0.01		0.09												0.50		0.13		5.25	
cu-zeman	0.41		0.42		4.36		0.50		-0.01		0.05												0.47		0.12		4.96	
dcu-combo	0.47		0.48		4.90		0.55		-0.01		0.14												0.54		0.19		5.96	
dcu	0.40		0.41		4.25		0.47		-0.01		0.05												0.46		0.13		4.95	
eurotrans	0.40		0.42		4.42		0.51		-0.01		0.04												0.46		0.10		4.44	
koc-combo	0.45		0.46		4.70		0.53		-0.01		0.02												0.51		0.17		5.58	
koc	0.38		0.40		4.24		0.43		-0.01		0.03												0.44		0.12		4.53	
onlineA	0.41		0.43		4.48		0.51		-0.01		0.06												0.47		0.12		4.65	
onlineB	0.46		0.48		4.87		0.54		-0.01		0.10												0.53		0.17		5.56	
pc-trans	0.41		0.43		4.52		0.50		-0.01		0.05												0.47		0.10		4.56	
potsdam	0.40		0.42		4.38		0.49		-0.01		0.03												0.46		0.12		4.74	
rwth-combo	0.46		0.47		4.81		0.55		-0.01		0.04												0.51		0.18		5.82	
sfu	0.41		0.43		4.44		0.50		-0.01		0.04												0.47		0.11		4.68	
uedin	0.45		0.46		4.73		0.54		-0.01		0.11												0.52		0.16		5.43	
upv-combo	0.46		0.48		4.84		0.54		-0.01		0.06												0.53		0.18		5.88	

English-French -- Metrics submitted to NIST MetricsMATR 2010, plus two baseline metrics (BLEU and NIST). Scores for "all" (entire WMT10 testset) and "sub" (subset of the humanly assessed data) are shown.

	rank		MT-NCD		MT-mNCD		Badger full		Badger lite		ATEC 2.1		METEOR adq		METEOR hter		METEOR rank		SEPIA		SemPOS		SemPOS BLEU		DCU-LFG		LRKB4		LRHB4	
	(all)	(sub)	(all)	(sub)	(all)	(sub)	(all)	(sub)	(all)	(sub)	(all)	(sub)	(all)	(sub)	(all)	(sub)	(all)	(sub)	(all)	(sub)	(all)	(sub)	(all)	(sub)	(all)	(sub)	(all)	(sub)	(all)	(sub)
cambridge	0.63		0.57		0.54		0.57		0.55		0.45						0.49										0.58		0.50	
cmu-HF-combo	0.74		0.58		0.55		0.57		0.56		0.47						0.51										0.60		0.52	
cu-zeman	0.26		0.51		0.53		0.47		0.46		0.38						0.43										0.54		0.43	
dfki	0.40		0.54		0.51		0.50		0.49		0.39						0.44										0.55		0.46	
eu	0.32		0.53		0.51		0.48		0.47		0.38						0.44										0.56		0.46	
geneva	0.35		0.55		0.51		0.49		0.48		0.37						0.42										0.54		0.44	
jhu	0.53		0.57		0.53		0.54		0.53		0.44						0.49										0.58		0.48	
koc-combo	0.68		0.59		0.55		0.57		0.56		0.47						0.51										0.60		0.52	
koc	0.26		0.53		0.51		0.49		0.48		0.37						0.43										0.55		0.46	
limsi	0.66		0.58		0.54		0.55		0.54		0.45						0.49										0.59		0.50	
lium	0.63		0.58		0.54		0.56		0.55		0.46						0.51										0.60		0.51	
nrc	0.62		0.57		0.54		0.54		0.53		0.45						0.49										0.58		0.49	
onlineA	0.55		0.57		0.53		0.54		0.53		0.44						0.48										0.58		0.49	
onlineB	0.68		0.58		0.54		0.57		0.55		0.46						0.51										0.60		0.51	
rali	0.66		0.58		0.54		0.56		0.55		0.46						0.50										0.60		0.51	
rwth-combo	0.75		0.59		0.55		0.57		0.56		0.47						0.51										0.60		0.52	
rwth	0.63		0.58		0.54		0.55		0.54		0.45						0.50										0.59		0.51	
uedin	0.70		0.58		0.54		0.56		0.55		0.45						0.50										0.60		0.51	
upv-combo	0.66		0.59		0.55		0.57		0.56		0.47						0.51										0.60		0.52	

	I letter BLEU		I letter recall		SVM Rank		TESLA M		TESLA		Stanford		TERp		DR		Drdoc		ULCh		BEwT-E		Bkars		BLEU 13a		NIST	
	(all)	(sub)	(all)	(sub)	(all)	(sub)	(all)	(sub)	(all)	(sub)	(all)	(sub)	(all)	(sub)	(all)	(sub)	(all)	(sub)	(all)	(sub)	(all)	(sub)	(all)	(sub)	(all)	(sub)	(all)	(sub)
cambridge	0.55		0.57		5.53		0.52		-0.02		0.06												0.58		0.28		7.47	
cmu-HF-combo	0.57		0.59		5.74		0.54		-0.01		0.03												0.60		0.30		7.52	
cu-zeman	0.50		0.52		5.03		0.40		-0.03		0.03												0.52		0.16		5.43	
dfki	0.51		0.54		5.29		0.46		-0.02		0.06												0.54		0.20		6.16	
eu	0.50		0.54		5.21		0.46		-0.02		0.03												0.53		0.19		5.94	
geneva	0.50		0.52		5.10		0.48		-0.03		0.05												0.52		0.18		6.04	
jhu	0.55		0.57		5.51		0.50		-0.02		0.05												0.57		0.24		6.65	
koc-combo	0.57		0.59		5.76		0.54		-0.01		0.00												0.60		0.29		7.53	
koc	0.49		0.51		5.06		0.45		-0.02		0.02												0.52		0.20		6.14	
limsi	0.56		0.58		5.67		0.54		-0.02		0.06												0.58		0.27		7.20	
lium	0.57		0.59		5.76		0.54		-0.01		0.07												0.59		0.29		7.38	
nrc	0.56		0.58		5.61		0.52		-0.01		0.06												0.58		0.27		7.22	
onlineA	0.55		0.57		5.58		0.52		-0.02		0.07												0.58		0.25		6.99	
onlineB	0.57		0.60		5.81		0.54		-0.02		0.14												0.60		0.28		7.32	
rali	0.57		0.59		5.73		0.54		-0.01		0.06												0.59		0.28		7.32	
rwth-combo	0.57		0.59		5.79		0.55		-0.01		0.04												0.60		0.30		7.62	
rwth	0.56		0.58		5.69		0.53		-0.01		0.06												0.59		0.28		7.28	
uedin	0.56		0.58		5.70		0.54		-0.01		0.09												0.59		0.28		7.24	
upv-combo	0.57		0.59		5.78		0.55		-0.01		0.05												0.60		0.30		7.65	

English-German -- Metrics submitted to NIST MetricsMATR 2010, plus two baseline metrics (BLEU and NIST). Scores for "all" (entire WMT10 testset) and "sub" (subset of the humanly assessed data) are shown.

	rank		MT-NCD		MT-mNCD		Badger full		Badger lite		ATEC 2.1		METEOR adq		METEOR hter		METEOR rank		SEPIA		SemPOS		SemPOS BLEU		DCU-LFG		LRKB4		LRHB4	
	(all)	(sub)	(all)	(sub)	(all)	(sub)	(all)	(sub)	(all)	(sub)	(all)	(sub)	(all)	(sub)	(all)	(sub)	(all)	(sub)	(all)	(sub)	(all)	(sub)	(all)	(sub)	(all)	(sub)	(all)	(sub)	(all)	(sub)
cmu-HF-combo	0.59		0.55		0.47		0.47		0.46		0.37						0.27										0.47		0.35	
cu-zeman	0.28		0.46		0.52		0.42		0.41		0.30						0.22										0.43		0.31	
dfki	0.62		0.53		0.46		0.44		0.44		0.34						0.24										0.45		0.33	
fbk	0.56		0.55		0.47		0.45		0.45		0.36						0.26										0.45		0.34	
jhu	0.46		0.53		0.47		0.46		0.45		0.34						0.25										0.43		0.31	
kit	0.60		0.55		0.47		0.47		0.46		0.36						0.26										0.45		0.33	
koc-combo	0.59		0.55		0.47		0.47		0.46		0.37						0.26										0.46		0.35	
koc	0.30		0.50		0.45		0.42		0.42		0.31						0.22										0.44		0.32	
limsi	0.51		0.54		0.46		0.45		0.44		0.35						0.25										0.45		0.33	
liu	0.55		0.54		0.47		0.46		0.45		0.35						0.25										0.44		0.33	
onlineA	0.59		0.54		0.46		0.46		0.45		0.35						0.25										0.44		0.32	
onlineB	0.70		0.56		0.48		0.48		0.47		0.39						0.28										0.47		0.35	
rwth-combo	0.65		0.55		0.47		0.47		0.46		0.37						0.27										0.46		0.35	
rwth	0.51		0.54		0.47		0.46		0.45		0.35						0.26										0.45		0.34	
sfu	0.34		0.51		0.45		0.44		0.43		0.29						0.21										0.39		0.28	
uedin	0.62		0.55		0.47		0.46		0.45		0.36						0.26										0.46		0.34	
uppsala	0.47		0.54		0.47		0.45		0.44		0.35						0.25										0.45		0.34	
upv-combo	0.55		0.55		0.47		0.47		0.47		0.37						0.27										0.45		0.34	

	I letter BLEU		I letter recall		SVM Rank		TESLA M		TESLA		Stanford		TERp		DR		Drdoc		ULCh		BEwT-E		Bkars			BLEU 13a		NIST	
	(all)	(sub)	(all)	(sub)	(all)	(sub)	(all)	(sub)	(all)	(sub)	(all)	(sub)	(all)	(sub)	(all)	(sub)	(all)	(sub)	(all)	(sub)	(all)	(sub)	(all)	(sub)		(all)	(sub)	(all)	(sub)
cmu-heafield-combo	0.47		0.48		4.86		0.45		0.03		0.05												0.53			0.18		5.98	
cu-zeman	0.41		0.42		4.32		0.33		0.03		0.03												0.47			0.12		5.03	
dfki	0.45		0.47		4.79		0.46		0.04		0.12												0.50			0.14		5.28	
fbk	0.46		0.47		4.76		0.45		0.03		0.03												0.52			0.16		5.85	
jhu	0.44		0.45		4.52		0.42		0.03		0.07												0.50			0.15		5.79	
kit	0.47		0.48		4.83		0.45		0.03		0.06												0.53			0.17		5.98	
koc-combo	0.46		0.47		4.77		0.45		0.03		0.00												0.53			0.17		5.98	
koc	0.41		0.42		4.40		0.39		0.03		0.02												0.46			0.14		5.19	
limsi	0.45		0.46		4.66		0.43		0.03		0.05												0.51			0.16		5.70	
liu	0.46		0.48		4.76		0.45		0.03		0.04												0.52			0.16		5.85	
onlineA	0.46		0.48		4.82		0.46		0.04		0.09												0.52			0.15		5.65	
onlineB	0.49		0.50		5.05		0.48		0.04		0.20												0.55			0.19		6.18	
rwth-combo	0.46		0.48		4.77		0.45		0.03		0.03												0.53			0.17		6.06	
rwth	0.45		0.47		4.71		0.44		0.03		0.05												0.52			0.16		5.86	
sfu	0.38		0.39		3.94		0.38		0.03		0.03												0.45			0.11		4.82	
uedin	0.47		0.48		4.85		0.46		0.03		0.08												0.53			0.17		5.94	
uppsala	0.45		0.46		4.65		0.43		0.03		0.03												0.51			0.16		5.74	
upv-combo	0.46		0.47		4.75		0.44		0.03		0.03												0.53			0.17		6.10	

English-Spanish -- Metrics submitted to NIST MetricsMATR 2010, plus two baseline metrics (BLEU and NIST). Scores for "all" (entire WMT10 testset) and "sub" (subset of the humanly assessed data) are shown.

	rank		MT-NCD		MT-mNCD		Badger full		Badger lite		ATEC 2.1		METEOR adq		METEOR hter		METEOR rank		SEPIA		SemPOS		SemPOS BLEU		DCU-LFG		LRKB4		LRHB4	
	(all)	(sub)	(all)	(sub)	(all)	(sub)	(all)	(sub)	(all)	(sub)	(all)	(sub)	(all)	(sub)	(all)	(sub)	(all)	(sub)	(all)	(sub)	(all)	(sub)	(all)	(sub)	(all)	(sub)	(all)	(sub)	(all)	(sub)
cambridge	0.54		0.59		0.56		0.57		0.55		0.45						0.25										0.57		0.50	
cmu-HF-combo	0.68		0.60		0.57		0.59		0.58		0.48						0.26										0.58		0.52	
cu-zeman	0.23		0.55		0.57		0.51		0.50		0.41						0.22										0.52		0.43	
dcu	0.61		0.60		0.57		0.58		0.57		0.47						0.25										0.58		0.51	
dfki	0.55		0.57		0.54		0.54		0.52		0.42						0.23										0.54		0.47	
jhu	0.55		0.59		0.56		0.57		0.55		0.45						0.25										0.56		0.48	
koc-combo	0.62		0.60		0.57		0.58		0.57		0.47						0.26										0.58		0.51	
koc	0.19		0.54		0.53		0.51		0.49		0.38						0.21										0.53		0.46	
onlineA	0.69		0.60		0.57		0.58		0.57		0.48						0.25										0.58		0.51	
onlineB	0.71		0.61		0.57		0.60		0.59		0.49						0.26										0.60		0.53	
rwth-combo	0.59		0.59		0.56		0.59		0.58		0.48						0.26										0.58		0.51	
sfu	0.40		0.58		0.55		0.55		0.54		0.42						0.24										0.53		0.45	
uedin	0.61		0.60		0.56		0.58		0.57		0.47						0.25										0.58		0.51	
upb-combo	0.60		0.60		0.57		0.59		0.58		0.48						0.26										0.58		0.51	
upv-nnlm	0.54		0.59		0.56		0.56		0.55		0.45						0.24										0.57		0.49	
upv	0.55		0.59		0.56		0.57		0.56		0.46						0.25										0.57		0.50	

	I letter BLEU		I letter recall		SVM Rank		TESLA M		TESLA		Stanford		TERp		DR		Drdoc		ULCh		BEwT-E		Bkars			BLEU 13a		NIST	
	(all)	(sub)	(all)	(sub)	(all)	(sub)	(all)	(sub)	(all)	(sub)	(all)	(sub)	(all)	(sub)	(all)	(sub)	(all)	(sub)	(all)	(sub)	(all)	(sub)	(all)	(sub)		(all)	(sub)	(all)	(sub)
cambridge	0.57		0.59		5.75		0.45		0.01		0.00												0.60			0.29		7.50	
cmu-HF-combo	0.59		0.61		5.90		0.48		0.01		0.00												0.62			0.32		7.96	
cu-zeman	0.54		0.56		5.41		0.40		0.00		0.00												0.56			0.21		6.54	
dcu	0.59		0.61		5.90		0.47		0.01		0.00												0.61			0.30		7.72	
dfki	0.54		0.57		5.55		0.42		0.00		0.00												0.57			0.24		6.83	
jhu	0.57		0.59		5.72		0.45		0.01		0.00												0.60			0.28		7.58	
koc-combo	0.58		0.60		5.84		0.46		0.01		0.00												0.61			0.30		7.79	
koc	0.51		0.53		5.19		0.36		0.00		0.00												0.53			0.21		6.37	
onlineA	0.59		0.62		5.97		0.48		0.01		0.00												0.62			0.30		7.65	
onlineB	0.60		0.63		6.12		0.49		0.01		0.00												0.64			0.32		7.87	
rwth-combo	0.59		0.61		5.89		0.47		0.01		0.00												0.60			0.31		7.97	
sfu	0.54		0.55		5.35		0.42		0.00		0.00												0.56			0.24		7.18	
uedin	0.58		0.61		5.86		0.47		0.01		0.01												0.61			0.30		7.66	
upb-combo	0.58		0.60		5.88		0.47		0.01		0.00												0.61			0.31		7.93	
upv-nnlm	0.57		0.59		5.71		0.44		0.01		0.00												0.59			0.28		7.39	
upv	0.58		0.60		5.80		0.45		0.01		0.00												0.60			0.29		7.48	

	REF	AALTO	CMU	CU-BOJAR	CU-ZEMAN	ONLINEA	ONLINEB	UEDIN	BBN-C	CMU-HEA-C	JHU-C	RWTH-C	UPV-C
REF	–	.03‡	.02‡	.03‡	.01‡	.03‡	.02‡	.05‡	.02‡	.06‡	.03‡	.05‡	.03‡
AALTO	**.93**‡	–	**.54**‡	**.54**‡	.23‡	.36	**.58**‡	**.56**‡	**.65**‡	**.69**‡	**.64**‡	**.67**‡	**.62**‡
CMU	**.94**‡	.30‡	–	**.47**	.14‡	.22‡	**.52**‡	**.41**	**.50**‡	**.57**‡	**.45**†	**.44**	.38
CU-BOJAR	**.94**‡	.26‡	.38	–	.10‡	.22‡	**.61**‡	**.47**†	**.46**	**.55**‡	**.42**	**.49**‡	**.44**
CU-ZEMAN	**.98**‡	**.58**‡	**.73**‡	**.77**‡	–	**.55**‡	**.79**‡	**.71**‡	**.84**‡	**.80**‡	**.77**‡	**.79**‡	**.75**‡
ONLINEA	**.94**‡	**.41**	**.61**‡	**.57**‡	.23‡	–	**.68**‡	**.63**‡	**.71**‡	**.71**‡	**.63**‡	**.54**‡	**.61**‡
ONLINEB	**.93**‡	.30‡	.31‡	.26‡	.10‡	.17‡	–	.32†	.35	.31	.22‡	.29*	.38
UEDIN	**.91**‡	.27‡	.35	.34†	.11‡	.18‡	**.47**†	–	**.54**‡	**.50**‡	**.35**	.29	**.35**
BBN-C	**.95**‡	.21‡	.22‡	.36	.06‡	.17‡	**.38**	.26‡	–	.32	.24‡	.31*	.26‡
CMU-HEA-C	**.90**‡	.17‡	.19‡	.23‡	.09‡	.18‡	**.32**	.27‡	**.34**	–	.31†	.31*	.30‡
JHU-C	**.93**‡	.19‡	.30†	.35	.09‡	.24‡	**.50**‡	.34	**.47**‡	**.45**†	–	**.41**‡	**.36**
RWTH-C	**.91**‡	.16‡	.35	.29‡	.12‡	.27‡	**.41***	**.37**	**.42***	**.42***	.23‡	–	.24†
UPV-C	**.94**‡	.24‡	**.40**	.36	.09‡	.28‡	**.39**	.32	**.46**‡	**.47**‡	.33	**.36**†	?
> others	.93	.26	.37	.38	.11	.24	.47	.40	.49	.49	.38	.41	.40
>= others	.97	.42	.56	.55	.25	.39	.67	.62	.70	.70	.61	.65	.62

Table 21: Sentence-level ranking for the WMT10 Czech-English News Task **(Combining expert and non-expert Mechanical Turk judgments)**

	REF	AALTO	CMU	CU-ZEMAN	DFKI	FBK	HUICONG	JHU	KIT	KOC	LIMSI	LIU	ONLINEA	ONLINEB	RWTH	UEDIN	UMD	UPPSALA	UU-MS	BBN-C	CMU-HEA-C	CMU-HYPO-C	JHU-C	KOC-C	RWTH-C	UPV-C
REF	–	.00‡	.02‡	.00‡	.07‡	.04‡	.03‡	.00‡	.06‡	.04‡	.00‡	.02‡	.07‡	.07‡	.07‡	.02‡	.09‡	.03‡	.03‡	.10‡	.04‡	.04‡	.03‡	.02‡	.07‡	.06‡
AALTO	**1.00**‡	–	**.43**	.39	**.48**	**.60**‡	**.38**	**.41**	**.74**‡	.18‡	**.42**	**.57**‡	**.50**†	**.63**‡	**.55**‡	**.68**‡	**.79**‡	**.42**	**.33**	**.71**‡	**.61**‡	**.66**‡	**.54**	**.51**‡	**.66**‡	**.56**‡
CMU	**.95**‡	.34	–	.19‡	**.45**	**.52**†	.38	**.50**	**.63**‡	.17‡	**.51**‡	**.55**‡	**.56**†	**.66**‡	**.55**‡	**.60**‡	**.56**‡	.30	.40	**.62**‡	**.64**‡	**.49**‡	**.58**‡	**.46**	**.64**‡	**.46**†
CU-ZEMAN	**1.00**‡	**.44**	**.64**‡	–	**.43**	**.72**‡	.31	**.45**†	**.69**‡	.36	**.55**	**.62**‡	**.75**‡	**.75**‡	**.78**‡	**.75**‡	**.75**‡	**.48**⋆	**.56**†	**.79**‡	**.82**‡	**.72**‡	**.68**‡	**.63**‡	**.67**‡	**.84**‡
DFKI	**.92**‡	.29	.33	.35	–	.37	**.40**	.34	**.59**	.08‡	.42	**.50**	**.49**	**.64**‡	.35	.44	**.44**	**.50**	.41	**.70**‡	**.61**†	**.57**	**.46**	**.47**	**.62**‡	**.44**
FBK	**.93**‡	.26‡	.23†	.17‡	**.49**	–	.12‡	.30	**.52**†	.08‡	.20‡	**.45**⋆	.41	**.62**‡	**.44**	**.44**	**.48**⋆	.18‡	.25†	**.53**‡	**.47**	**.38**	**.38**	.22†	**.41**	**.51**⋆
HUICONG	**.92**‡	.34	**.39**	**.37**	.38	**.71**‡	–	**.53**†	**.67**‡	.18‡	**.51**†	**.47**	**.60**‡	**.65**‡	**.49**⋆	**.55**‡	**.78**‡	**.35**	**.41**	**.56**‡	**.77**‡	**.74**‡	**.58**‡	**.41**	**.65**‡	**.57**‡
JHU	**.92**‡	.35	.30	.17†	**.52**	**.45**	.25†	–	**.58**‡	.16‡	**.43**	.38	**.57**†	**.60**‡	**.54**‡	**.60**‡	**.70**‡	.29	.25	**.65**‡	**.75**‡	**.56**‡	**.62**‡	**.49**⋆	**.66**‡	**.48**†
KIT	**.90**‡	.14‡	.16‡	.14‡	.35	.28†	.19‡	.16‡	–	.03‡	.29⋆	.20‡	.35	**.53**⋆	.21‡	.24†	.30	.20‡	.22‡	**.44**	.29	.38	**.35**	.24	**.40**	.24†
KOC	**.95**‡	**.66**‡	**.71**‡	**.51**	**.75**‡	**.80**‡	**.58**‡	**.68**‡	**.93**‡	–	**.75**‡	**.87**‡	**.72**‡	**.74**‡	**.74**‡	**.81**‡	**.81**‡	**.78**‡	**.66**‡	**.89**‡	**.85**‡	**.80**‡	**.80**‡	**.72**‡	**.91**‡	**.73**‡
LIMSI	**.99**‡	.26	.24‡	.32	**.45**	**.61**‡	.25†	.38	**.50**⋆	.10‡	–	**.50**⋆	**.55**⋆	**.69**‡	**.52**⋆	**.57**‡	**.57**‡	.29†	.22‡	**.60**‡	**.52**†	**.42**	**.47**†	.37	**.60**‡	**.56**‡
LIU	**.87**‡	.17‡	.20‡	.14‡	.34	.22⋆	.31	.38	**.66**‡	.04‡	.27⋆	–	**.51**⋆	**.53**†	**.52**⋆	**.53**⋆	**.51**	.20‡	.33	**.64**‡	**.59**‡	**.48**†	**.48**	**.51**	**.37**	**.53**⋆
ONLINEA	**.90**‡	.25†	.29†	.18‡	.34	**.43**	.23‡	.28†	**.49**	.08‡	.32⋆	.30⋆	–	**.44**	.38	.40	**.42**	.32†	.35⋆	**.39**	**.47**	**.51**	.27‡	.35	**.43**	**.40**
ONLINEB	**.76**‡	.22‡	.24‡	.14‡	.27‡	.27‡	.25‡	.25‡	.32⋆	.22‡	.21‡	.28†	.32	–	.27†	.21‡	.30†	.23‡	.15‡	.41	.31	.40	.23‡	.16‡	.42	.29
RWTH	**.89**‡	.22‡	.23‡	.13‡	**.49**	.35	.29⋆	.21‡	**.62**‡	.15‡	.32⋆	.29⋆	**.46**	**.57**†	–	.39	**.49**	.25	.38	**.41**	.27	**.34**	.36	.27	**.48**⋆	.22‡
UEDIN	**.91**‡	.15‡	.20‡	.12‡	**.49**	.35	.24‡	.22‡	**.49**†	.04‡	.22‡	.30⋆	**.46**	**.62**‡	**.43**	–	.39	.11‡	.15‡	**.45**	.33	**.40**	**.45**	.33	.34	.33
UMD	**.91**‡	.12‡	.23‡	.06‡	.35	.29⋆	.11‡	.16‡	**.47**	.14‡	.23‡	.35	.40	**.55**†	.36	**.47**	–	.16‡	.17‡	**.44**	.29†	.27	**.37**	.26	.27	.24†
UPPSALA	**.94**‡	.30	**.41**	.23⋆	.35	**.53**‡	.26	**.37**	**.66**‡	.03‡	**.54**†	**.71**‡	**.57**†	**.65**‡	**.45**	**.72**‡	**.67**‡	–	.25	**.59**‡	**.69**‡	**.49**‡	**.63**‡	.33	**.60**‡	**.64**‡
UU-MS	**.83**‡	.28	**.42**	.24†	.41	**.49**†	.28	**.42**	**.68**‡	.10‡	**.55**‡	**.48**	**.55**⋆	**.63**‡	**.49**	**.56**‡	**.60**‡	**.32**	–	**.52**†	**.58**‡	**.61**‡	**.64**‡	**.46**‡	**.64**‡	**.50**⋆
BBN-C	**.90**‡	.15‡	.16‡	.10‡	.22‡	.17‡	.22‡	.18‡	.41	.06‡	.16‡	.21‡	.35	**.45**	.30	.26	.34	.13‡	.20†	–	**.42**†	.14†	.27	.11‡	.25	.21†
CMU-HEA-C	**.83**‡	.20‡	.18‡	.07‡	.29†	.32	.06‡	.10‡	**.49**	.05‡	.26†	.21‡	.41	**.33**	**.37**	**.43**	**.58**†	.10‡	.14‡	.18†	–	**.33**	**.32**	.11‡	**.34**	.24⋆
CMU-HYPO-C	**.96**‡	.24‡	.20‡	.07‡	.37	.33	.12‡	.21‡	**.40**	.10‡	.41	.26†	.40	**.54**	.25	.37	**.44**	.13‡	.17‡	**.49**†	.31	–	.34	.23⋆	**.51**†	**.45**
JHU-C	**.97**‡	.33	.22‡	.18‡	.31	.30	.27‡	.18‡	.33	.12‡	.19†	.33	**.59**‡	**.60**‡	**.39**	.32	.30	.19‡	.20‡	**.44**	.29	.34	–	.21⋆	**.36**	.23
KOC-C	**.93**‡	.11‡	.31	.17‡	.41	**.50**†	.25	.27⋆	**.44**	.11‡	**.42**	.36	**.47**	**.68**‡	**.43**	**.41**	**.40**	.33	.18‡	**.59**‡	**.57**‡	**.46**⋆	**.47**⋆	–	**.52**†	**.43**
RWTH-C	**.87**‡	.20‡	.10‡	.21‡	.25‡	.27	.15‡	.23‡	.24	.02‡	.20‡	.30	.34	**.47**	.27⋆	.34	**.36**	.14‡	.20‡	**.33**	.26	.21†	.24	.20†	–	.17‡
UPV-C	**.93**‡	.14‡	.20†	.10‡	.42	.29⋆	.25‡	.25†	**.57**†	.20‡	.22‡	.33⋆	.39	**.45**	**.47**‡	**.40**	**.50**†	.24‡	.28⋆	**.44**†	**.42**⋆	.27	**.34**	.28	**.56**‡	?
> others	.92	.25	.28	.18	.39	.41	.25	.30	.52	.12	.34	.39	.47	.57	.42	.46	.51	.27	.28	.52	.49	.45	.44	.34	.50	.42
>= others	.96	.46	.49	.35	.53	.62	.45	.51	.71	.24	.54	.58	.63	.72	.63	.66	.70	.50	.51	.75	.73	.68	.67	.59	.74	.64

Table 22: Sentence-level ranking for the WMT10 German-English News Task **(Combining expert and non-expert Mechanical Turk judgments)**

	REF	CAMBRIDGE	COLUMBIA	CU-ZEMAN	DFKI	HUICONG	JHU	ONLINEA	ONLINEB	UEDIN	UPC	BBN-C	CMU-HEA-C	JHU-C	UPV-C
REF	–	.05‡	.01‡	.02‡	.03‡	.03‡	.01‡	.02‡	.04‡	.03‡	.04‡	.03‡	.07‡	.05‡	.04‡
CAMBRIDGE	**.90**‡	–	.24‡	.11‡	.35†	.26‡	**.43**	.35	**.50**†	**.45**†	.33⋆	**.40**	**.46**	.28⋆	**.41**
COLUMBIA	**.97**‡	**.61**‡	–	.25‡	**.47**	**.44**	**.61**‡	**.53**‡	**.62**‡	**.59**‡	**.48**†	**.59**‡	**.57**‡	**.45**†	**.57**‡
CU-ZEMAN	**.92**‡	**.73**‡	**.59**‡	–	**.62**‡	**.66**‡	**.71**‡	**.65**‡	**.75**‡	**.79**‡	**.58**‡	**.75**‡	**.78**‡	**.71**‡	**.72**‡
DFKI	**.95**‡	**.50**†	.41	.21‡	–	**.46**	**.56**‡	**.52**‡	**.65**‡	**.62**‡	**.47**	**.52**‡	**.56**‡	**.52**†	**.60**‡
HUICONG	**.93**‡	**.57**‡	.34	.21‡	.36	–	**.47**†	**.43**	**.67**‡	**.58**‡	**.40**	**.51**‡	**.62**‡	**.46**†	**.52**‡
JHU	**.94**‡	.39	.22‡	.16‡	.30‡	.32†	–	.41	**.52**‡	**.47**‡	.37	**.41**	**.33**†	.28	**.35**
ONLINEA	**.92**‡	**.45**	.35‡	.24‡	.34‡	.41	.41	–	**.60**‡	**.58**‡	.38	**.55**‡	**.46**	.36	**.57**‡
ONLINEB	**.87**‡	.34†	.24‡	.15‡	.21‡	.19‡	.33‡	.25‡	–	.34†	.26‡	.34†	.37⋆	.24‡	.40
UEDIN	**.94**‡	.33†	.26‡	.12‡	.24‡	.22‡	.25‡	.25‡	**.50**†	–	.25‡	.28†	.32⋆	.25‡	.26
UPC	**.89**‡	**.45**⋆	.36†	.23‡	.39	.37	**.42**	**.48**	**.62**‡	**.57**‡	–	**.54**‡	**.51**‡	**.50**‡	**.53**‡
BBN-C	**.91**‡	.33	.25‡	.11‡	.32‡	.30‡	.34	.31‡	**.51**†	**.41**†	.30‡	–	**.36**	.26‡	**.31**
CMU-HEA-C	**.89**‡	.37	.20‡	.10‡	.29‡	.23‡	.23†	.35	**.50**⋆	**.44**⋆	.31‡	.34	–	.23‡	**.31**
JHU-C	**.89**‡	**.39**⋆	.31†	.17‡	.37†	.33†	**.38**	**.42**	**.63**‡	**.47**‡	.31‡	**.42**‡	**.42**‡	–	**.37**†
UPV-C	**.91**‡	.35	.30‡	.16‡	.29‡	.26‡	.32	.28‡	**.44**	**.35**	.27‡	.27	.30	.24†	?
> others	.92	.42	.29	.16	.33	.32	.39	.37	.54	.48	.34	.42	.44	.35	.43
>= others	.97	.62	.45	.29	.46	.50	.61	.52	.68	.68	.51	.64	.65	.58	.66

Table 23: Sentence-level ranking for the WMT10 Spanish-English News Task **(Combining expert and non-expert Mechanical Turk judgments)**

	REF	CAMBRIDGE	CMU-STATXFER	CU-ZEMAN	DFKI	GENEVA	HUICONG	JHU	LIG	LIMSI	LIUM	NRC	ONLINEA	ONLINEB	RALI	RWTH	UEDIN	BBN-C	CMU-HEA-C	CMU-HYPO-C	DCU-C	JHU-C	LIUM-C	RWTH-C	UPV-C
REF	–	.02‡	.00‡	.00‡	.00‡	.00‡	.05‡	.02‡	.00‡	.00‡	.00‡	.02‡	.06‡	.02‡	.04‡	.02‡	.04‡	.03‡	.02‡	.05‡	.05‡	.04‡	.05‡	.06‡	.02‡
CAMBRIDGE	**.82**‡	–	.42	.16‡	.12‡	.35	.31	**.45**	.21‡	**.47**	.29	**.38**	.28†	**.54**	**.43**	.33	.38	.28	.39	**.45**†	.24	.25	.34	**.54**†	**.37**
CMU-STATXFER	**.91**‡	**.50**	–	.17‡	.41	.17‡	.28	**.44**	**.36**	**.48***	**.56**‡	**.57**‡	.47	**.56***	**.70**‡	**.49**	**.50**	**.47**	**.61**‡	**.68**‡	**.55**†	**.50**	.42	**.52**†	**.51**†
CU-ZEMAN	**1.00**‡	**.74**‡	**.71**‡	–	**.74**‡	**.46**	**.67**‡	**.73**‡	**.73**‡	**.74**‡	**.75**‡	**.76**‡	**.75**‡	**.89**‡	**.78**‡	**.66**‡	**.83**‡	**.74**‡	**.87**‡	**.73**‡	**.80**‡	**.83**‡	**.77**‡	**.95**‡	**.82**‡
DFKI	**1.00**‡	**.77**‡	**.48**	.17‡	–	.27†	**.49**	**.52**	**.48**	**.64**‡	**.69**‡	**.67**†	**.47**	**.62***	**.53**	.47	**.64**‡	**.60**†	**.73**‡	**.72**‡	**.79**‡	**.58***	**.66**‡	**.73**‡	**.74**‡
GENEVA	**.98**‡	**.58**	**.70**‡	.44	**.59**†	–	**.55***	**.67**‡	**.70**‡	**.70**‡	**.77**‡	**.73**‡	**.63**‡	**.81**‡	**.81**‡	**.69**†	**.77**‡	**.73**‡	**.62**†	**.66**‡	**.75**‡	**.60**‡	**.73**‡	**.88**‡	**.67**†
HUICONG	**.89**‡	**.53**	**.34**	.13‡	.34	.30*	–	**.41**	.36	**.43**	**.70**‡	**.56**‡	**.57**	**.59**†	**.56**‡	**.43**	**.55**†	**.45**	**.51***	**.64**‡	**.48**	**.49**	**.49**	**.53**†	**.57**†
JHU	**.88**‡	.36	.38	.11‡	.34	.25‡	.35	–	.33*	**.46**	**.49***	**.48**	.40	**.50**	.40	.34	**.36**	.39	**.33**	**.59**‡	**.54***	**.41**	.42	**.40**	**.41**
LIG	**.98**‡	**.65**‡	.34	.18‡	.44	.26‡	**.39**	**.56***	–	**.60**‡	**.55**‡	**.51**‡	**.45**	**.54**†	**.53**	.39	.38	**.52***	**.54**†	**.53**‡	**.51***	**.53**†	**.55**	**.51**	**.58**†
LIMSI	**.98**‡	.40	.24*	.23‡	.23‡	.15‡	.29	.38	.25‡	–	.28	.38	.27†	**.64**‡	.35	.30	**.41**	.27	.33	**.49**	**.45**	.37	.28	**.45**	**.39**
LIUM	**.90**‡	**.40**	.19‡	.12‡	.30‡	.11‡	.11‡	.26*	.15‡	**.36**	–	.36	.25†	.37	**.39**	.26	.29	.24	.34	**.49**†	.34	.33	.34	.31	.38
NRC	**.93**‡	.31	.06‡	.15‡	.29†	.23‡	.20‡	.32	.16‡	.38	.36	–	.23†	**.53**	.36	.24*	.31	**.44**	**.37**	**.47***	**.45***	.29	**.39**	**.38**	**.42**
ONLINEA	**.92**‡	**.60**†	.47	.15‡	.44	.22‡	.32	**.46**	.34	**.57**†	**.52**†	**.60**†	–	**.52***	.34	.44	**.57**†	**.56**	**.51**	**.51**	**.64**†	**.46**	**.51**	.41	**.60**
ONLINEB	**.85**‡	.35	.32*	.09‡	.33*	.10‡	.29†	.31	.25†	.17‡	**.40**	.34	.24*	–	.38	.32*	.28	.39	.30	**.42**	.37	**.41**	.35	.32	.22‡
RALI	**.90**‡	.31	.19‡	.10‡	.38	.10‡	.17‡	**.47**	.35	**.38**	.33	**.38**	**.48**	**.48**	–	.29*	.31	.29	**.38**	**.40**	**.38**	.34	.31	**.57**†	.21†
RWTH	**.93**‡	**.43**	.33	.12‡	.47	.26†	.39	**.40**	**.47**	**.35**	**.45**	**.49***	.44	**.53***	**.54***	–	**.44***	**.42**	**.48**	**.51***	**.54***	**.48**†	**.49**	**.50**‡	.26
UEDIN	**.92**‡	**.42**	.32	.10‡	.22‡	.10‡	.28†	.30	**.42**	.30	**.55**	**.36**	.23†	**.43**	**.33**	.20*	–	**.41**	.24	**.52**†	**.46**	.25	.22	.27	**.37**
BBN-C	**.92**‡	**.49**	.33	.24‡	.28†	.18‡	.40	.39	.28*	**.45**	**.27**	.27	.36	.39	**.35**	.35	.31	–	.26	**.45**‡	**.43**	.26	**.58**‡	**.36**	.28
CMU-HEA-C	**.90**‡	**.41**	.21‡	.06‡	.23‡	.29†	.28*	.27	.22†	**.39**	**.40**	.22	.39	**.43**	.29	.30	**.40**	**.28**	–	**.43**	**.28**	.15*	.25	.26	.16
CMU-HYPO-C	**.84**‡	.18†	.20‡	.14‡	.20‡	.22‡	.21‡	.19‡	.16‡	.31	.22†	.21*	.36	.38	.34	.27*	.22†	.16‡	.24	–	**.36**	.23	.10‡	**.33**	.24
DCU-C	**.92**‡	**.27**	.24†	.12‡	.17‡	.23‡	.30	.29*	.24*	.32	**.43**	.22*	.28†	**.41**	.23	.27*	.28	.22	.23	.25	–	.23	.23	**.24**	.17
JHU-C	**.88**‡	**.47**	.26	.10‡	.33*	.24‡	.36	.34	.24†	**.41**	**.39**	**.40**	.42	.39	.34	.25†	**.42**	**.28**	**.37***	**.38**	**.39**	–	.37	**.32**	**.38***
LIUM-C	**.90**‡	**.48**	.42	.13‡	.25‡	.20‡	.33	**.50**	.30	**.44**	**.37**	.34	.37	**.52**	**.43**	.34	**.33**	.22‡	**.34**	**.56**‡	**.33**	**.43**	–	**.49**‡	**.44**
RWTH-C	**.89**‡	.22†	.19†	.03‡	.23‡	.12‡	.19†	.23	.27	.30	**.36**	.19	**.47**	**.54**	.26†	.16‡	.27	.19	.26	.28	.16	.22	.16‡	–	.22
UPV-C	**.89**‡	.27	.15†	.10‡	.16‡	.29†	.30†	.31	.25†	.36	**.42**	.24	.32	**.64**‡	**.46**†	**.34**	.27	**.44**	**.33**	**.44**	**.23**	.17*	.31	**.24**	?
> others	.91	.43	.32	.14	.31	.21	.31	.39	.31	.42	.44	.40	.38	.52	.43	.33	.40	.37	.40	.49	.43	.38	.4	.44	.39
>= others	.97	.64	.51	.24	.40	.31	.50	.59	.50	.63	.68	.65	.51	.68	.65	.55	.66	.63	.69	.75	.71	.64	.62	.74	.67

Table 24: Sentence-level ranking for the WMT10 French-English News Task **(Combining expert and non-expert Mechanical Turk judgments)**

LIMSI's statistical translation systems for WMT'10

Alexandre Allauzen, Josep M. Crego, İlknur Durgar El-Kahlout and François Yvon
LIMSI/CNRS and Université Paris-Sud 11, France
BP 133, 91403 Orsay Cedex
Firstname.Lastname@limsi.fr

Abstract

This paper describes our Statistical Machine Translation systems for the WMT10 evaluation, where LIMSI participated for two language pairs (French-English and German-English, in both directions). For German-English, we concentrated on normalizing the German side through a proper preprocessing, aimed at reducing the lexical redundancy and at splitting complex compounds. For French-English, we studied two extensions of our in-house *N-code* decoder: firstly, the effect of integrating a new bilingual reordering model; second, the use of adaptation techniques for the translation model. For both set of experiments, we report the improvements obtained on the development and test data.

1 Introduction

LIMSI took part in the WMT 2010 evaluation campaign and developed systems for two languages pairs: French-English and German-English in both directions. For German-English, we focused on preprocessing issues and performed a series of experiments aimed at normalizing the German side by removing some of the lexical redundancy and by splitting compounds. For this pair, all the experiments were performed using the Moses decoder (Koehn et al., 2007). For French-English, we studied two extensions of our n-gram based system: first, the effect of integrating a new bilingual reordering model; second, the use of adaptation techniques for the translation model. Decoding is performed using our in-house *N-code* (Mariño et al., 2006) decoder.

2 System architecture and resources

In this section, we describe the main characteristics of the phrase-based systems developed for this evaluation and the resources that were used to train our models. As far as resources go, we used all the data supplied by the 2010 evaluation organizers. Based on our previous experiments (Déchelotte et al., 2008) which have demonstrated that better normalization tools provide better *BLEU* scores (Papineni et *al.*, 2002), we took advantage of our in-house text processing tools for the tokenization and detokenization steps. Only for German data did we used the TreeTagger (Schmid, 1994) tokenizer. Similar to last year's experiments, all of our systems are built in "true-case".

3 German-English systems

As German is morphologically more complex than English, the default policy which consists in treating each word form independently from the others is plagued with data sparsity, which poses a number of difficulties both at training and decoding time. When aligning parallel texts at the word level, German compound words typically tend to align with more than one English word; this, in turn, tends to increase the number of possible translation counterparts for each English type, and to make the corresponding alignment scores less reliable. In decoding, new compounds or unseen morphological variants of existing words artificially increase the number out-of-vocabulary (OOV) forms, which severely hurts the overall translation quality. Several researchers have proposed normalization (Niessen and Ney, 2004; Corston-oliver and Gamon, 2004; Goldwater and McClosky, 2005) and compound splitting (Koehn and Knight, 2003; Stymne, 2008; Stymne, 2009) methods. Our approach here is similar, yet uses different implementations; we also studied the joint effect of combining both techniques.

3.1 Reducing the lexical redundancy

In German, determiners, pronouns, nouns and adjectives carry inflection marks (typically suffixes)

Proceedings of the Joint 5th Workshop on Statistical Machine Translation and MetricsMATR, pages 54–59,
Uppsala, Sweden, 15-16 July 2010.

Input	POS	Lemma	Analysis
In	APPR	in	APPR.In
der*	ART	d	ART.Def.Dat.Sg.Fem
Folge	NN	Folge	N.Reg.Dat.Sg.Fem
befand	VVFIN	befinden	VFIN.Full.3.Sg.Past.Ind
die*	ART	d	ART.Def.Nom.Sg.Fem
derart	ADV	derart	ADV
gestärkte*	ADJA	gestärkt	ADJA.Pos.Nom.Sg.Fem
Justiz	NN	Justiz	N.Reg.Nom.Sg.Fem
wiederholt	ADJD	wiederholt	ADJD.Pos
gegen	APPR	gegen	APPR.Acc
die*	ART	d	ART.Def.Acc.Sg.Fem
Regierung	NN	Regierung	N.Reg.Acc.Sg.Fem
und	KON	und	CONJ.Coord.-2
insbesondere	ADV	insbesondere	ADV
gegen	APPR	gegen	APPR.Acc
deren*	PDAT	d	PRO.Dem.Subst.-3.Gen.Sg.Fem
Geheimdienste*	NN	Geheimdienst	N.Reg.Acc.Pl.Masc
.	$.	.	SYM.Pun.Sent

Table 1: TreeTagger and RFTagger outputs. Starred word forms are modified during preprocessing.

so as to satisfy agreement constraints. Inflections vary according to gender, case, and number information. For instance, the German definite determiner could be marked in sixteen different ways according to the possible combinations of genders (3), case (4) and number (2)[1], which are fused in six different tokens *der, das, die, den, dem, des*. With the exception of the plural and genitive cases, all these words translate to the same English word: *the*. In order to reduce the size of the German vocabulary and to improve the robustness of the alignment probabilities, we considered various normalization strategies for the different word classes. In a nutshell, normalizing amounts to collapsing several German forms of a given lemma into a unique representative, using manually written normalization patterns. A pattern typically specifies which forms of a given morphological paradigm should be considered equivalent when translating into English. These normalization patterns use the lemma information computed by the TreeTagger and the fine-grained POS information computed by the RFTagger (Schmid and Laws, 2008), which uses a tagset containing approximately 800 tags. Table 1 displays the analysis of an example sentence. [2]

In most cases, normalization patterns replace a word form by its lemma; in order to partially preserve some inflection marks, we introduced two generic suffixes, *+s* and *+en* which respectively denote plural and genitive wherever needed. Typical normalization rules take the following form:

- For articles, adjectives, and pronouns (Indefinite , possessive, demonstrative, relative and reflexive), if a token has;
  - Genitive case: replace with lemma+en (Ex. *des, der, des, der* → *d+en*)
  - Plural number: replace with lemma+s (Ex. *die, den* → *d+s*)
  - All other gender, case and number: replace with lemma (Ex. *der, die, das, die* → *d*)
- For nouns;
  - Plural number: replace with lemma+s (Ex. *Bilder, Bildern, Bilder* → *Bild+s*))
  - All other gender and case: replace with lemma (Ex *Bild, Bilde, Bildes* → *Bild*;

Using these tags, a normalized version of previous sentence is as follows: *In d Folge befand d derart gestärkt Justiz wiederholt gegen d Regierung und insbesondere gegen d+en Geheimdienst+s*. Several experiments were carried out to assess the effect of different normalization schemes. Removing all gender and case information, except for the genitive for articles, adjectives and pronouns, allowed to achieve the best *BLEU* scores.

3.2 Compound Splitting

Combining nouns, verbs and adjectives to forge new words is a very common process in German.

[1] For the plural forms, gender distinctions are neutralized and the same 4 forms are used for all genders .

[2] The English reference: *Subsequently , the energized judiciary continued ruling against government decisions , embarrassing the government – especially its intelligence agencies* .

It partly explains the difference between the number of types and tokens between English and German in parallel texts. In most cases, compounds are formed by a mere concatenation of existing word forms, and can easily be split into simpler units. As words are freely conjoined, the vocabulary size increases vastly, yielding to sparse data problems that turn into unreliable parameter estimates. We used the frequency-based segmentation algorithm initially introduced in (Koehn and Knight, 2003) to handle compounding. Our implementation extends this technique to handle the most common letter fillers at word junctions. In our experiments, we investigated different splitting schemes in a manner similar to the work of (Stymne, 2008).

4 French-English systems

4.1 Baseline N-coder systems

For this language pair, we used our in-house N-*code* system, which implements the n-gram-based approach to SMT. In a nutshell, the translation model is implemented as a stochastic finite-state transducer trained using a n-gram model of (source,target) pairs (Casacuberta and Vidal, 2004). Training this model requires to reorder source sentences so as to match the target word order. This is performed by a stochastic finite-state reordering model, which uses part-of-speech information[3] to generalize reordering patterns beyond lexical regularities.

In addition to the translation model, our system implements eight feature functions which are optimally combined using a discriminative training framework (Och, 2003): a *target-language model*; two *lexicon models*, which give complementary translation scores for each tuple; two *lexicalized reordering models* aiming at predicting the orientation of the next translation unit; a 'weak' distance-based *distortion model*; and finally a *word-bonus model* and a *tuple-bonus model* which compensate for the system preference for short translations. One novelty this year are the introduction of lexicalized reordering models (Tillmann, 2004). Such models require to estimate reordering probabilities for each phrase pairs, typically distinguishing three case, depending whether the current phrase is translated *monotone*, *swapped* or *discontiguous* with respect to the previous (respectively next phrase pair).

In our implementation, we modified the three orientation types originally introduced and consider: a *consecutive* type, where the original monotone and swap orientations are lumped together, a *forward* type, specifying a discontiguous forward orientation, and a *backward* type, specifying a discontiguous backward orientation. Empirical results showed that in our case, the new orientations slightly outperform the original ones. This may be explained by the fact that the model is applied over tuples instead of phrases.

Counts of these three types are updated for each unit collected during the training process. Given these counts, we can learn probability distributions of the form $p_r(orientation|(st))$ where $orientation \in \{c, f, b\}$ (consecutive, forward and backward) and (st) is a translation unit. Counts are typically smoothed for the estimation of the probability distribution.

The overall search process is performed by our in-house n-*code* decoder. It implements a beam-search strategy on top of a dynamic programming algorithm. Reordering hypotheses are computed in a preprocessing step, making use of reordering rules built from the word reorderings introduced in the tuple extraction process. The resulting reordering hypotheses are passed to the decoder in the form of word lattices (Crego and no, 2006).

4.2 A bilingual POS-based reordering model

For this year evaluation, we also experimented with an additional reordering model, which is estimated as a standard n-gram language model, over *generalized translation units*. In the experiments reported below, we generalized tuples using POS tags, instead of raw word forms. Figure 1 displays the same sequence of tuples when built from surface word forms (top), and from POS tags (bottom).

we	want	translations	perfect
nous	voulons	des_traductions	parfaites

pronoun	verb	noun	adjective
pronoun	verb	det_noun	adjective

Figure 1: *Sequence of units built from surface word forms (top) and POS-tags (bottom).*

Generalizing units greatly reduces the number of symbols in the model and enables to take larger

[3]Part-of-speech information for English and French is computed using the above mentioned TreeTagger.

n-gram contexts into account: in the experiments reported below, we used up to 6-grams. This new model is thus helping to capture the mid-range syntactic reorderings that are observed in the training corpus. This model can also be seen as a translation model of the sentence structure. It models the adequacy of translating sequences of source POS tags into target POS tags. Additional details on these new reordering models can be found in (Crego and Yvon, 2010).

4.3 Combining translation models

Our main translation model being a conventional n-gram model over bilingual units, it can directly take advantage of all the techniques that exist for these models. To take the diversity of the available parallel corpora into account, we independently trained several translation models on subpart of the training data. These translation models were then linearly interpolated, where the interpolation weights are chosen so as to minimize the perplexity on the development set.

5 Language Models

The English and French language models (LMs) are the same as for the last year's French-English task (Allauzen et al., 2009) and are heavily tuned to the newspaper/newswire genre, using the first part of the WMT09 official development data (dev2009a). We used all the authorized news corpora, including the French and English Gigaword corpora, for translating both into French (1.4 billion tokens) and English (3.7 billion tokens). To estimate such LMs, a vocabulary was defined for both languages by including all tokens in the WMT parallel data. This initial vocabulary of 130K words was then extended with the most frequent words observed in the training data, yielding a vocabulary of one million words in both languages. The training data was divided into several sets based on dates and genres (resp. 7 and 9 sets for English and French). On each set, a standard 4-gram LM was estimated from the 1M word vocabulary with in-house tools using Kneser-Ney discounting interpolated with lower order models (Kneser and Ney, 1995; Chen and Goodman, 1998)[4]. The resulting LMs were then linearly combined using interpolation coefficients chosen so as to minimize perplexity of the development set (dev2009a). The final LMs were finally pruned using perplexity as pruning criterion (Stolcke, 1998).

For German, since we have less training data, we only used the German monolingual texts (Europarl-v5, News Commentary and News Monolingual) provided by the organizers to train a single n-gram language model, with modified Kneser-Ney smoothing scheme (Chen and Goodman, 1998), using the SRILM toolkit (Stolcke, 2002).

[4]Given the amount of training data, the use of the modified Kneser-Ney smoothing is prohibitive while previous experiments did not show significant improvements.

6 Tuning

Moses-based systems were tuned using the implementation of minimum error rate training (MERT) (Och, 2003) distributed with the Moses decoder, using the development corpus (news-test2008).

The N-*code* systems were also tuned by the same implementation of *MERT*, which was slightly modified to match the requirements of our decoder. The *BLEU* score is used as objective function for MERT and to evaluate test performance. The interpolation experiment for French-English was tuned on news-test2008a (first 1025 lines). Optimization was carried out over newstest2008b (last 1026 lines).

7 Experiments

For each system, we used all the available parallel corpora distributed for this evaluation. We used *Europarl* and *News commentary* corpora for German-English task and *Europarl, News commentary, United Nations* and *Gigaword* corpora for the French-English tasks. All corpora were aligned with *GIZA++* for word-to-word alignments with *grow-diag-final-and* and default settings. For the German-English tasks, we applied normalization and compound splitting as a preprocessing step. For the French-English tasks, we used new POS-based reordering model and interpolation.

7.1 German-English Tasks

We combined our two preprocessing schemes (see Section 3) by applying compound splitting over normalized data. Our experiments showed that for German to English, using 4 characters as the minimum split length and 8 characters as the minimum compound candidate, and allowing the insertion of *-s -n -en -nen -e -es -er -ien)* and the truncation of

-e -en -n yielded the best *BLEU* scores. On the reverse direction, the best setting is different: 5 characters as minimum split length, 10 characters as minimum compound candidate, no truncation.

These processes are performed before alignment, training, tuning and decoding. Before decoding, we also replaced all OOV words with their lemma. We used the Moses (Koehn et al., 2007) decoder, with default settings, to obtain the translations. For translating from English to German, we used a two-level decoding. The first decoding step translates English to "preprocessed German", which is then turned into German by undoing the effect of normalization. In this second step, we thus aim at restoring inflection marks and at merging compounds. For this second "translation" step, we also use a Moses-based system. To point out the error rate of the second step, we also translated the preprocessed reference German text and computed the *BLEU* score as 97.05. Our experiments showed that this two-level decoding strategy was not improving the direct baseline systems. Table 2 reports the *BLEU* scores[5] on *newstest2010* of our official submissions.

System	*De* → *En*	*En* → *De*
Baseline	20.0	15.3
Norm+Split	21.3	15.0

Table 2: Results for German-English

7.2 French-English tasks

As explained above, in addition to the baseline system (**base**), two contrast systems were built. The first introduces an additional POS-based bilingual 6-gram reordering model (**bilrm**), the second implements the bilingual n-gram model after interpolating 4 models trained respectively on the news, epps, UNdoc and gigaword subparts of the parallel corpus (**interp**). Optimization was carried out over newstest2008b (last 1026 lines) and tested over newstest2010 (2489 lines). Table 3 reports translation accuracy for the three systems and for both translation directions.

As can be seen, the system using the new reordering model (base+bilrm) outperformed the baseline system when translating into French, while no difference was measured when translating into English. The interpolation experiments did not show any clear impact on performance.

[5]Scores are computed with the official script mteval-v11b.pl

System	*Fr* → *En*	*En* → *Fr*
base	26.52	27.22
base+bilrm	26.50	27.84
base+bilrm+interp	26.84	27.62

Table 3: Results for French-English

8 Conclusions

In this paper, we presented our statistical MT systems developed for the WMT'10 shared task, including several novelties, namely the preprocessing of German, and the integration of several new techniques in our n-gram based decoder.

Acknowledgments

This work was partly realized as part of the Quaero Program, funded by OSEO, the French agency for innovation.

References

Alexandre Allauzen, Josep M. Crego, Aurélien Max, and François Yvon. 2009. LIMSI's statistical translation systems for WMT'09. In *Proceedings of WMT'09*, Athens, Greece.

Francesco Casacuberta and Enrique Vidal. 2004. Machine translation with inferred stochastic finite-state transducers. *Computational Linguistics*, 30(3):205–225.

Stanley F. Chen and Joshua T. Goodman. 1998. An empirical study of smoothing techniques for language modeling. Technical Report TR-10-98, Computer Science Group, Harvard University.

Simon Corston-oliver and Michael Gamon. 2004. Normalizing german and english inflectional morphology to improve statistical word alignment. In *Proceedings of the Conference of the Association for Machine Translation in the Americas*, pages 48–57. Springer Verlag.

Josep M. Crego and José B. Mari no. 2006. Improving statistical MT by coupling reordering and decoding. *Machine Translation*, 20(3):199–215.

Daniel Déchelotte, Gilles Adda, Alexandre Allauzen, Olivier Galibert, Jean-Luc Gauvain, Hélène Meynard, and François Yvon. 2008. LIMSI's statistical translation systems for WMT'08. In *Proc. of the NAACL-HTL Statistical Machine Translation Workshop*, Columbus, Ohio.

Sharon Goldwater and David McClosky. 2005. Improving statistical MT through morphological analysis. In *Proceedings of Human Language Technology*

Conference and Conference on Empirical Methods in Natural Language Processing, pages 676–683, Vancouver, British Columbia, Canada, October.

Reinhard Kneser and Herman Ney. 1995. Improved backing-off for m-gram language modeling. In *Proceedings of the International Conference on Acoustics, Speech, and Signal Processing, ICASSP'95*, pages 181–184, Detroit, MI.

Philipp Koehn and Kevin Knight. 2003. Empirical methods for compound splitting. In *EACL '03: Proceedings of the tenth conference on European chapter of the Association for Computational Linguistics*, pages 187–193. Association for Computational Linguistics.

Philipp Koehn, Hieu Hoang, Alexandra Birch, Chris Callison-Burch, Marcello Federico, Nicola Bertoldi, Brooke Cowan, Wade Shen, Christine Moran, Richard Zens, Chris Dyer, Ondrej Bojar, Alexandra Constantin, and Evan Herbst. 2007. Moses: Open source toolkit for statistical machine translation. In *Proc. Annual Meeting of the Association for Computational Linguistics (ACL), demonstration session*, Prague, Czech Republic.

José B. Mariño, Rafael E. Banchs R, Josep M. Crego, Adrià de Gispert, Patrick Lambert, José A.R. Fonollosa, and Marta R. Costa-Jussà. 2006. N-gram-based machine translation. *Computational Linguistics*, 32(4):527–549.

Sonja Niessen and Hermann Ney. 2004. Statistical machine translation with scarce resources using morpho-syntatic information. *Computational Linguistics*, 30(2):181–204.

Franz J. Och. 2003. Minimum error rate training in statistical machine translation. In *Proceedings of the 41st Annual Meeting of the Association for Computational Linguistics*, pages 160–167, Sapporo, Japan.

Helmut Schmid and Florian Laws. 2008. Estimation of conditional probabilities with decision trees and an application to fine-grained POS tagging. In *Proceedings of the 22nd International Conference on Computational Linguistics (Coling 2008)*, pages 777–784, Manchester, UK, August. Coling 2008 Organizing Committee.

Helmut Schmid. 1994. Probabilistic part-of-speech tagging using decision trees. In *Proceedings of International Conference on New Methods in Language Processing*.

Andreas Stolcke. 1998. Entropy-based pruning of backoff language models. In *In Proceedings of the DARPA Broadcast News Transcription and Understanding Workshop*, pages 270–274.

Andreas Stolcke. 2002. SRILM – an extensible language modeling toolkit. In *Proceedings of the International Conference on Spoken Langage Processing (ICSLP)*, volume 2, pages 901–904, Denver, CO.

Sara Stymne. 2008. German compounds in factored statistical machine translation. In *GoTAL '08: Proceedings of the 6th international conference on Advances in Natural Language Processing*, pages 464–475, Berlin, Heidelberg. Springer-Verlag.

Sara Stymne. 2009. A comparison of merging strategies for translation of german compounds. In *EACL '09: Proceedings of the 12th Conference of the European Chapter of the Association for Computational Linguistics: Student Research Workshop*, pages 61–69, Morristown, NJ, USA. Association for Computational Linguistics.

Christoph Tillmann. 2004. A unigram orientation model for statistical machine translation. In *Proceedings of the Human Language Technology conference / North American chapter of the Association for Computational Linguistics 2004*, pages 101–104, Boston, MA, USA.

2010 Failures in English-Czech Phrase-Based MT *

Ondřej Bojar and Kamil Kos
Charles University in Prague, Institute of Formal and Applied Linguistics (ÚFAL)
Malostranské náměstí 25, Praha 1, CZ-11800, Czech Republic
bojar@ufal.mff.cuni.cz, kamilkos@email.cz

Abstract

The paper describes our experiments with English-Czech machine translation for WMT10[1] in 2010. Focusing primarily on the translation to Czech, our additions to the standard Moses phrase-based MT pipeline include two-step translation to overcome target-side data sparseness and optimization towards SemPOS, a metric better suited for evaluating Czech. Unfortunately, none of the approaches bring a significant improvement over our standard setup.

1 Introduction

Czech is a flective language with very rich morphological system. Translation between Czech and English poses different challenges for each of the directions.

When translating from Czech, the word order usually needs only minor changes (despite the issue of non-projectivity, a phenomenon occurring at 2% of words but in 23% of Czech sentences, see Hajičová et al. (2004) and Holan (2003)). A much more severe issue is caused by the Czech vocabulary size. Fortunately, this can be to a certain extent mitigated by backing-off to Czech lemmas if the exact forms are not available.

We are primarily interested in the harder task of translating to Czech and most of the paper deals with this direction. After a brief specification of data sets, pre-processing and evaluation method in this section, we provide details on the issue of Czech vocabulary size (Section 2). We describe our current attempts at generating Czech word forms in Section 3. Partly due to the large vocabulary size of Czech, BLEU score (Papineni et al., 2002) correlates rather poorly with human judgments. We summarize our efforts to use a better metric in the model optimization in Section 4. The final Section 5 lists the exact configurations of our English↔Czech primary submissions for WMT10, including the back-off to lemmas we use for Czech-to-English.

1.1 Data and Pre-Processing Pipeline

Throughout the paper, we use CzEng 0.9 (Bojar and Žabokrtský, 2009)[2] as our main parallel corpus. Following CzEng authors' request, we did not use sections 8* and 9* reserved for evaluation purposes.

As the baseline training dataset ("Small" in the following) only the news domain of CzEng (126k parallel sentences) is used. For large-scale experiments ("Large" in the following) and our primary WMT10 submissions, we use all CzEng domains except navajo and add the EMEA corpus (Tiedemann, 2009)[3,4] of 7.5M parallel sententes.

As our monolingual data we use by default only the target side of the parallel corpus. For experiments reported here, we also use the monolingual data provided by WMT10 organizers for Czech. Our primary WMT10 submission includes further monolingual data, see Section 5.1.

We use a slightly modified tokenization rules compared to CzEng export format. Most notably, we normalize English abbreviated negation and auxiliary verbs ("couldn't" → "could not") and attempt at normalizing quotation marks to distinguish between the opening and closing one follow-

* The work on this project was supported by the grants EuroMatrixPlus (FP7-ICT-2007-3-231720 of the EU and 7E09003 of the Czech Republic), GAČR P406/10/P259, and MSM 0021620838. Thanks to David Kolovratník for the help with manual evaluation.

[1] http://www.statmt.org/wmt10/

[2] http://ufal.mff.cuni.cz/czeng

[3] http://urd.let.rug.nl/tiedeman/OPUS

[4] Unfortunately, the EMEA corpus is badly tokenized on the Czech side. Most frequently, fractional numbers are split into several tokens (e.g. "3, 14"). We attempted to reconstruct the original detokenized form using a small set of regular expressions.

Proceedings of the Joint 5th Workshop on Statistical Machine Translation and MetricsMATR, pages 60–66,
Uppsala, Sweden, 15-16 July 2010. ©2010 Association for Computational Linguistics

	Large	Small	Dev
Sents	7.5M	126.1k	2.5k
Czech Tokens	79.2M	2.6M	55.8k
English Tokens	89.1M	2.9M	49.9k
Czech Vocabulary	923.1k	138.7k	15.4k
English Vocabulary	646.3k	64.7k	9.4k
Czech Lemmas	553.5k	60.3k	9.5k
English Lemmas	611.4k	53.8k	7.7k

Table 1: Corpus and vocabulary sizes.

ing proper typesetting rules.

The rest of our pre-processing pipeline matches the processing employed in CzEng (Bojar and Žabokrtský, 2009).[5] We use "supervised truecasing", meaning that we cast the case of the lemma to the form, relying on our morphological analyzers and taggers to identify proper names, all other words are lowercased.

The differences in relations between Czech and English Large and Small datasets can be attributed either to domain differences or possibly due to noise in CzEng.

1.2 Evaluation

We use WMT10 development sets for tuning (news-test2008) and evaluation (news-test2009). The official scores on news-test2010 are given only in the main WMT10 paper and not here.

The BLEU scores reported in this paper are based on truecased word forms in the original tokenization as provided by the decoder. Therefore they are likely to differ from figures reported elsewhere.

The $\pm$ value given with each BLEU score is the average of the distances to the lower and upper empirical 95% confidence bounds estimated using bootstrapping (Koehn, 2004).

2 Issues of Czech Vocabulary Size

Table 1 summarizes the differences of Czech and English vocabulary sizes in our parallel corpora. We see that the vocabulary size of Czech forms (truecased) is more than double compared to English in the Small dataset and significantly larger in the Large dataset as well. On the other hand, the number of distinct Czech and English lemmas is nearly identical.

[5]Due to the subsequent processing, incl. parsing, the tokenization of English follows PennTreebenk style. The rather unfortunate convention of treating hyphenated words as single tokens increases our out-of-vocabulary rate. Next time, we will surely post-tokenize the parsed text.

	Distortion Limit				
TOpts	3	6	10	30	40
1	0.2	0.3	0.3	0.3	0.3
5	0.8	0.9	1.0	1.0	1.0
10	1.1	1.3	1.5	1.5	1.5
20	1.2	1.5	1.7	1.7	1.7
50	1.2	1.5	1.7	1.7	1.7
100	1.2	1.5	1.7	1.7	1.7

Table 3: Percentage of sentences reachable in Czech-to-English small setting with various distortion limits and translation options per coverage (TOpts) (BLEU score 14.76$\pm$0.44).

2.1 Out-of-Vocabulary Rates

Table 2 lists out-of-vocabulary (OOV) rates of our Small and Large data setting given the development corpus. We calculate the rates for both the complete corpus and the restricted set of phrases extracted from the corpus. (Note that higher-order n-gram rates are estimated using phrases as independent units, no combination of phrases is performed.) We also list the effective OOV rate for English-to-Czech translation where all (English) words from each source sentence can be also produced in the hypothesis.

We see that in the small setting, the OOV rate is almost double for Czech than for English. The OOV is significantly decreased by enlarging the corpus or lemmatizing the word forms.

If we consider only the words available in the phrase tables, the issue of Czech with limited data is striking: 10–12% of devset tokens are not available in the training data.

2.2 Reachability of Training and Reference Translations

Schwartz (2008) extended Moses to support "constraint decoding", that is to perform an exhaustive search through the space of hypotheses in order to reach the reference translation (and get its score).

The current implementation of the exhaustive search in Moses is in fact subject to several configuration parameters, most importantly the number of translation options considered for each span (`-max-trans-opt-per-coverage`) and the distortion limit (`-distortion-limit`).

Given his aim, Schwartz (2008) uses the output of four MT systems translating from different languages to English as the references and notes that only around 10% of the reference translations are reachable by an independent Swedish-English MT system.

Dataset	Language	n-grams Out of Corpus Voc. 1	2	3	4	n-grams Out of Phrase-Table Voc. 1	2	3	4
Large	Czech	2.2%	30.5%	70.2%	90.3%	3.9%	44.1%	82.2%	95.6%
Large	English	1.5%	13.7%	47.3%	78.8%	2.1%	22.4%	63.5%	89.1%
Large	Czech + English input sent	1.5%	29.4%	69.6%	90.1%	3.1%	42.8%	81.5%	95.3%
Small	Czech	6.7%	48.1%	83.0%	95.5%	12.5%	65.4%	91.9%	98.6%
Small	English	3.6%	28.1%	68.3%	90.9%	6.3%	45.4%	84.3%	97.0%
Small	Czech + English input sent	5.2%	46.6%	82.4%	95.2%	10.6%	63.7%	91.2%	98.3%
Small	Czech lemmas	4.1%	36.3%	75.8%	92.8%	5.8%	52.6%	87.7%	97.4%
Small	English lemmas	3.4%	24.6%	64.6%	89.4%	6.9%	53.2%	87.9%	97.5%
Small	Czech + English input sent lemmas	3.1%	35.7%	75.6%	92.8%	5.1%	38.1%	80.8%	96.2%

Table 2: Out-of-vocabulary rates.

TOpts	Distortion Limit 3	6	10	30	40
1	0.4	0.4	0.4	0.4	0.4
5	1.5	1.9	2.0	2.0	2.0
10	2.5	3.2	3.5	3.5	3.5
20	3.7	5.0	5.5	5.6	5.6
50	4.9	6.7	8.0	8.6	8.6
100	5.3	7.6	9.1	9.4	9.4

Table 4: Percentage of sentences reachable in Czech-to-English large setting, two alternative decoding paths to translate from Czech lemma if the form is not available in the translation table (BLEU score 18.70±0.46).

We observe that reaching man-made reference translations in Czech-to-English translation is far harder. Table 3 provides the figures for small data setting (and no phrase table filtering). The best reachability we can hope for is given in Table 4 where we allow to use source word lemmas if the exact form is not available. We see that the default limits (50 translation options per span and distortion limit of 6) leave us with only 6.7% sentences reachable.

While not directly important for your training, the figures still underpin the issue of sparse data in Czech-English translation.

3 Targetting Czech Word Forms

Bojar (2007) experimented with several translation scenarios, including what we will call MorphG, i.e. the independent translation of lemma to lemma and tag to tag followed by a generation step to produce target-side word form. With the small training set available then, the MorphG model performed equally well as a simpler direct translation followed by target-side tagging and an additional n-gram model over morphological tags. Koehn and Hoang (2007) reports even a large loss with MorphG for German-to-English if the alternative of direct form-to-form translation is not available.

Bojar et al. (2009b) applied the two alternative decoding paths (direct form-to-form and MorphG, labelled "T+C+C&T+T+G") to English-Czech but they were able to use only 84k sentences. For the full training set of 2.2M sentences, the model was too big to fit in reasonable disk limits. More importantly, already in the small data setting, the complex model suffered from little stability due to abundance of features (5 features per phrase-table plus tree features for three LMs), so nearly the same performance on the development set gave largely varying quality on the independent test set.

The most important issue of the MorphG setup, however, is the explosion of translation options. Due to the "synchronous factors" approach of Moses (Koehn and Hoang, 2007), all translation options have to be fully constructed before the main search begins. The MorphG model however licenses too many possible combinations of lemmas, tags and final word forms, so the pruning of translation options strikes hard, causing search errors. For more details, see Bojar et al. (2009a) where a similar issue occurs for treelet-based translation.

3.1 Two-Step Translation

In order to avoid the explosion of the translation options[6], we experimented with two-step translation.

The first step translates from English to lemmatized Czech augmented to preserve important semantic properties known from the source phrase. The second step is a monotone translation from the lemmas to fully inflected Czech. The idea behind the delimitation is that all the morphological properties of Czech words that can be established

[6]and also motivated when we noticed that reading MT output to *lemmatized* Czech is sometimes more pleasant and informative than regular phrase-based output

Data Size		Simple		Two-Step	
Parallel	Mono	BLEU	SemPOS	BLEU	SemPOS
Small	Small	10.28±0.40	29.92	10.38±0.38	30.01
Small	Large	12.50±0.44	31.01	12.29±0.47	31.40
Large	Large	14.17±0.51	33.07	14.06±0.49	32.57

Table 5: Performance of direct (Simple) and two-step factored translation in small and large data setting.

regardless the English source should not cause parallel data sparseness and clutter the search. Instead, they should be decided based on context in the second phase only.

Specifically, the intermediate Czech represents most words as tuples containing only: lemma, negation, grade (of adjectives and adverbs), number (of nouns, adjectives, verbs) and detailed part of speech (constraining also e.g. verb tense of Czech verbs). Some words are handled separately:

- Pronouns, punctuation and the verbs "být" (to be) and "mít" (to have) are represented using their lowecased full forms because they are very frequent, often auxiliary to other words and their exact form best captures the available and necessary detail of many morphological and syntactic properties.
- Prepositions are represented using their lemmas and case because the case of a noun phrase is actually introduced by the governing word (e.g. the verb that subcategorized for the noun phrase or the preposition for prepositional phrases).

Table 5 compares the scores of the simple phrase-based and the two-step translation via augmented Czech lemmas as described above. The small and large parallel data denote the datasets described in Section 1.1. The small monolingual set means just the news domain of CzEng, while the large monolingual set means WMT10 monolingual Czech texts (and no CzEng data). Note that the monolingual data serve three purposes in the two-step approach: the language model for the first phase, the translation model in the second phase (monotone and restricted to phrase-length of 1; longer phrases did not bring significant improvement either), and the language model of the second phase. Ignoring the opportunity to use the monolingual set as the language model in the first phase already hurts the performance.

We see that the results as evaluated both by BLEU and SemPOS (see Section 4 below) are rather mixed but not that surprising. There is a negligible gain in the Small-Small setting, a mixed outcome in the Small-Large and a little loss in the

	Two- -Step	Both Fine	Both Wrong	Simple	Total
Two-Step	**23**	4	8	-	**35**
Both Fine	7	14	17	5	43
Both Wrong	8	1	28	2	39
Simple	-	3	7	**23**	33
Total	**38**	22	60	30	150

Table 6: Manual micro-evaluation of Simple (12.50±0.44) vs. Two-step (12.29±0.47) model in the Small-Large setting.

Large-Large setting.

The most interesting result is the Small-Large setting: BLEU (insignificantly) prefers the simple and SemPOS the two-step model. It thus seems that a large target-side LM is sufficient to improve the BLEU score, despite the untackled issue of bilingual data sparseness.

We carried out a quick manual evaluation of 150 sentences by two annotators (one of the authors and a third person; systems anonymized): for each input segment, either one of the outputs is distinguishably better or both are equally wrong or equally acceptable. As listed in the confusion matrix in Table 6, each annotator independently marginally prefers the two-step approach but the intersection does not confirm that.[7] One good thingis that the annotators do not completely contradict each other's preference.

Ultimately, we did not use the two-step approach in our primary submission, but we feel there is still some unexploited potential in this phrase-based approximation of the technique separating properties of words handled in the translation phase from properties implied by the target-side (grammatical) context only. Certainly, the representation of the intermediate language can

[7]Of the 23 sentences improved by the two-step setup, about three quarters indeed had an improvement in lexical coverage or better morphological choice of a word. Of the 23 sentences where the two-step model hurts, about a half suffered from errors related to superfluous auxiliary words in Czech that seem to be introduced by a bias towards word-for-word translation. This bias is not inherent to the model, only the (normalized) phrase penalty weight happened to get nearly three times bigger than in the simple model.

be still improved, and more importantly, the second phase of monotone decoding could be handled by a more appropriate model capable of including more additional (source) context features.[8]

4 Optimizing towards SemPOS

In our setup, we use minimum error-rate training (MERT, Och (2003)) to optimize weights of model components. In the standard implementation in Moses, BLEU (Papineni et al., 2002) is used as the objective function, despite its rather disputable correlation with human judgments of MT quality.

Kos and Bojar (2009) introduced SemPOS, a metric that performs much better in terms of correlation to human judgments when translating to Czech. Naturally, we wanted to optimize towards SemPOS.

SemPOS computes the overlapping of autosemantic (content-bearing) word lemmas in the candidate and reference translations given a fine-grained semantic part of speech (sempos[9]), as defined in Hajič et al. (2006), and outputs average overlapping score over all sempos types.

The SemPOS metric outperformed common metrics as BLEU, TER (Snover et al., 2006) or an adaptation of Meteor (Lavie and Agarwal, 2007) for Czech on test sets from WMT08 (Callison-Burch et al., 2008).

4.1 Integrating SemPOS to MERT

In our experiments we used Z-MERT (Zaidan, 2009), a recent implementation of the MERT algorithm, to optimize model parameters.

The SemPOS metric requires to remove all auxiliary words and to identify the (deep-syntactic) lemmas and semantic part of speech for autosemantic words. When employed in MERT training, the whole n-best list of candidates has to processed like this at each iteration.

We use the TectoMT platform (Žabokrtský and Bojar, 2008)[10] for the linguistic processing. TectoMT follows the complete pipeline of tagging, surface-syntactic analysis and deep-syntactic analysis, which is the best but rather costly way to obtain the required information.

Therefore, we use two different ways of obtaining lemmas and semantic parts of speech in the MERT loop:

- indeed apply TectoMT processing to the n-best list at each iteration (parallelized to 15 CPUs),
- apply TectoMT to the *training data*, express the (deep) lemma and sempos as additional factors using a blank value for auxiliary words, and using Moses factored translation to translate from English forms to triplets of Czech form, deep lemma and sempos.

	BLEU	SemPOS	Iters	Time
TectoMT	10.11±0.40	29.69	20	2d12.0h
in MERT	9.53±0.39	29.69	10	1d12.0h
Factored	9.46±0.37	29.36	10	2.4h
translation	8.20±0.37	29.68	-	-
	6.96±0.33	27.79	9	1.7h

Table 7: Five independent MERT runs optimizing towards SemPOS with semantic parts of speech and lemmas provided either by TectoMT on the fly or by Moses factored translation.

Table 7 lists several ZMERT runs when optimizing a simple form→form phrase-based model (small data setting) towards SemPOS. One observation is that using TectoMT in the MERT loop is unbearably costly and we avoided it in the subsequent experiments. More importantly, from the huge differences in the final BLEU as well as SemPOS scores (evaluated on the independent test set), we see how unstable the search is.

SemPOS, while good at comparing different MT systems, is very bad at comparing candidates from a single system in an n-best list. This can be easily explained by its low sensitivity to precision: SemPOS disregards word forms as well as all auxiliary words. This is a good thing to compare very different candidates (where each of the systems already struggled to produce a coherent output) but is of very little help when comparing candidates of a single system, because these candidates tend to differ rather in forms than in lexical choice.

4.2 Combination of SemPOS and BLEU

To compensate for some of the shortcomings of SemPOS, we also attempted to optimize towards a linear combination of SemPOS and BLEU. This should increase the suitability of the metric for MERT optimization because BLEU will take correct word forms into account while SemPOS should promote better lexical choice (possibly not confirmed by BLEU due to a different word form than in the reference).

Table 8 provides the results of various weight

[8] We are grateful to Trevor Cohn for the suggestion.

[9] In the following text we will use SemPOS to denote the SemPOS metric. When speaking about the semantic part of speech, we will write sempos type or sempos tag.

[10] `http://ufal.mff.cuni.cz/tectomt/`

W.	BLEU	SemPOS	W.	BLEU	SemPOS
1:0	10.42±0.38	29.91	3:1	10.30±0.39	30.03
1:1	10.15±0.39	29.81	10:1	10.17±0.40	29.58
1:1	9.42±0.37	29.30	1:2	10.11±0.38	29.80
2:1	10.37±0.38	29.95	1:10	9.44±0.40	29.74

Table 8: Optimizing towards a linear combination of BLEU and SemPOS (weights in this order), small data setting.

	BLEU	SemPOS
BLEU alone	14.08±0.50	32.44
SemPOS-BLEU (1:1)	13.79±0.55	33.17

Table 9: Optimizing towards BLEU and/or SemPOS in large data setting.

settings, including the optimization towards BLEU alone using ZMERT implementation. We see that the stability is much better, only few runs suffered a minor loss (including 1:1 in one case). Unfortunately, the differences in final BLEU and SemPOS scores are all within confidence intervals when trained on the small dataset.

Table 9 documents that in our large data setting, MERT indeed achieves slightly higher SemPOS (and lower BLEU) when optimizing towards it. This corresponds with the intuition that with more variance in lexical choices available in the phrase tables, SemPOS can help to balance model features. The current set of weights is rather limited, so our future experiments should focus on actually providing means to e.g. domain adaptation by using features indicating the applicability of a phrase in a specific domain.

5 Our Primary Submissions to WMT10

5.1 English-to-Czech Translation

Given the little or no improvements achieved by the many configurations we tried, our English-to-Czech primary submission is rather simple:

- Standard GIZA++ word alignment based on both source and target lemmas.
- Two alternative decoding paths; forms always truecased: form+tag→form & form→form.
  The first path is more specific and helps to preserve core syntactic elements in the sentence. Without the tag, ambiguous English words could often all translate as e.g. nouns, leading to no verb in the Czech sentence. The default path serves as a back-off.
- Significance filtering of the phrase tables (Johnson et al., 2007) implemented for Moses by Chris Dyer; default settings of filter value `a+e` and the cut-off 30.
- Two separate 5-gram Czech LMs of truecased forms each of which interpolates models trained on the following datasets; the interpolation weights were set automatically using SRILM (Stolcke, 2002) based on the target side of the development set:[11]
  - Interpolated CzEng domains: news, web, fiction. The rationale behind the selection of the domains is that we prefer prose-like texts for LM estimation (and not e.g. technical documentation) while we want as much parallel data as possible.
  - Interpolated monolingual corpora: WMT09 monolingual, WMT10 monolingual, Czech National Corpus (Kocek et al., 2000) sections SYN2000+2005+2006PUB.
- Lexicalized reordering (`or-bi-fe`) based on forms.
- Standard Moses MERT towards BLEU.

	Large	Small
Backed-off by source lemmas	18.95±0.45	14.95±0.48
form→form only	18.41±0.44	14.73±0.47

Table 10: Translation from Czech better when backed-off by source lemmas.

5.2 Czech-to-English Translation

For Czech-to-English translation we experimented with far fewer configuration options. Our primary submission is configured as follows:

- Two alternative decoding paths; forms always truecased: form→form & lemma→form.
- Significance filtering as in Section 5.1.
- 5-gram English LM based on CzEng English side only.[12]
- Lexicalized reordering (`or-bi-fe`) based on forms.
- Standard Moses MERT towards BLEU.

Table 10 documents the utility of the additional decoding path from Czech lemmas in both small and large setting, surprisingly less significant in the small setting. Later experiments with system combination by Kenneth Heafield indicated that while our system is not among the top three, it brings an advantage to the combination.

6 Conclusion

We provided an extensive documentation of Czech data sparseness issue for machine translation. We attempted to tackle the problem of constructing the target-side form by a two-step translation setup and the problem of unreliable automatic evaluation by employing a new metric in MERT loop, neither with much success so far. Both of the attempts however deserve further exploration. Additionally, we provide the exact configurations of our WMT10 primary submissions.

[11] The subsequent MERT training using the same development test may suffer from overestimating the language model weights, but we did not observe the issue, possibly due to only moderate overlap of the datasets.

[12] We attempted to use a second LM trained on English Gigaword by Chris Callison-Burch, but we observed a drop in BLEU score from 18.95±0.45 to 18.03±0.44 probably due to different tokenization guidelines applied.

References

Ondřej Bojar and Zdeněk Žabokrtský. 2009. CzEng 0.9: Large Parallel Treebank with Rich Annotation. *Prague Bulletin of Mathematical Linguistics*, 92.

Ondřej Bojar, Miroslav Janíček, and Miroslav Týnovský. 2009a. Evaluation of Tree Transfer System. Project Euromatrix - Deliverable 3.4, Institute of Formal and Applied Linguistics, Charles University in Prague.

Ondřej Bojar, David Mareček, Václav Novák, Martin Popel, Jan Ptáček, Jan Rouš, and Zdeněk Žabokrtský. 2009b. English-Czech MT in 2008. In *Proc. of Fourth Workshop on Statistical Machine Translation, ACL*, Athens, Greece.

Ondřej Bojar. 2007. English-to-Czech Factored Machine Translation. In *Proc. of the Second Workshop on Statistical Machine Translation, ACL*, Prague, Czech Republic, June.

Chris Callison-Burch, Cameron Fordyce, Philipp Koehn, Christof Monz, and Josh Schroeder. 2008. Further Meta-Evaluation of Machine Translation. In *Proc. of the Third Workshop on Statistical Machine Translation, ACL*, Columbus, Ohio.

Jan Hajič, Jarmila Panevová, Eva Hajičová, Petr Sgall, Petr Pajas, Jan Štěpánek, Jiří Havelka, Marie Mikulová, Zdeněk Žabokrtský, and Magda Ševčíková Razímová. 2006. Prague Dependency Treebank 2.0. LDC2006T01, ISBN: 1-58563-370-4.

Eva Hajičová, Jiří Havelka, Petr Sgall, Kateřina Veselá, and Daniel Zeman. 2004. Issues of Projectivity in the Prague Dependency Treebank. *The Prague Bulletin of Mathematical Linguistics*, 81.

Tomáš Holan. 2003. K syntaktické analýze českých(!) vět. In *MIS 2003*. MATFYZPRESS.

Howard Johnson, Joel Martin, George Foster, and Roland Kuhn. 2007. Improving translation quality by discarding most of the phrasetable. In *Proc. of EMNLP-CoNLL*, Prague, Czech Republic.

Jan Kocek, Marie Kopřivová, and Karel Kučera, editors. 2000. *Český národní korpus - úvod a příručka uživatele*. FF UK - ÚČNK, Prague.

Philipp Koehn and Hieu Hoang. 2007. Factored Translation Models. In *Proc. of EMNLP*.

Philipp Koehn. 2004. Statistical Significance Tests for Machine Translation Evaluation. In *Proc. of EMNLP*, Barcelona, Spain.

Kamil Kos and Ondřej Bojar. 2009. Evaluation of Machine Translation Metrics for Czech as the Target Language. *The Prague Bulletin of Mathematical Linguistics*, 92.

Alon Lavie and Abhaya Agarwal. 2007. Meteor: An Automatic Metric for MT Evaluation with High Levels of Correlation with Human Judgments. In *Proc. of the Second Workshop on Statistical Machine Translation, ACL*, Prague, Czech Republic.

Franz Josef Och. 2003. Minimum Error Rate Training in Statistical Machine Translation. In *Proc. of ACL*, Sapporo, Japan.

Kishore Papineni, Salim Roukos, Todd Ward, and Wei-Jing Zhu. 2002. BLEU: a Method for Automatic Evaluation of Machine Translation. In *Proc. of ACL*, Philadelphia, Pennsylvania.

Lane Schwartz. 2008. Multi-source translation methods. In *Proc. of AMTA*.

Matthew Snover, Bonnie Dorr, Richard Schwartz, Linnea Micciulla, and John Makhoul. 2006. A Study of Translation Edit Rate with Targeted Human Annotation. In *Proc. of AMTA*.

Andreas Stolcke. 2002. SRILM – An Extensible Language Modeling Toolkit. In *Proc. of Intl. Conf. on Spoken Language Processing*, volume 2.

Jörg Tiedemann. 2009. News from OPUS - A Collection of Multilingual Parallel Corpora with Tools and Interfaces. In *Proc. of Recent Advances in NLP (RANLP)*.

Zdeněk Žabokrtský and Ondřej Bojar. 2008. TectoMT, Developer's Guide. Technical Report TR-2008-39, Institute of Formal and Applied Linguistics, Charles University in Prague.

Omar F. Zaidan. 2009. Z-MERT: A Fully Configurable Open Source Tool for Minimum Error Rate Training of Machine Translation Systems. *The Prague Bulletin of Mathematical Linguistics*, 91.

An Empirical Study on Development Set Selection Strategy for Machine Translation Learning*

Cong Hui[1 2], **Hai Zhao**[1 2†], **Yan Song**[3], **Bao-Liang Lu**[1 2]
[1]Center for Brain-Like Computing and Machine Intelligence
Department of Computer Science and Engineering, Shanghai Jiao Tong University
[2]MOE-Microsoft Key Laboratory for Intelligent Computing and Intelligent Systems
Shanghai Jiao Tong University, 800 Dong Chuan Rd., Shanghai 200240, China
[3]Department of Chinese, Translation and Linguistics, City University of Hong Kong
huicong@sjtu.edu.cn, {zhaohai,blu}@cs.sjtu.edu.cn

Abstract

This paper describes a statistical machine translation system for our participation for the WMT10 shared task. Based on MOSES, our system is capable of translating German, French and Spanish into English. Our main contribution in this work is about effective parameter tuning. We discover that there is a significant performance gap as different development sets are adopted. Finally, ten groups of development sets are used to optimize the model weights, and this does help us obtain a stable evaluation result.

1 Introduction

We present a machine translation system that represents our participation for the WMT10 shared task from Brain-like Computing and Machine Intelligence Lab of Shanghai Jiao Tong University (SJTU-BCMI Lab). The system is based on the state-of-the-art SMT toolkit MOSES (Koehn et al., 2007). We use it to translate German, French and Spanish into English. Though different development sets used for training parameter tuning will certainly lead to quite different performance, we empirically find that the more sets we combine together, the more stable the performance is, and a development set similar with test set will help the performance improvement.

2 System Description

The basic model of the our system is a log-linear model (Och and Ney, 2002). For given source language strings, the target language string t will be obtained by the following equation,

$$\hat{t}_1^I = \arg\max_{t_1^I}\{p_{\lambda_1^m}(t_1^I \mid s_1^J)\}$$

$$= \arg\max_{t_1^I}\{\frac{\exp[\sum_{m=1}^{M}\lambda_m h_m(t_1^I, s_1^J)]}{\sum_{\bar{t}_1^I}\exp[\sum_{m=1}^{M}\lambda_m h_m(\bar{t}_1^I, s_1^J)]}\},$$

where h_m is the m-th feature function and λ_m is the m-th model weight. There are four main parts of features in the model: translation model, language model, reordering model and word penalty. The whole model has been well implemented by the state-of-the-art statistical machine translation toolkit MOSES.

For each language that is required to translated into English, two sets of bilingual corpora are provided by the shared task organizer. The first set is the new release (version 5) of Europarl corpus which is the smaller. The second is a combination of other available data sets which is the larger. In detail, two corpora, *europarl-v5* and *news-commentary10* are for German, *europarl-v5* and *news-commentary10* plus *undoc* for French and Spanish, respectively. Details of training data are in Table 1. Only sentences with length 1 to 40 are acceptable for our task. We used the larger set for our primary submission.

We adopt word alignment toolkit GIZA++ (Och and Ney, 2003) to learn word-level alignment with its default setting and *grow-diag-final-and* parameters. Given a sentence pair and its corresponding word-level alignment, phrases will be extracted by using the approach in (Och and Ney, 2004). Phrase probability is estimated by its relative frequency in the training corpus. Lexical reordering is determined by using the default setting of MOSES with *msd-bidirectional* parameter.

For training the only language model (English), the data sets are extracted from monolingual parts of both *europarl-v5* and *news-commentary10*,

*This work was partially supported by the National Natural Science Foundation of China (Grant No. 60903119, Grant No. 60773090 and Grant No. 90820018), the National Basic Research Program of China (Grant No. 2009CB320901), and the National High-Tech Research Program of China (Grant No.2008AA02Z315).

†corresponding author

Proceedings of the Joint 5th Workshop on Statistical Machine Translation and MetricsMATR, pages 67–71,
Uppsala, Sweden, 15-16 July 2010. ©2010 Association for Computational Linguistics

		sentences	words(s)	words(t)
de	small	1540549	35.76M	38.53M
	large	1640818	37.95M	40.64M
fr	small	1683156	44.02M	44.20M
	large	8997997	251.60M	228.50M
es	small	1650152	43.17M	41.25M
	large	7971200	236.24M	207.79M

Table 1: Bilingual training corpora from German(de), French(fr) and Spanish(es) to English.

which include 1968914 sentences and 47.48M words. And SRILM is adopted with *5-gram, interpolate* and *kndiscount* settings (Stolcke, 2002)
.

The next step is to estimate feature weights by optimizing translation performance on a development set. We consider various combinations of 10 development sets with 18207 sentences to get a stable performance in our primary submission.

We use the default toolkits which are provided by WMT10 organizers for preprocessing (i.e., tokenize) and postprocessing (i.e., detokenize, recaser).

3 Development Set Selection

3.1 Motivation

Given the previous feature functions, the model weights will be obtained by optimizing the following maximum mutual information criterion, which can be derived from the maximum entropy principle:

$$\hat{\lambda}_1^M = \arg\max_{\lambda_1^M}\{\sum_{i=1}^{S} \log p_{\lambda_1^M}(t_i \mid s_i)\}$$

As usual, minimum error rate training (MERT) is adopted for log-linear model parameter estimation (Och, 2003). There are many improvements on MERT in existing work (Bertoldi et al., 2009; Foster and Kuhn, 2009), but there no demonstration that the weights with better performance on the development set would lead to a better result on the unseen test set. In our experiments, we found that different development sets will cause significant BLEU score differences, even as high as one percent. Thus the remained problem will be how to effectively choose the development set to obtain a better and more stable performance.

3.2 Experimental Settings

Our empirical study will be demonstrated through German to English translation on the smaller corpus. The development sets are all development sets and test sets from the previous WMT shared translation task as shown in Table 2, and labeled as dev-0 to dev-9. Meanwhile, we denote 10 batch sets from batch-0 to batch-9 where the batch-i set is the combination of dev- sets from dev-0 to dev-i. The test set is *newstest2009*, which includes 2525 sentences, 54K German words and 58K English words, and *news-test2008*, which includes 2051 sentences, 41K German words and 43K English words.

id	name	sent	w(de)	w(en)
dev-0	dev2006	2000	49K	53K
dev-1	devtest2006	2000	48K	52K
dev-2	nc-dev2007	1057	23K	23K
dev-3	nc-devtest2007	1064	24K	23K
dev-4	nc-test2007	2007	45K	44K
dev-5	nc-test2008	2028	45K	44K
dev-6	news-dev2009	2051	41K	43K
dev-7	test2006	2000	49K	54K
dev-8	test2007	2000	49K	54K
dev-9	test2008	2000	50K	54K

Table 2: Development data.

3.3 On the Scale of Development Set

Having 20 different development sets (10 dev- sets and batch- sets), 20 models are correspondingly trained.The decode results on the test set are summarized in Table 3 and Figure 1. The dotted lines are the performances of 10 different development sets on the two test sets, we will see that there is a huge gap between the highest and the lowest score, and there is not an obvious rule to follow. It will bring about unsatisfied results if a poor development set is chosen. The solid lines represents the performances of 10 incremental batch sets on the two test sets, the batch processing still gives a poor performance at the beginning, but the results become better and more stable when the development sets are continuously enlarged. This sort of results suggest that a combined development set may produce reliable results in the worst case. Our primary submission used the combined development set and the results as Table 4.

id	09-dev	09-batch	08-dev	08-batch
0	16.46	16.46	16.38	16.38
1	16.67	16.25	16.66	16.44
2	16.74	16.20	16.94	16.22
3	16.15	16.83	16.18	17.02
4	16.44	16.73	16.64	16.89
5	16.50	16.97	16.75	17.13
6	17.15	17.03	17.67	17.24
7	16.51	17.00	16.34	17.09
8	17.03	16.97	17.15	17.22
9	16.25	16.99	16.24	17.26

Table 3: BLEU scores on the two test sets(*newstest2009* & *news-test2008*), which use two data set sequences(dev- sequence & batch- sequence) to optimize model weights.

de-en	fr-en	es-en
18.90	24.30	26.40

Table 4: BLEU scores of our primary submission.

3.4 On BLEU Score Difference

To compare BLEU score differences between test set and development set, we consider two groups of BLEU score differences, For each development set, dev-i, the BLEU score difference will be computed between b_1 from which adopts itself as the development set and b_2 from which adopts test set as the development set. For the test set, the BLEU score difference will be computed between b'_1 from which adopts each development set, dev-i, as the development set and b'_2 from which adopts itself as the development set.

These two groups of results are illustrated in Figure 2 (the best score of the test set under self tuning, *newstest2009* is 17.91). The dotted lines have the inverse trend with the dotted in Figure 1(because the addition of these two values is constant), and the solid lines have the same trend with the dotted, which means that the good performance is mutual between test set and development sets: if tuning using A set could make a good result over B set, then vice versa.

3.5 On the Similarity between Development Set and Test Set

This experiment is motivated by (Utiyama et al., 2009), where they used BLEU score to measure the similarity of a sentences pair and then extracted sentences similar with those in test set to

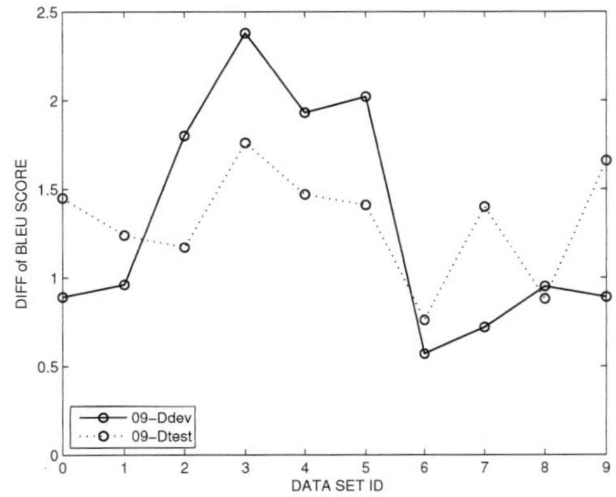

Figure 2: The trend of BLEU score differences

construct a specific tuning set. In our experiment, we will try to measure data set similarity instead. Given two sets of sentences, one is called as candidate(cnd) set and the other reference(ref) set. For any cnd sentence, we let the whole ref set to be its reference and then multi-references BLEU score is computed for cnd set. There comes a problem that the sentence penalty will be constant for any cnd sentence, we turn to calculate the average length of whose sentences which have common n-gram with the given cnd sentence.

Now we may define three measures. The measure which uses dev- and batch- sets as cnd sets and *news-test2009* set as ref set is defined as precision-BLEU , and the measure which uses the above sets on the contrary way is defined as recall-BLEU. Then F1-BLEU is defined as the harmonic mean of precision-BLEU and recall-BLEU. These results are illustrated in Figure 3. From the figure, we find that F1-BLEU plays an important role to predict the goodness of a development set, F1-BLEU scores of batch- sets have an ascending curve and batch data set sequence will cause a stable good test performance, the point on dev- sets which has high F1-BLEU(eg, dev-0,4,5) would also has a good test performance.

3.6 Related Work

The special challenge of the WMT shared task is domain adaptation, which is a hot topic in recent years and more relative to our experiments. Many existing works are about this topic (Koehn and Schroeder, 2007; Nakov, 2008; Nakov and Ng, 2009; Paul et al., 2009; Haque et al., 2009). However, most of previous works focus on language model, translation phrase table, lexicons model and factored translation model, few of them pay attention to the domain adaptation on the development set. For future work we consider to use some machine learning approaches to select sentences in development sets more relevant with the test set in order to further improve translation performance.

4 Conclusion

In this paper, we present our machine translation system for the WMT10 shared task and perform an empirical study on the development set selection. According to our experimental results, Choosing different development sets would play an important role for translation performance. We find that a development set with higher F1-BLEU yields better and more stable results.

References

Nicola Bertoldi, Barry Haddow, and Jean Baptiste Fouet. 2009. Improved Minimum Error Rate Training in Moses. *The Prague Bulletin of Mathematical Linguistics*, 91:7–16.

George Foster and Roland Kuhn. 2009. Stabilizing minimum error rate training. In *Proceedings of the 4th Workshop on Statistical Machine Translation(WMT)*, Boulder, Colorado, USA.

Rejwanul Haque, Sudip Kumar Naskar, Josef Van Genabith, and Andy Way. 2009. Experiments on Domain Adaptation for EnglishłHindi SMT. In *7th International Conference on Natural Language Processing(ICNLP)*, Hyderabad, India.

Philipp Koehn and Josh Schroeder. 2007. Experiments in domain adaptation for statistical machine translation. In *Proceedings of the 2nd Workshop on Statistical Machine Translation(WMT)*, Prague, Czech Republic.

Philipp Koehn, Hieu Hoang, Alexandra Birch, Chris Callison-Burch, Marcello Federico, Nicola Bertoldi, Brooke Cowan, Wade Shen, Christine Moran, Richard Zens, Chris Dyer, Ondrej Bojar, Alexandra Constantin, and Evan Herbst. 2007. Moses: Open source toolkit for statistical machine translation. In *Proceedings of the 45th Annual Meeting of the Association for Computational Linguistics(ACL)*, Prague, Czech Republic.

Preslav Nakov and Hwee Tou Ng. 2009. NUS at WMT09: domain adaptation experiments for English-Spanish machine translation of news commentary text. In *Proceedings of the 4th Workshop on Statistical Machine Translation(WMT)*, Singapore.

Preslav Nakov. 2008. Improving English-Spanish statistical machine translation: Experiments in domain adaptation, sentence paraphrasing, tokenization, and recasing. In *Proceedings of the 3rd Workshop on Statistical Machine Translation(WMT)*, Columbus, Ohio, USA.

Franz Josef Och and Hermann Ney. 2002. Discriminative training and maximum entropy models for statistical machine translation. In *Proceedings of the 40th Annual Meeting of the Association for Computational Linguistics(ACL)*, Philadelphia, Pennsylvanian, USA.

Franz Josef Och and Hermann Ney. 2003. A systematic comparison of various statistical alignment models. *Computational Linguistics*, 29(1):19–51.

Franz Josef Och and Hermann Ney. 2004. The alignment template approach to statistical machine translation. *Computational Linguistics*, 30(4):417–449.

Franz Josef Och. 2003. Minimum error rate training in statistical machine translation. In *Proceedings of the 41th Annual Meeting of the Association for Computational Linguistics(ACL)*, Sapporo, Japan.

Michael Paul, Andrew Finch, and Eiichiro Sumita. 2009. NICT@ WMT09: model adaptation and transliteration for Spanish-English SMT. In *Proceedings of the 4th Workshop on Statistical Machine Translation(WMT)*, Singapore.

Andreas Stolcke. 2002. SRILM: an extensible language modeling toolkit. In *7th International Conference on Spoken Language Processing(ICSLP)*, Denver, Colorado, USA.

Masao Utiyama, Hirofumi Yamamoto, and Eiichiro Sumita. 2009. Two methods for stabilizing MERT: NICT at IWSLT 2009. In *Proceedings of International Workshop on Spoken Language Translation(IWSLT)*, Tokyo, Japan.

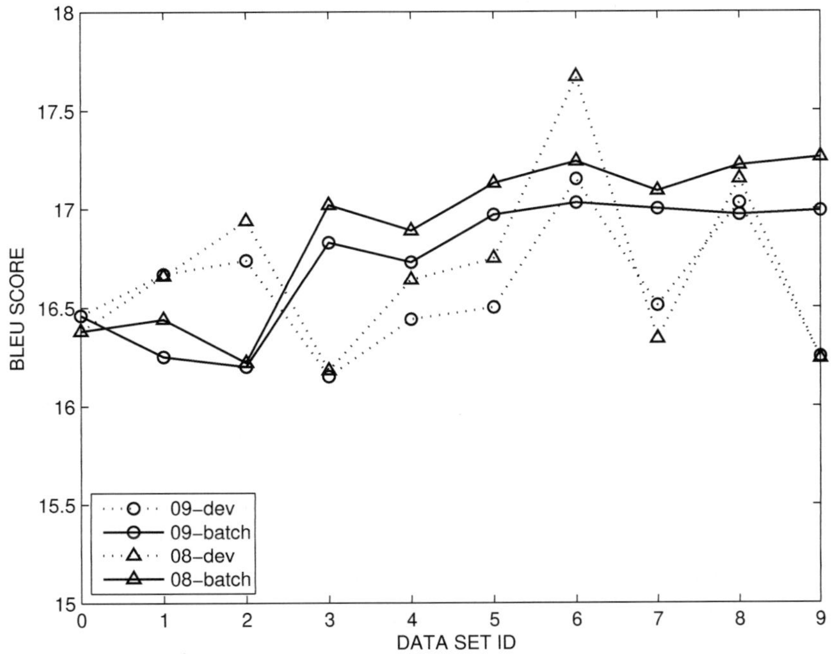

Figure 1: The BLEU score trend in Tabel 3, we will see that the batch lines output a stable and good performance.

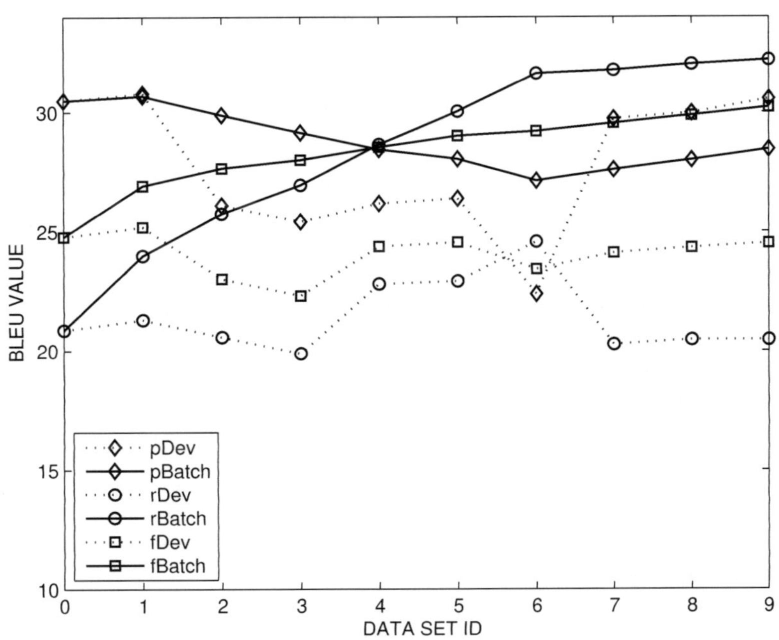

Figure 3: The precision(p), recall(r) and F1(f) BLEU score on the dev(Dev) and batch(Batch) sets based on the comparison with *news-test2009* set.

The University of Maryland Statistical Machine Translation System for the Fifth Workshop on Machine Translation

Vladimir Eidelman[†], **Chris Dyer**[†‡], **and Philip Resnik**[†‡]
[†]UMIACS Laboratory for Computational Linguistics and Information Processing
[‡]Department of Linguistics
University of Maryland, College Park
{vlad,redpony,resnik}@umiacs.umd.edu

Abstract

This paper describes the system we developed to improve German-English translation of News text for the shared task of the Fifth Workshop on Statistical Machine Translation. Working within cdec, an open source modular framework for machine translation, we explore the benefits of several modifications to our hierarchical phrase-based model, including segmentation lattices, minimum Bayes Risk decoding, grammar extraction methods, and varying language models. Furthermore, we analyze decoder speed and memory performance across our set of models and show there is an important trade-off that needs to be made.

1 Introduction

For the shared translation task of the Fifth Workshop on Machine Translation (WMT10), we participated in German to English translation under the constraint setting. We were especially interested in translating from German due to set of challenges it poses for translation. Namely, German possesses a rich inflectional morphology, productive compounding, and significant word reordering with respect to English. Therefore, we directed our system design and experimentation toward addressing these complications and minimizing their negative impact on translation quality.

The rest of this paper is structured as follows. After a brief description of the baseline system in Section 2, we detail the steps taken to improve upon it in Section 3, followed by experimental results and analysis of decoder performance metrics.

2 Baseline system

As our baseline system, we employ a hierarchical phrase-based translation model, which is formally based on the notion of a synchronous context-free grammar (SCFG) (Chiang, 2007). These grammars contain pairs of CFG rules with aligned nonterminals, and by introducing these nonterminals into the grammar, such a system is able to utilize both word and phrase level reordering to capture the hierarchical structure of language. SCFG translation models have been shown to be well suited for German-English translation, as they are able to both exploit lexical information for and efficiently compute all possible reorderings using a CKY-based decoder (Dyer et al., 2009).

Our system is implemented within cdec, an efficient and modular open source framework for aligning, training, and decoding with a number of different translation models, including SCFGs (Dyer et al., 2010).[1] cdec's modular framework facilitates seamless integration of a translation model with different language models, pruning strategies and inference algorithms. As input, cdec expects a string, lattice, or context-free forest, and uses it to generate a hypergraph representation, which represents the full translation forest without any pruning. The forest can now be rescored, by intersecting it with a language model for instance, to obtain output translations. The above capabilities of cdec allow us to perform the experiments described below, which would otherwise be quite cumbersome to carry out in another system.

The set of features used in our model were the rule translation relative frequency $P(e|f)$, a target n-gram language model $P(e)$, a 'pass-through' penalty when passing a source language word to the target side without translating it, lexical translation probabilities $P_{lex}(\overline{e}|\overline{f})$ and $P_{lex}(\overline{f}|\overline{e})$,

[1] http://cdec-decoder.org

Proceedings of the Joint 5th Workshop on Statistical Machine Translation and MetricsMATR, pages 72–76,
Uppsala, Sweden, 15-16 July 2010.

a count of the number of times that arity-0,1, or 2 SCFG rules were used, a count of the total number of rules used, a source word penalty, a target word penalty, the segmentation model cost, and a count of the number of times the glue rule is used. The number of non-terminals allowed in a synchronous grammar rule was restricted to two, and the non-terminal span limit was 12 for non-glue grammars. The hierarchical phrase-base translation grammar was extracted using a suffix array rule extractor (Lopez, 2007).

2.1 Data preparation

In order to extract the translation grammar necessary for our model, we used the provided Europarl and News Commentary parallel training data. The lowercased and tokenized training data was then filtered for length and aligned using the GIZA++ implementation of IBM Model 4 (Och and Ney, 2003) to obtain one-to-many alignments in both directions and symmetrized by combining both into a single alignment using the grow-diag-final-and method (Koehn et al., 2003). We constructed a 5-gram language model using the SRI language modeling toolkit (Stolcke, 2002) from the provided English monolingual training data and the non-Europarl portions of the parallel data with modified Kneser-Ney smoothing (Chen and Goodman, 1996). Since the beginnings and ends of sentences often display unique characteristics that are not easily captured within the context of the model, and have previously been demonstrated to significantly improve performance (Dyer et al., 2009), we explicitly annotate beginning and end of sentence markers as part of our translation process. We used the 2525 sentences in news-test2009 as our dev set on which we tuned the feature weights, and report results on the 2489 sentences of the news-test2010 test set.

2.2 Viterbi envelope semiring training

To optimize the feature weights for our model, we use Viterbi envelope semiring training (VEST), which is an implementation of the minimum error rate training (MERT) algorithm (Dyer et al., 2010; Och, 2003) for training with an arbitrary loss function. VEST reinterprets MERT within a semiring framework, which is a useful mathematical abstraction for defining two general operations, addition ($\oplus$) and multiplication ($\otimes$) over a set of values. Formally, a semiring is a 5-tuple $(\mathbb{K}, \oplus, \otimes, \overline{0}, \overline{1})$, where addition must be commutative and associative, multiplication must be associative and must distribute over addition, and an identity element exists for both. For VEST, having $\mathbb{K}$ be the set of line segments, $\oplus$ be the union of them, and $\otimes$ be Minkowski addition of the lines represented as points in the dual plane, allows us to compute the necessary MERT line search with the INSIDE algorithm.[2] The error function we use is BLEU (Papineni et al., 2002), and the decoder is configured to use cube pruning (Huang and Chiang, 2007) with a limit of 100 candidates at each node. During decoding of the test set, we raise the cube pruning limit to 1000 candidates at each node.

2.3 Compound segmentation lattices

To deal with the aforementioned problem in German of productive compounding, where words are formed by the concatenation of several morphemes and the orthography does not delineate the morpheme boundaries, we utilize word segmentation lattices. These lattices serve to encode alternative ways of segmenting compound words, and as such, when presented as the input to the system allow the decoder to automatically choose which segmentation is best for translation, leading to markedly improved results (Dyer, 2009).

In order to construct diverse and accurate segmentation lattices, we built a maximum entropy model of compound word splitting which makes use of a small number of dense features, such as frequency of hypothesized morphemes as separate units in a monolingual corpus, number of predicted morphemes, and number of letters in a predicted morpheme. The feature weights are tuned to maximize conditional log-likelihood using a small amount of manually created reference lattices which encode linguistically plausible segmentations for a selected set of compound words.[3]

To create lattices for the dev and test sets, a lattice consisting of all possible segmentations for every word consisting of more than 6 letters was created, and the paths were weighted by the posterior probability assigned by the segmentation model. Then, max-marginals were computed using the forward-backward algorithm and used to prune out paths that were greater than a factor of 2.3 from the best path, as recommended by Dyer

[2]This algorithm is equivalent to the hypergraph MERT algorithm described by Kumar et al. (2009).

[3]The reference segmentation lattices used for training are available in the cdec distribution.

(2009).[4] To create the translation model for lattice input, we segmented the training data using the 1-best segmentation predicted by the segmentation model, and word aligned this with the English side. This version of the parallel corpus was concatenated with the original training parallel corpus.

3 Experimental variation

This section describes the experiments we performed in attempting to assess the challenges posed by current methods and our exploration of new ones.

3.1 Bloom filter language model

Language models play a crucial role in translation performance, both in terms of quality, and in terms of practical aspects such as decoder memory usage and speed. Unfortunately, these two concerns tend to trade-off one another, as increasing to a higher-order more complex language model improves performance, but comes at the cost of increased size and difficulty in deployment. Ideally, the language model will be loaded into memory locally by the decoder, but given memory constraints, it is entirely possible that the only option is to resort to a remote language model server that needs to be queried, thus introducing significant decoding speed delays.

One possible alternative is a randomized language model (RandLM) (Talbot and Osborne, 2007). Using Bloom filters, which are a randomized data structure for set representation, we can construct language models which significantly decrease space requirements, thus becoming amenable to being stored locally in memory, while only introducing a quantifiable number of false positives. In order to assess what the impact on translation quality would be, we trained a system identical to the one described above, except using a RandLM. Conveniently, it is possible to construct a RandLM directly from an existing SRILM, which is the route we followed in using the SRILM described in Section 2.1 to create our RandLM.[5] Table 1 shows the comparison of SRILM and RandLM with respect to performance on BLEU and TER (Snover et al., 2006) on the test set.

[4] While normally the forward-backward algorithm computes sum-marginals, by changing the addition operator to max, we can obtain max-marginals.

[5] Default settings were used for constructing the RandLM.

Language Model	BLEU	TER
RandLM	22.4	69.1
SRILM	**23.1**	**68.0**

Table 1: Impact of language model on translation

3.2 Minimum Bayes risk decoding

During minimum error rate training, the decoder employs a maximum derivation decision rule. However, upon exploration of alternative strategies, we have found benefits to using a minimum risk decision rule (Kumar and Byrne, 2004), wherein we want the translation E of the input F that has the least expected loss, again as measured by some loss function L:

$$\begin{aligned}\widehat{E} &= \arg\min_{E'} \mathbb{E}_{P(E|F)}[L(E,E')] \\ &= \arg\min_{E'} \sum_{E} P(E|F) L(E,E')\end{aligned}$$

Using our system, we generate a unique 500-best list of translations to approximate the posterior distribution $P(E|F)$ and the set of possible translations. Assuming $H(E,F)$ is the weight of the decoder's current path, this can be written as:

$$P(E|F) \propto \exp \alpha H(E,F)$$

where α is a free parameter which depends on the models feature functions and weights as well as pruning method employed, and thus needs to be separately empirically optimized on a held out development set. For this submission, we used $\alpha = 0.5$ and BLEU as the loss function. Table 2 shows the results on the test set for MBR decoding.

Language Model	Decoder	BLEU	TER
RandLM	Max-D	22.4	69.1
	MBR	**22.7**	**68.8**
SRILM	Max-D	23.1	68.0
	MBR	**23.4**	**67.7**

Table 2: Comparison of maximum derivation versus MBR decoding

3.3 Grammar extraction

Although the grammars employed in a SCFG model allow increased expressivity and translation quality, they do so at the cost of having a large

Language Model	Grammar	Decoder Memory (GB)	Decoder time (Sec/Sentence)
Local SRILM	corpus	14.293 ± 1.228	$\mathbf{5.254 \pm 3.768}$
Local SRILM	sentence	$10.964 \pm .964$	5.517 ± 3.884
Remote SRILM	corpus	$3.771 \pm .235$	15.252 ± 10.878
Remote SRILM	sentence	$\mathbf{.443 \pm .235}$	14.751 ± 10.370
RandLM	corpus	$7.901 \pm .721$	9.398 ± 6.965
RandLM	sentence	$4.612 \pm .699$	9.561 ± 7.149

Table 3: Decoding memory and speed requirements for language model and grammar extraction variations

number of rules, thus efficiently storing and accessing grammar rules can become a major problem. Since a grammar consists of the set of rules extracted from a parallel corpus containing tens of millions of words, the resulting number of rules can be in the millions. Besides storing the whole grammar locally in memory, other approaches have been developed, such as suffix arrays, which lookup and extract rules on the fly from the phrase table (Lopez, 2007). Thus, the memory requirements for decoding have either been for the grammar, when extracted beforehand, or the corpus, for suffix arrays. In cdec, however, loading grammars for single sentences from a disk is very fast relative to decoding time, thus we explore the additional possibility of having sentence-specific grammars extracted and loaded on an as-needed basis by the decoder. This strategy is shown to massively reduce the memory footprint of the decoder, while having no observable impact on decoding speed, introducing the possibility of more computational resources for translation. Thus, in addition to the large corpus grammar extracted in Section 2.1, we extract sentence-specific grammars for each of the test sentences. We measure the performance across using both grammar extraction mechanisms and the three different language model configurations: local SRILM, remote SRILM, and RandLM.

As Table 3 shows, there is a marked trade-off between memory usage and decoding speed. Using a local SRILM regardless of grammar increases decoding speed by a factor of 3 compared to the remote SRILM, and approximately a factor of 2 against the RandLM. However, this speed comes at the cost of its memory footprint. With a corpus grammar, the memory footprint of the local SRILM is twice as large as the RandLM, and almost 4 times as large as the remote SRILM. Using sentence-specific grammars, the difference becomes increasingly glaring, as the remote SRILM memory footprint drops to $\approx$450MB, a factor of nearly 24 compared to the local SRILM and a factor of 10 compared to the process size with the RandLM. Thus, using the remote SRILM reduces the memory footprint substantially but at the cost of significantly slower decoding speed, and conversely, using the local SRILM produces increased decoder speed but introduces a substantial memory overhead. The RandLM provides a median between the two extremes: reduced memory and (relatively) fast decoding at the price of somewhat decreased translation quality. Since we are using a relatively large beam of 1000 candidates for decoding, the time presented in Table 3 does not represent an accurate basis for comparison of cdec to other decoders, which should be done using the results presented in Dyer et al. (2010).

We also tried one other grammar extraction configuration, which was with so-called 'loose' phrase extraction heuristics, which permit unaligned words at the edges of phrases (Ayan and Dorr, 2006). When decoded using the SRILM and MBR, this achieved the best performance for our system, with a BLEU score of 23.6 and TER of 67.7.

4 Conclusion

We presented the University of Maryland hierarchical phrase-based system for the WMT2010 shared translation task. Using cdec, we experimented with a number of methods that are shown above to lead to improved German-to-English translation quality over our baseline according to BLEU and TER evaluation. These include methods to directly address German morphological complexity, such as appropriate feature functions, segmentation lattices, and a model for automatically constructing the lattices, as well as alternative decoding strategies, such as MBR. We also presented several language model configuration alternatives, as well as grammar extraction methods, and emphasized the trade-off that must be made between decoding time, memory overhead, and translation quality in current statistical machine translation systems.

5 Acknowledgments

The authors gratefully acknowledge partial support from the GALE program of the Defense Advanced Research Projects Agency, Contract No. HR0011-06-2-001 and NSF award IIS0838801. Any opinions, findings, conclusions or recommendations expressed in this paper are those of the authors and do not necessarily reflect the view of the sponsors.

References

Necip Fazil Ayan and Bonnie J. Dorr. 2006. Going beyond AER: An extensive analysis of word alignments and their impact on MT. In *Proceedings of the Joint Conference of the International Committee on Computational Linguistics and the Association for Computational Linguistics (COLING-ACL'2006)*, pages 9–16, Sydney.

Stanley F. Chen and Joshua Goodman. 1996. An empirical study of smoothing techniques for language modeling. In *Proceedings of the 34th Annual Meeting of the Association for Computational Linguistics*, pages 310–318.

David Chiang. 2007. Hierarchical phrase-based translation. In *Computational Linguistics*, volume 33(2), pages 201–228.

Chris Dyer, Hendra Setiawan, Yuval Marton, and P. Resnik. 2009. The University of Maryland statistical machine translation system for the Fourth Workshop on Machine Translation. In *Proceedings of the EACL-2009 Workshop on Statistical Machine Translation*.

Chris Dyer, Adam Lopez, Juri Ganitkevitch, Jonathan Weese, Ferhan Ture, Phil Blunsom, Hendra Setiawan, Vladimir Eidelman, and Philip Resnik. 2010. cdec: A decoder, alignment, and learning framework for finite-state and context-free translation models. In *Proceedings of ACL System Demonstrations*.

Chris Dyer. 2009. Using a maximum entropy model to build segmentation lattices for mt. In *Proceedings of NAACL-HLT*.

Liang Huang and David Chiang. 2007. Forest rescoring: Faster decoding with integrated language models. In *Proceedings of the 45th Annual Meeting of the Association of Computational Linguistics*, pages 144–151.

Philipp Koehn, Franz Josef Och, and Daniel Marcu. 2003. Statistical phrase-based translation. In *NAACL '03: Proceedings of the 2003 Conference of the North American Chapter of the Association for Computational Linguistics on Human Language Technology*, pages 48–54.

Shankar Kumar and William Byrne. 2004. Minimum bayes-risk decoding for statistical machine translation. In *HLT-NAACL 2004: Main Proceedings*.

Shankar Kumar, Wolfgang Macherey, Chris Dyer, and Franz Och. 2009. Efficient minimum error rate training and minimum bayes-risk decoding for translation hypergraphs and lattices. In *Proceedings of the Joint Conference of the 47th Annual Meeting of the ACL and the 4th International Joint Conference on Natural Language Processing of the AFNLP*, pages 163–171.

Adam Lopez. 2007. Hierarchical phrase-based translation with suffix arrays. In *Proceedings of EMNLP*, pages 976–985.

Franz Och and Hermann Ney. 2003. A systematic comparison of various statistical alignment models. In *Computational Linguistics*, volume 29(21), pages 19–51.

Franz Josef Och. 2003. Minimum error rate training in statistical machine translation. In *Proceedings of the 41st Annual Meeting of the Association for Computational Linguistics*, pages 160–167.

Kishore Papineni, Salim Roukos, Todd Ward, and Wei-Jing Zhu. 2002. BLEU: a method for automatic evaluation of machine translation. In *Proceedings of 40th Annual Meeting of the Association for Computational Linguistics*, pages 311–318.

Matthew Snover, Bonnie Dorr, Richard Schwartz, Linnea Micciulla, and John Makhoul. 2006. A study of translation edit rate with targeted human annotation. In *In Proceedings of Association for Machine Translation in the Americas*, pages 223–231.

Andreas Stolcke. 2002. SRILM - an extensible language modeling toolkit. In *Intl. Conf. on Spoken Language Processing*.

David Talbot and Miles Osborne. 2007. Randomised language modelling for statistical machine translation. In *Proceedings of the 45th Annual Meeting of the Association of Computational Linguistics*, June.

Further Experiments with Shallow Hybrid MT Systems

Christian Federmann[1], **Andreas Eisele**[1], **Hans Uszkoreit**[1,2],
Yu Chen[1], **Sabine Hunsicker**[1], **Jia Xu**[1]
1: Deutsches Forschungszentrum für Künstliche Intelligenz GmbH, Saarbrücken, Germany
2: Universität des Saarlandes, Saarbrücken, Germany
{cfedermann,eisele,uszkoreit,yuchen,sabine.hunsicker,jia.xu}@dfki.de

Abstract

We describe our hybrid machine translation system which has been developed for and used in the WMT10 shared task. We compute translations from a rule-based MT system and combine the resulting translation "templates" with partial phrases from a state-of-the-art phrase-based, statistical MT engine. Phrase substitution is guided by several decision factors, a continuation of previous work within our group. For the shared task, we have computed translations for six language pairs including English, German, French and Spanish. Our experiments have shown that our shallow substitution approach can effectively improve the translation result from the RBMT system; however it has also become clear that a deeper integration is needed to further improve translation quality.

1 Introduction

In recent years the quality of machine translation (MT) output has improved greatly, although each paradigm suffers from its own particular kind of errors: statistical machine translation (SMT) often shows poor syntax, while rule-based engines (RBMT) experience a lack in vocabulary. Hybrid systems try to avoid these typical errors by combining techniques from both paradigms in a most useful manner.

In this paper we present the improved version of the hybrid system we developed last year's shared task (Federmann et al., 2009). We take the output from an RBMT engine as basis for our hybrid translations and substitute noun phrases by translations from an SMT engine. Even though a general increase in quality could be observed, our system introduced errors of its own during the substitution process. In an internal error analysis, these degradations were classified as follows:

- the translation by the SMT engine is incorrect
- the structure degrades through substitution (because of e.g. capitalization errors, double prepositions, etc.)
- the phrase substitution goes astray (caused by alignment problems, etc.)

Errors of the first class cannot be corrected, as we have no way of knowing when the translation by the SMT engine is incorrect. The other two classes could be eliminated, however, by introducing additional steps for pre- and post-processing as well as improving the hybrid algorithm itself. Our current error analysis based on the results of this year's shared task does not show these types of errors anymore.

Additionally, we extended our coverage to also include the language pairs English↔French and English↔Spanish in both directions as well as English→German, compared to last year's initial experiments for German→English only. We were able to achieve an increase in translation quality for this language set, which shows that the substitution method works for different language configurations.

2 Architecture

Our hybrid translation system takes translation output from a) the Lucy RBMT system (Alonso and Thurmair, 2003) and b) a Moses-based SMT system (Koehn et al., 2007). We then identify noun phrases inside the rule-based translation and compute the most likely correspondences in the statistical translation output. For these, we apply a factored substitution method that decides whether the original RBMT phrase should be kept or rather be replaced by the Moses phrase. As this shallow substitution process may introduce problems at

Proceedings of the Joint 5th Workshop on Statistical Machine Translation and MetricsMATR, pages 77–81,
Uppsala, Sweden, 15-16 July 2010.

phrase boundaries, we afterwards perform several post-processing steps to cleanup and finalize the hybrid translation result. A schematic overview of our hybrid system and its main components is given in figure 1.

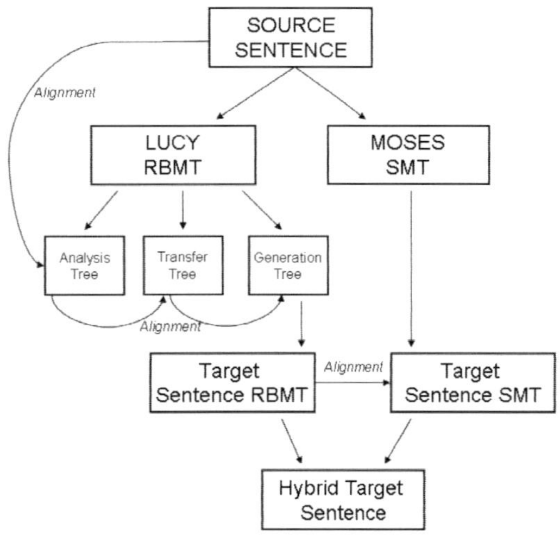

Figure 1: Schematic overview of the hybrid MT system architecture.

2.1 Input to the Hybrid System

Lucy RBMT System We obtain the translation as well as linguistic structures from the RBMT system. An internal evaluation has shown that these structures are usually of a high quality which supports our initial decision to consider the RBMT output as an appropriate "template" for our hybrid translation approach. The Lucy translation output can include additional markup that allows to identify unknown words or other, local phenomena.

The Lucy system is a transfer-based MT system that performs translation in three phases, namely *analysis*, *transfer*, and *generation*. Intermediate tree structures for each of the translation phases can be extracted from the Lucy system to guide the hybrid system. Sadly, only the 1-best path through these three phases is given, so no alternative translation possibilities can be extracted from the given data; a fact that clearly limits the potential for more deeply integrated hybrid translation approaches. Nevertheless, the availability of the 1-best trees already allows to improve the translation quality of the RBMT system as we will show in this paper.

Moses SMT System We used a state-of-the-art Moses SMT system to create statistical phrase-based translations of our input text. Moses has been modified so that it returns the translation results together with the bidirectional word alignments between the source texts and the translations. Again, we make use of markup which helps to identify unknown words as these will later guide the factored substitution method. Both of the translation models and the language models within our SMT systems were only trained with lower-cased and tokenized Europarl training data. The system used sets of feature weights determined using data sets also from Europarl (test2008). In addition, we used LDC gigaword corpus to train large scale n-gram language models to be used in our hybrid system. We tokenized the source texts using the standard tokenizers available from the shared task website. The SMT translations are recased before being fed into the hybrid system together with the word alignment information.The hybrid system can easily be adapted to support other statistical translation engines. If the alignment information is not available, a suitable alignment tool would be necessary to compute it as the alignment is a key requirement for the hybrid system.

2.2 Aligning RBMT and SMT Output

We compute alignment in several components of the hybrid system, namely:

source-text-to-tree: we first find an alignment between the source text and the corresponding analysis tree(s). As Lucy tends to subdivide large sentences into several smaller units, it sometimes becomes necessary to align more than one tree structure to a given source sentence.

analysis-transfer-generation: for each of the analysis trees, we re-construct the path from its tree nodes, via the transfer tree, and their corresponding generation tree nodes.

tree-to-target-text: similarly to the first alignment process, we find a mapping between generation tree nodes and the actual translation output of the RBMT system.

source-text-to-tokenized: as the Lucy RBMT system works on non-tokenized input text and our Moses system takes tokenized input, we need to align the source text to its tokenized form.

Given the aforementioned alignments, we can then correlate phrases from the rule-based translation with their counterparts from the statistical translation, both on source or target side. As our hybrid approach relies on the identification of such phrase pairs, the computation of the different alignments is critical to obtain good combination performance.

Please note that all these tree-based alignments can be computed with a very high accuracy. However, due to the nature of statistical word alignment, the same does not hold for the alignment obtained from the Moses system. If the alignment process has produced erroneous phrase tables, it is very likely that Lucy phrases and their "aligned" SMT matches simply will not fit. Or put the other way round: the better the underlying SMT word alignment, the greater the potential of the hybrid substitution approach.

2.3 Factored Substitution

Given the results of the alignment process, we can then identify "interesting" phrases for substitution. Following our experimental setup from last year's shared task, we again decided to focus on *noun phrases* as these seem to be best-suited for in-place swapping of phrases. Our initial assumption is that SMT phrases are better on a lexical level, hence we aim to replace Lucy's noun phrases by their Moses counterparts.

Still, we want to perform the substitution in a controlled manner in order to avoid problems or non-matching insertions. For this, we have (manually) derived a set of *factors* that are checked for each of the phrase pairs that are processed. The factors are described briefly below:

identical? simply checks whether two candidate phrases are identical.

too complex? a Lucy phrase is "too complex" to substitute if it contains more than 2 embedded noun phrases.

many-to-one? this factor checks if a Lucy phrase containing more than one word is mapped to a Moses phrase with only one token.

contains pronoun? checks if the Lucy phrase contains a pronoun.

contains verb? checks if the Lucy phrase contains a verb.

unknown? checks whether one of the phrases is marked as "unknown".

length mismatch computes the number of words for both phrases and checks if the absolute difference is too large.

language model computes language model scores for both phrases and checks which is more likely according to the LM.

All of these factors have been designed and adjusted during an internal development phase using data from previous shared tasks.

2.4 Post-processing Steps

After the hybrid translation has been computed, we perform several post-processing steps to clean up and finalize the result:

cleanup first, we perform basic cleanup operations such as whitespace normalization, capitalizing the first word in each sentence, etc.

multi-words then, we take care of proper handling of multi-word expressions. Using the tree structures from the RBMT system we eliminate superfluous whitespace and join multi-words, even if they were separated in the SMT phrase.

prepositions finally, we give prepositions a special treatment. Experience from last year's shared task had shown that things like double prepositions contributed to a large extent to the amount of avoidable errors. We tried to circumvent this class of error by identifying the correct prepositions; erroneous prepositions are removed.

3 Hybrid Translation Analysis

We evaluated the intermediate outputs using BLEU (Papineni et al., 2001) against human references as in table 3. The BLEU score is calculated in lower case after the text tokenization. The translation systems compared are Moses, Lucy, Google and our hybrid system with different configurations:

Hybrid: we use the language model with case information and substitute some NPs in Lucy outputs by Moses outputs.

Hybrid LLM: same as Hybrid but we use a larger language model.

Table 1: Intermediate results of BLEU[%] scores for WMT10 shared task.

System	de→en	en→de	fr→en	en→fr	es→en	en→es
Moses	18.32	12.66	22.26	20.06	24.28	24.72
Lucy	16.85	12.38	18.49	17.61	21.09	20.85
Google	25.64	18.51	28.53	28.70	32.77	32.20
Hybrid	17.29	13.05	18.92	19.58	22.53	23.55
Hybrid LLM	17.37	13.73	18.93	19.76	22.61	23.66
Hybrid SG	17.43	14.40	19.67	20.55	24.37	24.99
Hybrid NCLM	17.38	14.42	19.56	20.55	24.41	24.92

Hybrid SG: same as Hybrid but the NP substitutions are based on Google output instead of Moses translations.

Hybrid NCLM: same as Hybrid but we use the language model without case information.

We participated in the translation evaluation in six language pairs: German to English (de→en), English to German (en→de), French to English (fr→en), English to French (en→fr), Spanish to English (es→en) and English to Spanish (en→es). As shown in table 3, the Moses translation system achieves better results overall than the Lucy system does. Google's system outperforms other systems in all language pairs. The hybrid translation as described in section 2 improves the Lucy translation quality with a BLEU score up to 2.7% absolutely.

As we apply a larger language model or a language model without case information, the translation performance can be improved further. One major problem in the hybrid translation is that the Moses outputs are still not good enough to replace the Lucy outputs, therefore we experimented on a hybrid translation of Google and Lucy systems and substitute some unrelaible NP translations by the Google's translations. The results in the line of 'Hybrid SG' shows that the hybrid translation quality can be enhanced if the translation system where we select substitutions is better.

4 Internal Evaluation of Results

In the analysis of the remaining issues, the following main sources of problems can be distinguished:

- Lucy's output contains structural errors that cannot be fixed by the chosen approach.
- Lucy results contain errors that could have been corrected by alternative expressions from SMT, but the constraints in our system were too restrictive to let that happen.
- The SMT engine we use generates suboptimal results that find their way into the hybrid result.
- SMT results that are good are incorporated into the hybrid results in a wrong way.

We have inspected a part of the results and classified the problems according to these criteria. As this work is still ongoing, it is too early to report numerical results for the relative frequencies of the different causes of the error. However, we can already see that three of these four cases appear frequently enough to justify further attention. We observed several cases in which the parser in the Lucy system was confused by unknown expressions and delivered results that could have been significantly improved by a more robust parsing approach. We also encountered several cases in which an expression from SMT was used although the original Lucy output would have been better. Also we still observe problems finding to correct correspondences between Lucy output and SMT output, which leads to situations where material is inserted in the wrong place, which can lead to the loss of content words in the output.

5 Conclusion and Outlook

In our contribution to the shared task we have applied the hybrid architecture from (Federmann et al., 2009) to six language pairs. We have identified and fixed many of the problems we had observed last year, and we think that, in addition to the increased coverage in laguage pairs, the overall quality has been significantly increased.

However, in the last section we characterized three main sources of problems that will require further attention. We will address these problems in the near future in the following way:

1. We will investigate in more detail the alignment issue that leads to occasional loss of content words, and we expect that a careful inspection and correction of the code will in all likelihood give us a good remedy.

2. The problem of picking expressions from the SMT output that appear more probable to the language model although they are inferior to the original expression from the RBMT system is more difficult to fix. We will try to find better thresholds and biases that can at least reduce the number of cases in which this type of degradation happen.

3. Finally, we will also address the robustness issue that leads to suboptimal structures from the RBMT engine caused by parsing failures.

Our close collaboration with Lucy enables us to address these issues in a very effective way via the inspection and classification of intermediate structures and, if these structures indicate parsing problems, the generation of variants of the input sentence that facilitate correct parsing.

Acknowledgments

This work was supported by the EuroMatrixPlus project (IST-231720) which is funded by the European Commission under the Seventh Framework Programme. The authors want to thank Michael Jellinghaus and Bastian Simon for help with the inspection of intermediate results and classification of errors.

References

Juan A. Alonso and Gregor Thurmair. 2003. The Comprendium Translator system. In *Proc. of the Ninth MT Summit.*

Christian Federmann, Silke Theison, Andreas Eisele, Hans Uszkoreit, Yu Chen, Michael Jellinghaus, and Sabine Hunsicker. 2009. Translation combination using factored word substitution. In *Proceedings of the Fourth Workshop on Statistical Machine Transla tion*, pages 70–74, Athens, Greece, March. Association for Computational Linguistics.

Philipp Koehn, Hieu Hoang, Alexandra Birch, Chris Callison-Burch, Marcello Federico, Nicola Bertoldi, Brooke Cowan, Wade Shen, Christine Moran, Richard Zens, Chris Dyer, Ondrej Bojar, Alexandra Constantin, and Evan Herbst. 2007. Moses: Open source toolkit for statistical machine translation. In *Proc. of ACL Demo and Poster Sessions*, pages 177–180, June.

Kishore Papineni, Salim Roukos, Todd Ward, and Wei-Jing Zhu. 2001. Bleu: a method for automatic evaluation of machine translation. IBM Research Report RC22176(W0109-022), IBM.

Improved Features and Grammar Selection for Syntax-Based MT

Greg Hanneman and **Jonathan Clark** and **Alon Lavie**
Language Technologies Institute
Carnegie Mellon University
Pittsburgh, PA 15213 USA
{ghannema, jhclark, alavie}@cs.cmu.edu

Abstract

We present the Carnegie Mellon University Stat-XFER group submission to the WMT 2010 shared translation task. Updates to our syntax-based SMT system mainly fell in the areas of new feature formulations in the translation model and improved filtering of SCFG rules. Compared to our WMT 2009 submission, we report a gain of 1.73 BLEU by using the new features and decoding environment, and a gain of up to 0.52 BLEU from improved grammar selection.

1 Introduction

From its earlier focus on linguistically rich machine translation for resource-poor languages, the statistical transfer MT group at Carnegie Mellon University has expanded in recent years to the increasingly successful domain of syntax-based statistical MT in large-data scenarios. Our submission to the 2010 Workshop on Machine Translation is a syntax-based SMT system with a synchonous context-free grammar (SCFG), where the SCFG rules are derived from full constituency parse trees on both the source and target sides of parallel training sentences. We participated in the French-to-English shared translation task.

This year, we focused our efforts on making more and better use of syntactic grammar. Much of the work went into formulating a more expansive feature set in the translation model and a new method of assigning scores to phrase pairs and grammar rules. Following a change of decoder that allowed us to experiment with systems using much larger syntactic grammars than previously, we also adapted a technique to more intelligently pre-filter grammar rules to those most likely to be useful.

2 System Overview

We built our system on a partial selection of the provided French–English training data, using the Europarl, News Commentary, and UN sets, but ignoring the Giga-FrEn data. After tokenization and some pruning of our training data, this left us with a corpus of approximately 8.6 million sentence pairs. We word-aligned the corpus with MGIZA++ (Gao and Vogel, 2008), a multi-threaded implementation of the standard word alignment tool GIZA++ (Och and Ney, 2003). Word alignments were symmetrized with the "grow-diag-final-and" heuristic. We automatically parsed the French side of the corpus with the Berkeley parser (Petrov and Klein, 2007), while we used the fast vanilla PCFG model of the Stanford parser (Klein and Manning, 2003) for the English side. These steps resulted in a parallel parsed corpus from which to extract phrase pairs and grammar rules.

Phrase extraction involves three distinct steps. In the first, we perform standard (non-syntactic) phrase extraction according to the heuristics of phrase-based SMT (Koehn et al., 2003). In the second, we obtain syntactic phrase pairs using the tree-to-tree matching method of Lavie et al. (2008). Briefly, this method aligns nodes in parallel parse trees by projecting up from the word alignments. A source-tree node s will be aligned to a target-tree node t if the word alignments in the yield of s all land within the yield of t, and vice versa. This node alignment is similar in spirit to the subtree alignment method of Zhechev and Way (2008), except our method is based on the specific Viterbi word alignment links found for each

Proceedings of the Joint 5th Workshop on Statistical Machine Translation and MetricsMATR, pages 82–87,
Uppsala, Sweden, 15-16 July 2010.

sentence rather than on the general word translation probabilities computed for the corpus as a whole. This enables us to use efficient dynamic programming to infer node alignments, rather than resorting to a greedy search or the enumeration of all possible alignments. Finally, in the third step, we use the node alignments from syntactic phrase pair extraction to extract grammar rules. Each aligned node in a tree pair specifies a decomposition point for breaking the parallel trees into a series of SCFG rules. Like Galley et al. (2006), we allow "composed" (non-minimal) rules when they build entirely on lexical items. However, to control the size of the grammar, we do not produce composed rules that build on other non-terminals, nor do we produce multiple possible rules when we encounter unaligned words. Another difference is that we discard internal structure of composed lexical rules so that we produce SCFG rules rather than synchronous tree substitution grammar rules.

The extracted phrase pairs and grammar rules are collected together and scored according to a variety of features (Section 3). Instead of decoding with the very large complete set of extracted grammar rules, we select only a small number of rules meeting certain criteria (Section 4).

In contrast to previous years, when we used the Stat-XFER decoder, this year we switched to the the Joshua decoder (Li et al., 2009) to take advantage of its more efficient architecture and implementation of modern decoding techniques, such as cube pruning and multi-threading. We also managed system-building workflows with LoonyBin (Clark and Lavie, 2010), a toolkit for managing multi-step experiments across different servers or computing clusters. Section 5 details our experimental results.

3 Translation Model Construction

One major improvement in our system this year is the feature scores we applied to our grammar and phrase pairs. Inspired largely by the Syntax-Augmented MT system (Zollmann and Venugopal, 2006), our translation model contains 22 features in addition to the language model. In contrast to earlier formulations of our features (Hanneman and Lavie, 2009), our maximum-likelihood features are now based on a strict separation between counts drawn from non-syntactic phrase extraction heuristics and our syntactic rule extractor; no feature is estimated from counts in both spaces.

We define an aggregate rule instance as a 5-tuple $r = (L, S, T, C_{phr}, C_{syn})$ that contains a left-hand-side label L, a sequence of terminals and non-terminals for the source (S) and target (T) right-hand sides, and aggregated counts from phrase-based SMT extraction heuristics C_{phr} and the syntactic rule extractor C_{syn}.

In preparation for feature scoring, we:

1. Run phrase instance extraction using standard phrase-based SMT heuristics to obtain tuples $(\texttt{PHR}, S, T, C_{phr}, \emptyset)$ where S and T never contain non-terminals
2. Run syntactic rule instance extraction as described in Section 2 above to obtain tuples $(L, S, T, \emptyset, C_{syn})$
3. Share non-syntactic counts such that, for any two tuples $r_1 = (\texttt{PHR}, S, T, C_{phr}, \emptyset)$ and $r_2 = (L_2, S, T, \emptyset, C_{syn})$ with equivalent S and T values, we produce $r_2 = (L_2, S, T, C_{phr}, C_{syn})$

Note that there is no longer any need to retain PHR rules $(\texttt{PHR}, S, T)$ that have syntactic equivalents $(L \neq \texttt{PHR}, S, T)$ since they have the same features In addition, we assume there will be no tuples where S and T contain non-terminals while $C_{phr} = 0$ and $C_{syn} > 0$. That is, the syntactic phrases are a subset of non-syntactic phrases.

3.1 Maximum-Likelihood Features

Our most traditional features are $P_{phr}(T \mid S)$ and $P_{phr}(S \mid T)$, estimated using only counts C_{phr}. These features apply only to rules not containing any non-terminals. They are equivalent to the phrase $P(T \mid S)$ and $P(S \mid T)$ features from the Moses decoder, even when $L \neq$ PHR. In contrast, we used $P_{syn \cup phr}(L, S \mid T)$ and $P_{syn \cup phr}(L, T \mid S)$ last year, which applied to all rules. The new features are no longer subject to increased sparsity as the number of non-terminals in the grammar increases.

We also have grammar rule probabilities $P_{syn}(T \mid S)$, $P_{syn}(S \mid T)$, $P_{syn}(L \mid S)$, $P_{syn}(L \mid T)$, and $P_{syn}(L \mid S, T)$ estimated using C_{syn}; these apply only to rules where S and T contain non-terminals. By no longer including counts from phrase-based SMT extraction heuristics in these features, we encourage rules where $L \neq \texttt{PHR}$ since the smaller counts from the rule learner would have otherwise been overshadowed by the much larger counts from the phrase-based SMT heuristics.

Finally, we estimate "not labelable" (NL) features $P_{syn}(\text{NL} \mid S)$ and $P_{syn}(\text{NL} \mid T)$. With R denoting the set of all extracted rules,

$$P_{syn}(\text{NL} \mid S) = \frac{C_{syn}}{\sum_{r' \in R \text{ s.t. } S'=S} C'_{syn}} \quad (1)$$

$$P_{syn}(\text{NL} \mid T) = \frac{C_{syn}}{\sum_{r' \in R \text{ s.t. } T'=T} C'_{syn}} \quad (2)$$

We use additive smoothing (with $n = 1$ for our experiments) to avoid a probability of 0 when there is no syntactic label for an (S, T) pair. These features can encourage syntactic rules when syntax is likely given a particular string since probability mass is often distributed among several different syntactic labels.

3.2 Instance Features

We add several features that use sufficient statistics local to each rule. First, we add three binary low-count features that take on the value 1 when the frequency of the rule is exactly 1, 2, or 3. There are also two indicator features related to syntax: one each that fires when L = PHR and when $L \neq$ PHR. Other indicator features analyze the abstractness of grammar rules: $A_S = 1$ when the source side contains only non-terminals, $A_T = 1$ when the target side contains only non-terminals, TGTINSERTION $= 1$ when $A_S = 1, A_T = 0$, SRCDELETION $= 1$ when $A_S = 0, A_T = 1$, and INTERLEAVED $= 1$ when $A_S = 0, A_T = 0$.

Bidirectional lexical probabilities for each rule are calculated from a unigram lexicon MLE-estimated over aligned word pairs in the training corpus, as is the default in Moses.

Finally, we include a glue rule indicator feature that fires whenever a glue rule is applied during decoding. In the Joshua decoder, these monotonic rules stitch syntactic parse fragments together at no model cost.

4 Grammar Selection

With extracted grammars typically reaching tens of millions of unique rules — not to mention phrase pairs — our systems clearly face an engineering challenge when attempting to include the full grammar at decoding time. Iglesias et al. (2009) classified SCFG rules according to the pattern of terminals and non-terminals on the rules' right-hand sides, and found that certain patterns could be entirely left out of the grammar without loss of MT quality. In particular, large classes of monotonic rules could be removed without a loss in automatic metric scores, while small classes of reordering rules contributed much more to the success of the system. Inspired by that approach, we passed our full set of extracted grammar rule instances through a filter after scoring. Using the rule notation from Section 3, the filter retained only those rules that matched one of the following patterns:

$$\begin{aligned} S = X^1\, w, &\quad T = w\, X^1 \\ S = w\, X^1, &\quad T = X^1\, w \\ S = X^1\, X^2, &\quad T = X^2\, X^1 \\ S = X^1\, X^2, &\quad T = X^1\, X^2 \end{aligned}$$

where X represents any non-terminal and w represents any span of one or more terminals. The choice of the specific reordering patterns above captures our intuition that binary swaps are a fundamental ordering divergence between languages, while the inclusion of the abstract monotonic pattern $(X^1\, X^2, X^1\, X^2)$ ensures that the decoder is not disproportionately biased towards applying reordering rules without supporting lexical evidence merely because in-order rules are left out.

Orthogonally to the pattern-based pruning, we also selected grammars by sorting grammar rules in decreasing order of frequency count and using the top n in the decoder. We experimented with n = 0, 100, 1000, and 10,000. In all cases of grammar selection, we disallowed rules that inserted unaligned target-side terminals unless the inserted terminals were among the top 100 most frequent unigrams in the target-side vocabulary.

5 Results and Analysis

5.1 Comparison with WMT 2009 Results

We performed our initial development work on an updated version of our previous WMT submission (Hanneman et al., 2009) so that the effects of our changes could be directly compared. Our 2009 system was trained from the full Europarl and News Commentary data available that year, plus the pre-release version of the Giga-FrEn data, for a total of 9.4 million sentence pairs. We used the news-dev2009a set for minimum error-rate training and tested system performance on news-dev2009b. To maintain continuity with our previously reported scores, we report new scores here using the same training, tuning, and testing sets, using the uncased versions of IBM-style

System Configuration	METEOR	BLEU
1. WMT '09 submission	0.5263	0.2073
2. Joshua decoder	0.5231	0.2158
3. New TM features	0.5348	0.2246

Table 1: Dev test results (on news-dev2009b) from our WMT 2009 system when updating decoding environment and feature formulations.

System Configuration	METEOR	BLEU
1. n = 100	0.5314	0.2200
2. n = 100, filtered	0.5341	0.2242
3. n = 1000	0.5324	0.2206
4. n = 1000, filtered	0.5330	0.2233
5. n = 10,000	0.5332	0.2198
6. n = 10,000, filtered	0.5350	0.2250

Table 2: Dev test results (on news-dev2009b) from our WMT 2009 system with and without pattern-based grammar selection.

BLEU 1.04 (Papineni et al., 2002) and METEOR 0.6 (Lavie and Agarwal, 2007).

Table 1 shows the effect of our new scoring and decoding environment. Line 2 uses the same extracted phrase pairs and grammar rules as line 1, but the system is tuned and tested with the Joshua decoder instead of Stat-XFER. For line 3, we rescored the extracted phrase pairs from lines 1 and 2 using the updated features discussed in Section 3.[1] The difference in automatic metric scores shows a significant benefit from both the new decoder and the updated feature formulations: 0.8 BLEU points from the change in decoder, and 0.9 BLEU points from the expanded set of 22 translation model features.

Our next test was to examine the usefulness of the pattern-based grammar selection described in Section 4. For various numbers of rules n, Table 2 shows the scores obtained with and without filtering the grammar before the n most frequent rules are skimmed off for use. We observe a small but consistent gain in scores from the grammar selection process, up to half a BLEU point in the largest-grammar systems (lines 5 and 6).

[1]In line 2, we did not control for difference in formulation of the translation length feature: Stat-XFER uses a length ratio, while Joshua uses a target word count. Line 3 does not include 26 manually selected grammar rules present in lines 1 and 2; this is because our new feature scoring requires information from the grammar rules that was not present in our 2009 extracted resources.

Source	Target
un rôle AP^1	ADJP^1 roles
l' instabilité AP^1	ADJP^1 instability
l' argent PP^1	NP^1 money
une pression AP^1	ADJP^1 pressure
la gouvernance AP^1	ADJP^1 governance
la concurrence AP^1	ADJP^1 competition
des preuves AP^1	ADJP^1 evidence
les outils AP^1	ADJP^1 tools
des changements AP^1	ADJP^1 changes

Table 3: Rules fitting the pattern $(S = w\ X^1, T = X^1\ w)$ that applied on the news-test2010 test set.

5.2 WMT 2010 Results and Analysis

We built the WMT 2010 version of our system from the training data described in Section 2. (The system falls under the strictly constrained track: we used neither the Giga-FrEn data for training nor the LDC Gigaword corpora for language modeling.) We used the provided news-test2008 set for system tuning, while news-test2009 served as our 2010 dev test set. Based on the results in Table 2, our official submission to this year's shared task was constructed as in line 6, with 10,000 syntactic grammar rules chosen after a pattern-based grammar selection step. On the news-test2010 test set, this system scored 0.2327 on case-insensitive IBM-style BLEU 1.04, 0.5614 on METEOR 0.6, and 0.5519 on METEOR 1.0 (Lavie and Denkowski, 2009).

The actual application of grammar rules in the system is quite surprising. Despite having a grammar of 10,000 rules at its disposal, the decoder chose to only apply a total of 20 unique rules in 392 application instances in the 2489-sentence news-test2010 set. On a per-sentence basis, this is actually *fewer* rule applications than our system performed last year with a 26-rule handpicked grammar! The most frequently applied rules are fully abstract, monotonic structure-building rules, such as for stitching together compound noun phrases with adverbial phrases or prepositional phrases. Nine of the 20 rules, listed in Table 3, demonstrate the effect of our pattern-based grammar selection. These partially lexicalized rules fit the pattern $(S = w\ X^1, T = X^1\ w)$ and handle cases of lexicalized binary reordering between French and English. Though the overall impact of these rules on automatic metric scores is presumably quite small, we believe that the key to effective syntactic grammars in our MT approach lies in retaining precise rules of this type for common linguistically motivated reordering patterns.

The above pattern of rule applications is also observed in our dev test set, news-test2009, where 16 distinct rules apply a total of 352 times. Seven of the fully abstract rules and three of the lexicalized rules that applied on news-test2009 also applied on news-test2010, while a further two abstract and four lexicalized rules applied on news-test2009 alone. We thus have a general trend of a set of general rules applying with higher frequency across test sets, while the set of lexicalized rules used varies according to the particular set.

Since, overall, we still do not see as much grammar application in our systems as we would like, we plan to concentrate future work on further improving this aspect. This includes a more detailed study of grammar filtering or refinement to select the most useful rules. We would also like to explore the effect of the features of Section 3 individually, on different language pairs, and using different grammar types.

Acknowledgments

This research was supported in part by NSF grant IIS-0534217 (LETRAS) and the DARPA GALE program. We thank Yahoo! for the use of the M45 research computing cluster, where we ran many steps of our experimental pipeline.

References

Jonathan Clark and Alon Lavie. 2010. LoonyBin: Keeping language technologists sane through automated management of experimental (hyper)workflows. In *Proceedings of the Seventh International Language Resources and Evaluation (LREC '10)*, Valletta, Malta, May.

Michel Galley, Jonathan Graehl, Kevin Knight, Daniel Marcu, Steve DeNeefe, Wei Wang, and Ignacio Thayer. 2006. Scalable inference and training of context-rich syntactic translation models. In *Proceedings of the 21st International Conference on Computational Linguistics and 44th Annual Meeting of the ACL*, pages 961–968, Sydney, Australia, July.

Qin Gao and Stephan Vogel. 2008. Parallel implementations of word alignment tool. In *Software Engineering, Testing, and Quality Assurance for Natural Language Processing*, pages 49–57, Columbus, OH, June.

Greg Hanneman and Alon Lavie. 2009. Decoding with syntactic and non-syntactic phrases in a syntax-based machine translation system. In *Proceedings of the Third Workshop on Syntax and Structure in Statistical Translations*, pages 1–9, Boulder, CO, June.

Greg Hanneman, Vamshi Ambati, Jonathan H. Clark, Alok Parlikar, and Alon Lavie. 2009. An improved statistical transfer systems for French–English machine translation. In *Proceedings of the Fourth Workshop on Statistical Machine Translation*, pages 140–144, Athens, Greece, March.

Gonzalo Iglesias, Adrià de Gispert, Eduardo R. Banga, and William Byrne. 2009. Rule filtering by pattern for efficient hierarchical translation. In *Proceedings of the 12th Conference of the European Chapter of the ACL*, pages 380–388, Athens, Greece, March–April.

Dan Klein and Christopher D. Manning. 2003. Fast exact inference with a factored model for natural language parsing. In *Advances in Neural Information Processing Systems 15*, pages 3–10. MIT Press, Cambridge, MA.

Philipp Koehn, Franz Josef Och, and Daniel Marcu. 2003. Statistical phrase-based translation. In *Proceedings of HLT-NAACL 2003*, pages 48–54, Edmonton, Alberta, May–June.

Alon Lavie and Abhaya Agarwal. 2007. METEOR: An automatic metric for MT evaluation with high levels of correlation with human judgments. In *Proceedings of the Second Workshop on Statistical Machine Translation*, pages 228–231, Prague, Czech Republic, June.

Alon Lavie and Michael J. Denkowski. 2009. The METEOR metric for automatic evaluation of machine translation. *Machine Translation*, 23(2–3):105–115.

Alon Lavie, Alok Parlikar, and Vamshi Ambati. 2008. Syntax-driven learning of sub-sentential translation equivalents and translation rules from parsed parallel corpora. In *Proceedings of the Second ACL Workshop on Syntax and Structure in Statistical Translation*, pages 87–95, Columbus, OH, June.

Zhifei Li, Chris Callison-Burch, Chris Dyer, Juri Ganitkevitch, Sanjeev Khudanpur, Lane Schwartz, Wren N.G. Thornton, Jonathan Weese, and Omar F. Zaidan. 2009. Joshua: An open source toolkit for parsing-based machine translation. In *Proceedings of the Fourth Workshop on Statistical Machine Translation*, pages 135–139, Athens, Greece, March.

Franz Josef Och and Hermann Ney. 2003. A systematic comparison of various statistical alignment models. *Computational Linguistics*, 29(1):19–51.

Kishore Papineni, Salim Roukos, Todd Ward, and Wei-Jing Zhu. 2002. BLEU: A method for automatic evalution of machine translation. In *Proceedings of the 40th Annual Meeting of the Association for Computational Linguistics*, pages 311–318, Philadelphia, PA, July.

Slav Petrov and Dan Klein. 2007. Improved inference for unlexicalized parsing. In *Proceedings of NAACL HLT 2007*, pages 404–411, Rochester, NY, April.

Ventsislav Zhechev and Andy Way. 2008. Automatic generation of parallel treebanks. In *Proceedings of the 22nd International Conference on Computational Linguistics*, pages 1105–1112, Manchester, England, August.

Andreas Zollmann and Ashish Venugopal. 2006. Syntax augmented machine translation via chart parsing. In *Proceedings of the Workshop on Statistical Machine Translation*, pages 138–141, New York, NY, June.

FBK at WMT 2010: Word Lattices for Morphological Reduction and Chunk-based Reordering

Christian Hardmeier, Arianna Bisazza and Marcello Federico
Fondazione Bruno Kessler
Human Language Technologies
Trento, Italy
{hardmeier,bisazza,federico}@fbk.eu

Abstract

FBK participated in the WMT 2010 Machine Translation shared task with phrase-based Statistical Machine Translation systems based on the Moses decoder for English-German and German-English translation. Our work concentrates on exploiting the available language modelling resources by using linear mixtures of large 6-gram language models and on addressing linguistic differences between English and German with methods based on word lattices. In particular, we use lattices to integrate a morphological analyser for German into our system, and we present some initial work on rule-based word reordering.

1 System overview

The Human Language Technologies group at Fondazione Bruno Kessler (FBK) participated in the WMT 2010 Machine Translation (MT) evaluation with systems for English-German and German-English translation. While the English-German system we submitted was relatively simple, we put some more effort into the inverse translation direction to make better use of the abundance of language modelling data available for English and to address the richness of German morphology, which makes it hard for a Statistical Machine Translation (SMT) system to achieve good vocabulary coverage. In the remainder of this section, an overview of the common features of our systems will be given. The next two sections provide a more detailed description of our approaches to language modelling, morphological preprocessing and word reordering.

Both of our systems were based on the Moses decoder (Koehn et al., 2007). They were similar to the WMT 2010 Moses baseline system. Instead of lowercasing the training data and adding a recasing step, we retained the data in document case throughout our system, except for the morphologically normalised word forms described in section 3. Our phrase tables were trained with the standard Moses training script, then filtered based on statistical significance according to the method described by Johnson et al. (2007). Finally, we used Minimum Bayes Risk decoding (Kumar and Byrne, 2004) based on the BLEU score (Papineni et al., 2002).

2 Language modelling

At the 2009 NIST MT evaluation, our system obtained good results using a mixture of linearly interpolated language models (LMs) combining data from different sources. As the training data provided for the present evaluation campaign again included a large set of language modelling corpora from different sources, especially for English as a target language, we decided to adopt the same strategy. The partial corpora for English and their sizes can be found in table 1. Our base models of the English Gigaword texts were trained on version 3 of the corpus (LDC2007T07). We trained separate language models for the new data from the years 2007 and 2008 included in version 4 (LDC2009T13). Apart from the monolingual English data, we also included language models trained on the English part of the additional parallel datasets supplied for the French-English and Czech-English tasks. All the models were estimated as 6-gram models with Kneser-Ney smoothing using the IRSTLM language modelling toolkit (Federico et al., 2008).

For technical reasons, we were unable to use all the language models during decoding. We therefore selected a subset of the models with the following data selection procedure:

1. For a linear mixture of the complete set of 24 language models, we estimated a set of

Proceedings of the Joint 5th Workshop on Statistical Machine Translation and MetricsMATR, pages 88–92,
Uppsala, Sweden, 15-16 July 2010. ©2010 Association for Computational Linguistics

Corpus	*n-grams*
Europarl v5	115,702,157
News	1,437,562,740
News commentary 10	10,381,511
Gigaword v3: 6 models	7,990,828,834
Gigaword 2007/08: 6 models	1,418,281,597
10^9 fr-en	1,190,593,051
UNDOC fr-en	333,120,732
CzEng: 7 models	153,355,518
Total: 24 models	**12,649,826,140**

Table 1: Language modelling corpora for English

LMs	*Perplexity*	
	DEV	*EVAL*
2	188.57	181.38
5	163.68	158.99
10	156.43	151.73
15	154.71	144.98
20	154.39	144.91
24	154.42	144.92

Table 2: Perplexities of LM mixtures

optimal interpolation weights to minimise the perplexity of the mixture model on the `news-test2008` development set.

2. By sorting the mixture coefficients in descending order, we obtained an ordering of the language models by their importance with respect to the development set. We created partial mixtures by selecting the top n models according to this order and retraining the mixture weights with the same algorithm.

Computing the perplexities of these partial mixtures on the `news-test2008` (DEV) and `newstest2009` (EVAL) corpora shows that significant improvements can be obtained up to a mixtures size of about 15 elements. As this size still turned out to be too large to be managed by our systems, we used a 5-element mixture in our final submission (see table 3 for details about the mixture and table 4 for the evaluation results of the submitted systems).

For the English-German system, the only corpora available for the target language were Europarl v5, News commentary v10 and the monolingual News corpus. Similar experiments showed that the News corpus was by far the most important for the text genre to be translated and that including language models trained on the other

Weight	*Language model*
0.368023	News
0.188156	10^9 fr-en
0.174802	Gigaword v3: NYT
0.144465	Gigaword v3: AFP
0.124553	Gigaword v3: APW

Table 3: 5-element LM mixture used for decoding

	BLEU-cased	BLEU
en-de		
primary	15.5	15.8
secondary	15.3	15.6
primary: only News language model *secondary:* linear mixture of 3 LMs		
de-en		
primary	20.9	21.9
secondary	20.3	21.3
primary: morph. reduction, linear mixture of 5 LMs *secondary:* reordering, only News LM		

Table 4: Evaluation results of submitted systems

corpora could even degrade system performance. We therefore decided not to use Europarl or News commentary for language modelling in our primary submission. However, we submitted a secondary system using a mixture of language models based on all three corpora.

3 Morphological reduction and decompounding of German

Compounding is a highly productive part of German noun morphology. Unlike in English, German compound nouns are usually spelt as single words, which greatly increases the vocabulary. For a Machine Translation system, this property of the language causes a high number of out-of-vocabulary (OOV) words. It is likely that many compounds in an input text have not been seen in the training corpus. We addressed this problem by splitting compounds in the German source text.

Compound splitting was done using the Gertwol morphological analyser (Koskenniemi and Haapalainen, 1996), a linguistically informed system based on two-level finite state morphology. Since Gertwol outputs all possible analyses of a word form without taking into account the context, the output has to be disambiguated. For this purpose, we used part-of-speech (POS) tags obtained from the TreeTagger (Schmid, 1994) along with a set of POS-based heuristic disambiguation rules provided to us by the Institute of Computational Linguistics of the University of Zurich.

As a side effect, Gertwol outputs the base forms of all words that it processes: Nominative singular of nouns, infinitive of verbs etc. We decided to combine the tokens analysed by Gertwol, whether or not they had been decompounded and lowercased, in a further attempt to reduce data sparseness, with their original form in a word lattice (see fig. 1) and to let the decoder make the choice between the two according to the translations the phrase table can provide for each.

Our word lattices are similar to those used by Dyer et al. (2008) for handling word segmentation in Chinese and Arabic. For each word that was segmented by Gertwol, we provide exactly one alternative edge labelled with the component words and base forms as identified by Gertwol, after removing linking morphemes. The edge transition probabilities are used to identify the source of an edge: their values are $e^{-1} = 0.36788$ for edges deriving from Gertwol analysis and $e^0 = 1$ for edges carrying unprocessed words. Tokens whose decompounded base form according to Gertwol is identical to the surface form in the input are represented by a single edge with transition probability $e^{-0.5} = 0.606531$. These transition probabilities translate into a binary feature with values -1, -0.5 and 0 after taking logarithms in the decoder. The feature weight is determined by Minimum Error-Rate Training (Och, 2003), together with the weights of the other feature functions used in the decoder. During system training, the processed version of the training corpus was concatenated with the unprocessed text.

Experiments show that decompounding and morphological analysis have a significant impact on the performance of the MT system. After these steps, the OOV rate of the `newstest2009` test set decreases from 5.88 % to 3.21 %. Using only the News language model, the BLEU score of our development system (measured on the `newstest2009` corpus) increases from 18.77 to 19.31. There is an interesting interaction with the language models. While using a linear mixture of 15 language models instead of just the News LM does not improve the performance of the baseline system (BLEU score 18.78 instead of 18.77), the BLEU score of the 15-LM system increases to 20.08 when adding morphological reduction. In the baseline system, the additional language models did not have a noticeable effect on translation quality; however, their impact was realised in the decompounding system.

4 Word reordering

Current SMT systems are based on the assumption that the word order of the source and the target languages are fundamentally similar. While the models permit some local reordering, systematic differences in word order involving movements of more than a few words pose major problems. In particular, Statistical Machine Translation between German and English is notoriously impacted by the different fundamental word order in subordinate clauses, where German Subject–Object–Verb (SOV) order contrasts with English Subject–Verb–Object (SVO) order.

In our English-German system, we made the observation that the verb in an SVO subordinate clause following a punctuation mark frequently gets moved before the preceding punctuation. This movement is triggered by the German language model, which prefers verbs preceding punctuation as consistent with SOV order, and it is facilitated by the fact that the distance from the verb to the end of the preceding clause is often smaller than the distance to the end of the current phrase, so moving the verb backwards results in a better score from the distance-based reordering model. This tendency can be counteracted effectively by enabling the Moses decoder's `monotone-at-punctuation` feature, which makes sure that words are not reordered across punctuation marks. The result is a modest gain from 14.28 to 14.38 BLEU points (`newstest2009`).

In the German-English system, we applied a chunk-based technique to produce lattices representing multiple permutations of the test sentences in order to enable long-range reorderings of verb phrases. This approach is similar to the reordering technique based on part-of-speech tags presented by Niehues and Kolss (2009), which results in the addition of a large number of reordering paths to the lattices. By contrast, we assume that verb reorderings only occur between shallow syntax chunks, and not within them. This makes it possible to limit the number of long-range reordering options in an effective way.

We used the TreeTagger to perform shallow syntax chunking of the German text. By man-

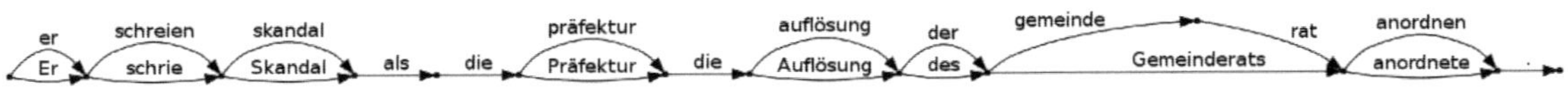

Figure 1: Word lattice for morphological reduction

Sonst [drohe]$_{VC}$, dass auch [weitere Länder]$_{NC}$ [vom Einbruch]$_{PC}$ [betroffen sein würden]$_{VC}$.

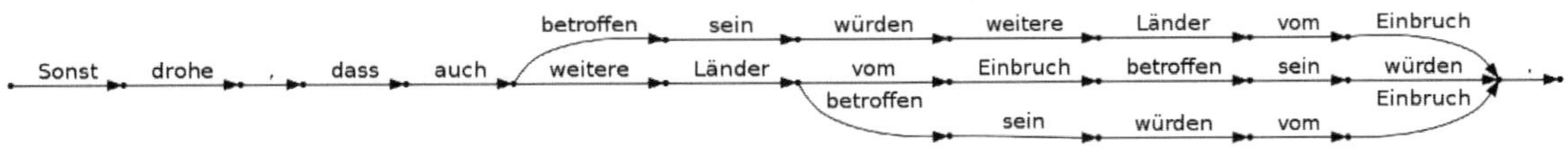

Figure 2: Chunk reordering lattice

	BLEU	
	test-09	test-10
Baseline	18.77	20.1
+ chunk-based reordering	18.94	20.3
Morphological reduction	19.31	20.6
+ chunk-based reordering	19.79	21.1

note: only News LM, case-sensitive evaluation

Table 5: Results with morphological reduction and chunk reordering on `newstest 2009/2010`

ual inspection of a data sample, we then identified a few recurrent patterns of long reorderings involving the verbs. In particular, we focused on clause-final verbs in German SOV clauses, which we move to the left in order to approximate the English SVO word order. For each sentence a chunk-based lattice is created, which is then expanded into a word lattice like the one shown in fig. 2. The lattice representation provides the decoder with up to three possible reorderings for a particular verb chunk. It always retains the original word order as an alternative input.

For technical reasons, we were unable to prepare a system with reordering, morphological reduction and all language models in time for the shared task. Our secondary submission with reordering is therefore not comparable with our best system, which includes more language models and morphological reduction. In subsequent experiments, we combined morphological reduction with chunk-based reordering (table 5). When morphological reduction is used, the reordering approach yields an improvement of about 0.5 BLEU percentage points.

5 Conclusions

There are three important features specific to the FBK systems at WMT 2010: mixtures of large language models, German morphological reduction and decompounding and word reordering. Our approach to using large language models proved successful at the 2009 NIST MT evaluation. In the present evaluation, its effectiveness was reduced by a number of technical problems, which were mostly due to the limitations of disk access throughput in our parallel computing environment. We are working on methods to reduce and distribute disk accesses to large language models, which will be implemented in the IRSTLM language modelling toolkit (Federico et al., 2008). By doing so, we hope to overcome the current limitations and exploit the power of language model mixtures more fully.

The Gertwol-based morphological reduction and decompounding component we used is a working solution that results in a significant improvement in translation quality. It is an alternative to the popular statistical compound splitting methods, such as the one by Koehn and Knight (2003), incorporating a greater amount of linguistic knowledge and offering morphological reduction even of simplex words to their base form in addition. It would be interesting to compare the relative performance of the two approaches systematically.

Word reordering between German and English is a complex problem. Encouraged by the success of chunk-based verb reordering lattices on Arabic-English (Bisazza and Federico, 2010), we tried to adapt the same approach to the German-English language pair. It turned out that there is a larger variety of long reordering patterns in this case. Nevertheless, some experiments performed after the official evaluation showed promising results. We plan to pursue this work in several directions: Defining a lattice weighting scheme that distinguishes between original word order and reordering paths could help the decoder select the more promising path through the lattice. Applying similar reordering rules to the training corpus would reduce the mismatch between the training data and the reordered input sentences. Finally, it would be useful to explore the impact of different distortion limits on the decoding of reordering lattices in order to find an optimal trade-off between decoder-driven short-range and lattice-driven long-range reordering.

Acknowledgements

This work was supported by the EuroMatrixPlus project (IST-231720), which is funded by the European Commission under the Seventh Framework Programme for Research and Technological Development.

References

Arianna Bisazza and Marcello Federico. 2010. Chunk-based verb reordering in VSO sentences for Arabic-English statistical machine translation. In *Proceedings of the Joint Fifth Workshop on Statistical Machine Translation and Metrics MATR*, Uppsala, Sweden, July. Association for Computational Linguistics.

Christopher Dyer, Smaranda Muresan, and Philip Resnik. 2008. Generalizing word lattice translation. In *Proceedings of ACL-08: HLT*, pages 1012–1020, Columbus, Ohio, June. Association for Computational Linguistics.

Marcello Federico, Nicola Bertoldi, and Mauro Cettolo. 2008. IRSTLM: an open source toolkit for handling large scale language models. In *Interspeech 2008*, pages 1618–1621. ISCA.

Howard Johnson, Joel Martin, George Foster, and Roland Kuhn. 2007. Improving translation quality by discarding most of the phrasetable. In *Proceedings of the 2007 Joint Conference on Empirical Methods in Natural Language Processing and Computational Natural Language Learning (EMNLP-CoNLL)*, pages 967–975, Prague, Czech Republic, June. Association for Computational Linguistics.

Philipp Koehn and Kevin Knight. 2003. Empirical methods for compound splitting. In *Proceedings of EACL*, pages 187–193.

Philipp Koehn, Hieu Hoang, Alexandra Birch, et al. 2007. Moses: open source toolkit for statistical machine translation. In *Annual meeting of the Association for Computational Linguistics: Demonstration session*, pages 177–180, Prague.

Kimmo Koskenniemi and Mariikka Haapalainen. 1996. GERTWOL – Lingsoft Oy. In Roland Hausser, editor, *Linguistische Verifikation. Dokumentation zur Ersten Morpholympics 1994*, chapter 11, pages 121–140. Niemeyer, Tübingen.

Shankar Kumar and William Byrne. 2004. Minimum bayes-risk decoding for statistical machine translation. In Daniel Marcu Susan Dumais and Salim Roukos, editors, *HLT-NAACL 2004: Main Proceedings*, pages 169–176, Boston, Massachusetts, USA, May 2 - May 7. Association for Computational Linguistics.

Jan Niehues and Muntsin Kolss. 2009. A POS-based model for long-range reorderings in SMT. In *Proceedings of the Fourth Workshop on Statistical Machine Translation*, pages 206–214, Athens, Greece, March. Association for Computational Linguistics.

Franz Josef Och. 2003. Minimum error rate training in statistical machine translation. In *Proceedings of the 41st annual meeting of the Association for Computational Linguistics*, pages 160–167, Sapporo (Japan).

Kishore Papineni, Salim Roukos, Todd Ward, and Wei-Jing Zhu. 2002. BLEU: a method for automatic evaluation of machine translation. In *Proceedings of the 40th annual meeting of the Association for Computational Linguistics*, pages 311–318, Philadelphia. ACL.

Helmut Schmid. 1994. Probabilistic part-of-speech tagging using decision trees. In *Proceedings of the International Conference on New Methods in Language Processing*, pages 44–49.

The RWTH Aachen Machine Translation System for WMT 2010

Carmen Heger, Joern Wuebker, Matthias Huck, Gregor Leusch, Saab Mansour, Daniel Stein and Hermann Ney
RWTH Aachen University
Aachen, Germany
surname@cs.rwth-aachen.de

Abstract

In this paper we describe the statistical machine translation system of the RWTH Aachen University developed for the translation task of the Fifth Workshop on Statistical Machine Translation. State-of-the-art phrase-based and hierarchical statistical MT systems are augmented with appropriate morpho-syntactic enhancements, as well as alternative phrase training methods and extended lexicon models. For some tasks, a system combination of the best systems was used to generate a final hypothesis. We participated in the constrained condition of German-English and French-English in each translation direction.

1 Introduction

This paper describes the statistical MT system used for our participation in the WMT 2010 shared translation task. We used it as an opportunity to incorporate novel methods which have been investigated at RWTH over the last year and which have proven to be successful in other evaluations.

For all tasks we used standard alignment and training tools as well as our in-house phrase-based and hierarchical statistical MT decoders. When German was involved, morpho-syntactic preprocessing was applied. An alternative phrase-training method and additional models were tested and investigated with respect to their effect for the different language pairs. For two of the language pairs we could improve performance by system combination.

An overview of the systems and models will follow in Section 2 and 3, which describe the baseline architecture, followed by descriptions of the additional system components. Morpho-syntactic analysis and other preprocessing issues are covered by Section 4. Finally, translation results for the different languages and system variants are presented in Section 5.

2 Translation Systems

For the WMT 2010 Evaluation we used standard phrase-based and hierarchical translation systems. Alignments were trained with a variant of GIZA++. Target language models are 4-gram language models trained with the SRI toolkit, using Kneser-Ney discounting with interpolation.

2.1 Phrase-Based System

Our phrase-based translation system is similar to the one described in (Zens and Ney, 2008). Phrase pairs are extracted from a word-aligned bilingual corpus and their translation probability in both directions is estimated by relative frequencies. Additional models include a standard n-gram language model, phrase-level IBM1, word-, phrase- and distortion-penalties and a discriminative reordering model as described in (Zens and Ney, 2006).

2.2 Hierarchical System

Our hierarchical phrase-based system is similar to the one described in (Chiang, 2007). It allows for gaps in the phrases by employing a context-free grammar and a CYK-like parsing during the decoding step. It has similar features as the phrase-based system mentioned above. For some systems, we only allowed the non-terminals in hierarchical phrases to be substituted with initial phrases as in (Iglesias et al., 2009), which gave better results on some language pairs. We will refer to this as "shallow rules".

2.3 System Combination

The RWTH approach to MT system combination of the French→English systems as well as the German→English systems is a refined version of the ROVER approach in ASR (Fiscus, 1997) with

Proceedings of the Joint 5th Workshop on Statistical Machine Translation and MetricsMATR, pages 93–97,
Uppsala, Sweden, 15-16 July 2010. ©2010 Association for Computational Linguistics

	German→English		French→English		English→French	
	BLEU	# Phrases	BLEU	# Phrases	BLEU	# Phrases
Standard	19.7	128M	25.5	225M	23.7	261M
FA	20.0	12M	25.9	35M	24.0	33M

Table 1: BLEU scores on Test and phrase table sizes with and without forced alignment (FA). For German→English and English→French phrase table interpolation was applied.

additional steps to cope with reordering between different hypotheses, and to use true casing information from the input hypotheses. The basic concept of the approach has been described by Matusov et al. (2006). Several improvements have been added later (Matusov et al., 2008). This approach includes an enhanced alignment and reordering framework. Alignments between the systems are learned by GIZA++, a one-to-one alignment is generated from the learned state occupation probabilities.

From these alignments, a confusion network (CN) is then built using one of the hypotheses as "skeleton" or "primary" hypothesis. We do not make a hard decision on which of the hypotheses to use for that, but instead combine all possible CNs into a single lattice. Majority voting on the generated lattice is performed using the prior probabilities for each system as well as other statistical models such as a special trigram language model. This language model is also learned on the input hypotheses. The intention is to favor longer phrases contained in individual hypotheses. The translation with the best total score within this lattice is selected as consensus translation. Scaling factors of these models are optimized similar to MERT using the Downhill Simplex algorithm. As the objective function for this optimization, we selected a linear combination of BLEU and TER with a weight of 2 on the former; a combination that has proven to deliver stable results on several MT evaluation measures in preceding experiments.

In contrast to previous years, we now include a separate consensus true casing step to exploit the true casing capabilities of some of the input systems: After generating a (lower cased) consensus translation from the CN, we sum up the counts of different casing variants of each word in a sentence over the input hypotheses, and use the majority casing over those. In previous experiments, this showed to work significantly better than using a fixed non-consensus true caser, and maintains flexibility on the input systems.

3 New Additional Models

3.1 Forced Alignment

For the German→English, French→English and English→French language tasks we applied a forced alignment procedure to train the phrase translation model with the EM algorithm, similar to the one described in (DeNero et al., 2006). Here, the phrase translation probabilities are estimated from their relative frequencies in the phrase-aligned training data. The phrase alignment is produced by a modified version of the translation decoder. In addition to providing a statistically well-founded phrase model, this has the benefit of producing smaller phrase tables and thus allowing more rapid experiments. For the language pairs German→English and English→French the best results were achieved by log-linear interpolation of the standard phrase table with the generative model. For French→English we directly used the model trained by forced alignment. A detailed description of the training procedure is given in (Wuebker et al., 2010). Table 1 shows the system performances and phrase table sizes with the standard phrase table and the one trained with forced alignment after the first EM iteration. We can see that the generative model reduces the phrase table size by 85-90% while increasing performance by 0.3% to 0.4% BLEU.

3.2 Extended Lexicon Models

In previous work, RWTH was able to show the positive impact of extended lexicon models that cope with lexical context beyond the limited horizon of phrase pairs and n-gram language models.

Mauser et al. (2009) report improvements of up to +1% in BLEU on large-scale systems for Chinese→English and Arabic→English by incorporating discriminative and trigger-based lexicon models into a state-of-the-art phrase-based decoder. They discuss how the two types of lexicon models help to select content words by capturing long-distance effects.

The triplet model is a straightforward extension of the IBM model 1 with a second trigger, and like the former is trained iteratively using the EM algorithm. In search, the triggers are usually on the source side, i.e., $p(e|f, f')$ is modeled. The path-constrained triplet model restricts the first source trigger to the aligned target word, whereas the second trigger can move along the whole source sentence. See (Hasan et al., 2008) for a detailed description and variants of the model and its training.

For the WMT 2010 evaluation, triplets modeling $p(e|f, f')$ were trained and applied directly in search for all relevant language pairs. Path-constrained models were trained on the in-domain news-commentary data only and on the news-commentary plus the Europarl data. Although experience from similar setups indicates that triplet lexicon models can be beneficial for machine translation between the languages English, French, and German, on this year's WMT translation tasks slight improvements on the development sets did not or only partially carry over to the held-out test sets. Nevertheless, systems with triplets were used for system combination, as extended lexicon models often help to predict content words and to capture long-range dependencies. Thus they can help to find a strong consensus hypothesis.

3.3 Unsupervised Training

Due to the small size of the English→German resources available for language modeling as well as for lexicon extraction, we decided to apply the unsupervised adaptation suggested in (Schwenk and Senellart, 2009). We use a baseline SMT system to translate in-domain monolingual source data, filter the translations according to a decoder score normalized by sentence length, add this synthetic bilingual data to the original one and rebuild the SMT system from scratch.

The motivation behind the method is that the phrase table will adapt to the genre, and thus let phrases which are domain related have higher probabilities. Two phenomena are observed from phrase tables and the corresponding translations:

- Phrase translation probabilities are changed, making the system choose better phrase translation candidates.

	Running Words	
	English	German
Bilingual	44.3M	43.4M
Dict.	1.4M	1.2M
AFP	610.7M	
AFP unsup.	152.0M	157.3M

Table 2: Overview on data for unsupervised training.

	BLEU	
	Dev	Test
baseline	15.0	14.7
+dict.	15.1	14.6
+unsup.+dict	15.4	14.9

Table 3: Results for unsupervised training method.

- Phrases which appear repeatedly in the domain get higher probabilities, so that the decoder can better segment the sentence.

To implement this idea, we translate the AFP part of the English LDC Gigaword v4.0 and obtain the synthetic data.

To decrease the number of OOV words, we use dictionaries from the stardict directory as additional bilingual data to translate the AFP corpus. We filter sentences with OOV words and sentences longer than 100 tokens. A summary of the additional data used is shown in Table 2.

We tried to use the best 10%, 20% and 40% of the synthetic data, where the 40% option worked best. A summary of the results is given in Table 3.

Although this is our best result for the English→German task, it was not submitted, because the use of the dictionary is not allowed in the constrained track.

4 Preprocessing

4.1 Large Parallel Data

In addition to the provided parallel Europarl and news-commentary corpora, also the large French-English news corpus (about 22.5 Mio. sentence pairs) and the French-English UN corpus (about 7.2 Mio. sentence pairs) were available. Since model training and tuning with such large corpora takes a very long time, we extracted about 2 Mio. sentence pairs of both of these corpora. We filter sentences with the following properties:

- Only sentences of minimum length of 4 tokens were considered.
- At least 92% of the vocabulary of each sentence occur in the development set.
- The ratio of the vocabulary size of a sentence and the number of its tokens is minimum 80%.

4.2 Morpho-Syntactic Analysis

German, as a flexible and morphologically rich language, raises a couple of problems in machine translation. We picked two major problems and tackled them with morpho-syntactic pre- and post-processing: compound splitting and long-range verb reordering.

For the translation from German into English, German compound words were split using the frequency-based method described in (Koehn and Knight, 2003). Thereby, we forbid certain words and syllables to be split. For the other translation direction, the English text was first translated into the modified German language with split compounds. The generated output was then postprocessed by re-merging the previously generated components using the method described in (Popović et al., 2006).

Additionally, for the German→English phrase-based system, the long-range POS-based reordering rules described in (Popović and Ney, 2006) were applied on the training and test corpora as a preprocessing step. Thereby, German verbs which occur at the end of a clause, like infinitives and past participles, are moved towards the beginning of that clause. With this, we improved our baseline phrase-based system by 0.6% BLEU.

5 Experimental Results

For all translation directions, we used the provided parallel corpora (Europarl, news) to train the translation models and the monolingual corpora to train the language models. We improved the French-English systems by enriching the data with parts of the large addional data, extracted with the method described in Section 4.1. Depending on the system this gave an improvement of 0.2-0.7% BLEU. We also made use of the large giga-news as well as the LDC Gigaword corpora for the French and English language models. All systems were optimized for BLEU score on the development data, `newstest2008`. The `newstest2009` data is used as a blind test set.

In the following, we will give the BLEU scores for all language tasks of the baseline system and the best setup for both, the phrase-based and the hierarchical system. We will use the following notations to indicate the several methods we used:

(+POS)	POS-based verb reordering
(+mero)	maximum entropy reordering
(+giga)	including giga-news and LDC Gigaword in LM
(fa)	trained by forced alignment
(shallow)	allow only shallow rules

We applied system combination of up to 6 systems with several setups. The submitted systems are marked in tables 4-7.

6 Conclusion

For the participation in the WMT 2010 shared translation task, RWTH used state-of-the-art phrase-based and hierarchical translation systems. To deal with the rich morphology and word order differences in German, compound splitting and long range verb reordering were applied in a preprocessing step. For the French-English language pairs, RWTH extracted parts of the large news corpus and the UN corpus as additional training data. Further, training the phrase translation model with forced alignment yielded improvements in BLEU. To obtain the final hypothesis for the French→English and German→English

	BLEU	
	Dev	Test
phrase-based baseline	19.9	19.2
phrase-based (+POS+mero+giga)	21.0	20.3
hierarchical baseline	20.2	19.6
hierarchical (+giga)	20.5	20.1
system combination	21.4	20.4

Table 4: Results for the German→English task.

	BLEU	
	Dev	Test
phrase-based baseline	14.8	14.5
phrase-based (+mero)	15.0	14.7
hierarchical baseline	14.2	13.9
hierarchical (shallow)	14.5	14.3

Table 5: Results for the English→German task.

	BLEU	
	Dev	Test
phrase-based baseline	21.8	25.1
phrase-based (fa+giga)	23.0	26.1
hierarchical baseline	21.9	25.0
hierarchical (shallow+giga)	22.7	25.6
system combination	23.1	26.1

Table 6: Results for the French→English task.

	BLEU	
	Dev	Test
phrase-based baseline	20.9	23.2
phrase-based (fa+mero+giga)	23.0	24.6
hierarchical baseline	20.6	22.5
hierarchical (shallow,+giga)	22.4	24.3

Table 7: Results for the English→French task.

language pairs, RWTH applied system combination. Altogether, by application of these methods RWTH was able to increase performance in BLEU by 0.8% for German→English, 0.2% for English→German, 1.0% for French→English and 1.4% for English→French on the test set over the respective baseline systems.

Acknowledgments

This work was realized as part of the Quaero Programme, funded by OSEO, French State agency for innovation.

References

D. Chiang. 2007. Hierarchical Phrase-Based Translation. *Computational Linguistics*, 33(2):201–228.

J. DeNero, D. Gillick, J. Zhang, and D. Klein. 2006. Why Generative Phrase Models Underperform Surface Heuristics. In *Proceedings of the Workshop on Statistical Machine Translation*, pages 31–38.

J.G. Fiscus. 1997. A Post-Processing System to Yield Reduced Word Error Rates: Recognizer Output Voting Error Reduction (ROVER). In *IEEE Workshop on Automatic Speech Recognition and Understanding*.

S. Hasan, J. Ganitkevitch, H. Ney, and J. Andrés-Ferrer. 2008. Triplet Lexicon Models for Statistical Machine Translation. In *Proceedings of Emperical Methods of Natural Language Processing*, pages 372–381.

G. Iglesias, A. de Gispert, E.R. Banga, and W. Byrne. 2009. Rule Filtering by Pattern for Efficient Hierarchical Translation. In *Proceedings of the 12th Conference of the European Chapter of the ACL (EACL 2009)*, pages 380–388.

P. Koehn and K. Knight. 2003. Empirical Methods for Compound Splitting. In *Proceedings of European Chapter of the ACL (EACL 2009)*, pages 187–194.

E. Matusov, N. Ueffing, and H. Ney. 2006. Computing consensus translation from multiple machine translation systems using enhanced hypotheses alignment. In *Conference of the European Chapter of the Association for Computational Linguistics (EACL)*, pages 33–40.

E. Matusov, G. Leusch, R.E. Banchs, N. Bertoldi, D. Dechelotte, M. Federico, M. Kolss, Y.-S. Lee, J.B. Marino, M. Paulik, S. Roukos, H. Schwenk, and H. Ney. 2008. System Combination for Machine Translation of Spoken and Written Language. *IEEE Transactions on Audio, Speech and Language Processing*, 16(7):1222–1237.

A. Mauser, S. Hasan, and H. Ney. 2009. Extending Statistical Machine Translation with Discriminative and Trigger-Based Lexicon Models. In *Conference on Empirical Methods in Natural Language Processing*, pages 210–217.

M. Popović and H. Ney. 2006. POS-based Word Reorderings for Statistical Machine Translation. In *International Conference on Language Resources and Evaluation*, pages 1278–1283.

M. Popović, D. Stein, and H. Ney. 2006. Statistical Machine Translation of German Compound Words. In *FinTAL - 5th International Conference on Natural Language Processing, Springer Verlag, LNCS*, pages 616–624.

H. Schwenk and J. Senellart. 2009. Translation Model Adaptation for an Arabic/French News Translation System by Lightly-Supervised Training. In *MT Summit XII*.

J. Wuebker, A. Mauser, and H. Ney. 2010. Training Phrase Translation Models with Leaving-One-Out. In *Proceedings of the 48th Annual Meeting of the Association for Computational Linguistics*. To appear.

R. Zens and H. Ney. 2006. Discriminative Reordering Models for Statistical Machine Translation. In *Workshop on Statistical Machine Translation*, pages 55–63.

R. Zens and H. Ney. 2008. Improvements in Dynamic Programming Beam Search for Phrase-based Statistical Machine Translation. In *International Workshop on Spoken Language Translation*.

Using collocation segmentation to augment the phrase table

Carlos A. Henríquez Q.*, **Marta R. Costa-jussà**[†], **Vidas Daudaravicius**‡

Rafael E. Banchs[†], **José B. Mariño***

*TALP Research Center, Universitat Politècnica de Catalunya, Barcelona, Spain
{carlos.henriquez,jose.marino}@upc.edu
[†]Barcelona Media Innovation Center, Barcelona, Spain
{marta.ruiz,rafael.banchs}@barcelonamedia.org
‡Faculty of Informatics, Vytautas Magnus University, Kaunas, Lithuania
vidas@donelaitis.vdu.lt

Abstract

This paper describes the 2010 phrase-based statistical machine translation system developed at the TALP Research Center of the UPC[1] in cooperation with BMIC[2] and VMU[3]. In phrase-based SMT, the phrase table is the main tool in translation. It is created extracting phrases from an aligned parallel corpus and then computing translation model scores with them. Performing a collocation segmentation over the source and target corpus before the alignment causes that different and larger phrases are extracted from the same original documents. We performed this segmentation and used the union of this phrase set with the phrase set extracted from the non-segmented corpus to compute the phrase table. We present the configurations considered and also report results obtained with internal and official test sets.

1 Introduction

The TALP Research Center of the UPC[1] in cooperation with BMIC[2] and VMU[3] participated in the Spanish-to-English WMT task. Our primary submission was a phrase-based SMT system enhanced with POS tags and our contrastive submission was an *augmented* phrase-based system using collocation segmentation (Costa-jussà et al., 2010), which mainly is a way of introducing new phrases in the translation table. This paper presents the description of both systems together with the results that we obtained in the evaluation task and is organized as follows: first, Section 2 and 3 present a brief description of a phrase-based SMT, followed by a general explanation of collocation segmentation. Section 4 presents the experimental framework, corpus used and a description of the different systems built for the translation task; the section ends showing the results we obtained over the official test set. Finally, section 5 presents the conclusions obtained from the experiments.

[1]Universitat Politècnica de Catalunya
[2]Barcelona Media Innovation Center
[3]Vytautas Magnus University

2 Phrase-based SMT

This approach to SMT performs the translation splitting the source sentence in segments and assigning to each segment a bilingual phrase from a phrase-table. Bilingual phrases are translation units that contain source words and target words, e.g. < *unidad de traducción* | *translation unit* >, and have different scores associated to them. These bilingual phrases are then sorted in order to maximize a linear combination of feature functions. Such strategy is known as the log-linear model (Och and Ney, 2003) and it is formally defined as:

$$\hat{e} = \arg\max_{e} \left[\sum_{m=1}^{M} \lambda_m h_m(e, f) \right] \tag{1}$$

where h_m are different feature functions with weights λ_m. The two main feature functions are the translation model (TM) and the target language model (LM). Additional models include POS target language models, lexical weights, word penalty and reordering models among others.

3 Collocation segmentation

Collocation segmentation is the process of detecting boundaries between collocation segments within a text (Daudaravicius and Marcinkeviciene, 2004). A collocation segment is a piece of text between boundaries. The boundaries are established in two steps using two different measures: the Dice score and a Average Minimum Law (AML).

The Dice score is used to measure the association strength between two words. It has been used before in the collocation compiler XTract (Smadja, 1993) and in the lexicon extraction system Champollion (Smadja et al., 1996). It is defined as follows:

$$Dice(x; y) = \frac{2f(x, y)}{f(x) + f(y)} \tag{2}$$

where $f(x, y)$ is the frequency of co-occurrence of x and y, and $f(x)$ and $f(y)$ the frequencies of occurrence of x and y anywhere in the text. It gives high scores when x and y occur in conjunction. The first step then establishes a boundary between

Proceedings of the Joint 5th Workshop on Statistical Machine Translation and MetricsMATR, pages 98–102,
Uppsala, Sweden, 15-16 July 2010.

two adjacent words when the Dice score is lower than a threshold $t = exp(-8)$. Such a threshold was established following the results obtained in (Costa-jussà et al., 2010), where an integration of this technique and a SMT system was performed over the Bible corpus.

The second step of the procedure uses the AML. It defines a boundary between words x_{i-1} and x_i when:

$$\frac{Dice(x_{i-2}; x_{i-1}) + Dice(x_i; x_{i+1})}{2} > Dice(x_{i-1}; x_i) \quad (3)$$

That is, the boundary is set when the Dice value between words x_i and x_{i-1} is lower than the average of preceding and following values.

4 Experimental Framework

All systems were built using Moses (Koehn et al., 2007), a state-of-the-art software for phrase-based SMT. For preprocessing Spanish, we used Freeling (Atserias et al., 2006), an open source library of natural language analyzers. For English, we used TnT (Brants, 2000) and Moses' tokenizer. The language models were built using SRILM (Stolcke, 2002).

4.1 Corpus

This year, the translation task provided four different sources to collect corpora for the Spanish-English pair. Bilingual corpora included version 5 of the Europarl Corpus (Koehn, 2005), the News Commentary corpus and the United Nations corpus. Additional English corpora was available from the News corpus. The organizers also allowed the use of the English Gigaword Third and Fourth Edition, released by the LDC. As for development and internal test, the test sets from 2008 and 2009 translation tasks were available.

For our experiments, we selected as training data the union of the Europarl and the News Commentary. Development was performed with a section of the 2008 test set and the 2009 test set was selected as internal test. We deleted all empty lines, removed pairs that were longer than 40 words, either in Spanish or English; and also removed pairs whose ratio between number of words were bigger than 3.

As a preprocess, all corpora were lower-cased and tokenized. The Spanish corpus was tokenized and POS tags were extracted using Freeling, which split clitics from verbs and also separated words like *"del"* into "de el". In order to build a POS target language model, we also obtained POS tags from the English corpus using the TnT tagger. Statistics of the selected corpus can be seen in Table 1.

Corpora	Spanish	English
Training sent	1,180,623	1,180,623
Running words	26,454,280	25,291,370
Vocabulary	118,073	89,248
Development sent	1,729	1,729
Running words	37,092	34,774
Vocabulary	7,025	6,199
Internal test sent	2,525	2,525
Running words	69,565	65,595
Vocabulary	10,539	8,907
Official test sent	2,489	-
Running words	66,714	-
Vocabulary	10,725	-

Table 1: Statistics for the training, development and test sets.

	Internal test	Official test
Adjectives	137	72
Common nouns	369	188
Proper nouns	408	2,106
Verbs	213	128
Others	119	168
Total	1246	2662

Table 2: Unknown words found in internal and official test sets

It is important to notice that neither the United Nations nor the Gigaword corpus were used for bilingual training. Nevertheless, the English part from the United Nations and the monolingual News corpus were used to build the language model of our systems.

4.1.1 Unknown words

We analyzed the content from the internal and official test and realized that they both contained many words that were not seen in the training data. Table 2 shows the number of unknown words found in both sets, classified according to their POS.

In average, we may expect an unknown word every two sentences in the internal test and more than one per sentence in the official test set. It can also be seen that most of those unknown words are proper nouns, representing 32% and 79% of the unknown sets, respectively. Common nouns were the second most frequent type of unknown words, followed by verbs and adjectives.

4.2 Systems

We submitted two different systems for the translation task. First a baseline using the training data mentioned before; and then an *augmented* system, where the baseline-extracted phrase list was extended with additional phrases coming from a segmented version of the training corpus.

We also considered an additional system built

with two different decoding path, a standard path from words to words and POS and an alternative path from stems to words and POS in the target side. At the end, we did not submit this system to the translation task because it did not provide better results than the previous two in our internal test.

The set of feature functions used include: source-to-target and target-to-source relative frequencies, source-to-target and target-to-source lexical weights, word and phrase penalties, a target language model, a POS target language model, and a lexicalized reordering model (Tillman, 2004).

4.2.1 Considering stems as an alternate decoding path.

Using Moses' framework for factored translation models we defined a system with two decoding paths: one decoding path using words and the other decoding path using stems in the source language and words in the target language. Both decoding paths only had a single translation step. The possibility of using multiple alternative decoding path was developed by Birch et. al. (2007).

This system tried to solve the problem with the unknown words. Because Spanish is morphologically richer than English, this alternative decoding path allowed the decoder translate words that were not seen in the training data and shared the same root with other known words.

4.2.2 Expanding the phrase table using collocation segmentation.

In order to build the augmented phrase table with the technique mentioned in section 3, we segmented each language of the bilingual corpus independently and then, using the collocation segments as words, we aligned the corpus and extracted the phrases from it. Once the phrases were extracted, the segments of each phrase were split again in words to have standard phrases. Finally, we use the union of this phrases and the phrases extracted from the baseline system to compute the final phrase table. A diagram of the whole procedure can be seen in figure 1.

The objective of this integration is to add new phrases in the translation table and to enhance the relative frequency of the phrases that were extracted from both methods.

4.2.3 Language model interpolation.

Because SMT systems are trained with a bilingual corpus, they ended highly tied to the domain the corpus belong to. Therefore, when the documents we want to translate belong to a different domain, additional domain adaptation techniques are recommended to build the system. Those techniques usually employ additional corpora that correspond to the domain we want to translate from.

	internal test
baseline	24.25
baseline+stem	23.45
augmented	23.9

Table 3: Internal test results.

	test	$\text{test}_{cased-detok}$
baseline	26.1	25.1
augmented	26.1	25.1

Table 4: Results from translation task

The test set for this translation task comes from the news domain, but most of our bilingual corpora belonged to a political domain, the Europarl. Therefore we use the additional monolingual corpus to adapt the language model to the news domain.

The strategy used followed the experiment performed last year in (R. Fonollosa et al., 2009). We used SRILM during the whole process. All language models were order five and used modified Kneser-Ney discount and interpolation. First, we build three different language models according to their domain: Europarl, United Nations and news; then, we obtained the perplexity of each language model over the News Commentary development corpus; next, we used `compute-best-mix` to obtain weights for each language model that diminish the global perplexity. Finally, the models were combined using those weights.

In our experiments all systems used the resulting language model, therefore the difference obtained in our results were cause only by the translation model.

4.3 Results

We present results from the three systems developed this year. First, the *baseline*, which included all the features mentioned in section 4.2; then, the system with an alternative decoding path, called *baseline+stem*; and finally the *augmented* system, which integrated collocation segmentation to the baseline. Internal test results can be seen in table 3. Automatic scores provided by the WMT 2010 organizers for the official test can be found in table 4. All BLEU scores are case-insensitive and tokenized except for the official test set which also contains case-sensitive and non-tokenized score.

We obtained a BLEU score of 26.1 and 25.1 for our case-insensitive and sensitive outputs, respectively. The highest score was obtained by University of Cambridge, with 30.5 and 29.1 BLEU points.

Figure 1: Example of the expansion of the phrase table using collocation segmentation. New phrases added by the collocation-based system are marked with a $**$.

4.3.1 Comparing systems

Once we obtained the translation outputs from the baseline and the *augmented* system, we performed a manual comparison of them. Even though we did not find any significant advantages of the *augmented* system over the baseline, the collocation segmentation strategy chose a better morphological structures in some cases as can be seen in Table 5 (only sentence sub-segments are shown):

5 Conclusion

We presented two different submissions for the Spanish-English language pair. The language model for both system was built interpolating two big out-of-domain language models and one smaller in-domain language model. The first system was a baseline with POS target language model; and the second one an *augmented* system, that integrates the baseline with collocation segmentation. Results over the official test set showed no difference in BLEU between these two, even though internal results showed that the baseline obtained a better score.

We also considered adding an additional decoding path from stems to words in the baseline but internal tests showed that it did not improve translation quality either. The high number of unknown words found in Spanish suggested us that considering in parallel the simple form of stems could help us achieve better results. Nevertheless, a deeper study of the unknown set showed us that most of those words were proper nouns, which do not have inflection and therefore cannot benefited from stems.

Finally, despite that internal test did not showed an improvement with the *augmented* system, we submitted it as a secondary run looking for the effect these phrases could have over human evaluation.

Acknowledgment

The research leading to these results has received funding from the European Community's Seventh Framework Programme (FP7/2007-2013) under grant agreement number 247762, from the Spanish Ministry of Science and Innovation through the Buceador project (TEC2009-14094-C04-01) and the *Juan de la Cierva* fellowship program. The authors also wants to thank the Barcelona Media Innovation Centre for its support and permission to publish this research.

References

Jordi Atserias, Bernardino Casas, Elisabet Comelles, Meritxell González, Lluís Padró, and Muntsa Padró. 2006. FreeLing 1.3: Syntactic and semantic services in an open-source NLP

Original:	sabiendo que **está recibiendo** el premio
Baseline:	knowing that **it receive** the prize
Augmented:	knowing that **he is receiving** the prize
Original:	muchos de mis amigos **prefieren no separarla**.
Baseline:	many of my friends **prefer not to separate them**.
Augmented:	many of my friends **prefer not to separate it**.
Original:	Los estadounidenses **contarán** con un teléfono móvil
Baseline:	The Americans **have** a mobile phone
Augmented:	The Americans **will have** a mobile phone
Original:	es plenamente consciente del camino más largo **que debe emprender**
Baseline:	is fully aware of the longest journey **must undertake**
Augmented:	is fully aware of the longest journey **that need to be taken**

Table 5: Comparison between baseline and augmented outputs

library. In *Proceedings of the fifth international conference on Language Resources and Evaluation (LREC 2006), ELRA*, Genoa, Italy, May.

Alexandra Birch, Miles Osborne, and Philipp Koehn. 2007. Ccg supertags in factored statistical machine translation. In *StatMT '07: Proceedings of the Second Workshop on Statistical Machine Translation*, pages 9–16, Morristown, NJ, USA. Association for Computational Linguistics.

Thorsten Brants. 2000. TnT – a statistical part-of-speech tagger. In *Proceedings of the Sixth Applied Natural Language Processing (ANLP-2000)*, Seattle, WA.

Marta R. Costa-jussà, Vidas Daudaravicius, and Rafael E. Banchs. 2010. Integration of statistical collocation segmentations in a phrase-based statistical machine translation system. In *14th Annual Conference of the European Association for Machine Translation.*

Vidas Daudaravicius and Ruta Marcinkeviciene. 2004. Gravity counts for the boundaries of collocations. *International Journal of Corpus Linguistics*, 9:321–348(28).

Philipp Koehn, Hieu Hoang, Alexandra Birch, Chris Callison-Burch, Marcello Federico, Nicola Bertoldi, Brooke Cowan, Wade Shen, Christine Moran, Richard Zens, Chris Dyer, Ondřej Bojar, Alexandra Constantin, and Evan Herbst. 2007. Moses: Open Source Toolkit for Statistical Machine Translation. In *ACL '07: Proceedings of the 45th Annual Meeting of the ACL on Interactive Poster and Demonstration Sessions*, pages 177–180, Morristown, NJ, USA. Association for Computational Linguistics.

Philipp Koehn. 2005. Europarl: A Parallel Corpus for Statistical Machine Translation. In *Machine Translation Summit.*

Franz Josef Och and Hermann Ney. 2003. A Systematic Comparison of Various Statistical Alignment Models. *Computational Linguistics*, 29:19–51.

José A. R. Fonollosa, Maxim Khalilov, Marta R. Costa-jussá, José B. Mariño, Carlos A. Henríquez Q., Adolfo Hernández H., and Rafael E. Banchs. 2009. The TALP-UPC phrase-based translation system for EACL-WMT 2009. In *Proceedings of the Fourth Workshop on Statistical Machine Translation*, pages 85–89, Athens, Greece, March. Association for Computational Linguistics.

Frank A. Smadja, Kathleen McKeown, and Vasileios Hatzivassiloglou. 1996. Translating collocations for bilingual lexicons: A statistical approach. *Computational Linguistics*, 22(1):1–38.

Frank Smadja. 1993. Retrieving collocations from text: Xtract. *Comput. Linguist.*, 19(1):143–177.

Andreas Stolcke. 2002. SRILM – an extensible language modeling toolkit. pages 901–904.

Christoph Tillman. 2004. A Unigram Orientation Model for Statistical Machine Translation. In *HLT-NAACL*.

The RALI Machine Translation System for WMT 2010

Stéphane Huet, Julien Bourdaillet, Alexandre Patry and Philippe Langlais
RALI - Université de Montréal
C.P. 6128, succursale Centre-ville
H3C 3J7, Montréal, Québec, Canada
{huetstep,bourdaij,patryale,felipe}@iro.umontreal.ca

Abstract

We describe our system for the translation task of WMT 2010. This system, developed for the English-French and French-English directions, is based on Moses and was trained using only the resources supplied for the workshop. We report experiments to enhance it with out-of-domain parallel corpora sub-sampling, N-best list post-processing and a French grammatical checker.

1 Introduction

This paper presents the phrase-based machine translation system developed at RALI in order to participate in both the French-English and English-French translation tasks. In these two tasks, we used all the corpora supplied for the constraint data condition apart from the LDC Gigaword corpora.

We describe its different components in Section 2. Section 3 reports our experiments to subsample the available out-of-domain corpora in order to adapt the translation models to the news domain. Section 4, dedicated to post-processing, presents how N-best lists are reranked and how the French 1-best output is corrected by a grammatical checker. Section 5 studies how the original source language of news acts upon translation quality. We conclude in Section 6.

2 System Architecture

2.1 Pre-processing

The available corpora were pre-processed using an in-house script that normalizes quotes, dashes, spaces and ligatures. We also reaccentuated French words starting with a capital letter. We significantly cleaned up the parallel `Giga word corpus` (noted as `gw` hereafter), keeping 18.1 M of the original 22.5 M sentence pairs. For example, sentence pairs with numerous numbers, non-alphanumeric characters or words starting with capital letters were removed.

Moreover, training material was tokenized with the tool provided for the workshop and truecased, meaning that the words occuring after a strong punctuation mark were lowercased when they belonged to a dictionary of common all-lowercased forms; the others were left unchanged. In order to reduce the number of words unknown to the translation models, all numbers were serialized, i.e. mapped to a special unique token. The original numbers are then placed back in the translation in the same order as they appear in the source sentence. Since translations are mostly monotonic between French and English, this simple algorithm works well most of the time.

2.2 Language Models

We trained Kneser-Ney discounted 5-gram language models (LMs) on each available corpus using the SRILM toolkit (Stolcke, 2002). These LMs were combined through linear interpolation: first, an out-of-domain LM was built from `Europarl`, `UN` and `gw`; then, this model was combined with the two in-domain LMs trained on `news-commentary` and `news.shuffled`, which will be referred to as `nc` and `ns` in the remainder of the article. Weights were fixed by optimizing the perplexity of a development corpus made of `news-test2008` and `news-syscomb2009` texts.

In order to reduce the size of the LMs, we limited the vocabulary of our models to 1 M words for English and French. The words of these vocabularies were selected from the computation of the number of their occurences using the method proposed by Venkataraman and Wang (2003). The out-of-vocabulary rate measured on `news-test2009` and `news-test2010` with a so-built vocabulary varies between 0.6 %

Proceedings of the Joint 5th Workshop on Statistical Machine Translation and MetricsMATR, pages 103–109,
Uppsala, Sweden, 15-16 July 2010. ©2010 Association for Computational Linguistics

and 0.8 % for both English and French, while it was between 0.4 % and 0.7 % before the vocabulary was pruned.

To train the LM on the 48 M-sentence English `ns` corpus, 32 Gb RAM were required and up to 16 Gb RAM, for the other corpora. To reduce the memory needs during decoding, LMs were pruned using the SRILM prune option.

2.3 Alignment and Translation Models

All parallel corpora were aligned with Giza++ (Och and Ney, 2003). Our translation models are phrase-based models (PBMs) built with Moses (Koehn et al., 2007) with the following non-default settings:

- maximum sentence length of 80 words,
- limit on the number of phrase translations loaded for each phrase fixed to 30.

Weights of LM, phrase table and lexicalized reordering model scores were optimized on the development corpus thanks to the MERT algorithm (Och, 2003).

2.4 Experiments

This section reports experiments done on the `news-test2009` corpus for testing various configurations. In these first experiments, we trained LMs and translation models on the `Europarl` corpus.

Case We tested two methods to handle case. The first one lowercases all training data and documents to translate, while the second one normalizes all training data and documents into their natural case. These two methods require a post-processing recapitalization but this last step is more basic for the truecase method. Training models on lowercased material led to a 23.15 % case-insensitive BLEU and a 21.61 % case-sensitive BLEU; from truecased corpora, we obtained a 23.24 % case-insensitive BLEU and a 22.13 % case-sensitive BLEU. As truecasing induces an increase of the two metrics, we built all our models in truecase. The results shown in the remainder of this paper are reported in terms of case-insensitive BLEU which showed last year a better correlation with human judgments than case-sensitive BLEU for the two languages we consider (Callison-Burch et al., 2009).

Tokenization Two tokenizers were tested: one provided for the workshop and another we developed. They differ mainly in the processing of compound words: our in-house tokenizer splits these words (e.g. *percentage-wise* is turned into *percentage - wise*), which improves the lexical coverage of the models trained on the corpus. This feature does not exist in the WMT tool. However, using the WMT tokenizer, we measured a 23.24 % BLEU, while our in-house tokenizer yielded a lower BLEU of 22.85 %. Follow these results prompted us to use the WMT tokenizer.

Serialization In order to test the effect of serialization, i.e. the mapping of all numbers to a special unique token, we measured the BLEU score obtained by a PBM trained on `Europarl` for English-French, when numbers are left unchanged (Table 1, line 1) or serialized (line 2). These results exhibit a slight decrease of BLEU when serialization is performed. Moreover, if BLEU is computed using a serialized reference (line 3), which is equivalent to ignoring deserialization errors, a minor gain of BLEU is observed, which validates our recovering method. Since resorting to serialization/deserialization yields comparable performance to a system not using it, while reducing the model's size, we chose to use it.

	BLEU
no serialization	23.24
corpus serialization	23.13
corpus and reference serialization	23.27

Table 1: BLEU measured for English-French on `news-test2009` when training on `Europarl`.

LM Table 2 reports the perplexity measured on `news-test2009` for French (column 1) and English (column 3) LMs learned on different corpora and interpolated using the development corpus. We also provide the BLEU score (column 2) for English-French obtained from translation models trained on `Europarl` and `nc`. As expected, using in-domain corpora (line 2) for English-French led to better results than using out-of-domain data (line 3). The best perplexities and BLEU score are obtained when LMs trained on all the available corpora are combined (line 4). The last three lines exhibit how LMs perform when they are trained on in-domain corpora without pruning them. While the gzipped 5-gram LM (last line) obtained in such a manner occupies 1.4 Gb on hard disk, the gzipped pruned 5-gram LM (line 4) trained using all corpora occupies 0.9 Gb and yields the same BLEU score. This last LM was used in all the experiments reported in the subsequent sections.

corpora	Fr		En
	ppl	BLEU	ppl
nc	327	22.44	454
nc + ns	125	25.69	166
Europarl + UN + Gw	156	24.91	225
all corpora	**113**	**26.01**	**151**
nc + ns (3g, unpruned)	138	25.32	-
nc + ns (4g, unpruned)	124	25.86	-
nc + ns (5g, unpruned)	120	26.04	-

Table 2: LMs perplexities and BLEU scores measured on news-test2009. Translation models used here were trained on nc and Europarl.

3 Domain adaptation

As the only news parallel corpus provided for the workshop contains 85k sentence pairs, we must resort to other parallel out-of-domain corpora in order to build reliable translation models. If in-domain and out-of-domain LMs are usually mixed with the well-studied interpolation techniques, training translation models from data of different domains has received less attention (Foster and Kuhn, 2007; Bertoldi and Federico, 2009). Therefore, there is still no widely accepted technique for this last purpose.

3.1 Effects of the training data size

We investigated how increasing training data acts upon BLEU score. Table 3 shows a high increase of 2.7 points w.r.t. the use of nc alone (line 1) when building the phrase table and the reordering model from nc and either the 1.7 M-sentence-pair Europarl (line 2) or a 1.7 M-sentence-pair corpus extracted from the 3 out-of-domain corpora: Europarl, UN and Gw (line 3). Training a PBM on merged parallel corpora is not necessarily the best way to combine data from different domains. We repeated 20 times nc before adding it to Europarl so as to have the same amount of out-of-domain and in-domain material. This method turned out to be less successful since it led to a minor 0.15 BLEU decrease (line 4) w.r.t. our previous system.

Following the motto "no data is better than more data", a PBM was built using all the parallel corpora at our disposal. Since the overall parallel sentences were too numerous for our computational resources to be simultaneously used, we randomly split out-of-domain corpora into 3 parts of 8.7 M sentence pairs each and then combined them with nc. PBMs were trained on each of these parts (lines 5 to 7), which yields respectively 0.5 and 0.8 BLEU gain for English-French and French-English w.r.t. the use of 1.7 M out-of-domain sentence pairs. The more significant improvement noticed for the French-English direction is probably explained by the fact that the French language is morphologically richer than English. The 3 PBMs were then combined by merging the 3 phrase tables. To do so, the 5 phrase table scores computed by Moses were mixed using the geometric average and a 6th score was added, which counts the number of phrase tables where the given phrase pair occurs. We ended up with a phrase table containing 623 M entries, only 9 % and 4 % of them being in 2 and 3 tables respectively. The resulting phrase table led to a slight improvement of BLEU scores (last line) w.r.t. the previous models, except for the model trained on part 0 for French-English.

corpora	En→Fr	Fr→En
nc	23.29	23.23
nc + Europarl	26.01	-
nc + 1.7 M random pairs	26.02	26.68
20×nc + Europarl	25.86	-
nc + 8.7 M pairs (part 0)	26.44	27.65
nc + 8.7 M pairs (part 1)	26.68	27.46
nc + 8.7 M pairs (part 2)	26.54	27.50
3 models merged	26.86	27.56

Table 3: BLEU (in %) measured on news-test2009 for English-French and French-English when translations models and lexicalized reordering models are built using various amount of data in addition to nc.

3.2 Corpus sub-sampling

Whereas using all corpora improves translation quality, it requires a huge amount of memory and disk space. We investigate in this section ways to select sentence pairs among large out-of-domain corpora.

Unknown words The main interest of adding new training material relies on the finding of words missing in the phrase table. According to this principle, nc was extended with new sentence pairs containing an unknown word (Table 4, line 2) or a word that belongs to our LM vocabulary and that occurs less than 3 times in the current corpus (line 3). This resulted in adding 400 k pairs in the first case and 950 k in the second one, with BLEU scores close or even better than those obtained with 1.7 M.

corpora	En→Fr	Fr→En
nc + 1.7 M random pairs	26.02	26.68
nc + 400k pairs (occ = 1)	25.67	-
nc + 950k pairs (occ = 3)	26.13	-
nc + Joshua sub-sampling	26.98	27.68
nc + IR (1-g q, w/ repet)	25.81	-
nc + IR (1-g q, no repet)	26.56	27.54
nc + IR (1,2-g q, w/ repet)	26.26	-
nc + IR (1,2-g q, no repet)	26.53	-
nc + 8.7 M pairs	26.68	27.65
+ IR score (1g q, no repet)	26.93	27.65
3 large models merged	26.86	27.56
+ IR score (1g q, no repet)	**26.98**	**27.74**

Table 4: BLEU measured on news-test2009 for English-French and French-English using translation models trained on nc and a subset of out-of-domain corpora.

Unknown n-grams We applied the sub-sampling method available in the Joshua toolkit (Li et al., 2009). This method adds a new sentence pair when it contains new n-grams (with $1 \leq n \leq 12$) occurring less than 20 times in the current corpus, which led us to add 1.5 M pairs for English-French and 1.4 M for French-English. A significant improvement of BLEU is observed using this method (0.8 for English-French and 1.0 for French-English) w.r.t. the use of 1.7 M randomly selected pairs. However, this method has the major drawback of needing to build a new phrase table for each document to translate.

Information retrieval Information retrieval (IR) methods have been used in the past to sub-sample parallel corpora (Hildebrand et al., 2005; Lü et al., 2007). These studies use sentences belonging to the development and test corpora as queries to select the k most similar source sentences in an indexed parallel corpus. The retrieved sentence pairs constitute a training corpus for the translation models. In order to alleviate the fact that a new PBM has to be learned for each new test corpus, we built queries using sentences contained in the monolingual ns corpus, leading to the selection of sentence pairs stylistically close to those in the news domain. The source sentences of the three out-of-domain corpora were indexed using Lemur.[1] Two types of queries were built from ns sentences after removing stop words: the first one is limited to unigrams, the second one contains both unigrams and bigrams, with a weight for bigrams twice as high as for unigrams. The interest of the latter query type is based on the hypothesis that bigrams are more domain-dependent than unigrams. Another choice that needs to be made when using IR methods is concerning the retention of redundant sentences in the final corpus.

Lines 5 to 8 of Table 4 show the results obtained when sentence pairs were gathered up to the size of Europarl, i.e. 1.7 M pairs. 10 sentences were retrieved per query in various configurations: with or without bigrams inside queries, with or without duplicate sentence pairs in the training corpus. Results demonstrate the interest of the approach since the BLEU scores are close to those obtained using the previous tested method based on n-grams of the test data. Taking bigrams into account does not improve results and adding only once new sentences is more relevant than duplicating them.

Since using all data led to even better performances (see last line of Table 3), we used information provided by the IR method in the PBMs trained on nc + 8.7 M out-of-domain sentence pairs or taking into account all the training material. To this end, we included a new score in the phrase tables which is fixed to 1 for entries that are in the phrase table trained on sentences retrieved with unigram queries without repetition (see line 6 of Table 4), and 0 otherwise. Therefore, this score aims at boosting the weight of phrases that were found in sentences close to the news domain. The results reported in the 4 last lines of Table 4 show minor but consistent gains when adding this score. The outputs of the PBMs trained on all the training corpus and which obtained the best BLEU scores on news-test2009 were submitted as contrastive runs. The two first lines of Table 5 report the results on this years's test data, when the score related to the retrieved corpus is incorporated or not. These results still exhibit a minor improvement when adding this score.

[1] www.lemurproject.org

	En→Fr			Fr→En		
	BLEU	BLEU-cased	TER	BLEU	BLEU-cased	TER
PBM	27.5	26.5	62.2	27.8	26.9	61.2
+IR score	27.7	26.6	62.1	28.0	27.0	61.0
+N-best list reranking	27.9	26.8	62.1	28.0	27.0	61.2
+grammatical checker	28.0	26.9	62.0	-	-	-

Table 5: Official results of our system on `news-test2010`.

4 Post-processing

4.1 N-best List Reranking

Our best PBM enhanced by IR methods was employed to generate 500-best lists. These lists were reranked combining the global decoder score with the length ratio between source and target sentences, and the proportions of source sentence n-grams that are in the news monolingual corpora (with $1 \leq n \leq 5$). Weights of these 7 scores are optimized via MERT on `news-test2009`. Lines 2 and 3 of Table 5 provide the results obtained before and after N-best list reranking. They show a tiny gain for all metrics for English-French, while the results remain constant for French-English. Nevertheless, we decided to use those translations for the French-English task as our primary run.

4.2 Grammatical Checker

PBM outputs contain a significant number of grammatical errors, even when LMs are trained on large data sets. We tested the use of a grammatical checker for the French language: Antidote RX distributed by Druide informatique inc.[2] This software was applied in a systematic way on the first translation generated after N-best reranking. Thus, as soon as the software suggests one or several choices that it considers as more correct than the original translation, the first proposal is kept. The checked translation is our first run for English-French.

Antidote RX changed at least one word in 26 % of the news-test2010 sentences. The most frequent type of corrections are agreement errors, like in the following example where the agreement between the subject *nombre* (*number*) is correctly made with the adjective *coupé* (*cut*), thanks to the full syntactic parsing of the French sentence.

Source: [...] *the number of revaccinations could then be* ***cut*** [...]

Reranking: [...] *le nombre de revaccinations pourrait alors être* ***coupées*** [...]

+Grammatical checker: [...] *le nombre de revaccinations pourrait alors être* ***coupé*** [...]

The example below exhibits a good decision made by the grammatical checker on the mood of the French verb *être* (*to be*).

Source: *It will be a long time before anything else* ***will be*** *on offer in Iraq.*

Reranking: *Il faudra beaucoup de temps avant que tout le reste* ***sera*** *offert en Irak.*

+Grammatical checker: *Il faudra beaucoup de temps avant que tout le reste* ***soit*** *offert en Irak.*

A last interesting type of corrected errors concerns negation. Antidote has indeed the capacity to add the French particle *ne* when it is missing in the expressions *ne ... pas*, *ne ... plus*, *aucun ne*, *personne ne* or *rien ne*. The results obtained using the grammatical checker are reported in the last line of Table 5. The automatic evaluation shows only a minor improvement but we expect the changes induced by this tool to be more significant for human annotators.

5 Effects of the Original Source Language of Articles on Translation

During our experiments, we found that translation quality is highly variable depending on the original source language of the news sentences. This phenomenon is correlated to the previous work of Kurokawa et al. (2009) that showed that whether or not a piece of text is an original or a translation has an impact on translation performance. The main reason that explains our observations is probably that the topics and the vocabulary of news originally expressed in languages other than French and English tend to differ more from those of the training materials used to train PBM models for these two languages. In order to take into account this phenomenon, MERT tuning was repeated for each original source language, using the

[2] `www.druide.com`

same PBM models trained on all parallel corpora and incorporating an IR score.

Columns 1 and 3 of Table 5 display the BLEU measured using our previous global MERT optimization made on 2553 sentence pairs, while columns 2 and 4 show the results obtained when running MERT on subsets of the development material, made of around 700 sentence pairs each. The BLEU measured on the whole 2010 test set is reported in the last line. As expected, language-dependent MERT tends to increase the LM weight for English and French. However, an absolute 0.35 % BLEU decrease is globally observed for English-French using this approach and a 0.21 % improvement for French-English.

	En→Fr		Fr→En	
MERT	global	lang dep	global	lang dep
Cz	21.95	21.45	21.84	21.85
En	30.80	29.84	33.73	35.00
Fr	37.59	36.96	31.59	32.62
De	16.60	16.73	17.41	17.76
Es	24.52	24.45	29.25	28.31
total	27.64	27.39	27.99	28.20

Table 6: BLEU scores measured on parts of `news-test2010` according to the original source language.

6 Conclusion

This paper presented our statistical machine translation system developed for the translation task using Moses. Our submitted runs were generated from models trained on all the corpora made available for the workshop, as this method had provided the best results in our experiments. This system was enhanced using IR methods which exploits news monolingual copora, N-best list reranking and a French grammatical checker.

This was our first participation where such a huge amount data was involved. Training models on so many sentences is challenging from an engineering point of view and requires important computational resources and storage capacities. The time spent in handling voluminous data prevented us from testing more approaches. We suggest that the next edition of the workshop could integrate a task restraining the number of parameters in the models trained.

References

Nicola Bertoldi and Marcello Federico. 2009. Domain adaptation for statistical machine translation with monolingual resources. In *4th EACL Workshop on Statistical Machine Translation (WMT)*, Athens, Greece.

Chris Callison-Burch, Philipp Koehn, Christof Monz, and Josh Schroeder. 2009. Findings of the 2009 workshop on statistical machine translation. In *4th EACL Workshop on Statistical Machine Translation (WMT)*, Athens, Greece.

George Foster and Roland Kuhn. 2007. Mixture-model adaptation for SMT. In *2nd ACL Workshop on Statistical Machine Translation (WMT)*, Prague, Czech Republic.

Almut Silja Hildebrand, Matthias Eck, Stephan Vogel, and Alex Waibel. 2005. Adaptation of the translation model for statistical machine translation based on information retrieval. In *10th conference of the European Association for Machine Translation (EAMT)*, Budapest, Hungary.

Philipp Koehn, Hieu Hoang, Alexandra Birch, Chris Callison-Burch, Marcello Federico, Nicola Bertoldi, Brooke Cowan, Wade Shen, Christine Moran, Richard Zens, Chris Dyer, Ondrej Bojar, Alexandra Constantin, and Evan Herbst. 2007. Moses: Open source toolkit for statistical machine translation. In *45th Annual Meeting of the Association for Computational Linguistics (ACL), Companion Volume*, Prague, Czech Republic.

David Kurokawa, Cyril Goutte, and Pierre Isabelle. 2009. Automatic detection of translated text and its impact on machine translation. In *12th Machine Translation Summit*, Ottawa, Canada.

Zhifei Li, Chris Callison-Burch, Chris Dyer, Juri Ganitkevitch, Sanjeev Khudanpur, Lane Schwartz, Wren N. G. Thornton, Jonathan Weese, and Omar F. Zaidan. 2009. Joshua: An open source toolkit for parsing-based machine translation. In *4th EACL Workshop on Statistical Machine Translation (WMT)*, Athens, Greece.

Yajuan Lü, Jin Huang, and Qun Liu. 2007. Improving statistical machine translation performance by training data selection and optimization. In *Join Conference on Empirical Methods in Natural Language Processing and Computational Natural Language Learning (EMNLP-CoNLL)*, Prague, Czech Republic.

Franz Josef Och and Hermann Ney. 2003. A systematic comparison of various statistical alignment models. *Computational Linguistics*, 29(1):19–51.

Franz Josef Och. 2003. Minimum error rate training in statistical machine translation. In *41st Annual Meeting of the Association for Computational Linguistics (ACL)*, Sapporo, Japan.

Andreas Stolcke. 2002. SRILM - an extensible language modeling toolkit. In *7th International Conference on Spoken Language Processing (ICSLP)*, Denver, CO, USA.

Arnand Venkataraman and Wen Wang. 2003. Techniques for effective vocabulary selection. In *8th European Conference on Speech Communication and Technology (Eurospeech)*, Geneva, Switzerland.

Exodus – Exploring SMT for EU Institutions

Michael Jellinghaus[1,2], Alexandros Poulis[1], David Kolovratník[3]
1: European Parliament, Luxembourg
2: Saarland University, Saarbrücken, Germany
3: Charles University in Prague, Czech Republic
micha@coli.uni-sb.de, apoulis@europarl.europa.eu, david@kolovratnik.net

Abstract

In this paper, we describe Exodus, a joint pilot project of the European Commission's Directorate-General for Translation (DGT) and the European Parliament's Directorate-General for Translation (DG TRAD) which explores the potential of deploying new approaches to machine translation in European institutions. We have participated in the English-to-French track of this year's WMT10 shared translation task using a system trained on data previously extracted from large in-house translation memories.

1 Project Background

1.1 Translation at EU Institutions

The European Union's policy on multilingualism[1] requires enormous amounts of documents to be translated into the 23 official languages (which yield 506 translation directions). To cope with this task, the EU has the biggest translation service in the world, employing almost 5000 internal staff as translators (out of which 1750 at the European Commission (EC) and 760 at the European Parliament (EP) alone), backed up by more than 2000 support staff. In 2009, the total output of the Commission's Directorate-General for Translation (DGT) and the Parliament's Directorate-General for Translation (DG TRAD) together was more than 3 million translated pages. Thus, it is not surprising that the cost of all translation and interpreting services of all the EU institutions amounts to 1% of the annual EU budget (2008 figures). According to our estimations, this is more than € 1 billion per year.

1.2 Machine Translation and Other Translation Technologies at EU Institutions

In order to make the translators' work more efficient so that they can translate more pages in the same time, a number of tools like terminology databases, bilingual concordancers, and, most importantly, translation memories are at their disposition, most of which are heavily used.

In real translation production scenarios, Machine Translation is usually used to complement translation memory tools (TM tool). Translation memories are databases that contain text segments (usually sentences) that are stored together with their translations. Each such pair of source and target language segments is called a translation unit. Translation units also contain useful meta-data (creation date, document type, client, etc.) that allow us to filter the data both for translation and machine translation purposes.

A TM tool tries to match the segments within a document that needs to be translated with segments in the translation memory and propose translations. If the memory contains an identical string then we have a so-called exact or 100% match which yields a very reliable translation. Approximate or partial matches are called fuzzy matches and usually, the minimum value of a fuzzy match is set to 65%–70%. Lower matches are not considered as usable since they demand more editing time than typing a translation from scratch. First experiments have shown that the quality of SMT output for certain language pairs is equal or similar to 70% fuzzy matches.

Consequently, the cases where machine translation can play a helpful role in this context is when, for a segment to be translated, there is no exact match and the available fuzzy matches do not exceed a certain threshold. This threshold in our case is expected to be 85% or lower. To this end, there exists a system called ECMT (European Commission Machine Translation; also accessible to other European institutions) which is a rule-based system.

However, only certain translation directions are covered by ECMT, and its maintenance is quite complicated and requires quite a lot of dedicated and specialized human resources. In the light of these facts and with the addition of the languages of (prospective) new member states, statistical approaches to machine translation seem to offer a viable alternative.

First of all, SMT is data-driven, i.e. it exploits parallel corpora of which there are plenty at the EU institutions in the form of translation memories. Translation memories have two main advantages over other parallel corpora. First of all, they contain almost exclusively perfectly aligned segments, as each segment is stored together with its translation, and secondly,

[1] http://ec.europa.eu/education/languages/eu-language-policy/index_en.htm

Proceedings of the Joint 5th Workshop on Statistical Machine Translation and MetricsMATR, pages 110–114,
Uppsala, Sweden, 15-16 July 2010.

they contain cleaner data since their content is regularly maintained by linguists and database administrators. SMT systems are quicker to develop and easier to maintain than rule-based systems. The availability of free, open-source software like Moses[2] (Koehn et al., 2007), GIZA++[3] (Och and Ney, 2003) and the like constitutes a further argument in their favor.

Early experiments with Moses were started by members of DGT's Portuguese Language Department as early as summer 2008 (Leal Fontes and Machado, 2009), then turned into a wider interinstitutional project with the codename Exodus, currently combining resources from European Commission's DGT and European Parliament's DGTRAD. Exodus is the first joint project of the interinstitutional Language Technology Watch group where a number of EU institutions join forces in the field of language technology.

2 Participation in WMT 2010 Shared Task

After the English-Portuguese experiments, the first language pair for which we developed a system with a sizeable amount of training data was English-to-French. This system has been developed for testing at the European Parliament. As English-to-French is also one of the eight translation directions evaluated in this year's shared translation task, we decided to participate. The reasons behind this decision are manifold: We would like to

- know where we stand in comparison to other systems,
- learn about what system adaptations are the most beneficial,
- make our project known to potential collaborators,
- compare the WMT10 evaluation results to the outcome of our in-house evaluation.

There is, however, one major difference between the evaluation as carried out in WMT10 and our in-house evaluation: The test data of WMT10 consists exclusively of news articles and is thus out-of-domain for our system intended for use within the European Parliament. This means that the impact of training our system on the in-domain data we obtain from our translation memories cannot be assessed properly, i.e. taking into consideration our specific translation production needs.

Therefore, we would like to invite other interested groups to also translate our in-domain test data with the goal of seeing how our translation scenario could benefit from their setups. Due to legal issues, however, we unfortunately cannot provide our internal training data at this moment.

[2]http://www.statmt.org/moses/

[3]http://www.fjoch.com/GIZA++.html

3 Data Used

To build our English-to-French MT system, we did not use any of the data provided by the organizers of the WMT10 shared translation task. Instead, we used data that was extracted from the translation memories at the core of EURAMIS (European Advanced Multilingual Information System; (Theologitis, 1997; Blatt, 1998)) which are the fruit of thousands of man-years contributed by translators at EU institutions who, each day, upload the majority of the segments they translate.

Initially (before pre-processing), our EN-FR corpus contained 10,446,450 segments and included documents both from the Commission and the EP from common legislative procedures. These segments were extracted in November 2009 from 7 translation memories hosted in Euramis. Currently, we do not have information about the exact document types coming from the Commission's databases. The Parliament's document types used include, among others:

- legislative documents such as draft reports, final reports, amendments, opinions, etc.,
- documents for the plenary such as questions, resolutions or session amendments,
- committee and delegation documents,
- documents concerning the ACP[4] and the EMPA[5],
- internal documents such as budget estimates, staff regulations, rules of procedure, etc.,
- calls for tender.

Any sensitive or classified documents or Commission-internal documents that do not belong to common legislative procedures have been excluded from the data.

In terms of preprocessing, we performed several steps. First, we obtained translation memory exchange (TMX) files from EURAMIS and converted them to UTF-8 text as the Euramis native character encoding is UCS-2. Then we removed certain control characters which otherwise would have halted processing, we extracted the two single-language corpora into a plaintext file, tokenized and lowercased the data. Finally, we separated the corpus into training data (9,300,682 segments), and data for tuning and testing – 500 segments each. These segments did not exceed a maximum length of 60 tokens and were excluded from the preparation of the translation and language models. The models were then trained on the remaining segments. The maximum length of 60 tokens was applied here as well.

[4]African, Caribbean and Pacific Group of States

[5]Euro-Mediterranean Parliamentary Assembly

Metric	Score
BLEU	18.8
BLEU-cased	16.9
TER	0.747

Table 1: Automatic scores calculated for Exodus in WMT10

	Evaluator A	Evaluator B	**Overall**
Reference	1.75	2.06	**1.97**
ECMT	3.34	3.31	**3.32**
Google	3.59	3.28	**3.37**
Exodus	3.52	3.45	**3.47**

Table 2: Average relative rank (on a scale from 1 to 5)

	OK	Edited	Bad
Reference	29	30	2
ECMT	8	57	2
Google	7	33	5
Exodus	13	62	12

Table 3: Results of Editing Task ("OK" means "No corrections needed"; "Bad" means "Unable to correct")

4 Building the Models and Decoding

The parallel data described above was used to train an English-to-French translation model and a French target language model. This was done on a server running Sun Solaris with 64 GB of RAM and 8 double core CPU's @1800 Mhz (albeit shared with other processes running simultaneously).

In general, we simply used a vanilla Moses installation at this point, leaving the integration of more sophisticated features to a later moment, i.e. after a thorough analysis of the results of the present evaluation campaign when we will know which adaptations yield the most significant improvements.

For the word alignments, we chose MGIZA (Gao and Vogel, 2008), using seven threads per MGIZA instance, with the parallel option, i.e. one MGIZA instance per pair direction running in parallel. The target language model is a 7-gram, binarized IRSTLM (Federico et al., 2008). The weights of the distortion, translation and language models were optimized with respect to BLEU scores (Papineni et al., 2002) on a given held-out set of sentences with Minimum Error Rate Training (MERT; (Och, 2003)) in 15 iterations.

After the actual translation with Moses, an additional recasing "translation" model was applied in the same manner. Finally, the translation output underwent minimal automatic postprocessing based on regular expression replacements. This was mainly undertaken in order to fix the distribution of whitespace and some remaining capitalization issues.

5 Results

5.1 WMT10 Evaluation

In one of the tasks of the WMT10 human evaluation campaign, people were asked to rank competing translations. From each 1-through-5 ranking of a set of 5 system outputs, 10 pairwise comparisons are extracted. Then, for each system, a score is computed that tells how often it was ranked equally or better than the other system. For our system, this score is 32.35%, meaning it ranked 17th out of 19 systems for English-to-French. A number of automatic scores were also calculated and appear in Table 1.

5.2 Evaluation at the European Parliament

As the goal behind building our system has been to provide a tool to translators at EU institutions, we have also had it evaluated by two of our colleagues, both native speakers of French and working as professional translators of the French Language Unit at the Parliament's DG TRAD.

For this purpose, we had 1742 sentences of in-house documents translated by our system as well as by the rule-based ECMT and the statistics-based Google Translate.[6,7] We developed an online evaluation tool based on the one used by the WMT evaluation campaign in the last years (Callison-Burch et al., 2009) where we asked the evaluators to perform three different tasks.

In the first one, they were shown the three automatic translations plus a human reference in random order and asked to rank the four versions relative to each other on a scale from 1 to 5. The average relative ranks can be seen in Table 2.

The second task consisted of post-editing a given translation. Again, the sentence might come from one of three MT systems, or be a human translation. The absolute number of items that did not need any corrections, had to be edited, or were impossible to correct are shown in Table 3.

For the third and last task, only translations of our own system were displayed. Here, the evaluators should simply assign them to one of four quality categories as proposed by (Roturier, 2009), and additionally tick boxes standing for the presence of 13 different types of errors in the sentence concerning word order, punctuation, or different types of syntactic/semantic problems. A total of 150 segments were judged. For the categorization results, see Tables 4 and 5.

5.3 Evaluation at the European Commission

On a side note, the Portuguese Language Department also performed a manual evaluation (Leal Fontes and Machado, 2009) which involved 14 of their managers and translators, comparing their Moses-based system to

[6] `http://translate.google.com`

[7] As about a third of the source documents are not public, we could not send those to Google Translate.

	Items	Proportion
Excellent	28	18.6%
Good	42	28%
Medium	45	30%
Poor	35	23.3%

Table 4: Results of Categorization Task: Quality Categories

Error type	Occurrences
Word order	
Single word	11
Sequence of words	42
Incorrect word(s)	
Wrong lexical choice	51
Wrong terminology choice	6
Incorrect form	77
Extra word(s)	21
Missing word(s)	14
Style	44
Idioms	1
Untranslated word(s)	5
Punctuation	24
Letter case	7
Other	5

Table 5: Results of Categorization Task: Error Types

ECMT and Google. Table 6 shows how many people considered Moses better, similar, or worse compared to ECMT and Google, respectively.

Moses-based SMT did well in fields where ECMT is systematically used (e.g. Justice and Home Affairs and Trade) and showed a big improvement over ECMT in terminology-intensive domains (e.g. Fisheries). As of early 2009, more than half of their translators (58%) now already use ECMT systematically in production, i.e. for all English and French originals. 85% use it for specific language combinations or for certain domains only. On a voluntary basis, they have been replacing ECMT with Moses-based SMT for the translation of day-to-day incoming documents. Over a three-month period, more than 2500 pages have been translated in this manner, and the translators of the Portuguese department declared themselves ready to switch over to an SMT system as soon as it should become available.

Compared to	Better	Similar	Worse
ECMT	7	5	2
Google	5	5	3

Table 6: Portuguese Language Department evaluation results of Moses-based MT system

6 Discussion of Results

As expected, our system did not rank among the top competitors in the WMT10 shared task. This is mainly due to the data we trained on, which is of a very specific domain (common legislative procedures of European Institutions) and relatively small in size when compared to what others used for this language combination. In addition, we more or less used Moses out-of-the-box with no sophisticated add-ons or optimization.

In the internal evaluation, our system beat neither Google Translate nor ECMT overall but it did show a similar performance. This is all the more encouraging as Exodus has been built within less than a month, while ECMT has been developed and maintained in excess of 30 years, and while Google Translate is based on manpower and computing resources that a public administration body usually cannot provide.

Finally, the successful trials of SMT software at the EC's Portuguese department seem to indicate that such a system holds enormous potential, especially when a serious adaptation to specific language combinations and domains is taken into consideration.

7 Outlook

Further use and development of SMT at EU institutions depends on the outcome of internal evaluations, among other factors. We plan to extend our activities to other language pairs, an English-to-Greek machine translation project already having started. Given a continuation of the currently promising results, Exodus will eventually be integrated into the CAT (computer-aided translation) tools used by EU translators.[8] Furthermore, we would like to release an extended EuroParl corpus not only containing parliamentary proceedings but also other types of public documents. We estimate that such a step should foster research to the benefit of both EU institutions and machine translation in general.

8 Conclusions

We have presented Exodus, a joint pilot project of the European Commission's Directorate-General for Translation (DGT) and the European Parliament's Directorate-General for Translation (DG TRAD) with the aim of exploring the potential of deploying new approaches to machine translation in European institutions.

Our system is based on a fairly vanilla Moses installation and trained on data extracted from large in-house translation memories covering a range of EU documents. The obtained models use 7-grams.

We applied the Exodus system to this year's WMT10 shared English-to-French translation task. As the test

[8] However, speed issues will have to be addressed before as the current system is not able to provide translations in real time.

data stems from a different domain than the one targeted by our system, we did not outperform the competitors. However, results from in-house evaluation are promising and indicate the big potential of SMT for European Institutions.

Acknowledgments

We would very much like to thank (in alphabetical order) Manuel Tomás Carrasco Benítez, Dirk De Paepe, Alfons De Vuyst, Peter Hjortsø, Herman Jenné, Hilário Leal Fontes, Maria José Machado, Spyridon Pilos, João Rosas, Helmut Spindler, Filiep Spyckerelle, and Angelika Vaasa for their invaluable help and support.

David Kolovratník was supported by the Czech Science Foundation under contract no. 201/09/H057 and by the Grant Agency of Charles University under contract no. 100008/2008.

References

A. Blatt. 1998. EURAMIS : Added value by integration. In *T&T Terminologie et Traduction, 1.1998*, pages 59–73.

Chris Callison-Burch, Philipp Koehn, Christof Monz, and Josh Schroeder. 2009. Findings of the 2009 Workshop on Statistical Machine Translation. In *Proceedings of the Fourth Workshop on Statistical Machine Translation*, pages 1–28, Athens, Greece, March. Association for Computational Linguistics.

Marcello Federico, Nicola Bertoldi, and Mauro Cettolo. 2008. IRSTLM: an Open Source Toolkit for Handling Large Scale Language Models. In *Proceedings of Interspeech*, Brisbane, Australia.

Qin Gao and Stephan Vogel. 2008. Parallel Implementations of Word Alignment Tool. In *Software Engineering, Testing, and Quality Assurance for Natural Language Processing*, pages 49–57, Columbus, Ohio, June. Association for Computational Linguistics.

Philipp Koehn, Hieu Hoang, Alexandra Birch, Chris Callison-Burch, Marcello Federico, Nicola Bertoldi, Brooke Cowan, Wade Shen, Christine Moran, Richard Zens, Chris Dyer, Ondrej Bojar, Alexandra Constantin, and Evan Herbst. 2007. Moses: Open Source Toolkit for Statistical Machine Translation. In *Proc. of ACL Demo and Poster Sessions*, pages 177–180, Jun.

Hilário Leal Fontes and Maria José Machado. 2009. Contribution of the Portuguese Langauge Department to the Evaluation of Moses Machine Translation System. Technical report, Portuguese Language Department, DGT, European Commission, December.

Franz Josef Och and Hermann Ney. 2003. A Systematic Comparison of Various Statistical Alignment Models. *Computational Linguistics*, 29(1):19–51, March.

Franz Josef Och. 2003. Minimum Error Rate Training for Statistical Machine Translation. In *Proceedings of ACL*, Sapporo, Japan, July.

Kishore Papineni, Salim Roukos, Todd Ward, and Wei-Jing Zhu. 2002. BLEU: A Method for Automatic Evaluation of Machine Translation. In *ACL '02: Proceedings of the 40th Annual Meeting on Association for Computational Linguistics*, pages 311–318, Morristown, NJ, USA. Association for Computational Linguistics.

Johann Roturier. 2009. Deploying novel MT technology to raise the bar for quality: A review of key advantages and challenges. In *The twelfth Machine Translation Summit*, Ottawa, Canada, August. International Association for Machine Translation.

D. Theologitis. 1997. EURAMIS, the platform of the EC translator. In *EAMT Workshop*, pages 17–32.

More Linguistic Annotation for Statistical Machine Translation

Philipp Koehn, Barry Haddow, Philip Williams, and Hieu Hoang
University of Edinburgh
Edinburgh, United Kingdom
{pkoehn,bhaddow,p.j.williams-2,h.hoang}@inf.ed.ac.uk

Abstract

We report on efforts to build large-scale translation systems for eight European language pairs. We achieve most gains from the use of larger training corpora and basic modeling, but also show promising results from integrating more linguistic annotation.

1 Introduction

We participated in the shared translation task of the ACL Workshop for Statistical Machine Translation 2010 in all language pairs. We continued our efforts to integrate linguistic annotation into the translation process, using factored and tree-based translation models. On average we outperformed our submission from last year by 2.16 BLEU points on the same newstest2009 test set.

While the submitted system follows the factored phrase-based approach, we also built hierarchical and syntax-based models for the English–German language pair and report on its performance on the development test sets. All our systems are based on the Moses toolkit (Koehn et al., 2007).

We achieved gains over the systems from last year by consistently exploiting all available training data, using large-scale domain-interpolated, and consistent use of the factored translation model to integrate n-gram models over speech tags. We also experimented with novel domain adaptation methods, with mixed results.

2 Baseline System

The baseline system uses all available training data, except for the large UN and 10^9 corpora, as well as the optional LDC Gigaword corpus. It uses a straight-forward setup of the Moses decoder.

Some relevant parameter settings are:

- maximum sentence length 80 words
- tokenization with hyphen splitting
- truecasing
- *grow-diag-final-and* alignment heuristic
- *msd-bidirectional-fe* lexicalized reordering
- interpolated 5-gram language model
- tuning on *newsdev2009*
- testing during development on *newstest2009*
- MBR decoding
- no reordering over punctuation
- cube pruning

We used most of these setting in our submission last year (Koehn and Haddow, 2009).

The main difference to our baseline system from the submission from last year is the use of additional training data: larger releases of the News Commentary, Europarl, Czeng, and monolingual news corpora. The first two parallel corpora increased roughly 10-20% in size, while the Czeng parallel corpus and the monolingual news corpora are five times and twice as big, respectively.

We also handled some of the corpus preparation steps with more care to avoid some data inconsistency problems from last year (affecting mostly the French language pairs).

An overview of the results is given in Table 1. The baseline outperforms our submission from last year by an average of +1.25 points. The gains for the individual language pairs track the increase in training data (most significantly for the Czech–English pairs), and the French–English data processing issue.

Note that last year's submission used special handling of the German–English language pair, which we did not replicate in the baseline system, but report on below.

The table also contains results on the extensions discussed in the next section.

Proceedings of the Joint 5th Workshop on Statistical Machine Translation and MetricsMATR, pages 115–120,
Uppsala, Sweden, 15-16 July 2010.

Language Pair	'09	Baseline	GT Smooth.	UN Data	Factored	Beam
Spanish-English	24.41	25.25 (+0.76)	25.48 (+0.23)	26.03 (+0.55)	26.20 (+0.17)	26.22 (+0.02)
French-English	23.88	25.23 (+1.35)	25.37 (+0.14)	25.92 (+0.55)	26.13 (+0.21)	26.07 (–0.08)
German-English	18.51	19.47 (+0.96)	19.51 (+0.04)	-	21.09 (+0.24)	21.10 (+0.01)
Czech-English	18.49	20.74 (+2.25)	21.19 (+0.45)	-	21.33 (+0.14)	21.32 (–0.01)
English-Spanish	23.27	24.20 (+0.93)	24.65 (+0.45)	24.65 (+0.30)	24.37 (–0.28)	24.42 (+0.05)
English-French	22.50	23.83 (+1.33)	23.72 (–0.11)	24.70 (+0.98)	24.74 (+0.04)	24.92 (+0.18)
English-German	14.22	14.68 (+0.46)	14.81 (+0.13)	-	15.28 (+0.47)	15.34 (+0.06)
English-Czech	12.64	14.63 (+1.99)	14.68 (+0.05)	-	-	-
avg		+1.25	+0.17	+0.60	+0.14	+0.03

Table 1: **Overview of results:** baseline system and extensions. On average we outperformed our submission from last year by 1.87 BLEU points on the same newstest2009 test set. For additional gains for French–English and German–English, please see Tables 7 and 8.

Czech–English

Corpus	Num. Tokens	Pplx.	Weight
EU	29,238,799	582	0.054
Fiction	15,441,105	429	0.028
Navajo	561,144	671	0.002
News (czeng)	2,909,322	288	0.127
News (mono)	1,148,480,525	175	0.599
Subtitles	23,914,244	526	0.019
Techdoc	8,322,958	851	0.099
Web	4,469,177	441	0.073

French–English

Corpus	Num. Tokens	Pplx.	Weight
Europarl	50,132,615	352	0.105
News Com.	2,101,921	311	0.204
UN	216,052,412	383	0.089
News	1,148,480,525	175	0.601

Table 2: English LM interpolation: number of tokens, perplexity, and interpolation weight for the different corpora

2.1 Interpolated Language Model

The WMT training data exhibits an increasing diversity of corpora: Europarl, News Commentary, UN, 10^9, News — and seven different sources within the Czeng corpus.

It is well known that domain adaptation is an important step in optimizing machine translation systems. A relatively simple and straight-forward method is the linear interpolation of the language model, as we explored previously (Koehn and Schroeder, 2007; Schwenk and Koehn, 2008).

We trained domain-specific language models separately and then linearly interpolated them using SRILM toolkit (Stolke, 2002) with weights optimized on the development set *newsdev2009*.

See Table 2 for numbers on perplexity, corpus sizes, and interpolation weights. Note, for instance, the relatively high weight for the News Commentary corpus (0.204) compared to the Europarl corpus (0.105) in the English language model for the French-English system, despite the latter being about 25 times bigger.

Language Pair	Cased	Uncased
Spanish-English	25.25	26.36 (+1.11)
French-English	25.23	26.29 (+1.06)
German-English	19.47	20.63 (+1.16)
Czech-English	20.74	21.76 (+1.02)
English-Spanish	24.20	25.47 (+1.27)
English-French	23.83	25.02 (+1.19)
English-German	14.68	15.18 (+0.50)
English-Czech	14.63	15.13 (+0.50)
avg		+0.98

Table 3: Effect of truecasing: cased and uncased BLEU scores

2.2 Truecasing

As last year, we deal with uppercase and lowercase forms of the same words by truecasing the corpus. This means that we change each surface word occurrence of a word to its natural case, e.g., *the, Europe*. During truecasing, we change the first word of a sentence to its most frequent casing. During de-truecasing, we uppercase the first letter of the first word of a sentence.

See Table 3 for the performance of this method. In this table, we compare the cased and uncased BLEU scores, and observe that we lose on average roughly one BLEU point due to wrong casing.

Count	Count of Count	Discount	Count*
1	357,929,182	0.140	0.140
2	24,966,751	0.487	0.975
3	8,112,930	0.671	2.014
4	4,084,365	0.714	2.858
5	2,334,274	0.817	4.088

Table 4: Good Turing smoothing, as in the French–English model: counts, counts of counts, discounting factor and discounted count

3 Extensions

In this section, we describe extensions over the baseline system. On average, these give us improvements of about 1 BLEU point over the baseline.

3.1 Good Turing Smoothing

Traditionally, we use raw counts to estimate conditional probabilities for phrase translation. However, this method gives dubious results for rare counts. The most blatant case is the single occurrence of a foreign phrase, whose sole English translation will receive the translation probability $\frac{1}{1} = 1$.

Foster et al. (2006) applied ideas from language model smoothing to the translation model. Good Turing smoothing (Good, 1953) uses counts of counts statistics to assess how likely we will see a word (or, in our case, a phrase) again, if we have seen it n times in the training corpus. Instead of using the raw counts, adapted (lower) counts are used in the estimation of the conditional probability distribution.

The count of counts are collected for the phrase pairs. See Table 4 for details on how this effects the French–English model. For instance, we find singleton 357,929,182 phrase pairs and 24,966,751 phrase pairs that occur twice. The Good Turing formula tells us to adapt singleton counts to $\frac{24,966,751}{357,929,182} = 0.14$. This means for our degenerate example of a single occurrence of a single French phrase that its single English translation has probability $\frac{0.14}{1} = 0.14$ (we do not adjust the denominator).

Good Turing smoothing of the translation table gives us a gain of +0.17 BLEU points on average, and improvements for 7 out of 8 language pairs. For details refer back to Table 1.

Model	BLEU
Baseline	14.81
Part-of-Speech	15.03 (+0.22)
Morphogical	15.28 (+0.47)

Table 5: English–German: use of morphological and part-of-speech n-gram models

3.2 UN Data

While we already used the UN data in the language model for the Spanish–English and French–English language pairs, we now also add it to the translation model.

The corpus is very large, four times bigger than the already used training data, but relatively out of domain, as indicated by the high perplexity and low interpolation weight during language model interpolation (recall Table 2).

Adding the corpus to the four systems gives improvements of +0.60 BLEU points on average. For details refer back to Table 1.

3.3 POS n-gram Model

The factored model approach (Koehn and Hoang, 2007) allows us to integrate 7-gram models over part-of-speech tags. The part-of-speech tags are produced during decoding by the phrase mapping of surface words on the source side to a factored representation of surface words and their part-of-speech tags on the target side in one translation step.

We previously used this additional scoring component for the German–English language pairs with success. Thus we now applied to it all other language pairs (except for English–Czech due to the lack of a Czech part-of-speech tagger).

We used the following part-of-speech taggers:

- English: mxpost[1]
- German: LoPar[2]
- French: TreeTagger[3]
- Spanish: TreeTagger

For English–German, we also used morphological tags, which give better performance than just basic part-of-speech tags (+0.46 vs. +0.22, see Table 5). We observe gains for all language pairs except for English–Spanish, possibly due to the

[1] www.inf.ed.ac.uk/resources/nlp/local_doc/MXPOST.html

[2] www.ims.uni-stuttgart.de/projekte/gramotron/SOFTWARE/LoPar.html

[3] www.ims.uni-stuttgart.de/projekte/corplex/TreeTagger/

Model	BLEU
Baseline	14.81
Part-of-Speech	15.03 (+0.22)
Morphogical	15.28 (+0.47)

Table 6: English–German: use of morphological and part-of-speech n-gram models

Language Pair	Baseline	with 10^9
French–English	25.92	27.15 (+1.23)
English–French	24.70	24.80 (+0.10)

Table 7: Use of large French–English corpus

faulty use of the Spanish part-of-speech tagger. We gain +0.14 BLEU points on average (including the –0.28 drop for Spanish). For details refer back to Table 1.

3.4 Bigger Beam Sizes

As a final general improvement, we adjusted the beam settings during decoding. We increased the pop-limit from 5,000 to 20,000 and the translation table limit from the default 20 to 50.

The decoder is quite fast, partly due to multi-threaded decoding using 4 cores machines (Haddow, 2010). Increasing the beam sizes slowed down decoding speed from about 2 seconds per sentence to about 8 sec/sentence.

However, this resulted only in minimal gains, on average +0.03 BLEU. For details refer back to Table 1.

3.5 10^9 Corpus

Last year, due to time constraints, we were not able to use the billion word 10^9 corpus for the French–English language pairs. This is largest publicly available parallel corpus, and it does strain computing resources, for instance forcing us to use multi-threaded GIZA++ (Gao and Vogel, 2008).

Table 7 shows the gains obtained from using this corpus in both the translation model and the language model opposed to a baseline system trained with otherwise the same settings. For French–English we see large gains (+1.23), but not for English–French (+0.10).

Our official submission for the French–English language pairs used these models. They did not include a part-of-speech language model and bigger beam sizes.

Model	BLEU
Baseline	19.51
+ compound splitting	20.09 (+0.58)
+ pre-reordering	20.03 (+0.52)
+ both	20.85 (+1.34)

Table 8: Special handling of German–English

Language Pair	Baseline	Weighted TM
Spanish-English	26.20	26.15 (–0.05)
French-English	26.11	26.30 (+0.19)
German-English	21.09	20.81 (–0.28)
Czech-English	21.33	21.21 (–0.12)
English-German	15.28	15.01 (–0.27)
avg.		–0.11

Table 9: Interpolating the translation model with language model weights

3.6 German–English

For the German–English language direction, we used two additional processing steps that have shown to be successful in the past, and again resulted in significant gains.

We split large words based on word frequencies to tackle the problem of word compounds in German (Koehn and Knight, 2003). Secondly, we re-order the German input to the decoder (and the German side of the training data) to align more closely to the English target language (Collins et al., 2005).

The two methods improve +0.58 and +0.52 over the baseline individually, and +1.34 when combined. See also Table 8.

3.7 Translation Model Interpolation

Finally, we explored a novel domain adaption method for the translation model. Since the interpolation of language models is very successful, we want to interpolate translation models similarly. Given interpolation weights, the resulting translation table is a weighted linear interpolation of the individual translation models trained separately for each domain.

However, while for language models we have a effective method to find the interpolation weights (optimizing perplexity on a development set), we do not have such a method for the translation model. Thus, we simply recycle the weights we obtained from language model interpolation (excluding the weighting for monolingual corpora).

Model	BLEU
phrase-based	14.81
factored phrase-based	15.28
hierarchical	14.86
target syntax	14.66

Table 10: Tree-based models for English–German

Over the Spanish–English baseline system, we obtained gains of +0.39 BLEU points. Unfortunately, we did not see comparable gains on the systems optimized by the preceding steps. In fact, in 4 out of 5 language pairs, we observed lower BLEU scores. See Table 9 for details.

We did not use this method in our submission.

4 Tree-Based Models

A major extension of the capabilities of the Moses system is the accommodation of tree-based models (Hoang et al., 2009). While we have not yet carried out sufficient experimentation and optimization of the implementation, we took the occasion of the shared translation task as a opportunity to build large-scale systems using such models.

We build two translation systems: One using tree-based models without additional linguistic annotation, which are known as hierarchical phrase-based models (Chiang, 2005), and another system that uses linguistic annotation on the target side, which are known under many names such as string-to-tree models or syntactified target models (Marcu et al., 2006).

Both models are trained using a very similar pipeline as for the phrase model. The main difference is that the translation rules do not have to be contiguous phrases, but may contain gaps with are labeled and co-ordinated by non-terminal symbols. Decoding with such models requires a very different algorithm, which is related to syntactic chart parsing.

In the target syntax model, the target gaps and the entire target phrase must map to constituents in the parse tree. This restriction may be relaxed by adding constituent labels such as DET+ADJ or NP\DET to group neighboring constituents or indicate constituents that lack an initial child, respectively (Zollmann and Venugopal, 2006).

We applied these models to the English–German language direction, which is of particular interest to us due to the rich target side morphology and large degree of reordering, resulting in relatively poor performance. See Table 10 for experimental results with the two traditional models (phrase-based model and a factored model that includes a 7-gram morphological tag model) and the two newer models (hierarchical and target syntax). The performance of the phrase-based, hierarchical, and target syntax model are close in terms of BLEU.

5 Conclusions

We obtained substantial gains over our systems from last year for all language pairs. To a large part, these gains are due to additional training data and our ability to exploit them.

We also saw gains from adding linguistic annotation (in form of 7-gram models over part-of-speech tags) and promising results for tree-based models. At this point, we are quite satisfied being able to build competitive systems with these new models, which opens up major new research directions.

Everything we described here is part of the open source Moses toolkit. Thus, all our experiments should be replicable with publicly available resources.

Acknowledgement

This work was supported by the EuroMatrixPlus project funded by the European Commission (7th Framework Programme).

References

Chiang, D. (2005). A hierarchical phrase-based model for statistical machine translation. In *Proceedings of the 43rd Annual Meeting of the Association for Computational Linguistics (ACL'05)*, pages 263–270, Ann Arbor, Michigan. Association for Computational Linguistics.

Collins, M., Koehn, P., and Kucerova, I. (2005). Clause restructuring for statistical machine translation. In *Proceedings of the 43rd Annual Meeting of the Association for Computational Linguistics (ACL'05)*, pages 531–540, Ann Arbor, Michigan. Association for Computational Linguistics.

Foster, G., Kuhn, R., and Johnson, H. (2006). Phrasetable smoothing for statistical machine translation. In *Proceedings of the 2006 Conference on Empirical Methods in Natural Language Processing*, pages 53–61, Sydney, Australia. Association for Computational Linguistics.

Gao, Q. and Vogel, S. (2008). Parallel implementations of word alignment tool. In *ACL Workshop on Software Engineering, Testing, and Quality Assurance for Natural Language Processing*, pages 49–57.

Good, I. J. (1953). The population frequency of species and the estimation of population parameters. *Biometrika*, 40:237–264.

Haddow, B. (2010). Adding multi-threaded decoding to moses. *The Prague Bulletin of Mathematical Linguistics*, (93):57–66.

Hoang, H., Koehn, P., and Lopez, A. (2009). A unified framework for phrase-based, hierarchical, and syntax-based statistical machine translation. In *Proceedings of IWSLT*.

Koehn, P. and Haddow, B. (2009). Edinburgh's submission to all tracks of the WMT2009 shared task with reordering and speed improvements to Moses. In *Proceedings of the Fourth Workshop on Statistical Machine Translation*, pages 160–164, Athens, Greece. Association for Computational Linguistics.

Koehn, P. and Hoang, H. (2007). Factored translation models. In *Proceedings of the 2007 Joint Conference on Empirical Methods in Natural Language Processing and Computational Natural Language Learning (EMNLP-CoNLL)*, pages 868–876.

Koehn, P., Hoang, H., Birch, A., Callison-Burch, C., Federico, M., Bertoldi, N., Cowan, B., Shen, W., Moran, C., Zens, R., Dyer, C. J., Bojar, O., Constantin, A., and Herbst, E. (2007). Moses: Open source toolkit for statistical machine translation. In *Proceedings of the 45th Annual Meeting of the Association for Computational Linguistics Companion Volume Proceedings of the Demo and Poster Sessions*, pages 177–180, Prague, Czech Republic. Association for Computational Linguistics.

Koehn, P. and Knight, K. (2003). Empirical methods for compound splitting. In *Proceedings of Meeting of the European Chapter of the Association of Computational Linguistics (EACL)*.

Koehn, P. and Schroeder, J. (2007). Experiments in domain adaptation for statistical machine translation. In *Proceedings of the Second Workshop on Statistical Machine Translation*, pages 224–227, Prague, Czech Republic. Association for Computational Linguistics.

Marcu, D., Wang, W., Echihabi, A., and Knight, K. (2006). Spmt: Statistical machine translation with syntactified target language phrases. In *Proceedings of the 2006 Conference on Empirical Methods in Natural Language Processing*, pages 44–52, Sydney, Australia. Association for Computational Linguistics.

Schwenk, H. and Koehn, P. (2008). Large and diverse language models for statistical machine translation. In *Proceedings of the 3rd International Joint Conference on Natural Language Processing (IJCNLP)*.

Stolke, A. (2002). SRILM - an extensible language modeling toolkit. In *Proceedings of the International Conference on Spoken Language Processing*.

Zollmann, A. and Venugopal, A. (2006). Syntax augmented machine translation via chart parsing. In *Proceedings on the Workshop on Statistical Machine Translation*, pages 138–141, New York City. Association for Computational Linguistics.

LIUM SMT Machine Translation System for WMT 2010

Patrik Lambert, Sadaf Abdul-Rauf and Holger Schwenk
LIUM, University of Le Mans
72085 Le Mans cedex 9, FRANCE
FirstName.LastName@lium.univ-lemans.fr

Abstract

This paper describes the development of French–English and English–French machine translation systems for the 2010 WMT shared task evaluation. These systems were standard phrase-based statistical systems based on the Moses decoder, trained on the provided data only. Most of our efforts were devoted to the choice and extraction of bilingual data used for training. We filtered out some bilingual corpora and pruned the phrase table. We also investigated the impact of adding two types of additional bilingual texts, extracted automatically from the available monolingual data. We first collected bilingual data by performing automatic translations of monolingual texts. The second type of bilingual text was harvested from comparable corpora with Information Retrieval techniques.

1 Introduction

This paper describes the machine translation systems developed by the Computer Science laboratory at the University of Le Mans (LIUM) for the 2010 WMT shared task evaluation. We only considered the translation between French and English (in both directions). The main differences with respect to previous year's system (Schwenk et al., 2009) are as follows: restriction to the data recommended for the workshop, usage of the (filtered) French–English gigaword bitext, pruning of the phrase table, and usage of automatic translations of the monolingual news corpus to improve the translation model. We also used a larger amount of bilingual data extracted from comparable corpora than was done in 2009. These different points are described in the rest of the paper, together with a summary of the experimental results showing the impact of each component.

2 Resources Used

The following sections describe how the resources provided or allowed in the shared task were used to train the translation and language models of the system.

2.1 Bilingual data

Our system was developed in two stages. First, a baseline system was built to generate automatic translations of some of the monolingual data available. These automatic translations may be used directly with the source texts to build additional bitexts, or as queries of an Information Retrieval (IR) system to extract new bitexts from comparable corpora. In a second stage, these additional bilingual data were incorporated to the system (see Section 4 and Tables 1 and 2).

The latest version of the News-Commentary (NC) corpus, of the Europarl (Eparl) corpus (version 5), and of the United Nations (UN) corpus were used. We also took as training data a subset of the French–English Gigaword (10^9) corpus. Since a significant part of the data was crawled from the web, we thought that many sentence pairs may be only approximate translations of each other. We applied a lexical filter to discard them. Furthermore, some sentences of this corpus were extracted from web page menus and are not grammatical. Although we could have used a part of the menu items as a dictionary, for simplicity we applied an n-gram language model (LM) filter to remove all non-grammatical sentences. Thanks to this filter, sentences out of the language model domain (in this case, mainly the news domain), may also have been discarded because they contain many unknown or unfrequent n-grams. The lexical filter was based on the IBM model 1 cost (Brown et al., 1993) of each side of a sentence pair given the other side, normalised with respect to both sentence lengths. This filter

Proceedings of the Joint 5th Workshop on Statistical Machine Translation and MetricsMATR, pages 121–126,
Uppsala, Sweden, 15-16 July 2010. ©2010 Association for Computational Linguistics

was trained on a corpus composed of Eparl, NC, and UN data. The language model filter was an n-gram LM cost of the target sentence (see Section 3), normalised with respect to its length. This filter was trained with all monolingual resources available except the 10^9 data. We generated a first subset, 10^9_1, selecting sentence pairs with a lexical cost inferior to 4 and an LM cost inferior to 2.3. The corpus selected in this way contains 115 million words in the English side (out of 580 million in the original corpus). Close to the evaluation deadline we decided to generate a second corpus (10^9_2) by raising the LM cost threshold to 2.6. The 10^9_2 corpus contains 232 million words on the English side (twice as much as in the 10^9_1 corpus).

In the French side of the bilingual corpora, for the French–English direction only, the contractions 'du' ('of the'), 'au' and 'aux' ('to the' singular and plural) were substituted by their expanded forms ('de le', 'à le' and 'à les').

2.2 Use of Automatic Translations and Comparable corpora

Available human translated bitexts such as the UN corpus seem to be out-of domain for this task. We used two types of automatically extracted resources to adapt our system to the task domain.

First, we generated automatic translations of the French News corpus provided (231M words), and selected the sentences with a normalised translation cost (returned by the decoder) inferior to a threshold. The resulting bitext has no new words in the English side, since all words of the translation output come from the translation model, but it contains new combinations (phrases) of known words, and reinforces the probability of some phrase pairs (Schwenk, 2008).

Second, as in last year's evaluation, we automatically extracted and aligned parallel sentences from comparable in-domain corpora. This year we used the AFP and APW news texts since there are available in the French and English LDC Gigaword corpora. The general architecture of our parallel sentence extraction system is described in detail by Abdul-Rauf and Schwenk (2009). We first translated 91M words from French into English using our first stage SMT system. These English sentences were then used to search for translations in the English AFP and APW texts of the Gigaword corpus using information retrieval techniques. The Lemur toolkit (Ogilvie and Callan, 2001) was used for this purpose. Search was limited to a window of ± 5 days of the date of the French news text. The retrieved candidate sentences were then filtered using the Translation Error Rate (TER) with respect to the automatic translations. In this study, sentences with a TER below 65% for the French–English system and 75% for the English–French system were kept. Sentences with a large length difference (French versus English) or containing a large fraction of numbers were also discarded. By these means, about 15M words of additional bitexts were obtained to include in the French–English system, and 21M words to include in the English–French system. Note that these additional bitexts do not depend on the translation direction. The most suitable amount of additional data was just different in the French–English and English–French translation directions.

2.3 Monolingual data

The French and English target language models were trained on all provided monolingual data. In addition, LDC's Gigaword collection was used for both languages. Data corresponding to the development and test periods were removed from the Gigaword collections.

2.4 Development data

All development was done on *news-test2008*, and *newstest2009* was used as internal test set. For all corpora except the French side of the bitexts used to train the French–English system (see above), the default Moses tokenization was used. However, we added abbreviations for the French tokenizer. All our models are case sensitive and include punctuation. The BLEU scores reported in this paper were calculated with the multi-bleu.perl tool and are case sensitive. The BLEU score was one of metrics with the best correlation with human ratings in last year evaluation (Callison-Burch et al., 2009) for the French–English and English–French directions.

3 Architecture of the SMT system

The goal of statistical machine translation (SMT) is to produce a target sentence e from a source sentence f. It is today common practice to use phrases as translation units (Koehn et al., 2003; Och and Ney, 2003) and a log linear framework in order to introduce several models explaining the translation process:

$$e^* = \arg\max_e p(e|f) = \arg\max_e \{exp(\sum_i \lambda_i h_i(e,f))\} \quad (1)$$

The feature functions h_i are the system models and the λ_i weights are typically optimized to maximize a scoring function on a development set (Och and Ney, 2002). In our system fourteen features functions were used, namely phrase and lexical translation probabilities in both directions, seven features for the lexicalized distortion model, a word and a phrase penalty and a target language model (LM).

The system is based on the Moses SMT toolkit (Koehn et al., 2007) and constructed as follows. First, word alignments in both directions are calculated. We used a multi-threaded version of the GIZA++ tool (Gao and Vogel, 2008).[1] This speeds up the process and corrects an error of GIZA++ that can appear with rare words.

Phrases and lexical reorderings are extracted using the default settings of the Moses toolkit. The parameters of Moses were tuned on *newstest2008*, using the 'new' MERT tool. We repeated the training process three times, each with a different seed value for the optimisation algorithm. In this way we have an rough idea of the error introduced by the tuning process.

4-gram back-off LMs were used. The word list contains all the words of the bitext used to train the translation model and all words that appear at least ten times in the monolingual corpora. Words of the monolingual corpora containing special characters or sequences of uppercase characters were not included in the word list. Separate LMs were build on each data source with the SRI LM toolkit (Stolcke, 2002) and then linearly interpolated, optimizing the coefficients with an EM procedure. The perplexities of these LMs were 103.4 for French and 149.2 for English.

4 Results and Discussion

The results of our SMT system for the French–English and English–French tasks are summarized in Tables 1 and 2, respectively. The MT metric scores are the average of three optimisations performed with different seeds (see Section 3). The numbers in parentheses are the standard deviation of these three values. The standard deviation gives a lower bound of the significance of the difference between two systems. If the difference between two average scores is less than the sum of the standard deviations, we can say that this difference is not significant. The reverse is not true. Note that most of the improvements shown in the tables are small and not significant. However many of the gains are cumulative and the sum of several small gains makes a significant difference.

Phrase-table Pruning

We tried to prune the phrase-table as proposed by Johnson et. al. (2007), and available in moses ('sigtest-filter'). We used the $\alpha - \epsilon$ filter[2]. As lines 3 and 4 of Table 1, and lines 3 and 4 of Table 2 reveal, in addition to the reduction 43% of the phrase-table, a small gain in BLEU score (0.15 and 0.11 respectively) was obtained with the pruning.

Baseline French–English System

The first section of Table 1 (lines 1 to 5) shows results of the development of the baseline SMT system, used to generate automatic translations. Although being out-of-domain data, the introduction of the UN corpus yields an improvement of one BLEU point with respect to Eparl+NC. Adding the 10^9_1 corpus, we gain 0.7 BLEU point more. Actually, we obtained the same score with the 10^9_1 added directly to Eparl+NC (line 5). However, we choose to include the UN corpus to generate translations to have a larger vocabulary. The system highlighted in bold (line 4) is the one we choose to generate our English translations.

Although no French translations were generated, we did similar experiments in the English–French direction (lines 1 to 4 of Table 2). In this direction, the 10^9_1 corpus is still more valuable than the UN corpus when added to Eparl+NC, but with less difference in terms of BLEU score. In this di-

[1]The source is available at `http://www.cs.cmu.edu/~qing/`

[2]The p-value of two-by-two contingency tables (describing the degree of association between a source and a target phrase) is calculated with Fisher exact test. This probability is interpreted as the probability of observing by chance an association that is at least as strong as the given one, and hence as its significance. An important special case of a table occurs when a phrase pair occurs exactly once in the corpus, and each of the component phrases occurs exactly once in its side of the parallel corpus (1-1-1 phrase pairs). In this case the negative log of the p-value is $\alpha = logN$ (N is number of sentence pairs in the corpus). $\alpha - \epsilon$ is the largest threshold that results in all of the 1-1-1 phrase pairs being included.

rection, we obtain a gain by adding the UN corpus to Eparl+NC+10^9_1.

Filtering the 10^9 Corpus

Lines 5 to 7 of Table 1 show the impact of filtering the 10^9 corpus. The system trained on the full 10^9 corpus added to Eparl+NC achieves a BLEU score of 26.83. Substituting the full 10^9 corpus by 10^9_1 (5 times smaller), i.e. using the first filtering settings, we gain 0.13 BLEU point. Using 10^9_2 instead of 10^9_1, we gain another 0.16 BLEU point, that is 0.3 in total. With respect to not using the 10^9 data at all (as we did last year), we gain 0.8 BLEU point.

Impact of the Additional Bitexts

With the baseline French–English SMT system (see above), we translated the French News corpus to generated an additional bitext (News). We also translated some parts of the French LDC Gigaword corpus, to serve as queries to our IR system (see section 2.2). The resulting additional bitext is referred to as IR. Lines 8 to 13 of Table 1 and lines 6 to 12 of Table 2 summarize the system development including the additional bitexts.

With the News additional bitext added to Eparl+NC, we obtain a system of similar performance as the baseline system used to generate the automatic translations, but with less than 30% of the data. This holds in both translation directions. Adding the News corpus to a larger corpus, such as Eparl+NC+10^9_1, has less impact but still yields some improvement: 0.15 BLEU point in French–English and 0.3 in English–French. Thus, the News bitext translated from French to English may have more impact when translating from English to French than in the opposite direction. Note that the number of additional phrase-table entries per additional running word is twice as high for the News bitext than for the other corpora. For example, with respect to Eparl+NC+UN+10^9_1 (Table 2), Eparl+NC+UN+10^9_1+News has 56M more words and 116M more entries in the phrase-table, thus the ratio is more than 2. For all other corpora, the ratio is equal to 1 or less. This is unexpected, particularly in this case where the News bitext has no new English vocabulary with respect to the Eparl+NC+UN+10^9_1 corpus, from which its English side was generated.

With the IR additional bitext added to Eparl+NC, we obtain a system of similar performance as the system trained on Eparl+NC+UN, while the IR bitext is 10 times smaller than the UN corpus. Added to Eparl+NC+10^9_1+News, the IR bitext allows gains of 0.13 and 0.2 BLEU point respectively in the French–English and English–French directions.

Comparing the systems trained on Eparl+NC+10^9_1 or Eparl+NC+10^9_2 to the systems trained on the same corpora plus News+IR, we can estimate the cumulative impact of the additional bitexts. The gain is around 0.3 BLEU point for French–English and around 0.5 BLEU point for English–French.

Final System

In both translation directions our best system was the one trained on Eparl+NC+10^9_2+News+IR. We further achieved small improvements (0.3 BLEU point) by pruning the phrase-table (as above) and by using a language model with no cut-off together with increasing the beam size and/or the maximum number of translation table entries per input phrase. Note that the English LM with cut-off had a size of 6G, and the one with no cut-off had a size of 29G. It was too much to fit in our 72G machines so we pruned it with the SRILM pruning tool down to a size of 19G. The French LM with cut-off had a size of 2G and the one with no cut-off had a size of 9G. These sizes correspond to the binary format. Taking as example the French–English direction, the running time went from 8600 seconds for the system of line 14 (with a threshold pruning coefficient of 0.4 and a LM with cut-off) to 28200 seconds for the system submitted (with the LM without cut-off pruned by the SRILM tool and a threshold pruning coefficient of 0.00001).

5 Conclusions and Further Work

We presented the development of our machine translation system for the French–English and English–French 2010 WMT shared task. Our system was actually a standard phrase-based SMT system based on the Moses decoder. Its originality mostly lied in the choice and extraction of the training data used.

We decided to use a part of the 10^9 French–English corpus. We found this resource useful, even without filtering. We nevertheless gained 0.3 BLEU point by selecting sentences based on an IBM Model 1 filter and a language model filter.

We pruned the phrase table with the 'sigtest-filter' distributed in Moses, yielding improve-

	Bitext	#Fr Words (M)	P-table size (M)	Mem (G)	news-test2008 BLEU	newstest2009 BLEU
1	Eparl+NC	52	66	19.3	22.80 (0.03)	25.31 (0.2)
2	Eparl+NC+UN	275	250	22.8	23.38 (0.1)	26.30 (0.2)
3	Eparl+NC+UN+10^9_1	406	376	25.1	23.81 (0.05)	27.0 (0.2)
4	**Eparl+NC+UN+10^9_1 pruned**	**406**	**215**	**21.4**	**23.96 (0.1)**	**27.15 (0.18)**
5	Eparl+NC+10^9_1	183	198	22.1	23.83 (0.07)	26.96 (0.04)
6	Eparl+NC+10^9_2	320	319	24.1	23.95 (0.03)	27.12 (0.1)
7	Eparl+NC+10^9	733	580	29.5	23.65 (0.09)	26.83 (0.2)
8	Eparl+NC+News	111	188	19.5	23.46 (0.1)	26.95 (0.2)
9	Eparl+NC+10^9_1+News	242	317	22.5	23.77 (0.04)	27.11 (0.04)
10	Eparl+NC+IR	68	78	19.5	22.97 (0.03)	26.20 (0.1)
11	Eparl+NC+News+IR	127	198	20.1	23.62 (0.01)	27.04 (0.06)
12	Eparl+NC+10^9_1+News+IR	258	327	22.8	23.75 (0.05)	27.24 (0.05)
13	Eparl+NC+10^9_2+News+IR	395	441	24.4	23.87 (0.03)	27.43 (0.08)
14	**Eparl+NC+10^9_2+News+IR pruned** (+larger beam, +no-cutoff LM)	**395**	**285**	**62.5**	**24.04**	**27.72**

Table 1: French–English results: number of French words (in million), number of entries in the phrase-table (in million), memory needed during decoding (in gigabytes) and BLEU scores in the development (news-test2008) and internal test (newstest2009) sets for the different systems developped. The BLEU scores and the number in parentheses are the average and standard deviation over 3 values (see Section 3.)

ments of 0.1 to 0.2 BLEU point for a 43% reduction of the phrase-table size.

We used additional bitexts extracted automatically from the available monolingual corpora. The first type of additional bitext is generated with automatic translations of the monolingual data with a baseline SMT system. The second one is extracted from comparable corpora, with Information Retrieval techniques. With the additional bitexts we gained 0.3 and 0.5 BLEU point for the French–English and English–French systems, respectively.

Next year we want to perform an improved selection of parallel training data with re-sampling techniques. We also want to use a continuous space language model (Schwenk, 2007) in an n-best list rescoring step after decoding. Finally, we plan to train different types of systems (such as a hierarchical SMT system and a Statistical Post-Editing system) and combine their outputs with the MANY open source system combination software (Barrault, 2010).

Acknowledgments

This work has been partially funded by the European Union under the EuroMatrix Plus project – Bringing Machine Translation for European Languages to the User – (http://www.euromatrixplus.net, IST-2007.2.2-FP7-231720).

References

Sadaf Abdul-Rauf and Holger Schwenk. 2009. On the use of comparable corpora to improve SMT performance. In *Proceedings of the 12th Conference of the European Chapter of the ACL (EACL 2009)*, pages 16–23, Athens, Greece.

Loïc Barrault. 2010. MANY : Open source machine translation system combination. *Prague Bulletin of Mathematical Linguistics, Special Issue on Open Source Tools for Machine Translation*, 93:147–155.

Peter F. Brown, Stephen A. Della Pietra, Vincent J. Della Pietra, and Robert L. Mercer. 1993. The mathematics of statistical machine translation: Parameter estimation. *Computational Linguistics*, 19(2):263–311.

Chris Callison-Burch, Philipp Koehn, Christof Monz, and Josh Schroeder. 2009. Findings of the 2009 Workshop on Statistical Machine Translation. In *Proceedings of the ACL Fourth Workshop on Statistical Machine Translation*, pages 1–28, Athens, Greece.

Qin Gao and Stephan Vogel. 2008. Parallel implementations of word alignment tool. In *Software Engineering, Testing, and Quality Assurance for Natural Language Processing*, pages 49–57, Columbus, Ohio, June. Association for Computational Linguistics.

	Bitext	#En Words (M)	Phrase-table size (M)	news-test2008 BLEU	newstest2009 BLEU
1	Eparl+NC+UN	242	258	24.21 (0.01)	25.29 (0.12)
2	Eparl+NC+10^9_1	163	203	24.24 (0.06)	25.51 (0.13)
3	Eparl+NC+UN+10^9_1	357	385	24.46 (0.08)	25.73 (0.20)
4	Eparl+NC+UN+10^9_1 pruned	357	221	24.42 (0.1)	25.84 (0.05)
5	Eparl+NC+10^9_2	280	330	24.43 (0.04)	25.68 (0.12)
6	Eparl+NC+News	103	188	24.27 (0.2)	25.70 (0.15)
7	Eparl+NC+10^9_1+News	218	321	24.51 (0.05)	25.83 (0.05)
8	Eparl+NC+UN+10^9_1+News	413	501	24.70 (0.1)	25.86 (0.14)
9	Eparl+NC+IR	69	81	24.14 (0.05)	25.17 (0.2)
10	Eparl+NC+News+IR	124	201	24.32 (0.12)	25.84 (0.17)
11	Eparl+NC+10^9_1+News+IR	239	333	24.54 (0.1)	26.03 (0.15)
12	Eparl+NC+10^9_2+News+IR	356	453	24.68 (0.04)	26.19 (0.05)
13	**Eparl+NC+10^9_2+News+IR pruned** (+larger beam, +no-cutoff LM)	**356**	**293**	**25.06**	**26.53**

Table 2: English–French results: number of English words (in million), number of entries in the phrase-table (in million) and BLEU scores in the development (news-test2008) and internal test (newstest2009) sets for the different systems developped. The BLEU scores and the number in parentheses are the average and standard deviation over 3 values (see Section 3.)

Howard Johnson, Joel Martin, George Foster, and Roland Kuhn. 2007. Improving translation quality by discarding most of the phrasetable. In *Proceedings of the 2007 Joint Conference on Empirical Methods in Natural Language Processing and Computational Natural Language Learning (EMNLP-CoNLL)*, pages 967–975, Prague, Czech Republic.

Philipp Koehn, Franz Josef Och, and Daniel Marcu. 2003. Statistical phrased-based machine translation. In *HLT/NACL*, pages 127–133.

Philipp Koehn et al. 2007. Moses: Open source toolkit for statistical machine translation. In *ACL, demonstration session.*

Franz Josef Och and Hermann Ney. 2002. Discriminative training and maximum entropy models for statistical machine translation. In *Proc. of the Annual Meeting of the Association for Computational Linguistics*, pages 295–302.

Franz Josef Och and Hermann Ney. 2003. A systematic comparison of various statistical alignement models. *Computational Linguistics*, 29(1):19–51.

Paul Ogilvie and Jamie Callan. 2001. Experiments using the Lemur toolkit. In *In Proceedings of the Tenth Text Retrieval Conference (TREC-10)*, pages 103–108.

Holger Schwenk, Sadaf Abdul Rauf, Loïc Barrault, and Jean Senellart. 2009. SMT and SPE machine translation systems for WMT'09. In *Proceedings of the Fourth Workshop on Statistical Machine Translation*, pages 130–134, Athens, Greece. Association for Computational Linguistics.

Holger Schwenk. 2007. Continuous space language models. *Computer Speech and Language*, 21:492–518.

Holger Schwenk. 2008. Investigations on large-scale lightly-supervised training for statistical machine translation. In *IWSLT*, pages 182–189.

A. Stolcke. 2002. SRILM: an extensible language modeling toolkit. In *Proc. of the Int. Conf. on Spoken Language Processing*, pages 901–904, Denver, CO.

Lessons from NRC's Portage System at WMT 2010

Samuel Larkin, Boxing Chen, George Foster, Ulrich Germann, Eric Joanis, Howard Johnson, and Roland Kuhn
National Research Council of Canada (NRC)
Gatineau, Québec, Canada.
Firstname.Lastname@cnrc-nrc.gc.ca

Abstract

NRC's Portage system participated in the English-French (E-F) and French-English (F-E) translation tasks of the ACL WMT 2010 evaluation. The most notable improvement over earlier versions of Portage is an efficient implementation of lattice MERT. While Portage has typically performed well in Chinese to English MT evaluations, most recently in the NIST09 evaluation, our participation in WMT 2010 revealed some interesting differences between Chinese-English and E-F/F-E translation, and alerted us to certain weak spots in our system. Most of this paper discusses the problems we found in our system and ways of fixing them. We learned several lessons that we think will be of general interest.

1 Introduction

Portage, the statistical machine translation system of the National Research Council of Canada (NRC), is a two-pass phrase-based system. The translation tasks to which it is most often applied are Chinese to English, English to French (henceforth "E-F"), and French to English (henceforth "F-E"): in recent years we worked on Chinese-English translation for the GALE project and for NIST evaluations, and English and French are Canada's two official languages. In WMT 2010, Portage scored 28.5 BLEU (uncased) for F-E, but only 27.0 BLEU (uncased) for E-F. For both language pairs, Portage truecasing caused a loss of 1.4 BLEU; other WMT systems typically lost around 1.0 BLEU after truecasing. In Canada, about 80% of translations between English and French are from English to French, so we would have preferred better results for that direction. This paper first describes the version of Portage that participated in WMT 2010. It then analyzes problems with the system and describes the solutions we found for some of them.

2 Portage system description

2.1 Core engine and training data

The NRC system uses a standard two-pass phrase-based approach. Major features in the first-pass loglinear model include phrase tables derived from symmetrized IBM2 alignments and symmetrized HMM alignments, a distance-based distortion model, a lexicalized distortion model, and language models (LMs) that can be either static or else dynamic mixtures. Each phrase table used was a merged one, created by separately training an IBM2-based and an HMM-based joint count table on the same data and then adding the counts. Each includes relative frequency estimates and lexical estimates (based on Zens and Ney, 2004) of forward and backward conditional probabilities. The lexicalized distortion probabilities are also obtained by adding IBM2 and HMM counts. They involve 6 features (monotone, swap and discontinuous features for following and preceding phrase) and are conditioned on phrase pairs in a model similar to that of Moses (Koehn *et al.*, 2005); a MAP-based backoff smoothing scheme is used to combat data sparseness when estimating these probabilities. Dynamic mixture LMs are linear mixtures of ngram models trained on parallel sub-corpora with weights set to minimize perplexity of the current source text as described in (Foster and Kuhn, 2007); henceforth, we'll call them "dynamic LMs".

Decoding uses the cube-pruning algorithm of (Huang and Chiang, 2007) with a 7-word distortion limit. Contrary to the usual implementation of distortion limits, we allow a new phrase to end

Proceedings of the Joint 5th Workshop on Statistical Machine Translation and MetricsMATR, pages 127–132,
Uppsala, Sweden, 15-16 July 2010.

more than 7 words past the first non-covered word, as long as the new phrase starts within 7 words from the first non-covered word. Notwithstanding the distortion limit, contiguous phrases can always be swapped. Out-of-vocabulary (OOV) source words are passed through unchanged to the target. Loglinear weights are tuned with Och's max-BLEU algorithm over lattices (Macherey *et al.*, 2008); more details about lattice MERT are given in the next section. The second pass rescores 1000-best lists produced by the first pass, with additional features including various LM and IBM-model probabilities; ngram, length, and reordering posterior probabilities and frequencies; and quote and parenthesis mismatch indicators. To improve the quality of the maxima found by MERT when using large sets of partially-overlapping rescoring features, we use greedy feature selection, first expanding from a baseline set, then pruning.

We restricted our training data to data that was directly available through the workshop's website; we didn't use the LDC resources mentioned on the website (*e.g.*, French Gigaword, English Gigaword). Below, "mono" refers to all monolingual data (Europarl, news-commentary, and shuffle); "mono" English is roughly three times bigger than "mono" French (50.6 M lines in "mono" English, 17.7 M lines in "mono" French). "Domain" refers to all WMT parallel training data except GigaFrEn (*i.e.*, Europarl, news-commentary, and UN).

2.2 Preprocessing and postprocessing

We used our own English and French pre- and post-processing tools, rather than those available from the WMT web site. For training, all English and French text is tokenized with a language-specific tokenizer and then mapped to lowercase. Truecasing uses an HMM approach, with lexical probabilities derived from "mono" and transition probabilities from a 3-gram LM trained on truecase "mono". A subsequent rule-based pass capitalizes sentence-initial words. A final detokenization step undoes the tokenization.

2.3 System configurations for WMT 2010

In the weeks preceding the evaluation, we tried several ways of arranging the resources available to us. We picked the configurations that gave the highest BLEU scores on WMT2009 Newstest. We found that tuning with lattice MERT rather than N-best MERT allowed us to employ more parameters and obtain better results.

E-F system components:

1. Phrase table trained on "domain";
2. Phrase table trained on GigaFrEn;
3. Lexicalized distortion model trained on "domain";
4. Distance-based distortion model;
5. 5-gram French LM trained on "mono";
6. 4-gram LM trained on French half of GigaFrEn;
7. Dynamic LM composed of 4 LMs, each trained on the French half of a parallel corpus (5-gram LM trained on "domain", 4-gram LM on GigaFrEn, 5-gram LM on news-commentary and 5-gram LM on UN).

The F-E system is a mirror image of the E-F system.

3 Details of lattice MERT (LMERT)

Our system's implementation of LMERT (Macherey *et al.*, 2008) is the most notable recent change in our system. As more and more features are included in the loglinear model, especially if they are correlated, N-best MERT (Och, 2003) shows more and more instability, because of convergence to local optima (Foster and Kuhn, 2009). We had been looking for methods that promise more stability and better convergence. LMERT seemed to fit the bill. It optimizes over the complete lattice of candidate translations after a decoding run. This avoids some of the problems of N-best lists, which lack variety, leading to poor local optima and the need for many decoder runs.

Though the algorithm is straightforward and is highly parallelizable, attention must be paid to space and time resource issues during implementation. Lattices output by our decoder were large and needed to be shrunk dramatically for the algorithm to function well. Fortunately, this could be achieved via the finite state equivalence algorithm for minimizing deterministic finite state machines. The second helpful idea was to separate out the features that were a function of the phrase associated with an arc (*e.g.*, translation length and translation model probability features). These features could then be stored in a smaller phrase-feature table. Features associated with language or distortion models could be handled in a larger transition-feature table.

The above ideas, plus careful coding of data structures, brought the memory footprint down sufficiently to allow us to use complete lattices from the decoder and optimize over the complete development set for NIST09 Chinese-English. However, combining lattices between decoder runs again resulted in excessive memory requirements. We achieved acceptable performance by searching only the lattice from the latest decoder run; perhaps information from earlier runs, though critical for convergence in N-best MERT, isn't as important for LMERT.

Until a reviewer suggested it, we had not thought of pruning lattices to a specified graph density as a solution for our memory problems. This is referred to in a single sentence in (Macherey *et al.*, 2008), which does not specify its implementation or its impact on performance, and is an option of OpenFst (we didn't use OpenFst). We will certainly experiment with lattice pruning in future.

Powell's algorithm (PA), which is at the core of MERT, has good convergence when features are mostly independent and do not depart much from a simple coordinate search; it can run into problems when there are many correlated features (as with multiple translation and language models). **Figure 1** shows the kind of case where PA works well. The contours of the function being optimized are relatively smooth, facilitating learning of new search directions from gradients.

Figure 2 shows a more difficult case: there is a single optimum, but noise dominates and PA has difficulty finding new directions. Search often iterates over the original co-ordinates, missing optima that are nearby but in directions not discoverable from local gradients. Probes in random directions can do better than iteration over the same directions (this is similar to the method proposed for N-best MERT by Cer *et al.*, 2008). Each 1-dimensional MERT optimization is exact, so if our probe stabs a region with better scores, it will be discovered. **Figures 1** and **2** only hint at the problem: in reality, 2-dimensional search isn't a problem. The difficulties occur as the dimension grows: in high dimensions, it is more important to get good directions and they are harder to find.

For WMT 2010, we crafted a compromise with the best properties of PA, yet allowing for a more aggressive search in more directions. We start with PA. As long as PA is adding new direction vectors, it is continued. When PA stops adding new directions, random rotation (orthogonal transformation) of the coordinates is performed and PA is restarted in the new space. PA almost always fails to introduce new directions within the new coordinates, then fails again, so another set of random coordinates is chosen. This process repeats until convergence. In future work, we will look at incorporating random restarts into the algorithm as additional insurance against premature convergence.

Our LMERT implementation has room for improvement: it may still run into over-fitting problems with many correlated features. However, during preparation for the evaluation, we noticed that LMERT converged better than N-best MERT, allowing models with more features and higher BLEU to be chosen.

After the WMT submission, we discovered that our LMERT implementation had a bug; our submission was tuned with this buggy LMERT. Comparison between our E-F submission tuned with N-best MERT and the same system tuned with bug-fixed LMERT shows BLEU gains of +1.5-3.5 for LMERT (on dev, WMT2009, and WMT2010, with no rescoring). However, N-best MERT performed very poorly in this particular case; we usually obtain a gain due to LMERT of +0.2-1.0 (*e.g.*, for the submitted F-E system).

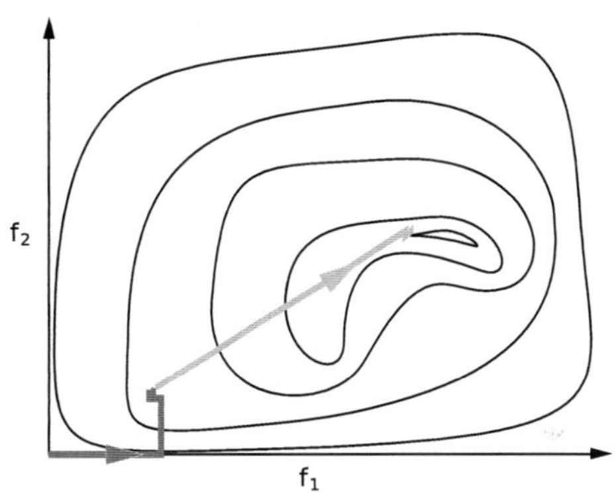

Figure 1: Convergence for PA (Smooth Feature Space)

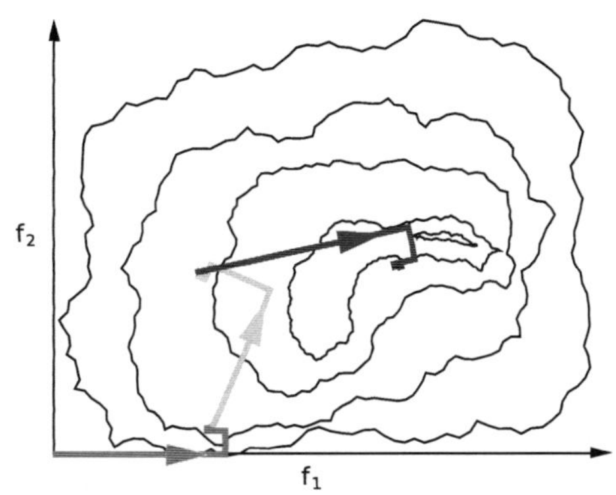

Figure 2: Convergence for PA with Random Rotation (Rough Feature Space)

4 Problems and Solutions

4.1 Fixing LMERT

Just after the evaluation, we noticed a discrepancy for E-F between BLEU scores computed during LMERT optimization and scores from the 1-best list immediately after decoding. Our LMERT code had a bug that garbled any accented word in the version of the French reference in memory; previous LMERT experiments had English as target language, so the bug hadn't showed up. The bug didn't affect characters in the 7-bit ASCII set, such as English ones, only accented characters. Words in candidate translations were not garbled, so correct translations with accents received a lower BLEU score than they should have. As **Table 1** shows, this bug cost us about 0.5 BLEU for WMT 2010 E-F after rescoring (according to NRC's internal version of BLEU, which differs slightly from WMT's BLEU). Despite this bug, the system tuned with buggy LMERT (and submitted) was still better than the best system we obtained with N-best MERT. The bug didn't affect F-E scores.

	Dev	WMT2009	WMT2010
LMERT (bug)	25.26	26.85	27.55
LMERT (no bug)	25.43	26.89	28.07

Table 1: LMERT bug fix (E-F BLEU after rescoring)

4.2 Fixing odd translations

After the evaluation, we carefully studied the system outputs on the WMT 2010 test data, particularly for E-F. Apart from truecasing errors, we noticed two kinds of bad behaviour: translations of proper names and apparent passthrough of English words to the French side.

Examples of E-F translations of proper names from our WMT 2010 submission (each from a different sentence):

Mr. Onderka → M. Roman, Lukáš Marvan → G. Lukáš, Janey → The, Janette Tozer → Janette, Aysel Tugluk → joints tugluk, Tawa Hallae → Ottawa, Oleson → production, Alcobendas → ;

When the LMERT bug was fixed, some but not all of these bad translations were corrected (*e.g.*, 3 of the 8 examples above were corrected).

Our system passes OOV words through unchanged. Thus, the names above aren't OOVs, but words that occur rarely in the training data, and for which bad alignments have a disproportionate effect. We realized that when a source word begins with a capital, that may be a signal that it should be passed through. We thus designed a passthrough feature function that applies to all capitalized forms not at the start of a sentence (and also to forms at the sentence start if they're capitalized elsewhere). Sequences of one or more capitalized forms are grouped into a phrase suggestion (*e.g.*, Barack Obama → barrack obama) which competes with phrase table entries and is assigned a weight by MERT.

The passthrough feature function yields a tiny improvement over the E-F system with the bug-fixed LMERT on the dev corpus (WMT2008): +0.06 BLEU (without rescoring). It yields a larger improvement on our test corpus: +0.27 BLEU (without rescoring). Furthermore, it corrects all the examples from the WMT 2010 test shown above (after the LMERT bug fix 5 of the 8 examples above still had problems, but when the passthrough function is incorporated all of them go away). Though the BLEU gain is small, we are happy to have almost eradicated this type of error, which human beings find very annoying.

The opposite type of error is apparent passthrough. For instance, "we're" appeared 12 times in the WMT 2010 test data, and was translated 6 times into French as "we're" - even though better translations had higher forward probabilities. The source of the problem is the backward probability P(E="we're"|F="we're"), which is 1.0; the backward probabilities for valid French translations of "we're" are lower. Because of the high probability P(E="we're"|F="we're") within the loglinear combination, the decoder often chooses "we're" as the French translation of "we're".

The (E="we're", F="we're") pair in WMT 2010 phrase tables arose from two sentence pairs where the "French" translation of an English sentence is a copy of that English sentence. In both, the original English sentence contains "we're". Naturally, the English words on the "French" side are word-aligned with their identical twins on the English side. Generally, if the training data has sentence pairs where the "French" sentence contains words from the English sentence, those words will get high backward probabilities of being translated as themselves. This problem may not show up as an apparent passthrough; instead, it may cause MERT to lower the weight of the backward probability component, thus hurting performance.

We estimated English contamination of the French side of the parallel training data by manually inspecting a random sample of "French" sentences containing common English function words. Manual inspection is needed for accurate estimation: a legitimate French sentence might contain mostly English words if, *e.g.*, it is short and cites the title of an English work (this wouldn't count as contamination). The degree of contamination is roughly 0.05% for Europarl, 0.5% for news-commentary, 0.5% for UN, and 1% for GigaFrEn (in these corpora the French is also contaminated by other languages, particularly German). Foreign contamination of English for these corpora appears to be much less frequent.

Contamination can take strange forms. We expected to see English sentences copied over intact to the French side, and we did, but we did not expect to see so many "French" sentences that interleaved short English word sequences with short French word sequences, apparently because text with an English and a French column had been copied by taking lines from alternate columns. We found many of these interleaved "French" sentences, and found some of them in exactly this form on the Web (*i.e.*, the corruption didn't occur during WMT data collection). The details may not matter: whenever the "French" training sentence contains words from its English twin, there can be serious damage via backward probabilities.

To test this hypothesis, we filtered all parallel and monolingual training data for the E-F system with a language guessing tool called text_cat (Cavnar and Trenkle, 1994). From parallel data, we filtered out sentence pairs whose French side had a high probability of not being French; from LM training data, sentences with a high non-French probability. We set the filtering level by inspecting the guesser's assessment of news-commentary sentences, choosing a rather aggressive level that eliminated 0.7% of news-commentary sentence pairs. We used the same level to filter Europarl (0.8% of sentence pairs removed), UN (3.4%), GigaFrEn (4.7%), and "mono" (4.3% of sentences).

	Dev	WMT2009	WMT2010
Baseline	25.23	26.47	27.72
Filtered	25.45	26.66	27.98

Table 2: Data filtering (E-F BLEU, no rescoring)

Table 2 shows the results: a small but consistent gain (about +0.2 BLEU without rescoring). We have not yet confirmed the hypothesis that copies of source-language words in the paired target sentence within training data can damage system performance via backward probabilities.

4.3 Fixing problems with LM training

Post-evaluation, we realized that our arrangement of the training data for the LMs for both language directions was flawed. The grouping together of disparate corpora in "mono" and "domain" didn't allow higher-quality, truly in-domain corpora to be weighted more heavily (*e.g.*, the news corpora should have higher weights than Europarl, but they are lumped together in "mono"). There are also potentially harmful overlaps between LMs (*e.g.*, GigaFrEn is used both inside and outside the dynamic LM).

We trained a new set of French LMs for the E-F system, which replaced all the French LMs (#5-7) described in section 2.3 in the E-F system:

1. 5-gram LM trained on news-commentary and shuffle;
2. Dynamic LM based on 4 5-gram LMs trained on French side of parallel data (LM trained on GigaFrEn, LM on UN, LM on Europarl, and LM on news-commentary).

We did not apply the passthrough function or language filtering (section 4.2) to any of the training data for any component (LMs, TMs, distortion models) of this system; we did use the bug-fixed version of LMERT (section 4.1).

The experiments with these new French LMs for the E-F system yielded a small decrease of NRC BLEU on dev (-0.15) and small increases on WMT Newstest 2009 and Newstest 2010 (+0.2 and +0.4 respectively without rescoring). We didn't do F-E experiments of this type.

4.4 Pooling improvements

The improvements above were (individual uncased E-F BLEU gains without rescoring in brackets): LMERT bug fix (about +0.5); passthrough feature function (+0.1-0.3); language filtering for French (+0.2). There was also a small gain on test data by rearranging E-F LM training data, though the loss on "dev" suggests this may be a statistical fluctuation. We built these four improvements into the evaluation E-F system, along with quote normalization: in all training and test data, diverse single quotes were mapped onto the ascii single quote, and diverse double quotes were mapped onto the ascii double quote. The average result on WMT2009 and WMT2010 was +1.7 BLEU points compared to the original system, so there may be synergy between the improvements. The original system had gained +0.3 from rescoring, while the final improved system only gained +0.1 from rescoring: a post-evaluation rescored gain of +1.5.

An experiment in which we dropped lexicalized distortion from the improved system showed that this component yields about +0.2 BLEU. Much earlier, when we were still training systems with N-best MERT, incorporation of the 6-feature lexicalized distortion often caused scores to go down (by as much as 2.8 BLEU). This illustrates how LMERT can make incorporation of many more features worthwhile.

4.5 Fixing truecasing

Our truecaser doesn't work as well as truecasers of other WMT groups: we lost 1.4 BLEU by truecasing in both language directions, while others lost 1.0 or less. To improve our truecaser, we tried: 1. Training it on all relevant data and 2. Collecting 3-gram case-pattern statistics instead of unigrams. Neither of these helped significantly. One way of improving the truecaser would be to let case information from source words influence the case of the corresponding target words. Alternatively, one of the reviewers stated that several labs involved in WMT have no separate truecaser and simply train on truecase text. We had previously tried this approach for NIST Chinese-English and discarded it because of its poor performance. We are currently re-trying it on WMT data; if it works better than having a separate truecaser, this was yet another area where lessons from Chinese-English were misleading.

5 Lessons

LMERT is an improvement over N-best MERT. The submitted system was one for which N-best MERT happened to work very badly, so we got ridiculously large gains of +1.5-3.5 BLEU for non-buggy LMERT over N-best MERT. These results are outliers: in experiments with similar configurations, we typically get +0.2-1.0 for LMERT over N-best MERT. Post-evaluation, four minor improvements – a case-based passthrough function, language filtering, LM rearrangement, and quote normalization – collectively gave a nice improvement. Nothing we tried helped truecaser performance significantly, though we have some ideas on how to proceed.

We learned some lessons from WMT 2010.

Always test your system on the relevant language pair. Our original version of LMERT was developed on Chinese-English and worked well there, but had a bug that surfaced only when the target language had accents.

European language pairs are more porous to information than Chinese-English. Our WMT system reflected design decisions for Chinese-English, and thus didn't exploit case information in the source: it passed through OOVs to the target, but didn't pass through upper-case words that are likely to be proper nouns.

It is beneficial to remove foreign-language contamination from the training data.

When entering an evaluation one hasn't participated in for several years, always read system papers from the previous year. Some of the WMT 2008 system papers mention passthrough of some non-OOVs, filtering out of noisy training data, and using the case of a source word to predict the case of the corresponding target word.

References

William Cavnar and John Trenkle. 1994. N-Gram-Based Text Categorization. *Proc. Symposium on Document Analysis and Information Retrieval*, UNLV Publications/Reprographics, pp. 161-175.

Daniel Cer, Daniel Jurafsky, and Christopher D. Manning. 2008. Regularization and search for minimum error rate training. *Proc. Workshop on SMT*, pp. 26-34.

George Foster and Roland Kuhn. 2009. Stabilizing Minimum Error Rate Training. *Proc. Workshop on SMT*, pp. 242-249.

George Foster and Roland Kuhn. 2007. Mixture-Model Adaptation for SMT. *Proc. Workshop on SMT*, pp. 128-135.

Liang Huang and David Chiang. 2007. Forest Rescoring: Faster Decoding with Integrated Language Models. *Proc. ACL*, pp. 144-151.

Philipp Koehn, Amittai Axelrod, Alexandra Birch Mayne, Chris Callison-Burch, Miles Osborne, and David Talbot. 2005. Edinburgh System Description for the 2005 IWSLT Speech Transcription Evaluation. *MT Eval. Workshop.*

Wolfgang Macherey, Franz Josef Och, Ignacio Thayer, and Jakob Uszkoreit. 2008. Lattice-based Minimum Error Rate Training for Statistical Machine-Translation. *Conf. EMNLP*, pp. 725-734.

Franz Josef Och. 2003. Minimum Error Rate Training in Statistical Machine Translation. *Proc. ACL*, pp. 160-167.

Richard Zens and Hermann Ney. 2004. Improvements in Phrase-Based Statistical Machine Translation. *Proc. HLT/NAACL*, pp. 257-264.

Joshua 2.0: A Toolkit for Parsing-Based Machine Translation with Syntax, Semirings, Discriminative Training and Other Goodies

Zhifei Li, Chris Callison-Burch, Chris Dyer,[†] Juri Ganitkevitch, Ann Irvine, Sanjeev Khudanpur, Lane Schwartz,[⋆] Wren N. G. Thornton, Ziyuan Wang, Jonathan Weese and **Omar F. Zaidan**

Center for Language and Speech Processing, Johns Hopkins University, Baltimore, MD

† Computational Linguistics and Information Processing Lab, University of Maryland, College Park, MD

⋆ Natural Language Processing Lab, University of Minnesota, Minneapolis, MN

Abstract

We describe the progress we have made in the past year on **Joshua** (Li et al., 2009a), an open source toolkit for parsing based machine translation. The new functionality includes: support for translation grammars with a rich set of syntactic nonterminals, the ability for external modules to posit constraints on how spans in the input sentence should be translated, lattice parsing for dealing with input uncertainty, a semiring framework that provides a unified way of doing various dynamic programming calculations, variational decoding for approximating the intractable MAP decoding, hypergraph-based discriminative training for better feature engineering, a parallelized MERT module, document-level and tail-based MERT, visualization of the derivation trees, and a cleaner pipeline for MT experiments.

1 Introduction

Joshua is an open-source toolkit for parsing-based machine translation that is written in Java. The initial release of **Joshua** (Li et al., 2009a) was a re-implementation of the Hiero system (Chiang, 2007) and all its associated algorithms, including: chart parsing, n-gram language model integration, beam and cube pruning, and k-best extraction. The **Joshua** 1.0 release also included re-implementations of suffix array grammar extraction (Lopez, 2007; Schwartz and Callison-Burch, 2010) and minimum error rate training (Och, 2003; Zaidan, 2009). Additionally, it included parallel and distributed computing techniques for scalability (Li and Khudanpur, 2008).

This paper describes the additions to the toolkit over the past year, which together form the 2.0 release. The software has been heavily used by the authors and several other groups in their daily research, and has been substantially refined since the first release. The most important new functions in the toolkit are:

- Support for any style of synchronous context free grammar (SCFG) including syntax augment machine translation (SAMT) grammars (Zollmann and Venugopal, 2006)
- Support for external modules to posit translations for spans in the input sentence that constrain decoding (Irvine et al., 2010)
- Lattice parsing for dealing with input uncertainty, including ambiguous output from speech recognizers or Chinese word segmenters (Dyer et al., 2008)
- A semiring architecture over hypergraphs that allows many inference operations to be implemented easily and elegantly (Li and Eisner, 2009)
- Improvements to decoding through variational decoding and other approximate methods that overcome intractable MAP decoding (Li et al., 2009b)
- Hypergraph-based discriminative training for better feature engineering (Li and Khudanpur, 2009b)
- A parallelization of MERT's computations, and supporting document-level and tail-based optimization (Zaidan, 2010)
- Visualization of the derivation trees and hypergraphs (Weese and Callison-Burch, 2010)
- A convenient framework for designing and running reproducible machine translation experiments (Schwartz, under review)

The sections below give short descriptions for each of these new functions.

Proceedings of the Joint 5th Workshop on Statistical Machine Translation and MetricsMATR, pages 133–137, Uppsala, Sweden, 15-16 July 2010.

2 Support for Syntax-based Translation

The initial release of **Joshua** supported only Hiero-style SCFGs, which use a single nonterminal symbol X. This release includes support for arbitrary SCFGs, including ones that use a rich set of linguistic nonterminal symbols. In particular we have added support for Zollmann and Venugopal (2006)'s syntax-augmented machine translation. SAMT grammar extraction is identical to Hiero grammar extraction, except that one side of the parallel corpus is parsed, and syntactic labels replace the X nonterminals in Hiero-style rules. Instead of extracting this Hiero rule from the bitext

`[X]` ⇒ `[X,1]` sans `[X,2]` | `[X,1]` without `[X,2]`

the nonterminals can be labeled according to which constituents cover the nonterminal span on the parsed side of the bitext. This constrains what types of phrases the decoder can use when producing a translation.

`[VP]` ⇒ `[VBN]` sans `[NP]` | `[VBN]` without `[NP]`

`[NP]` ⇒ `[NP]` sans `[NP]` | `[NP]` without `[NP]`

Unlike GHKM (Galley et al., 2004), SAMT has the same coverage as Hiero, because it allows non-constituent phrases to get syntactic labels using CCG-style slash notation. Experimentally, we have found that the derivations created using syntactically motivated grammars exhibit more coherent syntactic structure than Hiero and typically result in better reordering, especially for languages with word orders that diverge from English, like Urdu (Baker et al., 2009).

3 Specifying Constraints on Translation

Integrating output from specialized modules (like transliterators, morphological analyzers, and modality translators) into the MT pipeline can improve translation performance, particularly for low-resource languages. We have implemented an XML interface that allows external modules to propose alternate translation rules (constraints) for a particular word span to the decoder (Irvine et al., 2010). Processing that is separate from the MT engine can suggest translations for some set of source side words and phrases. The XML format allows for both hard constraints, which must be used, and soft constraints, which compete with standard extracted translation rules, as well as specifying associated feature weights. In addition to specifying translations, the XML format allows constraints on the lefthand side of SCFG rules, which allows constraints like forcing a particular span to be translated as an NP. We modified **Joshua**'s chart-based decoder to support these constraints.

4 Semiring Parsing

In **Joshua**, we use a hypergraph (or packed forest) to compactly represent the exponentially many derivation trees generated by the decoder for an input sentence. Given a hypergraph, we may perform many atomic inference operations, such as finding one-best or k-best translations, or computing expectations over the hypergraph. For each such operation, we could implement a dedicated dynamic programming algorithm. However, a more general framework to specify these algorithms is semiring-weighted parsing (Goodman, 1999). We have implemented the inside algorithm, the outside algorithm, and the inside-outside speedup described by Li and Eisner (2009), plut the first-order expectation semiring (Eisner, 2002) and its second-order version (Li and Eisner, 2009). All of these use our newly implemented semiring framework.

The first- and second-order expectation semirings can also be used to compute many interesting quantities over hypergraphs. These quantities include expected translation length, feature expectation, entropy, cross-entropy, Kullback-Leibler divergence, Bayes risk, variance of hypothesis length, gradient of entropy and Bayes risk, covariance and Hessian matrix, and so on.

5 Word Lattice Input

We generalized the bottom-up parsing algorithm that generates the translation hypergraph so that it supports translation of word lattices instead of just sentences. Our implementation's runtime and memory overhead is proportional to the size of the lattice, rather than the number of paths in the lattice (Dyer et al., 2008). Accepting lattice-based input allows the decoder to explore a distribution over input sentences, allowing it to select the best translation from among all of them. This is especially useful when **Joshua** is used to translate the output of statistical preprocessing components, such as speech recognizers or Chinese word segmenters, which can encode their alternative analyses as confusion networks or lattices.

6 Variational Decoding

Statistical models in machine translation exhibit spurious ambiguity. That is, the probability of an output string is split among many distinct derivations (e.g., trees or segmentations) that have the same yield. In principle, the goodness of a string is measured by the total probability of its many derivations. However, finding the best string during decoding is then NP-hard. The first version of **Joshua** implemented the Viterbi approximation, which measures the goodness of a translation using only its most probable derivation.

The Viterbi approximation is efficient, but it ignores most of the derivations in the hypergraph. We implemented variational decoding (Li et al., 2009b), which works as follows. First, given a foreign string (or lattice), the MT system produces a hypergraph, which encodes a probability distribution p over possible output strings and their derivations. Second, a distribution q is selected that approximates p as well as possible but comes from a family of distributions $\mathcal{Q}$ in which inference is tractable. Third, the best string according to q (instead of p) is found. In our implementation, the q distribution is parameterized by an n-gram model, under which the second and third steps can be performed efficiently and exactly via dynamic programming. In this way, variational decoding considers all derivations in the hypergraph but still allows tractable decoding.

7 Hypergraph-based Discriminative Training

Discriminative training with a large number of features has potential to improve the MT performance. We have implemented the hypergraph-based minimum risk training (Li and Eisner, 2009), which minimizes the *expected loss* of the reference translations. The minimum-risk objective can be optimized by a gradient-based method, where the risk and its gradient can be computed using a second-order expectation semiring. For optimization, we use both L-BFGS (Liu et al., 1989) and Rprop (Riedmiller and Braun, 1993).

We have also implemented the average Perceptron algorithm and forest-reranking (Li and Khudanpur, 2009b). Since the reference translation may not be in the hypergraph due to pruning or inherent defficiency of the translation grammar, we need to use an *oracle translation* (i.e., the translation in the hypergraph that is most simmilar to the reference translation) as a surrogate for training. We implemented the *oracle extraction* algorithm described by Li and Khudanpur (2009a) for this purpose.

Given the current infrastructure, other training methods (e.g., maximum conditional likelihood or MIRA as used by Chiang et al. (2009)) can also be easily supported with minimum coding. We plan to implement a large number of feature functions in **Joshua** so that exhaustive feature engineering is possible for MT.

8 Minimum Error Rate Training

Joshua's MERT module optimizes parameter weights so as to maximize performance on a development set as measuered by an automatic evaluation metric, such as Bleu (Och, 2003).

We have parallelized our MERT module in two ways: parallelizing the computation of metric scores, and parallelizing the search over parameters. The computation of metric scores is a computational concern when tuning to a metric that is slow to compute, such as translation edit rate (Snover et al., 2006). Since scoring a candidate is independent from scoring any other candidate, we parallelize this computation using a multi-threaded solution[1]. Similarly, we parallelize the optimization of the intermediate initial weight vectors, also using a multi-threaded solution.

Another feature is the module's awareness of document information, and the capability to perform optimization of *document-based* variants of the automatic metric (Zaidan, 2010). For example, in document-based Bleu, a Bleu score is calculated *for each document*, and the tuned score is the average of those document scores. The MERT module can furthermore be instructed to target a specific subset of those documents, namely the *tail* subset, where only the subset of documents with the lowest document Bleu scores are considered.[2]

More details on the MERT method and the implementation can be found in Zaidan (2009).[3]

[1] Based on sample code by Kenneth Heafield.

[2] This feature is of interest to GALE teams, for instance, since GALE's evaluation criteria place a lot of focus on translation quality of tail documents.

[3] The module is also available as a standalone application, *Z-MERT*, that can be used with other MT systems. (Software and documentation at: `http://cs.jhu.edu/~ozaidan/zmert`.)

9 Visualization

We created tools for visualizing two of the main data structures used in **Joshua** (Weese and Callison-Burch, 2010). The first visualizer displays hypergraphs. The user can choose from a set of input sentences, then call the decoder to build the hypergraph. The second visualizer displays derivation trees. Setting a flag in the configuration file causes the decoder to output parse trees instead of strings, where each nonterminal is annotated with its source-side span. The visualizer can read in multiple n-best lists in this format, then display the resulting derivation trees side-by-side. We have found that visually inspecting these derivation trees is useful for debugging grammars.

We would like to add visualization tools for more parts of the pipeline. For example, a chart visualizer would make it easier for researchers to tell where search errors were happening during decoding, and why. An alignment visualizer for aligned parallel corpora might help to determine how grammar extraction could be improved.

10 Pipeline for Running MT Experiments

Reproducing other researchers' machine translation experiments is difficult because the pipeline is too complex to fully detail in short conference papers. We have put together a workflow framework for designing and running reproducible machine translation experiments using **Joshua** (Schwartz, under review). Each step in the machine translation workflow (data preprocessing, grammar training, MERT, decoding, etc) is modeled by a Make script that defines how to run the tools used in that step, and an auxiliary configuration file that defines the exact parameters to be used in that step for a particular experimental setup. Workflows configured using this framework allow a complete experiment to be run – from downloading data and software through scoring the final translated results – by executing a single Makefile.

This framework encourages researchers to supplement research publications with links to the complete set of scripts and configurations that were actually used to run the experiment. The Johns Hopkins University submission for the WMT10 shared translation task was implemented in this framework, so it can be easily and exactly reproduced.

Acknowledgements

Research funding was provided by the NSF under grant IIS-0713448, by the European Commission through the EuroMatrixPlus project, and by the DARPA GALE program under Contract No. HR0011-06-2-0001. The views and findings are the authors' alone.

References

Kathy Baker, Steven Bethard, Michael Bloodgood, Ralf Brown, Chris Callison-Burch, Glen Coppersmith, Bonnie Dorr, Wes Filardo, Kendall Giles, Anni Irvine, Mike Kayser, Lori Levin, Justin Martineau, Jim Mayfield, Scott Miller, Aaron Phillips, Andrew Philpot, Christine Piatko, Lane Schwartz, and David Zajic. 2009. Semantically informed machine translation (SIMT). SCALE summer workshop final report, Human Language Technology Center Of Excellence.

David Chiang, Kevin Knight, and Wei Wang. 2009. 11,001 new features for statistical machine translation. In *NAACL*, pages 218–226.

David Chiang. 2007. Hierarchical phrase-based translation. *Computational Linguistics*, 33(2):201–228.

Christopher Dyer, Smaranda Muresan, and Philip Resnik. 2008. Generalizing word lattice translation. In *Proceedings of ACL-08: HLT*, pages 1012–1020, Columbus, Ohio, June. Association for Computational Linguistics.

Jason Eisner. 2002. Parameter estimation for probabilistic finite-state transducers. In *ACL*.

Michel Galley, Mark Hopkins, Kevin Knight, and Daniel Marcu. 2004. What's in a translation rule? In *HLT-NAACL*.

Joshua Goodman. 1999. Semiring parsing. *Computational Linguistics*, 25(4):573–605.

Ann Irvine, Mike Kayser, Zhifei Li, Wren Thornton, and Chris Callison-Burch. 2010. Integrating output from specialized modules in machine translation: Transliteration in joshua. *The Prague Bulletin of Mathematical Linguistics*, 93:107–116.

Zhifei Li and Jason Eisner. 2009. First- and second-order expectation semirings with applications to minimum-risk training on translation forests. In *EMNLP*, Singapore.

Zhifei Li and Sanjeev Khudanpur. 2008. A scalable decoder for parsing-based machine translation with equivalent language model state maintenance. In *ACL SSST*, pages 10–18.

Zhifei Li and Sanjeev Khudanpur. 2009a. Efficient extraction of oracle-best translations from hypergraphs. In *Proceedings of NAACL*.

Zhifei Li and Sanjeev Khudanpur. 2009b. Forest reranking for machine translation with the perceptron algorithm. In *GALE book chapter on "MT From Text"*.

Zhifei Li, Chris Callison-Burch, Chris Dyer, Juri Ganitkevitch, Sanjeev Khudanpur, Lane Schwartz, Wren Thornton, Jonathan Weese, and Omar. Zaidan. 2009a. Joshua: An open source toolkit for parsing-based machine translation. In *WMT09*.

Zhifei Li, Jason Eisner, and Sanjeev Khudanpur. 2009b. Variational decoding for statistical machine translation. In *ACL*.

Dong C. Liu, Jorge Nocedal, Dong C. Liu, and Jorge Nocedal. 1989. On the limited memory bfgs method for large scale optimization. *Mathematical Programming*, 45:503–528.

Adam Lopez. 2007. Hierarchical phrase-based translation with suffix arrays. In *EMNLP-CoNLL*.

Franz Josef Och. 2003. Minimum error rate training in statistical machine translation. In *ACL*.

Martin Riedmiller and Heinrich Braun. 1993. A direct adaptive method for faster backpropagation learning: The rprop algorithm. In *IEEE INTERNATIONAL CONFERENCE ON NEURAL NETWORKS*, pages 586–591.

Lane Schwartz and Chris Callison-Burch. 2010. Hierarchical phrase-based grammar extraction in joshua. *The Prague Bulletin of Mathematical Linguistics*, 93:157–166.

Lane Schwartz. under review. Reproducible results in parsing-based machine translation: The JHU shared task submission. In *WMT10*.

Matthew Snover, Bonnie J. Dorr, and Richard Schwartz. 2006. A study of translation edit rate with targeted human annotation. In *AMTA*.

Jonathan Weese and Chris Callison-Burch. 2010. Visualizing data structures in parsing-based machine translation. *The Prague Bulletin of Mathematical Linguistics*, 93:127–136.

Omar F. Zaidan. 2009. Z-MERT: A fully configurable open source tool for minimum error rate training of machine translation systems. *The Prague Bulletin of Mathematical Linguistics*, 91:79–88.

Omar F. Zaidan. 2010. Document- and tail-based minimum error rate training of machine translation systems. In preparation.

Andreas Zollmann and Ashish Venugopal. 2006. Syntax augmented machine translation via chart parsing. In *Proceedings of the NAACL-2006 Workshop on Statistical Machine Translation (WMT-06)*, New York, New York.

The Karlsruhe Institute for Technology Translation System for the ACL-WMT 2010

Jan Niehues, Teresa Herrmann, Mohammed Mediani and Alex Waibel
Karlsruhe Instiute of Technolgy
Karlsruhe, Germany
firstname.lastname@kit.edu

Abstract

This paper describes our phrase-based Statistical Machine Translation (SMT) system for the WMT10 Translation Task. We submitted translations for the German to English and English to German translation tasks. Compared to state-of-the-art phrase-based systems we preformed additional preprocessing and used a discriminative word alignment approach. The word reordering was modeled using POS information and we extended the translation model with additional features.

1 Introduction

In this paper we describe the systems that we built for our participation in the Shared Translation Task of the ACL 2010 Joint Fifth Workshop on Statistical Machine Translation and MetricsMATR. Our translations are generated using a state-of-the-art phrase-based translation system and applying different extensions and modifications including Discriminative Word Alignment, a POS-based reordering model and bilingual language models using POS and stem information.

Depending on the source and target languages, the proposed models differ in their benefit for the translation task and also expose different correlative effects. The Sections 2 to 4 introduce the characteristics of the baseline system and the supplementary models. In Section 5 we present the performance of the system variants applying the different models and chose the systems used for creating the submissions for the English-German and German-English translation task. Section 6 draws conclusions and suggests directions for future work.

2 Baseline System

The baseline systems for the translation directions German-English and English-German are both developed using Discriminative Word Alignment (Niehues and Vogel, 2008) and the Moses Toolkit (Koehn et al., 2007) for extracting phrase pairs and generating the phrase table from the discriminative word alignments. The difficult reordering between German and English was modeled using POS-based reordering rules. These rules were learned using a word-aligned parallel corpus. The POS tags for the reordering models are generated using the TreeTagger (Schmid, 1994) for all languages.

Translation is performed by the STTK Decoder (Vogel, 2003) and all systems are optimized towards BLEU using Minimum Error Rate Training as proposed in Venugopal et al. (2005).

2.1 Training, Development and Test Data

We used the data provided for the WMT for training, optimizing and testing our systems: Our training corpus consists of Europarl and News Commentary data, for optimization we use newstest2008 as development set and newstest2009 as test set.

The baseline language models are trained on the target language part of the Europarl and News Commentary corpora. Additional, bigger language models were trained on monolingual corpora. For both systems the News corpus was used while an English language model was also trained on the even bigger Gigaword corpus.

2.2 Preprocessing

The training data was preprocessed before used for training. In this step different normalizations were done like mapping different types of quotes. In the end the first word of every sentence was smart-cased.

Proceedings of the Joint 5th Workshop on Statistical Machine Translation and MetricsMATR, pages 138–142,
Uppsala, Sweden, 15-16 July 2010.

For the German text, additional preprocessing steps were applied. First, the older German data uses the old German orthography whereas the newer parts of the corpus use the new German orthography. We tried to normalize the text by converting the whole text to the new German orthography. In a first step, we search for words that are only correct according to the old writing rules. Therefore, we selected all words in the corpus, that are correct according to the hunspell lexicon[1] using the old rules, but not correct according to the hunspell lexicon using the new rules. In a second step we tried to find the correct spelling according to the new rules. We first applied rules describing how words changed from one spelling system to the other, for example replacing 'ß' by 'ss'. If the new word is a correct word according to the hunspell lexicon using the new spelling rules, we map the words.

When translating from German to English, we apply compound splitting as described in Koehn and Knight (2003) to the German corpus.

As a last preprocessing step we remove sentences that are too long and empty lines to obtain the final training corpus.

3 Word Reordering Model

Reordering was applied on the source side prior to decoding through the generation of lattices encoding possible reorderings of each source sentence that better match the word sequence in the target language. These possible reorderings were learned based on the POS of the source language words in the training corpus and the information about alignments between source and target language words in the corpus. For short-range reorderings, continuous reordering rules were applied to the test sentences (Rottmann and Vogel, 2007). To model the long-range reorderings between German and English, different types of non-continuous reordering rules were applied depending on the translation direction. (Niehues and Kolss, 2009). When translating from English to German, most of the changes in word order consist in a shift to the right while typical word shifts in German to English translations take place in the reverse direction.

[1] `http://hunspell.sourceforge.net/`

4 Translation Model

The translation model was trained on the parallel corpus and the word alignment was generated by a discriminative word alignment model, which is described below. The phrase table was trained using the Moses training scripts, but for the German to English system we used a different phrase extraction method described in detail in Section 4.2. In addition, we applied phrase table smoothing as described in Foster et al. (2006). Furthermore, we extended the translation model by additional features for unaligned words and introduced bilingual language models.

4.1 Word Alignment

In most phrase-based SMT systems the heuristic grow-diag-final-and is used to combine the alignments generated by GIZA++ from both directions. Then these alignments are used to extract the phrase pairs.

We used a discriminative word alignment model (*DWA*) to generate the alignments as described in Niehues and Vogel (2008) instead. This model is trained on a small amount of hand-aligned data and uses the lexical probability as well as the fertilities generated by the PGIZA++[2] Toolkit and POS information. We used all local features, the GIZA and indicator fertility features as well as first order features for 6 directions. The model was trained in three steps, first using maximum likelihood optimization and afterwards it was optimized towards the alignment error rate. For more details see Niehues and Vogel (2008).

4.2 Lattice Phrase Extraction

In translations from German to English, we often have the case that the English verb is aligned to both parts of the German verb. Since this phrase pair is not continuous on the German side, it cannot be extracted. The phrase could be extracted, if we also reorder the training corpus.

For the test sentences the POS-based reordering allows us to change the word order in the source sentence so that the sentence can be translated more easily. If we apply this also to the training sentences, we would be able to extract the phrase pairs for originally discontinuous phrases and could apply them during translation of the reordered test sentences.

[2] `http://www.cs.cmu.edu/~qing/`

Therefore, we build lattices that encode the different reorderings for every training sentence, as described in Niehues et al. (2009). Then we can not only extract phrase pairs from the monotone source path, but also from the reordered paths. So it would be possible to extract the example mentioned before, if both parts of the verb were put together by a reordering rule. To limit the number of extracted phrase pairs, we extract a source phrase only once per sentence even if it may be found on different paths. Furthermore, we do not use the weights in the lattice.

If we used the same rules as for reordering the test sets, the lattice would be so big that the number of extracted phrase pairs would be still too high. As mentioned before, the word reordering is mainly a problem at the phrase extraction stage if one word is aligned to two words which are far away from each other in the sentence. Therefore, the short-range reordering rules do not help much in this case. So, only the long-range reordering rules were used to generate the lattices for the training corpus.

4.3 Unaligned Word Feature

Guzman et al. (2009) analyzed the role of the word alignment in the phrase extraction process. To better model the relation between word alignment and the phrase extraction process, they introduced two new features into the log-linear model. One feature counts the number of unaligned words on the source side and the other one does the same for the target side. Using these additional features they showed improvements on the Chinese to English translation task. In order to investigate the impact on closer related languages like English and German, we incorporated those two features into our systems.

4.4 Bilingual Word language model

Motivated by the improvements in translation quality that could be achieved by using the n-gram based approach to statistical machine translation, for example by Allauzen et al. (2009), we tried to integrate a bilingual language model into our phrase-based translation system.

To be able to integrate the approach easily into a standard phrase-based SMT system, a token in the bilingual language model is defined to consist of a target word and all source words it is aligned to. The tokens are ordered according to the target language word order. Then the additional tokens can be introduced into the decoder as an additional target factor. Consequently, no additional implementation work is needed to integrate this feature.

If we have the German sentence *Ich bin nach Hause gegangen* with the English translation *I went home*, the resulting bilingual text would look like this: *I_Ich went_bin_gegangen home_Hause*.

As shown in the example, one problem with this approach is that unaligned source words are ignored in the model. One solution could be to have a second bilingual text ordered according to the source side. But since the target sentence and not the source sentence is generated from left to right during decoding, the integration of a source side language model is more complex. Therefore, as a first approach we only used a language model based on the target word order.

4.5 Bilingual POS language model

The main advantage of POS-based information is that there are less data sparsity problems and therefore a longer context can be considered. Consequently, if we want to use this information in the translation model of a phrase-based SMT system, the POS-based phrase pairs should be longer than the word-based ones. But this is not possible in many decoders or it leads to additional computation overhead.

If we instead use a bilingual POS-based language model, the context length of the language model is independent from the other models. Consequently, a longer context can be considered for the POS-based language model than for the word-based bilingual language model or the phrase pairs.

Instead of using POS-based information, this approach can also be applied with other additional linguistic word-level information like word stems.

5 Results

We submitted translations for English-German and German-English for the Shared Translation Task. In the following we present the experiments we conducted for both translation directions applying the aforementioned models and extensions to the baseline systems. The performance of each individual system configuration was measured applying the BLEU metric. All BLEU scores are calculated on the lower-cased translation hypotheses. The individual systems that were used to create the submission are indicated in bold.

5.1 English-German

The baseline system for English-German applies short-range reordering rules and discriminative word alignment. The language model is trained on the News corpus. By expanding the coverage of the rules to enable long-range reordering, the score on the test set could be slightly improved. We then combined the target language part of the Europarl and News Commentary corpora with the News corpus to build a bigger language model which resulted in an increase of 0.11 BLEU points on the development set and an increase of 0.25 points on the test set. Applying the bilingual language model as described above led to 0.04 points improvement on the test set.

Table 1: Translation results for English-German (BLEU Score)

System	Dev	Test
Baseline	15.30	15.40
+ Long-range Reordering	15.25	15.44
+ EPNC LM	15.36	15.69
+ bilingual Word LM	15.37	**15.73**
+ bilingual POS LM	15.42	15.67
+ unaligned Word Feature	15.65	15.66
+ bilingual Stem LM	15.57	15.74

This system was used to create the submission to the Shared Translation Task of the WMT 2010. After submission we performed additional experiments which only led to inconclusive results. Adding the bilingual POS language model and introducing the unaligned word feature to the phrase table only improved on the development set, while the scores on the test set decreased. A third bilingual language model based on stem information again only showed noteworthy effects on the development set.

5.2 German-English

For the German to English translation system, the baseline system already uses short-range reordering rules and the discriminative word alignment. This system applies only the language model trained on the News corpus. By adding the possibility to model long-range reorderings with POS-based rules, we could improve the system by 0.6 BLEU points. Adding the big language model using also the English Gigaword corpus we could improve by 0.3 BLEU points. We got an additional improvement by 0.1 BLEU points by adding lattice phrase extraction.

Both the word-based and POS-based bilingual language model could improve the translation quality measured in BLEU. Together they improved the system performance by 0.2 BLEU points.

The best results could be achieved by using also the unaligned word feature for source and target words leading to the best performance on the test set (22.09).

Table 2: Translation results for German-English (BLEU Score)

System	Dev	Test
Baseline	20.94	20.83
+ Long-range Reordering	21.52	21.43
+ Gigaword LM	21.90	21.71
+ Lattice Phrase Extraction	21.94	21.81
+ bilingual Word LM	21.94	21.87
+ bilingual POS LM	22.02	22.05
+ unaligned Word Feature	22.09	**22.09**

6 Conclusions

For our participation in the WMT 2010 we built translation systems for German to English and English to German. We addressed to the difficult word reordering when translating from or to German by using POS-based reordering rules during decoding and by using lattice-based phrase extraction during training. By applying those methods we achieved substantially better results for both translation directions.

Furthermore, we tried to improve the translation quality by introducing additional features to the translation model. On the one hand we included bilingual language models based on different word factors into the log-linear model. This led to very slight improvements which differed also with respect to language and data set. We will investigate in the future whether further improvements are achievable with this approach. On the other hand we included the unaligned word feature which has been applied successfully for other language pairs. The improvements we could gain with this method are not as big as the ones reported for other languages, but still the performance of our systems could be improved using this feature.

Acknowledgments

This work was realized as part of the Quaero Programme, funded by OSEO, French State agency for innovation.

References

Alexandre Allauzen, Josep Crego, Aurélien Max, and François Yvon. 2009. LIMSI's statistical translation system for WMT'09. In *Fourth Workshop on Statistical Machine Translation (WMT 2009)*, Athens, Greece.

George Foster, Roland Kuhn, and Howard Johnson. 2006. Phrasetable Smoothing for Statistical Machine Translation. In *Conference on Empirical Methods in Natural Language Processing (EMNLP 2006)*, Sydney, Australia.

Francisco Guzman, Qin Gao, and Stephan Vogel. 2009. Reassessment of the Role of Phrase Extraction in PBSMT. In *MT Summit XII*, Ottawa, Ontario, Canada.

Philipp Koehn and Kevin Knight. 2003. Empirical Methods for Compound Splitting. In *EACL*, Budapest, Hungary.

Philipp Koehn, Hieu Hoang, Alexandra Birch, Chris Callison-Burch, Marcello Federico, Nicola Bertoldi, Brooke Cowan, Wade Shen, Christine Moran, Richard Zens, Chris Dyer, Ondrej Bojar, Alexandra Constantin, and Evan Herbst. 2007. Moses: Open Source Toolkit for Statistical Machine Translation. In *ACL 2007, Demonstration Session*, Prague, Czech Republic, June 23.

Jan Niehues and Muntsin Kolss. 2009. A POS-Based Model for Long-Range Reorderings in SMT. In *Fourth Workshop on Statistical Machine Translation (WMT 2009)*, Athens, Greece.

Jan Niehues and Stephan Vogel. 2008. Discriminative Word Alignment via Alignment Matrix Modeling. In *Proc. of Third ACL Workshop on Statistical Machine Translation*, Columbus, USA.

Jan Niehues, Teresa Herrmann, Muntsin Kolss, and Alex Waibel. 2009. The Universität Karlsruhe Translation System for the EACL-WMT 2009. In *Fourth Workshop on Statistical Machine Translation (WMT 2009)*, Athens, Greece.

Kay Rottmann and Stephan Vogel. 2007. Word Reordering in Statistical Machine Translation with a POS-Based Distortion Model. In *TMI*, Skövde, Sweden.

Helmut Schmid. 1994. Probabilistic Part-of-Speech Tagging Using Decision Trees. In *International Conference on New Methods in Language Processing*, Manchester, UK.

Ashish Venugopal, Andreas Zollman, and Alex Waibel. 2005. Training and Evaluation Error Minimization Rules for Statistical Machine Translation. In *Workshop on Data-drive Machine Translation and Beyond (WPT-05)*, Ann Arbor, MI.

Stephan Vogel. 2003. SMT Decoder Dissected: Word Reordering. In *Int. Conf. on Natural Language Processing and Knowledge Engineering*, Beijing, China.

MaTrEx: The DCU MT System for WMT 2010

Sergio Penkale, Rejwanul Haque, Sandipan Dandapat, Pratyush Banerjee, Ankit K. Srivastava, Jinhua Du, Pavel Pecina, Sudip Kumar Naskar, Mikel L. Forcada, Andy Way

CNGL, School of Computing
Dublin City University, Dublin 9, Ireland

{ spenkale, rhaque, sdandapat, pbanerjee, asrivastava, jdu, ppecina, snaskar, mforcada, away }@computing.dcu.ie

Abstract

This paper describes the DCU machine translation system in the evaluation campaign of the Joint Fifth Workshop on Statistical Machine Translation and Metrics in ACL-2010. We describe the modular design of our multi-engine machine translation (MT) system with particular focus on the components used in this participation. We participated in the English–Spanish and English–Czech translation tasks, in which we employed our multi-engine architecture to translate. We also participated in the system combination task which was carried out by the MBR decoder and confusion network decoder.

1 Introduction

In this paper, we present the DCU multi-engine MT system MaTrEx (Machine Translation using Examples). This system exploits example-based MT, statistical MT (SMT), and system combination techniques.

We participated in the English–Spanish (`en–es`) and English–Czech (`en–cs`) translation tasks. For these two tasks, we employ several individual MT systems: 1) Baseline: phrase-based SMT (Koehn et al., 2007); 2) EBMT: Monolingually chunking both source and target sides of the dataset using a marker-based chunker (Gough and Way, 2004); 3) Factored translation model (Koehn and Hoang, 2007); 4) Source-side context-informed (SSCI) systems (Stroppa et al., 2007); 5) the `moses-chart` (a Moses implementation of the hierarchical phrase-based (HPB) approach of Chiang (2007)) and 6) Apertium (Forcada et al., 2009) rule-based machine translation (RBMT). Finally, we use a word-level combination framework (Rosti et al., 2007) to combine the multiple translation hypotheses and employ a new rescoring model to generate the final translation.

For the system combination task, we first use the minimum Bayes-risk (MBR) (Kumar and Byrne, 2004) decoder to select the best hypothesis as the alignment reference for the confusion network (CN) (Mangu et al., 2000). We then build the CN using the TER metric (Snover et al., 2006), and finally search for the best translation.

The remainder of this paper is organised as follows: Section 2 details the various components of our system, in particular the multi-engine strategies used for the shared task. In Section 3, we outline the complete system setup for the shared task and provide evaluation results on the test set. Section 4 concludes the paper.

2 The MaTrEx System

2.1 System Architecture

The MaTrEx system is a combination-based multi-engine architecture, which exploits aspects of both the EBMT and SMT paradigms. The architecture includes various individual systems: phrase-based, example-based, hierarchical phrase-based and tree-based MT.

The combination structure uses the MBR and CN decoders, and is based on a word-level combination strategy (Du et al., 2009). In the final stage, we use a new rescoring module to process the N-best list generated by the combination module. Figure 1 illustrates the architecture.

2.2 Example-Based Machine Translation

The EBMT system uses a language-specific, reduced set of closed-class *marker* morphemes or lexemes (Gough and Way, 2004) to define a way to segment sentences into *chunks*, which are then aligned using an edit-distance-style algorithm, in which edit costs depend on word-to-word transla-

Proceedings of the Joint 5th Workshop on Statistical Machine Translation and MetricsMATR, pages 143–148,
Uppsala, Sweden, 15-16 July 2010. ©2010 Association for Computational Linguistics

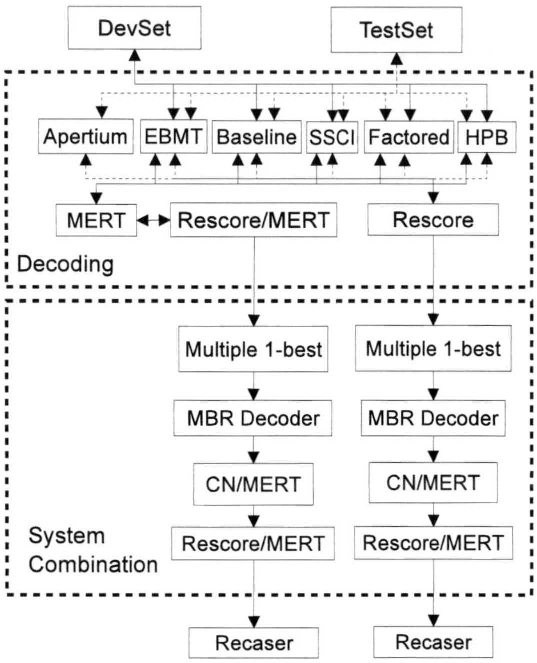

Figure 1: System Framework.

tion probabilities and the amount of word-to-word *cognates* (Stroppa and Way, 2006).

Once these phrase pairs were obtained they were merged with the phrase pairs extracted by the baseline system adding word alignment information.

2.3 Apertium RBMT

Apertium[1] is a free/open-source platform for RBMT. The current version of the en–es system in Apertium was used for the system combination task (section 2.7), and its morphological analysers and part-of-speech taggers were used to build a factored Moses model.

2.4 Factored Translation Model

We also used a factored model for the en–es translation task. Factored models (Koehn and Hoang, 2007) facilitate the translation by breaking it down into several factors which are further combined using a log-linear model (Och and Ney, 2002).

We used three factors in our factored translation model, which are used in two different decoding paths: a surface form (SF) to SF translation factor, a lemma to lemma translation factor, and a part-of-speech (PoS) to PoS translation factor.

Finally, we used two decoding paths based on the above three translation factors: an SF to SF decoding path and a path which maps lemma to lemma, PoS to PoS, and an SF generated using the TL lemma and PoS. The lemmas and PoS for en and es were obtained using Apertium (section 2.3).

2.5 Source-Side Context-informed PB-SMT

One natural way to express a context-informed feature ($\hat{h}_{\text{MBL}}$) is to view it as the conditional probability of the target phrases ($\hat{e}_k$) given the source phrase ($\hat{f}_k$) and its source-side *context information* (CI):

$$\hat{h}_{\text{MBL}} = \log P(\hat{e}_k|\hat{f}_k, \text{CI}(\hat{f}_k)) \quad (1)$$

We use a memory-based machine learning (MBL) classifier (TRIBL:[2] Daelemans and van den Bosch (2005)) that is able to estimate $P(\hat{e}_k|\hat{f}_k, \text{CI}(\hat{f}_k))$ by similarity-based reasoning over memorized nearest-neighbour examples of source–target phrase translations. In equation (1), SSCI may include any feature (lexical, syntactic, etc.), which can provide useful information to disambiguate a given source phrase. In addition to using local words and PoS-tags as features, as in (Stroppa et al., 2007), we incorporate grammatical dependency relations (Haque et al., 2009a) and supertags (Haque et al., 2009b) as syntactic source context features in the log-linear PB-SMT model.

In addition to the above feature, we derived a simple binary feature $\hat{h}_{\text{best}}$, defined in (2):

$$\hat{h}_{\text{best}} = \begin{cases} 1 & \text{if } \hat{e}_k \text{ maximizes } P(\hat{e}_k|\hat{f}_k, \text{CI}(\hat{f}_k)) \\ 0 & \text{otherwise} \end{cases} \quad (2)$$

We performed experiments by integrating these two features, $\hat{h}_{\text{MBL}}$ and $\hat{h}_{\text{best}}$, directly into the log-linear framework of Moses.

2.6 Hierarchical PB-SMT model

For the en–cs translation task, we built a weighted synchronous context-free grammar model (Chiang, 2007) of translation that uses the bilingual phrase pairs of PB-SMT as a starting point to learn hierarchical rules. We used the open-source Tree-Based translation system `moses-chart`[3] to perform this experiment.

[1] http://www.apertium.org

[2] An implementation of TRIBL is freely available as part of the TiMBL software package, which can be downloaded from http://ilk.uvt.nl/timbl

[3] http://www.statmt.org/moses/?n=Moses.SyntaxTutorial

2.7 System Combination

For multiple system combination, we used an MBR-CN framework (Du et al., 2009, 2010) as shown in Figure 1. Due to the varying word order in the MT hypotheses, it is essential to define the *backbone* which determines the general word order of the CN. Instead of using a single system output as the skeleton, we employ an MBR decoder to select the best single system output E_r from the merged N-best list by minimizing the BLEU (Papineni et al., 2002) loss, as in (3):

$$r = \arg\min_{i} \sum_{j=1}^{N_s} (1 - \text{BLEU}(E_j, E_i)) \qquad (3)$$

where N_s indicates the number of translations in the merged N-best list, and $\{E_i\}_{i=1}^{N_s}$ are the translations themselves. In our task, we only merge the 1-best output of each individual system.

The CN is built by aligning other hypotheses against the backbone, based on the TER metric. Null words are allowed in the alignment. Either votes or different confidence measures are assigned to each word in the network. Each arc in the CN represents an alternative word at that position in the sentence and the number of votes for each word is counted when constructing the network. The features we used are as follows:

- word posterior probability (Fiscus, 1997);
- 3, 4-gram target language model;
- word length penalty;
- Null word length penalty;

We use MERT (Och, 2003) to tune the weights of the CN.

2.8 Rescoring

Rescoring is a very important part in post-processing which can select a better hypothesis from the N-best list. We augmented our previous rescoring model (Du et al., 2009) with more large-scale data. The features we used include:

- Direct and inverse IBM model;
- 3, 4-gram target language model;
- 3, 4, 5-gram PoS language model (Schmid, 1994; Ratnaparkhi, 1996);
- Sentence length posterior probability (Zens and Ney, 2006);
- N-gram posterior probabilities within the N-Best list (Zens and Ney, 2006);
- Minimum Bayes Risk probability;
- Length ratio between source and target sentence;

The weights are optimized via MERT.

3 Experimental Setup

This section describes our experimental setup for the en–cs and en–es translation tasks.

3.1 Data

Bilingual data: In the experiments we used data sets provided by the workshop organizers. For the en–cs translation table extraction we employed both parallel corpora (News-Commentary10 and CzEng 0.9), and for the en–es experiments, we used the Europarl(Koehn, 2005), News Commentary and United Nations parallel data. We used a maximum sentence length of 80 for en–es and 40 for en–cs. Detailed statistics are shown in Table 1.

Corpus	Langs.	Sent.	Source tokens	Target tokens
Europarl	en–es	1.6M	43M	45M
News-comm	en–es	97k	2.4M	2.7M
UN	en–es	5.9M	160M	190M
News-Comm	en–cs	85k	1.8M	1.6M
CzEng	en–cs	7.8M	80M	69M

Table 1: Statistics of en–cs and en–es parallel data.

Monolingual data: For language modeling purposes, in addition to the target parts of the bilingual data, we used the monolingual News corpus for cs; and the Gigaword corpus for es. For both languages, we used the SRILM toolkit (Stolcke, 2002) to train a 5-gram language model using all monolingual data provided. However, for en–es we used the IRSTLM toolkit (Federico and Cettolo, 2007) to train a 5-gram language model using the es Gigaword corpus. Both language models use modified Kneser-Ney smoothing (Chen and Goodman, 1996). Statistics for the monolingual corpora are given in Table 2.

Corpus	Language	Sentences	Tokens
E/N/NC/UN	es	9,6M	290M
Gigaword	es	40M	1,2G
News	cs	13M	210M

Table 2: Statistics of Monolingual Data. *E/N/NC/UN* refers to Europarl/News/News_Commentary/United_Nations corpora.

For all the systems except Apertium, we first lowercase and tokenize all the monolingual and bilingual data using the tools provided by the WMT10 organizers. After translation, system combination output is detokenised and true-cased.

3.2 English–Czech (en–cs) Experiments

The CzEng corpus (Bojar and Žabokrtský, 2009) is a collection of parallel texts from sources of different quality and as such it contains some noise. As the first step, we discarded those sentence pairs having more than 10% of non-Latin characters.

The CzEng corpus is quite large (8M sentence pairs). Although we were able to build a vanilla SMT system on all parallel data available (News-Commentary + CzEng), we also attempted to build additional systems using News-Commentary data (which we considered in-domain) and various in-domain subsets of CzEng hoping to achieve better results on domain-specific data.

For our first system, we selected 128,218 sentence pairs from CzEng labeled as *news*. For the other two systems, we selected subsets of 2M and 4M sentence pairs identified as most similar to the development sets (as a sample of in-domain data) based on cosine similarity of their representation in a TF-IDF weighted vector space model (cf. Byrne et al. (2003)). We also applied the pseudo-relevavance-feedback technique for query expansion (Manning et al., 2008) to select another subset with 2M sentence pairs.

We used the output of 15 systems for system combination for the en–cs translation task. Among these, 5 systems were built using Moses and varying the size of the training data (DCU-All, DCU-Ex2M, DCU-4M, DCU-2M and DCU-News); 9 context-informed PB-SMT systems (DCU-SSCI-*) using (combinations of) various context features (word, PoS, supertags and dependency relations) trained only on the News Commentary data (marked with ‡ in Table 4); and one system using the `moses-chart` decoder, also trained on the news commentary data.

3.3 English–Spanish (en–es) Experiments

Three baseline systems using Moses were built, where we varied the amount of training data used:

- epn: This system uses all of the Europarl and News-Commentary parallel data.
- UN-half: This system uses the data suplied to "epn", plus an additional 2.1M sentences pairs randomly selected from the United Nations corpus.
- all: This system uses all of the available parallel data.

For en–es we also obtained output from the factored model (trained only on the news commentary corpus) and the Apertium RBMT system. We also derived phrase alignments using the MaTrEx EBMT system (Stroppa and Way, 2006), and added those phrase translations in the Moses phrase table. The systems marked with ⋆ use a language model built using the Spanish Gigaword corpus, in addition to the one built using the provided monolingual data. These 6 sets of system outputs are then used for system combination.

3.4 Experimental Results

The evaluation results for en–es and en–cs experiments are shown in Table 3 and Table 4 respectively. The output of the systems marked † were submitted in the shared tasks.

System	BLEU	NIST	METEOR	TER
DCU-half †⋆	29.77%	7.68	59.86%	59.55%
DCU-all †⋆	29.63%	7.66	59.82%	59.74%
DCU-epn †⋆	29.45%	7.66	59.71%	59.64%
DCU-ebmt †⋆	29.38%	7.62	59.59%	60.11%
DCU-factor	22.58%	6.56	54.94%	67.65%
DCU-apertium	19.22%	6.37	49.68%	67.68%
DCU-system-combination †	30.42%	7.78	60.56%	58.71%

Table 3: en–es experimental results.

System	BLEU	NIST	METEOR	TER
DCU-All	10.91%	4.60	39.18%	81.76%
DCU-Ex2M	10.63%	4.56	39.12%	81.96%
DCU-4M	10.61%	4.56	39.26%	82.04%
DCU-2M	10.48%	4.58	39.35%	81.56%
DCU-Chart	9.34%	4.25	37.04%	83.87%
DCU-News	8.64%	4.16	36.27%	84.96%
DCU-SSCI-ccg‡	8.26%	4.02	34.76%	85.58%
DCU-SSCI-supertag-pair‡	8.11%	3.95	34.93%	86.63%
DCU-SSCI-ccg-ltag‡	8.09%	3.96	34.90%	86.62%
DCU-SSCI-PR‡	8.06%	4.00	34.89%	85.99%
DCU-SSCI-base‡	8.05%	3.97	34.61%	86.02%
DCU-SSCI-PRIR‡	8.03%	3.99	34.81%	85.98%
DCU-SSCI-ltag‡	8.00%	3.95	34.57%	86.41%
DCU-SSCI-PoS‡	7.91%	3.94	34.57%	86.51%
DCU-SSCI-word‡	7.57%	3.88	34.16%	87.14%
DCU-system-combination †	13.22%	4.98	40.39%	78.59%

Table 4: en–cs experimental results.

4 Conclusion

This paper presents the Dublin City University MT system in WMT2010 shared task campaign. This was DCU's first attempt to translate from en to es and cs in any shared task. We developed a multi-engine framework which combined the outputs of several individual MT systems and generated a new N-best list after CN decoding. Then by using some global features, the rescoring model generated the final translation output. The experimental results demonstrated that the combination module and rescoring module are effective in our framework for both language pairs, and produce statistically significant improvements as measured by bootstrap resampling methods (Koehn, 2004) on BLEU over the single best system.

Acknowledgements: This work is supported by Science Foundation Ireland (Grant No. 07/CE/I1142) and by PANACEA, a 7th Framework Research Programme of the European Union, contract number 7FP-ITC-248064. M.L. Forcada's sabbatical stay at Dublin City University is supported by Science Foundation Ireland through ETS Walton Award 07/W.1/I1802 and by the Universitat d'Alacant (Spain).

References

Bojar, O. and Žabokrtský, Z. (2009). CzEng0.9: Large Parallel Treebank with Rich Annotation. *Prague Bulletin of Mathematical Linguistics*, 92:63–83.

Byrne, W., Khudanpur, S., Kim, W., Kumar, S., Pecina, P., Virga, P., Xu, P., and Yarowsky, D. (2003). The Johns Hopkins University 2003 Chinese–English machine translation system. In *Proceedings of MT Summit IX*, pages 447–450, New Orleans, LA.

Chen, S. F. and Goodman, J. (1996). An Empirical Study of Smoothing Techniques for Language Modeling. In *Proc. 34th Ann. Meeting of the Association for Computational Linguistics*, pages 310–318, San Francisco, CA.

Chiang, D. (2007). Hierarchical phrase-based translation. *Computational Linguistics*, 33(2):201–228.

Daelemans, W. and van den Bosch, A. (2005). *Memory-Based Language Processing (Studies in Natural Language Processing)*. Cambridge University Press, New York, NY.

Du, J., He, Y., Penkale, S., and Way, A. (2009). MaTrEx: The DCU MT System for WMT2009. In *Proc. 3rd Workshop on Statistical Machine Translation, EACL 2009*, pages 95–99, Athens, Greece.

Du, J., Pecina, P., and Way, A. (2010). An Augmented Three-Pass System Combination Framework: DCU Combination System for WMT 2010. In *Proc. ACL 2010 Joint Workshop in Statistical Machine Translation and Metrics Matr*, Uppsala, Greece.

Federico, M. and Cettolo, M. (2007). Efficient Handling of N-gram Language Models for Statistical Machine Translation. In *Proceedings of the Second Workshop on Statistical Machine Translation*, pages 88–95, Prague, Czech Republic.

Fiscus, J. G. (1997). A post-processing system to yield reduced word error rates: Recognizer output voting error reduction (ROVER). In *Proceedings 1997 IEEE Workshop on Automatic Speech Recognition and Understanding (ASRU)*, pages 347–352, Santa Barbara, CA.

Forcada, M. L., Tyers, F. M., and Ramírez-Sánchez, G. (2009). The free/open-source machine translation platform Apertium: Five years on. In *Proceedings of the First International Workshop on Free/Open-Source Rule-Based Machine Translation FreeRBMT'09*, pages 3–10.

Gough, N. and Way, A. (2004). Robust Large-Scale EBMT with Marker-Based Segmentation. In *Proceedings of the 10th International Conference on Theoretical and Methodological Issues in Machine Translation (TMI-04)*, pages 95–104, Baltimore, MD.

Haque, R., Naskar, S. K., Bosch, A. v. d., and Way, A. (2009a). Dependency relations as source context in phrase-based smt. In *Proc. 23rd Pacific Asia Conference on Language, Information and Computation*, pages 170–179, Hong Kong, China.

Haque, R., Naskar, S. K., Ma, Y., and Way, A. (2009b). Using supertags as source language context in SMT. In *EAMT-2009: Proceedings of the 13th Annual Conference of the European Association for Machine Translation*, pages 234–241, Barcelona, Spain.

Koehn, P. (2004). Statistical significance tests for machine translation evaluation. In *Proceedings of EMNLP*, volume 4, pages 388–395.

Koehn, P. (2005). Europarl: A Parallel Corpus for Statistical Machine Translation. In *Machine Translation Summit X*, pages 79–86, Phuket, Thailand.

Koehn, P. and Hoang, H. (2007). Factored Translation Models. In *Proceedings of the Joint Conference on Empirical Methods in Natural Language Processing and Computational Natural*

Language Learning (EMNLP-CoNLL), pages 868–876, Prague, Czech Republic.

Koehn, P., Hoang, H., Birch, A., Callison-Burch, C., Federico, M., Bertoldi, N., Cowan, B., Shen, W., Moran, C., Zens, R., Dyer, C., Bojar, O., Constantin, A., and Herbst, E. (2007). Moses: Open Source Toolkit for Statistical Machine Translation. In *Annual Meeting of the Association for Computational Linguistics (ACL), demonstration session*, pages 177–180, Prague, Czech Republic.

Kumar, S. and Byrne, W. (2004). Minimum Bayes-Risk Decoding for Statistical Machine Translation. In *Proceedings of the Joint Meeting of the Human Language Technology Conference and the North American Chapter of the Association for Computational Linguistics (HLT-NAACL 2004)*, pages 169–176, Boston, MA.

Mangu, L., Brill, E., and Stolcke, A. (2000). Finding consensus in speech recognition: Word error minimization and other applications of confusion networks. *Computer Speech and Language*, 14(4):373–400.

Manning, C. D., Raghavan, P., and Schütze, H. (2008). *Introduction to Information Retrieval*. Cambridge University Press.

Och, F. (2003). Minimum error rate training in statistical machine translation. In *Proceedings of the 41st Annual Meeting of the Association for Computational Linguistics (ACL)*, pages 160–167, Sapporo, Japan.

Och, F. and Ney, H. (2002). Discriminative training and maximum entropy models for statistical machine translation. In *Proceedings of ACL*, volume 2, pages 295–302.

Papineni, K., Roukos, S., Ward, T., and Zhu, W.-J. (2002). BLEU: a Method for Automatic Evaluation of Machine Translation. In *Proceedings of the 40th Annual Meeting of the Association for Computational Linguistics (ACL-02)*, pages 311–318, Philadelphia, PA.

Ratnaparkhi, A. (1996). A Maximum Entropy Model for Part-Of-Speech Tagging. In *Proceedings of the Empirical Methods in Natural Language Processing Conference (EMNLP)*, pages 133–142, Philadelphia, PA.

Rosti, A.-V. I., Xiang, B., Matsoukas, S., Schwartz, R., Ayan, N. F., and Dorr, B. J. (2007). Combining outputs from multiple machine translation systems. In *Proceedings of the Joint Meeting of the Human Language Technology Conference and the North American Chapter of the Association for Computational Linguistics (HLT-NAACL 2007)*, pages 228–235, Rochester, NY.

Schmid, H. (1994). Probabilistic Part-of-Speech Tagging Using Decision Trees. In *Proceedings of International Conference on New Methods in Language Processing*, pages 44–49, Manchester, UK.

Snover, M., Dorr, B., Schwartz, R., Micciula, L., and Makhoul, J. (2006). A study of translation edit rate with targeted human annotation. In *Proceedings of the 7th Conference of the Association for Machine Translation in the Americas (AMTA 2006)*, pages 223–231, Cambridge, MA.

Stolcke, A. (2002). SRILM - An Extensible Language Modeling Toolkit. In *Proceedings of the International Conference Spoken Language Processing*, pages 901–904, Denver, CO.

Stroppa, N., van den Bosch, A., and Way, A. (2007). Exploiting Source Similarity for SMT using Context-Informed Features. In *Proceedings of the 11th International Conference on Theoretical and Methodological Issues in Machine Translation (TMI-07)*, pages 231–240, Skövde, Sweden.

Stroppa, N. and Way, A. (2006). MaTrEx: the DCU machine translation system for IWSLT 2006. In *Proceedings of the International Workshop on Spoken Language Translation*, pages 31–36, Kyoto, Japan.

Zens, R. and Ney, H. (2006). N-gram Posterior Probabilities for Statistical Machine Translation. In *Proceedings of the Joint Meeting of the Human Language Technology Conference and the North American Chapter of the Association for Computational Linguistics (HLT-NAACL 2006)*, pages 72–77, New York, NY.

The Cunei Machine Translation Platform for WMT '10

Aaron B. Phillips
Carnegie Mellon
Pittsburgh, USA.
aphillips@cmu.edu

Abstract

This paper describes the Cunei Machine Translation Platform and how it was used in the WMT '10 German to English and Czech to English translation tasks.

1 The Cunei Machine Translation Platform

The Cunei Machine Translation Platform (Phillips and Brown, 2009) is open-source software and freely available at http://www.cunei.org/. Like Moses (Koehn et al., 2007) and Joshua (Li et al., 2009), Cunei provides a statistical decoder that combines partial translations (either phase pairs or grammar rules) in order to compose a coherent sentence in the target language. What makes Cunei unique is that it models the translation task with a non-parametric model that assesses the relevance of each translation instance.

The process begins by encoding in a lattice all possible contiguous phrases from the input.[1] For each source phrase in the lattice, Cunei locates instances of it in the corpus and then identifies the aligned target phrase(s). This much is standard to most data-driven MT systems. The typical step at this stage is to model a phrase pair by computing relative frequencies over the collection of translation instances. This model for the phrase pair will never change and knowledge of the translation instances can subsequently be discarded. In contrast to using a phrase pair as the basic unit of modeling, Cunei models each translation instance. A distance function, represented by a log-linear model, scores the relevance of each translation instance. Our model then sums the scores of translation instances that predict the same target hypothesis.

The advantage of this approach is that it provides a flexible framework for novel sources of information. The non-parametric model still uses information gleaned over all translation instances, but it permits us to define a distance function that operates over one translation instance at a time. This enables us to score a wide-variety of information represented by the translation instance with respect to the input and the target hypothesis under consideration. For example, we could compute how similar one translation instance's parse tree or morpho-syntactic information is to the input. Furthermore, this information will vary throughout the corpus with some translation instances exhibiting higher similarity to the input. Our approach captures that these instances are more relevant and they will have a larger effect on the model. For the WMT '10 task, we exploited instance-specific context and alignment features which will be discussed in more detail below.

1.1 Formalism

Cunei's model is a hybrid between the approaches of Statistical MT and Example-Based MT. A typical SMT model will score a phrase pair with source s, target t, log features ϕ, and weights λ using a log-linear model, as shown in Equation 1 of Figure 1. There is no prototypical model for EBMT, but Equation 2 demonstrates a reasonable framework where evidence for the phrase pair is accumulated over all instances of translation. Each instance of translation from the corpus has a source s' and target t'. In the most limited case $s = s'$ and $t = t'$, but typically an EBMT system will have some notion of similarity and use instances of translation that do not exactly match the input.

Cunei's model is defined in such a way that we maintain the distance function $\phi(s, s', t', t)$ from the EBMT model, but compute it in a much more efficient manner. In particular, we remove the real-space summation within a logarithm that makes it impractical to tune model weights. However, our

[1] Cunei offers limited support for non-contiguous phrases, similar in concept to grammar rules, but this setting was disabled in our experiments.

Proceedings of the Joint 5th Workshop on Statistical Machine Translation and MetricsMATR, pages 149–154,
Uppsala, Sweden, 15-16 July 2010. ©2010 Association for Computational Linguistics

$$score(s,t) = \sum_k \lambda_k \phi_k(s,t) \quad (1)$$

$$score(s,t) = \ln \sum_{s',t'} e^{\sum_k \lambda_k \phi_k(s,s',t',t)} \quad (2)$$

$$score(s,t) = \delta + \sum_k \lambda_k \left(\frac{\sum_{(s',t') \in C} \phi_k(s,s',t',t) e^{\sum_i \lambda_i \phi_i(s,s',t',t)}}{\sum_{(s',t') \in C} e^{\sum_i \lambda_i \phi_i(s,s',t',t)}} \right) \quad (3)$$

Figure 1: Translation model scores according to SMT (1), EBMT (2), and Cunei (2)

model preserves the first-order derivative of Equation 2, which is useful during optimization to locally approximate the hypothesis space. While the inner term initially appears complex, it is simply the expectation of each feature under the distribution of translation instances and can be efficiently computed with an online update. Last, the introduction of δ, a slack variable, is necessary to additionally ensure that the score of this model is equal to Equation 2. Specifying the model in this manner ties together the two different modeling approaches pursued by SMT and EBMT; the SMT model of Equation 1 is merely a special case of our model when the features for all instances of a translation are constant such that $\phi_k(s,s',t',t) = \phi_k(s,t)\ \forall s',t'$.

Indeed, this distinction illuminates the primary advantage of our model. Each feature is calculated particular to one translation instance in the corpus and each translation instance is scored individually. The model is then responsible for aggregating knowledge across multiple instances of translation. Unlike the SMT model, our aggregate model does not maintain feature independence. Each instance of translation represents a *joint* set of features. The higher the score of a translation instance, the more *all* its features inform the aggregate model. Thus, our model is biased toward feature values that represent relevant translation instances.

1.2 Context

Not all translations found in a corpus are equally useful. Often, when dealing with data of varying quality, training a SMT system on all of the data *degrades performance*. A common workaround is to perform some sort of sub-sampling that selects a small quantity of novel phrase pairs from the large out-of-domain corpus such that they do not overwhelm the number of phrase pairs extracted from the smaller in-domain corpus.

Instead of building our model from a heuristic sub-sample, we utilize Cunei's modeling approach to explicitly identify the relevance of each translation instance. We add features to the model that identify when a translation instance occurs within the same context as the input. This permits us to train on *all* available data by dynamically weighting each instance of a translation.

First, we capture the broader context or genre of a translation instance by comparing the document in the corpus from which it was extracted to the input document. These documents are modeled as a bag of words, and we use common document-level distance metrics from the field of information retrieval. Specifically, we implement as features document-level precision, recall, cosine distance and Jensen-Shannon distance (Lin, 1991).

In order to capture local, intra-sentential context, we compare the words immediately to the left and right of each translation instance with the input. We add one feature that counts the total number of adjacent words that match the input and a second feature that penalizes translation instances whose adjacent context only (or mostly) occurs in one direction. As a variation on the same concept, we also add four binary features that indicate when a *unigram* or *bigram* match is present on the *left* or *right* hand side.

The corpus in which an instance is located can also substantially alter the style of a translation. For example, both the German to English and the Czech to English corpora consisted of in-domain News Commenary and out-of-domain Europarl text. When creating the index, Cunei stores the name of the corpus that is associated with each sentence. From this information we create a set of binary features for each instance of translation that indicate from which corpus the instance originated. The weights for these origin features can be conceived as mixture weights specifying the relevance of each corpus.

1.3 Alignment

After a match is found on the source-side of the corpus, Cunei must determine the target phrase to which it aligns. The phrase alignment is treated as a hidden variable and not specified during training. Ideally, the full alignment process would be carried out dynamically at run-time. Unfortunately, even a simple word alignment such as IBM Model-1 is too expensive. Instead, we run a word aligner offline and our on-line phrase alignment computes features over the the word alignments. The phrase alignment features are then components of the model for each translation instance. While the calculations are not exactly the same, conceptually this work is modeled after (Vogel, 2005).

For each source-side match in the corpus, an alignment matrix is loaded for the complete sentence in which the match resides. This alignment matrix contains scores for all word correspondences in the sentence pair and can be created using GIZA++ (Och and Ney, 2003) or the Berkeley aligner (Liang et al., 2006). Intuitively, when a source phrase is aligned to a target phrase, this implies that the remainder of the source sentence that is not specified by the source phrase is aligned to the remainder of the target sentence not specified by the target phrase. Separate features compute the probability that the word alignments for tokens within the phrase are concentrated within the phrase boundaries and that the word alignments for tokens outside the phrase are concentrated outside the phrase boundaries. In addition, words with no alignment links or weak alignments links demonstrate uncertainty in modeling. To capture this effect, we incorporate two more features that count the number of uncertain alignments present in the source phrase and the target phrase.

The features described above assess the phrase alignment likelihood for a particular translation instance. Because they operate over all the word alignments present in a sentence, the alignment scores are contextual and usually vary from instance to instance. As the model weights change, so too will the phrase alignment scores. Each source phrase is modeled as having some probability of aligning to every possible target phrase within a given sentence. However, it is not practical to compute all possible phrase alignments, so we extract translation instances using only a few high-scoring phrase alignments for each occurrence of a source phrase in the corpus.[2] As discussed previously, these extracted translation instances form the basic modeling unit in Cunei.

1.4 Optimization

Cunei's built-in optimization code closely follows the approach of (Smith and Eisner, 2006), which minimizes the expectation of the loss function over the distribution of translations present in the n-best list. Following (Smith and Eisner, 2006), we implemented $\log(\text{BLEU})$ as the loss function such that the objective function can be decomposed as the expected value of BLEU's brevity penalty and the expected value of BLEU's precision score. The optimization process slowly anneals the distribution of the n-best list in order to avoid local minima. This begins with a near uniform distribution of translations and eventually reaches a distribution where, for each sentence, nearly all of the probability mass resides on the top translation (and corresponds closely with the actual 1-best BLEU score). In addition, Cunei supports the ability to decode sentences *toward* a particular set of references. This is used to prime the optimization process in the first iteration with high-scoring, obtainable translations.

2 The WMT '10 Translation Task

For the WMT '10 Translation Task we built two systems. The first translated from German to English and was trained with the provided News Commentary and Europarl (Koehn, 2005) corpora. The second system translated from Czech to English and used the CzEng 0.9 corpus (Bojar and Žabokrtský, 2009), which is a collection of many different texts and includes the Europarl. To validate our results, we also trained a Moses system with the same corpus, alignments, and language model.

2.1 Corpus Preparation

A large number of hand-crafted regular expressions were used to remove noise (control characters, null bytes, etc.), normalize (hard spaces vs. soft spaces, different forms of quotations,

[2] This is controlled by a score ratio that typically selects 2-6 translation instances per occurrence of a source phrase.

render XML codes as characters, etc.), and tokenize (abbreviations, numbers, punctuation, etc.). However, these rules are fairly generic and applicable to most Western languages. In particular, we did not perform any morphologically-sensitive segmentation. From the clean text we calculated the expected word and character ratios between the source language and the target language. Then we proceeded to remove sentence pairs according to the following heuristics:

- A sentence exceeded 125 words
- A sentence exceeded 1,000 characters
- The square of the difference between the actual and expected words divided by the square of the standard deviation exceeded 5
- The square of the difference between the actual and expected characters divided by the square of the standard deviation exceeded 5

All of these processing routines are included as part of the Cunei distribution and are configurable options. An overview of the resulting corpora is shown in Table 1.

Finally, we used the GIZA++ toolkit (Och and Ney, 2003) to induce word alignments in both directions for each language pair. The resulting corpus and word alignments were provided to Moses and Cunei for training. Each system used their respective phrase extraction and model estimation routines.

2.2 Language Model

We intentionally selected two language pairs that translated into English so that we could share one language model between them. We used the large monolingual English News text made available through the workshop and augmented this with the Xinhua and AFP sections of the English Gigaword corpus (Parker and others, 2009). In all, approximately one billion words of English text were fed to the SRILM toolkit (Stolcke, 2002) to construct a single English 5-gram language model with Kneser-Ney smoothing.

2.3 Experiments

The newswire evaluation sets from the prior two years were selected as development data. 636 sentences were sampled from WMT '09 for tuning and all 2,051 sentences from WMT '08 were reserved for testing. Finally, a blind evaluation was also performed with the new WMT '10 test set. All systems were tuned toward BLEU (Papineni et al., 2002) and all evaluation metrics were run on lowercased, tokenized text.

The results in Table 2 and Table 3 show the performance of Cunei[3] against the Moses system we also built with the same data. The first Cunei system we built included all the alignment features discussed in §1.3. These per-instance alignment features are essential to Cunei's run-time phrase extraction and cannot be disabled. The second, and complete, system added to this all the context features described in §1.2. Cunei, in general, performs significantly better than Moses in German and is competitive with Moses in Czech. However, we hoped to see a larger gain from the addition of the context features.

In order to better understand our results and see if there was greater potential for the context features, we selectively added a few of the features at a time to the German system. These experiments are reported in Table 4. What is interesting here is that most subsets of context features did better than the whole and none degraded the baseline (at least according to BLEU) on the test sets. We did not expect a fully additive gain from the combination, as many of the context features do represent different ways of capturing the same phenomena. However, we were still surprised to find an apparently *detrimental* interaction among the full set of context features.

Theoretically adding new features should only improve a system as a feature can always by ignored by assigning it a weight of zero. However, new features expand the hypothesis space and provide the model with more degrees of freedom which may make it easier to get stuck in local minima. While the gradient-based, annealing method for optimization that we use tends work better than MERT (Och, 2003), it is still susceptible to these issues. Indeed, the variation on the tuning set–while relatively inconsequential–is evidence that this is occurring and that we have not found the global optimum. Further investigation is necessary into the interaction between the context features and techniques for robust optimization.

[3]These results have been updated since the official WMT '10 submission as a result of minor bug-fixes and code improvements to Cunei.

	German	English	Czech	English
Tokens	41,245,188	43,064,069	63,776,164	72,325,831
Sentences	1574044		6181270	

Table 1: Corpus Statistics

2.4 Conclusion

We used the Cunei Machine Translation Platform to build German to English and Czech to English systems for the WMT '10 evaluation. In both systems we experimented with per-instance alignment and context features. Our addition of the context features resulted in only minor improvement, but a deeper analysis of the individual features suggests greater potential. Overall, Cunei performed strongly in our evaluation against a comparable Moses system. We acknowledge that the actual features we selected are not particularly novel. Instead, the importance of this work is the simplicity with which instance-specific features can be jointly modeled and integrated within Cunei as a result of its unique modeling approach.

Acknowledgements

The author would like to thank Ralf Brown for providing suggestions and feedback on this paper.

References

Ondřej Bojar and Zdeněk Žabokrtský. 2009. Czeng0.9: Large parallel treebank with rich annotation. *Prague Bulletin of Mathematical Linguistics*, 92.

Philipp Koehn, Hieu Hoang, Alexandra Birch, Chris Callison-Burch, Marcello Federico, Nicola Bertoldi, Brooke Cowan, Wade Shen, Christine Moran, Richard Zens, Chris Dyer, Ondrej Bojar, Alexandra Constantin, and Evan Herbst. 2007. Moses: Open source toolkit for statistical machine translation. In *Proceedings of the 45th Annual Meeting of the Association for Computational Linguistics*, pages 177–180, Prague, Czech Republic, June.

Philipp Koehn. 2005. Europarl: A parallel corpus for statistical machine translation. In *Machine Translation Summit X Proceedings* (mts, 2005), pages 79–86.

Zhifei Li, Chris Callison-Burch, Chris Dyer, Sanjeev Khudanpur, Lane Schwartz, Wren Thornton, Jonathan Weese, and Omar Zaidan. 2009. Joshua: An open source toolkit for parsing-based machine translation. In *Proceedings of the Fourth Workshop on Statistical Machine Translation*, pages 135–139, Athens, Greece, March.

Percy Liang, Ben Taskar, and Dan Klein. 2006. Alignment by agreement. In *Proceedings of the Human Language Technology Conference of the North American Chapter of the Association for Computational Linguistics*, pages 104–111, New York City, USA, June.

Jianhua Lin. 1991. Divergence measures based on the shannon entropy. *IEEE Transactions on Information Theory*, 37(1):145–151, January.

2005. Phuket, Thailand, September.

Franz Josef Och and Hermann Ney. 2003. A systematic comparison of various statistical alignment models. *Computational Linguistics*, 29(1):19–51.

Franz Josef Och. 2003. Minimum error rate training in statistical machine translation. In *Proceedings of the 41st Annual Meeting of the Association for Computational Linguistics*, pages 160–167, Sapporo, Japan, July.

Kishore Papineni, Salim Roukos, Todd Ward, and Wei-Jing Zhu. 2002. Bleu: a method for automatic evaluation of machine translation. In *Proceedings of the 40th Annual Meeting of the Association for Computational Linguistics*, pages 311–318, Philadelphia, USA, July.

Robert Parker et al. 2009. English gigaword fourth edition.

Aaron B. Phillips and Ralf D. Brown. 2009. Cunei machine translation platform: System description. In Mikel L. Forcada and Andy Way, editors, *Proceedings of the 3rd Workshop on Example-Based Machine Translation*, pages 29–36, Dublin, Ireland, November.

David A. Smith and Jason Eisner. 2006. Minimum risk annealing for training log-linear models. In *Proceedings of the 21st International Conference on Computational Linguistics and 44th Annual Meeting of the Association for Computational Linguistics*, pages 787–794, Sydney, Australia, July.

Andreas Stolcke. 2002. Srilm - an extensible language modeling toolkit. In *7th International Conference on Spoken Language Processing*, pages 901–904, Denver, USA, September.

Stephan Vogel. 2005. Pesa: Phrase pair extraction as sentence splitting. In *Machine Translation Summit X Proceedings* (mts, 2005), pages 251–258.

	Development Tuning				**Development Test**				**Blind Test**			
	BLEU	NIST	Meteor	TER	BLEU	NIST	Meteor	TER	BLEU	NIST	Meteor	TER
Moses	0.1916	5.9156	0.5286	0.6475	0.2046	6.2802	0.5330	0.6523	0.2097	6.5657	0.5591	0.6313
Cunei with Alignment	0.2018	5.9847	0.5326	0.6375	0.2125	6.3639	0.5342	0.6430	0.2210	6.6355	0.5573	0.6224
Cunei with Alignment & Context	0.2022	6.0021	0.5331	0.6362	0.2127	6.3753	0.5344	0.6408	0.2214	6.6467	0.5575	0.6198

Table 2: Overview of German to English Evaluations

	Development Tuning				**Development Test**				**Blind Test**			
	BLEU	NIST	Meteor	TER	BLEU	NIST	Meteor	TER	BLEU	NIST	Meteor	TER
Moses	0.2141	6.1969	0.5536	0.6170	0.2041	6.3574	0.5361	0.6422	0.2297	6.7916	0.5617	0.6054
Cunei with Alignment	0.2206	6.2634	0.5555	0.6128	0.2058	6.4116	0.5425	0.6391	0.2291	6.8464	0.5665	0.6003
Cunei with Alignment & Context	0.2170	6.2802	0.5567	0.6125	0.2065	6.4391	0.5398	0.6362	0.2315	6.8829	0.5676	0.5984

Table 3: Overview of Czech to English Evaluations

	Development Tuning				**Development Test**				**Blind Test**			
	BLEU	NIST	Meteor	TER	BLEU	NIST	Meteor	TER	BLEU	NIST	Meteor	TER
Cunei	0.2018	5.9847	0.5326	0.6375	0.2125	6.3639	0.5342	0.6430	0.2210	6.6355	0.5573	0.6224
+ Origins	0.2010	6.0233	0.5370	0.6353	0.2150	6.4154	0.5361	0.6391	0.2221	6.6719	0.5609	0.6208
+ Adjacent Length & Skew	0.2002	6.0080	0.5338	0.6402	0.2147	6.4183	0.5354	0.6431	0.2237	6.7336	0.5574	0.6172
+ Adjacent N-grams	0.2011	5.9648	0.5310	0.6410	0.2137	6.3598	0.5329	0.6434	0.2235	6.6656	0.5564	0.6202
+ Doc Cosine & JSD	0.1987	5.9514	0.5305	0.6422	0.2134	6.3498	0.5324	0.6456	0.2228	6.6647	0.5579	0.6209
+ Doc Precision & Recall	0.2007	5.9764	0.5315	0.6376	0.2145	6.3984	0.5361	0.6410	0.2244	6.6900	0.5608	0.6206

Table 4: Breakdown of Context Features in German to English

The CUED HiFST System for the WMT10 Translation Shared Task

Juan Pino Gonzalo Iglesias[‡1] Adrià de Gispert
Graeme Blackwood Jamie Brunning William Byrne
Department of Engineering, University of Cambridge, Cambridge, CB2 1PZ, U.K.
{jmp84,gi212,ad465,gwb24,jjjb2,wjb31}@eng.cam.ac.uk
[‡] Department of Signal Processing and Communications, University of Vigo, Vigo, Spain

Abstract

This paper describes the Cambridge University Engineering Department submission to the Fifth Workshop on Statistical Machine Translation. We report results for the French-English and Spanish-English shared translation tasks in both directions. The CUED system is based on HiFST, a hierarchical phrase-based decoder implemented using weighted finite-state transducers. In the French-English task, we investigate the use of context-dependent alignment models. We also show that lattice minimum Bayes-risk decoding is an effective framework for multi-source translation, leading to large gains in BLEU score.

1 Introduction

This paper describes the Cambridge University Engineering Department (CUED) system submission to the ACL 2010 Fifth Workshop on Statistical Machine Translation (WMT10). Our translation system is HiFST (Iglesias et al., 2009a), a hierarchical phrase-based decoder that generates translation lattices directly. Decoding is guided by a CYK parser based on a synchronous context-free grammar induced from automatic word alignments (Chiang, 2007). The decoder is implemented with Weighted Finite State Transducers (WFSTs) using standard operations available in the OpenFst libraries (Allauzen et al., 2007). The use of WFSTs allows fast and efficient exploration of a vast translation search space, avoiding search errors in decoding. It also allows better integration with other steps in our translation pipeline such as 5-gram language model (LM) rescoring and lattice minimum Bayes-risk (LMBR) decoding.

[1]Now a member of the Department of Engineering, University of Cambridge, Cambridge, CB2 1PZ, U.K.

	# Sentences	# Tokens	# Types
(A)Europarl+News-Commentary			
FR	1.7 M	52.4M	139.7k
EN		47.6M	121.6k
(B)Europarl+News-Commentary+UN			
FR	8.7 M	277.9M	421.0k
EN		241.4M	482.1k
(C)Europarl+News-Commentary+UN+Giga			
FR	30.2 M	962.4M	2.4M
EN		815.3M	2.7M

Table 1: Parallel data sets used for French-to-English experiments.

We participated in the French-English and Spanish-English translation shared tasks in each translation direction. This paper describes the development of these systems. Additionally, we report multi-source translation experiments that lead to very large gains in BLEU score.

The paper is organised as follows. Section 2 describes each step in the development of our system for submission, from pre-processing to post-processing. Section 3 presents and discusses results and Section 4 describes an additional experiment on multi-source translation.

2 System Development

We built three French-English and two Spanish-English systems, trained on different portions of the parallel data sets available for this shared task. Statistics for the different parallel sets are summarised in Tables 1 and 2. No additional parallel data was used. As will be shown, the largest parallel corpus gave the best results in French, but this was not the case in Spanish.

2.1 Pre-processing

The data was minimally cleaned by replacing HTML-related metatags by their corresponding

Proceedings of the Joint 5th Workshop on Statistical Machine Translation and MetricsMATR, pages 155–160,
Uppsala, Sweden, 15-16 July 2010. ©2010 Association for Computational Linguistics

	# Sentences	# Tokens	# Types
(A) Europarl + News-Commentary			
SP	1.7M	49.4M	167.2k
EN		47.0M	122.7k
(B) Europarl + News-Commentary + UN			
SP	6.5M	205.6M	420.8k
EN		192.0M	402.8k

Table 2: Parallel data sets used for Spanish-to-English experiments.

UTF8 token (e.g., replacing "&amp" by "&") as this interacts with tokenization. Data was then tokenized and lowercased, so mixed case is added as post-processing.

2.2 Alignments

Parallel data was aligned using the MTTK toolkit (Deng and Byrne, 2005). In the English-to-French and English-to-Spanish directions, we trained a word-to-phrase HMM model with maximum phrase length of 2. In the French to English and Spanish to English directions, we trained a word-to-phrase HMM Model with a bigram translation table and maximum phrase length of 4.

We also trained context-dependent alignment models (Brunning et al., 2009) for the French-English medium-size (B) dataset. The context of a word is based on its part-of-speech and the part-of-speech tags of the surrounding words. These tags were obtained by applying the TnT Tagger (Brants, 2000) for English and the TreeTagger (Schmid, 1994) for French. Decision tree clustering based on optimisation of the EM auxiliary function was used to group contexts that translate similarly. Unfortunately, time constraints prevented us from training context-dependent models for the larger (C) dataset.

2.3 Language Model

For each target language, we used the SRILM Toolkit (Stolcke, 2002) to estimate separate 4-gram LMs with Kneser-Ney smoothing (Kneser and Ney, 1995), for each of the corpora listed in Tables 3, 4 and 5. The LM vocabulary was adjusted to the parallel data set used. The component models of each language pair were then interpolated to form a single LM for use in first-pass translation decoding. For French-to-English translation, the interpolation weights were optimised for perplexity on a development set.

Corpus	# Sentences	# Tokens
EU + NC + UN	9.0M	246.4M
CNA	1.3M	34.8M
LTW	12.9M	298.7M
XIN	16.0M	352.5M
AFP	30.4M	710.6M
APW	62.1M	1268.6M
NYT	73.6M	1622.5M
Giga	21.4M	573.8M
News	48.7M	1128.4M
Total	275.4M	6236.4M

Table 3: English monolingual training corpora.

Corpus	# Sentences	# Tokens
EU + NC + UN	9.0M	282.8
AFP	25.2M	696.0M
APW	12.7M	300.6M
News	15.2M	373.5M
Giga	21.4M	684.4M
Total	83.5 M	2337.3M

Table 4: French monolingual training corpora.

Corpus	# Sentences	# Tokens
NC + News	4.0M	110.8M
EU + Gigaword (5g)	249.4M	1351.5M
Total	253.4 M	1462.3M

Table 5: Spanish monolingual training corpora.

The Spanish-English first pass LM was trained directly on the NC+News portion of monolingual data, as we did not find improvements by using Europarl. The second pass rescoring LM used all available data.

2.4 Grammar Extraction and Decoding

After unioning the Viterbi alignments, phrase-based rules of up to five source words in length were extracted, hierarchical rules with up to two non-contiguous non-terminals in the source side were then extracted applying the restrictions described in (Chiang, 2007). For Spanish-English and French-English tasks, we used a shallow-1 grammar where hierarchical rules are allowed to be applied only once on top of phrase-based rules. This has been shown to perform as well as a fully hierarchical grammar for a Europarl Spanish-English task (Iglesias et al., 2009b).

For translation, we used the HiFST decoder (Iglesias et al., 2009a). HiFST is a hierarchical decoder that builds target word lattices guided by a probabilistic synchronous context-free grammar. Assuming $\mathbf{N}$ to be the set of non-terminals and $\mathbf{T}$ the set of terminals or words, then we can define the grammar as a set $\mathbf{R} = \{R^r\}$ of rules $R^r : N \rightarrow \langle\gamma^r,\alpha^r\rangle$ / p^r, where $N \in \mathbf{N}$; and $\gamma, \alpha \in \{\mathbf{N} \cup \mathbf{T}\}^+$.

HiFST translates in three steps. The first step is a variant of the CYK algorithm (Chappelier and Rajman, 1998), in which we apply hypothesis recombination without pruning. Only the source language sentence is parsed using the corresponding source-side context-free grammar with rules $N \rightarrow \gamma$. Each cell in the CYK grid is specified by a non-terminal symbol and position: (N, x, y), spanning s_x^{x+y-1} on the source sentence $s_1...s_J$.

For the second step, we use a recursive algorithm to construct word lattices with all possible translations produced by the hierarchical rules. Construction proceeds by traversing the CYK grid along the back-pointers established in parsing. In each cell (N, x, y) of the CYK grid, we build a target language word lattice $\mathcal{L}(N, x, y)$ containing every translation of s_x^{x+y-1} from every derivation headed by N. For efficiency, this lattice can use pointers to lattices on other cells of the grid.

In the third step, we apply the word-based LM via standard WFST composition with failure transitions, and perform likelihood-based pruning (Allauzen et al., 2007) based on the combined translation and LM scores.

As explained before, we are using shallow-1 hierarchical grammars (de Gispert et al., 2010) in our experiments for WMT2010. One very interesting aspect is that HiFST is able to build exact search spaces with this model, i.e. there is no pruning in search that may lead to spurious undergeneration errors.

2.5 Parameter Optimisation

Minimum error rate training (MERT) (Och, 2003) under the BLEU score (Papineni et al., 2001) optimises the weights of the following decoder features with respect to the *newstest2008* development set: target LM, number of usages of the glue rule, word and rule insertion penalties, word deletion scale factor, source-to-target and target-to-source translation models, source-to-target and target-to-source lexical models, and three binary rule count features inspired by Bender et al. (2007) indicating whether a rule occurs once, twice, or more than twice in the parallel training data.

2.6 Lattice Rescoring

One of the advantages of HiFST is direct generation of large translation lattices encoding many alternative translation hypotheses. These first-pass lattices are rescored with second-pass higher-order LMs prior to LMBR.

2.6.1 5-gram LM Lattice Rescoring

We build sentence-specific, zero-cutoff stupid-backoff (Brants et al., 2007) 5-gram LMs estimated over approximately 6.2 billion words for English, 2.3 billion words for French, and 1.4 billion words for Spanish. For the English-French task, the second-pass LM training data is the same monolingual data used for the first-pass LMs (as summarised in Tables 3, 4). The Spanish second-pass 5-gram LM includes an additional 1.4 billion words of monolingual data from the Spanish GigaWord Second Edition (Mendonca et al., 2009) and Europarl, which were not included in the first-pass LM (see Table 5).

2.6.2 LMBR Decoding

Minimum Bayes-risk (MBR) decoding (Kumar and Byrne, 2004) over the full evidence space of the 5-gram rescored lattices was applied to select the translation hypothesis that maximises the conditional expected gain under the linearised sentence-level BLEU score (Tromble et al., 2008; Blackwood and Byrne, 2010). The unigram precision p and average recall ratio r were set as described in Tromble et al. (2008) using the *newstest2008* development set.

2.7 Hypothesis Combination

Linearised lattice minimum Bayes-risk decoding (Tromble et al., 2008) can also be used as an effective framework for multiple lattice combination (de Gispert et al., 2010). For the French-English language pair, we used LMBR to combine translation lattices produced by systems trained on alternative data sets.

2.8 Post-processing

For both Spanish-English and French-English systems, the recasing procedure was performed with the SRILM toolkit. For the Spanish-English system, we created models from the GigaWord set corresponding to each system output language.

Task	Configuration	*newstest2008*	*newstest2009*	*newstest2010*
FR → EN	HiFST (A)	23.4	26.4	–
	HiFST (B)	24.0	27.3	–
	HiFST (B)^{CD}	24.2	27.6	28.0
	+5g+LMBR	**24.6**	**28.4**	**28.9**
	HiFST (C)	24.7	28.4	28.5
	+5g+LMBR	**25.3**	**29.1**	**29.3**
	LMBR (B)^{CD}+(C)	**25.6**	**29.3**	**29.6**
EN → FR	HiFST (A)	22.5	24.2	–
	HiFST (B)	23.4	24.8	–
	HiFST (B)^{CD}	23.3	24.8	26.7
	+5g+LMBR	**23.7**	**25.3**	**27.1**
	HiFST (C)	23.6	25.6	27.4
	+5g+LMBR	**23.9**	**25.8**	**27.8**
	LMBR (B)^{CD}+(C)	**24.2**	**26.1**	**28.2**

Table 6: Translation Results for the French-English (FR-EN) language pair, shown in single-reference lowercase IBM BLEU. Bold results correspond to submitted systems.

For the French-English system, the English model was trained using the monolingual News corpus and the target side of the News-Commentary corpus, whereas the French model was trained using all available constrained French data.

English, Spanish and French outputs were also detokenized before submission. In French, words separated by apostrophes were joined.

3 Results and Discussion

French–English Language Pair

Results are reported in Table 6. We can see that using more parallel data consistently improves performance. In the French-to-English direction, the system HiFST (B) improves over HiFST (A) by +0.9 BLEU and HiFST (C) improves over HiFST (B) by +1.1 BLEU on the *newstest2009* development set prior to any rescoring. The same trend can be observed in the English-to-French direction (+0.6 BLEU and +0.8 BLEU improvement). The use of context dependent alignment models gives a small improvement in the French-to-English direction: system (B)^{CD} improves by +0.3 BLEU over system (B) on *newstest2009*. In the English-to-French direction, there is no improvement nor degradation in performance. 5-gram and LMBR rescoring also give consistent improvement throughout the datasets. Finally, combination between the medium-size system (B)^{CD} and the full-size system (C) gives further small gains in BLEU over LMBR on each individual system.

Spanish–English Language Pair

Results are reported in Table 7. We report experimental results on two systems. The HiFST(A) system is built on the Europarl + News-Commentary training set. Systems HiFST (B),(B2) and (B3) use UN data in different ways. System (B) simply uses all the data for the standard rule extraction procedure. System HiFST (B2) includes UN data to build alignment models and therefore reinforce alignments obtained from smaller dataset (A), but extracts rules only from dataset (A). HiFST (B3) combines hierarchical phrases extracted for system (A) with phrases extracted from system (B). Unfortunately, these three larger data strategies lead to degradation over using only the smaller dataset (A). For this reason, our best systems only use the Euparl + News-Commentary parallel data. This is surprising given that additional data was helpful for the French-English task. Solving this issue is left for future work.

4 Multi-Source Translation Experiments

Multi-source translation (Och and Ney, 2001; Schroeder et al., 2009) is possible whenever multiple translations of the source language input sentence are available. The motivation for multi-source translation is that some of the ambiguity that must be resolved in translating between one pair of languages may not be present in a different pair. In the following experiments, multiple LMBR is applied for the first time to the task of multi-source translation.

Task	Configuration	*newstest2008*	*newstest2009*	*newstest2010*
SP → EN	HiFST (A)	24.6	26.0	29.1
	+5g+LMBR	**25.4**	**27.0**	**30.5**
	HiFST (B)	23.7	25.4	–
	HiFST (B2)	24.3	25.7	–
	HiFST (B3)	24.2	25.6	–
EN → SP	HiFST (A)	23.9	24.5	28.0
	+5g+LMBR	**24.7**	**25.5**	**29.1**

Table 7: Translation Results for the Spanish-English (SP-EN) language pair, shown in lowercase IBM BLEU. Bold results correspond to submitted systems.

Configuration		*newstest2008*	*newstest2009*	*newstest2010*
FR→EN	HiFST+5g	24.8	28.5	28.8
	+LMBR	25.3	29.0	29.2
ES→EN	HiFST+5g	25.2	26.8	30.1
	+LMBR	25.4	26.9	30.3
FR→EN + ES→EN	LMBR	27.2	30.4	32.0

Table 8: Lowercase IBM BLEU for single-system LMBR and multiple LMBR multi-source translation of French (FR) and Spanish (ES) into English (EN).

Separate second-pass 5-gram rescored lattices $\mathcal{E}_{\text{FR}}$ and $\mathcal{E}_{\text{ES}}$ are generated for each test set sentence using the French-to-English and Spanish-to-English HiFST translation systems. The MBR hypothesis space is formed as the union of these lattices. In a similar manner to MBR decoding over multiple k-best lists in de Gispert et al. (2009), the path posterior probability of each n-gram u required for linearised LMBR is computed as a linear interpolation of the posterior probabilities according to each individual lattice so that $p(u|\mathcal{E}) = \lambda_{\text{FR}}\, p(u|\mathcal{E}_{\text{FR}}) + \lambda_{\text{ES}}\, p(u|\mathcal{E}_{\text{ES}})$, where $p(u|\mathcal{E})$ is the sum of the posterior probabilities of all paths containing the n-gram u. The interpolation weights $\lambda_{\text{FR}} + \lambda_{\text{ES}} = 1$ are optimised for BLEU score on the development set *newstest2008*.

The results of single-system and multi-source LMBR decoding are shown in Table 8. The optimised interpolation weights were $\lambda_{\text{FR}} = 0.55$ and $\lambda_{\text{ES}} = 0.45$. Single-system LMBR gives relatively small gains on these test sets. Much larger gains are obtained through multi-source MBR combination. Compared to the best of the single-system 5-gram rescored lattices, the BLEU score improves by +2.0 for *newstest2008*, +1.9 for *newstest2009*, and +1.9 for *newstest2010*. For scoring with respect to a single reference, these are very large gains indeed.

5 Summary

We have described the CUED submission to WMT10 using HiFST, a hierarchical phrase-based translation system. Results are very competitive in terms of automatic metric for both English-French and English-Spanish tasks in both directions. In the French-English task, we have seen that the UN and Giga additional parallel data are helpful. It is surprising that UN data did not help for the Spanish-English language pair.

Future work includes investigating this issue, developing detokenization tailored to each output language and applying context dependent alignment models to larger parallel datasets.

Acknowledgments

The research leading to these results has received funding from the European Union Seventh Framework Programme (FP7-ICT-2009-4) under grant agreement number 247762, and was supported in part by the GALE program of the Defense Advanced Research Projects Agency, Contract No. HR0011-06-C-0022. Gonzalo Iglesias was supported by the Spanish Government research grant BES-2007-15956 (projects TEC2006-13694-C03-03 and TEC2009-14094-C04-04).

References

Cyril Allauzen, Michael Riley, Johan Schalkwyk, Wojciech Skut, and Mehryar Mohri. 2007. OpenFst: A general and efficient weighted finite-state transducer library. In *Proceedings of CIAA*, pages 11–23.

Oliver Bender, Evgeny Matusov, Stefan Hahn, Sasa Hasan, Shahram Khadivi, and Hermann Ney. 2007. The RWTH Arabic-to-English spoken language translation system. In *Proceedings of ASRU*, pages 396–401.

Graeme Blackwood and William Byrne. 2010. Efficient Path Counting Transducers for Minimum Bayes-Risk Decoding of Statistical Machine Translation Lattices (to appear). In *Proceedings of the ACL*.

Thorsten Brants, Ashok C. Popat, Peng Xu, Franz J. Och, and Jeffrey Dean. 2007. Large language models in machine translation. In *Proceedings of EMNLP-ACL*, pages 858–867.

Thorsten Brants. 2000. Tnt – a statistical part-of-speech tagger. In *Proceedings of ANLP*, pages 224–231, April.

Jamie Brunning, Adrià de Gispert, and William Byrne. 2009. Context-dependent alignment models for statistical machine translation. In *Proceedings of HLT/NAACL*, pages 110–118.

Jean-Cédric Chappelier and Martin Rajman. 1998. A generalized CYK algorithm for parsing stochastic CFG. In *Proceedings of TAPD*, pages 133–137.

David Chiang. 2007. Hierarchical phrase-based translation. *Computational Linguistics*, 33(2):201–228.

Adrià de Gispert, Sami Virpioja, Mikko Kurimo, and William Byrne. 2009. Minimum Bayes Risk Combination of Translation Hypotheses from Alternative Morphological Decompositions. In *Proceedings of HLT/NAACL, Companion Volume: Short Papers*, pages 73–76.

Adrià de Gispert, Gonzalo Iglesias, Graeme Blackwood, Eduardo R. Banga, and William Byrne. 2010. Hierarchical phrase-based translation with weighted finite state transducers and shallow-n grammars (to appear). In *Computational Linguistics*.

Yonggang Deng and William Byrne. 2005. HMM Word and Phrase Alignment for Statistical Machine Translation. In *Proceedings of HLT/EMNLP*, pages 169–176.

Gonzalo Iglesias, Adrià de Gispert, Eduardo R. Banga, and William Byrne. 2009a. Hierarchical phrase-based translation with weighted finite state transducers. In *Proceedings of NAACL*, pages 433–441.

Gonzalo Iglesias, Adrià de Gispert, Eduardo R. Banga, and William Byrne. 2009b. The HiFST System for the EuroParl Spanish-to-English Task. In *Proceedings of SEPLN*, pages 207–214.

Reinhard Kneser and Hermann Ney. 1995. Improved backing-off for m-gram language modeling. In *Proceedings of ICASSP*, volume 1, pages 181–184.

Shankar Kumar and William Byrne. 2004. Minimum Bayes-risk decoding for statistical machine translation. In *Proceedings of HLT-NAACL*, pages 169–176.

Angelo Mendonca, David Graff, and Denise DiPersio. 2009. Spanish Gigaword Second Edition, Linguistic Data Consortium.

Franz Josef Och and Hermann Ney. 2001. Statistical multi-source translation. In *Machine Translation Summit 2001*, pages 253–258.

Franz J. Och. 2003. Minimum Error Rate Training in Statistical Machine Translation. In *Proceedings of ACL*, pages 160–167.

Kishore Papineni, Salim Roukos, Todd Ward, and Wei-Jing Zhu. 2001. BLEU: a method for automatic evaluation of machine translation. In *Proceedings of ACL*, pages 311–318.

Helmut Schmid. 1994. Probabilistic part-of-speech tagging using decision trees. In *Proceedings of International Conference on New Methods in Language Processing*, volume 12. Manchester, UK.

Josh Schroeder, Trevor Cohn, and Philipp Koehn. 2009. Word Lattices for Multi-Source Translation. In *Proceedings of EACL*, pages 719–727.

Andreas Stolcke. 2002. SRILM–An Extensible Language Modeling Toolkit. In *Proceedings of ICSLP*, volume 3, pages 901–904.

Roy W. Tromble, Shankar Kumar, Franz Och, and Wolfgang Macherey. 2008. Lattice Minimum Bayes-Risk decoding for statistical machine translation. In *Proceedings of EMNLP*, pages 620–629.

The LIG machine translation system for WMT 2010

Marion Potet, Laurent Besacier and Hervé Blanchon
LIG Laboratory, GETALP Team
University Joseph Fourier, Grenoble, France.
Marion.Potet@imag.fr
Laurent.Besacier@imag.fr
Herve.Blanchon@imag.fr

Abstract

This paper describes the system submitted by the Laboratory of Informatics of Grenoble (LIG) for the fifth Workshop on Statistical Machine Translation. We participated to the news shared translation task for the French-English language pair. We investigated differents techniques to simply deal with Out-Of-Vocabulary words in a statistical phrase-based machine translation system and analyze their impact on translation quality. The final submission is a combination between a standard phrase-based system using the Moses decoder, with appropriate setups and pre-processing, and a lemmatized system to deal with Out-Of-Vocabulary conjugated verbs.

1 Introduction

We participated, for the first time, to the shared news translation task of the fifth Workshop on Machine Translation (WMT 2010) for the French-English language pair. The submission was performed using a standard phrase-based translation system with appropriate setups and pre-processings in order to deal with system's unknown words. Indeed, as shown in (Carpuat, 2009), (Habash, 2008) and (Niessen, 2004), handling Ou-of-Vocabulary words with techniques like lemmatization, phrase table extension or morphological pre-processing is a way to improve translation quality. After a short presentation of our baseline system setups we discuss the effect of Out-Of-Vocabulary words in the system and introduce some ideas we chose to implement. In the last part, we evaluate their impact on translation quality using automatic and human evaluations.

2 Baseline System Setup

2.1 Used Resources

We used the provided Europarl and News parallel corpora (total 1,638,440 sentences) to train the translation model and the News monolingual corpora (48,653,884 sentences) to train the language model. The 2008 News test corpora (news-test2008; 2,028 sentences) was used to tune the produced system and last year's test corpora (news-test2009; 3,027 sentences) was used for evaluation purposes. These corpora will be refered to as *Dev* and *Test* later in the paper. As pre-processing steps, we applied the PERL scripts provided with the corpora to lowercase and tokenise the data.

2.2 Language modeling

The target language model is a standard n-gram language model trained using the SRI language modeling toolkit (Stocke, 2002) on the news monolingual corpus. The smoothing technique we applied is the modified Kneser-Ney discounting with interpolation.

2.3 Translation modeling

The translation model was trained using the parallel corpus described earlier (Europarl+News). First, the corpus was word aligned and then, the pairs of source and corresponding target phrases were extracted from the word-aligned bilingual training corpus using the scripts provided with the Moses decoder (Koehn et al., 2007). The result is a phrase-table containing all the aligned phrases. This phrase-table, produced by the translation modeling, is used to extract several translations models. In our experiment we used thirteen standard translation models: six distortion models, a lexicon word-based and a phrase-based translation model for both direction, and a phrase, word and distortion penalty.

Proceedings of the Joint 5th Workshop on Statistical Machine Translation and MetricsMATR, pages 161–166,
Uppsala, Sweden, 15-16 July 2010. ©2010 Association for Computational Linguistics

2.4 Tuning and decoding

For the decoding (i.e. translation of the test set), the system uses a log-linear combination of the previous target language model and the thirteen translation models extracted from the phrase-table. As the system can be beforehand tuned by adjusting log-linear combination weights on a developement corpus, we used the Minimum Error Rate Training (MERT) method, by (Och, 2003).

3 Ways of Improvements

3.1 Discussion about Out-Of-Vocabulary words in PBMT systems

Phrase-based statistical machine translation (PBMT) use phrases as units in the translation process. A phrase is a sequence of n consecutive words known by the system. During the training, these phrases are automaticaly learned and each source phrase is mapped with its corresponding target phrase. Throughout test set decoding, a word not being part of this vocabulary list is labeled as "Out-Of-Vocabulary" (OOV) and, as it doesn't appear in the translation table, the system is unable to translate it. During the decoding, Out-Of-Vocabulary words lead to "broken" phrases and degrade translation quality. For these reasons, we present some techniques to handle Out-Of-Vocabulary words in a PBMT system and combine these techniques before evaluating them.

In a preliminary study, we automatically extracted and manually analyzed OOVs of a 1000 sentences sample extracted from the test corpus (news-test2009). There were altogether 487 OOVs tokens wich include 64.34% proper nouns and words in foreign languages, 17.62% common nouns, 15.16% conjugated verbs, 1.84% errors in source corpus and 1.02% numbers. Note that, as our system is configured to copy systematically the OOVs in the produced translated sentence, the rewriting of proper nouns and words in foreign language is straightforward in that case. However, we still have to deal with common nouns and conjugated verbs.

Initial sentence:
"Cela ne marchera pas" *souligna-t-il* par la suite.
Normalised sentence:
"Cela ne marchera pas" *il souligna* par la suite

Figure 1: Normalisation of the euphonious "t"

3.2 Term expansion with dictionary

The first idea is to expand the vocabulary size, more specifically minimizing Out-Of-Vocabulary common nouns adding a French-English dictionary during the training process. In our experiment, we used a free dictionnary made available by the *Wiktionary*[1] collaborative project (wich aims to produce free-content multilingual dictionaries). The provided dictionnary, containing 15,200 entries, is added to the bilingual training corpus before phrase-table extraction.

3.3 Lemmatization of the French source verbs

To avoid Out-Of-Vocabulary conjugated verbs one idea is to lemmatize verbs in the source training and test corpus to train a so-called lemmatized system. We used the freely available French lemmatiser LIA_TAGG (Béchet, 2001). But, applying lemmatization leads to a loss of information (tense, person, number) which may affect deeply the translation quality. Thus, we decided to use the lematized system only when OOV verbs are present in the source sentence to be translated. Consequently, we differentiate two kinds of sentences: -sentences containing at least one OOV conjugated verb, and - sentences which do not have any conjugated verb (these latter sentences obviously don't need any lemmatization!). Thereby, we decided to build a combined translation system which call the lemmatized system only when the source sentence contains at least one Out-Of-Vocabulary conjugated verb (otherwise, the sentence will be translated by the standard system). To detect sentences with Out-Of-Vocabulary conjugated verb we translate each sentence with both systems (lemmatized and standard), count OOV and use the lemmatized translation only if it contains less OOV than the standard translation. For example, a translation containing k Out-Of-Vocabulary conjugated verbs and n others Out-Of-Vocabulary words (in total $k+n$ OOV) with the standard system, contains, most probably, only n Out-Of-Vocabulary words with the lemmatised system because the conjugated verbs will be lemmatized, recognized and translated by the system.

[1] http://wiki.webz.cz/dict/

3.4 Normalization of a special French form

We observed, in the French source corpra, a special French form which generates almost always Out-Of-Vocabulary words in the English translation. The special French form, named euphonious "t", consists of adding the letter "t" between a verb (ended by "a", "e" or "c") and a personal pronoun and, then, inverse them in order to facilitate the prononciation. The sequence is represented by: *verb*-t-*pronoun* like *annonca-t-elle*, *arrive-t-il*, *a-t-on*, etc. This form concerns 1.75% of the French sentences in the test corpus whereas these account for 0.66% and 0.78% respetively in the training and the developement corpora. The normalized proposed form, illustrated below in figure 1, contains the subject pronoun (in first posistion) and the verb (in the second position). This change has no influence on the French source sentence and accordingly on the correctness and fluency of the English translation.

3.5 Adaptation of the language model

Finally, for each system, we decided to apply different language models and to look at those who perfom well. In addition to the 5-gram language model, we trained and tested 3-gram and 4-gram language models with two different kinds of vocabularies : - the first one (conventional, refered to as n-gram in table 3) contains an open-vocabulary extracted from the monolingual English training data, and - the second one (refered to as n-gram-vocab in table 3) contains a closed-vocabulary extracted from the English part of the bilingual training data. In both cases, language model probabilities are trained from the monolingual LM training data but, in the second case, the lexicon is restricted to the one of the phrase-table.

4 Experimental results

In the automatic evaluation, the reported evaluation metric is the BLEU score (Papineni et al., 2002) computed by MTEval version 13a. The results are reported in table 1. Note that in our experiments, according to the resampling method of (Koehn, 2004), there are significative variations (improvement or deterioration), with 95% certainty, only if the difference between two BLEU scores represent, at least, 0.33 points. To complete this automatic evaluation, we performed a human analysis of the systems outputs.

4.1 Standard systems

4.1.1 Term expansion with dictionary

Regarding the results of automatic evaluation (table 1, system (2)), adding the dictionary do not leads to a significant improvement. The OOV rate and system perplexity are reduced but, ignoring the tuned system which presents lower performance, the BLEU score decreases significatly on the test set. The BLEU score of the system augmented with the dictionary is 24.50 whereas the baseline one is 24.94. So we can conclude that there is not a meaningfull positive contribution, probably because the size of the dictionary is very small regarding the bilingual training corpus. We found out very few Out-Of-Vocabulary words of the standard system recognized by the system with the dictionary, see figure 2 for example (among them : *coupon*, *cafard*, *blonde*, *retardataire*, *médicaments*, *pamplemousse*, etc.). But, as the dictionnary is very small, most OOV common words like *hôtesse* and *clignotant* are still unknown. Regarding the output sentences, we note that there are very few differences and the quality is equivalent. The dictionary used is to small to extend the system's vocabulary and most of words still Out-Of-Vocabulary are conjugated verbs and unrecognized forms.

Baseline system:
A *cafard* fled before the danger, but if he felt fear?
System with dictionary:
A *blues* fled before the danger, but if he felt fear?

Figure 2: Example of sentence with an OOV common noun

4.1.2 Normalisation of special French form

Considering the BLEU score, the normalization of French euphonious "t" have, apparently, very few repercussion on the translation result (table 1, system (3)) but the human analysis indicates that, in our context, the normalisation of euphonious "t" brings a clear improvement as seen in example 3. Consequently, this preprocessing is kept in the final system.

4.1.3 Tuning

We can see in table 1 that the usual tuning with Minimum Error Rate Training algorithm deteriorates systematically performance scores on the test set, for all systems. This can be explained by the

System	OOVs	ppl	Dev score	Test score
(1) Baseline	2.32%	207	29.72 (19.93)	23.77 (24.94)
(2) + dictionary	2.30%	204	30.01 (23.92)	24.32 (24.50)
(3) + normalization	2.31%	204	30.07 (19.90)	23.99 (24.98)
(4) + normalization + Dev data	2.30%	204	/ (/)	/ (25,05)

Table 1: Standard systems BLEU scores with tuning (without tuning)/ LM 5-gram

Baseline system:
"It will not work" *souligna-t-il* afterwards.
System with normalisation:
"It will not work" *he stressed* afterwards.

Figure 3: Example of sentence with a "*verb*-t-*pronoun*" form

gap between the developement and test corpora (ie the Dev set may be not representative of the Test set). So, even if it is recommanded in the standard process, we do not tune our system (we use the default weights proposed by the Moses decoder) and add the developement corpus to train it. In this case, the training set contains 1,640,468 sentences (the initial 1,638,440 sentences and the 2,028 sentences of the developement set). This slightly improves the system (from 24.98, the BLEU score raise to 25,05 after adding the developpement set to the training).

4.2 Lemmatised systems

Results of lemmatised systems are reported on table 2. First, we can notice that, in this particular case, the tuning (with MERT method) is mandatory to adapt the weights of the log linear model. Our analysis of the tuned weight of the lemmatised system shows that, in particular, the word penalty model has a very low weight (this favours short sentences) and the lexical word-based translation models have a very low weight (no use of the lexical translation probability). We also notice that the lemmatization leads to a real drop-off of OOV rate (fall from 2.32% for the baseline, to 2.23% for the lemmatized system) and perplexity (fall from 207 for the baseline, to 178 for the lemmatized system). We can observe a clear decrease of the performance with the lemmatized system (BLEU score of 20.50) compared with a non-lemmatized one (BLEU score of 24.94). This can be significatively improved applying euphonious "t" normalization to the source data (BLEU score of 22.14). Almost all French OOV conjugated verbs with the standard system were recognized by the lemmatized one (*trierait*, *joues*, *testaient*, *immergée*, *économiseraient*, *baisserait*, *prépares*, etc.) but the small decrease of the translation quality can be explained, among other things, by several tense errors. See illustration in figure 4. So, we conclude that the systematic normalization of French verbs, as a pre-process, reduce the Out-Of-Vocabulary conjugated verbs but decrease slighly the final translation quality. The use of such a system is helpfull especially when the sentence contains conjugated verbs (see example 5).

4.3 Adaptation of the language model

We applied five differents language models (3-gram and 4-gram language models with selected vocabulary or not and a 5-gram language model) to the four standard systems and the two lemmatised one. The results, reported in table 3, show that BLEU score can be significantly different depending on the language model used. For example, the fifth system (5) obtained a BLEU score of 21.48 with a 3-gram language model and a BLEU score of 22.84 with a 4-gram language model. We can also notice that five out of our six systems outperform using a language model with selected vocabulary (*n-gram-vocab*). One possible explanation is that with LM using selected vocabulary (*n-gram-vocab*), there is no loss of probability mass for english words not present in the translation table.

4.4 Final combined system

Considering the previous observations, we believe that the best choice is to apply the lemmatized system only if necessary i.e. only if the sentence contains OOV conjugated verbs, otherwise, a standard system should be used. We consider system (4), with 4-gram-vocab language model (selected vocabulary) without tuning, as the best standard system and system (6), with 3-gram-vocab language model (selected vocabulary) not tuned either, as the best lemmatized system. The final

System	OOVs	ppl	Dev score	Test score
(5) lemmatization	2.23%	178	20.97 (8.57)	20.50 (8.56)
(6) lemmatization + normalization	2.18%	175	27.81 (9.20)	22.14 (10.82)

Table 2: Lemmatised systems BLEU scores with tuning (without tuning)/ LM 5-gram

Baseline system: You *will be limited* by the absence of exit for headphones.
Lemmatised system: You *are limited* by the lack of exit for ordinary headphones.
reference: You *will be limited* by the absence of output on ordinary headphones.

Figure 4: Example of sentences without OOV verbs

system translations are those of the lemmatized system (6) when we translate sentences with one or more Out-Of-Vocabulary conjugated verbs and those of the un-lemmatized system (4) otherwise. Around 6% of test set sentences were translated by the lemmatized system. Considering the results reported in table 4, the combined system's BLEU score is comparable to the standard one (25.11 against 25.17).

System	Test score	sentences
(4) Standard sys.	25.17	94 %
(6) Lemmatised sys.	22.89	6%
(7) Combined	25.11	100 %

Table 4: Combined system's results and % translated sentences by each system

5 Human evaluation

We compared two data set. The first set (selected sent.) contains 301 sentences selected from test data by the combined system (7) to be translated by the lemmatized system (6) whereas the second set (random sent.) contains 301 sentences randomly picked up. The latter is our control data set. We compared for both groups the translation hypothesis given by the lemmatized system and the standard one.

We performed a subjective evaluation with the NIST five points scales to measure fluency and adequacy of each sentences through SECtra_w interface (Huynh et al., 2009).We involved a total of 6 volunteers judges (3 for each set). We evaluated the inter-annotator agreement using a generalized version of Kappa. The results show a *slight* to *fair* agreement according (Landis, 1977).

The evaluation results, detailled in table 5 and 6, showed that both fluency and adequacy were improved using our combined system. Indeed, for a random input (random sent.), the lemmatized system lowers the translations quality (fluency and adequacy are degraded for, respectively, 35.8% and 37.5% of the sentences), while it improves the quality for sentences selected by the combined system (for "selected sent.", fluency and adequacy are improved or stable for 81% of the sentences).

Adequacy	selected sent.	random sent.
(6) $\geq$ (4)	81%	62.4%
(6) $<$ (4)	18.9%	37.5%

Table 5: Subjective evaluation of sentences adequacy ((6) lemmatized system - (4) standard system)

Fluency	selected sent.	random sent.
(6) $\geq$ (4)	81%	64.1%
(6)$<$(4)	18.9%	35.8%

Table 6: Subjective evaluation of sentences fluency ((6) lemmatized system - (4) standard system)

6 Conclusion and Discussion

We have described the system used for our submission to the WMT'10 shared translation task for the French-English language pair.

We propose dsome very simple techniques to improve rapidely a statistical machine translation. Those techniques particularly aim at handling Out-Of-Vocabulary words in statistical phrase-based machine translation and lead an improved fluency in translation results. The submited system (see section 4.4) is a combination between a standard system and a lemmatized system with appropriate setup.

Baseline system: At the end of trade, the stock market in the negative *bascula*.
Lemmatised system: At the end of trade, the stock market exchange *stumbled* into the negative.

Baseline system: You can choose *conseillera*.
Lemmatised system: We would *advise* you, how to choose.

Figure 5: Example of sentences with OOV conjugated verbs

System	3-gram	3-gram-vocab	4-gram	4-gram-vocab	5-gram
(1)	24.60	24.95	24.94	**25.11**	24.94
(2)	25.14	**25.17**	24.50	23.49	24.50
(3)	24.88	25.00	24.98	**25.15**	24.98
(4)	24.92	24.99	25.05	**25.17**	25.05
(5)	21.48	19.48	**22.84**	20.18	20.50
(6)	22.60	**22.89**	22.14	22.24	22.14

Table 3: Systems's results on test set with differents language models

This system evaluation showed a positive influence on translation quality, indeed, while the improvements on automatic metrics are small, manual inspection suggests a significant improvements of translation fluency and adequacy.

In future work, we plan to investigate and develop more sophisticated methods to deal with Out-Of-Vocabulary words, still relying on the analyze of our system output. We believe, for example, that an appropriate way to use the dictionary, a sensible pre-processings of French source texts (in particular normalization of some specific French forms) and a factorial lemmatization with the tense information can highly reduce OOV rate and improve translation quality.

References

Philipp Koehn, Hieu Hoang, Alexandra Birch, Chris Callison-Burch, Marcello Federico, Nicola Bertoldi, Brooke Cowan, Wade Shen, Christine Moran, Richard Zens, Chris Dyer, Ondrej Bojar, Alexandra Constantin, Evan Herbst. 2007. Moses: Open Source Toolkit for Statistical Machine Translation. *Annual Meeting of the Association for Computational Linguistics (ACL)*. Prague, Czech Republic.

Papineni K., Roukos S., Ward T., and Zhu W.J. 2002. BLEU: a method for automatic evaluation of machine translation. *ACL-2002: 40th Annual meeting of the Association for Computational Linguistics*, pp. 311–318. Philadelphia, Pennsylvania, USA.

Andreas Stolcke. 2002. SRILM - An Extensible Language Modeling Toolkit. *International Conference on Spoken Language Processing*, Vol. 2, pp 901–904. Denver, Colorado, USA.

Frederic Béchet. 2001. LIA_TAGG. http://old.lia.univ-avignon.fr/chercheurs/bechet/download_fred.html.

Franz Josef Och. 2003. Minimum error rate training for statistical machine translation. *Annual Meeting of the Association for Computational Linguistics (ACL)*. Sapporo, July.

Philipp Koehn. 2004. Statistical significance tests for machine translation evaluation. *conference on Empirical Methods in Natural Language Processing (EMNLP)*, pp 388–395. Barcelona, Spain.

Marine Carpuat. 2009. Toward Using Morphology in French-English Phrase-based SMT. *Workshop on Machine Translation in European Association for Computational Linguistics (EACL-WMT)*, pp 150–154. Athens, Greece.

Sonja Niessen and Hermann Ney. 2004. Statistical Machine Translation with Scarce Resources Using Morpho-syntactic Information. *Computational Linguistics*, vol. 30, pp 181–204.

Nizar Habash. 2008. Four techniques for Online Handling of Out-Of-Vocabulary Words in Arabic-English Statistical Machine Translation. *Human Language Technology Workshop in Association for Computational Linguistics, (ACL-HTL)*, pp 57–60. Columbus, Ohio, USA.

Landis J. R. and Koch G. G.. 1977. The Measurement of Observer Agreement for Categorical Data. *Biometrics*, vol. 33, pp. 159–174.

Hervé Blanchon, Christian Boitet and Cong-Phap Huynh. 2009. A Web Service Enabling Gradable Post-edition of Pre-translations Produced by Existing Translation Tools: Practical Use to Provide High-quality Translation of an Online Encyclopedia. *MT Summit XII, Beyond Translation Memories: New Tools for Translators Workshop*, pp 20–27. Ottawa, Canada.

Linear Inversion Transduction Grammar Alignments as a Second Translation Path

Markus SAERS and **Joakim NIVRE**
Computational Linguistics Group
Dept. of Linguistics and Philology
Uppsala University
Sweden
first.last@lingfil.uu.se

Dekai WU
Human Language Technology Center
Dept. of Computer Science and Engineering
HKUST
Hong Kong
dekai@cs.ust.hk

Abstract

We explore the possibility of using Stochastic Bracketing Linear Inversion Transduction Grammars for a full-scale German–English translation task, both on their own and in conjunction with alignments induced with GIZA++. The rationale for transduction grammars, the details of the system and some results are presented.

1 Introduction

Lately, there has been some interest in using Inversion Transduction Grammars (ITGs) for alignment purposes. The main problem with ITGs is the time complexity, $\mathcal{O}(Gn^6)$ doesn't scale well. By limiting the grammar to a bracketing ITG (BITG), the grammar constant (G) can be eliminated, but $\mathcal{O}(n^6)$ is still prohibitive for large data sets.

There has been some work on approximate inference of ITGs. Zhang et al. (2008) present a method for evaluating spans in the sentence pair to determine whether they should be excluded or not. The algorithm has a best case time complexity of $\mathcal{O}(n^3)$. Saers, Nivre & Wu (2009) introduce a beam pruning scheme, which reduces time complexity to $\mathcal{O}(bn^3)$. They also show that severe pruning is possible without significant deterioration in alignment quality (as measured by downstream translation quality). Haghighi et al. (2009) use a simpler aligner as guidance for pruning, which reduces the time complexity by two orders of magnitude. Their work also partially implements the phrasal ITGs for translation-driven segmentation introduced in Wu (1997), although they only allow for one-to-many alignments, rather than many-to-many alignments. A more extreme approach is taken in Saers, Nivre & Wu (2010). Not only is the search severely pruned, but the grammar itself is limited to a linearized form, getting rid of branching within a single parse. Although a small deterioration in downstream translation quality is noted (compared to harshly pruned SBITGs), the grammar can be induced in linear time.

In this paper we apply SBLITGs to a full size German–English WMT'10 translation task. We also use differentiated translation paths to combine SBLITG translation models with a standard GIZA++ translation model.

2 Background

A transduction grammar is a grammar that generates a pair of languages. In a transduction grammar, the terminal symbols consist of pairs of tokens where the first is taken from the vocabulary of one of the languages, and the second from the vocabulary of the other. Transduction grammars have to our knowledge been restricted to transduce between languages no more complex than context-free languages (CFLs). Transduction between CFLs was first described in Lewis & Stearns (1968), and then further explored in Aho & Ullman (1972). The main motivation for exploring this was to build programming language compilers, which essentially translate between source code and machine code. There are two types of transduction grammars between CFLs described in the computer science literature: simple transduction grammars (STGs) and syntax-directed transduction grammars (SDTGs). The difference between them is that STGs are monotone, whereas SDTGs allow unlimited reordering in rule productions. Both allow the use of singletons to insert and delete tokens from either language. A singleton is a biterminal where one of the tokens is the empty string (ϵ). Neither STGs nor SDTGs are intuitively useful in translating natural languages, since STGs have no way to model reordering, and SDTGs require exponential time to be induced from examples (parallel corpora). Since

Proceedings of the Joint 5th Workshop on Statistical Machine Translation and MetricsMATR, pages 167–171,
Uppsala, Sweden, 15-16 July 2010.

compilers in general work on well defined, manually specified programming languages, there is no need to induce them from examples, so the exponential complexity is not a problem in this setting – SDTGs can transduce in $\mathcal{O}(n^3)$ time, so once the grammar is known they can be used to translate efficiently.

In natural language translation, the grammar is generally not known, in fact, state-of-the art translation systems rely heavily on machine learning. For transduction grammars, this means that they have to be induced from parallel corpora.

An inversion transduction grammar (ITG) strikes a good balance between STGs and SDTGs, as it allows some reordering, while requiring only polynomial time to be induced from parallel corpora. The allowed reordering is either the identity permutation of the production, or the inversion permutation. Restricting the permutations in this way ensures that an ITG can be expressed in two-normal form, which is the key property for avoiding exponential time complexity in biparsing (parsing of a sentence pair).

An ITG in two-normal form (representing the transduction between L_1 and L_2) is written with identity productions in square brackets, and inverted productions in angle brackets. Each such rule can be construed to represent two (one L_1 and one L_2) synchronized CFG rules:

ITG_{L_1,L_2}	CFG_{L_1}	CFG_{L_2}
$A \rightarrow [\, B\, C\,]$	$A \rightarrow B\, C$	$A \rightarrow B\, C$
$A \rightarrow \langle\, B\, C\, \rangle$	$A \rightarrow B\, C$	$A \rightarrow C\, B$
$A \rightarrow e/f$	$A \rightarrow e$	$A \rightarrow f$

Inducing an ITG from a parallel corpus is still slow, as the time complexity is $\mathcal{O}(Gn^6)$. Several ways to get around this has been proposed (Zhang et al., 2008; Haghighi et al., 2009; Saers et al., 2009; Saers et al., 2010).

Taking a closer look at the linear ITGs (Saers et al., 2010), there are five rules in normal form. Decomposing these five rule types into monolingual rule types reveals that the monolingual grammars are linear grammars (LGs):

LITG_{L_1,L_2}	LG_{L_1}	LG_{L_2}
$A \rightarrow [\, e/f\, C\,]$	$A \rightarrow e\, C$	$A \rightarrow f\, C$
$A \rightarrow [\, B\, e/f\,]$	$A \rightarrow B\, e$	$A \rightarrow B\, f$
$A \rightarrow \langle\, e/f\, C\, \rangle$	$A \rightarrow e\, C$	$A \rightarrow C\, f$
$A \rightarrow \langle\, B\, e/f\, \rangle$	$A \rightarrow B\, e$	$A \rightarrow f\, B$
$A \rightarrow \epsilon/\epsilon$	$A \rightarrow \epsilon$	$A \rightarrow \epsilon$

This means that LITGs are transduction grammars that transduce between linear languages.

There is also a nice parallel in search time complexities between CFGs and ITGs on the one hand, and LGs and LITGs on the other. Searching for all possible parses given a sentence is $\mathcal{O}(n^3)$ for CFGs, and $\mathcal{O}(n^2)$ for LGs. Searching for all possible biparses given a bisentence is $\mathcal{O}(n^6)$ for ITGs, and $\mathcal{O}(n^4)$ for LITGs. This is consistent with thinking of biparsing as finding every L_2 parse for every L_1 parse. Biparsing consists of assigning a joint structure to a sentence pair, rather than assigning a structure to a sentence.

In this paper, only stochastic bracketing grammars (SBITGs and SBLITGs) were used. A bracketing grammar has only one nonterminal symbol, denoted X. A stochastic grammar is one where each rule is associated with a probability, such that

$$\forall X \left[\sum_{\phi} p(X \rightarrow \phi) = 1 \right]$$

While training a Stochastic Bracketing ITG (SBITG) or LITG (SBLITG) with EM, expectations of probabilities over the biparse-forest are calculated. These expectations approach the true probabilities, and can be used as approximations. The probabilities over the biparse-forest can be used to select the one-best parse-tree, which in turn forces an alignment over the sentence pair. The alignments given by SBITGs and SBLITGs has been shown to give better translation quality than bidirectional IBM-models, when applied to short sentence corpora (Saers and Wu, 2009; Saers et al., 2009; Saers et al., 2010). In this paper we explore whether this hold for SBLITGs on standard sentence corpora.

3 Setup

The baseline system for the shared task was a phrase based translation model based on bidirectional IBM- (Brown et al., 1993) and HMM-models (Vogel et al., 1996) combined with the `grow-diag-final-and` heuristic. This is computed with the GIZA++ tool (Och and Ney, 2003) and the Moses toolkit (Koehn et al., 2007). The language model was a 5-gram SRILM (Stolcke, 2002). Parameters in the final translation system were determined with Minimum Error-Rate Training (Och, 2003), and translation quality was assessed with the automatic measures BLEU (Papineni et al., 2002) and NIST (Doddington, 2002).

Corpus	Type	Size
German–English Europarl	out of domain	1,219,343 sentence pairs
German–English news commentary	in-domain	86,941 sentence pairs
English news commentary	in-domain	48,653,884 sentences
German–English news commentary	in-domain tuning data	2,051 sentence pairs
German–English news commentary	in-domain test data	2,489 sentence pairs

Table 1: Corpora available for the German–English translation task after baseline cleaning.

System	BLEU	NIST
GIZA++	**17.88**	5.9748
SBLITG	17.61	5.8846
SBLITG (only Europarl)	17.46	5.8491
SBLITG (only news)	15.49	5.4987
GIZA++ and SBLITG	17.66	5.9650
GIZA++ and SBLITG (only Europarl)	17.58	**5.9819**
GIZA++ and SBLITG (only news)	17.48	5.9693

Table 2: Results for the German–English translation task.

We chose to focus on the German–English translation task. The corpora resources available for that task is summarized in Table 1. We used the entire news commentary monolingual data concatenated with the English side of the Europarl bilingual data to train the language model. In retrospect, this was probably a bad choice, as others seem to prefer the use of two language models instead.

We contrasted the baseline system with pure SBLITG systems trained on different parts of the training data, as well as combined systems, where the SBLITG systems were combined with the baseline system. The combination was done by adding the SBLITG translation model as a second translation path to the base line system.

To train our SBLITG systems, we used the algorithm described in Saers et al. (2010). We set the beam size parameter to 50, and ran expectation-maximization for 10 iterations or until the log-probability of the training corpus started deteriorating. After the grammar was induced we obtained the one-best parse for each sentence pair, which also dictates a word alignment over that sentence pair, which we used instead of the word alignments provided by GIZA++. From that point, training did not differ from the baseline procedure.

We trained a total of three pure SBLITG system, one with only the news commentary part of the corpus, one with only the Europarl part, and one with both. We also combined all three SBLITG systems with the baseline system to see whether the additional translation paths would help.

The system we submitted corresponds to the "GIZA++ and SBLITG (only news)" system, but with RandLM (Talbot and Osborne, 2007) as language model rather than SRILM. This was because we lacked the necessary RAM resources to calculate the full SRILM model before the system submission deadline.

4 Results

The results for the development test set are summarized in Table 2. The submitted system achieved a BLEU score of 0.1759 and a NIST score of 5.9579 for cased output on this year's test set (these numbers are not comparable to those in Table 2). To our surprise, adding the additional phrases as a second translation path does not seem to help. Instead a small deterioration in BLEU is noted (0.22–0.40 points), whereas the differences in NIST are mixed (-0.0098–+0.0071 points). Over all the variations were very small. The pure SBLITG systems perform consistently below baseline, which could indicate that the grammar class is unable to capture the reorderings found in longer sentence pairs adequately in one parse. The variation between the pure SBLITG systems can be explained by the size of the training data: more data – better quality.

5 Conclusions

We tried to use SBLITGs as word aligners on full size sentences, which has not been done to date, and noted that the formalism seems unable to account for the full complexity of longer sentence pairs. We also tried combining the translation models acquired with SBLITG alignments to the baseline system, and noted very small differences, tending to a deterioration in quality. The fact that SBLITGs seem unable to capture the complex relationship between an English and a German sentence in one parse means that we need to find either some more complex model or some way to use the entire parse forest to arrive at the alignment.

Acknowledgments

This work was funded by the Swedish National Graduate School of Language Technology (GSLT), the Defense Advanced Research Projects Agency (DARPA) under GALE Contract No. HR0011-06-C-0023, and the Hong Kong Research Grants Council (RGC) under research grants GRF621008, DAG03/04.EG09, RGC6256/00E, and RGC6083/99E. Any opinions, findings and conclusions or recommendations expressed in this material are those of the authors and do not necessarily reflect the views of the Defense Advanced Research Projects Agency. The computations were performed on UPPMAX resources under project p2007020.

References

Jeffrey D. Aho, Alfred V. Ullman. 1972. *The Theory of Parsing, Translation, and Compiling*. Prentice-Halll, Englewood Cliffs, NJ.

Peter F Brown, Stephen A Della Pietra, Vincent J Della Pietra, and Robert L Mercer. 1993. The mathematics of statistical machine translation: Parameter estimation. *Computational Linguistics*, 19(2):263–311.

George Doddington. 2002. Automatic evaluation of machine translation quality using n-gram cooccurrence statistics. In *Proceedings of Human Language Technology conference (HLT-2002)*, San Diego, California.

Aria Haghighi, John Blitzer, John DeNero, and Dan Klein. 2009. Better word alignments with supervised ITG models. In *Proceedings of the Joint Conference of the 47th Annual Meeting of the ACL and the 4th International Joint Conference on Natural Language Processing of the AFNLP*, pages 923–931, Suntec, Singapore, August.

Philipp Koehn, Hieu Hoang, Alexandra Birch, Chris Callison-Burch, Marcello Federico, Nicola Bertoldi, Brooke Cowan, Wade Shen, Christine Moran, Richard Zens, Chris Dyer, Ondrej Bojar, Alexandra Constantin, and Evan Herbst. 2007. Moses: Open source toolkit for statistical machine translation. In *Proceedings of the 45th Annual Meeting of the Association for Computational Linguistics Companion Volume Proceedings of the Demo and Poster Sessions*, pages 177–180, Prague, Czech Republic, June.

Philip M. Lewis and Richard E. Stearns. 1968. Syntax-directed transduction. *Journal of the Association for Computing Machinery*, 15(3):465–488.

Franz Josef Och and Hermann Ney. 2003. A systematic comparison of various statistical alignment models. *Computational Linguistics*, 29(1):19–51.

Franz Josef Och. 2003. Minimum error rate training in statistical machine translation. In *41st Annual Meeting of the Association for Computational Linguistics*, pages 160–167, Sapporo, Japan, Jul.

Kishore Papineni, Salim Roukos, Todd Ward, and Wei-Jing Zhu. 2002. Bleu: a method for automatic evaluation of machine translation. In *Proceedings of 40th Annual Meeting of the Association for Computational Linguistics*, pages 311–318, Philadelphia, Pennsylvania, July.

Markus Saers and Dekai Wu. 2009. Improving phrase-based translation via word alignments from Stochastic Inversion Transduction Grammars. In *Proceedings of the Third Workshop on Syntax and Structure in Statistical Translation (SSST-3) at NAACL HLT 2009*, pages 28–36, Boulder, Colorado, June.

Markus Saers, Joakim Nivre, and Dekai Wu. 2009. Learning Stochastic Bracketing Inversion Transduction Grammars with a cubic time biparsing algorithm. In *Proceedings of the 11th International Conference on Parsing Technologies (IWPT'09)*, pages 29–32, Paris, France, October.

Markus Saers, Joakim Nivre, and Dekai Wu. 2010. Word alignment with Stochastic Bracketing Linear Inversion Transduction Grammar. In *Proceedings of Human Language Technologies: The 11th Annual Conference of the North American Chapter of the Association for Computational Linguistics*, Los Angeles, California, June.

Andreas Stolcke. 2002. SRILM – an extensible language modeling toolkit. In *International Conference on Spoken Language Processing*, Denver, Colorado, September.

David Talbot and Miles Osborne. 2007. Randomised language modelling for statistical machine translation. In *Proceedings of the 45th Annual Meeting of the Association of Computational Linguistics*, pages 512–519, Prague, Czech Republic, June.

Stephan Vogel, Hermann Ney, and Christoph Tillmann. 1996. Hmm-based word alignment in statistical translation. In *Proceedings of the 16th conference on Computational linguistics*, pages 836–841, Morristown, New Jersey.

Dekai Wu. 1997. Stochastic inversion transduction grammars and bilingual parsing of parallel corpora. *Computational Linguistics*, 23(3):377–403.

Hao Zhang, Chris Quirk, Robert C. Moore, and Daniel Gildea. 2008. Bayesian learning of non-compositional phrases with synchronous parsing. In *Proceedings of ACL-08: HLT*, pages 97–105, Columbus, Ohio, June.

UPV-PRHLT English–Spanish system for WMT10

Germán Sanchis-Trilles and **Jesús Andrés-Ferrer** and **Guillem Gascó**
Jesús González-Rubio and **Pascual Martínez-Gómez** and **Martha-Alicia Rocha**
Joan-Andreu Sánchez and **Francisco Casacuberta**
Instituto Tecnológico de Informática
Departamento de Sistemas Informáticos y Computación
Universidad Politécnica de Valencia
{gsanchis|jandres|fcn}@dsic.upv.es
{ggasco|jegonzalez|pmartinez}@dsic.upv.es
{mrocha|jandreu}@dsic.upv.es

Abstract

In this paper, the system submitted by the PRHLT group for the Fifth Workshop on Statistical Machine Translation of ACL2010 is presented. On this evaluation campaign, we have worked on the English–Spanish language pair, putting special emphasis on two problems derived from the large amount of data available. The first one, how to optimize the use of the monolingual data within the language model, and the second one, how to make good use of all the bilingual data provided without making use of unnecessary computational resources.

1 Introduction

For this year's translation shared task, the Pattern Recognition and Human Language Technologies (PRHLT) research group of the Universidad Politécnica de Valencia submitted runs for the English–Spanish translation task. In this paper, we report the configuration of such a system, together with preliminary experiments performed to establish the final setup.

As in 2009, the central focus of the Shared Task is on Domain Adaptation, where a system typically trained using out-of-domain data is adjusted to translate news commentaries.

For the preliminary experiments, we used only a small amount of the largest available bilingual corpus, i.e. the United Nations corpus, by including into our system only those sentences which were considered similar.

Language model interpolation using a development set was explored in this work, together with a technique to cope with the problem of "out of vocabulary words".

Finally, a reordering constraint using walls and zones was used in order to improve the performance of the submitted system.

In the final evaluation, our system was ranked fifth, considering only primary runs.

2 Language Model interpolation

Nowadays, it is quite common to have very large amounts of monolingual data available from several different domains. Despite of this fact, in most of the cases we are only interested in translating from one specific domain, as is the case in this year's shared task, where the provided monolingual training data belonged to European parliamentary proceedings, news related domains, and the United Nations corpus, which consists of data crawled from the web.

Although the most obvious thing to do is to concatenate all the data available and train a single language model on the whole data, we also investigated a "smarter" use of such data, by training one language model for each of the available corpora.

3 Similar sentences selection

Currently, it is common to of huge bilingual corpora for SMT. For some common language pairs, corpora of millions of parallel sentences are available. In some of the cases big corpora are used as out-of-domain corpora. For example, in the case of the shared task, we try to translate a news text using a small in-domain bilingual news corpus (News Commentary) and two big out-of-domain corpora: Europarl and United Nations.

Europarl is a medium size corpus and can be completely incorporated to the training set. However, the use of the UN corpus requires a big computational effort. In order to alleviate this problem, we have chosen only those bilingual sentences from the United Nations that are similar to the in-domain corpus sentences. As a similarity measure, we have chosen the alignment score.

Alignment scores have already been used as a

Proceedings of the Joint 5th Workshop on Statistical Machine Translation and MetricsMATR, pages 172–176,
Uppsala, Sweden, 15-16 July 2010. ©2010 Association for Computational Linguistics

filter for noisy corpora (Khadivi and Ney, 2005). We trained an IBM model 4 using GIZA++ (Och and Ney, 2003) with the in-domain corpus and computed the alignment scores over the United Nations sentences. We assume that the alignment score is a good measure of similarity.

An important factor in the alignment score is the length of the sentences, so we clustered the bilingual sentences in groups with the same sum of source and target language sentence sizes. In each of the groups, the higher the alignment score is, the more similar the sentence is to the in-domain corpus sentences. Hence, we computed the average alignment score for each one of the clusters obtained for the corpus considered in-domain (i.e. the News-Commentary corpus). This being done, we assessed the similarity of a given sentence by computing the probability of such sentence with respect to the alignment model of the in-domain corpus, and established the following similarity levels:

- Level 1: Sentences with an alignment score equal or higher than the in-domain average.
- Level 2: Sentences with an alignment score equal or higher than the in-domain average, minus one standard deviation.
- Level 3: Sentences with an alignment score equal or higher than the in-domain average, minus two standard deviations.

Naturally, such similarity levels establish partitions of the out-of-domain corpus. Then, such partitions were included into the training set used for building the SMT system, and re-built the complete system from scratch.

4 Out of Vocabulary Recovery

As stated in the previous section, in order to avoid a big computational effort, we do not use the whole United Nations corpus to train the translation system. Out of vocabulary words are a common problem for machine translation systems. When translating the test set, there are test words that are not in the reduced training set (out of vocabulary words). Some of those out of vocabulary words are present in the sentences discarded from the United Nations Corpus. Thus, recovering the discarded sentences with out of vocabulary words is needed.

The out of vocabulary words recovery method is simple: the out of vocabulary words from the test, when taking into account the reduced training set, are obtained and then discarded sentences that contain at least one of them are retrieved. Then, those sentences are added to the reduced training set.

Finally, alignments with the resulting training set were computed and the usual training procedure for phrase-based systems was performed.

5 Walls and zones

In translation, as in other linguistics areas, punctuation marks are essential as they help to understand the intention of a message and organise the ideas to avoid ambiguity. They also indicate pauses, hierarchies and emphasis.

In our system, punctuation marks have been taken into account during decoding. Traditionally, in SMT punctuation marks are treated as words and this has undesirable effects (Koehn and Haddow, 2009). For example, commas have a high probability of occurrence and many possible translations are generated. Most of them are not consistent across languages. This introduces too much noise to the phrase tables.

(Koehn and Haddow, 2009) established a framework to specify reordering constraints with `walls` and `zones`, where commas and end of sentence are not mixed with various clauses. Gains between 0.1 and 0.2 of BLEU are reported. Specifying `zones` and `walls` with XML tags in input sentences allows us to identify structured fragments that the Moses decoder uses with the following restrictions:

1. If a <zone> tag is detected, then a block is identified and must be translated until a </zone> tag is found. The text between tags <zone> and </zone> is identified and translated as a block.

2. If the decoder detects a <wall/> tag, the text is divided into a prefix and suffix and Moses must translate all the words of the prefix before the suffix.

3. If both `zones` and `walls` are specified, then `local walls` are considered where the constraint 2 applies only to the area established by zones.

corpus	Language	$\|S\|$	$\|W\|$	$\|V\|$
Europarl v5	Spanish	1272K	28M	154K
	English		27M	106K
NC	Spanish	81K	1.8M	54K
	English		1.6M	39K

Table 1: Main figures of the Europarl v5 and News-Commentary (NC) corpora. K/M stands for thousands/millions. $|S|$ is the number of sentences, $|W|$ the number of running words, and $|V|$ the vocabulary size. Statistics are reported on the tokenised and lowercased corpora.

corpus	$\|S\|$	$\|W\|$	$\|V\|$
Europarl	1822K	51M	172K
NC	108K	3M	68K
UN	6.2M	214M	411K
News	3.9M	107M	512K

Table 2: Main figures of the Spanish resources provided: Europarl v5, News-Commentary (NC), United Nations (UN) and News-shuffled (News).

We used quotation marks, parentheses, brackets and dashes as zone delimiters. Quotation marks (when appearing once in the sentence), commas, colons, semicolons, exclamation and question marks and periods are used as wall delimiters.

The use of zone delimiters do not alter the performance. When using `walls`, a gain of 0.1 BLEU is obtained in our best model.

6 Experiments

6.1 Experimental setup

For building our SMT systems, the open-source SMT toolkit Moses (Koehn et al., 2007) was used in its standard setup. The decoder includes a log-linear model comprising a phrase-based translation model, a language model, a lexicalised distortion model and word and phrase penalties. The weights of the log-linear interpolation were optimised by means of MERT (Och, 2003). In addition, a 5-gram LM with Kneser-Ney (Kneser and Ney, 1995) smoothing and interpolation was built by means of the SRILM (Stolcke, 2002) toolkit.

For building our baseline system, the News-Commentary and Europarl v5 (Koehn, 2005) data were employed, with maximum sentence length set to 40 in the case of the data used to build the translation models, and without restriction in the case of the LM. Statistics of the bilingual data can be seen in Table 1.

In all the experiments reported, MERT was run on the 2008 test set, whereas the test set 2009 was considered as test set as such. In addition, all the experiments described below were performed in lowercase and tokenised conditions. For the final run, the detokenisation and recasing was performed according to the technique described in the Workshop baseline description.

6.2 Language Model interpolation

The final system submitted to the shared task included a linear interpolation of four language models, one for each of the monolingual resources available for Spanish (see Table 2). The results can be seen in Table 3. As a first experiment, only the in-domain corpus, i.e. the News-Commentary data (`NC data`) was used for building the LM. Then, all the available monolingual Spanish data was included into a single LM, by concatenating all the data together (`pooled`). Next, in `interpolated`, one LM for each one of the provided monolingual resources was trained, and then they were linearly interpolated so as to minimise the perplexity of the 2008 test set, and fed such interpolation to the SMT system. We found out that weights were distributed quite unevenly, since the News-shuffled LM received a weight of 0.67, whereas the other three corpora received a weight of 0.11 each. It must be noted that even the in-domain LM received a weight of 0.11 (less than the News-shuffled LM). The reason for this might be that, although the in-domain LM should be more appropriate and should receive a higher weight, the News-shuffled corpus is also news related (hence not really out-of-domain), but much larger. For this reason, the result of using only such LM (`News`) was also analysed. As expected, the translation quality dropped slightly. Nevertheless, since the differences are not statistically significant, we used the News-shuffled LM for internal development purposes, and the interpolated LM only whenever an improvement prooved to be useful.

6.3 Including UN data

We analysed the impact of the selection technique detailed in Section 3. In this case, the LM used was the interpolated LM described in the previous section. The result can be seen in Table 4. As it can be seen, translation quality as measured by

Table 3: Effect of considering different LMs

LM used	BLEU
NC data	21.86
pooled	23.53
interpolated	**24.97**
news	24.79

BLEU improves constantly as the number of sentences selected increases. However, further sentences were not included for computational reasons.

In the same table, we also report the effect of adding the UN sentences selected by our out-of-vocabulary technique described in Section 4. In this context, it should be noted that MERT was not rerun once such sentences had been selected, since such sentences are related with the test set, and not with the development set on which MERT is run.

Table 4: Effect of including selected sentences

system	BLEU
baseline	24.97
+ oovs	25.08
+ Level 1	24.98
+ Level 2	25.07
+ Level 3	25.13

6.4 Final system

Since the News-shuffled, UN and Europarl corpora are large corpora, a new LM interpolation was estimated by using a 6-gram LM on each one of these corpora, obtaining a gain of 0.17 BLEU points by doing so. Further increments in the n-gram order did not show further improvements.

In addition, preliminary experimentation revealed that the use of `walls`, as described in Section 5, also provided slight improvements, although using `zones` or combining both did not prove to improve further. Hence, only `walls` were included into the final system.

Lastly, the final system submitted to the Workshop was the result of combining all the techniques described above. Such combination yielded a final BLEU score of 25.31 on the 2009 test set, and 28.76 BLEU score on the 2010 test set, both in tokenised and lowercased conditions.

7 Conclusions and future work

In this paper, the SMT system presented by the UPV-PRHLT team for WMT 2010 has been described. Specifically, preliminary results about how to make use of larger data collections for translating more focused test sets have been presented.

In this context, there are still some things which need a deeper investigation, since the results presented here give only a small insight about the potential of the similar sentence selection technique described.

However, a deeper analysis is needed in order to assess the potential of such technique and other strategies should be implemented to explore new kids of reordering constraints.

Acknowledgments

This paper is based upon work supported by the EC (FEDER/FSE) and the Spanish MICINN under the MIPRCV "Consolider Ingenio 2010" program (CSD2007-00018),iTrans2 (TIN2009-14511) project, and the FPU scholarship AP2006-00691. This work was also supported by the Spanish MITyC under the erudito.com (TSI-020110-2009-439) project and by the Generalitat Valenciana under grant Prometeo/2009/014 and scholarships BFPI/2007/117 and ACIF/2010/226 and by the Mexican government under the PROMEP-DGEST program.

References

Shahram Khadivi and Hermann Ney. 2005. Automatic filtering of bilingual corpora for statistical machine translation. In *Natural Language Processing and Information Systems, 10th Int. Conf. on Applications of Natural Language to Information Systems*, volume 3513 of *Lecture Notes in Computer Science*, pages 263–274, Alicante, Spain, June. Springer.

R. Kneser and H. Ney. 1995. Improved backing-off for m-gram language modeling. *IEEE International Conference on Acoustics, Speech and Signal Processing*, II:181–184, May.

Philipp Koehn and Barry Haddow. 2009. Edinburgh's submission to all tracks of the WMT2009 shared task with reordering and speed improvements to Moses. In *The 4th EACL Workshop on Statistical Machine Translation*, ACL, pages 160–164, Athens, Greece, March. Springer.

P. Koehn et al. 2007. Moses: Open Source Toolkit for Statistical Machine Translation. In *Proceedings of the ACL Demo and Poster Sessions*, pages 177–180, Prague, Czech Republic.

P. Koehn. 2005. Europarl: A parallel corpus for statistical machine translation. In *MT Summit*.

Franz Josef Och and Hermann Ney. 2003. A systematic comparison of various statistical alignment models. *Computational Linguistics*, 29(1):19–51.

F.J. Och. 2003. Minimum Error Rate Training in Statistical Machine Translation. In *Proceedings of ACL*, pages 160–167, Sapporo, Japan.

A. Stolcke. 2002. SRILM – an extensible language modeling toolkit. In *Proc. of ICSLP'02*, pages 901–904, September.

Reproducible Results in Parsing-Based Machine Translation: The JHU Shared Task Submission

Lane Schwartz *
University of Minnesota
Minneapolis, MN
lane@cs.umn.edu

Abstract

We present the Johns Hopkins University submission to the 2010 WMT shared translation task. We describe processing steps using open data and open source software used in our submission, and provide the scripts and configurations required to train, tune, and test our machine translation system.

1 Introduction

Research investigating natural language processing and computational linguistics can and should have an extremely low barrier to entry. The data with which we work is customarily available in common electronic formats. The computational techniques which we apply can typically be performed on commodity computing resources which are widely available. In short, there should be no reason why small research groups and even lone researchers should not be able to join and make substantive contributions furthering our field. The reality is less encouraging.

Many published articles describe novel techniques and provide interesting results, yet fail to describe technical details in sufficient detail to allow their results to be reproduced by other researchers. While there are notable and laudable exceptions, many publications fail to provide the source code and scripts necessary to reproduce results. The use of restricted data, not freely available for download by any interested researcher only compounds these problems. Pedersen (2008) rightly argues that the implementation details so often ignored in publications are in fact essential for our research to be reproducible science.

Reproducibility in machine translation is made more challenging by the complexity of experimental workflows. Results in machine translation tasks are dependent on a cascade of processing steps and configurations. While interesting subsets of these usually appear in experimental descriptions, many steps (preprocessing techniques, alignment parameters, translation rule extraction parameters, language model parameters, list of features used) are invariably omitted, even though these configurations are often critical to reproducing results.

This paper describes the Johns Hopkins University submission to the 2010 Workshop on Statistical Machine Translation shared translation task. Links to the software, scripts, and configurations used to run the experiments described herein are provided. The remainder of this paper is structured as follows. Section 2 lists the major examples of publicly available open source machine translation systems, parallel corpora, and machine translation workflow management systems. Section 3 describes the experimental workflow used to run the shared task translations, with the corresponding experimental design in section 4. Section 5 presents the shared task results.

2 Related Work

The last four years have witnessed the implementation and release of numerous open source machine translation systems. The widely used Moses system (Koehn et al., 2007) implements the standard phrase-based translation model. Parsing-based translation models are implemented by Joshua (Li et al., 2009), SAMT (Zollmann and Venugopal, 2006), and cdec (Dyer et al., 2010). Cunei (Phillips and Brown, 2009) implements statistical example-based translation. Olteanu et al. (2006) and Schwartz (2008) respectively provide additional open-source implementations of phrase-based and hierarchical decoders.

The SRILM (Stolcke, 2002), IRSTLM (Federico et al., 2008), and RandLM (Talbot and Osborne, 2007) toolkits enable efficient training and

*Research conducted as a visiting researcher at Johns Hopkins University

Proceedings of the Joint 5th Workshop on Statistical Machine Translation and MetricsMATR, pages 177–182,
Uppsala, Sweden, 15-16 July 2010.

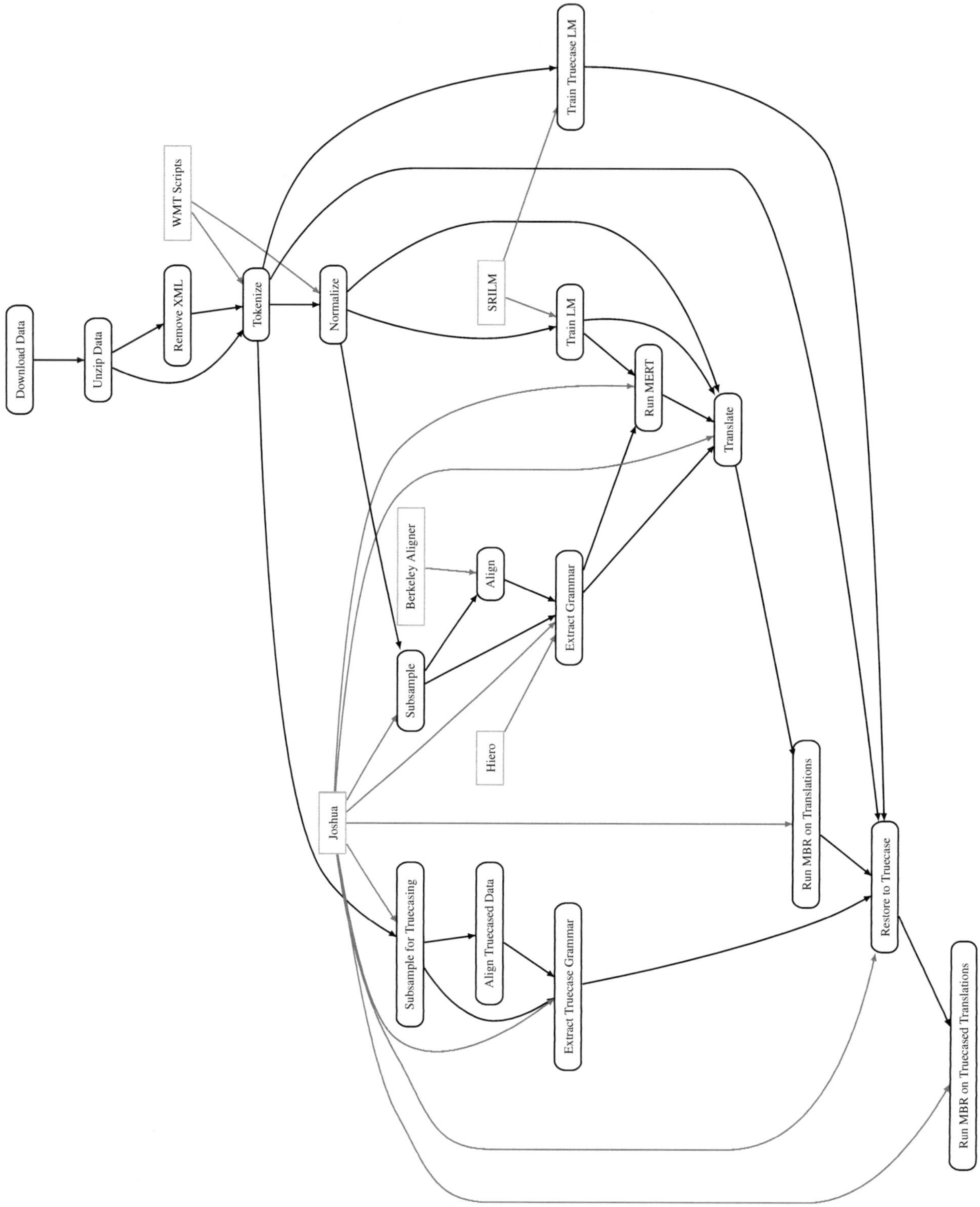

Figure 1: Machine translation workflow. Square nodes in grey indicate software and scripts. The scripts and configuration files used to implement and run this workflow are available for download at `http://sourceforge.net/projects/joshua/files/joshua/1.3/wmt2010-experiment.tgz/download`

querying of n-gram language models.

Freely available parallel corpora for numerous European languages have also been released in recent years. These include the Europarl (Koehn, 2005) and JRC-Acquis (Steinberger et al., 2006) legislative corpora, each of which includes data for most EU language pairs. The smaller News Commentary corpora (Callison-Burch et al., 2007; Callison-Burch et al., 2008) provide smaller amounts of parallel data in the news genre. The recent Fr-En 10^9 (Callison-Burch et al., 2009) corpus aggregates huge numbers of parallel French-English sentences from the web.

Open source systems to address the complex workflows required to run non-trivial machine translation experiments have also been developed. These include `experiment.perl` (Koehn et al., 2010), developed as a workflow management system at the University of Edinburgh, and LoonyBin (Clark et al., 2010), a general hyperworkflow management utility from Carnegie Melon University.

3 Managing Experiment Workflows

Running a statistical machine translation system to achieve state-of-the-art performance involves the configuration and execution of numerous interdependent intermediate tools. To manage task dependencies and tool configuration, our shared task workflow consists of a set of dependency scripts written for GNU Make (Stallman et al., 2006).

Figure 1 shows a graph depicting the steps in our experimental workflow, and the dependencies between steps. Each node in the graph represents a step in the workflow; each step is implemented as a Make script that defines how to run the tools required in that step. In each experiment, an additional configuration script is provided for each experimental step, defining the parameters to be used when running that step in the current experiment. Optional front-end wrapper scripts can also be provided, allowing for a complete experiment to be run - from downloading data and software through truecasing translated results - by executing a single make file.

This framework is also conducive to parallelization. Many tasks, such as preprocessing numerous training files, are not dependent on one another. In such cases `make` can be configured to execute multiple processes simultaneously on a single multi-processor machine. In cases where scheduled distributed computing environments such as the Sun Grid Engine are configured, make files can be processed by scheduler-aware `make` variants (`distmake`, SGE `qmake`, Sun Studio `dmake`) which distribute outstanding tasks to available distributed machines using the relevant distributed scheduler.

4 Experimental Configuration

Experimental workflows were configured[1] and run for six language pairs in the translation shared task: English-French, English-German, English-Spanish, French-English, German-English, and Spanish-English.

In all experiments, only data freely available for download was used. No restricted data from the LDC or other sources was used. Table 1 lists the parallel corpora used in training the translation model for each experiment. The monolingual corpora used in training each target language model are listed in table 2. In all experiments, newstest2008 was used as a development tuning corpus during minimum error rate training; newstest2009 was used as a development test set. The shared task data set newstest2010 was used as a final blind test set.

All data was automatically downloaded, unzipped, and preprocessed prior to use. Files provided in XML format were converted to plain text by selecting lines with `<seg>` tags, then removing the beginning and end tags for each segment; this processing was applied using GNU grep and sed. The `tokenize.perl` and `lowercase.perl` scripts provided for the shared task[2] were applied to all data.

Interpolated n-gram language models for the four target languages were built using the SRI Language Model Toolkit[3], with n-gram order set to 5. The Chen and Goodman (1998) technique for modified Kneser-Ney discounting (Kneser and Ney, 1995) was applied during language model training.

Following Li et al. (2009), a subset of the available training sentences was selected via subsam-

[1] http://sourceforge.net/projects/joshua/files/joshua/1.3/wmt2010-experiment.tgz/download

[2] http://www.statmt.org/wmt08/scripts.tgz with md5sum: `tokenize.perl` 45cd1832827131013245eca76481441a `lowercase.perl` a1958ab429b1e29d379063c3b9cd7062

[3] http://www-speech.sri.com/projects/srilm SRILM version 1.5.7. Our experimental workflow requires that SRILM be compiled separately, with the $SRILM environment variable set to the install location.

Source	Target	Parallel Corpora
German	English	news-commentary10.de-en europarl-v5.de-en
English	German	news-commentary10.de-en europarl-v5.de-en
French	English	news-commentary10.fr-en europarl-v5.fr-en giga-fren.release2 undoc.2000.en-fr
English	French	news-commentary10.fr-en europarl-v5.fr-en giga-fren.release2 undoc.2000.en-fr
Spanish	English	news-commentary10.es-en europarl-v5.es-en undoc.2000.en-es
English	Spanish	news-commentary10.es-en europarl-v5.es-en undoc.2000.en-es

Table 1: Parallel training data used for training translation model, per language pair

Target	Monolingual Corpora
English	europarl-v5.en news-commentary10.en news.en.shuffled undoc.2000.en-fr.en giga-fren.release2.en
French	europarl-v5.fr news-commentary10.fr news.fr.shuffled undoc.2000.en-fr.fr giga-fren.release2.fr
German	europarl-v5.de news-commentary10.de news.de.shuffled
Spanish	europarl-v5.es news-commentary10.es news.es.shuffled undoc.2000.en-es.es

Table 2: Monolingual training data used for training language model, per target language

pling; training sentences are selected based on the estimated likelihood of each sentence being useful later for translating a particular test corpus.

Given a subsampled parallel training corpus, word alignment is performed using the Berkeley aligner[4] (Liang et al., 2006).

For each language pair, a synchronous context free translation grammar is extracted for a particular test set, following the methods of Lopez (2008) as implemented in (Schwartz and Callison-Burch, 2010). For the largest training sets (French-English and English-French) the original (Lopez, 2008) implementation included with Hiero was used to save time during training[5].

Because of the use of subsampling, the extracted translation grammars are targeted for use with a specific test set. Our experiments were begun prior to the release of the blind newstest2010 shared task test set. Subsampling was performed for the development tuning set, news-test2008, and the development test set, newstest2009. Once the newstest2010 test set was released, the process of subsampling, alignment, and grammar extraction was repeated to obtain translation grammars targeted for use with the shared task test set.

Our experiments used hierarchical phrase-based grammars containing exactly two nonterminals - the wildcard nonterminal X, and S, used to glue together neighboring constituents. Recent work has shown that parsing-based machine translation using SAMT (Zollmann and Venugopal, 2006) grammars with rich nonterminal sets can demonstrate substantial gains over hierarchical grammars for certain language pairs (Baker et al., 2009). Joshua supports such grammars; the experimental workflow presented here could easily be extended in future research to incorporate the use of SAMT grammars with additional language pairs.

The Z-MERT implementation (Zaidan, 2009) of minimum error rate training (Och, 2003) was used for parameter tuning. Tuned grammars were used by Joshua to translate all test sets. The Joshua decoder produces n-best lists of translations.

Rather than simply selecting the top candidate from each list, we take the preferred candidate after perform minimum Bayes risk rescoring (Kumar and Byrne, 2004).

Once a single translation has been extracted for each sentence in the test set, we repeat the procedures described above to train language and translation models for use in translating lowercased results into a more human-readable truecased form. A truecase language model is trained as above, but on the tokenized (but not normalized) monolingual target language corpus. Monotone word alignments are deterministically created, mapping normalized lowercase training text to the original truecase text. As in bilingual translation, subsampling is performed for the training set, and a translation grammar for lowercase-to-truecase is extracted. No tuning is

[4]http://berkeleyaligner.googlecode.com/files/berkeleyaligner_unsupervised-2.1.tar.gz — Berkeley aligner version 2.1

[5]It is expected that using the Joshua implementation should result in nearly identical results, albeit with somewhat more time required to extract the grammar.

performed. The Joshua decoder is used to translate the lowercased target language test results into truecase format. The `detokenize.perl` and `wrap-xml.perl` scripts provided for the shared task were manually applied to truecased translation results prior to final submission of results.

The code used for subsampling, grammar extraction, decoding, minimum error rate training, and minimum Bayes risk rescoring is provided with Joshua[6], with the exception of the original (Lopez, 2008) grammar extraction implementation.

5 Experimental Results

The experiments described in sections 3 and 4 above provided truecased translations for six language pairs in the translation shared task: English-French, English-German, English-Spanish, French-English, German-English, and Spanish-English. Table 3 lists the automatic metric scores for the newstest2010 test set, according to the BLEU (Papineni et al., 2002) and TER (Snover et al., 2006) metrics.

Source	Target	BLEU	BLEU-cased	TER
German	English	21.3	19.5	0.660
English	German	15.2	14.6	0.738
French	English	27.7	26.4	0.614
English	French	23.8	22.8	0.681
Spanish	English	29.0	27.6	0.595
English	Spanish	28.1	26.5	0.596

Table 3: Automatic metric scores for the test set newstest2010

The submitted system ranked highest among shared task participants for the German-English task, according to TER.

In order to provide points of comparison with the 2009 Workshop on Statistical Machine Translation shared translation task participants, table 4 lists automatic metric scores for our systems' translations of the newstest2009 test set, which we used as a development test set.

6 Steps to Reproduce

The experiments in this paper can be reproduced by running the make scripts provided in the following file: `http://sourceforge.net/projects/joshua/files/joshua/1.3/wmt2010-experiment.tgz/download`. The README file details how to configure the workflow for your environment. Note that SRILM must be downloaded and compiled separately before running the experimental steps.

[6]http://sourceforge.net/projects/joshua/files/joshua/1.3/joshua-1.3.tgz/download — Joshua version 1.3

Source	Target	BLEU
German	English	18.19
English	German	13.57
French	English	26.41
English	French	25.28
Spanish	English	25.28
English	Spanish	24.02

Table 4: Automatic metric scores for the development test set newstest2009

Acknowledgements

This work was supported by the DARPA GALE program (Contract No HR0011-06-2-0001).

References

Kathy Baker, Steven Bethard, Michael Bloodgood, Ralf Brown, Chris Callison-Burch, Glen Coppersmith, Bonnie Dorr, Wes Filardo, Kendall Giles, Anni Irvine, Mike Kayser, Lori Levin, Justin Martineau, Jim Mayfield, Scott Miller, Aaron Phillips, Andrew Philpot, Christine Piatko, Lane Schwartz, and David Zajic. 2009. Semantically informed machine translation (SIMT). SCALE summer workshop final report, Human Language Technology Center Of Excellence.

Chris Callison-Burch, Cameron Fordyce, Philipp Koehn, Christof Monz, and Josh Schroeder. 2007. (Meta-) evaluation of machine translation. In *Proceedings of the Second Workshop on Statistical Machine Translation (WMT07)*.

Chris Callison-Burch, Cameron Fordyce, Philipp Koehn, Christof Monz, and Josh Schroeder. 2008. Further meta-evaluation of machine translation. In *Proceedings of the Third Workshop on Statistical Machine Translation (WMT08)*.

Chris Callison-Burch, Philipp Koehn, Christof Monz, and Josh Schroeder. 2009. Findings of the 2009 Workshop on Statistical Machine Translation. In *Proceedings of the Fourth Workshop on Statistical Machine Translation (WMT09)*, March.

Stanley Chen and Joshua Goodman. 1998. An empirical study of smoothing techniques for language modeling. Technical Report TR-10-98, Harvard University, Cambridge, MA, USA, August.

Jonathan Clark, Jonathan Weese, Byung Gyu Ahn, Andreas Zollman, Qin Gao, Kenneth Heafield, and Alon Lavie. 2010. The machine translation toolpack for LoonyBin: Automated management of experimental machine translation hyperworkflows. *The Prague Bulletin of Mathematical Linguistics*, 93:117–126, January.

C. Dyer, A. Lopez, J. Ganitkevitch, J. Weese, F. Ture, P. Blunsom, H. Setiawan, V. Eidelman, and P. Resnik. 2010. cdec: A decoder, alignment, and learning framework for finite-state and context-free translation models. In *Proc. ACL (Demonstration Track)*, Uppsala, Sweden.

Marcello Federico, Nicola Bertoldi, and Mauro Cettolo. 2008. IRSTLM: An open source toolkit for handling large scale language models. In *Proc. Interspeech*, Brisbane, Australia.

Reinhard Kneser and Hermann Ney. 1995. Improved smoothing for mgram language modeling. In *Proceedings of the International Conference on Acoustics, Speech and Signal Processing*.

Philipp Koehn, Hieu Hoang, Alexandra Birch, Chris Callison-Burch, Marcello Federico, Nicola Bertoldi, Brooke Cowan, Wade Shen, Christine Moran, Richard Zens, Chris Dyer, Ondrej Bojar, Alexandra Constantin, and Evan Herbst. 2007. Moses: Open source toolkit for statistical machine translation. In *Proc. ACL-2007 Demo and Poster Sessions*.

Philipp Koehn, Anthony Rousseau, Ben Gottesmann, Aurora Marsye, Frédéric Blain, and Eun-Jin Park, 2010. *An Experiment Management System*. Fourth Machine Translation Marathon, Dublin, Ireland, January.

Philipp Koehn. 2005. A parallel corpus for statistical machine translation. In *Proceedings of MT-Summit*, Phuket, Thailand.

Shankar Kumar and William Byrne. 2004. Minimum bayes-risk decoding for statistical machine translation. In *Proceedings of HLT/NAACL*.

Zhifei Li, Chris Callison-Burch, Chris Dyer, Juri Ganitkevitch, Sanjeev Khudanpur, Lane Schwartz, Wren Thornton, Jonathan Weese, and Omar Zaidan. 2009. Joshua: An open source toolkit for parsing-based machine translation. In *Proceedings of the Fourth Workshop on Statistical Machine Translation*, pages 135–139, Athens, Greece, March. Association for Computational Linguistics.

P. Liang, B. Taskar, and D. Klein. 2006. Alignment by agreement. In *North American Association for Computational Linguistics (NAACL)*, pages 104–111.

Adam Lopez. 2008. *Machine Translation by Pattern Matching*. Ph.D. thesis, University of Maryland.

Franz Josef Och. 2003. Minimum error rate training for statistical machine translation. In *Proceedings of ACL*.

Marian Olteanu, Chris Davis, Ionut Volosen, and Dan Moldovan. 2006. Phramer an open source statistical pharse-based translator. In *HLT-NAACL 2006: Proceedings of the Workshop on Statistical Machine Translation*, New York, June.

Kishore Papineni, Salim Roukos, Todd Ward, and Wei-Jing Zhu. 2002. Bleu: A method for automatic evaluation of machine translation. In *Proceedings of ACL*.

Ted Pedersen. 2008. Empiricism is not a matter of faith. *Computational Linguistics*, 34(3):465–470.

Aaron B. Phillips and Ralf D. Brown. 2009. Cunei machine translation platform: System description. In *3rd Workshop on Example-Based Machine Translation*, Dublin, Ireland.

Lane Schwartz and Chris Callison-Burch. 2010. Hierarchical phrase-based grammar extraction in joshua suix arrays and prex trees. *The Prague Bulletin of Mathematical Linguistics*, 93:157–166.

Lane Schwartz. 2008. An open-source hierarchical phrase-based translation system. In *Proceedings of the 5th Midwest Computational Linguistics Colloquium (MCLC'08)*, May.

Matthew Snover, Bonnie Dorr, Richard Schwartz, Linnea Micciulla, and John Makhoul. 2006. A study of translation edit rate with targeted human annotation. In *Proceedings of AMTA*.

Richard M. Stallman, Roland McGrath, and Paul D. Smith, 2006. *GNU Make*. Free Software Foundation, Boston, MA, 0.70 edition, April.

Ralf Steinberger, Bruno Pouliquen, Anna Widiger, Camelia Ignat, Tomaz Erjavec, Dan Tufis, and Daniel Varga. 2006. The JRC-acquis: A multilingual aligned parallel corpus with 20+ languages. In *Proceedings of the 5th International Conference on Language Resources and Evaluation (LREC)*, Genoa, Italy.

Andreas Stolcke. 2002. SRILM - an extensible language modeling toolkit. In *Proceedings of the International Conference on Spoken Language Processing*, Denver, Colorado, September.

David Talbot and Miles Osborne. 2007. Randomised language modelling for statistical machine translation. In *Proceedings of ACL*.

Omar F. Zaidan. 2009. Z-MERT: A fully configurable open source tool for minimum error rate training of machine translation systems. *The Prague Bulletin of Mathematical Linguistics*, 91:79–88.

Andreas Zollmann and Ashish Venugopal. 2006. Syntax augmented machine translation via chart parsing. In *Proceedings of the NAACL-2006 Workshop on Statistical Machine Translation (WMT-06)*, New York, New York.

Vs and OOVs: Two Problems for Translation between German and English

Sara Stymne, Maria Holmqvist, Lars Ahrenberg
Linköping University
Sweden
{sarst,marho,lah}@ida.liu.se

Abstract

In this paper we report on experiments with three preprocessing strategies for improving translation output in a statistical MT system. In training, two reordering strategies were studied: (i) reorder on the basis of the alignments from Giza++, and (ii) reorder by moving all verbs to the end of segments. In translation, out-of-vocabulary words were preprocessed in a knowledge-lite fashion to identify a likely equivalent. All three strategies were implemented for our English↔German system submitted to the WMT10 shared task. Combining them lead to improvements in both language directions.

1 Introduction

We present the Liu translation system for the constrained condition of the WMT10 shared translation task, between German and English in both directions. The system is based on the 2009 Liu submission (Holmqvist et al., 2009), that used compound processing, morphological sequence models, and improved alignment by reordering.

This year we have focused on two issues: translation of verbs, which is problematic for translation between English and German since the verb placement is different with German verbs often being placed at the end of sentences; and OOVs, out-of-vocabulary words, which are problematic for machine translation in general. Verb translation is targeted by trying to improve alignment, which we believe is a crucial step for verb translation since verbs that are far apart are often not aligned at all. We do this mainly by moving verbs to the end of sentences previous to alignment, which we also combine with other alignments. We transform OOVs into known words in a post-processing step, based on casing, stemming, and splitting of hyphenated compounds. In addition, we perform general compound splitting for German both before training and translation, which also reduces the OOV rate.

All results in this article are for the development test set newstest2009, on truecased output. We report Bleu scores (Papineni et al., 2002) and Meteor ranking (without WordNet) scores (Agarwal and Lavie, 2008), using percent notation. We also used other metrics, but as they gave similar results they are not reported. For significance testing we used approximate randomization (Riezler and Maxwell, 2005), with $p < 0.05$.

2 Baseline System

The 2010 Liu system is based on the PBSMT baseline system for the WMT shared translation task[1]. We use the Moses toolkit (Koehn et al., 2007) for decoding and to train translation models, Giza++ (Och and Ney, 2003) for word alignment, and the SRILM toolkit (Stolcke, 2002) to train language models. The main difference to the WMT baseline is that the Liu system is trained on truecased data, as in Koehn et al. (2008), instead of lowercased data. This means that there is no need for a full recasing step after translation, instead we only need to uppercase the first word in each sentence.

2.1 Corpus

We participated in the constrained task, where we only trained the Liu system on the news and Europarl corpora provided for the workshop. The translation and reordering models were trained using the bilingual Europarl and news commentary corpora, which we concatenated.

We used two sets of language models, one where we first trained two models on Europarl and news commentary, which we then interpolated

[1] http://www.statmt.org/wmt10/baseline.html

Proceedings of the Joint 5th Workshop on Statistical Machine Translation and MetricsMATR, pages 183–188,
Uppsala, Sweden, 15-16 July 2010.

with more weight given to the news commentary, using weights from Koehn and Schroeder (2007). The second set of language models were trained on monolingual news data. For tuning we used every second sentence, in total 1025 sentences, of news-test2008.

2.2 Training with Limited Computational Resources

One challenge for us was to train the translation sytem with limited computational resources. We trained all systems on one Intel Core 2 CPU, 3.0Ghz, 16 Gb of RAM, 64 bit Linux (RedHat) machine. This constrained the possibilities of using the data provided by the workshop to the full. The main problem was training the language models, since the monolingual data was very large compared to the bilingual data.

In order to train language models that were both fast at runtime, and possible to train with the available memory, we chose to use the SRILM toolkit (Stolcke, 2002), with entropy-based pruning, with 10^{-8} as a threshold. To reduce the model size we also used lower order models for the large corpus; 4-grams instead of 5-grams for words and 6-grams instead of 7-grams for the morphological models. It was still impossible to train on the monolingual English news corpus, with nearly 50 million sentences, so we split that corpus into three equal size parts, and trained three models, that were interpolated with equal weights.

3 Morphological Processing

We added morphological processing to the baseline system, by training additional sequence models on morphologically enriched part-of-speech tags, and by compound processing for German.

We utilized the factored translation framework in Moses, to enrich the baseline system with an additional target sequence model. For English we used part-of-speech tags obtained using TreeTagger (Schmid, 1994), enriched with more fine-grained tags for the number of determiners, in order to target more agreement issues, since nouns already have number in the tagset. For German we used morphologically rich tags from RFTagger (Schmid and Laws, 2008), that contains morphological information such as case, number, and gender for nouns and tense for verbs. We used the extra factor in an additional sequence model on the target side, which can improve word order and agreement between words. For German the factor was also used for compound merging.

System	Bleu	Meteor
Baseline	13.42	48.83
+ morph	13.85	49.69
+ comp	14.24	49.41

Table 1: Results for morphological processing, English→German

System	Bleu	Meteor
Baseline	18.34	38.13
+ morph	18.39	37.86
+ comp	18.50	38.47

Table 2: Results for morphological processing, German→English

Prior to training and translation, compound processing was performed, using an empirical method (Koehn and Knight, 2003; Stymne, 2008) that splits words if they can be split into parts that occur in a monolingual corpus, choosing the splitting option with the highest arithmetic mean of its part frequencies in the corpus. We split nouns, adjectives and verbs, into parts that are content words or particles. We imposed a length limit on parts of 3 characters for translation from German and of 6 characters for translation from English, and we had a stop list of parts that often led to errors, such as *arische* (*Aryan*) in *konsularische* (*consular*). We allowed 10 common letter changes (Langer, 1998) and hyphens at split points. Compound parts were given a special part-of-speech tag that matches the head word.

For translation into German, compound parts were merged into full compounds using a method described in Stymne and Holmqvist (2008), which is based on matching of the special part-of-speech tag for compound parts. A word with a compound POS-tag were merged with the next word, if their POS-tags were matching.

Tables 1 and 2 show the results of the additional morphological processing. Adding the sequence models on morphologically enriched part-of-speech tags gave a significant improvement for translation into German, but similar or worse results as the baseline for translation into English. This is not surprising, since German morphology is more complex than English morphology. The addition of compound processing significantly improved the results on Meteor for translation into

English, and it also reduced the number of OOVs in the translation output by 20.8%. For translation into German, compound processing gave a significant improvement on both metrics compared to the baseline, and on Bleu compared to the system with morphological sequence models. Overall, we believe that both compound splitting and morphology are useful; thus all experiments reported in the sequel are based on the baseline system with morphology models and compound splitting, which we will call *base*.

4 Improved Alignment by Reordering

Previous work has shown that translation quality can be improved by making the source language more similar to the target language, for instance in terms of word order (Wang et al., 2007; Xia and McCord, 2004). In order to harmonize the word order of the source and target sentence, they applied hand-crafted or automatically induced reordering rules to the source sentences of the training corpus. At decoding time, reordering rules were again applied to input sentences before translation. The positive effects of such methods seem to come from a combination of improved alignment and improved reordering during translation.

In contrast, we focus on improving the word alignment by reordering the training corpus. The training corpus is reordered prior to word alignment with Giza++ (Och and Ney, 2003) and then the word links are re-adjusted back to the original word positions. From the re-adjusted corpus, we create phrase tables that allow translation of non-reordered input text. Consequently, our reordering only affects the word alignment and the phrase tables extracted from it.

We investigated two ways of reordering. The first method is based on word alignments and the other method is based on moving verbs to similar positions in the source and target sentences. We also investigated different combinations of reorderings and alignments. All results for the systems with improved reordering are shown in Tables 3 and 4.

System	Bleu	Meteor
base	14.24	49.41
reorder	14.32	49.58
verb	13.93	49.22
base+verb	14.38	49.72
base+verb+reorder	14.39	49.39

Table 3: Results for improved alignment, English→German

System	Bleu	Meteor
base	18.50	38.47
reorder	18.77	38.53
verb	18.61	38.53
base+verb	18.66	38.61
base+verb+reorder	18.73	38.59

Table 4: Results for improved alignment, German→English

4.1 Reordering Based on Alignments

The first reordering method does not require any syntactic information or rules for reordering. We simply used symmetrized Giza++ word alignments to reorder the words in the source sentences to reflect the target word order and applied Giza++ again to the reordered training corpus. The following steps were performed to produce the final word alignment:

1. Word align the training corpus with Giza++.
2. Reorder the source words according to the order of the target words they are aligned to (store the original source word positions for later).
3. Word align the reordered source and original target corpus with Giza++.
4. Re-adjust the new word alignments so that they align source and target words in the original corpus.

The system built on this word alignment (reorder) had a significant improvement in Bleu score over the unreordered baseline (*base*) for translation into English, and small improvements otherwise.

4.2 Verb movement

The positions of finite verbs are often very different in English and German, where they are often placed at the end of sentences. In several cases we noted that finite verbs were misaligned by Giza++. To improve the alignment of verbs, we moved all verbs in both English and German to the end of the sentences prior to word alignment. The reordered sentences were word aligned with Giza++ and the resulting word links were then re-adjusted to align words in the original corpus.

The system created from this alignment (verb) resulted in significantly lower scores than *base* for translation into German, and similar scores as *base* for translation into English.

4.3 Combination Systems

The alignment based on reordered verbs did not produce a better alignment in terms of Bleu scores of the resulting translations, which led us to the conclusion that the alignment was noisy. However, it is possible that we did correctly align some words that were misaligned in the baseline alignment. To investigate this issue we concatenated first the baseline and verb alignments, and then all three alignments, and extracted phrase tables from the concatenated training sets.

All scores for both combined systems significantly outperformed the unfactored baseline, and were slightly better than *base*. For translation into German it was best to use the combination of only verb and *base*, which was significantly better than *base* on Meteor. This shows that even though the verb alignments were not good when used in a single system, they still could contribute in a combination system.

5 Preprocessing of OOVs

Out-of-vocabulary words, words that have not been seen in the training data, are a problem in statistical machine translation, since no translations have been observed for them. The standard strategy is to transfer them as is to the translation output, which, naive as it sounds, actually works well in some cases, since many OOVs are numbers or proper names (Stymne and Holmqvist, 2008). However, it still results in incomprehensible words in the output in many cases. We have investigated several ways of changing unknown words into similar words that have been seen in the training data, in a preprocessing step.

We also considered another OOV problem, number formatting, since it differs between English and German. To address this, we swapped decimal points/commas, and other delimeters for unknown numbers in a post-processing step.

In the preprocessing step, we applied a number of transformations to each OOV word, accepting the first applicable transformation that led to a known word:

Type	German	English
total OOVs	1833	1489
casing	124	26
stemming	270	72
hyphenated words	230	124
end hyphens	24	–

Table 5: Number of affected words by OOV-preprocessing

1. Change the word into a known cased version (since we trained a truecased system, this handles cased variations of words)
2. Stem the word, and if we know the stem, choose the most common realisation of that stem (using a Porter stemmer)
3. For hyphenated words, split at the hyphen (if any of the resulting parts are OOVs, they are recursively treated as well)
4. Remove hyphens at the end of German words (that could result from compound splitting)

The first two steps were based on frequency lists of truecased and stemmed words that we compiled from the monolingual training corpora.

Inspection of the initial results showed that proper names were often changed into other words in English, so we excluded them from the preprocessing by not applying it to words with an initial capital letter. This happened to a lesser extent for German, but here it was impossible to use the same simple heuristic for proper names, since German nouns also have an initial capital letter.

The number of affected words for the baseline using the final transformations are shown in Table 5. Even though we managed to transform some words, we still lack a transformation for the majority of OOVs. Despite this, there is a tendency of small improvements on both metrics in the majority of cases in both translation directions, as shown in Tables 6 and 7.

Figure 1 shows an example of how OOV processing affects one sentence for translation from German to English. In this case splitting a hyphenated compound gives a better translation, even though the word *opening* is chosen rather than *jack*. There is also a stemming change, where the adjective *ausgereiftesten* (*the most well-engineered*), is changed form superlative to positive. This results in a more understandable trans-

DE original	Die besten und technisch *ausgereiftesten* Telefone mit einer *3,5-mm-Öffnung* für normale Kopfhörer kosten bis zu fünfzehntausend Kronen.
DE preprocessed	die besten und technisch *ausgereifte* Telefone mit einer *3,5 mm Öffnung* für normale Kopf Hörer kosten bis zu fünfzehntausend Kronen .
base+verb+reorder	The best and technically *ausgereiftesten* phones with a *3,5-mm-Öffnung* for normal earphones cost up to fifteen thousand kronor.
base+verb+reorder +OOV	The best and technologically *advanced* phones with a *3.5 mm opening* for normal earphones cost up to fifteen thousand kronor.
EN reference	The best and most technically *well-equipped* telephones, with a *3.5 mm jack* for ordinary headphones, cost up to fifteen thousand crowns.

Figure 1: Example of the effects of OOV processing for German→English

System	Bleu	Meteor
base	14.24	49.41
+ OOV	14.26	49.43
base+verb	14.38	49.72
+ OOV	14.42	49.75
+ MBR	**14.41**	**49.77**

Table 6: Results for OOV-processing and MBR, English→German.

System	Bleu	Meteor
base	18.50	38.47
+ OOV	18.48	38.59
base+verb+reorder	18.73	38.59
+ OOV	18.81	38.70
+ MBR	**18.84**	**38.75**

Table 7: Results for OOV-processing and MBR, German→English.

lation, which, however, is harmful to automatic scores, since the preceding word, *technically*, which is identical to the reference, is changed into *technologically*.

This work is related to work by Arora et al. (2008), who transformed Hindi OOVs by using morphological analysers, before translation to Japanese. Our work has the advantage that it is more knowledge-lite, as it only needs a Porter stemmer and a monolingual corpus. Mirkin et al. (2009) used WordNet to replace OOVs by synonyms or hypernyms, and chose the best overall translation partly based on scoring of the source transformations. Our OOV handling could potentially be used in combination with both these strategies.

6 Final Submission

For the final Liu shared task submission we used the base+verb+reorder+OOV system for German→English and the base+verb+OOV system for English→German, which had the best overall scores considering all metrics. To these systems we added minimum Bayes risk (MBR) decoding (Kumar and Byrne, 2004). In standard decoding, the top suggestion of the translation system is chosen as the system output. In MBR decoding the risk is spread by choosing the translation that is most similar to the N highest scoring translation suggestions from the system, with $N = 100$, as suggested in Koehn et al. (2008). MBR decoding gave hardly any changes in automatic scores, as shown in Tables 6 and 7. The final system was significantly better than the baseline in all cases, and significantly better than *base* on Meteor in both translation directions, and on Bleu for translation into English.

7 Conclusions

As in Holmqvist et al. (2009) reordering by using Giza++ in two phases had a small, but consistent positive effect. Aligning verbs by co-locating them at the end of sentences had a largely negative effect. However, when output from this method was concatenated with the baseline alignment before extracting the phrase table, there were consistent improvements. Combining all three alignments, however, had mixed effects. Combining reordering in training with a knowledge-lite method for handling out-of-vocabulary words led to significant improvements on Meteor scores for translation between German and English in both directions.

References

Abhaya Agarwal and Alon Lavie. 2008. METEOR, M-BLEU and M-TER: Evaluation metrics for high-correlation with human rankings of machine translation output. In *Proceedings of the Third Workshop on Statistical Machine Translation*, pages 115–118, Columbus, Ohio, USA.

Karunesh Arora, Michael Paul, and Eiichiro Sumita. 2008. Translation of unknown words in phrase-based statistical machine translation for languages of rich morphology. In *Proceedings of the 1st International Workshop on Spoken Languages Technologies for Under-Resourced Languages*, pages 70–75, Hanoi, Vietnam.

Maria Holmqvist, Sara Stymne, Jody Foo, and Lars Ahrenberg. 2009. Improving alignment for SMT by reordering and augmenting the training corpus. In *Proceedings of the Fourth Workshop on Statistical Machine Translation*, pages 120–124, Athens, Greece.

Philipp Koehn and Kevin Knight. 2003. Empirical methods for compound splitting. In *Proceedings of the 10th Conference of the EACL*, pages 187–193, Budapest, Hungary.

Philipp Koehn and Josh Schroeder. 2007. Experiments in domain adaptation for statistical machine translation. In *Proceedings of the Second Workshop on Statistical Machine Translation*, pages 224–227, Prague, Czech Republic.

Philipp Koehn, Hieu Hoang, Alexandra Birch, Chris Callison-Burch, Marcello Federico, Nicola Bertoldi, Brooke Cowan, Wade Shen, Christine Moran, Richard Zens, Chris Dyer, Ondrej Bojar, Alexandra Constantin, and Evan Herbst. 2007. Moses: Open source toolkit for statistical machine translation. In *Proceedings of the 45th Annual Meeting of the ACL, demonstration session*, pages 177–180, Prague, Czech Republic.

Philipp Koehn, Abhishek Arun, and Hieu Hoang. 2008. Towards better machine translation quality for the German-English language pairs. In *Proceedings of the Third Workshop on Statistical Machine Translation*, pages 139–142, Columbus, Ohio, USA.

Shankar Kumar and William Byrne. 2004. Minimum Bayes-risk decoding for statistical machine translation. In *Proceedings of the 2004 Human Language Technology Conference of the NAACL*, pages 169–176, Boston, Massachusetts, USA.

Stefan Langer. 1998. Zur Morphologie und Semantik von Nominalkomposita. In *Tagungsband der 4. Konferenz zur Verarbeitung natürlicher Sprache (KONVENS)*, pages 83–97, Bonn, Germany.

Shachar Mirkin, Lucia Specia, Nicola Cancedda, Ido Dagan, Marc Dymetman, and Idan Szpektor. 2009. Source-language entailment modeling for translating unknown terms. In *Proceedings of the Joint Conference of the 47th Annual Meeting of the ACL and the 4th International Joint Conference on Natural Language Processing of the AFNLP*, pages 791–799, Suntec, Singapore.

Franz Josef Och and Hermann Ney. 2003. A systematic comparison of various statistical alignment models. *Computational Linguistics*, 29(1):19–51.

Kishore Papineni, Salim Roukos, Todd Ward, and Wei-Jing Zhu. 2002. BLEU: A method for automatic evaluation of machine translation. In *Proceedings of the 40th Annual Meeting of the ACL*, pages 311–318, Philadelphia, Pennsylvania, USA.

Stefan Riezler and John T. Maxwell. 2005. On some pitfalls in automatic evaluation and significance testing for MT. In *Proceedings of the Workshop on Intrinsic and Extrinsic Evaluation Measures for MT and/or Summarization at the 43th Annual Meeting of the ACL*, pages 57–64, Ann Arbor, Michigan, USA.

Helmut Schmid and Florian Laws. 2008. Estimation of conditional probabilities with decision trees and an application to fine-grained pos tagging. In *Proceedings of the 22th International Conference on Computational Linguistics*, pages 777–784, Manchester, UK.

Helmut Schmid. 1994. Probabilistic part-of-speech tagging using decision trees. In *Proceedings of the International Conference on New Methods in Language Processing*, pages 44–49, Manchester, UK.

Andreas Stolcke. 2002. SRILM – an extensible language modeling toolkit. In *Proceedings of the Seventh International Conference on Spoken Language Processing*, pages 901–904, Denver, Colorado, USA.

Sara Stymne and Maria Holmqvist. 2008. Processing of Swedish compounds for phrase-based statistical machine translation. In *Proceedings of the 12th Annual Conference of the European Association for Machine Translation*, pages 180–189, Hamburg, Germany.

Sara Stymne. 2008. German compounds in factored statistical machine translation. In *Proceedings of GoTAL – 6th International Conference on Natural Language Processing*, pages 464–475, Gothenburg, Sweden.

Chao Wang, Michael Collins, and Philipp Koehn. 2007. Chinese syntactic reordering for statistical machine translation. In *Proc. of the 2007 Joint Conference on Empirical Methods in Natural Language Processing and Computational Natural Language Learning*, pages 737–745, Prague, Czech Republic.

Fei Xia and Michael McCord. 2004. Improving a statistical MT system with automatically learned rewrite patterns. In *Proceedings of the 20th International Conference on Computational Linguistics*, pages 508–514, Geneva, Switzerland.

To Cache or not to Cache?
Experiments with Adaptive Models in Statistical Machine Translation

Jörg Tiedemann
Department of Linguistics and Philology
Uppsala University, Uppsala/Sweden
jorg.tiedemann@lingfil.uu.se

Abstract

We report results of our submissions to the WMT 2010 shared translation task in which we applied a system that includes adaptive language and translation models. Adaptation is implemented using exponentially decaying caches storing previous translations as the history for new predictions. Evidence from the cache is then mixed with the global background model. The main problem in this setup is error propagation and our submissions essentially failed to improve over the competitive baseline. There are slight improvements in lexical choice but the global performance decreases in terms of BLEU scores.

1 Motivation

The main motivation of our submission was to test the use of adaptive language and translation models in a standard phrase-based SMT setting for the adaptation to wider context beyond sentence boundaries. Adaptive language models have a long tradition in the speech recognition community and various approaches have been proposed to reduce model perplexity in this way. The general task is to adjust statistical models to essential properties of natural language which are usually not captured by standard n-gram models or other local dependency models. First of all, it is known that repetition is very common especially among content words (see, for example, words like "honey", "milk", "land" and "flowing" in figure 1). In most cases a repeated occurrence of a content word is much more likely than its first appearance, which is not predicted in this way by a static language model. Secondly, the use of expressions is related to the topic in the current discourse and the chance of using the same topic-related expressions again in running text is higher than a mixed-topic model would predict.

In translation another phenomenon can be observed, namely the consistency of translations. Polysemous terms are usually not ambiguous in their context and, hence, their translations become consistent according to the contextual sense. Even the choice between synonymous translations is rather consistent in translated texts as we can see in the example of subtitle translations in figure 1 (taken from the OPUS corpus (Tiedemann, 2009)).

The 10 commandments	**Kerd ma lui**
To some land flowing with milk and **honey**! Till ett land fullt av mjölk och **honung**. I've never tasted **honey**. Jag har aldrig smakat **honung**. ... But will sympathy lead us to this land flowing with milk and **honey**? Men kan sympati leda oss till detta mjölkens och **honungens** land?	Mari **honey** ... Mari, **gumman** **Sweetheart**, where are you going? **Älskling**, var ska du? ... Who was that, **honey**? Vem var det, **gumman**?

Figure 1: Repetition and translation consistency

Ambiguous terms like "honey" are consistently translated into the Swedish counterpart "honung" (in the sense of the actual substance) or "gumman" (in the metaphoric sense). Observe that this is true even in the latter case where synonymous translations such as "älskling" would be possible as well. In other words, deciding to stick to consistent lexical translations should be preferred in MT because the chance of alternative translations in repeated cases is low. Here again, common static translation models do not capture this property at all.

In the following we explain our attempt to integrate contextual dependencies using cache-based adaptive models in a standard SMT setup. We have already successfully applied this technique to a domain-adaptation task (Tiedemann, 2010).

Proceedings of the Joint 5th Workshop on Statistical Machine Translation and MetricsMATR, pages 189–194,
Uppsala, Sweden, 15-16 July 2010.

Now we would like to investigate the robustness of this model in a more general case where some in-domain training data is available and input data is less repetitive.

2 Cache-based Adaptive Models

The basic idea behind cache-based models is to mix a large static background model with a small local model that is dynamically estimated from recent items from the input stream. Dynamic cache language models have been introduced by (Kuhn and Mori, 1990) and are often implemented in the form of linear mixtures:

$$P(w_n|history) = (1-\lambda)P_{background}(w_n|history) + \lambda P_{cache}(w_n|history)$$

The background model is usually a standard n-gram model taking limited amount of local context from the history into account and the cache model is often implemented as a simple (unsmoothed) unigram model using the elements stored in a fixed-size cache (100-5000 words) to estimate its parameters. Another improvement can be achieved by making the importance of cached elements a function of recency. This can be done by introducing a decaying factor in the estimation of cache probabilities (Clarkson and Robinson, 1997):

$$P_{cache}(w_n|w_{n-k}..w_{n-1}) \approx \frac{1}{Z}\sum_{i=n-k}^{n-1} I(w_n = w_i)e^{-\alpha(n-i)}$$

This is basically the model that we applied in our experiments as it showed the largest perplexity reduction in our previous experiments on domain adaptation.

Similarly, translation models can be adapted as well. This is especially useful to account for translation consistency forcing the decoder to prefer identical translations for repeated terms. In our approach we try to model recency again using a decay factor to compute translation model scores from the cache in the following way (only for source language phrases f_n for which a translation option exist in the cache; we use a score of zero otherwise):

$$\phi_{cache}(e_n|f_n) = \frac{\sum_{i=1}^{K} I(\langle e_n, f_n\rangle = \langle e_i, f_i\rangle) * e^{-\alpha i}}{\sum_{i=1}^{K} I(f_n = f_i)}$$

The importance of a cached translation option exponentially decays and we normalize the sum of cached occurrences by the number of translation options with the same foreign language item that we condition on.

Plugging this in into a standard phrase-based SMT engine is rather straightforward. The use of cache-based language models in SMT have been investigated before (Raab, 2007). In our case we used Moses as the base decoder (Koehn et al., 2007). The cache-based language model can be integrated in the decoder by simply adjusting the call to the language modeling toolkit appropriately. We implemented the exponentially decaying cache model within the standard SRILM toolkit (Stolcke, 2002) and added command line arguments to Moses to switch to that model and to set cache parameters such as interpolation, cache size and decay. Adding the translation model cache is a bit more tricky. For this we added a new feature function to the global log-linear model and implemented the decaying cache as explained above within the decoder. Again, simple command-line arguments can be used to switch caching on or off and to adjust cache parameters.

One important issue is to decide when and what to cache. As we explore a lot of different options in decoding it is not feasible to adapt the cache continuously. This would mean a lot of cache operations trying to add and remove hypotheses from the cache memory. Therefore, we opted for a context model that considers history only from previous sentences. Once decoding is finished translation options from the best hypothesis found in decoding are put into language and translation model cache. This is arguably a strong approximation of the adaptive approach. However, considering our special concern about wider context across sentence boundaries this seems to be a reasonable compromise between completeness and efficiency.

Another issue is related to the selection of items to be cached. As discussed earlier repetition is most likely to be found among content words. Similarly, translation consistency is less likely to be true for function words. In the best case one would know the likelihood of specific terms to be repeated. This could be trained on some development data possibly in connection with word classes instead of fully lexicalized parameters in order to overcome data sparseness and to improve generality. Even though this idea is very tempting it would require a substantial extension of our model and would introduce language and domain-specific parameters. Therefore, we just added a simplistic approach filtering tokens by their length in characters instead. Assuming that longer items are more likely to be content words we simply set a threshold to decide whether to add a term to the cache or not. This threshold can be adjusted using command-line arguments.

Finally, we also need to be careful about noise in the cache. This is essential as the caching approach is prone to error propagation. However, detecting noise is difficult. If there would be a notion of noise in translation hypotheses, the decoder would avoid it. In related work (Nepveu et al., 2004) have studied cache-based translation models in connection with interactive machine translation. In that case, one can assume correct input after post-editing the translation suggestions. One way to approach noise reduction in non-interactive MT is to make use of transition costs in the translation lattice. Assuming that this cost (which is estimated internally within the decoder during the expansion of translation hypotheses) refers to some kind of confidence we can discard translation options above a certain threshold, which is what we did in the implementation of our translation model cache.

3 Experiments

We followed the setup proposed in the shared translation task. Primarily we concentrated our efforts on German-English (de-en) and English-German (en-de) using the constrained track, i.e. using the provided training and development data from Europarl and the News domain. Later we also added experiments for Spanish (es) and English using a similar setup.

Our baseline system incorporates the following components: We trained two separate 5-gram language models for each language with the standard smoothing strategies (interpolation and Kneser-Ney discounting), one for Europarl and one for the News data. All of them were estimated using the SRILM toolkit except the English News LM for which we applied RandLM (Talbot and Osborne, 2007) to cope with the large amount of training data. We also included two separate translation models, one for the combined Europarl and News data and one for the News data only. They were estimated using the standard tools GIZA++ (Och and Ney, 2003) and Moses (Koehn et al., 2007) applying default settings and lowercased training data. Lexicalized reordering was trained on the combined data set. All baseline models were then tuned on the News test data from 2008 using minimum error rate training (MERT) (Och, 2003). The results in terms of lower-case BLEU scores are listed in table 1.

		n-gram scores			
	BLEU	1	2	3	4
de-en baseline	21.3	57.4	27.8	15.1	8.6
de-en cache	21.5	58.1	28.1	15.2	8.7
en-de baseline	15.6	52.5	21.7	10.6	5.5
en-de cache	14.4	52.6	21.0	9.9	4.9
es-en baseline	26.7	61.7	32.7	19.9	12.6
es-en cache	26.1	62.6	32.7	19.8	12.5
en-es baseline	26.9	61.5	33.3	20.5	12.9
en-es cache	23.0	60.6	30.4	17.6	10.4

Table 1: Results on the WMT10 test set.

In the adaptation experiments we applied exactly the same models using the feature weights from the baseline with the addition of the caching components in both, language models and translation models. Cache parameters are not particularly tuned for the task in our initial experiments which could be one reason for the disappointing results we obtained. Some of them can be integrated in the MERT procedure, for example, the interpolation weight of the translation cache. However, tuning these parameters with the standard procedures appears to be difficult as we will see in later experiments presented in section 3.2. Initially we used settings that appeared to be useful in previous experiments. In particular, we used a language model cache of 10,000 words with a decay of $\alpha = 0.0005$ and an interpolation weight of 0.001. A cache was used in all language models except the English News model for which caching was not available (because we did not implement this feature for RandLM). The translation cache size was set to 5,000 with a decay factor of 0.001. The weight for the translation cache was set to 0.001. Furthermore, we filtered items for the translation cache using a length constraint of 4 characters or more and a transition cost threshold (log score) of -4.

The final results of the adaptive runs are shown in table 1. In all but one case the cache-based result is below the baseline which is, of course, quite disappointing. For German-English a small improvement can be observed. However, this may be rather accidental. In general, it seems that the adaptive approach cannot cope with the noise added to the cache.

3.1 Discussion

There are two important observations that should be mentioned here. First of all, the adaptive approach assumes coherent text input. However, the WMT test-set is composed of many short news headlines with various topics involved. We, therefore, also ran the adaptive approach on individual news segments. The results are illustrated in figure 2.

Basically, the results do not change compared to the previous run. Still, cache-based models perform worse on average except for the German-English test-set for which we obtained a slight but insignificant improvement. Figure 2 plots the BLEU score differences between standard models and cached models for the individual news items. We can see a very blurred picture of these individual scores and the general conclusion is that caching failed. One problem is that the individual news items are very short (around 20 sentences each) which is probably too little for caching to show any positive effect. Surprising, however, is the negative influence of caching even on these small documents which is quite similar to the runs on the entire sets. The drop in performance for English-Spanish is especially striking. We have no explanation at this point for this exceptional behavior.

A second observation is the variation in individual n-gram precision scores (see table 1). In all but one case the unigram precision goes up which indicates that the cache models often improve lexical choice at least in terms of individual words. The first example in figure 2 could be seen as a slight improvement due to a consistent lexical choice of "missile" (instead of "rocket").

The main problem, however, in the adaptive approach seems to appear in local contexts which might be due to the simplistic language modeling cache. It would be interesting to study possibilities of integrating local dependencies into the cache models. However, there are serious problems with data sparseness. Initial experiments with a bigram LM cache did not produce any improvements so far.

Another crucial problem with the cache-based model is of course error propagation. An example which is probably due to this issue can be seen in table 2 in the last two translations (propagation of the translation option "extortion"). This problem is difficult to get around especially in case of bad baseline translations. One possible idea would be to implement a two-pass procedure to run over the entire input first only to fill the cache and to identify reliable evidence for certain translation options (possibly focusing on simple translation tasks such as short sentences). Then, in the second pass the adaptive model can be applied to prefer repetition and consistency according to the parameters learned in the first pass.

baseline	until the end of the journey , are , in turn , technical damage to the rocket .
cache	until the end of the journey , in turn , technical damage to the missile .
reference	but near the end of the flight there was technical damage to the missile .
baseline	iran has earlier criticism of its human rights record .
cache	iran rejected previous criticism of its human rights record .
reference	iran has dismissed previous criticism of its human rights record .
baseline	facing conservationists is accused of extortion
cache	facing conservationists is accused of extortion
reference	Nature protection officers accused of blackmail
baseline	the leitmeritz-polizei accused the chairman of the bürgervereinigung " naturschutzgemeinschaft leitmeritz " because of blackmail .
cache	the leitmeritz-polizei accused the chairman of the bürgervereinigung " naturschutzgemeinschaft leitmeritz " because of extortion .
reference	The Litomerice police have accused the chairman of the Litomerice Nature Protection Society civil association of blackmail.

Table 2: German to English example translations.

3.2 Parameter Optimization

Another question is if the cache parameters require careful optimization in order to make this approach effective. An attempt to investigate the influence of the cache components by simply varying the interpolation weights gave us the following results for English-German (see table 3).

fixed cache TM parameters		fixed cache LM parameters	
λ_{LM}	BLEU	λ_{TM}	BLEU
0.1	14.12	0.1	12.75
0.01	14.39	0.01	13.04
0.005	14.40	0.005	13.57
0.001	14.44	0.001	14.42
0.0005	14.43	0.0005	14.57

Table 3: Results for English to German with varying mixture weights.

Looking at these results the tendency of the scores

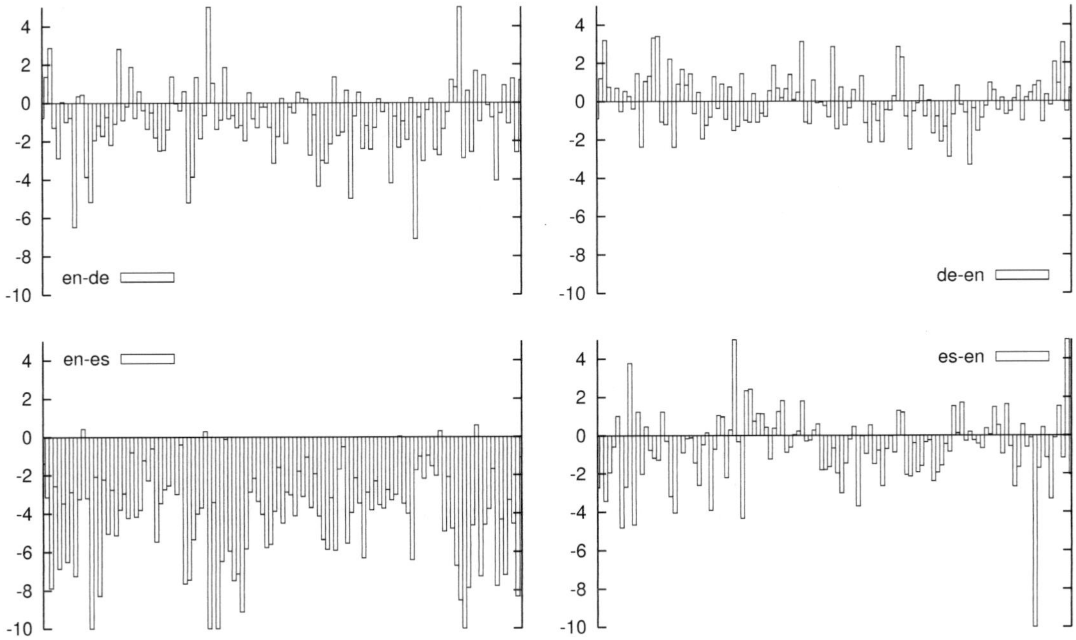

Figure 2: BLEU score differences between a standard model and a cached model for individual news segments from the WMT test-set.

seems to suggest that switching off caching is the right thing to do (as one might have expected already from the initial experimental results). We did not perform the same type of investigation for the other language pairs but we expect a similar behavior.

Even though these results did not encourage us very much to investigate the possibilities of cache parameter optimization any further we still tried to look at the integration of the interpolation weights into the MERT procedure. The weight of the TM cache is especially suited for MERT as this component is implemented in terms of a separate feature function within the global log-linear model used in decoding. The LM mixture model, on the other hand, is implemented internally within SRILM and therefore not so straightforward to integrate into standard MERT. We, therefore, doubled the number of LM's included in the SMT model using two standard LM's and two LM's with cache (one for Europarl and one for News in both cases). The latter are actually mixtures as well using a fixed interpolation weight of $\lambda_{LM} = 0.5$ between the cached component and the background model. In this way the cached LM's benefit from the smoothing with the static background model. Individual weights for all four LM's are then learned in the global MERT procedure. Unfortunately, other cache parameters cannot be optimized in this way as they do not produce any particular values for individual translation hypotheses in decoding.

We applied this tuning setup to the English-German translation task and ran MERT on the same development data as before. Actually, caching slows down translation quite substantially which makes MERT very slow. Due to the sequential caching procedure it is also not possible to parallelize tuning. Furthermore, the extra parameters seem to cause problems in convergence and we had to stop the optimization after 30 iterations when BLEU scores seemed to start stabilizing around 14.9 (in the standard setup only 12 iterations were required to complete tuning). Unfortunately, the result is again quite disappointing (see table 4).

Actually, the final BLEU score after tuning is even lower than in our initial runs with fixed cache parameters taken from previous unrelated experiments. This is very surprising and it looks like that MERT just failed to find settings close to the global optimum because of some strong local suboptimal points in the search space. One would expect that it should be possible to obtain at least the

BLEU on dev-set (no caching)	15.2
BLEU on dev-set (with caching)	14.9
Europarl LM	0.000417
News LM	0.057042
Europarl LM (with cache)	0.002429
News LM (with cache)	-0.000604
λ_{TM}	0.000749
BLEU on test-set (no caching)	15.6
BLEU on test-set (with caching)	12.7

Table 4: Tuning cache parameters.

same score on the development set which was not the case in our experiment. However, as already mentioned, we had to interrupt tuning and there is still some chance that MERT would have improved in later iterations. At least intuitively, there seems to be some logic behind the tuned weights (shown in table 4). The out-of-domain LM (Europarl) obtains a higher weight with caching than without and the in-domain LM (News) is better without it and, therefore, the cached version obtains a negative weight. Furthermore, the TM cache weight is quite similar to the one we used in the initial experiments. However, applying these settings to the test-set did not work at all.

4 Conclusions

In our WMT10 experiments cache-based adaptive models failed to improve translation quality. Previous experiments have shown that they can be useful in adapting SMT models to new domains. However, they seem to have their limitations in the general case with mixed topics involved. A general problem is error propagation and the corruption of local dependencies due to over-simplified cache models. Parameter optimization seems to be difficult as well. These issues should be investigated further in future research.

References

P.R. Clarkson and A. J. Robinson. 1997. Language model adaptation using mixtures and an exponentially decaying cache. In *International Conference on Acoustics, Speech, and Signal Processing (ICASSP)*, pages 799–802, Munich, Germany.

Philipp Koehn, Hieu Hoang, Alexandra Birch, Chris Callison-Burch, Marcello Federico, Nicola Bertoldi, Brooke Cowan, Wade Shen, Christine Moran, Richard Zens, Chris Dyer, Ondřej Bojar, Alexandra Constantin, and Evan Herbst. 2007. Moses: open source toolkit for statistical machine translation. In *ACL '07: Proceedings of the 45th Annual Meeting of the ACL*, pages 177–180, Morristown, NJ, USA.

Roland Kuhn and Renato De Mori. 1990. A cache-based natural language model for speech recognition. *IEEE Transactions on Pattern Analysis and Machine Intelligence*, 12(6):570–583.

Laurent Nepveu, Lapalme, Guy, Langlais, Philippe, and George Foster. 2004. Adaptive Language and Translation Models for Interactive Machine Translation. In *Proceedings of the 9th Conference on Empirical Methods in Natural Language Processing (EMNLP)*, pages 190–197, Barcelona, Spain.

Franz Josef Och and Hermann Ney. 2003. A systematic comparison of various statistical alignment models. *Computational Linguistics*, 29(1):19–51.

Franz Josef Och. 2003. Minimum error rate training in statistical machine translation. In *ACL '03: Proceedings of the 41st Annual Meeting on Association for Computational Linguistics*, pages 160–167, Morristown, NJ, USA.

Martin Raab. 2007. *Language Modeling for Machine Translation*. VDM Verlag, Saarbrücken, Germany.

Andreas Stolcke. 2002. SRILM - an extensible language modeling toolkit. In *Proceedings of the 7th international conference on spoken language processing (ICSLP 2002)*, pages 901–904, Denver, CO, USA.

David Talbot and Miles Osborne. 2007. Randomised language modelling for statistical machine translation. In *ACL '07: Proceedings of the 45th Annual Meeting of the ACL*, Prague, Czech Republic. Association for Computational Linguistics.

Jörg Tiedemann. 2009. News from OPUS - A collection of multilingual parallel corpora with tools and interfaces. In *Recent Advances in Natural Language Processing*, volume V, pages 237–248. John Benjamins, Amsterdam/Philadelphia.

Jörg Tiedemann. 2010. Context adaptation in statistical machine translation using models with exponentially decaying cache. In *ACL 2010 Workshop on Domain Adaptation for Natural Language Processing (DANLP)*.

Applying morphological decomposition to statistical machine translation

Sami Virpioja and **Jaakko Väyrynen** and **André Mansikkaniemi** and **Mikko Kurimo**
Aalto University School of Science and Technology
Department of Information and Computer Science
PO BOX 15400, 00076 Aalto, Finland
{svirpioj,jjvayryn,ammansik,mikkok}@cis.hut.fi

Abstract

This paper describes the Aalto submission for the German-to-English and the Czech-to-English translation tasks of the ACL 2010 Joint Fifth Workshop on Statistical Machine Translation and MetricsMATR. Statistical machine translation has focused on using words, and longer phrases constructed from words, as tokens in the system. In contrast, we apply different morphological decompositions of words using the unsupervised Morfessor algorithms. While translation models trained using the morphological decompositions did not improve the BLEU scores, we show that the Minimum Bayes Risk combination with a word-based translation model produces significant improvements for the German-to-English translation. However, we did not see improvements for the Czech-to-English translations.

1 Introduction

The effect of morphological variation in languages can be alleviated by using word analysis schemes, which may include morpheme discovery, part-of-speech tagging, or other linguistic information. Words are very convenient and even efficient representation in statistical natural language processing, especially with English, but morphologically rich languages can benefit from more fine-grained information. For instance, statistical morphs discovered with unsupervised methods result in better performance in automatic speech recognition for highly-inflecting and agglutinative languages (Hirsimäki et al., 2006; Kurimo et al., 2006).

Virpioja et al. (2007) applied morph-based models in statistical machine translation (SMT) between several language pairs without gaining improvement in BLEU score, but obtaining reductions in out-of-vocabulary rates. They utilized morphs both in the source and in the target language. Later, de Gispert et al. (2009) showed that Minimum Bayes Risk (MBR) combination of word-based and morph-based translation models improves translation with Arabic-to-English and Finnish-to-English language pairs, where only the source language utilized morph-based models. Similar results have been shown for Finnish-to-English and Finnish-to-German in performance evaluation of various unsupervised morpheme analysis algorithms in Morpho Challenge 2009 competition (Kurimo et al., 2009).

We continue the research described above and examine how the level of decomposition affects both the individual morph-based systems and MBR combinations with the baseline word-based model. Experiments are conducted with the WMT10 shared task data for German-to-English and Czech-to-English language pairs.

2 Methods

In this work, morphological analyses are conducted on the source language data, and each different analysis is applied to create a unique segmentation of words into morphemes. Translation systems are trained with the Moses toolkit (Koehn et al., 2007) from each differently segmented version of the same source language to the target language. Evaluation with BLEU is performed on both the individual systems and system combinations, using different levels of decomposition.

2.1 Morphological models for words

Morfessor (Creutz and Lagus, 2002; Creutz and Lagus, 2007, etc.) is a family of methods for unsupervised morphological segmentation. Morfessor does not limit the number of morphemes for each word, making it suitable for agglutinative and compounding languages. An analysis of a single word is a list of non-overlapping segments,

Proceedings of the Joint 5th Workshop on Statistical Machine Translation and MetricsMATR, pages 195–200,
Uppsala, Sweden, 15-16 July 2010.

morphs, stored in the model lexicon. We use both the Morfessor Baseline (Creutz and Lagus, 2005b) and the Morfessor Categories-MAP (Creutz and Lagus, 2005a) algorithms.[1] Both are formulated in a maximum a posteriori (MAP) framework, i.e., the learning algorithm tries to optimize the product of the model prior and the data likelihood.

The generative model applied by Morfessor Baseline assumes that the morphs are independent. The resulting segmentation can be influenced by using explicit priors for the morph lengths and frequencies, but their effect is usually minimal. The training data has a larger effect on the results: A larger data set allows a larger lexicon, and thus longer morphs and less morphs per word (Creutz and Lagus, 2007). Moreover, the model can be trained with or without taking into account the word frequencies. If the frequencies are included, the more frequent words are usually undersegmented compared to a linguistic analysis, whereas the rare words are oversegmented (Creutz and Lagus, 2005b). An easy way to control the amount of segmentation is to weight the training data likelihood by a positive factor α. If $\alpha > 1$, the increased likelihood results in longer morphs. If $\alpha < 1$, the morphs will be shorter and the words more segmented.

Words that are not present in the training data can be segmented using an algorithm similar to Viterbi. The algorithm can be modified to allow new morphs types to be used by using an approximative cost of adding them into the lexicon (Virpioja and Kohonen, 2009). The modification prevents oversegmentation of unseen word forms. In machine translation, this is important especially for proper nouns, for which there is usually no need for translation.

The Morfessor Categories-MAP algorithm extends the model by imposing morph categories of stems, prefixes and suffixes, as well as transition probabilities between them. In addition, it applies a hierarchical segmentation model that allows it to construct new stems from smaller pieces of "non-morphemes" (Creutz and Lagus, 2007). Due to these features, it can provide reasonable segmentations also for those words that contain new morphemes. The drawback of the more sophisticated model is the slower and more complex training algorithm. In addition, the amount of the segmentation is harder to control.

Morfessor Categories-MAP was applied to statistical machine translation by Virpioja et al. (2007) and de Gispert et al. (2009). However, Kurimo et al. (2009) report that Morfessor Baseline outperformed Categories-MAP in Finnish-to-English and German-to-English tasks both with and without MBR combination, although the differences were not statistically significant. In all the previous cases, the models were trained on word types, i.e., without using their frequencies. Here, we also test models trained on word tokens.

2.2 Statistical machine translation

We utilize the Moses toolkit (Koehn et al., 2007) for statistical machine translation. The default parameter values are used except with the segmented source language, where the maximum sentence length is increased from 80 to 100 tokens to compensate for the larger number of tokens in text.

2.3 Morphological model combination

For combining individual models, we apply Minimum Bayes Risk (MBR) system combination (Sim et al., 2007). N-best lists from multiple SMT systems trained with different morphological analysis methods are merged; the posterior distributions over the individual lists are interpolated to form a new distribution over the merged list. MBR hypotheses selection is then performed using sentence-level BLEU score (Kumar and Byrne, 2004).

In this work, the focus of the system combination is not to combine different translation systems (e.g., Moses and Systran), but to combine systems trained with the same translation algorithm using the same source language data with with different morphological decompositions.

3 Experiments

The German-to-English and Czech-to-English parts of the ACL WMT10 shared task data were investigated. Vanilla SMT models were trained with Moses using word tokens for MBR combination and comparison purposes. Several different morphological segmentation models for German and Czech were trained with Morfessor. Each segmentation model corresponds to a morph-based SMT model trained with Moses. The word-based vanilla Moses model is compared to each morph-based model as well as to several MBR com-

[1] The respective software is available at `http://www.cis.hut.fi/projects/morpho/`

binations between word-based translation models and morph-based translation models. Quantitative evaluation is carried out using the BLEU score with re-cased and re-tokenized translations.

4 Data

The data used in the experiments consisted of Czech-to-English (CZ-EN) and German-to-English (DE-EN) parallel language data from ACL WMT10. The data was divided into distinct training, development, and evaluation sets. Statistics and details are shown in Table 1.

Aligned data from Europarl v5 and News Commentary corpora were included in training German-to-English SMT models. The English part from the same data sets was used for training a 5-gram language model, which was used in all translation tasks. The Czech-to-English translation model was trained with CzEng v0.9 (training section 0) and News Commentary data. The monolingual German and Czech parts of the training data sets were used for training the morph segmentation models with Morfessor.

The data sets news-test2009, news-syscomb2009 and news-syscombtune2010 from the ACL WMT 2009 and WMT 2010, were used for development. The news-test2008, news-test2010, and news-syscombtest2010 data sets were used for evaluation.

4.1 Preprocessing

All data sets were preprocessed before use. XML-tags were removed, text was tokenized and characters were lowercased for every training, development and evaluation set.

Morphological models for German and Czech were trained using a corpus that was a combination of the respective training sets. Then the models were used for segmenting all the data sets, including development and evaluation sets, with the Viterbi algorithm discussed in Section 2.1. The modification of allowing new morph types for out-of-vocabulary words was not applied.

The Moses cleaning script performed additional filtering on the parallel language training data. Specifically, sentences with over 80 words were removed from the vanilla Moses word-based models. For morph-based models the limit was set to 100 morphs, which is the maximum limit of the Giza++ alignment tool. After filtering with a threshold of 100 tokens, the different morph segmentations for DE-EN training data from combined Europarl and News Commentary data sets ranged from 1 613 556 to 1 624 070 sentences. Similarly, segmented CZ-EN training data ranged from 896 163 to 897 744 sentences. The vanilla words-based model was trained with 1 609 998 sentences for DE-EN and 897 497 sentences for CZ-EN.

5 Results

The details of the ACL WMT10 submissions are shown in Table 2. The results of experiments with different morphological decompositions and MBR system combinations are shown in Table 3. The significances of the differences in BLEU scores between the word-based model (Words) and models with different morphological decompositions was measured by dividing each evaluation data set into 49 subsets of 41–51 sentences, and using the one-sided Wilcoxon signed rank test ($p < 0.05$).

5.1 Segmentation

We created several word segmentations with Morfessor baseline and Morfessor Categories-MAP (CatMAP). Statistics for the different segmentations are given in Table 3. The amount of segmentation was measured as the average number of morphs per word (m/w) and as the percentage of segmented words (s-%) in the training data. Increasing the data likelihood weight α in Morfessor Baseline increases the amount of segmentation for both languages. However, it had little effect on the proportion of segmented words in the three evaluation data sets: The proportion of segmented word tokens was 10–11 % for German and 8–9 % for Czech, whereas the out-of-vocabulary rate was 7.5–7.8 % for German and 4.8–5.6 % for Czech.

Disregarding the word frequency information in Morfessor Baseline (nofreq) produced more morphs per word type and segmented nearly all words in the training data. The Morfessor CatMAP algorithm created segmentations with the largest number of morphs per word, but did not segment as many words as the Morfessor Baseline without the frequencies.

5.2 Morph-based translation systems

The models with segmented source language performed worse individually than the word-based models. The change in the BLEU score was statistically significant in almost all segmentations and

Data set	Statistics				Training					Development	Evaluation
	Sentences	Words per sentence			SM		LM	TM			
		DE	CZ	EN	DE	CZ	EN	DE-EN	CZ-EN	{DE,CZ}-EN	{DE,CZ}-EN
Europarl v5	1 540 549	23.2		25.2	x		x	x			
News Commentary	100 269	21.9	18.9	21.5	x	x	x	x	x		
CzEng v0.9 (training section 0)	803 286		8.3	9.9		x			x		
news-test2009	2 525	21.7	18.8	23.2						x	
news-syscomb2009	502	19.7	17.2	21.1						x	
news-syscombtune2010	455	20.2	17.3	21.0						x	
news-test2008	2 051	20.3	17.8	21.7							x
news-test2010	2 489	21.7	18.4	22.3							x
news-syscombtest2010	2 034	22.0	18.6	22.6							x

Table 1: Data sets for the Czech-to-English and German-to-English SMT experiments, including the number of aligned sentences and the average number of words per sentence in each language. The data sets used for model training, development and evaluation are marked. Training is divided into German (DE) and Czech (CZ) segmentation model (SM) training, English (EN) language model (LM) training and German-to-English (DE-EN) and Czech-to-English (CZ-EN) translation model (TM) training.

Submission	Segmentation model for source language	BLEU-cased (news-test2010)
aalto DE-EN WMT10	Morfessor Baseline ($\alpha = 0.5$)	17.0
aalto DE-EN WMT10 CatMAP	Morfessor Categories-MAP	16.5
aalto CZ-EN WMT10	Morfessor Baseline ($\alpha = 0.5$)	16.2
aalto CZ-EN WMT10 CatMAP	Morfessor Categories-MAP	15.9

Table 2: Our submissions for the ACL WMT10 shared task in translation. The translation models are trained from the segmented source language into unsegmented target language with Moses.

all evaluation sets. Morfessor Baseline ($\alpha = 0.5$) was the best individual segmented model for both German and Czech in the sense that it had the lowest number of significant decreases the BLEU score compared to the word-based model. Removing word frequency information with Morfessor Baseline and using Morfessor CatMAP gave the lowest BLEU scores with both source languages.

5.3 Translation system combination

For the DE-EN language pair, all MBR system combinations between each segmented model and the word-based model had slightly higher BLUE scores than the individual word-based model. Nearly all improvements were statistically significant.

The BLEU scores for the MBR combinations in the CZ-EN language pair were mostly not significantly different from the individual word-based model. Two scores were significantly lower.

6 Discussion

We have applied concatenative morphological analysis, in which each original word token is segmented into one or more non-overlapping morph tokens. Our results with different levels of segmentation with Morfessor suggest that the optimal level of segmentation is language pair dependent in machine translation.

Our approach for handling rich morphology has not been able to directly improve the translation quality. We assume that improvements might still be possible by carefully tuning the amount of segmentation. The experiments in this paper with different values of the α parameter for Morfessor Baseline were conducted with the word frequencies. The parameter had little effect on the proportion of segmented words in the evaluation data sets, as frequent words were not segmented at all, and out-of-vocabulary words were likely to be oversegmented by the Viterbi algorithm. Future work includes testing a larger range of values for α, also for models trained without the word frequencies, and using the modification of the Viterbi algorithm proposed in Virpioja and Kohonen (2009).

It might also be helpful to only segment selected words, where the selection would be based on the potential benefit in the translation process. In general, the direct segmentation of words into morphs is problematic because it increases the number of tokens in the text and directly increases both model training and decoding complexity. However, an efficient segmentation decreases the number of types and the out-of-vocabulary rate (Virpioja et al., 2007).

We have replicated here the result that an MBR combination of a morph-based MT system with

Segmentation (DE)	Statistics (DE)		BLEU-cased (DE-EN)				
			news-test2008		news-test2010	news-syscombtest2010	
	m/w	s-%	No MBR	MBR with Words	No MBR	No MBR	MBR with Words
Words	1.00	0.0%	16.37	-	17.28	13.22	-
Morfessor Baseline ($\alpha = 0.5$)	1.82	72.4%	**15.19**$^{-}$	16.47^{+}	**17.04**$^{\circ}$	**13.28**$^{\circ}$	**13.70**$^{+}$
Morfessor Baseline ($\alpha = 1.0$)	1.65	61.0%	15.14^{-}	**16.54**$^{+}$	16.87^{-}	11.95^{-}	13.66^{+}
Morfessor Baseline ($\alpha = 5.0$)	1.24	23.7%	15.04^{-}	16.44°	16.63^{-}	11.78^{-}	13.43^{+}
Morfessor CatMAP	2.25	67.5%	14.21^{-}	16.42°	16.53^{-}	11.15^{-}	13.61^{+}
Morfessor Baseline nofreq	2.24	91.6%	13.98^{-}	16.47^{+}	16.36^{-}	10.66^{-}	13.58^{+}

Segmentation (CZ)	Statistics (CZ)		BLEU-cased (CZ-EN)				
			news-test2008		news-test2010	news-syscombtest2010	
	m/w	s-%	No MBR	MBR with Words	No MBR	No MBR	MBR with Words
Words	1.00	0.0%	14.91	-	16.73	12.75	-
Morfessor Baseline ($\alpha = 0.5$)	1.19	17.7%	13.22^{-}	14.87°	16.01^{-}	**12.60**$^{\circ}$	12.53^{-}
Morfessor Baseline ($\alpha = 1.0$)	1.09	8.1%	13.33^{-}	14.88°	**16.10**$^{-}$	11.29^{-}	12.84°
Morfessor Baseline ($\alpha = 5.0$)	1.03	2.9%	**13.53**$^{-}$	14.83°	15.92^{-}	11.17^{-}	12.85°
Morfessor CatMAP	2.29	71.9%	11.93^{-}	14.86°	15.79^{-}	10.12^{-}	10.79^{-}
Morfessor Baseline nofreq	2.18	90.3%	12.43^{-}	**14.96**$^{\circ}$	15.82^{-}	10.13^{-}	**12.89**$^{\circ}$

Table 3: Results for German-to-English (DE-EN) and Czech-to-English (CZ-EN) translation models. The source language is segmented with the shown algorithms. The amount of segmentation in the training data is measured with the average number of morphs per word (m/w) and as proportion of segmented words (s-%) against the word-based model (Words). The trained translation systems are evaluated independently (No MBR) and in Minimum Bayes Risk system combination of word-based translation systems (MBR). Unchanged ($^{\circ}$), significantly higher ($^{+}$) and lower ($^{-}$) BLEU scores compared to the word-based translation model (Words) are marked. The best morph-based model for each column is emphasized.

a word-based MT system can produce a BLEU score that is higher than from either of the individual systems (de Gispert et al., 2009; Kurimo et al., 2009). With the DE-EN language pair, the improvement was statistically significant with all tested segmentation models. However, the improvements were not as large as those obtained before and the results for the CZ-EN language pair were not significantly different in most cases. Whether this is due to the different languages, training data sets, the domain of the evaluation data sets, or some problems in the model training, is currently uncertain.

One very different approach for applying different levels of linguistic analysis is factor models for SMT (Koehn and Hoang, 2007), where pre-determined factors (e.g., surface form, lemma and part-of-speech) are stored as vectors for each word. This provides better integration of morphosyntactic information and more control of the process, but the translation models are more complex and the number and factor types in each word must be fixed.

Our submissions to the ACL WMT10 shared task utilize unsupervised morphological decomposition models in a straightforward manner. The individual morph-based models trained with the source language words segmented into morphs did not improve the vanilla word-based models trained with the unsegmented source language. We have replicated the result for the German-to-English language pair that an MBR combination of a word-based and a segmented morph-based model gives significant improvements to the BLEU score. However, we did not see improvements for the Czech-to-English translations.

Acknowledgments

This work was supported by the Academy of Finland in the project *Adaptive Informatics*, the Finnish graduate school in Language Technology, and the IST Programme of the European Community, under the FP7 project EMIME (213845).

References

Mathias Creutz and Krista Lagus. 2002. Unsupervised discovery of morphemes. In *Proceedings of the Workshop on Morphological and Phonological Learning of ACL'02*, pages 21–30, Philadelphia, Pennsylvania, USA.

Mathias Creutz and Krista Lagus. 2005a. Inducing the morphological lexicon of a natural language from unannotated text. In *Proceedings of the AKRR'05*, Espoo, Finland.

Mathias Creutz and Krista Lagus. 2005b. Unsupervised morpheme segmentation and morphology induction from text corpora using Morfessor 1.0. Technical Report A81, Publications in Computer and Information Science, Helsinki University of Technology.

Mathias Creutz and Krista Lagus. 2007. Unsupervised models for morpheme segmentation and morphology learning. *ACM Transactions on Speech and Language Processing*, 4(1), January.

Adrià de Gispert, Sami Virpioja, Mikko Kurimo, and William Byrne. 2009. Minimum Bayes risk combination of translation hypotheses from alternative morphological decompositions. In *Proceedings of Human Language Technologies: The 2009 Annual Conference of the North American Chapter of the Association for Computational Linguistics, Companion Volume: Short Papers*, pages 73–76, Boulder, USA, June. Association for Computational Linguistics.

Teemu Hirsimäki, Mathias Creutz, Vesa Siivola, Mikko Kurimo, Sami Virpioja, and Janne Pylkkönen. 2006. Unlimited vocabulary speech recognition with morph language models applied to Finnish. *Computer Speech and Language*, 20(4):515–541.

Philipp Koehn and Hieu Hoang. 2007. Factored translation models. In *Proceedings of the EMNLP 2007*, pages 868–876, Prague, Czech Republic, June.

Philipp Koehn, Hieu Hoang, Alexandra Birch, Chris Callison-Burch, Marcello Federico, Nicola Bertoldi, Brooke Cowan, Wade Shen, Christine Moran, Richard Zens, Chris Dyer, Ondrej Bojar, Alexandra Constantin, and Evan Herbst. 2007. Moses: Open source toolkit for statistical machine translation. In *Annual Meeting of ACL, demonstration session*, pages 177–180, Czech Republic, June.

Shankar Kumar and William Byrne. 2004. Minimum bayes-risk decoding for statistical machine translation. In *Proceedings of the HLT-NAACL 2004*, pages 169–176.

Mikko Kurimo, Antti Puurula, Ebru Arisoy, Vesa Siivola, Teemu Hirsimäki, Janne Pylkkönen, Tanel Alumäe, and Murat Saraclar. 2006. Unlimited vocabulary speech recognition for agglutinative languages. In *Proceedings of the HLT-NAACL 2006*, pages 487–494, New York, USA.

Mikko Kurimo, Sami Virpioja, Ville T. Turunen, Graeme W. Blackwood, and William Byrne. 2009. Overview and results of Morpho Challenge 2009. In *Working Notes for the CLEF 2009 Workshop*, Corfu, Greece, September.

K. C. Sim, W. J. Byrne, M. J. F. Gales, H. Sahbi, and P. C. Woodl. 2007. Consensus network decoding for statistical machine translation system combination. In *IEEE Int. Conf. on Acoustics, Speech, and Signal Processing*.

Sami Virpioja and Oskar Kohonen. 2009. Unsupervised morpheme analysis with Allomorfessor. In *Working notes for the CLEF 2009 Workshop*, Corfu, Greece.

Sami Virpioja, Jaakko J. Väyrynen, Mathias Creutz, and Markus Sadeniemi. 2007. Morphology-aware statistical machine translation based on morphs induced in an unsupervised manner. In *Proceedings of the Machine Translation Summit XI*, pages 491–498, Copenhagen, Denmark, September.

Maximum Entropy Translation Model in Dependency-Based MT Framework

David Mareček, Martin Popel, Zdeněk Žabokrtský
Charles University in Prague, Institute of Formal and Applied Linguistics
Malostranské nám. 25, Praha 1, CZ-118 00, Czech Republic
{marecek,popel,zabokrtsky}@ufal.mff.cuni.cz

Abstract

Maximum Entropy Principle has been used successfully in various NLP tasks. In this paper we propose a forward translation model consisting of a set of maximum entropy classifiers: a separate classifier is trained for each (sufficiently frequent) source-side lemma. In this way the estimates of translation probabilities can be sensitive to a large number of features derived from the source sentence (including non-local features, features making use of sentence syntactic structure, etc.). When integrated into English-to-Czech dependency-based translation scenario implemented in the TectoMT framework, the new translation model significantly outperforms the baseline model (MLE) in terms of BLEU. The performance is further boosted in a configuration inspired by Hidden Tree Markov Models which combines the maximum entropy translation model with the target-language dependency tree model.

1 Introduction

The principle of maximum entropy states that, given known constraints, the probability distribution which best represents the current state of knowledge is the one with the largest entropy. Maximum entropy models based on this principle have been widely used in Natural Language Processing, e.g. for tagging (Ratnaparkhi, 1996), parsing (Charniak, 2000), and named entity recognition (Bender et al., 2003). Maximum entropy models have the following form

$$p(y|x) = \frac{1}{Z(x)} exp \sum_i \lambda_i f_i(x, y)$$

where f_i is a feature function, λ_i is its weight, and $Z(x)$ is the normalizing factor

$$Z(x) = \sum_y exp \sum_i \lambda_i f_i(x, y)$$

In statistical machine translation (SMT), translation model (TM) $p(t|s)$ is the probability that the string t from the target language is the translation of the string s from the source language. Typical approach in SMT is to use backward translation model $p(s|t)$ according to Bayes' rule and noisy-channel model. However, in this paper we deal only with the forward (direct) model.[1]

The idea of using maximum entropy for constructing forward translation models is not new. It naturally allows to make use of various features potentially important for correct choice of target-language expressions. Let us adopt a motivating example of such a feature from (Berger et al., 1996) (which contains the first usage of maxent translation model we are aware of): "If *house* appears within the next three words (e.g., the phrases *in the house* and *in the red house*), then *dans* might be a more likely [French] translation [of *in*]."

Incorporating non-local features extracted from the source sentence into the standard noisy-channel model in which only the backward translation model is available, is not possible. This drawback of the noisy-channel approach is typically compensated by using large target-language n-gram models, which can – in a result – play a role similar to that of a more elaborate (more context sensitive) forward translation model. However, we expect that it would be more beneficial to exploit both the parallel data and the monolingual data in a more balance fashion, rather than extract only a reduced amount of information from the parallel data and compensate it by large language model on the target side.

[1]A backward translation model is used only for pruning training data in this paper.

Proceedings of the Joint 5th Workshop on Statistical Machine Translation and MetricsMATR, pages 201–206,
Uppsala, Sweden, 15-16 July 2010.

A deeper discussion on the potential advantages of maximum entropy approach over the noisy-channel approach can be found in (Foster, 2000) and (Och and Ney, 2002), in which another successful applications of maxent translation models are shown. Log-linear translation models (instead of MLE) with rich feature sets are used also in (Ittycheriah and Roukos, 2007) and (Gimpel and Smith, 2009); the idea can be traced back to (Papineni et al., 1997).

What makes our approach different from the previously published works is that

1. we show how the maximum entropy translation model can be used in a dependency framework; we use deep-syntactic dependency trees (as defined in the Prague Dependency Treebank (Hajič et al., 2006)) as the transfer layer,

2. we combine the maximum entropy translation model with target-language dependency tree model and use tree-modified Viterbi search for finding the optimal lemmas labeling of the target-tree nodes.

The rest of the paper is structured as follows. In Section 2 we give a brief overview of the translation framework TectoMT in which the experiments are implemented. In Section 3 we describe how our translation models are constructed. Section 4 summarizes the experimental results, and Section 5 contains a summary.

2 Translation framework

We use tectogrammatical (deep-syntactic) layer of language representation as the transfer layer in the presented MT experiments. Tectogrammatics was introduced in (Sgall, 1967) and further elaborated within the Prague Dependency Treebank project (Hajič et al., 2006). On this layer, each sentence is represented as a tectogrammatical tree, whose main properties (from the MT viewpoint) are following: (1) nodes represent autosemantic words, (2) edges represent semantic dependencies (a node is an argument or a modifier of its parent), (3) there are no functional words (prepositions, auxiliary words) in the tree, and the autosemantic words appear only in their base forms (lemmas). Morphologically indispensable categories (such as number with nouns or tense with verbs, but not number with verbs as it is only imposed by agreement) are stored in separate node attributes (grammatemes).

The intuition behind the decision to use tectogrammatics for MT is the following: we believe that (1) tectogrammatics largely abstracts from language-specific means (inflection, agglutination, functional words etc.) of expressing non-lexical meanings and thus tectogrammatical trees are supposed to be highly similar across languages,[2] (2) it enables a natural transfer factorization,[3] (3) and local tree contexts in tectogrammatical trees carry more information (especially for lexical choice) than local linear contexts in the original sentences.[4]

In order to facilitate transfer of sentence 'syntactization', we work with tectogrammatical nodes enhanced with the formeme attribute (Žabokrtský et al., 2008), which captures the surface morphosyntactic form of a given tectogrammatical node in a compact fashion. For example, the value n:před+4 is used to label semantic nouns that should appear in an accusative form in a prepositional group with the preposition před in Czech. For English we use formemes such as n:subj (semantic noun (SN) in subject position), n:for+X (SN with preposition *for*), n:X+ago (SN with postposition *ago*), n:poss (possessive form of SN), v:because+fin (semantic verb (SV) as a subordinating finite clause introduced by *because*), v:without+ger (SV as a gerund after *without*), adj:attr (semantic adjective (SA) in attributive position), adj:compl (SA in complement position).

We have implemented our experiments in the TectoMT software framework, which already offers tool chains for analysis and synthesis of Czech and English sentences (Žabokrtský et al., 2008). The translation scenario proceeds as follows.

1. The input English text is segmented into sentences and tokens.

2. The tokens are lemmatized and tagged with Penn Treebank tags using the Morce tagger (Spoustová et al., 2007).

[2] This claim is supported by error analysis of output of tectogrammatics-based MT system presented in (Popel and Žabok/rtský, 2009), which shows that only 8 % of translation errors are caused by the (obviously too strong) assumption that the tectogrammatical tree of a sentence and the tree representing its translation are isomorphic.

[3] Morphological categories can be translated almost independently from lemmas, which makes parallel training data 'denser', especially when translating from/to a language with rich inflection such as Czech.

[4] Recall the house-is-somewhere-around feature in the introduction; again, the fact that we know the dominating (or dependent) word should allow to construct a more compact translation model, compared to n-gram models.

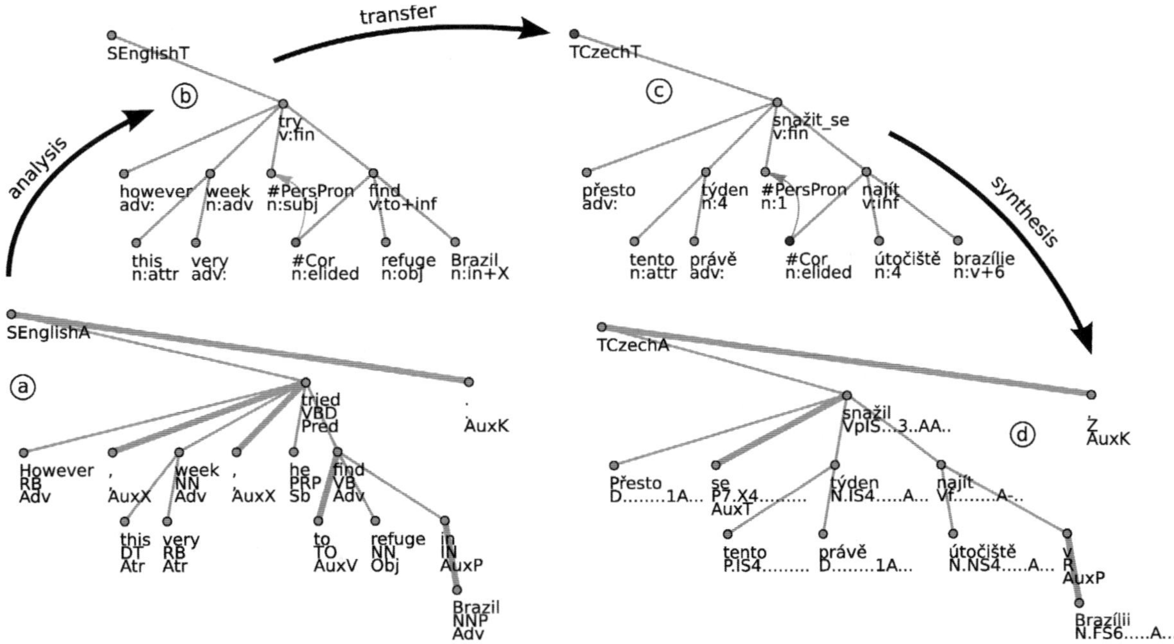

Figure 1: Intermediate sentence representations when translating the English sentence *"However, this very week, he tried to find refuge in Brazil."*, leading to the Czech translation *"Přesto se tento právě týden snažil najít útočiště v Brazílii."*.

3. Then the Maximum Spanning Tree parser (McDonald et al., 2005) is applied and a surface-syntax dependency tree (analytical tree in the PDT terminology) is created for each sentence (Figure 1a).

4. This tree is converted to a tectogrammatical tree (Figure 1b). Each autosemantic word with its associated functional words is collapsed into a single tectogrammatical node, labeled with lemma, formeme, and semantically indispensable morphologically categories; coreference is also resolved. Collapsing edges are depicted by wider lines in the Figure 1a.

5. The transfer phase follows, whose most difficult part consists in labeling the tree with target-side lemmas and formemes[5] (changes of tree topology are required relatively infrequently). See Figure 1c.

6. Finally, surface sentence shape (Figure 1d) is synthesized from the tectogrammatical tree, which is basically a reverse operation for the tectogrammatical analysis: adding punctuation and functional words, spreading morphological categories according to grammatical agreement, performing inflection (using Czech morphology database (Hajič, 2004)), arranging word order etc.

[5]In this paper we focus on using maximum entropy for translating lemmas, but it can be used for translating formemes as well.

3 Training the two models

In this section we describe two translation models used in the experiments: a baseline translation model based on maximum likelihood estimates (3.2), and a maximum entropy based model (3.3). Both models are trained using the same data (3.1).

In addition, we describe a target-language tree model (3.4), which can be combined with both the translation models using the Hidden Tree Markov Model approach and tree-modified Viterbi search, similarly to the approach of (Žabokrtský and Popel, 2009).

3.1 Data preprocessing common for both models

We used Czech-English parallel corpus CzEng 0.9 (Bojar and Žabokrtský, 2009) for training the translation models. CzEng 0.9 contains about 8 million sentence pairs, and also their tectogrammatical analyses and node-wise alignment.

We used only trees from training sections (about 80 % of the whole data), which contain around 30 million pairs of aligned tectogrammatical nodes.

From each pair of aligned tectogrammatical nodes, we extracted triples containing the source (English) lemma, the target (Czech) lemma, and the feature vector.

In order to reduce noise in the training data, we pruned the data in two ways. First, we disregarded all triples whose lemma pair did not occur at least twice in the whole data. Second, we computed forward and backward maximum likelihood (ML) translation models (target lemma given source lemma and vice versa) and deleted all triples whose probability according to one of the two models was lower than the threshold 0.01.

Then the forward ML translation model was reestimated using only the remaining data.

For a given pair of aligned nodes, the feature vector was of course derived only from the source-side node or from the tree which it belongs to. As already mentioned in the introduction, the advantage of the maximum entropy approach is that a rich and diverse set of features can be used, without limiting oneself to linearly local context. The following features (or, better to say, feature templates, as each categorical feature is in fact converted to a number of 0-1 features) were used:

- formeme and morphological categories of the given node,
- lemma, formeme and morphological categories of the governing node,
- lemmas and formemes of all child nodes,
- lemmas and formemes of the nearest linearly preceding and following nodes.

3.2 Baseline translation model

The baseline TM is basically the ML translation model resulting from the previous section, linearly interpolated with several translation models making use of regular word-formative derivations, which can be helpful for translating some less frequent (but regularly derived) lemmas. For example, one of the derivation-based models estimates the probability $p(\textit{zajímavě}|\textit{interestingly})$ (possibly unseen pair of deadjectival adverbs) by the value of $p(\textit{zajímavý}|\textit{interesting})$. More detailed description of these models goes beyond the scope of this paper; their weights in the interpolation are very small anyway.

3.3 MaxEnt translation model

The MaxEnt TM was created as follows:

1. training triples (source lemma, target lemma, feature vector) were disregarded if the source lemma was not seen at least 50 times (only the baseline model will be used for such lemmas),
2. the remaining triples were grouped by the English lemma (over 16 000 groups),
3. due to computational issues, the maximum number of triples in a group was reduced to 1000 by random selection,
4. a separate maximum entropy classifier was trained for each group (i.e., one classifier per source-side lemma) using `AI::MaxEntropy` Perl module,[6]
5. due to the more aggressive pruning of the training data, coverage of this model is smaller than that of the baseline model; in order not to loose the coverage, the two models were combined using linear interpolation (1:1).

Selected properties of the maximum entropy translation model (before the linear interpolation with the baseline model) are shown in Figure 2. We increased the size of the training data from 10 000 training triples up to 31 million and evaluated three relative quantities characterizing the translation models:

- *coverage* - relative frequency of source lemmas for which the translation model offers at least one translation,
- *first* - relative frequency of source lemmas for which the target lemmas offered as the first by the model ($argmax$) are the correct ones,
- *oracle* - relative frequency of source lemmas for which the correct target lemma is among the lemmas offered by the translation model.

As mentioned in Section 3.1, there are context features making use both of local linear context and local tree context. After training the MaxEnt model, there are about 4.5 million features with non-zero weight, out of which 1.1 million features

[6] `http://search.cpan.org/perldoc?AI::MaxEntropy`

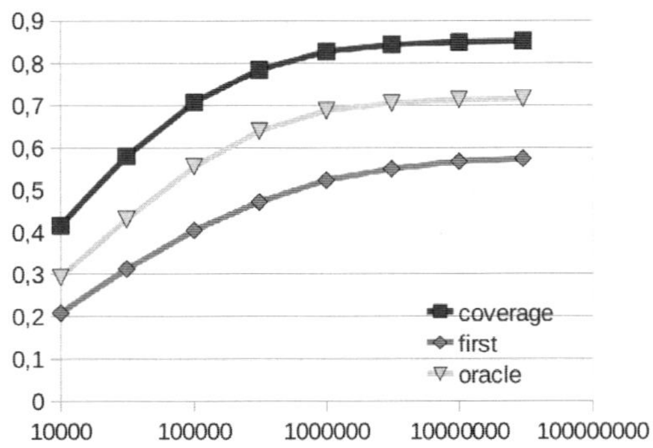

Figure 2: Three measures characterizing the MaxEnt translation model performance, depending on the training data size. Evaluated on aligned node pairs from the `dtest` portion of CzEng 0.9.

are derived from the linear context and 2.4 million features are derived from the tree context. This shows that the MaxEnt translation model employs the dependency structure intensively.

A preliminary analysis of feature weights seems to support our intuition that the linear context is preferred especially in the case of more stable collocations. For example, the most important features for translating the lemma *bare* are based on the lemma of the following noun: target lemma *bosý* (barefooted) is preferred if the following noun on the source side is *foot*, while *holý* (naked, unprotected) is preferred if *hand* follows.

The contribution of dependency-based features can be illustrated on translating the word *drop*. The greatest weight for choosing *kapka* (a droplet) as the translation is assigned to the feature capturing the presence of a node with formeme n:of+X among the node's children. The greatest weights in favor of *odhodit* (throw aside) are assigned to features capturing the presence of words such as *gun* or *weapon*, while the greatest weights in favor of *klesnout* (to come down) are assigned to features saying that there is the lemma *percent* or the percent sign among the children.

Of course, the lexical choice is influenced also by the governing lemmas, as can be illustrated with the word *native*. One can find a high-value feature for *rodilý* (native-born) saying that the source-side parent is *speaker*; similarly for *mateřský* (mother) with governing *tongue*, and *rodný* (home) with *land*.

Linear and tree features are occasionally used simultaneously: there are high-valued positive weights for translating *order* as *objednat* (reserve, give an order for st.) assigned both to tree-based features saying that there are words such as *pizza*, *meal* or *goods* and to linear features saying that the very following word is *some* or *two*.

configuration	BLEU	NIST
baseline TM	10.44	4.795
MaxEnt TM	11.77	5.135
baseline TM + TreeLM	11.77	5.038
MaxEnt TM + TreeLM	12.58	5.250

Table 1: BLEU and NIST evaluation of four configurations of our MT system; the WMT 2010 test set was used.

3.4 Target-language tree model

Although the MaxEnt TM captures some contextual dependencies that are covered by language models in the standard noisy-channel SMT, it may still be beneficial to exploit target-language models, because these can be trained on huge monolingual corpora. We use a target-language dependency tree model differing from standard n-gram model in two aspects:

- it uses tree context instead of linear context,
- it predicts tectogrammatical attributes (lemmas and formemes) instead of word forms.

In particular, our target-language tree model (TreeLM) predicts the probability of node's lemma and formeme given its parent's lemma and formeme. The optimal (lemma and formeme) labeling is found by tree-modified Viterbi search; for details see (Žabokrtský and Popel, 2009).

4 Experiments

When included into the above described translation scenario, the MaxEnt TM outperforms the baseline TM, be it used together with or without TreeLM. The results are summarized in Table 1. The improvement is statistically significant according to paired bootstrap resampling test (Koehn, 2004). In the configuration without TreeLM the improvement is greater (1.33 BLEU) than with TreeLM (0.81 BLEU), which confirms our hypothesis that MaxEnt TM captures some of the contextual dependencies resolved otherwise by language models.

5 Conclusions

We have introduced a maximum entropy translation model in dependency-based MT which enables exploiting a large number of feature functions in order to obtain more accurate translations. The BLEU evaluation proved significant improvement over the baseline solution based on the translation model with maximum likelihood estimates. However, the performance of this system still below the state of the art (which is around BLEU 16 for the English-to-Czech direction).

Acknowledgments

This research was supported by the grants MSM0021620838, MŠMT ČR LC536, FP7-ICT-2009-4-247762 (Faust), FP7-ICT-2007-3-231720 (EuroMatrix Plus), GA201/09/H057, and GAUK 116310. We thank two anonymous reviewers for helpful comments.

References

Oliver Bender, Franz Josef Och, and Hermann Ney. 2003. Maximum entropy models for named entity recognition. In *Proceedings of CoNLL 2003*, pages 148–151.

Adam L. Berger, Vincent J. Della Pietra, and Stephen A. Della Pietra. 1996. A maximum entropy approach to natural language processing. *Computational linguistics*, 22(1):39–71.

Ondřej Bojar and Zdeněk Žabokrtský. 2009. CzEng 0.9, Building a Large Czech-English Automatic Parallel Treebank. *The Prague Bulletin of Mathematical Linguistics*, 92:63–83.

Eugene Charniak. 2000. A maximum-entropy-inspired parser. In *Proceedings of the 1st North American chapter of the ACL conference*, pages 132–139, San Francisco, USA.

George Foster. 2000. A maximum entropy/minimum divergence translation model. In *Proceedings of the 38th Annual Meeting on Association for Computational Linguistics*, pages 45–52, Morristown, USA. Association for Computational Linguistics.

Kevin Gimpel and Noah A. Smith. 2009. Feature-rich translation by quasi-synchronous lattice parsing. In *Proceedings of the 2009 Conference on Empirical Methods in Natural Language Processing*, pages 219–228, Morristown, USA. Association for Computational Linguistics.

Jan Hajič et al. 2006. Prague Dependency Treebank 2.0. CD-ROM, Linguistic Data Consortium, LDC Catalog No.: LDC2006T01, Philadelphia.

Jan Hajič. 2004. *Disambiguation of Rich Inflection – Computational Morphology of Czech*. Charles University – The Karolinum Press, Prague.

Abraham Ittycheriah and Salim Roukos. 2007. Direct translation model 2. In Candace L. Sidner, Tanja Schultz, Matthew Stone, and ChengXiang Zhai, editors, *HLT-NAACL*, pages 57–64. The Association for Computational Linguistics.

Philipp Koehn. 2004. Statistical significance tests for machine translation evaluation. In *Proceedings of EMNLP*, volume 4, pages 388–395.

Ryan McDonald, Fernando Pereira, Kiril Ribarov, and Jan Hajič. 2005. Non-projective dependency parsing using spanning tree algorithms. In *Proceedings of HLT / EMNLP*, pages 523–530, Vancouver, Canada.

Franz Josef Och and Hermann Ney. 2002. Discriminative training and maximum entropy models for statistical machine translation. In *Proceedings of ACL*, pages 295–302.

Kishore A. Papineni, Salim Roukos, and Todd R. Ward. 1997. Feature-based language understanding. In *European Conference on Speech Communication and Technology (EUROSPEECH)*, pages 1435–1438, Rhodes, Greece, September.

Martin Popel and Zdeněk Žabok/rtský. 2009. Improving English-Czech Tectogrammatical MT. *The Prague Bulletin of Mathematical Linguistics*, (92):1–20.

Adwait Ratnaparkhi. 1996. A maximum entropy model for part-of-speech tagging. In *In Proceedings of EMNLP'96*, pages 133–142.

Petr Sgall. 1967. *Generativní popis jazyka a česká deklinace*. Academia, Prague.

Drahomíra Spoustová, Jan Hajič, Jan Votrubec, Pavel Krbec, and Pavel Květoň. 2007. The Best of Two Worlds: Cooperation of Statistical and Rule-Based Taggers for Czech. In *Proceedings of the Workshop on Balto-Slavonic Natural Language Processing, ACL 2007*, pages 67–74, Praha.

Zdeněk Žabokrtský and Martin Popel. 2009. Hidden markov tree model in dependency-based machine translation. In *Proceedings of the ACL-IJCNLP 2009 Conference Short Papers*, pages 145–148, Suntec, Singapore.

Zdeněk Žabokrtský, Jan Ptáček, and Petr Pajas. 2008. TectoMT: Highly Modular MT System with Tectogrammatics Used as Transfer Layer. In *Proceedings of the 3rd Workshop on Statistical Machine Translation, ACL*, pages 167–170.

UCH-UPV English–Spanish system for WMT10

Francisco Zamora-Martínez
Dep. de Física, Matemáticas y Computación
Universidad CEU-Cardenal Herrera
Alfara del Patriarca (Valencia), Spain
fzamora@dsic.upv.es

Germán Sanchis-Trilles
Instituto Tecnológico de Informática
Universidad Politécnica de Valencia
Valencia, Spain
gsanchis@dsic.upv.es

Abstract

This paper describes the system developed in collabaration between UCH and UPV for the 2010 WMT. For this year's workshop, we present a system for English-Spanish translation. Output N-best lists were rescored via a target Neural Network Language Model, yielding improvements in the final translation quality as measured by BLEU and TER.

1 Introduction

In Statistical Machine Translation (SMT), the goal is to translate a sentence $\mathbf{f}$ from a given source language into an equivalent sentence $\hat{\mathbf{e}}$ from a certain target language. Such statement is typically formalised by means of the so-called log-linear models (Papineni et al., 1998; Och and Ney, 2002) as follows:

$$\hat{\mathbf{e}} = \underset{\mathbf{e}}{\text{argmax}} \sum_{k=1}^{K} \lambda_k h_k(\mathbf{f}, \mathbf{e}) \qquad (1)$$

where $h_k(\mathbf{f}, \mathbf{e})$ is a score function representing an important feature for the translation of $\mathbf{f}$ into $\mathbf{e}$, K is the number of models (or features) and λ_k are the weights of the log-linear combination. Typically, the weights λ_k are optimised during the tuning stage with the use of a development set. Such features typically include the *target language model* $p(\mathbf{e})$, which is one of the core components of an SMT system. In fact, most of the times it is assigned a relatively high weight in the log-linear combination described above. Traditionally, language modelling techniques have been classified into two main groups, the first one including traditional grammars such as context-free grammars, and the second one comprising more statistical, corpus-based models, such as n-gram models. In order to assign a probability to a given word, such models rely on the assumption that such probability depends on the previous *history*, i.e. the $n-1$ preceding words in the utterance. Nowadays, n-gram models have become a "de facto" standard for language modelling in state-of-the-art SMT systems.

In the present work, we present a system which follows a coherent and natural evolution of probabilistic Language Models. Specifically, we propose the use of a continuous space language model trained in the form of a Neural Network Language Model (NN LM).

The use of continuous space representation of language has been successfully applied in recent NN approaches to language modelling (Bengio et al., 2003; Schwenk and Gauvain, 2002; Castro-Bleda and Prat, 2003; Schwenk et al., 2006). However, the use of Neural Network Language Models (NN LMs) (Bengio, 2008) in state-of-the-art SMT systems is not so popular. The only comprehensive work refers to (Schwenk, 2010), where the target LM is presented in the form of a fully-connected Multilayer Perceptron.

The presented system combines a standard, state-of-the-art SMT system with a NN LM via log-linear combination and N-best output re-scoring. We chose to participate in the English-Spanish direction.

2 Neural Network Language Models

In SMT the most extended language models are n-grams (Bahl et al., 1983; Jelinek, 1997; Bahl et al., 1983). They compute the probability of each word given the context of the $n-1$ previous words:

$$p(s_1 \dots s_{|S|}) \approx \prod_{i=1}^{|S|} p(s_i | s_{i-n+1} \dots s_{i-1}) \,. \qquad (2)$$

where S is the sequence of words for which we want compute the probability, and $s_i \in S$, from a vocabulary Ω.

Proceedings of the Joint 5th Workshop on Statistical Machine Translation and MetricsMATR, pages 207–211,
Uppsala, Sweden, 15-16 July 2010.

A NN LM is a statistical LM which follows equation (2) as n-grams do, but where the probabilities that appear in that expression are estimated with a NN (Bengio et al., 2003; Castro-Bleda and Prat, 2003; Schwenk, 2007; Bengio, 2008). The model naturally fits under the probabilistic interpretation of the outputs of the NNs: if a NN, in this case a MLP, is trained as a classifier, the outputs associated to each class are estimations of the posterior probabilities of the defined classes (Bishop, 1995).

The training set for a LM is a sequence $s_1 s_2 \ldots s_{|S|}$ of words from a vocabulary Ω. In order to train a NN to predict the next word given a history of length $n-1$, each input word must be encoded. A natural representation is a local encoding following a "1-of-$|\Omega|$" scheme. The problem of this encoding for tasks with large vocabularies (as is typically the case) is the huge size of the resulting NN. We have solved this problem following the ideas of (Bengio et al., 2003; Schwenk, 2007), learning a distributed representation for each word. Figure 1 illustrates the architecture of the feed-forward NN used to estimate the NN LM:

- The input is composed of words $s_{i-n+1}, \ldots, s_{i-1}$ of equation (2). Each word is represented using a local encoding.

- P is the projection layer of the input words, formed by $P_{i-n+1}, \ldots, P_{i-1}$ subsets of projection units. The subset of projection units P_j represents the distributed encoding of input word s_j. The weights of this projection layer are linked, that is, the weights from each local encoding of input word s_j to the corresponding subset of projection units P_j are the same for all input words. After training, the codification layer is removed from the network by pre-computing a table of size $|\Omega|$ which serves as a distributed encoding.

- H denotes the hidden layer.

- The output layer O has $|\Omega|$ units, one for each word of the vocabulary.

This n-gram NN LM predicts the posterior probability of each word of the vocabulary given the $n-1$ previous words. A single forward pass of the MLP gives $p(\omega|s_{i-n+1} \ldots s_{i-1})$ for every word $\omega \in \Omega$.

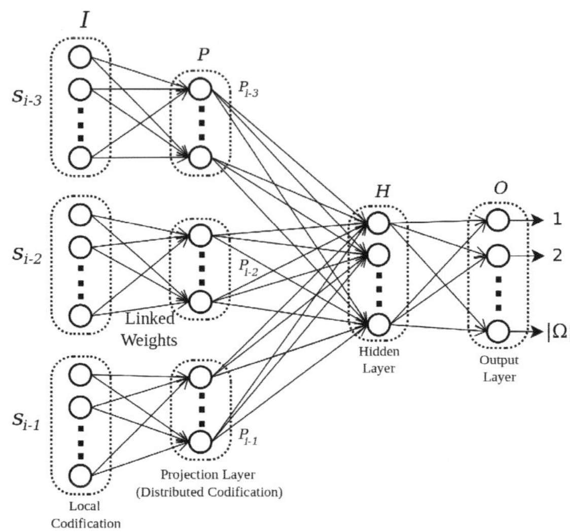

Figure 1: Architecture of the continuous space NN LM during training. The input words are $s_{i-n+1}, \ldots, s_{i-1}$ (in this example, the input words are s_{i-3}, s_{i-2}, and s_{i-1} for a 4-gram). I, P, H, and O are the input, projection, hidden, and output layer, respectively, of the MLP.

The major advantage of the connectionist approach is the automatic smoothing performed by the neural network estimators. This smoothing is done via a continuous space representation of the input words. Learning the probability of n-grams, together with their representation in a continous space (Bengio et al., 2003), is an appropriate approximation for large vocabulary tasks. However, one of the drawbacks of such approach is the high computational cost entailed whenever the NN LM is computed directly, with no simplification whatsoever. For this reason, in this paper we will be restricting vocabulary size.

3 Experiments

3.1 Baseline system

For building the baseline SMT system, we used the open-source SMT toolkit Moses (Koehn et al., 2007), in its standard setup. The decoder includes a log-linear model comprising a phrase-based translation model, a language model, a lexicalised distortion model and word and phrase penalties. The weights of the log-linear interpolation were optimised by means of MERT (Och, 2003).

For the baseline LM, we computed a regular n-gram LM with Kneser-Ney smoothing (Kneser and Ney, 1995) and interpolation by means of the SRILM (Stolcke, 2002) toolkit. Specifically, we trained a 6-gram LM on the larger Spanish corpora available (i.e. UN, News-Shuffled and Europarl), and a 5-gram LM on the News-Commentary corpus. Once these LMs had been built, they were finally interpolated so as to maximise the perplexity of the News-Commentary test set of the 2008 shared task. This was done so according to preliminary investigation.

3.2 NN LM system architecture

The presented systems follow previous works of (Schwenk et al., 2006; Khalilov et al., 2008; Schwenk and Koehn, 2008; Schwenk, 2010) where the use of a NN LM helps achieving better performance in the final system.

The NN LM was incorporated to the baseline system via log-linear combination, adding a new feature to the output N-best list generated by the baseline system (in this case $N = 1\,000$). Specifically, the NN LM was used to compute the log-probability of each sentence within the N-best list. Then, the scores of such list were extended with our new, NN LM-based feature. This being done, we optimised the coefficients of the log-linear interpolation by means of MERT, taking into account the newly introduced feature. Finally the list was re-scored and the best hypothesis was extracted and returned as final output. Figure 2 shows a diagram of the system structure.

3.3 Experimental setup and results

NN LM was trained with the concatenation of the News-shuffled and News-Commentary10 Spanish corpora. Other language resources were discarded due to the large amount of computational resources that would have been needed for training a NN LM with such material. Table 1 shows some statistics of the corpora. In order to reduce the complexity of the model, the vocabulary was restricted to the 20K more frequent words in the concatenation of news corpora. Using this restricted vocabulary implies that 6.4% of the running words of the news-test2008 set, and 7.3% of the running words within the official 2010 test set, will be considered as unknown for our system. In addition, the vocabulary includes a special token for unknown words used for compute probabilities when an unknown word appears, as described in Equation 2.

Table 1: Spanish corpora statistics. NC stands for News-Commentary and UN for United Nations, while $|\Omega|$ stands for vocabulary size, and M/K for millions/thousands of elements.

Set	# Lines	# Words	$\|\Omega\|$
NC	108K	2.96M	67K
News-Shuffled	3.86M	107M	512K
Europarl	1.82M	51M	172K
UN	6.22M	214M	411K
Total	3.96M	110M	521K

A 6-gram NN LM was trained for this task, based in previous works (Khalilov et al., 2008). The distributed encoding input layer consists of 640 units (128 for each word), the hidden layer has 500 units, and the output layer has 20K units, one for each word in the restricted vocabulary. The total number of weights in the network was 10 342 003. The training procedure was conducted by means of the stochastic back-propagation algorithm with weight decay, with a replacement of 300K training samples and 200K validation samples in each training epoch. The training and validation sets were randomly extracted from the concatenation of news corpora. The training set consisted of 102M words (3M sentences) and validation set 8M words (300K sentences). The network needed 129 epochs for achieving convergence, resulting in 38.7M and 25.8M training and validation samples respectively. For training the NN LM we used the April toolkit (España-Boquera et al., 2007; Zamora-Martínez et al., 2009), which implements a pattern recognition and neural networks toolkit. The perplexity achieved by the 6-gram NN LM in the Spanish news-test08 development set was 116, versus 94 obtained with a standard 6-gram language model with interpolation and Kneser-Ney smoothing (Kneser and Ney, 1995).

The number of sentences in the N-best list was set to 1 000 unique output sentences. Results can be seen in Table 2. In order to assess the reliability of such results, we computed pairwise improvement intervals as described in (Koehn, 2004), by means of bootstrapping with 1000 bootstrap iterations and at a 95% confidence level. Such confidence test reported the improvements to be statistically significant.

Four more experiments have done in order to study the influence of the N-best list size in the

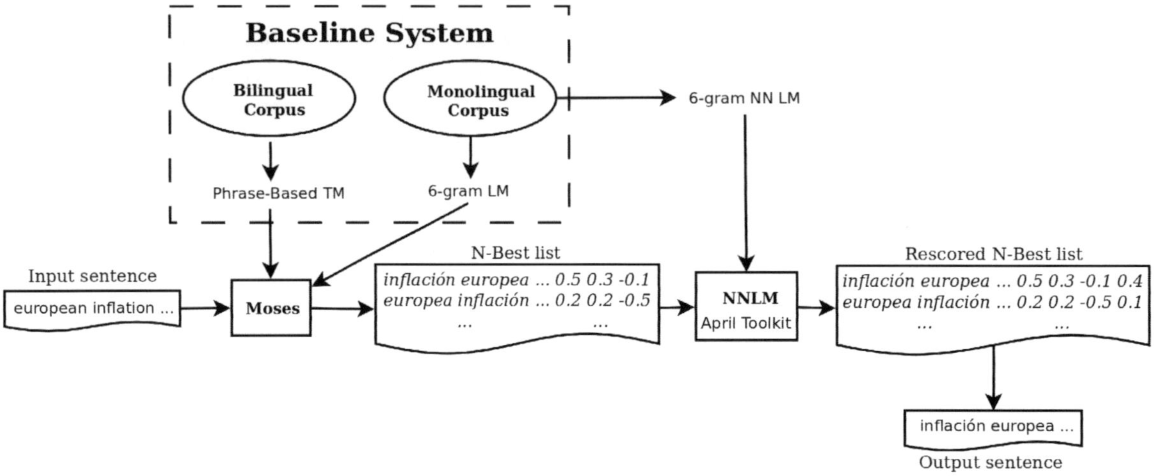

Figure 2: Architecture of the system.

Table 2: English-Spanish translation quality for development and official test set. Results are given in BLEU/TER.

	test08 (dev)	test10 (test)
Baseline	24.8/60.0	26.7/55.1
NN LM	25.2/59.6	27.8/54.0

Table 3: Test set BLEU/TER performance for each N-best list size.

N-best list size	BLEU	TER
200	27.5	54.2
400	27.6	54.2
600	27.7	54.1
800	27.6	54.2
1000	27.8	54.0

performance achieved by the NN LM rescoring. For each N-best list size (200, 400, 600 and 800) the weights of the log-linear interpolation were optimised by means of MERT over the test08 set. Table 3 shows the test results for each N-best list size using the correspondent optimised weights. As it can be seen, the size of the N-best list seems to have an impact on the final translation quality produced. Although in this case the results are not statistically significant for each size step, the final difference (from 27.5 to 27.8) is already significant.

4 Conclusions

In this paper, an improved SMT system by using a NN LM was presented. Specifically, it has been shown that the final translation quality, as measured by BLEU and TER, is improved over the quality obtained with a state-of-the-art SMT system. Such improvements, of 1.1 BLEU points, were found to be statistically significant. The system presented uses a neural network only for computing the language model probabilities. As an immediate future work, we intend to compute the language model by means of a linear interpolation of several neural networks. Another interesting idea is to integrate the NN LM within the decoder itself, instead of performing a subsequent rescoring step. This can be done extending the ideas presented in a previous work (Zamora-Martínez et al., 2009), in which the evaluation of NN LM is significantly sped-up.

Acknowledgments

This paper was partially supported by the EC (FEDER/FSE) and by the Spanish Government (MICINN and MITyC) under the MIPRCV "Consolider Ingenio 2010" program (CSD2007-00018), iTrans2 (TIN2009-14511) project and the erudito.com (TSI-020110-2009-439) project.

References

L. R. Bahl, F. Jelinek, and R. L. Mercer. 1983. A Maximum Likelihood Approach to Continuous Speech Recognition. *IEEE Trans. on Pat. Anal. and Mach. Intel.*, 5(2):179–190.

Y. Bengio, R. Ducharme, P. Vincent, and C. Jauvin. 2003. A Neural Probabilistic Language Model. *Journal of Machine Learning Research*, 3(2):1137–1155.

Y. Bengio. 2008. Neural net language models. *Scholarpedia*, 3(1):3881.

C. M. Bishop. 1995. *Neural networks for pattern recognition*. Oxford University Press.

M.J. Castro-Bleda and F. Prat. 2003. New Directions in Connectionist Language Modeling. In *Computational Methods in Neural Modeling*, volume 2686 of *LNCS*, pages 598–605. Springer-Verlag.

S. España-Boquera, F. Zamora-Martínez, M.J. Castro-Bleda, and J. Gorbe-Moya. 2007. Efficient BP Algorithms for General Feedforward Neural Networks. In *Bio-inspired Modeling of Cognitive Tasks*, volume 4527 of *LNCS*, pages 327–336. Springer.

F. Jelinek. 1997. *Statistical Methods for Speech Recognition*. Language, Speech, and Communication. The MIT Press.

M. Khalilov, J. A. R. Fonollosa, F. Zamora-Martínez, M. J. Castro-Bleda, and S. España-Boquera. 2008. Neural network language models for translation with limited data. In *20th International Conference on Tools with Artificial Intelligence, ICTAI'08*, pages 445–451, november.

R. Kneser and H. Ney. 1995. Improved backing-off for m-gram language modeling. *IEEE Int. Conf. on Acoustics, Speech and Signal Processing*, II:181–184, May.

P. Koehn et al. 2007. Moses: Open Source Toolkit for Statistical Machine Translation. In *Proc. of the ACL Demo and Poster Sessions*, pages 177–180, Prague, Czech Republic.

P. Koehn. 2004. Statistical significance tests for machine translation evaluation. In *Proc. of EMNLP*, pages 388–395.

F. Och and H. Ney. 2002. Discriminative training and maximum entropy models for statistical machine translation. In *Proc. of ACL'02*, pages 295–302.

F.J. Och. 2003. Minimum Error Rate Training in Statistical Machine Translation. In *Proc. of ACL*, pages 160–167, Sapporo, Japan.

K. Papineni, S. Roukos, and T. Ward. 1998. Maximum likelihood and discriminative training of direct translation models. In *Proc. of ICASSP*, pages 189–192.

H. Schwenk and J. L. Gauvain. 2002. Connectionist language modeling for large vocabulary continuous speech recognition. In *Proceedings of the International Conference on Acoustics, Speech, and Signal Processing (ICASSP'02)*, pages 765–768, Orlando, Florida (USA), May.

H. Schwenk and P. Koehn. 2008. Large and diverse language models for statistical machine translation. In *International Joint Conference on Natural Language Processing*, pages 661–668.

H. Schwenk, D. Déchelotte, and J. L. Gauvain. 2006. Continuous space language models for statistical machine translation. In *Proceedings of the COLING/ACL 2006 Main Conference Poster Sessions*, pages 723–730.

H. Schwenk. 2007. Continuous space language models. *Computer Speech and Language*, 21(3):492–518.

H. Schwenk. 2010. Continuous space language models for statistical machine translation. *The Prague Bulletin of Mathematical Linguistics*, 93.

A. Stolcke. 2002. SRILM – an extensible language modeling toolkit. In *Proc. of ICSLP'02*, pages 901–904, September.

F. Zamora-Martínez, M.J. Castro-Bleda, and S. España-Boquera. 2009. Fast Evaluation of Connectionist Language Models. In *International Work-Conference on Artificial Neural Networks*, volume 5517 of *LNCS*, pages 33–40. Springer.

Hierarchical Phrase-Based MT at the Charles University for the WMT 2010 Shared Task

Daniel Zeman
Charles University in Prague, Institute of Formal and Applied Linguistics (ÚFAL)
Univerzita Karlova v Praze, Ústav formální a aplikované lingvistiky (ÚFAL)
Malostranské náměstí 25, Praha, CZ-11800, Czechia
zeman@ufal.mff.cuni.cz

Abstract

We describe our experiments with hierarchical phrase-based machine translation for WMT 2010 Shared Task. We provide a detailed description of our configuration and data so the results are replicable. For English-to-Czech translation, we experiment with several datasets of various sizes and with various preprocessing sequences. For the other 7 translation directions, we just present the baseline results.

1 Introduction

Czech is a language with rich morphology (both inflectional and derivational) and relatively free word order. In fact, the predicate-argument structure, often encoded by fixed word order in English, is usually captured by inflection (especially the system of 7 grammatical cases) in Czech. While the free word order of Czech is a problem when translating to English (the text should be parsed first in order to determine the syntactic functions and the English word order), generating correct inflectional affixes is indeed a challenge for English-to-Czech systems. Furthermore, the multitude of possible Czech word forms (at least order of magnitude higher than in English) makes the data sparseness problem really severe, hindering both directions.

There are numerous ways how these issues could be addressed. For instance, parsing and syntax-aware reordering of the source-language sentences can help with the word order differences (same goal could be achieved by a reordering model or a synchronous context-free grammar in a hierarchical system). Factored translation, a secondary language model of morphological tags or even a morphological generator are some of the possible solutions to the poor-to-rich translation issues.

Our submission to the shared task should reveal where a pure hierarchical system stands in this jungle and what of the above mentioned ideas match the phenomena the system suffers from. Although our primary focus lies on English-to-Czech translation, we also report the accuracy of the same system on moderately-sized corpora for the other three languages and seven translation directions.

2 The Translation System

Our translation system belongs to the hierarchical phrase-based class (Chiang, 2007), i.e. phrase pairs with nonterminals (rules of a synchronous context-free grammar) are extracted from symmetrized word alignments and subsequently used by the decoder. We use Joshua, a Java-based open-source implementation of the hierarchical decoder (Li et al., 2009), release 1.1.[1]

Word alignment was computed using the first three steps of the `train-factored-phrase-model.perl` script packed with Moses[2] (Koehn et al., 2007). This includes the usual combination of word clustering using `mkcls`[3] (Och, 1999), two-way word alignment using GIZA++[4] (Och and Ney, 2003), and alignment symmetrization using the *grow-diag-final-and* heuristic (Koehn et al., 2003).

For language modeling we use the SRILM toolkit[5] (Stolcke, 2002) with modified Kneser-Ney smoothing (Kneser and Ney, 1995; Chen and Goodman, 1998).

We use the Z-MERT implementation of minimum error rate training (Zaidan, 2009). The following settings have been used for Joshua and Z-MERT:

[1] http://sourceforge.net/projects/joshua/
[2] http://www.statmt.org/moses/
[3] http://fjoch.com/mkcls.html
[4] http://fjoch.com/GIZA++.html
[5] http://www-speech.sri.com/projects/srilm/

Proceedings of the Joint 5th Workshop on Statistical Machine Translation and MetricsMATR, pages 212–215,
Uppsala, Sweden, 15-16 July 2010.

- Grammar extraction: `--maxPhraseLength=5`
- Decoding: `span_limit=10` `fuzz1=0.1` `fuzz2=0.1` `max_n_items=30` `relative_threshold=10.0` `max_n_rules=50` `rule_relative_threshold=10.0`
- N-best decoding: `use_unique_nbest=true` `use_tree_nbest=false` `add_combined_cost=true` `top_n=300`
- Z-MERT: `-m BLEU 4 closest -maxIt 5 -ipi 20`

3 Data and Pre-processing Pipeline

3.1 Baseline Experiments

We applied our system to all eight language pairs. However, for all but one we ran only a baseline experiment. From the data point of view the baseline experiments were even more constrained than the organizers of the shared task suggested. We did not use the Europarl corpus, we only used the News Commentary corpus[6] for training. The target side of the News Commentary corpus was also the only source to train the language model. Table 1 shows the size of the corpus.

Corpus	SentPairs	Tokens xx	Tokens en
cs-en	94,742	2,077,947	2,327,656
de-en	100,269	2,524,909	2,484,445
es-en	98,598	2,742,935	2,472,860
fr-en	84,624	2,595,165	2,137,407

Table 1: Number of sentence pairs and tokens for every language pair in the News Commentary corpus. Unlike the organizers of the shared task, we stick with the standard ISO 639 language codes: cs = Czech, de = German, en = English, es = Spanish, fr = French.

Note that in some cases the grammar extraction algorithm in Joshua fails if the training corpus contains sentences that are too long. Removing sentences of 100 or more tokens (per advice by Joshua developers) effectively healed all failures. Unfortunately, for the baseline corpora the loss of training material was still considerable and resulted in drop of BLEU score, though usually insignificant.[7]

The News Test 2008 data set (2051 sentences in each language) was used as development data for MERT. BLEU scores reported in this paper were computed on the News Test 2009 set (2525 sentences each language). The official scores on News Test 2010 are given only in the main WMT 2010 paper.

Only lowercased data were used for the baseline experiments.

3.2 English-to-Czech

A separate set of experiments has been conducted for the English-to-Czech direction and larger data were used. We used CzEng 0.9 (Bojar and Žabokrtský, 2009)[8] as our main parallel corpus. Following CzEng authors' request, we did not use sections 8* and 9* reserved for evaluation purposes.

As the baseline training dataset ("Small" in the following) only the news section of CzEng was used. For large-scale experiments ("Large" in the following), we used all CzEng together with the EMEA corpus[9] (Tiedemann, 2009).[10]

As our monolingual data we use the monolingual data provided by WMT10 organizers for Czech. Table 2 shows the sizes of these corpora.

Corpus	SentPairs	Tokens cs	Tokens en
Small	126,144	2,645,665	2,883,893
Large	7,543,152	79,057,403	89,018,033
Mono	13,042,040	210,507,305	

Table 2: Number of sentences and tokens in the Czech-English corpora.

Again, the official WMT 2010[11] development set (News Test 2008, 2051 sentences each language) and test set (News Test 2009, 2525 sentences each language) are used for MERT and evaluation, respectively. The official scores on News Test 2010 are given only in the main WMT 2010 paper.

We use a slightly modified tokenization rules compared to CzEng export format. Most notably, we normalize English abbreviated negation and auxiliary verbs ("couldn't" → "could not") and

[6] Available for download at `http://www.statmt.org/wmt10/translation-task.html` using the link "Parallel corpus training data".

[7] Table 1 and Table 2 present statistics *before* removing the long sentences.

[8] `http://ufal.mff.cuni.cz/czeng/`

[9] `http://urd.let.rug.nl/tiedeman/OPUS/EMEA.php`

[10] Unfortunately, the EMEA corpus is badly tokenized on the Czech side with fractional numbers split into several tokens (e.g. "3, 14"). We attempted to reconstruct the original detokenized form using a small set of regular expressions.

[11] `http://www.statmt.org/wmt10`

attempt at normalizing quotation marks to distinguish between opening and closing one following proper typesetting rules.

The rest of our pre-processing pipeline matches the processing employed in CzEng (Bojar and Žabokrtský, 2009).[12] We use "supervised truecasing", meaning that we cast the case of the lemma to the form, relying on our morphological analyzers and taggers to identify proper names, all other words are lowercased.

4 Experiments

All BLEU scores were computed directly by Joshua on the News Test 2009 set. Note that they differ from what the official evaluation script would report, due to different tokenization.

4.1 Baseline Experiments

The set of baseline experiments with all translation directions involved running the system on lowercased News Commentary corpora. Word alignments were computed on 4-character stems (including the en-cs and cs-en directions). A trigram language model was trained on the target side of the parallel corpus.

Direction	BLEU
en-cs	0.0905
en-de	0.1114
cs-en	0.1471
de-en	0.1617
en-es	0.1966
en-fr	0.2001
fr-en	0.2020
es-en	0.2025

Table 3: Lowercased BLEU scores of the baseline experiments on News Test 2009 data.

4.2 English-to-Czech

The extended (non-baseline) English-to-Czech experiments were trained on larger parallel and monolingual data, described in Section 3.2. Note that the dataset denoted as "Small" still falls into the constrained task because it only uses CzEng 0.9 and the WMT 2010 monolingual data.

Word alignments were computed on lemmatized version of the parallel corpus. Hexagram language model was trained on the monolingual data. Truecased data were used for training, as described above; the BLEU scores of these experiments in Table 4 are computed on truecased system output.

Setup	BLEU
Baseline	0.0905
Small	0.1012
Large	0.1300

Table 4: BLEU scores (lowercased baseline, truecased rest) of the English-to-Czech experiments, including the baseline experiment with News Commentary, mentioned earlier.

As for the official evaluation on News Test 2010, we used the Small setup as our *primary submission*, and the Large setup as *secondary* despite its better results. The reason was that it was not clear whether the experiment would be finished in time for the official evaluation.[13]

An interesting perspective on the three en-cs models is provided by the feature weights optimized during MERT. We can see in Table 5 that the small and relatively weak baseline LM is trusted less than the most influential translation feature while for large parallel data and even much larger LM the weights are distributed more evenly.

Setup	LM	Pt_0	Pt_1	Pt_2	WP
Baseline	1.0	1.55	0.51	0.63	−2.63
Small	1.0	1.03	0.72	−0.09	−0.34
Large	1.0	0.98	0.97	−0.02	−0.82

Table 5: Feature weights are relative to the weight of LM, the score by the language model. Then there are the three translation features: $Pt_0 = P(e|f)$, $Pt_1 = P_{lex}(f|e)$ and $Pt_2 = P_{lex}(e|f)$. WP is the word penalty.

4.3 Efficiency

The machines on which the experiments were conducted are 64bit Intel Xeon dual core 2.8 GHz CPUs with 32 GB RAM.

Word alignment of each baseline corpus took about 1 hour, time needed for data preprocessing

[12] Due to the subsequent processing, incl. parsing, the tokenization of English follows PennTreebenk style. The rather unfortunate convention of treating hyphenated words as single tokens increases our out-of-vocabulary rate.

[13] In fact, it was not finished in time. Due to a failure of a MERT run, we used feature weights from the primary submission for the secondary one, too.

and training of the language model was negligible. Grammar extraction took about four hours but it could be parallelized. For decoding the test data were split into 20 chunks that were processed in parallel. One MERT iteration, including decoding, took from 30 minutes to 1 hour.

Training the large en-cs models requires more careful engineering. The grammar extraction easily consumes over 20 GB memory so it is important to make sure Java really has access to it. We parallelized the extraction in the same way as we had done with the decoding; even so, about 5 hours were needed to complete the extraction. The decoder now must use the SWIG-linked SRILM library because Java-based language modeling is too slow and memory-consuming. Otherwise, the decoding times are comparable to the baseline experiments.

5 Conclusion

We have described the hierarchical phrase-based SMT system we used for the WMT 2010 shared task. For English-to-Czech translation, we discussed experiments with large data from the point of view of both the translation accuracy and efficiency.

This has been our first attempt to switch to hierarchical SMT and we have not gone too far beyond just putting together the infrastructure and applying it to the available data. Nevertheless, our en-cs experiments not only confirm that more data helps; in the Small and Large setup, the data was not only larger than in Baseline, it also underwent a more refined preprocessing. In particular, we took advantage of the Czeng corpus being lemmatized to produce better word alignment; also, the truecasing technique helped to better target named entities.

Acknowledgements

The work on this project was supported by the grant MSM0021620838 by the Czech Ministry of Education.

References

Ondřej Bojar and Zdeněk Žabokrtský. 2009. Czeng 0.9: Large parallel treebank with rich annotation. *The Prague Bulletin of Mathematical Linguistics*, 92:63–83.

Stanley F. Chen and Joshua Goodman. 1998. An empirical study of smoothing techniques for language modeling. In *Technical report TR-10-98, Computer Science Group*, Harvard, MA, USA, August. Harvard University.

David Chiang. 2007. Hierarchical Phrase-Based Translation. *Computational Linguistics*, 33(2):201–228.

Reinhard Kneser and Hermann Ney. 1995. Improved backing-off for m-gram language modeling. In *Proceedings of the IEEE International Conference on Acoustics, Speech and Signal Processing*, pages 181–184, Los Alamitos, California, USA. IEEE Computer Society Press.

Philipp Koehn, Franz Josef Och, and Daniel Marcu. 2003. Statistical phrase-based translation. In *NAACL '03: Proceedings of the 2003 Conference of the North American Chapter of the Association for Computational Linguistics on Human Language Technology*, pages 48–54, Morristown, NJ, USA. Association for Computational Linguistics.

Philipp Koehn, Hieu Hoang, Alexandra Birch, Chris Callison-Burch, Marcello Federico, Nicola Bertoldi, Brooke Cowan, Wade Shen, Christine Moran, Richard Zens, Chris Dyer, Ondřej Bojar, Alexandra Constantin, and Evan Herbst. 2007. Moses: Open Source Toolkit for Statistical Machine Translation. In *Proceedings of the 45th Annual Meeting of the Association for Computational Linguistics Companion Volume Proceedings of the Demo and Poster Sessions*, pages 177–180, Praha, Czechia, June. Association for Computational Linguistics.

Zhifei Li, Chris Callison-Burch, Sanjeev Khudanpur, and Wren Thornton. 2009. Decoding in Joshua: Open Source, Parsing-Based Machine Translation. *The Prague Bulletin of Mathematical Linguistics*, 91:47–56, 1.

Franz Josef Och and Hermann Ney. 2003. A systematic comparison of various statistical alignment models. *Computational Linguistics*, 29(1):19–51.

Franz Josef Och. 1999. An efficient method for determining bilingual word classes. In *Proceedings of the Ninth Conference of the European Chapter of the Association for Computational Linguistics (EACL'99)*, pages 71–76, Bergen, Norway, June. Association for Computational Linguistics.

Andreas Stolcke. 2002. Srilm – an extensible language modeling toolkit. In *Proceedings of International Conference on Spoken Language Processing*, Denver, Colorado, USA.

Jörg Tiedemann. 2009. News from opus – a collection of multilingual parallel corpora with tools and interfaces. In *Recent Advances in Natural Language Processing (vol. V)*, pages 237–248. John Benjamins.

Omar F. Zaidan. 2009. Z-mert: A fully configurable open source tool for minimum error rate training of machine translation systems. *The Prague Bulletin of Mathematical Linguistics*, 91:79–88.

Incremental Decoding for Phrase-based Statistical Machine Translation

Baskaran Sankaran, Ajeet Grewal and Anoop Sarkar
School of Computing Science
Simon Fraser University
8888 University Drive
Burnaby BC. V5A 2Y1. Canada
{baskaran, asg10, anoop}@cs.sfu.ca

Abstract

In this paper we focus on the *incremental decoding* for a statistical phrase-based machine translation system. In incremental decoding, translations are generated incrementally for every word typed by a user, instead of waiting for the entire sentence as input. We introduce a novel modification to the beam-search decoding algorithm for phrase-based MT to address this issue, aimed at efficient computation of future costs and avoiding search errors. Our objective is to do a faster translation during incremental decoding without significant reduction in the translation quality.

1 Introduction

Statistical Machine Translation has matured significantly in the past decade and half, resulting in the proliferation of several web-based and commercial translation services. Most of these services work on sentence or document level, where a user enters a sentence or chooses a document for translation, which are then translated by the servers. Translation in such typical scenarios is still offline in the sense that the user input and translation happen sequentially without any interaction between the two phases.

In this paper we study decoding for SMT with the constraint that translations are to be generated incrementally for every word typed in by the user. Such a translation service can be used for language learning, where the user is fluent in the target language and experiments with many different source language sentences interactively, or in real-time translation environments such as speech-speech translation or translation during interactive chats.

We use a phrase-based decoder similar to Moses (Koehn et al., 2007) and propose novel modifications in the decoding algorithm to tackle incremental decoding. Our system maintains a partial decoder state at every stage and uses it while decoding for each newly added word. As the decoder has access only to the partial sentence at every stage, the future costs change with every additional word and this has to be taken into account while continuing from an existing partial decoder state. Another major issue is that as incremental decoding is provided new input one word at at time, some of the entries that were pruned out at an earlier decoder state might later turn out to better candidates resulting in search errors compared to decoding the entire sentence at once. It is to be noted that, the search error problem is related to the inability to compute full future cost in incremental decoding. Our proposed modifications address these twin challenges and allow for efficient incremental decoding.

2 Incremental Decoding

2.1 Beam Search for Phrase-based SMT

In this section we review the usual beam search decoder for phrase-based MT because we present our modifications for incremental decoding using the same notation. Beam search decoding for phrase-based SMT (Koehn, 2004) begins by collecting the translation options from the phrase table for all possible phrases of a given input sentence and precomputes the future cost for all possible contiguous sequences in the sentence. The pseudo-code for the usual beam-search decoding algorithm is illustrated in Algorithm 1.

The decoder creates n bins for storing hypotheses grouped by the number of source words covered. Starting from a null hypothesis in bin 0, the decoder iterates through bins 1 though n filling them with new hypotheses by extending the entries in the earlier bins.

A hypothesis contains the target words generated (e), the source positions translated so far (f) commonly known as *coverage set* and the score of the current translation (p) computed by the weighted log-linear combination of different feature functions. It also contains a back-pointer to

Proceedings of the Joint 5th Workshop on Statistical Machine Translation and MetricsMATR, pages 216–223,
Uppsala, Sweden, 15-16 July 2010. ©2010 Association for Computational Linguistics

Algorithm 1 Phrase-based Decoder pseudocode (Koehn, 2004)

Given: sentence S_n: $s_1 s_2 ... s_n$ of length n
Pre-compute future costs for all contiguous sequences
Initialize bins b_i where $i = 1 \ldots n$
Create initial hypothesis: $\{e : (), f : (), p : 1.0\}$
for $i = 1$ to n **do**
  for *hyp* $\in b_i$ **do**
    for *newHyp* that extends *hyp* **do**
      nf := num src words covered by *newHyp*
      Add *newHyp* to bin b_{nf}
      Prune bin b_{nf} using future costs
Find best hypothesis in b_n
Output best path that leads to best hypothesis

its parent hypothesis in the previous state and other information used for pruning and computing cost in later iterations.

As a new hypothesis is generated by extending an existing hypothesis with a new phrase pair, decoder updates the associated information such as coverage set, the target words generated, future cost (for translating rest of the source words) and its translation score. For example, consider Spanish to English translation: for the source sentence *Maria no daba una bofetada*, the hypothesis $\{e : (\text{Mary}), f : (1), p : 0.534\}$ which is the hypothesis that covers *Maria* can be extended to a new hypothesis $\{e : (\text{Mary, slap}), f : (1, 3, 4, 5), p : 0.043\}$ by choosing a new phrase pair *(daba una bofetada, slap)* covering the source phrases *Maria* and *daba una bofetada*. The probability score is obtained by weighted log-linear sum of the features of the phrases contained in the derivation so far.

An important aspect of beam search decoding is the pruning away of low-scoring hypotheses in each bin to reduce the search space and thus making the decoding faster. To do this effectively, beam search decoding uses the future cost of a hypothesis together with its current cost. The future cost is an estimate of the translation cost of the input words that are yet to be translated, and is typically pre-computed for all possible contiguous sequences in the input sentence before the decoding step. The future cost prevents the any hypotheses that are low-scoring, but potentially promising, from being pruned.

2.2 Incremental Decoder - Challenges

Our goal for the *incremental decoder* (ID) is to generate output translations incrementally for partial phrases as the source sentence is being input by the user. We assume *white-space* to be the word delimiter and the partial sentence is decoded for every encounter of the space character. We further assume the *return* key to mark *end-of-sentence* (EOS) and use it to compute language model score for the entire sentence.

As we noted above, future costs cannot be pre-computed as in regular decoding because the complete input sentence is not known while decoding incrementally. Thus the incremental decoder can only use a partial future cost until the EOS is reached. The partial future cost could result in some of the potentially better candidates being pruned away in earlier stages. This leads to search errors and result in lower translation quality.

2.3 Approach

We use a modified beam search for incremental decoding (ID) and the two key modifications are aimed at addressing the issues of future cost and search errors. Beam search for ID begins with a single bin for the first word and more bins are added as the sentence is completed by the user. Our approach requires that the decoder states for the partial source sentence can be stored in a way that allows efficient retrieval. It also maintains a current decoder state, which includes all the bins and the hypotheses contained in them, all pertaining to the present sentence.

At each step ID goes through a pre-process phase, where it recomputes the partial future costs for all the spans accounting for the new word and updates the current decoder state with new partial future costs. It then generates new hypotheses into all the earlier bins and in the newly created using any new phrases (resulting from the new word added by the user) not used earlier.

Algorithm 2 shows the pseudocode of our incremental decoder. Given a partial sentence S_i[1] ID starts with the pre-process phase illustrated separately in algorithm 3. We use $P_{type}(l)$ to denote phrases of length l words and H_{type} to denote the set of hypotheses; in both cases *type* correspond to either *old* or *new*, indicating if it was not known in the previous decoding state or not.

[1] we use S_i and s_i to denote a i word partial sentence and i^{th} word in a (partial) sentence respectively

Algorithm 2 Incremental Decoder pseudocode

```
1: Input: (partial) sentence S_p: s_1 s_2 ... s_{i-1} s_i
   with l_s words where s_i is the new word
2: PreProcess(S_p) (Algorithm 3)
3: for every bin b_j in (1 ... i) do
4:    Update future cost and cover set ∀ H_old
5:    Add any new phrase of length b_j (subject to
      d)
6:    for bin b_k in (b_{j-MaxPhrLen} ... b_{j-1}) do
7:       Generate H_new for b_j by extending:
8:       every H_old with every other P_new(b_j −
         b_k)
9:       every H_new with every other P_any(b_j −
         b_k)
10:   Prune bin b_j
```

Algorithm 3 PreProcess subroutine

```
Input: partial sentence S_p of length l_s
Retrieve partial decoder object for S_{p-1}
Identify possible P_new (subject to MaxPhrLen)
Recompute f_c for all spans in 1...l_s
for every P_new in local phrase table do
   Load translation options to table
for every P_old in local phrase table do
   Update f_c with the recomputed cost
```

Given S_i, the pre-process phase extracts the new set of phrases (P_{new}) for the ith word and adds them to the existing phrases (P_{old}). It then recomputes the future-cost (f_c) for all the contiguous sequences in the partial input and updates existing entries in the local copy of phrase table with new f_c.

In decoding phase, ID generates new hypotheses in two ways: i) by extending the existing hypotheses H_{old} in the previous decoder state S_{i-1} with new phrases P_{new} and ii) by generating new hypotheses H_{new} that are unknown in the previous state.

The main difference between incremental decoding and regular beam-search decoding is inside the two 'for' loops corresponding to lines $3 - 9$ in algorithm 2. In the outer loop each of the existing hypotheses are updated to reflect the recomputed f_c and coverage set. Any new phrases belonging to the current bin are also added to it[2].

[2]Based on our implementation of lazier cube pruning they are added to a priority queue, the contents of which are flushed into the bin at the end of inner for-loop and before the pruning step

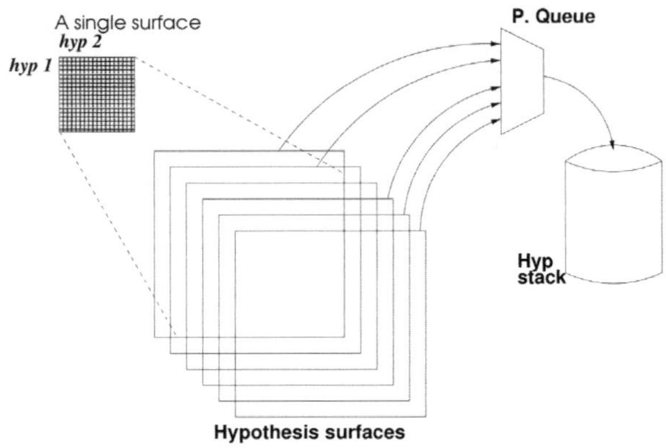

Figure 1: Illustration of Lazier Cube Pruning

The inner for-loop corresponds to the extension of hypotheses sets (grouped by same coverage set) to generate new hypotheses. Here a distinction is made between hypotheses H_{old} corresponding to previous decoder state S_{p-1} and hypotheses H_{new} resulting from the addition of word s_i. H_{old} is extended only using the newly found phrases P_{new}, whereas the newer hypotheses are processed as in regular beam-search.

2.4 Lazier Cube Pruning

We have adapted the pervasive lazy algorithm (or 'lazier cube pruning') proposed originally for Hiero-style systems by (Pust and Knight, 2009) for our phrase-based system. This step corresponds to the lines $5 - 9$ of algorithm 2 and allows us to only generate as many hypotheses as specified by the configurable parameters, beam size and beam threshold. Figure 1 illustrates the process of lazier cube pruning for a single bin.

At the highest level it uses a priority queue, which is populated by the different *hyper-edges* or *surfaces*[3], each corresponding to a *pair* of hypotheses that are being merged to create a new hypothesis. New hypotheses are generated iteratively, such that the hypothesis with the highest score is chosen in each iteration from among different hyper-edges bundles.

However, this will lead to search errors as have been observed earlier. Any hyper-edge that has been discarded due to poor score in an early stage might later become a better candidate. The problem worsens further when using smaller beam sizes (for interactive decoding in real-time settings, we even consider a beam size of 3). In

[3]Unlike Hiero-style systems, only two hypotheses are merged in a phrase-based system and hence the term *surface*

the next section, we introduce the idea of delayed pruning to reduce search errors.

3 Delayed Pruning

Delayed pruning (DP) in our decoder was inspired by the well known fable about the race between a *tortoise* and a *hare*. If the decoding is considered to be a race between competing candidate hypotheses with the winner being the best hypothesis for Viterbi decoding or among the top-n candidates for n-best decoding.[4]

In this analogy, a hypothesis having a poor score, might just be a tortoise having a slow start (due to a bad estimate of the true future cost for what the user intends to type in the future) as opposed to a high scoring hare in the same state. Pruning such hypotheses early on is not risk-free and might result in search errors. We hypothesize that, given enough chance it might improve its score and move ahead of a hare in terms of translation score.

We implement DP by relaxing the lazier cube pruning step to generate a small, fixed number of hypotheses for coverage sets that are not represented in the priority queue and place them in the bin. These hypotheses are distinct from the usual top-k derivations. Thus, the resulting bin will have entries from all possible hyper-edge bundles. Though this reduces the search error problem, it leads to increasing number of possibilities to be explored at later stages with vast majority of them being *worse* hypotheses that should be pruned away.

We use a two level strategy of *delay* and then *prune*, to avoid such exponentially increasing search space and at the same time to reduce search error. At the delay level, the idea is to delay the pruning for few promising tortoises, instead of retaining a fixed number of hypotheses from all unrepresented hyper-edges. We use the normalized language model scores of the top-hypotheses in each hyper-edge that is not represented in cube pruning and based on a threshold (which is obtained using a development test set), we selectively choose few hyper-edge bundles and generate a small number (typically 1-3) of hypotheses from each of them and flag them as *tortoises*. These tortoises are extended minimally at each iteration subject to their normalized LM score.

While this significantly reduces the total number of hypotheses at initial bins, many of these tortoises might not show improvement even after several bins. Thus at the prune level, we prune out tortoises that does not improve beyond a threshold number of bins called *race course* limit. The race course limit signifies the number of steps a tortoise has in order to get into the decoder beam.

When a tortoise improves in score and breaks into the beam during cube pruning, it is deflagged as a tortoise and enters the regular decoding stream. We found DP to be effective in reducing the search error for incremental decoder in our experiments.

4 Evaluation and Discussion

The evaluation was performed using our own implementation of the beam-search decoding algorithms. The architecture of our system is similar to Moses, which we also use for training and for minimum error rate training (MERT) of the log-linear model for translation (Och, 2003; Koehn et al., 2007). Our features include 7 standard phrase-based features: 4 translation model features, i.e. $p(f|e)$, $p(e|f)$, $p_{lex}(f|e)$ and $p_{lex}(e|f)$, where e and f are target and source phrases respectively; features for phrase penalty, word penalty and language model, and we do not include the reordering feature. We used Giza++ and Moses respectively for aligning the sentences and training the system. The decoder was written in Java and includes *cube pruning* (Huang and Chiang, 2007) and *lazier cube pruning* (Pust and Knight, 2009) functionalities as part of the decoder. Our decoder supports both regular beam search (similar to Moses) and incremental decoding.

In our experiments we experimented various approaches for storing partial decoder states including memcache and transactional persistence using JDBM but found that the serialization and deserialization of decoder objects directly into and from the memory to work better in terms of speed and memory requirements. The partial object is retrieved and deserialized from the memory when required by the incremental decoder.

We evaluated the incremental decoder for translations between French and English (in both directions). We used the Workshop on Machine Translation shared task (WMT07) dataset for training,

[4]The analogy is used to compare two or more hypotheses in terms of their translation scores and *not* speed. Though our objective is faster incremental decoding, we use the analogy here to compare the scores.

optimizing and testing. The system was trained using Moses and the feature weights were optimized using MERT. To benchmark our Java decoder, we compare it with Moses by running it in regular beam search mode. The Moses systems were also optimized separately on the WMT07 devsets.

Apart from comparing our decoder with Moses in regular beam search, we also compared the incremental decoding with regular regular beam using our decoder. To make it comparable with incremental decoding, we used the regular beam search to *re-decode* the sentence fragments for every additional word in the input sentence. We measured the following parameters in our empirical analysis: translation quality (as measured by BLEU (Papineni et al., 2002) and TER (Snover et al., 2006)), search errors and translation speed. Finally, we also measured the effect of different race course limits on BLEU and decoding speed for incremental decoding.

4.1 Benchmarking our decoder

In this section we compare our decoder with Moses for regular beam search decoding. Table 1 gives the BLEU and TER for the two language pairs. Our decoder implementation compares favourably with Moses for Fr-En: the slightly better BLEU and TER for our decoder in Fr-En is possibly due to the minor differences in the configuration settings. For En-Fr translation, Moses performs better in both metrics. There are differences in the beam size between the two decoders, in our system the beam size is set to 100 compared to the default value of 1000 (the cube pruning pop limit) in Moses; we are planning to explore this and remove any other differences between them. However based on our understanding of the Moses implementation and our experiments, we believe our decoder to be comparable in accuracy with the Moses implementation. The numbers in the boldface are statistically significant at 95% confidence interval.

4.2 Re-decoding v.s. Incremental decoding

We test our hypothesis that incremental decoding can benefit by using partial decoder states for decoding every additional word in the input sentence. In order to do this, we run our incremental decoder in both regular beam search mode and in incremental decoding mode. In regular beam search mode, we forced the beam search decoder to re-decode the sentence fragments for every additional word and in incremental decoding mode, we used the partial decoding states to incrementally decode lastly added word. We then compare the BLEU and TER scores between them to validate our hypothesis.

We further test effectiveness of delayed pruning (DP) in incremental decoding by comparing it to the case where we turn off the DP. For incremental decoding, we set the beam size and the race course limit (for DP) to be 3. Additionally, we used a threshold of -2.0 (in log-scale) for normalized LM in the delay phase of DP, which was obtained by testing on a separate development test set.

We would like to highlight two observations from the results in Table 2. First the regular beam search indicate possible search errors due to the small beam size (cube pruning pop limit) and the BLEU scores has decreased by 0.56 for Fr-En and by over 2.5 for En-Fr, than the scores corresponding to a beam size of 100 shown in Table 1. Secondly, we find the incremental decoding to perform better for the same beam size. However, incremental decoding without delay pruning still seems to incur search errors when compared with the regular decoding with a larger beam. Delayed pruning alleviates this issue and improves the BLEU and TER significantly. This we believe, is mainly because the strategy to delay the pruning retains the potentially better partial hypotheses for every coverage set. It should be noted that results in Table 2 pertain only to our decoder implementation and not with Moses.

We now give a comparative note between our approach and the pruning strategy in regular beam search. Delaying the hypothesis pruning is the important aspect in our approach to incremental decoding. In the case of regular beam search, the hypotheses are pruned when they fall out of the beam and the idea is to have a larger beam size to avoid the early pruning of potentially good candidates. With the advent of cube pruning (Huang and Chiang, 2007), the 'cube pruning pop limit' (in Moses) determines the number of hypotheses retained in each stack. In both the cases, it is possible that some of the coverage sets go unrepresented in the stack due to poor candidate scores. This is not desirable in the incremental decoding setting as this might lead to search errors while decoding a partial sentence.

Additionally, Moses offers an option (cube

Decoder	Fr-En		En-Fr	
	BLEU	TER	BLEU	TER
Moses	**26.98**	0.551	**27.24**	0.610
Our decoder	**27.53**	0.541	26.96	0.657

Table 1: Regular beam search: Moses v.s. Our decoder

Decoder	Fr-En		En-Fr	
	BLEU	TER	BLEU	TER
Re-decode w/ beam search	26.96	0.548	24.33	0.635
ID w/o delay pruning	27.01	0.547	25.00	0.618
ID w/ delay pruning	**27.62**	0.545	**25.45**	0.616

Table 2: BLEU and TER: Re-decoding v.s. Incremental Decoding (ID)

pruning diversity) to control the number of hypotheses generated for each coverage set (though set to '0' by default). It might be possible to use this in conjunction with cube pruning pop limit as an alternative to our delayed pruning in the incremental decoding setting (with the risk of combinatorial explosion in the search space).

In contrast, the delayed pruning not only avoids search errors but also provides a dynamically manageable search space (refer section 4.2.2) by retaining the best of the potential candidates. In a practical scenario like real-time translation of internet chat, translation speed is an important consideration. Furthermore, it is better to avoid large number of candidates and generate only few best ones, as only the top few translations will be used by the system. Thus we believe our delayed pruning approach to be a principled pruning strategy that combines the different factors in an elegant framework.

4.2.1 Search Errors

As BLEU only indirectly indicates the number of search errors made by algorithm, we used a more direct way of quantifying the search errors incurred by the ID in comparison to regular beam search. We define the search error to be the difference between the translation scores of the best hypotheses produced by the ID and the regular beam search and then compute the mean squared error (MSE) for the entire test set. We use this method to compare ID in the two settings of delayed pruning being turned off (using a smaller beam size of 3 to simulate the requirements of near instantaneous translations in real-time environments) and delayed pruning turned on. We compare the model score in these cases with the model score for the best result obtained from the regular beam search decoder (using a larger beam of size 100).

Direction	Beam search against Incremental Decoding	
	w/o DP	*w/ DP*
Fr-En	0.3823	0.3235
En-Fr	1.1559	0.6755

Table 3: Search Errors in Incremental Decoding

The results are shown in Table 3 and as can be clearly seen, ID shows much lesser mean square error with the DP turned on than when it is turned off. Together the BLEU and TER numbers and the mean square search error show that delayed pruning is useful in the incremental decoding setting. Comparing the En-Fr and Fr-En results show that the two language pairs show slightly different characteristics but the experiments in both directions support our overall conclusions.

4.2.2 Speed

In this experiment, we set out to evaluate the ID against the regular beam-search in which sentence fragments are incrementally decoded for additional words. In order compare with the incremental decoder, we modified the regular decoder to decode the partial phrases, so that it *re-decodes* the partial phrase from the scratch instead of reusing the earlier state.

We ran the timing experiments on a Dell machine with an Intel Core i7 processor and 12 GB memory, clocking 2.67 GHz and running Linux (CentOS 5.3). We measured the time taken for decoding the fragment with every word added and averaged it first over the sentence and then the entire test set. The average time (in msecs) includes the future cost computation for both. We also measured the average number of hypotheses for every bin at the end of decoding a complete sentence, which was also averaged over the test set.

The results in Table 4 show that the incremental decoder was significantly faster than the beam search in re-decoding mode almost by a factor of 9 in the best case (for Fr-En). The speedup is primarily due to two factors, i) computing the future cost for the new phrases as opposed to computing it for all the phrases and ii) using partial decoder states without having to re-generate hypotheses through the cube pruning step and the latencies associated with computing LM scores for them. The addition of delayed pruning slowed down the speed at most by 7 msecs (for En-Fr). In addition, delayed pruning can be seen generating far more hypotheses than the other two cases. Clearly, this is because of the delay in pruning the tortoises until the race course limit. Even with such significantly large number of hypotheses being retained for every bin, DP results in improved speed (over re-decoding from scratch) and better performance by avoiding search errors (compared to the incremental decoder that does not use DP).

4.3 Effect of Race course limit

Table 5 shows the effect of different race course limits on translation quality measured using BLEU. We generally expect the race course limit to behave similar to the beam size as they both allow more hypotheses in the bin thereby reducing search error although at the expense of increasing decoding time.

However, in our experiments for Fr-En, we did not find significant variations in BLEU for different race course limits. This could be due to the absence of long distance re-orderings between English and French and that the smallest race course limit of 3 is sufficient for capturing all cases of local re-ordering. As expected, we find the decoding speed to slightly decrease and the average number of hypotheses per bin to increase with the increasing race course limit.

5 Related Work

Google[5] does seem to perform incremental decoding, but the underlying algorithms are not public knowledge. They may be simply re-translating the input each time using a fast decoder or re-using prior decoder states as we do here.

Intereactive translation using text prediction strategies have been studied well (Foster et al., 1997; Foster et al., 2002; Och et al., 2003). They all attempt to interactively help the human user in the *postediting* process, by suggesting completion of the word/phrase based on the user accepted prefix and the source sentece. Incremental feedback is part of *Caitra* (Koehn, 2009) an interactive tool for human-aided MT and works on a similar setting to interactive MT. In *Caitra*, the source text is pre-translated first and during the interactions it dynamically generates user suggestions.

Our incremental decoder work differs from these text prediction based approaches, in the sense that the input text is not available to the decoder beforehand and the decoding is being done dynamically for every source word as opposed to generating suggestions dynamically for completing target sentece.

6 Conclusion and Future Work

We presented a modified beam search algorithm for an efficient *incremental decoder* (ID), which will allow translations to be generated incrementally for every word typed by a user, instead of waiting for the entire sentence as input by reusing the partial decoder state. Our proposed modifications help us to efficiently compute partial future costs in the incremental setting. We introduced the notion of *delayed pruning* (DP) to avoid search errors in incremental decoding. We showed that reusing the partial decoder states is faster than re-decoding the input from the scratch every time a new word is typed by the user. Our exhaustive experiments further demonstrated DP to be highly effective in avoiding search errors under the incremental decoding setting. In our experiments in this paper we used a very tight beam size; in future work, we would like to explore the tradeoff between speed, accuracy and the utility of delayed pruning by varying the beam size in our experiments.

[5] *translate.google.com*

References

George Foster, Pierre Isabelle, and Pierre Plamondon. 1997. Target-text mediated interactive machine translation. *Machine Translation*, 12(1/2):175–194.

Decoder	Fr-En		En-Fr	
	Avg time	*Avg Hyp/ bin*	*Avg time*	*Avg Hyp/ bin*
Re-decode	724.46	2.21	130.29	2.32
ID w/o DP	84.85	2.89	27.58	2.89
ID w/ DP	87.01	85.11	34.35	60.46

Table 4: Speed: Re-decoding v.s. Incremental Decoding (ID)

Race Course Limit	Fr-En			En-Fr		
	BLEU	*Avg time*	*Avg Hyp/ bin*	*BLEU*	*Avg time*	*Avg Hyp/ bin*
3	26.75	87.83	85.11	25.39	36.15	75.03
4	26.77	91.14	86.35	25.37	36.21	77.69
5	26.77	90.81	86.52	25.37	36.25	78.47
6	26.77	95.91	86.56	25.37	37.34	78.71
7	26.77	91.67	86.57	25.37	36.26	78.81

Table 5: Effect of different race course limits

George Foster, Philippe Langlais, and Guy Lapalme. 2002. User-friendly text prediction for translators. In *EMNLP '02: Proceedings of the ACL-02 conference on Empirical methods in natural language processing*, pages 148–155, Morristown, NJ, USA. Association for Computational Linguistics.

Liang Huang and David Chiang. 2007. Forest rescoring: Faster decoding with integrated language models. In *Proceedings of the 45th Annual Meeting of the Association of Computational Linguistics*, pages 144–151, Prague, Czech Republic, June. Association for Computational Linguistics.

Philipp Koehn, Hieu Hoang, Alexandra Birch, Chris Callison-Burch, Marcello Federico, Nicola Bertoldi, Brooke Cowan, Wade Shen, Christine Moran, Richard Zens, Chris Dyer, Ondrej Bojar, Alexandra Constantin, and Evan Herbst. 2007. Moses: Open source toolkit for statistical machine translation. In *Proceedings of the 45th Annual Meeting of the Association for Computational Linguistics Companion Volume Proceedings of the Demo and Poster Sessions*, pages 177–180, Prague, Czech Republic, June. Association for Computational Linguistics.

Philipp Koehn. 2004. Pharaoh: A beam search decoder for phrase-based statistical machine translation models. In Robert E. Frederking and Kathryn Taylor, editors, *AMTA*, volume 3265 of *Lecture Notes in Computer Science*, pages 115–124. Springer.

Philipp Koehn. 2009. A web-based interactive computer aided translation tool. In *In Proceedings of ACL-IJCNLP 2009: Software Demonstrations*, Suntec, Singapore, August.

Franz Josef Och, Richard Zens, and Hermann Ney. 2003. Efficient search for interactive statistical machine translation. In *EACL '03: Proceedings of the tenth conference on European chapter of the Association for Computational Linguistics*, pages 387–393, Morristown, NJ, USA. Association for Computational Linguistics.

Franz Josef Och. 2003. Minimum error rate training in statistical machine translation. In *Proceedings of the 41st Annual Meeting of the Association for Computational Linguistics*, pages 160–167, Sapporo, Japan, July. Association for Computational Linguistics.

Kishore Papineni, Salim Roukos, Todd Ward, and Wie-Jing Zhu. 2002. BLEU: a method for automatic evaluation of machine translation. In *Proc. ACL*.

Michael Pust and Kevin Knight. 2009. Faster mt decoding through pervasive laziness. In *Proceedings of Human Language Technologies: The 2009 Annual Conference of the North American Chapter of the Association for Computational Linguistics, Companion Volume: Short Papers*, pages 141–144, Boulder, Colorado, June. Association for Computational Linguistics.

Matthew Snover, Bonnie Dorr, Richard Schwartz, Linnea Micciulla, and John Makhoul. 2006. A study of translation edit rate with targeted human annotation. In *Proceedings of Association for Machine Translation in the Americas: AMTA 2006*.

How to Avoid Burning Ducks: Combining Linguistic Analysis and Corpus Statistics for German Compound Processing

Fabienne Fritzinger and Alexander Fraser
Institute for Natural Language Processing
University of Stuttgart
{fritzife, fraser}@ims.uni-stuttgart.de

Abstract

Compound splitting is an important problem in many NLP applications which must be solved in order to address issues of data sparsity. Previous work has shown that linguistic approaches for German compound splitting produce a correct splitting more often, but corpus-driven approaches work best for phrase-based statistical machine translation from German to English, a worrisome contradiction. We address this situation by combining linguistic analysis with corpus-driven statistics and obtaining better results in terms of both producing splittings according to a gold standard and statistical machine translation performance.

1 Introduction

Compounds are highly productive in German and cause problems of data sparsity in data-driven systems. Compound splitting is an important component of German to English statistical machine translation systems. The central result of work by (Koehn and Knight, 2003) is that corpus-driven approaches to compound splitting perform better than approaches based on linguistic analysis, and this result has since been confirmed by other researchers (Popović et al., 2006; Stymne, 2008). This is despite the fact that linguistic analysis performs better in terms of matching a gold standard splitting. Our work shows that integrating these two approaches, by employing high-recall linguistic analysis disambiguated using corpus statistics, effectively combines the benefits of both approaches. This is important due to the wide usage of the Koehn and Knight approach in statistical machine translation systems.

The splittings we produce are best in terms of both end-to-end machine translation performance (resulting in an improvement of 0.59 BLEU and 0.84 METEOR over the corpus-driven approach of Koehn and Knight on the development test set used for WMT 2009[1]) and two gold standard evaluations (see section 4). We provide an extensive analysis of the improvements of our approach over the corpus-driven approach. The approach we have developed may help show how to improve previous approaches to handling compounds in such applications as speech recognition (e.g., (Larson et al., 2000)) or information retrieval (e.g., (Braschler and Ripplinger, 2004)).

The organization of the paper is as follows. Section 2 discusses previous work on compound splitting for statistical machine translation. Section 3 presents approaches for compound splitting and also presents SMOR, the morphological analyzer that is a key knowledge source for our approach. Section 4 presents a comparison of compound splitting techniques using two gold standard corpora and an error analysis. Section 5 presents phrase-based statistical machine translation (SMT) results. Section 6 concludes.

2 Related Work on German Compound Splitting

Rule-based compound splitting for SMT has been addressed by Nießen and Ney (2000), where GERTWOL was used for morphological analysis and the GERCG parser for lexical analysis and disambiguation. Their results showed that morpho-syntactic analysis could reduce the subjective sentence error rate.

The empirical approach of Koehn and Knight (2003) splits German compounds into words found in a training corpus. A minimal amount of linguistic knowledge is included in that the filler letters "s" and "es" are allowed to be introduced between any two words while "n" might be

[1] See Table 6 in section 5 for details.

Proceedings of the Joint 5th Workshop on Statistical Machine Translation and MetricsMATR, pages 224–234,
Uppsala, Sweden, 15-16 July 2010.

dropped. A scoring function based on the average log frequency of the resulting words is used to find the best splitting option, see section 3.2 for details. SMT experiments with additional knowledge sources (parallel corpus, part-of-speech tagger) for compound splitting performed worse than using only the simple frequency metric. Stymne (2008) varies the Koehn and Knight approach by examining the effect of a number of parameters: e.g. word length, scoring method, filler letters.

Popović et al. (2006), compared the approach of Nießen and Ney (2000) with the corpus-driven splitting of Koehn and Knight (2003) in terms of performance on an SMT task. Both systems yield similar results for a large training corpus, while the linguistic-based approach is slightly superior when the amount of training data is drastically reduced.

There has recently been a large amount of interest in the use of input lattices in SMT. One use of lattices is to defer disambiguation of word-level phenomena such as inflection and compounds to decoding. Dyer (2009) applied this to German using a lattice encoding different segmentations of German words. The work is evaluated by using the 1-best output of a weak segmenter[2] on the training data and then using a lattice of the N-best output of the same segmenter on the test set to decode, which was 0.6 BLEU better than the unsegmented baseline. It would be of interest to test whether deferral of disambiguation to decoding still produces an improvement when used in combination with a high-performance segmenter such as the one we present, an issue we leave for future work.

3 Compound Processing

Previous work has shown a positive impact of compound splitting on translation quality of SMT systems. The splitting reduces data sparsity and enhances word alignment performance. An example is given in Figure 1.

Previous approaches for compound splitting can be characterized as following two basic approaches: the use of morphological analyzers to find split points based on linguistic knowledge and corpus-driven approaches combining large

[2]The use of the 1-best output of the segmenter for German to English decoding results in a degradation of 0.3 BLEU, showing that it is worse in performance than the corpus-driven method of Koehn and Knight, which improves performance (see the evaluation section). However, this segmenter is interesting because it is language neutral.

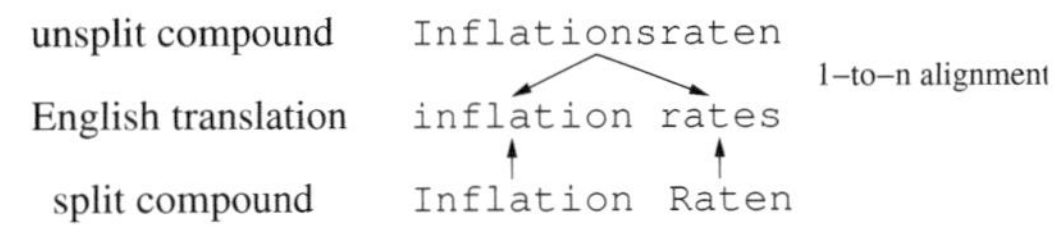

Figure 1: Compound splitting enhances the number of 1-to-1 word alignments.

amounts of data and scoring metrics.

We briefly introduce the computational morphology SMOR (section 3.1) and the corpus-driven approach of Koehn and Knight (2003) (section 3.2), before we present our hybrid approach that combines the benefits of both in section 3.3.

3.1 SMOR Morphological Analyzer

SMOR is a finite-state based morphological analyzer covering the productive word formation processes of German, namely inflection, derivation and compounding (Schmid et al., 2004). Word formation is implemented as a concatenation of morphemes filtered according to selectional restrictions. These restrictions are based on feature decorations of stems and affixes encoded in the lexicon. Inflection is realized using inflection classes.

An abbreviated[3] SMOR analysis of the word *Durchschnittsauto* ("standard car")[4] is given in Figure 2 (a). The hierarchical structure of the word formation process is given in Figure 2 (b). Implemented with finite-state technology, SMOR is not able to produce this hierarchy: in our example it outputs two (correct) analyses of different depths and does not perform disambiguation.

3.2 Corpus-Driven Approach

Koehn and Knight (2003) describe a method requiring no linguistically motivated morphological analysis to split compounds. Instead, a compound is broken into parts (words) that are found in a large German monolingual training corpus.

We re-implemented this approach with an extended list of filler letters that are allowed to oc-

[3]We show analyses for nominative, and analyses for the other cases *genitive, ,dative, accusative* are left out as they are identical.

[4]*durch* = "through", *schneiden* = "to cut", *Schnitt* = "(the) cut", *Durchschnitt* = "average", *Auto* = "car"
part-of-speech: <NN>/<V> (noun/verb)
gender: <Neu> (neutrum)
case: <Nom> (nominative)
number: <Sg> (singular)
suffixation: <SUFF> (suffix)
prefixation: <VPART> (verb particle)

```
analyze> Durchschnittsauto
Durchschnitt<NN>Auto<+NN><Neut><Nom><Sg>
durch<VPART>schneiden<V><NN><SUFF>Auto<+NN><Neut><Nom><Sg>
```

(a) SMOR output format

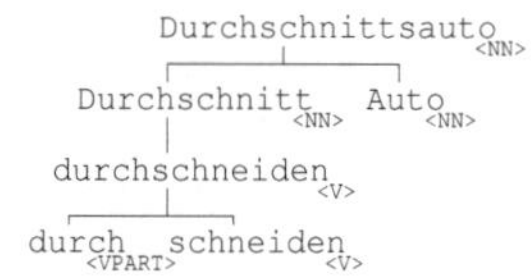

(b) Morphological analysis

Figure 2: Morphological analysis of *Durchschnittsauto* ("standard car").

cur between any two parts (*nen, ien, en, es, er, s, n*) such as *s* in *Inflationsrate* (cf. Figure 1) and deletable letters (*e, n*), required for compounds such as *Kirchturm* = *Kirche+Turm* ("steeple", "church+tower"). Filler letters are dropped only in cases where the part is more frequent without the letter than with it (an example is that the frequency of the word *Inflation* is greater than the frequency of the word *Inflations*); the same holds for deletable letters and hyphens ("-"). The minimal part size was set to 3 characters. Word frequencies are derived from the true-cased corpus using case insensitive matching. In order to reduce wrong splittings, infrequent words (frequency $\leq$ 3) are removed from the training corpus and a stop list was used[5]. These are similar choices to those found to be best in work by Stymne (2008).

The splitting that maximizes the geometric mean of part frequencies using the following formula[6] is chosen:

$$\text{argmax}\, S\left(\prod_{p_i \in S} count(p_i)\right)^{\frac{1}{n}}$$

Figure 3 contains all splitting options of the corpus-driven approach for *Ministerpräsident* ("prime minister"). As can be seen, the desired splitting *Minister|Präsident* is among the options, but in the end *Min|ist|Präsident* ("Min|is|president") is picked by the corpus-driven approach because this splitting maximizes the geometric mean score (mainly due to the highly frequent verb *ist* "is"). This is linguistically implausible, and the system we introduce in the next section splits this correctly.

Even though this corpus-driven approach tends to oversplit it works well for phrase-based SMT because adjacent words (or word parts) are likely

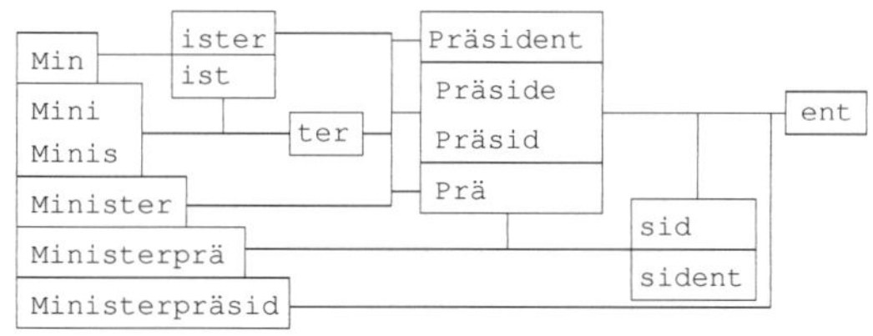

Figure 3: Corpus-driven splittings of *Ministerpräsident* ("prime minister").

to be learned as phrases. We will refer to the corpus-driven approach using the abbreviation *cd*.

3.3 Hybrid Approach

We present a novel approach to compound splitting: based on linguistically motivated split points gained from SMOR, we search word frequencies in a large training corpus (the same corpus as we will use for the corpus-driven approach) in order to determine the best splitting option for a word (or to leave it unsplit). This approach needs no explicit definition of filler letters or deletable letters, as this knowledge is encoded in SMOR.

In contrast to the corpus-driven approach described in the previous section, the hybrid approach uses neither a minimal part size constraint, nor a stop-list. Instead, we make use of the linguistic knowledge encoded in SMOR, i.e. we allow the hybrid approach to split only into parts that can appear as free morphemes, such as stems and separatable particles. An example is *auf|gibt* ("to give up"), where the particle *auf* may occur separated from the verb, as in *Er* ***gibt*** *nicht* ***auf*** ("he gives not up"). Bound morphemes, such as prefixes and suffixes cannot be split from the stem, e.g. *verhandelbar* ("negotiable") which consists of the prefix *ver-*, the stem *handeln* and the suffix *-bar*, is left unsplit by the hybrid approach.

For N-ary compounds (with N>2), we use not only the split points proposed by SMOR, but we also search the training corpus for recombinations of the compound parts: e.g. SMOR provides the parts A|B|C for the compound ABC, and we addi-

[5]The stop list contains the following units, which occur in the corpus as separate words (e.g., as names, function words, etc.), and frequently occur in incorrect splittings: *adr, and, bes, che, chen, den, der, des, eng, ein, fue, ige, igen, iger, kund, sen, ses, tel, ten, trips, ung, ver*.

[6]Taken from (Koehn and Knight, 2003): S = split, p_i = part, n = number of parts. The original word is also considered, it has 1 part and a minimal count of 1.

(a) SMOR splitting options

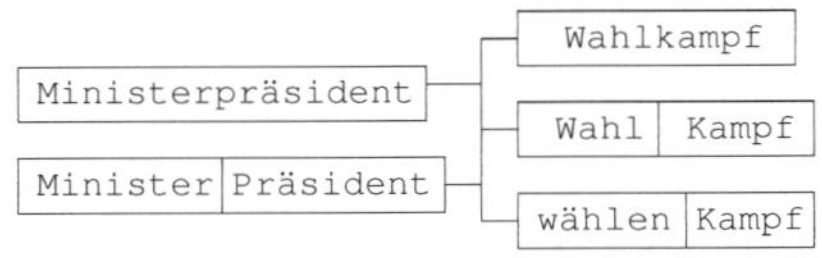

(b) Part frequencies

word part	frequency
Kampf	30,546
Minister	12,742
Ministerpräsident	22,244
Ministerpräsidentwahl	111
Ministerpräsidentwahlkampf	1
Präsident	125,747
Präsidentenwahl	2,482
Präsidentenwahlkampf	25
Wahl	29,255
Wahlkampf	23,335

(c) Log-based geometric mean scores

splitting option	score
Ministerpräsidentenwahlkampf	0
Ministerpräsident|Wahlkampf	10.04
Ministerpräsident|Wahl|Kampf	10.21
Ministerpräsident|wählen|Kampf	9.85
Minister|Präsident|Wahlkampf	10.38
Minister|Präsident|Wahl|Kampf	10.42
Minister|Präsident|wählen|Kampf	10.15
Ministerpräsidentenwahl|Kampf	7.52
Minister|Präsidentenwahl|Kampf	9.19
Minister|Präsidentenwahlkampf	6.34

Table 1: Splitting options for *Ministerpräsidentenwahlkampf* ("election campaign of the prime minister") (a) with part frequencies derived from the corpus (b) and log-based geometric mean scores (c).

tionally search for `AB|C` and `A|BC`.

Even though SMOR lemmatizes along with compound splitting, only the information about possible split points is used in our splitting approach. The compound *Beitrittsländer* ("accession countries"), for example, is reduced to *Beitritt|Land* by SMOR, but is retransformed to *Beitritt|Länder* in our approach. This holds also for adjectives, e.g. *firmeninterne* "company-internal" which is split to *firma|interne* (*interne* is the female form of the adjective *intern*) and verbs, such as the participle *wasser|gebunden* "water bound", where the lemma is *Wasser|binden*.

Hyphenated words can also be split with SMOR, as long as the rightmost part of the word is in its lexicon. However, the word parts which are to the left of hyphen(s) are left unanalyzed. The SMOR analyses for *NATO-Berichts* ("NATO report") and the nonsense *XYZabc-Berichts* ("XYZabc report") are given below:

```
analyze> NATO-Berichts
NATO-<TRUNC>Bericht<+NN><Masc><Gen><Sg>
analyze> XYZabc-Berichts
XYZabc-<TRUNC>Bericht<+NN><Masc><Gen><Sg>
```

Such Words where the rightmost part is unknown to SMOR are left completely unanalyzed by SMOR. Examples include *NATO-Berxchts* (which is a typo of *NATO-Berichts*) or *al-Qaeda* (a proper name). If such words occurred less than 5 times in the training corpus, they were split at the hyphens. This procedure splits *NATO|Berxchts*, while it leaves *al-Qaeda* unsplit.

Table 1(a) shows the different splittings[7] that SMOR returns for the ambiguous ad-hoc compound *Ministerpräsidentenwahlkampf* ("election campaign of the prime minister"). All of them are morphologically sound compounds of German.

The corpus frequencies of the parts provided by SMOR (and their recombinations) are given in Table 1 (b). The average natural log frequencies of the SMOR splittings in Table 1 (c), with the recombinations of their parts in the last three rows. We set the minimal frequency for each part to 1 (which gives a log frequency of 0) even if it was not seen in the training corpus.

Even though "prime" is not a literal translation of *Präsident*, the best splitting (out of the given options) is *Minister|Präsident|Wahl|Kampf* ("minister|president|election|campaign"). It is scored highest and thus chosen by the hybrid approach.

For the purpose of SMT, we want to split compounds into parts that have a translational correspondent in the target language. To accomplish that, it is often sufficient to consider the split at the highest linguistic analysis level. For

[7] *Ministerpräsident* = "prime minister", *Wahlkampf* = "election campaign", *Minister* = "minister", *Präsident* = "president", *Wahl* = "election", *wählen* = "to elect", *Kampf* = "fight"

the example *Durchschnittsauto* ("standard car") (cf. Figure 2 above), where the ideal split is *Durchschnitt|Auto* ("average|car"). Here, the deeper analysis of *Durchschnitt* as a nominalisation of the particle verb *durch|schneiden* ("to cut through") is not relevant. The same holds for *Ministerpräsidentenwahlkampf* of Table 1, where in one of the splittings *Wahl* is further reduced to the verb *wählen*.

In order to prevent such analyses from being picked, we investigate the use of restricting SMOR's splitting options to analyses having a minimal number of component parts. On the other hand, there are many lexicalized compounds in German, that, besides being analyzed as a compound also appear as a free word stem in SMOR's lexicon (e.g. both *Geländewagen* "all-terrain vehicle" and *Gelände|wagen* "terrain vehicle" are returned by SMOR). Therefore, we keep both variants for our subsequent experiments: the constrained version that uses only analyses with a minimal number of parts (and thus performs a more conservative splitting) is referred to as *smc*, while using all of SMOR's analyses is named *sm*. In addition to these, we use a constraint that splits only nouns. To do so, the text to be split was POS-tagged with TreeTagger (Schmid, 1994) to determine the nouns in the context of the whole sentence. Splitting only nouns will be referred to as *@nn* in the remainder of this paper.

Compared to the purely corpus-driven approach, hybrid compound splitting substantially reduces the number of false splitting options, because only splittings that are linguistically motivated are looked up in the training corpus. We will show that this restriction of splitting options enhances the number of correct splittings being picked. The purely corpus-driven approach considers the correct splitting in most cases, but often does not choose it because there is another higher scoring splitting option (cf. section 4.3).

The main shortcoming of the hybrid approach is its dependence on SMOR's lexical coverage. SMOR incorporates numerous word formation rules and thousands of word stems (e.g. over 16,000 noun base stems), but our approach will leave all words unsplit that cannot be analyzed with SMOR. However, we will show in both the gold standard evaluations (section 4) and the SMT evaluation (section 5) that the recall of SMOR is sufficient to result in substantial gains over the corpus-driven approach.

4 Gold Standard Evaluation

The accuracies of the compound splitting approaches are evaluated against two hand-crafted gold standards: one that includes linguistically motivated split points (section 4.1), and one indicating compounds that were translated compositionally by a human translator (section 4.2). We found that the hybrid approach performs best for both. In section 5, we will show the impact of the different splitting approaches on translation performance, with the result that the hybrid approach outperforms the corpus-driven approach even for translation quality (in contrast to previous work, where the best system according to the gold standard was not the best system for translation quality). In order to better understand the divergent results of the splitting approaches, we perform a detailed error analysis in section 4.3.

The accuracy of compound splitting is measured using the same terminology and metrics as described in (Koehn and Knight, 2003):

correct split: should be split and was split correctly
correct not: should not be split and was not
wrong split: should not be split but was split
wrong not: should be split but was not
wrong faulty (fty): should be split, but was split wrongly

precision: $\frac{correctsplit}{correctsplit+wrongfaulty+wrongsplit}$

recall: $\frac{correctsplit}{correctsplit+wrongfaulty+wrongnot}$

accuracy: $\frac{correct}{correct+wrong}$

The results of the following splitting approaches were investigated:

raw	= baseline without splitting
cd	= corpus-driven splitting
sm	= hybrid approach using all SMOR analyses
smc	= hybrid approach using the SMOR analysis with the minimal number of parts
@nn	= split only nouns

The word frequencies required for all splitting approaches were derived from the German monolingual language model training data ($\sim$ 225 million tokens) of the shared task of the 2009 ACL workshop on machine translation.

4.1 Linguistically Motivated Gold Standard

In the course of developing the hybrid approach, we used a hand-crafted gold standard for testing, which contains 6,187 distinct word types extracted

	Correct		Wrong			Metrics		
	split	not	split	not	fty	prec.	recall	acc.
raw	0	5073	0	1114	0	-	0.00%	81.99%
cd	679	4192	883	120	313	36.21%	61.06%	78.73%
sm	912	4534	541	35	165	56.37%	**82.01%**	88.02%
sm@nn	628	4845	230	337	147	62.49%	56.73%	88.46%
smc	884	4826	249	135	93	72.10%	79.50%	**92.29%**
smc@nn	648	4981	94	380	84	**78.45%**	58.27%	90.98%

Table 2: Linguistically motivated gold standard: 6,187 distinct word types. **Bold-face** font indicates the best result of each column.

from the development set of the 2009 shared MT task. The most plausible split points were annotated by a native speaker of German, allowing for splits into word stems or particles, but not into bound morphemes such as prefixes or suffixes.

Splits were annotated at the highest word formation level only, see also *Durchschnittsauto* in Figure 2 (section 3.1 above), where only the split point *Durchschnitt|Auto* would be annotated in the gold standard. Another example is the complex derivative *Untersuchungshäftling* ("person being imprisoned on remand"), where the inherent word structure looks as follows: *[Untersuchung+Haft]+ling* ("[investigation+imprisonment]+being a person"). The splitting into *Untersuchung|Häftling* is semantically not correct and the word is thus left unsplit in the gold standard. Finally, particles are only split if these can be used separately from the verb in a grammatically sound sentence, as is the case in the example mentioned in section 3.3, *auf|gibt*: *Er gibt nicht auf* ("he gives not up"). In contrast, the particle cannot be separated in a past participle construction like *aufgegeben*: **Er gegeben nicht auf* ("he given not up"), because in this example, *-ge-* is an infix introduced between the particle and the verb in order to form the past participle form. Constructions of this kind are thus left unsplit in the gold standard.

We found that 1,114 of the 6,187 types we investigated were compounds, of which 837 were nouns. The detailed results are given in Table 2. Due to the fact that the majority of words should not be split, the *raw* method reaches a considerable accuracy of 81.99%.

As can be seen from Table 2, 679 of the 1,114 compounds are split correctly by the corpus-driven approach (*cd*). However, the high number of wrong splits (883), which is the main shortcoming of the corpus-driven approach, leads to an accuracy below the *raw* system (78.73% vs. 81.99%).

Out of the variants of the hybrid approach, the less constrained one, *sm* achieves the highest recall (82.01%), while the most constrained one *smc@nn* has the highest precision (78.45%). The *smc* variant yields the most accurate splitting *92.29%*. The higher precision of the *@nn*-variants comes from the fact that most of the compounds are nouns (837 of 1,114) and that these approaches (*sm@nn, smc@nn*) leave more words incorrectly unsplit than oversplit.

Note that the gold standard we presented in this section was measured on a few times during development of the hybrid approach and there might be some danger of overfitting. Therefore, we used another gold standard based on human translations to confirm the high accuracy of the hybrid approach. We introduce it in the next section.

4.2 One-to-one Correspondence Gold Standard

The one-to-one correspondence gold standard (Koehn and Knight, 2003) indicates only compounds that were translated compositionally by a human translator. Such translations need not always be consistent: the human translator might decide to translate a compound compositionally in one sentence and using a different concept in another sentence. As a consequence, a linguistically correct split might or might not be considered correct, depending on how it was translated. This is therefore a harsh metric.

We used data from the 2009 shared MT task[8] for this evaluation. The first 5,000 words of the test text (*news-dev2009b*) were annotated manually with respect to compounds that are translated compositionally into more than one English word. This is the same data set as used for the evaluation of SMT performance in section 5, but the compound annotation was done only after all SMT experiments were completed, to ensure unbiased translation results. The use of the same data set facilitates the comparison of the splitting approaches in terms of the one-to-one gold standard vs. translation quality.

The results are given in Table 3. In this set, only 155 compounds with one-to-one correspondences are found amongst the 5,000 word tokens, which leads to a very high accuracy of 96.90% with no splitting (*raw*).

[8] http://www.statmt.org/wmt09/translation-task.html

	Correct		Wrong			Metrics		
	split	not	split	not	fty	prec.	recall	acc.
raw	0	4,845	0	155	0	——	0.00%	96.90%
cd	81	4,435	404	14	59	14,89%	52.60%	90.32%
sm	112	4,563	283	8	34	26.11%	72.73%	93.50%
sm@nn	107	4,677	169	15	32	34.74%	69.48%	95.68%
smc	128	4,666	180	12	14	39,75%	**83,12%**	95,88%
smc@nn	123	4,744	102	18	13	**51.68%**	79.87%	**97.34%**

Table 3: Evaluation of splitting approaches with respect to one-to-one correspondences. **Bold-face** font indicates the best result of each column.

The corpus-driven approach (*cd*) splits 81 of the 155 compounds correctly (52.60% recall), but also splits 404 words that should have been left unsplit, which leads to a low precision of only 14.89%.

As can be seen from Table 3, all variants of the hybrid splitting approach, reach higher accuracies than the corpus-driven approach, and again, the most restrictive one (*smc@nn*) performs best: it is the only one that achieves a slightly higher accuracy than *raw* (97.34% vs. 96.90%). Even though the number of correct splits of *smc@nn* (123) is lower than for e.g. *smc* (with 128, the highest recall 83.12%), the number of correct not splittings is higher (4,744 vs. 4,666).

Generally speaking, the results of both gold standards show that linguistic knowledge enhances the number of correct splits, while at the same time it considerably reduces oversplitting, which is the main shortcoming of the corpus-driven approach. A detailed error analysis is provided in the following section 4.3.

4.3 Error Analysis

4.3.1 Errors of the Corpus-Driven Approach

In gold standard evaluation, the purely corpus-driven approach exhibited a number of erroneous splits. These splits are not linguistically motivated and are thus filtered out a priori by the SMOR-based systems. In the following, we give some examples for wrong splits that are typical for the corpus-driven approach.

In Table 4 we divide typical errors into two categories: *frequency-based* where wrong splitting is solely due to higher frequencies of the parts from the wrong splitting and *insertions/deletions* where filler letters or deletions of letters lead to wrong splittings of which the parts are again more frequent than for the correct splitting.

The adjective *lebenstreuen* ("true-to-life") is the only true compound of Table 4. Its correct split is *Leben|treuen* ("life|true"). All other words in Table 4 should be left unsplit.

error type	word	splitting
frequency based	lebenstreuen *true-to-life*	Leben|streuen *life|spread*
	traumatisch *traumatic*	Trauma|Tisch *trauma|table*
	Themen *themes*	the|men *the|men*
insertions/deletions	entbrannte *broke out*	Ente|brannte *duck|burned*
	Belangen *aspect*	Bela|Gen *Bela|gene*
	Toynbeesche *Toynbeean*	toy|been|sche *toy|been|*sche*

Table 4: Typical errors of the corpus-driven approach. The only true compound in this table is *Leben|treuen* ("life|true").

The lookup of word frequencies is done case-insensitively, i.e. the casing variant with the highest frequency is chosen. This leads to cases like *traumatisch* ("traumatic"), where adjectives are split into nominal head words (namely *Trauma|Tisch* = "trauma|table"), which is impossible from a linguistic point of view. If, however, *Traumatisch* occurs uppercased and is thus to be interpreted as a noun, the splitting into *Trauma|Tisch* is correct.

The splitting accuracy of the corpus-driven method is highly dependent on the quality of the monolingual training corpus from which word frequencies are derived. The examples *Themen* ("themes") and *Toynbeesche* ("Toynbeean") in Table 4 show how foreign language material from a language like English in the training corpus can lead to severe splitting errors.

In order to account for the lack of linguistic knowledge, the corpus-driven approach has to allow for a high flexibility of filler letters, deletion of letters and combinations of both. The examples in the lower part of Table 4 show that this flexibility often leads to erroneous splits that completely modify the semantic content of the original word. For example, the verb participle form of "to break out", *entbrannte* is split into *Ente|brannte* ("duck|burned"), because the corpus-driven approach allows to add an "e" at the end of each but the rightmost part. This transformation is required to cover compounds like *Kirchturm* ("church tower" (or also "steeple")) that are composed of the words *Kirche* ("church") and *Turm* ("tower").

Often, one high frequent part of the (possible)

compound determines the split of a word, even though the other part(s) are much less frequent. This is the case for *Belangen* (442 occurrences), where the high frequent *Gen* ("gene", 1,397 occurrences) leads to a splitting of the word, even though the proper name *Bela* is much less frequent (165 occurrences).

The case of *Toynbeesche* (which is a proper noun used as an adjective) shows that the corpus-driven approach splits everything into parts, as long as they are more frequent than the unsplit word. In contrast, all words that are unknown to SMOR are left unsplit by the hybrid approach.

Finally, the corpus-driven approach often identifies content-free syllables such as *-sche* (see last row of Table 4) as compound parts. These syllables frequently occur in the training corpus due to syllabification, making them a prevalent source for corpus-driven splitting errors. Such wrong splittings could be blocked by extending the stopword list of the corpus-driven approach. See footnote 5 in section 3.2, for the list of stopwords we used in our implementation.

Previous approaches to corpus-driven compound splitting used a part-of-speech (POS) tagger to reduce the number of erroneous analyses (e.g. (Koehn and Knight, 2003), (Stymne, 2008)): the word class of the rightmost (possible) part of the compound is restricted to match the word class of the whole compound, which is coherent to German compositional morphology. This constraint lead to higher accuracies in gold standard evaluations, but it did not improve translation quality in the experiments of Koehn and Knight (2003) and Stymne (2008), and therefore, we did not re-implement the corpus-driven approach with this POS-constraint. However, some of the errors presented in this section could have been prevented if the POS-constraint was used: the erroneous splits of *lebenstreuen* and *traumatisch* were avoided, but for the splittings of *Belangen* and *entbrannte*, the POS-constraint would not help. A more restrictive POS-constraint proposed by Stymne (2008), allows splitting only into parts belonging to content-bearing word classes. This works for *Belangen*, but not for *entbrannte*. In the case of *Themen* and *Toynbeesche*, the output of a POS-tagger for the last part are not trustworthy, as these are not correct German words: *men* belongs to foreign language material or it is a content-free syllable, such as *sche*.

4.3.2 Errors of the Hybrid Approach

During the development of the hybrid splitting approach, we did an extensive gold standard evaluation along the way, as described in section 4.1 above. The performance of the hybrid approach is limited by the performance of its constituents, namely the coverage of SMOR and the quality of the corpus from which part frequencies are derived. In the gold standard evaluation, we distinguished three error categories: **wrong split** (should not be split but was), **wrong not** (should be split but was not) and **wrong faulty** (should be split, and was split, but wrongly). Table 2 (cf. Section 4.1) contains the results of the gold standard we used as development set for our approach. In Table 5, we give a detailed distribution of the wrong splittings of the less constrained hybrid approach *sm*, into the following categories:

frequency-based:	SMOR found the correct split, but a wrong split was scored higher
unknown to SMOR:	lexeme or rule missing in SMOR
lexicalized in SMOR:	lexeme exists in SMOR, but fully lexicalized (no splitting possible)

It can be seen from Table 5 that most of the errors are due to corpus frequencies of the component parts. An example is *Nachteil* ("disadvantage"), which is lexicalized in German, but can also be correctly divided (even though it is semantically less plausible) into *nach|Teil* ("after|part"), and as both of these parts are high frequent, *Nachteil* is split.

As the corpus-driven approach uses the same disambiguation component, there must be an overlap of the frequency-based errors of the two approaches.

error type	Wrong		
	split	not	faulty
frequency-based	538	26	155
unknown to SMOR	3	7	0
lexicalized in SMOR	0	2	10
total number of errors	541	35	165

Table 5: Error analysis of *sm* with respect to the gold standard in Table 2 above.

The remaining two categories contain errors that are attributed to wrong or missing analyses in SMOR. Compared to the total number of errors, there are very few such errors. Most of the unknown words are proper names or compounds with proper names, such as *Petrischale* ("petri dish"). Here, the corpus-driven approach is able to correctly the compound into *Petri|Schale*.

There are a number of compounds in German that originally consisted of two words, but are now lexicalized. For some of them SMOR does not provide any splitting option. An example is *Sackgasse* ("dead end street") which contains the words *Sack* ("sack") and *Gasse* ("narrow street"), where SMOR leaves the word unsplit (but not unanalyzed: it is encoded as one lexeme), while the corpus-driven approach correctly splits it.

5 Translation Performance

5.1 System Description

The Moses toolkit (Koehn et al., 2007) was used to construct a baseline PBSMT system (with default parameters), following the instructions of the shared task[9]. The baseline system is Moses built exactly as described for the shared task baseline. Contrastive systems are also built identically, except for the use of preprocessing on the German training, tuning and testing data; this ensures that all measured effects on translation quality are attributable to the preprocessing. We used data from the EACL 2009 workshop on statistical machine translation[10]. The data include ∼1.2 million parallel sentences for training (EUROPARL and news), 1,025 sentences for tuning and 1,026 sentences for testing. All data was lowercased and tokenized, using the shared task tokenizer. We used the English side of the parallel data for the language model. As specified in the instructions, sentences longer than 40 words were removed from the bilingual training corpus, but not from the language model corpus. The monolingual language model training data (containing roughly 227 million words[11]) was used to derive corpus frequencies for the splitting approaches.

For tuning of feature weights we ran Minimum Error Rate Training (Och, 2003) until convergence, individually for each system (optimizing BLEU). The experiments were evaluated using BLEU (Papineni et al., 2002) and METEOR (Lavie and Agarwal, 2007)[12]. Tuning scores are calculated on lowercased, tokenized text; all test scores are case sensitive and performed on automatically recapitalized, detokenized text.

system	tuning BLEU	test BLEU	test METEOR
raw	18.10	15.72	47.65
cd	18.52	**16.17**	**49.29**
sm	19.47	**16.59**	**<u>49.98</u>**
sm@nn	19.42	**16.76**	**<u>49.77</u>**
smc	19.53	**16.63**	**<u>50.13</u>**
smc@nn	19.61	**16.40**	**<u>49.64</u>**

Table 6: Effects of compound splitting:
raw = without preprocessing, *cd* = corpus-driven,
sm = hybrid approach using all SMOR analyses,
smc = hybrid approach with minimal SMOR splits
**@nn* = split only nouns.
bold-face = significant wrt. *raw*
<u>underlined</u> = significant wrt. *cd*

5.2 Translation Results

The BLEU and METEOR scores of our experiments are summarized in Table 6. Results that are significantly better than the baseline are boldfaced[13]. Underlining indicates that a result is significantly better than corpus-driven.

Compared to not-splitting (*raw*), the corpus-driven approach (*cd*) gains 0.45 BLEU points and +1.64 in METEOR for testing. All variants of the hybrid approach (*sm**) score higher than *cd*, reaching up to +0.59 BLEU compared to *cd* and +1.04 BLEU compared to *raw* for *sm@nn*. In terms of METEOR, gains of up to +0.84 compared to *cd* and +2.48 compared to *raw* are observable for *smc*, all of them being significant with respect to both, *raw* and *cd*. The *smc* variant of the hybrid approach yielded the highest METEOR score and it was also found to be the most accurate one when evaluated against the linguistic gold standard in section 4.1.

The restriction to split only nouns (*@nn*) leads to a slightly improved performance of *sm* (+0.17) BLEU, while METEOR is slightly worse when the *@nn* constraint is used: -0.21. Despite the fact that it had a high precision in the gold standard evaluation of section 4.1 above, *smc*, when used with the *@nn* constraint, decreases in performance versus *smc* without the constraint, because the *@nn* variant leaves many compounds unsplit (cf. row "Wrong not", Table 2), Secion 4.1).

[9] http://www.statmt.org/wmt09/baseline.html

[10] http://www.statmt.org/wmt09/translation-task.html

[11] http://www.statmt.org/wmt09/training-monolingual.tar

[12] The version of METEOR used is 0.7, we use "exact porter-stem wn-synonmy", weights are "0.8 0.83 0.28".

[13] We used pair-wise bootstrap resampling using sample size 1,000 and p-value 0.05, code obtained from http://www.ark.cs.cmu.edu/MT

5.3 Vocabulary Reduction Through Compound Splitting

One of the main issues in translating from a compounding and/or highly inflected language into a morphologically less complex language is data sparsity: many source words occur very rarely, which makes it difficult to learn the correct translations. Compound splitting aims at making the vocabulary as small as possible but at the same time keeping as much of the morphological information as necessary to ensure translation quality. Table 7 shows the vocabulary sizes of our translation experiments, where "types" and "singles" refer to the training data and "unknown" refers to the test set. It can be seen that the vocabulary is smallest for the corpus-driven approach (*cd*). However, as the translation experiments in the previous section have shown, the *cd* approach was outperformed by the hybrid approaches, despite their larger vocabularies.

system	types	singles	unknown
raw	267,392	135,328	1,032
cd	97,378	36,928	506
sm	100,836	37,433	593
sm@nn	130,574	51,799	644
smc	109,837	39,908	608
smc@nn	133,755	52,505	650

Table 7: Measuring Vocabulary Reduction for Compound Splitting.

6 Conclusion

We combined linguistic analysis with corpus-based statistics and obtained better results in terms of both producing splittings and statistical machine translation performance. We provided an extensive analysis showing where our approach improves on corpus-driven splitting.

We believe that our work helps to validate the utility of SMOR. The unsupervised morphology induction community has already begun to evaluate using SMT (Viripioja et al., 2007). Developers of high recall hand-crafted morphologies should also consider statistical machine translation as a useful extrinsic evaluation.

Acknowledgments

This work was supported by Deutsche Forschungsgemeinschaft grant "Models of Morphosyntax for Statistical Machine Translation". We would like to thank Helmut Schmid.

References

Martin Braschler and Bärbel Ripplinger. 2004. How effective is stemming and decompounding for German text retrieval? *Information Retrieval*, 7(3-4):291–316.

Chris Dyer. 2009. Using a maximum entropy model to build segmentation lattices for MT. In *HLT-NAACL'09: Proceedings of the Human Language Technology Conference of the North American Chapter of the Association for Computational Linguistics*.

Philipp Koehn and Kevin Knight. 2003. Empirical methods for compound splitting. In *EACL '03: Proceedings of the 10th Conference of the European Chapter of the Association for Computational Linguistics*, pages 187–193, Morristown, NJ, USA. Association for Computational Linguistics.

Philipp Koehn, Hieu Hoang, Alexandra Birch, Chris Callison-Burch, Marcello Federico, Nicola Bertoldi, Brooke Cowan, Wade Shen, Christine Moran, Richard Zens, Chris Dyer, Ondrej Bojar, Alexandra Constantin, and Evan Herbst. 2007. Moses: Open source toolkit for statistical machine translation. In *ACL'07: Proceedings of the 45th Annual Meeting of the Association for Computational Linguistics, Demonstration Session*, pages 177–180.

Martha Larson, Daniel Willett, Joachim Köhler, and Gerhard Rigoll. 2000. Compound splitting and lexical unit recombination for improved performance of a speech recognition system for German parliamentary speeches. In *ICSLP'00: Proceedings of the 6th International Conference on Spoken Language Processing*, pages 945–948.

Alon Lavie and Abhaya Agarwal. 2007. Meteor: An automatic metric for MT evaluation with high levels of correlation with human judgements. In *ACL'07: Proceedings of the 2nd Workshop on Statistical Machine Translation within the 45th Annual Meeting of the Association for Computational Linguistics*, pages 228–231.

Sonja Nießen and Hermann Ney. 2000. Improving SMT quality with morpho-syntactic analysis. In *COLING'00: Proceedings of the 18th International Conference on Computational Linguistics*, pages 1081–1085. Morgan Kaufmann.

Franz Josef Och. 2003. Minimum error rate training in statistical machine translation. In *ACL'03: Proceedings of the 41st Annual Meeting of the Association for Compuational Linguistics*, pages 160–167.

Kishore Papineni, Salim Roukos, Todd Ward, and Wei-Jing Zhu. 2002. Bleu: A method for automatic evaluation of machine translation. In *ACL'02: Proceedings of the 40th Annual Meeting of the Association for Computational Linguistics*, pages 311–318.

Maja Popović, Daniel Stein, and Hermann Ney. 2006. Statistical machine translation of German compound words. In *FinTAL'06: Proceedings of the 5th International Conference on Natural Language Processing*, pages 616–624. Springer Verlag.

Helmut Schmid, Arne Fitschen, and Ulrich Heid. 2004. Smor: A German computational morphology covering derivation, composition and inflection. In *LREC '04: Proceedings of the 4th Conference on Language Resources and Evaluation*, pages 1263–1266.

Helmut Schmid. 1994. Probabilistic part-of-speech tagging using decision trees. In *Proceedings of the International Conference on New Methods in Language Processing*, pages 44–49.

Sara Stymne. 2008. German compounds in factored statistical machine translation. In *GoTAL '08: Proceedings of the 6th International Conference on Natural Language Processing*, pages 464–475. Springer Verlag.

Sami Virpioja, Jaakko J. Väyrynen, Mathias Creutz, and Markus Sadeniemi. 2007. Morphology-aware statistical machine translation based on morphs induced in an unsupervised manner. In *MT Summit '07: Proceedings of the 11th Machine Translation Summit*, pages 491–498.

Chunk-based Verb Reordering in VSO Sentences for Arabic-English Statistical Machine Translation

Arianna Bisazza and Marcello Federico
Fondazione Bruno Kessler
Human Language Technologies
Trento, Italy
{bisazza,federico}@fbk.eu

Abstract

In Arabic-to-English phrase-based statistical machine translation, a large number of syntactic disfluencies are due to wrong long-range reordering of the verb in VSO sentences, where the verb is anticipated with respect to the English word order. In this paper, we propose a chunk-based reordering technique to automatically detect and displace clause-initial verbs in the Arabic side of a word-aligned parallel corpus. This method is applied to preprocess the training data, and to collect statistics about verb movements. From this analysis, specific verb reordering lattices are then built on the test sentences before decoding them. The application of our reordering methods on the training and test sets results in consistent BLEU score improvements on the NIST-MT 2009 Arabic-English benchmark.

1 Introduction

Shortcomings of phrase-based statistical machine translation (PSMT) with respect to word reordering have been recently shown on the Arabic-English pair by Birch et al. (2009). An empirical investigation of the output of a strong baseline we developed with the Moses toolkit (Koehn et al., 2007) for the NIST 2009 evaluation, revealed that an evident cause of syntactic disfluency is the anticipation of the verb in Arabic Verb-Subject-Object (VSO) sentences – a class that is highly represented in the news genre[1].

Fig. 1 shows two examples where the Arabic main verb phrase comes before the subject. In such sentences, the subject can be followed by adjectives, adverbs, coordinations, or appositions that further increase the distance between the verb and its object. When translating into English – a primarily SVO language – the resulting long verb reorderings are often missed by the PSMT decoder either because of pure modeling errors or because of search errors (Germann et al., 2001): i.e. their span is longer than the maximum allowed distortion distance, or the correct reordering hypothesis does not emerge from the explored search space because of a low score. In the two examples, the missed verb reorderings result in different translation errors by the decoder, respectively, the introduction of a subject pronoun before the verb and, even worse, a verbless sentence.

In Arabic-English machine translation, other kinds of reordering are of course very frequent: for instance, adjectival modifiers following their noun and head-initial genitive constructions (*Idafa*). These, however, appear to be mostly local, therefore more likely to be modeled through phrase internal alignments, or to be captured by the reordering capabilities of the decoder. In general there is a quite uneven distribution of word-reordering phenomena in Arabic-English, and long-range movements concentrate on few patterns.

Reordering in PSMT is typically performed by *(i)* constraining the maximum allowed word movement and exponentially penalizing long reorderings (distortion limit and penalty), and *(ii)* through so-called lexicalized orientation models (Och et al., 2004; Koehn et al., 2007; Galley and Manning, 2008). While the former is mainly aimed at reducing the computational complexity of the decoding algorithm, the latter assigns at each decoding step a score to the next source phrase to cover, according to its orientation with respect to the last translated phrase. In fact, neither method discriminates among different reordering distances for a specific word or syntactic class. To our view, this could be a reason for their inadequacy to properly deal with the reordering peculiarities of the Arabic-English language pair. In

[1] In fact, Arabic syntax admits both SVO and VSO orders.

Proceedings of the Joint 5th Workshop on Statistical Machine Translation and MetricsMATR, pages 235–243,
Uppsala, Sweden, 15-16 July 2010. ©2010 Association for Computational Linguistics

src:	w **AstdEt** kl mn AlsEwdyp w lybyA w swryA$_{Subj}$ sfrA' hA$_{Obj}$ fy AldnmArk .
ref:	*Each of Saudi Arabia , Libya and Syria*$_{Subj}$ ***recalled*** *their ambassadors*$_{Obj}$ *from Denmark .*
MT:	He recalled all from Saudi Arabia , Libya and Syria ambassadors in Denmark .
src:	**jdd** AlEAhl Almgrby Almlk mHmd AlsAds$_{Subj}$ dEm h$_{Obj}$ l m$rwE Alr}ys Alfrnsy
ref:	*The Moroccan monarch King Mohamed VI*$_{Subj}$ ***renewed*** *his support*$_{Obj}$ *to the project of French President*
MT:	The Moroccan monarch King Mohamed VI his support to the French President

Figure 1: Examples of problematic SMT outputs due to verb anticipation in the Arabic source.

this work, we introduce a reordering technique that addresses this limitation.

The remainder of the paper is organized as follows. In Sect. 2 we describe our verb reordering technique and in Sect. 3 we present statistics about verb movement collected through this technique. We then discuss the results of preliminary MT experiments involving verb reordering of the training based on these findings (Sect. 4). Afterwards, we explain our lattice approach to verb reordering in the test and provide evaluation on a well-known MT benchmark (Sect. 5). In the last two sections we review some related work and draw the final conclusions.

2 Chunk-based Verb Reordering

The goal of our work is to displace Arabic verbs from their clause-initial position to a position that minimizes the amount of word reordering needed to produce a correct translation. In order to restrict the set of possible movements of a verb and to abstract from the usual token-based movement length measure, we decided to use shallow syntax chunking of the source language. Full syntactic parsing is another option which we have not tried so far mainly because popular parsers that are available for Arabic do not mark grammatical relations such as the ones we are interested in.

We assume that Arabic verb reordering only occurs between shallow syntax chunks, and not within them. For this purpose we annotated our Arabic data with the AMIRA chunker by Diab et al. (2004)[2]. The resulting chunks are generally short (1.6 words on average). We then consider a specific type of reordering by defining a production rule of the kind: *"move a chunk of type* T *along with its* L *left neighbours and* R *right neighbours by a shift of* S *chunks"*. A basic set of rules that displaces the verbal chunk to the right by at most 10 positions corresponds to the setting:

T='VP', L=0, R=0, S=1..10

In order to address cases where the verb is moved along with its adverbial, we also add a set of rules that include a one-chunk right context in the movement:

T='VP', L=0, R=1, S=1..10

To prevent verb reordering from overlapping with the scope of the following clause, we always limit the maximum movement to the position of the next verb. Thus, for each verb occurrence, the number of allowed movements for our setting is at most $2 \times 10 = 20$.

Assuming that a word-aligned translation of the sentence is available, the best movement, if any, will be the one that reduces the amount of distortion in the alignment, that is: *(i)* it reduces the number of swaps by 1 or more, and *(ii)* it minimizes the sum of distances between source positions aligned to consecutive target positions, i.e. $\sum_i |a_i - (a_{i-1} + 1)|$ where a_i is the index of the foreign word aligned to the ith English word. In case several movements are optimal according to these two criteria, e.g. because of missing word-alignment links, only the shortest good movement is retained.

The proposed reordering method has been applied to various parallel data sets in order to perform a quantitative analysis of verb anticipation, and to train a PSMT system on more monotonic alignments.

3 Analysis of Verb Reordering

We applied the above technique to two parallel corpora[3] provided by the organizers of the NIST-MT09 Evaluation. The first corpus (Gale-NW) contains human-made alignments. As these refer to non-segmented text, they were adjusted to

[2]This tool implies morphological segmentation of the Arabic text. All word statistics in this paper refer to AMIRA-segmented text.

[3]Newswire sections of LDC2006E93 and LDC2009E08, respectively 4337 and 777 sentence pairs.

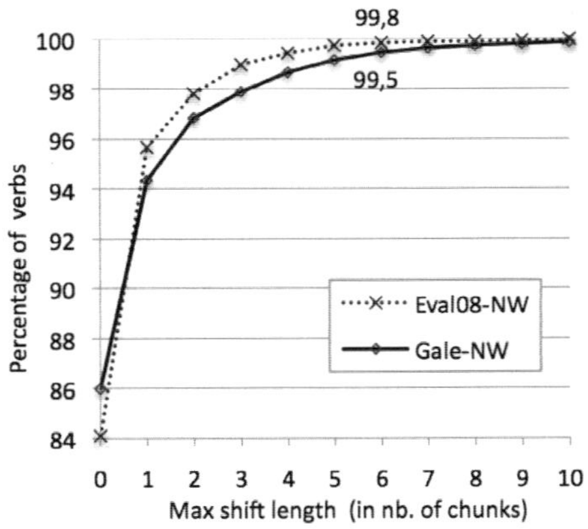

Figure 2: Percentage of verb reorderings by maximum shift (0 stands for no movement).

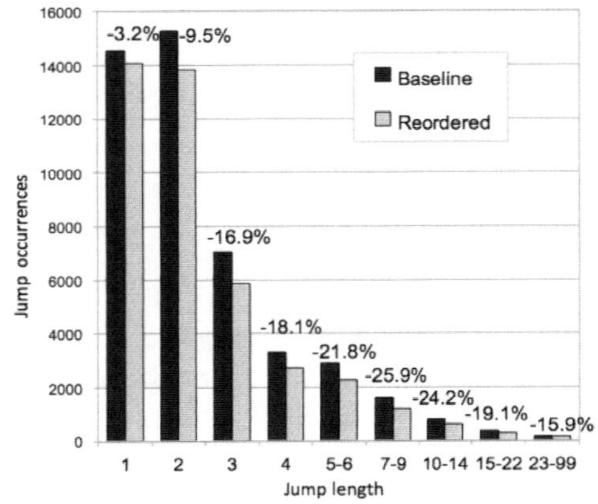

Figure 3: Distortion reduction in the GALE-NW corpus: jump occurrences grouped by length range (in nb. of words).

agree with AMIRA-style segmentation. For the second corpus (Eval08-NW), we filtered out sentences longer than 80 tokens in order to make word alignment feasible with GIZA++ (Och and Ney, 2003). We then used the *Intersection* of the direct and inverse alignments, as computed by Moses. The choice of such a high-precision, low-recall alignment set is supported by the findings of Habash (2007) on syntactic rule extraction from parallel corpora.

3.1 The *Verb's Dance*

There are 1,955 verb phrases in Gale-NW and 11,833 in Eval08-NW. Respectively 86% and 84% of these do not need to be moved according to the alignments. The remaining 14% and 16% are distributed by movement length as shown in Fig. 2: most verb reorderings consist in a 1-chunk long jump to the right (8.3% in Gale-NW and 11.6% in Eval08-NW). The rest of the distribution is similar in the two corpora, which indicates a good correspondence between verb reordering observed in automatic and manual alignments. By increasing the maximum movement length from 1 to 2, we can cover an additional 3% of verb reorderings, and around 1% when passing from 2 to 3. We recall that the length measured in chunks doesn't necessarily correspond to the number of jumped tokens. These figures are useful to determine an optimal set of reordering rules. From now on we will focus on verb movements of at most 6 chunks, as these account for about 99.5% of the verb occurrences.

3.2 Impact on Corpus Global Distortion

We tried to measure the impact of chunk-based verb reordering on the total word distortion found in parallel data. For the sake of reliability, this investigation was carried out on the manually aligned corpus (Gale-NW) only. Fig. 3 shows the positive effect of verb reordering on the total distortion, which is measured as the number of *words* that have to be *jumped* on the source side in order to cover the sentence in the target order (that is $|a_i - (a_{i-1} + 1)|$). Jumps have been grouped by length and the relative decrease of jumps per length is shown on top of each double column.

These figures do not prove as we hoped that verb reordering resolves *most* of the long range reorderings. Thus we manually inspected a sample of verb-reordered sentences that still contain long jumps, and found out that many of these were due to what we could call "unnecessary" reordering. In fact, human translations that are free to some extent, often display a global sentence restructuring that makes distortion dramatically increase. We believe this phenomenon introduces noise in our analysis since these are not reorderings that an MT system needs to capture to produce an accurate and fluent translation.

Nevertheless, we can see from the relative decrease percentages shown in the plot, that although short jumps are by far the most frequent, verb reordering affects especially medium and long range distortion. More precisely, our selective reordering technique solves 21.8% of the 5-to-6-words jumps, 25.9% of the 7-to-9-words jumps and 24.2% of the 10-to-14-words jumps, against only 9.5% of the 2-words jumps, for example. Since our primary goal is to improve the handling of long reorderings, this makes us think that we are advancing in a promising direction.

4 Preliminary Experiments

In this section we investigate how verb reordering on the source language can affect translation quality. We apply verb reordering both on the training and the test data. However, while the parallel corpus used for training can be reordered by exploiting word alignments, for the test corpus we need a verb reordering "prediction model". For these preliminary experiments, we assumed that optimal verb-reordering of the test data is provided by an *oracle* that has access to the word alignments with the reference translations.

4.1 Setup

We trained a Moses-based system on a subset of the NIST-MT09 Evaluation data[4] for a total of 981K sentences, 30M words. We first aligned the data with GIZA++ and use the resulting *Intersection* set to apply the technique explained in Sect. 2. We then retrained the whole system – from word alignment to phrase scoring – on the reordered data and evaluated it on two different versions of Eval08-NW: plain and oracle verb-reordered, obtained by exploiting word alignments with the first of the four available English references. The first experiment is meant to measure the impact of the verb reordering procedure on training only. The latter will provide an estimate of the maximum improvement we can expect from the application to the test of an optimal verb reordering prediction technique. Given our experimental setting, one could argue that our BLEU score is biased because one of the references was also used to generate the verb reordering. However, in a series of experiments not reported here, we evaluated the same systems using only the remaining three references and observed similar trends as when all four references are used.

Feature weights were optimized through MERT (Och, 2003) on the newswire section of the NIST-MT06 evaluation set (Dev06-NW), in the original version for the baseline system, in the verb-reordered version for the reordered system.

[4]LDC2007T08, 2003T07, 2004E72, 2004T17, 2004T18, 2005E46, 2006E25, 2006E44 and LDC2006E39 – the two last with first reference only.

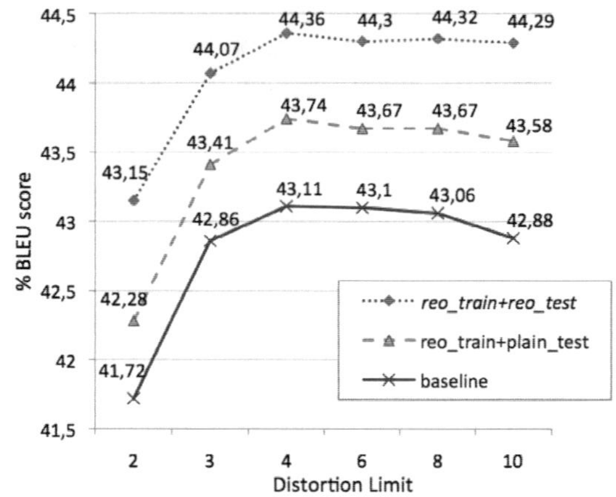

Figure 4: BLEU scores of baseline and reordered system on plain and oracle reordered Eval08-NW.

Fig. 4 shows the results in terms of BLEU score for *(i)* the baseline system, *(ii)* the reordered system on a plain version of Eval08-NW and *(iii)* the reordered system on the reordered test. The scores are plotted against the distortion limit (DL) used in decoding. Because high DL values (8-10) imply a larger search space and because we want to give Moses the best possible conditions to properly handle long reordering, we relaxed for these conditions the default pruning parameter to the point that led the highest BLEU score[5].

4.2 Discussion

The first observation is that the reordered system always performs better (0.5∼0.6 points) than the baseline on the plain test, despite the mismatch between training and test ordering. This may be due to the fact that automatic word alignments are more accurate when less reordering is present in the data, although previous work (Lopez and Resnik, 2006) showed that even large gains in alignment accuracy seldom lead to better translation performances. Moreover phrase extraction may benefit from a distortion reduction, since its heuristics rely on word order in order to expand the context of alignment links.

The results on the oracle reordered test are also interesting: a gain of at least 1.2 point absolute over the baseline is reported in all tested DL conditions. These improvements are remarkable, keeping in mind that only 31% of the train and 33% of the test sentences get modified by verb reordering.

[5]That is, the histogram pruning maximum stack size was set to 1000 instead of the default 200.

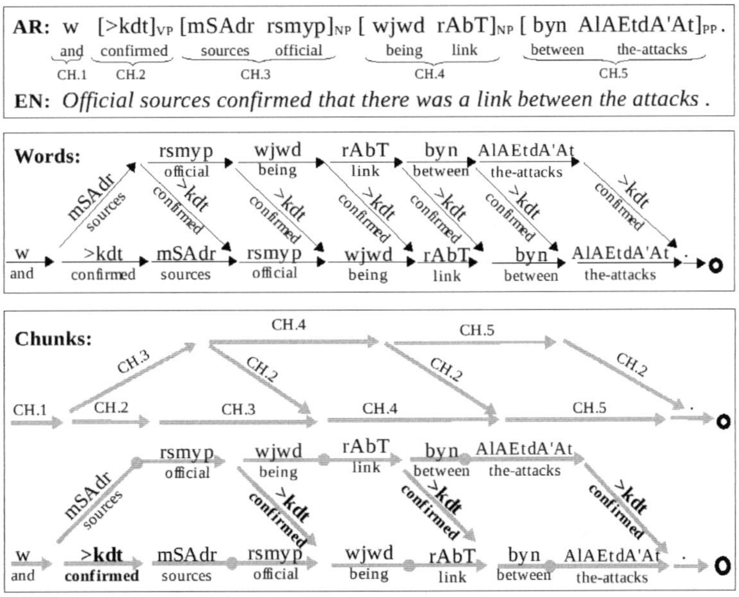

Figure 5: Reordering lattices for Arabic VSO sentences: word-based and chunk-based.

Concerning distortion, although long verb movements are often observed in parallel corpora, relaxing the DL to high values does not benefit the translation, even with our 'generous' setting (wider beam search). This is probably due to the fact that, with weakly constrained distortion, the risk of search errors increases as the reordering model fails to properly rank an exponentially growing set of permutations. Therefore many correct reordering hypotheses receive low scores and get lost in pruning or recombination.

5 Verb Reordering Lattices

Having assessed the negative impact of VSO sentences on Arabic-English translation performance, we now propose a method to improve the handling of this phenomenon at decoding time. As in real working conditions word alignments of the input text are not available, we explore a reordering lattice approach.

5.1 Lattice Construction

Firstly conceived to optimally encode multiple transcription hypothesis produced by a speech recognizer, word lattices have later been used to represent various forms of input ambiguity, mainly at the level of token boundaries (e.g. word segmentation, morphological decomposition, word decompounding (Dyer et al., 2008)).

A main problem when dealing with permutations is that the lattice size can grow very quickly when medium to long reorderings are represented. We are particularly concerned with this issue because our decoding will perform additional reordering on the lattice input. Thanks to the restrictions we set on our verb movement reordering rules described in Sect. 2 – i.e. only reordering between chunks and no overlap between consecutive verb chunks movement – we are able to produce quite compact word lattices.

Fig. 5 illustrates how a chunk-based reordering lattice is generated. Suppose we want to translate the Arabic sentence *"w >kdt mSAdr rsmyp wjwd rAbT byn AlAEtdA'At"*, whose English meaning is *"Official sources confirmed that there was a link between the attacks"*. The Arabic main verb *>kdt (confirmed)* is in pre-subject position. If we applied word-based rather than chunk-based rules to move the verb to the right, we would produce the first lattice of the figure, containing 7 paths (the original plus 6 verb movements). With the chunk-based rules, we treat instead chunks as units and get the second lattice. Then, by expanding each chunk, we obtain the final, less dense lattice, that compared to the first does not contain 3 (unlikely) reordering edges.

To be consistent with the reordering applied to the training data, we use a set of rules that move each verb phrase alone or with its following chunk by 1 to 6 chunks to the right. With this settings,

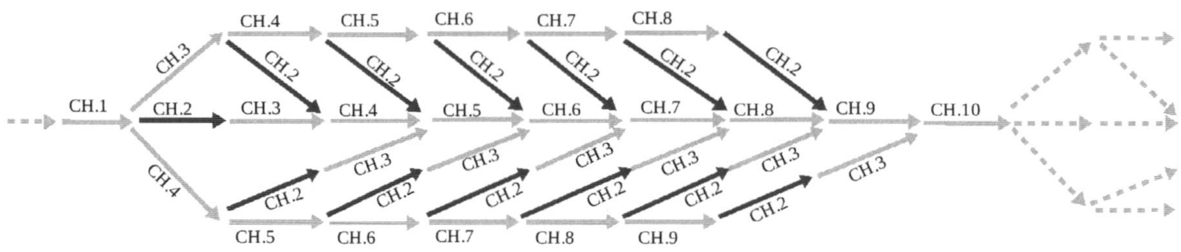

Figure 6: Structure of a chunk-based reordering lattice for verb reordering, before word expansion. Edges in boldface represent the verbal chunk.

our lattice generation algorithm computes a compact lattice (Fig. 6) that introduces at most $5 \times \Delta S$ chunk edges for each verb chunk, where ΔS is the permitted movement range (6 in this case).

Before translation, each edge has to be associated with a weight that the decoder will use as additional feature. To differentiate between the original word order and verb reordering we assign a fixed weight of 1 to the edges of the plain path, and 0.25 to the other edges. As future work we will devise more discriminative weighting schemes.

5.2 Evaluation

For the experiments, we relied on the existing Moses-implementation of non-monotonic decoding for word lattices (Dyer et al., 2008) with some fixes concerning the computation of reordering distance. The translation system is the same as the one presented in Sect. 4, to which we added an additional feature function evaluating the lattice weights (*weight-i*). Instead of rerunning MERT, we directly estimated the additional feature-function weight over a suitable interval (0.002 to 0.5), by running the decoder several times on the development set. The resulting optimal weight was 0.05.

Table 1 presents results on three test sets: **Eval08-NW** which was used to calibrate the reordering rules, **Reo08-NW** a specific test set consisting of the 33% of Eval08-NW sentences that actually require verb reordering, and **Eval09-NW** a yet unseen dataset (newswire section of the NIST-MT09 evaluation set, 586 sentences). Best results with lattice decoding were obtained with a distortion limit (DL) of 4, while best performance of text decoding was obtained with a DL of 6.

As we hoped, translating a verb reordering lattice yields an additional improvement to the reordering of the training corpus: from 43.67% to 44.04% on Eval08-NW and from 48.53% to 48.96% on Eval09-NW. The gap between the baseline and the score obtainable by oracle verb reordering, as estimated in the preliminary experiments on Eval08-NW (44.36%), has been largely filled.

On the specific test set – Reo08-NW – we observe a performance drop when reordered models are applied to non-reordered (plain) input: from 46.90% to 46.64%. Hence it seems that the mismatch between training and test data is significantly impacting on the reordering capabilities of the system with respect to verbs. We speculate that such negative effect is diluted in the full test set (Eval08-NW) and compensated by the positive influence of verb reordering on phrase extraction. Indeed, when the lattice technique is applied we get an improvement of about 0.6 point over the baseline, which is still a fair result, but not as good as the one obtained on the general test sets.

Finally, our approach led to an overall gain of 0.8 point BLEU over the baseline, on Eval09-NW. We believe this is a satisfactory result, given the fairly good starting performance, and given that the BLEU metric is known not to be very sensitive to word order variations (Callison-Burch et al., 2006). For the future, we plan to also use specific evaluation metrics that will allow us to isolate the impact of our approach on reordering, like the ones by Birch et al. (2010).

System	DL	eval08nw	reo08nw	eval09nw
baseline	6	43.10	46.90	48.13
reord. training +				
plain input	6	43.67	46.64	48.53
lattice	4	44.04	47.51	48.96
oracle reord.	*4*	*44.36*	*48.25*	*na*

Table 1: BLEU scores of baseline and reordered system on plain test and on reordering lattices.

6 Related Work

Linguistically motivated word reordering for Arabic-English has been proposed in several recent works. Habash (2007) extracts syntactic reordering rules from a word-aligned parallel corpus whose Arabic side has been fully parsed. The rules involve reordering of syntactic constituents and are applied in a deterministic way (always the most probable) as preprocessing of training and test data. The technique achieves consistent improvements only in very restrictive conditions: maximum phrase size of 1 and monotonic decoding, thus failing to enhance the existing reordering capabilities of PSMT. In (Crego and Habash, 2008; Elming and Habash, 2009) possible input permutations are represented through a word graph, which is then processed by a monotonic phrase- or n-gram-based decoder. Thus, these approaches are conceived as alternatives, rather than integrations, to PSMT reordering. On the contrary, we focused on a single type of significant long reorderings, in order to integrate class-specific reordering methods into a standard PSMT system.

To our knowledge, the work by Niehues and Kolss (2009) on German-English is the only example of a lattice-based reordering approach being coupled with reordering at decoding time. In their paper, discontinuous non-deterministic POS-based rules learned from a word-aligned corpus are applied to German sentences in the form of weighted edges in a word lattice. Their phrase-based decoder admits local reordering within a fixed window of 2 words, while, in our work, we performed experiments up to a distortion limit of 10. Another major difference is that we used shallow syntax annotation to effectively reduce the number of possible permutations. A first attempt to adapt our technique to the German language is described in Hardmeier et al. (2010).

Our work is also tightly related to the problem of noun-phrase subject detection, recently addressed by Green et al. (2009). In fact, detecting the extension of the subject can be a sufficient condition to guess the optimal reordering of the verb. In their paper, a discriminative classifier was trained on a rich variety of linguistic features to detect the full scope of Arabic NP subjects in verb-initial clauses. The authors reported an F-score of 61.3%, showing that the problem is hard to solve even when more linguistic information is available. In order to integrate the output of the classifier into a PSMT decoder, a specific translation feature was designed to reward hypotheses in which the subject is translated as a contiguous block. Unfortunately, no improvement in translation quality was obtained.

7 Conclusions

Word reordering remains one of the hardest problems in statistical machine translation. Based on the intuition that few reordering patterns would suffice to handle the most significant cases of long reorderings in Arabic-English, we decided to focus on the problem of VSO sentences.

Thanks to simple linguistic assumptions on verb movement, we developed an efficient, low-cost technique to reorder the training data, on the one hand, and to better handle verb reordering at decoding time, on the other. In particular, translation is performed on a compact word lattice that represents likely verb movements. The resulting system outperforms a strong baseline in terms of BLEU, and produces globally more readable translations. However, the problem is not totally solved because many verb reorderings are still missed, despite the suggestions provided by the lattice. Different factors can explain these errors: poor interaction between lattice and distortion/orientation models used by the decoder; poor discriminative power of the target language model with respect to different reorderings of the source.

As a first step to improvement, we will devise a discriminative weighting scheme based on the length of the reorderings represented in the lattice. For the longer term we are working towards bringing linguistically informed reordering constraints inside decoding, as an alternative to the lattice solution. In addition, we plan to couple our reordering technique with more informative language models, including for instance syntactic analysis of the hypothesis under construction. Finally we would like to compare the proposed chunk-based technique with one that exploits full syntactic parsing of the Arabic sentence to further decrease the reordering possibilities of the verb.

Acknowledgments

This work was supported by the EuroMatrixPlus project (IST-231720) which is funded by the European Commission under the Seventh Framework Programme for Research and Technological Development.

src:	w A$Ar AlsnAtwr AlY dEm h m$rwEA ErD ElY mjls Al$ywx
ref:	*The Senator referred to his support for a project proposed to the Senate*
base MT:	The Senator to support projects presented to the Senate
new MT:	Senator noted his support projects presented to the Senate

src:	mn jAnb h hdd >bw mSEb EbdAlwdwd Amyr AlqAEdp b blAd Almgrb AlAslAmy fy nfs Al$ryT b AlqyAm b slslp AEtdA'At w >EmAl <rhAbyp Dd AlmSAlH w Alm&ssAt AljzA}ryp fy AlEdyd mn AlmnATq AljzA}ryp
ref:	*For his part , Abu Musab Abd al-Wadud , the commander of al-Qaeda in the Islamic Maghreb Countries , threatened in the same tape to carry out a series of attacks and terrorist actions against Algerian interests and organizations in many parts of Algeria*
base MT:	For his part threatened Abu Musab EbdAlwdwd Amir al-Qaeda Islamic Morocco country in the same tape to carry out a series of attacks and terrorist acts against the interests and the Algerian institutions in many areas of Algiers
new MT:	For his part , Abu Musab EbdAlwdwd Amir al Qaida threatened to Morocco Islamic country in the same tape to carry out a series of attacks and terrorist acts against the interests of the Algerian and institutions in many areas of Algiers

src:	w ymtd Alm$rwE 500 km mtr w yrbT Almdyntyn Almqdstyn b mdynp jdp ElY sAHl AlbHr Al>Hmr .
ref:	*The project is 500 kilometers long and connects the two holy cities with the city of Jeddah on the Red Sea coast.*
base MT:	It extends the project 500 km and linking the two holy cities in the city of Jeddah on the Red Sea coast .
new MT:	The project extends 500 km , linking the two holy cities in the city of Jeddah on the Red Sea coast .

Figure 7: Examples showing MT improvements coming from chunk-based verb-reordering.

References

Alexandra Birch, Phil Blunsom, and Miles Osborne. 2009. A quantitative analysis of reordering phenomena. In *StatMT '09: Proceedings of the Fourth Workshop on Statistical Machine Translation*, pages 197–205, Morristown, NJ, USA. Association for Computational Linguistics.

Alexandra Birch, Miles Osborne, and Phil Blunsom. 2010. Metrics for MT evaluation: evaluating reordering. *Machine Translation*, Published online.

Chris Callison-Burch, Miles Osborne, and Philipp Koehn. 2006. Re-evaluation the role of BLEU in machine translation research. In *Proceedings of the 11th Conference of the European Chapter of the Association for Computational Linguistics*, Trento, Italy, April.

Josep M. Crego and Nizar Habash. 2008. Using shallow syntax information to improve word alignment and reordering for smt. In *StatMT '08: Proceedings of the Third Workshop on Statistical Machine Translation*, pages 53–61, Morristown, NJ, USA. Association for Computational Linguistics.

Mona Diab, Kadri Hacioglu, and Daniel Jurafsky. 2004. Automatic Tagging of Arabic Text: From Raw Text to Base Phrase Chunks. In Daniel Marcu Susan Dumais and Salim Roukos, editors, *HLT-NAACL 2004: Short Papers*, pages 149–152, Boston, Massachusetts, USA, May 2 - May 7. Association for Computational Linguistics.

Christopher Dyer, Smaranda Muresan, and Philip Resnik. 2008. Generalizing word lattice translation. In *Proceedings of ACL-08: HLT*, pages 1012–1020, Columbus, Ohio, June. Association for Computational Linguistics.

Jakob Elming and Nizar Habash. 2009. Syntactic reordering for English-Arabic phrase-based machine translation. In *Proceedings of the EACL 2009 Workshop on Computational Approaches to Semitic Languages*, pages 69–77, Athens, Greece, March. Association for Computational Linguistics.

Michel Galley and Christopher D. Manning. 2008. A simple and effective hierarchical phrase reordering model. In *EMNLP '08: Proceedings of the Conference on Empirical Methods in Natural Language Processing*, pages 848–856, Morristown, NJ, USA. Association for Computational Linguistics.

Ulrich Germann, Michael Jahr, Kevin Knight, Daniel Marcu, and Kenji Yamada. 2001. Fast decoding and optimal decoding for machine translation. In *Proceedings of the 39th Annual Meeting of the Association for Computational Linguistics (ACL)*, pages 228–335, Toulouse, France.

Spence Green, Conal Sathi, and Christopher D. Manning. 2009. NP subject detection in verb-initial Arabic clauses. In *Proceedings of the Third Workshop on Computational Approaches to Arabic Script-based Languages (CAASL3)*, Ottawa, Canada.

Nizar Habash. 2007. Syntactic preprocessing for statistical machine translation. In Bente Maegaard, editor, *Proceedings of the Machine Translation Summit XI*, pages 215–222, Copenhagen, Denmark.

Christian Hardmeier, Arianna Bisazza, and Marcello Federico. 2010. FBK at WMT 2010: Word lattices for morphological reduction and chunk-based reordering. In *Proceedings of the Joint Fifth Workshop on Statistical Machine Translation and Metrics MATR*, Uppsala, Sweden, July. Association for Computational Linguistics.

P. Koehn, H. Hoang, A. Birch, C. Callison-Burch, M. Federico, N. Bertoldi, B. Cowan, W. Shen, C. Moran, R. Zens, C. Dyer, O. Bojar, A. Constantin, and E. Herbst. 2007. Moses: Open source toolkit for statistical machine translation. In *Proceedings of the 45th Annual Meeting of the Association for Computational Linguistics Companion Volume Proceedings of the Demo and Poster Sessions*, pages 177–180, Prague, Czech Republic.

Adam Lopez and Philip Resnik. 2006. Word-based alignment, phrase-based translation: What's the link? In *5th Conference of the Association for Machine Translation in the Americas (AMTA)*, Boston, Massachusetts, August.

Jan Niehues and Muntsin Kolss. 2009. A POS-based model for long-range reorderings in SMT. In *Proceedings of the Fourth Workshop on Statistical Machine Translation*, pages 206–214, Athens, Greece, March. Association for Computational Linguistics.

Franz Josef Och and Hermann Ney. 2003. A systematic comparison of various statistical alignment models. *Computational Linguistics*, 29(1):19–51.

F. J. Och, D. Gildea, S. Khudanpur, A. Sarkar, K. Yamada, A. Fraser, S. Kumar, L. Shen, D. Smith, K. Eng, V. Jain, Z. Jin, and D. Radev. 2004. A smorgasbord of features for statistical machine translation. In *Proceedings of the Joint Conference on Human Language Technologies and the Annual Meeting of the North American Chapter of the Association of Computational Linguistics (HLT-NAACL)*, Boston, MA.

Franz Josef Och. 2003. Minimum error rate training in statistical machine translation. In Erhard Hinrichs and Dan Roth, editors, *Proceedings of the 41st Annual Meeting of the Association for Computational Linguistics*, pages 160–167.

Head Finalization: A Simple Reordering Rule for SOV Languages

Hideki Isozaki, Katsuhito Sudoh, Hajime Tsukada, Kevin Duh
NTT Communication Science Laboratories, NTT Corporation
2-4 Hikaridai, Seikacho, Sorakugun, Kyoto, 619-0237, Japan
{isozaki,sudoh,tsukada,kevinduh}@cslab.kecl.ntt.co.jp

Abstract

English is a typical SVO (Subject-Verb-Object) language, while Japanese is a typical SOV language. Conventional Statistical Machine Translation (SMT) systems work well within each of these language families. However, SMT-based translation from an SVO language to an SOV language does not work well because their word orders are completely different. Recently, a few groups have proposed rule-based preprocessing methods to mitigate this problem (Xu et al., 2009; Hong et al., 2009). These methods rewrite SVO sentences to derive more SOV-like sentences by using a set of handcrafted rules. In this paper, we propose an alternative single reordering rule: **Head Finalization**. This is a syntax-based preprocessing approach that offers the advantage of simplicity. We do not have to be concerned about part-of-speech tags or rule weights because the powerful Enju parser allows us to implement the rule at a general level. Our experiments show that its result, **Head Final English (HFE)**, follows almost the same order as Japanese. We also show that this rule improves automatic evaluation scores.

1 Introduction

Statistical Machine Translation (SMT) is useful for building a machine translator between a pair of languages that follow similar word orders. However, SMT does not work well for distant language pairs such as English and Japanese, since English is an SVO language and Japanese is an SOV language.

Some existing methods try to solve this word-order problem in language-independent ways. They usually parse input sentences and learn a reordering decision at each node of the parse trees. For example, Yamada and Knight (2001), Quirk et al. (2005), Xia and McCord (2004), and Li et al. (2007) proposed such methods.

Other methods tackle this problem in language-dependent ways (Katz-Brown and Collins, 2008; Collins et al., 2005; Nguyen and Shimazu, 2006). Recently, Xu et al. (2009) and Hong et al. (2009) proposed rule-based preprocessing methods for SOV languages. These methods parse input sentences and reorder the words using a set of handcrafted rules to get SOV-like sentences.

If we could completely reorder the words in input sentences by preprocessing to match the word order of the target language, we would be able to greatly reduce the computational cost of SMT systems.

In this paper, we introduce a single reordering rule: **Head Finalization**. *We simply move syntactic heads to the end of the corresponding syntactic constituents (e.g., phrases and clauses).* We use only this reordering rule, and we do not have to consider part-of-speech tags or rule weights because the powerful Enju parser allows us to implement the rule at a general level.

Why do we think this works? The reason is simple: Japanese is a typical **head-final** language. That is, a syntactic head word comes after non-head (dependent) words. SOV is just one aspect of head-final languages. In order to implement this idea, we need a parser that outputs **syntactic heads**. **Enju** is such a parser from the University of Tokyo (`http://www-tsujii.is.s.u-tokyo.ac.jp/enju`). We discuss other parsers in section 5.

There is another kind of head: **semantic heads**. Hong et al. (2009) used Stanford parser (de Marneffe et al., 2006), which outputs semantic head-based dependencies; Xu et al. (2009) also used the same representation.

The use of syntactic heads and the number of **dependents** are essential for the simplicity of

Proceedings of the Joint 5th Workshop on Statistical Machine Translation and MetricsMATR, pages 244–251,
Uppsala, Sweden, 15-16 July 2010.

Head Finalization (See Discussion). Our method simply checks whether a tree node is a syntactic head. We do not have to consider what we are moving and how to move it. On the other hand, Xu et al. had to introduce dozens of weighted rules, probably because they used the semantic head-based dependency representation without restriction on the number of dependents.

The major difference between our method and the above conventional methods, other than its simplicity, is that our method moves not only verbs and adjectives but also functional words such as prepositions.

2 Head Finalization

Figure 1 shows Enju's XML output for the simple sentence: "`John hit a ball.`" The tag `<cons>` indicates a nonterminal node and `<tok>` indicates a terminal node or a word (token). Each node has a unique `id`. Head information is given by the node's `head` attribute. For instance, node `c0`'s head is node `c3`, and `c3` is a `VP`, or verb phrase. Thus, Enju treats not only words but also non-terminal nodes as heads.

Enju outputs at most two child nodes for each node. One child is a head and the other is a dependent. `c3`'s head is `c4`, which is `VX`, or a fragment of a verb phrase. `c4`'s head is `t1` or `hit`, which is `VBD` or a past-tense verb. The upper picture of Figure 2 shows the parse tree graphically. Here, $\star$ indicates an edge that is linked from a 'head.'

Our **Head Finalization** rule simply swaps two children when the head child appears before the dependent child. In the upper picture of Fig. 2, `c3` has two children `c4` and `c5`. Here, `c3`'s head `c4` appears before `c5`, so `c4` and `c5` are swapped.

The lower picture shows the swapped result. Then we get `John a ball hit`, which has the same word order as its Japanese translation *jon wa bohru wo utta* except for the functional words `a`, *wa*, and *wo*.

We have to add Japanese particles *wa* (topic marker) or *ga* (nominative case marker) for `John` and *wo* (objective case marker) for `ball` to get an acceptable Japanese sentence.

It is well known that SMT is not good at generating appropriate particles from English, whitch does not have particles. Particle generation was tackled by a few research groups (Toutanova and Suzuki, 2007; Hong et al., 2009).

Here, we use Enju's output to generate seeds

```
⟨sentence id="s0" parse_status="success"⟩
  ⟨cons id="c0" cat="S" xcat="" head="c3"⟩
    ⟨cons id="c1" cat="NP" xcat="" head="c2"⟩
      ⟨cons id="c2" cat="NX" xcat="" head="t0"⟩
        ⟨tok id="t0" cat="N" pos="NNP"
                  base="john"⟩John⟨/tok⟩
      ⟨/cons⟩
    ⟨/cons⟩
    ⟨cons id="c3" cat="VP" xcat="" head="c4"⟩
      ⟨cons id="c4" cat="VX" xcat="" head="t1"⟩
        ⟨tok id="t1" cat="V" pos="VBD" base="hit"
                  arg1="c1" arg2="c5"⟩hit⟨/tok⟩
      ⟨/cons⟩
      ⟨cons id="c5" cat="NP" xcat="" head="c7"⟩
        ⟨cons id="c6" cat="DP" xcat="" head="t2⟩
          ⟨tok id="t2" cat="D" pos="DT" base="a"
                  arg1="c7"⟩a⟨/tok⟩
        ⟨/cons⟩
        ⟨cons id="c7" cat="NX" xcat="" head="t3"⟩
          ⟨tok id="t3" cat="N" pos="NN"
                  base="ball"⟩ball⟨/tok⟩
        ⟨/cons⟩
      ⟨/cons⟩
    ⟨/cons⟩
  ⟨/cons⟩
.⟨/sentence⟩
```

Figure 1: Enju's XML output (some attributes are removed for readability).

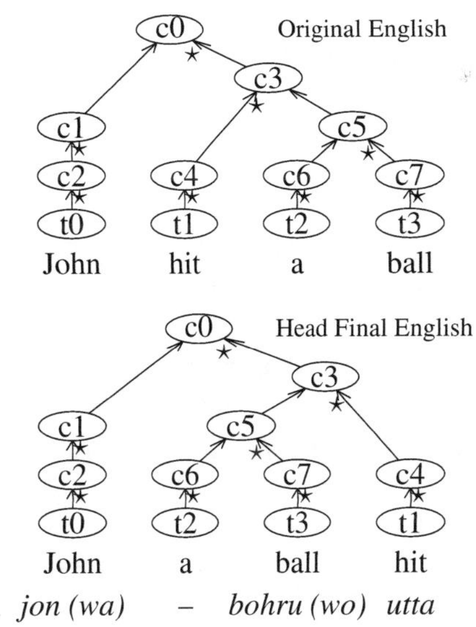

Figure 2: Head Finalization of a simple sentence ($\star$ indicates a head).

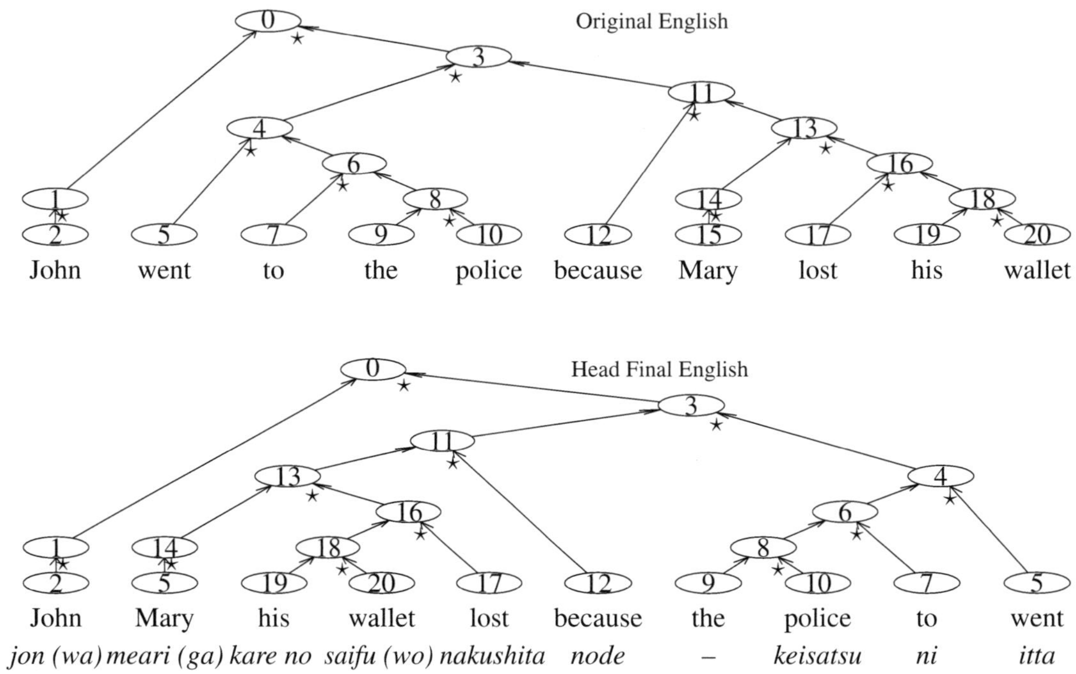

Figure 3: Head-Finalizing a complex sentence.

for particles. As Fig. 1 shows, the verb `hit` has `arg1="c1"` and `arg2="c5"`. This indicates that `c1 (John)` is the subject of `hit` and `c5 (a ball)` is the object of `hit`. We add seed words `va1` after `arg1` and `va2` after `arg2`. Then, we obtain `John va1 a ball va2 hit`. We do not have to add `arg2` for `be` because `be`'s `arg2` is not an object but a complement. We introduced the idea of particle seed words independently but found that it is very similar to Hong et al. (2009)'s method for Korean.

Figure 3 shows Enju's parse tree for a more complicated sentence "`John went to the police because Mary lost his wallet.`" For brevity, we hide the terminal nodes, and we removed the nonterminal nodes' prefix `c`.

Conventional Rule-Based Machine Translation (RBMT) systems swap X and Y of "X because Y" and move verbs to the end of each clause. Then we get "Mary his wallet lost because John the police to went." Its word-to-word translation is a fluent Japanese sentence: *meari (ga) kare no saifu (wo) nakushita node jon (wa) keisatsu ni itta*.

On the other hand, our Head Finalization with particle seed words yields a slightly different word order "John va1 Mary va1 his wallet va2 lost because the police to went." Its word-to-word translation is *jon wa meari ga kare no saifu wo nakushita node keisatsu ni itta*. This is also an acceptable Japanese sentence.

This difference comes from the syntactic role of '`because`.' In our method, Enju states that `because` is a dependent of `went`, whereas RBMT systems treat `because` as a clause conjunction.

When we use Xu et al.'s preprocessing method, '`because`' moves to the beginning of the sentence. We do not know a good monotonic translation of the result.

Preliminary experiments show that HFE looks good as a first approximiation of Japanese word order. However, we can make it better by introducing some heuristic rules. (We did not see the test set to develop these heuristic rules.)

From a preliminary experiment, we found that **coordination** expressions such as `A and B` and `A or B` are reordered as `B and A` and `B or A`. Although `A` and `B` have syntactically equal positions, the order of these elements sometimes matters. Therefore, we decided to stop swapping them at coordination nodes, which are indicated `cat` and `xcat` attributes of the Enju output. We call this the **coordination exception rule**. In addition, we avoid Enju's splitting of numerical expressions such as "`12,345`" and "`(1)`" because this splitting leads to inappropriate word orders.

3 Experiments

In order to show how closely our Head Finalization makes English follow Japanese word order, we measured Kendall's τ, a rank correlation coefficient. We also measured BLEU (Papineni et al., 2002) and other automatic evaluation scores to show that Head Finalization can actually improve the translation quality.

We used NTCIR7 PAT-MT's Patent corpus (Fujii et al., 2008). Its training corpus has 1.8 million sentence pairs. We used MeCab (`http://mecab.sourceforge.net/`) to segment Japanese sentences.

3.1 Rough evaluation of reordering

First, we examined rank correlation between Head Final English sentences produced by the Head Finalization rule and Japanese reference sentences. Since we do not have handcrafted word alignment data for an English-to-Japanese bilingual corpus, we used GIZA++ (Och and Ney, 2003) to get automatic word alignment.

Based on this automatic word alignment, we measured Kendall's τ for the word order between HFE sentences and Japanese sentences. Kendall's τ is a kind of rank correlation measure defined as follows. Suppose a list of integers such as L = [2, 1, 3, 4]. The number of all integer pairs in this list is ${}_4C_2 = 4 \times 3/(2 \times 1) = 6$. The number of increasing pairs is five: $(2,3)$, $(2,4)$, $(1,3)$, $(1,4)$, and $(3,4)$. Kendall's τ is defined by

$$\tau = \frac{\#\text{increasing pairs}}{\#\text{all pairs}} \times 2 - 1.$$

In this case, we get $\tau = 5/6 \times 2 - 1 = 0.667$.

For each sentence in the training data, we calculate τ based on a GIZA++ alignment file, `en-ja.A3.final`. (We also tried `ja-en.A3.final`, but we got similar results.) It looks something like this:

`John hit a ball .`
`NULL` ({3}) *jon* ({1}) *wa* ({}) *bohru* ({4})
wo ({}) *utta* ({2}) . ({5})

Numbers in `({ })` indicate corresponding English words. The article '`a`' has no corresponding word in Japanese, and such words are listed in `NULL ({ })`. From this alignment information, we get an integer list [1, 4, 2, 5]. Then, we get $\tau = 5/{}_4C_2 \times 2 - 1 = 0.667$.

For HFE in Figure 2, we will get the following alignment.

`John va1 a ball va2 hit .`
`NULL` ({3}) *jon* ({1}) *wa* ({2}) *bohru* ({4})
wo ({5}) *utta* ({6}) . ({7})

Then, we get [1, 2, 4, 5, 6, 7] and $\tau = 1.0$. We use $\overline{\tau}$ or the average of τ over all training sentences to observe the tendency.

Sometimes, one Japanese word corresponds to an English phrase:

`John went to Costa Rica .`
`NULL` ({}) *jon* ({1}) *wa* ({}) *kosutarika* ({4 5})
ni ({3}) *itta* ({2}) . ({6})

We get [1, 4, 5, 3, 2, 6] from this alignment.

When the same word (or derivative words) appears twice or more in a single English sentence, two or more non-consecutive words in the English sentence are aligned to a single Japanese word:

`rate of change of speed`
`NULL` ({}) *sokudo* ({5}) *henka* ({3})
no ({2 4}) *wariai* ({1})

We excluded the ambiguously aligned words `(2 4)` from the calculation of τ. We use only [5, 3, 1] and get $\tau = -1.0$. The exclusion of these words will be criticized by statisticians, but even this rough calculation of τ sheds light on the weak points of Head Finalization.

Because of this exclusion, the best value $\tau = 1.0$ does not mean that we obtained the perfect word ordering, but low τ values imply failures. In section 4, we use τ to analyze failures.

By examining low τ sentences, we found that patent documents have a lot of expressions such as "`motor 2`." These are reordered (`2 motor`) and slightly degrade τ. We did not notice this problem until we handled the patent corpus because these expressions are rare in other documents such as news articles. Here, we added a rule to keep these expressions.

We did not use any dictionary in our experiment, but if we add dictionary entries to the training data, it raises $\overline{\tau}$ because most entries are short. One-word entries do not affect $\overline{\tau}$ because we cannot calculate τ. Most multi-word entries are short noun phrases that are not reordered (τ = 1.0). Therefore, we should exclude dictionary entries from the calculation of $\overline{\tau}$.

3.2 Quality of translation

It must be noted that the rank correlation does not directly measure the quality of translation. Therefore, we also measured BLEU and other automatic evaluation scores of the translated sentences. We used Moses (Koehn, 2010) for Minimum Error Rate Training and decoding.

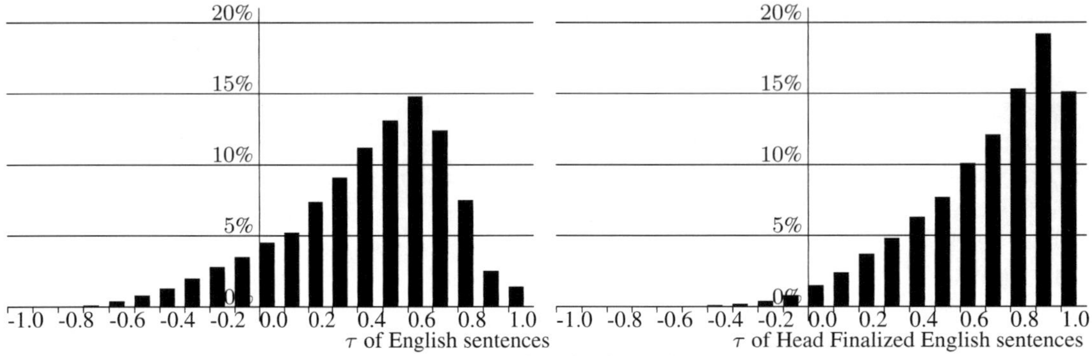

Figure 4: Distribution of τ

We used the development set (915 sentences) in the NTCIR7 PAT-MT PSD data as well as the formal run test set (1,381 sentences).

In the NTCIR7 PAT-MT workshop held in 2008, its participants used different methods such as hierarchical phrase-based SMT, RBMT, and EBMT (Example-Based Machine Translation). However, the organizers' Moses-based baseline system obtained the best BLEU score.

4 Results

First, we show τ values to evaluate word order, and then we show BLEU and other automatic evaluation scores.

4.1 Rank correlation

The original English sentences have $\overline{\tau} = 0.451$. Head Finalization improved it to 0.722. Figure 4 shows the distribution of τ for all training sentences. HFE reduces the percentage of low τ sentences: **49.6% of the 1.8 million HFE sentences have $\tau \geq 0.8$ and 15.1% have $\tau = 1.0$.**

We also implemented Xu et al.'s method with the Stanford parser 1.6.2. Its $\overline{\tau}$ was 0.624. The rate of the sentences with $\tau \geq 0.8$ was 30.6% and the rate of $\tau = 1.0$ was 4.3%.

We examined low τ sentences of our method and found the following reasons for low τ values.

- The sentence pair is not an exact one-to-one translation. A Japanese reference sentence for "`I bought the cake.`" can be something like "`The cake I bought.`" or "`The person who bought the cake is me.`"
- Mistakes in Enju's tagging or parsing. We encountered certain POS tag mistakes:
  - VBZ/NNS mistake: '`advances`' of "`... device advances along ...`" is VBZ, but NNS is assigned.
  - VBN/VBD mistake: '`encoded`' of "`... the error correction encoded data is supplied ...`" is VBN, but VBD is assigned.

  These tagging mistakes lead to global parsing mistakes. In addition, just like other parsers, Enju tends to make mistakes when a sentence has a comma or '`and`.'
- Mistakes/Ambiguity of GIZA++ automatic word alignment. Ambiguity happens when a single sentence has two or more occurrences of a word or derivatives of a word (e.g., difference/different/differential). As we described above, ambiguously aligned words are removed from calculation of τ, and small reordering mistakes in other words are emphasized.

main cause	count
tagging/parsing mistakes	12
VBN/VBD mistake	(4)
VBZ/NNS mistake	(2)
comma or `and`	(2)
inexact translation	7
wrong alignment	1

Table 1: Main causes of 20 worst sentences

We analyzed the 20 worst sentences with $\tau < -0.5$ when we used only 400,000 sentences for GIZA++. Their causes are summarized in Table 1. In general, low τ sentences have two or more causes, but here we show only the most influential cause for each sentence. This table shows that mistakes in tagging and parsing are major causes of low τ values. When we used all of 1.8 million

Method	BLEU	WER	TER
proposed (0)	30.79	0.663	0.554
proposed (3)	30.97	0.665	0.554
proposed (6)	**31.21**	**0.660**	**0.549**
proposed (9)	31.11	0.661	**0.549**
proposed (12)	30.98	0.662	0.551
proposed (15)	31.00	0.662	0.552
no va (6)	30.99	0.669	0.559
Organizer	*30.58*	*0.755*	*0.592*

Table 2: Automatic Evaluation of Translation Quality (Numbers in parentheses indicate distortion limits).

sentence pairs, only 11 sentences had $\tau < -0.5$ among the 1.8 million sentences.

4.2 Automatic Evaluation of Translation Quality

In general, it is believed that translation between English and Japanese requires a large *distortion limit* (dl), which restricts how far a phrase can move. SMT reasearchers working on E-J or J-E translation often use **dl=-1 (unlimited) as a default value, and this takes a long translation time.**

For PATMT J-E translation, Katz-Brown and Collins (2008) showed that dl=unlimited is the best and it requires a very long translation time. For PATMT E-J translation, Kumai et al. (2008) claimed that they achieved the best result "*when the distortion limit was 20 instead of* -1."

Table 2 compares the single-reference BLEU score of the proposed method and that of the Moses-based system by the NTCIR-7 PATMT organizers. This organizers' system was better than all participants (Fujii et al., 2008) in terms of BLEU. Here, we used Bleu Kit (`http://www.mibel.cs.tsukuba.ac.jp/norimatsu/bleu_kit/`) following the PATMT's overview paper (Fujii et al., 2008). The table shows that dl=6 gives the best result, and even dl=0 (no reordering in Moses) gives better scores than the organizers' Moses.

Table 2 also shows Word Error Rates (WER) and Translation Error Rates (TER) (Snover et al., 2006). Since they are error rates, smaller is better. Although the improvement of BLEU is not very impressive, the score of WER is greatly reduced. This difference comes from the fact that BLEU measures only local word order, while WER measures global word order. Another line 'no va' stands for our method without `vas` or particle seeds. Without particle seeds, all scores slightly drop.

Method	ROUGE-L	IMPACT	PER
proposed (6)	**0.480**	**0.369**	0.390
no va (6)	0.475	0.368	0.398
Organizer	*0.403*	*0.339*	**0.384**

Table 3: Improvement in word order

Echizen-ya et al. (2009) showed that IMPACT and ROUGE-L are highly correlated to human evaluation in evaluating J-E patent translation. Therefore, we also used these evaluation methods here for E-J translation. Table 3 shows that the proposed method is also much better than the organizers' Moses in terms of these measures. Without particle seeds, these scores also drop slightly.

On the other hand, Position-independent Word Error Rate (PER), which completely disregards word order, does not change very much. These facts indicate that our method improves word order, which is the most important problem in E-J translation.

The organizers' Moses uses dl=unlimited, and it has been reported that its MERT training took two weeks. On the other hand, our MERT training with dl=6 took only eight hours on a PC: Xeon X5570 2.93 GHz. Our method takes extra time to parse sentences by Enju, but it is easy to run the parser in parallel.

5 Discussion

Our method used an HPSG parser, which gives rich information, but it is not easy to build such a parser. It is much easier to build word dependency parsers and Penn Treebank-style parsers. In order use these parsers, we have to add some heuristic rules.

5.1 Word Dependency Parsers

At first, we thought that we could substitute a word dependency parser for Enju by simply rephrasing a **head** with a **modified word**. Xu et al. (2009) used a semantic head-based dependency parser for a similar purpose. Even when we use a syntactic head-based dependency parser instead, we encountered their 'excessive movement' problem.

A straightforward application of their rules changes

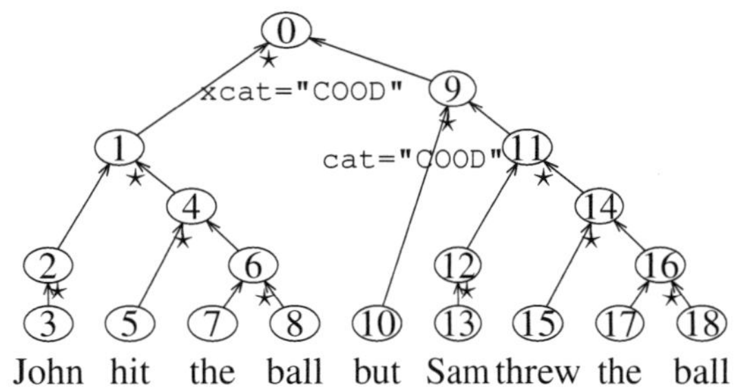

Figure 5: Head Finilization does not mix up clauses

(0) John hit the ball but Sam threw the ball.

to

(1) John the ball but Sam the ball threw hit.

Here, the two clauses are mixed up. To prevent this, they disallow any movement across punctuation and conjunctions. Then they get a better result:

(2) John the ball hit but Sam the ball threw.

When we used Enju, these clauses were not mixed up. Enju-based Head Finalization gave the same word order as (2):

(3) John va1 ball va2 hit but Sam va1 ball va2 throw.

Figure 5 shows Enju's parse tree. When Head Finalization swaps the children of a mother node, the children do not move beyond the range of the mother node. Therefore, Head Finalization based on Enju does not mix up the first clause `John hit the ball` covered by Node 1 with the second clause `Sam threw the ball` covered by Node 11. Moreover, our coordination exception rule keeps the order of these clauses. Thus, non-terminal nodes in Enju's output are useful to protect clauses.

When we use a word-dependency parser, we assume that the modified words are heads. Furthermore, the Head Finalization rule is rephrased as "move modified words after modifiers." Therefore, `hit` is moved after `threw` just like (2), and the two clauses become mixed up. Consequently, we need a heuristic rule like Xu's.

5.2 Penn Treebank-style parsers

We also tried Charniak-Johnson's parser (Charniak and Johnson, 2005). PyInputTree (`http://www.cs.brown.edu/~dmcc/software/PyInputTree/`) gives heads. Enju outputs at most two children for a mother node, but Penn Treebank-style parsers do not have such a limitation on the number of children. This fact causes a problem.

When we use Enju, '`This toy is popular in Japan`' is reordered as '`This toy va1 Japan in popular is`.' Its monotonic translation is fluent: *kono omocha wa nihon de ninki ga aru.*

On the other hand, Charniak-Johnson's parser outputs the following S-expression for this sentence (we added asterisks (⋆) to indicate heads).

```
(S (NP (DT This) (NN⋆ toy))
  (VP⋆ (AUX⋆ is)
     (ADJP (JJ⋆ popular))
     (PP (IN⋆ in) (NP (NNP⋆ Japan)))))
```

Simply moving heads to the end introduces '`Japan in`' between '`is`' and '`popular`': *this toy va1 popular Japan in is.* It is difficult to translate this monotonically because of this interruption.

Reversing the children order (Xu et al., 2009) reconnects `is` and `popular`. We get '`This toy (va1) Japan in popular is`' from the following reversed S-expression.

```
(S (NP (DT This) (NN⋆ toy))
  (VP⋆ (PP (IN⋆ in) (NP (NNP⋆ Japan)))
     (ADJP (JJ⋆ popular))
     (AUX⋆ is)))
```

5.3 Limitation of Head Finalization

Head Finalization gives a good first approximation of Japanese word order in spite of its simplicity. However, it is not perfect. In fact, a small distortion limit improved the performance.

Sometimes, the Japanese language does not have an appropriate word for monotonic translation. For instance, '`I have no time`' becomes '`I va1 no time va2 have`.' Its monotonic translation is '`watashi wa nai jikan wo motteiru`,' but this sentence is not acceptable. An acceptable literal translation is '`watashi wa jikan ga nai`.' Here, '`no`' corresponds to '`nai`' at the end of the sentence.

6 Conclusion

To solve the word-order problem between SVO languages and SOV langugages, we introduced a new reordering rule called **Head Finalization**. This rule is simple, and we do not have to consider POS tags or rule weights. We also showed that this reordering improved automatic evaluation scores of English-to-Japanese translation. Improvement of the BLEU score is not very impressive, but other evaluation scores (WER, TER, LOUGE-L, and IMPACT) are greatly improved.

However, Head Finalization requires a sophisticated HPSG tagger such as Enju. We showed that severe failures are caused by Enju's POS tagging mistakes. We discussed the problems of other parsers and how to solve them.

Our future work is to build our own parser that makes fewer errors and to apply Head Finalization to other SOV languages such as Korean.

Acknowledgements

We would like to thank Dr. Yusuke Miyao for his useful advice on the usage of Enju. We also thank anonymous reviewers for their valuable suggestions.

References

Eugene Charniak and Mark Johnson. 2005. Coarse-to-fine n-best parsing and MaxEnt discriminative reranking. In *Proc. of the Annual Meeting of the Association of Computational Linguistics (ACL)*, pages 173–180.

Michael Collins, Philipp Koehn, and Ivona Kucerova. 2005. Clause restructuring for statistical machine translation. In *Proc. of the Annual Meeting of the Association of Computational Linguistics (ACL)*.

Marie-Catherine de Marneffe, Bill MacCartney, and Christopher D. Manning. 2006. Generating typed dependency parses from phrase structure parses. In *Proc. of the Language Resources and Evaluation Conference (LREC)*, pages 449–454.

Hiroshi Echizen-ya, Terumasa Ehara, Sayori Shimohata, Atsushi Fujii, Masao Utiyama, Mikio Yamamoto, Takehito Utsuro, and Noriko Kando. 2009. Meta-evaluation of automatic evaluation methods for machine translation using patent translation data in NTCIR-7. In *Proceedings of the 3rd Workshop on Patent Translation*, pages 9–16.

Atsushi Fujii, Masao Utiyama, Mikio Yamamoto, and Takehito Utsuro. 2008. Overview of the patent translation task at the NTCIR-7 workshop. In *Working Notes of the NTCIR Workshop Meeting (NTCIR)*, pages 389–400.

Gumwon Hong, Seung-Wook Lee, and Hae-Chang Rim. 2009. Bridging morpho-syntactic gap between source and target sentences for English-Korean statistical machine translation. In *Proc. of ACL-IJCNLP*, pages 233–236.

Jason Katz-Brown and Michael Collins. 2008. Syntactic reordering in preprocessing for Japanese → English translation: MIT system description for NTCIR-7 patent translation task. In *Working Notes of the NTCIR Workshop Meeting (NTCIR)*.

Philipp Koehn, 2010. *MOSES, Statistical Machine Translation System, User Manual and Code Guide*.

Hiroyuki Kumai, Hirohiko Segawa, and Yasutsugu Morimoto. 2008. NTCIR-7 patent translation experiments at Hitachi. In *Working Notes of the NTCIR Workshop Meeting (NTCIR)*, pages 441–444.

Chi-Ho Li, Dongdong Zhang, Mu Li, Ming Zhou, Minghui Li, and Yi Guan. 2007. A probabilistic approach to syntax-based reordering for statistical machine translation. In *Proc. of the Annual Meeting of the Association of Computational Linguistics (ACL)*, pages 720–727.

Thai Phuong Nguyen and Akira Shimazu. 2006. Improving phrase-based statistical machine translation with morphosyntactic transformation. *Machine Translation*, 20(3):147–166.

Franz Josef Och and Hermann Ney. 2003. A systematic comparison of various statistical alignment models. *Computational Linguistics*, 29(1):19–51.

Kishore Papineni, Salim Roukos, Todd Ward, and Wei-Jing Zhu. 2002. BLEU: a method for automatic evaluation of machine translation. In *Proc. of the Annual Meeting of the Association of Computational Linguistics (ACL)*, pages 311–318.

Chris Quirk, Arul Menezes, and Colin Cherry. 2005. Dependency treelet translation: Syntactically informed phrasal SMT. In *Proc. of the Annual Meeting of the Association of Computational Linguistics (ACL)*, pages 271–279.

Matthew Snover, Bonnie Dorr, Richard Schwartz, Linnea Micciulla, and John Makhoul. 2006. A study of translation edit rate with targeted human annotation. In *Proceedings of Association for Machine Translation in the Americas*.

Kristina Toutanova and Hisami Suzuki. 2007. Generating case markers in machine translation. In *Proc. of NAACL-HLT*, pages 49–56.

Fei Xia and Michael McCord. 2004. Improving a statistical MT system with automatically learned rewrite patterns. In *Proc. of the International Conference on Computational Linguistics (COLING)*, pages 508–514.

Peng Xu, Jaeho Kang, Michael Ringgaard, and Franz Och. 2009. Using a dependency parser to improve SMT for Subject-Object-Verb languages. In *Proc. of NAACL-HLT*, pages 245–253.

Kenji Yamada and Kevin Knight. 2001. A syntax-based statistical translation model. In *Proc. of the Annual Meeting of the Association of Computational Linguistics (ACL)*, pages 523–530.

Aiding Pronoun Translation with Co-Reference Resolution

Ronan Le Nagard and Philipp Koehn
University of Edinburgh
Edinburgh, United Kingdom
s0678231@sms.ed.ac.uk, pkoehn@inf.ed.ac.uk

Abstract

We propose a method to improve the translation of pronouns by resolving their co-reference to prior mentions. We report results using two different co-reference resolution methods and point to remaining challenges.

1 Introduction

While machine translation research has made great progress over the last years, including the increasing exploitation of linguistic annotation, the problems are mainly framed as the translation of isolated sentences. This restriction of the task ignores several discourse-level problems, such as the translation of pronouns.

Pronouns typically refer to earlier mention of entities, and the nature of these entities may matter for translation. A glaring case is the translation of the English *it* and *they* into languages with grammatical gender (as for instance, most European languages). If *it* refers to an object that has a male grammatical gender in the target language, then its translation is a male pronoun (e.g., *il* in French), while referring to a female object requires a female pronoun (e.g., *elle* in French).

Figure 1 illustrates the problem. Given a pair of sentence such as

The window is open. It is blue.

the translation of *it* cannot be determined given only the sentence it occurs in. It is essential that we connect it to the entity *the window* in the previous sentence.

Making such a connection between references to the same entity is called co-reference resolution, or anaphora resolution.[1] While this problem has motivated significant research in the field of natural language processing, the integration of co-reference resolution methods into machine translation has been lacking. The recent wave of work on statistical machine translation has essentially not moved beyond sentence-level and has not touched co-reference resolution.

Our approach to aiding pronoun translation with co-reference resolution can be outlined as follows. On both training and test data, we identify the anaphoric noun of each occurrence of *it* and *they* on the source side (English). We then identify the noun's translation into the target language (in our experiments, French), and identify the target noun's grammatical gender. Based on that gender, we replace *it* with *it-masculine, it-feminine* or *it-neutral* (ditto for *they*). We train a statistical machine translation system with a thusly annotated corpus and apply it to the annotated test sentences.

Our experiments show some degree of success of the method, but also highlight that current co-reference resolution methods (we implemented Hobbs and Lappin/Laess) have not yet achieved sufficient performance to significantly reduce the number of errors in pronoun translation.

2 Related Work

2.1 Co-Reference and Machine Translation

The problem of anaphora resolution applied to machine translation has not been treated much in the literature. Although some papers refer to the problem, their content is mostly concerned with the problem of anaphora resolution and speak very little about the integration of such an algorithm in the bigger theme of machine translation.

Mitkov et al. [1995] deplore the lack of study of the question and try to address it with the implementation of an anaphora resolution model and its integration into the CAT2 translation system [Sharp, 1988], a transfer system that uses an ab-

[1] In the context of pronouns, anaphora resolution and co-reference resolution are identical, but they differ in other contexts.

Proceedings of the Joint 5th Workshop on Statistical Machine Translation and MetricsMATR, pages 252–261,
Uppsala, Sweden, 15-16 July 2010.

The window is open. **It** *is blue.*	*La fenêtre est ouverte.* **Elle** *est bleue.*	CORRECT
The window is open. **It** *is black.*	*La fenêtre est ouverte.* **Il** *est noir.*	WRONG
The oven is open. **It** *is new.*	*Le four est ouverte.* **Elle** *est neuve.*	WRONG
The door is open. **It** *is new.*	*La porte est ouverte.* **Elle** *est neuve.*	CORRECT

Figure 1: Translation errors due to lack of co-reference resolution (created with Google Translate).

stract intermediate representation. The anaphora resolution step adds additional features to the intermediate representation.

Leass and Schwall [1991] present a list of rules to be implemented directly into the machine translation system. These rules seem to work mostly like a dictionary and are checked in a priority order. They state what should be the translation of a pronoun in each special case. Being specific to the problem of translating anaphors into Korean, these are of little interest to our current work.

2.2 Co-Reference : Syntactic Method

The first work on the resolution of pronouns was done in the 1970s, largely based on a syntactic approach. This work was based on empirical data and observations about natural languages. For example, Winograd [1972] uses the notion of co-reference chains when stating that if a single pronoun is used several times in a sentence or a group of adjunct sentences, all instances of this pronoun should refer to the same entity.

Others have also stated that antecedents of a pronoun should be found in one of the n sentences preceding the pronouns, where n should be small [Klapholz and Lockman, 1975]. Hobbs [1978] showed that this number was close to one, although no actual limit could be really imposed.

In work by both Hobbs [1978] and Winograd [1972], the resolution of pronouns also involves a syntactic study of the parse tree of sentences. The order with which candidate antecedents are prioritized is similar in both studies. They first look for the antecedent to be a subject, then the direct object of a noun and finally an indirect object. Only thereafter previous sentences are checked for an antecedent, in no particular order, although the left to right order seems to be preferred in the literature as it implicitly preserves the order just mentioned. Winograd uses focus values of noun phrases in sentences to choose the appropriate antecedent.

Hobbs also refers to the work by Charniak [1972] and Wilks [1975] for the problem of anaphora resolution. However, they do not offer a complete solution to the problem. For this reason Hobbs [1978] is often considered to be the most comprehensive early syntactic study of the problem, and as such, often used as a baseline to evaluate anaphora resolution methods. We use his work and comment on it in a later section.

Another approach to anaphora resolution is based on the centering theory first proposed by Grosz et al. [1995]. Brennan et al. [1987] propose an algorithm for pronoun resolution based on centering theory. Once again, the entities are ranked according to their grammatical role, where subject is more salient than existential constructs, which are more salient than direct and indirect objects. Walker [1998] further improves the theory of centering theory for anaphora resolution, proposing the idea of cache model to replace the stack model described originally.

Another syntactic approach to the problem of co-reference resolution is the use of weighted features by Lappin and Leass [1994] which we present in more details in a further section. This algorithm is based on two modules, a syntactic filter followed by a system of salience weighting. The algorithm gathers all potential noun phrase antecedents of a pronoun from the current and close previous sentences. The syntactic filter then filters out the ones that are unlikely to be antecedents, according to different rules, including general agreement rules. The remaining candidate noun phrases are weighted according to salience factors. The authors demonstrate a higher success rate with their algorithm (86%) than with their implementation of the Hobbs algorithm (82%).

2.3 Co-Reference : Statistical Approach

Machine Learning has also been applied to the problem of anaphora resolution. Ng [2005] gives a survey of the research carried out in this area.

The work by Aone and Bennett [1995] is among the first in this field. It applies machine learning to anaphora resolution on Japanese text. The authors use a set of 66 features, related to both the referent itself and to the relation between the referent and its antecedent. They include "lexical (e.g. category), syntactic (e.g. grammatical role), semantic (e.g. semantic class), and positional (e.g. distance between anaphor and antecedent)" information.

Ge et al. [1998] also present a statistical algorithm based on the study of statistical data in a large corpus and the application of a naive Bayes model. The authors report an accuracy rate of 82.9%, or 84.2% with the addition of statistical data on gender categorization of words.

In more recent work, Kehler et al. [2004] show a move towards the use of common-sense knowledge to help the resolution of anaphors. They use referring probabilities taken from a large annotated corpus as a knowledge base.

2.4 Shared Tasks and Evaluation

Although a fairly large amount of research has been done in the field, it is often reported [Mitkov et al., 1995] that there does not yet exist a method to resolve pronouns which is entirely satisfactory and effective. Different kinds of texts (novel, newspaper,...) pose problems [Hobbs, 1978] and the field is also victim of lack of standardization.

Algorithms are evaluated on different texts and large annotated corpora with co-reference information is lacking to check results. A response to these problems came with the creation of shared tasks, such as the MUC [Grishman and Sundheim, 1996] which included a co-reference subtask [Chinchor and Hirschmann, 1997] and led to the creation of the MUC-6 and MUC-7 corpora.

There are other annotation efforts worth mentioning, such as the ARRAU corpus [Poesio and Artstein, 2008] which include texts from various sources and deals with previous problems in annotation such as anaphora ambiguity and annotation of information on agreement, grammatical function and reference. The Anaphoric Bank and the Phrase Detectives are both part of the Anawiki project [Poesio et al., 2008] and also promise the creation of a standardized corpus. The first one allows for the sharing of annotated corpora. The second is a collaborative effort to annotate large corpora through the Web. In its first year of use, the system saw the resolution of 700,000 pronouns.

3 Method

The method has two main aspects: the application of co-reference to annotate pronouns and the subsequent integration into statistical machine translation. We begin our description with the latter aspect.

3.1 Integration into Machine Translation

English pronouns such as *it* (and *they*) do not have a unique French translation, but rather several words are potential translations. Note that for simplicity we comment here on the pronoun *it*, but the same conclusions can be drawn from the study of the plural pronoun *they*.

In most cases, the translation ambiguity cannot be resolved in the context of a single sentence because the pronoun refers to an antecedent in a previous sentence. Statistical machine translation focuses on single sentences and therefore cannot deal with antecedents in previous sentences. Our approach does not fundamentally change the statistical machine translation approach, but treats the necessary pronoun classification as a external task.

Hence, the pronoun *it* is annotated, resulting in the three different surface forms presented to the translation system: *it-neutral*, *it-feminine*, *it-masculine*. These therefore encode the gender information of the pronoun and each of them will be match to its corresponding French translation in the translation table.

An interesting point to note is the fact that these pronouns only encode gender information about the pronouns and omit number and person information. This has two reasons.

Firstly, study of the lexical translation table for the baseline system shows that the probability of having the singular pronoun *it* translated into the plural pronouns *ils* and *elles* is 10 times smaller than the one for the singular/singular translation pair. This means that the number of times a singular pronoun in English translates into a plural pronoun in French is negligible.

The other reason to omit the cases when a singular pronoun is translated into a plural pronoun is due to the performance of our algorithm. Indeed, the detection of number information in the algorithm is not good enough and returns many false results which would reduce the performance of the final system. Also, adding the number agreement to the pronoun would mean a high segmentation between all the different possibilities, which we assumed would result in worse performance of the translation system.

Once we have created a way to tag the pronouns with gender information, the system needs to learn

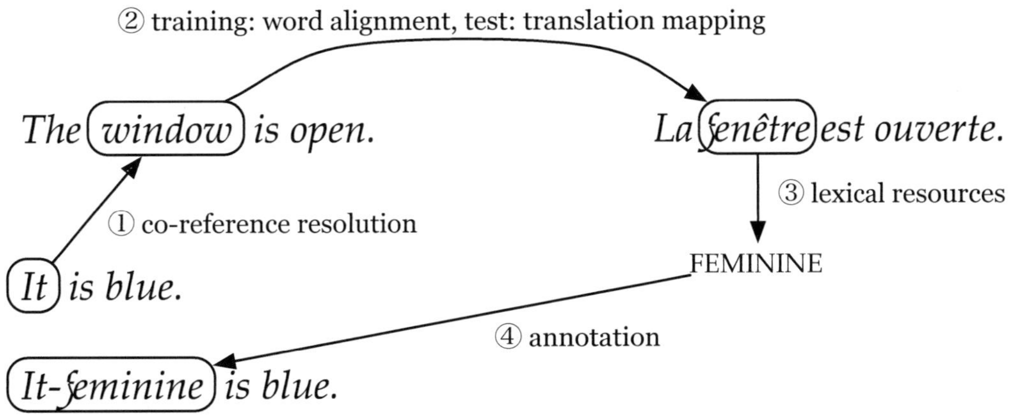

Figure 2: Overview of the process to annotate pronouns: The word *it* is connected to the antecedent *window* which was translated as *fenêtre*, a feminine noun. Thus, the pronoun is annotated as *it-feminine*.

the new probabilities that link the source language pronoun to the target language pronouns. That is all instances of *it* in the training data, which can be found at any position in the corpus sentences, should be replaced by one of its three declension. However, it is important to stress that the gender information that should be encoded in the English corpus is the one which corresponds to the gender of the French translation of the antecedent.

In order to find the correct gender information for the pronoun, we execute the co-reference resolution algorithm on the English text which returns the antecedent of the pronoun (more on this in the next section). Note that we are not interested in the English gender of the antecedent, but in gender of its translation.

Thus, we need to detect the French translation of the English antecedent. For the training data, we rely on the word alignment that is produced as a by-product of the training of a statistical machine translation system. For the test data, we rely on the implicit word mapping performed during the translation process.

Note that this requires in practice the translation of all preceding sentences before we can annotate the current sentence. To avoid this practical burden in our experiments, we simply use the mapping in the baseline translation. The performance of the sentence alignment (88

Once the French word is obtained, it is used as the input of a module which returns the gender of the entity in French. This is then used to replace the original pronoun with the new gendered pronoun.

The entire process is illustrated in Figure 2.

3.2 The Hobbs Algorithm

The Hobbs algorithm is considered to be the baseline algorithm for co-reference resolution. The algorithm uses the syntactic parse tree of the sentences as input.

The algorithm traverses the parse tree and selects appropriate candidate referents to the pronoun. It goes up sentence nodes and checks all NP nodes encountered for agreement with the pronoun. The order in which the algorithm traverses the tree ensures that some priorities are respected, to make sure the most probable antecedent is returned first. By doing this, the algorithm tends to enforces some of the constraints that apply to co-reference [Jurafsky et al., 2000]. The recency constraint is enforced thanks to the order in which the algorithm traverses the sentences and both the binding and grammatical role constraints are enforced by the use of the syntactic tree and Part-Of-Speech tags on the words.

Because the algorithm only uses the parse tree of the sentences, the semantic meaning of words is completely omitted in the process of selecting candidate antecedents and no knowledge is required except for the implicit knowledge contained within agreement features.

As mentioned earlier, the Hobbs algorithm goes up the tree from the given pronoun to the top of the tree and stops at each sentence or noun node on its way. In each of these nodes, it performs breadth first search of the sub tree and returns any noun phrase node encountered as a potential antecedent. If the antecedent is genuine (according to gender, number, and person agreement), it is returned.

In case no antecedent was found in the current sentence, the algorithm goes back up in the text, looking at each sentence separately, in a left-to-right breadth first fashion. This ensures that the subject/object/indirect object priorities and hierarchy are respected. Again, if a candidate NP has matching agreement features, it is returned as the antecedent of the pronoun. Otherwise the algorithm goes one sentence higher.

The original algorithm uses limited knowledge because it assumes that:

- Dates do not move.
- Places do not move.
- Large fixed objects don't move.

This add limited semantic restrictions for the antecedent chosen. Indeed, if the pronoun is followed by a motion verb, the antecedent could not be a date, a place or a large fixed object. However, as Hobbs states himself, those constraints help little since they do not apply in most cases.

3.3 The Lappin and Leass Algorithm

Lappin and Leass [1994] proposed an anaphora resolution algorithm for third person pronouns and lexical anaphors. It is based on slot grammar and uses syntax combined with a system of weights to select the appropriate antecedent of a pronoun. The implementation of the algorithm we deal with here is fairly different from the one presented in the original paper, and is largely inspired from the JavaRAP implementation [Qiu et al., 2004].

The first important variation was mentioned earlier and concerns the application of co-reference resolution to machine translation. We concentrate in this work on the resolution of third person pronouns, and we omit reflexive pronouns (*itself, themselves*) (referred to as lexical anaphora in some works).

Another variation comes from the use of the Collins parser [Collins, 2003]. Although work on the original algorithm uses McCord's Slot Grammar parser [McCord, 1990], work on JavaRAP shows that rules can be created to simulate the categories and predicates used in slot grammar. Also, Preiss [2002] evaluates the use of different parsers for the Lappin and Leass algorithm, showing that performance of the algorithm is not related to the performance of the parser itself. The JavaRAP implementation uses a Charniak parser, which performs worse than the Collins parser in Preiss' research.

For these reasons and in order to allow for reuse of the code used previously in the implementation of the Hobbs algorithm, the input to the Lappin and Leass algorithm is text parsed with the Collins parser.

It should be noted that the Lappin and Leass algorithm (also called RAP for Resolution of Anaphora Procedure) has been used in the original research for the application of machine translation.

The algorithm processes sentence by sentence, keeping in memory the information regarding the last four sentences. In the first step of the algorithm, all noun phrases (NPs) are extracted and classified. Definite and indefinite NPs are separated, and pleonastic pronouns are segregated from other pronouns.

The notion of salience is very important in RAP, as it allows the algorithm to choose between competing NPs. All candidate NPs are given a "salience weighting", which represents the importance and visibility of the phrase in the sentence, and in relation to the pronoun that is being resolved.

Salience weighting is based on the syntactic form of the sentence and the value for an NP is calculated through the contribution, or not, of different salience factors, to which weights are associated. This calculation ensures that different importance will be given to a subject noun phrase in a sentence, and a noun phrase that is embedded in another or that represents the indirect object of a verb.

There are a number of salience factors such as sentence recency, subject emphasis, existential emphasis, accusative emphasis, etc. Each factor is associated with a predefined weight.

Once the weight of each candidate has been calculated, the algorithm uses syntactic information to filter out the noun phrases that the pronoun is unlikely to refer to. This includes agreement and other checks.

The list of candidate NPs obtained after this processing is then cleared of all NPs that fall under a given threshold. The original algorithm then deals with singular and plural pronouns in different ways. The JavaRAP implementation however does not use these differences and we refer the reader to Lappin and Leass' paper for further information.

Finally, the candidate NPs mentioned in the previous list are ranked according to their salience weights and the highest scoring one is returned as the antecedent of the pronoun. In case several NPs have the same salience weight, the one closest to the pronoun is returned.

3.4 Pleonastic It

English makes an extensive use of the pronoun *it* in a pleonastic fashion. That is, many times, *it* is considered to be structural and does not refer to any entity previously mentioned. The following are examples of pleonastic uses of *it*:

- *It is raining.*
- *It seems important that I see him.*
- *The session is opened, it was announced.*

Being able to discriminate the use of a structural *it* from the use of a referential use of *it* is very important for the success of the co-reference algorithm. Indeed, resolving a pleonastic *it* will be a waste of time for the algorithm, and more importantly, it will increase the chance of errors and will result in poorer performances. Moreover, the pleonastic *it* is most times translated masculine in French, meaning any other resolution by the algorithm will yield errors.

In the past, the importance given to the detection of the pleonastic use of *it* has varied from author to author. As an example, Rush et al. [1971], in their work on automatic summarization, only mentioned the problem. Others formed a set of rules to detect them, such as Liddy et al. [1987] with 142 rules, or Lappin and Leass [1994] who propose a very restricted set of rules for the detection of the structural *it*.

Paice and Husk [1987] carried out extensive research on the topic and their paper defines various categories for the pronoun *it* as well as proposing a set of rules that allow to differentiate when the pronoun *it* is used as a relational pronoun or as a pleonastic pronoun.

Their method categorise words according to the presence of given words around the pronoun it. They distinguish constructs such as *it VERB STATUS to TASK* ; construct expressing doubt containing words such as *whether*, *if*, *how* ; parenthetical it such as *it seems*, *it was said*. The original article identifies seven categories for pleonastic pronouns.

Since their own results showed a success rate of 92.2% on a test section of the LOBC corpus and the implementation of their technique yields results similar to the implementation of a machine learning technique, this method seemed appropriate for our purpose.

4 Experiments

In this section, we comment on the tools used for the implementation of the algorithms, as well as support tools and corpora.

The implementation of both of the algorithms was done using the Python programming language, which was chosen for its simplicity in processing text files and because it is the language in which the Natural Language Toolkit is developed.

The Natural Language Toolkit (NLTK) is a suite of Python modules used for research into natural language processing. We mostly used its Tree and ParentedTree modules which enable the representation of parse trees into tree structures. NLTK also includes a naive Bayes classifier, which we used in association with the names corpus in order to classify proper names into gender categories according to a set of features. We also use NLTK for its named entity capacities, in order to find animacity information of entities.

English sentences were annotated with the MXPOST Part of Speech tagger and the Collins syntactic parser.

The Lefff lexicon, introduced by Sagot et al. [2006] was used to get agreement features of French words. It contains over 80,000 French words,[2] along with gender and number information.

We used the open source Moses toolkit [Koehn et al., 2007] and trained standard phrase-based translation models.

As training data, we used the Europarl corpus [Koehn, 2005], a commonly used parallel corpus in statistical machine translation research. While there are also commonly used Europarl test sets, these do not contain sentences in sequence for complete documents. Instead, we used as test set the proceedings from October 5, 2000 - a set of 1742 sentences from the held-out portion of the corpus. We translated the test set both with a baseline system and a system trained on the annotated training data and tested on an annotated test set.

[2]The original version version of the lexicon is available from http://www.labri.fr/perso/clement/lefff/.

	Word	Count
English singular	*he*	17,181
	she	4,575
	it	214,047
French singular	*il*	187,921
	elle	45,682
English plural	*they*	54,776
French plural	*ils*	32,350
	elles	16,238

Table 1: Number of sentences in the training corpus containing third person personal pronouns.

Truth	Method	
	Pleonastic	Referential
Pleonastic	**42**	20
Referential	19	**98**

Table 2: Detection of pleonastic pronouns

5 Results

5.1 Corpus Statistics for Pronouns

Personal pronouns are among the most frequent words in text. In the training corpus of 1,393,452 sentences, about a 6th contain third person personal pronouns. See Table 1 for detailed statistics.

The English pronoun *it* is much more frequent than *he* or *she*. For both languages, the masculine forms are more frequent than the feminine forms.

There are then a total of 233,603 sentences containing a third person pronoun in French, and 235,803 sentences containing a third person pronoun in English. This means that over 2,000 of those pronouns in English do not have equivalent in French. Similarly for plural: A total of 48,588 sentences contain a plural pronoun in French, against 54,776 in English. That shows that over 6,000 of the English ones are not translated into French.

5.2 Detection of the Pleonastic *it*

We checked, how well our method for pleonastic *it* detection works on a section of the test set. We achieved both recall and precision of 83% for the categorization of the referential *it*. For details, please see Table 2.

5.3 Translation Probabilities

Let us now examine the translation probabilities for the annotated and un-annotated pronouns. Details are given in Table 3.

correct annotation	33/59	56%
correct translation:		
annotated	40/59	68%
correctly annotated	27/33	82%
baseline	41/59	69%

Table 4: **Translation Results:** On a manually examined portion of the test set, only 33 of 59 pronouns are labeled correctly. The translation results of our method does not differ significantly from the baseline. Most of the correctly annotated pronouns are translated correctly.

In the baseline system, both *it* and *they* have a strong translation preference for the masculine over the feminine form of the French pronoun. *It* translates with probability 0.307 to *il* and with probability *0.090* to *elle*. The rest of the probability mass is taken up by the NULL token, punctuation, and a long tail of unlikely choices.

For both the Hobbs and the Lappin/Laess algorithm, the probability distribution is shifted to the desired French pronoun. The shift is strongest for the masculine marked *they*, which prefers the masculine *ils* with 0.431 over the feminine *elles* with 0.053 (numbers for Hobbs, Lappin/Laess numbers are 0.435 and 0.054, respectively).

Feminine marked pronouns now slightly prefer feminine French forms, overcoming the original bias. The neutrally marked pronouns shift slightly in favor of masculine translations.

The pronoun *they-neutral* appears in 12,424 sentences in the corpus, which all represent failed resolution of the co-reference. Indeed, French does not have neutral gender and the plural third person pronoun is never pleonastic. These results therefore show that a lot of noise is added to the system.

5.4 Translation Results

The BLEU scores for our method is almost identical to the baseline performance. This is not surprising, since we only expect to change the translation of a small number of words (however, important words for understanding the meaning of the text).

A better evaluation metric is the number of correctly translated pronouns. This requires manual inspection of the translation results. Results are given in Table 4.

While the shift of the translation probabilities

Unannotated				Hobbs				Lappin and Laess		
English	French	p		English	French	p		English	French	p
it	*il*	0.307		*it-neutral*	*il*	0.369		*it-neutral*	*il*	0.372
it	*elle*	0.090		*it-neutral*	*elle*	0.065		*it-neutral*	*elle*	0.064
				it-masculine	*il*	0.230		*it-masculine*	*il*	0.211
				it-masculine	*elle*	0.060		*it-masculine*	*elle*	0.051
				it-feminine	*il*	0.144		*it-feminine*	*il*	0.142
				it-feminine	*elle*	0.168		*it-feminine*	*elle*	0.156
they	*ils*	0.341		*they-neutral*	*ils*	0.344		*they-neutral*	*ils*	0.354
they	*elles*	0.130		*they-neutral*	*elles*	0.102		*they-neutral*	*elles*	0.090
				they-masc.	*ils*	0.435		*they-masc.*	*ils*	0.431
				they-masc.	*elles*	0.053		*they-masc.*	*elles*	0.054
				they-feminine	*ils*	0.208		*they-feminine*	*ils*	0.207
				they-feminine	*elles*	0.259		*they-feminine*	*elles*	0.255

Table 3: **Translation probabilities.** The probabilities of gender-marked pronouns are shifted to the corresponding gender in the two cases the text was annotated with the co-reference resolution methods mentionned earlier.

suggests that we are moving the translation of pronouns in the right direction, this is not reflected by the sample of pronoun translations we inspected. In fact, the performance for our method is almost identical to the baseline (68% and 69%, respectively).

One cause for this is the poor performance of the co-reference resolution method, which labels only 56% of pronouns correctly. On this sub-sample of correctly annotated pronouns, we achieve 82% correct translations. However, the baseline method also performs well on this subset.

6 Conclusion

We presented a method to aid pronoun translation for statistical machine translation by using co-reference resolution. This is to our knowledge the first such work.

While our method works in principle, the results are not yet convincing. The main problem is the low performance of the co-reference resolution algorithm we used. The method works well when the co-reference resolution algorithm provides correct results.

Future work should concentrate on better co-reference algorithms. The context of machine translation also provides an interesting testbed for such algorithms, since it offers standard test sets for many language pairs.

7 Acknowledgements

This work was supported by the EuroMatrixPlus project funded by the European Commission (7th Framework Programme).

References

C. Aone and S.W. Bennett. Evaluating automated and manual acquisition of anaphora resolution strategies. In *Proceedings of the 33rd annual meeting on Association for Computational Linguistics*, pages 122–129. Association for Computational Linguistics Morristown, NJ, USA, 1995.

S. E. Brennan, M. W. Friedman, and C. J. Pollard. A centering approach to pronouns. In *Proceedings of the 25th annual meeting on Association for Computational Linguistics*, pages 155–162, 1987.

E. Charniak. *Toward a model of children's story comprehension*. MIT, 1972.

N. Chinchor and L. Hirschmann. MUC-7 coreference task definition, version 3.0. In *Proceedings of MUC*, volume 7, 1997.

M. Collins. Head-driven statistical models for natural language parsing. *Computational Linguistics*, 29(4):589–637, 2003.

N. Ge, J. Hale, and E. Charniak. A statistical approach to anaphora resolution. In *Proceedings of the Sixth Workshop on Very Large Corpora*, pages 161–170, 1998.

R. Grishman and B. Sundheim. Message understanding conference-6: A brief history. In *Proceedings of the 16th conference on Computational Linguistics-Volume 1*, pages 466–471. Association for Computational Linguistics Morristown, NJ, USA, 1996.

B. J. Grosz, S. Weinstein, and A. K. Joshi. Centering: A framework for modeling the local coherence of discourse. *Computational Linguistics*, 21(2):203–225, 1995.

J. R. Hobbs. Resolving Pronoun References. *Lingua*, 44:339–352, 1978.

D. Jurafsky, J. H. Martin, A. Kehler, K. Vander Linden, and N. Ward. *Speech and language processing*. Prentice Hall New York, 2000.

A. Kehler, D. Appelt, L. Taylor, and A. Simma. The (non) utility of predicate-argument frequencies for pronoun interpretation. In *Proc. of HLT-NAACL*, volume 4, pages 289–296, 2004.

D. Klapholz and A. Lockman. Contextual reference resolution. *American Journal of Computational Linguistics, microfiche 36*, 1975.

Philipp Koehn. Europarl: A parallel corpus for statistical machine translation. In *Proceedings of the Tenth Machine Translation Summit (MT Summit X)*, Phuket, Thailand, September 2005.

Philipp Koehn, Hieu Hoang, Alexandra Birch, Chris Callison-Burch, Marcello Federico, Nicola Bertoldi, Brooke Cowan, Wade Shen, Christine Moran, Richard Zens, Christopher J. Dyer, Ondřej Bojar, Alexandra Constantin, and Evan Herbst. Moses: Open source toolkit for statistical machine translation. In *Proceedings of the 45th Annual Meeting of the Association for Computational Linguistics Companion Volume Proceedings of the Demo and Poster Sessions*, pages 177–180, Prague, Czech Republic, June 2007. Association for Computational Linguistics.

S. Lappin and H.J. Leass. An algorithm for pronominal anaphora resolution. *Computational Linguistics*, 20(4):561, 1994.

Herbert Leass and Ulrike Schwall. An Anaphora Resolution Procedure for Machine Translation. Technical Report Report 172, IBM Germany Science Center, Institute for Knowledge Based Systems, 1991.

E. Liddy, S. Bonzi, J. Katzer, and E. Oddy. A study of discourse anaphora in scientific abstracts. *Journal of the American Society for Information Science*, 38(4):255–261, 1987.

Michael C. McCord. Slot grammar: A system for simpler construction of practical natural language grammars. In *Proceedings of the International Symposium on Natural Language and Logic*, pages 118–145, London, UK, 1990. Springer-Verlag. ISBN 3-540-53082-7.

R. Mitkov, S. K. Choi, and R. Sharp. Anaphora resolution in Machine Translation. In *Proceedings of the Sixth International Conference on Theoretical and Methodological Issues in Machine Translation, TMI'95*, 1995.

V. Ng. Machine learning for coreference resolution: From local classification to global ranking. In *Proceedings of the 43rd Annual Meeting on Association for Computational Linguistics*, page 164. Association for Computational Linguistics, 2005.

C. D. Paice and G. D. Husk. Towards the automatic recognition of anaphoric features in English text: the impersonal pronoun. *Computer Speech & Language*, 2(2):109–132, 1987.

M. Poesio and R. Artstein. Anaphoric annotation in the ARRAU corpus. In *Proceedings of the International Conference on Language Resources and Evaluation (LREC)*, 2008.

M. Poesio, U. Kruschwitz, and J. Chamberlain. ANAWIKI: Creating anaphorically annotated resources through Web cooperation. In *Proceedings of the International Conference on Language Resources and Evaluation (LREC)*, volume 8. Citeseer, 2008.

Judita Preiss. Choosing a parser for anaphora resolution. In *4th Discourse Anaphora and Anaphor Resolution Colloquium (DAARC)*, pages 175–180. Edi cões Colibri, 2002.

Long Qiu, Min yen Kan, and Tat seng Chua. A public reference implementation of the rap anaphora resolution algorithm. In *Proceedings of the International Conference on Language Resources and Evaluation (LREC)*, pages 291–294, 2004.

J. E. Rush, R. Salvador, and A. Zamora. Automatic abstracting and indexing. II. Production of indicative abstracts by application of contextual inference and syntactic coherence criteria. *Journal of the American Society for Information Science and Technology*, 22(4):260–274, 1971.

B. Sagot, L. Clément, E. V. de La Clergerie, and P. Boullier. The Lefff 2 syntactic lexicon for French: architecture, acquisition, use. In *Proceedings of the International Conference on Language Resources and Evaluation (LREC)*, 2006.

Randall Sharp. CAT2 – implementing a formalism for multi-lingual MT. In *2nd International Conference on Theoretical and Methodological Issues in Machine Translation of Natural Language*, pages 3–6, 1988.

M. A. Walker. Centering, anaphora resolution, and discourse structure. *Centering theory in discourse*, pages 401–435, 1998.

Y. Wilks. A preferential, pattern-seeking, semantics for natural language inference. *Words and Intelligence I*, pages 83–102, 1975.

T. Winograd. Understanding natural language. *Cognitive Psychology*, 3(1):1–191, 1972.

Jane: Open Source Hierarchical Translation, Extended with Reordering and Lexicon Models

David Vilar, Daniel Stein, Matthias Huck and Hermann Ney
Lehrstuhl für Informatik 6
RWTH Aachen University
Aachen, Germany
{vilar,stein,huck,ney}@cs.rwth-aachen.de

Abstract

We present Jane, RWTH's hierarchical phrase-based translation system, which has been open sourced for the scientific community. This system has been in development at RWTH for the last two years and has been successfully applied in different machine translation evaluations. It includes extensions to the hierarchical approach developed by RWTH as well as other research institutions. In this paper we give an overview of its main features.

We also introduce a novel reordering model for the hierarchical phrase-based approach which further enhances translation performance, and analyze the effect some recent extended lexicon models have on the performance of the system.

1 Introduction

We present a new open source toolkit for hierarchical phrase-based translation, as described in (Chiang, 2007). The hierarchical phrase model is an extension of the standard phrase model, where the phrases are allowed to have "gaps". In this way, long-distance dependencies and reorderings can be modelled in a consistent way. As in nearly all current statistical approaches to machine translation, this model is embedded in a log-linear model combination.

RWTH has been developing this tool during the last two years and it was used successfully in numerous machine translation evaluations. It is developed in C++ with special attention to clean code, extensibility and efficiency. The toolkit is available under an open source non-commercial license and downloadable from `http://www.hltpr.rwth-aachen.de/jane`.

In this paper we give an overview of the main features of the toolkit and introduce two new extensions to the hierarchical model. The first one is an additional reordering model inspired by the reordering widely used in phrase-based translation systems and the second one comprises two extended lexicon models which further improve translation performance.

2 Related Work

Jane implements many features presented in previous work developed both at RWTH and other groups. As we go over the features of the system we will provide the corresponding references.

Jane is not the first system of its kind, although it provides some unique features. There are other open source hierarchical decoders available. These include

- SAMT (Zollmann and Venugopal, 2006): The original version is not maintained any more and we had problems working on big corpora. A new version which requires Hadoop has just been released, however the documentation is still missing.
- Joshua (Li et al., 2009): A decoder written in Java by the John Hopkins University. This project is the most similar to our own, however both were developed independently and each one has some unique features. A brief comparison between these two systems is included in Section 5.1.
- Moses (Koehn et al., 2007): The de-facto standard phrase-based translation decoder has now been extended to support hierarchical translation. This is still in an experimental branch, however.

3 Features

In this section we will only give a brief overview of the features implemented in Jane. For detailed explanation of previously published algo-

Proceedings of the Joint 5th Workshop on Statistical Machine Translation and MetricsMATR, pages 262–270,
Uppsala, Sweden, 15-16 July 2010.

rithms and methods, we refer to the given literature.

3.1 Search Algorithms

The search for the best translation proceeds in two steps. First, a monolingual parsing of the input sentence is carried out using the CYK+ algorithm (Chappelier and Rajman, 1998), a generalization of the CYK algorithm which relaxes the requirement for the grammar to be in Chomsky normal form. From the CYK+ chart we extract a hypergraph representing the parsing space.

In a second step the translations are generated, computing the language model scores in an integrated fashion. Both the cube pruning and cube growing algorithms (Huang and Chiang, 2007) are implemented. For the latter case, the extensions concerning the language model heuristics similar to (Vilar and Ney, 2009) have also been included.

3.2 Language Models

Jane supports four formats for n-gram language models:

- The ARPA format for language models. We use the SRI toolkit (Stolcke, 2002) to support this format.

- The binary language model format supported by the SRI toolkit. This format allows for a more efficient language model storage, which reduces loading times. In order to reduce memory consumption, the language model can be reloaded for every sentence, filtering the n-grams that will be needed for scoring the possible translations. This format is specially useful for this case.

- Randomized LMs as described in (Talbot and Osborne, 2007), using the open source implementation made available by the authors of the paper. This approach uses a space efficient but approximate representation of the set of n-grams in the language model. In particular the probability for unseen n-grams may be overestimated.

- An in-house, exact representation format with on-demand loading of n-grams, using the internal prefix-tree implementation which is also used for phrase storage (see also Section 3.9).

Several language models (also of mixed formats) can be used during search. Their scores are combined in the log-linear framework.

3.3 Syntactic Features

Soft syntactic features comparable to (Vilar et al., 2008) are implemented in the extraction step of the toolkit. In search, they are considered as additional feature functions of the translation rules.

The decoder is able to handle an arbitrary number of non-terminal symbols. The extraction has been extended so that the extraction of SAMT-rules is included (Zollmann and Venugopal, 2006) but this approach is not fully supported (there may be empty parses due to the extended number of non-terminals). We instead opted to support the generalization presented in (Venugopal et al., 2009), where the information about the new non-terminals is included as an additional feature in the log-linear model.

In addition, dependency information in the spirit of (Shen et al., 2008) is included. Jane features models for string-to-dependency language models and computes various scores based on the well-formedness of the resulting dependency tree. Jane supports the Stanford parsing format,[1] but can be easily extended to other parsers.

3.4 Additional Reordering Models

In the standard formulation of the hierarchical phrase-based translation model two additional rules are added:

$$
\begin{aligned}
S &\rightarrow \langle S^{\sim 0} X^{\sim 1}, S^{\sim 0} X^{\sim 1} \rangle \\
S &\rightarrow \langle X^{\sim 0}, X^{\sim 0} \rangle
\end{aligned}
\qquad (1)
$$

This allows for a monotonic concatenation of phrases, very much in the way monotonic phrase-based translation is carried out.

It is a well-known fact that for phrase-based translation, the use of additional reordering models is a key component, essential for achieving good translation quality. In the hierarchical model, the reordering is already integrated in the translation formalism, but there are still cases where the required reorderings are not captured by the hierarchical phrases alone.

The flexibility of the grammar formalism allows us to add additional reordering models without the need to explicitely modify the code for supporting them. The most straightforward example would

[1] http://nlp.stanford.edu/software/lex-parser.shtml

be to include the ITG-Reorderings (Wu, 1997), by adding following rule

$$S \rightarrow \langle S^{\sim 0} S^{\sim 1}, S^{\sim 1} S^{\sim 0} \rangle \quad (2)$$

We can also model other reordering constraints. As an example, phrase-level IBM reordering constraints with a window length of 1 can be included substituting the rules in Equation (1) with following rules

$$\begin{aligned} S &\rightarrow \langle M^{\sim 0}, M^{\sim 0} \rangle \\ S &\rightarrow \langle M^{\sim 0} S^{\sim 1}, M^{\sim 0} S^{\sim 1} \rangle \\ S &\rightarrow \langle B^{\sim 0} M^{\sim 1}, M^{\sim 1} B^{\sim 0} \rangle \\ M &\rightarrow \langle X^{\sim 0}, X^{\sim 0} \rangle \\ M &\rightarrow \langle M^{\sim 0} X^{\sim 1}, M^{\sim 0} X^{\sim 1} \rangle \\ B &\rightarrow \langle X^{\sim 0}, X^{\sim 0} \rangle \\ B &\rightarrow \langle B^{\sim 0} X^{\sim 1}, X^{\sim 1} B^{\sim 0} \rangle \end{aligned} \quad (3)$$

In these rules we have added two additional non-terminals. The M non-terminal denotes a *monotonic block* and the B non-terminal a *back jump*. Actually both of them represent monotonic translations and the grammar could be simplified by using only one of them. Separating them allows for more flexibility, e.g. when restricting the jump width, where we only have to restrict the maximum span width of the non-terminal B. These rules can be generalized for other reordering constraints or window lengths.

Additionally distance-based costs can be computed for these reorderings. To the best of our knowledge, this is the first time such additional reorderings have been applied to the hierarchical phrase-based approach.

3.5 Extended Lexicon Models

We enriched Jane with the ability to score hypotheses with discriminative and trigger-based lexicon models that use global source sentence context and are capable of predicting context-specific target words. This approach has recently been shown to improve the translation results of conventional phrase-based systems. In this section, we briefly review the basic aspects of these extended lexicon models. They are similar to (Mauser et al., 2009), and we refer there for a more detailed exposition on the training procedures and results in conventional phrase-based decoding.

Note that the training for these models is not distributed together with Jane.

3.5.1 Discriminative Word Lexicon

The first of the two lexicon models is denoted as *discriminative word lexicon* (DWL) and acts as a statistical classifier that decides whether a word from the target vocabulary should be included in a translation hypothesis. For that purpose, it considers all the words from the source sentence, but does not take any position information into account, i.e. it operates on sets, not on sequences or even trees. The probability of a word being part of the target sentence, given a set of source words, are decomposed into binary features, one for each source vocabulary entry. These binary features are combined in a log-linear fashion with corresponding feature weights. The discriminative word lexicon is trained independently for each target word using the L-BFGS (Byrd et al., 1995) algorithm. For regularization, Gaussian priors are utilized.

DWL model probabilities are computed as

$$p(\mathbf{e}|\mathbf{f}) = \prod_{e \in \mathbf{V_E}} p(e^-|\mathbf{f}) \cdot \prod_{e \in \mathbf{e}} \frac{p(e^+|\mathbf{f})}{p(e^-|\mathbf{f})} \quad (4)$$

with $\mathbf{V_E}$ being the target vocabulary, $\mathbf{e}$ the set of target words in a sentence, and $\mathbf{f}$ the set of source words, respectively. Here, the event e^+ is used when the target word e is included in the target sentence and e^- if not. As the left part of the product in Equation (4) is constant given a source sentence, it can be dropped, which enables us to score partial hypotheses during search.

3.5.2 Triplet Lexicon

The second lexicon model we employ in Jane, the *triplet lexicon model*, is in many aspects related to IBM model 1 (Brown et al., 1993), but extends it with an additional word in the conditioning part of the lexical probabilities. This introduces a means for an improved representation of long-range dependencies in the data. Like IBM model 1, the triplets are trained iteratively with the Expectation-Maximization (EM) algorithm (Dempster et al., 1977). Jane implements the so-called inverse triplet model $p(e|f, f')$.

The triplet lexicon model score $t(\cdot)$ of the application of a rule $X \rightarrow \langle \alpha, \beta \rangle$ where (α, β) is a bilingual phrase pair that may contain symbols from the non-terminal set is computed as

$$\begin{aligned} t(\alpha, \beta, f_0^J) &= \quad (5) \\ -\sum_e \log &\left(\frac{2}{J \cdot (J+1)} \sum_j \sum_{j'>j} p(e|f_j, f_{j'}) \right) \end{aligned}$$

with e ranging over all terminal symbols in the target part β of the rule. The second sum selects all words from the source sentence f_0^J (including the empty word that is denoted as f_0 here). The third sum incorporates the rest of the source sentence right of the first triggering word. The order of the triggers is not relevant because per definition $p(e|f, f') = p(e|f', f)$, i.e. the model is symmetric. Non-terminals in β have to be skipped when the rule is scored.

In Jane, we also implemented scoring for a variant of the triplet lexicon model called the *path-constrained* (or *path-aligned*) triplet model. The characteristic of path-constrained triplets is that the first trigger f is restricted to the aligned target word e. The second trigger f' is allowed to move along the whole remaining source sentence. For the training of the model, we use word alignment information obtained by GIZA++ (Och and Ney, 2003). To be able to apply the model in search, Jane has to be run with a phrase table that contains word alignment for each phrase, too, with the exception of phrases which are composed purely of non-terminals. Jane's phrase extraction can optionally supply this information from the training data.

(Hasan et al., 2008) and (Hasan and Ney, 2009) employ similar techniques and provide some more discussion on the path-aligned variant of the model and other possible restrictions.

3.6 Forced Alignments

Jane has also preliminary support for forced alignments between a given source and target sentence. Given a sentence in the source language and its translation in the target language, we find the best way the source sentence can be translated into the given target sentence, using the available inventory of phrases. This is needed for more advanced training approaches like the ones presented in (Blunsom et al., 2008) or (Cmejrek et al., 2009). As reported in these papers, due to the restrictions in the phrase extraction process, not all sentences in the training corpus can be aligned in this way.

3.7 Optimization Methods

Two method based on n-best for minimum error rate training (MERT) of the parameters of the log-linear model are included in Jane. The first one is the procedure described in (Och, 2003), which has become a standard in the machine translation community. We use an in-house implementation of the method.

The second one is the MIRA algorithm, first applied for machine translation in (Chiang et al., 2009). This algorithm is more adequate when the number of parameters to optimize is large.

If the Numerical Recipes library (Press et al., 2002) is available, an additional general purpose optimization tool is also compiled. Using this tool a single-best optimization procedure based on the downhill simplex method (Nelder and Mead, 1965) is included. This method, however, can be considered deprecated in favour of the above mentioned methods.

3.8 Parallelized operation

If the Sun Grid Engine[2] is available, all operations of Jane can be parallelized. For the extraction process, the corpus is split into chunks (the granularity being user-controlled) which are distributed in the computer cluster. Count collection, marginal computation and count normalization all happens in an automatic and parallel manner.

For the translation process a batch job is started on a number of computers. A server distributes the sentences to translate to the computers that have been made available to the translation job.

The optimization process also benefits from the parallelized optimization. Additionally, for the minimum error rate training methods, random restarts may be performed on different computers in a parallel fashion.

The same client-server infrastructure used for parallel translation may also be reused for interactive systems. Although no code in this direction is provided, one would only need to implement a corresponding frontend which communicates with the translation server (which may be located on another machine).

3.9 Extensibility

One of the goals when implementing the toolkit was to make it easy to extend it with new features. For this, an abstract class was created which we called *secondary model*. New models need only to derive from this class and implement the abstract methods for data reading and costs computation. This allows for an encapsulation of the computations, which can be activated and deactivated on demand. The models described in Sections 3.3

[2]http://www.sun.com/software/sge/

through 3.5 are implemented in this way. We thus try to achieve loose coupling in the implementation.

In addition a flexible prefix tree implementation with on-demand loading capabilities is included as part of the code. This class has been used for implementing on-demand loading of phrases in the spirit of (Zens and Ney, 2007) and the on-demand n-gram format described in Section 3.2, in addition to some intermediate steps in the phrase extraction process. The code may also be reused in other, independent projects.

3.10 Code

The main core of Jane has been implemented in C++. Our guideline was to write code that was correct, maintainable and efficient. We tried to achieve correctness by means of unit tests integrated in the source as well as regression tests. We also defined a set of coding guidelines, which we try to enforce in order to have readable and maintainable code. Examples include using descriptive variable names, appending an underscore to private members of classes or having each class name start with an uppercase letter while variable names start with lowercase letters.

The code is documented at great length using the doxygen system,[3] and the filling up of the missing parts is an ongoing effort. Every tool comes with an extensive help functionality, and the main tools also have their own man pages.

As for efficiency we always try to speed up the code and reduce memory consumption by implementing better algorithms. We try to avoid "dark magic programming methods" and hard to follow optimizations are only applied in critical parts of the code. We try to document every such occurrence.

4 Experimental Results

In this section we will present some experimental results obtained using Jane. We will pay special attention to the performance of the new reordering and lexicon models presented in this paper. We will present results on three different large-scale tasks and language pairs.

Additionally RWTH participated in this year's WMT evaluation, where Jane was one of the submitted systems. We refer to the system description for supplementary experimental results.

[3] http://www.doxygen.org

	dev		test	
System	BLEU	TER	BLEU	TER
Jane baseline	24.2	59.5	25.4	57.4
+ reordering	25.2	58.2	26.5	56.1

Table 1: Results for Europarl German-English data. BLEU and TER results are in percentage.

4.1 Europarl Data

The first task is the Europarl as defined in the Quaero project. The main part of the corpus in this task consists of the Europarl corpus as used in the WMT evaluation (Callison-Burch et al., 2009), with some additional data collected in the scope of the project.

We tried the reordering approach presented in Section 3.4 on the German-English language pair. The results are shown in Table 1. As can be seen from these results, the additional reorderings obtain nearly 1% improvement both in BLEU and TER scores. Regrettably for this corpus the extended lexicon models did not bring any improvements.

Table 2 shows the results for the French-English language pair of the Europarl task. On this task the extended lexicon models yield an improvement over the baseline system of 0.9% in BLEU and 0.9% in TER on the test set.

4.2 NIST Arabic-English

We also show results on the Arabic-English NIST'08 task, using the NIST'06 set as development set. It has been reported in other work that the hierarchical system is not competitive with a phrase-based system for this language pair (Birch et al., 2009). We report the figures of our state-of-the-art phrase-based system as comparison (denoted as PBT).

As can be seen from Table 3, the baseline Jane system is in fact 0.6% worse in BLEU and 1.0% worse in TER than the baseline PBT system. When we include the extended lexicon models we see that the difference in performance is reduced. For Jane the extended lexicon models give an improvement of up to 1.9% in BLEU and 1.7% in TER, respectively, bringing the system on par with the PBT system extended with the same lexicon models, and obtaining an even slightly better BLEU score.

	dev		test	
	BLEU	TER	BLEU	TER
Baseline	30.0	52.6	31.1	50.0
DWL	30.4	52.2	31.4	49.6
Triplets	30.4	52.0	31.7	49.4
path-constrained Triplets	30.3	52.1	31.6	49.3
DWL + Triplets	30.7	52.0	32.0	49.1
DWL + path-constrained Triplets	30.8	51.7	31.6	49.3

Table 2: Results for the French-English task. BLEU and TER results are in percentage.

	dev (MT'06)				test (MT'08)			
	Jane		PBT		Jane		PBT	
	BLEU	TER	BLEU	TER	BLEU	TER	BLEU	TER
Baseline	43.2	50.8	44.1	49.4	44.1	50.1	44.7	49.1
DWL	45.3	48.7	45.1	48.4	45.6	48.4	45.6	48.4
Triplets	44.4	49.1	44.6	49.2	45.3	48.8	44.9	49.0
path-constrained Triplets	44.3	49.4	44.7	49.1	44.9	49.3	45.3	48.7
DWL + Triplets	45.0	48.9	45.1	48.5	45.3	48.6	45.5	48.5
DWL + path-constrained Triplets	45.2	48.8	45.1	48.6	46.0	48.5	45.8	48.3

Table 3: Results for the Arabic-English task. BLEU and TER results are in percentage.

5 Discussion

We feel that the hierarchical phrase-based translation approach still shares some shortcomings concerning lexical selection with conventional phrase-based translation. Bilingual lexical context beyond the phrase boundaries is barely taken into account by the base model. In particular, if only one generic non-terminal is used, the selection of a sub-phrase that fills the gap of a hierarchical phrase is not affected by the words composing the phrase it is embedded in – except for the language model score. This shortcoming is one of the issues syntactically motivated models try to address.

The extended lexicon models analyzed in this work also try to address this issue. One can consider that they complement the efforts that are being made on a deep structural level within the hierarchical approach. Though they are trained on surface forms only, without any syntactic information, they still operate at a scope that exceeds the capability of common feature sets of standard hierarchical phrase-based SMT systems.

As the experiments in Section 4 show, the effect of these extended lexicon models is more important for the hierarchical phrase-based approach than for the phrase-based approach. In our opinion this is probably mainly due to the higher flexibility of the hierarchical system, both because of its intrinsic nature and because of the higher number of phrases extracted by the system. The scoring of the phrases is still carried out by simple relative frequencies, which seem to be insufficient. The additional lexicon models seem to help in this respect.

5.1 Short Comparison with Joshua

As mentioned in Section 2, Joshua is the most similar decoder to our own. It was developed in parallel at the Johns Hopkins University and it is

System	words/sec
Joshua	11.6
Jane cube prune	15.9
Jane cube grow	60.3

Table 4: Speed comparison Jane vs. Joshua. We measure the translated words per second.

currently used by a number of groups around the world.

Jane was started separately and independently. In their basic working mode, both systems implement parsing using a synchronous grammar and include language model information. Each of the projects then progressed independently, most of the features described in Section 3 being only available in Jane.

Efficiency is one of the points where we think Jane outperforms Joshua. One of the reasons can well be the fact that it is written in C++ while Joshua is written in Java. In order to compare running times we converted a grammar extracted by Jane to Joshua's format and adapted the parameters accordingly. To the best of our knowledge we configured both decoders to perform the same task (cube pruning, 300-best generation, same pruning parameters). Except for some minor differences[4] the results were equal.

We tried this setup on the IWSLT'08 Arabic to English translation task. The speed results (measured in translated words per second) can be seen in Table 4. Jane operating with cube prune is nearly 50% faster than Joshua, at the same level of translation performance. If we switch to cube grow, the speed difference is even bigger, with a speedup of nearly 4 times. However this usually comes with a penalty in BLEU score (normally under 0.5% BLEU in our experience). This increased speed can be specially interesting for applications like interactive machine translation or online translation services, where the response time is critical and sometimes even more important than a small (and often hardly noticeable) loss in translation quality.

Another important point concerning efficiency is the startup time. Thanks to the binary format described in Section 3.9, there is virtually no delay in the loading of the phrase table in Jane.[5] In fact Joshua's long phrase table loading times were the main reason the performance measures were done on a small corpus like IWSLT instead of one of the large tasks described in Section 4.

We want to make clear that we did not go into great depth in the workings of Joshua, just stayed at the basic level described in the manual. This tool is used also for large-scale evaluations and hence there certainly are settings for dealing with these big tasks. Therefore this comparison has to be taken with a grain of salt.

We also want to stress that we explicitly chose to leave translation results out of this comparison. Several different components have great impact on translation quality, including phrase extraction, minimum error training and additional parameter settings of the decoder. As we pointed out we do not have the expertise in Joshua to perform all these tasks in an optimal way, and for that reason we did not include such a comparison. However, both JHU and RWTH participated in this year's WMT evaluation, where the systems, applied by their respective authors, can be directly compared.

And in no way do we see Joshua and Jane as "competing" systems. Having different systems is always enriching, and particularly as system combination shows great improvements in translation quality, having several alternative systems can only be considered a positive situation.

6 Licensing

Jane is distributed under a custom open source license. This includes free usage for non-commercial purposes as long as any changes made to the original software are published under the terms of the same license. The exact formulation is available at the download page for Jane.

7 Conclusion

With Jane, we release a state-of-the-art hierarchical toolkit to the scientific community and hope to provide a good starting point for fellow researchers, allowing them to have a solid system even if the research field is new to them. It is available for download from `http://www.hltpr.rwth-aachen.de/jane`. The system in its current state is stable and efficient enough to handle even large-scale tasks such as

[4]E.g. the OOVs seem to be handled in a slightly different way, as the placement was sometimes different.

[5]There is, however, still some delay when loading the language model for some of the supported formats.

the WMT and NIST evaluations, while producing highly competitive results.

Moreover, we presented additional reordering and lexicon models that further enhance the performance of the system.

And in case you are wondering, Jane is **J**ust an **A**cronym, **N**othing **E**lse. The name comes from the character in the Ender's Game series (Card, 1986).

Acknowledgments

Special thanks to the people who have contributed code to Jane: Markus Freitag, Stephan Peitz, Carmen Heger, Arne Mauser and Niklas Hoppe.

This work was partly realized as part of the Quaero Programme, funded by OSEO, French State agency for innovation, and also partly based upon work supported by the Defense Advanced Research Projects Agency (DARPA) under Contract No. HR001-06-C-0023. Any opinions, findings and conclusions or recommendations expressed in this material are those of the authors and do not necessarily reflect the views of the DARPA.

References

Alexandra Birch, Phil Blunsom, and Miles Osborne. 2009. A Quantitative Analysis of Reordering Phenomena. In *Proc. of the Workshop on Statistical Machine Translation*, pages 197–205, Athens, Greece, March.

Phil Blunsom, Trevor Cohn, and Miles Osborne. 2008. A Discriminative Latent Variable Model for Statistical Machine Translation. In *Proc. of the Annual Meeting of the Association for Computational Linguistics (ACL)*, pages 200–208, Columbus, Ohio, June.

Peter F. Brown, Stephan A. Della Pietra, Vincent J. Della Pietra, and Robert L. Mercer. 1993. The Mathematics of Statistical Machine Translation: Parameter Estimation. *Computational Linguistics*, 19(2):263–311, June.

Richard H. Byrd, Peihuang Lu, Jorge Nocedal, and Ciyou Zhu. 1995. A Limited Memory Algorithm for Bound Constrained Optimization. *SIAM Journal on Scientific Computing*, 16(5):1190–1208.

Chris Callison-Burch, Philipp Koehn, Christof Monz, and Josh Schroeder. 2009. Findings of the 2009 Workshop on Statistical Machine Translation. In *Proc. of the Workshop on Statistical Machine Translation*, pages 1–28, Athens, Greece, March.

Orson Scott Card. 1986. *Speaker for the Dead*. Tor Books.

Jean-Cédric Chappelier and Martin Rajman. 1998. A Generalized CYK Algorithm for Parsing Stochastic CFG. In *Proc. of the First Workshop on Tabulation in Parsing and Deduction*, pages 133–137, Paris, France, April.

David Chiang, Kevin Knight, and Wei Wang. 2009. 11,001 new Features for Statistical Machine Translation. In *Proc. of the Human Language Technology Conference / North American Chapter of the Association for Computational Linguistics (HLT-NAACL)*, pages 218–226, Boulder, Colorado, June.

David Chiang. 2007. Hierarchical Phrase-based Translation. *Computational Linguistics*, 33(2):201–228, June.

Martin Cmejrek, Bowen Zhou, and Bing Xiang. 2009. Enriching SCFG Rules Directly From Efficient Bilingual Chart Parsing. In *Proc. of the International Workshop on Spoken Language Translation (IWSLT)*, pages 136–143, Tokyo, Japan.

Arthur P. Dempster, Nan M. Laird, and Donald B. Rubin. 1977. Maximum Likelihood from Incomplete Data via the EM Algorithm. *Journal of the Royal Statistical Society Series B*, 39(1):1–22.

Saša Hasan and Hermann Ney. 2009. Comparison of Extended Lexicon Models in Search and Rescoring for SMT. In *Proc. of the Annual Meeting of the Association for Computational Linguistics (ACL)*, volume short papers, pages 17–20, Boulder, CO, USA, June.

Saša Hasan, Juri Ganitkevitch, Hermann Ney, and Jesús Andrés-Ferrer. 2008. Triplet Lexicon Models for Statistical Machine Translation. In *Proc. of the Conference on Empirical Methods for Natural Language Processing (EMNLP)*, pages 372–381.

Liang Huang and David Chiang. 2007. Forest Rescoring: Faster Decoding with Integrated Language Models. In *Proc. of the Annual Meeting of the Association for Computational Linguistics (ACL)*, pages 144–151, Prague, Czech Republic, June.

Philipp Koehn, Hieu Hoang, Alexandra Birch, Chris Callison-Burch, Marcello Federico, Nicola Bertoldi, Brooke Cowan, Wade Shen, Christine Moran, Richard Zens, Chris Dyer, Ondej Bojar, Alexandra Constantin, and Evan Herbst. 2007. Moses: Open Source Toolkit for Statistical Machine Translation. In *Proc. of the Annual Meeting of the Association for Computational Linguistics (ACL)*, pages 177–180, Prague, Czech Republic, June.

Zhifei Li, Chris Callison-Burch, Chris Dyer, Sanjeev Khudanpur, Lane Schwartz, Wren Thornton, Jonathan Weese, and Omar Zaidan. 2009. Joshua: An Open Source Toolkit for Parsing-Based Machine Translation. In *Proc. of the Workshop on Statistical Machine Translation*, pages 135–139, Athens, Greece, March.

Arne Mauser, Saša Hasan, and Hermann Ney. 2009. Extending Statistical Machine Translation with Discriminative and Trigger-Based Lexicon Models. In *Proc. of the Conference on Empirical Methods for Natural Language Processing (EMNLP)*, pages 210–218, Singapore, August.

John A. Nelder and Roger Mead. 1965. The Downhill Simplex Method. *Computer Journal*, 7:308.

Franz Josef Och and Hermann Ney. 2003. A Systematic Comparison of Various Statistical Alignment Models. *Computational Linguistics*, 29(1):19–51.

Franz Josef Och. 2003. Minimum Error Rate Training for Statistical Machine Translation. In *Proc. of the Annual Meeting of the Association for Computational Linguistics (ACL)*, pages 160–167, Sapporo, Japan, July.

William H. Press, Saul A. Teukolsky, William T. Vetterling, and Brian P. Flannery. 2002. *Numerical Recipes in C++*. Cambridge University Press, Cambridge, UK.

Libin Shen, Jinxi Xu, and Ralph Weischedel. 2008. A New String-to-Dependency Machine Translation Algorithm with a Target Dependency Language Model. In *Proc. of the Annual Meeting of the Association for Computational Linguistics (ACL)*, pages 577–585, Columbus, Ohio, June.

Andreas Stolcke. 2002. SRILM – an Extensible Language Modeling Toolkit. In *Proc. of the International Conference on Spoken Language Processing (ICSLP)*, volume 3, pages 901–904, Denver, Colorado, September.

David Talbot and Miles Osborne. 2007. Smoothed Bloom Filter Language Models: Tera-scale LMs on the Cheap. In *Proc. of the Joint Conference on Empirical Methods in Natural Language Processing and Computational Natural Language Learning (EMNLP-CoNLL)*, pages 468–476, Prague, Czech Republic, June.

Ashish Venugopal, Andreas Zollmann, N.A. Smith, and Stephan Vogel. 2009. Preference Grammars: Softening Syntactic Constraints to Improve Statistical Machine Translation. In *Proc. of the Human Language Technology Conference / North American Chapter of the Association for Computational Linguistics (HLT-NAACL)*, pages 236–244, Boulder, Colorado, June.

David Vilar and Hermann Ney. 2009. On LM Heuristics for the Cube Growing Algorithm. In *Proc. of the Annual Conference of the European Association for Machine Translation (EAMT)*, pages 242–249, Barcelona, Spain, May.

David Vilar, Daniel Stein, and Hermann Ney. 2008. Analysing Soft Syntax Features and Heuristics for Hierarchical Phrase Based Machine Translation. In *Proc. of the International Workshop on Spoken Language Translation (IWSLT)*, pages 190–197, Waikiki, Hawaii, October.

Dekai Wu. 1997. Stochastic inversion transduction grammars and bilingual parsing of parallel corpora. *Computational Linguistics*, 23(3):377–403.

Richard Zens and Hermann Ney. 2007. Efficient Phrase-Table Representation for Machine Translation with Applications to Online MT and Speech Translation. In *Proc. of the Annual Meeting of the Association for Computational Linguistics (ACL)*, pages 492–499, Rochester, New York, April.

Andreas Zollmann and Ashish Venugopal. 2006. Syntax Augmented Machine Translation via Chart Parsing. In *Proc. of the Human Language Technology Conference / North American Chapter of the Association for Computational Linguistics (HLT-NAACL)*, pages 138–141, New York, June.

MANY : Open Source MT System Combination at WMT'10

Loïc Barrault
LIUM, University of Le Mans
Le Mans, France.
FirstName.LastName@lium.univ-lemans.fr

Abstract

LIUM participated in the System Combination task of the Fifth Workshop on Statistical Machine Translation (WMT 2010). Hypotheses from 5 French/English MT systems were combined with MANY, an open source system combination software based on confusion networks currently developed at LIUM.

The system combination yielded significant improvements in BLEU score when applied on WMT'09 data. The same behavior has been observed when tuning is performed on development data of this year evaluation.

1 Introduction

This year, the LIUM computer science laboratory has participated in the French-English system combination task at WMT'10 evaluation campaign. The system used for this task is MANY[1] (Barrault, 2010), an open source system combination software based on Confusion Networks (CN). Several improvements have been made in order to being able to combine many systems outputs in a decent time.

The focus has been put on the tuning step, and more precisely how to perform system parameter tuning. Two methods have been experimented corresponding to two different representations of system combination. In the first one, system combination is considered as a whole : fed by system hypotheses as input and generating a new hypothesis as output. The second method considers that the alignment module is independent from the decoder, so that the parameters from each module can be tuned separately.

Those tuning approaches are described in section 3. Before that, a quick description of MANY, including recent developments, can be found in section 2. Results on WMT'09 data are presented in section 4 along results of tuning on newssyscombtune2010.

2 System description

MANY is a system combination software (Barrault, 2010) based on the decoding of a lattice made of several Confusion Networks (CN). This is a widespread approach in MT system combination (Rosti et al., 2007); (Shen et al., 2008); (Karakos et al., 2008). MANY can be decomposed in two main modules. The first one is the alignment module which actually is a modified version of TERp (Snover et al., 2009). Its role is to incrementally align the hypotheses against a backbone in order to create a confusion network. Those confusion networks are then connected together to create a lattice. This module uses different costs (which corresponds to a match, an insertion, a deletion, a substitution, a shift, a synonym and a stem) to compute the best alignment and incrementally build a confusion network. In the case of confusion network, the match (substitution, synonyms, and stems) costs are considered when the word in the hypothesis matches (is a substitution, a synonyms or a stems of) at least one word of the considered confusion sets in the CN, as shown in Figure 1.

The second module is the decoder. This decoder is based on the token pass algorithm and it accepts as input the lattice previously created. The probabilities computed in the decoder can be expressed as follow :

$$log(P_W) = \sum_{n=0}^{Len(W)} \Big\{ \alpha_1 logP_{ws}(n) + \alpha_2 logP_{lm}(n) + \alpha_3 L_{pen}(n) + \alpha_4 N_{pen}(n) \Big\} \quad (1)$$

where $Len(W)$ is the length of the hypothesis,

[1] MANY is available at the following address http://www-lium.univ-lemans.fr/~barrault/MANY

Proceedings of the Joint 5th Workshop on Statistical Machine Translation and MetricsMATR, pages 271–275,
Uppsala, Sweden, 15-16 July 2010.

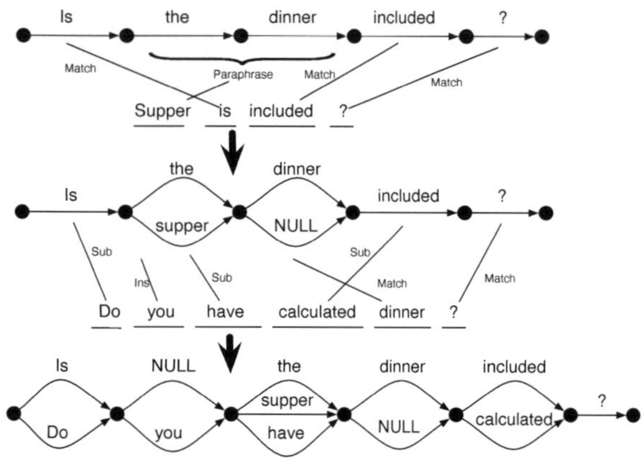

Figure 1: Incremental alignment with TERp resulting in a confusion network.

$P_{ws}(n)$ is the score of the nth word in the lattice, $P_{lm}(n)$ is its LM probability, $L_{pen}(n)$ is the length penalty (which apply when W_n is not a null-arc), $N_{pen}(n)$ is the penalty applied when crossing a null-arc, and the α_i are the features weights.

Multithreading

One major issue with system combination concerns scaling. Indeed, in order to not lose information about word order, all system hypotheses are considered as backbone and all other hypotheses are aligned to it to create a CN. Consequently, if we consider N system outputs, then to build N confusion networks, $N * (N-1)$ alignments with modified TERp have to be performed. Moreover, in order to get better results, the TERp costs have to be optimized, which requires a lot of iterations, all of which calculate $N * (N-1)$ alignments. However, the building of a CN with system i as backbone does not depend on the building of CN with other system as backbone. Therefore multithreading has been integrated into MANY so that multiple CNs can be created in parallel. From now on, the number of thread can be specified in the configuration file.

3 Tuning

As mentioned before, MANY is made of two main modules : the alignment module based on a modified version of TERp and the decoder. Considering 10 systems, 19 parameters in total have to be optimized in order to get better results. By default, TERp costs are set to 0.0 for match and 1.0 for everything else. These costs are not correct, since a shift in that case will hardly be possible. TERp costs, system priors, fudge factor, null-arc penalty, length penalty are tuned with Condor (a global optimizer based on the Powell's algorithm, (Berghen and Bersini, 2005)).

Two ways of tuning have been experimented. The first one consists in optimizing the whole set of parameters together (see section 3.1). The second one rely on the (maybe likely) independence of the TERp parameters towards those of the decoder and consists in tuning TERp parameters in a first step and then using the optimized TERp costs when tuning the decoder parameters (see section 3.2).

3.1 Tuning all parameters together

Condor is an optimizer which aims at minimizing a certain objective function. In our case, the objective function is the whole system combination. As input, it takes the whole set of parameters (*i.e.* TERp costs except match costs (which is always set to 0), system priors, the fudge factor, and null-arc and length penalty) and outputs -BLEU score. The BLEU score is one of the most robust metrics as presented in (Leusch et al., 2009), which is consequently an obvious target for optimization.

Such a tuning protocol has the disadvantage to be slower as all the confusion networks have to be regenerated at each step because the TERp costs provided by the optimizer will hardly be the same for two iterations (thus, confusion networks computed during previous iterations can hardly be reused). Another issue with this approach is that it is hard to converge when the parameter set is that large. This is mainly due to the fact that we cannot guarantee the convexity of the problem. However, one advantage is that the possible correlation between all parameters are taken into account during the optimization process, which is not the case when optimizing in several steps.

3.2 Two-step tuning

Tuning TERp parameters : In order to optimize TERp parameters (*i.e.* del, ins, sub, shift, stem and syn costs), we have to determine which measure to use to evaluate a certain configuration. We naturally considered the minimization of the TERp score. To do so, the confusion networks are built using the set of parameters given by the optimizer. TERp scores are then calculated between the reference and each CN, and summed up.

The goal of this step is to guide the confusion networks generation process to produce sentences similar to the reference. Consequently, if the confusion networks generated at this step have a lower TERp score, then this means that the decoder is more likely to find a better hypothesis inside.

Tuning decoder parameters : Based on the TERp configuration determined at the previous step, this step aims at finding good parameter values. Those parameters control the final hypothesis size and the importance given to the language model probabilities compared to the translation scores (occurring on words). The metric which is minimized is -BLEU for the same reasons mentioned in section 3.1.

4 Experiments and Results

During experiments, data from last year evaluation campaign are used for testing the tuning approach. news-dev2009a is used as development set, and news-dev2009b as internal test, these corpora are described in Table 1.

NAME	#sent.	#words	#tok
news-dev2009a	1025	21583	24595
news-dev2009b	1026	21837	24940

Table 1: WMT'09 corpora : number of sentences, words and tokens calculated on the reference.

For the sake of speed and simplicity, the five best systems (ranking given by score on dev) are considered only. Baseline systems performances on dev and test are presented in Table 2.

Corpus	Sys0	Sys1	Sys2	Sys3	Sys4
Dev	18.20	17.83	20.14	21.06	17.72
Test	18.53	18.33	20.43	21.35	18.15

Table 2: Baseline systems performance on WMT'09 data (%BLEU).

When tuning all parameters together, the set obtained is presented in Table 3. The 2-step tuning protocol applied on news-dev2009a provides the set of parameters presented in Table 4.

Costs :	Del	Stem	Syn	Ins	Sub	Shift
	0.89	0.94	1.04	0.98	0.94	0.94
Dec. :	Fudge		$Null_{pen}$		Len_{pen}	
	0.01		0.25		1.46	
Weights :	Sys0	Sys1	Sys2	Sys3	Sys4	
	0.04	0.04	0.16	0.26	0.04	

Table 3: Parameters obtained with 1-step tuning.

Costs :	Del	Stem	Syn	Ins	Sub	Shift
	9e-6	0.89	1.22	0.26	0.44	1.76
Dec. :	Fudge		$Null_{pen}$		Len_{pen}	
	0.1		0.27		2.1	
Weights :	Sys0	Sys1	Sys2	Sys3	Sys4	
	0.07	0.09	0.09	0.09	0.11	

Table 4: Parameters obtained with 2-step tuning.

Results on development corpus of WMT'09 (used as test set) are presented in Table 5. We can observe that 2-step tuning provides almost 0.9 BLEU point improvement on development corpus which is well reflected on test set with a gain of more than 0.7 BLEU. The best results are obtain when tuning all parameters together, which give more than 1 BLEU point improvement on dev and more than 0.9 on test.

System	Dev	Test
Best single	21.06	21.35
MANY	**22.08**	**22.28**
MANY-2steps	**21.94**	**22.09**

Table 5: System Combination results on WMT'09 data.

4.1 Discussion

Choosing a measure to optimize the TERp costs is not something easy. One important remark is that default (equal) costs are not suitable to get good confusion networks. The goal of the confusion networks is to make possible the generation of a new hypothesis which can be different from those provided by each individual system.

In these experiments, TERp calculated between the CNs and the reference is used as the distance to be minimized by the optimizer. We can notice that for the 2-step optimization, the deletion cost is very small. This is probably not a value which is expected, because in this case, this means that deletions can occur in an hypothesis without penalizing it a lot. However, this parameter set has a beneficial impact on the system combination performance. Another comment is that the system weights are not directly proportional to the results. This suggests that some phrases proposed by weaker systems can have a higher importance for system combination.

By contrast, optimizing parameters all together provides more fair weights, according to the results of the single systems.

4.2 2010 evaluation campaign

For this year system combination tasks, a development corpus (syscombtune) and the test (syscombtest), described in Table 6, were provided to participants.

NAME	#sentences	#words	#words tok
syscombtune	455	9348	10755
syscombtest	2034	-	-

Table 6: Description of WMT'10 corpora.

Language model : The English target language models has been trained on all monolingual data provided for the translation tasks. In addition, LDC's Gigaword collection was used for both languages. Data corresponding to the development and test periods were removed from the Gigaword collections.

Tuning on syscombdev2010 corpus produced the parameter set presented in Table 7

Costs :	Del	Stem	Syn	Ins	Sub	Shift
Dec. :	Fudge		Null$_{pen}$		Len$_{pen}$	
	0.01		0.33		1.6	
Weights :	Sys0	Sys1	Sys2	Sys3	Sys4	
	0.11	0.21	0.04	0.15	0.15	

Table 7: Parameters obtained with tuning.

The result provided by the system with this configuration can be compared to the single systems in Table 8.

System	newssyscombtune2010
Sys0	27.74
Sys1	27.26
Sys2	27.15
Sys3	27.06
Sys4	27.04
MANY	**28.63**

Table 8: Baseline systems performance on WMT'10 development data (%BLEU).

A behavior comparable to WMT'09 evaluation campaign is observed, which suggests that the approach is correct.

5 Conclusion and future work

We have shown that tuning all parameters together is better than 2-step tuning. However, the second method has not been fully explored. Tuning TERp parameters targeting minimum TERp score is not satisfying. Therefore, an alternative measure, like ngram agreement which would be more related to BLEU, can be considered in order to obtain better parameters.

Further improvement for MANY will be considered like case insensitive combination then recasing the output using majority vote on the confusion networks. This is currently a work in progress.

6 Acknowledgement

This work has been partially funded by the European Union under the EuroMatrix Plus project (http://www.euromatrixplus.net, IST-2007.2.2-FP7-231720)

References

Barrault, L. (2010). MANY : Open source machine translation system combination. *Prague Bulletin of Mathematical Linguistics, Special Issue on Open Source Tools for Machine Translation*, 93:147–155.

Berghen, F. V. and Bersini, H. (2005). CONDOR, a new parallel, constrained extension of Powell's UOBYQA algorithm: Experimental results and comparison with the DFO algorithm. *Journal of Computational and Applied Mathematics*, 181:157–175.

Karakos, D., Eisner, J., Khudanpur, S., and Dreyer, M. (2008). Machine translation system combination using ITG-based alignments. In *46th Annual Meeting of the Association for Computational Linguistics: Human Language Technologies.*, pages 81–84, Columbus, Ohio, USA.

Leusch, G., Matusov, E., and Ney, H. (2009). The RWTH system combination system for WMT 2009. In *Proceedings of the Fourth Workshop on Statistical Machine Translation*, pages 61–65, Athens, Greece.

Rosti, A.-V., Matsoukas, S., and Schwartz, R. (2007). Improved word-level system combination for machine translation. In *Association for Computational Linguistics*, pages 312–319.

Shen, W., Delaney, B., Anderson, T., and Slyh, R. (2008). The MIT-LL/AFRL IWSLT-2008 MT System. In *International Workshop on Spoken Language Translation*, Hawaii, U.S.A.

Snover, M., Madnani, N., Dorr, B., and Schwartz, R. (2009). TER-Plus: Paraphrase, semantic, and alignment enhancements to translation edit rate. *Machine Translation Journal*.

Adaptive Model Weighting and Transductive Regression for Predicting Best System Combinations

Ergun Biçici
Koç University
34450 Sariyer, Istanbul, Turkey
ebicici@ku.edu.tr

S. Serdar Kozat
Koç University
34450 Sariyer, Istanbul, Turkey
skozat@ku.edu.tr

Abstract

We analyze adaptive model weighting techniques for reranking using instance scores obtained by L_1 regularized transductive regression. Competitive statistical machine translation is an on-line learning technique for sequential translation tasks where we try to select the best among competing statistical machine translators. The competitive predictor assigns a probability per model weighted by the sequential performance. We define additive, multiplicative, and loss-based weight updates with exponential loss functions for competitive statistical machine translation. Without any pre-knowledge of the performance of the translation models, we succeed in achieving the performance of the best model in all systems and surpass their performance in most of the language pairs we considered.

1 Introduction

When seen as independent instances, system combination task can be solved with a sequential learning algorithm. Online learning algorithms enable us to benefit from previous good model choices to estimate the next best model. We use transductive regression based machine translation model to estimate the scores for each sentence.

We analyze adaptive model weighting techniques for system combination when the competing translators are SMT models. We use separate model weights weighted by the sequential performance. We use additive, multiplicative, or loss based weight updates to update model weights. Without any pre-knowledge of the performance of the translation models, we are able to achieve the performance of the best model in all systems and we can surpass its performance as well as the regression based machine translation's performance.

The next section reviews the transductive regression approach for machine translation, which we use to obtain instance scores. In section 3 we present competitive statistical machine translation model for solving sequential translation tasks with competing translation models. Section 4 presents our results and experiments and the last section gives a summary of our contributions.

2 Transductive Regression Based Machine Translation

Transduction uses test instances, which can sometimes be accessible at training time, to learn specific models tailored towards the test set. Transduction has computational advantages since we are not using the full training set and a smaller set of constraints exist to satisfy. Transductive regression based machine translation (TRegMT) aims to reduce the computational burden of the regression approach by reducing the dimensionality of the training set and the feature set and also improve the translation quality by using transduction.

Regression Based Machine Translation: Let n training instances be represented as $(\mathbf{x}_1, \mathbf{y}_1), \ldots, (\mathbf{x}_n, \mathbf{y}_n) \in X^* \times Y^*$, where $(\mathbf{x}_i, \mathbf{y}_i)$ corresponds to a pair of source and target language token sequences. Our goal is to find a mapping $f : X^* \rightarrow Y^*$ that can convert a given set of source tokens to a set of target tokens that share the same meaning in the target language.

Proceedings of the Joint 5th Workshop on Statistical Machine Translation and MetricsMATR, pages 276–281,
Uppsala, Sweden, 15-16 July 2010. ©2010 Association for Computational Linguistics

We use feature mappers $\Phi_X : X^* \rightarrow F_X = \mathbb{R}^{N_X}$ and $\Phi_Y : Y^* \rightarrow F_Y = \mathbb{R}^{N_Y}$ to represent the training set. Then, $\mathbf{M}_X \in \mathbb{R}^{N_X \times n}$ and $\mathbf{M}_Y \in \mathbb{R}^{N_Y \times n}$ such that $\mathbf{M}_X = [\Phi_X(\mathbf{x}_1), \ldots, \Phi_X(\mathbf{x}_n)]$ and $\mathbf{M}_Y = [\Phi_Y(\mathbf{y}_1), \ldots, \Phi_Y(\mathbf{y}_n)]$. The ridge regression solution using L_2 regularization is found as:

$$\mathbf{H}_{L_2} = \underset{\mathbf{H} \in \mathbb{R}^{N_Y \times N_X}}{\arg\min} \parallel \mathbf{M}_Y - \mathbf{H}\mathbf{M}_X \parallel_F^2 + \lambda \parallel \mathbf{H} \parallel_F^2 . \quad (1)$$

Two main challenges of the regression based machine translation (RegMT) approach are learning the regression function, $g : X^* \rightarrow F_Y$, and solving the *pre-image problem*, which, given the features of the estimated target string sequence, $g(\mathbf{x}) = \Phi_Y(\hat{\mathbf{y}})$, attempts to find $\mathbf{y} \in Y^*$: $f(\mathbf{x}) = \arg\min_{\mathbf{y} \in Y^*} ||g(\mathbf{x}) - \Phi_Y(\mathbf{y})||^2$. Pre-image calculation involves a search over possible translations minimizing the cost function:

$$f(\mathbf{x}) = \underset{\mathbf{y} \in Y^*}{\arg\min} \parallel \Phi_Y(\mathbf{y}) - \mathbf{H}\Phi_X(\mathbf{x}) \parallel^2 . \quad (2)$$

We use n-spectrum weighted word feature mappers (Taylor and Cristianini, 2004) which consider all word sequences up to order n.

L_1 Regularized Regression for Learning: $\mathbf{H}_{L_2}$ is not a sparse solution as most of the coefficients remain non-zero. L_1 norm behaves both as a feature selection technique and a method for reducing coefficient values.

$$\mathbf{H}_{L_1} = \underset{\mathbf{H} \in \mathbb{R}^{N_Y \times N_X}}{\arg\min} \parallel \mathbf{M}_Y - \mathbf{H}\mathbf{M}_X \parallel_F^2 + \lambda \parallel \mathbf{H} \parallel_1 . (3)$$

Equation 3 presents the *lasso* (least absolute shrinkage and selection operator) (Tibshirani, 1996) solution where the regularization term is defined as $\|\mathbf{H}\|_1 = \sum_{i,j} |H_{i,j}|$. We use forward stagewise regression (FSR) (Hastie et al., 2006) and quadratic programming (QP) to find $\mathbf{H}_{L_1}$. The details of the TRegMT model can be read in a separate submission to the translation task (Bicici and Yuret, 2010).

3 Competitive Statistical Machine Translation

We develop the Competitive Statistical Machine Translation (CSMT) framework for sequential translation tasks when the competing models are statistical machine translators. CSMT uses the output of different translation models to achieve a translation performance that surpasses the translation performance of all of the component models or achieves the performance of the best.

CSMT uses online learning to update the weights used for estimating the best performing translation model. Competitive predictor assigns a weight per model estimated by their sequential performance. At each step, m component translation models are executed in parallel over the input source sentence sequence and the loss $l_p[n]$ of model p at observation n is calculated by comparing the desired data $y[n]$ with the output of model p, $\hat{y_p}[n]$. CSMT model selects a model based on the weights and the performance of the selected model as well as the remaining models to adaptively update the weights given for each model. This corresponds to learning in *full information setting* where we have access to the loss for each action (Blum and Mansour, 2007). CSMT learning involves two main steps: *estimation* and *weight update*:

$$\begin{aligned}
\hat{y_c}[n] &= E(\mathbf{w}[n], \mathbf{x}[n]), && \texttt{(estimation)} \\
l_p[n] &= y[n] - \hat{y_p}[n], && \texttt{(instance loss)} \\
\mathcal{L}_p[n] &= \textstyle\sum_{i=1}^{n} l_p[i]^2, && \texttt{(cumulative loss)} \\
\mathbf{w}[n+1] &= U(\mathbf{w}[n], \hat{y_c}[n], \boldsymbol{\mathcal{L}}[n]), && \texttt{(update)}
\end{aligned} \quad (4)$$

where $\mathbf{w}[n] = (w_1[n], \ldots, w_m[n])$ for m models, $\mathcal{L}_p$ is the cumulative squared loss of model p, $\boldsymbol{\mathcal{L}}[n]$ stores cumulative and instance losses, and $\hat{y_c}[n]$ is the competitive model estimated for instance n. The learning problem is finding an adaptive $\mathbf{w}$ that minimizes the cumulative squared error with appropriate estimation and update methods.

Related Work: Multistage adaptive filtering (Kozat and Singer, 2002) combines the output of multiple adaptive filters to outperform the best among them where the first stage executes models in parallel and the second stage updates parameters using the performance of the combined prediction, $\hat{y_c}[n]$. Macherey and Och (2007) investigate different approaches for system combination including candidate selection that maximize a weighted combination of BLEU scores among different system outputs. Their system uses a fixed weight vector trained on the development set to be multiplied with instance BLEU scores.

3.1 Estimating the Best Performing Translation Model

We use additive, multiplicative, or loss based updates to estimate model weights. We measure instance loss with $\texttt{trLoss}(y[i], \hat{y_p}[i])$, which is a function that returns the translation performance of the output translation of model p with respect to the reference translation at instance i. 1-BLEU (Papineni et al., 2001) is one such function with outputs in the range $[0, 1]$. Cumulative squared loss of the p-th translation model is defined as:

$$\mathcal{L}_p[n] = \sum_{i=1}^{n} \texttt{trLoss}(y[i], \hat{y_p}[i])^2. \qquad (5)$$

We use *exponentially re-weighted prediction* to estimate model performances, which uses exponentially re-weighted losses based on the outputs of the m different translation models.

We define the *additive* exponential weight update as follows:

$$w_p[n+1] = \frac{w_p[n] + e^{-\eta\, l_p[n]}}{\sum_{k=1}^{m} \left(w_k[n] + e^{-\eta\, l_k[n]} \right)}, \qquad (6)$$

where $\eta > 0$ is the learning rate and the denominator is used for normalization. The update amount, $e^{-\eta\, l_p[n]}$ is 1 when $l_p[n] = 0$ and it approaches zero with increasing instance loss. Perceptrons, gradient descent, and Widrow-Huff learning have additive weight updates.

We define the *multiplicative* exponential weight update as follows:

$$w_p[n+1] = w_p[n] \times \frac{e^{-\eta\, l_p[n]^2}}{\sum_{k=1}^{m} w_k[n]\; e^{-\eta\, l_k[n]^2}}, \qquad (7)$$

where we use the squared instance loss. Equation 7 is similar to the update of Weighted Majority Algorithm (Littlestone and Warmuth, 1992) where the weights of the models that make a mistake are multiplied by a fixed β such that $0 \leq \beta < 1$.

We use *Bayesian Information Criterion (BIC)* as a *loss based* re-weighting technique. Assuming that instance losses are normally distributed with variance σ^2, BIC score is obtained as (Hastie et al., 2009):

$$\text{BIC}_p[n] = \frac{\mathcal{L}_p[n]}{\sigma^2} + d_p \log(n), \qquad (8)$$

where σ^2 is estimated by the average of model sample variances of squared instance loss and d_p is the number of parameters used in model p which we assume to be the same for all models; therefore we can discard the second term. The model with the minimum BIC value becomes the one with the highest posterior probability where the posterior probability of model p can be estimated as (Hastie et al., 2009):

$$w_p[n+1] = \frac{e^{-\frac{1}{2}\text{BIC}_p[n]}}{\sum_{k=1}^{m} e^{-\frac{1}{2}\text{BIC}_k[n]}}. \qquad (9)$$

The posterior probabilities become model weights and we basically forget about the previous weights, whose information is presumably contained in the cumulative loss, $\mathcal{L}_p$. We define multiplicative re-weighting with BIC scores as follows:

$$w_p[n+1] = w_p[n] \times \frac{e^{-\frac{1}{2}\text{BIC}_p}}{\sum_{k=1}^{m} w_k[n]\; e^{-\frac{1}{2}\text{BIC}_k}}. \qquad (10)$$

Model selection: We use *stochastic* or *deterministic* selection to choose the competitive model for each instance. Deterministic choice randomly selects among the maximum scoring models with minimum translation length whereas stochastic choice draws model p with probability proportional to $w_p[n]$. Randomization with the stochastic model selection decreases expected mistake bounds in the weighted majority algorithm (Littlestone and Warmuth, 1992; Blum, 1996).

Auer et al. (2002) show that optimal fixed learning rate for the weighted majority algorithm is found as $\eta[n] = \sqrt{m/\mathcal{L}_*[n]}$ where $\mathcal{L}_*[n] = \min_{1 \leq i \leq m} \mathcal{L}_i[n]$, which requires prior knowledge of the cumulative losses. We use $\eta = \sqrt{m/(0.05n)}$ for constant η.

4 Experiments and Discussion

We perform experiments on the system combination task for the English-German (*en-de*), German-English (*de-en*), English-French (*en-fr*), English-Spanish (*en-es*), and English-Czech (*en-cz*) language pairs using the translation outputs for all the competing systems provided in WMT10. We experiment in a *simulated online learning* setting where only the scores obtained from the TRegMT system are used during both tuning and testing. We do not use reference translations in measuring instance performance in this simulated setting for the results we obtain be in line with system combination challenge's goals.

4.1 Datasets

We use the training set provided in WMT10 to index and select transductive instances from. The challenge split the test set for the translation task of 2489 sentences into a tuning set of 455 sentences and a test set with the remaining 2034 sentences. Translation outputs for each system is given in a separate file and the number of system outputs per translation pair varies. We have tokenized and lowercased each of the system outputs and combined these in a single N-best file per language pair. We use BLEU (Papineni et al., 2001) and NIST (Doddington, 2002) evaluation metrics for measuring the performance of translations automatically.

4.2 Reranking Scores

The problem we are solving is online learning with prior information, which comes from the comparative BLEU scores, LM scores, and TRegMT scores at each step n. The scoring functions are explained below:

1. TRegMT: Transductive regression based machine translation scores as found by Equation 2. We use the TRegMT scores obtained by the FSR model.
2. CBLEU: Comparative BLEU scores we obtain by measuring the average BLEU performance of each translation relative to the other systems' translations in the N-best list.
3. LM: We calculate 5-gram language model scores for each translation using the language model trained over the target corpus provided in the translation task.

To make things simpler, we use a single prior TRegMT system score linearly combining the three scores mentioned with weights learned on the tuning set. The overall TRegMT system score for instance n, model i is referred as $\texttt{TRegScore}_i[n]$.

Since we do not have access to the reference translations nor to the translation model scores each system obtained for each sentence, we estimate translation model performance by measuring the average BLEU performance of each translation relative to other translations in the N-best list. Thus, each possible translation in the N-best list is BLEU scored against other translations and the average of these scores is selected as the CBLEU score for the sentence. Sentence level BLEU score calculation avoids singularities in n-gram precisions by taking the maximum of the match count and $\frac{1}{2|s_i|}$ for $|s_i|$ denoting the length of the source sentence s_i as used in (Macherey and Och, 2007).

4.3 Adaptive Model Weighting

We initialize model weights to $1/m$ for all models, which are updated after each instance according to the losses based on the TRegMT model. Table 1 presents the performance of the algorithms on the *en-de* development set. We have measured their performances with stochastic (stoc.) or deterministic (det.) model selection when using only the weights or mixture weights obtained when instance scores are also considered. Mixture weights are obtained as: $w_i[n] = w_i[n]\ \texttt{TRegScore}_i[n]$, for instance n, model i.

Baseline performance obtained with random selection has .1407 BLEU and 4.9832 NIST scores. TRegMT model obtains a performance of .1661 BLEU and 5.3283 NIST with reranking. The best model performance among the 12 *en-de* translation models has .1644 BLEU and 5.2647 NIST scores. Therefore, by using TRegMT score, we are able to achieve better scores.

Not all of the settings are meaningful. For instance, stochastic model selection is used for algorithms having multiplicative weight updates. This is reflected in the Table 1 by low performance on the additive and BIC models. Similarly, using mixture weights may not result in better scores for algorithms with multiplicative updates, which resulted in decreased

	Additive		Multiplicative		BIC		BIC Weighting	
Setting	BLEU	NIST	BLEU	NIST	BLEU	NIST	BLEU	NIST
Stoc., W	.1419	5.0016 ±.003	.1528	5.1710 ±.001	.1442	5.0468	.1568 ±.001	5.2052 ±.005
Stoc., M	.1415	5.0001	.1525	5.1601 ±.001	.1459	5.0619 ±.004	.1566 ±.001	5.2030 ±.006
Det., W	.1644	5.3208	.1638	5.2571	.1638	5.2542	.1646	5.2535
Det., M	.1643	5.3173	.1536	5.1756	.1530	5.1871	.1507	5.1973

Table 1: Performances of the algorithms on the development set over 100 repetitions. W: Weights, M: Mixture.

performance in Table 1. Decreased performance with BIC hints that we may use other techniques for mixture weights.

Table 2 presents reranking results on all of the language pairs we considered with the random, TRegMT, and CSMT models. Random model score lists the random model performance selected among the competing translations randomly and it can be used as a baseline. Best model score lists the performance of the best model performance. CSMT models are named with the weighting model used (Add for additive, Mul for multiplicative, BICW for BIC weighting), model selection technique (S for stochastic, D for deterministic), and mixtures model (W for using only weights, M for using mixture weights) with hyphens in between. Our challenge submission is given in the last row of Table 2 where we used multiplicative exponential weight updates, deterministic model selection, and only the weights during model selection. For the challenge results, we initialized the weights to the weights obtained in the development set.

We have presented scores that are better than or close to the best model in **bold**. We observe that the additive model performs the best by achieving the performance of the best competing translation model and performing better than the best in most of the language pairs. For the *en-de* language pair, additive model score achieves even better than the TRegMT model, which is used for evaluating instance scores.

5 Contributions

We have analyzed adaptive model weighting techniques for system combination when the competing translators are statistical machine translation models. We defined additive, multiplicative, and loss-based weight updates with exponential loss functions for the competitive statistical machine translation framework.

Competitive SMT via adaptive weighting of various translators is shown to be a powerful technique for sequential translation tasks. We have demonstrated its use in the system combination task by using the instance scores obtained by the TRegMT model. Without any pre-knowledge of the performance of the translation models, we have been able to achieve the performance of the best model in all systems and we are able to surpass its performance as well as TRegMT's performance with the additive model.

Acknowledgments

The research reported here was supported in part by the Scientific and Technological Research Council of Turkey (TUBITAK). The first author would like to thank Deniz Yuret for helpful discussions and for guidance and support during the term of this research.

References

Auer, Cesa-Bianchi, and Gentile. 2002. Adaptive and self-confident on-line learning algorithms. *JCSS: Journal of Computer and System Sciences*, 64.

Ergun Bicici and Deniz Yuret. 2010. L_1 regularized regression for reranking and system combination in machine translation. In *Proceedings of the ACL 2010 Joint Fifth Workshop on Statistical Machine Translation and Metrics MATR*, Uppsala, Sweden, July. Association for Computational Linguistics.

Avrim Blum and Yishay Mansour. 2007. Learning, regret minimization and equilibria. In Noam Nisan, Tim Roughgarden, Eva Tardos, and Vijay V. Vazirani, editors, *Algorithmic Game Theory (Cambridge University Press, 2007)*.

Avrim Blum. 1996. On-line algorithms in machine learning. In *In Proceedings of the Workshop on On-Line Algorithms, Dagstuhl*, pages 306–325. Springer.

Model	*en-de* BLEU	*en-de* NIST	*de-en* BLEU	*de-en* NIST	*en-fr* BLEU	*en-fr* NIST	*en-es* BLEU	*en-es* NIST	*en-cz* BLEU	*en-cz* NIST
Random	.1490	5.6555	.2088	6.4886	.2415	6.8948	.2648	7.2563	.1283	4.9238
Best model	.1658	5.9610	.2408	6.9861	.2864	7.5272	.3047	7.7559	.1576	5.4480
TRegMT	.1689	5.9638	.2357	6.9254	.2947	7.7107	.3049	7.8156	.1657	5.5632
Add-D-W	<u>**.1697**</u>	<u>**5.9821**</u>	**.2354**	**6.9175**	**.2948**	**7.7094**	**.3043**	**7.8093**	**.1642**	**5.5463**
Add-D-M	<u>**.1698**</u>	<u>**5.9824**</u>	**.2353**	**6.9152**	**.2949**	**7.7103**	**.3044**	**7.8091**	**.1642**	**5.5461**
Mul-S-W	.1574	5.7564	.2161	6.5950	.2805	7.4599	**.2961**	**.7.6870**	**.1572**	**5.4394**
Mul-D-W	.1618	5.8912	**.2408**	**6.9854**	**.2847**	**7.5085**	.2785	7.4133	.1612	5.5119
BIC-D-W	.1614	5.8852	**.2408**	**6.9853**	**.2842**	**7.5022**	.2785	7.4132	**.1623**	**5.5236**
BIC-D-M	.1580	5.7614	.2141	6.5597	.2791	7.4309	.2876	7.5138	**.1577**	**5.4488**
BICW-S-W	.1621	5.8795	.2274	6.8142	.2802	7.4873	.2892	7.5569	**.1565**	**5.4126**
BICW-S-M	.1618	5.8730	.2196	6.6493	.2806	7.4948	.2849	7.4845	.1561	5.4099
BICW-D-W	**.1648**	**5.9298**	**.2355**	**6.9112**	.2807	7.4648	.2785	7.4134	.1534	5.3458
Challenge	.1567	5.73	**.2394**	**6.9627**	.2758	7.4333	**.3047**	**7.7559**	**.1641**	**5.5435**

Table 2: CSMT results where **bold** corresponds to scores better than or close to the best model. <u>Underlined</u> scores are better than both the TregMT model and the best model.

George Doddington. 2002. Automatic evaluation of machine translation quality using n-gram co-occurrence statistics. In *Human Language Technology Research*, pages 138–145.

Trevor Hastie, Jonathan Taylor, Robert Tibshirani, and Guenther Walther. 2006. Forward stagewise regression and the monotone lasso. *Electronic Journal of Statistics*, 1.

Trevor Hastie, Robert Tibshirani, and Jerome Friedman. 2009. *The Elements of Statistical Learning: Data Mining, Inference and Prediction*. Springer-Verlag, 2nd edition.

S.S. Kozat and A.C. Singer. 2002. Further results in multistage adaptive filtering. *ICASSP*, 2:1329–1332.

Nick Littlestone and Manfred K. Warmuth. 1992. The Weighted Majority Algorithm. Technical Report UCSC-CRL-91-28, University of California, Santa Cruz, Jack Baskin School of Engineering, October 26,.

Wolfgang Macherey and Franz J. Och. 2007. An empirical study on computing consensus translations from multiple machine translation systems. In *EMNLP-CoNLL*, pages 986–995.

Kishore Papineni, Salim Roukos, Todd Ward, and Wei-Jing Zhu. 2001. Bleu: a method for automatic evaluation of machine translation. In *ACL*, pages 311–318. ACL.

J. Shawe Taylor and N. Cristianini. 2004. *Kernel Methods for Pattern Analysis*. Cambridge University Press.

Robert J. Tibshirani. 1996. Regression shrinkage and selection via the lasso. *Journal of the Royal Statistical Society, Series B*, 58(1):267–288.

L_1 Regularized Regression for Reranking and System Combination in Machine Translation

Ergun Biçici
Koç University
34450 Sariyer, Istanbul, Turkey
ebicici@ku.edu.tr

Deniz Yuret
Koç University
34450 Sariyer, Istanbul, Turkey
dyuret@ku.edu.tr

Abstract

We use L_1 regularized transductive regression to learn mappings between source and target features of the training sets derived for each test sentence and use these mappings to rerank translation outputs. We compare the effectiveness of L_1 regularization techniques for regression to learn mappings between features given in a sparse feature matrix. The results show the effectiveness of using L_1 regularization versus L_2 used in ridge regression. We show that regression mapping is effective in reranking translation outputs and in selecting the best system combinations with encouraging results on different language pairs.

1 Introduction

Regression can be used to find mappings between the source and target feature sets derived from given parallel corpora. Transduction learning uses a subset of the training examples that are closely related to the test set without using the model induced by the full training set. In the context of SMT, we select a few training instances for each test instance to guide the translation process. This also gives us a computational advantage when considering the high dimensionality of the problem. The goal in transductive regression based machine translation (TRegMT) is both reducing the computational burden of the regression approach by reducing the dimensionality of the training set and the feature set and also improving the translation quality by using transduction. Transductive regression is shown to achieve higher accuracy than L_2 regularized ridge regression on some machine learning benchmark datasets (Chapelle et al., 1999).

In an idealized feature mapping matrix where features are word sequences, we would like to observe few target features for each source feature derived from a source sentence. In this setting, we can think of feature mappings being close to permutation matrices with one nonzero item for each column. L_1 regularization helps us achieve solutions close to the permutation matrices by increasing sparsity.

We show that L_1 regularized regression mapping is effective in reranking translation outputs and present encouraging results on different language pairs in the translation task of WMT10. In the system combination task, different translation outputs of different translation systems are combined to find a better translation. We model system combination task as a reranking problem among the competing translation models and present encouraging results with the TRegMT system.

Related Work: Regression techniques can be used to model the relationship between strings (Cortes et al., 2007). Wang et al. (2007) applies a string-to-string mapping approach to machine translation by using ordinary least squares regression and n-gram string kernels to a small dataset. Later they use L_2 regularized least squares regression (Wang and Shawe-Taylor, 2008). Although the translation quality they achieve is not better than Moses (Koehn et al., 2007), which is accepted to be the state-of-the-art, they show the feasibility of the approach. Serrano et al. (2009) use kernel regression to find translation mappings from source to target feature vectors and experiment with translating hotel front desk requests. Ueffing (2007) approaches the transductive learning problem for SMT by bootstrapping the training using the translations produced by the SMT system that have a scoring performance above some threshold as estimated by the SMT system itself.

Proceedings of the Joint 5th Workshop on Statistical Machine Translation and MetricsMATR, pages 282–289,
Uppsala, Sweden, 15-16 July 2010.

Outline: Section 2 gives an overview of regression based machine translation, which is used to find the mappings between the source and target features of the training set. In section 3 we present L_1 regularized transductive regression for alignment learning. Section 4 presents our experiments, instance selection techniques, and results on the translation task for WMT10. In section 5, we present the results on the system combination task using reranking. The last section concludes.

2 An Overview of Regression Based Machine Translation

Let X and Y correspond to the token sets used to represent source and target strings, then a training sample of m inputs can be represented as $(\mathbf{x}_1, \mathbf{y}_1), \ldots, (\mathbf{x}_m, \mathbf{y}_m) \in X^* \times Y^*$, where $(\mathbf{x}_i, \mathbf{y}_i)$ corresponds to a pair of source and target language token sequences. Our goal is to find a mapping $f : X^* \rightarrow Y^*$ that can convert a given set of source tokens to a set of target tokens that share the same meaning in the target language.

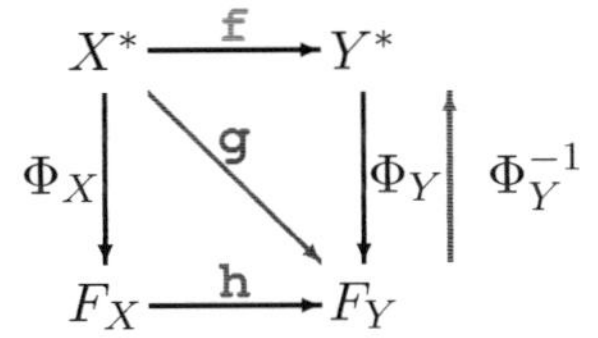

Figure 1: String-to-string mapping.

Figure 1 depicts the mappings between different representations. $\Phi_X : X^* \rightarrow F_X = \mathbb{R}^{N_X}$ and $\Phi_Y : Y^* \rightarrow F_Y = \mathbb{R}^{N_Y}$ map each string sequence to a point in high dimensional real number space where $dim(F_X) = N_X$ and $dim(F_Y) = N_Y$.

Let $\mathbf{M}_X \in \mathbb{R}^{N_X \times m}$ and $\mathbf{M}_Y \in \mathbb{R}^{N_Y \times m}$ such that $\mathbf{M}_X = [\Phi_X(\mathbf{x}_1), \ldots, \Phi_X(\mathbf{x}_m)]$ and $\mathbf{M}_Y = [\Phi_Y(\mathbf{y}_1), \ldots, \Phi_Y(\mathbf{y}_m)]$. The ridge regression solution using L_2 regularization is found as:

$$\mathbf{H}_{L_2} = \underset{\mathbf{H} \in \mathbb{R}^{N_Y \times N_X}}{\arg\min} \| \mathbf{M}_Y - \mathbf{H}\mathbf{M}_X \|_F^2 + \lambda \| \mathbf{H} \|_F^2 \ . \quad (1)$$

Proposition 1 *Solution to the cost function given in Equation 1 is found by the following identities:*

$$\begin{aligned} \boldsymbol{H} &= \boldsymbol{M}_Y \boldsymbol{M}_X^T (\boldsymbol{M}_X \boldsymbol{M}_X^T + \lambda \boldsymbol{I}_{N_X})^{-1} \quad \textit{(primal)} \\ \boldsymbol{H} &= \boldsymbol{M}_Y (\boldsymbol{K}_X + \lambda \boldsymbol{I}_m)^{-1} \boldsymbol{M}_X^T \quad \textit{(dual)} \end{aligned} \quad (2)$$

where $\boldsymbol{K}_X = \boldsymbol{M}_X^T \boldsymbol{M}_X$ *is the Gram matrix with* $\boldsymbol{K}_X(i,j) = k_X(\boldsymbol{x}_i, \boldsymbol{x}_j)$ *and* $k_X(\boldsymbol{x}_i, \boldsymbol{x}_j)$ *is the kernel function defined as* $k_X(\boldsymbol{x}_i, \boldsymbol{x}_j) = \phi(\boldsymbol{x}_i)^T \phi(\boldsymbol{x}_j)$.

The primal solution involves the inversion of the covariance matrix in the feature space ($O(N_X^3)$) and the dual solution involves the inversion of the kernel matrix in the instance space ($O(m^3)$) and L_2 regularization term prevents the normal equations to be singular. We use the dual solution when computing $\mathbf{H}_{L_2}$.

Two main challenges of the RegMT approach are learning the regression function, $g : X^* \rightarrow F_Y$, and solving the *pre-image problem*, which, given the features of the estimated target string sequence, $g(\mathbf{x}) = \Phi_Y(\hat{\mathbf{y}})$, attempts to find $\mathbf{y} \in Y^*$: $f(\mathbf{x}) = \arg\min_{\mathbf{y} \in Y^*} ||g(\mathbf{x}) - \Phi_Y(\mathbf{y})||^2$. Pre-image calculation involves a search over possible translations minimizing the cost function:

$$\begin{aligned} f(\mathbf{x}) &= \underset{\mathbf{y} \in Y^*}{\arg\min} \| \Phi_Y(\mathbf{y}) - \mathbf{H}\Phi_X(\mathbf{x}) \|^2 \\ &= \underset{\mathbf{y} \in Y^*}{\arg\min}\, k_Y(\mathbf{y}, \mathbf{y}) - 2(\mathbf{K}_Y^{\mathbf{y}})^T (\mathbf{K}_X + \lambda \mathbf{I}_m)^{-1} \mathbf{K}_X^{\mathbf{x}}, \end{aligned} \quad (3)$$

where $\mathbf{K}_Y^{\mathbf{y}} = [k_Y(\mathbf{y}, \mathbf{y}_1), \ldots, k_Y(\mathbf{y}, \mathbf{y}_m)]^T \in \mathbb{R}^{m \times 1}$ and $\mathbf{K}_X^{\mathbf{x}} \in \mathbb{R}^{m \times 1}$ is defined similarly.

We use n-spectrum weighted word kernel (Shawe-Taylor and Cristianini, 2004) as feature mappers which consider all word sequences up to order n:

$$k(\mathbf{x}, \mathbf{x}') = \sum_{p=1}^{n} \sum_{i=1}^{|x|-p+1} \sum_{j=1}^{|x'|-p+1} p\, I(\mathbf{x}[i:i+p-1] = \mathbf{x}'[j:j+p-1]) \quad (4)$$

where $\mathbf{x}[i:j]$ denotes a substring of $\mathbf{x}$ with the words in the range $[i, j]$, $I(.)$ is the indicator function, and p is the number of words in the feature.

3 L_1 Regularized Regression

In statistical machine translation, parallel corpora, which contain translations of the same documents in source and target languages, are used to estimate a likely target translation for a given source sentence based on the observed translations. String kernels lead to very sparse representations of the feature space and we examine the effectiveness of L_1 regularized regression to find the mappings between sparsely observed feature sets.

3.1 Sparsity in Translation Mappings

We would like to observe only a few nonzero target feature coefficients corresponding to a source feature in the coefficient matrix. An example solution matrix representing a possible alignment between unigram source and target features could be the following:

$\mathbf{H}$	e_1	e_2	e_3
f_1	1	1	
f_2		1	
f_3			1

Here e_i represents unigram source features and f_i represent unigram target features. e_1 and e_3 have unambiguous translations whereas e_2 is ambiguous. Even if unigram features lead to ambiguity, we expect higher order features like bigrams and trigrams to help us resolve the ambiguity. Typical $\mathbf{H}$ matrices have thousands of features. L_1 regularization helps us achieve solutions close to permutation matrices by increasing sparsity (Bishop, 2006). In contrast, L_2 solutions give us dense matrices.

3.2 L_1 Regularized Regression for Learning

$\mathbf{H}_{L_2}$ does not give us a sparse solution and most of the coefficients remain non-zero. L_1 norm behaves both as a feature selection technique and a method for reducing coefficient values.

$$\mathbf{H}_{L_1} = \underset{\mathbf{H}\in\mathbb{R}^{N_Y\times N_X}}{\arg\min} \parallel \mathbf{M}_Y - \mathbf{H}\mathbf{M}_X \parallel_F^2 + \lambda \parallel \mathbf{H} \parallel_1 . (5)$$

Equation 5 presents the *lasso* (least absolute shrinkage and selection operator) (Tibshirani, 1996) solution where the regularization term is now the L_1 matrix norm defined as $\parallel \mathbf{H} \parallel_1 = \sum_{i,j} |H_{i,j}|$. Since L_1 regularization cost is not differentiable, $\mathbf{H}_{L_1}$ is found by optimization or approximation techniques. We briefly describe three techniques to obtain L_1 regularized regression coefficients.

Forward Stagewise Regression (FSR): We experiment with forward stagewise regression (FSR) (Hastie et al., 2006), which approximates the *lasso*. The incremental forward stagewise regression algorithm increases the weight of the predictor variable that is most correlated with the residual by a small amount, ϵ, multiplied with the sign of the correlation at each step. As $\epsilon \to 0$, the profile of the coefficients resemble the *lasso* (Hastie et al., 2009).

Quadratic Programming (QP): We also use quadratic programming (QP) to find $\mathbf{H}_{L_1}$. We can pose *lasso* as a QP problem as follows (Mørup and Clemmensen, 2007). We assume that the rows of $\mathbf{M}_Y$ are independent and solve for each row i, $\mathbf{M}_{y_i} \in \mathbb{R}^{1\times m}$, using non-negative variables $\mathbf{h}_i^+, \mathbf{h}_i^- \in \mathbb{R}^{N_X\times 1}$ such that $\mathbf{h}_i = \mathbf{h}_i^+ - \mathbf{h}_i^-$:

$$\mathbf{h}_i = \underset{\mathbf{h}}{\arg\min} \ \| \mathbf{M}_{y_i} - \mathbf{h}\mathbf{M}_X \|_F^2 + \lambda \sum_{k=1}^{N_X} |h_k|, \quad (6)$$

$$\mathbf{h}_i = \underset{\tilde{\mathbf{h}_i}}{\arg\min} \ \frac{1}{2}\tilde{\mathbf{h}}_i \widetilde{\mathbf{M}_X} \widetilde{\mathbf{M}_X}^T \tilde{\mathbf{h}}_i^T - \tilde{\mathbf{h}}_i(\widetilde{\mathbf{M}_X} \mathbf{M}_{y_i}^T - \lambda \mathbf{1}), \quad (7)$$

$$\text{s.t. } \tilde{\mathbf{h}}_i > 0, \ \widetilde{\mathbf{M}_X} = \begin{bmatrix} \mathbf{M}_X \\ -\mathbf{M}_X \end{bmatrix}, \ \tilde{\mathbf{h}}_i = \begin{bmatrix} \mathbf{h}_i^+ & \mathbf{h}_i^- \end{bmatrix}.$$

Linear Programming (LP): L_1 minimization can also be posed as a linear programming (LP) problem by interpreting the error term as the constraint (Chen et al., 1998) and solving for each row i:

$$\mathbf{h}_i = \underset{\mathbf{h}}{\arg\min} \ \| \mathbf{h} \|_1 \ \text{subject to } \mathbf{M}_{y_i} = \mathbf{h}\mathbf{M}_X, \quad (8)$$

which can again be solved using non-negative variables. This is a slightly different optimization and the results can be different but linear programming solvers offer computational advantages.

3.3 Transductive Regression

Transduction uses test instances, which can sometimes be accessible at training time, to learn specific models tailored towards the test set. Transduction has computational advantages by not using the full training set and by having to satisfy a smaller set of constraints. For each test sentence, we pick a limited number of training instances designed to improve the coverage of correct features to build a regression model. Section 4.2 details our instance selection methods.

4 Translation Experiments

We perform experiments on the translation task of the English-German, German-English, English-French, English-Spanish, and English-Czech language pairs using the training corpus provided in WMT10.

4.1 Datasets and Baseline

We developed separate SMT models using Moses (Koehn et al., 2007) with default settings with maximum sentence length set to 80 using 5-gram language model and obtained distinct 100-best lists for the test sets. All systems were tuned with 2051 sentences and tested with 2525 sentences. We have randomly picked 100 instances from the development set to be used in tuning the regression experiments (*dev.100*). The translation challenge test set contains 2489 sentences. Number of sentences in the training set of each system and baseline performances for uncased output (test set BLEU, challenge test set BLEU) are given in Table 1.

Corpus	# sent	BLEU	BLEU Challenge
en-de	1609988	.1471	.1309
de-en	1609988	.1943	.1556
en-fr	1728965	.2281	.2049
en-es	1715158	.2237	.2106
en-cz	7320238	.1452	.1145

Table 1: Initial uncased performances of the translation systems.

Feature mappers used are 3-spectrum counting word kernels, which consider all N-grams up to order 3 weighted by the number of tokens in the feature. We segment sentences using some of the punctuation for managing the feature set better and do not consider N-grams that cross segments.

We use BLEU (Papineni et al., 2001) and NIST (Doddington, 2002) evaluation metrics for measuring the performance of translations automatically.

4.2 Instance Selection

Proper selection of training instances plays an important role to learn feature mappings with limited computational resources accurately. In previous work (Wang and Shawe-Taylor, 2008), sentence based training instances were selected using *tf-idf* retrieval. We transform test sentences to feature sets obtained by the kernel mapping before measuring their similarities and index the sentences based on the features. Given a source sentence of length 20, its feature representation would have a total of 57 uni/bi/tri-gram features. If we select closest sentences from the training set, we may not have translations for all the features in this representation. But if we search for translations of each feature, then we have a higher chance of covering all the features found in the sentence we are trying to translate. The index acts as a dictionary of source phrases storing training set entries whose source sentence match the given source phrase.

The number of instances per feature is chosen inversely proportional to the frequency of the feature determined by the following formula:

$$\textit{\#instance}(f) = n / \ln(1 + \text{idfScore}(f)/9.0), \quad (9)$$

where $\text{idfScore}(f)$ sums the *idf* (inverse document frequency) of the tokens in feature f and n is a small number.

4.3 Addition of Brevity Penalty

Detailed analysis of the results shows TRegMT score achieves better N-gram match percentages than Moses translation but suffers from the brevity penalty due to selecting shorter translations. Due to using a cost function that minimizes the squared loss, TRegMT score tends to select shorter translations when the coverage is low. We also observe that we are able to achieve higher scores for NIST, which suggests the addition of a brevity penalty to the score.

Precision based BLEU scoring divides N-gram match counts to N-gram counts found in the translation and this gives an advantage to shorter translations. Therefore, a brevity penalty (BP) is added to penalize short translations:

$$BP = \min(1 - \frac{\text{ref-length}}{\text{trans-length}}, 0) \quad (10)$$

$$BLEU = e^{(\log(\mathtt{ngram}_{prec}) + BP)} \quad (11)$$

where $\mathtt{ngram}_{prec}$ represent the sum of n-gram precisions. Moses rarely incurs BP as it has a word penalty parameter optimized against BLEU which penalizes translations that are too long or too short. For instance, Moses 1-best translation for *en-de* system achieves .1309 BLEU versus .1320 BLEU without BP.

We handle short translations in two ways. We optimize the λ parameter of QP, which manages the sparsity of the solution (larger λ values correspond to sparser solutions) against BLEU score rather than the squared loss. Optimization yields λ = 20.744. We alternatively add a BP cost to the squared loss:

$$BP = e^{\left(\min(1 - \frac{|\Phi_Y(\mathbf{y})|}{|\ulcorner \mathbf{H}\Phi_X(\mathbf{x}) + \alpha_{BP} \urcorner|}, 0)\right)} \quad (12)$$

$$f(\mathbf{x}) = \arg\min_{\mathbf{y} \in Y^*} \| \Phi_Y(\mathbf{y}) - \mathbf{H}\Phi_X(\mathbf{x}) \|^2 + \lambda_{BP} BP \quad (13)$$

where $|.|$ denotes the length of the feature vector, $\ulcorner . \urcorner$ rounds feature weights to integers, α_{BP} is a constant weight added to the estimation, and λ_{BP} is the weight given for the BP cost. $|\ulcorner \mathbf{H}\Phi_X(\mathbf{x}) + \alpha_{BP} \urcorner|$ represents an estimate of the length of the reference as found by the TRegMT system. This BP cost estimate is similar to the cost used in (Serrano et al., 2009) normalized by the length of the reference. We found $\alpha_{BP} = 0.1316$ and $\lambda_{BP} = -13.68$ when optimized on the *en-de* system. We add a BP penalty to all of the reranking results given in the next section and QP results also use optimized λ.

	en-de		*de-en*		*en-fr*		*en-es*		*en-cz*	
Score	**BLEU**	**NIST**	**BLEU**	**NIST**	**BLEU**	**NIST**	**BLEU**	**NIST**	**BLEU**	**NIST**
Baseline	.1309	5.1417	.1556	5.4164	.2049	6.3194	.2106	6.3611	.1145	4.5008
Oracle	.1811	6.0252	.2101	6.2103	.2683	7.2409	.2770	7.3190	.1628	5.4501
L2	**.1319**	**5.1680**	.1555	**5.4344**	.2044	**6.3370**	**.2132**	**6.4093**	.1148	**4.5187**
FSR	*.1317**	**5.1639**	.1559	**5.4383**	.2053	**6.3458**	**.2144**	**6.4168**	.1150	**4.5172**
LP	.1317	**5.1695**	.1561	**5.4304**	.2048	6.3245	.2109	**6.4176**	.1124	4.5143
QP	.1309	**5.1664**	.1550	**5.4553**	.2033	*6.3354**	**.2121**	**6.4271**	.1150	**4.5264**

Table 2: Reranking results using TRegMT, TM, and LM scores. We use approximate randomization test (Riezler and Maxwell, 2005) with 1000 repetitions to determine score difference significance: results in **bold** are significant with $p \leq 0.01$ and *italic* results with (*) are significant with $p \leq .05$. The difference of the remaining from the baseline are not statistically significant.

4.4 Reranking Experiments

We rerank N-best lists by using linear combinations of the following scoring functions:

1. TRegMT: Transductive regression based machine translation scores as found by Equation 3.
2. TM: Translation model scores we obtain from the baseline SMT system that is used to generate the N-best lists.
3. LM: 5-gram language model scores that the baseline SMT system uses when calculating the translation model scores.

The training set we obtain may not contain all of the features of the reference target due to low coverage. Therefore, when performing reranking, we also add the cost coming from the features of $\Phi_Y(\mathbf{y})$ that are not represented in the training set to the squared loss as in:

$$\| \Phi_Y(\mathbf{y}) \setminus F_Y \|^2 + \| \Phi_Y(\mathbf{y}) - \mathbf{H}\Phi_X(\mathbf{x}) \|^2, \quad (14)$$

where $\Phi_Y(\mathbf{y}) \setminus F_Y$ represent the features of $\mathbf{y}$ not represented in the training set.

We note that TRegMT score only contains ordering information as present in the bi/tri-gram features in the training set. Therefore, the addition of a 5-gram LM score as well as the TM score, which also incorporates the LM score in itself, improves the performance. We are not able to improve the BLEU score when we use TRegMT score by itself however we are able to achieve improvements in the NIST and 1-WER scores. The performance increase is important for two reasons. First of all, we are able to improve the performance using blended spectrum 3-gram features against translations obtained with 5-gram language model and higher order features. Outperforming higher order n-gram models is known to be a difficult task (Galley and Manning, 2009). Secondly, increasing the performance with reranking itself is a hard task since possible translations are already constrained by the ones observed in N-best lists. Therefore, an increase in the N-best list size may increase the score gaps.

Table 2 presents reranking results on all of the language pairs we considered, using TRegMT, TM, and LM scores with the combination weights learned in the development set. We are able to achieve better BLEU and NIST scores on all of the listed systems. We are able to see up to .38 BLEU points increase for the *en-es* pair. Oracle reranking performances are obtained by using BLEU scoring metric.

If we used only the TM and LM scores when reranking with the *en-de* system, then we would obtain .1309 BLEU and 5.1472 NIST scores. We only see a minor increase in the NIST score and no change in the BLEU score with this setting when compared with the baseline given in Table 2.

Due to computational reasons, we do not use the same number of instances to train different models. In our experiments, we used $n = 3$ for L2, $n = 1.5$ for FSR, and $n = 1.2$ for QP and LP solutions to select the number of instances in Equation 9. The average number of instances used per sentence in training corresponding to these choices are approximately 140, 74, and 61. Even with these decreased number of training instances, L_1 regularized regression techniques are able to achieve comparable scores to L_2 regularized regression model in Table 2.

5 System Combination Experiments

We perform experiments on the system combination task for the English-German, German-English, English-French, English-Spanish, and English-Czech language pairs using the training

Score	*en-de* BLEU	*en-de* NIST	*de-en* BLEU	*de-en* NIST	*en-fr* BLEU	*en-fr* NIST	*en-es* BLEU	*en-es* NIST	*en-cz* BLEU	*en-cz* NIST
Random	.1490	5.6555	.2088	6.4886	.2415	6.8948	.2648	7.2563	.1283	4.9238
Best model	.1658	5.9610	.2408	6.9861	.2864	7.5272	.3047	7.7559	.1576	5.4480
L2	**.1694**	5.9974	.2336	**6.9398**	**.2948**	7.7037	.3036	7.8120	.1657	5.5654
FSR	.1689	5.9638	.2357	6.9254	.2947	7.7107	**.3049**	**7.8156**	.1657	5.5632
LP	**.1694**	5.9954	**.2368**	6.8850	.2928	**7.7157**	.3027	7.7838	.1659	5.5680
QP	.1692	**5.9983**	**.2368**	6.9172	.2913	7.6949	.3040	7.8086	**.1662**	**5.5785**

Table 3: Reranking results using TRegMT, TM, and LM scores. **bold** correspond to the best score in each rectangle of scores.

corpus provided in WMT10.

5.1 Datasets

We use the training set provided in WMT10 to index and select transductive instances from. The challenge split the test set for the translation task of 2489 sentences into a tuning set of 455 sentences and a test set with the remaining 2034 sentences. Translation outputs for each system is given in a separate file and the number of system outputs per translation pair varies. We have tokenized and lowercased each of the system outputs and combined these in a single N-best file per language pair. We also segment sentences using some of the punctuation for managing the feature set better. We use these N-best lists for TRegMT reranking to select the best translation model. Feature mappers used are 3-spectrum counting word kernels, which consider all n-grams up to order 3 weighted by the number of tokens in the feature.

5.2 Experiments

We rerank N-best lists by using combinations of the following scoring functions:

1. TRegMT: Transductive regression based machine translation scores as found by Equation 3.
2. TM': Translation model scores are obtained by measuring the average BLEU performance of each translation relative to the other translations in the N-best list.
3. LM: We calculate 5-gram language model scores for each translation using the language model trained over the target corpus provided in the translation task.

Since we do not have access to the reference translations nor to the translation model scores each system obtained for each sentence, we estimate translation model performance (TM') by measuring the average BLEU performance of each translation relative to the other translations in the N-best list. Thus, each possible translation in the N-best list is BLEU scored against other translations and the average of these scores is selected as the TM score for the sentence. Sentence level BLEU score calculation avoids singularities in n-gram precisions by taking the maximum of the match count and $\frac{1}{2|s_i|}$ for $|s_i|$ denoting the length of the source sentence s_i as used in (Macherey and Och, 2007).

Table 3 presents reranking results on all of the language pairs we considered, using TRegMT, TM, and LM scores with the same combination weights as above. Random model score lists the random model performance selected among the competing translations randomly and it is used as a baseline. Best model score lists the performance of the best model performance. We are able to achieve better BLEU and NIST scores in all of the listed systems except for the *de-en* language pair when compared with the performance of the best competing translation system. The lower performance in the *de-en* language pair may be due to having a single best translation system that outperforms others significantly. The difference between the best model performance and the mean as well as the variance of the scores in the *de-en* language pair is about twice their counterparts in *en-de* language pair.

Due to computational reasons, we do not use the same number of instances to train different models. In our experiments, we used $n = 4$ for L2, $n = 1.5$ for FSR, and $n = 1.2$ for QP and LP solutions to select the number of instances in Equation 9. The average number of instances used per sentence in training corresponding to these choices are approximately 189, 78, and 64.

6 Contributions

We use transductive regression to learn mappings between source and target features of given parallel corpora and use these mappings to rerank translation outputs. We compare the effectiveness of L_1 regularization techniques for regression. TRegMT score has a tendency to select shorter translations when the coverage is low. We incorporate a brevity penalty to the squared loss and optimize λ parameter of QP to tackle this problem and further improve the performance of the system.

The results show the effectiveness of using L_1 regularization versus L_2 used in ridge regression. Proper selection of training instances plays an important role to learn correct feature mappings with limited computational resources accurately. We plan to investigate better instance selection methods for improving the translation performance. TRegMT score has a tendency to select shorter translations when the coverage is low. We incorporate a brevity penalty to the score and optimize the λ parameter of QP to tackle this problem.

Acknowledgments

The research reported here was supported in part by the Scientific and Technological Research Council of Turkey (TUBITAK).

References

Christopher M. Bishop. 2006. *Pattern Recognition and Machine Learning*. Springer.

Olivier Chapelle, Vladimir Vapnik, and Jason Weston. 1999. Transductive inference for estimating values of functions. In *NIPS*, pages 421–427.

Scott Shaobing Chen, David L. Donoho, and Michael A. Saunders. 1998. Atomic decomposition by basis pursuit. *SIAM Journal on Scientific Computing*, 20(1):33–61.

Corinna Cortes, Mehryar Mohri, and Jason Weston. 2007. A general regression framework for learning string-to-string mappings. In Gokhan H. Bakir, Thomas Hofmann, and Bernhard Sch editors, *Predicting Structured Data*, pages 143–168. The MIT Press, September.

George Doddington. 2002. Automatic evaluation of machine translation quality using n-gram co-occurrence statistics. In *Proceedings of the second international conference on Human Language Technology Research*, pages 138–145, San Francisco, CA, USA. Morgan Kaufmann Publishers Inc.

Michel Galley and Christopher D. Manning. 2009. Quadratic-time dependency parsing for machine translation. In *Proceedings of the Joint Conference of the 47th Annual Meeting of the ACL and the 4th International Joint Conference on Natural Language Processing of the AFNLP*, pages 773–781, Suntec, Singapore, August. Association for Computational Linguistics.

Trevor Hastie, Jonathan Taylor, Robert Tibshirani, and Guenther Walther. 2006. Forward stagewise regression and the monotone lasso. *Electronic Journal of Statistics*, 1.

Trevor Hastie, Robert Tibshirani, and Jerome Friedman. 2009. *The Elements of Statistical Learning: Data Mining, Inference and Prediction*. Springer-Verlag, 2nd edition.

Philipp Koehn, Hieu Hoang, Alexandra Birch, Chris Callison-Burch, Marcello Federico, Nicola Bertoldi, Brooke Cowan, Wade Shen, Christine Moran, Richard Zens, Chris Dyer, Ondrej Bojar, Alexandra Constantin, and Evan Herbst. 2007. Moses: Open source toolkit for statistical machine translation. In *Annual Meeting of the Assoc. for Computational Linguistics*, pages 177–180, Prague, Czech Republic, June.

Wolfgang Macherey and Franz J. Och. 2007. An empirical study on computing consensus translations from multiple machine translation systems. In *EMNLP-CoNLL*, pages 986–995.

M. Mørup and L. H. Clemmensen. 2007. Multiplicative updates for the lasso. In *Machine Learning for Signal Processing MLSP, IEEE Workshop on*, pages 33 –38, Aug.

Kishore Papineni, Salim Roukos, Todd Ward, and Wei-Jing Zhu. 2001. BLEU: a method for automatic evaluation of machine translation. In *ACL '02: Proceedings of the 40th Annual Meeting on Association for Computational Linguistics*, pages 311–318, Morristown, NJ, USA. Association for Computational Linguistics.

Stefan Riezler and John T. Maxwell. 2005. On some pitfalls in automatic evaluation and significance testing for MT. In *Proceedings of the ACL Workshop on Intrinsic and Extrinsic Evaluation Measures for Machine Translation and/or Summarization*, pages 57–64, Ann Arbor, Michigan, June. Association for Computational Linguistics.

Nicolas Serrano, Jesus Andres-Ferrer, and Francisco Casacuberta. 2009. On a kernel regression approach to machine translation. In *Iberian Conference on Pattern Recognition and Image Analysis*, pages 394–401.

John Shawe-Taylor and Nello Cristianini. 2004. *Kernel Methods for Pattern Analysis*. Cambridge University Press.

Robert J. Tibshirani. 1996. Regression shrinkage and selection via the lasso. *Journal of the Royal Statistical Society, Series B*, 58(1):267–288.

Nicola Ueffing, Gholamreza Haffari, and Anoop Sarkar. 2007. Transductive learning for statistical machine translation. In *Proceedings of the 45th Annual Meeting of the Association of Computational Linguistics*, pages 25–32, Prague, Czech Republic, June. The Association for Computer Linguistics.

Zhuoran Wang and John Shawe-Taylor. 2008. Kernel regression framework for machine translation: UCL system description for WMT 2008 shared translation task. In *Proceedings of the Third Workshop on Statistical Machine Translation*, pages 155–158, Columbus, Ohio, June. Association for Computational Linguistics.

Zhuoran Wang, John Shawe-Taylor, and Sandor Szedmak. 2007. Kernel regression based machine translation. In *Human Language Technologies 2007: The Conference of the North American Chapter of the Association for Computational Linguistics; Companion Volume, Short Papers*, pages 185–188, Rochester, New York, April. Association for Computational Linguistics.

An Augmented Three-Pass System Combination Framework: DCU Combination System for WMT 2010

Jinhua Du, Pavel Pecina, Andy Way
CNGL, School of Computing
Dublin City University
Dublin 9, Ireland
{jdu, ppecina, away}@computing.dcu.ie

Abstract

This paper describes the augmented three-pass system combination framework of the Dublin City University (DCU) MT group for the WMT 2010 system combination task. The basic three-pass framework includes building individual confusion networks (CNs), a super network, and a modified Minimum Bayes-risk (mConMBR) decoder. The augmented parts for WMT2010 tasks include 1) a rescoring component which is used to re-rank the N-best lists generated from the individual CNs and the super network, 2) a new hypothesis alignment metric – TERp – that is used to carry out English-targeted hypothesis alignment, and 3) more different backbone-based CNs which are employed to increase the diversity of the mConMBR decoding phase. We took part in the combination tasks of English-to-Czech and French-to-English. Experimental results show that our proposed combination framework achieved 2.17 absolute points (13.36 relative points) and 1.52 absolute points (5.37 relative points) in terms of BLEU score on English-to-Czech and French-to-English tasks respectively than the best single system. We also achieved better performance on human evaluation.

1 Introduction

In several recent years, system combination has become not only a research focus, but also a popular evaluation task due to its help in improving machine translation quality. Generally, most combination approaches are based on a confusion network (CN) which can effectively re-shuffle the translation hypotheses and generate a new target sentence. A CN is essentially a directed acyclic graph built from a set of translation hypotheses against a reference or "backbone". Each arc between two nodes in the CN denotes a word or token, possibly a *null* item, with an associated posterior probability.

Typically, the dominant CN is constructed at the word level by a state-of-the-art framework: firstly, a minimum Bayes-risk (MBR) decoder (Kumar and Byrne, 2004) is utilised to choose the backbone from a merged set of hypotheses, and then the remaining hypotheses are aligned against the backbone by a specific alignment approach. Currently, most research in system combination has focused on hypothesis alignment due to its significant influence on combination quality.

A multiple CN or "super-network" framework was firstly proposed in Rosti et al. (2007) who used each of all individual system results as the backbone to build CNs based on the same alignment metric, TER (Snover et al., 2006). A consensus network MBR (ConMBR) approach was presented in (Sim et al., 2007), where MBR decoding is employed to select the best hypothesis with the minimum cost from the original single system outputs compared to the consensus output.

Du and Way (2009) proposed a combination strategy that employs MBR, super network, and a modified ConMBR (mConMBR) approach to construct a three-pass system combination framework which can effectively combine different hypothesis alignment results and easily be extended to more alignment metrics. Firstly, a number of individual CNs are built based on different backbones and different kinds of alignment metrics. Each network generates a 1-best output. Secondly, a super network is constructed combining all the individual networks, and a consensus is generated based on a weighted search model. In the third

Proceedings of the Joint 5th Workshop on Statistical Machine Translation and MetricsMATR, pages 290–295,
Uppsala, Sweden, 15-16 July 2010.

pass, all the 1-best hypotheses coming from single MT systems, individual networks, and the super network are combined to select the final result using the mConMBR decoder.

In the system combination task of WMT 2010, we adopted an augmented framework by extending the strategy in (Du and Way, 2009). In addition to the basic three-pass architecture, we augment our combination system as follows:

- We add a rescoring component in Pass 1 and Pass 2.
- We introduce the TERp (Snover et al., 2009) alignment metric for the English-targeted combination.
- We employ different backbones and hypothesis alignment metrics to increase the diversity of candidates for our mConMBR decoding.

The remainder of this paper is organised as follows. In Section 2, we introduce the three hypothesis alignment methods used in our framework. Section 3 details the steps for building our augmented three-pass combination framework. In Section 4, a rescoring model with rich features is described. Then, Sections 5 and 6 respectively report the experimental settings and experimental results on English-to-Czech and French-to-English combination tasks. Section 7 gives our conclusions.

2 Hypothesis Alignment Methods

Hypothesis alignment plays a vital role in the CN, as the backbone sentence determines the skeleton and the word order of the consensus output.

In the combination evaluation task, we integrated TER (Snover et al., 2006), HMM (Matusov et al., 2006) and TERp (Snover et al., 2009) into our augmented three-pass combination framework. In this section, we briefly describe these three methods.

2.1 TER

The TER (Translation Edit Rate) metric measures the ratio of the number of edit operations between the hypothesis E' and the reference E_b to the total number of words in E_b. Here the backbone E_b is assumed to be the reference. The allowable edits include insertions (Ins), deletions (Del), substitutions (Sub), and phrase shifts (Shft). The TER of E' compared to E_b is computed as in (1):

$$TER(E', E_b) = \frac{\text{Ins} + \text{Del} + \text{Sub} + \text{Shft}}{N_b} \times 100\% \quad (1)$$

where N_b is the total number of words in E_b. The difference between TER and Levenshtein edit distance (or WER) is the sequence shift operation allowing phrasal shifts in the output to be captured.

The phrase shift edit is carried out by a greedy algorithm and restricted by three constraints: 1) The shifted words must exactly match the reference words in the destination position. 2) The word sequence of the hypothesis in the original position and the corresponding reference words must not exactly match. 3) The word sequence of the reference that corresponds to the destination position must be misaligned before the shift (Snover et al., 2006).

2.2 HMM

The hypothesis alignment model based on HMM (Hidden Markov Model) considers the alignment between the backbone and the hypothesis as a hidden variable in the conditional probability $P_r(E'|E_b)$. Given the backbone $E_b = \{e_1, \ldots, e_I\}$ and the hypothesis $E' = \{e'_1, \ldots, e'_J\}$, which are both in the same language, the probability $P_r(E'|E_b)$ is defined as in (2):

$$P_r(E'|E_b) = \sum_{A} P_r(E', A|E_b) \quad (2)$$

where the alignemnt $A \subseteq \{(j, i) : 1 \leq j \leq J; 1 \leq i \leq I\}$, i and j represent the word position in E_b and E' respectively. Hence, the alignment issue is to seek the optimum alignment $\hat{A}$ such that:

$$\hat{A} = \arg\max_{A} P(A|e_1^I, e_1'^J) \quad (3)$$

For the HMM-based model, equation (2) can be represented as in (4):

$$P_r(E'|E_b) = \sum_{a_j^J} \prod_{j=1}^{J} [p(a_j|a_{j-1}, I) \cdot p(e'_j|e_{a_j})] \quad (4)$$

where $p(a_j|a_{j-1}, I)$ is the alignment probability and $p(e'_j|e_i)$ is the translation probability.

2.3 TER-Plus

TER-Plus (TERp) is an extension of TER that aligns words in the hypothesis and reference not only when they are exact matches but also when the words share a stem or are synonyms (Snover et al., 2009). In addition, it uses probabilistic phrasal substitutions to align phrases in the hypothesis and referencc. In contrast to the use of the constant edit cost for all operations such as shifts, insertion, deleting or substituting in TER, all edit costs in TERp are optimized to maximize correlation with human judgments.

TERp uses all the edit operations of TER – matches, insertions, deletions, substitutions, and shifts – as well as three new edit operations: stem matches, synonym matches, and phrase substitutions (Snover et al., 2009). TERp employs the Porter stemming algorithm (Porter, 1980) and WordNet (Fellbaum, 1998) to perform the "stem match" and "synonym match" respectively. Sequences of words in the reference are considered to be paraphrases of a sequence of words in the hypothesis if that phrase pair occurs in the TERp phrase table (Snover et al., 2009).

In our experiments, TERp was used for the French-English system combination task, and we used the default configuration of optimised edit costs.

3 Augmented Three-Pass Combination Framework

The construction of the augmented three-pass combination framework is shown in Figure 1.

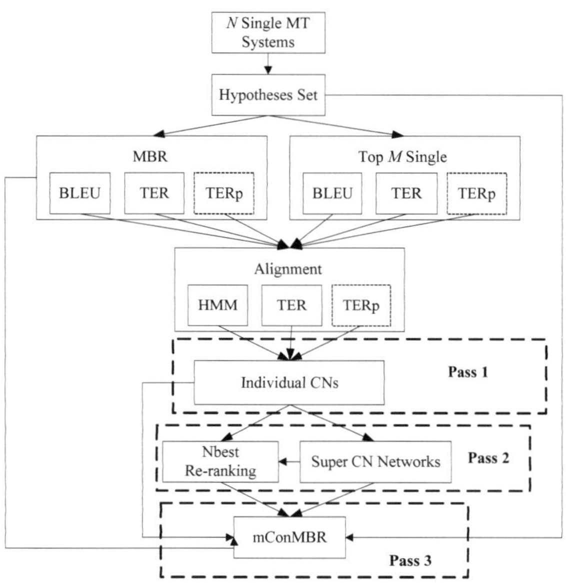

Figure 1: Three-Pass Combination Framework

In Figure 1, the dashed boxes labeled "TERp" indicate that the TERp alignment is only applicable for English-targeted hypothesis alignment. The lines with arrows pointing to "mConMBR" represent adding outputs into the mConMBR decoding component. "Top M Single" indicates that the 1-best results from the best M individual MT systems are also used as backbones to build individual CNs under different alignment metrics. The three dashed boxes represent Pass 1, Pass 2 and Pass 3 respectively. The steps can be summarised as follows:

Pass 1: Specific Metric-based Single Networks

1. Merge all the 1-best hypotheses from single MT systems into a new N-best set N_s.

2. Utilise the standard MBR decoder to select one from the N_s as the backbone given some specific loss function such as TER, BLEU (Papineni et al., 2002) and TERp; Additionally, in order to increase the diversity of candidates used for Pass 2 and Pass 3, we also use the 1-best hypotheses from the top M single MT systems as the backbone. Add the backbones generated by MBR into N_s.

3. Perform the word alignment between the different backbones and the other hypotheses via the TER, HMM, TERp (only for English) metrics.

4. Carry out word reordering based on word alignment (TER and TERp have completed the reordering in the process of scoring) and build individual CNs (Rosti et al., 2007);

5. Decode the single networks and export the 1-best outputs and the N-best lists separately. Add these 1-best outputs into N_s.

Pass 2: Super-Network

1. Connect the single networks using a start node and an end node to form a super-network based on multiple hypothesis alignment and different backbones. In this evaluation, we set uniform weights for these different individual networks when building the super network(Du and Way, 2009).

2. Decode the super network and generate a consensus output as well as the N-best list. Add the 1-best result into N_s.

3. Rescore the N-best lists from all individual networks and super network and add the new 1-best results into N_s.

Pass 3: mConMBR

1. Rename the set N_s as a new set N_{con};

2. Use mConMBR decoding to search for the best final result from N_{con}. In this step, we set a uniform distribution between the candidates in N_{con}.

4 Rescoring Model

We adapted our previous rescoring model (Du et al., 2009) to larger-scale data. The features we used are as follows:

- Direct and inverse IBM model;
- 4-gram and 5-gram target language model;
- 3, 4, and 5-gram Part-of-Speech (POS) language model (Schmid, 1994; Ratnaparkhi, 1996);
- Sentence-length posterior probability (Zens and Ney, 2006);
- N-gram posterior probabilities within the N-best list (Zens and Ney, 2006);
- Minimum Bayes Risk cost. This process is similar to the calculation of the MBR decoding in which we take the current hypothesis in the N-best list as the "backbone", and then calculate and sum up all the Bayes risk cost between the backbone and each of the rest of the N-best list using BLEU metric as the loss function;
- Length ratio between source and target sentence.

The weights are optimized via the MERT algorithm (Och, 2003).

5 Experimental Settings

We participated in the English–Czech and French–English system combination tasks.

In our system combination framework, we use a large-scale monolingual data to train language models and carry out POS-tagging.

5.1 English-Czech

Training Data

The statistics of the data used for language models training are shown in Table 1.

Corpus	*Monolingual tokens (Cz)*	*Number of sentences*
News-Comm	2,214,757	84,706
CzEng	81,161,278	8,027,391
News	205,600,053	13,042,040
Total	288,976,088	21,154,137

Table 1: Statistics of data in the En–Cz task

All the data are provided by the workshop organisers. [1] In Table 1, "News-Comm" indicates the data set of News-Commentary v1.0 and "CzEng" is the Czech–English corpus v0.9 (Bojar and Žabokrtský, 2009). "News" is the Czech monolingual News corpus.

As to our CN and rescoring components, we use "News-Comm+CzEng" to train a 4-gram language model and use "News-Comm+CzEng+News" to train a 5-gram language model. Additionally, we perform POS tagging (Hajič, 2004) for 'News-Comm+CzEng+News" data, and train 3-gram, 4-gram, and 5-gram POS-tag language models.

Devset and Testset

The devset includes 455 sentences and the testset contains 2,034 sentences. Both data sets are provided by the workshop organizers. Each source sentence has only one reference. There are 11 MT systems in the En-Cz track and we use all of them in our combination experiments.

5.2 French-English

Training Data

The statistics of the data used for language models training and POS tagging are shown in Table 2.

Corpus	*Monolingual tokens (En)*	*Number of sentences*
News-Comm	2,973,711	125,879
Europarl	50,738,215	1,843,035
News	1,131,527,255	48,648,160
Total	1,184,234,384	50,617,074

Table 2: Statistics of data in the Fr–En task

"News" is the English monolingual News corpus. We use "News-Comm+Europarl" to train a 4-gram language model and use "News-Comm+Europarl+News" to train a 5-gram language model. We also perform POS tagging (Ratnaparkhi, 1996) for all available data, and train 3-gram, 4-gram and, 5-gram POS-tag language models.

Devset and Testset

We also use all the 1-best results to carry out system combination. There are 14 MT systems in the Fr-En track and we use all of them in our combination experiments.

6 Experimental Results

In this section, all the results are reported on devsets in terms of BLEU and NIST scores.

6.1 English–Czech

In this task, we only used one hypothesis alignment method – TER – to carry out hypothesis

[1] http://www.statmt.org/wmt10/translation-task.html

alignment. However, in order to increase diversity for our 3-pass framework, in addition to using the output from MBR decoding as the backbone, we also separately selected the top 4 individual systems (SYS1, SYS4, SYS6, and SYS11 in our system set) in terms of BLEU scores on the devset as the backbones so that we can build multiple individual CNs for the super network. All the results are shown in Table 3.

SYS	BLEU4	NIST
Worst	9.09	3.83
Best	**17.28**	4.99
SYS1	15.11	4.76
SYS4	12.67	4.40
SYS6	17.28	4.99
SYS11	15.75	4.81
CN-SYS1	17.36	5.12
CN-SYS4	16.94	5.10
CN-SYS6	17.91	5.13
CN-SYS11	17.45	5.09
CN-MBR	**18.29**	5.15
SuperCN	**18.44**	5.17
mConMBR-BAS	**18.60**	5.18
mConMBR-New	**18.84**	5.11

Table 3: Automatic evaluation of the combination results on the En-Cz devset.

"Worst" indicates the 1-best hypothesis from the worst single system, the "Best" is the 1-best hypothesis from the best single system (SYS11)). "CN-SYSX" denotes that we use SYSX ($X = 1, 4, 6, 11$ and MBR) as the backbone to build an individual CN. "mConMBR-BAS" stands for the original three-pass combination framework without rescoring component, while "mConMBR-New" indicates the proposed augmented combination framework. It can be seen from Table 3 that 1) in all individual CNs, the CN-MBR achieved the best performance; 2) SuperCN and mConMBR-New improved by 1.16 (6.71% relative) and 1.56 (9.03% relative) absolute BLEU points compared to the best single MT system. 3) our new three-pass combination framework achieved the improvement of 0.24 absolute (1.29% relative) BLEU points than the original framework.

The final results on the test set are shown in Table 4.

SYS	BLEU4	human eval.(%win)
Best	**16.24**	70.38
mConMBR-BAS	17.91	-
mConMBR-New	**18.41** [2]	**75.17**

Table 4: Evaluation of the combination results on the En-Cz testset.

It can be seen that our "mConMBR-New" framework performs better than the best single system and our original framework "mConMBR-BAS" in terms of automatic BLEU scores and human evaluation for the English-to-Czech task. In this task campaign, we achieved top 1 in terms of the human evaluation.

6.2 French–English

We used three hypothesis alignment methods – TER, TERp and HMM – to carry out word alignment between the backbone and the rest of the hypotheses. Apart from the backbone generated from MBR, we separately select the top 5 individual systems (SYS1, SYS10, SYS11, SYS12, and SYS13 in our system set) respectively as the backbones using HMM, TER and TERp to carry out hypothesis alignment so that we can build more individual CNs for the super network to increase the diversity of candidates for mConMBR. The results are shown in Table 5.[3]

SYS	BLEU4(%)	NIST
Worst	15.04	4.97
Best	**28.88**	6.71
CN-SYS1-TER	29.56	6.78
CN-SYS1-HMM	29.60	6.84
CN-SYS1-TERp	**29.77**	6.83
CN-MBR-TER	30.16	6.91
CN-MBR-HMM	30.19	6.92
CN-MBR-TERp	**30.27**	6.92
SuperCN	**30.58**	6.90
mConMBR-BAS	30.74	7.01
mConMBR-New	**31.02**	6.96

Table 5: Automatic evaluation of the combination results on the Fr-En devset.

"CN-MBR-X" represents the different possible hypothesis alignment methods ($X = \{$TER, HMM, TERp$\}$) which are used to build individual CNs using the output from MBR decoding as the backbone. We can see that the SuperCN and mConMBR-New respectively improved by 1.7 absolute (5.89% relative) and 2.88 absolute (9.97% relative) BLEU points compared to the best single system. Furthermore, our augmented framework "mConMBR-New" achieved the improvement of 0.28 absolute (0.91% relative) BLEU points than the original three-pass framework as well.

[2] This score was measured in-house on the reference provided by the organizer using metric mteval-v13 (ftp://jaguar.ncsl.nist.gov/mt/resources/mteval-v13.pl).

[3] In this Table, we take SYS1 as an example to show the results using a single MT system as the backbone under the three alignment metrics.

The final results on the test set are shown in Table 6.

SYS	BLEU4	human eval.(%win)
Best	**28.30**	66.84
mConMBR-BAS	29.21	-
mConMBR-New	**29.82** [2]	**72.15**

Table 6: Evaluation of the combination results on Fr-En test set.

It can be seen that our "mConMBR-New" framework performs the best than the best single system and our original framework "mConMBR-BAS" in terms of automatic BLEU scores and human evaluation for the French–English task.

7 Conclusions and Future Work

We proposed an augmented three-pass multiple system combination framework for the WMT2010 system combination shared task. The augmented parts include 1) a rescoring model to select the potential 1-best result from the individual CNs and super network to increase the diversity for "mConMBR" decoding; 2) a new hypothesis alignment metric "TERp" for English-targeted alignment; 3) 1-best results from the top M individual systems employed to build CNs to augment the "mConMBR" decoding. We took part in the English-to-Czech and French-to-English tasks. Experimental results reported on test set of these two tasks showed that our augmented framework performed better than the best single system in terms of BLEU scores and human evaluation. Furthermore, the proposed augmented framework achieved better results than our basic three-pass combination framework (Du and Way, 2009) as well in terms of automatic evaluation scores. In the released preliminary results, we achieved top 1 and top 3 for the English-to-Czech and French-to-English tasks respectively in terms of human evaluation.

As for future work, firstly we plan to do further experiments using automatic weight-tuning algorithm to tune our framework. Secondly, we plan to examine how the differences between the hypothesis alignment metrics impact on the accuracy of the super network. We also intend to integrate more alignment metrics to the networks and verify on the other language pairs.

Acknowledgments

This research is supported by the Science Foundation Ireland (Grant 07/CE/I1142) as part of the Centre for Next Generation Localisation (www.cngl.ie) at Dublin City University and has been partially funded by PANACEA, a 7th Framework Research Programme of the European Union (contract number: 7FP-ITC-248064) as well as partially supported by the project *GA405/09/0278* of the Grant Agency of the Czech Republic. Thanks also to the reviewers for their insightful comments.

References

Bojar, O. and Žabokrtský, Z. (2009). CzEng0.9: Large Parallel Treebank with Rich Annotation. *Prague Bulletin of Mathematical Linguistics*, 92.

Du, J., He, Y., Penkale, S., and Way, A. (2009). MaTrEx: The DCU MT System for WMT2009. In *Proceedings of the EACL-WMT 2009*, pages 95–99, Athens, Greece.

Du, J. and Way, A. (2009). A Three-pass System Combination Framework by Combining Multiple Hypothesis Alignment Methods. In *Proceedings of the International Conference on Asian Language Processing (IALP)*, pages 172–176, Singapore.

Fellbaum, C., editor (1998). *WordNet: an electronic lexical database*. MIT Press.

Hajič, J. (2004). *Disambiguation of Rich Inflection (Computational Morphology of Czech)*, volume 1. Charles University Press, Prague.

Kumar, S. and Byrne, W. (2004). Minimum Bayes-Risk Decoding for Statistical Machine Translation. In *Proceedings of the HLT-NAACL 2004*, pages 169–176, Boston, MA.

Matusov, E., Ueffing, N., and Ney, H. (2006). Computing consensus translation from multiple machine translation systems using enhanced hypotheses alignment. In *Proceedings of EACL'06*, pages 33–40.

Och, F. (2003). Minimum error rate training in statistical machine translation. In *Proceedings of the 41st Annual Meeting of the Association for Computational Linguistics (ACL)*, pages 160–167, Sapporo, Japan.

Papineni, K., Roukos, S., Ward, T., and Zhu, W.-J. (2002). BLEU: a Method for Automatic Evaluation of Machine Translation. In *Proceedings of the ACL-02*, pages 311–318, Philadelphia, PA.

Porter, M. F. (1980). An algorithm for suffix stripping, program.

Ratnaparkhi, A. (1996). A Maximum Entropy Model for Part-of-Speech Tagging. In *Proceedings of the EMNLP'96*, pages 133–142, Philadelphia, PA.

Rosti, A., Matsoukas, S., and Schwartz, R. (2007). Improved Word-Level System Combination for Machine Translation. In *Proceedings of ACL'07*, pages 312–319.

Schmid, H. (1994). Probabilistic Part-of-Speech Tagging Using Decision Trees. In *Proceedings of International Conference on New Methods in Language Processing*, pages 44–49, Manchester, UK.

Sim, K., Byrne, W., Gales, M., Sahbi, H., and Woodland, P. (2007). Consensus network decoding for statistical machine translation system combination. In *Proceedings of the ICASSP'07*, pages 105–108.

Snover, M., Dorr, B., Schwartz, R., Micciula, L., and Makhoul, J. (2006). A study of translation edit rate with targeted human annotation. In *Proceedings of the AMTA'06)*, pages 223–231, Cambridge, MA.

Snover, M., Madnani, N., J.Dorr, B., and Schwartz, R. (2009). Fluency, adequacy, or HTER? Exploring different human judgments with a tunable MT metric. In *Proceedings of the WMT'09*, pages 259–268, Athens, Greece.

Zens, R. and Ney, H. (2006). N-gram Posterior Probabilities for Statistical Machine Translation. In *Proceedings of the HLT NAACL'06)*, pages 72–77, New York, USA.

The UPV-PRHLT Combination System for WMT 2010

Jesús González-Rubio and **Jesús Andrés-Ferrer** and **Germán Sanchis-Trilles**
Guillem Gascó and **Pascual Martínez-Gómez** and **Martha-Alicia Rocha**
Joan-Andreu Sánchez and **Francisco Casacuberta**
Instituto Tecnológico de Informática
Departamento de Sistemas Informáticos y Computación
Universidad Politécnica de Valencia
{jegonzalez|jandres|gsanchis}@dsic.upv.es
{ggasco|pmartinez|mrocha}@dsic.upv.es
{jandreu|fcn}@dsic.upv.es

Abstract

UPV-PRHLT participated in the System Combination task of the Fifth Workshop on Statistical Machine Translation (WMT 2010). On each translation direction, all the submitted systems were combined into a consensus translation. These consensus translations always improve translation quality of the best individual system.

1 Introduction

The UPV-PRHLT approach to MT system combination is based on a refined version of the algorithm described in (González-Rubio and Casacuberta, 2010), with additional information to cope with hypotheses of different quality.

In contrast to most of the previous approaches to combine the outputs of multiple MT systems (Bangalore et al., 2001; Jayaraman and Lavie, 2005; Matusov et al., 2006; Schroeder et al., 2009), which are variations over the ROVER voting scheme (Fiscus, 1997), we consider the problem of computing a consensus translation as the problem of modelling a set of string patterns with an adequate prototype. Under this framework, the translation hypotheses of each of the MT systems are considered as individual patterns in a set of string patterns. The *(generalised) median string*, which is the optimal prototype of a set of strings (Fu, 1982), is the chosen prototype to model the set of strings.

2 System Combination Algorithm

The median string of a set is defined as the string that minimises the sum of distances to the strings in the set. Therefore, defining a distance between strings is the primary problem to deal with.

The most common definition of distance between two strings is the Levenshtein distance, also known as edit distance (ED). This metric computes the optimal sequence of edit operations (insertions, deletions and substitutions of words) needed to transform one string into the other. The main problem with the ED is its dependence on the length of the compared strings. This fact led to the definition of a new distance whose value is independent from the length of the strings compared. This *normalised edit distance* (NED) (Vidal et al., 1995) is computed by averaging the number of edit operations by the length of the edit path. The experimentation in this work was carried out using the NED.

2.1 Median String

Given a set $E = \mathbf{e}_1, \ldots, \mathbf{e}_n, \ldots, \mathbf{e}_N$ of translation hypotheses from N MT systems, let Σ be the vocabulary in the target language and Σ^* be the free monoid over that vocabulary ($E \subseteq \Sigma^*$). The median string of the set E (noted as $\mathcal{M}(E)$) can be formally defined as:

$$\mathcal{M}(E) = \underset{\mathbf{e}' \in \Sigma^*}{\text{argmin}} \sum_{n=1}^{N} \left[w_n \cdot \mathcal{D}(\mathbf{e}', \mathbf{e}_n) \right] , \quad (1)$$

where $\mathcal{D}$ is the distance used to compare two strings and the value w_n, $1 \leq n \leq N$ weights the contribution of the hypothesis n to the sum of distances, and therefore, it denotes the significance of hypothesis n in the computation of the median string. The value w_n can be seen as a measure of the "quality" of hypothesis n.

Computing the median string is a NP-Hard problem (de la Higuera and Casacuberta, 2000), therefore we can only build approximations to the median string by using several heuristics. In this work, we follow two different approximations: the *set median* string (Fu, 1982) and the *approximate median* string (Martínez et al., 2000).

Proceedings of the Joint 5th Workshop on Statistical Machine Translation and MetricsMATR, pages 296–300,
Uppsala, Sweden, 15-16 July 2010. ©2010 Association for Computational Linguistics

2.2 Set Median String

The most straightforward approximation to the median string corresponds to the search of a *set median* string. Under this approximation, the search is constrained to the strings in the given input set. The set median string can be informally defined as the most "centred" string in the set. The set median string of the set E (noted as $\mathcal{M}_s(E)$) is given by:

$$\mathcal{M}_s(E) = \underset{\mathbf{e}' \in E}{\text{argmin}} \sum_{n=1}^{N} [w_n \cdot \mathcal{D}(\mathbf{e}', \mathbf{e}_n)] \ . \quad (2)$$

The set median string can be computed in polynomial time (Fu, 1982; Juan and Vidal, 1998). Unfortunately, in some cases, the set median may not be a good approximation to the median string. For example, in the extreme case of a set of two strings, either achieves the minimum accumulated distance to the set. However, the set median string is a useful initialisation in the computation of the approximate median string.

2.3 Approximate Median String

A good approximation to efficiently compute the median string is proposed in (Martínez et al., 2000). To compute the approximate median string of the set E, the algorithm starts with an initial string $\mathbf{e}$ which is improved by successive refinements in an iterative process. This iterative process is based on the application of different edit operations over each position of the string $\mathbf{e}$ looking for a reduction of the accumulated distance to the strings in the set. Algorithm 1 describes this iterative process.

The initial string can be a random string or a string computed from the set E. Martinez et al. (2000) proposed two kinds of initial strings: the set median string of E and a string computed by a greedy algorithm, both of them obtained similar results. In this work, we start with the set median string in the initialisation of the computation of the approximate median string of the set E. Over this initial string we apply the iterative procedure described in Algorithm 1 until there is no improvement. The final median string may be different from the original hypotheses.

The computational time cost of Algorithm 1 is linear with the number of hypotheses in the combination, and usually only a moderate number of iterations is needed to converge.

For each position i in the string $\mathbf{e}$:

1. Build alternatives:

   Substitution: Make $\mathbf{x} = \mathbf{e}$. For each word $a \in \Sigma$:

   - Make $\mathbf{x}'$ the result string of substituting the ith word of $\mathbf{x}$ by a.
   - If the accumulated distance of $\mathbf{x}'$ to E is lower than the accumulated distance from $\mathbf{x}$ to E, then make $\mathbf{x} = \mathbf{x}'$.

   Deletion: Make $\mathbf{y}$ the result string of deleting the ith word of $\mathbf{e}$.

   Insertion: Make $\mathbf{z} = \mathbf{e}$. For each word $a \in \Sigma$:

   - Make $\mathbf{z}'$ the result of inserting a at position i of $\mathbf{e}$.
   - If the accumulated distance from $\mathbf{z}'$ to E is lower than the accumulated distance from $\mathbf{z}$ to E, then make $\mathbf{z} = \mathbf{z}'$.

2. Choose an alternative:

   - From the set $\{\mathbf{e}, \mathbf{x}, \mathbf{y}, \mathbf{z}\}$ take the string $\mathbf{e}'$ with less accumulated distance to E. Make $\mathbf{e} = \mathbf{e}'$.

Algorithm 1: Iterative process to refine a string $\mathbf{e}$ in order to reduce its accumulated distance to a given set E.

3 Experiments

Experiments were conducted on all the 8 translation directions cz→en, en→cz, de→en, en→de, es→en, en→es, fr→en and en→fr. Some of the entrants to the shared translation task submit lists of n-best translations, but, in our experience, if a large number of systems is available, using n-best translations does not allow to obtain better consensus translations than using single best translations, but raises computation time significantly. Consequently, we compute consensus translations only using the single best translation of each individual MT system. Table 1 shows the number of systems submitted and gives an overview of the test corpus on each translation direction. The number of running words is the average number of running words in the test corpora, from where the consensus translations were computed; the vocabulary is the merged vocabulary of these test corpora. All the experiments were carried out with the true-cased, detokenised version of the tuning and test corpora, following the WMT 2010 submission guidelines.

3.1 Evaluation Criteria

We will present translation quality results in terms of *translation edit rate* (TER) (Snover et al., 2006) and *bilingual evaluation understudy* (BLEU) (Pa-

	cz→en	en→cz	de→en	en→de	es→en	en→es	fr→en	en→fr
Submitted systems	6	11	16	12	8	10	14	13
Avg. Running words	45K	37K	47K	41K	47K	47K	47K	49K
Distinct words	24K	51K	38K	40K	23K	30K	27K	37K

Table 1: Number of systems submitted and main figures of test corpora on each translation direction. K stands for thousands of elements.

pineni et al., 2002). TER is computed as the number of edit operations (insertions, deletions and substitutions of single words and shifts of word sequences) to convert the system hypothesis into the reference translation. BLEU computes a geometric mean of the precision of n-grams multiplied by a factor to penalise short sentences.

3.2 Weighted Sum of Distances

In section 2, we define the median string of a set as the string which minimises a weighted sum of distances to the strings in the set (Eq. (1)). The weights w_n in the sum can be tuned. We compute a weight value for each MT system as a whole, i.e. all the hypotheses of a given MT system share the same weight value. We study the performance of different sets of weight looking for improvements in the quality of the consensus translations. These weight values are derived from different automatic MT evaluation measures:

- BLEU score of each system.
- 1.0 minus TER score of each system.
- Number of times the hypothesis of each system is the best TER-scoring translation.

We estimate these scores on the tuning corpora. A normalisation is performed to transform these scores into the range $[0.0, 1.0]$. After the normalisation, a weight value of 0.0 is assigned to the lowest-scoring hypothesis, i.e. the lowest-scoring hypothesis is not taking into account in the computation of the median string.

3.3 System Combination Results

Our framework to compute consensus translations allows multiple combinations varying the median string algorithm or the set of weight values used in the weighted sum of distances. To assure the soundness of our submission to the WMT 2010 system combination task, the experiments on the tuning corpora were carried out in a leaving-one-out fashion dividing the tuning data into 5 parts and averaging translation results over these 5 partitions. On each of the experiments, 4 of the partitions are devoted to obtain the weight values for the weighted sum of distances while BLEU and TER scores are calculated on the consensus translations of the remaining partition.

Table 2 shows, on each translation direction, the performance of the consensus translations on the tuning corpora. The consensus translations were computed with the set median string and the approximated median string using different sets of weight values: Uniform, all weights are set to 1.0, BLEU-based weights, TER-based weights and oracle-based weights. In addition, we display the performance of the best of the individual MT systems for comparison purposes. The number of MT systems combined for each translation direction is displayed between parentheses.

On all the translation directions under study, the consensus translations improved the results of the best individual systems. E.g. TER improved from 66.0 to 63.3 when translating from German into English. On average, the set median strings performed better than the best individual system, but its results were always below the performance of the approximate median string. The use of weight values computed from MT quality measures allows to improve the quality of the consensus translation computed. Specially, oracle-based weight values that, except for the cz→en task, always perform equal or better than the other sets of weight values. We have observed that no improvements can be achieved with uniform weight values; it is necessary to penalise low quality hypotheses.

To compute our primary submission to the WMT 2010 system combination task we choose the configurations that obtain consensus translations with highest BLEU score on the tuning corpora. The approximate median string using oracle-based scores is the chosen configuration for all translation directions, except on the cz→en translation direction for which TER-based weights performed better. As our secondary submission we

		Single best	Set median				Approximated median			
			Uniform	Bleu	Ter	Oracle	Uniform	Bleu	Ter	Oracle
cz→en (6)	BLEU	17.6	16.5	17.8	18.2	17.6	17.1	**18.5**	**18.5**	18.0
	TER	64.5	68.7	67.6	65.2	64.5	67.0	65.9	65.4	**64.4**
en→cz (11)	BLEU	11.4	10.1	10.9	10.7	**11.0**	10.1	10.7	10.7	**11.0**
	TER	75.3	75.1	74.3	74.2	74.2	73.9	73.4	73.3	**73.0**
de→en (16)	BLEU	19.0	19.0	19.1	19.3	19.7	19.3	19.8	19.9	**20.1**
	TER	66.0	65.4	65.2	65.0	64.6	64.4	63.4	63.4	**63.3**
en→de (12)	BLEU	11.9	11.6	11.7	11.7	**12.0**	11.6	11.8	11.8	**12.0**
	TER	74.3	74.1	74.1	74.0	73.7	72.7	72.9	72.7	**72.6**
es→en (8)	BLEU	23.2	23.0	23.3	23.2	23.6	23.1	23.9	23.8	**24.2**
	TER	60.2	60.6	59.8	59.8	59.5	60.0	59.2	59.4	**59.1**
en→es (10)	BLEU	23.3	23.0	23.3	23.4	24.0	23.6	23.8	23.8	**24.2**
	TER	60.1	60.1	59.9	59.7	59.5	59.0	59.1	58.9	**58.6**
fr→en (14)	BLEU	23.3	22.9	23.2	23.2	23.4	23.4	23.8	23.8	**23.9**
	TER	61.1	61.2	60.9	60.9	60.7	60.6	60.0	60.1	**59.9**
en→fr (13)	BLEU	22.7	23.4	23.5	23.6	**23.8**	23.3	23.6	23.7	**23.8**
	TER	62.3	61.0	61.0	60.9	60.6	60.2	60.1	**60.0**	**60.0**

Table 2: Consensus translation results (case-sensitive) on the tuning corpora with the set median string and the approximate median string using different sets of weights: Uniform, BLEU-based, TER-based and oracle-based. The number of systems being combined for each translation direction is in parentheses. Best consensus translation scores are in bold.

	Best		Secondary		Primary	
	BLEU	TER	BLEU	TER	BLEU	TER
cz→en	18.2	63.9	18.3	66.7	19.0	65.1
en→cz	10.8	75.2	11.3	73.6	11.6	71.9
de→en	18.3	66.6	19.1	65.4	19.6	63.9
en→de	11.6	73.4	11.7	72.9	11.9	71.7
es→en	24.7	59.0	24.9	58.9	25.0	58.2
en→es	24.3	58.4	24.9	57.3	25.3	56.3
fr→en	23.7	59.7	23.6	59.8	23.9	59.4
en→fr	23.3	61.3	23.6	59.9	24.1	58.9

Table 3: Translation scores (case-sensitive) on the test corpora of our primary and secondary submissions to the WMT 2010 system combination task.

chose the set median string using the same set of weight values chosen for the primary submission.

We compute MT quality scores on the WMT 2010 test corpora to verify the results on the tuning data. Table 3 displays, on each translation direction, the results on the test corpora of our primary and secondary submissions and of the best individual system. These results confirm the results on the tuning data. On all translation directions, our submissions perform better than the best individual systems as measured by BLEU and TER.

4 Summary

We have studied the performance of two consensus translation algorithms that based in the computation of two different approximations to the median string. Our algorithms use a weighted sum of distances whose weight values can be tuned. We show that using weight values derived from automatic MT quality measures computed on the tuning corpora allow to improve the performance of the best individual system on all the translation directions under study.

Acknowledgements

This paper is based upon work supported by the EC (FEDER/FSE) and the Spanish MICINN under the MIPRCV "Consolider Ingenio 2010" program (CSD2007-00018), the iTransDoc (TIN2006-15694-CO2-01) and iTrans2 (TIN2009-14511) projects and the FPU scholarship AP2006-00691. This work was also supported by the Spanish MITyC under the erudito.com (TSI-020110-2009-439) project and by the Generalitat Valenciana under grant Prometeo/2009/014 and scholarships BFPI/2007/117 and ACIF/2010/226 and by the Mexican government under the PROMEP-DGEST program.

References

S. Bangalore, G. Bodel, and G. Riccardi. 2001. Computing consensus translation from multiple machine translation systems. In *IEEE Workshop on ASRU*, pages 351–354.

C. de la Higuera and F. Casacuberta. 2000. Topology of strings: Median string is np-complete. *Theoretical Computer Science*, 230:39–48.

J. Fiscus. 1997. A post-processing system to yield reduced word error rates: Recogniser output voting error reduction (rover).

K.S. Fu. 1982. *Syntactic Pattern Recognition and Applications*. Prentice Hall.

J. González-Rubio and F. Casacuberta. 2010. On the use of median string for multi-source translation. In *Proceedings of 20th International Conference on Pattern Recognition*, Istambul, Turkey, May 27-28.

S. Jayaraman and A. Lavie. 2005. Multi-engine machine translation guided by explicit word matching. In *Proc. of EAMT*, pages 143–152.

A. Juan and E. Vidal. 1998. Fast Median Search in Metric Spaces. In *Proc. of SPR*, volume 1451 of *Lecture Notes in Computer Science*, pages 905–912.

C. D. Martínez, A. Juan, and F. Casacuberta. 2000. Use of Median String for Classification. In *Proc. of ICPR*, volume 2, pages 907–910.

E. Matusov, N. Ueffing, and H-Ney. 2006. Computing consensus translation from multiple machine translation systems using enhanced hypotheses alignment. In *Proc. of EACL*, pages 33–40.

K. Papineni, S. Roukos, T. Ward, and W. Zhu. 2002. Bleu: a method for automatic evaluation of machine translation. In *Proc. of ACL*, pages 311–318.

J. Schroeder, T. Cohn, and P. Koehn. 2009. Word lattices for multi-source translation. In *Proc. of EACL*, pages 719–727.

M. Snover, B. Dorr, R. Schwartz, L. Micciulla, and J. Makhoul. 2006. A study of TER with targeted human annotation. In *Proc. of AMTA*, pages 223–231.

E. Vidal, A. Marzal, and P. Aibar. 1995. Fast computation of normalized edit distances. *IEEE Transactions on PAMI*, 17(9):899–902.

CMU Multi-Engine Machine Translation for WMT 2010

Kenneth Heafield
Carnegie Mellon University
Pittsburgh, PA, USA.
heafield@cs.cmu.edu

Alon Lavie
Carnegie Mellon University
Pittsburgh, PA, USA.
alavie@cs.cmu.edu

Abstract

This paper describes our submission, cmu-heafield-combo, to the WMT 2010 machine translation system combination task. Using constrained resources, we participated in all nine language pairs, namely translating English to and from Czech, French, German, and Spanish as well as combining English translations from multiple languages. Combination proceeds by aligning all pairs of system outputs then navigating the aligned outputs from left to right where each path is a candidate combination. Candidate combinations are scored by their length, agreement with the underlying systems, and a language model. On tuning data, improvement in BLEU over the best system depends on the language pair and ranges from 0.89% to 5.57% with mean 2.37%.

1 Introduction

System combination merges the output of several machine translation systems into a single improved output. Our system combination scheme, submitted to the Workshop on Statistical Machine Translation (WMT) 2010 as cmu-heafield-combo, is an improvement over our previous system (Heafield et al., 2009), called cmu-combo in WMT 2009. The scheme consists of aligning 1-best outputs from each system using the METEOR (Denkowski and Lavie, 2010) aligner, identifying candidate combinations by forming left-to-right paths through the aligned system outputs, and scoring these candidates using a battery of features. Improvements this year include unigram paraphrase alignment, support for all target languages, new features, language modeling without pruning, and more parameter optimization. This paper describes our scheme with emphasis on improved areas.

2 Related Work

Confusion networks (Rosti et al., 2008) are the most popular form of system combination. In this approach, a single system output acts as a backbone to which the other outputs are aligned. This backbone determines word order while other outputs vote for substitution, deletion, and insertion operations. Essentially, the backbone is edited to produce a combined output which largely preserves word order. Our approach differs in that we allow paths to switch between sentences, effectively permitting the backbone to switch at every word.

Other system combination techniques typically use TER (Snover et al., 2006) or ITGs (Karakos et al., 2008) to align system outputs, meaning they depend solely on positional information to find approximate matches; we explicitly use stem, synonym, and paraphrase data to find alignments. Our use of paraphrases is similar to Leusch et al. (2009), though they learn a monolingual phrase table while we apply cross-lingual pivoting (Bannard and Callison-Burch, 2005).

3 Alignment

System outputs are aligned at the token level using a variant of the METEOR (Denkowski and Lavie, 2010) aligner. This identifies, in decreasing order of priority: exact, stem, synonym, and unigram paraphrase matches. Stems (Porter, 2001) are available for all languages except Czech, though this is planned for future work and expected to produce significant improvement. Synonyms come from WordNet (Fellbaum, 1998) and are only available in English. Unigram paraphrases are automatically generated using phrase table pivoting (Bannard and Callison-Burch, 2005). The phrase tables are trained using parallel data from Europarl (fr-en, es-en, and de-en), news commentary (fr-en, es-en, de-en, and cz-en), United Na-

Proceedings of the Joint 5th Workshop on Statistical Machine Translation and MetricsMATR, pages 301–306,
Uppsala, Sweden, 15-16 July 2010.

tions (fr-en and es-en), and CzEng (cz-en) (Bojar and Žabokrtský, 2009) sections 0–8. The German and Spanish tables also use the German-Spanish Europarl corpus released for WMT08 (Callison-Burch et al., 2008). Currently, the generated paraphrases are filtered to solely unigram matches; full use of this table is planned for future work. When alignment is ambiguous (i.e. "that" appears twice in a system output), an alignment is chosen to minimize crossing with other alignments. Figure 1 shows an example alignment. Compared to our previous system, this replaces heuristic "artificial" alignments with automatically learned unigram paraphrases.

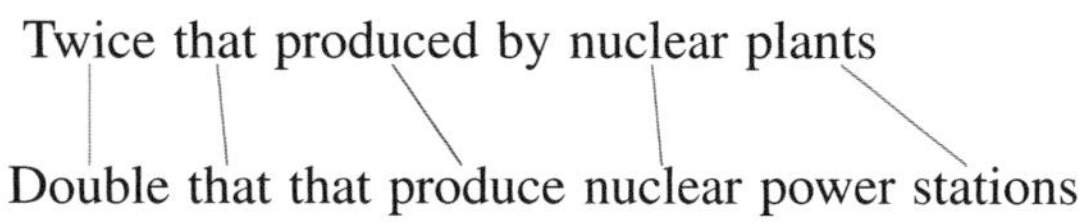

Figure 1: Alignment generated by METEOR showing exact (that–that and nuclear–nuclear), stem (produced–produce), synonym (twice–double), and unigram paraphrase (plants–stations) alignments.

4 Search Space

A candidate combination consists of a string of tokens (words and punctuation) output by the underlying systems. Unconstrained, the string could repeat tokens and assemble them in any order. We therefore have several constraints:

Sentence The string starts with the beginning of sentence token and finishes with the end of sentence token. These tokens implicitly appear in each system's output.

Repetition A token may be used at most once. Tokens that METEOR aligned are alternatives and cannot both be used.

Weak Monotonicity This prevents the scheme from reordering too much. Specifically, the path cannot jump backwards more than r tokens, where positions are measured relative to the beginning of sentence. It cannot make a series of smaller jumps that add up to more than r either. Equivalently, once a token in the ith position of some system output is used, all tokens before the $i - r$th position in their respective system outputs become unusable. The value of r is a hyperparameter considered in Section 6.

Completeness Tokens may not be skipped unless the sentence ends or another constraint would be violated. Specifically, when a token from some system is used, it must be the first (leftmost in the system output) available token from that system. For example, the first decoded token must be the first token output by some system.

Together, these define the search space. The candidate starts at the beginning of sentence by choosing the first token from any system. Then it can either continue with the next token from the same system or switch to another one. When it switches to another system, it does so to the first available token from the new system. The repetition constraint requires that the token does not repeat content. The weak monotonicity constraint ensures that the jump to the new system goes at most r words back. The process repeats until the end of sentence token is encountered.

The previous version (Heafield et al., 2009) also had a hard phrase constraint and heuristics to define a phrase; this has been replaced with new match features.

Search is performed using beam search where the beam contains partial candidates of the same length, each of which starts with the beginning of sentence token. In our experiments, the beam size is 500. When two partial candidates will extend in the same way (namely, the set of available tokens is the same) and have the same feature state (i.e. language model history), they are recombined. The recombined partial candidate subsequently acts like its highest scoring element, until k-best list extraction when it is lazily unpacked.

5 Scoring Features

Candidates are scored using three feature classes:

Length Number of tokens in the candidate. This compensates, to first order, for the impact of length on other features.

Match For each system s and small n, feature $m_{s,n}$ is the number of n-grams in the candidate matching the sentence output by system s. This is detailed in Section 5.1.

Language Model Log probability from a n-gram language model and backoff statistics. Section 5.2 details our training data and backoff features.

Features are combined into a score using a linear model. Equivalently, the score is the dot product of a weight vector with the vector of our feature values. The weight vector is a parameter optimized in Section 6.

5.1 Match Features

The n-gram match features reward agreement between the candidate combination and underlying system outputs. For example, feature $m_{1,1}$ counts tokens in the candidate that also appear in system 1's output for the sentence being combined. Feature $m_{1,2}$ counts bigrams appearing in both the candidate and the translation suggested by system 1. Figure 2 shows example feature values.

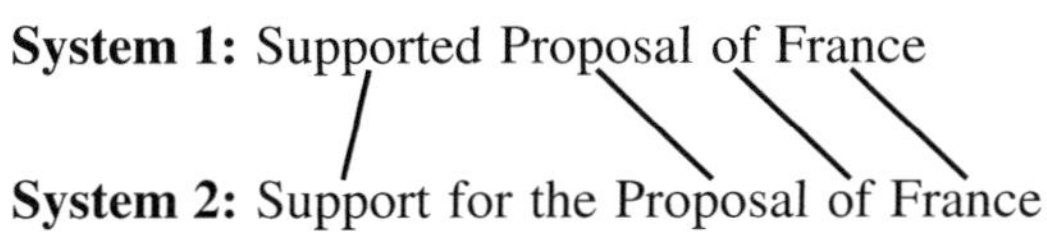

Candidate: Support for Proposal of France

	Unigram	Bigram	Trigram
System 1	4	2	1
System 2	5	3	1

Figure 2: Example match feature values with two systems and matches up to length three. Here, "Supported" counts because it aligns with "Support".

The match features count n-gram matches between the candidate and each system. These matches are defined in terms of alignments. A token matches the system that supplied it as well as the systems to which it aligns. This can be seen in Figure 2 where System 1's unigram match count includes "Supported" even though the candidate chose "Support". Longer matches are defined similarly: a bigram match consists of two consecutive alignments without reordering. Since METEOR generates several types of alignments as shown in Figure 1, we wonder whether all alignment types should count as matches. If we count all types of alignment, then the match features are blind to lexical choice, leaving only the language model to discriminate. If only exact alignments count, then less systems are able to vote on a word order decision mediated by the bigram and trigram features. We find that both versions have their advantages, and therefore include two sets of match features: one that counts only exact alignments and another that counts all alignments. We also tried copies of the match features at the stem and synonym level but found these impose additional tuning cost with no measurable improvement in quality.

Since systems have different strengths and weaknesses, we avoid assigning a single system confidence (Rosti et al., 2008) or counting n-gram matches with uniform system confidence (Hildebrand and Vogel, 2009). The weight on match feature $m_{s,n}$ corresponds to our confidence in n-grams from system s. These weights are fully tunable. However, there is another hyperparameter: the maximum length of n-gram considered; we typically use 2 or 3 with little gain seen above this.

5.2 Language Model

We built language models for each of the five target languages with the aim of using all constrained data. For each language, we used the provided Europarl (Koehn, 2005) except for Czech, News Commentary, and News monolingual corpora. In addition, we used:

Czech CzEng (Bojar and Žabokrtský, 2009) sections 0–7

English Gigaword Fourth Edition (Parker et al., 2009), Giga-FrEn, and CzEng (Bojar and Žabokrtský, 2009) sections 0–7

French Gigaword Second Edition (Mendonca et al., 2009a), Giga-FrEn

Spanish Gigaword Second Edition (Mendonca et al., 2009b)

Paragraphs in the Gigaword corpora were split into sentences using the script provided with Europarl (Koehn, 2005); parenthesized formatting notes were removed from the NYT portion. We discarded Giga-FrEn lines containing invalid UTF8, control characters, or less than 90% Latin characters or punctuation. Czech training data and system outputs were preprocessed using TectoMT (Žabokrtský and Bojar, 2008) following the CzEng 0.9 pipeline (Bojar and Žabokrtský, 2009). English training data and system outputs were tokenized with the IBM tokenizer. French, German, and Spanish used the provided tokenizer.

Czech words were truecased based on automatically identified lemmas marking names; for other languages, training data was lowercased and systems voted, with uniform weight, on capitalization of each character in the final output.

With the exception of Czech (for which we used an existing model), all models were built with no lossy pruning whatsoever, including our English model with 5.8 billion tokens (i.e. after IBM tokenization). Using the stock SRILM (Stolcke, 2002) toolkit with modified Kneser-Ney smoothing, the only step that takes unbounded memory is final model estimation from n-gram counts. Since key parameters have already been estimated at this stage, this final step requires only counts for the desired n-grams and all of their single token extensions. We can therefore filter the n-grams on all but the last token. Our scheme will only query an n-gram if all of the tokens appear in the union of system outputs for some sentence; this strict filtering criterion is further described and released as open source in Heafield and Lavie (2010). The same technique applies to machine translation systems, with phrase table expansion taking the place of system outputs.

For each language, we built one model by appending all data. Another model interpolates smaller models built on the individual sources where each Gigaword provider counts as a distinct source. Interpolation weights were learned on the WMT 2009 references. For English, we also tried an existing model built solely on Gigaword using interpolation. The choice of model is a hyperparameter we consider in Section 6.

In the combination scheme, we use the log language model probability as a feature. Another feature reports the length of the n-gram matched by the model; this exposes limited tunable control over backoff behavior. For Czech, the model was built with a closed vocabulary; when an out-of-vocabulary (OOV) word is encountered, it is skipped for purposes of log probability and a third feature counts how often this happens. This amounts to making the OOV probability a tunable parameter.

6 Parameter Optimization

6.1 Feature Weights

Feature weights are tuned using Minimum Error Rate Training (MERT) (Och, 2003) on the 455 provided references. Our largest submission, xx-en primary, combines 17 systems with five match features each plus three other features for a total of 88 features. This immediately raises two concerns. First, there is overfitting and we expect to see a loss in the test results, although our experience in the NIST Open MT evaluation is that the amount of overfitting does not significantly increase at this number of parameters. Second, MERT is poor at fitting this many feature weights. We present one modification to MERT that addresses part of this problem, leaving other tuning methods as future work.

MERT is prone to local maxima, so we apply a simple form of simulated annealing. As usual, the zeroth iteration decodes with some initial feature weights. Afterward, the weights $\{\lambda_f\}$ learned from iteration $0 \leq j < 10$ are perturbed to produce new feature weights

$$\mu_f \sim U\left[\frac{j}{10}\lambda_f, \left(2 - \frac{j}{10}\right)\lambda_f\right]$$

where U is the uniform distribution. This sampling is done on a per-sentence basis, so the first sentence is decoded with different weights than the second sentence. The amount of random perturbation decreases linearly each iteration until the 10th and subsequent iterations whose learned weights are not perturbed. We emphasize that the point is to introduce randomness in sentences decoded during MERT, and therefore considered during parameter tuning, and not on the specific formula presented in this system description. In practice, this technique increases the number of iterations and decreases the difference in tuning scores following MERT. In our experiments, weights are tuned towards uncased BLEU (Papineni et al., 2002) or the combined metric TER-BLEU (Snover et al., 2006).

6.2 Hyperparameters

In total, we tried 1167 hyperparameter configurations, limited by CPU time during the evaluation period. For each of these configurations, the feature weights were fully trained with MERT and scored on the same tuning set, which we used to select the submitted combinations. Because these configurations represent a small fraction of the hyperparameter space, we focused on values that work well based on prior experience and tuning scores as they became available:

Set of systems Top systems by BLEU. The number of top systems included ranged from 3 to

Pair	Entry	#Sys	r	Match	LM	Objective	ΔBLEU	ΔTER	ΔMETE
cz-en	main	5	4	2	Append	BLEU	2.38	0.99	1.50
de-en	main	6	4	2	Append	TER-BLEU	2.63	-2.38	1.36
	contrast	7	3	2	Append	BLEU	2.60	-2.62	1.09
es-en	main	7	5	3	Append	BLEU	1.22	-0.74	0.70
	contrast	5	6	2	Gigaword	BLEU	1.08	-0.80	0.97
fr-en	main	9	5	3	Append	BLEU	2.28	-2.26	0.78
	contrast	8	5	3	Append	BLEU	2.19	-1.81	0.63
xx-en	main	17	5	3	Append	BLEU	5.57	-5.60	4.33
	contrast	16	5	3	Append	BLEU	5.45	-5.38	4.22
en-cz	main	7	5	3	Append	TER-BLEU	0.74	-0.26	0.68
en-de	main	6	6	2	Interpolate	BLEU	1.26	0.16	1.14
	contrast	5	4	2	Interpolate	BLEU	1.26	0.30	1.00
en-es	main	8	5	3	Interpolate	BLEU	2.38	-2.20	0.96
	contrast	6	7	2	Append	BLEU	2.40	-1.85	1.02
en-fr	main	6	7	2	Append	BLEU	2.64	-0.50	1.55

Table 1: Submitted combinations chosen from among 1167 hyperparameter settings by tuning data scores. Uncased BLEU, uncased TER, and METEOR 1.0 with adequacy-fluency parameters are shown relative to top system by BLEU. Improvement is seen in all pairs on all metrics except for TER on cz-en and en-de where the top systems are 5% and 2% shorter than the references, respectively. TER has a well known preference for shorter hypotheses. The #Sys column indicates the number of systems combined, using the top scoring systems by BLEU. The Match column indicates the maximum n-gram length considered for matching on all alignments; we separately counted unigram and bigram exact matches. In some cases, we made a contrastive submission where metrics disagreed or length behavior differed near the top; contrastive submissions are not our 2009 scheme.

all of them, except on xx-en where we combined up to 17.

Jump limit Mostly $r = 5$, with some experiments ranging from 3 to 7.

Match features Usually unigram and bigram features, sometimes trigrams as well.

Language model Balanced between the appended and interpolated models, with the occasional baseline Gigaword model for English.

Tuning objective Usually BLEU for speed reasons; occasional TER-BLEU with typical values for other hyperparameters.

7 Conclusion

Table 1 shows the submitted combinations and their performance. Our submissions this year improve over last year (Heafield et al., 2009) in overall performance and support for multiple languages. The improvement in performance we primarily attribute to the new match features, which account for most of the gain and allowed us to include lower quality systems. We also trained language models without pruning, replaced heuristic alignments with unigram paraphrases, tweaked the other features, and improved the parameter optimization process. We hope that the improvements seen on tuning scores generalize to significantly improved test scores, especially human evaluation.

Acknowledgments

Ondřej Bojar made the Czech language model and preprocessed Czech system outputs. Michael Denkowski provided the paraphrase tables and wrote the version of METEOR used. This work was supported in part by the DARPA GALE program and by a NSF Graduate Research Fellowship.

References

Colin Bannard and Chris Callison-Burch. 2005. Paraphrasing with bilingual parallel corpora. In *Proceedings ACL*.

Ondřej Bojar and Zdeněk Žabokrtský. 2009. CzEng

0.9, building a large Czech-English automatic parallel treebank. *The Prague Bulletin of Mathematical Linguistics*, (92):63–83.

Chris Callison-Burch, Cameron Fordyce, Philipp Koehn, Christof Monz, and Josh Schroeder. 2008. Further meta-evaluation of machine translation. In *Proceedings of the Third Workshop on Statistical Machine Translation*, pages 70–106, Columbus, Ohio, June. Association for Computational Linguistics.

Michael Denkowski and Alon Lavie. 2010. Extending the METEOR machine translation metric to the phrase level. In *Proceedings NAACL 2010*, Los Angeles, CA, June.

Christiane Fellbaum. 1998. *WordNet: An Electronic Lexical Database*. MIT Press.

Kenneth Heafield and Alon Lavie. 2010. Combining machine translation output with open source: The Carnegie Mellon multi-engine machine translation scheme. In *The Prague Bulletin of Mathematical Linguistics*, number 93, pages 27–36, Dublin.

Kenneth Heafield, Greg Hanneman, and Alon Lavie. 2009. Machine translation system combination with flexible word ordering. In *Proceedings of the Fourth Workshop on Statistical Machine Translation*, pages 56–60, Athens, Greece, March. Association for Computational Linguistics.

Almut Silja Hildebrand and Stephan Vogel. 2009. CMU system combination for WMT'09. In *Proceedings of the Fourth Workshop on Statistical Machine Translation*, pages 47–50, Athens, Greece, March. Association for Computational Linguistics.

Damianos Karakos, Jason Eisner, Sanjeev Khudanpur, and Markus Dreyer. 2008. Machine translation system combination using ITG-based alignments. In *Proceedings ACL-08: HLT, Short Papers (Companion Volume)*, pages 81–84.

Philipp Koehn. 2005. Europarl: A parallel corpus for statistical machine translation. In *Proceedings of MT Summit*.

Gregor Leusch, Evgeny Matusov, and Hermann Ney. 2009. The RWTH system combination system for WMT 2009. In *Proceedings of the Fourth Workshop on Statistical Machine Translation*, pages 51–55, Athens, Greece, March. Association for Computational Linguistics.

Angelo Mendonca, David Graff, and Denise DiPersio. 2009a. French gigaword second edition. LDC2009T28.

Angelo Mendonca, David Graff, and Denise DiPersio. 2009b. Spanish gigaword second edition. LDC2009T21.

Franz Josef Och. 2003. Minimum error rate training in statistical machine translation. In *ACL '03: Proceedings of the 41st Annual Meeting on Association for Computational Linguistics*, pages 160–167, Morristown, NJ, USA. Association for Computational Linguistics.

Kishore Papineni, Salim Roukos, Todd Ward, and Wei-Jing Zhu. 2002. BLEU: a method for automatic evaluation of machine translation. In *Proceedings of 40th Annual Meeting of the Association for Computational Linguistics (ACL)*, pages 311–318, Philadelphia, PA, July.

Robert Parker, David Graff, Junbo Kong, Ke Chen, and Kazuaki Maeda. 2009. English gigaword fourth edition. LDC2009T13.

Martin Porter. 2001. Snowball: A language for stemming algorithms. http://snowball.tartarus.org/.

Antti-Veikko I. Rosti, Bing Zhang, Spyros Matsoukas, and Richard Schwartz. 2008. Incremental hypothesis alignment for building confusion networks with application to machine translation system combination. In *Proceedings Third Workshop on Statistical Machine Translation*, pages 183–186.

Matthew Snover, Bonnie Dorr, Richard Schwartz, Linnea Micciulla, and John Makhoul. 2006. A study of translation edit rate with targeted human annotation. In *Proceedings Seventh Conference of the Association for Machine Translation in the Americas*, pages 223–231, Cambridge, MA, August.

Andreas Stolcke. 2002. SRILM - an extensible language modeling toolkit. In *Proceedings of the Seventh International Conference on Spoken Language Processing*, pages 901–904.

Zdeněk Žabokrtský and Ondřej Bojar. 2008. TectoMT, Developer's Guide. Technical Report TR-2008-39, Institute of Formal and Applied Linguistics, Faculty of Mathematics and Physics, Charles University in Prague, December.

CMU System Combination via Hypothesis Selection for WMT'10

Almut Silja Hildebrand
Carnegie Mellon University
Pittsburgh, USA
silja@cs.cmu.edu

Stephan Vogel
Carnegie Mellon University
Pittsburgh, USA
vogel@cs.cmu.edu

Abstract

This paper describes the CMU entry for the system combination shared task at WMT'10. Our combination method is hypothesis selection, which uses information from n-best lists from the input MT systems, where available. The sentence level features used are independent from the MT systems involved. Compared to the baseline we added source-to-target word alignment based features and trained system weights to our feature set. We combined MT systems for French - English and German - English using provided data only.

1 Introduction

For the combination of machine translation systems there have been several approaches described in recent publications. One uses confusion networks formed along a skeleton sentence to combine translation systems as described in (Rosti et al., 2008) and (Karakos et al., 2008). A different approach described in (Heafield et al., 2009) is not keeping the skeleton fixed when aligning the systems. Another approach selects whole hypotheses from a combined n-best list (Hildebrand and Vogel, 2008).

Our setup follows the latter approach. We combine the output from the submitted translation systems, including n-best lists where available, into one joint n-best list, then calculate a set of features consistently for all hypotheses. We use MER training on the provided development data to determine feature weights and re-rank the joint n-best list. We train to maximize BLEU.

2 Features

For our entries to the WMT'09 we used the following feature groups (in parenthesis are the number of separate feature values per group):

- Language model scores (3)
- Word lexicon scores (6)
- Sentence length features (3)
- Rank feature (1)
- Normalized n-gram agreement (6)
- Source-target word alignment features (6)
- Trained system weights (no. of systems)

The details on language model and word lexicon scores can be found in (Hildebrand and Vogel, 2008) and details on the rank feature and the normalized n-gram agreement can be found in (Hildebrand and Vogel, 2009). We use three sentence length features, which are the ratio of the hypothesis length to the length of the source sentence, the diversion of this ratio from the overall length ratio of the bilingual training data and the difference between the hypothesis length and the average length of the hypotheses in the n-best list for the respective source sentence. The system weights are trained together with the other feature weights during MERT using a binary feature per system. To the feature vector for each hypothesis one feature per input system is added; for each hypothesis one of the features is one, indicating which system it came from, all others are zero.

2.1 Source-Target Word Alignment Features

We trained the IBM word alignment models up to model 4 using the GIZA++ toolkit (Och and Ney, 2003) on the bilingual training corpus. Then a forced alignment algorithm utilizes the trained models to align each source sentence to each translation hypothesis in its respective n-best list.

We use the alignment score given by the word alignment models, the number of unaligned words

Proceedings of the Joint 5th Workshop on Statistical Machine Translation and MetricsMATR, pages 307–310,
Uppsala, Sweden, 15-16 July 2010.

and the number of NULL aligned words, all normalized by the sentence length, as three separate features. We calculate these alignability features for both language directions.

3 Experiments

In the WMT shared translation task only a very small number of participants submitted n-best lists, e.g. in the German-English track there were only four n-best lists among the 16 submissions. Our combination method is proven to work significantly better when n-best lists are available.

For all our experiments on the data from WMT'09, which was available for system combination development as well as the WMT'10 shared task data we used the same setup and the same statistical models.

To train our language models and word lexica we only used provided data. We trained the statistical word lexica on the parallel data provided for each language pair[1]. For each combination we used three language models: a 4-gram language model trained on the English part of the parallel training data, a 1.2 giga-word 3-gram language model trained on the provided monolingual English data, and an interpolated 5-gram language model trained on the English GigaWord corpus. We used the SRILM toolkit (Stolcke, 2002) for training. We chose to train three separate LMs for the three corpora, so the feature weight training can automatically determine the importance of each corpus for this task. The reason for training only a 3-gram LM from the wmt10 monolingual data was simply that there were not sufficient time and resources available to train a bigger model.

For each of the two language pairs we compared a combination that used the word alignment features, or trained system weights or both of these feature groups in addition to the features described in (Hildebrand and Vogel, 2009) which serves a baseline for this set of experiments.

For combination we tokenized and lowercased all data, because the n-best lists were submitted in various formats. Therefore we report the case insensitive scores here. The combination was optimized toward the BLEU metric, therefore TER results might not be very meaningful here and are only reported for completeness.

[1] http://www.statmt.org/wmt10/translation-task.html#training

3.1 French-English data from WMT'09

We used 14 systems from the restricted data track of the WMT'09 including five n-best lists. The scores of the individual systems for the combination tuning set range from BLEU 27.93 for the best to 15.09 for the lowest ranked individual system (case insensitive evaluation).

system	tune	test
best single	27.93 / 56.53	27.21 / 56.99
baseline	30.17 / 54.76	28.89 / 55.74
+ wrd al	30.67 / 54.34	28.69 / 55.67
+ sys weights	29.71 / 55.45	28.07 / 56.18
all features	30.30 / 54.53	28.37 / 55.77

Table 1: French-English Results: BLEU / TER

The combination outperforms the best single system by 1.7 BLEU points. Here adding the 14 binary features for training system weights with MERT hurts the combinations performance on the unseen data. The reason for this might be the rather small tuning set of 502 sentences with one reference. Adding the word alignment features does not improve the result either, the difference to the baseline is at the noise level.

3.2 German-English data from WMT'09

For our experiments on the development data for German-English we used the top 12 systems, scoring between BLEU 23.01 and BLEU 16.06, excluding systems known to use data beyond the provided data. Within those 12 system outputs were four n-best lists, three of which were 100-best and one was 10-best.

system	tune	test
best single	23.01 / 60.52	21.44 / 62.33
baseline	26.28 / 58.69	23.62 / 60.49
+ wrd al	26.25 / 59.13	23.42 / 61.11
+ sys weights	26.78 / 58.48	23.28 / 60.80
all features	26.81 / 58.12	23.51 / 60.25

Table 2: German-English Results: BLEU / TER

Our system combination via hypothesis selection could improve translation quality by +2.2 BLEU over the best single system on the unseen test set. Again, the differences between the four different feature sets are not significant on the unseen test set.

3.3 French-English WMT'10 system combination shared task

Out of 14 systems submitted to the French-English translation task, we combined the top 11 systems, the best of which scored 28.58 BLEU and the last 24.16 BLEU on the tuning set. There were only three n-best lists among the submissions. We included up to 100 hypotheses per system in our joint n-best list.

system	tune	test
best sys.	28.58 / 54.17	29.98 / 52.62 / 53.88
baseline	30.67 / 52.62	29.94 / 52.53 / -
+ w. al	30.69 / 52.76	29.97 / 52.76 / 53.76
+ sys w.	30.90 / 52.44	29.79 / 52.84 / 54.05
all feat.	31.10 / 52.06	29.80 / 52.86 / 53.67

Table 3: French-English Results: BLEU / TER / MaxSim

Our system combination via hypothesis selection could not improve the translation quality compared to the best single system on the unseen data. Adding any of the new feature groups to the baseline does not change the result of the combination significantly. This result could be explained by the fact, that due to computational problems and time constraints we were not able to train our models on the whole provided French-English training data. This should only affect the lexicon and word alignment feature groups though.

3.4 German-English WMT'10 system combination shared task

For the German-English combination we used 13 out of the 16 submitted systems, which scored between BLEU 25.01 to BLEU 19.76 on the tuning set. Our combination could improve translation quality by +1.64 BLEU compared to the best system.

system	tune	test
best sys.	25.01 / 58.34	23.89 / 59.14 / 51.10
baseline	26.47 / 56.89	25.44 / 57.96 / -
+ w. al	26.37 / 57.02	25.25 / 58.34 / 50.72
+ sys w.	27.67 / 56.05	25.53 / 57.70 / 51.06
all feat.	27.66 / 56.35	25.25 / 57.86 / 50.83

Table 4: German-English Results: BLEU / TER / MaxSim

The word alignment features seem to hurt performance slightly, which might be due to the more difficult word alignment between German and English compared to other language pairs. But this is not really a strong conclusion, because all differences of the results on the unseen data are not significant.

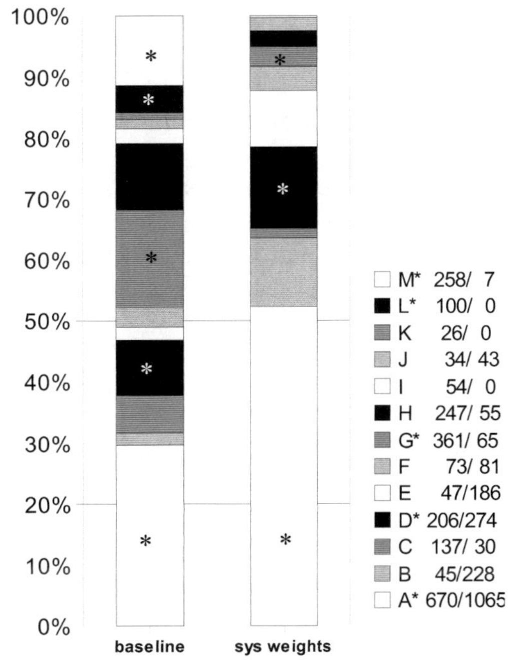

Figure 1: German-English '10: Contributions of the individual systems to the final translation, percentages and absolute number of hyps chosen.

Figure 1 shows, how many hypotheses were contributed by the individual systems to the final translation (unseen data) in the baseline combination compared with the one with trained system weights. The systems A to M are ordered by their BLEU score on the development set. The bars show percentages of the test set, the numbers listed next to the systems A to M give the absolute number of hypotheses chosen from the system for the two depicted combinations. The systems which provided n-best lists, marked with a star in the diagram, clearly dominate the selection in the baseline, but this effect is gone when system weights are used. The dominance of system A in the latter is to be expected, because it is a whole BLEU point ahead of the next ranking system on the system combination tuning set. In the baseline combination identical hypotheses contributed by different systems have an identical total score. In that case the hypothesis is attributed to all systems which contributed it. This accounts for the higher total number of hypotheses shown in the graphic for the baseline as well as for part of the contributions of the low ranking systems. For example 35 hypotheses were provided identically from two systems and still four hypotheses were produced by all 13 systems, for example the sentence: "aber es geht auch um wirtschaftliche beziehungen ." - "but it is also about economic relations .".

4 Conclusions

In this paper we explored new features in our system combination system, which performs hypothesis selection. We used hypothesis to source sentence alignment scores as well system weight features.

Most systems available for combination did not submit n-best lists, which decreases the effectiveness of our combination method significantly.

The reason for not getting an improvement from word alignment features might be that the top systems might be using more clever word alignment strategies than running the GIZA++ toolkit out of the box. Therefore the alignability according to these weaker models does not give useful ranking information for rescoring.

Experiments on different language pairs and data sets have shown improvements for training system weights in the past for certain setups. Combining up to 14 individual translation systems adds that many features to the feature set for which weights have to optimized via MERT. The provided tuning set of 455 sentences with only one reference is extremely small. It is possible, that MERT could not reliably determine feature weights here. In the setup where this feature set was used successfully, a tuning set of close to 2000 lines with four references was available. It is not possible to improve the tuning data situation by using the provided data from last years workshop as additional tuning data, because the set of systems submitted is not the same and even the systems submitted by the same sites might have changed significantly.

Interesting to note is that looking at the numbers, the German-English combination with an improvement of +1.64 BLEU over the best single system seems to have worked much better than the French-English one with no improvement. But looking at the preliminary human evaluation result the picture is opposite: For German-English our combination is ranked below several of the single systems and most of the combinations, while for French-English it tops the list of all systems and combinations in the workshop.

Acknowledgments

We would like to thank the participants in the WMT'10 shared translation task for providing their data, especially n-best lists. This work was partly funded by DARPA under the project GALE (Grant number #HR0011-06-2-0001).

References

Kenneth Heafield, Greg Hanneman, and Alon Lavie. 2009. Machine translation system combination with flexible word ordering. In *StatMT '09: Proceedings of the Fourth Workshop on Statistical Machine Translation*, pages 56–60, Morristown, NJ, USA. Association for Computational Linguistics.

Almut Silja Hildebrand and Stephan Vogel. 2008. Combination of machine translation systems via hypothesis selection from combined n-best lists. In *MT at work: Proceedings of the Eighth Conference of the Association for Machine Translation in the Americas*, pages 254–261, Waikiki, Hawaii, October. Association for Machine Translation in the Americas.

Almut Silja Hildebrand and Stephan Vogel. 2009. CMU system combination for WMT'09. In *Proceedings of the Fourth Workshop on Statistical Machine Translation*, pages 47–50, Athens, Greece, March. Association for Computational Linguistics.

Damianos Karakos, Jason Eisner, Sanjeev Khudanpur, and Markus Dreyer. 2008. Machine translation system combination using itg-based alignments. In *Proceedings of ACL-08: HLT, Short Papers*, pages 81–84, Columbus, Ohio, June. Association for Computational Linguistics.

Franz Josef Och and Hermann Ney. 2003. A systematic comparison of various statistical alignment models. *Computational Linguistics*, 29(1):19–51.

Antti-Veikko Rosti, Bing Zhang, Spyros Matsoukas, and Richard Schwartz. 2008. Incremental hypothesis alignment for building confusion networks with application to machine translation system combination. In *Proceedings of the Third Workshop on Statistical Machine Translation*, pages 183–186, Columbus, Ohio, June. Association for Computational Linguistics.

Andreas Stolcke. 2002. Srilm - an extensible language modeling toolkit. In *Proceedings International Conference for Spoken Language Processing*, Denver, Colorado, September.

JHU System Combination Scheme for WMT 2010

Sushant Narsale
Johns Hopkins University
Baltimore, USA.
sushant@jhu.edu

Abstract

This paper describes the JHU system combination scheme that was used in the WMT 2010 submission. The incremental alignment scheme of (Karakos et.al, 2008) was used for confusion network generation. The system order in the alignment of each sentence was learned using SVMs, following the work of (Karakos et.al, 2010). Additionally, web-scale n-grams from the Google corpus were used to build language models that improved the quality of the combination output. Experiments in Spanish-English, French-English, German-English and Czech-English language pairs were conducted, and the results show approximately 1 BLEU point and 2 TER points improvement over the best individual system.

1 Introduction

System Combination refers to the method of combining output of multiple MT systems, to produce a output better than each individual system. Currently, there are several approaches to machine translation which can be classified as phrase-based, hierarchical, syntax-based (Hildebrand and Vogel, 2008) which are equally good in their translation quality even though the underlying frameworks are completely different. The motivation behind System Combination arises from this diversity in the state-of-art MT systems, which suggests that systems with different paradigms make different errors, and can be made better by combining their strengths.

One approach of combining translations is based on representing translations by confusion network and then aligning these confusion networks using string alignment algorithms (Rosti et.al, 2009), (Karakos and Khudanpur, 2008). Another approach generates features for every translation to train algorithms for ranking systems based on their quality and the top ranking output is considered to be a candidate translation, (Hildebrand and Vogel, 2008) is an example of ranking based combination. We use ideas from ranking based approaches to learn order in which systems should be aligned in a confusion network based approach.

Our approach is based on incremental alignment of confusion networks (Karakos et.al, 2008), wherein each system output is represented by a confusion network. The confusion networks are then aligned in a pre-defined order to generate a combination output. This paper contributes two enhancements to (Karakos et.al, 2008). First, use of Support Vector Machines to learn order in which the system outputs should be aligned. Second, we explore use of Google n-grams for building dynamic language model and interpolate the resulting language model with a large static language model for rescoring of system combination outputs.

The rest of the paper is organized as follows: Section 2 illustrates the idea and pipeline of the baseline combination system; Section 3 gives details of SVM ranking for learning system order for combination; Section 4 explains use of Google n-gram based language models; Results are discussed in Section 5; Concluding remarks are given in Section 6;

2 Baseline System Combination

This section summarizes the algorithm for baseline combination. The baseline combination pipeline includes three stages:

1. Representing translations by confusion networks.

Proceedings of the Joint 5th Workshop on Statistical Machine Translation and MetricsMATR, pages 311–314,
Uppsala, Sweden, 15-16 July 2010. ©2010 Association for Computational Linguistics

2. Generating between system confusion networks.

3. Rescoring the final confusion network.

Confusion networks are compressed form of lattices with a constraint that all paths should pass through all nodes. Each system output is represented by an equivalent confusion network. The per-system confusion networks are aligned one at a time. The order in which systems are aligned is usually decided by evaluation of system's performance. Two alternatives for deciding the system order are discussed in Section 3. Inversion-Transduction Grammar (Wu, 1997) is used for alignments and the cost function for aligning two confusion networks is

$$cost(b_1, b_2) = \frac{1}{|b_1||b_2|} \sum_{w \in b_1} \sum_{v \in b_2} c(v)c(w)\mathbf{1}(w \neq v)$$

where b_1 and b_2 are two different bins, $|b_1|$ and $|b_2|$ is the number of tokens in b_1 and b_2 respectively, $c(v)$ and $c(w)$ are the number of words of token v and token w. which are in b_1 and b_2 separately. The idea of this cost is to compute the probability that a word from bin b_1 is not equal to a word from bin b_2.

$$cost(b_1, b_2) = Prob(v \neq w, v \in b_1, w \in b_2)$$

The final confusion network is rescored with a 5-gram language model with Kneser-Ney smoothing. To generate the final output, we need to find the best (minimum-cost) path through the rescored confusion network. In the best path every bin in the network contributes only one word to the output.

Ordering the systems for incremental combination and use of different language models were the two components of the pipeline that were experimented with for WMT'2010 shared task. The following sections describe these variations in detail.

3 Learning to Order Systems for Combination

Determining the order in which systems are aligned is critical step in our system combination process. The first few aligned translations/systems determine the word ordering in the final output and have a significant influence on the final translation quality. For the baseline combination the systems are aligned in the increasing order of (TER-BLEU) scores. TER and BLEU (Papineni et.al, 2002) scores are calculated over all the sentences in the training set. This approach to ordering of systems is static and results in a global order for all the source segments. An alternative approach is to learn local order of systems for every source sentence using a SVM ranker.

3.1 SVM Rank Method

This section describes an approach to order systems for alignment using SVMs (Karakos et.al, 2010). For each system output a number of features are generated, the features fall broadly under the following three categories:

N-gram Agreements

These features capture the percentage of hypothesis for a source sentence that contain same n-grams as the candidate translation under consideration. The n-gram matching is position independent because phrases often appear in different orders in sentences with same meaning and correct grammar. The scores for each n-gram are summed and normalized by sentence length. N-grams of length $1 \cdots 5$ are used as five features.

Length Feature

The ratio of length of the translation to the source sentence is a good indication of quality of the translation, for a lengthy source sentence a short translation is most likely to be bad. Here, the ratio of source sentence length to length of the target sentence is calculated.

Language Model Features

Language models for target language are used to calculate perplexity of a given translation. The lower the perplexity the better is the translation quality. We use two different language models: (i) a large static 5-gram language model and (ii)a dynamic language model generated from all the translations of the same source segment. The perplexity values are normalized by sentence length.

Translations in training set are ranked based on (TER-BLEU) scores. An SVM ranker is then trained on this set. The SVM ranker (Joachims, 2002) returns a score for each translation, based on its signed distance from the separating hyperplane. This value is used in the combination process to weight the contribution of systems to the final confusion network scores.

Table 1: Results for all Language pairs on development set

	es-en		fr-en		cz-en		de-en	
Combination	BLEU	TER	BLEU	TER	BLEU	TER	BLEU	TER
BEST SYSTEM	29.27	52.38	26.74	56.88	21.56	58.24	26.53	56.87
BASELINE	28.57	51.61	27.65	55.20	21.01	58.79	26.80	54.54
SVM	28.68	51.99	27.53	55.35	21.56	58.24	26.85	54.9
SVM+NGRAM	29.92	50.92	27.86	55.06	21.80	57.78	27.24	54.86

4 Language Models

In the system combination process, the final confusion networks are rescored with language models. Language models are widely used to ensure a fluent output translation. I explored use of two language models. The first language model was trained on the English side of French-English corpus, UN corpus and English Gigaword corpus made available by WMT. The second language model used counts generated from Google n-grams. It was trained by generating all 1-gram to 5-grams in the system outputs for a source segment and then using the N-gram search engine (Lin et.al, 2010) built over Google n-grams to get the corresponding n-gram counts. The n-gram counts were used to train a 5-gram language model with Kneser-Ney smoothing. SRILM toolkit (Stockle, 2002) was used for training the language models.

The baseline combinations were rescored only with the static language model. I always did a weighted interpolation of the two language models when using n-gram based language model.

5 Results

Results for four language pairs: Spanish-English, French-English, Czech-English and German-English are presented. The training data for WMT'10 was divided into development and test set, consisting of 208 and 247 segments respectively. Table 1 shows TER and BLEU scores on the TEST set for all the four language pairs in the following settings: (i) *Baseline* corresponds to procedure described in section 2, (ii) *SVM* corresponds to using SVM ranker for learning order of systems as described in section 3.1 (iii)*SVM+N-Grams* corresponds to the use of a SVM ranker along with weighted interpolation of n-gram language model and the large static language model. The ranking SVM was trained using SVM-light (Joachims, 2002) with a RBF kernel. Two-fold cross-validation was done to prevent over-fitting on development data. All the scores are with lower-cased outputs, a tri-gram language model was used to true-case the output before the final submission. 1-best output from only the primary systems were used for combination. The number of systems used for combination in each language pair are: 6 for Czech-English, 8 in Spanish-English, 14 in French-English and 16 in German-English. The best results for baseline combination were obtained with 3 systems for Czech-English, 6 systems for German-English, 3 systems for Spanish-English and 9 systems for French-English.

From the results, we conclude that for all language pairs the combinations with SVM and n-gram language models show gain over all the other settings in both TER and BLEU evaluations. However, use of SVM with only one large language model shows performance degradation on three out of four language pairs. Size of training data (208 segments) could be one reason for the degradation and this issue needs further investigation. For the final submission, the settings that performed the best on $\frac{(TER-BLEU)}{2}$ scale were chosen.

6 Conclusion

The system combination task gave us an opportunity to evaluate enhancements added to the JHU system combination pipeline. Experimental results show that web-scale language models can be used to improve translation quality, this further underlines the usefulness of web-scale resources like Google n-grams. Further investigation is needed to completely understand the reasons for inconsistency in the magnitude of gain across different language pairs. Specifically the impact of training data on SVMs for ranking in system combination scenario needs to be analysed.

Acknowledgments

This work was partially supported by the DARPA GALE program Grant No HR0022-06-2-0001. I would like to thank all the participants of WMT 2010 for their system outputs. I would also like to thank Prof. Damianos Karakos for his guidance and support. Many thanks go to the Center for Language and Speech Processing at Johns Hopkins University for availability of their computer clusters.

References

Almut Silja Hildebrand and Stephan Vogel. 2008. *Combination of Machine Translation Systems via Hypothesis Selection from Combined N-Best Lists.* In MT at work: Proceedings of the Eight Conference of Association of Machine Translation in the Americas, pages 254-261, Waikiki, Hawaii, October. Association for Machine Translations in the Americas.

Almut Silja Hildebrand and Stephan Vogel. 2009. *CMU System Combination for WMT'09.* Proceedings of Fourth Workshop on Statistical Machine Translation,Athen,Greece, March 2009.

Andreas Stockle. 2002. *Srilm - an extensible language modeling toolkit.* In Proceedings International Conference for Spoken Language Processing, Denver, Colarado, September.

Antti-Veikko I. Rosti and Necip Fazil Ayan and Bing Xiang and Spyros Matsoukas and Richard Schwartz and Bonnie J. Dorr 2007. *Combining Outputs from Multiple Machine Translation Systems.* In Proceedings of the Third Workshop on Statistical Machine Transaltion, pages 183-186, Colombus, Ohio, June. Association for Computational Linguistics.

Damianos Karakos and Sanjeev Khudanpur 2008. *Sequential System Combination for Machine Translation of Speech.* In Proceedings of IEEE SLT-08, December 2008.

Damianos Karakos and Jason Smith and Sanjeev Khudanpur 2010. *Hypothesis Ranking and Two-pass Approaches for Machine Translation System Combination.* In Proceedings of ICASSP-2010, Dallas, Texas, March 14-19 2010.

Damianos Karakos and Jason Eisner and Sanjeev Khudanpur and Markus Dreyer. 2008. *Machine Translation system combination using ITG-based alignments.* In Proceedings of ACL-08: HLT, Short Papers, pages 81-84, Colombus, Ohio, June. Association for Computational Linguistics.

Dekang Lin and Kenneth Church and Heng Ji and Satoshi Sekine and David Yarowsky and Shane Bergsma and Kailash Patil and Emily Pitler Rachel Lathbury and Vikram Rao and Kapil Dalwani and Sushant Narsale 2010. *New Tools for Web-Scale N-grams.* In the Proceedings of LREC, 2010.

D. Wu 1997. *Stochastic inversion transduction grammars and bilingual parsing of parallel corpora.* Computational Linguistics, vol.23,no.3,pp.377-403, September 1997.

Kishore Papineni and Salim Roukos and Todd Ward and Wei-Jing Zhu. 2002. *BLEU: A method for automatic evaluation of machine translation.* In Proceedings of 40th Annual Meeting of Association for Computational Linguistics, pages 311-318. Philadelphia, PA, July.

Thorsten Joachims 2002. *Optimizing Search Engines using Clickthrough Data.* In Proceedings of ACM Conference on Knowledge Discovery and Data Mining(KDD), 2002.

The RWTH System Combination System for WMT 2010

Gregor Leusch and Hermann Ney
RWTH Aachen University
Aachen, Germany
{leusch,ney}@cs.rwth-aachen.de

Abstract

RWTH participated in the System Combination task of the Fifth Workshop on Statistical Machine Translation (WMT 2010). For 7 of the 8 language pairs, we combine 5 to 13 systems into a single consensus translation, using additional n-best reranking techniques in two of these language pairs. Depending on the language pair, improvements versus the best single system are in the range of $+0.5$ and $+1.7$ on BLEU, and between -0.4 and -2.3 on TER. Novel techniques compared with RWTH's submission to WMT 2009 include the utilization of n-best reranking techniques, a consensus true casing approach, a different tuning algorithm, and the separate selection of input systems for CN construction, primary/skeleton hypotheses, HypLM, and true casing.

1 Introduction

The RWTH approach to MT system combination is a refined version of the ROVER approach in ASR (Fiscus, 1997), with additional steps to cope with reordering between different hypotheses, and to use true casing information from the input hypotheses. The basic concept of the approach has been described by Matusov et al. (2006). Several improvements have been added later (Matusov et al., 2008). This approach includes an enhanced alignment and reordering framework. In contrast to existing approaches (Jayaraman and Lavie, 2005; Rosti et al., 2007), the context of the whole corpus rather than a single sentence is considered in this iterative, unsupervised procedure, yielding a more reliable alignment. Majority voting on the generated lattice is performed using prior weights for each system as well as other statistical models such as a special n-gram language model. In addition to lattice rescoring, n-best list reranking techniques can be applied to n best paths of this lattice. True casing is considered a separate step in RWTH's approach, which also takes the input hypotheses into account.

The pipeline, and consequently the description of the pipeline given in this paper, is based on our pipeline for WMT 2009 (Leusch et al., 2009), with several extensions as described.

2 System Combination Algorithm

In this section we present the details of our system combination method. Figure 1 gives an overview of the system combination architecture described in this section. After preprocessing the MT hypotheses, pairwise alignments between the hypotheses are calculated. The hypotheses are then reordered to match the word order of a selected *primary* or *skeleton* hypothesis. From this, we create a lattice which we then rescore using system prior weights and a language model (LM). The single best path in this CN then constitutes the consensus translation; alternatively the n best paths are generated and reranked using additional statistical models. The consensus translation is then true cased and postprocessed.

2.1 Word Alignment

The proposed alignment approach is a statistical one. It takes advantage of multiple translations for a whole corpus to compute a consensus translation for each sentence in this corpus. It also takes advantage of the fact that the sentences to be aligned are in the same language.

For each of the K source sentences in the test corpus, we select one of its translations $E_n, n = 1, \ldots, M$, as the *primary* hypothesis. Then we align the *secondary* hypotheses $E_m (m = 1, \ldots, M; n \neq m)$ with E_n to match the word order in E_n. Since it is not clear which hypothesis should be primary, i. e. has the "best" word order, we let several or all hypothesis play the role of the primary translation, and align all pairs of hypotheses (E_n, E_m); $n \neq m$. In this paper, we denote the number of possible primary hypotheses by N.

The word alignment is *trained* in analogy to the alignment training procedure in statistical MT. The difference is that the two sentences that have to be aligned are in the same language. We use the IBM Model 1 (Brown et al., 1993) and the Hidden Markov Model (HMM, (Vogel et al., 1996))

Proceedings of the Joint 5th Workshop on Statistical Machine Translation and MetricsMATR, pages 315–320,
Uppsala, Sweden, 15-16 July 2010. ©2010 Association for Computational Linguistics

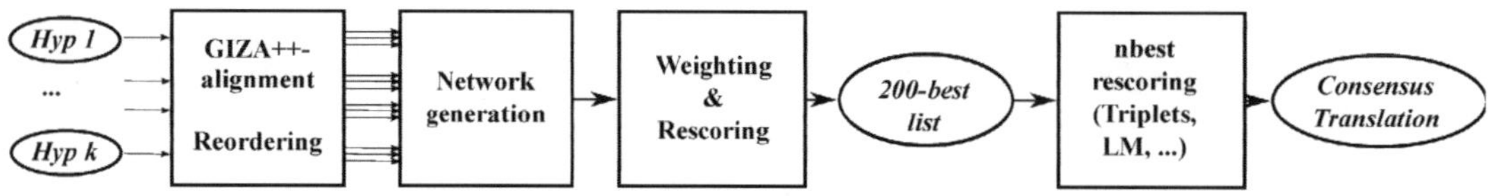

Figure 1: The system combination architecture.

to estimate the alignment model.

The alignment training corpus is created from a test corpus of effectively $N \cdot (M-1) \cdot K$ sentences translated by the involved MT engines. Model parameters are trained iteratively using the GIZA++ toolkit (Och and Ney, 2003). The training is performed in the directions $E_m \rightarrow E_n$ and $E_n \rightarrow E_m$. The final alignments are determined using a cost matrix C for each sentence pair (E_m, E_n). Elements of this matrix are the local costs $C(j, i)$ of aligning a word $e_{m,j}$ from E_m to a word $e_{n,i}$ from E_n. Following Matusov et al. (2004), we compute these local costs by interpolating the negated logarithms of the state occupation probabilities from the "source-to-target" and "target-to-source" training of the HMM model.

2.2 Word Reordering and Confusion Network Generation

After reordering each secondary hypothesis E_m and the rows of the corresponding alignment cost matrix, we determine $M-1$ monotone *one-to-one* alignments between E_n as the primary translation and $E_m, m = 1, \ldots, M; m \neq n$. We then construct the confusion network.

We consider words without a correspondence to the primary translation (and vice versa) to have a null alignment with the empty word ε, which will be transformed to an ε-arc in the corresponding confusion network.

The $M-1$ monotone one-to-one alignments can then be transformed into a confusion network, as described by Matusov et al. (2008).

2.3 Voting in the Confusion Network

Instead of choosing a fixed sentence to define the word order for the consensus translation, we generate confusion networks for N possible hypotheses as primary, and unite them into a single lattice. In our experience, this approach is advantageous in terms of translation quality compared to a minimum Bayes risk primary (Rosti et al., 2007).

Weighted majority voting on a single confusion network is straightforward and analogous to ROVER (Fiscus, 1997). We sum up the probabilities of the arcs which are labeled with the same word and have the same start state and the same end state. This can also be regarded as having a binary system feature in a log-linear model.

2.4 Language Models

The lattice representing a union of several confusion networks can then be directly rescored with an n-gram language model (LM). A transformation of the lattice is required, since LM history has to be memorized.

We train a trigram LM on the outputs of the systems involved in system combination. For LM training, we take the system hypotheses for the same test corpus for which the consensus translations are to be produced. Using this "adapted" LM for lattice rescoring thus gives bonus to n-grams from the original system hypotheses, in most cases from the original phrases. Presumably, many of these phrases have a correct word order. Previous experimental results show that using this LM in rescoring together with a word penalty notably improves translation quality. This even results in better translations than using a "classical" LM trained on a monolingual training corpus. We attribute this to the fact that most of the systems we combine already include such general LMs.

2.5 Extracting Consensus Translations

To generate our consensus translation, we extract the single-best path from the rescored lattice, using "classical" decoding as in MT. Alternatively, we can extract the n best paths for n-best list rescoring.

2.6 n-best-List Reranking

If n-best lists were generated in the previous steps, additional sentence-based features can be calculated on these sentences, and combined in a log-linear way. These scores can then be used to rerank the sentences.

For the WMT 2010 FR–EN and the DE–EN task, we generated 200-best lists, and calculated the following features:

1. Total score from the lattice rescoring
2. NGram posterior weights on those (Zens and Ney, 2006)
3. Word Penalty
4. HypLM trained on a different set of hypotheses (FR–EN only)
5. Large fourgram model trained on Gigaword (DE–EN) or Europarl (FR–EN)
6. IBM1 scores and deletion counts based on a word lexicon trained on WMT training data

7. Discriminative word lexicon score (Mauser et al., 2009)
8. Triplet lexicon score (Hasan et al., 2008)

Other features were also calculated, but did not seem to give an improvement on the DEV set.

2.7 Consensus True Casing

Previous approaches to achieve true cased output in system combination operated on true-cased lattices, used a separate input-independent true caser, or used a general true-cased LM to differentiate between alternative arcs in the lattice, as in (Leusch et al., 2009). For WMT 2010, we use per-sentence information from the input systems to determine the consensus case of each output word. Lattice generation, rescoring, and reranking are performed on lower-cased input, with a lower-cased consensus hypothesis as their result. For each word in this hypothesis, we count how often each casing variant occurs in the input hypotheses for this sentence. We then use the variant with the highest support for the final consensus output. One advantage is that the set of systems used to determine the consensus case does not have to be identical to those used for building the lattice: Assuming that each word from the consensus hypothesis also occurs in one or several of the true casing input hypotheses, we can focus on systems that show a good true casing performance.

3 Tuning

3.1 Tuning Weights for Lattice and n-best Rescoring

For lattice rescoring, we need to tune system weights, LM factor, and word penalty to produce good consensus translations. The same holds for the log-linear weights in n-best reranking.

For the WMT 2010 Workshop, we selected a linear combination of BLEU (Papineni et al., 2002) and TER (Snover et al., 2006) as optimization criterion, $\hat{\Theta} := \text{argmax}_{\Theta} \{BLEU - TER\}$, based on previous experience (Mauser et al., 2008). For more stable results, we use the case-insensitive variants for both measures, despite the explicit use of case information in the pipeline.

System weights were tuned to this criterion using the Downhill Simplex method. Because we considered the number of segments in the tuning set to be too small to allow for a further split into an actual tuning and a control (dev) part, we went for a method closely related to 5-fold cross validation: We randomly split the tuning set into 5 equal-sized parts, and tune parameters on four fifth of the set, measuring progress on the remaining fifth. This was repeated for the other four choices for the "dev" part. Only settings which reliably showed progress on these five different versions were used later on the test set. For the actual weights and numerical parameters to be used on the test set, we calculate the median of the five variants, which lowered the risk of outliers and overfitting.

3.2 System Selection

With the large numbers of input systems – e.g., 17 for DE–EN – and their large spread in translation quality – e.g. 10% abs. in BLEU – not all systems should participate in the system combination process. For the generation of lattices, we considered several variants of systems, often starting from the top, and either replacing some of the systems very similar to others with systems further down the list, or not considering those as primary, adding further systems as additional secondaries.

For true casing, and the additional HypLM for FR–EN, we selected a set of 8 to 12 promising systems, and ran an exhaustive search on all combinations of those to optimize the LM perplexity on the dev set (LM) or the true case BLEU/TER score on a consensus translation (TC). Further research may include a weighted combination here, followed by an optimization of the weights as described in the previous paragraph.

4 Experimental Results

Each language pair and each direction in WMT 2010 had its own set of systems, so we selected and tuned for each direction separately. After submission of our system combination output to WMT 2010, we also calculated scores on the test set (TEST), to validate our results, and as a preparation for this report. Note that the scores reported for DEV are calculated on the full DEV set, but not on any combination of the one-fifth "cross validation" subcorpora.

4.1 FR–EN and EN–FR

For French–English, we selected a set of eight systems for the primary submission, and eleven systems for the contrastive system, of which six served as skeleton. Six different systems were used for an additional HypLM, five for consensus true casing. Table 1 shows the distribution of these systems. We see the results of system combination on DEV and TEST (the latter calculated after submission) in Table 2. System combination itself turns out to have the largest improvement, +0.5 in BLEU and -0.7 in TER on TEST over the best single system. n-best reranking improves this result even more, by +0.3/-0.3. The influence of tuning and of TC selection is measurable on DEV, but rather small on TEST.

For English–French, 13 systems were used to construct the lattice, 5 serving as skeleton. Five different systems were used for true casing. No n-best list reranking was performed here, as preliminary experiments did not show any significant

Table 1: Overview of systems used for FR/EN.

System	FR–EN A	FR–EN B	EN–FR A	EN–FR B
cambridge	P L C	p	P	p
cu-zeman			S	
cmu-statxfer	L	s		
dfki			S	
eu			S	
geneva			S	
huicong		s		
jhu	P L	p	S	p
koc			S	
lig		s		
limsi	P C	p	S C	p
lium	P L C	s	P C	p
nrc	P C	s	S	p
rali	P L	p	P C	p
rwth	P	p	P C	p
uedin	P L C	p	P C	p

"A" is the primary, "B" the contrastive submission.
"P" denotes a system that served as skeleton.
"S" a system that was only aligned to others.
"L" denotes a system used for a larger HypLM-n-best-rescoring.
"C" is a system used for consensus true casing.

Table 2: Results for FR–EN.

	TUNE BLEU	TUNE TER	TEST BLEU	TEST TER
Best single	27.9	55.4	28.5	54.0
Lattice SC	28.4	55.0	29.0	53.3
+ tuning	28.8	54.5	29.1	53.3
+ CV tuning	28.6	54.7	29.1	53.3
+ nbest rerank.	29.0	54.4	29.4	53.0
+ sel. for TC	**29.1**	**54.3**	**29.3**	**53.0**
Contrast. SC	**28.9**	**54.3**	**28.8**	**53.4**

"SC" stands for System Combination output.
"CV" denotes the split into five different tuning and validation parts.
"sel. TC" is the separate selection for consensus true casing.
Systems in bold were submitted for WMT 2010.

Table 3: Results for EN–FR.

	TUNE BLEU	TUNE TER	TEST BLEU	TEST TER
Best single	27.1	55.7	26.5	56.1
Primary SC	**28.3**	**55.2**	**28.2**	**54.7**
Contrast. SC	**28.5**	**54.7**	**28.1**	**54.6**

Table 4: Overview of systems used for DE/EN.

System	DE–EN A	DE–EN B	EN–DE A	EN–DE B
cu-zeman			S	
cmu	C		P	
dfki			S	p
fbk	P C	p	P	
jhu				p
kit	P C	p	P C	p
koc			S C	p
limsi	P	p	P C	p
liu	C		S C	p
rwth	P	p	P C	p
sfu			S	
uedin	P C	p	P C	p
umd	P	p		
uppsala		p	S	

For abbreviations see Table 1.

Table 5: Results for DE–EN.

	TUNE BLEU	TUNE TER	TEST BLEU	TEST TER
Best single	23.8	59.7	23.5	59.7
Lattice SC	24.7	58.5	25.0	57.9
+ tuning	25.1	57.6	25.0	57.6
+ CV tuning	24.8	58.0	24.9	57.8
+ nbest rerank.	25.3	57.6	24.9	57.6
+ sel. for TC	**25.5**	**57.5**	**24.9**	**57.6**
Contrast. SC	**25.2**	**57.7**	**24.8**	**57.7**

For abbreviations see Table 2.

gain in this direction. As a contrastive submission, we submitted the consensus of 8 systems. These are also listed in Table 1. The results can be found in Table 3. Note that the contrastive system was not tuned using the "cross validation" approach; as a result, we expected it to be sensitive to overfitting. We see improvements around +1.7/-1.4 on TEST.

4.2 DE–EN and EN–DE

In the German–English language pair, 17 systems were available, but incorporating only six of them turned out to deliver optimal results on DEV. As shown in Table 4, we used a combination of seven systems in the contrastive submission. While a

Table 6: Results for EN–DE.

	TUNE BLEU	TUNE TER	TEST BLEU	TEST TER
Best single	16.1	66.3	16.4	65.7
Primary SC	**16.4**	**64.9**	**17.0**	**63.7**
Contrast. SC	**16.4**	**64.9**	**17.3**	**63.4**

Table 7: Overview of systems used for CZ/EN.

System	CZ–EN	EN–CZ
aalto	P	
cmu	P C	
cu-bojar	P	P
cu-tecto		S
cu-zeman	P	S C
dcu		P
eurotrans		S
google	P C	P C
koc		P C
pc-trans		S
potsdam		P C
sfu		S
uedin	P C	P C

For abbreviations see Table 1.
No contrastive systems were built for this language pair.

Table 8: Results for CZ–EN and EN–CZ.

	TUNE		TEST	
	BLEU	TER	BLEU	TER
CZ–EN				
Best single	21.8	58.4	22.9	57.5
Primary SC	**22.4**	**59.1**	**23.4**	**57.9**
EN–CZ				
Best single	17.0	67.1	16.6	66.4
Primary SC	**16.7**	**65.4**	**17.4**	**63.6**

Table 9: Overview of systems used for ES/EN.

System	EN–ES	
	A	B
cambridge	P C	p
dcu	P	p
dfki	P C	p
jhu	P C	p
sfu	P C	p
uedin	P C	p
upv		p
upv-nnlm	P	p

Table 10: Results for EN–ES.

	TUNE		TEST	
	BLEU	TER	BLEU	TER
ES–EN				
Best single	28.7	53.6	–	–
SC	29.0	53.3	–	–
EN–ES				
Best single	27.8	55.2	28.7	54.0
Primary SC	**29.5**	**52.9**	**30.0**	**51.4**
Contrast. SC	**29.6**	**52.8**	**30.1**	**51.7**

different set of five systems was used for consensus true casing, it turned out that using the same six systems for the "additional" HypLM as for the lattice seemed to be optimal in our approach. Table 5 shows the outcome of our experiments: Again, we see that the largest effect on TEST results from system combination as such (+1.5/-1.8). The other steps, in particular tuning and selection for TC, seem to help on DEV, but make hardly a difference on TEST. n-best reranking brings an improvement of -0.2 in TER, but at a minor deterioration (-0.1) in BLEU.

In the opposite direction, English–German, we combined all twelve systems, five of them serving as skeleton. The contrastive submission consists of a combination of eight systems. Six systems were used for true casing. Again, n-best list rescoring did not result in any improvement in preliminary experiments, and was skipped. Results are shown in Table 6: We see that even though both versions perform equally well on DEV (+0.4/-1.4), the contrastive system performs better by +0.3/-0.3 on TEST (+0.9/-2.3).

4.3 CZ–EN and EN–CZ

In both directions involving Czech, the number of systems was rather limited, so no additional selection turned out to be necessary, and we did not build a contrastive system. For Czech–English, all six systems were used; three of them for true casing. For English–Czech, all eleven systems were used in building the lattice, six of them also as skeleton. Five systems were used in the true casing step. Table 7 lists these systems. From the results in Table 8, we see that for CZ–EN, system combination gains around +0.5 in BLEU, but at costs of +0.4 to +0.7 in TER. For EN–CZ, the results look more positive: While we see only -0.3/-1.7 on DEV, there is a significant improvement of +1.2/-2.8 on TEST.

4.4 ES–EN and EN–ES

In the Spanish–English language pair, we did not see any improvement at all on the direction with English as target in preliminary experiments. Consequently, and given the time constraints, we did not further investigate on this language pair. Post-eval experiments revealed that improvements of +0.3/-0.3 are possible, with far off-center weights favoring the top three systems.

On English–Spanish, where these preliminary experiments showed a gain, we used seven out of the available ten systems in building the lattice for the primary system, eight for the contrastive. Five of those were uses for consensus true casing. Table 9 lists these systems. Table 10 shows the results on this language pair: For both the primary and the contrastive systems we see improvements of around +1.7/-2.3 on DEV, and +1.3/-2.6 on TEST. Except for the TER on TEST, these two submissions differ only by ± 0.1 from each other.

5 Conclusions

We have shown that our system combination system can lead to significant improvements over single best MT output where a significant number of comparably good translations is available on a single language pair. n-best reranking can further improve the quality of the consensus translation; results vary though. While consensus true casing turned out to be very useful despite of its simplicity, we were unable to find significant improvements on TEST from the selection of a separate set of true casing input systems.

Acknowledgments

This work was partly realized as part of the Quaero Programme, funded by OSEO, French State agency for innovation. This work was partly supported by the Defense Advanced Research Projects Agency (DARPA) under Contract No. HR0011-06-C-0023.

References

P. F. Brown, S. A. Della Pietra, V. J. Della Pietra, and R. L. Mercer. 1993. The mathematics of statistical machine translation: parameter estimation. *Computational Linguistics*, 19(2):263–311, June.

J. Fiscus. 1997. A post-processing system to yield reduced word error rates: Recognizer output voting error reduction (ROVER). In *IEEE Workshop on Automatic Speech Recognition and Understanding*.

S. Hasan, J. Ganitkevitch, H. Ney, and J. Andrés-Ferrer. 2008. Triplet lexicon models for statistical machine translation. In *Conference on Empirical Methods in Natural Language Processing*, pages 372–381, Honolulu, Hawaii, October. Association for Computational Linguistics.

S. Jayaraman and A. Lavie. 2005. Multi-engine machine translation guided by explicit word matching. In *Proc. of the 10th Annual Conf. of the European Association for Machine Translation (EAMT)*, pages 143–152, Budapest, Hungary, May.

G. Leusch, E. Matusov, and H. Ney. 2009. The RWTH system combination system for WMT 2009. In *Fourth Workshop on Statistical Machine Translation*, pages 56–60, Athens, Greece, March. Association for Computational Linguistics.

E. Matusov, R. Zens, and H. Ney. 2004. Symmetric word alignments for statistical machine translation. In *COLING '04: The 20th Int. Conf. on Computational Linguistics*, pages 219–225, Geneva, Switzerland, August.

E. Matusov, N. Ueffing, and H. Ney. 2006. Computing consensus translation from multiple machine translation systems using enhanced hypotheses alignment. In *Conference of the European Chapter of the Association for Computational Linguistics (EACL)*, pages 33–40, Trento, Italy, April.

E. Matusov, G. Leusch, R. E. Banchs, N. Bertoldi, D. Dechelotte, M. Federico, M. Kolss, Y. S. Lee, J. B. Marino, M. Paulik, S. Roukos, H. Schwenk, and H. Ney. 2008. System combination for machine translation of spoken and written language. *IEEE Transactions on Audio, Speech and Language Processing*, 16(7):1222–1237, September.

A. Mauser, S. Hasan, and H. Ney. 2008. Automatic evaluation measures for statistical machine translation system optimization. In *International Conference on Language Resources and Evaluation*, Marrakech, Morocco, May.

A. Mauser, S. Hasan, and H. Ney. 2009. Extending statistical machine translation with discriminative and trigger-based lexicon models. In *Conference on Empirical Methods in Natural Language Processing*, pages 210–217, Singapore, August.

F. J. Och and H. Ney. 2003. A systematic comparison of various statistical alignment models. *Computational Linguistics*, 29(1):19–51, March.

K. Papineni, S. Roukos, T. Ward, and W. J. Zhu. 2002. BLEU: a Method for Automatic Evaluation of Machine Translation. In *Proc. of the 40th Annual Meeting of the Association for Computational Linguistics (ACL)*, pages 311–318, Philadelphia, PA, July.

A. V. Rosti, S. Matsoukas, and R. Schwartz. 2007. Improved word-level system combination for machine translation. In *Proceedings of the 45th Annual Meeting of the Association of Computational Linguistics (ACL)*, pages 312–319, Prague, Czech Republic, June.

M. Snover, B. Dorr, R. Schwartz, L. Micciulla, and J. Makhoul. 2006. A Study of Translation Error Rate with Targeted Human Annotation. In *Proc. of the 7th Conf. of the Association for Machine Translation in the Americas (AMTA)*, pages 223–231, Boston, MA, August.

S. Vogel, H. Ney, and C. Tillmann. 1996. HMM-based word alignment in statistical translation. In *COLING '96: The 16th Int. Conf. on Computational Linguistics*, pages 836–841, Copenhagen, Denmark, August.

R. Zens and H. Ney. 2006. N-gram posterior probabilities for statistical machine translation. In *Human Language Technology Conf. / North American Chapter of the Assoc. for Computational Linguistics Annual Meeting (HLT-NAACL), Workshop on Statistical Machine Translation*, pages 72–77, New York City, June.

BBN System Description for WMT10 System Combination Task

Antti-Veikko I. Rosti and **Bing Zhang** and **Spyros Matsoukas** and **Richard Schwartz**
Raytheon BBN Technologies, 10 Moulton Street, Cambridge, MA 02138, USA
{arosti,bzhang,smatsouk,schwartz}@bbn.com

Abstract

BBN submitted system combination outputs for Czech-English, German-English, Spanish-English, French-English, and All-English language pairs. All combinations were based on confusion network decoding. An incremental hypothesis alignment algorithm with flexible matching was used to build the networks. The bi-gram decoding weights for the single source language translations were tuned directly to maximize the BLEU score of the decoding output. Approximate expected BLEU was used as the objective function in gradient based optimization of the combination weights for a 44 system multi-source language combination (All-English). The system combination gained around 0.4-2.0 BLEU points over the best individual systems on the single source conditions. On the multi-source condition, the system combination gained 6.6 BLEU points.

1 Introduction

The BBN submissions to the WMT10 system combination task were based on confusion network decoding. The confusion networks were built using the incremental hypothesis alignment algorithm with flexible matching introduced in the BBN submission for the WMT09 system combination task (Rosti et al., 2009). This year, the system combination weights were tuned to maximize the BLEU score (Papineni et al., 2002) of the 1-best decoding output (lattice based BLEU tuning) using downhill simplex method (Press et al., 2007). A 44 system multi-source combination was also submitted. Since the gradient-free optimization algorithms do not seem to be able to handle more than 20-30 weights, a gradient ascent to maximize an approximate expected BLEU objective was used to optimize the larger number of weights.

The lattice based BLEU tuning may be implemented using any optimization algorithm that does not require the gradient of the objective function. Due to the size of the lattices, the objective function evaluation may have to be distributed to multiple servers. The optimizer client accumulates the BLEU statistics of the 1-best hypotheses from the servers for given search weights, computes the final BLEU score, and passes it to the optimization algorithm which returns a new set of search weights. The lattice based tuning explores the entire search space and does not require multiple decoding iterations with N-best list merging to approximate the search space as in the standard minimum error rate training (Och, 2003). This allows much faster turnaround in weight tuning.

Differentiable approximations of BLEU have been proposed for consensus decoding. Tromble et al. (2008) used a linear approximation and Pauls et al. (2009) used a closer approximation called CoBLEU. CoBLEU is based on the BLEU formula but the n-gram counts are replaced by expected counts over a translation forest. Due to the min-functions required in converting the n-gram counts to matches and a non-differentiable brevity penalty, a sub-gradient ascent must be used. In this work, an approximate expected BLEU (ExpBLEU) defined over N-best lists was used as a differentiable objective function. ExpBLEU uses expected BLEU statistics where the min-function is not needed as the statistics are computed offline and the brevity penalty is replaced by a differentiable approximation. The ExpBLEU tuning yields comparable results to direct BLEU tuning using gradient-free algorithms on combinations of small number of systems (fewer than 20-30 weights). Results on a 44 system combination show that the gradient based optimization is more robust with larger number of weights.

Proceedings of the Joint 5th Workshop on Statistical Machine Translation and MetricsMATR, pages 321–326,
Uppsala, Sweden, 15-16 July 2010.

This paper is organized as follows. Section 2 reviews the incremental hypothesis alignment algorithm used to built the confusion networks. Decoding weight optimization using direct lattice 1-best BLEU tuning and N-best list based ExpBLEU tuning are presented in Section 3. Experimental results on combining single source language to English outputs and all 44 English outputs are detailed in Section 4. Finally, Section 5 concludes this paper with some ideas for future work.

2 Hypothesis Alignment

The confusion networks were built by using the incremental hypothesis alignment algorithm with flexible matching introduced in Rosti et al. (2009). The algorithm is reviewed in more detail here. It is loosely related to the alignment performed in the calculation of the translation edit rate (TER) (Snover et al., 2006) which estimates the edit distance between two strings allowing shifts of blocks of words in addition to insertions, deletions, and substitutions. Calculating an exact TER for strings longer than a few tokens[1] is not computationally feasible, so the `tercom`[2] software uses heuristic shift constraints and pruning to find an upper bound of TER. In this work, the hypotheses were aligned incrementally with the confusion network, thus using tokens from all previously aligned hypotheses in computing the edit distance. Lower substitution costs were assigned to tokens considered equivalent and the heuristic shift constraints of `tercom` were relaxed[3].

First, tokens from all hypotheses are put into equivalence classes if they belong to the same WordNet (Fellbaum, 1998) synonym set or have the same stem. The 1-best hypothesis from each system is used as the confusion network skeleton which defines the final word order of the decoding output. Second, a trivial confusion network is generated from the skeleton hypothesis by generating a single arc for each token. The alignment algorithm explores shifts of blocks of words that minimize the edit distance between the current confusion network and an unaligned hypothesis. Third, the hypothesis with the lowest edit distance to the current confusion network is aligned into the network. The heuristically selected edit costs used in the WMT10 system were 1.0 for insertions, deletions, and shifts, 0.2 for substitutions of tokens in the same equivalence class, and 1.0001 for substitutions of non-equivalent tokens. An insertion with respect to the network always results in a new node and two new arcs. The first arc contains the inserted token and the second arc contains a NULL token representing the missing token from all previously aligned hypotheses. A substitution/deletion results in a new token/NULL arc or increase in the confidence of an existing token/NULL arc. The process is repeated until all hypotheses are aligned into the network.

For example, given the following hypotheses from four systems: "cat sat mat", "cat sat on mat", "sat mat", and "cat sat hat", an initial network in Figure 1(a) is generated. The following two hypotheses have a distance of one edit from the initial network, so the second can be aligned next. Figure 1(b) shows the additional node created and the two new arcs for 'on' and 'NULL' tokens. The third hypothesis has deleted token 'cat' and matches the

(a) Skeleton hypothesis.

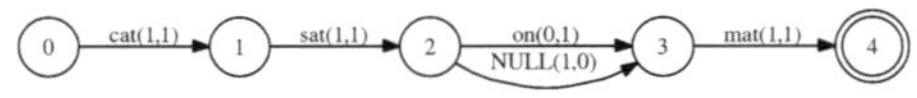

(b) Two hypotheses (insertion).

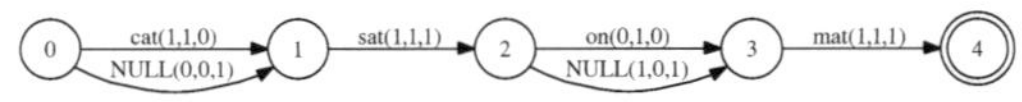

(c) Three hypotheses (deletion).

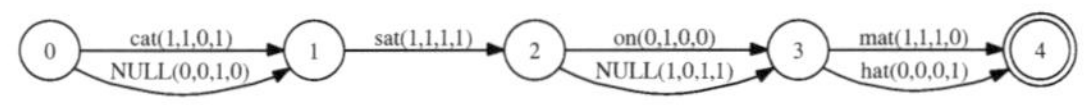

(d) Four hypotheses (substitution).

Figure 1: Example of incrementally aligning "cat sat mat", "cat sat on mat", "sat mat", and "cat sat hat".

[1] Hypotheses are tokenized and lower-cased prior to alignment. Tokens generally refer to words and punctuation.

[2] `http://www.cs.umd.edu/~snover/tercom/` current version 0.7.25.

[3] This algorithm is not equivalent to an incremental TER-Plus (Snover et al., 2009) due to different shift constraints and the lack of paraphrase matching

'NULL' token between nodes 2 and 3 as seen in Figure 1(c). The fourth hypothesis matches all but the final token 'hat' which becomes a substitution for 'mat' in Figure 1(d). The binary vectors in the parentheses following each token show which system generated the token aligned to that arc. If the systems generated N-best hypotheses, a fractional increment could be added to these vectors as in (Rosti et al., 2007). Given these system specific scores are normalized to sum to one over all arcs connecting two consecutive nodes, they may be viewed as system specific word arc posterior estimates. Note, for 1-best hypotheses the scores sum to one without normalization.

Given system outputs $\mathcal{E} = \{E_1, \ldots, E_{N_s}\}$, an algorithm to build a set of N_s confusion networks $\mathcal{C} = \{C_1, \ldots, C_{N_s}\}$ may be written as:

for $n = 1$ to N_s **do**
  $C_n \Leftarrow \text{Init}(E_n)$ {initialize confusion network from the skeleton}
  $\mathcal{E}' \Leftarrow \mathcal{E} - E_n$ {set of unaligned hypotheses}
  while $\mathcal{E}' \neq \emptyset$ **do**
    $E_m \Leftarrow \arg\min_{E \in \mathcal{E}'} \text{Dist}(E, C_n)$ {compute edit distances}
    $C_n \Leftarrow \text{Align}(E_m, C_n)$ {align closest hypothesis}
    $\mathcal{E}' \Leftarrow \mathcal{E}' - E_m$ {update set of unaligned hypotheses}
  end while
end for

The set of N_s confusion networks are expanded to separate paths with distinct bi-gram contexts and connected in parallel into a big lattice with common start and end nodes with NULL token arcs. A prior probability estimate is assigned to the system specific word arc confidences connecting the common start node and the first node in each subnetwork. A heuristic prior is estimated as:

$$p_n = \frac{1}{Z} \exp(-100 \frac{e_n}{N_n}) \qquad (1)$$

where e_n is the total cost of aligning all hypotheses when using system n as the skeleton, N_n is the number of nodes in the confusion network before bi-gram expansion, and Z is a scaling factor to guarantee p_n sum to one. This gives a higher prior for a network with fewer alignment errors and longer expected decoding output.

3 Weight Optimization

Standard search algorithms may be used to find N-best hypotheses from the final lattice. The score for arc l is computed as:

$$s_l = \log\Big(\sum_{n=1}^{N_s} \sigma_n s_{nl}\Big) + \lambda L(w_l | w_{P(l)}) + \omega S(w_l) \qquad (2)$$

where σ_n are the system weights constrained to sum to one, s_{nl} are the system specific arc posteriors, λ is a language model (LM) scaling factor, $L(w_l|w_{P(l)})$ is the bi-gram log-probability for the token w_l on the arc l given the token $w_{P(l)}$ on the arc $P(l)$ preceding the arc l, ω is the word insertion scaling factor, and $S(w_l)$ is zero if w_l is a NULL token and one otherwise. The path with the highest total score under summation is the 1-best decoding output. The decoding weights $\theta = \{\sigma_1, \ldots, \sigma_{N_s}, \lambda, \omega\}$ are tuned to optimize two objective functions described next.

3.1 Lattice Based BLEU Optimization

Powell's method (Press et al., 2007) on N-best lists was used in system combination weight tuning in Rosti et al. (2007). This requires multiple decoding iterations and merging the N-best lists between tuning runs to approximate the full search space as in Och (2003). To speed up the tuning process, a distributed optimization method can be used. The lattices are divided into multiple chunks each of which are loaded into memory by a server. A client runs the optimization algorithm relying on the servers for parallelized objective function evaluation. The client sends a new set of search weights to the servers which decode the chunks of lattices and return the 1-best hypothesis BLEU statistics back to the client. The client accumulates the BLEU statistics from all servers and computes the final BLEU score used as the objective function by the optimization algorithm. Results similar to Powell's method can be obtained with fewer iterations by using the downhill simplex method in multi-dimensions (Amoeba) (Press et al., 2007). To enforce the sum to one constraint of the system weights σ_n, the search weights are restricted to $[0, 1]$ by assigning a large penalty if any corresponding search weight breaches the limits and these restricted search weights are scaled to sum to one before the objective function evaluation.

After optimizing the bi-gram decoding weights directly on the lattices, a 300-best list are generated. The 300-best hypotheses are re-scored using a 5-gram LM and another set of re-scoring weights are tuned on the development set using the standard N-best list based method. Multiple random restarts may be used in both lattice and N-best list based optimization to decrease chances of finding a local minimum. Twenty sets of initial weights (the weights from the previous tuning and 19 randomly perturbed weights) were used in all experiments.

3.2 Approximate Expected BLEU Optimization

The gradient-free optimization algorithms like Powell's method and downhill simplex work well for up to around 20-30 weights. When the number of weights is larger, the algorithms often get stuck in local optima even if multiple random restarts are used. The BLEU score for a 1-best output is defined as follows:

$$\text{BLEU} = \prod_{n=1}^{4} \left(\frac{\sum_i m_i^n}{\sum_i h_i^n} \right)^{\frac{1}{4}} \phi\left(1 - \frac{\sum_i r_i}{\sum_i h_i^1}\right) \quad (3)$$

where m_i^n is the number of n-gram matches between the hypothesis and reference for segment i, h_i^n is the number of n-grams in the hypothesis, r_i is the reference length (or the reference length closest to the hypothesis if multiple references are available), and $\phi(x) = \min(1.0, e^x)$ is the brevity penalty. The first term in Equation 3 is a harmonic mean of the n-gram precisions up to $n = 4$. The selection of 1-best hypotheses is discrete and the brevity penalty is not continuous, so the BLEU score is not differentiable and gradient based optimization cannot be used. Given a posterior distribution over all possible decoding outputs could be defined, an expected BLEU could be optimized using gradient ascent. However, this posterior distribution can only be approximated by expensive sampling methods.

A differentiable objective function over N-best lists to approximate the BLEU score can be defined using expected BLEU statistics and a continuous approximation of the brevity penalty. The posterior probability for hypothesis j of segment i is simply the normalized decoder score:

$$p_{ij} = \frac{e^{\gamma S_{ij}}}{\sum_k e^{\gamma S_{ik}}} \quad (4)$$

where γ is a posterior scaling factor and S_{ij} is the total score of hypothesis j of segment i. The posterior scaling factor controls the shape of the posterior distribution: $\gamma > 1.0$ moves the probability mass toward the 1-best hypothesis and $\gamma < 1.0$ flattens the distribution. The BLEU statistics in Equation 3 are replaced by the expected statistics; for example, $\hat{m}_i^n = \sum_j p_{ij} m_{ij}$, and the brevity penalty $\phi(x)$ is approximated by:

$$\varphi(x) = \frac{e^x - 1}{e^{1000x} + 1} + 1 \quad (5)$$

ExpBLEU has a closed form solution for the gradient, provided the total decoder score is differentiable.

The penalty used to restrict the search weights corresponding to the system weights σ_n in gradient-free BLEU tuning is not differentiable. For expected BLEU tuning, the search weights ς_n are unrestricted but the system weights are obtained by a sigmoid transform and normalized to sum to one:

$$\sigma_n = \frac{\delta(\varsigma_n)}{\sum_m \delta(\varsigma_m)} \quad (6)$$

where $\delta(\varsigma_n) = 1/(1 + e^{-\varsigma_n})$.

The expected BLEU tuning is performed on N-best lists in similar fashion to direct BLEU tuning. Tuned weights from one decoding iteration are used to generate a new N-best list, the new N-best list is merged with the N-best list from the previous tuning run, and a new set of weights are optimized using limited memory Broyden-Fletcher-Goldfarb-Shanno method (lBFGS) (Liu and Nocedal, 1989). Since the posterior distribution is affected by the size of the N-best list and different decoding weights, the posterior scaling factor can be set for each tuning run so that the perplexity of the posterior distribution given the merged N-best list is constant. A target perplexity of 5.0 was used in the experiments. Four iterations of bi-gram decoding weight tuning were performed using 300-best lists. The final 300-best list was re-scored with a 5-gram and another set of re-scoring weights was tuned on the development set.

4 Experimental Evaluation

System outputs for all language pairs with English as the target were combined. Unpruned English bi-gram and 5-gram language model components were trained using the WMT10 corpora: `EuroParl`, `GigaFrEn`, `NewsCommentary`, and `News`. Additional six Gigaword v4 components were trained: `AFP`, `APW`, `XIN+CNA`,

tune	cz-en		de-en		es-en		fr-en	
System	TER	BLEU	TER	BLEU	TER	BLEU	TER	BLEU
worst	68.99	13.85	68.45	15.07	60.86	21.02	71.17	15.00
best	56.77	22.84	57.76	25.05	51.81	30.10	53.66	28.64
syscomb	57.31	25.11	54.97	27.75	50.46	31.54	51.35	31.16

test	cz-en		de-en		es-en		fr-en	
System	TER	BLEU	TER	BLEU	TER	BLEU	TER	BLEU
worst	68.65	14.29	67.50	15.66	60.52	21.86	68.36	16.82
best	56.13	23.56	58.12	24.34	51.45	30.56	52.16	29.79
syscomb	56.89	25.12	55.60	26.38	50.33	31.59	51.36	30.16

Table 1: Case insensitive TER and BLEU scores on syscombtune (tune) and syscombtest (test) for combinations of outputs from four source languages.

LTW, NYT, and Headlines+Datelines. Interpolation weights for the ten components were tuned so as to minimize perplexity on the newstest2009-ref.en development set. The LMs used modified Kneser-Ney smoothing. On the multi-source condition (xx-en) another LM was trained from the system outputs and interpolated with the general LM using an interpolation weight 0.3 for the LM trained on the system outputs. This LM is referred to as biasLM later. A tri-gram true casing model was trained using all available English data. This model was used to restore the case of the lower-case system combination output.

All six 1-best system outputs on cz-en, 16 outputs on de-en, 8 outputs on es-en, and 14 outputs on fr-en were combined. The lattice based BLEU tuning was used to optimize the bi-gram decoding weights and N-best list based BLEU tuning was used to optimize the 5-gram rescoring weights. Results for these single source language experiments are shown in Table 1. The gains on syscombtune were similar to those on syscombtest for all but French-English. The tuning set contained only 455 segments but appeared to be well matched with the larger (2034 segments) test set. The characteristics of the individual system outputs were probably different for the tuning and test sets on French-English translation. In our experience, optimizing system combination weights using the ExpBLEU tuning for a small number of systems yields similar results to lattice based BLEU tuning. The lattice based BLEU tuning is faster as there is no need for multiple decoding and tuning iterations. Using the biasLM on the single source combinations did not yield any gains. The output for these conditions probably did not contain enough data for biasLM training given the small tuning set and small number of systems.

xx-en	**tune**		**test**	
System	TER	BLEU	TER	BLEU
worst	71.17	13.85	68.65	14.29
best	51.81	30.10	51.45	30.56
lattice	43.15	35.72	43.79	35.29
expBLEU	44.07	36.91	44.35	36.62
+biasLM	43.63	**37.61**	44.50	**37.12**

Table 2: Case insensitive TER and BLEU scores on syscombtune (tune) and syscombtest (test) for xx-en combination. Combinations using lattice BLEU tuning, expected BLEU tuning, and after adding the system output biased LM are shown.

Finally, experiments combining all 44 1-best system outputs were performed to produce a multi-source combination output. The first experiment used the lattice based BLEU tuning and gave a 5.6 BLEU point gain on the tuning set as seen in Table 2. The ExpBLEU tuning gave an additional 1.2 point gain which suggests that the direct lattice based BLEU tuning got stuck in a local optimum. Using the system output biased LM gave an additional 0.7 point gain. The gains on the test set were similar and the best combination gave a 6.6 point gain over the best individual system.

5 Conclusions

The BBN submissions for WMT10 system combination task were described in this paper. The combination was based on confusion network decoding. The confusion networks were built using an incremental hypothesis alignment algorithm with flexible matching. The bi-gram decoding weights for the single source conditions were optimized directly to maximize the BLEU scores of the 1-best decoding outputs and the 5-gram re-scoring weights were tuned on 300-best lists. The BLEU gains over the best individual system outputs were around 1.5 points on `cz-en`, 2.0 points on `de-en`, 1.0 points on `es-en`, and 0.4 points on `fr-en`. The system combination weights on `xx-en` were tuned to maximize ExpBLEU, and a system output biased LM was used. The BLEU gain over the best individual system was 6.6 points. Future work will investigate tuning of the edit costs used in the alignment. A lattice based ExpBLEU tuning will be investigated. Also, weights for more complicated functions with additional features may be tuned using ExpBLEU.

Acknowledgments

This work was supported by DARPA/IPTO Contract No. HR0011-06-C-0022 under the GALE program.

References

Christiane Fellbaum, editor. 1998. *WordNet: An Electronic Lexical Database*. MIT Press.

Dong C. Liu and Jorge Nocedal. 1989. On the limited memory method for large scale optimization. *Mathematical Programming*, 45(3):503–528.

Franz J. Och. 2003. Minimum error rate training in statistical machine translation. In *Proceedings of the 41st Annual Meeting of the Association for Computational Linguistics*, pages 160–167.

Kishore Papineni, Salim Roukos, Todd Ward, and Wei-Jing Zhu. 2002. BLEU: a method for automatic evaluation of machine translation. In *Proceedings of the 40th Annual Meeting of the Association for Computational Linguistics*, pages 311–318.

Adam Pauls, John DeNero, and DanKlein. 2009. Consensus training for consensus decoding in machine translation. In *Proceedings of the 2009 Conference on Empirical Methods in Natural Language Processing*, pages 1418–1427.

William H. Press, Saul A. Teukolsky, William T. Vetterling, and Brian P. Flannery. 2007. *Numerical recipes: the art of scientific computing*. Cambridge University Press, 3rd edition.

Antti-Veikko I. Rosti, Spyros Matsoukas, and Richard Schwartz. 2007. Improved word-level system combination for machine translation. In *Proceedings of the 45th Annual Meeting of the Association of Computational Linguistics*, pages 312–319.

Antti-Veikko I. Rosti, Bing Zhang, Spyros Matsoukas, and Richard Schwartz. 2009. Incremental hypothesis alignment with flexible matching for building confusion networks: BBN system description for WMT09 system combination task. In *Proceedings of the Fourth Workshop on Statistical Machine Translation*, pages 61–65.

Matthew Snover, Bonnie Dorr, Richard Schwartz, Linnea Micciula, and John Makhoul. 2006. A study of translation edit rate with targeted human annotation. In *Proceedings of the 7th Conference of the Association for Machine Translation in the Americas*, pages 223–231.

Matthew Snover, Nitin Madnani, Bonnie Dorr, and Richard Schwartz. 2009. Fluency, adequacy, or HTER? exploring different human judgments with a tunable MT metric. In *Proceedings of the Fourth Workshop on Statistical Machine Translation*, pages 259–268.

Roy W. Tromble, Shankar Kumar, Franz Och, and Wolfgang Macherey. 2008. Lattice minimum bayes-risk decoding for statistical machine translation. In *Proceedings of the 2008 Conference on Empirical Methods in Natural Language Processing*, pages 620–629.

LRscore for Evaluating Lexical and Reordering Quality in MT

Alexandra Birch
University of Edinburgh
United Kingdom
a.c.birch-mayne@s0454866.ed.ac.uk

Miles Osborne
University of Edinburgh
United Kingdom
miles@inf.ed.ac.uk

Abstract

The ability to measure the quality of word order in translations is an important goal for research in machine translation. Current machine translation metrics do not adequately measure the reordering performance of translation systems. We present a novel metric, the LRscore, which directly measures reordering success. The reordering component is balanced by a lexical metric. Capturing the two most important elements of translation success in a simple combined metric with only one parameter results in an intuitive, shallow, language independent metric.

1 Introduction

The main purpose of MT evaluation is to determine "to what extent the makers of a system have succeeded in mimicking the human translator" (Krauwer, 1993). But machine translation has no "ground truth" as there are many possible correct translations. It is impossible to judge whether a translation is incorrect or simply unknown and it is even harder to judge the the degree to which it is incorrect. Even so, automatic metrics are necessary. It is nearly impossible to collect enough human judgments for evaluating incremental improvements in research systems, or for tuning statistical machine translation system parameters. Automatic metrics are also much faster and cheaper than human evaluation and they produce reproducible results.

Machine translation research relies heavily upon automatic metrics to evaluate the performance of models. However, current metrics rely upon indirect methods for measuring the quality of the word order, and their ability to capture reordering performance has been demonstrated to be poor (Birch et al., 2010). There are two main approaches to capturing reordering. The first way to measure the quality of word order is to count the number of matching n-grams between the reference and the hypothesis. This is the approach taken by the BLEU score (Papineni et al., 2002). This method discounts any n-gram which is not identical to a reference n-gram, and also does not consider the relative position of the strings. They can be anywhere in the sentence. Another common approach is typified by METEOR (Banerjee and Lavie, 2005) and TER (Snover et al., 2006). They calculate an ordering penalty for a hypothesis based on the minimum number of chunks the translation needs to be broken into in order to align it to the reference. The disadvantage of the second approach is that aligning sentences with very different words can be inaccurate. Also there is no notion of how far these blocks are out of order. More sophisticated metrics, such as the RTE metric (Padó et al., 2009), use higher level syntactic or even semantic analysis to determine the quality of the translation. These approaches are useful, but can be very slow, require annotation, they are language dependent and their parameters are hard to train. For most research work shallow metrics are more appropriate.

Apart from failing to capture reordering performance, another common criticism of most current automatic MT metrics is that a particular score value reported does not give insights into quality (Przybocki et al., 2009). This is because there is no intrinsic significance of a difference in scores. Ideally, the scores that the metrics report would be meaningful and stand on their own. However, the most one can say is that higher is better for accuracy metrics and lower is better for error metrics.

We present a novel metric, the LRscore, which explicitly measures the quality of word order in machine translations. It then combines the reordering metric with a metric measuring lexical success. This results in a comprehensive met-

Proceedings of the Joint 5th Workshop on Statistical Machine Translation and MetricsMATR, pages 327–332,
Uppsala, Sweden, 15-16 July 2010.

ric which measures the two most fundamental aspects of translation. We argue that the LRscore is intuitive and meaningful because it is a simple, decomposable metric with only one parameter to train.

The LRscore has many of the properties that are deemed to be desirable in a recent metric evaluation campaign (Przybocki et al., 2009). The LRscore is language independent. The reordering component relies on abstract alignments and word positions and not on words at all. The lexical component of the system can be any meaningful metric for a particular target language. In our experiments we use 1-gram BLEU and 4-gram BLEU, however, if a researcher was interested in morphologically rich languages, a different metric which scores partially correct words might be more appropriate. The LRscore is a shallow metric, which means that it is reasonably fast to run. This is important in order to be useful for training of the translation model parameters. A final advantage is that the LRscore is a sentence level metric. This means that human judgments can be directly compared to system scores and helps researchers to understand what changes they are seeing between systems.

In this paper we start by describing the reordering metrics and then we present the LRscore. Finally we discuss related work and conclude.

2 Reordering Metrics

The relative ordering of words in the source and target sentences is encoded in alignments. We can interpret alignments as permutations. This allows us to apply research into metrics for ordered encodings to our primary tasks of measuring and evaluating reorderings. A word alignment over a sentence pair allows us to transcribe the source word positions in the order of the aligned target words. Permutations have already been used to describe reorderings (Eisner and Tromble, 2006), primarily to develop a reordering model which uses ordering costs to score possible permutations. Here we use permutations to evaluate reordering performance based on the methods presented in (Birch et al., 2010).

The ordering of the words in the target sentence can be seen as a permutation of the words in the source sentence. The source sentence s of length N consists of the word positions $s_0 \cdots s_i \cdots s_N$. Using an alignment function where a source word at position i is mapped to a target word at position j with the function $a : i \rightarrow j$, we can reorder the source word positions to reflect the order of the words in the target. This gives us a permutation.

A **permutation** is a bijective function from a set of natural numbers $1, 2, \cdots, N$ to itself. We will name our permutations π and σ. The ith symbol of a permutation π will be denoted as $\pi(i)$, and the inverse of the permutation π^{-1} is defined so that if $\pi(i) = j$ then $\pi^{-1}(j) = i$. The identity, or monotone, permutation id is the permutation for which $id(i) = i$ for all i. Table 1 shows the permutations associated with the example alignments in Figure 1. The permutations are calculated by iterating over the source words, and recording the ordering of the aligned target words.

Permutations encode one-one relations, whereas alignments contain null alignments and one-many, many-one and many-many relations. For now, we make some simplifying assumptions to allow us to work with permutations. Source words aligned to null ($a(i) \rightarrow null$) are assigned the target word position immediately after the target word position of the previous source word ($\pi(i) = \pi(i-1) + 1$). Where multiple source words are aligned to the same target word or phrase, a many-to-one relation, the target ordering is assumed to be monotone. When one source word is aligned to multiple target words, a one-to-many relation, the source word is assumed to be aligned to the first target word.

A translation can potentially have many valid word orderings. However, we can be reasonably certain that the ordering of reference sentence must be acceptable. We therefore compare the ordering of a translation with that of the reference sentence. The underlying assumption is that most reasonable word orderings should be fairly similar to the reference. The assumption that the reference is somehow similar to the translation is necessary for all automatic machine translation metrics. We propose using permutation distance metrics to perform the comparison.

There are many different ways of measuring distance between two permutations, with different solutions originating in different domains (statistics, computer science, molecular biology, ...). Real numbered data leads to measures such as Euclidean distance, binary data to measures such as Hamming distance. But for ordered sets, there are many different options, and the best one de-

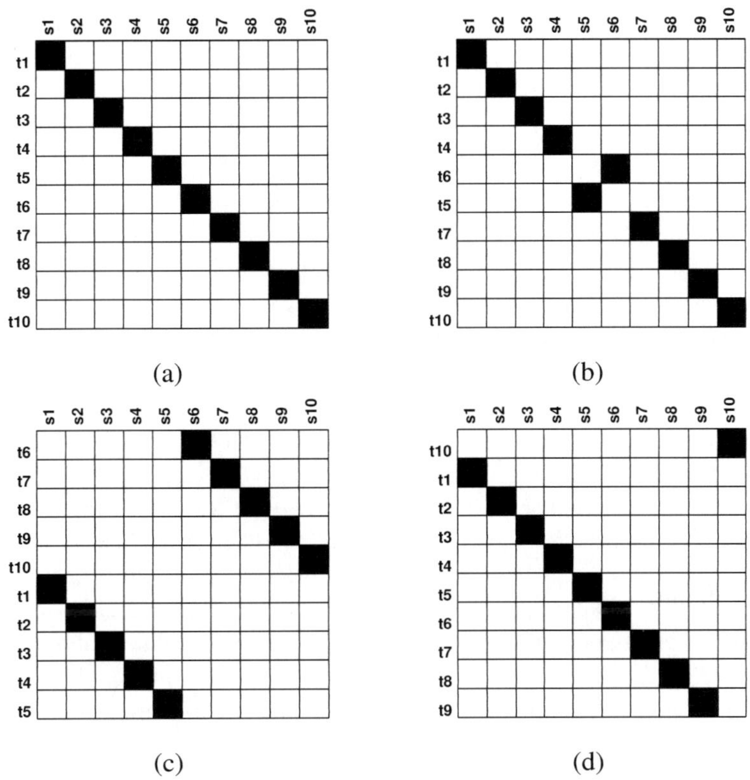

Figure 1: Synthetic examples: a translation and three reference scenarios. (a) is a monotone translation, (b) is a reference with one short distance word order difference, (c) is a reference where the order of the two halves has been swapped, and (d) is a reference with a long distance reordering of the first target word.

pends on the task at hand. We choose a few metrics which are widely used, efficient to calculate and capture certain properties of the reordering. In particular, they are sensitive to the number of words that are out of order. Three of the metrics, Kendall's tau, Spearman's rho and Spearman's footrule distances also take into account the distance between positions in the reference and translation sentences, or the size of the reordering.

An obvious disadvantage of this approach is the fact that we need alignments, either between the source and the reference, and the source and the translation, or directly between the reference and the translation. If accuracy is paramount, the test set could include manual alignments and the systems could directly output the source-translation alignments. Outputting the alignment information should require a trivial change to the decoder. Alignments can also be automatically generated using the alignment model that aligns the training data.

Distance metrics increase as the quality of translation decreases. We invert the scale of the distance metrics in order to easily compare them with other metrics where increases in the metrics mean increases in translation quality. All permutation distance metrics are thus subtracted from 1. Note that the two permutations we refer to π and σ are relative to the source sentence, and not to the reference: the source-reference permutation is compared to the source-translation permutation.

(a)	(1 2 3 4 5 6 7 8 9 10)
(b)	(1 2 3 4 •6 •5 •7 8 9 10)
(c)	(6 7 8 9 10 •1 2 3 4 5)
(d)	(2 3 4 5 6 7 8 9 10 •1)

Table 1: Permutations extracted from the sentence pairs shown in Figure 1: (a) is a monotone permutation and (b), (c) and (d) are permutations with different amounts of disorder, where bullet points highlight non-sequential neighbors.

2.1 Hamming Distance

The Hamming distance (Hamming, 1950) measures the number of disagreements between two permutations. The Hamming distance for permutations was proposed by (Ronald, 1998) and is also known as the **exact match distance**. It is defined as follows:

$$d_H(\pi, \sigma) = 1 - \frac{\sum_{i=1}^{n} x_i}{n} \text{ where } x_i = \begin{cases} 0 \text{ if } \pi(i) = \sigma(i) \\ 1 \text{ otherwise} \end{cases}$$

Where π, σ are the two permutations and the normalization constant Z is n, the length of the permutation. We are interested in the Hamming distance for its ability to capture the amount of absolute disorder that exists between two permutations. The Hamming distance is widely utilized in coding theory to measure the discrepancy between two binary sequences.

2.2 Kendall's Tau Distance

Kendall's tau distance is the minimum number of transpositions of two *adjacent* symbols necessary to transform one permutation into another (Kendall, 1938; Kendall and Gibbons, 1990). This is sometimes known as the **swap distance** or the **inversion distance** and can be interpreted as a function of the probability of observing concordant and discordant pairs (Kerridge, 1975). It is defined as follows:

$$\begin{aligned} d_\tau(\pi, \sigma) &= 1 - \frac{\sum_{i=1}^{n} \sum_{j=1}^{n} z_{ij}}{Z} \\ \text{where } z_{ij} &= \begin{cases} 1 \text{ if } \pi(i) < \pi(j) \text{ and } \sigma(i) > \sigma(j) \\ 0 \text{ otherwise} \end{cases} \\ Z &= \frac{(n^2 - n)}{2} \end{aligned}$$

The Kendall's tau metric is possibly the most interesting for measuring reordering as it is sensitive to all relative orderings. It consequently measures not only how many reordering there are but also the distance that words are reordered.

In statistics, Spearman's rho and Kendall's tau are widely used non-parametric measures of association for two rankings. In natural language processing research, Kendall's tau has been used as a means of estimating the distance between a system-generated and a human-generated gold-standard order for the sentence ordering task (Lapata, 2003). Kendall's tau has also been used in machine translation as a cost function in a reordering model (Eisner and Tromble, 2006) and an MT metric called ROUGE-S (Lin and Och, 2004) is similar to a Kendall's tau metric on lexical items. ROUGE-S is an F-measure of ordered pairs of words in the translation. As far as we know, Kendall's tau has not been used as a reordering metric before.

3 LRscore

The goal of much machine translation research is either to improve the quality of the words used in the output, or their ordering. We use the reordering metrics and combine them with a measurement of lexical performance to produce a comprehensive metric, the LRscore. The LRscore is a linear interpolation of a reordering metric with the BLEU score. If we use the 1-gram BLEU score, BLEU1, then the LRscore relies purely upon the reordering metric for all word ordering evaluation. We also use the 4-gram BLEU score, BLEU4, as it is an important baseline and the values it reports are very familiar to machine translation researchers. BLEU4 also contains a notion of word ordering based on longer matching n-grams. However, it is aware only of very local orderings. It does not measure the magnitude of the orderings like the reordering metrics do, and it is dependent on exact lexical overlap which does not affect the reordering metric. The two components are therefore largely orthogonal and there is a benefit in combining them. Both the BLEU score and the reordering distance metric apply a brevity penalty to account for translations of different lengths.

The formula for calculating the LRscore is as follows:

$$LRscore = \alpha * R + (1 - \alpha) BLEU$$

Where the reordering metric R is calculated as follows:

$$R = d * BP$$

Where we either take the Hamming distance d_H or the Kendall's tau distance d_τ as the reordering distance d and then we apply the brevity penalty BP. The brevity penalty is calculated as:

$$BP = \begin{cases} 1 & \text{if } t > r \\ e^{1-r/t} & \text{if } t \leq r \end{cases}$$

where t is the length of the translation, and r is the closest reference length. R is calculated at the sentence level, and the scores are averaged over a test set. This average is then combined with the system level lexical score. The Lexical metric is the BLEU score which sums the log precision of n-grams. In our paper we set the n-gram length to either be one or four.

The only parameter in the metric α balances the contribution of reordering and the lexical components. There is no analytic solution for optimizing this parameter, and we use greedy hillclimbing in order to find the optimal setting. We optimize the sentence level correlation of the metric to human judgments of accuracy as provided by the WMT 2010 shared task. As hillclimbing can end up in a local minima, we perform 20 random restarts, and retaining only the parameter value with the best consistency result. Random-restart hill climbing is a surprisingly effective algorithm in many cases. It turns out that it is often better to spend CPU time exploring the space, rather than carefully optimizing from an initial condition.

The brevity penalty applies to both the reordering metric and the BLEU score. We do not set a parameter to regulate the impact of the brevity penalty, as we want to retain BLEU scores that are comparable with BLEU scores computed in published research. And as we do not regulate the brevity penalty in the BLEU score, we do not wish to do so for the reordering metric either. It therefore impacts on both the reordering and the lexical components equally.

4 Correlation with Human Judgments

It has been common to use seven-point fluency and adequacy scores as the main human evaluation task. These scores are intended to be absolute scores and comparable across sentences. Seven-point fluency and adequacy judgements are quite unreliable at a sentence level and so it seems dubious that they would be reliable across sentences. However, having absolute scores does have the advantage of making it easy to calculate the correlation coefficients of the metric with human judgements. Using rank judgements, we do not have absolute scores and thus we cannot compare translations across different sentences.

We therefore take the method adopted in the 2009 workshop on machine translation (Callison-Burch et al., 2009). We ascertained how consistent the automatic metrics were with the human judgements by calculating consistency in the following manner. We take each pairwise comparison of translation output for single sentences by a particular judge, and we recorded whether or not the metrics were consistent with the human rank. Ie. we counted cases where both the metric and the human judged agree that one system is better than another. We divided this by the total umber of pairwise comparisons to get a percentage. There were many ties in the human data, but metrics rarely give the same score to two different translations. We therefore excluded pairs that the human annotators ranked as ties. The human ranking data and the system outputs from the 2009 Workshop on Machine Translation (Callison-Burch et al., 2009) have been used to evaluate the LRscore.

Metric	de-en	es-en	fr-en	cz-en
BLEU4	58.72	55.48	57.71	57.24
LR-HB1	60.37	**60.55**	58.59	53.70
LR-HB4	60.49	58.88	**58.80**	57.74
LR-KB1	60.67	58.54	58.46	54.20
LR-KB4	**61.07**	59.86	58.59	**58.92**

Table 2: The percentage consistency between human judgements of rank and metrics. The LRscore variations (LR-*) are optimised for consistency for each language pair.

We optimise the sentence level consistency of the metric. As hillclimbing can end up in a local minima, we perform 20 random restarts, and retaining only the parameter value with the best consistency result. Random-restart hill climbing is a surprisingly effective algorithm in many cases. It turns out that it is often better to spend CPU time exploring the space, rather than carefully optimising from an initial condition.

Table 2 reports the optimal consistency of the LRscore and baseline metrics with human judgements for each language pair. The table also reports the individual component results. The LRscore variations are named as follows: LR refers to the LRscore, "H" refers to the Hamming distance and "K" to Kendall's tau distance. "B1" and "B4" refer to the smoothed BLEU score with the 1-gram and 4-gram scores. The LRscore is the metric which is most consistent with human judgement. This is an important result which shows that combining lexical and reordering information makes for a stronger metric.

5 Related Work

(Wong and Kit, 2009) also suggest a metric which combines a word choice and a word order component. They propose a type of F-measure which uses a matching function M to calculate precision and recall. M combines the number of matched words, weighted by their *tfidf* importance, with their position difference score, and finally subtracting a score for unmatched words. Including unmatched words in the in M function undermines the interpretation of the supposed F-measure. The reordering component is the average difference of absolute and relative word positions which has no clear meaning. This score is not intuitive or easily decomposable and it is more similar to METEOR, with synonym and stem functionality mixed with a reordering penalty, than to our metric.

6 Conclusion

We propose the LRscore which combines a lexical and a reordering metric. This results in a metric which is both meaningful and accurately measures the word order performance of the translation model.

References

Satanjeev Banerjee and Alon Lavie. 2005. Meteor: An automatic metric for MT evaluation with improved correlation with human judgments. In *Workshop on Intrinsic and Extrinsic Evaluation Measures for MT and/or Summarization.*

Alexandra Birch, Phil Blunsom, and Miles Osborne. 2010. Metrics for MT Evaluation: Evaluating Reordering. *Machine Translation (to appear).*

Chris Callison-Burch, Philipp Koehn, Christof Monz, and Josh Schroeder. 2009. Findings of the 2009 Workshop on Statistical Machine Translation. In *Proceedings of the Fourth Workshop on Statistical Machine Translation*, pages 1–28, Athens, Greece, March. Association for Computational Linguistics.

Jason Eisner and Roy W. Tromble. 2006. Local search with very large-scale neighborhoods for optimal permutations in machine translation. In *Proceedings of the HLT-NAACL Workshop on Computationally Hard Problems and Joint Inference in Speech and Language Processing*, pages 57–75, New York, June.

Richard Hamming. 1950. Error detecting and error correcting codes. *Bell System Technical Journal*, 26(2):147–160.

M. Kendall and J. Dickinson Gibbons. 1990. *Rank Correlation Methods.* Oxford University Press, New York.

Maurice Kendall. 1938. A new measure of rank correlation. *Biometrika*, 30:81–89.

D Kerridge. 1975. The interpretation of rank correlations. *Applied Statistics*, 2:257–258.

S. Krauwer. 1993. Evaluation of MT systems: a programmatic view. *Machine Translation*, 8(1):59–66.

Mirella Lapata. 2003. Probabilistic text structuring: Experiments with sentence ordering. *Computational Linguistics*, 29(2):263–317.

Chin-Yew Lin and Franz Josef Och. 2004. Automatic evaluation of machine translation quality using longest common subsequence and skip-bigram statistics. In *Proceedings of the 42nd Meeting of the Association for Computational Linguistics (ACL'04), Main Volume*, pages 605–612, Barcelona, Spain, July.

Sebastian Padó, Daniel Cer, Michel Galley, Dan Jurafsky, and Christopher D. Manning. 2009. Measuring machine translation quality as semantic equivalence: A metric based on entailment features. *Machine Translation.*

Kishore Papineni, Salim Roukos, Todd Ward, and Wei-Jing Zhu. 2002. BLEU: a method for automatic evaluation of machine translation. In *Proceedings of the Association for Computational Linguistics*, pages 311–318, Philadelphia, USA.

Mark Przybocki, Kay Peterson, Sébastien Bronsart, and Gregory Sanders. 2009. The nist 2008 metrics for machine translation challengeoverview, methodology, metrics, and results. *Machine Translation.*

S Ronald. 1998. More distance functions for order-based encodings. In *the IEEE Conference on Evolutionary Computation*, pages 558–563.

Matthew Snover, Bonnie Dorr, R Schwartz, L Micciulla, and J Makhoul. 2006. A study of translation edit rate with targeted human annotation. In *AMTA.*

B. Wong and C. Kit. 2009. ATEC: automatic evaluation of machine translation via word choice and word order. *Machine Translation*, pages 1–15.

Document-level Automatic MT Evaluation based on Discourse Representations

Jesús Giménez and **Lluís Màrquez**
TALP UPC
Barcelona, Spain
{jgimenez, lluism}@lsi.upc.edu

Elisabet Comelles and **Irene Castellón**
Universitat de Barcelona
Barcelona, Spain
{elicomelles, icastellon}@ub.edu

Victoria Arranz
ELDA/ELRA
Paris, France
arranz@elda.org

Abstract

This paper describes the joint submission of Universitat Politècnica de Catalunya and Universitat de Barcelona to the Metrics MaTr 2010 evaluation challenge, in collaboration with ELDA/ELRA. Our work is aimed at widening the scope of current automatic evaluation measures from sentence to document level. Preliminary experiments, based on an extension of the metrics by Giménez and Màrquez (2009) operating over discourse representations, are presented.

1 Introduction

Current automatic similarity measures for Machine Translation (MT) evaluation operate all, without exception, at the segment level. Translations are analyzed on a segment-by-segment[1] fashion, ignoring the text structure. Document and system scores are obtained using aggregate statistics over individual segments. This strategy presents the main disadvantage of ignoring cross-sentential/discursive phenomena.

In this work we suggest widening the scope of evaluation methods. We have defined genuine document-level measures which are able to exploit the structure of text to provide more informed evaluation scores. For that purpose we take advantage of two coincidental facts. First, test beds employed in recent MT evaluation campaigns include a document structure grouping sentences related to the same event, story or topic (Przybocki et al., 2008; Przybocki et al., 2009; Callison-Burch et al., 2009). Second, we count on automatic linguistic processors which provide very detailed discourse-level representations of text (Curran et al., 2007).

Discourse representations allow us to focus on relevant pieces of information, such as the agent (who), location (where), time (when), and theme (what), which may be spread all over the text. Counting on a means of discerning the events, the individuals taking part in each of them, and their role, is crucial to determine the semantic equivalence between a reference document and a candidate translation.

Moreover, the discourse analysis of a document is not a mere concatenation of the analyses of its individual sentences. There are some phenomena which may go beyond the scope of a sentence and can only be explained within the context of the whole document. For instance, in a newspaper article, facts and entities are progressively added to the discourse and then referred to anaphorically later on. The following extract from the development set illustrates the importance of such a phenomenon in the discourse analysis: *'Among the current or underlying crises in the Middle East, Rod Larsen mentioned the Arab-Israeli conflict and the Iranian nuclear portfolio, as well as the crisis between Lebanon and Syria. He stated: "All this leads us back to crucial values and opinions, which render the situation prone at any moment to getting out of control, more so than it was in past days."'*. The subject pronoun *"he"* works as an anaphoric pronoun whose antecedent is the proper noun *"Rod Larson"*. The anaphoric relation established between these two elements can only be identified by analyzing the text as a whole, thus considering the gender agreement between the third person singular masculine subject pronoun *"he"* and the masculine proper noun *"Rod Larson"*. However, if the two sentences were analyzed separately, the identification of this anaphoric relation would not be feasible due to the lack of connection between the two elements. Discourse representations allow us to trace links across sentences between the different facts and entities appearing in them. Therefore, providing an approach to the text more similar to that of

[1] A segment typically consists of one or two sentences.

Proceedings of the Joint 5th Workshop on Statistical Machine Translation and MetricsMATR, pages 333–338, Uppsala, Sweden, 15-16 July 2010.

a human, which implies taking into account the whole text structure instead of considering each sentence separately.

The rest of the paper is organized as follows. Section 2 describes our evaluation methods and the linguistic theory upon which they are based. Experimental results are reported and discussed in Section 3. Section 4 presents the metric submitted to the evaluation challenge. Future work is outlined in Section 5.

As an additional result, document-level metrics generated in this study have been incorporated to the IQMT package for automatic MT evaluation[2].

2 Metric Description

This section provides a brief description of our approach. First, in Section 2.1, we describe the underlying theory and give examples on its capabilities. Then, in Section 2.2, we describe the associated similarity measures.

2.1 Discourse Representations

As previously mentioned in Section 1, a document has some features which need to be analyzed considering it as a whole instead of dividing it up into sentences. The anaphoric relation between a subject pronoun and a proper noun has already been exemplified. However, this is not the only anaphoric relation which can be found inside a text, there are some others which are worth mentioning:

- the connection between a possessive adjective and a proper noun or a subject pronoun, as exemplified in the sentences *"Maria bought a new sweater. Her new sweater is blue."*, where the possessive feminine adjective *"her"* refers to the proper noun *"Maria"*.

- the link between a demonstrative pronoun and its referent, which is exemplified in the sentences *"He developed a new theory on grammar. However, this is not the only theory he developed"*. In the second sentence, the demonstrative pronoun *"this"* refers back to the noun phrase *"new theory on grammar"* which occurs in the previous sentence.

- the relation between a main verb and an auxiliary verb in certain contexts, as illustrated in the following pair of sentences *"Would you like more sugar? Yes, I would"*. In this example, the auxiliary verb *"would"* used in the short answer substitutes the verb phrase *"would like"*.

In addition to anaphoric relations, other features need to be highlighted, such as the use of discourse markers which help to give cohesion to the text, link parts of a discourse and show the relations established between them. Below, some examples are given:

- "Moreover", "Furthermore", "In addition" indicate that the upcoming sentence adds more information.

- "However", "Nonetheless", "Nevertheless" show contrast with previous ideas.

- "Therefore", "As a result", "Consequently" show a cause and effect relation.

- "For instance", "For example" clarify or illustrate the previous idea.

It is worth noticing that anaphora, as well as discourse markers, are key features in the interface between syntax, semantics and pragmatics. Thus, when dealing with these phenomena at a text level we are not just looking separately at the different language levels, but we are trying to give a complete representation of both the surface and the deep structures of a text.

2.2 Definition of Similarity Measures

In this work, as a first proposal, instead of elaborating on novel similarity measures, we have borrowed and extended the Discourse Representation *(DR)* metrics defined by Giménez and Màrquez (2009). These metrics analyze similarities between automatic and reference translations by comparing their respective discourse representations over individual sentences.

For the discursive analysis of texts, DR metrics rely on the C&C Tools (Curran et al., 2007), specifically on the Boxer component (Bos, 2008). This software is based on the Discourse Representation Theory (DRT) by Kamp and Reyle (1993). DRT is a theoretical framework offering a representation language for the examination of contextually dependent meaning in discourse. A discourse is represented in a discourse representation structure (DRS), which is essentially a variation of first-order predicate calculus —its forms are pairs

[2] `http://www.lsi.upc.edu/~nlp/IQMT`

of first-order formulae and the free variables that occur in them.

DRSs are viewed as semantic trees, built through the application of two types of DRS conditions:

basic conditions: one-place properties (predicates), two-place properties (relations), named entities, time-expressions, cardinal expressions and equalities.

complex conditions: disjunction, implication, negation, question, and propositional attitude operations.

For instance, the DRS representation for the sentence *"Every man loves Mary."* is as follows: $\exists y\ named(y, mary, per) \wedge (\forall x\ man(x) \rightarrow \exists z\ love(z) \wedge event(z) \wedge agent(z,x) \wedge patient(z,y))$. DR integrates three different kinds of metrics:

DR-STM These metrics are similar to the *Syntactic Tree Matching* metric defined by Liu and Gildea (2005), in this case applied to DRSs instead of constituent trees. All semantic subpaths in the candidate and reference trees are retrieved. The fraction of matching subpaths of a given length (*l*=4 in our experiments) is computed.

DR-$O_r(\star)$ Average lexical overlap between discourse representation structures of the same type. Overlap is measured according to the formulae and definitions by Giménez and Màrquez (2007).

DR-$O_{rp}(\star)$ Average morphosyntactic overlap, i.e., between grammatical categories –parts-of-speech– associated to lexical items, between discourse representation structures of the same type.

We have extended these metrics to operate at document level. For that purpose, instead of running the C&C Tools in a sentence-by-sentence fashion, we run them document by document. This is as simple as introducing a "<META>" tag at the beginning of each document to denote document boundaries[3].

[3]Details on the advanced use of Boxer are available at `http://svn.ask.it.usyd.edu.au/trac/candc/wiki/BoxerComplex`.

3 Experimental Work

In this section, we analyze the behavior of the new DR metrics operating at document level with respect to their sentence-level counterparts.

3.1 Settings

We have used the 'mt06' part of the development set provided by the Metrics MaTr 2010 organization, which corresponds to a subset of 25 documents from the NIST 2006 Open MT Evaluation Campaign Arabic-to-English translation. The total number of segments is 249. The average number of segments per document is, thus, 9.96. The number of segments per document varies between 2 and 30. For the purpose of automatic evaluation, 4 human reference translations and automatic outputs by 8 different MT systems are available. In addition, we count on the results of a process of manual evaluation. Each translation segment was assessed by two judges. After independently and completely assessing the entire set, the judges reviewed their individual assessments together and settled on a single final score. Average system adequacy is 5.38.

In our experiments, metrics are evaluated in terms of their correlation with human assessments. We have computed Pearson, Spearman and Kendall correlation coefficients between metric scores and adequacy assessments. Document-level and system-level assessments have been obtained by averaging over segment-level assessments. We have computed correlation coefficients and confidence intervals applying bootstrap resampling at a 99% statistical significance (Efron and Tibshirani, 1986; Koehn, 2004). Since the cost of exhaustive resampling was prohibitive, we have limited to 1,000 resamplings. Confidence intervals, not shown in the tables, are in all cases lower than 10^{-3}.

3.2 Metric Performance

Table 1 shows correlation coefficients at the document level for several DR metric representatives, and their document-level counterparts (DR_{doc}). For the sake of comparison, the performance of the METEOR metric is also reported[4].

Contrary to our expectations, DR_{doc} variants obtain lower levels of correlation than their DR

[4]We have used METEOR version 1.0 with default parameters optimized by its developers over adequacy and fluency assessments. The METEOR metric is publicly available at `http://www.cs.cmu.edu/~alavie/METEOR/`

Metric	Pearson$_\rho$	Spearman$_\rho$	Kendall$_\tau$
METEOR	**0.9182**	**0.8478**	**0.6728**
DR-$O_r(\star)$	0.8567	0.8061	0.6193
DR-$O_{rp}(\star)$	0.8286	0.7790	0.5875
DR-STM	0.7880	0.7468	0.5554
DR$_{doc}$-$O_r(\star)$	0.7936	0.7784	0.5875
DR$_{doc}$-$O_{rp}(\star)$	0.7219	0.6737	0.4929
DR$_{doc}$-STM	0.7553	0.7421	0.5458

Table 1: Meta-evaluation results at document level

Metric	Pearson$_\rho$	Spearman$_\rho$	Kendall$_\tau$
METEOR	**0.9669**	0.9151	0.8533
DR-$O_r(\star)$	0.9100	0.6549	0.5764
DR-$O_{rp}(\star)$	0.9471	0.7918	0.7261
DR-STM	0.9295	0.7676	0.7165
DR$_{doc}$-$O_r(\star)$	0.9534	0.8434	0.7828
DR$_{doc}$-$O_{rp}(\star)$	0.9595	0.9101	0.8518
DR$_{doc}$-STM	**0.9676**	**0.9655**	**0.9272**
DR-$O_r(\star)'$	0.9836	0.9594	0.9296
DR-$O_{rp}(\star)'$	**0.9959**	**1.0000**	**1.0000**
DR-STM$'$	0.9933	0.9634	0.9307

Table 2: Meta-evaluation results at system level

counterparts. There are three different factors which could provide a possible explanation for this negative result. First, the C&C Tools, like any other automatic linguistic processor are not perfect. Parsing errors could be causing the metric to confer less informed scores. This is especially relevant taking into account that candidate translations are not always well-formed. Secondly, we argue that the way in which we have obtained document-level quality assessments, as an average of segment-level assessments, may be biasing the correlation. Thirdly, perhaps the similarity measures employed are not able to take advantage of the document-level features provided by the discourse analysis. In the following subsection we show some error analysis we have conducted by inspecting particular cases.

Table 2 shows correlation coefficients at system level. In the case of DR and DR$_{doc}$ metrics, system scores are computed by simple average over individual documents. Interestingly, in this case DR$_{doc}$ variants seem to obtain higher correlation than their DR counterparts. The improvement is especially substantial in terms of Spearman and Kendall coefficients, which do not consider absolute values but ranking positions. However, it could be the case that it was just an average effect. While DR metrics compute system scores as an average of segment scores, DR$_{doc}$ metrics average directly document scores. In order to clarify this result, we have modified DR metrics so as to compute system scores as an average of document scores (DR$'$ variants, the last three rows in the table). It can be observed that DR' variants outperform their DR$_{doc}$ counterparts, thus confirming our suspicion about the averaging effect.

3.3 Analysis

It is worth noting that DR$_{doc}$ metrics are able to detect and deal with several linguistic phenomena related to both syntax and semantics at sentence and document level. Below, several examples illustrating the potential of this metric are presented.

Control structures. Control structures (either subject or object control) are always a difficult issue as they mix both syntactic and semantic knowledge. In Example 1 a couple of control structures must be identified and DR$_{doc}$ metrics deal correctly with the argument structure of all the verbs involved. Thus, in the first part of the sentence, a subject control verb can be identified being *"the minister"* the agent of both verb forms *"go"* and *"say"*. On the other hand, in the quoted question, the verb *"invite"* works as an object control verb because its patient *"Chechen representatives"* is also the agent of the verb *visit*.

Example 1: *The minister went on to say, "What would Moscow say if we were to invite Chechen representatives to visit Jerusalem?"*

Anaphora and pronoun resolution. Whenever there is a pronoun whose antecedent is a named entity (NE), the metric identifies correctly its antecedent. This feature is highly valuable because a relationship between syntax and semantics is established. Moreover, when dealing with Semantic Roles the roles of Agent or Patient are given to the antecedents instead of the pronouns. Thus, in Example 2 the antecedent of the relative pronoun *"who"* is the NE *"Putin"* and the patient of the verb *"classified"* is also the NE *"Putin"* instead of the relative pronoun *"who"*.

Example 2: *Putin, who was not classified as his country Hamas as "terrorist organizations", recently said that the European Union is "a big mistake" if it decided to suspend financial aid to the Palestinians.*

Nevertheless, although Boxer was expected to deal with long-distance anaphoric relations beyond the sentence, after analyzing several cases, results show that it did not succeed in capturing this type of relations as shown in Example 3. In this example, the antecedent of the pronoun *"he"* in the second sentence is the NE *"Roberto Calderoli"* which appears in the first sentence. DR_{doc} metrics should be capable of showing this connection. However, although the proper noun *"Roberto Calderoli"* is identified as a NE, it does not share the same reference as the third person singular pronoun *"he"*.

Example 3: *Roberto Calderoli does not intend to apologize. The newspaper Corriere Della Sera reported today, Saturday, that he said "I don't feel responsible for those deaths."*

4 Our Submission

Instead of participating with individual metrics, we have combined them by averaging their scores as described in (Giménez and Màrquez, 2008). This strategy has proven as an effective means of combining the scores conferred by different metrics (Callison-Burch et al., 2008; Callison-Burch et al., 2009). Metrics submitted are:

DR_{doc} an arithmetic mean over a heuristically-defined set of DR_{doc} metric variants, respectively computing lexical overlap, morphosyntactic overlap, and semantic tree matching ($M = \{$'DR_{doc}-$O_r(\star)$', 'DR_{doc}-$O_{rp}(\star)$', 'DR_{doc}-STM_4'$\}$). Since DR_{doc} metrics do not operate over individual segments, we have assigned each segment the score of the document in which it is contained.

DR a measure analog to DR_{doc} but using the default version of DR metrics operating at the segment level ($M = \{$'DR-$O_r(\star)$', 'DR-$O_{rp}(\star)$', 'DR-STM_4'$\}$).

ULC_h an arithmetic mean over a heuristically-defined set of metrics operating at different linguistic levels, including lexical metrics, and measures of overlap between constituent parses, dependency parses, semantic roles, and discourse representations ($M = \{$'$ROUGE_W$', 'METEOR', 'DP-HWC_r', 'DP-$O_c(\star)$', 'DP-$O_l(\star)$', 'DP-$O_r(\star)$', 'CP-STM_4', 'SR-$O_r(\star)$', 'SR-O_{rv}', 'DR-$O_{rp}(\star)$'$\}$). This metric corresponds exactly to the metric submitted in our previous participation.

The performance of these metrics at the document and system levels is shown in Table 3.

5 Conclusions and Future Work

We have presented a modified version of the DR metrics by Giménez and Màrquez (2009) which, instead of limiting their scope to the segment level, are able to capture and exploit document-level features. However, results in terms of correlation with human assessments have not reported any improvement of these metrics over their sentence-level counterparts as document and system quality predictors. It must be clarified whether the problem is on the side of the linguistic tools, in the similarity measure, or in the way in which we have built document-level human assessments.

For future work, we plan to continue the error analysis to clarify why DR_{doc} metrics do not outperform their DR counterparts at the document level, and how to improve their behavior. This

Metric	Document level			System level		
	Pearson$_\rho$	Spearman$_\rho$	Kendall$_\tau$	Pearson$_\rho$	Spearman$_\rho$	Kendall$_\tau$
ULC$_{DR}$	0.8418	0.8066	0.6135	0.9349	0.7936	0.7145
ULC$_{DRdoc}$	0.7739	0.7358	0.5474	0.9655	0.9062	0.8435
ULC$_h$	0.8963	0.8614	0.6848	0.9842	0.9088	0.8638

Table 3: Meta-evaluation results at document and system level for submitted metrics

may imply defining new metrics possibly using alternative linguistic processors. In addition, we plan to work on the identification and analysis of discourse markers. Finally, we plan to repeat this experiment over other test beds with document structure, such as those from the 2009 Workshop on Statistical Machine Translation shared task (Callison-Burch et al., 2009) and the 2009 NIST MT Evaluation Campaign (Przybocki et al., 2009). In the case that document-level assessments are not provided, we will also explore the possibility of producing them ourselves.

Acknowledgments

This work has been partially funded by the Spanish Government (projects OpenMT-2, TIN2009-14675-C03, and KNOW, TIN-2009-14715-C0403) and the European Community's Seventh Framework Programme (FP7/2007-2013) under grant agreement numbers 247762 (FAUST project, FP7-ICT-2009-4-247762) and 247914 (MOLTO project, FP7-ICT-2009-4-247914). We are also thankful to anonymous reviewers for their comments and suggestions.

References

Johan Bos. 2008. Wide-coverage semantic analysis with boxer. In Johan Bos and Rodolfo Delmonte, editors, *Semantics in Text Processing. STEP 2008 Conference Proceedings*, Research in Computational Semantics, pages 277–286. College Publications.

Chris Callison-Burch, Cameron Fordyce, Philipp Koehn, Christof Monz, and Josh Schroeder. 2008. Further meta-evaluation of machine translation. In *Proceedings of the Third Workshop on Statistical Machine Translation*, pages 70–106.

Chris Callison-Burch, Philipp Koehn, Christof Monz, and Josh Schroeder. 2009. Findings of the 2009 Workshop on Statistical Machine Translation. In *Proceedings of the Fourth Workshop on Statistical Machine Translation*, pages 1–28.

James Curran, Stephen Clark, and Johan Bos. 2007. Linguistically motivated large-scale nlp with c&c and boxer. In *Proceedings of the 45th Annual Meeting of the Association for Computational Linguistics Companion Volume Proceedings of the Demo and Poster Sessions*, pages 33–36.

Bradley Efron and Robert Tibshirani. 1986. Bootstrap Methods for Standard Errors, Confidence Intervals, and Other Measures of Statistical Accuracy. *Statistical Science*, 1(1):54–77.

Jesús Giménez and Lluís Màrquez. 2007. Linguistic Features for Automatic Evaluation of Heterogeneous MT Systems. In *Proceedings of the ACL Workshop on Statistical Machine Translation*, pages 256–264.

Jesús Giménez and Lluís Màrquez. 2008. A Smorgasbord of Features for Automatic MT Evaluation. In *Proceedings of the Third Workshop on Statistical Machine Translation*, pages 195–198.

Jesús Giménez and Lluís Màrquez. 2009. On the Robustness of Syntactic and Semantic Features for Automatic MT Evaluation. In *Proceedings of the 4th Workshop on Statistical Machine Translation (EACL 2009)*.

Hans Kamp and Uwe Reyle. 1993. *From Discourse to Logic: An Introduction to Modeltheoretic Semantics of Natural Language, Formal Logic and Discourse Representation Theory*. Dordrecht: Kluwer.

Philipp Koehn. 2004. Statistical Significance Tests for Machine Translation Evaluation. In *Proceedings of the Conference on Empirical Methods in Natural Language Processing (EMNLP)*, pages 388–395.

Ding Liu and Daniel Gildea. 2005. Syntactic Features for Evaluation of Machine Translation. In *Proceedings of ACL Workshop on Intrinsic and Extrinsic Evaluation Measures for MT and/or Summarization*, pages 25–32.

Mark Przybocki, Kay Peterson, and Sébastien Bronsart. 2008. NIST Metrics for Machine Translation 2008 Evaluation (MetricsMATR08). Technical report, National Institute of Standards and Technology.

Mark Przybocki, Kay Peterson, and Sébastien Bronsart. 2009. NIST Open Machine Translation 2009 Evaluation (MT09). Technical report, National Institute of Standards and Technology.

METEOR-NEXT and the METEOR Paraphrase Tables: Improved Evaluation Support for Five Target Languages

Michael Denkowski and **Alon Lavie**
Language Technologies Institute
School of Computer Science
Carnegie Mellon University
Pittsburgh, PA 15232, USA
{mdenkows,alavie}@cs.cmu.edu

Abstract

This paper describes our submission to the WMT10 Shared Evaluation Task and MetricsMATR10. We present a version of the METEOR-NEXT metric with paraphrase tables for five target languages. We describe the creation of these paraphrase tables and conduct a tuning experiment that demonstrates consistent improvement across all languages over baseline versions of the metric without paraphrase resources.

1 Introduction

Workshops such as WMT (Callison-Burch et al., 2009) and MetricsMATR (Przybocki et al., 2008) focus on the need for accurate automatic metrics for evaluating the quality of machine translation (MT) output. While these workshops evaluate metric performance on many target languages, most metrics are limited to English due to the relative lack of lexical resources for other languages.

This paper describes a language-independent method for adding paraphrase support to the METEOR-NEXT metric for all WMT10 target languages. Taking advantage of the large parallel corpora released for the translation tasks often accompanying evaluation tasks, we automatically construct paraphrase tables using the *pivot* method (Bannard and Callison-Burch, 2005). We use the WMT09 human evaluation data to tune versions of METEOR-NEXT with and without paraphrases and report significantly better performance for versions with paraphrase support.

2 The METEOR-NEXT Metric

The METEOR-NEXT metric (Denkowski and Lavie, 2010) evaluates a machine translation hypothesis against a reference translation by calculating a similarity score based on an alignment between the two strings. When multiple references are provided, the hypothesis is scored against each and the reference producing the highest score is used. Alignments are formed in two stages: search space construction and alignment selection.

For a single hypothesis-reference pair, the space of possible alignments is constructed by identifying all possible word and phrase matches between the strings according to the following matchers:

Exact: Words are matched if and only if their surface forms are identical.

Stem: Words are stemmed using a language-appropriate Snowball Stemmer (Porter, 2001) and matched if the stems are identical.

Synonym: Words are matched if they are both members of a synonym set according to the WordNet (Miller and Fellbaum, 2007) database.

Paraphrase: Phrases are matched if they are listed as paraphrases in a paraphrase table. The tables used are described in Section 3.

Previously, full support has been limited to English, with French, German, and Spanish having exact and stem match support only, and Czech having exact match support only.

Although the exact, stem, and synonym matchers identify *word* matches while the paraphrase matcher identifies *phrase* matches, all matches can be generalized to phrase matches with a start position and phrase length in each string. A word occurring less than *length* positions after a match start is considered *covered* by the match. Exact, stem, and synonym matches always cover one word in each string.

Once the search space is constructed, the final alignment is identified as the largest possible subset of all matches meeting the following criteria in order of importance:

1. Each word in each sentence is covered by zero or one matches

2. Largest number of covered words across both

Proceedings of the Joint 5th Workshop on Statistical Machine Translation and MetricsMATR, pages 339–342,
Uppsala, Sweden, 15-16 July 2010.

sentences

3. Smallest number of chunks, where a chunk is defined as a series of matched phrases that is contiguous and identically ordered in both sentences

4. Smallest sum of absolute distances between match start positions in the two sentences (prefer to align words and phrases that occur at similar positions in both sentences)

Once an alignment is selected, the METEOR-NEXT score is calculated as follows. The number of words in the translation hypothesis (t) and reference (r) are counted. For each of the matchers (m_i), count the number of words covered by matches of this type in the hypothesis ($m_i(t)$) and reference ($m_i(r)$) and apply matcher weight (w_i). The weighted Precision and Recall are then calculated:

$$P = \frac{\sum_i w_i \cdot m_i(t)}{|t|} \qquad R = \frac{\sum_i w_i \cdot m_i(r)}{|r|}$$

The parameterized harmonic mean of P and R (van Rijsbergen, 1979) is then calculated:

$$F_{mean} = \frac{P \cdot R}{\alpha \cdot P + (1 - \alpha) \cdot R}$$

To account for gaps and differences in word order, a fragmentation penalty (Lavie and Agarwal, 2007) is calculated using the total number of matched words (m) and number of chunks (ch):

$$Pen = \gamma \cdot \left(\frac{ch}{m}\right)^{\beta}$$

The final METEOR-NEXT score is then calculated:

$$Score = (1 - Pen) \cdot F_{mean}$$

The parameters α, β, γ, and $w_i \ldots w_n$ can be tuned to maximize correlation with various types of human judgments.

3 The METEOR Paraphrase Tables

To extend support for WMT10 target languages, we use released parallel corpora to construct paraphrase tables for English, Czech, German, Spanish, and French. These tables are used by the METEOR-NEXT paraphrase matcher to identify additional phrase matches in each language.

3.1 Paraphrasing with Parallel Corpora

Following Bannard and Callison-Burch (2005), we extract paraphrases automatically from bilingual corpora using a *pivot phrase* method. For a given language pair, word alignment, phrase extraction, and phrase scoring are conducted on parallel corpora to build a single bilingual phrase table for the language pair. For each native phrase (n_1) in the table, we identify each foreign phrase (f) that translates n_1. Each alternate native phrase ($n_2 \neq n_1$) that translates f is considered a paraphrase of n_1 with probability $P(f|n_1) \cdot P(n_2|f)$. The total probability of n_2 paraphrasing n_1 is given as the sum over all f:

$$P(n_2|n_1) = \sum_f P(f|n_1) \cdot P(n_2|f)$$

The same method can be used to identify foreign paraphrases (f_1, f_2) given native pivot phrases n. To merge same-language paraphrases extracted from different parallel corpora, we take the mean of the corpus-specific paraphrase probabilities (P_C) weighted by the size of the corpora (C) used for paraphrase extraction:

$$P(n_2|n_1) = \frac{\sum_C |C| \cdot P_C(n_2|n_1)}{\sum_C |C|} \quad .$$

To improve paraphrase accuracy, we apply multiple filtering techniques during paraphrase extraction. The following are applied to each paraphrase *instance* (n_1, f, n_2):

1. Discard paraphrases with very low probability ($P(f|n_1) \cdot P(n_2|f) < 0.001$)

2. Discard paraphrases for which n_1, f, or n_2 contain *any* punctuation characters.

3. Discard paraphrases for which n_1, f, or n_2 contain *only* common words. Common words are defined as having relative frequency of 0.001 or greater in the parallel corpus.

Remaining phrase instances are summed to construct corpus-specific paraphrase tables. Same-language paraphrase tables are selectively merged as part of the tuning process described in Section 4.2. Final paraphrase tables are further filtered to include only paraphrases with probabilities above a final threshold (0.01).

Language Pair		Corpus	Phrase Table
Target	Source	Sentences	Phrase Pairs
English	Czech	7,321,950	128,326,269
English	German	1,630,132	84,035,599
English	Spanish	7,965,250	363,714,779
English	French	8,993,161	404,883,736
German	Spanish	1,305,650	70,992,157

Table 1: Sizes of training corpora and phrase tables used for paraphrase extraction

Language	Pivot Languages	Phrase Pairs
English	German, Spanish, French	6,236,236
Czech	English	756,113
German	English, Spanish	3,521,052
Spanish	English, German	6,352,690
French	English	3,382,847

Table 2: Sizes of final paraphrase tables

3.2 Available Data

We conduct paraphrase extraction using parallel corpora released for the WMT10 Shared Translation Task. This includes Europarl corpora (French-English, Spanish-English, and German-English), news commentary (French-English, Spanish-English, German-English, and Czech-English), United Nations corpora (French-English and Spanish-English), and the CzEng (Bojar and Žabokrtský, 2009) corpus sections 0-8 (Czech-English). In addition, we use the German-Spanish Europarl corpus released for WMT08 (Callison-Burch et al., 2008).

3.3 Paraphrase Table Construction

Using all available data for each language pair, we create bilingual phrase tables for the following: French-English, Spanish-English, German-English, Czech-English, and German-Spanish. The full training corpora and resulting phrase tables are described in Table 1. For each phrase table, both foreign and native paraphrases are extracted. Same-language paraphrases are selectively merged as described in Section 4.2 to produce the final paraphrase tables described in Table 2. To keep table size reasonable, we only extract paraphrases for phrases occurring in target corpora consisting of the pooled development data from the WMT08, WMT09, and WMT10 translation tasks (10,158 sentences for Czech, 20,258 sentences for all other languages).

Target	Systems	Usable Judgments
English	45	20,357
Czech	5	11,242
German	11	6,563
Spanish	9	3,249
French	12	2,967

Table 3: Human ranking judgment data from WMT09

4 Tuning METEOR-NEXT

4.1 Development Data

As part of the WMT10 Shared Evaluation Task, data from WMT09 (Callison-Burch et al., 2009), including system output, reference translations, and human judgments, is available for metric development. As metrics are evaluated primarily on their ability to rank system output on the segment level, we select the human ranking judgments from WMT09 as our development set (described in Table 3).

4.2 Tuning Procedure

Tuning a version of METEOR-NEXT consists of selecting parameters (α, β, γ, $w_i...w_n$) that optimize an objective function for a given language. If multiple paraphrase tables exist for a language, tuning also requires selecting the optimal set of tables to merge.

For WMT10, we tune to rank consistency on the WMT09 data. Following Callison-Burch et. al (2009), we discard judgments where system outputs are deemed equivalent and calculate the proportion of remaining judgments preserved when system outputs are ranked by automatic metric scores. For each target language, tuning is conducted as an exhaustive grid search over metric parameters and possible paraphrase tables, resulting in global optima for both.

5 Experiments

To evaluate the impact of our paraphrase tables on metric performance, we tune versions of METEOR-NEXT with and without the paraphrase matchers for each language. For further comparison, we tune a version of METEOR-NEXT using the TERp English paraphrase table (Snover et al., 2009) used by previous versions of the metric.

As shown in Table 4, the addition of paraphrases leads to a better tuning point for every target language. The best scoring subset of paraphrase ta-

Language	Paraphrases	Rank Consistency	α	β	γ	w_{exact}	w_{stem}	w_{syn}	w_{par}
English	none	0.619	0.85	2.35	0.45	1.00	0.80	0.60	–
	TERp	0.625	0.70	1.40	0.25	1.00	0.80	0.80	0.60
	de+es+fr	**0.629**	0.75	0.60	0.35	1.00	0.80	0.80	0.60
Czech	none	0.564	0.95	0.20	0.70	1.00	–	–	–
	en	**0.574**	0.95	2.15	0.35	1.00	–	–	0.40
German	none	0.550	0.20	0.75	0.25	1.00	0.80	–	–
	en+es	**0.576**	0.75	0.80	0.90	1.00	0.20	–	0.80
Spanish	none	0.586	0.95	0.55	0.90	1.00	0.80	–	–
	en+de	**0.608**	0.15	0.25	0.75	1.00	0.80	–	0.40
French	none	0.696	0.95	0.80	0.35	1.00	0.60	–	–
	en	**0.707**	0.90	0.85	0.45	1.00	0.00	–	0.60

Table 4: Optimal METEOR-NEXT parameters with and without paraphrases for WMT10 target languages

bles for English also outperforms the TERp paraphrase table.

Analysis of the phrase matches contributed by the paraphrase matchers reveals an interesting point about the task of paraphrasing for MT evaluation. Despite filtering techniques, the final paraphrase tables include some unusual, inaccurate, or highly context-dependent paraphrases. However, the vast majority of matches identified between actual system output and reference translations correspond to valid paraphrases. In many cases, the evaluation task itself acts as a final filter; to produce a phrase that can match a spurious paraphrase, not only must a MT system produce incorrect output, but it must produce output that overlaps exactly with an obscure paraphrase of some phrase in the reference translation. As systems are far more likely to produce phrases with similar words to those in reference translations, far more valid paraphrases exist in typical system output.

6 Conclusions

We have presented versions of METEOR-NEXT and paraphrase tables for five target languages. Tuning experiments indicate consistent improvements across all languages over baseline versions of the metric. Created for MT evaluation, the METEOR paraphrase tables can also be used for other tasks in MT and natural language processing. Further, the techniques used to build the paraphrase tables are language-independent and can be used to improve evaluation support for other target languages. METEOR-NEXT, the METEOR paraphrase tables, and the software used to generate paraphrases are released under an open source license and made available via the METEOR website.

References

Colin Bannard and Chris Callison-Burch. 2005. Paraphrasing with bilingual parallel corpora. In *Proc. of ACL05*.

Ondřej Bojar and Zdeněk Žabokrtský. 2009. CzEng 0.9: Large Parallel Treebank with Rich Annotation. *Prague Bulletin of Mathematical Linguistics*.

Chris Callison-Burch, Cameron Fordyce, Philipp Koehn, Christof Monz, and Josh Schroeder. 2008. Further meta-evaluation of machine translation. In *Proc. of WMT08*.

Chris Callison-Burch, Philipp Koehn, Christof Monz, and Josh Schroeder. 2009. Findings of WMT09. In *Proc. of WMT09*.

Michael Denkowski and Alon Lavie. 2010. Extending the METEOR Machine Translation Metric to the Phrase Level for Improved Correlation with Human Post-Editing Judgments. In *Proc. NAACL/HLT 2010*.

Alon Lavie and Abhaya Agarwal. 2007. METEOR: An Automatic Metric for MT Evaluation with High Levels of Correlation with Human Judgments. In *Proc. of WMT07*.

George Miller and Christiane Fellbaum. 2007. WordNet. http://wordnet.princeton.edu/.

Martin Porter. 2001. Snowball: A language for stemming algorithms. http://snowball.tartarus.org/texts/.

M. Przybocki, K. Peterson, and S Bronsart. 2008. Official results of the NIST 2008 "Metrics for MAchine TRanslation" Challenge (MetricsMATR08).

Matthew Snover, Nitin Madnani, Bonnie Dorr, and Richard Schwartz. 2009. Fluency, Adequacy, or HTER? Exploring Different Human Judgments with a Tunable MT Metric. In *Proc. of WMT09*.

C. van Rijsbergen, 1979. *Information Retrieval*, chapter 7. 2nd edition.

Normalized Compression Distance Based Measures for MetricsMATR 2010

Marcus Dobrinkat and **Jaakko Väyrynen** and **Tero Tapiovaara**
Adaptive Informatics Research Centre
Aalto University School of Science and Technology
P.O. Box 15400, FI-00076 Aalto, Finland
{marcus.dobrinkat,jaakko.j.vayrynen,tero.tapiovaara}@tkk.fi

Kimmo Kettunen
Kymenlaakso University of Applied Sciences
P.O. Box 9, FI-48401 Kotka, Finland
Kimmo.kettunen@kyamk.fi

Abstract

We present the MT-NCD and MT-mNCD machine translation evaluation metrics as submission to the machine translation evaluation shared task (MetricsMATR 2010). The metrics are based on normalized compression distance (NCD), a general information theoretic measure of string similarity, and evaluated against human judgments from the WMT08 shared task. The experiments show that 1) our metric improves correlation to human judgments by using flexible matching, 2) segment replication is effective, and 3) our NCD-inspired method for multiple references indicates improved results. Generally, the proposed MT-NCD and MT-mNCD methods correlate competitively with human judgments compared to commonly used machine translations evaluation metrics, for instance, BLEU.

1 Introduction

The quality of automatic machine translation (MT) evaluation metrics plays an important role in the development of MT systems. Human evaluation would no longer be necessary if automatic MT metrics correlated perfectly with manual judgments. Besides high correlation with human judgments of translation quality, a good metric should be language independent, fast to compute and sensitive enough to reliably detect small improvements in MT systems.

Recently there have been some experiments with normalized compression distance (NCD) as a method for automatic evaluation of machine translation. NCD is a general string similarity measure that has been useful for clustering in various tasks (Cilibrasi and Vitanyi, 2005).

Parker (2008) introduced BADGER, a machine translation evaluation metric that uses NCD together with a language independent word normalization method. Kettunen (2009) independently applied NCD to the direct evaluation of translations. He showed with a small corpus of three language pairs that the scores of NCD and METEOR (v0.6) from translations of 10–12 MT systems were highly correlated.

Väyrynen et al. (2010) have extended the work by showing that NCD can be used to rank translations of different MT systems so that the ranking order correlates with human rankings at the same level as BLEU (Papineni et al., 2001). For translations into English, NCD had an overall system-level correlation of 0.66 whereas the best method, ULC had an overall correlation of 0.76, and BLEU had an overall correlation of 0.65. NCD presents a viable alternative to the de facto standard BLEU. Both metrics are language independent, simple and efficient to compute. However, NCD is a general measure of similarity that has been applied in many domains. More advanced methods achieve better correlation with human judgments, but typically use additional language specific linguistic resources. Dobrinkat et al. (2010) experimented with relaxed word matching, adding language specific resources to NCD. The metric called mNCD, which works similarly to mBLEU (Agarwal and Lavie, 2008), showed improved correlation to human judgments in English, the only language where a METEOR synonym module was used.

The motivation for this challenge submission is to evaluate the MT-NCD and MT-mNCD metric performance in an open competition with state-of-

Proceedings of the Joint 5th Workshop on Statistical Machine Translation and MetricsMATR, pages 343–348,
Uppsala, Sweden, 15-16 July 2010. ©2010 Association for Computational Linguistics

the-art MT evaluation metrics. Our experiments and submission build on NCD and mNCD. We expand NCD to handle multiple references and report experimental results for replicating segments as a preprocessing step that improves the NCD as an MT evaluation metric.

2 NCD-based MT evaluation metrics

NCD-based MT evaluation metrics build on the idea that a string x is similar to another string y, when both share common substrings. When describing y, common substrings do not have to be repeated, but can be referenced to x. This is done when compressing the concatenation of x and y, which results in smaller output when more information of y is already included in x.

2.1 Normalized Compression Distance

The normalized compression distance, as defined by Cilibrasi and Vitanyi (2005) is given in Equation 1, in which $C(x)$ is the length of the compression of x and $C(x, y)$ is the length of the compression of the concatenation of x and y.

$$\text{NCD}(x, y) = \frac{C(x, y) - \min\{C(x), C(y)\}}{\max\{C(x), C(y)\}} \quad (1)$$

NCD computes the distance as a score closer to one for very different strings and closer to zero for more similar strings. Most MT evaluation metrics are defined as similarity measures in contrast to NCD, which is a distance measure. For easier comparison with other MT evaluation metrics, we define the NCD based MT evaluation similarity metric MT-NCD as $1 - \text{NCD}$.

NCD is a practically usable form of the uncomputable normalized information distance (NID), a general metric for the similarity of two objects. NID is based on the notion of Kolmogorov complexity $K(x)$, a theoretical measure for the algorithmic information content of a string x. It is defined as the shortest universal Turing machine that prints x and stops (Solomonoff, 1964). NCD approximates NID by the use of a compressor $C(x)$ that presents a computable approximation of the Kolmogorov complexity $K(x)$.

2.2 NCD with multiple references

Most ideas can be described with in different ways, therefore using only one reference translation for the evaluation of a candidate sentence is not ideal and the exploitation of knowledge in several different reference translations is helpful for automatic MT evaluation.

One simple way for handling multiple references is to evaluate against each reference individually and select the maximum score. Although this works, it is clearly not optimal. We developed the NCD_m metric, which is inspired by NCD. It considers all references simultaneously and the quality of a translation t against multiple references $R = \{r_1, \ldots, r_m\}$ is assessed as

$$\text{NCD}_m(t, R) = \frac{\max\{C(t|R), \min_{r \in R} C(r|t)\}}{\max\{C(t), \min_{r \in R} C(r)\}} \quad (2)$$

where $C(x|y) = C(x, y) - C(y)$ approximates conditional algorithmic information with the compressor C. The NCD_m similarity metric with a single reference ($m = 1$) is equal to NCD in Equation 1. Again, we define MT-NCD_m as $1-\text{NCD}_m$.

Figure 1 shows how both, the MT-NCD_m and the BLEU metric change with a different number of references when the translation is varied from correct to a random sequence of words. The scores are computed with 249 sentences from the LDC2010E28Dev data set using the first reference as the correct translation. A higher score with multiple references against the correct translation indicates that the measure is able to take into account information from multiple references at the same time.

The words in the candidate translation are replaced with probability p with a word randomly selected with uniform probability from a lexicon created from all reference translations. This simulates partially correct translations. The words are changed in a simple way without deletions, insertions or word order permutations. The MT-NCD_m score increases with more than one reference translation and random changes to the sentence reduce the score roughly proportional to the number of changed words. With BLEU, the score is affected more by a small number of changes.

2.3 mNCD

One enhancement to the basic NCD as automatic evaluation metric is mNCD (Dobrinkat et al., 2010), which provides relaxed word matching based on the flexible matching modules of METEOR (Agarwal and Lavie, 2008).

What mNCD does is that it changes the reference sentence to be more similar to the candi-

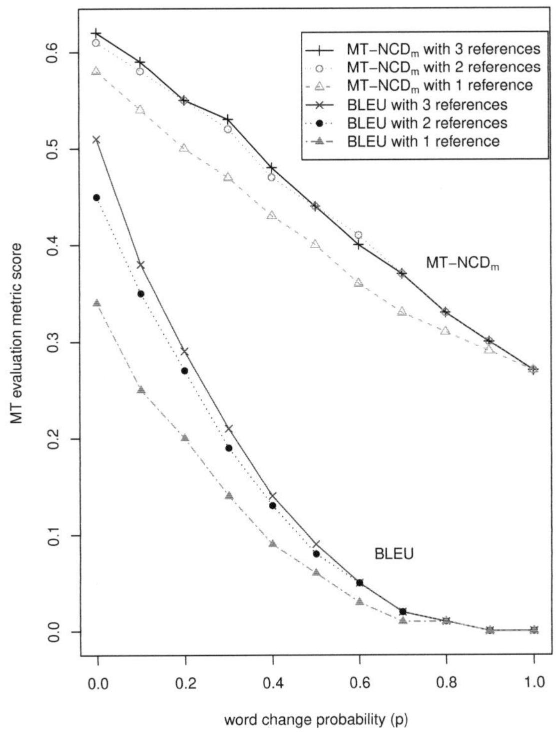

Figure 1: The MT-NCD$_m$ and BLEU scores with a different number of multiple references against correct translation with random word change probability (p).

date, given that some of the words are synonyms or share the same stem. Subsequent analysis using any n-gram based automatic analysis should result in a larger similarity score in the hope that this reflects more than just the surface similarity between the candidate and the reference.

Given suitable Wordnet resources, mNCD should alleviate the problem of translation variability especially in absence of multiple reference translations. Our submission uses the default METEOR `exact stem synonym` modules, which provide synonyms only for English. We base our submission metric on the MT-NCD metric and therefore define MT-mNCD as $1 -$ mNCD.

3 MT Evaluation System Description

3.1 System Parameters

The system parameters for the submission metrics include how candidates and references are preprocessed, the choice of compressor for the NCD itself, as well as the granularity of how large segments are evaluated by NCD and how they are combined into a final score.

Partly due to time constraints we decided not to introduce language specific parameters, therefore we chose those parameter values that perform well in overall and are simple to compute.

3.1.1 Preprocessing

Character casing For MT-NCD, we did experiments without preprocessing and with lower-casing candidates and references. On average over all tasks for language pairs into English, lower-casing consistently decreased the RANK correlation scores but increased the CONST correlation scores. No consistent effect could be found for the language pairs from English. In our submission metrics we use no preprocessing.

For MT-mNCD the used METEOR matching module lower-cases the adapted words by default. After adapting a synonym in a reference, we tried to keep the casing as it was in the candidate, which we called real-casing. We use no real-casing for our submitted MT-mNCD metric as this did not improve results consistently over all task into English.

Segment Replication Compression algorithms may not work optimally with short strings, which would deteriorate the approximation of Kolmogorov complexity. Our hypothesis was that a replication of a string ($"abc"$) multiple times ($3 \times "abc" = "abcabcabc"$) could help the compression algorithm to produce a better estimate of the algorithmic information. This was tested in the MT evaluation framework, and correlation between MT-NCD and human judgments improved when the segments were replicated two times. Further replication did not produce improvements.

Results for the MT-NCD metric with replications one, two and three times are shown in Table 1. The results are averages over all used languages. With two compared to one replication, the details for each language show that RANK correlation is improved for the target languages English and French, but degrades for German and Spanish. CONST andYES/NO correlation improve for all languages except German. We did not use replication in our submissions.

3.1.2 Block size

The block size parameter governs the number of joined segments that are compared with NCD as a single string. On one extreme, with block size one,

		RANK	CONST	YES/NO	TOTAL
MT-NCD	rep 1	.61	.71	.73	.68
MT-NCD	rep 2	.62	.73	.75	.70
MT-NCD	rep 3	.61	.72	.74	.69

Table 1: Effect of the replication factor on MT-NCD correlation scores for the bz2 compressor with block size one as average over all languages.

each segment is evaluated separately and the segment scores are aggregated to a document score. This is similar to how other MT metrics, for example, BLEU, work. The other extreme is to join all segments together, with block size equal to the number of segments, and evaluate it as a single string, which is similar to document comparison. For block aggregation we experimented with arithmetic and geometric mean and obtained very similar results. We selected arithmetic mean for the submission metrics.

Figure 2 shows the block size effect on the correlation between MT-NCD and human judgments for different target languages. Except for Spanish, our experiments indicate that the block size value has little effect. Therefore, and given how other evaluation metrics work, we chose a block size of one for our submission metrics. We noticed inconsistencies with Spanish in other settings as well and will investigate these issues further.

3.1.3 Compressor

There are several universal compressors that can be utilized with NCD, for instance, zlib/gzip, bz2 and PPMZ, which represent different approaches to compression. In terms of compression rate, PPMZ is the best of the mentioned methods, but it is considerably slower to compute compared to the other methods. In terms of correlation with human judgments, NCD using bz2 performs slightly worse than using PPMZ. Given much shorter compression times for bz2 with very little correlation performance degradation, our choice for the submission is the more standard bz2 compressor.

3.1.4 Segment Interleaving

Computation of NCD between longer texts (e.g. documents) may exceed the internal compressor window size that is present in some compression algorithms (Cebrian et al., 2005). In this case, only a part of the texts to be compared are visible at any time to the compressor and similarities to the text outside the window will be missed. One solution for the MT evaluation task is to use utilize the known parallel segments of candidate and reference translations. The two segment lists can be interleaved so that the corresponding segments are always adjacent and the compression window size is not exceeded for matching segments.

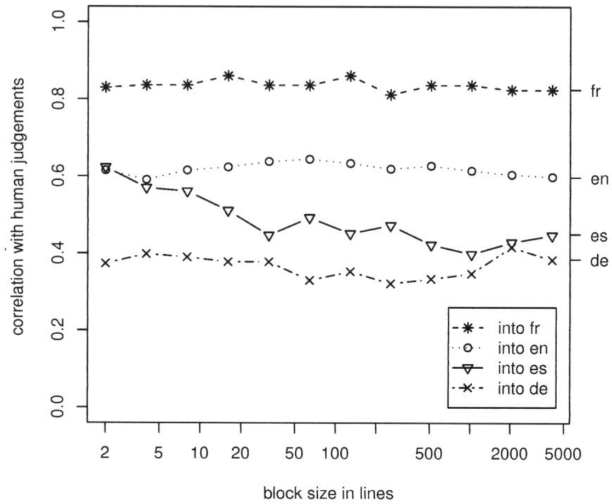

Figure 2: Effect of the block size on the correlation of MT-NCD to human judgments for the system level evaluation.

For our submission, we chose a block size of one, therefore every segment is evaluated individually. As a result, segment interleaving does not have any effect. Segment interleaving is affective in the block size evaluation and results shown in Figure 2.

3.2 Evaluation Experiments

We chose parameters and evaluated our metrics using the WMT08 part of the MetricsMATR 2010 development data, which contains human judgments of the 2008 ACL Workshop on Statistical Machine Translation (Callison-Burch et al., 2008) for translations from a total of 30 MT systems between English and five other European languages. There are human evaluations and several automatic evaluations for the translations, divided into several tasks defined by the language pair and the domain of the translated sentences. For each of these tasks, the WMT08 data contains about 2 000 reference sentences (segments) plus their aligned translations for 12 to 17 different translation systems, depending on the language pair.

The human judgments include three categories which contain evaluations for at most one segment at a time, not whole documents. In the RANK category, humans had to rank the output of five MT systems according to quality. The CONST category contains rankings for short phrases (constituents), and the YES/NO category contains binary answers to judge if a short phrase is an acceptable translation or not.

We report RANK, CONST and YES/NO system level correlations to human judgments as results of our metrics for French, Spanish and German both from and to English. The English–Spanish news task was left out as most metrics had negative correlation with human judgments.

The evaluation methodology used in Callison-Burch et al. (2008) allows us to measure how each MT evaluation metric correlates with human judgments on the system level, in which all translations from each MT system are aggregated into a single score. The system rankings based on the scores are compared to human judgments.

Spearman's rank correlation coefficient ρ was calculated between each MT metric and human judgment category using the simplified equation:

$$\rho = 1 - \frac{6 \sum_i d_i}{n(n^2 - 1)} \quad (3)$$

where for each system i, d_i is the difference between the rank derived from annotators' input and the rank obtained from the metric. From the annotators' input, the n MT systems were ranked based on the number of times each system's output was selected as the best translation divided by the number of times each system was part of a judgment.

3.3 Results

The results for WMT08 data for our submitted metrics are shown in Table 2 and are sorted by the RANK category separately for language pairs from English and into English.

For tasks into English, the correlations show that MT-mNCD improves over the MT-NCD metric in all categories. Also the flexible matching seems to work better for NCD-based metrics than for BLEU, where mBLEU only improves the CONST correlation scores. For tasks from English, MT-mNCD shows slightly higher correlation compared to MT-NCD, except for the YES/NO category. The standard BLEU correlation score is best of the shown evaluation metrics. Relaxed matching using mBLEU does not improve BLEU's RANK correlation scores here either, but CONST and YES/NO correlation performs better relative to BLEU than MT-mNCD compared to MT-NCD.

		RANK	CONST	YES/NO	TOTAL
INTO EN	MT-mNCD	.61	.74	.75	.70
	MT-NCD	.57	.69	.71	.66
	mBLEU	.50	.76	.70	.65
	BLEU	.50	.72	.74	.65
FROM EN	BLEU	.68	.79	.79	.75
	MT-mNCD	.67	.76	.74	.72
	MT-NCD	.65	.73	.75	.71
	mBLEU	.63	.81	.81	.75

Table 2: Average system-level correlations for the WMT08 data sorted by RANK into English and from English for our submitted metrics MT-NCD and MT-mNCD and for BLEU and mBLEU

4 Conclusions

In our submissions, we applied MT-NCD and MT-mNCD metrics and extended the NCD MT evaluation metric to handle multiple references. The reported experiment indicate a possible improvement for the multiple references.

We showed that a replication of segments as a preprocessing step improves the correlation to human judgments. The string replication might alleviate problems in the compressor for short strings and thus could provide better estimates of the algorithmic information.

The results of our experiments show that relaxed matching in MT-mNCD works well with proper synonym dictionaries, but is less effective for tasks from English, which only use stemming.

MT-mNCD and MT-NCD are reasonably simple to compute and utilize standard and widely used resources, such as the bz2 compression algorithm and WordNet. The metrics perform comparable to the de facto standard BLEU. Improvements with language dependent resources, in particular relaxed matching using synonym dictionaries proved to be useful.

References

Abhaya Agarwal and Alon Lavie. 2008. METEOR, M-BLEU and M-TER: evaluation metrics for high-correlation with human rankings of machine translation output. In *StatMT '08: Proceedings of the Third Workshop on Statistical Machine Translation*, pages 115–118, Morristown, NJ, USA. Association for Computational Linguistics.

Chris Callison-Burch, Cameron Fordyce, Philipp Koehn, Christof Monz, and Josh Schroeder. 2008. Further meta-evaluation of machine translation. In *StatMT '08: Proceedings of the Third Workshop on Statistical Machine Translation*, pages 70–106, Morristown, NJ, USA. Association for Computational Linguistics.

Manuel Cebrian, Manuel Alfonseca, and Alfonso Ortega. 2005. Common pitfalls using the normalized compression distance: What to watch out for in a compressor. *Communications in Information and Systems*, 5(4):367–384.

Rudi Cilibrasi and Paul Vitanyi. 2005. Clustering by compression. *IEEE Transactions on Information Theory*, 51:1523–1545.

Marcus Dobrinkat, Tero Tapiovaara, Jaakko J. Väyrynen, and Kimmo Kettunen. 2010. Evaluating machine translations using mNCD. In *Proceedings of the ACL-2010 (to appear)*, Uppsala, Sweden.

Kimmo Kettunen. 2009. Packing it all up in search for a language independent MT quality measure tool. In *Proceedings of LTC-09, 4th Language and Technology Conference*, pages 280–284, Poznan.

K. Papineni, S. Roukos, T. Ward, and W. Zhu. 2001. BLEU: a method for automatic evaluation of machine translation. Technical Report RC22176 (W0109-022), IBM Research Division, Thomas J. Watson Research Center.

Steven Parker. 2008. BADGER: A new machine translation metric. In *Metrics for Machine Translation Challenge 2008*, Waikiki, Hawai'i, October. AMTA.

Ray Solomonoff. 1964. Formal theory of inductive inference. Part I. *Information and Control*, 7(1):1–22.

Jaakko J. Väyrynen, Tero Tapiovaara, Kimmo Kettunen, and Marcus Dobrinkat. 2010. Normalized compression distance as an automatic MT evaluation metric. In *Proceedings of MT 25 years on*. To appear.

The DCU Dependency-Based Metric in WMT-MetricsMATR 2010

Yifan He **Jinhua Du** **Andy Way** **Josef van Genabith**
Centre for Next Generation Localisation
School of Computing
Dublin City University
Dublin 9, Ireland
{yhe,jdu,away,josef}@computing.dcu.ie

Abstract

We describe DCU's LFG dependency-based metric submitted to the shared evaluation task of WMT-MetricsMATR 2010.

The metric is built on the LFG F-structure-based approach presented in (Owczarzak et al., 2007). We explore the following improvements on the original metric: 1) we replace the in-house LFG parser with an open source dependency parser that directly parses strings into LFG dependencies; 2) we add a stemming module and unigram paraphrases to strengthen the aligner; 3) we introduce a chunk penalty following the practice of METEOR to reward continuous matches; and 4) we introduce and tune parameters to maximize the correlation with human judgement. Experiments show that these enhancements improve the dependency-based metric's correlation with human judgement.

1 Introduction

String-based automatic evaluation metrics such as BLEU (Papineni et al., 2002) have led directly to quality improvements in machine translation (MT). These metrics provide an alternative to expensive human evaluations, and enable tuning of MT systems based on automatic evaluation results.

However, there is widespread recognition in the MT community that string-based metrics are not discriminative enough to reflect the translation quality of today's MT systems, many of which have gone beyond pure string-based approaches (cf. (Callison-Burch et al., 2006)).

With that in mind, a number of researchers have come up with metrics which incorporate more sophisticated and linguistically motivated resources. Examples include METEOR (Banerjee and Lavie, 2005; Lavie and Denkowski, 2009) and TERP (Snover et al., 2010), both of which now utilize stemming, WordNet and paraphrase information. Experimental and evaluation campaign results have shown that these metrics can obtain better correlation with human judgements than metrics that only use surface-level information.

Given that many of today's MT systems incorporate some kind of syntactic information, it was perhaps natural to use syntax in automatic MT evaluation as well. This direction was first explored by (Liu and Gildea, 2005), who used syntactic structure and dependency information to go beyond the surface level matching.

Owczarzak et al. (2007) extended this line of research with the use of a term-based encoding of Lexical Functional Grammar (LFG:(Kaplan and Bresnan, 1982)) *labelled* dependency graphs into unordered sets of dependency triples, and calculating precision, recall, and F-score on the triple sets corresponding to the translation and reference sentences. With the addition of partial matching and *n*-best parses, Owczarzak et al. (2007)'s method considerably outperforms Liu and Gildea's (2005) w.r.t. correlation with human judgement.

The EDPM metric (Kahn et al., 2010) improves this line of research by using arc labels derived from a Probabilistic Context-Free Grammar (PCFG) parse to replace the LFG labels, showing that a PCFG parser is sufficient for preprocessing, compared to a dependency parser in (Liu and Gildea, 2005) and (Owczarzak et al., 2007). EDPM also incorporates more information sources: e.g. the parser confidence, the Porter stemmer, WordNet synonyms and paraphrases.

Besides the metrics that rely solely on the dependency structures, information from the dependency parser is a component of some other metrics that use more diverse resources, such as the textual entailment-based metric of (Pado et al., 2009).

In this paper we extend the work of (Owczarzak et al., 2007) in a different manner: we use an

Proceedings of the Joint 5th Workshop on Statistical Machine Translation and MetricsMATR, pages 349–353,
Uppsala, Sweden, 15-16 July 2010.

adapted version of the Malt parser (Nivre et al., 2006) to produce 1-best LFG dependencies and allow triple matches where the dependency labels are different. We incorporate stemming, synonym and paraphrase information as in (Kahn et al., 2010), and at the same time introduce a chunk penalty in the spirit of METEOR to penalize discontinuous matches. We sort the matches according to the match level and the dependency type, and weight the matches to maximize correlation with human judgement.

The remainder of the paper is organized as follows. Section 2 reviews the dependency-based metric. Sections 3, 4, 5 and 6 introduce our improvements on this metric. We report experimental results in Section 7 and conclude in Section 8.

2 The Dependency-Based Metric

In this section, we briefly review the metric presented in (Owczarzak et al., 2007).

2.1 C-Structure and F-Structure in LFG

In Lexical Functional Grammar (Kaplan and Bresnan, 1982), a sentence is represented as both a hierarchical c-(onstituent) structure which captures the phrasal organization of a sentence, and a f-(unctional) structure which captures the functional relations between different parts of the sentence. Our metric currently only relies on the f-structure, which is encoded as labeled dependencies in our metric.

2.2 MT Evaluation as Dependency Triple Matching

The basic method of (Owczarzak et al., 2007) can be illustrated by the example in Table 1.

The metric in (Owczarzak et al., 2007) performs triple matching over the Hyp- and Ref-Triples and calculates the metric score using the F-score of matching precision and recall. Let m be the number of matches, h be the number of triples in the hypothesis and e be the number of triples in the reference. Then we have the matching precision $P = m/h$ and recall $R = m/e$. The score of the hypothesis in (Owczarzak et al., 2007) is the F-score based on the precision and recall of matching as in (1):

$$Fscore = \frac{2PR}{P + R} \tag{1}$$

Table 1: Sample Hypothesis and Reference

Hypothesis
rice will be held talks in egypt next week
Hyp-Triples
`adjunct(will, rice)`
`xcomp(will, be)`
`adjunct(talks, held)`
`xcomp(be, talks)`
`adjunct(talks, in)`
`obj(in, egypt)`
`adjunct(week, next)`
`adjunct(talks, week)`
Reference
rice to hold talks in egypt next week
Ref-Triples
`obl(rice, to)`
`obj(hold, to)`
`adjunct(week, talks)`
`adjunct(talks, in)`
`obj(in, egypt)`
`adjunct(week, next)`
`obj(hold, week)`

2.3 Details of the Matching Strategy

(Owczarzak et al., 2007) uses several techniques to facilitate triple matching. First of all, considering that the MT-generated hypotheses have variable quality and are sometimes ungrammatical, the metric will search the 50-best parses of both the hypothesis and reference and use the pair that has the highest F-score to compensate for parser noise.

Secondly, the metric performs *complete* or *partial* matching according to the dependency labels, so the metric will find more matches on dependency structures that are presumably more informative.

More specifically, for all except the LFG `Predicate-Only` labeled triples of the form `dep(head, modifier)`, the method does not allow a match if the dependency labels (`deps`) are different, thus enforcing a *complete* match. For the `Predicate-Only` dependencies, *partial* matching is allowed: i.e. two triples are considered identical even if only the `head` or the `modifier` are the same.

Finally, the metric also uses linguistic resources for better coverage. Besides using WordNet synonyms, the method also uses the lemmatized output of the LFG parser, which is equivalent to using an English lemmatizer.

If we do not consider these additional linguistic resources, the metric would find the following matches in the example in Table 1: `adjunct(talks, in)`, `obj(in, egypt)` and `adjunct(week, next)`, as these three triples appear both in the reference and in the hypothesis.

2.4 Points for Improvement

We see several points for improvement from Table 1 and the analysis above.

- More linguistic resources: we can use more linguistic resources than WordNet in pursuit of better coverage.
- Using the 1-best parse instead of 50-best parses: the parsing model we currently use does not produce k-best parses and using only the 1-best parse significantly improves the speed of triple matching. We allow 'soft' triple matches to capture the triple matches which we might otherwise miss using the 1-best parse.
- Rewarding continuous matches: it would be more desirable to reflect the fact that the 3 matching triples `adjunct(talks, in)`, `obj(in, egypt)` and `adjunct(week, next)` are continuous in Table 1.

We introduce our improvements to the metric in response to these observations in the following sections.

3 Producing and Matching LFG Dependency Triples

3.1 The LFG Parser

The metric described in (Owczarzak et al., 2007) uses the DCU LFG parser (Cahill et al., 2004) to produce LFG dependency triples. The parser uses a Penn treebank-trained parser to produce c-structures (constituency trees) and an LFG f-structure annotation algorithm on the c-structure to obtain f-structures. In (Owczarzak et al., 2007), triple matching on f-structures produced by this paradigm correlates well with human judgement, but this paradigm is not adequate for the WMT-MetricsMatr evaluation in two respects: 1) the in-house LFG annotation algorithm is not publicly available and 2) the speed of this paradigm is not satisfactory.

We instead use the Malt Parser[1] (Nivre et al., 2006) with a parsing model trained on LFG dependencies to produce the f-structure triples. Our collaborators[2] first apply the LFG annotation algorithm to the Penn Treebank training data to obtain f-structures, and then the f-structures are converted into dependency trees in CoNLL format to train the parsing model. We use the *liblinear* (Fan et al., 2008) classification module to for fast parsing speed.

3.2 Hard and Soft Dependency Matching

Currently our parser produces only the 1-best outputs. Compared to the 50-best parses in (Owczarzak et al., 2007), the 1-best parse limits the number of triple matches that can be found. To compensate for this, we allow triple matches that have the same `Head` and `Modifier` to constitute a match, even if their dependency labels are different. Therefore for triples `Dep1(Head1, Mod1)` and `Dep2(Head2, Mod2)`, we allow three types of match: a *complete* match if the two triples are identical, a *partial* match if `Dep1=Dep2` and `Head1=Head2`, and a *soft* match if `Head1=Head2` and `Mod1=Mod2`.

4 Capturing Variations in Language

In (Owczarzak et al., 2007), lexical variations at the word-level are captured by WordNet. We use a Porter stemmer and a unigram paraphrase database to allow more lexical variations.

With these two resources combined, there are four stages of word level matching in our system: *exact* match, *stem* match, *WordNet* match and unigram *paraphrase* match. The stemming module uses Porter's stemmer implementation[3] and the WordNet module uses the JAWS WordNet interface.[4] Our metric only considers unigram paraphrases, which are extracted from the paraphrase database in TERP[5] using the script in the METEOR[6] metric.

[1] http://maltparser.org/index.html

[2] Özlem Çetinoğlu and Jennifer Foster at the National Centre for Language Technology, Dublin City University

[3] http://tartarus.org/~martin/PorterStemmer/

[4] http://lyle.smu.edu/~tspell/jaws/index.html

[5] http://www.umiacs.umd.edu/~snover/terp/

[6] http://www.cs.cmu.edu/~alavie/METEOR/

5 Adding Chunk Penalty to the Dependency-Based Metric

The metric described in (Owczarzak et al., 2007) does not explicitly consider word order and fluency. METEOR, on the other hand, utilizes this information through a chunk penalty. We introduce a chunk penalty to our dependency-based metric following METEOR's string-based approach.

Given a reference $r = w_{r1}...w_{rn}$, we denote w_{ri} as 'covered' if it is the head or modifier of a matched triple. We only consider the w_{ri}s that appear as `head` or `modifier` in the reference triples. After this notation, we follow METEOR's approach by counting the number of chunks in the reference string, where a chunk $w_{rj}...w_{rk}$ is a sequence of adjacent covered words in the reference. Using the hypothesis and reference in Table 1 as an example, the three matched triples `adjunct(talks, in)`, `obj(in, egypt)` and `adjunct(week, next)` will *cover* a continuous word sequence in the reference (underlined), constituting one single chunk:

rice to hold talks (in) egypt next week

Based on this observation, we introduce a similar chunk penalty Pen as in METEOR in our metric, as in 2:

$$Pen = \gamma \cdot (\frac{\#chunks}{\#matches})^{\beta} \tag{2}$$

where β and γ are free parameters, which we tune in Section 6.2. We add this penalty to the dependency based metric (cf. Eq. (1)), as in Eq. (3).

$$score = (1 - Pen) \cdot Fscore \tag{3}$$

6 Parameter Tuning

6.1 Parameters of the Metric

In our metric, dependency triple matches can be categorized according to many criteria. We assume that some matches are more critical than others and encode the importance of matches by weighting them differently. The final match will be the sum of weighted matches, as in (4):

$$m = \sum \lambda_t m_t \tag{4}$$

where λ_t and m_t are the weight and number of match category t. We categorize a triple match according to three perspectives: 1) the level of match L={*complete, partial*}; 2) the linguistic resource used in matching R={*exact, stem, WordNet, paraphrase*}; and 3) the type of dependency D. To avoid too large a number of parameters, we only allow a set of frequent dependency types, along with the type *other*, which represents all the other types and the type *soft* for *soft* matches. We have D={*app, subj, obj, poss, adjunct, topicrel, other, soft*}.

Therefore for each triple match m, we can have the type of the match $t \in L \times R \times D$.

6.2 Tuning

In sum, we have the following parameters to tune in our metric: precision weight α, chunk penalty parameters β, γ, and the match type weights $\lambda_1...\lambda_n$. We perform Powell's line search (Press et al., 2007) on the sufficient statistics of our metric to find the set of parameters that maximizes Pearson's ρ on the segment level. We perform the optimization on the MT06 portion of the NIST MetricsMATR 2010 development set with 2-fold cross validation.

7 Experiments

We experiment with four settings of the metric: HARD, SOFT, SOFTALL and WEIGHTED in order to validate our enhancements. The first two settings compare the effect of allowing/not allowing *soft* matches, but only uses WordNet as in (Owczarzak et al., 2007). The third setting applies our additional linguistic features and the final setting tunes parameter weights for higher correlation with human judgement.

We report Pearson's r, Spearman's ρ and Kendall's τ on segment and system levels on the NIST MetricsMATR 2010 development set using Snover's scoring tool.[7]

Table 2: Correlation on the Segment Level

	r	ρ	τ
HARD	0.557	0.586	0.176
SOFT	0.600	0.634	0.213
SOFTALL	0.633	0.662	0.235
WEIGHTED	0.673	0.709	0.277

Table 2 shows that allowing *soft* triple matches and using more linguistic features all lead to higher correlation with human judgement. Though the parameters might somehow overfit on

[7] http://www.umiacs.umd.edu/~snover/terp/scoring/

the data set even if we apply cross validation, this certainly confirms the necessity of weighing dependency matches according to their types.

Table 3: Correlation on the System Level

	r	ρ	τ
HARD	0.948	0.905	0.786
SOFT	0.964	0.905	0.786
SOFTALL	0.975	0.976	0.929
WEIGHTED	0.989	1.000	1.000

When considering the system-level correlation in Table 3, the trend is very similar to that of the segment level. The improvements we introduce all lead to improvements in correlation with human judgement.

8 Conclusions and Future Work

In this paper we describe DCU's dependency-based MT evaluation metric submitted to WMT-MetricsMATR 2010. Building upon the LFG-based metric described in (Owczarzak et al., 2007), we use a publicly available parser instead of an in-house parser to produce dependency labels, so that the metric can run on a third party machine. We improve the metric by allowing more lexical variations and weighting dependency triple matches depending on their importance according to correlation with human judgement.

For future work, we hope to apply this method to languages other than English, and perform more refinement on dependency type labels and linguistic resources.

Acknowledgements

This research is supported by the Science Foundation Ireland (Grant 07/CE/I1142) as part of the Centre for Next Generation Localisation (www.cngl.ie) at Dublin City University. We thank Özlem Çetinoğlu and Jennifer Foster for providing us with the LFG parsing model for the Malt Parser, as well as the anonymous reviewers for their insightful comments.

References

Satanjeev Banerjee and Alon Lavie. 2005. METEOR: An automatic metric for MT evaluation with improved correlation with human judgments. In *Proceedings of the ACL Workshop on Intrinsic and Extrinsic Evaluation Measures for Machine Translation and/or Summarization*, pages 65–72, Ann Arbor, MI.

Aoife Cahill, Michael Burke, Ruth O'Donovan, Josef van Genabith, and Andy Way. 2004. Long-distance dependency resolution in automatically acquired wide-coverage PCFG-based LFG approximations. In *Proceedings of the 42nd Meeting of the Association for Computational Linguistics (ACL-2004)*, pages 319–326, Barcelona, Spain.

Chris Callison-Burch, Miles Osborne, and Philipp Koehn. 2006. Re-evaluation the role of bleu in machine translation research. In *Proceedings of 11th Conference of the European Chapter of the Association for Computational Linguistics*, pages 249–256, Trento, Italy.

Rong-En Fan, Kai-Wei Chang, Cho-Jui Hsieh, Xiang-Rui Wang, and Chih-Jen Lin. 2008. Liblinear: A library for large linear classification. *Journal of Machine Learning Research*, 9:1871–1874.

Jeremy G. Kahn, Matthew Snover, and Mari Ostendorf. 2010. Expected dependency pair match: predicting translation quality with expected syntactic structure. *Machine Translation*.

Ronald M. Kaplan and Joan Bresnan. 1982. Lexical-functional grammar: A formal system for grammatical representation. *The mental representation of grammatical relations*, pages 173–281.

Alon Lavie and Michael J. Denkowski. 2009. he meteor metric for automatic evaluation of machine translation. *Machine Translation*, 23(2-3).

Ding Liu and Daniel Gildea. 2005. Syntactic features for evaluation of machine translation. In *Proceedings of the ACL Workshop on Intrinsic and Extrinsic Evaluation Measures for Machine Translation and/or Summarization*, pages 25–32, Ann Arbor, MI.

Joakim Nivre, Johan Hall, and Jens Nilsson. 2006. Maltparser: A data-driven parser-generator for dependency parsing. In *In The fifth international conference on Language Resources and Evaluation (LREC-2006)*, pages 2216–2219, Genoa, Italy.

Karolina Owczarzak, Josef van Genabith, and Andy Way. 2007. Labelled dependencies in machine translation evaluation. In *Proceedings of the Second Workshop on Statistical Machine Translation*, pages 104–111, Prague, Czech Republic.

Sebastian Pado, Michel Galley, Dan Jurafsky, and Christopher D. Manning. 2009. Robust machine translation evaluation with entailment features. In *Proceedings of the Joint Conference of the 47th Annual Meeting of the ACL and the 4th International Joint Conference on Natural Language Processing of the AFNLP*, pages 297–305, Suntec, Singapore.

Kishore Papineni, Salim Roukos, Todd Ward, and Wei-Jing Zhu. 2002. Bleu: a method for automatic evaluation of machine translation. In *Proceedings of 40th Annual Meeting of the Association for Computational Linguistics (ACL-2002)*, pages 311–318, Philadelphia, PA.

William H. Press, Saul A. Teukolsky, William T. Vetterling, and Brian P. Flannery. 2007. *Numerical Recipes 3rd Edition: The Art of Scientific Computing*. Cambridge University Press, New York, NY.

Matthew Snover, Nitin Madnani, Bonnie Dorr, and Richard Schwartz. 2010. Ter-plus: paraphrase, semantic, and alignment enhancements to translation edit rate. *Machine Translation*.

TESLA: Translation Evaluation of Sentences with Linear-programming-based Analysis

Chang Liu[1] and **Daniel Dahlmeier**[2] and **Hwee Tou Ng**[1,2]
[1]Department of Computer Science, National University of Singapore
[2]NUS Graduate School for Integrative Sciences and Engineering
{liuchan1,danielhe,nght}@comp.nus.edu.sg

Abstract

We present TESLA-M and TESLA, two novel automatic machine translation evaluation metrics with state-of-the-art performances. TESLA-M builds on the success of METEOR and MaxSim, but employs a more expressive linear programming framework. TESLA further exploits parallel texts to build a shallow semantic representation. We evaluate both on the WMT 2009 shared evaluation task and show that they outperform all participating systems in most tasks.

1 Introduction

In recent years, many machine translation (MT) evaluation metrics have been proposed, exploiting varying amounts of linguistic resources.

Heavyweight linguistic approaches including RTE (Pado et al., 2009) and ULC (Giménez and Màrquez, 2008) performed the best in the WMT 2009 shared evaluation task. They exploit an extensive array of linguistic features such as parsing, semantic role labeling, textual entailment, and discourse representation, which may also limit their practical applications.

Lightweight linguistic approaches such as METEOR (Banerjee and Lavie, 2005), MaxSim (Chan and Ng, 2008), wpF and wpBleu (Popović and Ney, 2009) exploit a limited range of linguistic information that is relatively cheap to acquire and to compute, including lemmatization, part-of-speech (POS) tagging, and synonym dictionaries.

Non-linguistic approaches include BLEU (Papineni et al., 2002) and its variants, TER (Snover et al., 2006), among others. They operate purely at the surface word level and no linguistic resources are required. Although still very popular with MT researchers, they have generally shown inferior performances than the linguistic approaches.

We believe that the lightweight linguistic approaches are a good compromise given the current state of computational linguistics research and resources. In this paper, we devise TESLA-M and TESLA, two lightweight approaches to MT evaluation. Specifically: (1) the core features are F-measures derived by matching bags of N-grams; (2) both recall and precision are considered, with more emphasis on recall; and (3) WordNet synonyms feature prominently.

The main novelty of TESLA-M compared to METEOR and MaxSim is that we match the N-grams under a very expressive linear programming framework, which allows us to assign weights to the N-grams. This is in contrast to the greedy approach of METEOR, and the more restrictive maximum bipartite matching formulation of MaxSim.

In addition, we present a heavier version TESLA, which combines the features using a linear model trained on development data, making it easy to exploit features not on the same scale, and leaving open the possibility of domain adaptation. It also exploits parallel texts of the target language with other languages as a shallow semantic representation, which allows us to model phrase synonyms and idioms. In contrast, METEOR and MaxSim are capable of processing only word synonyms from WordNet.

The rest of this paper is organized as follows. Section 2 gives a high level overview of the evaluation task. Sections 3 and 4 describe TESLA-M and TESLA, respectively. Section 5 presents experimental results in the setting of the WMT 2009 shared evaluation task. Finally, Section 6 concludes the paper.

2 Overview

We consider the task of evaluating machine translation systems in the direction of translating the *source language* to the *target language*. Given a *reference translation* and a *system translation*, the

Proceedings of the Joint 5th Workshop on Statistical Machine Translation and MetricsMATR, pages 354–359, Uppsala, Sweden, 15-16 July 2010.

goal of an automatic machine translation evaluation algorithm such as TESLA(-M) is to output a score predicting the quality of the system translation. Neither TESLA-M nor TESLA requires the source text, but as additional linguistic resources, TESLA makes use of phrase tables generated from parallel texts of the target language and other languages, which we refer to as *pivot languages*. The source language may or may not be one of the pivot languages.

3 TESLA-M

This section describes TESLA-M, the lighter one among the two metrics. At the highest level, TESLA-M is the *arithmetic average* of F-measures between *bags of N-grams* (BNGs). A BNG is a multiset of weighted N-grams. Mathematically, a BNG B consists of tuples (b_i, b_i^W), where each b_i is an N-gram and b_i^W is a positive real number representing its weight. In the simplest case, a BNG contains every N-gram in a translated sentence, and the weights are just the counts of the respective N-grams. However, to emphasize the content words over the function words, we discount the weight of an N-gram by a factor of 0.1 for every function word in the N-gram. We decide whether a word is a function word based on its POS tag.

In TESLA-M, the BNGs are extracted in the target language, so we call them *bags of target language N-grams* (BTNGs).

3.1 Similarity functions

To match two BNGs, we first need a similarity measure between N-grams. In this section, we define the similarity measures used in our experiments.

We adopt the similarity measure from MaxSim as s_{ms}. For unigrams x and y,

- If $\text{lemma}(x) = \text{lemma}(y)$, then $s_{ms} = 1$.
- Otherwise, let

  $$a = I(\text{synsets}(x) \text{ overlap with synsets}(y))$$
  $$b = I(\text{POS}(x) = \text{POS}(y))$$

  where $I(\cdot)$ is the indicator function, then $s_{ms} = (a + b)/2$.

The synsets are obtained by querying WordNet (Fellbaum, 1998). For languages other than English, a synonym dictionary is used instead.

We define two other similarity functions between unigrams:

$$s_{lem}(x, y) = I(\text{lemma}(x) = \text{lemma}(y))$$
$$s_{pos}(x, y) = I(\text{POS}(x) = \text{POS}(y))$$

All the three unigram similarity functions generalize to N-grams in the same way. For two N-grams $x = x^{1,2,\ldots,n}$ and $y = y^{1,2,\ldots,n}$,

$$s(x, y) = \begin{cases} 0 & \text{if } \exists i,\ s(x^i, y^i) = 0 \\ \frac{1}{n}\sum_{i=1}^{n} s(x^i, y^i) & \text{otherwise} \end{cases}$$

3.2 Matching two BNGs

Now we describe the procedure of matching two BNGs. We take as input the following:

1. Two BNGs, X and Y. The ith entry in X is x_i and has weight x_i^W (analogously for y_j and y_j^W).
2. A similarity measure, s, that gives a similarity score between any two entries in the range of 0 to 1.

Intuitively, we wish to align the entries of the two BNGs in a way that maximizes the overall similarity. As translations often contain one-to-many or many-to-many alignments, we allow one entry to split its weight among multiple alignments. An example matching problem is shown in Figure 1a, where the weight of each node is shown, along with the similarity for each edge. Edges with a similarity of zero are not shown. The solution to the matching problem is shown in Figure 1b, and the overall similarity is $0.5 \times 1.0 + 0.5 \times 0.6 + 1.0 \times 0.2 + 1.0 \times 0.1 = 1.1$.

Mathematically, we formulate this as a (real-valued) linear programming problem[1]. The variables are the allocated weights for the edges

$$w(x_i, y_j) \quad \forall i, j$$

We maximize

$$\sum_{i,j} s(x_i, y_j) w(x_i, y_j)$$

subject to

$$w(x_i, y_j) \geq 0 \quad \forall i, j$$
$$\sum_j w(x_i, y_j) \leq x_i^W \quad \forall i$$
$$\sum_i w(x_i, y_j) \leq y_j^W \quad \forall j$$

[1]While integer linear programming is NP-complete, real-valued linear programming can be solved efficiently.

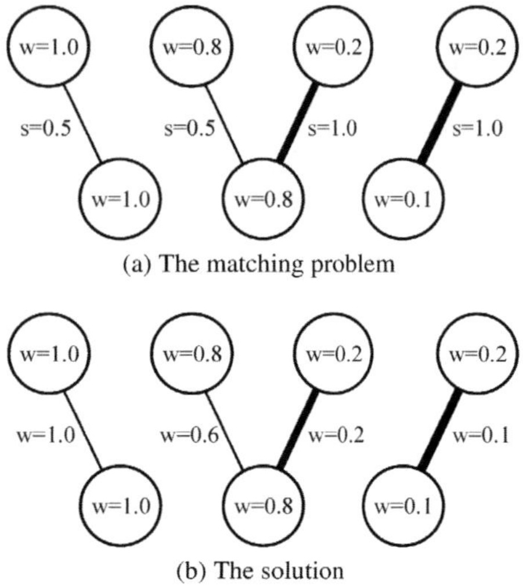

(a) The matching problem

(b) The solution

Figure 1: A BNG matching problem

The value of the objective function is the overall similarity S. Assuming X is the reference and Y is the system translation, we have

$$\text{Precision} = \frac{S}{\sum_j y_j^W}$$

$$\text{Recall} = \frac{S}{\sum_i x_i^W}$$

The F-measure is derived from the precision and the recall:

$$F = \frac{\text{Precision} \times \text{Recall}}{\alpha \times \text{Precision} + (1 - \alpha) \times \text{Recall}}$$

In this work, we set $\alpha = 0.8$, following MaxSim. The value gives more importance to the recall than the precision.

3.3 Scoring

The TESLA-M sentence-level score for a reference and a system translation is the arithmetic average of the BTNG F-measures for unigrams, bigrams, and trigrams based on similarity functions s_{ms} and s_{pos}. We thus have $3 \times 2 = 6$ features for TESLA-M.

We can compute a system-level score for a machine translation system by averaging its sentence-level scores over the complete test set.

3.4 Reduction

When every x_i^W and y_j^W is 1, the linear programming problem proposed above reduces to *weighted bipartite matching*. This is a well known result; see for example, Cormen et al. (2001) for details. This is the formalism of MaxSim, which precludes the use of fractional weights.

If the similarity function is binary-valued and transitive, such as s_{lem} and s_{pos}, then we can use a much simpler and faster greedy matching procedure: the best match is simply $\sum_g \min(\sum_{x_i=g} x_i^W, \sum_{y_i=g} y_i^W)$.

4 TESLA

Unlike the simple arithmetic average used in TESLA-M, TESLA uses a general linear combination of three types of features: BTNG F-measures as in TESLA-M, F-measures between bags of N-grams in each of the pivot languages, called *bags of pivot language N-grams* (BPNGs), and normalized language model scores of the system translation, defined as $\frac{1}{n} \log P$, where n is the length of the translation, and P the language model probability. The method of training the linear model depends on the development data. In the case of WMT, the development data is in the form of manual rankings, so we train SVM^{rank} (Joachims, 2006) on these instances to build the linear model. In other scenarios, some form of regression can be more appropriate.

The rest of this section focuses on the *generation* of the BPNGs. Their matching is done in the same way as described for BTNGs in the previous section.

4.1 Phrase level semantic representation

Given a sentence-aligned bitext between the target language and a pivot language, we can align the text at the word level using well known tools such as GIZA++ (Och and Ney, 2003) or the Berkeley aligner (Liang et al., 2006; Haghighi et al., 2009).

We observe that the distribution of aligned phrases in a pivot language can serve as a semantic representation of a target language phrase. That is, if two target language phrases are often aligned to the same pivot language phrase, then they can be inferred to be similar in meaning. Similar observations have been made by previous researchers (Bannard and Callison-Burch, 2005; Callison-Burch et al., 2006; Snover et al., 2009).

We note here two differences from WordNet synonyms: (1) the relationship is not restricted to the word level only, and (2) the relationship is not binary. The degree of similarity can be measured by the percentage of overlap between the semantic representations. For example, at the word level, the phrases *good morning* and *hello* are unrelated even with a synonym dictionary, but they both very often align to the same French phrase *bonjour*, and we conclude they are semantically related to a high degree.

4.2 Segmenting a sentence into phrases

To extend the concept of this semantic representation of phrases to sentences, we segment a sentence in the target language into phrases. Given a phrase table, we can approximate the probability of a phrase p by:

$$Pr(p) = \frac{N(p)}{\sum_{p'} N(p')} \quad (1)$$

where $N(\cdot)$ is the count of a phrase in the phrase table. We then define the likelihood of segmenting a sentence S into a sequence of phrases $(p_1, p_2, \ldots, p_n)$ by:

$$Pr(p_1, p_2, \ldots, p_n | S) = \frac{1}{Z(S)} \prod_{i=1}^{n} Pr(p_i) \quad (2)$$

where $Z(S)$ is a normalizing constant. The segmentation of S that maximizes the probability can be determined efficiently using a dynamic programming algorithm. The formula has a strong preference for longer phrases, as every $Pr(p)$ is a small fraction. To deal with out-of-vocabulary (OOV) words, we allow any single word w to be considered a phrase, and if $N(w) = 0$, we set $N(w) = 0.5$ instead.

4.3 BPNGs as sentence level semantic representation

Simply merging the phrase-level semantic representation is insufficient to produce a sensible sentence-level semantic representation. As an example, we consider two target language (English) sentences segmented as follows:

1. ||| *Hello ,* ||| *Querrien* ||| . |||

2. ||| *Morning , sir .* |||

A naive comparison of the bags of aligned pivot language (French) phrases would likely conclude that the two sentences are completely unrelated, as the bags of aligned phrases are likely to be completely disjoint. We tackle this problem by constructing a confusion network representation of the aligned phrases, as shown in Figures 2 and

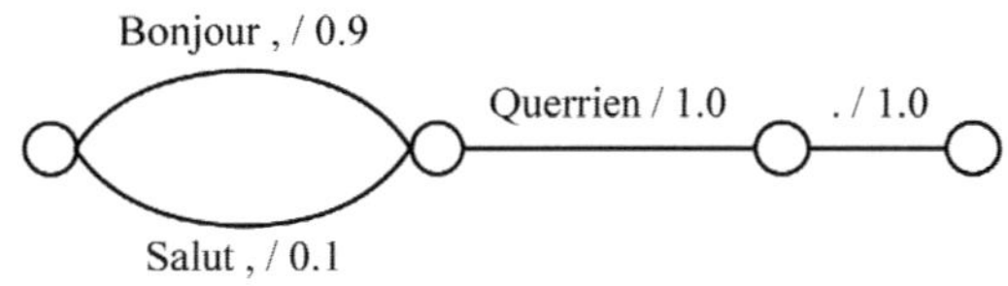

Figure 2: A confusion network as a semantic representation

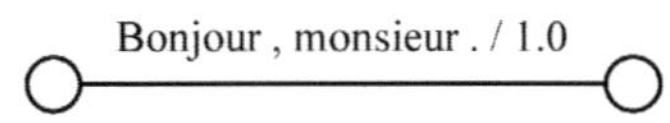

Figure 3: A degenerate confusion network as a semantic representation

3. A confusion network is a compact representation of a potentially exponentially large number of weighted and likely malformed French sentences. We can collect the N-gram statistics of this ensemble of French sentences efficiently from the confusion network representation. For example, the trigram *Bonjour , Querrien* [2] would receive a weight of $0.9 \times 1.0 = 0.9$ in Figure 2. As with BTNGs, we discount the weight of an N-gram by a factor of 0.1 for every function word in the N-gram, so as to place more emphasis on the content words.

The collection of all such N-grams and their corresponding weights forms the BPNG of a sentence. The reference and system BPNGs are then matched using the algorithm outlined in Section 3.2.

4.4 Scoring

The TESLA sentence-level score is a linear combination of (1) BTNG F-measures for unigrams, bigrams, and trigrams based on similarity functions s_{ms} and s_{pos}, (2) BPNG F-measures for unigrams, bigrams, and trigrams based on similarity functions s_{lem} and s_{pos} for each pivot language, and (3) normalized language model scores. In this work, we use two language models. We thus have 3×2 features from the BTNGs, $3 \times 2 \times$ *#pivot languages* features from the BPNGs, and 2 features from the language models. Again, we can compute system-level scores by averaging the sentence-level scores.

5 Experiments

5.1 Setup

We test our metrics in the setting of the WMT 2009 evaluation task (Callison-Burch et al., 2009). The manual judgments from WMT 2008 are used

[2]Note that the N-gram can span more than one segment.

as the development data and the metric is evaluated on WMT 2009 manual judgments with respect to two criteria: sentence level consistency and system level correlation.

The sentence level consistency is defined as the percentage of correctly predicted pairs among all the manually judged pairs. Pairs judged as ties by humans are excluded from the evaluation. The system level correlation is defined as the average Spearman's rank correlation coefficient across all translation tracks.

5.2 Pre-processing

We POS tag and lemmatize the texts using the following tools: for English, OpenNLP POS-tagger[3] and WordNet lemmatizer; for French and German, TreeTagger[4]; for Spanish, the FreeLing toolkit (Atserias et al., 2006); and for Czech, the Morce morphological tagger[5].

For German, we additionally perform noun compound splitting. For each noun, we choose the split that maximizes the geometric mean of the frequency counts of its parts, following the method in (Koehn and Knight, 2003):

$$\max_{n,p_1,p_2,\ldots,p_n} \left[\prod_{i=1}^{n} N(p_i) \right]^{\frac{1}{n}}$$

The resulting compound split sentence is then POS tagged and lemmatized.

Finally, we remove all non-alphanumeric tokens from the text in all languages. To generate the language model features, we train SRILM (Stolcke, 2002) trigram models with modified Kneser-Ney discounting on the supplied monolingual Europarl and news commentary texts.

We build phrase tables from the supplied news commentary bitexts. Word alignments are produced by the Berkeley aligner. The widely used phrase extraction heuristic in (Koehn et al., 2003) is used to extract phrase pairs and phrases of up to 4 words are collected.

5.3 Into-English task

For each of the BNG features, we generate three scores, for unigrams, bigrams, and trigrams respectively. For BPNGs, we generate one such triple for each of the four pivot languages supplied, namely Czech, French, German, and Spanish.

	System correlation	Sentence consistency
TESLA	0.8993	0.6324
TESLA-M	0.8718	0.6097
ulc	0.83	0.63
maxsim	0.80	0.62
meteor-0.6	0.72	0.50

Table 1: Into-English task on WMT 2009 data

Table 1 compares the scores of TESLA and TESLA-M against three participants in WMT 2009 under identical settings[6]: ULC (a heavyweight linguistic approach with the best performance in WMT 2009), MaxSim, and METEOR. The results show that TESLA outperforms all these systems by a substantial margin, and TESLA-M is very competitive too.

5.4 Out-of-English task

A synonym dictionary is required for target languages other than English. We use the freely available Wiktionary dictionary[7] for each language. For Spanish, we additionally use the Spanish WordNet, a component of FreeLing.

Only one pivot language (English) is used for the BPNG. For the English-Czech task, we only have one language model instead of two, as the Europarl language model is not available.

Tables 2 and 3 show the sentence-level consistency and system-level correlation respectively of TESLA and TESLA-M against the best reported results in WMT 2009 under identical setting. The results show that both TESLA and TESLA-M give very competitive performances. Interestingly, TESLA and TESLA-M obtain similar scores in the out-of-English task. This could be because we use only one pivot language (English), compared to four in the into-English task. We plan to investigate this phenomenon in our future work.

6 Conclusion

This paper describes TESLA-M and TESLA. Our main contributions are: (1) we generalize the bipartite matching formalism of MaxSim into a more expressive linear programming framework;

[3] opennlp.sourceforge.net

[4] www.ims.uni-stuttgart.de/projekte/corplex/TreeTagger

[5] ufal.mff.cuni.cz/morce/index.php

[6] The original WMT09 report contained erroneous results. The scores here are the corrected results released after publication.

[7] www.wiktionary.org

	en-fr	en-de	en-es	en-cz	Overall
TESLA	0.6828	0.5734	0.5940	0.5519	0.5796
TESLA-M	0.6390	0.5890	0.5927	0.5656	0.5847
wcd6p4er	0.67	0.58	0.61	0.59	0.60
wpF	0.66	0.60	0.61	n/a	0.61
terp	0.62	0.50	0.54	0.31	0.43

Table 2: Out-of-English task sentence-level consistency on WMT 2009 data

	en-fr	en-de	en-es	en-cz	Overall
TESLA	0.8529	0.7857	0.7272	0.3141	0.6700
TESLA-M	0.9294	0.8571	0.7909	0.0857	0.6657
wcd6p4er	-0.89	0.54	-0.45	-0.1	-0.22
wpF	0.90	-0.06	0.58	n/a	n/a
terp	-0.89	0.03	-0.58	-0.40	-0.46

Table 3: Out-of-English task system-level correlation on WMT 2009 data

(2) we exploit parallel texts to create a shallow semantic representation of the sentences; and (3) we show that they outperform all participants in most WMT 2009 shared evaluation tasks.

Acknowledgments

This research was done for CSIDM Project No. CSIDM-200804 partially funded by a grant from the National Research Foundation (NRF) administered by the Media Development Authority (MDA) of Singapore.

References

J. Atserias, B. Casas, E. Comelles, M. González, L. Padró, and M. Padró. 2006. Freeling 1.3: Syntactic and semantic services in an open-source NLP library. In *Proceedings of LREC*.

S. Banerjee and A. Lavie. 2005. METEOR: An automatic metric for MT evaluation with improved correlation with human judgments. In *Proceedings of the ACL Workshop on Intrinsic and Extrinsic Evaluation Measures for Machine Translation and/or Summarization*.

C. Bannard and C. Callison-Burch. 2005. Paraphrasing with bilingual parallel corpora. In *Proceedings of ACL*.

C. Callison-Burch, P. Koehn, and M. Osborne. 2006. Improved statistical machine translation using paraphrases. In *Proceedings of HLT-NAACL*.

C. Callison-Burch, P. Koehn, C. Monz, and J. Schroeder. 2009. Findings of the 2009 Workshop on Statistical Machine Translation. In *Proceedings of WMT*.

Y.S. Chan and H.T. Ng. 2008. MAXSIM: A maximum similarity metric for machine translation evaluation. In *Proceedings of ACL*.

T. Cormen, C.E. Leiserson, R.L. Rivest, and C. Stein, 2001. *Introduction to Algorithms*. MIT Press, Cambridge, MA.

C. Fellbaum, editor. 1998. *WordNet: An electronic lexical database*. MIT Press, Cambridge, MA.

J. Giménez and L. Màrquez. 2008. A smorgasbord of features for automatic MT evaluation. In *Proceedings of the Third WMT*.

A. Haghighi, J. Blitzer, J. DeNero, and D. Klein. 2009. Better word alignments with supervised ITG models. In *Proceedings of ACL-IJCNLP*.

T. Joachims. 2006. Training linear svms in linear time. In *Proceedings of KDD*.

P. Koehn and K. Knight. 2003. Empirical methods for compound splitting. In *Proceedings of EACL*.

P. Koehn, F.J. Och, and D. Marcu. 2003. Statistical phrase-based translation. In *Proceedings of HLT-NAACL*.

P. Liang, B. Taskar, and D. Klein. 2006. Alignment by agreement. In *Proceedings of HLT-NAACL*.

F.J. Och and N. Ney. 2003. A systematic comparison of various statistical alignment models. *Computational Linguistics*, 29(1).

S. Pado, M. Galley, D. Jurafsky, and C.D. Manning. 2009. Robust machine translation evaluation with entailment features. In *Proceedings of ACL-IJCNLP*.

K. Papineni, S. Roukos, T. Ward, and W.-J. Zhu. 2002. BLEU: A method for automatic evaluation of machine translation. In *Proceedings of ACL*.

M. Popović and H. Ney. 2009. Syntax-oriented evaluation measures for machine translation output. In *Proceedings of WMT*.

M. Snover, B. Dorr, R. Schwartz, L. Micciulla, and J. Makhoul. 2006. A study of translation edit rate with targeted human annotation. In *Proceedings of AMTA*.

M. Snover, N. Madnani, B. Dorr, and R. Schwartz. 2009. Fluency, adequacy, or HTER? Exploring different human judgments with a tunable MT metric. In *Proceedings of WMT*.

A. Stolcke. 2002. SRILM - an extensible language modeling toolkit. In *Proceedings of ICSLP*.

The Parameter-optimized ATEC Metric for MT Evaluation

Billy T-M Wong **Chunyu Kit**
Department of Chinese, Translation and Linguistics
City University of Hong Kong
Tat Chee Avenue, Kowloon, Hong Kong
{ctbwong, ctckit}@cityu.edu.hk

Abstract

This paper describes the latest version of the ATEC metric for automatic MT evaluation, with parameters optimized for word choice and word order, the two fundamental features of language that the metric relies on. The former is assessed by matching at various linguistic levels and weighting the informativeness of both matched and unmatched words. The latter is quantified in term of word position and information flow. We also discuss those aspects of language not yet covered by other existing evaluation metrics but carefully considered in the formulation of our metric.

1 Introduction

It is recognized that the proposal of the BLEU metric (Papineni et al., 2002) has piloted a paradigm evolution to MT evaluation. It provides a computable solution to the task and turns it into an engineering problem of measuring text similarity and simulating human judgments of translation quality. Related studies in recent years have extensively revealed more essential characteristics of BLEU, including its strengths and weaknesses. This has aroused the proposal of different new evaluation metrics aimed at addressing such weaknesses so as to find some other hopefully better alternatives for the task. Effort in this direction brings up some advanced metrics such as METEOR (Banerjee and Lavie, 2005) and TERp (Snover et al., 2009) that seem to have already achieved considerably strong correlations with human judgments. Nevertheless, few metrics have really nurtured our understanding of possible parameters involved in our language comprehension and text quality judgment. This inadequacy limits, inevitably, the application of the existing metrics.

The ATEC metric (Wong and Kit, 2008) was developed as a response to this inadequacy, with a focus to account for the process of human comprehension of sentences via two fundamental features of text, namely word choice and word order. It integrates various explicit measures for these two features in order to provide an intuitive and informative evaluation result. Its previous version (Wong and Kit, 2009b) has already illustrated a highly comparable performance to the few state-of-the-art evaluation metrics, showing a great improvement over its initial version for participation in MetricsMATR08[1]. It is also applied to evaluate online MT systems for legal translation, to examine its applicability for lay users' use to select appropriate MT systems (Wong and Kit, 2009a).

In this paper we describe the formulation of ATEC, including its new features and optimization of parameters. In particular we will discuss how the design of this metric can complement the inadequacies of other metrics in terms of its treatment of word choice and word order and its utilization of multiple references in the evaluation process.

2 The ATEC Metric

2.1 Word Choice

In general, word is the basic meaning bearing unit of language. In a semantic theory such as Latent Semantic Analysis (LSA) (Landauer et al., 1998), lexical selection is even the sole consideration of the meaning of a text. A recent study of the major errors in MT outputs by Vilar et al. (2006) also reveals that different kinds of error related to word choices constitute a majority of error types. It is therefore of prime importance

[1] http://www.itl.nist.gov/iad/mig/tests/metricsmatr/2008/

Proceedings of the Joint 5th Workshop on Statistical Machine Translation and MetricsMATR, pages 360–364,
Uppsala, Sweden, 15-16 July 2010.

for MT evaluation metrics to diagnose the adequacy of word selection by an MT system.

It is a general consensus that the performance of an evaluation metric can be improved by matching more words between MT outputs and human references. Linguistic resources like stemmer and WordNet are widely applied by many metrics for matching word stems and synonyms. ATEC is equipped with these two modules as well, and furthermore, with two measures for word similarity, including a WordNet-based (Wu and Palmer, 1994) and a corpus-based measure (Landauer et al., 1998) for matching word pairs of similar meanings. Our previous work (Wong, 2010) shows that the inclusion of semantically similar words results in a positive correlation gain comparable to the use of WordNet for synonym identification.

In addition to increasing the number of legitimate matches, we also consider the importance of each match. Although most metrics score every matched word with equal weight, different words indeed contribute different amount of information to the meaning of a sentence. In Example 1 below, both *C1* and *C2* contain the same number of words matched with *Ref*, but the matches in *C1* are more informative and therefore should be assigned higher weights.

Example 1
C1: it was <u>not</u> <u>first</u> <u>time</u> that <u>prime</u> <u>minister</u> confronts <u>northern</u> <u>league</u> ...
C2: <u>this</u> <u>is</u> <u>not</u> <u>the</u> <u>prime</u> <u>the</u> operation with <u>the</u> north ...
Ref: this is not the first time the prime minister has faced the northern league ...

The informativeness of a match is weighted by the *tf-idf* measure, which has been widely used in information retrieval to assess the relative importance of a word as an indexing term for a document. A word is more important to a document when it occurs more frequently in this document and less in others. In ATEC, we have "document" to refer to "sentence", the basic text unit in MT evaluation. This allows a more sensitive measure for words in different sentences, and gets around the problem of an evaluation dataset containing only one or a few long documents. Accordingly, the *tf-idf* measure is formulated as:

$$tfidf(i,j) = tf_{i,j} \cdot \log(\frac{N}{sf_i})$$

where $tf_{i,j}$ is the occurrences of word w_i in sentence s_j, sf_i the number of sentences containing word w_i, and N the total number of sentences in the evaluation set. In case of a high-frequency word whose *tf-idf* weight is less than 1, it is then rounded up to 1.

In addition to matched words, unmatched words are also considered to have a role to play in determining the quality of word choices of an MT output. As illustrated in Example 1, the unmatched words in *Ref* for *C1* and *C2* are [this | is | the | the | has | faced | the] and [first | time | minister | has | faced | northern | league] respectively. One can see that the words missing in *C2* are more significant. It is therefore necessary to apply the *tf-idf* weighting to unmatched reference words so as to quantify the information missed in the MT outputs in question.

2.2 Word Order

In MT evaluation, word order refers to the extent to which an MT output is interpretable following the information flow of its reference translation. It is not rare that an MT output has many matched words but does not make sense because of a problematic word order. Currently it is observed that consecutive matches represent a legitimate local ordering, causing some metrics to extend the unit of matching from word to phrase. Birch et al. (2010) show, however, that the current metrics including BLEU, METEOR and TER are highly lexical oriented and still cannot distinguish between sentences of different word orders. This is a serious problem in MT evaluation, for many MT systems have become capable of generating more and more suitable words in translations, resulting in that the quality difference of their outputs lies more and more crucially in the variances of word order.

ATEC uses three explicit features for word order, namely position distance, order distance and phrase size. Position distance refers to the divergence of the locations of matches in an MT output and its reference. Example 2 illustrates two candidates with the same match, whose position in *C1* is closer to its corresponding position in *Ref* than that in *C2*. We conceive this as a significant indicator of the accuracy of word order: the closer the positions of a matched word in the candidate and reference, the better match it is.

Example 2
C1: non-signatories these acts <u>victims</u> but it caused to incursion transcendant
C2: non-signatories but it caused to incursion transcendant these acts <u>victims</u>
Ref: there were no <u>victims</u> in this incident but they did cause massive damage

The calculation of position distance is based on the position indices of words in a sentence. In particular, we align every word in a candidate to its closest counterpart in a reference. In Example 3, all the candidate words have a match in the reference. As illustrated by the two "*a*" in the candidate, the shortest alignments (strict lines) are preferred over any farther alternatives (dash lines). In a case like this, only two matches, i.e., *thief* and *police*, vary in position by a distance of 3.

Example 3

Candidate:	a	thief	chases	a	police
Pos distance:	0	3	0	0	3
Pos index:	1	2	3	4	5
Reference:	a	police	chases	a	thief
Pos index:	1	2	3	4	5

This position distance is sensitive to sentence length as it simply makes use of word position indices without any normalization. Example 4 illustrates two cases of different lengths. The position distance of the bold matched words is 3 in *C1* but 14 in *C2*. Indeed, the divergence of word order in *C1* does not hinder our understanding, but in *C2* it poses a serious problem. This excessive length inevitably magnifies the interference effect of word order divergence.

Example 4

C1: Short$_1$ and$_2$ various$_3$ **international$_4$** news$_5$

R1: **International$_1$** news$_2$ brief$_3$

C2: Is$_1$ on$_2$ a$_3$ popular$_4$ the$_5$ very$_6$ in$_7$ Iraq$_8$ to$_9$ those$_{10}$ just$_{11}$ like$_{12}$ other$_{13}$ world$_{14}$ in$_{15}$ which$_{16}$ young$_{17}$ people$_{18}$ with$_{19}$ the$_{20}$ and$_{21}$ flowers$_{22}$ while$_{23}$ awareness$_{24}$ by$_{25}$ other$_{26}$ times$_{27}$ of$_{28}$ the$_{29}$ **countries$_{30}$** of$_{31}$ the$_{32}$

R2: Valentine's$_1$ day$_2$ is$_3$ a$_4$ very$_5$ popular$_6$ day$_7$ in$_8$ Iraq$_9$ as$_{10}$ it$_{11}$ is$_{12}$ in$_{13}$ the$_{14}$ other$_{15}$ **countries$_{16}$** of$_{17}$ the$_{18}$ world$_{19}$. Young$_{20}$ men$_{21}$ exchange$_{22}$ with$_{23}$ their$_{24}$ girlfriends$_{25}$ sweets$_{26}$, flowers$_{27}$, perfumes$_{28}$ and$_{29}$ other$_{30}$ gifts$_{31}$.

Another feature, the order distance, concerns the information flow of a sentence in the form of the sequence of matches. Each match in a candidate and a reference is first assigned an order index in a sequential manner. Then, the difference of two counterpart indices is measured, so as to see if a variance exists. Examples 5a and 5b exemplify two kinds of order distance and their corresponding position distance. Both cases have two matches with the same sum of position distance. However, the matches are in an identical sequence in 5a but cause a cross in 5b, resulting in a larger order distance for the latter.

Example 5a

Position index	1	2	3	4
Order index		1		2
Candidate:	A	B	C	D
Reference:	B	E	D	F
Order index	1		2	
Position index	1	2	3	4

Position distance (2-1) + (4-3) = 2

Order distance (1-1) + (2-2) = 0

Example 5b

Position index	1	2	3	4
Order index		1	2	
Candidate:	A	B	C	D
Reference:	C	B	E	F
Order index	1	2		
Position index	1	2	3	4

Position distance (2-2) + (3-1) = 2

Order distance (2-1) + (2-1) = 2

In practice, ATEC operates on phrases like many other metrics. But unlike these metrics that count only the number of matched phrases, ATEC gives extra credit to a longer phrase to reward its valid word sequence. In Example 6, *C1* and *C2* represent two MT outputs of the same length, with matched words underlined. Both have 10 matches in 3 phrases, and will receive the same evaluation score from a metric like METEOR or TERp, ignoring the subtle difference in the sizes of the matched phrases, which are [8,1,1] and [4,3,3] words for *C1* and *C2* respectively. In contrast, ATEC uses the size of a phrase as a reduction factor to its position distance, so as to raise the contribution of a larger phrase to the metric score.

Example 6

C1: $\underline{w_1}$ $\underline{w_2}$ $\underline{w_3}$ $\underline{w_4}$ $\underline{w_5}$ $\underline{w_6}$ $\underline{w_7}$ $\underline{w_8}$ w_9 w_{10} $\underline{w_{11}}$ w_{12} $\underline{w_{13}}$

C2: $\underline{w_1}$ $\underline{w_2}$ $\underline{w_3}$ $\underline{w_4}$ w_5 w_6 $\underline{w_7}$ $\underline{w_8}$ $\underline{w_9}$ w_{10} $\underline{w_{11}}$ $\underline{w_{12}}$ $\underline{w_{13}}$

2.3 Multiple References

The availability of multiple references allows more legitimate word choices and word order of an MT output to be accounted. Some existing metrics only compute the scores of a candidate against each reference and select the highest one.

This deficit can be illustrated by a well-known example from Papineni et al. (2002), as replicated in Example 7 with slight modification. It shows that nearly all candidate words can find their matches in either reference. However, if we resort to single reference, only around half of them can have a match, which would seriously underrate the quality of the candidate.

Example 7

C: It is a guide to action which ensures that the military always obeys the commands of the party.

R1: It is a guide to action that ensures that the military will forever heed Party commands.

R2: It is the guiding principle which guarantees the military forces always being under the commands of the party.

ATEC exploits multiple references in this fashion to maximize the number of matches in a candidate. It begins with aligning the longest matches with either reference. The one with the shortest position distance is preferred if more than one alternative available in the same phrase size. This process repeats until no more candidate word can find a match.

2.4 Formulation of ATEC

The computation of an ATEC score begins with alignment of phrases, as described above. For each matched phase, we first sum up the score of each word i in the phrase as

$$W_{match} = \sum_{i \in \{phrase\}} (w_{type} - \frac{Info_{match}}{tfidf_i})$$

where w_{type} refers to a basic score of a matched word depending on its match type. It is then minus its information load, i.e., the *tf-idf* score of the matched word with a weight factor, $Info_{match}$.

There is also a distance penalty for a phrase,

$$Dis = w_{pos} dis_{pos} (1 - \frac{|p|^e}{|c|}) + w_{order} dis_{order}$$

,

where dis_{pos} and dis_{order} refer to the position distance and order distance, and w_{pos} and w_{order} are their corresponding weight factors, respectively. The position distance is further weighted according to the size of phrase $|p|$ with an exponential factor e, in proportion to the length of candidate $|c|$.

The score of a matched phrase is then computed by

$$Phrase = \begin{cases} W_{match} \cdot Limit_{dis}, & \text{if } Dis > W_{match} \cdot Limit_{dis}; \\ W_{match} - Dis, & \text{otherwise,} \end{cases}$$

$Limit_{dis}$ is an upper limit for the distance penalty. Accordingly, the score C of all phrases in a candidate is

$$C = \sum_{j \in \{candidate\}} Phrase_j$$

.

Then, we move on to calculating the information load of unmatched reference words $W_{unmatch}$, approximated as

$$W_{unmatch} = \sum_{k \in \{unmatch\}} (w_{type} - \frac{Info_{unmatch}}{tfidf_k})$$

.

The overall score M accounting for both the matched and unmatched is defined as

$$M = \begin{cases} C \cdot Limit_{Info}, & \text{if } W_{unmatch} > C \cdot Limit_{Info}; \\ C - W_{unmatch}, & \text{otherwise,} \end{cases}$$

$Limit_{Info}$ is an upper limit for the information penalty of the unmatched words.

Finally, the ATEC score is computed using the conventional F-measure in terms of precision P and recall R as

$$ATEC = \frac{PR}{\alpha P + (1-\alpha)R}$$

where

$$P = \frac{M}{|c|}, \qquad R = \frac{M}{|r|}.$$

The parameter α adjusts the weights of P and R, and |c| and |r| refer to the length of candidate and reference, respectively. In the case of multiple references, $|r|$ refers to the average length of references.

We have derived the optimized values for the parameters involved in ATEC calculation using the development data of NIST MetricsMATR10 with adequacy assessments by a simple hill climbing approach. The optimal parameter setting is presented in Table 1 below.

3 Conclusion

In the above sections we have presented the latest version of our ATEC metric with particular emphasis on word choice and word order as two fundamental features of language. Each of these features contains multiple parameters intended to

Parameters	Values	
w_{type}	1	(exact match),
	0.95	(stem / synonym / semantically close),
	0.15	(unmatch)
$Info_{match}$	0.34	
$Info_{unmatch}$	0.26	
w_{pos}	0.02	
w_{order}	0.15	
e	1.1	
$Limit_{dis}$	0.95	
$Limit_{Info}$	0.5	
α	0.5	

Table 1 Optimal parameter values for ATEC

have a comprehensive coverage of different textual factors involved in our interpretation of a sentence. The optimal offsetting for the parameters is expected to report an empirical observation of the relative merits of each factor in adequacy assessment. We are currently exploring their relation with the errors of MT outputs, to examine the potential of automatic error analysis. The ATEC package is obtainable at:
http://mega.ctl.cityu.edu.hk/ctbwong/ATEC/

Acknowledgments

The research work described in this paper was supported by City University of Hong Kong through the Strategic Research Grant (SRG) 7002267.

References

Satanjeev Banerjee and Alon Lavie. 2005. METEOR: An Automatic Metric for MT Evaluation with Improved Correlation with Human Judgments. *Proceedings of Workshop on Intrinsic and Extrinsic Evaluation Measures for MT and/or Summarization at the 43th Annual Meeting of the Association of Computational Linguistics (ACL)*, pages 65-72, Ann Arbor, Michigan, June 2005.

Alexandra Birch, Miles Osborne and Phil Blunsom. 2010. Metrics for MT Evaluation: Evaluating Reordering. *Machine Translation* (forthcoming).

Thomas Landauer, Peter W. Foltz and Darrell Laham. 1998. Introduction to Latent Semantic Analysis. *Discourse Processes* 25: 259–284.

Kishore Papineni, Salim Roukos, Todd Ward, and Wei-Jing Zhu. 2002. BLEU: A Method for Automatic Evaluation of Machine Translation. *Proceedings of 40th Annual Meeting of the Association for Computational Linguistics (ACL)*, pages 311–318, Philadelphia, PA, July 2002.

Matthew Snover, Nitin Madnani, Bonnie Dorr, and Richard Schwartz. 2009. Fluency, Adequacy, or HTER? Exploring Different Human Judgments with a Tunable MT Metric. *Proceedings of the Fourth Workshop on Statistical Machine Translation at the 12th Meeting of the European Chapter of the Association for Computational Linguistics (EACL)*, pages 259-268, Athens, Greece, March, 2009.

David Vilar, Jia Xu, Luis Fernando D'Haro and Hermann Ney. 2006. Error Analysis of Statistical Machine Translation Output. *Proceedings of the 5th International Conference on Language Resources and Evaluation (LREC)*, pages 697-702, Genova, Italy, May 2006.

Billy T-M Wong. 2010. Semantic Evaluation of Machine Translation. *Proceedings of the 7th International Conference on Language Resources and Evaluation (LREC)*, Valletta, Malta, May, 2010.

Billy T-M Wong and Chunyu Kit. 2008. Word choice and Word Position for Automatic MT Evaluation. *AMTA 2008 Workshop: MetricsMATR*, 3 pages, Waikiki, Hawai'i, October, 2008.

Billy T-M Wong and Chunyu Kit. 2009a. Meta-Evaluation of Machine Translation on Legal Texts. *Proceedings of the 22nd International Conference on the Computer Processing of Oriental Languages (ICCPOL)*, pages 343-350, Hong Kong, March, 2009.

Billy Wong and Chunyu Kit. 2009b. ATEC: Automatic Evaluation of Machine Translation via Word Choice and Word Order. *Machine Translation*, 23(2):141-155.

Zhibiao Wu and Martha Palmer. 1994. Verb Semantics and Lexical Selection. *Proceedings of the 32nd Annual Meeting of the Association for Computational Linguistics*, pages 133-138, Las Cruces, New Mexico.

A Unified Approach to Minimum Risk Training and Decoding

Abhishek Arun, Barry Haddow and Philipp Koehn
School of Informatics
University of Edinburgh
Edinburgh, EH8 9AB, UK
a.arun@sms.ed.ac.uk, {bhaddow,pkoehn}@inf.ed.ac.uk

Abstract

We present a unified approach to performing minimum risk training and minimum Bayes risk (MBR) decoding with BLEU in a phrase-based model. Key to our approach is the use of a Gibbs sampler that allows us to explore the *entire probability distribution* and maintain a strict probabilistic formulation across the pipeline. We also describe a new sampling algorithm called *corpus sampling* which allows us at training time to use BLEU instead of an approximation thereof. Our approach is theoretically sound and gives better (up to +0.6%BLEU) and more stable results than the standard MERT optimization algorithm. By comparing our approach to lattice MBR, we are also able to gain crucial insights about both methods.

1 Introduction

According to statistical decision theory, the optimal decision rule for any statistical model is the solution that minimizes its risk (expected loss). This solution is often referred to as the Minimum Bayes Risk (MBR) solution (Kumar and Byrne, 2004). Since machine translation (MT) models are typically evaluated by BLEU (Papineni et al., 2002), a loss function which rewards partial matches, the MBR solution is to be preferred to the Maximum A Posteriori (MAP) solution.

In most statistical MT (SMT) systems, MBR is implemented as a reranker of a list[1] of translations generated by a first-pass decoder. This decoder typically assigns unnormalised log probabilities (known as *scores*) to each translation hypothesis, so these scores must be converted to probabilities in order to apply MBR. In order to perform this conversion, it is first necessary to compute the normalization function Z. Since Z is defined as an intractable sum over all possible translations, it is approximated by summing over the translations in the list. The second step is to find the correct scale factor for the scores using a hyper-parameter search over held-out data. This is needed because the model parameters for the first-pass decoder are normally learnt using MERT (Och, 2003), which is invariant under scaling of the scores.

Both these steps are theoretically unsatisfactory methods of estimating the posterior probability distribution since the approximation to Z is an unbounded term and the scaling factor is an artificial way of inducing a probability distribution.

Recently, (Tromble et al., 2008; Kumar et al., 2009) have shown that using a search lattice to improve the estimation of the true probability distribution can lead to improved MBR performance. However, these approaches still rely on MERT for training the base model, and in fact introduce several extra parameters which must also be estimated using either grid search or a second MERT run. The lattice pruning required to make these techniques tractable is quite drastic, and is in addition to the pruning already performed during the search. Such extensive pruning is liable to render any probability estimates heavily biased (Blunsom and Osborne, 2008; Bouchard-Côté et al., 2009).

Here, we present a unified approach to training and decoding in a phrase-based translation model (Koehn et al., 2003) which keeps the objective constant across the translation pipeline and so obviates the need for any extra hyper-parameter fitting. We use the phrase-based Gibbs sampler of Arun et al. (2009) at training time to compute the gradient of our *minimum risk training* objective in order to apply first-order optimization techniques,

[1] We use the term list to denote any enumerable representation of translation hypotheses e.g n-best list, translation lattice or forest.

Proceedings of the Joint 5th Workshop on Statistical Machine Translation and MetricsMATR, pages 365–374,
Uppsala, Sweden, 15-16 July 2010.

and at test time we use it to estimate the posterior distribution required by MBR (Section 3).

We experimented with two different objective functions for training (Section 4). First, following (Arun et al., 2009), we define our objective at the sentence-level using a sentence-level variant of BLEU. Then, in order to reduce the mismatch between training and test loss functions, we also tried directly optimising the expected corpus level BLEU, where we introduce a novel sampling technique, which we call *corpus sampling* to calculate the required expectations.

The methods presented in this paper are theoretically sound. Moreover, experimental evidence on three language pairs shows that our training regime is more stable than MERT, able to generalize better and generally leads to improvement in translation when used with sampling based MBR (Section 5). An added benefit is that the trained weights also lead to better performance when used with a beam-search based decoder.

2 Inference methods for MT

We assume a phrase-based machine translation model, defined with a log-linear form, with feature function vector $\mathbf{h}$ and parametrized by weight vector $\boldsymbol{\theta}$, as described in Koehn et al. (2003). The input sentence, f, is segmented into phrases, which are sequences of adjacent words. Each source phrase is translated into the target language, to produce an output sentence e and an alignment a representing the mapping from source to target phrases. Phrases are allowed to be reordered.

$$p(e,a|f;\boldsymbol{\theta}) = \frac{\exp\left[\boldsymbol{\theta}\cdot\mathbf{h}(e,a,f)\right]}{\sum_{\langle e',a'\rangle}\exp\left[\boldsymbol{\theta}\cdot\mathbf{h}(e',a',f)\right]} \quad (1)$$

MAP decoding under this model consists of finding the most likely output string, e^*:

$$e^* = \text{argmax}_e \sum_{a\in\triangle(e,f)} p(e,a|f) \quad (2)$$

where $\triangle(e,f)$ is the set of all derivations of output string e given source string f.

Summing over all the derivations is intractable, making approximations necessary. The most common of these approximations is the *Viterbi* approximation, which simply chooses the most likely derivation $\langle e^*, a^*\rangle$. This approximation can be computed in polynomial time via dynamic programming (DP). Though fast and effective for many problems, it has two serious drawbacks for probabilistic inference. First, the error incurred by the Viterbi maximum with respect to the true model maximum is unbounded. Second, the DP solution requires substantial pruning and restricts the use of non-local features. The latter problem persists even in the *variational* approximations of Li et al. (2009), which attempt to solve the former.

2.1 Gibbs sampling for phrase-based MT

An alternate approximate inference method for phrase-based MT without any of the previously mentioned drawbacks is the Gibbs sampler (Geman and Geman, 1984) of Arun et al. (2009) which draws samples from the posterior distribution of the translation model. For the work presented in this paper, we use this sampler.

The sampler produces a sequence of samples, $\mathcal{S}_1^N = (e_1, a_1)\ldots(e_N, a_N)$, that are drawn from the distribution $p(e,a|f)$. These samples can be used to estimate the expectation of a function $h(e,a,f)$ as follows:

$$\mathbb{E}_{p(a,e|f)}[h] = \lim_{N\to\infty}\frac{1}{N}\sum_{i=1}^{N} h(a_i, e_i, f) \quad (3)$$

3 Decoding

In this work, we are interested in performing MBR decoding with BLEU. We define the MBR decision rule following Tromble et al. (2008):

$$e^* = \arg\max_{e\in\epsilon_H}\sum_{e'\in\epsilon_E}\text{BLEU}_e(e')p(e'|f) \quad (4)$$

where ϵ_H refers to the hypothesis space from which translations are chosen, ϵ_E refers to the evidence space used for calculating risk and $\text{BLEU}_e(e')$ is a gain function that indicates the reward of hypothesising e' when the reference solution is e.

To perform MBR decoding using the sampler, let the function h in Equation 3 be the indicator function $h = \delta(a,\hat{a})\delta(e,\hat{e})$. Then, Equation 3 provides an estimate of $p(\hat{a},\hat{e}|f)$, and using $h = \delta(e,\hat{e})$ marginalizes over all derivations a', yielding an estimate of $p(\hat{e}|f)$. MBR is computed at the sentence-level while BLEU is a corpus-level metric, so instead we use a sentence-level approximation of BLEU.[2]

The sampler can be used to perform two other decoding tasks: the mode of the estimated distribution $p(\hat{a},\hat{e}|f)$ is the maximum derivation (MaxDeriv) solution while the mode of $p(\hat{e}|f)$ is the maximum translation (MaxTrans) solution.

[2]The ngram precision counts are smoothed by adding 0.01 for n > 1

4 Minimum Risk Training

In order to train models suitable for use with Max-Trans or MBR decoding, we need to employ a training method which takes account of the whole distribution. To this end, we employ minimum risk training to find weights θ for Equation 1 that minimize the expected loss on the training set. We consider two variants of minimum risk training: *sentence sampling* optimizes an objective defined at the sentence level and *corpus sampling* a corpus-based objective.

4.1 Sentence sampling

Since BLEU, the metric we care about, is a gain function, our objective function maximizes the expected gain of our model. The expected gain, $\mathcal{G}$ of a probabilistic translation model on a corpus $\mathcal{D}$, defined with respect to the gain function $\text{BLEU}_{\hat{e}}(e)$ is given by

$$\mathcal{G} = \sum_{\langle \hat{e}, f \rangle \in \mathcal{D}} \sum_{e,a} p(e, a|f) \text{BLEU}_{\hat{e}}(e) \qquad (5)$$

where $\hat{e}$ is the reference translation, e is a hypothesis translation and BLEU refers to the sentence-level approximation of the metric.

Using the probabilistic formulation of Equation 1, the optimization of the objective in (5) is facilitated by the fact that it is continuous and differentiable with respect to the model parameters θ to give

$$\frac{\partial \mathcal{G}}{\partial \theta_k} = \sum_{\substack{\langle \hat{e}, f \rangle \\ \in \mathcal{D}}} \sum_{e,a} \text{BLEU}_{\hat{e}}(e) \frac{\partial p}{\partial \theta_k} \qquad (6)$$

$$\text{where } \frac{\partial p}{\partial \theta_k} = \left(h_k - \mathbb{E}_{p(e,a|f)}[h_k]\right) p(e, a|f)$$

Since the gradient is expressed in terms of expectations of feature values, it can easily be calculated using the sampler and then first-order optimization techniques can be applied to find optimal values of θ. Because of the noise introduced by the sampler, we used stochastic gradient descent (SGD), with a learning rate that gets updated after each step proportionally to difference in successive gradients (Schraudolph, 1999).

While our initial formulation of minimum risk training is similar to that of Arun et al. (2009), in preliminary experiments we observed a tendency for translation performance on held-out data to quickly increase to a maximum and then plateau. Hypothesizing that we were being trapped in local maxima as $\mathcal{G}$ is non-convex, we decided to employ *deterministic annealing* (Rose, 1998) to smooth the objective function to ensure that the optimizer explored as large a region as possible of the space before it settled on an optimal weight set. Our instantiation of deterministic annealing (DA) is based on the work of Smith and Eisner (2006), and involves the addition of an entropic prior to the objective in Equation 5 to give

$$\hat{\mathcal{G}} = \sum_{\langle \hat{e}, f \rangle \in \mathcal{D}} \left[\left(\sum_{e,a} p(e, a|f) \text{BLEU}_{\hat{e}}(e) \right) + T.H(p) \right]$$

where $H(p)$ is the entropy of the probability distribution $p(e, a|f)$, and $T > 0$ is a temperature paramater which is gradually lowered as the optimization progresses according to some *annealing schedule*.

Differentiating with respect to θ_k then shows that the annealed gradient is given by the following expression:

$$\sum_{\substack{\langle \hat{e}, f \rangle \\ \in \mathcal{D}}} \sum_{e,a} (\text{BLEU}_{\hat{e}}(e) - T(1 + \log p)) \frac{\partial p}{\partial \theta_k}$$

$$\text{where } \frac{\partial p}{\partial \theta_k} = \left(h_k - \mathbb{E}_{p(e,a|f)}[h_k]\right) p(e, a|f)$$

A high value of T leads the optimizer to find weights which describe a fairly flat distribution, whereas a lower value of T pushes the optimizer towards a more peaked distribution. We perform 10 to 20 iterations of SGD at each temperature.

In their deterministic annealing formulation, (Smith and Eisner, 2006; Li and Eisner, 2009), express the parameterization of the distribution $\boldsymbol{\theta}$ as $\gamma\hat{\boldsymbol{\theta}}$ (where γ is the *scaling factor*) and perform optimization in two steps, the first optimizing $\hat{\boldsymbol{\theta}}$ and the second optimizing γ. We experimented with this two stage optimization process, but found that simply performing an unconstrained optimization on $\boldsymbol{\theta}$ gave better results.

4.2 Corpus sampling

While the objective functions in Equations 5 and 4.1 use a sentence-level variant of BLEU, the model's test-time performance is evaluated with corpus level BLEU. The lack of correlation between sentence-level BLEU and corpus BLEU is well-known (Chiang et al., 2008a). Therefore, in an effort to address this issue, we tried maximizing expected corpus BLEU directly.

In other words, given a training corpus of the form $\langle \mathcal{C}_F, \mathcal{C}_{\hat{E}} \rangle$ where $\mathcal{C}_F$ is a set of source sentences and $\mathcal{C}_{\hat{E}}$ its corresponding reference translations, we consider a gain function defined on the hypothesized translation $\mathcal{C}_E$ of the input $\mathcal{C}_F$ with respect to $\mathcal{C}_{\hat{E}}$.

The objective in equation 5 therefore becomes:

$$\mathcal{G} = \sum_{\mathcal{C}_E} P(\mathcal{C}_E|\mathcal{C}_F)\text{BLEU}_{\mathcal{C}_{\hat{E}}}(\mathcal{C}_E) \quad (7)$$

The pair $(\mathcal{C}_E, \mathcal{C}_F)$ is denoted as a *corpus sample* corresponding to a sequence $(e^1, a^1), \ldots, (e^N, a^N)$ of derivations of the corresponding source strings $f^1, \ldots, f^N$ of source corpus $\mathcal{C}_F$.

Although the sampler described in Section 2 generates samples at the sentence level, we can use it to generate corpus samples by applying the following procedure (see Figure 1). For each source sentence f^i in the corpus, we generate a sequence of samples $(e^i_1, a^i_1), \ldots, (e^i_n, a^i_n)$ using the sampler. From each of these sequences of samples, we then *resample* new sequences of derivation samples, one for each source sentence in the corpus. The first corpus sample is then obtained by iterating through the source sentences and taking the first resampled derivation for each sentence, then the second corpus sample by taking the second resampled derivation, and so on. The resampling step is necessary to eliminate any biases due to the order of the generated samples.

The corpus sampling procedure invariably generates a set of samples which are all distinct and so would give us a uniform estimate of the probability distribution $P(\mathcal{C}_E|\mathcal{C}_F)$. However this is not a problem since we are not interested in evaluating the actual distribution; we just need to calculate expectations of feature values and BLEU scores over the distribution. The feature values of a corpus sample are the average of the feature values of its constituting derivations and its BLEU score is computed based on the yield of its derivations.

When training using corpus sampling we process the training corpus in batches $\langle \mathcal{C}_F, \mathcal{C}_{\hat{E}} \rangle$, treating each batch as a corpus in its own right, and updating the weights after each batch.

The gradient for the objective function in (7) is:

$$\frac{\partial \mathcal{G}}{\partial \theta_k} = \sum_{\mathcal{C}_E} \text{BLEU}_{\mathcal{C}_{\hat{E}}}(\mathcal{C}_E) \frac{\partial P}{\partial \theta_k}$$

$$\text{where } \frac{\partial P}{\partial \theta_k} = \left(h^{\mathcal{C}}_k - \mathbb{E}_{P(\mathcal{C}_E|\mathcal{C}_F)}[h^{\mathcal{C}}_k]\right) P(\mathcal{C}_E|\mathcal{C}_F)$$

where $h^{\mathcal{C}}_k$ is the k-th component of a corpus sample feature vector.

During deterministic annealing for sentence sampling, the entropy term is computed over the distribution $p(e, a|f)$ of each individual sentence. While corpus sampling, we are considering the distribution $P(\mathcal{C}_E|\mathcal{C}_F)$ but the estimated distribution is always uniform. So we define the entropic prior term over the distribution $p(e, a|f)$ of the sentences making up the corpus sample.

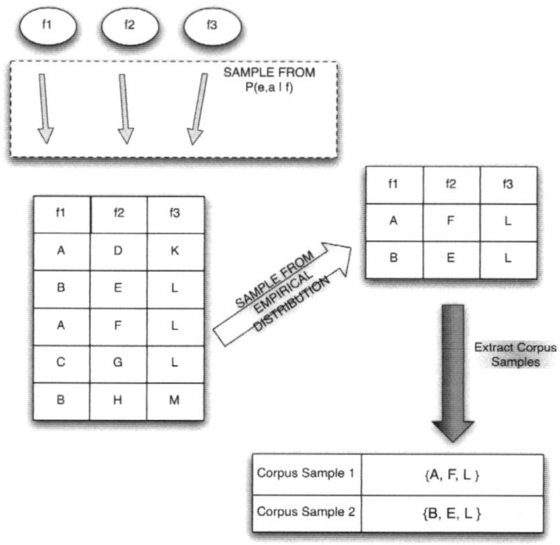

Figure 1: Example illustrating the extraction of 2 corpus samples for a corpus of source sentences f1, f2, f3. In the first step, we sample 5 derivations for each source sentence. We then resample 2 derivations from the empirical distributions of each source sentence.

The annealed corpus sampling objective is therefore:

$$\sum_{\mathcal{C}_E} P(\mathcal{C}_E|\mathcal{C}_F)\text{BLEU}_{\mathcal{C}_{\hat{E}}}(\mathcal{C}_E) + \frac{T}{|\mathcal{C}_F|} \sum_{f \in \mathcal{C}_F} H(p(e, a|f))$$

The gradient of this objective is of similar form to the sentence sampling gradient in Equation (6).

5 Experiments

5.1 Training Data and Preparation

The experiments in this section were performed using the Europarl section of the French-English and German-English parallel corpora from the WMT09 shared translation task (Callison-Burch et al., 2009), as well as 300k parallel Arabic-English sentences from the NIST MT evaluation training data.[3] For all language pairs, we constructed

[3]The Arabic-English training data consists of the eTIRR corpus (LDC2004E72), the Arabic news corpus (LDC2004T17), the Ummah corpus (LDC2004T18), and the

a phrase-based translation model as described in Koehn et al. (2003), limiting the phrase length to 5. The target side of the parallel corpus was used to train 3-gram language models. For the German and French systems, the DEV2006 set was used for model tuning and the first half of TEST2007 (in-domain) for heldout testing. Final testing was performed on NEWS-DEV2009B (out-of-domain) and the first half of TEST2008 (in-domain). For the Arabic system, the MT02 set (10 reference translations) was used for tuning and MT03 and MT05 (4 reference translations, each) were used for held-out testing and final testing respectively. To reduce the size of the phrase table, we used the association-score technique suggested by Johnson et al. (2007). Translation quality is reported using case-insensitive BLEU.

5.2 Baseline

Our baseline system is phrase-based Moses (Koehn et al., 2007) with feature weights trained using MERT. Moses and the Gibbs sampler use identical feature sets.[4]

The MERT optimization algorithm uses multiple random restarts to avoid getting stuck in a poor local optima. Therefore, every time MERT is run, it produces a slightly different final weight vector leading to varying test set results. While this characteristic of MERT is typically ignored, we account for it by performing MERT training 10 times for each of the 3 language pairs, decoding the test sets with each of the 10 optimized weight sets. We present the best and the worst test set results along with the mean and the standard deviation (σ) of these results in Table 1. We report results using the Moses implementation of Viterbi, nbest MBR and lattice MBR decoding (Kumar et al., 2009). [5] For both nbest and lattice MBR decoding, the hypothesis set was composed of the top 1000 unique translations produced by the Viterbi decoder, and the same 1000 translations were used as evidence set for nbest MBR.

As Table 1 shows, translation results using MERT optimized weights vary markedly from one tuning run to the other, with results varying from a range of 0.3% BLEU to 1.3% BLEU when using Viterbi decoding. We also see that, bar in-domain German to English, MBR decoding gives a small improvement on all other datasets.

Surprisingly, lattice MBR only gives improvements on two datasets and actually leads to a *drop* in performance on the other 3 datasets. We discuss possible reasons for this in Section 6.

5.3 Sentence sampling

At training time, the optimization algorithm is initialized with zero weights and the sampler is initialized with a random derivation from Moses. To get rid of any initialization biases, the first 100 samples are discarded.[6] We then run the sampler for 1000 iterations after which we perform *reheating* whereby the distribution is progressively flattened. Samples are not collected during this period. Reheating allows the sampler more mobility around the search space thus possibly escaping any local optima it might be trapped in. We subsequently run the sampler for 1000 more iterations. We denote this procedure as running 2 *chains* of the sampler. We use batch sizes of 96 randomly selected sentences for SGD optimization.

During DA, our cooling schedule is an exponentially decaying one with decay rate set to 0.9, performing 20 iterations of SGD optimization at each temperature setting. Five training runs were performed and the BLEU scores averaged. The feature weights were output every 50 iterations and performance measured on the heldout set by running the sampler as a decoder. At decode time, we use the same sampler configurations as during training but run 2 chains each for 5000 iterations.

For MBR decoding, we use the entirety of this sample set as our evidence set and use the top 1000 most probable translations as the hypothesis set.

5.4 Corpus sampling

For our corpus sampling experiments, we sample using the same procedure as in sentence sampling but using 2 chains of 2000 iterations. We then resample 2000 corpus samples from the empirical distribution estimated from the first 4000 samples. For Arabic-English training, we used batch sizes of 100 randomly selected sentences for experiments without DA and batches of 400 random

sentences with confidence $c > 0.995$ in the ISI automatically extracted web parallel corpus (LDC2006T02).

[4]We use 5 translation model scores, distance-based distortion, language model and word penalty. The reordering limit is set to 6 for all experiments.

[5]For nbest and lattice MBR decoding, we optimized for the scaling factor using a grid-search on held-out data. For lattice MBR decoding, we optimized the lattice density and set the p and r parameters as per Tromble et al. (2008).

[6]This procedure is referred to as *burn-in* in the MCMC literature.

	Viterbi				nMBR				lMBR			
	min	max	mean	σ	min	max	mean	σ	min	max	mean	σ
AR-EN MT05	43.7	44.3	44.0	0.17	44.2	44.5	44.4	0.13	44.2	44.6	**44.5**	0.12
FR-EN In	33.1	33.4	33.3	0.10	33.2	33.6	**33.4**	0.12	32.3	32.7	32.6	0.13
FR-EN Out	19.1	19.6	19.4	0.18	19.3	19.7	**19.5**	0.12	19.1	19.4	19.3	0.12
DE-EN In	27.6	27.9	**27.8**	0.10	27.6	27.9	27.7	0.10	27.2	27.5	27.4	0.10
DE-EN Out	14.9	16.2	15.7	0.33	15.0	16.3	15.7	0.33	15.3	16.4	**16.0**	0.30

Table 1: Baseline results - MERT trained models decoded using Viterbi, nbest MBR (nMBR) and lattice MBR (lMBR). MERT was run 10 times for each language pair. We report minimum, maximum, mean and standard deviation of test set BLEU scores across the 10 runs.

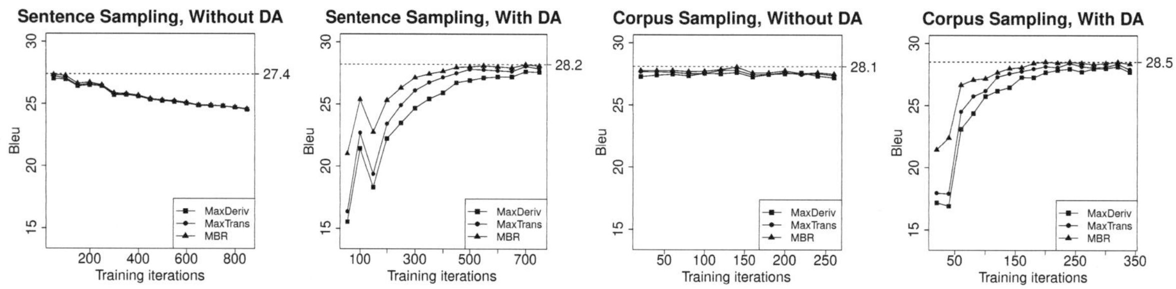

Figure 2: Heldout performance for German-English training averaged across 5 minimum risk training runs. Best scores achieved are indicated by dotted line.

sentences with DA. The size of the batches corresponds to the number of sentences that form a corpus sample. For German/French to English experiments, we used batches of 100 random sentences for training with and without DA. We perform 10 optimizations at each temperature setting during deterministic annealing. Test time conditions are identical to the sentence sampling ones and we measure performance on a held-out set after every 20 iterations of the learner.

5.5 Results

Figures 2 and 3 show the scores on the German-English and Arabic-English held-out sets respectively comparing all four training regimes: corpus vs sentence sampling, DA vs without DA. Results for French-English training are similar.

We focus our analysis on the Arabic-English experimental setup. Without deterministic annealing, the learner converges quickly, usually after just 20 iterations, after which performance degrades steadily. The magnitudes of the weights are large, sharpening the distribution. There is not much diversity amongst the sampled derivations, i.e. the entropy of the sample set is low. Therefore, all 3 decoding regimes give very similar results. With the addition of the entropic prior, the model is slow to converge before the so-called *phase transition* occurs (usually after around 50 iterations), after which performance goes up to reach a peak (45.2 BLEU) higher than that without the prior (44.2 BLEU), before steadily declining. The entropic prior encourages diversity among the sample set, especially at high temperature settings.

In the presence of diversity, the benefits of marginalization over derivations is clear: MaxTrans does better than MaxDeriv and MBR does best, confirm recent findings of (Blunsom et al., 2008; Arun et al., 2009) that MaxTrans improves over MaxDeriv decoding for models trained to account for multiple derivations. As the temperature decreases to zero, the model sharpens, effectively intent on maximizing one-best performance and thus voiding the benefits of MaxTrans and MBR. Figures 2 and 3 also show that corpus sampling improves over sentence sampling, although not by much (+ 0.3 BLEU).

5.6 Comparison with MERT baseline

Having established the superiority of the pipeline of expected corpus BLEU training with DA followed by MBR decoding over other alternatives considered, we compare it to the best results obtained with MERT optimized Moses (bold scores from Table 1). To account for sampler variance during both training and decoding, we average scores across 50 runs; 10 decoding runs each using the best weight set from 5 training runs. Results

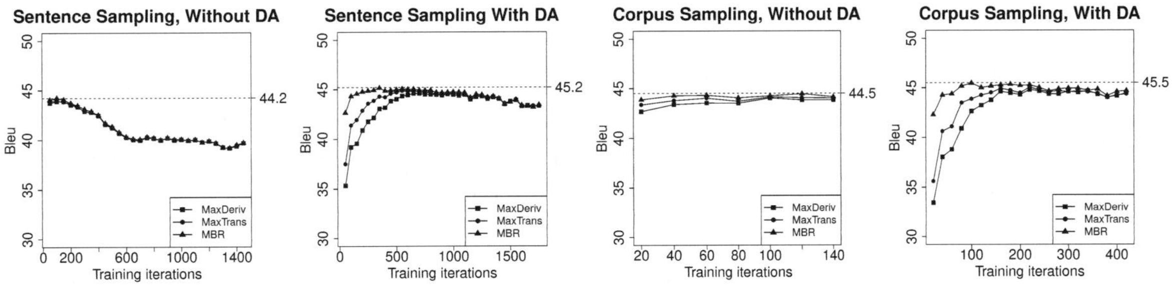

Figure 3: Heldout performance for Arabic-English training averaged across 5 minimum risk training runs. Best scores achieved are indicated by dotted line.

are shown in Table 2.[7]

We observe that on 3 out of 5 datasets, the sampler results are much more stable than MERT and as stable on the other 2 datasets. We attribute the improved stability to the more powerful optimization algorithm used by the sampler which uses gradient information to steer the model towards better weights. MERT, alternatively, optimizes one feature at a time using line search and therefore does not explore the full feature space as thoroughly.

Translation results with the sampler are better than with MERT on 2 datasets, are equal on another 2 and worse in one case. The improvements withe the sampler are obtained in the case of out-of-domain data suggesting that the minimum risk training objective generalizes better than the 1-best objective of MERT.

Test set	MERT/Moses		Sampler	
	Best	σ	MBR	σ
AR-EN MT05	**44.5** (lMBR)	0.12	**44.5**	0.14
FR-EN In	**33.4** (nMBR)	0.12	33.2	0.06
FR-EN Out	19.5 (nMBR)	0.12	**19.8**	0.05
DE-EN In	**27.8** (Viterbi)	0.10	**27.8**	0.11
DE-EN Out	16.0 (lMBR)	0.30	**16.6**	0.12

Table 2: *Final* results comparing MERT/Moses pipeline with unified sampler pipeline. Sampler uses corpus sampling during training and MBR decoding at test time. Moses results are averaged across decoding runs using weights from 10 MERT runs and sampler results are averaged across 10 decoding runs for each of 5 different training runs. We report BLEU scores and standard deviation (σ).

[7]The MBR decoding times, averaged over 10 decoding runs of 50 sentences each, are 10 secs/sent for Moses nbest MBR, 40 secs/sent for Moses lattice MBR and 180 secs/sent for the sampler.

	Viterbi	nMBR	lMBR	Sampler MBR
AR-EN MT05	44.2	44.4	**44.8**	**44.8**
FR-EN In	33.1	33.2	**33.3**	**33.3**
FR-EN Out	19.6	19.8	**19.9**	**19.9**
DE-EN In	27.7	27.9	**28.0**	**28.0**
DE-EN Out	16.0	16.3	**16.6**	**16.6**

Table 3: Comparison of decoding methods using expected BLEU trained weights. We report Viterbi, nbest MBR (nMBR) and lattice MBR (lMBR) decoding scores vs *best* sampler MBR decoding performance. We selected the best weight set based on performance on heldout data.

5.7 Moses with expected BLEU weights

In a final set of experiments, we reran the Moses decoder this time using weights obtained through expected BLEU optimization. Here, for each language pair, we picked the weight set that gave the best results on held-out data. Note that the results which we show in Table 3 are over one run only, so are not strictly comparable to those in Table 2 which are averaged over several training and decoding runs. We also report the best results obtained with the sampler MBR decoder using these weights.

In contrast to Table 1, here we see a consistent improvement across all test-sets when going from Viterbi decoding to n-best then to lattice MBR. Except for in-domain French-English, the translation results are superior to the best scores shown (in bold) in Table 1, confirming that the minimum risk training objective is able to find good weight sets. Interestingly, we also observe that sampler MBR gets the same exact results for all test sets as lattice MBR.

6 Discussion

We have shown that the sampler of Arun et al. (2009) can be used to perform minimum risk training over an unpruned search space. Our proposed corpus sampling technique, like MERT, is able to optimize corpus BLEU directly whereas alternate parameter estimation techniques usually employed in SMT optimize *approximations* of BLEU. Chiang et al. (2008b) accounts for the online nature of the MIRA optimization algorithm by smoothing the sentence-level BLEU precision counts of a translation with a weighted average of the precision counts of previously decoded sentences, thus approximating corpus BLEU. As for minimum risk training, prior implementations have either used sentence-level BLEU (Zens et al., 2007) or a linear approximation to BLEU (Smith and Eisner, 2006; Li and Eisner, 2009).

At test time, the sampler works best as an MBR decoder, but also allows us to verify past claims about the benefits of marginalizing over alignments during decoding. We compare the sampler MBR decoder's performance against MERT-optimized Moses run under three different decoding regimes, finding that the sampler does as well or better on 4 out of 5 datasets.

Our training and testing pipeline has the advantage of being able to handle a large number of both local and global features so we expect in the future to outperform the standard MERT and dynamic programming-based search pipeline further.

As shown in Section 5.2, lattice MBR in some cases leads to a marked drop in performance. (Kumar et al., 2009) mention that the linear approximation to BLEU used in their lattice MBR algorithm is not guaranteed to match corpus BLEU, especially on unseen test sets. To account for these cases, they allow their algorithm to *back-off to the MAP* solution. One possible reason for the drop in performance in our lattice MBR experiments is that the implementation we use does not employ this back-off strategy.

Table 3 provides valuable insights as to the merits of the lattice MBR approach versus our own sampling based pipeline. Firstly, whereas with MERT optimized weights, the benefits of lattice MBR are debatable (Table 1), running Moses with minimum risk trained weights gives results that are in line with what we would expect - lattice MBR does systematically better than competing decoding algorithms. This suggests that the unbiased minimum risk training criterion used by the sampler is a better fit for lattice MBR than the MERT criterion, and also that the mismatch between linear and corpus BLEU mentioned before might not be the reason for the results in Table 1.

Secondly, we find that sampling MBR matches lattice MBR on the minimum risk trained weights. The MBR sampler uses samples drawn from the distribution as hypothesis and evidence sets, typically 1000 samples for the former and 10000 samples for the latter. In the lattice MBR experiments of Tromble et al. (2008), it is shown that this size of hypothesis set is sufficient. Their evidence set, however, is significantly larger than ours.[8] Table 3 suggests that, since it is not biased by heuristic pruning, the sampler's limited evidence set is enough to give a good estimate of the probability distribution whereas beam-search based MBR needs to scale from using n-best lists to lattices to get equivalent results.

Sampling the phrase-based model is expensive, meaning that lattice MBR is still faster (around 4x) to run than sampler MBR. However, due to the *unified* nature of the training and decoding criterion in our approach, the minimum risk trained weights can be plugged *directly* into the sampler MBR decoder, whereas lattice MBR requires an additional expensive step of tuning the model hyper-parameters (Kumar et al., 2009).

In future work, we also intend to look at more efficient ways of generating samples. One possibility is to interleave Gibbs sampling steps using low order ngram language model distributions with Metropolis-Hasting steps that use higher order language model distributions.

7 Related Work

Expected BLEU training for phrase-based models has been successfully attempted by (Smith and Eisner, 2006; Zens et al., 2007), however they both used biased n-best lists to approximate the posterior distribution. Li and Eisner (2009) present work on performing expected BLEU training with deterministic annealing on translation forests generated by Hiero (Chiang, 2007). Since BLEU does not factorize over the search graph, they use the linear approximation of Tromble et al. (2008) instead.

Pauls et al. (2009) present an alternate training criterion over translation forests called CoBLEU,

[8] up to 10^{81} as per Tromble et al. (2008)

similar in spirit to expected BLEU training, but aimed to maximize the *expected counts* of n-grams appearing in reference translations. This training criterion is used in conjunction with consensus decoding (DeNero et al., 2009), a linear-time approximation of MBR.

In contrast to the approaches above, the algorithms presented in this paper are able to explore an *unpruned* search space. By using corpus sampling, we can perform minimum risk training with corpus BLEU rather than any approximations of this metric. Also, since we maintain a probabilistic formulation across training and decoding, our approach does not require a grid-search for a scaling factor as in Tromble et al. (2008).

8 Conclusions

We have presented a unified approach to the task of parameter estimation and decoding for a phrase-based system using the standard translation evaluation metric, BLEU. Using a Gibbs sampler to explore the entire probability distribution allows us to implement two probabilistic sound algorithms, minimum risk training and its equivalent, MBR decoding, in an unbiased way. The probabilistic formulation also allows us to use gradient based optimization techniques which produce stable model parameters. At decoding time, we show the benefits of marginalizing over derivations and that MBR gives better results than other decoding criteria.

Since our optimization algorithm can cope with a large number of features, in future work, we plan to incorporate more expressive features in the model. We use a Gibbs sampler for inference so there is scope for exploring non-local features which might not easily be added to dynamic programming based models.

Acknowledgments

This research was supported in part by the GALE program of the Defense Advanced Research Projects Agency, Contract No. HR0011-06-2-001; and by the EuroMatrix project funded by the European Commission (6th Framework Programme). The project made use of the resources provided by the Edinburgh Compute and Data Facility (http://www.ecdf.ed.ac.uk/). The ECDF is partially supported by the eDIKT initiative (http://www.edikt.org.uk/).

References

Abhishek Arun, Chris Dyer, Barry Haddow, Phil Blunsom, Adam Lopez, and Philipp Koehn. 2009. Monte carlo inference and maximization for phrase-based translation. In *Proceedings of CoNLL*, pages 102–110.

Phil Blunsom and Miles Osborne. 2008. Probabilistic inference for machine translation. In *Proc. of EMNLP 2008*.

Phil Blunsom, Trevor Cohn, and Miles Osborne. 2008. A discriminative latent variable model for statistical machine translation. In *Proc. of ACL-HLT*.

Alexandre Bouchard-Côté, Slav Petrov, and Dan Klein. 2009. Randomized pruning: Efficiently calculating expectations in large dynamic programs. In *Advances in Neural Information Processing Systems 22*, pages 144–152.

Chris Callison-Burch, Philipp Koehn, Christoph Monz, and Josh Schroeder, editors. 2009. *Proc. of Workshop on Machine Translations*.

David Chiang, Steve DeNeefe, Yee Seng Chan, and Hwee Tou Ng. 2008a. Decomposability of translation metrics for improved evaluation and efficient algorithms. In *Proceedings of the 2008 Conference on Empirical Methods in Natural Language Processing*, pages 610–619, Honolulu, Hawaii, October. Association for Computational Linguistics.

David Chiang, Yuval Marton, and Philip Resnik. 2008b. Online large-margin training of syntactic and structural translation features. In *Proceedings of the 2008 Conference on Empirical Methods in Natural Language Processing*, pages 224–233, Honolulu, Hawaii, October. Association for Computational Linguistics.

D. Chiang. 2007. Hierarchical phrase-based translation. *Computational Linguistics*, 33(2):201–228.

John DeNero, David Chiang, and Kevin Knight. 2009. Fast consensus decoding over translation forests. In *Proceedings of ACL/AFNLP*, pages 567–575.

Stuart Geman and Donald Geman. 1984. Stochastic relaxation, Gibbs distributions and the Bayesian restoration of images. *IEEE Transactions on Pattern Analysis and Machine Intelligence*, 6:721–741.

J.H. Johnson, J. Martin, G. Foster, and R. Kuhn. 2007. Improving translation quality by discarding most of the phrasetable. In *Proc. of EMNLP-CoNLL*, Prague.

P. Koehn, F.J. Och, and D. Marcu. 2003. Statistical phrase-based translation. In *Proc. of HLT-NAACL*, pages 48–54, Morristown, NJ, USA.

P. Koehn, H. Hoang, A. Birch Mayne, C. Callison-Burch, M. Federico, N. Bertoldi, B. Cowan, W. Shen, C. Moran, R. Zens, C. Dyer, O. Bojar, A. Constantin, and E. Herbst. 2007. Moses: Open source toolkit for statistical machine translation. In *Proceedings of ACL Demos*, pages 177–180.

S. Kumar and W. Byrne. 2004. Minimum Bayes-risk decoding for statistical machine translation. In *Processings of HLT-NAACL*.

Shankar Kumar, Wolfgang Macherey, Chris Dyer, and Franz Och. 2009. Efficient minimum error rate training and minimum bayes-risk decoding for translation hypergraphs and lattices. In *Proceedings of ACL/AFNLP*, pages 163–171.

Zhifei Li and Jason Eisner. 2009. First- and second-order expectation semirings with applications to minimum-risk training on translation forests. In *Proceedings of EMNLP*, pages 40–51.

Zhifei Li, Jason Eisner, and Sanjeev Khudanpur. 2009. Variational decoding for statistical machine translation. In *Proceedings of ACL/AFNLP*, pages 593–601.

F. Och. 2003. Minimum error rate training in statistical machine translation. In *Proceedings of ACL*, pages 160–167.

K. Papineni, S. Roukos, T. Ward, and W.-J. Zhu. 2002. BLEU: a method for automatic evaluation of machine translation. In *Proceedings of ACL*, pages 311–318.

Adam Pauls, John Denero, and Dan Klein. 2009. Consensus training for consensus decoding in machine translation. In *Proceedings of EMNLP*, pages 1418–1427.

Kenneth Rose. 1998. Deterministic annealing for clustering, compression, classification, regression, and related optimization problems. In *Proceedings of the IEEE*, pages 2210–2239.

Nicol N. Schraudolph. 1999. Local gain adaptation in stochastic gradient descent. Technical Report IDSIA-09-99, IDSIA.

David A. Smith and Jason Eisner. 2006. Minimum risk annealing for training log-linear models. In *Proceedings of COLING-ACL*, pages 787–794.

Roy Tromble, Shankar Kumar, Franz Och, and Wolfgang Macherey. 2008. Lattice Minimum Bayes-Risk decoding for statistical machine translation. In *Proceedings of EMNLP*, pages 620–629.

Richard Zens, Sasa Hasan, and Hermann Ney. 2007. A systematic comparison of training criteria for statistical machine translation. In *Proceedings of EMNLP*, pages 524–532.

N-best Reranking by Multitask Learning

Kevin Duh **Katsuhito Sudoh** **Hajime Tsukada** **Hideki Isozaki** **Masaaki Nagata**
NTT Communication Science Laboratories
2-4 Hikaridai, Seika-cho, Soraku-gun, Kyoto, 619-0237, Japan
{kevinduh,sudoh,tsukada,isozaki}@cslab.kecl.ntt.co.jp
nagata.masaaki@lab.ntt.co.jp

Abstract

We propose a new framework for N-best reranking on sparse feature sets. The idea is to reformulate the reranking problem as a Multitask Learning problem, where each N-best list corresponds to a distinct task.

This is motivated by the observation that N-best lists often show significant differences in feature distributions. Training a single reranker directly on this heterogenous data can be difficult.

Our proposed meta-algorithm solves this challenge by using multitask learning (such as ℓ_1/ℓ_2 regularization) to discover common feature representations across N-best lists. This meta-algorithm is simple to implement, and its modular approach allows one to plug-in different learning algorithms from existing literature. As a proof of concept, we show statistically significant improvements on a machine translation system involving millions of features.

1 Introduction

Many natural language processing applications, such as machine translation (MT), parsing, and language modeling, benefit from the N-best reranking framework (Shen et al., 2004; Collins and Koo, 2005; Roark et al., 2007). The advantage of N-best reranking is that it abstracts away the complexities of first-pass decoding, allowing the researcher to try new features and learning algorithms with fast experimental turnover.

In the N-best reranking scenario, the training data consists of sets of hypotheses (i.e. N-best lists) generated by a first-pass system, along with their labels. Given a new N-best list, the goal is to rerank it such that the best hypothesis appears near the top of the list. Existing research have focused on training a *single* reranker directly on the entire data. This approach is reasonable if the data is homogenous, but it fails when features vary significantly across different N-best lists. In particular, when one employs *sparse* feature sets, one seldom finds features that are simultaneously active on multiple N-best lists.

In this case, we believe it is more advantageous to view the N-best reranking problem as a *multitask learning* problem, where each N-best list corresponds to a distinct task. Multitask learning, a subfield of machine learning, focuses on how to effectively train on a set of different but related datasets (tasks). Our heterogenous N-best list data fits nicely with this assumption.

The contribution of this work is three-fold:

1. We introduce the idea of viewing N-best reranking as a multitask learning problem. This view is particularly apt to any general reranking problem with sparse feature sets.

2. We propose a simple meta-algorithm that first discovers common feature representations across N-bests (via multitask learning) before training a conventional reranker. Thus it is easily applicable to existing systems.

3. We demonstrate that our proposed method outperforms the conventional reranking approach on a English-Japanese biomedical machine translation task involving millions of features.

The paper is organized as follows: Section 2 describes the feature sparsity problem and Section 3 presents our multitask solution. The effectiveness of our proposed approach is validated by experiments demonstrated in Section 4. Finally, Sections 5 and 6 discuss related work and conclusions.

2 The Problem of Sparse Feature Sets

For concreteness, we will describe N-best reranking in terms of machine translation (MT), though

Proceedings of the Joint 5th Workshop on Statistical Machine Translation and MetricsMATR, pages 375–383,
Uppsala, Sweden, 15-16 July 2010.

our approach is agnostic to the application. In MT reranking, the goal is to translate a foreign language sentence f into an English sentence e by picking from a set of likely translations. A standard approach is to use a linear model:

$$\hat{e} = \arg\max_{e \in N(f)} \mathbf{w}^T \cdot \mathbf{h}(e, f) \quad (1)$$

where $\mathbf{h}(e, f)$ is a D-dimensional feature vector, $\mathbf{w}$ is the weight vector to be trained, and $N(f)$ is the set of likely translations of f, i.e. the N-best list. The feature $\mathbf{h}(e, f)$ can be any quantity defined in terms of the sentence pair, such as translation model and language model probabilities.

Here we are interested in situations where the feature definitions can be quite sparse. A common methodology in reranking is to first design *feature templates* based on linguistic intuition and domain knowledge. Then, numerous features are instantiated based on the training data seen. For example, the work of (Watanabe et al., 2007) defines feature templates based on bilingual word alignments, which lead to extraction of heavily-lexicalized features of the form:

$$h(e, f) = \begin{cases} 1 & \text{if foreign word "Monsieur"} \\ & \text{and English word "Mr."} \\ & \text{co-occur in } e, f \\ 0 & \text{otherwise} \end{cases} \quad (2)$$

One can imagine that such features are sparse because it may only fire for input sentences that contain the word "Monsieur". For all other input sentences, it is an useless, inactive feature.

Another common feature involves word ngram templates, for example:

$$h(e, f) = \begin{cases} 1 & \text{if English trigram} \\ & \text{"Mr. Smith said" occurs in } e \\ 0 & \text{otherwise} \end{cases} \quad (3)$$

In this case, all possible trigrams seen in the N-best list are extracted as features. One can see that this kind of feature can be very sensitive to the first-pass decoder: if the decoder has loose reordering constraints, then we may extract exponentially many nonsense ngram features such as "Smith said Mr." and "said Smith Mr.". Granted, the reranker training algorithm may learn that these nonsense ngrams are indicative of poor hypotheses, but it is unlikely that the exact same nonsense ngrams will appear given a different test sentence.

In summary, the following issues compound to create extremely sparse feature sets:

1. Feature templates are heavily-lexicalized, which causes the number of features to grow unbounded as the the amount of data increases.

2. The input (f) has high variability (e.g. large vocabulary size), so that features for different inputs are rarely shared.

3. The N-best list output also exhibits high variability (e.g. many different word reorderings). Larger N may improve reranking performance, but may also increase feature sparsity.

When the number of features is too large, even popular reranking algorithms such as SVM (Shen et al., 2004) and MIRA (Watanabe et al., 2007; Chiang et al., 2009) may fail. Our goal here is to address this situation.

3 Proposed Reranking Framework

In the following, we first give an intuitive comparison between single vs. multiple task learning (Section 3.1), before presenting the general meta-algorithm (Section 3.2) and particular instantiations (Section 3.3).

3.1 Single vs. Multiple Tasks

Given a set of I input sentences $\{f^i\}$, the training data for reranking consists of a set of I N-best lists $\{(\mathbf{H}^i, \mathbf{y}^i)\}_{i=1,\ldots,I}$, where $\mathbf{H}^i$ are features and $\mathbf{y}^i$ are labels.

To clarify the notation:[1] for an input sentence f^i, there is a N-best list $N(f^i)$. For a N-best list $N(f^i)$, there are N feature vectors corresponding to the N hypotheses, each with dimension D. The collection of feature vectors for $N(f^i)$ is represented by $\mathbf{H}^i$, which can be seen as a $D \times N$ matrix. Finally, the N-dimensional vector of labels $\mathbf{y}^i$ indicates the translation quality of each hypothesis in $N(f^i)$. The purpose of the reranker training algorithm is to find good parameters from $\{(\mathbf{H}^i, \mathbf{y}^i)\}$.

[1]Generally we use bold font $\mathbf{h}$ to represent a vector, bold-capital font $\mathbf{H}$ to represent a matrix. Script h and $h(\cdot)$ may be scalar, function, or sentence (depends on context).

The conventional method of training a single reranker (single task formulation) involves optimizing a generic objective such as:

$$\arg\min_{\mathbf{w}} \sum_{i=1}^{I} L(\mathbf{w}, \mathbf{H}^i, \mathbf{y}^i) + \lambda\Omega(\mathbf{w}) \quad (4)$$

where $\mathbf{w} \in \mathbb{R}^D$ is the reranker trained on all lists, and $L(\cdot)$ is some loss function. $\Omega(\mathbf{w})$ is an optional regularizer, whose effect is traded-off by the constant λ. For example, the SVM reranker for MT (Shen et al., 2004) defines $L(\cdot)$ to be some function of sentence-level BLEU score, and $\Omega(\mathbf{w})$ to be the large margin regularizer.[2]

On the other hand, multitask learning involves solving for multiple weights, $\mathbf{w}^1, \mathbf{w}^2, \ldots, \mathbf{w}^I$, one for each N-best list. One class of multitask learning algorithms, Joint Regularization, solves the following objective:

$$\arg\min_{\mathbf{w}^1,..,\mathbf{w}^I} \sum_{i=1}^{I} L(\mathbf{w}^i, \mathbf{H}^i, \mathbf{y}^i) + \lambda\Omega(\mathbf{w}^1, .., \mathbf{w}^I) \quad (5)$$

The loss decomposes by task but the joint regularizer $\Omega(\mathbf{w}^1, .., \mathbf{w}^I)$ couples together the different weight parameters. The key is to note that multiple weights allow the algorithm to fit the heterogenous data better, compared to a single weight vector. Yet these weights are still tied together so that some information can be shared across N-best lists (tasks).

One instantiation of Eq. 5 is ℓ_1/ℓ_2 regularization: $\Omega(\mathbf{w}^1, .., \mathbf{w}^I) \triangleq ||\mathbf{W}||_{1,2}$, where $\mathbf{W} = [\mathbf{w}^1|\mathbf{w}^2|\ldots|\mathbf{w}^I]^T$ is a I-by-D matrix of stacked weight vectors. The norm is computed by first taking the 2-norm on columns of $\mathbf{W}$, then taking a 1-norm on the resulting D-length vector. This encourages the optimizer to choose a small subset of features that are useful across all tasks.

For example, suppose two different sets of weight vectors $\mathbf{W_a}$ and $\mathbf{W_b}$ for a 2 lists, 4 features reranking problem. The ℓ_1/ℓ_2 norm for $\mathbf{W_a}$ is 14; the ℓ_1/ℓ_2 norm for $\mathbf{W_b}$ is 12. If both have the same loss $L(\cdot)$ in Eq. 5, the multitask optimizer would prefer $\mathbf{W_b}$ since more features are shared:

$$\mathbf{W_a}: \begin{bmatrix} 4 & 0 & 0 & 3 \\ 0 & 4 & 3 & 0 \end{bmatrix} \qquad \mathbf{W_b}: \begin{bmatrix} 4 & 3 & 0 & 0 \\ 0 & 4 & 3 & 0 \end{bmatrix}$$

$$4 \quad 4 \quad 3 \quad 3 \rightarrow 14 \qquad\qquad 4 \quad 5 \quad 3 \quad 0 \rightarrow 12$$

[2]In MT, evaluation metrics like BLEU do not exactly decompose across sentences, so for some training algorithms this loss is an approximation.

3.2 Proposed Meta-algorithm

We are now ready to present our general reranking meta-algorithm (see Algorithm 1), termed Reranking by Multitask Learning (RML).

Algorithm 1 Reranking by Multitask Learning

Input: N-best data $\{(\mathbf{H}^i, \mathbf{y}^i)\}_{i=1,\ldots,I}$
Output: Common feature representation $h_c(e, f)$ and weight vector $\mathbf{w}_c$

1: [optional] RandomHashing($\{\mathbf{H}^i\}$)
2: $\mathbf{W}$ = MultitaskLearn($\{(\mathbf{H}^i, \mathbf{y}^i)\}$)
3: h_c = ExtractCommonFeature($\mathbf{W}$)
4: $\{\mathbf{H}^i_c\}$ = RemapFeature($\{\mathbf{H}^i\}, h_c$)
5: $\mathbf{w}_c$ = ConventionalReranker($\{(\mathbf{H}^i_c, \mathbf{y}^i)\}$)

The first step, random hashing, is optional. Random hashing is an effective trick for reducing the dimension of sparse feature sets without suffering losses in fidelity (Weinberger et al., 2009; Ganchev and Dredze, 2008). It works by collapsing random subsets of features. This step can be performed to speed-up multitask learning later. In some cases, the original feature dimension may be so large that hashed representations may be necessary.

The next two steps are key. A multitask learning algorithm is run on the N-best lists, and a common feature space shared by all lists is extracted. For example, if one uses the multitask objective of Eq. 5, the result of step 2 is a set of weights $\mathbf{W}$. ExtractCommonFeature($\mathbf{W}$) then returns the feature id's (either from original or hashed representation) that receive nonzero weight in any of $\mathbf{W}$.[3] The new features $h_c(e, f)$ are expected to have lower dimension than the original features $h(e, f)$. Section 3.3 describes in detail different multitask methods that can be plugged-in to this step.

The final two steps involve a conventional reranker. In step 4, we remap the N-best list data according to the new feature representations $h_c(e, f)$. In step 5, we train a conventional reranker on this common representation, which by now should have overcome sparsity issues. Using a conventional reranker at the end allows us to exploit existing rerankers designed for specific NLP applications. In a sense, our meta-algorithm simply involves a change of representation for the conventional reranking scenario, where the

[3]For example in $\mathbf{W_b}$, features 1-3 have nonzero weights and are extracted. Feature 4 is discarded.

new representation is found by multitask methods which are well-suited to heterogenous data.

3.3 Multitask Objective Functions

Here, we describe various multitask methods that can be plugged in Step 2 of Algorithm 1. Our goal is to demonstrate that a wide range of existing methods from the multitask learning literature can be brought to our problem. We categorize multitask methods into two major approaches:

1. Joint Regularization: Eq. 5 is an example of joint regularization, with ℓ_1/ℓ_2 norm being a particular regularizer. The idea is to use the regularizer to ensure that the learned functions of related tasks are close to each other. The popular ℓ_1/ℓ_2 objective can be optimized by various methods, such as boosting (Obozinski et al., 2009) and convex programming (Argyriou et al., 2008). Yet another regularizer is the ℓ_1/ℓ_∞ norm (Quattoni et al., 2009), which replaces the 2-norm with a max.

One could also define a regularizer to ensure that each task-specific $\mathbf{w}^i$ is close to some average parameter, e.g. $\sum_i ||\mathbf{w}^i - \mathbf{w}^{avg}||_2$. If we interpret $\mathbf{w}^{avg}$ as a prior, we begin to see links to **Hierarchical Bayesian** methods for multitask learning (Finkel and Manning, 2009; Daume, 2009).

2. Shared Subspace: This approach assumes that there is an underlying feature subspace that is common to all tasks. Early works on multitask learning implement this by neural networks, where different tasks have different output layers but share the same hidden layer (Caruana, 1997).

Another method is to write the weight vector as two parts $\mathbf{w} = [\mathbf{u}; \mathbf{v}]$ and let the task-specific function be $\mathbf{u}^T \cdot \mathbf{h}(e, f) + \mathbf{v}^T \cdot \Theta \cdot \mathbf{h}(e, f)$ (Ando and Zhang, 2005). Θ is a $D' \times D$ matrix that maps the original features to a subspace common to all tasks. The new feature representation is computed by the projection $\mathbf{h}_c(e, f) \triangleq \Theta \cdot \mathbf{h}(e, f)$.

Multitask learning is a vast field and relates to areas like collaborative filtering (Yu and Tresp, 2005) and domain adaptation. Most methods assume some common representation and is thus applicable to our framework. The reader is urged to refer to citations in, e.g. (Argyriou et al., 2008) for a survey.

4 Experiments and Results

As a proof of concept, we perform experiments on a MT system with millions of features. We use a hierarchical phrase-based system (Chiang, 2007) to generate N-best lists (N=100). Sparse features used in reranking are extracted according to (Watanabe et al., 2007). Specifically, the majority are lexical features involving joint occurrences of words within the N-best lists and source sentences.

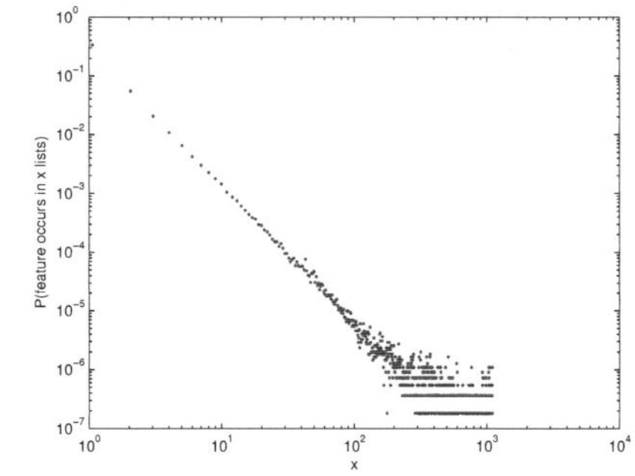

Figure 1: This log-log plot shows that there are many rare features and few common features. The probability that a feature occurs in x number of N-best lists behaves according to the power-law $x^{-\alpha}$, where $\alpha = 2.28$.

It is worth noting that the fact that the first pass system is a hierarchical system is not essential to the feature extraction step; similar features can be extracted with other systems as first-pass, e.g. a phrase-based system. That said, the extent of the feature sparsity problem may depend on the performance of the first-pass system.

We experiment with medical domain MT, where large numbers of technical vocabulary cause sparsity challenges. Our corpora consists of English abstracts from PubMed[4] with their Japanese translations. The first-pass system is built on hierarchical phrases extracted from 17k sentence pairs and target (Japanese) language models trained on 800k medical-domain sentences. For our reranking experiments, we used 500 lists as the training set[5], 500 lists as held-out, and another 500 for test.

4.1 Data Characteristics

We present some statistics to illustrate the feature sparsity problem: From 500 N-best lists, we extracted a total of 2.4 million distinct features. By type, 75% of these features occur in *only one* N-best list in the dataset. Less than 3% of features

[4] A database of the U.S. National Library of Medicine.

[5] In MT, training data for reranking is sometimes referred to as "dev set" to distinguish from the data used in first-pass. Also, while the 17k bitext may seem small compared to other MT work, we note that 1st pass translation quality (around 28 BLEU) is high enough to evaluate reranking methods.

occur in ten or more lists. The distribution of feature occurrence is clearly Zipfian, as seen in the power-law plot in Figure 1.

We can also observe the *feature growth rate* (Table 1). This is the number of new features introduced when an additional N-best list is seen. It is important to note that on average, 2599 new features are added everytime a new N-best list is seen. This is as much as $2599/4188 = 62\%$ of the active features. Imagine an online training algorithm (e.g. MIRA or perceptron) on this kind of data: whenever a loss occurs and we update the weight vector, less than half of the weight vector update applies to data we have seen thus far. Herein lies the potential for overfitting.

From observing the feature grow rate, one may hypothesize that adding large numbers of N-best lists to the training set (500 in the experiments here) may not necessarily improve results. While adding data potentially improves the estimation process, it also increases the feature space dramatically. Thus we see the need for a feature extraction procedure.

(Watanabe et al., 2007) also reports the possibility of overfitting in their dataset (Arabic-English newswire translation), especially when domain differences are present. Here we observe this tendency already on the same domain, which is likely due to the highly-specialized vocabulary and the complex sentence structures common in research paper abstracts.

Nbest id	#NewFt	#SoFar	#Active
1	3900	3900	3900
2	7535	11435	7913
3	6078	17513	7087
4	3868	21381	4747
5	1896	23277	2645
6	3542	26819	4747
....			
100	2440	289118	4299
101	1639	290757	2390
102	3468	294225	4755
103	2350	296575	3824
Average	2599	–	4188

Table 1: Feature growth rate: For N-best list i in the table, we have (#NewFt = number of new features introduced since N-best $i-1$) ; (#SoFar = Total number of features defined so far); and (#Active = number of active features for N-best i). E.g., we extracted 7535 new features from N-best 2; combined with the 3900 from N-best 1, the total features so far is 11435.

4.2 MT Results

Our goal is to compare different feature representations in reranking: The **baseline** reranker uses the original sparse feature representation. This is compared to feature representations discovered by three different multitask learning methods:

- Joint Regularization (Obozinski et al., 2009)
- Shared Subspace (Ando and Zhang, 2005)
- Unsupervised Multitask Feature Selection (Abernethy et al., 2007).[6]

We use existing implementations of the above methods.[7] The conventional reranker (Step 5, Algorithm 1) used in all cases is SVM^{rank}.[8] Our initial experiments show that the SVM baseline performance is comparable to MIRA training, so we use SVM throughout. The labels for the SVM are derived as in (Shen et al., 2004), where top 10% of hypotheses by smoothed sentence-BLEU is ranked before the bottom 90%. All multitask learning methods work on hashed features of dimension 4000 (Step 1, Algorithm 1). This speeds up the training process.

All hyperparameters of the multitask method are tuned on the held-out set. In particular, the most important is the number of common features to extract, which we pick from $\{250, 500, 1000\}$.

Table 2 shows the results by BLEU (Papineni et al., 2002) and PER. The Oracle results are obtained by choosing the best hypothesis per N-best list by sentence-level BLEU, which achieved 36.9 BLEU in both Train and Test. A summary of our observations is:

1. The baseline (All sparse features) overfits. It achieves the oracle BLEU score on the train set (36.9) but performs poorly on the test (28.6).

2. Similar overfitting occurs when traditional ℓ_1 regularization is used to select features on

[6]This is not a standard multitask algorithm since most multitask algorithms are supervised. We include it to see if unsupervised or semi-supervised multitask algorithms is promising. Intuitively, the method tries to select subsets of features that are correlated across multiple tasks using random sampling (MCMC). Features that co-occur in different tasks form a high probability path.

[7]Available at http://multitask.cs.berkeley.edu

[8]Available at http://svmlight.joachims.org

the sparse feature representation[9]. ℓ_1 regularization is a good method of handling sparse features for classification problems, but in reranking the lack of tying between lists makes this regularizer inappropriate. A small set of around 1200 features are chosen: they perform well independently on each task in the training data, but there is little sharing with the test data.

3. All three multitask methods obtained features that outperformed the baseline. The BLEU scores are 28.8, 28.9, 29.1 for Unsupervised Feature Selection, Joint Regularization, and Shared Subspace, respectively, which all outperform the 28.6 baseline. All improvements are statistically significant by bootstrap sampling test (1000 samples, $p < 0.05$) (Zhang et al., 2004).

4. Shared Subspace performed the best. We conjecture this is because its feature projection can create new feature combinations that is more expressive than the feature selection used by the two other methods.

5. PER results are qualitatively similar to BLEU results.

6. As a further analysis, we are interested in seeing whether multitask learning extracts novel features, especially those that have low frequency. Thus, we tried an additional feature representation (feature threshold) which only keeps features that occur in more than x N-bests, and concatenate these high-frequency features to the multitask features. The feature threshold alone achieves nice BLEU results (29.0 for $x > 10$), but the combination outperforms it by statistically significant margins (29.3-29.6). This implies that multitask learning is extracting features that complement well with high frequency features.

For the multitask features, improvements of 0.2 to 1.0 BLEU are modest but *consistent*. Figure 2 shows the BLEU of bootstrap samples obtained as part of the statistical significance test. We see that **multitask** almost never underperform **baseline** in any random sampling of the data. This implies that the proposed meta-algorithm is very stable, i.e. it is not a method that sometimes improves and sometimes degrades.

Finally, a potential question to ask is: what kinds of features are being selected by the multitask learning algorithms? We found that that two kinds of features are usually selected: one is general features that are not lexicalized, such as "count of phrases", "count of deletions/insertions", "number of punctuation marks". The other kind is lexicalized features, such as those in Equations 2 and 3, but involving functions words (like the Japanese characters "wa", "ga", "ni", "de") or special characters (such as numeral symbol and punctuation). These are features that can be expected to be widely applicable, and it is promising that multitask learning is able to recover these from the millions of potential features. [10]

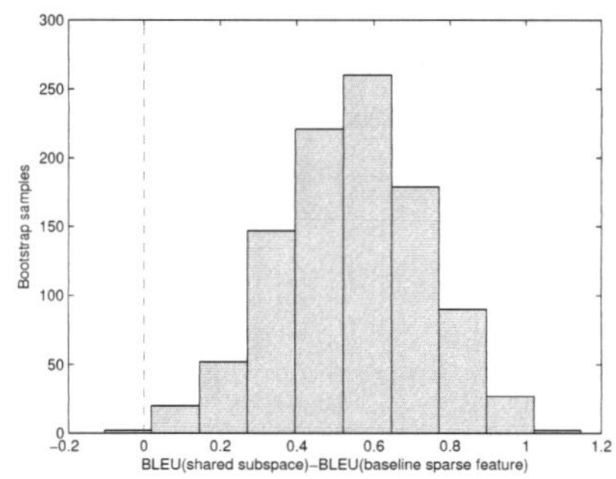

Figure 2: BLEU difference of 1000 bootstrap samples. 95% confidence interval is $[.15, .90]$ The proposed approach therefore seems to be a stable method.

5 Related Work in NLP

Previous reranking work in NLP can be classified into two different research focuses:

1. Engineering better features: In MT, (Och and others, 2004) investigates features extracted from a wide variety of syntactic representations, such as parse tree probability on the outputs. Although their results show that the proposed syntactic features gave little improvements, they point to some potential reasons, such as domain mismatch for the parser and overfitting by the reranking

[9]Optimized by the Vowpal Wabbit toolkit: http://hunch.net/vw/

[10]Note: In order to do this analysis, we needed to run Joint Regularization on the original feature representation, since the hashed representations are less interpretable. This turns out to be computationally prohibitive in the time being so we only ran on a smaller data set of 50 lists. Recently new optimization methods that are orders of magnitude faster have been developed (Liu et al., 2009), which makes larger-scale experiments possible.

Feature Representation	#Feature	Train BLEU	Test BLEU	Test PER
(baselines)				
First pass	20	29.5	28.5	38.3
All sparse features (Main baseline)	2.4M	36.9	28.6	38.2
All sparse features w/ ℓ_1 regularization	1200	36.5	28.5	38.6
Random hash representation	4000	33.0	28.5	38.2
(multitask learning)				
Unsupervised FeatureSelect	500	32.0	**28.8**	**37.7**
Joint Regularization	250	31.8	**28.9**	**37.5**
Shared Subspace	1000	32.9	**29.1**	**37.3**
(combination w/ high-frequency features)				
(a) Feature threshold $x > 100$	3k	31.7	27.9	38.2
(b) Feature threshold $x > 10$	60k	35.8	29.0	37.9
Unsupervised FeatureSelect + (b)	60.5k	36.2	**29.3**	**37.6**
Joint Regularization + (b)	60.25k	36.1	**29.4**	**37.5**
Shared Subspace + (b)	61k	36.2	**29.6**	**37.3**
Oracle (best possible)	–	36.9	36.9	33.1

Table 2: Results for different feature sets, with corresponding feature size and train/test BLEU/PER. All multitask features give statistically significant improvements over the baselines (boldfaced), e.g. Shared Subspace: 29.1 BLEU vs Baseline: 28.6 BLEU. Combinations of multitask features with high frequency features also give significant improvements over the high frequency features alone.

method. Recent work by (Chiang et al., 2009) describes new features for hierarchical phrase-based MT, while (Collins and Koo, 2005) describes features for parsing. Evaluation campaigns like WMT (Callison-Burch et al., 2009) and IWSLT (Paul, 2009) also contains a wealth of information for feature engineering in various MT tasks.

2. Designing better training algorithms: N-best reranking can be seen as a subproblem of structured prediction, so many general structured prediction algorithms (c.f. (Bakir et al., 2007)) can be applied. In fact, some structured prediction algorithms, such as the MIRA algorithm used in dependency parsing (McDonald et al., 2005) and MT (Watanabe et al., 2007) uses iterative sets of N-best lists in its training process. Other training algorithms include perceptron-style algorithms (Liang et al., 2006), MaxEnt (Charniak and Johnson, 2005), and boosting variants (Kudo et al., 2005).

The division into two research focuses is convenient, but may be suboptimal if the training algorithm and features do not match well together. Our work can be seen as re-connecting the two focuses, where the training algorithm is explicitly used to help discover better features.

Multitask learning is currently an active subfield within machine learning. There has already been some applications in NLP: For example, (Collobert and Weston, 2008) uses a deep neural network architecture for multitask learning on part-of-speech tagging, chunking, semantic role labeling, etc. They showed that jointly learning these related tasks lead to overall improvements. (Deselaers et al., 2009) applies similar methods for machine transliteration. In information extraction, learning different relation types can be naturally cast as a multitask problem (Jiang, 2009; Carlson et al., 2009). Our work can be seen as following the same philosophy, but applied to N-best lists.

In other areas, (Reichart et al., 2008) introduced an active learning strategy for annotating multitask linguistic data. (Blitzer et al., 2006) applies the multitask algorithm of (Ando and Zhang, 2005) to domain adaptation problems in NLP. We expect that more novel applications of multitask learning will appear in NLP as the techniques become scalable and standard.

6 Discussion and Conclusion

N-best reranking is a beneficial framework for experimenting with large feature sets, but unfortunately feature sparsity leads to overfitting. We addressed this by re-casting N-best lists as multitask learning data. Our MT experiments show consistent statistically significant improvements.

From the Bayesian view, multitask formulation of N-best lists is actually very natural: Each N-best is generated by a different data-generating distribution since the input sentences are different, i.e. $p(e|f^1) \neq p(e|f^2)$. Yet these N-bests are related since the general $p(e|f)$ distribution depends on the same first-pass models.

The multitask learning perspective opens up interesting new possibilities for future work, e.g.:

- Different ways to partition data into tasks, e.g. clustering lists by document structure, or hierarchical clustering of data
- Multitask learning on lattices or N-best lists with larger N. It is possible that a larger hypothesis space may improve the estimation of task-specific weights.
- Comparing multitask learning to sparse online learning of batch data, e.g. (Tsuruoka et al., 2009).
- Modifying the multitask objective to incorporate application-specific loss/decoding, such as Minimum Bayes Risk (Kumar and Byrne, 2004)
- Using multitask learning to aid large-scale feature engineering and visualization.

Acknowledgments

We have received numerous helpful comments throughout the course of this work. In particular, we would like to thank Albert Au Yeung, Jun Suzuki, Shinji Watanabe, and the three anonymous reviewers for their valuable suggestions.

References

Jacob Abernethy, Peter Bartlett, and Alexander Rakhlin. 2007. Multitask learning with expert advice. In *COLT*.

Rie Ando and Tong Zhang. 2005. A framework for learning predictive structures from multiple tasks and unlabeled data. *JMLR*.

Andreas Argyriou, Theodoros Evgeniou, and Massimiliano Pontil. 2008. Convex multitask feature learning. *Machine Learning*, 73(3).

G. Bakir, T. Hofmann, B. Scholkopf, A. Smola, B. Taskar, and S. V. N. Vishwanathan, editors. 2007. *Predicting structured data*. MIT Press.

J. Blitzer, R. McDonald, and F. Pereira. 2006. Domain adaptation with structural correspondence learning. In *EMNLP*.

Chris Callison-Burch, Philipp Koehn, Christof Monz, and Josh Schroeder. 2009. Findings of the 2009 workshop on statistical machine translation. In *WMT*.

Andrew Carlson, Justin Betteridge, Estevam Hruschka, and Tom Mitchell. 2009. Coupling semi-supervised learning of categories and relations. In *NAACL Workshop on Semi-supervised learning for NLP (SSLNLP)*.

Rich Caruana. 1997. Multitask learning. *Machine Learning*, 28.

Eugene Charniak and Mark Johnson. 2005. Coarse-to-fine n-best parsing and maxent discriminative reranking. In *ACL*.

David Chiang, Wei Wang, and Kevin Knight. 2009. 11,001 new features for statistical machine translation. In *NAACL*.

David Chiang. 2007. Hierarchical phrase-based translation. *Computational Linguistics*, 33(2).

Michael Collins and Terry Koo. 2005. Discriminative reranking for natural langauge parsing. *Computational Linguistics*, 31(1).

Ronan Collobert and Jason Weston. 2008. A unified architecture for natural language processing: deep neural networks with multitask learning. In *ICML*.

Hal Daume. 2009. Bayesian multitask learning with latent hierarchies. In *UAI*.

Thomas Deselaers, Sasa Hasan, Oliver Bender, and Hermann Ney. 2009. A deep learning approach to machine transliteration. In *WMT*.

Jenny Rose Finkel and Chris Manning. 2009. Hierarchical Bayesian domain adaptation. In *NAACL-HLT*.

Kuzman Ganchev and Mark Dredze. 2008. Small statistical models by random feature mixing. In *ACL-2008 Workshop on Mobile Language Processing*.

Jing Jiang. 2009. Multitask transfer learning for weakly-supervised relation extraction. In *ACL*.

Taku Kudo, Jun Suzuki, and Hideki Isozaki. 2005. Boosting-based parse reranking with subtree features. In *ACL*.

Shankar Kumar and William Byrne. 2004. Minimum bayes-risk decoding for statistical machine translation. In *HLT-NAACL*.

P. Liang, A. Bouchard-Cote, D. Klein, and B. Taskar. 2006. An end-to-end discriminative approach to machine translation. In *ACL*.

J. Liu, S. Ji, and J. Ye. 2009. Multi-task feature learning via efficient l2,1-norm minimization. In *UAI*.

Ryan McDonald, Koby Crammer, and Fernando Pereira. 2005. Online large margin training of dependency parsers. In *ACL*.

Guillaume Obozinski, Ben Taskar, and Michael Jordan. 2009. Joint covariate selection and joint subspace selection for multiple classification problems. *Statistics and Computing*.

F.J. Och et al. 2004. A smorgasbord of features for statistical machine translation. In *HLT/NAACL*.

Kishore Papineni, Salim Roukos, Todd Ward, and Wei-Jing Zhu. 2002. BLEU: A method for automatic evaluation of machine translation. In *ACL*.

Michael Paul. 2009. Overview of the iwslt 2009 evaluation campaign. In *IWSLT*.

Ariadna Quattoni, Xavier Carreras, Michael Collins, and Trevor Darrell. 2009. An efficient projection for L1-Linfinity regularization. In *ICML*.

Roi Reichart, Katrin Tomanek, Udo Hahn, and Ari Rappoport. 2008. Multi-task active learning for linguistic annotations. In *ACL*.

Brian Roark, Murat Saraclar, and Michael Collins. 2007. Discriminative n-gram language modeling. *Computer Speech and Language*, 21(2).

Libin Shen, Anoop Sarkar, and Franz Och. 2004. Discriminative reranking for machine translation. In *HLT-NAACL*.

Yoshimasa Tsuruoka, Jun'ichi Tsujii, and Sophia Ananiadou. 2009. Stochastic gradient descent training for l1-regularized log-linear models with cumulative penalty. In *ACL-IJCNLP*.

Taro Watanabe, Jun Suzuki, Hajime Tsukada, and Hideki Isozaki. 2007. Online large-margin training for statistical machine translation. In *EMNLP-CoNLL*.

Kilian Weinberger, Anirban Dasgupta, John Langford, Alex Smola, and Josh Attenberg. 2009. Feature hashing for large scale multitask learning. In *ICML*.

Kai Yu and Volker Tresp. 2005. Learning to learn and collaborative filtering. In *NIPS-2005 Workshop on Inductive Transfer*.

Ying Zhang, Stephan Vogel, and Alex Waibel. 2004. Interpreting BLEU/NIST scores: How much improvement do we need to have a better system? In *LREC*.

Taming Structured Perceptrons on Wild Feature Vectors

Ralf D. Brown
Carnegie Mellon University Language Technologies Institute
5000 Forbes Avenue, Pittsburgh PA 15213 USA
ralf+@cs.cmu.edu

Abstract

Structured perceptrons are attractive due to their simplicity and speed, and have been used successfully for tuning the weights of binary features in a machine translation system. In attempting to apply them to tuning the weights of real-valued features with highly skewed distributions, we found that they did not work well. This paper describes a modification to the update step and compares the performance of the resulting algorithm to standard minimum error-rate training (MERT). In addition, preliminary results for combining MERT or structured-perceptron tuning of the log-linear feature weights with coordinate ascent of other translation system parameters are presented.

1 Introduction

Structured perceptrons are a relatively recent (Collins, 2002) update of the classic perceptron algorithm which permit the prediction of vectors of values. Initially developed for part of speech taggers, they have been applied to tuning the weights of the features in the log-linear models used by statistical machine translation (Arun and Koehn, 2007), and found to have performance similar to the Margin-Infused Relaxed Algorithm (MIRA) by Crammer and Singer (2003; 2006) and Minimum-Error Rate Training (MERT) by Och (2003). Parameter tuning is an important aspect of current data-driven machine translation systems, as an improper selection of feature weights can dramatically reduce scores on evaluation metrics such as BLEU (Papineni et al., 2002) or METEOR (Banerjee and Lavie, 2005).

When we recently added new features to the CMU-EBMT translation system (Brown, 1996; Brown, 2008)[1], in addition to splitting a number of composite features into their components, our previous method of parameter tuning via coordinate ascent[2] became impractical. With now more than 50 features partaking in the scoring model, MERT no longer seemed a good choice, as the common wisdom is that it is not able to reliably optimize more than about 20 features (Chiang et al., 2008).

We had been using coordinate ascent because of a need to tune a substantial number of parameters which are not directly part of the log-linear model which can be tuned by MERT or similar methods. Our system generates a translation lattice by runtime lookup in the training corpus rather than using a precomputed phrase table, so important parameters include

- the size of the sample of retrieved training instances for a given input phrase which are aligned,
- the weight of source features for ranking training instances during sampling, and
- the minimum alignment score to accept a translation instance

Decoder parameters which are important to tune, but which are generally not mentioned in the literature include

- how many alternative translations of a phrase to consider during decoding,
- the size of the reordering window, and
- the rank of the language model (4-gram, 5-gram, etc.)

In addition, it is desirable to tune parameters such as beam width to minimize translation time without degrading performance.

[1] Source code for CMU-EBMT is available from http://cmu-ebmt.sourceforge.net.

[2] Coordinate ascent is described in more detail in Section 7.

Proceedings of the Joint 5th Workshop on Statistical Machine Translation and MetricsMATR, pages 384–391,
Uppsala, Sweden, 15-16 July 2010.

As a result of the non-model parameters, a full system tuning will involve multiple runs of the tuning algorithm for the feature weights, since the other parameters will affect the optimal weights. Thus, speed is an important consideration for any method to be used in this setting. The structured perceptron algorithm is ideally suited due to its speed, provided that it can produce competitive results.

2 Related Work

The perceptron algorithm (Rosenblatt, 1958) itself is over 50 years old, but variations such as voted and averaged perceptrons have gained popularity in the past ten years. In particular, Collins (2002) adapted the perceptron algorithm to structured prediction tasks such as part of speech tagging and noun phrase chunking. Arun and Koehn (2007) subsequently applied Collins' structured perceptron algorithm to the task of tuning feature weights in a statistical machine translation system, demonstrating the extreme scalability of the algorithm by applying it to vectors containing four to six million binary features. However, their work left open the question of how well structured perceptrons would deal with continuous-valued features. They were unable to apply a language model due to the lack of continuous-valued features and hence had to compare performance against a standard statistical machine translation (SMT) system which had been stripped of its language model, with a consequent loss of several BLEU points in performance.

During the same period, Crammer et al (2003; 2006) developed a number of "ultraconservative" learning algorithms, including MIRA, the Margin-Infused Relaxed Algorithm (which was also applied to large binary feature vectors by Arun and Koehn) and variations of what they referred to as Passive-Aggressive algorithms including PA-I and PA-II. These algorithms have in common the notion of updating a weight vector "just enough" to account for a new training instance which is incorrectly predicted by the existing weight vector. In contrast, the perceptron algorithm aggressively updates the weight vector and relies on averaging effects over the whole of the training set.

3 Structured Perceptrons

The structured perceptron algorithm can be applied to tasks where the goal is to select the best among competing hypotheses, where each hypothesis has an associated vector of feature values and the score for a hypothesis is a linear combination of its feature values.

Beginning with a zero vector for the feature weights, the structured perceptron algorithm iterates through each element of the training set, updating the weight vector after processing each training instance. The training set is processed repeatedly (each pass is known as a *training epoch*) until convergence. The update step is very simple: if the best hypothesis according to the product of feature vector and weight vector is not the correct answer, add the difference between the feature vectors of the correct answer and the model's selected answer to the weight vector.

Thus, the entire algorithm may be summarized with just two equations:

$$\vec{w} \leftarrow 0 \tag{1}$$

$$\vec{w} \leftarrow \vec{w} + (\Phi_{oracle} - \Phi_{top1}) \tag{2}$$

where Φ_x is the feature vector $(\phi_1, \phi_2, ..., \phi_n)$ for hypothesis x.

Repeated application of Equation 2 results in a weight vector which reflects the relative importance (on average) of each feature to making the correct selection. Since selecting the best hypothesis is an `arg max` operation, the absolute magnitudes of the weights are not important.

4 More Conservative Updates for Structured Perceptrons

One issue which arises in using learning algorithms for machine translation is that there is no one correct answer. In addition, it may not even be possible for the MT system to generate the reference translation at all. This is commonly addressed by using the highest-scoring (by some metric such as BLEU) translation which the system *can* generate as a pseudo-oracle.

Our initial implementation closely followed the description in (Arun and Koehn, 2007), including the refinement of using the objective-function score of the pseudo-oracle translation from the n-best list to modulate the learning rate of the update step, i.e.

$$\vec{w} \leftarrow \vec{w} + S_{\Phi_{oracle}} \times (\Phi_{oracle} - \Phi_{top1}) \tag{3}$$

As can be seen, the difference between Equations 2 and 3 is simply the additional factor of $S_{\Phi_{oracle}}$.

While we initially used sentence-level smoothed BLEU as the objective function, we found it to perform very poorly (the full BLEU scores on the Haitian Creole tuning set were well below 0.10), and instead adopted the Rouge-S (skip bigrams) metric by Lin and Och (2004a) with a maximum skip distance of four words, which was found to best correlate with human quality judgements (Lin and Och, 2004b).

In early testing, we found that both the feature weights and performance as measured by the average objective score over the tuning set oscillated wildly. Analyzing the results, it became apparent that the update function was overly aggressive. Unlike the binary features used in (Arun and Koehn, 2007), our continuous-valued features have different operating ranges for each feature, e.g. the total distance moved as a result of reordering could reach 100 on a long sentence, while the proportion of training instances with at least six words of adjacent context in the bilingual corpus is unlikely to exceed 0.05, even where sampling is biased toward training instances with adjacent context.

The first attempt to address the disparity in operating ranges was to perform feature-wise normalization on the update. Instead of taking the simple difference in feature vectors between the n-best entry with the highest log-linear score and the one with the highest objective score, we construct Φ_{diff} such that

$$\phi_i(diff) \leftarrow \frac{(\phi_i(oracle) - \phi_i(top1))}{r^2} \quad (4)$$

where

$$r \leftarrow max(0.01, max_j|\phi_i(j)|) \quad (5)$$

i.e. we estimate the operating range by finding the n-best entry with the highest magnitude value of the feature, and then divide by the square of that magnitude since large feature values also magnify the effects of weight changes. Normalization is limited by clipping the normalization factor to be at least 0.01 so that features whose values are always very near zero do not dominate the overall score.

While the feature-wise normalization did largely control the wild swings in feature weights, it did not curb the oscillations in the objective scores and produced only a minor improvement in tuning results.

We next looked at MIRA and related work on so-called Passive-Aggressive algorithms, and in particular at the update functions described in (Crammer et al., 2006). We decided on their PA-II update rule (PA-II being akin to 1-best MIRA), with which the learning step becomes

$$\vec{w} \leftarrow \vec{w} + \delta \times (\Phi_{oracle} - \Phi_{top1}) \quad (6)$$

where

$$loss \leftarrow S_{\Phi_{oracle}} - S_{\Phi_{top1}} \quad (7)$$

$$\delta \leftarrow \frac{loss}{||\Phi_{oracle} - \Phi_{top1}||^2 + \frac{1}{2C}} \quad (8)$$

with C an "aggressiveness" parameter.

This version of the update function produced the desired smooth changes in feature weights from iteration to iteration, though objective scores still do not converge. Allowing multiple passes through the tuning set before re-decoding with updated feature weights now frequently results in weights where the pseudo-oracle is the top-ranked translation in 80 to 90 percent of all sentences. None of our previous experiments had achieved even a fraction of this level due to the erratic behavior of the feature weights. However, as the extreme overfitting necessary to achieve such high rankings of the oracle translation results in poor BLEU scores, we have since used only one pass over the tuning set before re-decoding with updated weights.

5 The Final Algorithm

After the various attempts at taming the behavior of the structured perceptron approach just described, the final algorithm used for the experiments described below was

1. Structured perceptron, with
2. passive-aggressive updates,
3. run in semi-batch mode,
4. using sentence-level modified Rouge-S4 as the objective function

Semi-batch mode here means that while the perceptron algorithm updates the weight vector after each sentence, those updates are not communicated to the decoder until the end of a complete pass through the tuning set. An exception is made for the very first iteration, as it starts with uniform weights of 10^{-9} (rather than the conventional zero, which would cause problems with decoding). This permits the exact determination of the overall objective score for the weight vector which is eventually returned as the tuned optimal weights, and permits parallelization of the decoding (though the latter has not yet been implemented).

We slightly modified the Rouge-S scoring function to use the generalized F-measure

$$F_\beta = \frac{(1+\beta^2) \times precision \times recall}{\beta^2 \times precision + recall} \quad (9)$$

instead of the standard F_1, allowing us to give more weight to recall over precision by increasing β above 1.0. This change was prompted by the observation that the tuning process strongly favored shorter outputs, resulting in substantial brevity penalties from BLEU.

6 Experiments

We present the results of experiments on three data sets in the next section. The data sets are English-to-Haitian, French-to-English, and Czech-to-English.

The English-to-Haitian system was built using the data released by Carnegie Mellon University (2010). It consists of a medical phrasebook, a glossary, and a modest amount of newswire text, each available as a set of sentence pairs in English and Haitian Creole. For training, we used all of the glossary, all but the last 300 phrase pairs of the medical phrasebook (these had previously been used for development and testing of a "toy" system), and the first 12,500 sentence pairs of the newswire text. Tuning was performed using the next 217 sentence pairs of the newswire text, and the test set consisted of the final 800 sentence pairs of the newswire text. The target language model was built solely from the target half of the training corpus, as we did not have any additional Haitian Creole text.

The French-to-English system was built using the Europarl (Koehn, 2005) version 3 data for French and English. As is usual practice, text from the fourth quarter of 2000 was omitted from the training set. Tuning was performed using 200 sentences from the "devtest2006" file and all 2000 sentences of "test2007" were used as the final test set. Two target language models were built and interpolated during decoding; the first was trained on the target half of the bilingal corpus, and the second was built using the Canadian Hansards text released by ISI (Natural Language Group, 2001).

The Czech-to-English system was built using the parallel data made available for the 2010 Workshop on Statistical Machine Translation (WMT10). The target language model was built from the target half of the bilingual training corpus. Tuning was performed on a 200-sentence subset of the "news-2008-test" data, and all 2525 sentences of the "news-2009-test" data were used as unseen test data. As these experiments were the very first time that the CMU-EBMT system was applied to Czech, there are undoubtedly numerous pre-processing and training improvements which will increase scores above the values presented here.

Parameter tuning was performed using CMERT 0.5, the reimplemented MERT program included with recent releases of the MOSES translation system (specifically, the version included with the 2010-04-01 release), the annealing-based optimizer included with Cunei (Phillips and Brown, 2009; Phillips, 2010), and the Structured Perceptron optimizer. Feature weights were initialized to a uniform value of 1.0 for MERT and 10^{-9} for annealing and Perceptron (since the usual zero causes problems for the decoder). Both versions of MERT were permitted to run for 15 iterations or until features weights converged and remained (nearly) unchanged from one iteration to the next, using merged n-best lists from the current and the three most recent prior iterations. Annealing was run with gamma values from 0.25 to 4.0, skipping the entropy phase. The Structured Perceptron was allowed to run for 18 iterations and to choose the weights from the iteration which resulted in the highest average Rouge-S score for the top translation in the n-best list. For French-English, this proved to be the sixth iteration, while for English-Haitian it was the twelfth. We have found that the objective score increases for the first six to eight iterations of SP, after which it fluctuates with no trend up or down (but occasionally setting a new high, which is why we decided to run 18 iterations).

For French-English, we determined the best value of β for the Rouge-S scoring to be 1.5, and the best value of the aggressiveness parameter C to be 0.1, using a 40-sentence subset of the French-English tuning set, and then applied those value for the full tuning set. For English-Haitian, we used $\beta = 1.2$ and $C = 0.01$ (lower values of C provide more smoothing and overall smaller updates, which is necessary for sparse or noisy data). Due to limited time prior to submission, the English-Haitian values for β and C were re-used for Czech, with no attempt at tuning.

7 Combining Log-Linear Tuning with Coordinate Ascent

As noted in the introduction, translation systems using SMT-style decoders incorporate various features that affect performance (and/or speed), but which do not contribute directly to the log-linear scoring model. Thus, neither MERT nor the structured perceptron training presented in this paper is a complete solution for parameter tuning.

The CMU-EBMT system has long used a coordinate ascent approach to parameter tuning. Each parameter is varied in turn, with the MT system performing a translation for each setting, and the value which produces the best score is retained while the next parameter is varied. If the best scoring value is the highest or lowest in the list of values to be checked, the range is extended; likewise, unless the interval between adjacent values is already very small, the intervals on each side of the highest-scoring value (which is not one of the extremes) is divided in half and the two additional points are evaluated. This process continues until convergence (cycling through all parameters without changing any of them) or until a pre-set maximum number of parameter combinations is scored. Naturally, the approach becomes slower as the number of parameters increases, but it was still (barely) practical with 20 to 25 parameters.

A recent change in the internals of CMU-EBMT led to a decomposition of multiple composite scores and the addition of numerous others, ballooning the total number of tunable parameters to more than 60. Fortunately, most of the tunable parameters are feature weights, which can all be treated as a unit, leaving only about a dozen features for coordinate ascent.

The tuning program operates by calling an evaluation script which in turn invokes the machine translation on a modified configuration file provided by the tuner and returns the score corresponding to the given parameter settings. When given an optional flag, the evaluation script first invokes either MERT or SP to further adjust the parameters before performing the actual evaluation, and modifies the given configuration file accordingly. The tuner reads the modified parameters from the configuration file and stores then for further use.

Both MERT and SP can produce settings which actually *decrease* the resulting BLEU score, since they are optimizing toward a surrogate metric. If the evaluation score after an invocation of MERT or SP is less than 0.98 times the previous best score, the parameter settings are rolled back; otherwise, the best score is set to the evaluation score. This permits MERT/SP to move the parameters to a different space if necessary, without allowing them to substantially degrade overall scores.

There was time for only one experiment involving complete tuning, as summarized in Table 4. Starting with the Haitian-Creole feature weights found for the results in Table 1, the tuner randomly perturbed the non-feature-weight parameters by a small amount (up to 2% relative) twenty times, then started coordinate ascent from the best-scoring of those 20 trials. The tuner requested a MERT/SP run before ascending on the first parameter, and after every fourth parameter was processed thereafter. Because both MERT and SP started from previously-tuned feature weights, the number of iterations was reduced from 15 to 4 for MERT and from 18 to 5 for SP. The maximum number of parameter combinations for coordinate ascent was set to 750, which is approximately four cycles through all parameters (the exact number of combinations per cycle varies, as the tuner can add new combinations by extended the range which is searched or adding intermediate points around a maximum).

In Table 4, the three different Perceptron entries refer to the results starting from the previous experiment's feature weights ("Perceptron 1"), starting from the results of the complete tuning ("Perceptron 2"), and starting from uniform feature weights ("Perceptron 3"). The third run was stopped before convergence due to the looming submission deadline.

8 Results

Tables 1, 2, and 3 present the results of running the tuning methods on the English-Haitian, French-English, and Czech-English data sets, respectively. Performance is shown both in terms of the time required to perform a tuning run as well as the BLEU score achieved using the resulting feature weights.

Structured perceptrons are the clear winner for speed, thanks to the simplicity of the algorithm.

Method	Run-Time	Iter	BLEU (dev)	BLEU (test)	#words / ratio
CMERT 0.5	73m	5	0.0993	–	
new MERT	58m	3	0.0964	–	
CMERT 0.5[1]	138m	15	0.1073	0.0966	22298 / 1.213x
new MERT[1]	187m	15	0.1516	0.1347	17375 / 0.945x
Perceptron	22m	18	0.1619	0.1534	15565 / 0.847x

[1] omitting several unused features, as noted in the text

Table 1: English-to-Haitian tuning performance

Method	Run-Time	Iter	BLEU (dev)	BLEU (test)	#words / ratio
CMERT 0.5	3h53m	15	0.12952	0.13927	100875 / 1.709x
new MERT	5h52m	15	0.22533	0.23315	60354 / 1.023x
Annealing	6h46m	-	0.25017	0.25943	58518 / 0.992x
Perceptron	1h23m	18	0.24214	0.26048	57408 / 0.973x

Table 2: French-to-English tuning performance

While MERT takes two to three times as long to process ten random starting points as it does to decode the test set, SP is three orders of magnitude faster than decoding. As a result, SP tuning requires one-third or less of the time that MERT does, even though we used 18 iterations of SP compared to 15 for MERT. Note that the time difference between the two versions of MERT is in part due to different amounts of time spent decoding as a result of the different feature weights.

MERT unexpectedly has considerable difficulty with our new feature set, as can be seen by its much lower BLEU scores, particularly in the case of CMERT. An analysis of the actual feature weights produced by MERT shows that it places nearly all of the mass on a single feature, and that the feature receiving the bulk of the mass *changes from iteration to iteration*. In contrast, SP produces BLEU scores consistent with those produced by pure coordinate ascent prior to the proliferation of features.

We believe that the difference in performance between the two versions of MERT is due primarily to the simple difference in output format: CMERT 0.5 prints its tuned weights using a fixed-point format having six digits after the decimal point, while the new MERT program prints using scientific notation. Because the tuned weight vector is highly skewed, most features have low weights after L_1 normalization, and thus CMERT truncated many weights to zero (and indeed, loses significant digits for any features assigned weights less than 0.1), including such critical weights as length features and language model scores. We suspect that this preservation of significant digits contributes substantially to the improved BLEU scores Bertoldi et al (2009) reported for the new implementation compared to CMERT.

The features which, at one time or another, receive the bulk of the mass have one thing in common: for most translations, they have a default value, and in a small proportion of cases they have a value which varies from the default by only a small amount. Initially, most such features had a default value of zero in CMU-EBMT, but this meant that the line optimization in MERT had absolutely no constraint on raising the weight of the feature, and thus obtaining feature vectors where one feature has 10^{18} or even 10^{20} times the weight of any other feature. The same problem occurs with features that are unused but have a small jitter in their values due to rounding errors, for example, if there are no document boundaries (as is the case for the Haitian data described previously), the document-similarity score may be 1.000000 for 99% of the arcs in the translation lattices and 0.999999 for the remainder. Offsetting the mostly-zero features so that their default value is 1 or -1 (depending on the sense of the feature) and eliminating unused features mitigated but did not entirely solve the problem. In Table 1, two results are shown for both CMERT and new MERT; the first includes all 52 features while the second excludes five features which are not used in a baseline-trained CMU-EBMT system. In the former case, both programs placed all the mass on a single fea-

Method	Run-Time	Iter	BLEU (dev)	BLEU (test)
new MERT	56m	15	0.0584	0.0743
Perceptron	14m	18	0.0830	0.1163

Table 3: Czech-to-English tuning performance

Method	Run-Time	BLEU (dev)	BLEU (test)	length ratio
new MERT	48h	0.1821	0.1633	0.942
Perceptron 1	25h	0.1675	0.1547	0.833
Perceptron 2	38h	0.1738	0.1597	0.837
Perceptron 3	12h*	0.1705	0.1647	0.939

* truncated run (see text)

Table 4: English-to-Haitian tuning performance (including coordinate ascent)

ture and left all the others at 10^{-14} or less (displayed as 0.000000 in the case of CMERT).

The full tuning runs summarized in Table 4 show that SP is often competitive with MERT while running more quickly, but still requires further analysis to determine the causes of variability in its performance. One initial conclusion from examining the logs of the SP runs is that weight updates are perhaps *too* conservative when applied in conjunction with coordinate ascent. While MERT frequently shifted settings in response to changes in the non-feature parameters, SP rarely does so, typically preferring to retain the existing feature weights as the best setting encountered during the five iterations performed at each invocation. The "Perceptron 3" run starting with small uniform feature weights resulted from the observation that a first, buggy attempt at integration reached tuning-set BLEU scores in excess of 0.18 before early termination. The bug in question was that many of the feature weights were initially read in from the configuration file as zero rather than the correct value.

As shown in the rightmost column of Tables 1, 2 and 4, the Perceptron algorithm tends toward short output, yielding translations which are about 97% as long as the reference translation in French-English, a mere 85% as long for English-Haitian, and even shorter than that in two of three Czech runs. This tendency towards short translations prompted the inclusion of the β parameter – the French-English output was originally much shorter, but β has little effect on Haitian given the sparse training data. The extremely long output for CMERT on French-English is due to a large number of zero weights, including those for length features.

9 Conclusion and Future Work

Structured perceptrons with passive-aggressive updates are a viable alternative to the usual MERT feature-weight tuning, particularly where the number of features exceeds that which MERT can reliably handle, or when some of the features have characteristics which confuse MERT. Structured perceptrons are also a good alternative where speed is important, such as in a hybrid tuning scheme which alternates between (re-)tuning the log-linear model and performing coordinate ascent on parameters which do not directly contribute weight to the log-linear model.

We have thus far implemented two objective functions which operate on individual sentences without regard for choices made on other sentences. When the final evaluation metric incorporates global statistics, however, an objective function which takes them into account is desirable. For example, when using BLEU, it makes a big difference whether individual sentences are both longer and shorter than the reference or systematically shorter than the reference, but these two cases can not be distinguished by single-sentence objective functions. Our plan is to implement a windowed or moving-average version of BLEU as in (Chiang et al., 2008).

We also plan to further speed up the tuning process by parallelizing the decoding of the sentences in the tuning set. As we have used a semi-batch update method which leaves the decoder's weights unchanged for an entire pass through the tuning set, there is no data dependency between individual sentences, allowing them to be decoded in parallel. The perceptron algorithm itself remains sequential, but as it is three orders of magnitude faster than the decoding, this will have negligible impact on overall speedup factors until hundreds of CPUs are used for simultaneous decoding.

References

Abhishek Arun and Phillip Koehn. 2007. Online Learning Methods for Discriminative Training of Phrase Based Statistical Machine Translation. In *Proceedings of the Eleventh Machine Translation Summit (MT Summit XI)*.

Satanjeev Banerjee and Alon Lavie. 2005. METEOR: An Automatic Metric for MT Evaluation with Improved Correlation with Human Judgements. In *Proceedings of the Workshop on Intrinsic and Extrinsic Evaluation Measures for MT and/or Summarization at the 43rd Annual Meeting of the Association for Computational Linguistics (ACL-2005)*, June.

Nicola Bertoldi, Barry Haddow, and Jean-Baptiste Fouet. 2009. Improved Minimum Error Rate Training in Moses. *The Prague Bulletin of Mathematical Linguistics*, pages 1–11, February.

Ralf D. Brown. 1996. Example-Based Machine Translation in the PANGLOSS System. In *Proceedings of the Sixteenth International Conference on Computational Linguistics*, pages 169–174, Copenhagen, Denmark. `http://www.cs.cmu.edu/~ralf/papers.html`.

Ralf D. Brown. 2008. Exploiting Document-Level Context for Data-Driven Machine Translation. In *Proceedings of the Eighth Conference of the Association for Machine Translation in the Americas (AMTA-2008)*, October. `http://www.amtaweb.org/papers/2.02_Brown.pdf`.

Carnegie Mellon University. 2010. Public release of haitian-creole language data, January. `http://www.speech.cs.cmu.edu/haitian/text`.

David Chiang, Yuval Marton, and Philis Resnik. 2008. Online Large-Margin Training of Syntactic and Structural Translation Features. In *Proceedings of the Conference on Empirical Methods in Natural Langauge Processing (EMNLP-2008)*, pages 224–233, October.

Michael Collins. 2002. Discriminative Training Methods for Hidden Markov Models: Theory and Experiments with Perceptron Algorithms. In *Proceedings of EMNLP-2002*. `http://people.csail.mit.edu/mcollins/papers/tagperc.pdf`.

Koby Crammer, Ofer Deke, Joseph Keshet, Shai Shalev-Shwartz, and Yoram Singer. 2006. Online Passive-Aggressive Algorithms. *The Journal of Machine Learning Research*, 7:551–585, December.

Koby Cranmer and Yoram Singer. 2003. Ultraconservative Online Algorithms for Multiclass Problems. *The Journal of Machine Learning Research*, 3:951–991, March.

Philipp Koehn. 2005. Europarl: A Parallel Corpus for Statistical Machine Translation. In *Proceedings of the Tenth Machine Translation Summit (MT Summix X)*, pages 79–86.

Chin-Yew Lin and Franz Joseph Och. 2004a. Automatic Evaluation of Machine Translation Quality using Longest Common Subsequence and Skip-Bigram Statistics. In *Proceedings of ACL-2004*.

Chin-Yew Lin and Franz Joseph Och. 2004b. ORANGE: A Method for Evaluating Automatic Evaluation Metrics for Machine Translation. In *Proceedings of the 20th International Conference on Computational Linguistics (COLING 2004)*.

USC Information Sciences Institute Natural Language Group. 2001. Aligned *Hansards* of the 36th Parliament of Canada, Release 2001-1a. `http://www.isi.edu/natural-language/download/hansard/`.

Franz Josef Och. 2003. Minimum Error Rate Training in Statistical Machine Translation. In *Proceedings of the 41st Meeting of the Association for Computational Linguistics (ACL-2003)*, Sapporo, Japan, July 6–7.

Kishore Papineni, Salim Roukos, Todd Ward, and Wei-Jing Zhu. 2002. BLEU: a Method for Automatic Evaluation of Machine Translation. In *Proceedings of the 40th Annual Meeting of the Association for Computational Linguistics*, July. `http://acl.ldc.upenn.edu/P/P02/`.

Aaron B. Phillips and Ralf D. Brown. 2009. Cunei Machine Translation Platform: System Description. In *Proceedings of the Third Workshop on Example-Based Machine Translation*, Dublin, Ireland, November.

Aaron B. Phillips. 2010. The Cunei Machine Translation Platform for WMT'10. In *Proceedings of the ACL 2010 Joint Fifth Workshop on Statistical Machine Translation and Metrics MATR*, July.

F. Rosenblatt. 1958. The Perceptron: A Probabilistic Model for Information Storage and Organization in the Brain. *Psychological Review*, 65:386–408.

Translation Model Adaptation by Resampling

Kashif Shah, Loïc Barrault, Holger Schwenk
LIUM, University of Le Mans
Le Mans, France.
FirstName.LastName@lium.univ-lemans.fr

Abstract

The translation model of statistical machine translation systems is trained on parallel data coming from various sources and domains. These corpora are usually concatenated, word alignments are calculated and phrases are extracted. This means that the corpora are not weighted according to their importance to the domain of the translation task. This is in contrast to the training of the language model for which well known techniques are used to weight the various sources of texts. On a smaller granularity, the automatic calculated word alignments differ in quality. This is usually not considered when extracting phrases either.

In this paper we propose a method to automatically weight the different corpora and alignments. This is achieved with a resampling technique. We report experimental results for a small (IWSLT) and large (NIST) Arabic/English translation tasks. In both cases, significant improvements in the BLEU score were observed.

1 Introduction

Two types of resources are needed to train statistical machine translation (SMT) systems: parallel corpora to train the translation model and monolingual texts in the target language to build the language model. The performance of both models depends of course on the quality and quantity of the available resources.

Today, most SMT systems are generic, *i.e.* the same system is used to translate texts of all kinds. Therefore, it is the domain of the training resources that influences the translations that are selected among several choices. While monolingual texts are in general easily available in many domains, the freely available parallel texts mainly come from international organisations, like the European Union or the United Nations. These texts, written in particular jargon, are usually much larger than in-domain bitexts. As an example we can cite the development of an NIST Arabic/English phrase-based translation system. The current NIST test sets are composed of a news wire part and a second part of web-style texts. For both domains, there is only a small number of in-domain bitexts available, in comparison to almost 200 millions words of out-of-domain UN texts. The later corpus is therefore likely to dominate the estimation of the probability distributions of the translation model.

It is common practice to use a mixture language model with coefficients that are optimized on the development data, *i.e.* by these means on the domain of the translation task. Domain adaptation seems to be more tricky for the translation model and it seems that very little research has been done that seeks to apply similar ideas to the translation model. To the best of our knowledge, there is no commonly accepted method to weight the bitexts coming from different sources so that the translation model is best optimized to the domain of the task. Mixture models are possible when only two different bitexts are available, but are rarely used for more corpora (see discussion in the next section).

In this work we propose a new method to adapt the translation model of an SMT system. We only perform experiments with phrase-based systems, but the method is generic and could be easily applied to an hierarchical or syntax-based system. We first associate a weighting coefficient to each bitext. The main idea is to use resampling to produce a new collection of weighted alignment files, followed by the standard procedure to extract the phrases. In a second step, we also consider the

Proceedings of the Joint 5th Workshop on Statistical Machine Translation and MetricsMATR, pages 392–399,
Uppsala, Sweden, 15-16 July 2010.

alignment score of each parallel sentence pair, emphasizing by these means good alignments and down-weighting less reliable ones. All the parameters of our procedure are automatically tuned by optimizing the BLEU score on the development data.

The paper is organized as follows. The next section describes related work on weighting the corpora and model adaptation. Section 3 describes the architecture allowing to resample and to weight the bitexts. Experimental results are presented in section 4 and the paper concludes with a discussion.

2 Related Work

Adaptation of SMT systems is a topic of increasing interest since few years. In previous work, adaptation is done by using mixture models, by exploiting comparable corpora and by self-enhancement of translation models.

Mixture models were used to optimize the coefficients to the adaptation domain. (Civera and Juan, 2007) proposed a model that can be used to generate topic-dependent alignments by extension of the HMM alignment model and derivation of Viterbi alignments. (Zhao et al., 2004) constructed specific language models by using machine translation output as queries to extract similar sentences from large monolingual corpora. (Foster and Kuhn, 2007) applied a mixture model approach to adapt the system to a new domain by using weights that depend on text distances to mixture components. The training corpus was divided into different components, a model was trained on each part and then weighted appropriately for the given context. (Koehn and Schroeder, 2007) used two language models and two translation models: one in-domain and other out-of-domain to adapt the system. Two decoding paths were used to translate the text.

Comparable corpora are exploited to find additional parallel texts. Information retrieval techniques are used to identify candidate sentences (Hildebrand et al., 2005). (Snover et al., 2008) used cross-lingual information retrieval to find texts in the target language that are related to the domain of the source texts.

A self-enhancing approach was applied by (Ueffing, 2006) to filter the translations of the test set with the help of a confidence score and to use reliable alignments to train an additional phrase table. This additional table was used with the existing generic phrase table. (Ueffing, 2007) further refined this approach by using transductive semi-supervised methods for effective use of monolingual data from the source text. (Chen et al., 2008) performed domain adaptation simultaneously for the translation, language and reordering model by learning posterior knowledge from N-best hypothesis. A related approach was investigated in (Schwenk, 2008) and (Schwenk and Senellart, 2009) in which lightly supervised training was used. An SMT system was used to translate large collections of monolingual texts, which were then filtered and added to the training data.

(Matsoukas et al., 2009) propose to weight each sentence in the training bitext by optimizing a discriminative function on a given tuning set. Sentence level features were extracted to estimate the weights that are relevant to the given task. Then certain parts of the training bitexts were down-weighted to optimize an objective function on the development data. This can lead to parameter over-fitting if the function that maps sentence features to weights is complex.

The technique proposed in this paper is somehow related to the above approach of weighting the texts. Our method does not require an explicit specification of the in-domain and out-of-domain training data. The weights of the corpora are directly optimized on the development data using a numerical method, similar to the techniques used in the standard minimum error training of the weights of the feature functions in the log-linear criterion. All the alignments of the bitexts are resampled and given equal chance to be selected and therefore, influence the translation model in a different way. Our proposed technique does not require the calculation of extra sentence level features, however, it may use the alignments score associated with each aligned sentence pair as a confidence score.

3 Description of the algorithm

The architecture of the algorithm is summarized in figure 1. The starting point is an (arbitrary) number of parallel corpora. We first concatenate these bitexts and perform word alignments in both directions using GIZA++. This is done on the concatenated bitexts since GIZA++ may perform badly if some of the individual bitexts are rather small. Next, the alignments are separated in parts corre-

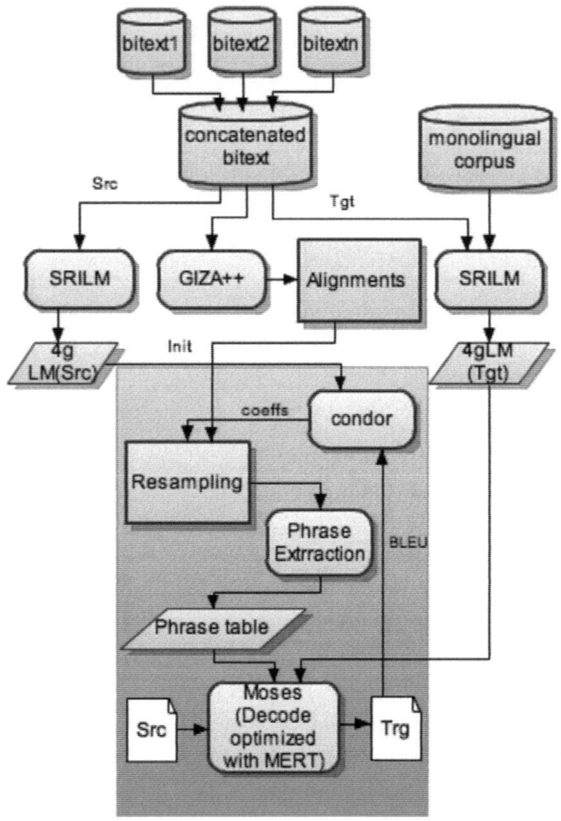

Figure 1: Architecture of SMT Weighting System

sponding to the individual bitexts and a weighting coefficient is associated to each one. We are not aware of a procedure to calculate these coefficients in an easy and fast way without building an actual SMT system. Note that there is an EM procedure to do this for language modeling.

In the next section, we will experimentally compare equal coefficients, coefficients set to the same values than those obtained when building an interpolated language model on the source language, and a new method to determine the coefficients by optimizing the BLEU score on the development data.

One could imagine to directly use these coefficients when calculating the various probabilities of the extracted phrases. In this work, we propose a different procedure that makes no assumptions on how the phrases are extracted and probabilities are calculated. The idea is to *resample alignments* from the alignment file corresponding to the individual bitexts according to their weighting coefficients. By these means, we create a new, potentially larger alignment file, which then in turn will be used by the standard phrase extraction procedure.

3.1 Resampling the alignments

In statistics, resampling is based upon repeated sampling within the same sample until a sample is obtained which better represents a given data set (Yu, 2003). Resampling is used for validating models on given data set by using random subsets. It overcomes the limitations to make assumptions about the distribution of the data. Usually resampling is done several times to better estimate and select the samples which better represents the target data set. The more often we resample, the closer we get to the true probability distribution.

In our case we performed resampling with replacement according to the following algorithm:

Algorithm 1 *Resampling*

```
for i = 0 to required size do
    Select any alignment randomly
    Al_score ← normalized alignment score
    Threshold ← rand[0, 1]
    if Al_score > Threshold then
        keep it
    end if
end for
```

Let us call resampling factor, the number of times resampling should be done. An interesting question is to determine the optimal value of this resampling factor.

It actually depends upon the task or data we are experimenting on. We may start with one time resampling and could stop when results becomes stable. Figure 2 plots a typical curve of the BLEU score as a function of the number of times we resample. It can be observed that the curve is growing proportionally to the resampling factor until it becomes stable after a certain point.

3.2 Weighting Schemes

We concentrated on translation model adaptation when the bitexts are heterogeneous, *e.g.* in-domain and out-of-domain or of different sizes. In this case, weighting these bitexts seems interesting and can be used in order to select data which better represent the target domain. Secondly when sentences are aligned, some alignments are reliable and some are less. Using unreliable alignments can put negative effect on the translation quality. So we need to exclude or down-weight

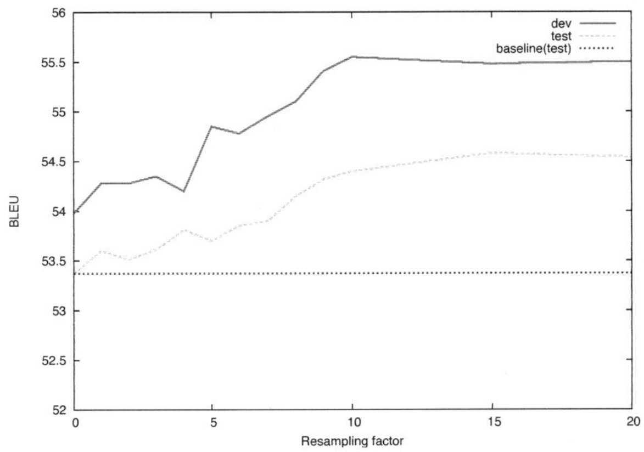

Figure 2: The curve shows that by increasing the resampling factor we get better and stable results on Dev and Test.

unreliable alignments and keep or up-weight the good ones. We conceptually divided the weighting in two parts that is (i) weighting the corpora and (ii) weighting the alignments

3.2.1 Weighting Corpora

We started to resample the bitexts with equal weights to see the effect of resampling. This gives equal importance to each bitext without taking into account the domain of the text to be translated. However, it should be better to give appropriate weights according to a given domain as shown in equation 1

$$\alpha_1 bitext_1 + \alpha_2 bitext_2 + .. + \alpha_n bitext_n \quad (1)$$

where the α_n are the coefficients to optimize. One important question is how to find out the appropriate coefficient for each corpus. We investigated a technique similar to the algorithm used to minimize the perplexity of an interpolated target LM. Alternatively, it is also possible to construct a interpolated language model on the source side of bitexts. This approach was implemented and these coefficients were used as the weights for each bitext. One can certainly ask the question whether the perplexity is a good criterion for weighting bitexts. Therefore, we worked on direct optimization of these coefficients by CONDOR (Berghen and Bersini, 2005). This freely available tool is a numerical optimizer based on Powell's UOBYQA algorithm (Powell, 1994). The aim of CONDOR is to minimize a objective function using the least number of function evaluations. Formally, it is used to find $x^* \in R^n$ with given constraints which satisfies

$$F(x^*) = \min_x F(x) \quad (2)$$

where n is the dimension of search space and x^* is the optimum of x. The following algorithm was used to weight the bitexts.

Algorithm 2 $WeightingCorpora$

Determine word to word alignment with GIZA++ on concatenated bitext.
while Not converged **do**
  Run Condor initialized with LM weights.
  Create new alignment file by resampling according to weights given by Condor.
  Use the alignment file to extract phrases and build the translation table (phrase table)
  Tune the system with MERT (this step can be skipped until weights are optimized to save time)
  Calculate the BLEU score
end while

3.2.2 Weighting Alignments

Alignments produced by GIZA++ have alignment scores associated with each sentence pair in both direction, *i.e.* source to target and target to source. We used these alignment scores as confidence measurement for each sentence pair. Alignment scores depend upon the length of each sentence, therefore, they must be normalized regarding the size of the sentence. Alignment scores have a very large dynamic range and we have applied a logarithmic mapping in order to flatten the probability distribution :

$$\log(\lambda \cdot \frac{(\sqrt[n_{trg}]{a_{src\_trg}} + \sqrt[n_{src}]{a_{trg\_src}})}{2}) \quad (3)$$

where *a* is the alignment score, *n* the size of a sentence and λ a coefficient to optimize. This is also done by Condor.

Of course, some alignments will appear several times, but this will increase the probability of certain phrase-pairs which are supposed to be more related to the target domain. We have observed that the weights of an interpolated LM build on the source side of the bitext are good initial values for CONDOR. Moreover, weights optimized by Condor are in the same order than these "LM weights". Therefore, we do not perform MERT of the SMT systems build at each step of the optimization of the weights α_i and λ by CONDOR,

	IWSLT Task		NIST Task	
	Dev (Dev6)	Test (Dev7)	Dev (NIST06)	Test (NIST08)
Baseline	53.98	53.37	43.16	42.21
With equal weights	53.71	53.20	43.10	42.11
With LM weights	54.20	53.71	43.42	42.22
Condor weights	54.80	53.98	43.49	42.28

Table 1: BLEU scores when weighting corpora (one time resampling)

	IWSLT Task		NIST Task	
	Dev (Dev6)	Test (Dev7)	Dev (NIST06)	Test (NIST08)
Baseline	53.98	53.37	43.16	42.21
With equal weights	53.80	53.30	43.13	42.15
With LM weights	54.32	53.91	43.54	42.37
Condor weights	55.10	54.13	43.80	42.40

Table 2: BLEU scores when weighting corpora (optimum number of resampling)

	IWSLT Task			NIST Task		
	Dev (Dev6)	Test (Dev7)	TER(Test)	Dev (NIST06)	Test (NIST08)	TER(Test)
Baseline	53.98	53.37	32.75	43.16	42.21	51.69
With equal weights	53.85	53.33	32.80	43.28	42.21	51.72
With LM weights	54.80	54.10	31.50	43.42	42.41	51.50
Condor weights	55.48	54.58	31.31	43.95	42.54	51.35

Table 3: BLEU and TER scores when weighting corpora and alignments (optimum number of resampling)

but use the values obtained by running MERT on a system obtained by using the "LM weights" to weight the alignments. Once CONDOR has converged to optimal weights, we can then tune our system by MERT. This saves lot of time taken by the tuning process and it had no impact on the results.

4 Experimental evaluation

The baseline system is a standard phrase-based SMT system based on the Moses SMT toolkit (Koehn and et al., 2007). In our system we used fourteen features functions. These features functions include phrase and lexical translation probabilities in both directions, seven features for lexicalized distortion model, a word and phrase penalty, and a target language model. The MERT tool is used to tune the coefficients of these feature functions. We considered Arabic to English translation. Tokenization of the Arabic source texts is done by a tool provided by SYSTRAN which also performs a morphological decomposition. We considered two well known official evaluation tasks to evaluate our approach, namely NIST and IWSLT.

For IWSLT, we used the BTEC bitexts (194M words), Dev1, Dev2, Dev3 (60M words each) as training data, Dev6 as development set and Dev7 as test set. From previous experiments, we have evidence that the various development corpora are not equally important and weighting them correctly should improve the SMT system. We analyze the translation quality as measured by the BLEU score for the three methods: equal weights, LM weights and Condor weights and considering one time resampling. Further experiments were performed using the optimized number of resampling with and without weighting the alignments. We have realized that it is beneficial to always include the original alignments. Even if we resample many times there is a chance that some alignments might never be selected but we do not want to loose any information. By keeping original alignments, all alignments are given a chance to be selected at least once. All these results are summarized in tables 1, 2 and 3.

One time resampling along with equal weights gave worse results than the baseline system while improvements in the BLEU score were observed with LM and Condor weights for the IWSLT task, as shown in table 1. Resampling many times always gave more stable results, as already shown in figure 2 and as theoretically expected. For this task, we resampled 15 times. The improvements in the BLEU score are shown in table 2. Furthermore, using the alignment scores resulted in additional improvements in the BLEU score. For the IWSLT task, we achieved and overall improvement of 1.5 BLEU points on the development set and 1.2 BLEU points on the test set as shown in table 3

To validate our approach we further experimented with the NIST evaluation task. Most of the training data used in our experiments for the NIST task is made available through the LDC. The bitexts consist of texts from the GALE project[1] (1.6M words), various news wire translations[2] (8.0M words) on development data from previous years (1.6M words), LDC treebank data (0.4M words) and the ISI extracted bitexts (43.7M words). The official NIST06 evaluation data was used as development set and the NIST08 evaluation data was used as test set. The same procedure was adapted for the NIST task as for the IWSLT task. Results are shown in table 1 by using different weights and one time resampling. Further improvements in the results are shown in table 2 with the optimum number of resampling which is 10 for this task. Finally, results by weighting alignments along with weighting corpora are shown in table 3. Our final system achieved an improvement of 0.79 BLEU points on the development set and 0.33 BLEU points on the test set. TER scores are also shown on test set of our final system in table 3. Note that these results are state-of-the-art when compared to the official results of the 2008 NIST evaluation[3].

The weights of the different corpora are shown in table 4 for the IWSLT and NIST task. In both cases, the weights optimized by CONDOR are substantially different form those obtained when creating an interpolated LM on the source side of the bitexts. In any case, the weights are clearly non uniform, showing that our algorithm has focused on in-domain data. This can be nicely seen for the NIST task. The Gale texts were explictely created to contain in-domain news wire and WEB texts and actually get a high weight despite their small size, in comparison to the more general news wire collection from LDC.

5 Conclusion and future work

We have proposed a new technique to adapt the translation model by resampling the alignments, giving a weight to each corpus and using the alignment score as confidence measurement of each aligned phrase pair. Our technique does not change the phrase pairs that are extracted,[4] but only the corresponding probability distributions. By these means we hope to adapt the translation model in order to increase the weight of translations that are important to the task, and to down-weight the phrase pairs which result from unreliable alignments.

We experimentally verified the new method on the low-resource IWSLT and the resource-rich NIST'08 tasks. We observed significant improvement on both tasks over state-of-the-art baseline systems. This weighting scheme is generic and it can be applied to any language pair and target domain. We made no assumptions on how the phrases are extracted and it should be possible to apply the same technique to other SMT systems which rely on word-to-word alignments.

On the other hand, our method is computationally expensive since the optimisation of the coefficients requires the creation of a new phrase table and the evaluation of the resulting system in the tuning loop. Note however, that we run GIZA++ only once.

In future work, we will try to directly use the weights of the corpora and the alignments in the algorithm that extracts the phrase pairs and calculates their probabilities. This would answer the interesting question whether resampling itself is needed or whether weighting the corpora and alignments is the key to the observed improvements in the BLEU score.

Finally, it is straight forward to consider more feature functions when resampling the alignments. This may be a way to integrate linguistic knowl-

[1] LDC2005E83, 2006E24, E34, E85 and E92

[2] LDC2003T07, 2004E72, T17, T18, 2005E46 and 2006E25.

[3] `http://www.nist.gov/speech/tests/mt/2008/`

[4] when also including the original alignments

IWSLT Task	BTEC	Dev1	Dev2	Dev3
# of Words	194K	60K	60K	60K
LM Coeffs	0.7233	0.1030	0.0743	0.0994
Condor Coeffs	0.6572	0.1058	0.1118	0.1253

NIST TASK	Gale	NewsWire	TreeBank	Dev	ISI
# of words	1.6M	8.1M	0.4M	1.7M	43.7M
LM Coeffs	0.3215	0.1634	0.0323	0.1102	0.3726
Condor Coeffs	0.4278	0.1053	0.0489	0.1763	0.2417

Table 4: Weights of the different bitexts.

edge into the SMT system, *e.g.* giving low scores to word alignments that are *"grammatically not reasonable"*.

Acknowledgments

This work has been partially funded by the European Commission under the project Euromatrix and by the Higher Education Commission(HEC) Pakistan as Overseas scholarship. We are very thankful to SYSTRAN who provided support for the Arabic tokenization.

References

Frank Vanden Berghen and Hugues Bersini. 2005. CONDOR, a new parallel, constrained extension of Powell's UOBYQA algorithm: Experimental results and comparison with the DFO algorithm. *Journal of Computational and Applied Mathematics*, 181:157–175, September.

Boxing Chen, Min Zhang, Aiti Aw, and Haizhou Li. 2008. Exploiting n-best hypotheses for SMT self- enhancement. In *Association for Computational Linguistics*, pages 157–160.

Jorge Civera and Alfons Juan. 2007. Domain adaptation in statistical machine translation with mixture modelling. In *Second Workshop on SMT*, pages 177–180.

George Foster and Roland Kuhn. 2007. Mixture-model adaptation for SMT. In *Proceedings of the Second Workshop on Statistical Machine Translation*, pages 128–135. Association for Computational Linguistics.

Almut Silja Hildebrand, Matthias Eck, Stephan Vogel, and Alex Waibel. 2005. Adaptation of the translation model for statistical machine translation based on information retrieval. In *EAMT*, pages 133–142.

Philipp Koehn and et al. 2007. Moses: Open source toolkit for statistical machine translation. In *Association for Computational Linguistics, demonstration session.*, pages 224–227.

Philipp Koehn and Josh Schroeder. 2007. Experiments in domain adaptation for statistical machine translation. In *Proceedings of the Second Workshop on Statistical Machine Translation*, pages 224–227. Association for Computational Linguistics.

Spyros Matsoukas, Antti-Veikko I. Rosti, and Bing Zhang. 2009. Discriminative corpus weight estimation for machine translation. In *Proceedings of the 2009 Conference on Empirical Methods in Natural Language Processing*, pages 708–717.

M.J.D. Powell. 1994. A direct search optimization method that models the objective and constraint functions by linar interpolation. In *In Advances in Optimization and Numerical Analysis, Proceedings of the sixth Workshop on Optimization and Numerical Analysis, Oaxaca, Mexico, volume 275*, pages 51–67. Kluwer Academic Publishers.

Holger Schwenk and Jean Senellart. 2009. Translation model adaptation for an Arabic/French news translation system by lightly-supervised training. In *MT Summit*.

Holger Schwenk. 2008. Investigations on large-scale lightly-supervised training for statistical machine translation. In *IWSLT*, pages 182–189.

Matthew Snover, Bonnie Dorr, and Richard Schwartz. 2008. Language and translation model adaptation using comparalble corpora. In *Proceedings of the 2008 Conference on Empirical Methods in Natural Language Processing*, pages 857–866.

Nicola Ueffing. 2006. Using monolingual sourcce language data to improve MT performance. In *IWSLT*, pages 174–181.

Nicola Ueffing. 2007. Transductive learning for statistical machine translation. In *Association for Computational Linguistics*, pages 25–32.

Chong Ho Yu. 2003. Resampling methods: Concepts, applications, and justification. In *Practical Assessment Research and Evaluation*.

Bing Zhao, Matthias Ech, and Stephen Vogal. 2004. Language model adaptation for statistical machine translation with structured query models. In *Proceedings of the 20th international conference on Computational Linguistics*. Association for Computational Linguistics.

Integration of Multiple Bilingually-Learned Segmentation Schemes into Statistical Machine Translation

Michael Paul and Andrew Finch and Eiichiro Sumita
MASTAR Project
National Institute of Information and Communications Technology
Hikaridai 2-2-2, Keihanna Science City
619-0288 Kyoto, Japan
michael.paul@nict.go.jp

Abstract

This paper proposes an unsupervised word segmentation algorithm that identifies word boundaries in continuous source language text in order to improve the translation quality of statistical machine translation (SMT) approaches. The method can be applied to any language pair where the source language is unsegmented and the target language segmentation is known. First, an iterative bootstrap method is applied to learn multiple segmentation schemes that are consistent with the phrasal segmentations of an SMT system trained on the resegmented bitext. In the second step, multiple segmentation schemes are integrated into a single SMT system by characterizing the source language side and merging identical translation pairs of differently segmented SMT models. Experimental results translating five Asian languages into English revealed that the method of integrating multiple segmentation schemes outperforms SMT models trained on any of the learned word segmentations and performs comparably to available state-of-the-art monolingually-built segmentation tools.

1 Introduction

The task of *word segmentation*, i.e., identifying word boundaries in continuous text, is one of the fundamental preprocessing steps of data-driven NLP applications like *Machine Translation* (MT). In contrast to Indo-European languages like English, many Asian languages like Chinese do not use a whitespace character to separate meaningful word units. The problems of word segmentation are:

(1) *ambiguity*, e.g., for Chinese, a single character can be a word component in one context, but a word by itself in another context.

(2) *unknown words*, i.e., existing words can be combined into new words such as proper nouns, e.g. "*White House*".

Purely dictionary-based approaches like (Cheng et al., 1999) addressed these problems by maximum matching heuristics. Recent research on unsupervised word segmentation focuses on approaches based on probabilistic methods. For example, (Brent, 1999) proposes a probabilistic segmentation model based on unigram word distributions, whereas (Venkataraman, 2001) uses standard n-gram language models. An alternative nonparametric Bayesian inference approach based on the Dirichlet process incorporating unigram and bigram word dependencies is introduced in (Goldwater et al., 2006).

The focus of this paper, however, is to learn word segmentations that are *consistent with phrasal segmentations of SMT translation models*. In case of small translation units, e.g. single Chinese or Japanese characters, it is likely that such tokens have been seen in the training corpus, thus these tokens can be translated by an SMT engine. However, the contextual information provided by these tokens might not be enough to obtain a good translation. For example, a Japanese-English SMT engine might translate the two successive characters "白" ("white") and "鳥" ("bird") as "*white bird*", while a human would translate "白鳥" as "*swan*". Therefore, the longer the translation unit, the more context can be exploited to find a meaningful translation. On the other hand, the longer the translation unit, the less likely it is that such a token will occur in the training data due to *data sparseness* of the language resources utilized to train the statistical translation models. Therefore, a word segmentation that is

Proceedings of the Joint 5th Workshop on Statistical Machine Translation and MetricsMATR, pages 400–408,
Uppsala, Sweden, 15-16 July 2010. ©2010 Association for Computational Linguistics

"consistent with SMT models" is one that identifies translation units that are small enough to be translatable, but large enough to be meaningful in the context of the given input sentence, achieving a trade-off between the *coverage* and the *translation task complexity* of the statistical models in order to improve translation quality.

The use of monolingual probabilistic models does not necessarily yield a better MT performance (Chang et al., 2008). However, improvements have been reported for approaches taking into account not only monolingual, but also bilingual information, to derive a word segmentation suitable for SMT. Due to the availability of language resources, most recent research has focused on optimizing Chinese word segmentation (CWS) for Chinese-to-English SMT. For example, (Xu et al., 2008) proposes a Bayesian Semi-Supervised approach for CWS that builds on (Goldwater et al., 2006). The generative model first segments Chinese text using an off-the-shelf segmenter and then learns new word types and word distributions suitable for SMT. Similarly, a dynamic programming-based variational Bayes approach using bilingual information to improve MT is proposed in (Chung and Gildea, 2009). Concerning other languages, for example, (Kikui and Yamamoto, 2002) extended Hidden-Markov-Models, where hidden n-gram probabilities were affected by co-occurring words in the target language part for Japanese word segmentation.

Recent research on SMT is also focusing on the usage of multiple word segmentation schemes for the source language to improve translation quality. For example, (Zhang et al., 2008) combines dictionary-based and CRF-based approaches for Chinese word segmentation in order to avoid *out-of-vocabulary* (OOV) words. Moreover, the combination of different morphological decomposition of highly inflected languages like Arabic or Finnish is proposed in (de Gispert et al., 2009) to reduce the data sparseness problem of SMT approaches. Similarly, (Nakov et al., 2009) utilizes SMT engines trained on different word segmentation schemes and combines the translation outputs using system combination techniques as a post-process to SMT decoding.

In order to integrate multiple word segmentation schemes into the SMT decoder, (Dyer et al., 2008) proposed to generate word lattices covering all possible segmentations of the input sentence and to decode the lattice input. An extended version of the lattice approach that does not require the use (and existence) of monolingual segmentation tools was proposed in (Dyer, 2009) where a maximum entropy model is used to assign probabilities to the segmentations of an input word to generate diverse segmentation lattices from a single automatically learned model.

The method of (Ma and Way, 2009) also uses a word lattice decoding approach, but they iteratively extract multiple word segmentation schemes from the training bitext. This dictionary-based approach uses heuristics based on the maximum matching algorithm to obtain an agglomeration of segments that are covered by the dictionary. It uses all possible source segmentations that are consistent with the extracted dictionary to create a word lattice for decoding.

The method proposed in this papers differs from previous approaches in the following points:

- it works for any language pair where the source language is unsegmented and the target language segmentation is known.
- it can be applied for the translation of a source language where no linguistically motivated word segmentation tools are available.
- it applies machine learning techniques to identify segmentation schemes that improve translation quality for a given language pair.
- it decodes directly from unsegmented text using segmentation information implicit in the phrase-table to generate the target and thus avoids issues of consistency between phrase-table and input representation.
- it uses segmentations at all iterative levels of the bootstrap process, rather than only those from the final iteration allowing the consideration of segmentations from many levels of granularity.

Word segmentations are learned using a parallel corpus by aligning character-wise source language sentences to word units separated by a white-space in the target language. Successive characters aligned to the same target words are merged into a larger source language unit. Therefore, the granularity of the translation unit is defined in the given bitext context. In order to minimize the side effects of alignment errors and to achieve segmentation consistency, a Maximum-Entropy (ME) algorithm is applied to learn the source language word segmentation that is consistent with the translation model of an SMT system trained on the resegmented bitext. The process is iterated until no further improvement in translation quality is achieved. In order to integrate multiple word segmentation into a single SMT system, the statistical translation models trained on differently segmented source language corpora are merged by characterizing the source side of each translation model, summing up the probabilities of identical phrase translation pairs, and rescoring the merged translation model (see Section 2).

The proposed segmentation method is applied to the translation of five Asian languages, i.e., Japanese, Korean, Thai, and two Chinese dialects (Standard Mandarin and Taiwanese Mandarin), into English. The utilized language resources and the outline of the experiments are summarized in Section 3. The experimental results revealed that the proposed method outperforms not only a baseline system that translates characterized source language sentences, but also all SMT models trained on any of the learned word segmentations. In addition, the proposed method achieves translation results comparable to SMT models trained on linguistically segmented bitext.

2 Word Segmentation

The word segmentation method proposed in this paper is an unsupervised, language-independent approach that treats the task of word segmentation as a *phrase-boundary tagging* task. This method uses a parallel text corpus consisting of initially unigram segmented source language character sequences and whitespace-separated target language words. The initial bitext is used to train a standard phrase-based SMT system (SMT_{chr}). The character-to-word alignment results of the SMT training procedure[1] are exploited to identify successive source language characters aligned to the same target language word in the respective bitext and to merge these characters into larger translation units, defining its granularity in the given bitext context.

The obtained translation units are then used to learn the word segmentation that is most consistent with the phrase alignments of the given SMT system. First, each character of the source language text is annotated with a word-boundary indicator where only two tags are used, i.e, *"E"* (end-of-word character tag) and *"I"* (in-word character tag). The annotations are derived from the SMT training corpus as described in Figure 1.

```
proc annotate-phrase-boundaries( Bitext ) ;
begin
   for each (Src, Trg) in {Bitext} do
      A ← align(Src, Trg) ;
      for each i in {1, ..., len(Src)-1} do
         Trg_i ← get-target(Src[i], A) ;
         Trg_{i+1} ← get-target(Src[i+1], A) ;
         if null(Trg_i) or Trg_i ≠ Trg_{i+1} then
            (* aligned to none or different target *)
            Src_ME ← assign-tag(Src[i], 'E') ;
         else
            (* aligned to the same target *)
            Src_ME ← assign-tag(Src[i], 'I') ;
         fi ;
         Corpus_ME ← add(Src_ME) ;
      od ;
      (* last source token *)
      LastSrc_ME ← assign-tag(Src[len(Src)], 'E') ;
      Corpus_ME ← add(LastSrc_ME) ;
   od ;
   return( Corpus_ME ) ;
end ;
```

Figure 1: ME Training Data Annotation

Using these alignment-based word boundary annotations, a Maximum-Entropy (ME) method is applied to learn the word segmentation consistent with the SMT translation model (see Section 2.1), to resegment the original source language corpus, and to retrain a phrase-based SMT engine that will hopefully achieve a better translation performance than the initial SMT engine. This process should be repeated as long as an improvement in translation quality is achieved. Eventually, the concatenation of succeeding translation units will result in overfitting, i.e., the newly created token can only be translated in the context of rare training data examples. Therefore, a lower translation quality due to an increase of untranslatable source language phrases is to be expected (see Section 2.2).

However, in order to increase the *coverage* and to reduce the *translation task complexity* of the statistical models, the proposed method integrates multiple segmentation schemes into the statistical translation models of a single SMT engine so that longer translation units are preferred for translation, if available, and smaller translation units can be used otherwise (see Section 2.3).

2.1 Maximum-Entropy Tagging Model

ME models provide a general purpose machine learning technique for classification and predic-

[1] For the experiments presented in Section 3, the GIZA++ toolkit was used.

Lexical Context Features	$< t_0, w_{-2} >$ $< t_0, w_{-1} >$ $< t_0, w_0 >$ $< t_0, w_{+1} >$ $< t_0, w_{+2} >$
Tag Context Features	$< t_0, t_{-1} >$ $< t_0, t_{-1}, t_{-2} >$

Table 1: Feature Set of ME Tagging Model

tion. They are versatile tools that can handle large numbers of features, and have shown themselves to be highly effective in a broad range of NLP tasks including sentence boundary detection or part-of-speech tagging (Berger et al., 1996).

A *maximum entropy classifier* is an exponential model consisting of a number of binary feature functions and their weights (Pietra et al., 1997). The model is trained by adjusting the weights to maximize the entropy of the probabilistic model given constraints imposed by the training data. In our experiments, we use a *conditional maximum entropy* model, where the conditional probability of the outcome given the set of features is modeled (Ratnaparkhi, 1996). The model has the form:

$$p(t, c) = \gamma \prod_{k=0}^{K} \alpha_k^{f_k(c,t)} \cdot p_0$$

where:

- t is the tag being predicted;
- c is the context of t;
- γ is a normalization coefficient;
- K is the number of features in the model;
- f_k are binary feature functions;
- a_k is the weight of feature function f_k;
- p_0 is the default model.

The feature set is given in Table 1. The *lexical context features* consist of target words annotated with a tag t. w_0 denotes the word being tagged and $w_{-2}, \ldots, w_{+2}$ the surrounding words. t_0 denotes the current tag, t_{-1} the previous tag, etc. The *tag context features* supply information about the context of previous tag sequences. This conditional model can be used as a classifier. The model is trained iteratively, and we used the improved iterative scaling algorithm (IIS) (Berger et al., 1996) for the experiments presented in Section 3.

2.2 Iterative Bootstrap Method

The proposed iterative bootstrap method to learn the word segmentation that is consistent with an SMT engine is summarized in Figure 2. After the ME tagging model is learned from the initial character-to-word alignments of the respective bitext ((1)-(4)), the obtained ME tagger is

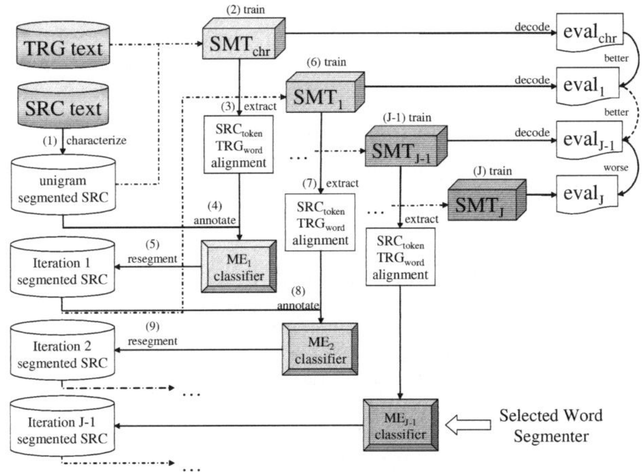

Figure 2: Iterative Bootstrap Method

applied to resegment the source language side of the unsegmented parallel text corpus ((5)). This results in a resegmented bitext that can be used to retrain and reevaluate another engine SMT_1 ((6)), achieving what is hoped to be a better translation performance than the initial SMT engine (SMT_{chr}).

The unsupervised ME tagging method can also be applied to the token-to-word alignments extracted during the training of the SMT_1 engine to obtain an ME tagging model ME_1 capable of handling longer translation units ((7)-(8)). Such a bootstrap method iteratively creates a sequence of SMT engines SMT_i ((9)-(J)), each of which reduces the translation complexity, because larger chunks can be translated in a single step leading to fewer word order or word disambiguation errors. However, at some point, the increased length of translation units learned from the training corpus will lead to overfitting, resulting in reduced translation performance when translating unseen sentences. Therefore, the bootstrap method stops when the Jth resegmentation of the training corpus results in a lower automatic evaluation score for the unseen sentences than the one for the previous iteration. The ME tagging model ME_{J-1} that achieved the highest automatic translation scores is then selected as the best single-iteration word segmenter.

2.3 Integration of Multiple Segmentations

The integration of multiple word segmentation schemes is carried out by merging the translation models of the SMT engines trained on the characterized and iteratively learned segmentation schemes. This process is performed by linearly interpolating the model probabilities of each of the models. In our experiments, equal weights were used; however, it might be interesting to investigate varying the weights according to iteration number, as the latter iterations may contain more useful segmentations.

In addition, we also remove the internal segmentation of the source phrases. The advantages are twofold. Primarily it allows decoding directly from unsegmented text. Moreover, the segmentation of the source phrase can differ between models at differing iterations; removing the source segmentation at this stage makes the phrase pairs in the translations models at various stages in the iterative process consistent with one another. Consequently, duplicate bilingual phrase pairs appear in the phrase table. These duplicates are combined by normalizing their model probabilities prior to model interpolation.

The rescored translation model covers all translation pairs that were learned by any of the iterative models. Therefore, the selection of longer translation units during decoding can reduce the complexity of the translation task. On the other hand, overfitting problems of single-iteration models can be avoided because multiple smaller source language translation units can be exploited to cover the given input parts and to generate translation hypotheses based on the concatenation of associated target phrase expressions. Moreover, the merging process increases the translation probabilities of the source/target translation parts that cover the same surface string but differ only in the segmentation of the source language phrase. Therefore, the more often such a translation pair is learned by different iterative models, the more often the respective target language expression will be exploited by the SMT decoder.

The translation of unseen data using the merged translation models is carried out by (1) characterizing the input text and (2) applying the SMT decoding in a standard way.

3 Experiments

The effects of using different word segmentations and integrating them into an SMT engine are investigated using the multilingual *Basic Travel Expressions Corpus* (BTEC), which is a collection of sentences that bilingual travel experts consider useful for people going to or coming from other countries (Kikui et al., 2006). For the word segmentation experiments, we selected five Asian languages that do not naturally separate word units, i.e., Japanese (ja), Korean (ko), Thai (th), and two dialects of Chinese (Standard Mandarin (zh) and Taiwanese Mandarin (tw)).

BTEC		train set	dev set	test set
# of sen		160,000	1,000	1,000
en	voc	15,390	1,262	1,292
	len	7.5	7.1	7.2
ja	voc	17,168	1,407	1,408
	len	8.5	8.2	8.2
ko	voc	17,246	1,366	1,365
	len	8.0	7.7	7.8
th	voc	7,354	1,081	1,053
	len	7.8	7.3	7.4
zh	voc	11,084	1,312	1,301
	len	7.1	6.4	6.5

Table 2: Language Resources

Table 2 summarizes the characteristics of the BTEC corpus used for the training (*train*) of the SMT models, the tuning of model weights and stop conditions of the iterative bootstrap method (*dev*), and the evaluation of translation quality (*test*). Besides the number of sentences (*sen*) and the vocabulary (*voc*), the sentence length (*len*) is also given as the average number of words per sentence. The given statistics are obtained using commonly-used linguistic segmentation tools available for the respective language, i.e., CHASEN (ja), WORDCUT (th), ICTCLAS (zh), HanTagger (ko). No segmentation was available for Taiwanese Mandarin and therefore no meaningful statistics could be obtained.

For the training of the SMT models, standard word alignment (Och and Ney, 2003) and language modeling (Stolcke, 2002) tools were used. Minimum error rate training (MERT) was used to tune the decoder's parameters and performed on the *dev* set using the technique proposed in (Och and Ney, 2003). For the translation, a multi-stack phrase-based decoder was used.

For the evaluation of translation quality, we applied standard automatic metrics, i.e., BLEU (Papineni et al., 2002) and METEOR (Lavie and Agarwal, 2007). We have tested the statistical significance of our results[2] using the bootstrap method reported in (Zhang et al., 2004) that (1) performs a random sampling with replacement from the evaluation data set, (2) calculates the evaluation metric score of each engine for the sampled test sentences and the difference between the two MT system scores, (3) repeats the sampling/scoring step itera-

[2]2000 iterations were used for the analysis of the automatic evaluation results in this paper. All reported differences in evaluation scores are statistically significant.

tively, and (4) applies the *Student's t-test* at a significance level of 95% confidence to test whether the score differences are significant.

In addition, human assessment of translation quality was carried out using the *Ranking* metrics. For the *Ranking* evaluation, a human grader was asked to *"rank each whole sentence translation from Best to Worst relative to the other choices (ties are allowed)"* (Callison-Burch et al., 2007). The *Ranking* scores were obtained as the average number of times that a system was judged better than any other system and the normalized ranks (*NormRank*) were calculated on a per-judge basis for each translation task using the method of (Blatz et al., 2003).

Section 3.1 compares the proposed method to the baseline system that translates characterized source language sentences and to the SMT engines that are trained on iteratively learned as well as language-dependent linguistic word segmentations. The effects of the iterative learning method are summarized in Section 3.2.

3.1 Effects of Word Segmentation

The automatic evaluation scores of the SMT engines trained on the differently segmented source language resources are given in Table 3, where "*character*" refers to the baseline system of using character-segmented source text; "*single-best*"[3] is the SMT engine that is trained on the corpus segmented by the best-performing iteration of the bootstrap approach; "*proposed*" is the SMT engine whose models integrate multiple word segmentation schemes; and "*linguistic*" uses language-dependent linguistically motivated word segmentation tools. The reported scores are calculated as the mean score of all metric scores obtained for the iterative sampling method used for statistical significance testing and listed as percentage figures.

The results show that the proposed method outperforms the *character* (*single-best*) system for each of the involved languages achieving gains of 2.0 to 9.1 (0.4 to 1.6) BLEU points and 2.0 to 5.9 (0.7 to 4.6) METEOR points, respectively. However, the improvements depend on the source language. For example, the smallest gains were obtained for Standard Mandarin, because single characters frequently form words of their own, thus resulting in more ambiguity than Japanese, where consecutive *hiragana* or *katakana* characters can form larger meaningful units.

Comparing the proposed method towards linguistically motivated segmenters, the results show that the proposed method outperforms the SMT engines using linguistic segmentation tools for tasks such as translating Korean and Standard Mandarin into English. Slightly lower evaluation scores were achieved for the automatically learned word segmentation for Japanese, although the results of the proposed method are quite similar. This is a suprisingly strong result, given the maturity of the linguistically motivated segmenters, and given that our segmenters use only the bilingual corpus used to train the SMT systems.

The Thai-English experiments expose some issues that are related to the definition of what a "character" is. Our segmentation schemes are learned directly from the bitext without any language-specific information, and can cope well with most languages. However, Thai seems to be an exceptional case in our experiments, because (1) the Thai script is a segmental writing system which is based on consonants but in which vowel notation is obligatory, so that the characterization of the baseline system affects vowel dependencies, (2) it uses tone markers that are placed above the consonant, but are treated as a single character in our approach, and (3) vowels sounding after a consonant are non-sequential and can occur before, after, above, or below a consonant increasing the number of word form variations in the training corpus and reducing the accuracy of the learned ME tagging models. This is an interesting result that motivates further study on how to incorporate features on language scripts into our machine learning framework. For example, Japanese is written in three different scripts (*kanji, hiragana, katakana*). Therefore, the script class of each character could be used as an additional feature to obtain the initial segmentation of the training corpus.

Finally, the results for Taiwanese Mandarin, where no linguistic tool was available to segment the source language text, shows that the proposed method can be applied successfully for the translation of any language where no linguistically-motivated segmentation tools are available.

Table 4 summarizes the subjective evaluation results which were carried out by a paid evaluation expert who is a native speaker of English. The *NormRank* results confirm the findings of the au-

[3] This approximates the approach of (Ma and Way, 2009) and is given as a way of showing the effect of segmentation at multiple levels of granularity.

BLEU

source language	word segmentation character	single-best	proposed	linguistic
ja	36.93	39.65	41.25	**41.46**
ko	34.72	37.32	**38.51**	37.19
th	41.42	50.16	50.53	**56.68**
zh	36.59	37.02	**38.61**	38.13
tw	45.71	50.95	**52.21**	–

METEOR

source language	word segmentation character	single-best	proposed	linguistic
ja	59.78	60.95	65.45	**66.03**
ko	58.45	60.06	**64.31**	63.04
th	67.22	71.22	72.58	**79.02**
zh	61.77	62.38	**63.80**	62.72
tw	70.14	73.64	**74.38**	–

Table 3: Automatic Evaluation

NormRank

source language	word segmentation character	single-best	proposed	linguistic
ja	2.76	2.85	**3.18**	3.12
ko	2.68	2.90	**3.17**	3.09
th	2.65	2.95	3.05	**3.43**
zh	2.87	3.01	**3.07**	3.04
tw	2.83	2.86	**3.24**	–

Table 4: Subjective Evaluation

tomatic evaluation. In addition, for Japanese, the translation outputs of the proposed method were judged better than those of the linguistically segmented SMT model.

3.2 Effects of Bootstrap Iteration

In order to get an idea of the robustness of the proposed method, the changes in system performance for each source language during the iterative bootstrap method is given in Figure 3. The results for BLEU and METEOR show that all languages reach their best performance after the first or second iteration and then slightly, but consistently decrease with the increased number of iterations. The reason for this is the effect of overfitting caused by the concatenation of source tokens that are aligned to longer target phrases, resulting in the segmentation of longer translation units.

The changes in the vocabulary size and the word length are summarized in Figure 4. The amount of words extracted by the proposed method is much larger than the one of the baseline system, increasing the vocabulary size by a factor of 10 for Standard Mandarin and Taiwanese Mandarin, 30 for Japanese and Korean, and 100 for Thai. It is also larger than the vocabulary obtained for the linguistic tools by a factor of 1.5 to 2.5 for all investigated

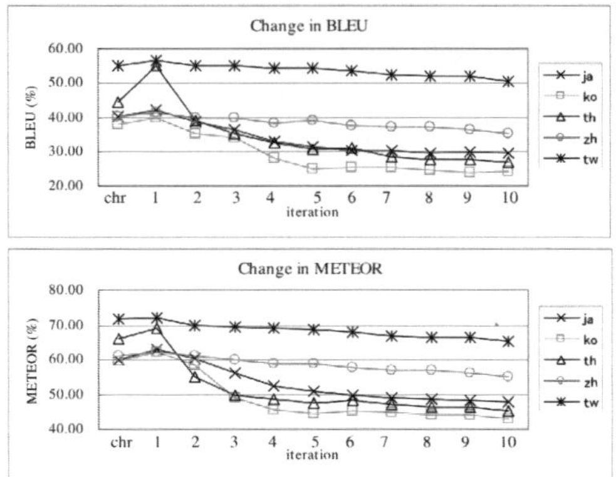

Figure 3: Change in System Performance

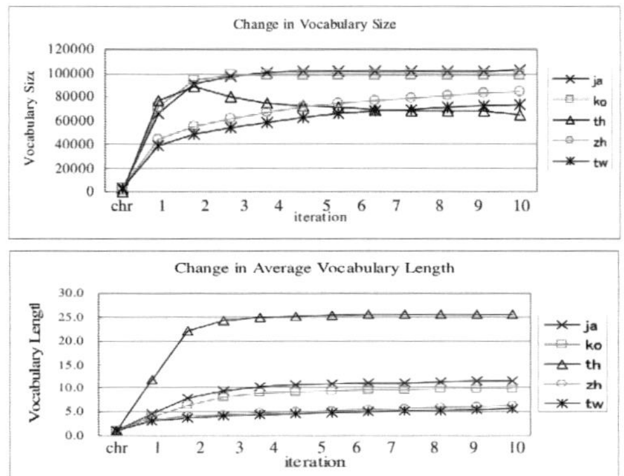

Figure 4: Change in Vocabulary Size and Length

languages. The average vocabulary length also increased for each iteration whereby the length of the translation units learned after 10 iterations almost doubles the word size of the initial iteration.

The overfitting problem of the iterative bootstrap method is illustrated in the increase of *out-of-vocabulary* words, i.e. source language words contained in the unseen evaluation data set that cannot be translated by the respective SMT. The results given in Figure 5 show a large increase in OOV for the first three iterations, resulting in lower translation qualities as listed in Figure 3.

Table 5 illustrates translation examples using different segmentation schemes for the Japanese-English translation task. The SMT engines that output the best translations are marked with an asterisk. In the first example, the concatenation of "もう真夜中" (*already midnight*) by the *single-best* segmentation scheme leads to an OOV word, thus only a partial translation can be achieved. However, the problem can be resolved using the proposed method. The second example is best translated using the *single-best* word segmentation that correctly handles the sentence coordination. The

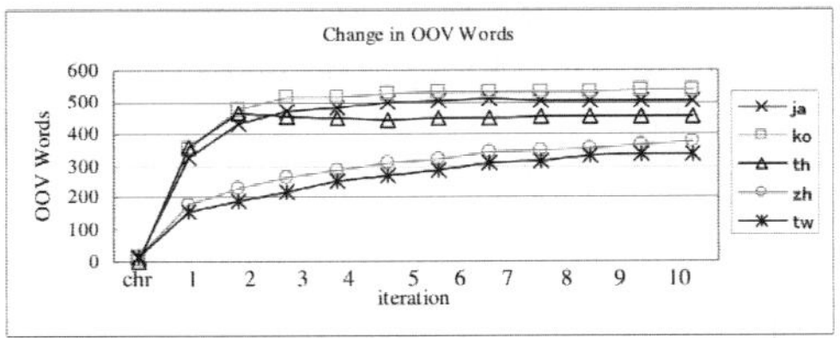

Figure 5: Change in Out-of-Vocabulary Size

baseline system omits the sentence coordination information, resulting in an unacceptable translation. The third examples illustrates that longer tokens reduce the translation complexity and thus can be translated better than the other segmentation that cause more ambiguities.

linguistic	*seg:*	ええ/。/えーと/、/もう/真夜中/です/ね 。
	trans:	Yes. Let's see. It's midnight.
character*	*seg:*	え/え/。/え/ー/と/、/も/う/真/夜/中/で/ す/ね/。
	trans:	Yes. Well, it's already midnight.
single-best	*seg:*	ええ。/えーと/、/もう真夜中/で/すね。
	trans:	Yes. Let 's see.
proposed*	*seg:*	え/え/。/え/ー/と/、/も/う/真/夜/中/で/ す/ね/。
	trans:	Yes. Well, it's already midnight.
linguistic	*seg:*	ジーンズ/が/欲しい/の/です/が/、/ いい/店/を/教え/て/ください/。
	trans:	I'd like a pair of jeans. Could you recommend a good shop?
character	*seg:*	ジ/ー/ン/ズ/が/欲/し/い/の/で/す/が/、/ い/い/店/を/教/え/て/く/だ/さ/い/。
	trans:	Could you recommend a good 'd like a pair of jeans.
single-best*	*seg:*	ジーンズ/が欲し/い/のですが、/ いい/店/を教え/てください/。
	trans:	I'd like some jeans. Could you recommend a good shop?
proposed	*seg:*	ジ/ー/ン/ズ/が/欲/し/い/の/で/す/が/、/ い/い/店/を/教/え/て/く/だ/さ/い/。
	trans:	I 'd like a pair of jeans and could you recommend a good shop?
linguistic	*seg:*	今日/の/午後/までに/できます/か/。
	trans:	Will it be ready by this afternoon?
character	*seg:*	今/日/の/午/後/ま/で/に/で/き/ま/す/ か/。
	trans:	It'll be ready by this afternoon?
single-best	*seg:*	今日の/午後まで/に/できま/すか。
	trans:	Will it be ready by this afternoon?
proposed*	*seg:*	今/日/の/午/後/ま/で/に/で/き/ま/す/ か/。
	trans:	Can you have these ready by this afternoon?

Table 5: Sample Translations

The experiments using Thai are interesting because the script is a segmental writing system using tone markers and vowel dependencies. This exposed some issues that are related to the definition of what a "character" is and motivates further study on how to incorporate features on language scripts into our machine learning framework.

4 Conclusions

This paper proposes a new language-independent method to segment languages that do not use whitespace characters to separate meaningful word units in an unsupervised manner in order to improve the performance of a state-of-the-art SMT system. The proposed method does not need any linguistic information about the source language which is important when building SMT systems for the translation of relatively resource-poor languages which frequently lack morphological analysis tools. In addition, the development costs are far less than those for developing linguistic word segmentation tools or even paying humans to segment the data sets manually, since only the bilingual corpus used to train the SMT system is needed to train the segmenter.

The effectiveness of the proposed method was investigated for the translation of Japanese, Korean, Thai, and two Chinese dialects (Standard Mandarin and Taiwanese Mandarin) into English for the domain of travel conversations. The automatic evaluation of the translation results showed consistent improvements of 2.0 to 9.1 BLEU points and 2.0 to 5.9 METEOR points compared to a baseline system that translates characterized input. Moreover, it improves the best performing SMT engine of the iterative learning procedure by 0.4 to 1.6 BLEU points and 0.7 to 4.6 METEOR points.

In addition, the proposed method achieved translation results similar to SMT models trained on bitext segmented with linguistically motivated tools, even outperforming these for Korean, Chinese, and Japanese in the human evaluation, although no external information and only the given bitext was used to train the segmentation models.

References

Adam Berger, Stephen Della Pietra, and Vincent Della Pietra. 1996. A maximum entropy approach to NLP. *Computational Linguistics*, 22(1):39–71.

John Blatz, Erin Fitzgerald, George Foster, Simona Gandrabur, Cyril Goutte, Alex Kulesza, Alberto Sanchis, and Nicola Ueffing. 2003. Confidence estimation for statistical machine translation. In *Final Report of the JHU Summer Workshop*.

Michael Brent. 1999. An efficient, probabilistically sound algorithm for segmentation and word discovery. *Machine Learning*, 34:71–105.

Chris Callison-Burch, Cameron Fordyce, Philipp Koehn, Christof Monz, and Jan Schroeder. 2007. (Meta-) Evaluation of Machine Translation. In *Proceedings of the 2nd Workshop on SMT*, pages 136–158, Prague, Czech Republic.

Pi-Chuan Chang, Michel Galley, and Christopher Manning. 2008. Optimizing Chinese Word Segmentation for Machine Translation Performance. In *Proc. of the 3rd Workshop on SMT*, pages 224–232, Columbus, USA.

Kwok-Shing Cheng, Gilbert Young, and Kam-Fai Wong. 1999. A study on word-based and integratbit Chinese text compression algorithms. *American Society of Information Science*, 50(3):218–228.

Tagyoung Chung and Daniel Gildea. 2009. Unsupervised Tokenization for Machine Translation. In *Proc. of the EMNLP*, pages 718–726, Singapore.

Adrian de Gispert, Sami Virpioja, Mikko Kurimo, and William Byrne. 2009. Minimum Bayes Risk Combination of Translation Hypotheses from Alternative Morphological Decompositions. In *Proc. of HLT, Companion Volume*, pages 73–76, Boulder, USA.

Christopher Dyer, Smaranda Muresan, and Philip Resnik. 2008. Generalizing Word Lattice Translation. In *Proc. of ACL*, pages 1012–1020, Columbus, USA.

Christopher Dyer. 2009. Using a maximum entropy model to build segmentation lattices for MT. In *Proc. of HLT*, pages 406–414, Boulder, USA.

Sharon Goldwater, Thomas Griffith, and Mark Johnson. 2006. Contextual Dependencies in Unsupervised Word Segmentation. In *Proc. of the ACL*, pages 673–680, Sydney, Australia.

Geninchiro Kikui and Hirofumi Yamamoto. 2002. Finding Translation Pairs from English-Japanese Untokenized Aligned Corpora. In *Proc. of the Workshop on Speech-to-Speech Translation*, pages 23–30, Philadephia, USA.

Geninchiro Kikui, Seiichi Yamamoto, Toshiyuki Takezawa, and Eiichiro Sumita. 2006. Comparative study on corpora for speech translation. *IEEE Transactions on Audio, Speech and Language*, 14(5):1674–1682.

Alon Lavie and Abhaya Agarwal. 2007. METEOR: An automatic metric for MT evaluation with high levels of correlation with human judgments. In *Proc. of the 2nd Workshop on SMT*, pages 228–231, Prague, Czech Republic.

Yanjun Ma and Andy Way. 2009. Bilingually Motivated Domain-Adapted Word Segmentation for Statistical Machine Translation. In *Proc. of the 12th EACL*, pages 549–557, Athens, Greece.

Preslav Nakov, Chang Liu, Wei Lu, and Hwee Tou Ng. 2009. The NUS SMT System for IWSLT 2009. In *Proc. of IWSLT*, pages 91–98, Tokyo, Japan.

Franz J. Och and Hermann Ney. 2003. A Systematic Comparison of Statistical Alignment Models. *Computational Linguistics*, 29(1):19–51.

Kishore Papineni, Salim Roukos, Todd Ward, and Wei-Jing Zhu. 2002. BLEU: a Method for Automatic Evaluation of Machine Translation. In *Proc. of the 40th ACL*, pages 311–318, Philadelphia, USA.

Stephen Della Pietra, Vincent Della Pietra, and John Lafferty. 1997. Inducing Features of Random Fields. *IEEE Transactions on Pattern Analysis and Machine Intelligence*, 19(4):380–393.

Adwait Ratnaparkhi. 1996. A Maximum Entropy Model for Part-Of-Speech Tagging. In *Proc. of the EMNLP*, pages 133–142, Pennsylvania, USA.

Andreas Stolcke. 2002. SRILM an extensible language modeling toolkit. In *Proc. of ICSLP*, pages 901–904, Denver, USA.

Anand Venkataraman. 2001. A statistical model for word discovery in transcribed speech. *Computational Linguistics*, 27(3):351–372.

Jia Xu, Jianfeng Gao, Kristina Toutanova, and Hermann Ney. 2008. Bayesian Semi-Supervised Chinese Word Segmentation for SMT. In *Proc. of the COLING*, pages 1017–1024, Manchester, UK.

Ying Zhang, Stephan Vogel, and Alex Waibel. 2004. Interpreting Bleu/NIST Scores: How Much Improvement do We Need to Have a Better System? In *Proc. of the LREC*, pages 2051–2054, Lisbon, Portugal.

Ruiqiang Zhang, Keiji Yasuda, and Eiichiro Sumita. 2008. Improved Statistical Machine Translation by Multiple Chinese Word Segmentation. In *Proc. of the 3rd Workshop on SMT*, pages 216–223, Columbus, USA.

Improved Translation with Source Syntax Labels

Hieu Hoang
School of Informatics
University of Edinburgh
h.hoang@sms.ed.ac.uk

Philipp Koehn
School of Informatics
University of Edinburgh
pkoehn@inf.ed.ac.uk

Abstract

We present a new translation model that include undecorated hierarchical-style phrase rules, decorated source-syntax rules, and partially decorated rules.

Results show an increase in translation performance of up to 0.8% BLEU for German–English translation when trained on the news-commentary corpus, using syntactic annotation from a source language parser. We also experimented with annotation from shallow taggers and found this increased performance by 0.5% BLEU.

1 Introduction

Hierarchical decoding is usually described as a formally syntactic model without linguistic commitments, in contrast with syntactic decoding which constrains rules and production with linguistically motivated labels. However, the decoding mechanism for both hierarchical and syntactic systems are identical and the rule extraction are similar.

Hierarchical and syntax statistical machine translation have made great progress in the last few years and can claim to represent the state of the art in the field. Both use synchronous context free grammar (SCFG) formalism, consisting of rewrite rules which simultaneously parse the input sentence and generate the output sentence. The most common algorithm for decoding with SCFG is currently CKY+ with cube pruning works for both hierarchical and syntactic systems, as implemented in Hiero (Chiang, 2005), Joshua (Li et al., 2009), and Moses (Hoang et al., 2009)

Rewrite rules in hierarchical systems have general applicability as their non-terminals are undecorated, giving hierarchical system broad coverage. However, rules may be used in inappropriate situations without the labeled constraints. The general applicability of undecorated rules create spurious ambiguity which decreases translation performance by causing the decoder to spend more time sifting through duplicate hypotheses. Syntactic systems makes use of linguistically motivated information to bias the search space at the expense of limiting model coverage.

This paper presents work on combining hierarchical and syntax translation, utilizing the high coverage of hierarchical decoding and the insights that syntactic information can bring. We seek to balance the generality of using undecorated non-terminals with the specificity of labeled non-terminals. Specifically, we will use syntactic labels from a source language parser to label non-terminal in production rules. However, other source span information, such as chunk tags, can also be used.

We investigate two methods for combining the hierarchical and syntactic approach. In the first method, syntactic translation rules are used concurrently with a hierarchical phrase rules. Each ruleset is trained independently and used concurrently to decode sentences. However, results for this method do not improve.

The second method uses one translation model containing both hierarchical and syntactic rules. Moreover, an individual rule can contain both decorated syntactic non-terminals, and undecorated hierarchical-style non-terminals (also, the left-hand-side non-terminal may, or may not be decorated). This results in a 0.8% improvement over the hierarchical baseline and analysis suggest that long-range ordering has been improved.

We then applied the same methods but using linguistic annotation from a chunk tagger (Abney, 1991) instead of a parser and obtained an improvement of 0.5% BLEU over the hierarchical baseline, showing that gains with additional source-side annotation can be obtained with simpler tools.

2 Past Work

Hierarchical machine translation (Chiang, 2005) extends the phrase-based model by allowing the use of non-contiguous phrase pairs ('production rules'). It promises better re-ordering of translation as the reordering rules are an implicit part of the translation model. Also, hierarchical rules follow the recursive structure of the sentence, reflecting the linguistic notion of language.

However, the hierarchical model has several limitations. The model makes no use of linguistic information, thus creating a simple model with broad coverage. However, (Chiang, 2005) also describe heuristic constraints that are used during

Proceedings of the Joint 5th Workshop on Statistical Machine Translation and MetricsMATR, pages 409–417,
Uppsala, Sweden, 15-16 July 2010.

rule extraction to reduce spurious ambiguity. The resulting translation model does reduces spurious ambiguity but also reduces the search space in an arbitrary manner which adversely affects translation quality.

Syntactic labels from parse trees can be used to annotate non-terminals in the translation model. This reduces incorrect rule application by restricting rule extraction and application. However, as noted in (Ambati and Lavie, 2008) and elsewhere,the naïve approach of constraining every non-terminal to a syntactic constituent severely limits the coverage of the resulting grammar, therefore, several approaches have been used to improve coverage when using syntactic information.

Zollmann and Venugopal (2006) allow rules to be extracted where non-terminals do not exactly span a target constituent. The non-terminals are then labeled with complex labels which amalgamates multiple labels in the span. This increase coverage at the expense of increasing data sparsity as the non-terminal symbol set increases dramatically. Huang and Chiang (2008) use parse information of the source language, production rules consists of source tree fragments and target languages strings. During decoding, a packed forest of the source sentence is used as input, the production rule tree fragments are applied to the packed forest. Liu et al. (2009) uses joint decoding with a hierarchical and tree-to-string model and find that translation performance increase for a Chinese-English task. Galley et al. (2004) creates minimal translation rules which can explain a parallel sentence pair but the rules generated are not optimized to produce good translations or coverage in any SMT system. This work was extended and described in (Galley et al., 2006) which creates rules composed of smaller, minimal rules, as well as dealing with unaligned words. These measures are essential for creating good SMT systems, but again, the rules syntax are strictly constrained by a parser.

Others have sought to add soft linguistic constraints to hierarchical models using addition feature functions. Marton and Resnik (2008) add feature functions to penalize or reward non-terminals which cross constituent boundaries of the source sentence. This follows on from earlier work in (Chiang, 2005) but they see gains when finer grain feature functions which different constituency types. The weights for feature function is tuned in batches due to the deficiency of MERT when presented with many features. Chiang et al. (2008) rectified this deficiency by using the MIRA to tune all feature function weights in combination. However, the translation model continues to be hierarchical.

Chiang et al. (2009) added thousands of linguistically-motivated features to hierarchical and syntax systems, however, the source syntax features are derived from the research above. The translation model remain constant but the parameterization changes.

Shen et al. (2009) discusses soft syntax constraints and context features in a dependency tree translation model. The POS tag of the target head word is used as a soft constraint when applying rules. Also, a source context language model and a dependency language model are also used as features.

Most SMT systems uses the Viterbi approximation whereby the derivations in the log-linear model is not marginalized, but the maximum derivation is returned. String-to-tree models build on this so that the most probable derivation, including syntactic labels, is assumed to the most probable translation. This fragments the derivation probability and the further partition the search space, leading to pruning errors. Venugopal et al. (2009) attempts to address this by efficiently estimating the score over an equivalent unlabeled derivation from a target syntax model.

Ambati and Lavie (2008); Ambati et al. (2009) notes that tree-to-tree often underperform models with parse tree only on one side due to the non-isomorphic structure of languages. This motivates the creation of an isomorphic backbone into the target parse tree, while leaving the source parse unchanged.

3 Model

In extending the phrase-based model to the hierarchical model, non-terminals are used in translation rules to denote subphrases. Hierarchical non-terminals are undecorated so are unrestricted to the span they cover. In contrast, SCFG-based syntactic models restrict the extraction and application of non-terminals, typically to constituency spans of a parse tree or forest. Our soft syntax model combine the hierarchical and source-syntactic approaches, allowing translation rules with undecorated and decorated non-terminals with information from a source language tool.

We give an example of the rules extracted from an aligned sentence in Figure 1, with a parse tree on the source side.

Lexicalized rules with decorated non-terminals are extracted, we list five (non-exhaustive) examples below.

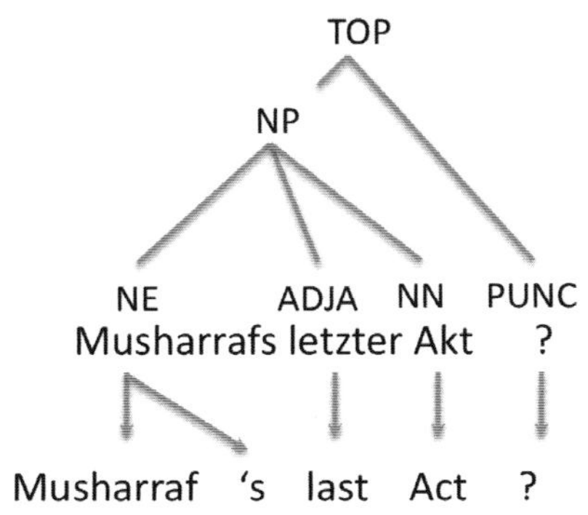

Figure 1: Aligned parsed sentence

$$
\begin{array}{lll}
NP & \rightarrow & Musharrafs\ letzter\ Akt \\
 & & \#\ Musharraf\ 's\ Last\ Act \\
NP & \rightarrow & NE_1\ letzter\ Akt\ \#\ X_1\ Last\ Act \\
NP & \rightarrow & NE_1\ ADJA_2\ Akt\ \#\ X_1\ X_2\ Act \\
NP & \rightarrow & NE_1\ letzter\ NN_2\ \#\ X_1\ Last\ X_2 \\
TOP & \rightarrow & NE_1\ ADJA_2\ Akt\ ?\ \#\ X_1\ X_2\ Act\ ?
\end{array}
$$

Hierarchical style rules are also extracted where the span doesn't exactly match a parse constituent. We list 2 below.

$$
\begin{array}{lll}
X & \rightarrow & letzter\ Akt\ \#\ Last\ Act \\
X & \rightarrow & letzter\ X_1\ \#\ Last\ X_1
\end{array}
$$

Unlexicalized rules with decorated non-terminals are also extracted:

$$
\begin{array}{lll}
TOP & \rightarrow & NP_1\ PUNC_2\ \#\ X_1\ X_2 \\
NP & \rightarrow & NE_1\ ADJA_2\ NN_3\ \#\ X_1\ X_2\ X_3
\end{array}
$$

Rules are also extracted which contains a mixture of decorated and undecorated non-terminals. These rules can also be lexicalized or unlexicalized. A non-exhaustive sample is given below:

$$
\begin{array}{lll}
X & \rightarrow & ADJA_1\ Akt\ \#\ X_1\ Act \\
NP & \rightarrow & NE_1\ X_2\ \#\ X_1\ X_2 \\
TOP & \rightarrow & NE_1\ letzter\ X_2\ \#\ X_1\ Last\ X_2
\end{array}
$$

At decoding time, the parse tree of the input sentence is available to the decoder. Decorated non-terminals in rules must match the constituent span in the input sentence but the undecorated X symbol can match any span.

Formally, we model translation as a string-to-string translation using a synchronous CFG that constrain the application of non-terminals to matching source span labels. The source words and span labels are represented as an unweighted word lattice, $< V, E >$, where each edge in the lattice correspond to a word or non-terminal label over the corresponding source span. In the soft syntax experiments, edges with the default source label, X, are also created for all spans. Nodes in the lattice represent word positions in the sentence.

We encode the lattice in a chart, as described in (Dyer et al., 2008). A chart is is a tuple of 2-dimensional matrices $< F, R >$. $F_{i,j}$ is the word or non-terminal label of the jth transition starting word position i. $R_{i,j}$ is the end word position of the node on the right of the jth transition leaving word position i.

The input sentence is decoded with a set of translation rules of the form

$$X \rightarrow < \alpha L_s, \gamma, \sim >$$

where α and γ and strings of terminals and non-terminals. L_s and the string α are drawn from the same source alphabet, Δ_s. γ is the target string, also consisting of terminals and non-terminals. $\sim$ is the one-to-one correspondence between non-terminals in α and γ. L_s is the left-hand-side of the source. As a string-to-string model, the left-hand-side of the target is always the default target non-terminal label, X.

Decoding follows the CKY+ algorithms which process contiguous spans of the source sentence bottom up. We describe the algorithm as inference rules, below, omitting the target side for brevity.

Initialization

$$\frac{}{[X \rightarrow \bullet \alpha L_s, i, i]} \qquad (X \rightarrow \alpha L_s) \in G$$

Terminal Symbol

$$\frac{[X \rightarrow \alpha \bullet F_{j,k} \beta L_s, i, j]}{[X \rightarrow \alpha F_{j,k} \bullet \beta L_s, i, j+1]}$$

Non-Terminal Symbol

$$\frac{[X \rightarrow \alpha \bullet F_{j,k} \beta L_s, i, j] \qquad [X, j, R_{j,k}]}{[X \rightarrow \alpha F_{j,k} \bullet \beta L_s, i, R_{j,k}]}$$

Left Hand Side

$$\frac{[X \rightarrow \alpha \bullet L_s, i, R_{i,j}] \quad [F_{i,j} = L_s]}{[X \rightarrow \alpha L_s \bullet, i, R_{i,j}]}$$

Goal

$$[X \rightarrow \alpha L_s \bullet, 0, |V| - 1]$$

This model allows translation rules to take advantage of both syntactic label and word context. The presence of default label edges between every node allows undecorated non-terminals to be applied to any span, allowing flexibility in the translation model.

This contrasts with the approach by (Zollmann and Venugopal, 2006) in attempting to improve the coverage of syntactic translation. Rather than creating ad-hoc schemes to categories non-terminals with syntactic labels when they do not span syntactic constituencies, we only use labels that are presented by the parser or shallow tagger. Nor do we try to expand the space where rules can apply by propagating uncertainty from the parser in building input forests, as in (Mi et al., 2008), but we build ambiguity into the translation rule.

The model also differs from (Marton and Resnik, 2008; Chiang et al., 2008, 2009) by adding informative labels to rule non-terminals and requiring them to match the source span label. The soft constraint in our model pertain not to a additional feature functions based on syntactic information, but to the availability of syntactic and non-syntactic informed rules.

4 Parameterization

In common with most current SMT systems, the decoding goal of finding the most probable target language sentence $\hat{\mathbf{t}}$, given a source language sentence $\mathbf{s}$

$$\hat{\mathbf{t}} = \text{argmax}_{\mathbf{t}} \; p(\mathbf{t}|\mathbf{s}) \qquad (1)$$

The argmax function defines the search objective of the decoder. We estimate $p(\mathbf{t}|\mathbf{s})$ by decomposing it into component models

$$p(\mathbf{t}|\mathbf{s}) = \frac{1}{Z} \prod_m h'_m(\mathbf{t}, \mathbf{s})^{\lambda_m} \qquad (2)$$

where $h'_m(\mathbf{t}, \mathbf{s})$ is the feature function for component m and λ_m is the weight given to component m. Z is a normalization factor which is ignored in practice. Components are translation model scoring functions, language model, and other features.

The problem is typically presented in log-space, which simplifies computations, but otherwise does not change the problem due to the monotonicity of the log function ($h_m = \log h'_m$)

$$\log p(\mathbf{t}|\mathbf{s}) = \sum_m \lambda_m \, h_m(\mathbf{t}, \mathbf{s}) \qquad (3)$$

An advantage of our model over (Marton and Resnik, 2008; Chiang et al., 2008, 2009) is the number of feature functions remains the same, therefore, the tuning algorithm does not need to be replaced; we continue to use MERT (Och, 2003).

5 Rule Extraction

Rule extraction follows the algorithm described in (Chiang, 2005). We note the heuristics used for hierarchical phrases extraction include the following constraints:

1. all rules must be at least partially lexicalized,
2. non-terminals cannot be consecutive,
3. a maximum of two non-terminals per rule,
4. maximum source and target span width of 10 word
5. maximum of 5 source symbols

In the source syntax model, non-terminals are restricted to source spans that are syntactic phrases which severely limits the rules that can be extracted or applied during decoding. Therefore, we can adapt the heuristics, dropping some of the constraints, without introducing too much complexity.

1. consecutive non-terminals are allowed
2. a maximum of three non-terminals,
3. all non-terminals and LHS must span a parse constituent

In the soft syntax model, we relax the constraint of requiring all non-terminals to span parse constituents. Where there is no constituency spans, the default symbol X is used to denote an undecorated non-terminal. This gives rise to rules which mixes decorated and undecorated non-terminals.

To maintain decoding speed and minimize spurious ambiguity, item (1) in the syntactic extraction heuristics is adapted to prohibit consecutive undecorated non-terminals. This combines the strength of syntactic rules but also gives the translation model more flexibility and higher coverage from having undecorated non-terminals. Therefore, the heuristics become:

1. consecutive non-terminals are allowed, but consecutive undecorated non-terminals are prohibited
2. a maximum of three non-terminals,
3. all non-terminals and LHS must span a parse constituent

5.1 Rule probabilities

Maximum likelihood phrase probabilities, $p(\bar{\mathbf{t}}|\bar{\mathbf{s}})$, are calculated for phrase pairs, using fractional counts as described in (Chiang, 2005). The maximum likelihood estimates are smoothed using Good-Turing discounting (Foster et al., 2006). A phrase count feature function is also create for each translation model, however, the lexical and backward probabilities are not used.

6 Decoding

We use the Moses implementation of the SCFG-based approach (Hoang et al., 2009) which support hierarchical and syntactic training and decoding used in this paper. The decoder implements the CKY+ algorithm with cube pruning, as well as histogram and beam pruning, all pruning parameters were identical for all experiments for fairer comparison.

All non-terminals can cover a maximum of 7 source words, similar to the maximum rule span feature other hierarchical decoders to speed up decoding time.

7 Experiments

We trained on the New Commentary 2009 corpus[1], tuning on a hold-out set. Table 1 gives more details on the corpus. *nc_test2007* was used for testing.

		German	English
Train	Sentences	82,306	
	Words	2,034,373	1,965,325
Tune	Sentences	2000	
Test	Sentences	1026	

Table 1: Training, tuning, and test conditions

The training corpus was cleaned and filtered using standard methods found in the Moses toolkit (Koehn et al., 2007) and aligned using GIZA++ (Och and Ney, 2003). Standard MERT weight tuning was used throughout. The English half of the training data was also used to create a trigram language model which was used for each experiment. All experiments use truecase data and results are reported in case-sensitive BLEU scores (Papineni et al., 2001).

The German side was parsed with the Bitpar parser[2]. 2042 sentences in the training corpus failed to parse and were discarded from the training for both hierarchical and syntactic models to ensure that train on identical amounts of data. Similarly, 991 out of 1026 sentences were parsable in the test set. To compare like-for-like, the baseline translates the same 991 sentences, but evaluated over 1026 sentences. (In the experiments with chunk tags below, all 1026 sentences are used).

[1]http://www.statmt.org/wmt09/

[2]http://www.ims.uni-stuttgart.de/tcl/SOFTWARE/BitPar.html

#	Model	% BLEU
	Using parse tree	
1	Hierarchical	15.9
2	Syntax rules	14.9
3	Joint hier. + syntax rules	16.1
4	Soft syntax rules	16.7
	Using chunk tags	
5	Hierarchical	16.3
6	Soft syntax	16.8

Table 2: German–English results for hierarchical and syntactic models, in %BLEU

We use as a baseline the vanilla hierarchical model which obtained a BLEU score of 15.9% (see Table 2, line 1).

7.1 Syntactic translation

Using the naïve translation model constrained with syntactic non-terminals significantly decreases translation quality, Table 2, line 2. We then ran hierarchical concurrently with the syntactic models, line 3, but see little improvement over the hierarchical baseline. However, we see a gain of 0.8% BLEU when using the soft syntax model.

7.2 Reachability

The increased performance using the soft syntax model can be partially explained by studying the effect of changes to the extraction and decoding algorithms has to the capacity of the translation pipeline. We run some analysis in which we trained the phrase models with a corpus of one sentence and attempt to decode the same sentence. Pruning and recombination were disabled during decoding to negate the effect of language model context and model scores.

The first thousand sentences of the training corpus was analyzed, Table 3. The hierarchical model successfully decode over half of the sentences while a translation model constrained by a source syntax parse tree manages only 113 sentences, illustrating the severe degradation in coverage when a naive syntax model is used.

Decoding with a hierarchical and syntax model jointly (line 3) only decode one extra sentence over the hierarchical model, suggesting that the expressive power of the hierarchical model almost

#	Model	Reachable sentences
1	Hierarchical	57.8%
2	Syntax rules	11.3%
3	Joint hier. + syntax rules	57.9%
4	Soft syntax rules	58.5%

Table 3: Reachability of 1000 training sentences: can they be translated with the model?

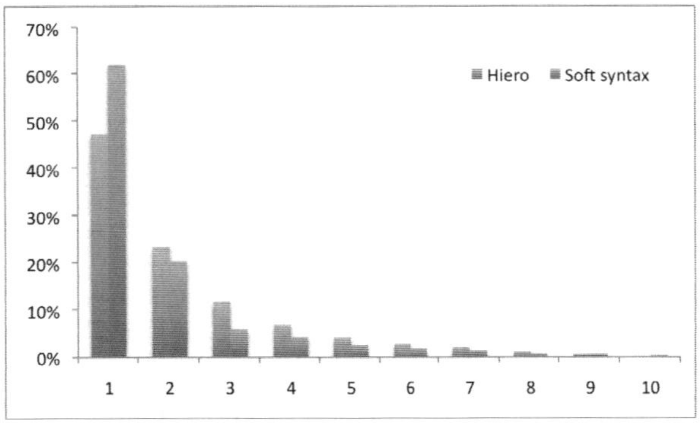

Figure 2: Source span lengths

completely subsumes that of the syntactic model. The MERT tuning adjust the weights so that the syntactic model is very rarely applied during joint decoding, suggesting that the tuning stage prefers the broader coverage of the hierarchical model over the precision of the syntactic model.

However, the soft syntax model slightly increases the reachability of the target sentences, lines 4.

7.3 Rule Span Width

The soft syntactic model contains rules with three non-terminals, as opposed to 2 in the hierarchical model, and consecutive non-terminals in the hope that the rules will have the context and linguistic information to apply over longer spans. Therefore, it is surprising that when decoding with a soft syntactic grammar, significantly more words are translated singularly and the use of long spanning rules is reduced, Figure 2.

However, looking at the usage of the glue rules paints a different picture. There is significantly less usage of the glue rules when decoding with the soft syntax model, Figure 3. The use of the glue rule indicates a failure of the translation model to explain the translation so the decrease in its usage is evidence of the better explanatory power of the soft syntactic model.

An example of an input sentence, and the best translation found by the hierarchical and soft syntax model can be seen in Table 4. Figure 4 is the

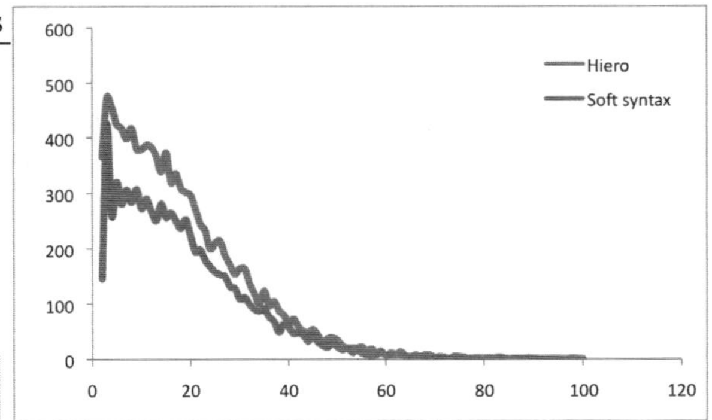

Figure 3: Length and count of glue rules used decoding test set

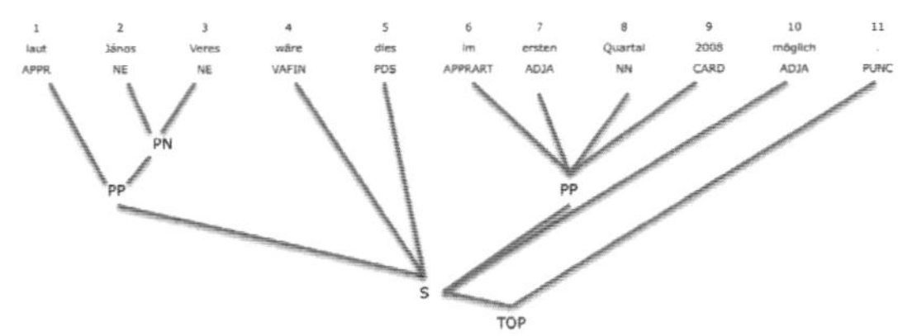

Figure 4: Example input parse tree

parse tree given to the soft syntax model.

Input laut János Veres wäre dies im ersten Quartal 2008 möglich .
Hierarchical output according to János Veres this in the first quarter of 2008 would be possible .
Soft Syntax according to János Veres this would be possible in the first quarter of 2008 .

Table 4: Example input and best output found

Both output are lexically identical but the output of the hierarchical model needs to be reordered to be grammatically correct. Contrast the derivations produced by the hierarchical grammar, Figure 5, with that produced with the soft syntax model, Figure 6. The soft syntax derivation makes use of several non-lexicalized to dictate word order, shown below.

$$X \rightarrow NE_1\ NE_2 \# X_1\ X_2$$
$$X \rightarrow VAFIN_1\ PDS_2 \# X_1\ X_2$$
$$X \rightarrow ADJA_1\ NN_2 \# X_1\ X_2$$
$$X \rightarrow APPRART_1\ X_2\ CARD_3 \# X_1\ X_2\ X_3$$
$$X \rightarrow PP_1\ X_2\ PUNC_3 \# X_2\ X_1\ X_3$$

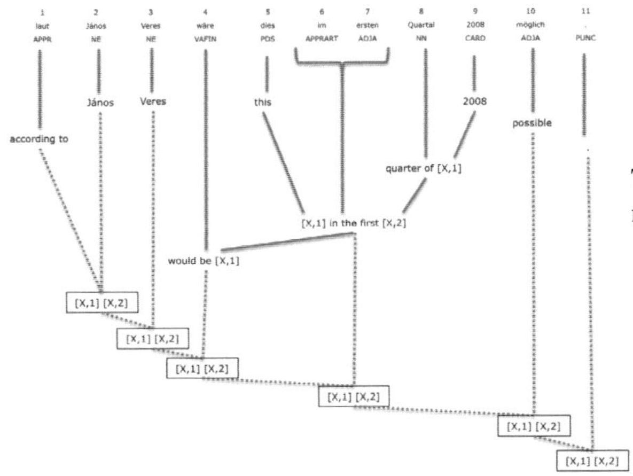

Figure 5: Derivation with Hierarchical model

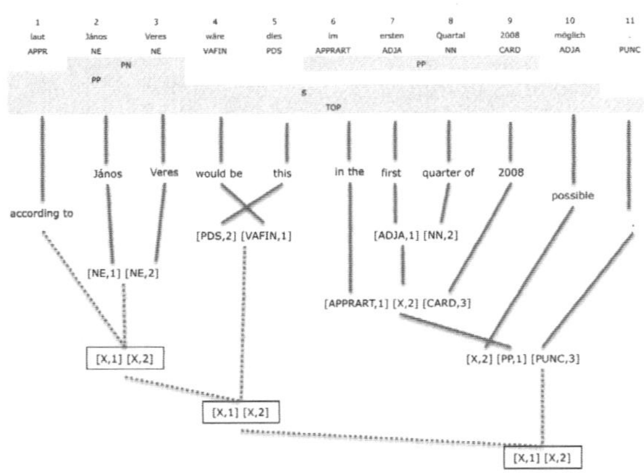

Figure 6: Derivation with soft syntax model

The soft syntax derivation include several rules which are partially decorated. Crucially, the last rule in the list above reorders the *PP* phrase and the non-syntactic phrase *X* to generate the grammatically correct output. The other non-lexicalized rules monotonically concatenate the output. This can be performed by the glue rule, but nevertheless, the use of empirically backed rules allows the decoder to better compare hypotheses. The derivation also rely less on the glue rules than the hierarchical model (shown in solid rectangles).

Reducing the maximum number of non-terminals per rule reduces translation quality but increasing it has little effect on the soft syntax model, Table 5. This seems to indicate that non-terminals are useful as context when applying rules up to a certain extent.

7.4 English to German

We experimented with the reverse language direction to see if the soft syntax model still increased translation quality. The results were positive but less pronounced, Table 6.

# non-terms	% BLEU
2	16.5
3	16.8
5	16.8

Table 5: Effect on %BLEU of varying number of non-terminals

#	Model	% BLEU
1	Hierarchical	10.2
2	Soft syntax	10.6

Table 6: English–German results in %BLEU

7.5 Using Chunk Tags

Parse trees of the source language provide useful information that we have exploited to create a better translation model. However, parsers are an expensive resource as they frequently need manually annotated training treebanks. Parse accuracy is also problematic and particularly brittle when given sentences not in the same domain as the training corpus. This also causes some sentences to be unparseable. For example, our original test corpus of 1026 sentences contained 35 unparsable sentences. Thus, high quality parsers are unavailable for many source languages of interest.

Parse forests can be used to mitigate the accuracy problem, allowing the decoder to choose from many alternative parses, (Mi et al., 2008).

The soft syntax translation model is not dependent on the linguistic information being in a tree structure, only that the labels identify contiguous spans. Chunk taggers (Abney, 1991) does just that. They offer higher accuracy than syntactic parser, are not so brittle to out-of-domain data and identify chunk phrases similar to parser-based syntactic phrases that may be useful in guiding reordering.

We apply the soft syntax approach as in the previous sections but replacing the use of parse constituents with chunk phrases.

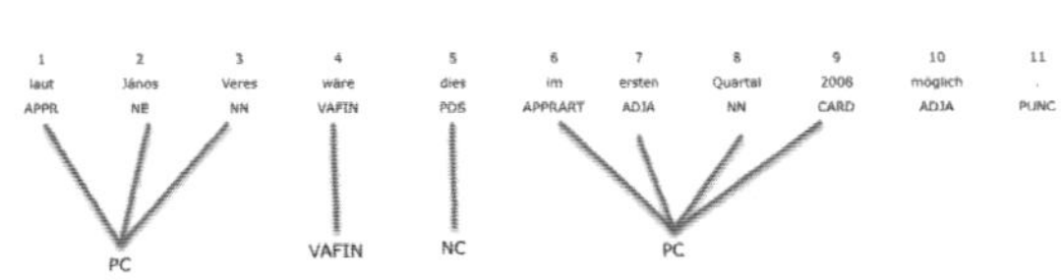

Figure 7: Chunked sentence

7.6 Experiments with Chunk Tags

We use the same data as described earlier in this chapter to train, tune and test our approach. The Treetagger chunker (Schmidt and Schulte im Walde, 2000) was used to tag the source (German) side of the corpus. The chunker successfully processed all sentences in the training and test dataset so no sentences were excluded. The increase training data, as well as the ability to translate all sentences in the test set, explains the higher hierarchical baseline than the previous experiments with parser data. We use the noun, verb and prepositional chunks, as well as part-of-speech tags, emitted by the chunker.

Results are shown in Table 2, line 5 & 6. Using chunk tags, we see a modest gain of 0.5% BLEU.

The same example sentence in Table 4 is shown with chunk tags in Figure 7. The soft syntax model with chunk tags produced the derivation tree shown in Figure 8. The derivation make use of an unlexicalized rule local reordering. In this example, it uses the same number of glue rule as the hierarchical derivation but the output is grammatically correct.

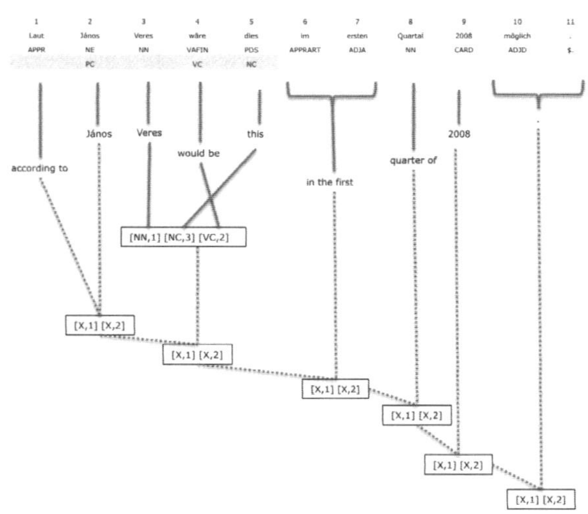

Figure 8: Translated chunked sentence

However, overall, the number of glue rules used shows the same reduction that we saw using soft syntax in the earlier section, as can be seen in Figure 9. Again, the soft syntax model, this time using chunk tags, is able to reduce the use of the glue rule with empirically informed rules.

8 Conclusion

We show in this paper that combining the generality of the hierarchical approach with the specificity of syntactic approach can improve translation. A reason for the improvement is the better long-range reordering made possible by the increase capacity of the translation model.

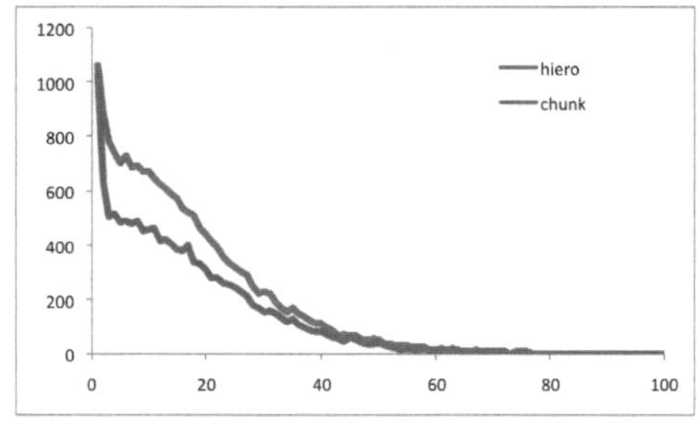

Figure 9: Chunk - Length and count of glue rules used decoding test set

Future work in this direction includes using tree-to-tree approaches, automatically created constituency labels, and back-off methods between decorated and undecorated rules.

9 Acknowledgement

This work was supported in part by the EuroMatrixPlus project funded by the European Commission (7th Framework Programme) and in part under the GALE program of the Defense Advanced Research Projects Agency, Contract No. HR0011-06-C-0022.

References

Abney, S. (1991). Parsing by chunks. In *Robert Berwick, Steven Abney, and Carol Tenny: Principle-Based Parsing*. Kluwer Academic Publishers.

Ambati, V. and Lavie, A. (2008). Improving syntax driven translation models by re-structuring divergent and non-isomorphic parse tree structures. In *AMTA*.

Ambati, V., Lavie, A., and Carbonell, J. (2009). Extraction of syntactic translation models from parallel data using syntax from source and target languages. In *MT Summit*.

Chiang, D. (2005). A hierarchical phrase-based model for statistical machine translation. In *Proceedings of the 43rd Annual Meeting of the Association for Computational Linguistics (ACL'05)*, pages 263–270, Ann Arbor, Michigan. Association for Computational Linguistics.

Chiang, D., Knight, K., and Wang, W. (2009). 11,001 new features for statistical machine translation. In *Proceedings of Human Language Technologies: The 2009 Annual Conference of the North American Chapter of the Association for Computational Linguistics*, pages 218–226, Boulder, Colorado. Association for Computational Linguistics.

Chiang, D., Marton, Y., and Resnik, P. (2008). Online large-margin training of syntactic and structural translation features. In *Proceedings of the 2008 Conference on Empirical Methods in Natural Language Processing*, pages 224–233, Honolulu, Hawaii. Association for Computational Linguistics.

Dyer, C., Muresan, S., and Resnik, P. (2008). Generalizing word lattice translation. In *Proceedings of ACL-08: HLT*, pages 1012–1020, Columbus, Ohio. Association for Computational Linguistics.

Foster, G., Kuhn, R., and Johnson, H. (2006). Phrasetable smoothing for statistical machine translation. In *Proceedings of the 2006 Conference on Empirical Methods in Natural Language Processing*, pages 53–61, Sydney, Australia. Association for Computational Linguistics.

Galley, M., Graehl, J., Knight, K., Marcu, D., DeNeefe, S., Wang, W., and Thayer, I. (2006). Scalable inference and training of context-rich syntactic translation models. In *Proceedings of the 21st International Conference on Computational Linguistics and 44th Annual Meeting of the Association for Computational Linguistics*, pages 961–968, Sydney, Australia. Association for Computational Linguistics.

Galley, M., Hopkins, M., Knight, K., and Marcu, D. (2004). What's in a translation rule? In *Proceedings of the Joint Conference on Human Language Technologies and the Annual Meeting of the North American Chapter of the Association of Computational Linguistics (HLT-NAACL)*.

Hoang, H., Koehn, P., and Lopez, A. (2009). A Unified Framework for Phrase-Based, Hierarchical, and Syntax-Based Statistical Machine Translation. In *Proc. of the International Workshop on Spoken Language Translation*, pages 152–159, Tokyo, Japan.

Huang, L. and Chiang, D. (2008). Forest-based translation rule extraction. In *EMNLP*, Honolulu, Hawaii.

Koehn, P., Hoang, H., Birch, A., Callison-Burch, C., Federico, M., Bertoldi, N., Cowan, B., Shen, W., Moran, C., Zens, R., Dyer, C., Bojar, O., Constantin, A., and Herbst, E. (2007). Moses: Open source toolkit for statistical machine translation. In *Proceedings of the 45th Annual Meeting of the Association for Computational Linguistics Companion Volume Proceedings of the Demo and Poster Sessions*, pages 177–180, Prague, Czech Republic. Association for Computational Linguistics.

Li, Z., Callison-Burch, C., Dyer, C., Khudanpur, S., Schwartz, L., Thornton, W., Weese, J., and Zaidan, O. (2009). Joshua: An open source toolkit for parsing-based machine translation. In *Proceedings of the Fourth Workshop on Statistical Machine Translation*, pages 135–139, Athens, Greece. Association for Computational Linguistics.

Liu, Y., Mi, H., Feng, Y., and Liu, Q. (2009). Joint decoding with multiple translation models. In *In Proceedings of ACL/IJCNLP 2009*, pages 576–584, Singapore.

Marton, Y. and Resnik, P. (2008). Soft syntactic constraints for hierarchical phrased-based translation. In *Proceedings of ACL-08: HLT*, pages 1003–1011, Columbus, Ohio. Association for Computational Linguistics.

Mi, H., Huang, L., and Liu, Q. (2008). Forest-based translation. In *Proceedings of ACL-08: HLT*, pages 192–199, Columbus, Ohio. Association for Computational Linguistics.

Och, F. J. (2003). Minimum error rate training for statistical machine translation. In *Proceedings of the 41st Annual Meeting of the Association of Computational Linguistics (ACL)*.

Och, F. J. and Ney, H. (2003). A systematic comparison of various statistical alignment models. *Computational Linguistics*, 29(1):19–52.

Papineni, K., Roukos, S., Ward, T., and Zhu, W.-J. (2001). BLEU: a method for automatic evaluation of machine translation. Technical Report RC22176(W0109-022), IBM Research Report.

Schmidt, H. and Schulte im Walde, S. (2000). Robust German noun chunking with a probabilistic context-free grammar. In *Proceedings of the International Conference on Computational Linguistics (COLING)*.

Shen, L., Xu, J., Zhang, B., Matsoukas, S., and Weischedel, R. (2009). Effective use of linguistic and contextual information for statistical machine translation. In *Proceedings of the 2009 Conference on Empirical Methods in Natural Language Processing*, pages 72–80, Singapore. Association for Computational Linguistics.

Venugopal, A., Zollmann, A., Smith, N. A., and Vogel, S. (2009). Preference grammars: Softening syntactic constraints to improve statistical machine translation. In *Proceedings of Human Language Technologies: The 2009 Annual Conference of the North American Chapter of the Association for Computational Linguistics*, pages 236–244, Boulder, Colorado. Association for Computational Linguistics.

Zollmann, A. and Venugopal, A. (2006). Syntax augmented machine translation via chart parsing. In *Proceedings on the Workshop on Statistical Machine Translation*, pages 138–141, New York City. Association for Computational Linguistics.

Divide and Translate: Improving Long Distance Reordering in Statistical Machine Translation

Katsuhito Sudoh, Kevin Duh, Hajime Tsukada, Tsutomu Hirao, Masaaki Nagata
NTT Communication Science Laboratories
2-4 Hikaridai, Seika-cho, Soraku-gun, Kyoto 619-0237, Japan
sudoh@cslab.kecl.ntt.co.jp

Abstract

This paper proposes a novel method for long distance, clause-level reordering in statistical machine translation (SMT). The proposed method separately translates clauses in the source sentence and reconstructs the target sentence using the clause translations with non-terminals. The non-terminals are placeholders of embedded clauses, by which we reduce complicated clause-level reordering into simple word-level reordering. Its translation model is trained using a bilingual corpus with clause-level alignment, which can be automatically annotated by our alignment algorithm with a syntactic parser in the source language. We achieved significant improvements of 1.4% in BLEU and 1.3% in TER by using Moses, and 2.2% in BLEU and 3.5% in TER by using our hierarchical phrase-based SMT, for the English-to-Japanese translation of research paper abstracts in the medical domain.

1 Introduction

One of the common problems of statistical machine translation (SMT) is to overcome the differences in word order between the source and target languages. This *reordering* problem is especially serious for language pairs with very different word orders, such as English-Japanese. Many previous studies on SMT have addressed the problem by incorporating probabilistic models into SMT reordering. This approach faces the very large computational cost of searching over many possibilities, especially for long sentences. In practice the search can be made tractable by limiting its reordering distance, but this also renders long distance movements impossible. Some recent studies avoid the problem by reordering source words prior to decoding. This approach faces difficulties when the input phrases are long and require significant word reordering, mainly because their reordering model is not very accurate.

In this paper, we propose a novel method for translating long sentences that is different from the above approaches. Problematic long sentences often include embedded clauses[1] such as relative clauses. Such an embedded (subordinate) clause can usually be translated almost independently of words outside the clause. From this viewpoint, we propose a *divide-and-conquer* approach: we aim to translate the clauses separately and reconstruct the target sentence using the clause translations. We first segment a source sentence into clauses using a syntactic parser. The clauses can include non-terminals as placeholders for nested clauses. Then we translate the clauses with a standard SMT method, in which the non-terminals are reordered as words. Finally we reconstruct the target sentence by replacing the non-terminals with their corresponding clause translations. With this method, clause-level reordering is reduced to word-level reordering and can be dealt with efficiently. The models for clause translation are trained using a bilingual corpus with clause-level alignment. We also present an automatic clause alignment algorithm that can be applied to sentence-aligned bilingual corpora.

In our experiment on the English-to-Japanese translation of multi-clause sentences, the proposed method improved the translation performance by 1.4% in BLEU and 1.3% in TER by using Moses, and by 2.2% in BLEU and 3.5% in TER by using our hierarchical phrase-based SMT.

The main contribution of this paper is two-fold:

[1]Although various definitions of a *clause* can be considered, this paper follows the definition of "S" (sentence) in Enju. It basically follows the Penn Treebank II scheme but also includes SINV, SQ, SBAR. See http://www-tsujii.is.s.u-tokyo.ac.jp/enju/enju-manual/enju-output-spec.html#correspondence for details.

Proceedings of the Joint 5th Workshop on Statistical Machine Translation and MetricsMATR, pages 418–427,
Uppsala, Sweden, 15-16 July 2010. ©2010 Association for Computational Linguistics

1. We introduce the idea of explicit separation of in-clause and outside-clause reordering and reduction of outside-clause reordering into common word-level reordering.

2. We propose an automatic clause alignment algorithm, by which our approach can be used without manual clause-level alignment.

This paper is organized as follows. The next section reviews related studies on reordering. Section 3 describes the proposed method in detail. Section 4 presents and discusses our experimental results. Finally, we conclude this paper with our thoughts on future studies.

2 Related Work

Reordering in SMT can be roughly classified into two approaches, namely a search in SMT decoding and preprocessing.

The former approach is a straightforward way that models reordering in noisy channel translation, and has been studied from the early period of SMT research. Distance-based reordering is a typical approach used in many previous studies related to word-based SMT (Brown et al., 1993) and phrase-based SMT (Koehn et al., 2003). Along with the advances in phrase-based SMT, lexicalized reordering with a block orientation model was proposed (Tillmann, 2004; Koehn et al., 2005). This kind of reordering is suitable and commonly used in phrase-based SMT. On the other hand, a syntax-based SMT naturally includes reordering in its translation model. A lot of research work undertaken in this decade has used syntactic parsing for linguistically-motivated translation. (Yamada and Knight, 2001; Graehl and Knight, 2004; Galley et al., 2004; Liu et al., 2006). Wu (1997) and Chiang (2007) focus on formal structures that can be extracted from parallel corpora, instead of a syntactic parser trained using treebanks. These syntactic approaches can theoretically model reordering over an arbitrary length, however, long distance reordering still faces the difficulty of searching over an extremely large search space.

The preprocessing approach employs deterministic reordering so that the following translation process requires only short distance reordering (or even a monotone). Several previous studies have proposed syntax-driven reordering based on source-side parse trees. Xia and McCord (2004) extracted reordering rules automatically from bilingual corpora for English-to-French translation; Collins et al. (2005) used linguistically-motivated clause restructuring rules for German-to-English translation; Li et al. (2007) modeled reordering on parse tree nodes by using a maximum entropy model with surface and syntactic features for Chinese-to-English translation; Katz-Brown and Collins (2008) applied a very simple reverse ordering to Japanese-to-English translation, which reversed the word order in Japanese segments separated by a few simple cues; Xu et al. (2009) utilized a dependency parser with several hand-labeled precedence rules for reordering English to subject-object-verb order like Korean and Japanese. Tromble and Eisner (2009) proposed another reordering approach based on a linear ordering problem over source words without a linguistically syntactic structure. These preprocessing methods reorder source words close to the target-side order by employing language-dependent rules or statistical reordering models based on automatic word alignment. Although the use of language-dependent rules is a natural and promising way of bridging gaps between languages with large syntactic differences, the rules are usually unsuitable for other language groups. On the other hand, statistical methods can be applied to any language pairs. However, it is very difficult to reorder all source words so that they are monotonic with the target words. This is because automatic word alignment is not usually reliable owing to data sparseness and the weak modeling of many-to-many word alignments. Since such a reordering is not complete or may even harm word ordering consistency in the source language, these previous methods further applied reordering in their decoding. Li et al. (2007) used N-best reordering hypotheses to overcome the reordering ambiguity.

Our approach is different from those of previous studies that aim to perform both short and long distance reordering at the same time. The proposed method distinguishes the reordering of embedded clauses from others and efficiently accomplishes it by using a divide-and-conquer framework. The remaining (relatively short distance) reordering can be realized in decoding and preprocessing by the methods described above. The proposed framework itself does not depend on a certain language pair. It is based on the assumption that a source language clause is translated to the corresponding target language clause as a continuous segment. The only language-dependent resource we need is a syntactic parser of the source language. Note that clause translation in the proposed method is a standard MT problem and therefore any reordering method can be employed for further improvement.

This work is inspired by syntax-based methods with respect to the use of non-terminals. Our method can be seen as a variant of tree-to-string translation that focuses only on the clause structure in parse trees and independently translates the clauses. Although previous syntax-based methods can theoretically model this kind of derivation, it is practically difficult to decode long multi-clause sentences as described above.

Our approach is also related to sentence simplification and is intended to obtain simple and short source sentences for better translation. Kim and Ehara (1994) proposed a rule-based method for splitting long Japanese sentences for Japanese-to-English translation; Furuse et al. (1998) used a syntactic structure to split ill-formed inputs in speech translation. Their splitting approach splits a sentence sequentially to obtain short segments, and does not undertake their reordering.

Another related field is clause identification (Tjong et al., 2001). The proposed method is not limited to a specific clause identification method and any method can be employed, if their clause definition matches the proposed method where clauses are independently translated.

3 Proposed Method

The proposed method consists of the following steps illustrated in Figure 1.

During training:

1) clause segmentation of source sentences with a syntactic parser (section 3.1)

2) alignment of target words with source clauses to develop a clause-level aligned corpus (section 3.2)

3) training the clause translation models using the corpus (section 3.3)

During testing:

1) clause translation with the clause translation models (section 3.4)

2) sentence reconstruction based on non-terminals (section 3.5)

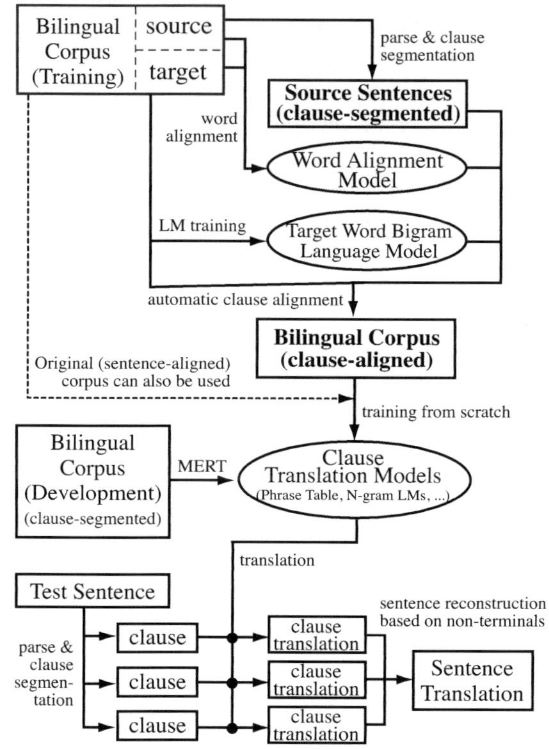

Figure 1: Overview of proposed method.

3.1 Clause Segmentation of Source Sentences

Clauses in source sentences are identified by a syntactic parser. Figure 2 shows a parse tree for the example sentence below. The example sentence has a relative clause modifying the noun *book*. Figure 3 shows the word alignment of this example.

English: *John lost the book that was borrowed last week from Mary.*

Japanese: *john wa* (topic marker) *senshu* (last week) *mary kara* (from) *kari* (borrow) *ta* (past tense marker) *hon* (book) *o* (direct object marker) *nakushi* (lose) *ta* (past tense marker) .

We segment the source sentence at the clause level and the example is rewritten with two clauses as follows.

- John lost the book *_s0* .
- that was borrowed last week from Mary

_s0 is a non-terminal symbol the serves as a placeholder of the relative clause. We allow an arbitrary

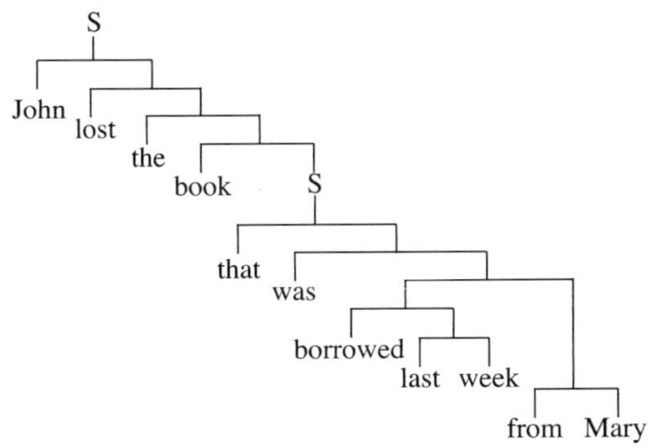

Figure 2: Parse tree for example English sentence. Node labels are omitted except S.

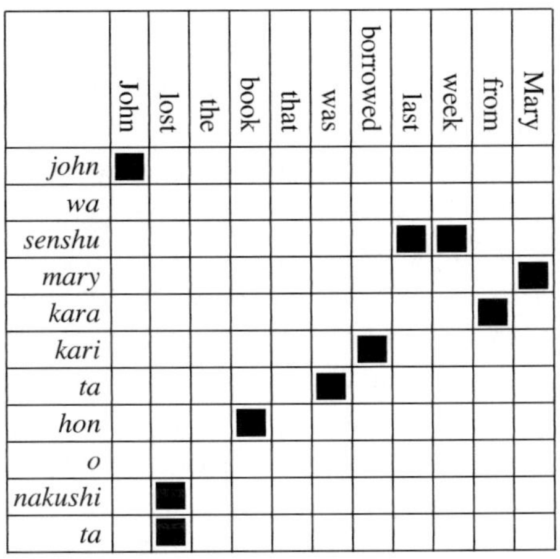

Figure 3: Word alignment for example bilingual sentence.

number of non-terminals in each clause[2]. A nested clause structure can be represented in the same manner using such non-terminals recursively.

3.2 Alignment of Target Words with Source Clauses

To translate source clauses with non-terminal symbols, we need models trained using a clause-level aligned bilingual corpus. A clause-level aligned corpus is defined as a set of parallel, bilingual clause pairs including non-terminals that represent embedded clauses.

We assume that a sentence-aligned bilingual corpus is available and consider the alignment of target words with source clauses. We can manually align these Japanese words with the English clauses as follows.

- *john wa _s0 hon o nakushi ta .*
  John lost the book _s0 .
- *senshu mary kara kari ta*
  that was borrowed last week from Mary

Since the cost of manual clause alignment is high especially for a large-scale corpus, a natural question to ask is whether this resource can be obtained from a sentence-aligned bilingual corpus *automatically with no human input*. To answer this, we now describe a simple method for dealing with clause alignment data from scratch, using only the word alignment and language model probabilities inferred from bilingual and monolingual corpora.

Our method is based on the idea that automatic clause alignment can be viewed as a classification problem: for an English sentence with N words ($\mathbf{e} = (e_1, e_2, \ldots, e_N)$) and K clauses ($\tilde{e}^1, \tilde{e}^2, \ldots, \tilde{e}^K$), and its Japanese translation with M words ($\mathbf{f} = (f_1, f_2, \ldots, f_M)$), the goal is to classify each Japanese word into one of $\{1, \ldots, K\}$ classes. Intuitively, the probability that a Japanese word f_m is assigned to class $k \in \{1, \ldots, K\}$ depends on two factors:

1. The probability of translating f_m into the English words of clause k (i.e. $\sum_{e \in \tilde{e}^k} p(e|f_m)$). We expect f_m to be assigned to a clause where this value is high.
2. The language model probability (i.e. $p(f_m|f_{m-1})$). If this value is high, we expect f_m and f_{m-1} to be assigned to the same clause.

We implement this intuition using a graph-based method. For each English-Japanese sentence pair, we construct a graph with K *clause nodes* (representing English clauses) and M *word nodes* (representing Japanese words). The edge weights between word and clause nodes are defined as the sum of lexical translation probabilities $\sum_{e \in \tilde{e}^k} p(e|f_m)$. The edge weights between words are defined as the bigram probability $p(f_m|f_{m-1})$. Each clause node is labeled with a class ID $k \in \{1, \ldots, K\}$. We then *propagate* these K labels along the graph to label the M word nodes. Figure 4 shows the graph for the example sentence.

Many label propagation algorithms are available. The important thing is to use an algorithm that encourages node pairs with strong edge weights to receive the same label. We use the label propagation algorithm of (Zhu et al., 2003). If we

[2] In practice not so many clauses are embedded in a single sentence but we found some examples with nine embedded clauses for coordination in our corpora.

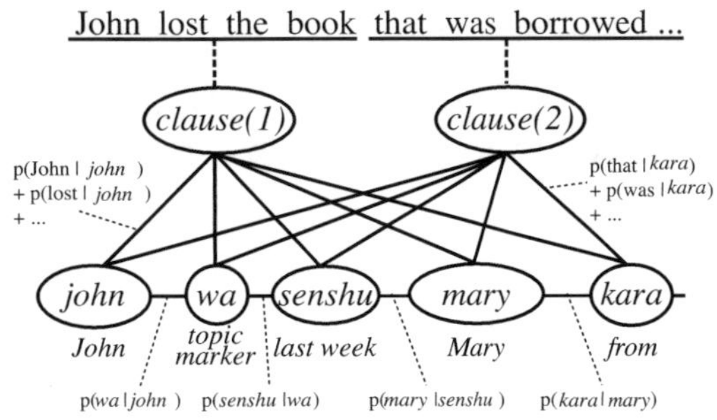

Figure 4: Graph-based representation of the example sentence. We propagate the clause labels to the Japanese word nodes on this graph to form the clause alignments.

assume the labels are binary, the following objective is minimized:

$$\underset{\boldsymbol{l} \in \mathcal{R}^{K+M}}{\operatorname{argmin}} \sum_{i,j} w_{ij}(l_i - l_j)^2 \quad (1)$$

where w_{ij} is the edge weight between nodes i and j ($1 \leq i \leq K+M$, $1 \leq j \leq K+M$), and $\boldsymbol{l}$ ($l_i \in \{0,1\}$) is a vector of labels on the nodes. The first K elements of $\boldsymbol{l}$, $\boldsymbol{l}_c = (l_1, l_2, ..., l_K)^T$, are constant because the clause nodes are pre-labeled. The remaining M elements, $\boldsymbol{l}_f = (l_{K+1}, l_{K+2}, ..., l_{K+M})^T$, are unknown and to be determined. Here, we consider the decomposition of the weight matrix $\boldsymbol{W} = [w_{ij}]$ into four blocks after the K-th row and column as follows:

$$\boldsymbol{W} = \begin{bmatrix} \boldsymbol{W}_{cc} & \boldsymbol{W}_{cf} \\ \boldsymbol{W}_{fc} & \boldsymbol{W}_{ff} \end{bmatrix} \quad (2)$$

The solution of eqn. (1), namely $\boldsymbol{l}_f$, is given by the following equation:

$$\boldsymbol{l}_f = (\boldsymbol{D}_{ff} - \boldsymbol{W}_{ff})^{-1} \boldsymbol{W}_{fc} \, \boldsymbol{l}_c \quad (3)$$

where $\boldsymbol{D}$ is the diagonal matrix with $d_i = \sum_j w_{ij}$ and is decomposed similarly to $\boldsymbol{W}$. Each element of $\boldsymbol{l}_f$ is in the interval $(0,1)$ and can be regarded as the label propagation probability. A detailed explanation of this solution can be found in Section 2 of (Zhu et al., 2003). For our multi-label problem with K labels, we slightly modified the algorithm by expanding the vector $\boldsymbol{l}$ to an $(M+K) \times K$ binary matrix $\boldsymbol{L} = [\, \boldsymbol{l}_1 \, \boldsymbol{l}_2 \, ... \, \boldsymbol{l}_K \,]$.

After the optimization, we can normalize $\boldsymbol{L}_f$ to obtain the clause alignment scores $t(l_m = k|f_m)$ between each Japanese word f_m and English clause k. Theoretically, we can simply output the clause id k' for each f_m by finding $k' = \arg\max_k t(l_m = k|f_m)$. In practice, this may sometimes lead to Japanese clauses that have too many gaps, so we employ a two-stage procedure to extract clauses that are more contiguous.

First, we segment the Japanese sentence into K clauses based on a dynamic programming algorithm proposed by Malioutov and Barzilay (2006). We define an $M \times M$ similarity matrix $\boldsymbol{S} = [s_{ij}]$ with $s_{ij} = \exp(-||\boldsymbol{l}^i - \boldsymbol{l}^j||)$ where $\boldsymbol{l}^i$ is $(K+i)$-th row vector in the label matrix $\boldsymbol{L}$. s_{ij} represents the similarity between the i-th and j-th Japanese words with respect to their clause alignment score distributions; if the score distributions are similar then s_{ij} is large. The details of this algorithm can be found in (Malioutov and Barzilay, 2006). The clause segmentation gives us contiguous Japanese clauses $\tilde{\boldsymbol{f}}^1$, $\tilde{\boldsymbol{f}}^2$, ..., $\tilde{\boldsymbol{f}}^K$, thus minimizing inter-segment similarity and maximizing intra-segment similarity. Second, we determine the clause labels of the segmented clauses, based on clause alignment scores $\boldsymbol{T} = [T_{kk'}]$ for English and automatically-segmented Japanese clauses:

$$T_{kk'} = \sum_{f_m \in \tilde{\boldsymbol{f}}_{k'}} t(l_m = k|f_m) \quad (4)$$

where $\tilde{\boldsymbol{f}}_{k'}$ is the j'-th Japanese clause. In descending order of the clause alignment score, we greedily determine the clause label [3].

3.3 Training Clause Translation Models

We train clause translation models using the clause-level aligned corpus. In addition we can also include the original sentence-aligned corpus. We emphasize that we can use standard techniques for heuristically extracted phrase tables, word n-gram language models, and so on.

3.4 Clause Translation

By using the source language parser, a multi-clause source sentence is reduced to a set of clauses. We translate these clauses with a common SMT method using the clause translation models.

Here we present another English example *I bought the magazine which Tom recommended yesterday.* This sentence is segmented into clauses as follows.

[3] Although a full search is available when the number of clauses is small, we employ a greedy search in this paper.

- I bought the magazine _s0 .
- which Tom recommended yersterday

These clauses are translated into Japanese:

- *watashi* (I) *wa* (topic marker) _s0 *zasshi* (magazine) *o* (direct object marker) *kat* (buy) *ta* (past tense marker).
- tom *ga* (subject marker) *kino* (yesterday) *susume* (recommend) *ta* (past tense marker)

3.5 Sentence Reconstruction

We reconstruct the target sentence from the clause translations, based on non-terminals. Starting from the clause translation of the top clause, we recursively replace non-terminal symbols with their corresponding clause translations. Here, if a non-terminal is eventually deleted in SMT decoding, we simply concatenate the translation behind its parent clause.

Using the example above, we replace the non-terminal symbol _s0 with the second clause and obtain the Japanese sentence:
watashi wa tom ga kino susume ta zasshi o kat ta .

4 Experiment

We conducted the following experiments on the English-to-Japanese translation of research paper abstracts in the medical domain. Such technical documents are logically and formally written, and sentences are often so long and syntactically complex that their translation needs long distance reordering. We believe that the medical domain is suitable as regards evaluating the proposed method.

4.1 Resources

Our bilingual resources were taken from the medical domain. The parallel corpus consisted of research paper abstracts in English taken from PubMed[4] and the corresponding Japanese translations.

The training portion consisted of 25,500 sentences (*no-clause-seg.*; original sentences without clause segmentation). 4,132 English sentences in the corpus were composed of multiple clauses and were separated at the clause level by the procedure in section 3.1. As the syntactic parser, we used the Enju[5] (Miyao and Tsujii, 2008) English HPSG parser. For these training sentences, we automatically aligned Japanese words with each English clause as described in section 3.2 and developed a clause-level aligned corpus, called *auto-aligned* corpus. We prepared manually-aligned (oracle) clauses for reference, called *oracle-aligned* clauses. The clause alignment error rate of the auto-aligned corpus was 14% (number of wrong clause assignments divided by total number of words). The development and test portions each consisted of 1,032 multi-clause sentences. because this paper focuses only on multi-clause sentences. Their English-side was segmented into clauses in the same manner as the training sentences, and the development sentences had oracle clause alignment for MERT.

We also used the Life Science Dictionary[6] for training. We extracted 100,606 unique English entries from the dictionary including entries with multiple translation options, which we expanded to one-to-one entries, and finally we obtained 155,692 entries.

English-side tokenization was obtained using Enju, and we applied a simple preprocessing that removed articles (a, an, the) and normalized plural forms to singular ones. Japanese-side tokenization was obtained using MeCab[7] with ComeJisyo[8] (dictionary for Japanese medical document tokenization). Our resource statistics are summarized in Table 1.

4.2 Model and Decoder

We used two decoders in the experiments, Moses[9] (Koehn et al., 2007) and our in-house hierarchical phrase-based SMT (almost equivalent to Hiero (Chiang, 2007)). Moses used a phrase table with a maximum phrase length of 7, a lexicalized reordering model with `msd-bidirectional-fe`, and a distortion limit of 12[10]. Our hierarchical phrase-based SMT used a phrase table with a maximum rule length of 7 and a window size (Hiero's Λ) of 12 [11]. Both

[4] http://www.ncbi.nlm.nih.gov/pubmed/

[5] http://www-tsujii.is.s.u-tokyo.ac.jp/enju/index.html

[6] http://lsd.pharm.kyoto-u.ac.jp/en/index.html

[7] http://mecab.sourceforge.net/

[8] http://sourceforge.jp/projects/comedic/ (in Japanese)

[9] http://www.statmt.org/moses/

[10] Unlimited distortion was also tested but the results were worse.

[11] A larger window size could not be used due to its memory requirements.

Table 1: Data statistics on training, development, and test sets. All development and test sentences are multi-clause sentences.

Training			
Corpus Type		#words	#sentences
Parallel (no-clause-seg.)	E	690,536	25,550
	J	942,913	
Parallel (auto-aligned)	E	135,698	4,132 (10,766 clauses)
(auto-aligned)	J	183,043	
(oracle-aligned)	J	183,147	
Dictionary	E	263,175	155.692 (entries)
	J	291,455	
Development			
Corpus Type		#words	#sentences
Parallel (oracle-aligned)	E	34,417	1,032 (2,683 clauses)
	J	46,480	
Test			
Corpus Type		#words	#sentences
Parallel (clause-seg.)	E	34,433	1,032 (2,737 clauses)
	J	45,975	

decoders employed two language models: a word 5-gram language model from the Japanese sentences in the parallel corpus and a word 4-gram language model from the Japanese entries in the dictionary. The feature weights were optimized for BLEU (Papineni et al., 2002) by MERT, using the development sentences.

4.3 Compared Methods

We compared four different training and test conditions with respect to the use of clauses in training and testing. The development (i.e., MERT) conditions followed the test conditions. Two additional conditions with oracle clause alignment were also tested for reference.

Table 2 lists the compared methods. First, the proposed method (*proposed*) used the auto-aligned corpus in training and clause segmentation in testing. Second, the baseline method (*baseline*) did not use clause segmentation in either training or testing. Using this standard baseline method, we focused on the advantages of the divide-and-conquer translation itself. Third, we tested the same translation models as used with the proposed method for test sentences without clause segmentation, (*comp.(1)*). Although this comparison method cannot employ the proposed clause-level reordering, it was expected to be better than the baseline method because its translation model can be trained more precisely using the finely aligned clause-level corpus. Finally, the second comparison method (*comp.(2)*) translated segmented clauses with the baseline (without clause segmentation) model, as if each of them was a single sentence. Its translation of each clause was expected to be better than that of the baseline because of the efficient search over shortened inputs, while its reordering of clauses (non-terminals) was unreliable due to the lack of clause information in training. Its sentence reconstruction based on non-terminals was the same as with the proposed method. Although non-terminals in the second comparison method were out-of-vocabulary words and may be deleted in decoding, all of them survived and we could reconstruct sentences from translated clauses throughout the experiments. In addition, two other conditions were tested: using oracle-aligned clauses in training: the proposed method trained using oracle-aligned (*oracle*) clauses and the first comparison method using oracle-aligned (*oracle-comp.*) clauses.

4.4 Results

Table 3 shows the results in BLEU, Translation Edit Rate (TER) (Snover et al., 2006), and Position-independent Word-error Rate (PER) (Och et al., 2001), obtained with Moses and our hierarchical phrase-based SMT, respectively. Bold face results indicate the best scores obtained with the compared methods (excluding oracles).

The proposed method consistently outperformed the baseline. The BLEU improvements with the proposed method over the baseline and comparison methods were statistically significant according to the bootstrap sampling test ($p < 0.05$, 1,000 samples) (Zhang et al., 2004). With Moses, the improvement when using the proposed method was 1.4% (33.19% to 34.60%) in BLEU and 1.3% (57.83% to 56.50%) in TER, with a slight improvement in PER (35.84% to 35.61%). We observed: $oracle \gg proposed \gg comp.(1) \gg baseline \gg comp.(2)$ by the Bonferroni method, where the symbol $A \gg B$ means "A's improvement over B is statistically significant." With the hierarchical phrase-based SMT, the improvement was 2.2% (32.39% to 34.55%) in BLEU, 3.5% (58.36% to 54.87%) in TER, and 1.5% in PER (36.42% to 34.79%). We observed: $oracle \gg proposed \gg$

Table 2: Compared methods.

Test \ Training	w/ auto-aligned	w/o aligned	w/ oracle-aligned
clause-seg.	**proposed**	comp.(2)	oracle
no-clause-seg.	comp.(1)	baseline	oracle-comp.

$\{comp.(1), comp.(2)\} \gg baseline$ by the Bonferroni method. The oracle results were better than these obtained with the proposed method but the differences were not very large.

4.5 Discussion

We think the advantage of the proposed method arises from three possibilities: 1) better translation model training using the fine-aligned corpus, 2) an efficient decoder search over shortened inputs, and 3) an effective clause-level reordering model realized by using non-terminals.

First, the results of the first comparison method (comp.(1)) indicate an advantage of the translation models trained using the auto-aligned corpus. The training of the translation models, namely word alignment and phrase extraction, is difficult for long sentences due to their large ambiguity. This result suggests that the use of clause-level alignment provides fine-grained word alignments and precise translation models. We can also expect that the model of the proposed method will work better for the translation of single-clause sentences.

Second, the average and median lengths (including non-terminals) of the clause-seg. test set were 13.2 and 10 words, respectively. They were much smaller than those of no-clause-seg. at 33.4 and 30 words and are expected to help realize an efficient SMT search. Another observation is the relationship between the number of clauses and translation performance, as shown in Figure 5. The proposed method achieved a greater improvement in sentences with a greater number of clauses. This suggests that our divide-and-conquer approach works effectively for multi-clause sentences. Here, the results of the second comparison method (comp.(2)) with Moses were worse than the baseline results, while there was an improvement with our hierarchical phrase-based SMT. This probably arose from the difference between the decoders when translating out-of-vocabulary words. The non-terminals were handled as out-of-vocabulary words under the comp.(2) condition.

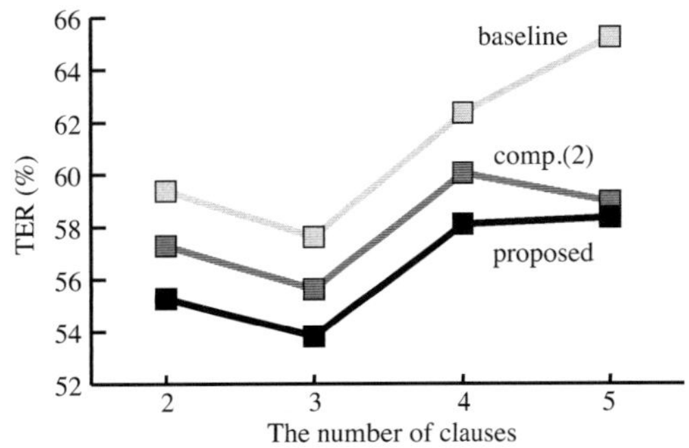

Figure 5: Relationship between TER and number of clauses for proposed, baseline, and comp.(2) when using our hierarchical phrase-based SMT.

Moses generated erroneous translations around such non-terminals that can be identified at a glance, while our hierarchical phrase-based SMT generated relatively good translations. This may be a decoder-dependent issue and is not an essential problem.

Third, the results obtained with the proposed method reveal an advantage in reordering in addition to the previous two advantages. The difference between the PERs with the proposed method and the baseline with Moses was small (0.2%) in spite of the large differences in BLEU and TER (about 1.5%). This suggests that the proposed method is better in word ordering and implies our method is also effective in reordering. With the hierarchical phrase-based SMT, the proposed method showed a large improvement from the baseline and comparison methods, especially in TER which was better than the best Moses configuration (proposed). This suggests that the decoding of long sentences with long-distance reordering is not easy even for the hierarchical phrase-based SMT due to its limited window size, while the hierarchical framework itself can naturally model a long-distance reordering. If we try to find a derivation with such long-distance reordering, we will probably be faced with an intractable search space and computation time. Therefore, we can conclude that the proposed divide-and-

Table 3: Experimental results obtained with Moses and our hierarchical phrase-based SMT, in BLEU, TER, and PER.

Moses : BLEU (%) / TER (%) / PER (%)			
Test \ Training	w/ auto-aligned	w/o aligned	w/ oracle-aligned
clause-seg.	**34.60 / 56.50** / 35.61	32.14 / 58.78 / 36.08	35.31 / 55.12 / 34.42
no-clause-seg.	34.22 / 56.90 / **35.20**	33.19 / 57.83 / 35.84	34.24 / 56.67 / 35.03
Hierarchical : BLEU (%) / TER (%) / PER (%)			
Test \ Training	w/ auto-aligned	w/o aligned	w/ oracle-aligned
clause-seg.	**34.55 / 54.87 / 34.79**	33.03 / 56.70 / 36.03	35.08 / 54.22 / 34.77
no-clause-seg.	33.41 / 57.02 / 35.86	32.39 / 58.36 / 36.42	33.83 / 56.26 / 34.96

conquer approach provides more practical long-distance reordering at the clause level.

We also analyzed the difference between automatic and manual clause alignment. Since auto-aligned corpus had many obvious alignment errors, we suspected these noisy clauses hurt the clause translation model. However, they were not serious in terms of final translation performance. So we can conclude that our proposed divide-and-conquer approach is promising for long sentence translation. Although we aimed to see whether we could bootstrap using existing bilingual corpora in this paper, we imagine better clause alignment can be obtained with some supervised classifiers.

One problem with the divide-and-conquer approach is that its independently-translated clauses potentially cause disfluencies in final sentence translations, mainly due to wrong inflections. A promising solution is to optimize a whole sentence translation by integrating search of each clause translation but this may require a much larger search space for decoding. More simply, we may be able to approximate it using n-best clause translations. This problem should be addressed for further improvement in future studies.

5 Conclusion

In this paper we proposed a clause-based divide-and-conquer approach for SMT that can reduce complicated clause-level reordering to simple word-level reordering. The proposed method separately translates clauses with non-terminals by using a well-known SMT method and reconstructs a sentence based on the non-terminals, to reorder long clauses. The clause translation models are trained using a bilingual corpus with clause-level alignment, which can be obtained with an unsupervised graph-based method using sentence-aligned corpora. The proposed method improves the translation of long, multi-clause sentences and is especially effective for language pairs with large word order differences, such as English-to-Japanese.

This paper focused only on clauses as segments for division. However, other long segments such as prepositional phrases are similarly difficult to reorder correctly. The divide-and-conquer approach itself can be applied to long phrases, and it is worth pursuing such an extension. As another future direction, we must develop a more sophisticated method for automatic clause alignment if we are to use the proposed method for various language pairs and domains.

Acknowledgments

We thank the U. S. National Library of Medicine for the use of PubMed abstracts and Prof. Shuji Kaneko of Kyoto University for the use of Life Science Dictionary. We also thank the anonymous reviewers for their valuable comments.

References

Peter F. Brown, Stephen A. Della Pietra, Vincent J. Della Pietra, and Robert L. Mercer. 1993. The mathematics of statistical machine translation: Parameter estimation. *Computational Linguistics*, 19(2):263–311.

David Chiang. 2007. Hierarchical phrase-based translation. *Computational Linguistics*, 33(2):201–228.

Michael Collins, Philipp Koehn, and Ivona Kuĉerová. 2005. Clause restructuring for statistical machine translation. In *Proc. ACL*, pages 531–540.

Osamu Furuse, Setsuo Yamada, and Kazuhide Yamamoto. 1998. Splitting long or ill-formed input for robust spoken-language translation. In *Proc. COLING-ACL*, pages 421–427.

Michel Galley, Mark Hopkins, Kevin Knight, and Daniel Marcu. 2004. What's in a translation rule? In *Proc. NAACL*, pages 273–280.

Jonathan Graehl and Kevin Knight. 2004. Training tree transducers. In *Proc. HLT-NAACL*, pages 105–112.

Jason Katz-Brown and Michael Collins. 2008. Syntactic reordering in preprocessing for Japanese-English translation: MIT system description for NTCIR-7 patent translation task. In *Proc. NTCIR-7*, pages 409–414.

Yeun-Bae Kim and Terumasa Ehara. 1994. A method for partitioning of long Japanese sentences with subject resolution in J/E machine translation. In *Proc. International Conference on Computer Processing of Oriental Languages*, pages 467–473.

Phillip Koehn, Franz Josef Och, and Daniel Marcu. 2003. Statistical phrase-based translation. In *Proc. HLT-NAACL*, pages 263–270.

Philipp Koehn, Amittai Axelrod, Alexandra Birch Mayne, Chris Callison-Burch, Miles Osborne, and David Talbot. 2005. Edinburgh system description for the 2005 IWSLT speech translation evaluation. In *Proc. IWSLT*.

Philipp Koehn, Hieu Hoang, Alexandra Birch, Chris Callison-Burch, Marcello Federico, Nicola Bertoldi, Brooke Cowan, Wade Shen, Christine Moran, Richard Zens, Chris Dyer, Ondrej Bojar, Alexandra Constantin, and Evan Herbst. 2007. Moses: Open source toolkit for statistical machine translation. In *Proc. ACL Companion Volume Proceedings of the Demo and Poster Sessions*, pages 177–180.

Chi-Ho Li, Dongdong Zhang, Mu Li, Ming Zhou, Minghui Li, and Yi Guan. 2007. A probabilistic approach to syntax-based reordering for statistical machine translation. In *Proc. ACL*, pages 720–727.

Yang Liu, Qun Liu, and Shouxun Lin. 2006. Tree-to-String alignment template for statistical machine translation. In *Proc. Coling-ACL*, pages 609–616.

Igor Malioutov and Regina Barzilay. 2006. Minimum cut model for spoken lecture segmentation. In *Proc. Coling-ACL*, pages 25–32.

Yusuke Miyao and Jun'ichi Tsujii. 2008. Feature forest models for probabilistic HPSG parsing. *Computational Linguistics*, 34(1):35–80.

Franz Josef Och, Nicola Ueffing, and Hermann Ney. 2001. An efficient A* search algorithm for statistical machine translation. In *Proc. the ACL Workshop on Data-Driven Methods in Machine Translation*, pages 55–62.

Kishore Papineni, Salim Roukos, Todd Ward, and Wei Jing Zhu. 2002. BLEU: a method for automatic evaluation of machine translation. In *Proc. ACL*, pages 311–318.

Matthew Snover, Bonnie Dorr, Richard Schwartz, Linnea Micciulla, and John Makhoul. 2006. A study of translation edit rate with targeted human annotation. In *Proc. AMTA*, pages 223–231.

Christoph Tillmann. 2004. A unigram orientation model for statistical machine translation. In *Proc. HLT-NAACL*, pages 101–104.

Erik F. Tjong, Kim Sang, and Hervé Déjean. 2001. Introduction to the CoNLL-2001 shared task: Clause identification. In *Proc. CoNLL*, pages 53–57.

Roy Tromble and Jason Eisner. 2009. Learning linear ordering problems for better translation. In *Proc. EMNLP*, pages 1007–1016.

Dekai Wu. 1997. Stochastic inversion transduction grammars and bilingual parsing of parallel corpora. *Computational Linguistics*, 23(3):377–404.

Fei Xia and Michael McCord. 2004. Improving a statistical MT system with automatically learned rewrite patterns. In *Proc. COLING*, pages 508–514.

Peng Xu, Jaeho Kang, Michael Ringgaard, and Franz Och. 2009. Using a dependency parser to improve SMT for Subject-Object-Verb languages. In *Proc. HLT-NAACL*, pages 245–253.

Kenji Yamada and Kevin Knight. 2001. A syntax-based statistical translation model. In *Proc. ACL*, pages 523–530.

Ying Zhang, Stephan Vogel, and Alex Weibel. 2004. Interpreting BLEU/NIST scores: How much improvement do we need to have a better system? In *Proc. LREC*, pages 2051–2054.

Xiaojin Zhu, Zoubin Ghahramani, and John Lafferty. 2003. Semi-supervised learning using gaussian fields and harmonic functions. In *Proc. ICML*, pages 912–919.

Decision Trees for Lexical Smoothing in Statistical Machine Translation

Rabih Zbib[†] and **Spyros Matsoukas** and **Richard Schwartz** and **John Makhoul**
BBN Technologies, 10 Moulton Street, Cambridge, MA 02138, USA
† Massachusetts Institute of Technology, 77 Massachusetts Ave., Cambridge, MA 02139, USA

Abstract

We present a method for incorporating arbitrary context-informed word attributes into statistical machine translation by clustering attribute-qualified source words, and smoothing their word translation probabilities using binary decision trees. We describe two ways in which the decision trees are used in machine translation: by using the attribute-qualified source word clusters directly, or by using attribute-dependent lexical translation probabilities that are obtained from the trees, as a lexical smoothing feature in the decoder model. We present experiments using Arabic-to-English newswire data, and using Arabic diacritics and part-of-speech as source word attributes, and show that the proposed method improves on a state-of-the-art translation system.

1 Introduction

Modern statistical machine translation (SMT) models, such as phrase-based SMT or hierarchical SMT, implicitly incorporate source language context. It has been shown, however, that such systems can still benefit from the explicit addition of lexical, syntactic or other kinds of context-informed word features (Vickrey et al., 2005; Gimpel and Smith, 2008; Brunning et al., 2009; Devlin, 2009). But the benefit obtained from the addition of attribute information is in general countered by the increase in the model complexity, which in turn results in a sparser translation model when estimated from the same corpus of data. The increase in model sparsity usually results in a deterioration of translation quality.

In this paper, we present a method for using arbitrary types of source-side context-informed word attributes, using binary decision trees to deal with the sparsity side-effect. The decision trees cluster attribute-dependent source words by reducing the entropy of the lexical translation probabilities. We also present another method where, instead of clustering the attribute-dependent source words, the decision trees are used to interpolate attribute-dependent lexical translation probability models, and use those probabilities to compute a feature in the decoder log-linear model.

The experiments we present in this paper were conducted on the translation of Arabic-to-English newswire data using a hierarchical system based on (Shen et al., 2008), and using Arabic diacritics (see section 2.3) and part-of-speech (POS) as source word attributes. Previous work that attempts to use Arabic diacritics in machine translation runs against the sparsity problem, and appears to lose most of the useful information contained in the diacritics when using partial diacritization (Diab et al., 2007). Using the methods proposed in this paper, we manage to obtain consistent improvements from diacritics against a strong baseline. The methods we propose, though, are not restrictive to Arabic-to-English translation. The same techniques can also be used with other language pairs and arbitrary word attribute types. The attributes we use in the described experiments are local; but long distance features can also be used.

In the next section, we review relevant previous work in three areas: Lexical smoothing and lexical disambiguation techniques in machine translation; using decision trees in natural language processing, and especially machine translation; and Arabic diacritics. We present a brief exposition of Arabic orthogra-

Proceedings of the Joint 5th Workshop on Statistical Machine Translation and MetricsMATR, pages 428–437,
Uppsala, Sweden, 15-16 July 2010. ©2010 Association for Computational Linguistics

phy, and refer to previous work on automatic diacritization of Arabic text. Section 3 describes the procedure for constructing the decision trees, and the two methods for using them in machine translation. In section 4 we describe the experimental setup and present experimental results. Finally, section 5 concludes the paper and discusses future directions.

2 Previous Work

2.1 Lexical Disambiguation and Lexical Smoothing

Various ways have been proposed to improve the lexical translation choices of SMT systems. These approaches typically incorporate local context information, either directly or indirectly.

The use of Word Sense Disambiguation (WSD) has been proposed to enhance machine translation by disambiguating the source words (Cabezas and Resnick, 2005; Carpuat and Wu, 2007; Chan et al., 2007). WSD usually requires that the training data be labeled with senses, which might not be available for many languages. Also, WSD is traditionally formulated as a classification problem, and therefore does not naturally lend itself to be integrated into the generative framework of machine translation. Carpuat and Wu (2007) formulate the SMT lexical disambiguation problem as a WSD task. Instead of learning from word sense corpora, they use the SMT training data, and use local context features to enhance the lexical disambiguation of phrase-based SMT.

Sarikaya et al. (2007) incorporate context more directly by using POS tags on the target side to model word context. They augmented the target words with POS tags of the word itself and its surrounding words, and used the augmented words in decoding and for language model rescoring. They reported gains on Iraqi-Arabic-to-English translation.

Finally, using word-to-word context-free lexical translation probabilities has been shown to improve the performance of machine translation systems, even those using much more sophisticated models. This feature, usually called lexical smoothing, has been used in phrase-based systems (Koehn et al., 2003). Och et al. (2004) also found that including IBM Model 1 (Brown et al., 1993) word probabilities in their log-linear model works better than most other higher-level syntactic features at improving the baseline. The incorporation of context on the source or target side enhances the gain obtained from lexical smoothing. Gimpel and Smith (2008) proposed using source-side lexical features in phrase-based SMT by conditioning the phrase probabilities on those features. They used word context, syntactic features or positional features. The features were added as components into the log-linear decoder model, each with a tunable weight. Devlin (2009) used context lexical features in a hierarchical SMT system, interpolating lexical counts based on multiple contexts. It also used target-side lexical features.

The work in the paper incorporates context information based on the reduction of the translation probability entropy.

2.2 Decision Trees

Decision trees have been used extensively in various areas of machine learning, typically as a way to cluster patterns in order to improve classification (Duda et al., 2000). They have, for instance, been long used successfully in speech recognition to cluster context-dependent phoneme model states (Young et al., 1994).

Decision trees have also been used in machine translation, although to a lesser extent. In this respect, our work is most similar to (Brunning et al., 2009), where the authors extended word alignment models for IBM Model 1 and Hidden Markov Model (HMM) alignments. They used decision trees to cluster the context-dependent source words. Contexts belonging to the same cluster were grouped together during Expectation Maximization (EM) training, thus providing a more robust probability estimate. While Brunning et al. (2009) used the source context clusters for word alignments, we use the attribute-dependent source words directly in decoding. The approach we propose can be readily used with any alignment model.

Stroppa et al. (2007) presented a generalization of phrase-based SMT (Koehn et al., 2003) that also takes into account source-side context information. They conditioned the target phrase probability on the source phrase as well as source phrase context, such as bordering words, or part-of-speech of bordering words. They built a decision tree for each source phrase extracted from the training data. The branching of the tree nodes was based on the different context features, branching on the most class-discriminative features first. Each node is associated with the set of aligned target phrases and corresponding context-conditioned probabilities. The decision tree thus smoothes the phrase probabilities based on the different features, allowing the model to back off to less context, or no context at all depending on the presence of that context-dependent source phrase in the training data. The model, however, did not provide for a back-off mechanism if the phrase pair was not found in the extracted phrase table. The method presented in this paper differs in various aspects. We use context-dependent information at the source word level, rather than the phrase level, thus making it readily applicable to any translation model and not just phrase-based translation. By incorporating context at the word level, we can decode directly with attribute-augmented source data (see section 3.2).

2.3 Arabic Diacritics

Since an important part of the experiments described in this paper use diacritized Arabic source, we present a brief description of Arabic orthography, and specifically diacritics.

The Arabic script, like that of most other Semitic languages, only represents consonants and long vowels using letters [1]. Short vowels can be written as small marks written above or below the preceding consonant, called diacritics. The diacritics are, however, omitted from written text, except in special cases, thus creating an additional level of lexical ambiguity. Readers can usually guess the correct pronunciation of words in non-diacritized text from the sentence and discourse context. Grammatical case on nouns and adjectives are also marked using diacritics at the end of words. Arabic MT systems use undiacritized text, since most available Arabic data is undiacritized.

Automatic diacritization of Arabic has been done with high accuracy, using various generative and discriminative modeling techniques. For example, Ananthakrishnan et al. (2005) used a generative model that incorporates word level n-grams, sub-word level n-grams and part-of-speech information to perform diacritization. Nelken and Shieber (2005) modeled the generative process of dropping diacritics using weighted transducers, then used Viterbi decoding to find the most likely generator. Zitouni et al. (2006) presented a method based on maximum entropy classifiers, using features like character n-grams, word n-grams, POS and morphological segmentation. Habash and Rambow (2007) determined various morpho-syntactic features of the word using SVM classifiers, then chose the corresponding diacritization. The experiments in this paper use the automatic diacritizer by Sakhr Software. The diacritizer determines word diacritics through rule-based morphological and syntactic analysis. It outputs a diacritization for both the internal stem and case ending markers of the word, with an accuracy of 97% for stem diacritization and 91% for full diacritization (i.e., including case endings).

There has been work done on using diacritics in Automatic Speech Recognition, e.g. (Vergyri and Kirchhoff, 2004). However, the only previous work on using diacritization for MT is (Diab et al., 2007), which used the diacritization system described in (Habash and Rambow, 2007). It investigated the effect of using full diacritization as well as partial diacritization on MT results. The authors found that using full diacritics deteriorates MT performance. They used partial diacritization schemes, such as diacritizing only passive verbs, keeping the case endings diacritics, or only gemination diacritics. They also saw no gain in most configurations. The authors argued that the deterioration in performance is caused by the increase in the size of the vocabulary, which in turn makes the translation model sparser; as well as by errors during the automatic diacritization process.

[1] Such writing systems are sometimes referred to as *Abjads* (See Daniels, Peter T., et al. eds. The World's Writing Systems Oxford. (1996), p.4.)

3 Decision Trees for Source Word Attributes

3.1 Growing the Decision Tree

In this section, we describe the procedure for growing the decision trees using context-informed source word attributes.

The attribute-qualified source-side of the parallel training data is first aligned to the target-side data. If S is the set of attribute-dependent forms of source word s, and t_j is a target word aligned to $s_i \in S$, then we define:

$$p(t_j|s_i) = \frac{\text{count}(s_i,t_j)}{\text{count}(s_i)} \quad (1)$$

where $\text{count}(s_i, t_j)$ is the count of alignment links between s_i and t_j.

A separate binary decision tree is grown for each source word. We start by including all the attribute-dependent forms of the source word at the root of the tree. We split the set of attributes at each node into two child nodes, by choosing the splitting that maximizes the reduction in weighted entropy of the probability distribution in (1). In other words, at node **n**, we choose the partition $(S_1^\star, S_2^\star)$ such that:

$$(S_1^\star, S_2^\star) = \underset{\substack{(S_1,S_2) \\ S_1 \cup S_2 = S}}{\text{argmax}} \{h(S) - (h(S_1) + h(S_2))\} \quad (2)$$

where $h(S)$ is the entropy of the probability distribution $p(t_j|s_i \in S)$, weighted by the number of samples in the training data of the source words in S. We only split a node if the entropy is reduced by more than a threshold θ_h. This step is repeated recursively until the tree cannot be grown anymore.

Weighting the entropy by the source word counts gives more weight to the context-dependent source words with a higher number of samples in the training data, sine the lexical translation probability estimates for frequent words can be trusted better. The rationale behind the splitting criterion used is that the split that reduces the entropy of the lexical translation probability distribution the most is also the split that best separates the list of forms of the source word in terms of the target word translation. For a source word that has multiple meanings, depending on its context, the decision tree will tend to implicitly separate those meanings using the information in the lexical translation probabilities.

Although we describe this method as growing one decision tree for each word, and using one attribute type at a time, a decision tree can clearly be constructed for multiple words, and more than one attribute type can be used in the same decision tree.

3.2 Trees for Source Word Clustering

The source words could be augmented to explicitly incorporate the word attributes (diacritics or other attribute types). The augmented source will be less ambiguous if the attributes do in fact contain disambiguating information. This, in principle, helps machine translation performance. The flip side is that the resulting increase in vocabulary size increases the translation model sparsity, usually with a detrimental effect on translation.

To mitigate the effect of the increase in vocabulary, decision trees can be use to cluster the attribute-augmented source words. More specifically, a decision tree is grown for each source word as described in the previous section, using a predefined entropy threshold θ_h. When the tree cannot be expanded anymore, its leaf nodes will contain a multi-set partitioning of the list of attribute-dependent forms of that source word. Each of the clusters is treated as an equivalence class, and all forms in that class are mapped to a unique form (e.g. an arbitrarily chosen member of the cluster). The mappings are used to map the tokens in the parallel training data before alignment is run on the mapped data. The test data is also mapped consistently. This clustering procedure will only keep the attribute-dependent forms of the source words that decrease the uncertainty in the translation probabilities, and are thus useful for translation.

The experiments we report on use diacritics as an attribute type. The various diacritized forms of a source word are thus used to train the decision trees. The resulting clusters are used to map the data into a subset of the vocabulary that is used in translation training and decoding (see section 4.2 for results). Diacritics are obviously specific to Arabic. But this method can be used with other attribute types, by first appending the source words with

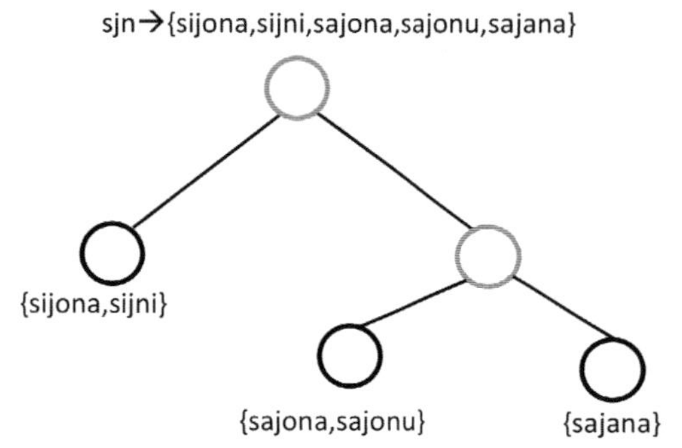

Figure 1: Decision tree for source word *sjn* using diacritics as an attribute.

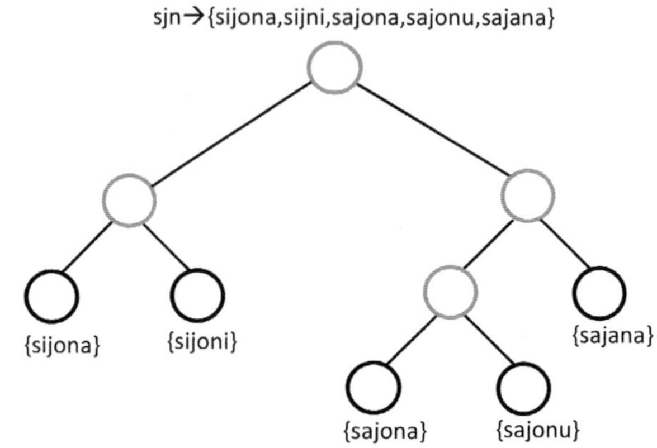

Figure 2: Decision tree for source word *sjn* grown fully using diacritics.

their context (e.g. attach to each source word its part-of-speech tag or context), and then training decision trees and mapping the source side of the data.

Figure 1 shows an example of a decision tree for the Arabic word *sjn*[2] using diacritics as a source attribute. The root contains the various diacritized forms (*sijona 'prison ACCUSATIVE', sijoni 'prison DATIVE', sajona 'imprisonment ACCUSATIVE.', sajoni 'imprisonment ACCUSATIVE.', sajana 'he imprisoned'*). The leaf nodes contain the attribute-dependent clusters.

3.3 Trees for Lexical Smoothing

As mentioned in section 2.1, lexical smoothing, computed from word-to-word translation probabilities, is a useful feature, even in SMT systems that use sophisticated translation models. This is likely due to the robustness of context-free word-to-word translation probability estimates compared to the probabilities of more complicated models. In those models, the rules and probabilities are estimated from much larger sample spaces.

In our system, the lexical smoothing feature is computed as follows:

$$f(\mathbf{U})=\prod_{t_j\in T(\mathbf{U})}\left(1-\prod_{s_i\in\{S(\mathbf{U})\cup\text{NULL}\}}(1-\bar{p}(t_j|s_i))\right) \quad (3)$$

where **U** is the modeling unit specific to the translation model used. For a phrase-based system, **U** is the phrase pair, and for a hierarchical system **U** is the translation rule. $S(\mathbf{U})$ is the set of terminals on the source side of **U**, and $T(\mathbf{U})$ is the set of terminals on its target. The NULL term in the equation above accounts for unaligned target words, which we found in our experiments to be beneficial. One way of interpreting equation (3) is that $f(\mathbf{U})$ is the probability that for each target word t_j in **U**, t_j is a likely translation of at least one word s_i on the source side. The feature value is then used as a component in the log-linear model, with a tunable weight.

In this work, we generalize the lexical smoothing feature to incorporate the source word attributes. A tree is grown for each source word as described in section 3.1, but using an entropy threshold $\theta_h = 0$. In other words, the tree is grown all the way until each leaf node contains one attribute-dependent form of the source word. Each node in the tree contains a cluster of attribute-dependent forms of the source word, and a corresponding attribute-dependent lexical translation probability distribution. The lexical translation probability models at the root nodes are those of the regular attribute-independent lexical translation probabilities. The models at the leaf nodes are the most fine-grained, since they are conditioned on only one attribute value. Figure 2 shows a fully grown decision tree for the same source word as the example in Figure 1.

The lexical probability distribution at the leafs are from sparser data than the original distributions, and are therefore less robust. To address this, the attribute-dependent lexical

[2]Examples are written using Buckwalter transliteration.

smoothing feature is estimated by recursively interpolating the lexical translation probabilities up the tree. The probability distribution $p_{\mathbf{n}}$ at each node $\mathbf{n}$ is interpolated with the probability of its parent node as follows:

$$\overline{p}_{\mathbf{n}} = \begin{cases} p_{\mathbf{n}} & \text{if } \mathbf{n} \text{ is root,} \\ w_{\mathbf{n}} p_{\mathbf{n}} + (1 - w_{\mathbf{n}}) \overline{p}_{\mathbf{m}} & \text{otherwise} \end{cases}$$

where $\mathbf{m}$ is the parent of $\mathbf{n}$ (4)

A fraction of the parent probability mass is thus given to the probability of the child node. If the probability estimate of an attribute-dependent form of a source word with a certain target word t is not reliable, or if the probability estimate is 0 (because the source word in this context is not aligned with t), then the model gracefully backs off by using the probability estimates from other attribute-dependent lexical translation probability models of the source word.

The interpolation weight is a logistic regression function of the source word count at a node $\mathbf{n}$:

$$w_{\mathbf{n}} = \frac{1}{1 + e^{-\alpha - \beta \log(\text{count}(S_{\mathbf{n}}))}} \quad (5)$$

The weight varies depending on the count of the attribute-qualified source word in each node, thus reflecting the confidence in the estimates of each node's distribution. The two global parameters of the function, a bias α and a scale β are tuned to maximize the likelihood of a set of alignment counts from a heldout data set of 179K sentences. The tuning is done using Powell's method (Brent, 1973).

During decoding, we use the probability distribution at the leaves to compute the feature value $f(\mathbf{R})$ for each hierarchical rule $\mathbf{R}$. We train and decode using the regular, attribute-independent source. The source word attributes are used in the decoder only to index the interpolated probability distribution needed to compute $f(\mathbf{R})$.

4 Experiments

4.1 Experimental Setup

As mentioned before, the experiments we report on use a string-to-dependency-tree hierarchical translation system based on the model described in (Shen et al., 2008). Forward and backward context-free lexical smoothing are used as decoder features in all the experiments. Other features such as rule probabilities and dependency tree language model (Shen et al., 2008) are also used. We use GIZA++ (Och and Ney, 2003) for word alignments. The decoder model parameters are tuned using Minimum Error Rate training (Och, 2003) to maximize the IBM BLEU score (Papineni et al., 2002).

	Likelihood	**%**
baseline	-1.29	-
Diacs. dec. trees	-1.25	+2.98%
POS dec. trees	-1.24	+3.41%

Table 1: Normalized likelihood of the test set alignments without decision trees, then with decision trees using diacritics and part-of-speech respectively.

For training the alignments, we use 27M words from the Sakhr Arabic-English Parallel Corpus (SSUSAC27). The language model uses 7B words from the English Gigaword and from data collected from the web. A 3-gram language model is used during decoding. The decoder produces an N-best list that is reranked using a 5-gram language model.

We tune and test on two separate data sets consisting of documents from the following collections: the newswire portion of NIST MT04, MT05, MT06, and MT08 evaluation sets, the GALE Phase 1 (P1) and Phase 2 (P2) evaluation sets, and the GALE P2 and P3 development sets. The tuning set contains 1994 sentences and the test set contains 3149 sentences. The average length of sentences is 36 words. Most of the documents in the two data sets have 4 reference translations, but some have only one. The average number of reference translations per sentence is 3.94 for the tuning set and 3.67 for the test set.

In the next section, we report on measurements of the likelihood of test data, and describe the translation experiments in detail.

4.2 Results

In order to assess whether the decision trees are in fact helpful in decreasing the uncertainty in the lexical translation probabilities

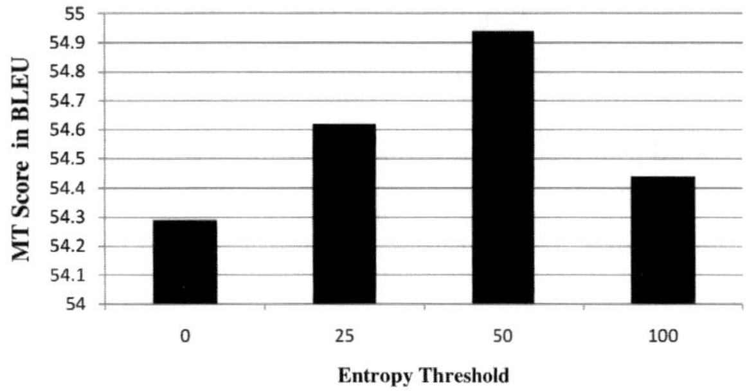

Figure 3: BLEU scores of the clustering experiments as a function of the entropy threshold on tuning set.

on unseen data, we compute the likelihood of the test data with respect to these probabilities with and without the decision tree splitting. We align the test set with its reference using GIZA++, and then obtain the link count $l\_count(s_i, t_j)$ for each alignment link $i = (s_i, t_i)$ in the set of alignment links I. We calculate the normalized likelihood of the alignments:

$$L = \log\left[\left(\prod_i \bar{p}(t_i \mid s_i)^{l\_count(s_i,t_i)}\right)^{\frac{1}{|I|}}\right] = \frac{1}{|I|}\sum_{i\in I} l\_count(s_i, t_i) \log \bar{p}\,(t_i \mid s_i) \quad (6)$$

where $\bar{p}\,(t_i \mid s_i)$ is the probability for the word pair (t_i, s_i) in equation (4). If the same instance of source word s_i is aligned to two target words t_i and t_j, then these two links are counted separately. If a source in the test set is out-of-vocabulary, or if a word pair (t_i, s_i) is aligned in the test alignment but not in the training alignments (and thus has no probability estimate), then it is ignored in the calculation of the log-likelihood.

Table 1 shows the likelihood for the baseline case, where one lexical translation probability distribution is used per source word. It also shows the likelihoods calculated using the lexical distributions in the leaf nodes of the decision trees, when either diacritics or part-of-speech are used as an attribute type. The table shows an increase in the likelihood of 2.98% using diacritics, and 3.41% using part-of-speech.

The translation result tables present MT scores in two different metrics: Translation Edit Rate (Snover et al., 2006) and IBM

	TER	**BLEU**
	Test	
baseline	**40.14**	**52.05**
full diacritics	40.31	52.39
	+0.17	+0.34
dec. trees, diac ($\theta_h = 50$)	39.75	52.60
	-0.39	+0.55

Table 2: Results of experiments using decision trees to cluster source words.

BLEU. The reader is reminded that a higher BLEU score and a lower TER are desired. The tables also show the difference in scores between the baseline and each experiment. It is worth noting that the gains reported are relative to a strong baseline that uses a state-of-the-art system with many features, and a fairly large training corpus.

The decision tree clustering experiment as described in section **3.2** depends on a global parameter, namely the threshold in entropy reduction θ_h. We tune this parameter manually on a tuning set. Figure 3 shows the BLEU scores as a function of the threshold value, with diacritics as an attribute type. The most gain is obtained for an entropy threshold of 50.

The fully diacritized data has an average of 1.78 diacritized forms per source word. The average weighted by the number of occurrences is 6.28, which indicates that words with more diacritized forms tend to occur more frequently. After clustering using a value of $\theta_h = 50$, the average number of diacritized forms becomes 1.11, and the occurrence weighted average becomes 3.69. The clustering procedure thus seems to eliminate most diacritized forms, which likely do not contain helpful disambiguating information.

Table 2 lists the detailed results of experiments using diacritics. In the first experiment, we show that using full diacritization results in a small gain on the BLEU score and no gain on TER, which is somewhat consistent with the result obtained by Diab et al. (2007). The next experiment shows the results of clustering the diacritized source words using decision trees for the entropy threshold of 50. The TER loss of the full diacritics becomes a gain, and the BLEU gain increases. This confirms our speculation that the use of fully diacritized data in-

	TER	BLEU
	Test	
baseline	**40.14**	**52.05**
dec. trees, diacs	39.75	52.55
	-0.39	+0.50
dec. trees, POS	40.05	52.40
	-0.09	+0.35
dec. trees, diacs, no interpolation	39.98	52.09
	-0.16	+0.04

Table 3: Results of experiments using the word attribute-dependent lexical smoothing feature.

creases the model sparsity, which undoes most of the benefit obtained from the disambiguating information that the diacritics contain. Using the decision trees to cluster the diacritized source data prunes diacritized forms that do not decrease the entropy of the lexical translation probability distributions. It thus finds a sweet-spot between the negative effect of increasing the vocabulary size and the positive effect of disambiguation.

In our experiments, using diacritics with case endings gave consistently better score than using diacritics with no case endings, despite the fact that they result in a higher vocabulary size. One possible explanation is that diacritics not only help in lexical disambiguation, but they might also be indirectly helping in phrase reordering, since the diacritics on the final letter indicate the word's grammatical function.

The results from using decision trees to interpolate attribute-dependent lexical smoothing features are summarized in table 3. In the first experiment, we show the results of using diacritics to estimate the interpolated lexical translation probabilities. The results show a gain of +0.5 BLEU points and 0.39 TER points. The gain is statistically significant with a 95% confidence level. Using part-of-speech as an attribute gives a smaller, but still statistically significant gain. We also ran a control experiment, where we used diacritic-dependent lexical translation probabilities obtained from the decision trees, but did not perform the probability interpolation of equation (4). The gains mostly disappear, especially on BLEU, showing the importance of the interpolation step for the proper estimation of the lexical smoothing feature.

5 Conclusion and Future Directions

We presented in this paper a new method for incorporating explicit context-informed word attributes into SMT using binary decision trees. We reported on experiments on Arabic-to-English translation using diacritized Arabic and part-of-speech as word attributes, and showed that the use of these attributes increases the likelihood of source-target word pairs of unseen data. We proposed two specific ways in which the results of the decision tree training process are used in machine translation, and showed that they result in better translation results.

For future work, we plan on using multiple source-side attributes at the same time. Different attributes could have different disambiguating information, which could provide more benefit than using any of the attributes alone. We also plan on investigating the use of multi-word trees; trees for word clusters can for instance be grown instead of growing a separate tree for each source word. Although the experiments presented in this paper use local word attributes, nothing in principle prevents this method from being used with long-distance sentence context, or even with document-level or discourse-level features. Our future plans include the investigation of using such features as well.

Acknowledgment

This work was supported by DARPA/IPTO Contract No. HR0011-06-C-0022 under the GALE program.

The views, opinions, and/or findings contained in this article are those of the author and should not be interpreted as representing the official views or policies, either expressed or implied, of the Defense Advanced Research Projects Agency or the Department of Defense. A pproved for Public Release, Distribution Unlimited.

References

S. Ananthakrishnan, S. Narayanan, and S. Bangalore. 2005. Automatic diacritization of arabic transcripts for automatic speech recognition. Kanpur, India.

R. Brent. 1973. *Algorithms for Minimization Without Derivatives.* Prentice-Hall.

P. Brown, V. Della Pietra, S. Della Pietra, and R. L. Mercer. 1993. The mathematics of statistical machine translation: Parameter estimation. *Computational Linguistics*, 19:263–311.

J. Brunning, A. de Gispert, and W. Byrne. 2009. Context-dependent alignment models for statistical machine translation. In *NAACL '09: Proceedings of the 2009 Human Language Technology Conference of the North American Chapter of the Association for Computational Linguistics*, pages 110–118.

C. Cabezas and P. Resnick. 2005. Using WSD techniques for lexical selection in statistical machine translation. In *Technical report, Institute for Advanced Computer Studies (CS-TR-4736, LAMP-TR-124, UMIACS-TR-2005-42)*, College Park, MD.

M. Carpuat and D. Wu. 2007. Improving statistical machine translation using word sense disambiguation. In *EMNLP-CoNLL-2007: Proceedings of the 2007 Joint Conference on Empirical Methods in Natural Language Processing and Computational Natural Language Learning*, Prague, Czech Republic.

Y. Chan, H. Ng, and D. Chiang. 2007. Word sense disambiguation improves statistical machine translation. In *Proceedings of the 45th Annual Meeting of the Association for Computational Linguistics (ACL).*

J. Devlin. 2009. Lexical features for statistical machine translation. Master's thesis, University of Maryland, December 2009.

M. Diab, M. Ghoneim, and N. Habash. 2007. Arabic diacritization in the context of statistical machine translation. In *MT Summit XI*, pages 143–149, Copenhagen, Denmark.

R. O. Duda, P. E. Hart, and D. G. Stork. 2000. *Pattern Classification.* Wiley-Interscience Publication.

K. Gimpel and N. A. Smith. 2008. Rich source-side context for statistical machine translation. In *StatMT '08: Proceedings of the Third Workshop on Statistical Machine Translation*, pages 9–17, Columbus, Ohio.

N. Habash and O. Rambow. 2007. Arabic diacritization through full morphological tagging. In *Proceedings of the 2007 Human Language Technology Conference of the North American Chapter of the Association for Computational Linguistics*, pages 53–56, Rochester, New York.

P. Koehn, F. J. Och, and D. Marcu. 2003. Statistical phrase-based translation. In *Proceedings of the 2003 Human Language Technology Conference of the North American Chapter of the Association for Computational Linguistics*, pages 48–54, Edmonton, Canada.

R. Nelken and S. M. Shieber. 2005. Arabic diacritization using weighted finite-state transducers. In *Proceedings of the 2005 ACL Workshop on Computational Approaches to Semitic Languages*, Ann Arbor, Michigan.

F. J. Och and H. Ney. 2003. A systematic comparison of various statistical alignment models. *Computational Linguistics*, 29(1):19–51.

F. J. Och, D. Gildea, S. Khudanpur, A. Sarkar, K. Yamada, A. Fraser, S. Kumar, L. Shen, D. Smith, K. Eng, V. Jain, Z. Jin, and D. R. Radev. 2004. A smorgasbord of features for statistical machine translation. In *HLT-NAACL*, pages 161–168.

F. J. Och. 2003. Minimum error rate training in statistical machine translation. In *Proceedings of the 41st Annual Meeting of the Association for Computational Linguistics (ACL)*, Sapporo, Japan.

K. Papineni, S. Roukos, T. Ward, and W. Zhu. 2002. Bleu: a method for automatic evaluation of machine translation. In *Proceedings of the 40th Annual Meeting of the Association for Computational Linguistics (ACL)*, Philadelphia, PA.

Ruhi Sarikaya, Yonggang Deng, and Yuqing Gao. 2007. Context dependent word modeling for statistical machine translation using part-of-speech tags. In *Proceedings of INTERSPEECH 2007fs*, Antwerp, Belgium.

L. Shen, J. Xu, and R. Weischedel. 2008. A new string-to-dependency machine translation algorithm with a target dependency language model. In *Proceedings of the 46th Annual Meeting of the Association for Computational Linguistics (ACL)*, Columbus, Ohio.

M. Snover, B. Dorr, R. Schwartz, J. Makhoul, and L. Micciulla. 2006. A study of translation error rate with targeted human annotation. In *Proceedings of the 7th Conf. of the Association for Machine Translation in the Americas (AMTA 2006)*, pages 223–231, Cambridge, MA.

N. Stroppa, A. van den Bosch, and A Way. 2007. Exploiting source similarity for SMT using context-informed features. In *Proceedings of the 11th International Conference on Theoretical and Methodological Issues in Machine Translation (TMI-07)*, pages 231–240.

D. Vergyri and K. Kirchhoff. 2004. Automatic diacritization of arabic for acoustic modeling in speech recognition. In *Semitic '04: Proceedings of the Workshop on Computational Approaches to Arabic Script-based Languages*, pages 66–73, Geneva, Switzerland.

D. Vickrey, L. Biewald, M. Teyssier, and D. Koller. 2005. Word-sense disambiguation for machine translation. In *HLT '05: Proceedings of the conference on Human Language Technology and Empirical Methods in Natural Language Processing*, Vancouser, BC, Canada.

S.J. Young, J.J. Odell, and P.C. Woodland. 1994. Tree-based state tying for high accuracy acoustic modelling. In *HLT'94: Proceedings of the Workshop on Human Language Technology*, pages 307–312.

I. Zitouni, J. S. Sorensen, and Ruhi Sarikaya. 2006. Maximum entropy based restoration of arabic diacritics. In *Proceedings of the 21st International Conference on Computational Linguistics and the 44th annual meeting of the Association for Computational Linguistics*, pages 577–584, Sydney, Australia.

Author Index

Association for Computational Linguistics
209 N. Eighth Street
Stroudsburg, Pennsylvania 18360

CURRAN ASSOCIATES INC
proceedings
.com